Introduction to Special Education

Introduction to Special Education

TEACHING IN AN AGE OF OPPORTUNITY

Fifth Edition

Deborah Deutsch Smith

Peabody College
Vanderbilt University

Boston · New York · San Francisco ·
Mexico City · Montreal · Toronto ·
London · Madrid · Munich · Paris ·
Hong Kong · Singapore · Tokyo ·
Cape Town · Sydney

Executive Editor: Virginia Lanigan

Editorial Assistant: Robert Champagne

Developmental Editor: Alicia R. Reilly

Executive Marketing Manager: Amy Cronin Jordan

Production Manager: Elaine Ober

Composition and Prepress Buyer: Linda Cox

Manufacturing Buyer: Andrew Turso

Cover Administrator: Linda Knowles

Photo and Fine Art Researcher: Helane M. Prottas/ Posh Pictures

Editorial Production Service: Barbara Gracia

Interior Designer: Carolyn Deacy

Electronic Composition: Schneck-DePippo Graphics

Library of Congress Cataloging-in-Publication Data

Smith, Deborah Deutsch
      Introduction to special education: teaching in an age of
opportunity/Deborah Deutsch Smith—5th ed.
          p.   cm.
      Includes bibliographical references and indexes.
      ISBN 0-205-37616-9
      1. Special education—United States. I. Title.
      LC3981.S56 2003
      371.9'0971–dc   2003040428

Printed in the United States of America

10 9 8 7 6 5 4 3 2 1—VHP—07 06 05 04 03

Photo Credits:
Chapter 1: P. 8, © Kate Brooks/SABA; p. 10, Lyle Ahern (left), Evans Picture Library (right); p. 15, Courtesy of the National Easter Seal Society; p. 16, Associated Press/Stuart Ramson; p. 17, BARBIE(r), BECKY ® and associated trademarks are owned by and used with permission of Mattel, Inc. © 2002, Mattel, Inc. All rights reserved. p. 18, Associated Press/Bob Galbraith; p. 24, (left) Associated Press, (right) Associated Press/Hillery Smith Garrison; p. 26, Noel Saltzman/PBS; p. 28, Courtesy of Easter Seals A.B.L.E. of Tennessee. **Chapter 2:** P. 40, Courtesy of Easter Seals A.B.L.E. of Tennessee; p. 42, Mary Kate Denny/PhotoEdit; p. 47, T. Lindfors/Lindfors Photography; p. 53, Tony Freeman/ PhotoEdit; p. 58, Michael Newman/PhotoEdit; p. 62, James Shaffe/PhotoEdit. **Chapter 3:** P. 73, Paul Conklin/PhotoEdit; p. 75, T. Lindfors/Lindfors Photography; p. 78, Myrleen Ferguson Cate/PhotoEdit; p. 85, Tony Freeman/PhotoEdit; p. 91, Associated Press, United Cerebral Palsy; p. 93, Will Hart; p. 97, Richard Hutchins/PhotoEdit; **Chapter 4:** Pp. 115, 122, 128, 141, T. Lindfors/Lindfors Photography; p. 117, Courtesy of the Council for Exceptional Children; p. 126, Bernard Wolf/Monkmeyer; pp. 131, 135, David Young-Wolff/PhotoEdit; p. 144 © Lernout & Hauspie Speech Products, Burlington, MA. **Chapter 5:** Pp. 153, 164, 177, T. Lindfors/Lindfors Photography; p. 157, Ellen Senisi/The Image Works; p. 162, Courtesy of the American Speech-Language-Hearing Association; p. 168, Mary Kate Denny/PhotoEdit; p. 171, David Young-Wolff/PhotoEdit;

Photo credits are continued on page 564 and are considered an extension of the copyright page.

Life is fragile. While most of us don't think about it much, some of us continually face this fact.

To Steve Smith, Rock McLean, and Drew Allen, who truly understand and demonstrate the resolve, courage, resilience, spirit, generosity, and sense of humor that most of us only wish for. The world is a better place because of people like them.

ON BEING A CHAMPION

A Champion is a winner,
A hero . . .
Someone who never gives up
Even when the going gets rough.
A champion is a member of
A winning team . . .
Someone who overcomes challenges
Even when it requires creative solutions
A champion is an optimist,
A hopeful spirit . . .
Someone who plays the game,
Even when the game is called life . . .
Especially when the game is called life.
There can be a champion in each of us,
If we live as a winner,
If we live as a member of the team,
If we live with a hopeful spirit,
For life.

BRIEF CONTENTS

SPECIAL FEATURES

CONTENTS

CHAPTER 5

Speech or Language Impairments 149

CHAPTER 6

Mental Retardation 185

CHAPTER 7

Giftedness and Talent Development 223

CHAPTER 8

Emotional or Behavioral Disorders 257

Contents

CHAPTER 9

Physical Impairments and Special Health Care Needs 299

CHAPTER 10

Deafness and Hard of Hearing 343

CHAPTER 11

Low Vision or Blindness 383

CHAPTER 12

Autistic Spectrum Disorders 415

CHAPTER 13

Very Low Incidence Disabilities: Multiple-Severe Disabilities, Deafblindness, and Traumatic Brain Injury 445

Children with special needs and their families demand, and deserve, a unique educational experience. They are entitled to a learning experience that is fashioned by excited, dedicated professionals who see the opportunities and meet the challenges that come with making a difference. However, making the "right difference" is not a simple accomplishment. Assuming this responsibility calls for commitment, an understanding of schools and their intricate systems, an appreciation for the diversity of perspectives that children with special needs and their families require, up-to-date knowledge about validated practices, the ability to arrive at informed decisions, and the courage to test those decisions and respond accordingly. The course that introduces college students to special education provides some of the necessary "first steps" in adopting appropriate attitudes, mastering important skills and content, and becoming a responsible and truly special educator.

Each time I revise and rewrite this text, I try to figure out a better way to introduce people to the field of special education and how more effectively to contribute to the development of the "next generation" of professionals who *will* make the "right difference." I attempt to create an inviting and intriguing introduction to students with special needs in order to encourage college students to learn more about gifted students, individuals with disabilities, their families, and their communities. Every time I create a new edition, I deliberately consider ways to present the most current content in such a way that the foundation for future intensive study of special education is solid. I also think about the process of initiating professionals whose first concern may not be the education of students with special needs. Because this course may be the only one these educators take before assuming the shared responsibility of teaching very diverse learners, this book offers information about a wide range of topics, including proven practices, making accommodations, and the delivery of individualized instruction tailored to the specific needs of individual students. Finally, I carefully consider how conversations are initiated among those who must develop effective partnerships so that an appropriate education in the least restrictive environment possible can become a reality for all students.

Becoming a professional (or an informed citizen) who can make the "right difference" requires intensive study and training. This text will help the reader begin to develop the awareness, sensitivity, knowledge, skills, and competence necessary to be one of the agents of positive change who work on behalf of people with disabilities. My hope is that, with a greater emphasis on methods and proven practices, together we can seize the opportunity to create a better future for a very diverse set of special learners.

UNDERLYING THEMES

What features and components of an introductory course are critical to the education of special and general educators who can make the "right difference"? Finding the perfect mix of content, human-interest stories, applications and examples, and issues is one of a textbook author's greatest challenges. Specifically, I was intent on including

- The voices of people with disabilities, of their friends, and of their family members (to bring their perspectives to the forefront)
- The most current research findings, verified practices, and policies
- Practical applications and examples of instructional methods and interventions
- A comprehensive focus on diversity and the components of cultural competence
- Pedagogical features, integrated throughout the text, that make learning thorough, efficient, accessible, and challenge-based via a problem solving orientation

FEATURES TO SUPPORT THE THEMES

Theme 1: The Voices of People with Disabilities

Stories about people with disabilities appear throughout the text. They feature people taking their places in American society, participating in community programs, and facing everyday challenges. Many of these stories come to life through photos, such as those of Michael Henson, who was working in one of the Twin Towers on September 11, 2001. He and his dog, Roselle, helped many of his co-workers escape the building. We also meet Marla Runyan, a blind athlete who made the 2002 U.S. Olympic Team. And we watch Michael Naranjo, whose art opens Chapter 3, as he climbs the statue of David to "see" Michelangelo's creative masterpiece through his hands.

- **Chapter-Opening Art** Artistic masterpieces created by well-known artists (such as, van Gogh, Toulouse-Lautrec, Manet, and Munch) who have the exceptionality presented in the chapter. These beautiful works of art enable us to see the world from the perspectives of artists with special needs.

- **Personal Perspectives** Stories told by people with disabilities, by their family members, or by advocates open every chapter. These opening vignettes were written for this text by individuals willing to talk about the challenges they have faced, the solutions they have discovered, people who have made a difference in their lives, and their hopes and dreams for the future.

Theme 2: Current Policies, Issues, Research, and Validated Practices

This edition has been revised and updated substantially to reflect the most current issues, thinking, and knowledge base about students with special needs and the education they require. Emphasis is placed on methods and instructional procedures—along with examples of how these are implemented through practical classroom applications. Important changes in national policy are presented in this edition. Students are encouraged to think about the implications of

- *Recent legislation,* such as the No Child Left Behind Act of 2001
- The national call for accountability for students' academic progress through *high stakes testing* and *alternative assessments*
- The 2002 American Association on Mental Retardation (AAMR) *definition of mental retardation* and the implementation of *"systems of supports"*
- Efforts to reconceptualize learning disabilities through a new key feature or characteristic—*"resistance to treatment"*
- *Attention deficit/hyperactivity disorder* (ADHD) being called out as a disability or condition within the "other health impairments" category of special education, with some students qualifying for special services and others not
- Early identification of preschoolers at risk for *reading* problems, new interventions to correct phonological processing deficits in very young children, intensive efforts to treat *reading disabilities* in school children, and the development of *literacy* in youth with disabilities

 Chapter 12 on Autistic Spectrum Disorders (ASD) In 1997, Congress made autism a separate special education category when it renewed the Individuals with Disabilities Education Act (IDEA). The media and researchers have given autism and the other disorders included in ASD considerable attention recently. Topics that are currently of special interest range from different theories about the causes of autism, and the reasons for its increased prevalence, to the advantages of one treatment program over another. Accordingly, this edition allots a full chapter to ASD.

In Chapter 13, Coverage of Multiple Severe Disabilities An entirely new, major section in the chapter about very low incidence disabilities explains the special educational needs of students who have more than one significant disability. This chapter also covers traumatic brain injury (TBI) and deafblindnesss. Now, with the addition of multiple severe disabilities, all disability categories included in IDEA have comprehensive coverage.

- *What IDEA Says About . . .* These boxes, which are found throughout the text, summarize key requirements of the special education law, (IDEA) and how this important legislation affects policies and practices.

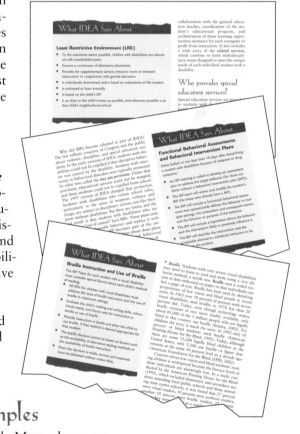

Theme 3: Practical Applications and Examples

The methods orientation of this edition has been strengthened. More classroom applications and examples help readers understand positive learning environments

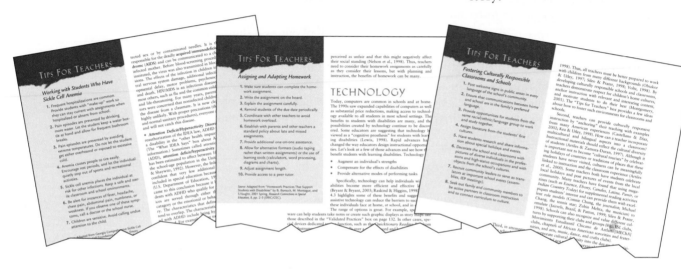

and how they are created. Illustrations of instructional procedures are woven into the text and highlighted through supporting boxes.

- **Achieving Discipline** These boxes provide different scenarios of classroom situations wherein a behavior problem needs to be resolved. Each presents a specific tactic that has proved effective in school settings. These boxes conclude with key steps involved in the application of the intervention described in the story.

NEW *Tips for Teachers* These boxes list simple, practical procedures to apply in specific teaching situations. The tactics selected, however, have broad applicability.

NEW *Validated Practices* These boxes focus on effective teaching methods that have been proved to benefit students with diverse learning needs across content areas (reading, reading comprehension, communication). Included in the boxed text are brief descriptions of the method, as well as step-by-step guidelines for implementing it in classroom settings. Whenever possible, an illustration of the tactic's execution is provided.

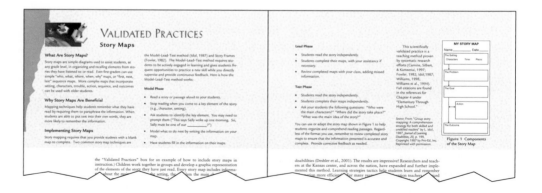

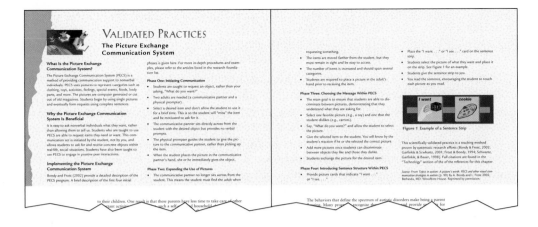

- ***Accommodating for Inclusive Environments*** These boxes give practical ideas for adapting or modifying instruction or adjusting the curriculum or the learning environment to enhance the success of students, with disabilities. Emphases is placed on the steps needed for effective integration of children with disabilities and improved access to the general education curriculum.

Theme 4: Cultural and Linguistic Diversity

The increasing diversity of America's schoolchildren presents both challenges and opportunities to those responsible for their education and to school systems. "Minority" students represent a majority in more and more school districts across the nation, and the number of schoolchildren who are not native speakers of English increases annually. These students and their families bring diverse cultures and perspectives to their learning environments, and educators have a great opportunity to tap this richness to enhance instruction. This edition is dedicated to helping teachers gain insight into special considerations that arise in the instruction of diverse students.

- This edition provides a full chapter on multicultural and bilingual special education.
- Topics related to correcting the overrepresentation of culturally and linguistically diverse learners with disabilities in special education, and their underrepresentation in programs for gifted students, are discussed throughout the text. These topics include

  Nondiscriminatory testing

  Cultural competence

  Fostering culturally sensitive learning environments to reduce these students' disproportional representation

Theme 5: Learning Aids Make for Efficient Mastery of Information

This edition incorporates many pedagogical aids designed to make the contents of this text more accessible, more engaging, and easier to master. Features, such as straightforward readability, consistency in organization, and inviting design enable students to focus on the most important material. Proven learning strategies are also incorporated into the text's conceptual design to help readers master the information presented. For example, the text incorporates a problem solving approach wherein students are challenged to think about current special education dilemmas and challenges and to consider possible solutions. This approach is especially notable in the "Opportunities for a Better Future" sections found at the beginning of each chapter. Also, to help students think critically, section headings are worded as questions that focus their attention on the essential points raised in the section that follows. Here are some highlights of these learning aids.

- *Standard Chapter Outlines* Chapters 3-13 are all organized into the following sections so that readers will always know what major topics to expect and exactly where to find information.

- Opportunities for a Better Future
- Definition
- History
- Prevalence
- Causes and Prevention
- Characteristics
- Early Childhood Education
- Elementary Through High School
- Collaboration for Inclusion
- Transition Through Adulthood
- Families
- Technology
- In Conclusion

- *Advance Organizers* Each chapter is introduced with an Overview and Self-Test Questions (five Focus Questions and a Challenge Question) that were designed to guide students' thinking as they read the chapter. These advance organizers are linked to a chapter summary, and bulleted answers to the Self-Test Questions are supplied at the end of each chapter as a study aid and for the purpose of reinforcing the chapter's content.

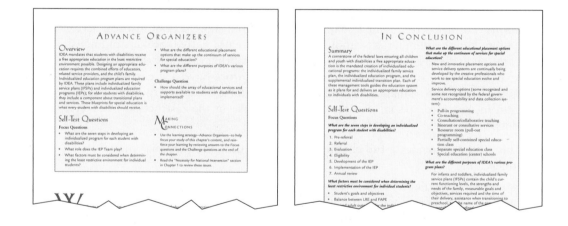

INTASC Principles and CEC Standards Another feature highlights important content. At the end of every chapter, information essential to meeting the professional standards and principles endorsed for entry-level teachers by two professional teacher associations—the Council for Exceptional Children

(CEC) and the Interstate New Teacher Assessment and Support Consortium (INTASC)—is presented and tied to the chapter's content. These principles and standards are those that influence the contents of the PRAXIS II™ and of many state-level licensure examinations for general education and special education teachers. General education teachers should pay particular attention to the INTASC principles, and special education teachers should focus on the CEC standards.

End-of-Chapter Film Critiques In the "Supplementary Resources" section of Chapters 3–13, brief descriptions and critiques of popular films, videos, and DVDs are found. The films included in these sections are readily available from video rental stores or from the Internet (e.g., amazon.com or moviesunlimited.com). In these films, a central character has the disability discussed in that chapter. In some cases, the portrayal is appropriate, but in other cases, for comparisons, the portrayal is insensitive or even cruel. One purpose of these sections is to draw students' attention to the impact that the media have on reinforcing or reducing stereotypes.

• *Making Connections* These marginal notations help students see the connections and relationships among ideas presented within and across chapters. These features provide a quick reminder that facts, information, and policies in special education are often related and are seldom confined to a particular disability.

COMPONENTS OF THE TEACHING PACKAGE

Our team has created a complete instructional package for this introduction to the field of special education[1]. The text is central to the course, and its supplements were created to support the text and the learning activities for the academic term. These supplements provide an outstanding array of resources that facilitate learning about students with disabilities and their families.

Resources for Instructors

• Online Web Resource Directory for Faculty. This searchable directory provides up-to-date listings of organizations' and agencies' web sites.

• Instructor's Resource Manual and Test Bank. The Instructor's Resource Manual includes a wealth of interesting ideas and activities designed to help instructors teach the course. Each chapter of the Manual includes: outline and lecture notes, discussion questions, web activities, handout masters (including case studies), and additional resources. The Test Bank includes hundreds of essay, multiple-choice, and true/false questions.

---

[1]For more information about the instructor and student supplements that accompany and support the text, ask your local Allyn and Bacon representative, or contact Allyn and Bacon, Sales Support Department.

- Computerized Test Bank. The printed Test Bank is also available electronically through the Allyn and Bacon computerized testing system: TestGen EQ. Instructors can use TestGen EQ to create exams in just minutes by selecting from the existing database of questions, editing questions, or writing original questions.

- PowerPoint™ Presentation. Ideal for lecture presentations or student handouts, the PowerPoint™ presentation created for this text provides dozens of ready-to-use graphic and text images (available on the Web at ablongman.com/ppt).

- The "Snapshots" Video Series for Special Education

- Snapshots: Inclusion Video (© 1995, 22 minutes in length). This profiles three students of differing ages and with various levels of disability in inclusive class settings. In each case, parents, classroom teachers, special education teachers, and school administrators talk about the steps they have taken to help the students succeed in inclusive settings.

- Snapshots 2: Video for Special Education (categorical organization) (© 1995, 20–25 minutes in length). This two-video set of six segments (traumatic brain injury, behavior disorders, learning disabilities, mental retardation, hearing impairments, and visual impairments) is designed specifically for use in college classrooms. Each segment profiles three individuals, and their families, teachers, and experiences. These programs are of high interest to students; instructors who have used the tapes in their courses have found that they help disabuse students of stereotypical viewpoints and put a "human face" on the course material.

- Professionals in Action Videotape: Teaching Students with Special Needs (© 2000, 120 minutes in length). This *Professionals in Action* video consists of five 15- to 30-minute modules presenting viewpoints and approaches to teaching students with various disabilities in general education classrooms, in separate education settings, and in various combinations of the two. Each module explores its topic via actual classroom footage and includes interviews with general and special education teachers, parents, and students themselves.

- Allyn and Bacon Transparencies for Special Education. This package includes 100 acetates, over half of which are full-color.

- Digital Media Archive for Special Education. This CD-ROM contains a variety of media elements that instructors can use to create electronic presentations in the classroom. It includes hundreds of original images, as well as selected art from Allyn and Bacon special education texts, providing instructors with a broad selection of graphs, charts, and tables. For classrooms with full multimedia capability, it also contains video segments and Web links.

Resources for Students

- Online Web Resource Directory for Students. This searchable directory provides up-to-date listings of organizations' and agencies' web sites.

- Study Guide. The Study Guide that accompanies the text contains proven learning strategies such as mnemonics, clustering information into main ideas, and study organizers. The Guide features numerous ways of helping students apply and practice what they have learned in the text, including: a timeline, define-the-terms activities, web activities, alphabet soup, mini case studies, practice tests, and crossword puzzles.

- Companion Website Plus. Students who visit the Companion Website that accompanies the text (ablongman.com/smith5e) will find many features and activities to help them in their studies: web links, learning activities, practice tests, video and audio clips, text correlations to national and state professional standards and the Praxis II™ exams, and vocabulary flash cards. The website also features an interactive Special Education Timeline that highlights the people and events that have shaped special education through history. The website also features Syllabus Manager, an online syllabus creation and management tool. Instructors can easily create syllabi with direct links to the companion website, links to other online resources, and student assignments. Students may access the syllabus at any time to help them with research projects and to complete the assignments.

- VideoWorkshop: A Course-Tailored Video Learning System. www.ablongman.com/videoworkshop
  VideoWorkshop for Special Education is a new way to bring video into your course for maximized learning. This total teaching and learning system includes quality video footage on an easy-to-use CD-ROM plus a Student Learning Guide and an Instructor's Teaching Guide—both with textbook-specific correlation grids. The result? A program that brings textbook concepts to life with ease and that helps your students understand, analyze, and apply the objectives of the course. VideoWorkshop is available for your students as a value-pack option with this textbook.

- "What's Best for Matthew?" Interactive CD-ROM Case Study for Learning to Develop IEPs, Version 2.0. This CD-ROM helps pre-service and in-service teachers develop their IEP writing skills through the case study of Matthew, a nine-year-old boy with autism. It is sold separately, and is also available at a reduced price as a "value package" with the textbook.

- Research Navigator™. Allyn & Bacon's new Research Navigator™ is the easiest way for students to start a research assignment or research paper. Complete with extensive help on the research process and three exclusive databases of credible and reliable source material, including EBSCO's ContentSelect Academic Journal Database, *New York Times* Search by Subject Archive, and "Best of the Web" Link Library, Research Navigator™ helps students quickly and efficiently make the most of their research time.

- iSearch Guide for Special Education (with Research Navigator™). This free reference guide includes tips, resources, activities, and URLs to help students use the Internet for their research projects. The first part introduces students to the basics of the Internet and the World Wide Web. Part II includes many Net activities that tie into the content of the text. Part III lists hundreds of special education Internet resources. Part IV outlines how to use the Research Navigator™ resources. The guide also includes information on how to cite research correctly and a guide to building an online glossary. Includes Access Code for Research Navigator™.

ACKNOWLEDGEMENTS

While it may take a village to raise a child, it definitely takes teams of villagers to create and produce an introductory textbook. The journey this revision took clearly drew every resource possible from individuals and teams from many "villages."

The Home Team

The support, work, and expertise of my Nashville team are incredible. Is there a word that exceeds "thanks?" My thesaurus doesn't show one, but clearly a new word is needed in the English language.

No one understands what it takes to write a text like this one better than the person who has to live with the writer along with the stress, the mess, and the missed events. Jim Smith, my husband and my Henry Higgins, has had to endure five such events, and to his credit complains remarkably little and seems proud of his Eliza almost all of the time. Naomi Chowdhuri Tyler coordinated the preparation of many of the supplements that accompany this text, created the Test Bank, and developed many of the activities included in the Instructor's and Students' Resource Manuals. We have worked together on many projects over quite a few years, and everything about Naomi is exceptionally outstanding. Everyone should be so lucky, and have such a friend and a colleague. Naomi, thanks. I also extend my appreciation to Kim Paulsen for writing the strand of Validated Practices boxes found in chapters 3 through 13; Ann Garfinkle who contributed to the chapter about autistic spectrum disorders, new to this edition; and Steve Smith who created and wrote the film critiques found at the end of chapters 3 through 13. Two non-Nashvilleans (maybe they should be honorary citizens) were members of this edition's home team: Nancy Halmhuber of Eastern Michigan University who researched and wrote the sections about how the text's content links to CEC and NTAS standards; and Rebecca Evers of Winthrop University who contributed the Video Workshop segments found at the end of most chapters.

My thanks is also extended to Amy Elleman who not only helped search out background information for several chapters, but also generated this edition's *Instructor's Resource Manual* and to Susan Saunders who improved upon previous editions of the *Students' Resource Manual*. Recognition for their excellence, acknowledgement for extraordinary dedication to me and this project, and my very special thanks is owed to some other wonderful people as well: Pamela Dismuke who helped prepare the manuscript for submission; Jen Vail, Katie Whelan, Clarissa Gaff and Steve Smith who assisted with reference list development and citation checking; and Merrilee Webb for ensuring that the agency and organization information found at the end of each chapter is accurate and as up-to-date as possible. Without the wonderful people at the Alliance and IRIS Projects at Peabody College at Vanderbilt University, work at my "real" jobs would have suffered and life would have been even nuttier than it was. For all of your help and support, my thanks: Janet Church, Clarissa Gaff, Judy Smith-Davis, Alicia Stark, Debbie Whelan, and Zina Yzquierdo. And, finally, but certainly not least, a special "hat's off" goes to the dedicated student workers whose attention to details guaranteed that references actually match citations, "lost" articles were only temporarily misplaced, location of that "very safe place" from where important figures and tables always eventually re-surfaced was remembered, and resource information was at my fingertips: Laura Burkhart, Kristen Quirk, and Mary Hamilton.

Members of the Peabody College of Vanderbilt University community demonstrated what true collegiality is all about, every academic should be so lucky to find themselves in such a supportive environment. My dean, Camilla Benbow, and my department chairperson, Dan Reschly, provide the support and leadership that creates such as climate. Also, I am blessed with many close friends and colleagues who were always standing by, ready to lend a hand, help make a connection, remember that reference, or offer needed guidance. In particular, I would like to mention just a few of these colleagues here at Vanderbilt who without hesitation went the very extra mile: Alfredo Artiles, Anne Corn, Lynn Fuchs, Doug Fuchs, Craig Kennedy, Kathleen Lane, Joe Wehby, and Mark Wolery.

Disability Advocates

Voices from the disability community—people with disabilities, their family members, and special education professionals—resonate throughout this text. They are heard most loudly in the Personal Perspective sections found at the beginning of each chapter. To those who so generously shared their individual stories and "spoke" for so many others, a special thanks is extended to: Norma Lopez-Reyna, Megan Askim, Amy Harris-Soloman, Jean Gibson, Tom Catron, Bethany Hoppe, Ann Corn, Susan

Acknowledgements

Saunders, Belinda Pandy, and Tom Hehir. And, thanks also goes to Lilly Cheng of San Diego State University who first told me the very special Starfish Story (which you find at the beginning of this text).

And, I'd like to share a little story about how this edition's effort introduced me to some incredible and generous people who give of themselves unselfishly. The half-time entertainment at a Vanderbilt Woman's basketball game was a local boy's team and their cheerleaders. The team was a group of wheelchair athletes from the A.B.L.E. program of Easter Seals of Nashville, and their cheerleaders were from the Music City Wheelcheerleaders (see pictures of both groups in Chapter 9). The director of the A.B.L.E. program and the boys' basketball coach, Rick Slaughter, took many of the photos included in this edition; Bethany Hoppe, the director of the cheerleaders, shared her story with you through the personal perspective that opens Chapter 9; and Lizzy B. is one of the cheerleaders in Bethany's troupe and her mom told their story at the beginning of Chapter 5. Besides being people who make real differences in the lives of individuals with disabilities and their families, they left their "footprints" on this edition while the thread of their connections bind this book.

Reviewers

I want to extend special appreciation to those professionals who assisted specifically with the development of this fifth edition by providing valuable input and reviews about the previous edition and ideas about new features that could be developed for this edition: Karen Ezaki, Mt. San Antonio College; Terry Jentsch, University of Idaho; Carolyn D. Boyles, University of North Carolina, Greensboro; Phyllis M. Robertson, University of Texas at Austin; Debra A. Ahola, Schenectady County Community College; Rayma Davis, Umpqua Community College; Peggy Reeder Moore, University of North Carolina at Charlotte; Barbara J. Davis, Olivet College; Sharon M. Daniels, Tennessee Tech. University; Kathleen M. Chinn, New Mexico State University; Thomas W. Willis, Tennessee Tech. University; Karen Bonewitz, Bethel College; Glenn Buck, Lynchburg College; Charles Neufiled, East Carolina University; Connie Lambert, Central Washington University; Festus E. Obiakor, University of Wisconsin—Milwaukee; James M. Alarid, New Mexico Highlands University; Carol Hughes, Brigham Young University—Idaho; Helen Brantley, South Carolina State University; Su-Je Cho, University of Hartford; Cheryle Crosby, Delta State University; Susan Leonard-Giesen, California State University, Long Beach; Deborah Metcalf, East Carolina University; Annette Oliver, Florida A&M University; Sheila Pemberton, Tennessee Technological University; David A. Powers, East Carolina University; Janice Seabrooks, University of North Florida; John Venn, University of North Florida; Kristine Webb, University of North Florida; Moon K. Chang, Alabama State University; Bobbie Sferra, Scottsdale Community College; Holy Pae, University of South Carolina Spartanburg; Dan Fennerty, Central Washington University; Vernon L. Clark, The University of the District of Columbia; Nancy T. Cupolo, Hudson Valley Community College.

The Allyn and Bacon Team

Once again, the team at Allyn and Bacon exceeded expectations for expertise and support. The development of this edition was fraught with challenges beyond what could ever be imagined. Without the incredible support and extra assistance from these fantastic, wonderful folks, who knows what jibberish you all would be reading! Virginia Lanigan—friend, colleague, and editor (and yes, those three words can go together, even though Somerset Maugham would disagree)—paved the way and guided the process needed to achieve the high standards and excellent product you find in this text and its supplements. It is an honor and always a learning experience to collaborate with Elaine Ober of Allyn and Bacon, production manager, who treated the development of this edition as if it were "her own" authored work. Elaine immediately caught my vision and added her creativity and sense of aesthetics to the project; the outcome is wonderful and apparent.

How can you ever thank enough the person who answers e-mails and telephone calls on evenings, weekends, and holidays; is always cheerful, even when things seem impossible; solves problems and doesn't ever create them; quickly gets questions answered; and is also a heck of a lot of fun to work with? Well, maybe these sentences do so in some small way. If any of you elect to create a personal nightmare and write an intro text, may you have a developmental editor as wonderful as Alicia Reilly.

Toward the end of a big book project like this one, nothing is more important to an author than to work with a production packager who is professional and efficient, attends to details from the beginning to the end, is available, always pleasant and positive we'll make that next important deadline, and is tireless. Barbara Gracia sets the highest quality standard for those in her business. Barbara and I have become a real team; one that works together well because we respect each other to the highest level. Barbara, once again, thanks. And, to those wonderful people who made this edition interesting to look at and easier for you to use, I thank them on your behalf. Connie Day, copy editor, who did an outstanding and thorough job to make this edition clear. Helene Prottas, photo researcher, took my sketchy ideas and found illustrations that were obviously just what I imagined. She also followed her own creative lead and enhanced this edition immeasurably with wonderful photos that tell important stories about children with disabilities and their families. Carolyn Deacy beautifully designed this edition, and Deborah Schneck and her team executed it well. At the end of the day, you have what we all hope is an enticing, inviting, and contemporary text that provides you with up-to-date content, where you hear the voices of the disability community, and you understand what it takes to make provide a good and effective education to students with disabilities.

Deborah Deutsch Smith

My career in special education is long, beginning when I was a teenager. What has sustained me over the years is the excitement of watching a child with disabilities achieve an important goal, perform a task that seemed impossible to accomplish only a few weeks before, and share a funny happening with everyone in class. In no way would I intend to minimize disabilities, but I also would not describe them as so complex and difficult that many cannot be compensated for or even reduced. One important message I want to convey is that people with disabilities can assume their places, alongside people without significant disabilities, in modern society when special education is truly special. May a child's laughter and joy over an accomplishment entice you, too, to devote your career to the field of disabilities as it did me.

Another message is that every school, not just isolated examples, are places where all children—those with and without disabilities—are engaged and excited by learning. Schools should be places where students learn with and from each other, helped by excellent teachers and other professionals—places where families are integral to the educational process and their famiy traditions, culture, and language are respected and reflected in educational programs. I realize that this vision is just that: a vision of what schools should and could be.

Lilly Cheng of San Diego State University often tells the following story. Think of the possibilities if each of us stops to save just one starfish!

An old man was walking on a beach one morning and saw some movements from a distance. He was very curious about the movements and as he walked closer, he saw a young girl picking something from the beach and throwing it into the ocean. When he got very near, he saw that the girl was throwing starfish that had washed up on the beach into the ocean. The old man said to the girl, "The sun is out and there are hundreds of starfish on the beach. You can't save them all. They'll all perish." The young girl picked up one more starfish, and while she was throwing the starfish into the ocean, she said, "This one won't."

Vincent van Gogh, *Self-Portrait with Bandaged Ear.*
Courtauld Institute Galleries, London. Giraudon/Art Resource, NY.

VINCENT VAN GOGH, the son of a Dutch pastor, was drawn to
the pulpit early in life. At the same time, his three uncles who
were very active in the art world also influenced him. His many
remaining letters give much insight into his early career indecision
and his continuing loneliness, melancholy, and emotional disturbance. Yet the impact and beauty of his most productive artistic
life are almost beyond comparison (Murdoch, 1998; Walther &
Metzger, 1993).

Van Gogh left many self-portraits. This painting, *Self-Portrait
with Bandaged Ear* (1889) is one made during the last years of his
life, and sends a message about his state of well-being.

1 The Context of Special Education

A Time of Opportunity

A PERSONAL PERSPECTIVE

My Turn

Toward the beginning of every chapter in this text you will find a section called "A Personal Perspective." A person with a special need, a family member of an individual with disabilities, or a professional who has devoted his or her career to special education wrote each story. I took the opportunity to share my own perspective in this opening chapter.

I began working with children with disabilities as a teenage volunteer. The Individuals with Disabilities Education Act (IDEA)—the law that guarantees children with disabilities a right to a free appropriate education—had not yet been passed, and many such children were denied access to schools. It is hard to believe today that not so long ago, parents were turned away from schools and told that "no children like yours go to school in this district." But it's true! It was commonplace for children who were not toilet trained, or could not walk, or could not talk, or acted very differently to be excluded. Many states in the late 1960s and early 1970s had "permissive" education laws. (Permissive education meant that school districts did not have to provide schooling to all of their students with disabilities.) This is when I began in special education, and it was a time of great energy because there were so many "wrongs" to be "righted" and so many opportunities to make a difference. Special education was a movement, and the excitement surrounding it was irresistible.

As a teenager, I volunteered at a private school specifically for children with learning disabilities, the Marianne Frostig School in Los Angeles. After earning a bachelor's degree in psychology from Pitzer College, I pursued general and special education teaching certificates at California State University–Northridge. Instead of taking a job, I accepted a fellowship at the University of Missouri–Columbia and received a master's degree in special education. Soon after that, I enrolled in a doctoral program at the University of Washington in Seattle.

Those of us training at that time learned from very different models of special education. My field experience, student teaching, internship, and teaching assignments were in self-contained special education classes, many of which were housed in separate special education schools. Some of these programs were even considered experimental, because they served students who at that time were not typically provided education in the public system. One was even housed in an old rural farmhouse where nearly all of the students traveled long distances from the same city to attend school out in the country. All the children who participated in that program were toilet trained and able to walk; those who did not meet these requirements either stayed home or went to institutions.

By the end of the 1970s, battles about the rights of children with disabilities to a public education were won. Such students now had a right to an education in public school systems across the nation. Still, for many, coming to school meant attending separate schools far from home or separate classes in portable buildings erected on the back side of playgrounds. Since then, parents and professionals have advocated for more integrated settings and for an education better suited to each child with a disability. While some focused on placement issues, I concentrated on instruction. I decided that my contribution would be to prepare new university faculty members who would generate knowledge about instructional methods, and to train special education teachers who would implement quality education programs for children with disabilities. I am also a committed advocate for culturally and linguistically diverse children with disabilities and their very special educational needs.

With the same passion I felt as a teenager, I remain committed to the concept of special education today. Individual-ized instruction and special techniques (proven through years of systematic research and application) do make a real difference in the outcomes of students with disabilities. Many more adults with disabilities are able to participate fully in American society because of the educational experiences they received. I continue to be excited about the future and the possibilities it holds. I hope the stories you read this academic term—written by people with disabilities, their family members, and friends—will engage you. Possibly, the challenges faced by students with disabilities and those who work with them will attract you to this exciting field. And maybe the knowledge that you can make a real difference in the lives of people will convince you, as it did me so long ago, that special education is a wonderful career opportunity. Please share my enthusiasm for the field of special education, the education of students with disabilities, and the people who constitute this community.

1. **Why do you think students with disabilities were excluded from schools?**

2. **What do you think the future holds for students and for adults with disabilities?**

ADVANCE ORGANIZERS

Overview

Special education and the related services it provides to students and families with disabilities, have become controversial, even contentious. Special education was developed to help students with disabilities gain the skills and knowledge they will need as adults to participate alongside people without disabilities in mainstream society. And special education has made a real difference in the lives of children and youth with disabilities and in the lives of their families. However, it has received criticism for not meeting all its goals, for being too expensive, for being a major source of discipline problems at schools, for discriminating against the very students it is meant to help, and for being administratively burdensome. The time is right to resolve these problems and make special education truly special.

Self-Test Questions

Focus Questions

- What does it mean to have a disability?
- Where did special education come from, and why did it develop?

- Why did the federal government and the public call for national intervention?
- What are some defining features of special education?
- Why is special education controversial?

Challenge Question

- What are some solutions to problems faced by students with disabilities and the educators charged with meeting their needs?

Making Connections

- Use the learning strategy—Advance Organizers—to help focus your study of this chapter's content, and reinforce your learning by reviewing answers to the Focus questions and the Challenge questions at the end of the chapter.

- Beginning with Chapter 2, the "Opportunities for a Better Future" sections should help you think about how the problems of special education can be solved.

D espite great advances in results experienced by children with disabilities and their families, special education has been criticized for some time as being immoral, ineffective, racist, too costly, and inequitable (Berman et al., 2001; Finn, Rotherham, & Hokanson, 2001; Gartner & Lipsky, 1987; Lyon et al., 2001; Stainback et al., 1994; Townsend & Patton, 2001). Very public attacks are mounted on all fronts, leveled by politicians, family members of students with disabilities, people with disabilities themselves, members of the press, and the entire education community. Debates about special education's effectiveness—who should receive special education services, how and where they should be delivered, and who should deliver them—rage. Concerns about the number of America's children identified as having disabilities and the number failing at school have surfaced. Policy makers and advocates have been alerted to the disproportionate number of students of color who are identified as having disabilities and are consequently educated as special education students. Although agreement has not been reached about what actions to take to address special education's problems, many professionals, members of the press, and the disability community believe its problems can be solved (Clayton, 2001). To respond intelligently to such charges will require deliberation and informed debate.

Across this academic term, consider and then consider again questions raised about the education of students with disabilities, and try to form your own conclusions about the merits of what we as a society call special education. At first glance, many of these questions seem simple and straightforward, but resist the temptation to be deceived by that illusion. They are complicated and complex. Resist the tendency to think in terms of "black and white," to assume that all questions can be answered "yes or no," and to expect debate issues to be clearly articulated "on one side or the other." Remember, people and cultures have different perspectives on complex issues. None of us truly lives in a world of black and white; for most issues, we live in "gray-space." As Hungerford wisely pointed out over half a century ago, "only the brave dare look upon the gray—upon the things which cannot be explained easily" (1950, p. 417). Take the time to ponder all possibilities as you spend the academic term developing your own understanding of special education and the students and families it serves. As we ponder these important issues, let's not lose sight of the fact that we are thinking about people, people who are important members of society.

THE ESSENCE OF DISABILITIES

To be an active participant in improving outcomes for students with disabilities, it is important to understand the services that students with disabilities and their families need. One place to begin is to think about the concept of disability and the challenges it can present.

What is a disability?

You might think that a question like "What is a disability?" has a simple and straightforward answer. It does not. Nothing is absolute in the human condition, and not all concepts are consistent across cultures. Many answers have been suggested to resolve this question. Definitions of disability differ because of differences in attitudes, beliefs, orientation, discipline, and culture. For example, different disciplines offer different definitions of disabilities; some definitions include analyses of a group of individuals' common characteristics (e.g., cognitive abilities, stereotypic behaviors). Other perspectives take a more sociological view and present differences as socially constructed—as more a function of the social system than of the individual (Danforth & Rhodes, 1997; Longmore, 2002).

Explanations of the concept of disability vary, as do opinions on whether disability must always impair a person's ability to participate in mainstream society. Some concepts of disability hold that disability would disappear if society were organized some other way. Evidence from other cultures, such as many American

M AKING C ONNECTIONS

In every chapter about an exceptionality, you will find a section devoted to definitions.

Indian cultures, supports this position (Jim Green, 2002 February, personal communication). Why would the response to disability be different across cultures? Some scholars propose that the concept of disabilities is a political and economic necessity of societies that require a class structure (Erevelles, 1996; Grossman, 1998). Other scholars do not accept the position that disability is the result of a stratified society and reject the idea that everyone should be treated alike (Kauffman, 1997). According to Jim Kauffman, an extreme need for "sameness" forces people to minimize disability—even to deny its existence. Another explanation is people's need to focus on the concept of "difference" and the related necessity of making value judgments (Artiles, 1998). And yet another explanation for the way people with disabilities are treated in American society is institutional discrimination and bias (Longmore, 2002).

Simple questions do not always have simple answers. Think about these points by comparing the terms often used to describe or refer to disability: able–disabled, normal–abnormal, typical–atypical, perfect–defective, functioning–dysfunctional, usual–unusual, ordinary–exceptional. The terms we use reflect how we think about disabilities and send clear messages to the individuals involved.

Is having a disability necessarily a handicap?

We learned from the civil rights movements of the 1960s that discrimination and bias can "handicap" groups of individuals, or keep them from participating fully in society. A discussion about the relationship between disabilities and being handicapped is not only an important concept but an interesting one as well. The way people are treated can limit their independence and opportunities. But we are still left with the question of whether the terms *disability* and *handicap* are synonymous. If they are, disability could then be viewed as a difference, a characteristic that sets an individual apart from everyone else, something that makes the individual less able or inferior. Many professions (medicine, psychology) view disabilities in terms of deviance—a model whereby the majority of the population is considered normal and a disability sets the individual apart. In that view, it is the disability that restricts an individual's ability to reach his or her potential, rather than the individual being handicapped by society's attitudes. And what of gifted individuals with exceptional talents and outstanding intellect? Do people's attitudes about their differences handicap them and prevent them from achieving their potential?

Some evidence exists that may help resolve this dilemma, or may blur the issue even more. Read the story, in the box about the settlers of Martha's Vineyard, of deaf Americans who were not stigmatized by their immediate society (Groce, 1985). Unencumbered by bias, they exhibited rates of success and failure similar to everyone else's, showing that how people are treated does influence their lives.

Now, however, we must consider whether the experience of the early settlers of Martha's Vineyard is an aberration. Is it so peculiar that we should not generalize from this case to other situations? Perhaps the story would have been different if these early settlers had had a genetically caused cognitive disability instead of deafness. Clearly, what happened at Martha's Vineyard was not commonplace. Regardless, it is information you should consider as you develop your own perspective on disability, its meaning, its impact, and its implications for social response. Thinking about the Martha's Vineyard experience, is it possible that disability and a response to it—special education—are phenomena of the twentieth century?

Is the notion of disabilities a modern-day invention?

The answer to this question is quite straightforward: No. Evidence abounds that disabilities are part of the human condition. The earliest written records note the existence of people with disabilities. Some, particularly those who were blind, or deaf,

MAKING CONNECTIONS

For other discussions about Deaf Culture and its history, see the "History of the Field" and "Deaf Culture" sections of Chapter 10.

MAKING CONNECTIONS

To learn more about how people with disabilities have been treated across time, see the "History of the Field" sections in Chapters 3—13.

CHAPTER 1 *The Context of Special Education*

DISABILITY DOES NOT EQUAL HANDICAP: THE CASE OF MARTHA'S VINEYARD

The 17th-Century settlers of Martha's Vineyard came from Kent, England. Apparently, they carried with them both a recessive gene for deafness and the ability to use sign language. The hearing people living on the island were bilingual, developing their oral and sign language skills simultaneously early in life. Generation after generation, the prevalence of deafness on the island was exceptionally high, being 1:4 in one small community and 1:25 in several others. Probably because deafness occurred at such a high rate and in almost everyone's family, people who were deaf were not treated like deaf people who lived on the mainland. They were integrated into society and were included in all of the community's work and play situations.

So what were the results of such integration and of society's adapting to the needs of people with this disability, rather than requiring them to adapt to the ways of those without it? These individuals were free to marry whomever they wished. Of those born before 1817, 73% of the Vineyard Deaf* married, whereas only 45% of deaf Americans married. Only 35% of the Vineyard Deaf married other deaf people, compared to 79% of deaf mainlanders. According to tax records, they generally earned average or above-average incomes, and some Deaf people became quite wealthy. Also, these individuals were active in all aspects of church affairs. Deaf individuals did have some advantages over their hearing neighbors and family members. They were better educated than the general population because they received tuition assistance to attend the school for the deaf in Connecticut. According to the reports of their descendants, these people were able to read and write, and there are numerous accounts about hearing people asking their Deaf neighbors to read something to them or write a letter for them.

The story of the English settlers on Martha's Vineyard shows how deafness, a disability historically considered to be extremely serious, did not affect the way of life or achievement of those who lived on the island. For more than two hundred years, life in this relatively restricted and

*A capital D is used here because the Deaf people on Martha's Vineyard represent an important historical group in Deaf culture. See Chapter 10.

Thomas Hart Benton often spent his summers on Martha's Vineyard where some of his neighbors were the Deaf residents of the island. Two of them appear in this painting.

Thomas Hart Benton, *The Lord Is My Sheperd*, 1926. Tempera on canvas. 33 × 27 3/8 in. (84.46 × 69.53 cm) Whitney Museum of Art, New York; purchase 31.100. Photograph copyright © 1996: Whitney Museum of American Art, New York. © T. H. Benton and R. P. Benton Testamentary Trust/Licensed by VAGA, New York, N.Y. Photo by Robert E. Mates

confined environment was much the same for those who had this disability and those who did not. Groce (1985) provides an explanation:

> The most striking fact about these deaf men and women is that they were not handicapped, because no one perceived their deafness as a handicap. As one woman said to me, "You know we didn't think anything special about them. They were just like anyone else. When you think about it, the Island was an awfully nice place to live." Indeed it was. (p. 110)

or "a bit eccentric," or who acquired their disability while adults, fared well and are part of the written record (Bragg, 1997). In fact, some (such as Aesop, the blind Greek poet of ancient times) were respected as wise. Aesop's morality lessons—Aesop's fables—are still read in schools today. Is it possible that disabilities do not signal a social problem worthy of concern? Could it be that the important issue is not whether disabilities exist but, rather, how people react to them? If people are treated fairly and can realize their potential without considerable support from others, maybe as a society we are expending considerable energy where it is not necessary. So let's examine how people with disabilities have been treated historically. This analysis might also help us better understand the nature of disabilities, and the situation in which people with disabilities find themselves.

How have people with disabilities been treated over the course of history?

The answer to this question is inconsistently, but often badly. As you have learned, examples of humane treatment can be documented. Here's another perspective to consider: People with disabilities served as court jesters in palaces and royal courts of the Middle Ages and Renaissance. Although we might think they were unfairly treated because they were kept for the amusement of royalty, they were protected, and they lived better than most common people of their times. Was this situation good or bad? Typically, however, people with disabilities were victims of discrimination and cruelty. It was common practice to leave defective babies in the woods or to throw them into rivers to die. For most who lived to adulthood, their treatment was harsh. For example, Balbus Balaesus the Stutterer, who lived during ancient Roman times, was caged and displayed along the Appian Way to amuse travelers who thought his speech was funny. Some people with disabilities were locked away in asylums or monasteries; others were thought to be possessed by demons, and some were tried as witches (Bragg, 1997).

You might think that such stories are confined to ancient history. Certainly, many people with disabilities are included in today's mainstream society. They now have access to public buildings, find suitable accommodations when they travel, and assume active roles in society. Unfortunately, modern history does not offer only positive stories. For example, around the middle of the last century, Nazi Germany sent millions of Jews, people with disabilities, and members of other targeted groups to their deaths in concentration camps. But that was over 50 years ago; certainly, you might think, such inhumane acts no longer occur. Well, many documented cases of abuse and neglect of children with disabilities do occur today. Exposé after exposé, particularly in Third World and developing countries (including members of the former Soviet union) reveals horrible conditions in orphanages and institutions where imperfect children are kept until they die (Bennett, 1997; Powell & Dlugy, 1998). However, inhumane treatment of people with disabilities is not just a problem that arises in other countries. Think about adults in the United States with mental illness who are left to wander the streets, have few supports to assist them, and remain in jail for nuisance crimes.

As you construct a concept of disabilities, think about the information

Without guarantees of civil and human rights around the world, many children with disabilities are forced to live in deplorable conditions. Such treatment is not "a thing-of-the past."

CHAPTER 1 *The Context of Special Education*

you can use to advocate for good solutions, and consider what educational programs should include, keep in mind the following:

1. Definitions of disability vary across cultures because people do not share the same attitudes, beliefs, orientation, discipline, and culture. Thus there is not an absolute nature to disabilities.

2. Bias and discrimination influence people's **outcomes** in such a way that what is thought of as a severe disability in one society might not handicap a person's efforts to achieve his or her potential in another society.

3. Disabilities have existed since the beginning of time. They are not a construct or phenomenon created by current American society.

4. The plight for many children with disabilities has been terrible, and cruel treatment continues today.

ORIGINS OF SPECIAL EDUCATION

Although many Americans believe that special education began in the United States in 1975 with the passage of the national law we now call IDEA, special education actually began over 200 years ago.

How did special education begin?

The legend of special education's beginnings is not only famous, it's true! A short synopsis of the story of Itard and Victor is presented in the accompanying box. Although Itard did not evaluate his long-term efforts with Victor positively, his work did spawn a new era for children with disabilities. His work heralded the beginning of a positive period when education was thought to be one answer to the problems associated with disabilities.

Edouard Seguin, a student of Itard, brought the movement to the United States. In 1846 Seguin published *The Moral Treatment, Hygiene, and Education of Idiots and Other Backward Children*, the first special education treatise addressing the needs of children with disabilities. He believed that sensorimotor exercises could help stimulate learning for children with disabilities (a belief that has alternately gained and lost popularity ever since). In 1876 Sequin also helped found the oldest and largest interdisciplinary professional association in the field of mental retardation, which is now called the American Association on Mental Retardation (AAMR). Attitudes gradually changed. Professionals and the public shifted from the belief that people with disabilities should be shunned to the position that they should be protected, cared for, and instructed, even if it took an extraordinary effort, to the concept that they should be unfettered and empowered and should take their places alongside peers without disabilities, even if it means hardship and challenges. For example, Paul Marchant, of The Arc (an organization founded by parents to advocate for services for their children with mental retardation) believes that today all segregated work settings for people with disabilities should be closed, even if individuals with disabilities would prefer to work in isolated placements (personal communication, October 22, 2001). He believes this even though some adults with disabilities find it more comfortable to work alongside other people with disabilities in settings where the climate is more nurturing and supportive than in competitive business places of work. What do you think about this idea?

While the special education effort gained steam in the United States, it also became popular across Europe. In Italy, Montessori worked first with children with

MAKING CONNECTIONS

For more on the importance of Itard and Victor, see the "History of the Field" section of Chapter 6.

THE ORIGINS OF SPECIAL EDUCATION:
THE STORY OF ITARD AND VICTOR

In 1799 a young child, who had probably been left to die in the woods of southern France because he was "defective," was found by some farmers. These farmers were concerned about the child's welfare and had heard of a doctor in Paris who was specializing in the treatment of deaf children. They took the child to this physician, Jean-Marc-Gaspard Itard, who is now considered to be the father of special education. Itard named the young boy Victor, but because he was thought to be a "wild child," untouched by civilization, he was often referred to as the Wild Boy of Aveyron. It is likely that he had mental retardation as well as environmental deprivation. Most people thought the case was hopeless. But Itard, believing in the power of education, took on the task of teaching Victor all the things that typical children learn from their families and in school. He used carefully designed techniques to teach Victor to speak a few words, to walk upright, to eat with dishes and utensils, and to interact with other people.

Fortunately, Itard wrote detailed reports of his techniques and his philosophy, as well as of Victor's progress. Many of these techniques are still used in modern special education. Here are Itard's five aims for Victor's "mental and moral education."

First aim: To interest him in social life ...

Second aim: To awaken his nervous sensibility ...

Third aim: To extend the range of his ideas ...

Fourth aim: To lead him to the use of speech ...

Fifth aim: To make him exercise the simplest mental operations ...

(*Itard*, 1806/1962, pp. 10–11)

Measures of success are subjective. Today we would credit Itard with the achievement of making great gains with Victor. Victor learned many basic skills of life, but he never became "normal." He was unable to develop oral language beyond a few words, and he did not learn all forms of socially acceptable behavior. Itard thought himself a failure, perhaps because his goals were unrealistic, and Victor lived out his life on Itard's country estate with a housekeeper attending to his needs.

Jean-Marc-Gaspard Itard, considered the father of special education, kept a detailed diary on his teaching of Victor.

Victor, the wild boy of Aveyron, contributed to the development of special education theory and techniques as a student of Itard.

CHAPTER 1 *The Context of Special Education*

cognitive disabilities. She showed that children could learn at young ages through concrete experiences offered in environments rich in manipulative materials. In 1817 Thomas Hopkins Gallaudet went to Europe to bring experts in deaf education back to the United States to implement model education programs. Samuel Gridley Howe, the famous American reformer and abolitionist, founded the New England Asylum for the Blind (later the Perkins Institute) in 1832 and created the Massachusetts School for Idiotic and Feeble-Minded Children in 1848. And so it continued: In state after state, educational programs for students with disabilities were initiated. Many of these programs followed Howe's and Gallaudet's model and established residential schools; others followed the example of those begun by Elizabeth Farrell (1898), offering programs for students with disabilities in public schools. Regardless, the 1800s were exciting and represented a positive change in the attitudes encountered by many students with disabilities and their families.

Have special education opportunities been consistently available?

Like most of us today, professionals in the late 19th Century believed in the individual worth of each student, regardless of that student's special learning needs. They were prepared to work hard to make achievement a reality for all students. And it became widely accepted that special education teachers needed special training to do this important work. The first training opportunity for teachers of special classes was offered in 1905 at the New Jersey Training School for Feebleminded Boys and Girls (Kanner, 1964). In 1907 the tuition for a 6-week summer course in special education was $25. (See Figure 1.1.)

The era of optimism, however, did not last. Public school classes were not widespread, and residential schools took on the nature of repressive institutions. To develop a lasting vision about the education of students with disabilities, it might help to understand the reasons for these shifting attitudes. First, there were not enough classes. Second, many children were excluded from public schools because they did not meet entrance criteria—because they were not toilet trained, could not walk, or could not speak. What happened to them? Many functioned to some degree in their home communities, rarely found employment, and lived with their parents. Others were forced to enter isolated, segregated institutions. Certainly, some died from lack of care, and others were hidden by families fearing discrimination and prejudice.

Although the residential schools established at the end of the 19th Century were considered "educational," they became warehouses where people were isolated from society. Possibly, like Itard, professionals and the public grew disillusioned about special education, for it was unable to "remove" disabilities, "cure" children, or make them "normal." Children with disabilities apparently were not worthy of investment. Rather, people with disabilities came to be viewed as the source of problems in society: one source of crime, a group that could bring society down (Winzer, 1993). Negative beliefs about people with disabilities took hold in the first decades of the 20th Century. Children without disabilities were now required to attend school under compulsory school attendance laws, but children with disabilities were prevented from attending school. The excuses presented for excluding these children from school are shocking by today's standards. One state supreme court justified excluding a young boy with cerebral palsy because he "produces a depressing and nauseating effect upon the teachers and school children" (*State ex rel. Beattie* v. *Board of Education*, 1919).

Bias against people with disabilities lasted throughout the first half of the 20th Century. The purpose of residential special education programs had changed; it no longer was to provide intensive education. From the beginning of the 20th Century

MAKING CONNECTIONS

For more stories of these and other special education pioneers, see the "History of the Field" sections in each chapter, beginning with Chapter 3.

Figure 1.1 Newsletter from the Training School in Vineland, New Jersey.

The Training School

Entered March 14, 1904, at Vineland, N. J., as second-class matter,
under act of Congress of July 16, 1894.

No. 36.　　　FEBRUARY 1907.　　　25c. per Annum.

*"I gave a beggar from my little store
Of well-earned gold. He spent the
　　　shining ore
And came again, and yet again, still
　　　cold
　　　And hungry as before.*

*I gave a thought and through that
　　　thought of mine
He found himself a man, supreme,
　　　divine,
Bold, clothed, and crowned with bless-
　　　ings manifold,
　　　And now he begs no more."*

THE SUMMER SCHOOL FOR TEACHERS.

The announcements of our Summer School for 1907 are now ready for distribution. The purpose of the School is to give professional training to those who desire to teach in the special classes in the public schools and to fit teachers and others to better understand peculiar, backward and "special" children. We have unusual facilities for this work, a splendid general equipment and quite a complete laboratory. The plan of work includes observation and teaching, laboratory work, lectures and reading. The tuition fee is $25 and those students who first apply may be boarded at the School at an additional cost of $25. The course extends from July 15th to August 24th.

Information concerning the Summer School may be obtained by addressing E. R. Johnstone, Vineland, N. J.

AS IT APPEARS TO THE PSYCHOLOGIST.

You remember the fable of the lion looking at the picture of a man conquering a lion and saying: "if a lion had painted the picture the man would have gotten the worst of it." It makes a difference who paints the picture.

Men strong of intellect have for long had a monopoly of painting the picture of the feeble-minded. While at times the feeble-minded child has been regarded as a supernatural being possessed of a spirit either good or bad, he has been among the more intellectual races more often treated much as the Spartans treated him—regarded as an outcast and either exposed to die or, where some reverence for human life as such has developed, been preserved from death indeed, but preserved for a life that is possibly worse than death. He has been not only useless, but a drag on society, an incurable disease, a horrible nightmare, one of God's blunders.

But how would the picture look if the lion and not the man painted it?

The feeble-minded child is a human being. He differs from those who call themselves normal, in degree, not in kind. No one of us but might have been of his grade had any one of a score of very possible contingencies taken place. Not one of us but might tomorrow become as "defective" as any of these by the slightest change in our organism. (It is true we should call it insanity, but that is only a matter of terminology.)

What then are we and who is this child? He is somewhere near the

MAKING CONNECTIONS

For more about the 20th Century reaction to people with disabilities and how they were shunned, see the "History of the Field" section of Chapter 6.

until the end of World War II, the primary purpose of institutions was to protect society from those who were different.

Thankfully, attitudes changed again during the last half of the 20th Century. The end of World War II saw a time of increased opportunities for all Americans, eventually leading to the civil rights movement of the 1960s and to advocacy for people with disabilities during the 1970s. Concern about how to guarantee fair treatment to people with disabilities—and to those who are gifted as well—then emerged.

Table 1.1 Landmark Court Cases That Set the Stage for the National Special Education Law

Case	Date	Ruling	Importance
Brown v. *Board of Education*	1954	Ended White "separate but equal" schools	Basis for future rulings that children with disabilities cannot be excluded from school
Pennsylvania Association for Retarded Children (PARC) v. *Commonwealth of Pennsylvania*	1972	Guaranteed special education to children with mental retardation	Court case that signaled a new era for special education
Mills v. *Board of Education of the District of Columbia*	1972	Extended the right to special education to all children with disabilities	Reinforced the right of all children with disabilities to a free public education

NECESSITY FOR NATIONAL INTERVENTION

By 1975 the stage was clearly set for a national special education law. Before then, the courts had been dealing with issues of discrimination and people's civil rights, and concerns about unfair treatment of children with disabilities and their access to education were being brought to the courts and legislatures state by state. Table 1.1 summarizes early landmark court cases that prepared the way for national special education consistently offered to all children with disabilities.

Why did Congress pass a national special education law?

Years of exclusion, segregation, and denial of basic educational opportunities to students with disabilities and their families made imperative a national civil rights law guaranteeing these students access to the education system. Why was this so? In 1948 only 12 percent of all children with disabilities received special education (Ballard, Ramirez, & Weintraub, 1982). As late as 1962, only 16 states had laws that included students with even mild mental retardation under mandatory school attendance requirements (Roos, 1970). In most states, even those children with the mildest levels of disabilities were not allowed to attend school. Children with more severe disabilities were routinely excluded.

Clearly, Congress, when first considering passage of a national special education law, recognized the importance of special education for children with disabilities. It was also concerned about widespread discrimination. It pointed out that many students with disabilities were excluded from education and that frequently, those who did attend school failed to benefit because their disabilities went undetected or ignored. Congress realized that special education, with proper financial assistance and educational support, could make a positive difference in the lives of these children and their families. Here are some of the findings that compelled Congress to pass a national law:

- One million of the children with disabilities in the U.S. were excluded entirely from the public school system.
- More than half of the eight million children with disabilities in the U.S. were not receiving appropriate educational services.
- The special educational needs of these children were not being fully met because they were not receiving necessary related services.

- The lack of adequate services within the public school system forced families to find services outside the public school system, often at great distance from their residence and at their own expense.
- Given appropriate funding, state and local educational agencies could provide effective special education and related services to meet the needs of children with disabilities.

What federal laws protect the civil rights of children and adults with disabilities?

The nation's policymakers reacted to injustices by passing laws to protect the civil rights of individuals with disabilities. The first law was part of a larger act. In 1973 Congress passed **Section 504 of the Rehabilitation Act**, which required accommodations, such as access to public buildings, for people with disabilities. Section 504 also set the stage for IDEA, because it included some protection of the rights of students with disabilities to public education. Most other laws address children's rights to an education separately from laws that address adults' civil rights and access to American society. Table 1.2 lists some of the important laws, or **legislation**, passed by Congress.

Congress decided that all children with disabilities should be guaranteed an appropriate education and that a national law was necessary to ensure that this

Table 1.2 Landmark Legislation

Date	Number of Law or Section	Name (and any Abbreviation)	Key Provisions
1973	Section 504	Section 504 of the Rehabilitation Act	• Set the stage for IDEA and ADA • Guarantees basic civil rights to people with disabilities • Requires accommodations in schools and in society
1975	PL 94-142	Education for All Handicapped Children Act (EHA)	• Guaranteed a free appropriate education in the least restrictive environment
1986	PL 99-457	EHA (reauthorized)	• Added infants and toddlers • Provided IFSPs
1990	PL 101-476	Individuals with Disabilities Education Act (IDEA)	• Changed name to IDEA • Added transition plans (ITPs) • Added autism as a special education category • Added traumatic brain injury as a category
1990	PL 101-336	Americans with Disabilities Act (ADA)	• Barred discrimination in employment, transportation, public accommodations, and telecommunications • Implements the concept of normalization across American life
1997	PL 105-17	IDEA (reauthorized)	• Added ADHD to the "other health impairments" category • Added Functional Behavioral Assessments and Behavior Intervention Plans
2001	PL 107-110	Elementary and Secondary Education (No Child Left Behind) Act of 2001: (ESEA)	• Required that all schoolchildren participate in state and district testing • Called for the 100 percent proficiency of all students in reading and math by 2012

CHAPTER 1 *The Context of Special Education*

guarantee would be universally available. This first special education law was passed in 1975 and was called **Public Law (PL) 94-142, Education for All Handicapped Children Act (EHA)**. (The first set of numbers refers to the session of Congress in which the law was passed, the second set to the number of the law. Thus, EHA was the 142nd law passed in the 94th session of Congress.) Congress gave the states 2 years to get ready to implement this new special education law, so it was actually initiated in 1977. That law was to be in effect for 10 years, and for it to continue, a **reauthorization** process was to be necessary. After the first 10-year period, the law would have to be reauthorized every 3 years.

EHA was reauthorized the first time in 1986. (Congress gives itself a couple of extra years to reauthorize laws so that they do not expire before the congressional committee can complete the job of rewriting the law.) Congress added services to infants, toddlers, and their families in this version of the special education law. In its next reauthorization, Congress (retroactively) changed the name of the law to PL 101-476, the **Individuals with Disabilities Education Act (IDEA)**. Besides changing the name, Congress called out two conditions (autism and traumatic brain injury) as special education categories and strengthened transitional services for adolescents with disabilities. IDEA was once

again reauthorized in 1997, and issues like access to the general education curriculum, participation in statewide and district-wide testing, and discipline assumed prominence in this version of the law.

Let's direct our attention away from students for a moment and think about the civil rights of all people with disabilities. Remember that Congress first considered these issues when it passed Section 504 of the Rehabilitation Act of 1973. However, after almost 20 years of implementation, Congress felt that Section 504 was not sufficient and did not end discrimination for adults with disabilities. It took stronger measures by passing yet another law.

On July 26, 1990, President Bush signed the **Americans with Disabilities Act (ADA)**, which bars discrimination in employment, transportation, public accommodations, and telecommunications. He said, "Let the shameful walls of exclusion finally come tumbling down." Senator Tom Harkin (D-IA), the chief sponsor of the act, spoke of this law as the "emancipation proclamation" for people with disabilities (West, 1994). ADA guarantees access to all aspects of life—not just those that are federally funded—to people with disabilities and implements the concept of normalization across all aspects of American life. Both Section 504 of the Rehabilitation Act of 1973 and ADA are considered civil rights and antidiscrimination laws (de Bettencourt, 2002). ADA supports and extends Section 504 and provides adults with disabilities greater access to employment and participation in everyday activities that adults without disabilities enjoy. ADA requires employers not to discriminate against qualified applicants or employees with disabilities. It requires new public transportation (buses, trains, subways) and new or remodeled public accommodations (hotels, stores, restaurants, banks, theaters) to be accessible to persons with disabilities. It also requires telephone companies to provide relay services so that deaf individuals and people with speech impairments can use ordinary telephones. For students who are making the transition from school to adult life, these improvements in access and nondiscrimination should help them achieve genuine participation in their communities.

MAKING CONNECTIONS

For specific IDEA requirements, see the "What IDEA Says" boxes throughout the text.

Now let's turn our attention back to the schools. In the last reauthorization of the Elementary and Secondary Education Act, which is known as the *No Child Left Behind Act of 2001*, students with disabilities were included in many ways. This law requires that 95 percent of all schoolchildren be full participants in state and district testing. It also includes as a goal that *all* students demonstrate proficiency in reading and mathematics by 2012 (Ziegler, 2002).

Normalization and the ADA have risks and benefits for everyone. Because of this principal and law, Michael Hingson (right) was working on the 78th floor of the World Trade Center on September 11. He and his yellow labrador guide dog Roselle helped many people working in Tower One get to safety. Hal Wilson (left) and Tsuanami were members of one of the 300 search and rescue teams that also helped save people at ground zero.

Have the protections of national laws made a difference in the lives of people with disabilities?

Here the answer is a resounding *yes!* ADA, and American attitudes that allowed its passage, have brought many personal benefits to people with disabilities. Businesses have made **accommodations** that enable all employees, including those with disabilities, to perform at levels they might not otherwise have achieved. Equipment is now available in the workplace to support people with disabilities: voice-activated computers, closed-circuit TV equipment that magnifies printed material, and such physical accommodations as ramps. Of course, the ADA law alone cannot be credited with all these changes and benefits, but it is clearly one part of the civil rights movement for citizens with disabilities that has made a real difference.

For many people with disabilities, access to and participation in mainstream society are readily available today. These adults actively participate in all aspects of daily life, from employment to recreation. Many people with disabilities—such as Omar Rivera and his dog Salty, and Michael Hingson and his dog Roselle (Hu, 2001, October, 7)—were working in the World Trade Center on September 11 and, alongside nondisabled co-workers, walked down many flights of stairs to escape the buildings' collapse.

Many examples illustrate improved access and participation for people with disabilities: wheelchair marathon races, tactile museum exhibits for blind people, accessible trails in national and state parks, captioned television and movies, and audio descriptions of visual images for people with limited visual abilities (DVS, 2002). Even Barbie® has doll-friends: Share a Smile Becky®, who uses a wheelchair and paralympic Becky®, who was created in honor of the 2000 Paralympic Games, help to promote inclusion of people with physical disabilities. People with disabilities also appear in TV and magazine advertisements and hold down jobs in the entertainment industry as newscasters, actors, and comedians. All of these examples demonstrate how attitudes have changed, improving the quality of life for many people with disabilities.

Accommodations now enable people with disabilities to travel, visit state and national parks, cruise to exotic places, and enjoy holidays like their friends without disabilities. Of course, we do not always "get it right." As I was checking into a hotel with a blind colleague recently, the term *accessible* took on new meaning for me. My colleague had asked for an accessible room, but when he arrived at the

MAKING CONNECTIONS

- More about high stakes testing is found in Chapter 2.

- For more about employment and adult outcomes for people with visual disabilities, see the "Defined" and "Transition" sections of Chapter 11.

MAKING CONNECTIONS

Please notice the series of photos throughout this text showing dolls with disabilities.

CHAPTER 1 *The Context of Special Education*

room, he found that the light switches and other fixtures were all at a level convenient for a person using a wheelchair. Thus the room was quite inaccessible to a blind person, who found no fixtures where he expected them to be! Clearly, just using the term *accessible* oversimplifies the concept.

Making accommodations for people with disabilities has stimulated thought about how everyone could benefit from different approaches to accessibility and access. For example, architects are now using a concept called **universal design** to remodel and build homes that are accessible to everyone (Leibrock & Terry, 1999). Lever handles on doors are easier to use for those whose arms are laden with shopping bags, for those who have arthritis, and for those with restricted mobility. Sinks are designed so that wheelchairs can roll under. Driveways gradually slope to the level of the front door, which eliminates the need for steps and is also aesthetically pleasing. The principles of universal design can greatly benefit almost everyone, not just those with disabilities.

Barbie® now has a friend, Share a Smile Becky®, who provides a role model for girls with disabilities in a fashion similar to the one Barbie® provides for girls without disabilities.

Section 504 and ADA also affect the education system, but there are some important differences between them and IDEA. Section 504 and ADA have a broader definition of disabilities than does IDEA, for they guarantee the right to accommodations even to those who do not need special education services and to those beyond school age. For example, it is under the authority of ADA that college students with special needs are entitled to special testing situations (untimed tests, someone to read the questions to the test taker, a braille version) and that schoolchildren with attention deficit/hyperactivity disorder who do not qualify for special education receive special accommodations.

Like IDEA, the ADA law has sparked controversy. On the one hand, many individuals with disabilities do not believe that the law is being implemented or enforced (West, 1994). Some members of the disability community are disappointed because they still cannot find jobs suited to their interests, training, or skills. On the other hand, many small-business owners claim that ADA requires them to make accommodations to their businesses that are expensive and rarely used.

Disagreement about what is fair and what the ADA law intended enter into almost every facet of American life. For example, considerable controversy surrounded Casey Martin's use of a golf cart during professional golfing events (Freedman, June 15, 2001). Casey Martin has a degenerative circulatory disorder that constitutes a disability under the ADA, and using a golf cart (which is not allowed at professional golf tournaments) is considered a necessary accommodation enabling Martin to participate. However, other professionals competing, and the PGA itself, maintain that this accommodation gives Martin an unfair advantage. The Supreme Court ruled that Martin's use of a golf cart was a reasonable accommodation, necessary for him to participate.

MAKING
CONNECTIONS

For more about universal design and related accommodations, see Chapter 9.

Why did the courts have to further interpret and define IDEA?

Although Congress thought it was clear in its intentions about the educational guarantees it believed were necessary for children with disabilities and their families, no legal language is perfect. It is the role of the courts to clarify laws passed by Congress and implemented by the administration (implementation of IDEA is the

Not without controversy, Casey Martin rides his golf cart as his caddy follows behind during the Bob Hope Chrysler Classic at Indian Wells Country Club in California. Martin was able to use a cart, instead of walking the course, because under the ADA law the cart was an accommodation for his disability.

responsibility of the U.S. Department of Education). Since 1975, when PL 94-142 (IDEA) became law, a very small percentage of all the children who have been served have been involved in formal disputes. Those disputes concern the identification of children with disabilities, evaluations, educational placements, and the provision of a free appropriate public education. Many of these disputes are resolved in noncourt proceedings (due process hearings).

Some disputes, however, must be settled in courts of law—a few even in the U.S. Supreme Court. Through such **litigation**, many different questions about special education have been addressed and clarified. The ramifications of the highest courts' decisions can be significant. Let's look at one recent example of a Supreme Court decision about a student with a disability and whether his school district had the obligation to pay for continuous one-on-one nursing care while he attended school. Garret F. was paralyzed as the result of a motorcycle accident at the age of 4. He required an electric ventilator (or someone manually pumping an air bag) to continue breathing and to stay alive. When Garret was in middle school, his mother requested that the school pick up the expenses of his physical care while he was in school. The district refused the request. Most school district administrators believed that providing "complex health services" to students was not a related service (and hence the district's responsibility) but rather a medical service (excluded under IDEA regulations). In other words, across the country, districts had interpreted the IDEA law and its regulations to mean that schools were not responsible for the cost of health services. The Supreme Court, however, disagreed and interpreted IDEA differently. The justices decided that if a doctor is not necessary to provide the health service, and the service is necessary to keep a student in an educational program, then it is the school's obligation to provide the "related service." The implications of this decision are enormous (Katsiyannis & Yell, 2000). Not only are the costs for additional personnel expensive—potentially between $20,000 and $40,000 per school year—but increased liability for schools, additional considerations for individualized education program (IEP) teams, the administrative costs for increased staff, and the complications of yet another adult in a classroom all make IDEA even more unpopular with many educators.

Who advocates for children and adults with disabilities?

Parents and family members of people with disabilities, special education professionals, and individuals with disabilities are usually the people who ask that the rights of people with disabilities be protected and that needed services be offered. The laws and court cases you have just learned about were, in part, stimulated by organized advocacy efforts. In the early 20th Century, the job of raising America's consciousness about the problems facing people with disabilities rested primarily with professional organizations, but in the latter part of the century, people with disabilities began to speak on their own behalf. Let's look at a bit of this history to understand an important aspect of the disability advocacy movement in America.

In 1922 the International Council for the Education of Exceptional Children (CEC) was founded (Aiello, 1976) when members of a summer special education class conducted at Teachers College, Columbia University, decided to meet annually to continue sharing exciting ideas about special education. Their professor, Elizabeth Farrell, became the group's first president. Membership grew, and today, with about 61,000 members, CEC remains the largest special education professional organization in the United States. CEC was not the only professional organization concerned about people with disabilities. The American Speech-Language-Hearing Association (ASHA) was established in 1935 and has a current membership of about 85,000 professionals. The American Occupational Therapy Association (AOTA), the National Association of Social Workers (NASW), and the American Physical Therapy Association (APTA) have all been instrumental in advocating for the availability of related services for every student with disabilities who needs those services.

Many volunteer and parent organizations began to organize after World War II to fight for the provision of educational services in the public schools for students with disabilities. The Arc (formerly the Association for Retarded Citizens of the United States), founded in 1950 as the National Association of Parents and Friends of Mentally Retarded Children, worked to have special education services provided through the public education system to all students with disabilities. Other influential groups were the United Cerebral Palsy Associations, Inc. (UCP), which began in 1949; the National Society for Autistic Children, formed in 1961; the Learning Disability Association of America (LDA), founded in 1963 as the Association for Children with Learning Disabilities; and the Epilepsy Foundation of America, which grew out of several earlier epilepsy groups in 1968. The power and importance of these parent advocacy groups must be recognized and applauded. It continues to be the strength of the parent movement that improves federal laws. Parents argue successfully for funding at the state and national levels, and they serve as "watchdogs" over local education programs to ensure that each student with a disability has access to a free appropriate public education.

People with disabilities have also formed their own advocacy groups, becoming effectively organized during the late 1980s and 1990s. The first phase was a quest for civil rights; the second phase is focusing on the development of a disability culture (Longmore, 1995; Treanor, 1993). Ed Roberts, founder of the World Institute on Disability and himself a person with disabilities, was a catalyst in organizing people with disabilities to demand access to mainstream U.S. society and the fulfillment of basic civil rights. Justin Dart organized people with disabilities across the nation and used his connections in the business community to ensure the ultimate passage of the ADA law. Because of all of these efforts, the National Council on Disability, which directly reports to the U.S. president and to Congress, was formed to ensure that the rights of people with disabilities are safeguarded. Today, parents, professionals, and people with disabilities have formed powerful lobbying groups and political action organizations that work to improve the opportunities available to all individuals with disabilities.

What basic principle guides special education and disability advocacy efforts?

One of the formative principles that guide advocacy efforts is the notion of normalization. Normalization is an essential dimension of special education and a

MAKING CONNECTIONS

The stories of Ed Roberts and Justin Dart are found in Chapter 9.

MAKING
CONNECTIONS

Normalization and its evolution are also discussed in Chapter 6.

guiding concept for adults with disabilities. Although the concept was suggested in 1959 by Bank-Mikkelsen of Denmark (Biklen, 1985), the word itself was coined by Bengt Nirje of Sweden (1969, 1976), who, along with Wolf Wolfensberger, encouraged the United States to incorporate this principle in services to people with disabilities (Wolfensberger, 1972, 1995). According to Nirje (1985), **normalization** means "making available to all persons with disabilities or other handicaps, patterns of life and conditions of everyday living which are as close as possible to or indeed the *same* as the regular circumstances and ways of life of society" (p. 67; emphasis in original). The principle of normalization applies to every aspect of a student's life. Nirje referred to a set of normal life patterns: the normal rhythm of the day, the normal rhythm of the week, the normal rhythm of the year, and the normal development of the life cycle. Until the 1970s, much of the day-to-day work in institutions—such as caring for individuals with severe disabilities or performing farm or laundry work—was provided by residents with mild and moderate disabilities. Because of the widely held belief that individuals with disabilities would contaminate the "normal" population, many people spent their entire lives in these institutions, isolated from mainstream society. Institutional living conflicts with the principle of normalization, and advocacy efforts have resulted in most people, even those with severe disabilities, living in community settings and having a voice about issues like how and where they live (Johnson, 1998). As you think about what the American response to children and adults with disabilities should be, remember the normalization principle.

SPECIAL EDUCATION TODAY

Special education is an evolving concept that has been described, defined, and explained in many ways. These different perceptions about what special education is result from people's diverse orientations and experiences. Special education should be thought of as setting the stage for better services and improved outcomes for students with disabilities.

What is special education?

One way in which special education is defined is by the teachers who have dedicated themselves to the field. However, as you can see from the accompanying story about who would be an "ideal teacher," perceptions of the educator's role have changed across time. Special education could also be defined as a service or supportive part of the educational system wherein professionals either consult with teachers or provide a considerable amount of direct instruction and collaborate with others who also teach and work with students with disabilities. Just as we have found in seeking answers to many of the questions we've investigated so far, special education means different things to different people. Let's look at a couple of other definitions of special education.

Congress explained what it meant by special education when it originally passed the Individuals with Disabilities Education Act in 1975:

> *It is the purpose of this chapter to assure that all handicapped children have available to them ... a free appropriate public education which emphasizes special education and related services designed to meet their unique needs, to assure that the rights of handicapped children and their parents or guardians are protected, to assist States and localities to provide for the education of all handicapped children, and to assess and assure the effectiveness of efforts to educate handicapped children. (20 U.S.C. section 1400[c])*

SPECIAL EDUCATION IN 1891: AS DEFINED BY ITS TEACHERS

In 1891 one superintendent of a residential school described the perfect special education teacher. He urged the teachers to be "sweet-tempered":

The ideal teacher is well educated, refined, intensely interested in her pupils, and has a professional zeal to grow in her work: she is original, striving to introduce new and bright methods, but not passing hastily from subject to subject before *the child has grasped the first. She is patient but energetic, sweet-tempered but persistent, and to the influences of her education and character she adds the charms of personal neatness and attractive manners. She possesses naturally a well grounded religious sense, which finds its best expression in self-sacrifice, conscientious duty, and instinctive kindness. (Isaac N. Kerlin,* Manual of Elwyn, *1891, quoted in Nazzaro, 1977, p. 11)*

The United States Department of Education, in its regulations implementing IDEA, says that special education means

specially designed instruction, at no cost to the parent, to meet the unique needs of a child with a disability, including instruction conducted in the classroom, in the home, in hospitals and institutions, and in other settings; and instruction in physical education. (1999, p. 12425)

These passages suggest three defining features of special education. Two important components of special education for every student with a disability are **free appropriate public education (FAPE)** and **least restrictive environment (LRE)**. The essential concepts here are that students with disabilities must be educated at no additional cost to their families and that their education must be delivered in the least restrictive environment possible, where they have access to the general education curriculum and role models of typically developing classmates. To determine what education is appropriate for each student and where such services should be delivered requires application of the third principle: an *individually determined* educational program.

FAPE, LRE, and an individually determined program affect both curriculum and instructional interventions. These features add to the controversy and confusion surrounding special education. Balancing the principles FAPE and LRE takes on particular meaning for students with severe disabilities, where questions arise about whether inclusion in general education classes is more important than participation in community based settings (Dymond & Orelove, 2001). The tension here is between those who believe that the benefits of social skills and access to role models provided by nondisabled classmates is more important than learning functional skills (such as work-related skills) in real-life employment situations. Because IDEA mandates access to the general education curriculum, should the special education curriculum default to the general education curriculum whether students can profit from age-appropriate classes or not?

Another way to conceptualize special education is by looking at the wide variety of services it provides to children with disabilities and their families. Special education is supposed to be individualized and to provide a tailor-made education for each child with a special need. These programs are also supposed to hold high expectations that lead to reasonable outcomes achieved by students with disabilities. Special education includes direct instruction in the classroom, consultation and

M AKING C ONNECTIONS

More discussion about FAPE and LRE is found in Chapter 2.

M AKING C ONNECTIONS

More about special education and the individualized education it offers is found in Chapter 2.

Least Restrictive Environment (LRE)

- To the maximum extent possible, children with disabilities are educated with nondisabled peers
- Ensures a continuum of alternative placements
- Provides for supplementary services (resource room or itinerant instruction) in conjunction with general education
- Is individually determined and is based on evaluations of the student
- Is evaluated at least annually
- Is based on the child's IEP
- Is as close to the child's home as possible, and whenever possible is at that child's neighborhood school

collaboration with the general education teacher, coordination of the student's educational program, and orchestration of those learning opportunities necessary for each youngster to profit from instruction. It also includes a wide array of the **related services**, which combine to form multidisciplinary teams designed to meet the unique needs of each individual student with a disability.

Who provides special education services?

Special education services are provided to students with disabilities and their families by an array of outstanding professionals who come from many different disciplines. The largest group of these professionals is special education teachers, who have the primary responsibility to ensure that students with disabilities are receiving an appropriate education. The second largest group of professionals is **speech/language pathologists (SLPs)**, who provide services to remediate students' speech or language impairments. Other related services are provided by adaptive PE teachers, **assistive technology specialists**, **audiologists**, diagnostic and evaluation staff, interpreters for the deaf, family therapists, **occupational therapists (OTs)**, orientation and mobility specialists, paraprofessionals (paraeducators, teacher aides), **physical therapists (PTs)**, psychologists, recreation and therapeutic-recreation therapists, rehabilitative counselors, school counselors, **school nurses**, school social workers, supervisors and administrators, transportation specialists, vocational education teachers, and work study coordinators.

How are disabilities classified for special education?

When it comes to schoolchildren, the government has elected to define disabilities by using a **categorical approach** and in terms of whether a child needs special services (U.S. Department of Education, 1999). Although many states use terms slightly different from those used by the federal government, the similarities are clear (Müller & Linehan, 2001, July). Within the 13 disability categories defined as disabilities in IDEA are many additional conditions. For example, attention deficit/hyperactivity disorder (ADHD) is part of the "other health impairments" category. Here—using the federal terminology—are the 13 major special education categories called out in IDEA:

Autism	Orthopedic impairment
Deaf-blindness	Other health impairment
Deafness	Specific learning disability
Emotional disturbance	Speech or language impairment
Hearing impairment	Traumatic brain injury
Mental retardation	Visual impairment
Multiple disabilities	

What are the fundamental provisions of special education?

Special education can also be defined in terms of the eight fundamental provisions outlined in IDEA. These provisions are listed here, and the two most often misunderstood are clarified in their respective "What IDEA Says" boxes.

- Free appropriate public education (FAPE)
- Parental rights to notification of evaluation and placement decisions, including the rights to due process hearings in the case of disagreements
- Individualized education and services to all children with disabilities
- Provision of necessary related services
- Individualized assessments
- Individualized education program (IEP) plans
- Education provided to the fullest extent possible in the least restrictive environment (LRE)
- Federal assistance to state and school districts to ease the burden of the excess costs for special education

What IDEA Says About

Free Appropriate Public Education (FAPE)

- Must be based on each child's identified special education and related service needs
- Guarantees parents that special education services will be at no cost to them
- Is determined by the child's unique needs, not on what is assumed by the special education category the child's been assigned to
- Ensures that there is no delay in implementing a child's individualized education plan, once it has been developed

OPPORTUNITIES FOR A BETTER 21ST CENTURY

Although much work remains to be done for people with disabilities to gain full participation in schools and in American society, considerable progress has been made. And many signals of a new era are visible. For example, one sign is the establishment of **disabilities studies** as a bona fide major at many colleges and universities. As with women's studies, Latino(a) studies, and Black studies, this major represents an interdisciplinary study of the history and culture of a group of people. Paul Longmore, a pioneer in the disability advocacy movement, established the Institute on Disabilities at San Francisco State University (Longmore, 2002). Longmore's perspective is that people with disabilities experience institutional bias and discrimination. Courses that focus on the history of people with disabilities, on issues contained in the ADA law, and on Congress's intentions about the rights of people with disabilities will better inform society about the issues and social policies that need to be addressed. Other universities, such as Syracuse University and the University of Illinois-Chicago, offer graduate degrees in disabilities studies (Mitchell, 2002). And surely more programs will become available. An interesting and emerging attitude is that one must have disability status (that is, must be a person with a disability) to be seen as an expert in the field of disabilities studies (Cassuto, 1999).

*During the time of Franklin D. Roosevelt's presidency, his disability was hidden from the public.
Times have changed, however, and the new statue of him in Washington, DC shows him using a wheelchair.*

Is society more sensitive to people with disabilities and their needs?

Perhaps stimulated by national policies, society now reflects a more sensitive and understanding way of regarding and talking about the minority group that includes children and adults with disabilities. People with disabilities are visible members of communities, a situation very different from that prevailing some 50 years ago when great efforts were made to hide from the public President Franklin D. Roosevelt's use of crutches and a wheelchair (Gallagher, 1994). The new statue of President Roosevelt demonstrates changes in attitudes toward disabilities and the people who have them.

People with disabilities express some strong feelings about the words and phrases used to describe them. Language evolves to reflect changing concepts and beliefs. What is socially acceptable at one point in history can be viewed as funny or offensive at another. For example, at the beginning of the 20th Century, such terms as *imbecile, moron,* and *mental retardate* were commonly used, and at the time they were not offensive. Other references, which we think of today as cruel, came and went. In most cases, they were not originally thought of as harmful, but they took on negative connotations. As a result of grassroots advocacy, people with disabilities and their families have influenced the language we use to talk about members of this minority group. This issue is very important to people with disabilities because words send a message to others about our respect for them. Although most of us try to "get it right" all of the time, we occasionally use language offensive to others. The language preferred by people with disabilities can be confusing because different groups and individuals have very different preferences. Although there are some exceptions (especially for the Deaf), there are two basic rules to follow:

1. Put people first.
2. Do not make the person equal the disability.

In light of these rules, therefore, it is proper to use phrases such as the following: students *with* mental retardation, individuals *who have* learning disabilities. Two groups of individuals with disabilities prefer a different descriptive approach:

CHAPTER 1 *The Context of Special Education*

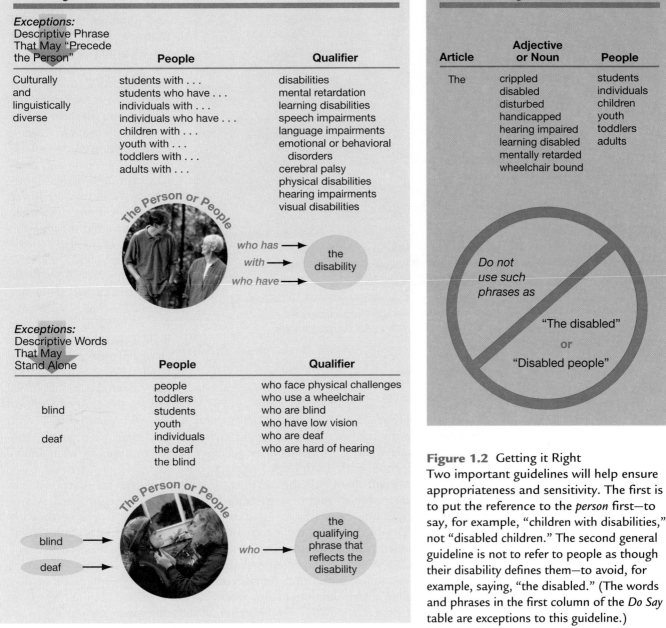

Do Say

Exceptions:
Descriptive Phrase That May "Precede the Person"

Exceptions: Descriptive Phrase That May "Precede the Person"	People	Qualifier
Culturally and linguistically diverse	students with . . . students who have . . . individuals with . . . individuals who have . . . children with . . . youth with . . . toddlers with . . . adults with . . .	disabilities mental retardation learning disabilities speech impairments language impairments emotional or behavioral disorders cerebral palsy physical disabilities hearing impairments visual disabilities

The Person or People

who has →
 with → the disability <br> who have →

Exceptions:
Descriptive Words That May Stand Alone

Exceptions: Descriptive Words That May Stand Alone	People	Qualifier
blind deaf	people toddlers students youth individuals the deaf the blind	who face physical challenges who use a wheelchair who are blind who have low vision who are deaf who are hard of hearing

The Person or People

blind →
 deaf → who → the qualifying phrase that reflects the disability

Don't Say

Article	Adjective or Noun	People
The	crippled disabled disturbed handicapped hearing impaired learning disabled mentally retarded wheelchair bound	students individuals children youth toddlers adults

Do not use such phrases as

"The disabled"

or

"Disabled people"

Figure 1.2 Getting it Right
Two important guidelines will help ensure appropriateness and sensitivity. The first is to put the reference to the *person* first—to say, for example, "children with disabilities," not "disabled children." The second general guideline is not to refer to people as though their disability defines them—to avoid, for example, saying, "the disabled." (The words and phrases in the first column of the *Do Say* table are exceptions to this guideline.)

Specifically, the Deaf (who prefer this term as a reflection of their heritage and culture) and those who are blind account for most of the exceptions found in accepted disability terminology. You might find the "Do Say" and "Don't Say" examples in Figure 1.2 helpful as you use the language of disabilities and its exceptions properly—at least for today! Remember, however, that not all members of any group agree unanimously on every issue; some people with disabilities might not agree with the rules of language described here. And the rules will certainly change over time. Remember that it is everyone's responsibility to remain sensitive to these issues.

Another way to measure and evaluate how any group of people is perceived by a society is to analyze how that group is portrayed in film. Film both reflects

Filmmaker Walter Brock and Arthur Campbell, Jr. discuss the impact of their film, If I Can't Do It, *which was part of the PBS series P.O.V. The film portrays both Brock's striving for independence and the history of the disability rights movement before and after the passage of the Americans with Disabilities Act.*

public attitudes and has the potential to influence the way people think and interact with others (Safran, 1998, 2000). It can also perpetuate stereotypes. Films produced at the beginning of the last century rarely depicted people with disabilities in a positive light. They were people who were villainous or evil, were being punished through their disabilities by God, or were bitter and self-pitying. Another theme was that through the miracles of modern medicine, people with paralysis or blindness could be cured. Comparisons of some acclaimed and Academy Award-winning films make it clear that the message has changed over a century of movies: *Frankenstein* (1931), *The Best Years of Our Lives* (1946), *My Left Foot* (1989), *Shine* (1996), *Girl Interrupted* (1999), and *A Beautiful Mind* (2001). Not all of the disability themes found in motion pictures across time are negative, and some films made worthy efforts to offer accurate representations of what life is like for many people with disabilities.

Despite important changes in the ways people with disabilities are portrayed and included in society, stigma and bias are a long way from being eliminated. Many people with disabilities and observers of societies across the world agree with Kitchin that "Disabled people are marginalized and excluded from 'mainstream' society.... Disabled people represent one of the poorest groups in Western society" (1998, p. 343). Most definitely, people with disabilities drop out of school at alarming rates, are unemployed and underemployed far more than people without disabilities, and face discrimination in the workplace and in the community (U.S. Department of Education, 2001). Think again about adults with mental illness in this country who are left homeless on the streets because changes in public policy made them vulnerable to neglect.

The climate of advocacy, the atmosphere of sensitivity, and the acknowledgement that as a minority group, people with disabilities have had to fight for their places in American society should now be clear. But to achieve the level of participation people with disabilities deserve and desire requires preparation for these responsibilities, which begins at school with an education. So let's return our attention to what actually is the focus of this text: the special educational opportunities available to students with disabilities.

Making Connections

In the "Supplementary Resources" sections at the ends of Chapters 3 through 13, annotated listings of films that include people with disabilities as central characters are provided as examples of different perspectives and portrayals of these individuals in society.

Why has special education become controversial?

It is impossible to ignore the fact that special education is controversial in America and internationally (Horn & Tynan, 2001; Rouse & Florian, 2001). Criticisms come from all sectors of society. This program, which had once been so widely acclaimed, appears to be falling out of favor. Here are a few examples:

An education is an investment.... If that is so, and I believe it because it makes sense, why should millions of dollars of our tax money be spent attempting to educate persons who will never use that learning for any reason whatsoever?... Well, forgive me, but if they had money to invest would those same people put it into an account that would not draw one cent of interest and would in fact cost them millions of dollars just to maintain? (Gatley, 2001, April 30, p. 14A)

Kudos to Pat Gatley for her letter on special needs kids. She said so well what most of us would like to say. (Lannon, 2001, May 2, p. 10A)

For too long, most politicians, policymakers, and others involved with the IDEA ... considered it taboo to discuss these programs and challenges. It seemed at times as if anything less than unadulterated praise for the IDEA was indicative of hostility towards its goals or—worse—towards children with special needs. Thus, the IDEA has come to be viewed as the "third rail" issue of education policy. (Finn, Rotherham, & Hokanson, 2001, p. v)

Although schooling is no longer denied to any child, and although the outcomes of students with disabilities are significantly improved over previous times, complaints about special education, its costs, and its practices continue to be pervasive in the press, in public conversations, and in Congress (Gotsch, 2001, December 19). Special education is blamed for many problems found in the public schools.

Clearly, the fairly recent but overwhelmingly negative feelings about special education held by many in American society are one of the significant legacies of the 20th Century. Here are some of the major concerns and issues that must be resolved.

Many are concerned about whether special education

- Is ineffective and unnecessary
- Is discriminatory
- Unnecessarily segregates students with disabilities from their nondisabled peers
- Includes too many students
- Is too costly and places too great a financial burden on states and local schools
- Imposes an administrative burden when school officials must address disruptive or violent behavior

Let's briefly look at these concerns to gain perspectives that might lead to effective solutions.

- ***Concern: Is Special Education Ineffective and Unnecessary?*** Debates about special education's effectiveness are often emotional and irrational. There is great confusion about what standards should be applied to measure special education's effectiveness. The goals for special education are implied, not specific. Many policymakers, educators, and parents also seem unclear about their expectations for special education. Many of them believe that special education is effective only if it "cures" or "fixes" disabilities—if it makes them go away (Lovitt & Cushing, 1999). If this becomes the standard by which to measure the effectiveness of special education services, then possibly the graduation rate of students with disabilities is the **outcome** to watch. These data are dismal: although this figure is gradually increasing, only 57 percent of students with disabilities presently leave the educational system with a standard high school diploma, compared to some 83 percent of students without disabilities (U.S. Department of Education, 2001; Young, 2002). Graduation rates vary considerably by disability category (e.g., 75 percent for students with visual disabilities, 63 percent for those with learning disabilities, 47 percent for students with autism, 42 percent for those with mental retardation).

Remember, the No Child Left Behind Act of 2001 requires that eventually all children become proficient in reading and mathematics. Even though some

MAKING CONNECTIONS

As a problem solving exercise, study the "Opportunities for a Better Future" sections, starting with Chapter 2.

Programs like Nashville's A.B.L.E. program at Easter Seals helps youngsters with disabilities begin a life-long pattern of exercise and recreation that should be part of every child's experience.

5 percent of students can be excused from state and district assessments, will this ambitious goal become an unreasonable expectation for special education, resulting in its always being judged ineffective? The related attitude of minimizing the impact of disabilities leads to arguments that "good teaching" and "high expectations" in general education classes ("the mainstream") *alone* can meet the needs of students with disabilities. Others, however, recognize that special education teachers work with students who are "difficult to teach" and who present some of the most serious challenges to the educational system, but the goals for their efforts are not clearly articulated. For example, some experts believe that general education teachers have been asked to include too many students who are increasingly diverse in learning ability, particularly students with emotional or behavioral disorders (White et al., 2001). Regardless, evidence does exist that the long-term effects of educating students with disabilities are positive (Hehir, 1996).

● *Concern: Is Special Education Discriminatory?* A commonly held belief and a widely held concern is that too many students of color are placed in special education programs (Artiles, Aguirre-Muñoza, & Abedi, 1998; ERIC Clearinghouse on Disabilities and Gifted Education, 2001; Oswald et al., 1999; Townsend, 2000; Townsend & Patton, 2001). The concern stems from the belief that special education is equivalent to placement in a lower academic track, to removal from the academic mainstream, and to a renewing of a cycle of poverty (Ewing, 2001). It is a fact that students of color have rates of placement in special education that exceed their proportions in the school population. Many different explanations for their disproportionate representation exist, ranging from documentation of these youngsters' low academic achievement and disruptive behaviors, to expected outcomes of being raised in poverty and having limited access to health care, to institutional racism, and to white teachers having little understanding or tolerance for diverse students' culture and behavior patterns (Cartledge, Tillman, & Johnson, 2001; MacMillan, Gresham, & Bocian, 1998; Patton, 1998; Reschly, 1997; Williams, 2001). Thus to some educators, special education is being provided to students who are not succeeding in the general education curriculum, and it is giving them the extra assistance and supports they require. To others, special education is a means to remove disruptive or undesirable students from the general education classroom. And still others perceive it as a sentence to low achievement and a "watered down" curriculum guaranteeing poor lifetime opportunities.

● *Concern: Does Special Education Unnecessarily Segregate Students with Disabilities from Their Nondisabled Peers?* There is no question that this was historically a problem; to many, it remains a problem today (Danforth & Rhodes,

MAKING **C**ONNECTIONS

Disproportionate representation of students of color in disability categories of special education, and underrepresentation in gifted education, are discussed in Chapters 3, 4, 6, 7, and 8.

CHAPTER 1 *The Context of Special Education*

1997; Gardner & Lipsky, 1987). When the field of special education began, the few services that were available were offered primarily in segregated settings. Sometimes these services were provided in special schools within a school district, but more often they were provided in residential schools, which in many cases became terrible institutions, geographically isolated in the rural parts of a state. As public school programs became more readily available and **mainstreaming** was limited, students with disabilities often found themselves in separate schools or separate classes, removed from their neighborhood peers. The concepts of least restrictive environment (review again the IDEA box about LRE) and fully inclusive education are guided by the principle of normalization. The result is that most students with disabilities (some 96 percent) attend neighborhood schools, and almost half receive more than 79 percent of their education in the general education class (U.S. Department of Education, 2001). The percentage of students with disabilities who are being included for the vast majority of the school day has consistently increased since 1985, growing from 25 percent in 1985 to 47 percent in 1999. To many professionals and parents, this participation rate is insufficient. However, views on placement (where students receive their education) vary wildly, ranging from support for full inclusion in general education classes to endorsement of full-time placement in center (residential) schools. On the one hand is the argument that being educated in classes with nondisabled peers of the same age provides students who have disabilities with the opportunity to learn age-appropriate social skills from their classmates. The extremely opposite position centers on the impossibility of offering a truly individualized education entirely within the constraints of the general education classroom and curriculum (Hockenbury, Kauffman, & Hallahan, 1999–2000). As debate continues about placement, particularly among professionals and federal policymakers, it is important to listen to the other voices. For example, according to a Gallup/Kappan public opinion poll, two-thirds (66 percent) of Americans believe that students with learning problems belong in separate classes (Rose & Gallup, 1998). And many (though not all) such students themselves prefer to receive their instruction outside of the general education setting (Klingner, Vaughn, Schumm et al., 1998; Lovitt, Plavins, & Cushing, 1999).

- *Concern: Does Special Education Include Too Many Students?* Clearly, the number of students participating in special education has increased since the initial passage of IDEA in 1975. While the overall student population in America increased in the last decade of the 20th Century by some 14 percent, special education enrollment increased by 30 percent. Is this growth unreasonable? First, let's think about students identified as having disabilities. **Prevalence** is the term professionals use to refer to the total number of cases at a given time, but to make fair comparisons, it is usually better to think in terms of the proportion or percentage of these individuals, rather than in terms of absolute numbers. When Congress passed IDEA in 1975, estimates were that special education would not serve any more than 12 percent of schoolchildren. According to the federal government, 5,383,009 children and youth from age 6 through age 17 are currently served in special education programs (U.S. Department of Education, 2001). This total represents a bit more than 11 percent of all children and youth in this age group. Although the percentage of students served through special education is still below original estimates, many administrators and policymakers think the number served is too high (Berman et al., 2001). And some fear that the number and proportion will rise for the following reasons:

- Medical advances are resulting in the survival of more infants with moderate and severe disabilities.
- More children with disabilities who might formerly have been educated at state-run residential institutions have been shifted to local public schools.
- Increasing numbers of preschoolers with disabilities will age into regular school programs.

For more information about inclusion and educational placements, see
· The "Collaboration for Inclusion" sections in Chapters 3—12
· Discussions about FAPE and LRE in Chapter 2.

For specific prevalence figures for each exceptionality, see the "Prevalence" sections in Chapters 3—12.

With the costs of education rising and the number of special needs students rising, many school districts are searching for ways to save money. One alternative used is to reduce the number of special education programs, particularly resource room programs.

- Raising general education standards and expectations will lead to more school failure.

Concerns about the growth in the number of students receiving special education could result in a lower cap, or limit, for the percentage of students who can be included or could lead to more alternatives to the present general education and special education options.

• *Concern: Is Special Education Too Costly, Placing Too Great a Financial Burden on States and Local School Districts?* Many state and school district officials believe that the costs for special education services reduce funding available for general education students because the current federal contribution toward special education costs is insufficient. In 1975 when IDEA was first passed, Congress authorized the federal government to pay up to 40 percent of the extra funds, **excess cost**, needed to provide special education services. (Note that Congress used the phrase *up to* in the original law.) Although federal appropriations have increased considerably over the last few years, the federal share of costs is only about 12 percent (Chambers, Parrish, & Harr, 2002). Many school administrators and the media believe that schools are left with an unfair burden (Clayton, 2001). Today, the costs of educating a student with disabilities is about 1.9 times greater than the cost of educating a student without disabilities. If facilities are included, this cost rises to 2.08 times greater. Thus, the nation spends about twice as much to educate a student with a disability as it does to educate a typical learner. Of course, the costs vary by state and also by the severity of the student's disability. It is interesting that these costs have actually decreased over recent years: In 1985, the cost of educating a student with disabilities was 2.28 times greater than the cost of educating a student without disabilities.

Why are special education costs greater? Many factors cause these increased expenses. For example, legal costs stemming from disputes between parents and school districts about services that children with disabilities are entitled to receive have increased costs. More expensive health care costs are now the obligation of schools because the Supreme Court ruled that schools must provide, as a related service, attendant care for students with significant health care needs (*Cedar Rapids School District* v. *Garret*). This action will probably result in increased liability costs as well (Katsiyannis & Yell, 2000). And the courts have ruled (*Wayzata Independent School District No. 284* v. *A.C.*) that school districts can be responsible for expensive private school tuition (Gotsch, 2001, August 15).

The nation must evaluate its educational investments in all children. It is impossible to know whether expenditures made on students with disabilities actually reduce the amount available for students without disabilities, but we do know that special education costs have risen at a far greater pace than the costs of general education (Chambers, Parrish, & Harr, 2002). A study conducted in Massachusetts helps us understand some reasons for the increased costs of educating students with disabilities (Berman et al., 2001). Increased numbers of students with moderate to severe disabilities, who cost more to educated, are the primary reason. Other factors include shifting expenditures for these children's education from institutions to public schools, expensive private school and out-of-district placements, and the provision of medical services by school personnel. We do know, however, that improved academic achievement is associated with school expenditures and reduced class size, particularly for low-income and diverse students (Grissmer et al., 1998). We also

CHAPTER 1 *The Context of Special Education*

know that many believe that special education expenditures are not in the best interests of students without disabilities (Finn et al., 2001).

• **Concern: Does Special Education Impose an Administrative Burden When School Officials Must Address Disruptive or Violent Behavior?** According to the federal government, acts of serious misconduct are three times higher for special education students, and 7 out of 10 of those actions are fights (U.S. General Accounting Office, 2001). School administrators, the public, the press, and many members of Congress still think that children with special needs, particularly those with emotional or behavioral disorders, are responsible for increased violence and disruption in the public schools (Perlstein, 2001, July 11). To what degree students with disabilities are responsible for major acts of violence is not clear, though at times public opinion places much of the blame squarely on special education students.

During the 1997 reauthorization of IDEA, many congressional leaders took the position that what had been known as the **stay-put provision** of IDEA was unfair and unequal. Up until then, students with disabilities could not be expelled or removed from school, or from the educational program specified in their individualized education plans, because of their disabilities or behaviors relating to them. With the 1997 reinterpretation of IDEA, (see the "What IDEA Says" box for a summary), the rules changed (U.S. Department of Education, 1999). Although students with disabilities—even those with emotional or behavioral disorders—may now be suspended and even expelled, they must have a Behavior Intervention Plan (BIP) included with their Individualized Educational Program. Some experts believe that these complicated and involved procedures can sometimes be a burden for general educators to develop (Yell, Bradley, Katsiyannis, & Rozalski, 2000). Regardless of these changes, many in Congress remain unsatisfied with these discipline regulations, and they continue to propose more legislation to tighten standards (Jane West, personal communication, August, 2002).

What IDEA Says About

The Stay-Put Provision and Discipline

- Placement decisions may be made without consulting with the student's IEP committee.

- Students with disabilities can be removed from school for a total of ten days for minor disciplinary infractions.

- Services must resume after the tenth day of expulsion.

- Students with disabilities can be removed from their school placements for up to forty-five days for major infractions, like involvement with drugs or weapons, and placed in alternative programs or schools.

- An IEP meeting does not have to be held each time the child is suspended.

MAKING CONNECTIONS

Issues related to discipline are included throughout the text, but see in particular

- The sections on the IEP process in Chapter 2

- The "Achieving Discipline" boxes in Chapters 3–12

What might be some informed and effective solutions to special education's problems?

Although individuals with disabilities have made great strides, much dissatisfaction and confusion surrounds the special education endeavor. Possibly, one general answer to this problem is for special education to become more accountable for its outcomes and to its constituents.

Consumer satisfaction is important, and like all good businesses, the special education community must find ways to listen to the voices of all its constituents: taxpayers, general educators, school administrators, students with disabilities, families of students with disabilities, and school alumni (Berman et al. 2001; Kortering & Braziel, 1999; Lovitt & Cushing, 1999). Many responsibilities are associated with satisfying the consumer. The consumer must be informed about services provided, must believe they are worthy and affordable, and feel confident that they make a difference. The consumer must also believe that the costs are fair to everyone.

Special education must become truly special (Finn et al., 2001). This educational option must make a difference. The interventions and strategies used must be effective. Research findings are available that document the power and effectiveness of many intervention strategies (Hockenbury, Kauffman, & Hallahan, 1999-2000). Here's an example. It is now clear that class size matters: The larger the class (or the teacher's caseload), the lower students' academic achievement in reading and mathematics (Russ et al., 2001). Despite this finding, special education's average teacher-to-student ratio is rising to levels close to that of general education. Even with the low class size for students with severe disabilities included in the averages, special education's average teacher-to-student ratio has risen from 15:1 to 17:1 in just 4 years, while general education's current ratio is 18:1 (Carlson, Schroll, & Klein, 2001).

Outcomes of students are greatly improved when they are taught by certified teachers (Smith et al., 2002). Besides class size and qualified teachers, interventions have been developed and verified specifically for students with disabilities. But if special education is to become special, educators (and related service providers) must use them. The use of unproven methods must be avoided. Scientifically validated practices (such as those found in the "Validated Practices" boxes throughout this text) make a difference in students' outcomes. Obviously, not all procedures or methods associated with the education of students with disabilities are effective. Special educators, early childhood specialists, speech/language pathologists, and all professionals who work with students with disabilities must become sophisticated consumers of research. Tolerance for using unproven or ineffective educational practices should be zero! The growing special education research base allows professionals and parents to make educational decisions with some confidence, and nothing less should be expected (West & Hardman, 2003). Special education professionals, then, must avoid such bad practices as adopting one educational fad after another, making widespread policy decisions before research can guide practice, and using unproven techniques because they "make sense."

A vast amount of knowledge is available and should be used (Forness et al., 1997; Lloyd et al., 1998). Here are some special education approaches that have been proven effective through research: mnemonic strategies, enhanced reading comprehension, behavior modification, direct instruction, cognitive behavior modification, formative evaluation (curriculum based measurement), and early intervention. Community based instruction, where students learn functional skills in the community and in job situations, can make real differences in their learning and generalizing of skills that they will need in employment and for independent living (Dymond & Orelove, 2001), Here are some practices that are often associated with special education, and are used by many teachers, but that research has shown *not* to be effective or to improve academic learning: modality instruction, diet, and perceptual training (Lloyd et al., 1998).

Another solution might be to develop reasonable expectations for the pursuit itself. Quite likely, one major source of the problems special education faces is confusion about its purpose. Without clear articulation of what it is supposed to accomplish, no standards to judge its effectiveness can be developed. Just as it is a tragic error to have low expectations for students with disabilities, it is also a mistake to minimize disabilities. If disabilities were not serious, why would the nation spend so much money on prevention, treatment, education, and supports? What are special education's goals? Certainly, the outcomes for special education cannot be to "cure" disabilities, but this expectation may be the unspoken understanding of many parents and thus may account for some dissatisfaction (Lovitt & Cushing, 1999). Many general educators, parents of nondisabled students, and members of the press resent special education because they think that special services for these children are provided at the expense of children without disabilities (Berman et al., 2001). A popular solution to this problem is for the federal government to pay more of the costs for special education (Clayton, 2001, July 30). A solution to this problem must be found.

Possibly a more reasonable expectation is for special education to result in adults with disabilities being able to compensate for their disabilities by drawing strength

MAKING CONNECTIONS

See the "Validated Practices" boxes in Chapters 3 through 13.

CHAPTER 1 *The Context of Special Education*

from developed abilities. But evaluation of this expectation must be left until a time when it is too late to adjust instruction. Hence, we will have opportunities to "get it right," but we must first decide what "it" is. And maybe "it" is the wrong referent. Remember the overriding principle of special education: First and foremost it is individualized, where each student's performance guides the selection and application of interventions. This approach demands an array of services offered both flexibly and responsibly.

Think again about the range of issues presented in this chapter. What should be clear is that we are left with no single "right answer" to any of the questions we considered. To many of us, exceptionality is a difference that demands an extraordinary response (Kauffman, 1997). Special education is a dynamic, changing, exciting, and controversial field. Although great strides have been made in the past 50 years, much work remains to be done as we strive to "get it right" and provide wonderful educational programs that truly meet the needs of each student with a disability. This job requires everyone to work together to arrive at solutions whereby all children have the access and opportunities they deserve.

Making Connections

Look again at the Advance Organizers at the beginning of the chapter; answers to the Focus and Challenge questions are found here. Also review the questions found throughout this chapter.

In Conclusion

Summary

After centuries of neglect and exclusion, all children and youth with disabilities today have the right to receive a free appropriate public school education. Thus many children receive special education services for at least part of their school careers. However, special education has come under attack in recent years, and the issues that surround it and the concept of disabilities are complex. The time for important questions to be addressed, and for solutions to the special education dilemma to be developed, is now.

Self-Test Questions

Focus Questions

What does it mean to have a disability?

The significance of a disability is related to whether it handicaps the individual.

Disability is a relative concept depending on culture, attitudes, beliefs, discipline, and orientation.

Disability has been part of the human condition since its beginning, and throughout history, people with disabilities typically have been treated harshly.

Where did special education come from and why did it develop?

Special education began

- in France in the late 1700s
- when farmers found a young, abandoned boy in the woods
- the boy was brought to Paris and given to Jean-Marc-Gaspard Itard, a doctor
- Itard spent years trying to teach Victor to speak, read, write, and exhibit the social skills required in French society

Special education developed in America

- through the efforts of Seguin, a student of Itard's
- with residential and public day schools
- but was restricted to some children with disabilities until 1977
- because of the passage of the first Individuals with Disabilities Education Act (IDEA) and of PL 94-142, the Education for All Handicapped Children Act (EHA).

Why did the federal government and the public call for national intervention?

In 1975, Congress found that
- Millions of children with disabilities

were not receiving a free appropriate public education.

- A million children were excluded from educational opportunities.
- Many students with disabilities were not identified and therefore were not being adequately served.
- Special education and related services could be effective.
- States needed federal assistance to pay for special education.

What are some defining features of special education?

FAPE

LRE

Individualized education

Why is special education controversial?

During the last decade, special education was accused of being ineffective, being discriminatory, segregating children from their peers, serving too many students, costing too much and placing a financial burden on local schools, and imposing on schools the administrative burden of protecting and dealing with violent and unruly children.

Debates about the efficacy of special education rage about who should be included, where students with disabilities should be educated, what should their curriculum should be, and to what extent they should participate in the general education curriculum and methodology.

Challenge Question

What are some solutions to the problems faced by students with disabilities and by educators charged with meeting their needs?

Solutions must be developed through responsive, flexible, and creative problem solving techniques.

Educators must be responsive to students and families, listening to multiple perspectives about how satisfied they are about the services provided.

Special education professionals need to develop goals for the field by determining and articulating its purpose, expectations for its outcomes, and standards against which to measure its effectiveness.

Special educators must become sophisticated evaluators of research and must apply only those methods, approaches, techniques, and practices that have been verified through stringent research trials.

MEETING THE STANDARDS AND PREPARING FOR LICENSURE EXAMS

After reading this chapter, you should be able to demonstrate basic knowledge and skills described in the CEC standards listed below. The section of this chapter most applicable to each standard is shown in parentheses at the end of the knowledge or skill statement.

 Council for Exceptional Children   **Content Standard 1: Foundations**

- **Current Practice** Understanding of models, theories, and practices that form the basis for special education practice. (Essence of Disabilities)
- **Rights and Responsibilities** Understanding of laws, policies and ethical principles including rights and responsibilities of students, parents, teachers, other professionals and schools related to exceptional learning needs. (Opportunities for a Better 21st Century)

- **History of the Field** Historical points of view. (Origins of Special Education)

Standards in Practice

You often will be asked to articulate your personal philosophy of teaching when you interview for a teaching position, when you are competing for a promotion or new position, and in your discussions with collaborating professionals. Having a clear understanding of the history of special education, the instructional practices and models on which current exceptional education is based, and the rights and responsibilities of all involved in the educational process is the *backbone* to an informed philosophy.

 Companion Website

Go to the companion website (ablongman.com/smith5e) for detailed text correlations to CEC and INTASC standards, PRAXIS II™ exams, and other state-sponsored licensure exams.

Supplementary Resources

Professional Readings and Resources

Artiles, A. J. (1998). The dilemma of difference: Enriching the disproportionality discourse with theory and context. *The Journal of Special Education, 32,* 32–36.

Finn, Jr., C. E., Rotherham, A. J., & Hokanson, Jr., C. R. (Eds.). (2001). *Rethinking special education for a new century.* Washington, DC: Thomas B. Fordham Foundation and the Progressive Policy Institute.

Kauffman, J. M., Hallahan, D. P., & Ford, D. Y. (Eds.). (1998). Special issue. *The Journal of Special Education, 32,* 3–62.

Lloyd, J. W., Forness, S. R., & Kavale, K. A. (1998). Some methods are more effective than others. *Intervention in School and Clinic, 33,* 195–200.

National Research Council (2002). *Minority students in special education and gifted education.* Committee on Minority Representation in Special Education. M. Suzanne Donovan and Christoper T. Cross, editors. Washington, DC: National Academy Press.

Oswald, D. P., Coutinho, M. J., Best, A. M., & Singh, N. N. (1999). Ethnic representation in special education: The influence of school-related economic and demographic variables. *The Journal of Special Education, 32,* 194–206.

Safford, P. L., & Safford, E. J. (1996). *A history of childhood and disability.* New York: Teachers College Press.

Popular Books

Bauby, J. -D. (1997). *The diving bell and the butterfly.* New York: Knopf.

Gallagher, H. G. (1994). *FDR's splendid deception* (Rev. ed.). Arlington, VA: Vandamere Press.

Hockenberry, J. (1996). *Moving violations: War zones, wheelchairs, and declarations of independence.* NY: Hyperion Press.

Treanor, R. B. (1993). *We overcame: The story of civil rights for disabled people.* Falls Church, VA: Regal Direct Publishing.

Parent, Professional, and Consumer Organizations and Agencies

Council for Exceptional Children (CEC)
1110 North Glebe Road, Suite 300
Arlington, VA 22201-5704
Phone: (703) 620-3660
(888) CEC-SPED
TTY: (703) 264-9446
Web site: http://www.cec.sped.org

ERIC Clearinghouse on Disabilities and Gifted Education (CEC)
1110 North Glebe Road
Arlington, VA 22201-5704
(888) CEC-SPED
V/TTY: (800) 328-0272
Web site: http://www.ericec.org

NICHY National Information Center for Children and Youth with Disabilities
P.O. Box 1492
Washington, DC 20013
Voice/TTY: (800) 695-0285 and (202) 884-8200
E-mail: nichy@aed.org
Web site: http://www.nichy.org

Office of Special Education Programs
U.S. Office of Special Education and Rehabilitative Services
U.S. Department of Education
400 Maryland Ave. SW
Washington, DC 20202-2641
Phone: (202) 205-5465; (202) 205-5507
Web site: www.ed.gov/offices/osers/osep

National Clearinghouse for Professions in Special Education (CEC)
1110 North Glebe Road
Arlington, VA 22201-5704
Phone: (800) 641-7824
TTY: (866) 915-5000
E-mail: ncpse@cec.sped.org
Web site: www.specialedcareers.org/

President's Committee on Employment of People with Disabilities
1331 F Street NW
Washington, DC 20002
Phone: (202) 376-6200
TTY: (202) 376-6205
Web site: http://www.dol.gov/dol/odep/

Video**Workshop** Extra

If the VideoWorkshop package was included with your textbook, go to Chapter 1 of the Companion Website (www.ablongman.com/smith5e) and click on the VideoWorkshop button. Follow the instructions for viewing Video clip 2. Consider this information along with what you have read in Chapter 1 while answering the following questions.

Video Clip 2: Inclusion (Time 3:28)

1. The text explains that society's attitude towards persons with disabilities can be a deterrent to full inclusion of all persons with differences. How is the teacher in the video, Ms. Roberts, helping change attitudes? What else might be done in our schools?

2. Nondisabled peers often benefit from inclusion. How does Lily benefit positively from inclusion in this class? How do the other students, but specifically the peer tutors, Anita and Amy, benefit positively from working with Lily?

Henri de Toulouse-Lautrec, *At the Moulin Rouge*, oil on canvas, 1893–95, 123 × 141 cm, Helen Birch Bartlett Memorial Collection, 1928.610. Photograph courtesy of The Art Insitute of Chicago.

HENRI DE TOULOUSE-LAUTREC, born into a noble French family, was closely related to the royal families of France and England. His childhood was privileged, but also tragic. Probably due to a hereditary condition, he had a speech impairment and was frail. He was highly intelligent but missed months of school. His bones were weak and he used a wheelchair for many long periods during his childhood. Early on Lautrec retreated to painting and became highly productive and success-ful. However, because of his disabilities, his adult life was often in tur-moil and plagued by alcoholism. (Art Institute of Chicago, 1999; Denvir, 1991; Perruchot, 1962).

At the Moulin Rouge was painted in 1895, and is now on display at the Art Institute of Chicago. This painting follows a typical theme of Lautrec, who was fascinated by the nightlife of Paris. Here, he included himself in the background.

2 Individualized Special Educational Programs:

Planning and Delivering Services

A PERSONAL PERSPECTIVE

So What's Gone Wrong Here?

In Vermont, a state where inclusive practices are long-standing and considered exemplary by experts across the nation, some parents are expressing their frustration with the special education process. They are even organizing a group, Citizens Against Unfair Special Education (CAUSE), to speak out against the way the educational system is dealing with them and their children. Here are some of the things they have to say about the special education services their children with disabilities are receiving and the IEP process they are experiencing.

"Parents of special needs kids have to participate in a process set up by federal law to develop an IEP (individualized education plan). This involves an indefinite amount of meetings in which the parents have to negotiate with sometimes up to a dozen school staff and administrators for services."

"Raising a child with special needs can be very challenging, but it pales in comparison with the frustration of the IEP process."

"When you talk about educating special needs kids, it varies in severity up to self-care and behavioral skills that are critical for a family to survive together. Parents are asking for help with education and training. Many of these children will be living with their parents for the rest of the parents' lives."

They say that changes are needed in the way the state's educational system approaches the education of students with disabilities. These parents feel that the state's inclusion policies—which place students of all abilities and developmental stages together— do have some benefits. However, they do not believe that these policies meet the needs of all students with disabilities and their families.

These parents also believe that the costs of implementing the state's inclusion model (which requires many specialists and expensive equipment) are causing the school districts' budgets to sky-rocket.

"It's pitting parents of kids without special needs against the parents of kids with special needs."

Source: From "Parents Form Special-Needs Group" by Eve Thorsen. *Burlington* (Vermont) *Free Press*, Towns section, October 18, 2002, p. 4B. Selections reprinted with permission.

1. **What do you think has gone wrong that parents of students with disabilities are complaining about services designed specifically to meet their needs and those of their children?**

2. **How do these parents' comments fit with information in Chapter 1 of this text relating to national problems surrounding special education and the services it provides?**

3. **How should this situation be resolved?**

Overview

IDEA mandates that students with disabilities receive a free appropriate education in the least restrictive environment possible. Designing an appropriate education requires the combined efforts of educators, related service providers, and the child's family. Individualized education program plans are required by IDEA. These plans include individualized family service plans (IFSPs) and individualized education programs (IEPs); for older students with disabilities, they include a component about transitional plans and services. These blueprints for special education is what every student with disabilities should receive.

Self-Test Questions

Focus Questions

- What are the seven steps in developing an individualized program for each student with disabilities?
- What role does the IEP Team play?
- What factors must be considered when determining the least restrictive environment for individual students?

- What are the different educational placement options that make up the continuum of services for special education?
- What are the different purposes of IDEA's various program plans?

Challenge Question

- How should the array of educational services and supports available to students with disabilities be implemented?

MAKING CONNECTIONS

- Use the learning strategy—Advance Organizers—to help focus your study of this chapter's content, and reinforce your learning by reviewing answers to the Focus questions and the Challenge questions at the end of the chapter.
- Read the "Necessity for National Intervention" section in Chapter 1 to review these issues.

While you read this chapter, consider our discussions in Chapter 1. Think about the basic rights that the Individuals with Disabilities Education Act (IDEA) guarantees to students with disabilities and their families. In this chapter, we will see how those civil rights are exercised through a balance of two important concepts: a free appropriate public education (FAPE) and least restrictive environment (LRE).

OPPORTUNITIES FOR A BETTER FUTURE

IDEA is a very important civil rights law, a national law that imposes many requirements on states and local school systems with the intention of guaranteeing children with disabilities their rights and access to an appropriate education. The protections that IDEA provides were codified into law as a reaction to injustices (such as exclusion from school or the provision of education in a restrictive setting) experienced by children with disabilities and their families during most of the 20th Century. IDEA safeguards these children's rights, and at the heart of these safeguards is the IEP process. Despite promises to the contrary, with each passage of IDEA, the IEP process and its components seem to become more and more cumbersome because more and more requirements have been added. Many of its features are at the root of criticism and complaints about special education. We now have the opportunity to find ways to streamline the process and guarantee students' rights to an appropriate education in the least restrictive environment without burdening teachers and family members with increased duties and responsibilities that yield few benefits.

Turning Legacies into Lessons

Complaints about special education and the requirements of the IEP process come from all quarters. Special education teachers believe that IEPs burdened them with too much paperwork, reducing the amount of instructional time available to work with students. Some special educators believed that students with disabilities were excluded from large-scale achievement assessments and therefore were not part of the education reform movement. General education teachers feel they are ill prepared to teach students with disabilities. They also do not have enough time to collaborate with special educators and related service providers in planning programs for students with disabilities included in their classrooms. Many principals and other administrators think IDEA regulations have negatively changed relationships between parents and schools because of the "legal atmosphere" created by mediation, due process, and civil actions used to resolve disputes with families about services and placement. Administrators complain that the IDEA regulations are too complicated and confusing. Superintendents and state officials are concerned that the increasing costs of educating students with disabilities sap funds that would otherwise be available for nondisabled students. And Congress and other policymakers have felt that the IEP results in unequal treatment of students with disabilities because, unlike their nondisabled classmates, they cannot be expelled from school for violent, disruptive, or potentially dangerous behaviors at school.

Thinking About Dilemmas to Solve

As you read this chapter, think about ways to guarantee the education rights of students with disabilities and yet address the issues listed here. Think about how to

- Reduce the paperwork burden.

- Encourage Congress to increase the federal contribution to the education costs of students with disabilities.

- Increase planning time for general education teachers to collaborate with special educators and related service providers.

- Streamline the legal requirements of IDEA.

- Make the IEP process less contentious.

SPECIAL EDUCATION SERVICES

As discussed in Chapter 1, IDEA is the law that provides the framework for special education. Originally passed as Public Law (PL) 94-142 in 1975, IDEA remains first a civil rights law, guaranteeing a free appropriate public education (FAPE), from birth through age 21, for all youngsters with disabilities. The law also requires states and local school districts to provide individualized education programs in the least restrictive environment (LRE) possible. **Special education** should always be based on the individual needs of the student and his or her family, not on what might be currently available at a neighborhood school. This individualized instruction is delivered by many different professionals who provide a broad array of services. Special education should not be defined by place, because its services are delivered in a wide range of settings, including the **general education** classroom. It is also not defined by any single curriculum or instructional program; however, to the greatest extent possible, students with special needs should participate in the general education curriculum. Like that of their nondisabled peers, the progress of students with disabilities in the curriculum in which they are participating should be evaluated, as is mandated in the reauthorization of the Elementary and Secondary Education Act: No Child Left Behind (Ziegler, 2002). All children, in whatever way is appropriate, must participate in state and district testing.

Here is another way of thinking about special education: It is an array of educational services, a consortium of professionals from a variety of disciplines, the availability of specialized expertise, and individualized educational programs that are directed toward specific goals and objectives and evaluated in terms of curriculum based benchmarks. Let's first look at the services special education provides to students with disabilities and their families.

MAKING **C**ONNECTIONS

For background about IDEA and other laws protecting the rights of persons with disabilities, see the "Necessity for National Intervention" section in Chapter 1.

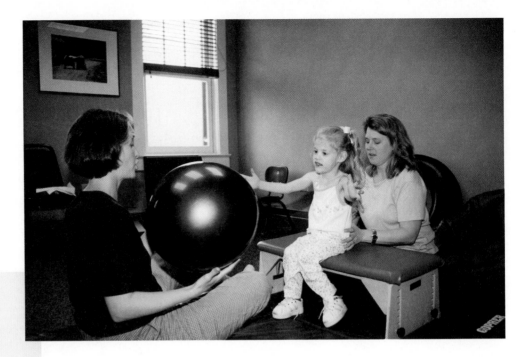

Some children require the services of professionals from different disciplines, such as physical therapy.

What services does special education offer?

Special education is an evolving concept, so the services that special education offers continue to expand and change. Special education includes classroom as well as related services. Special education services should be flexible and responsive to the needs of each student. Children and youth with special needs should have access to a variety of services that offer the support they need to achieve their potential. This support varies with the type, intensity, location, personnel, and duration of special education. One way to think about special education and related services is to envision a support system that contains a rich **array of services** consisting of components that are individually determined and applied. The term *array of services* implies that students do not have to travel, step by step, up and down a ladder of services but rather have available many selections. For example, in some cases, with support from a consulting teacher or specialist (for instance, an SLP), the general education classroom can meet the needs of the student. Other cases require more intensive services from many different specialists.

What are the critical features of special education programs?

Six fundamental principles are integral to the implementation of IDEA and are stressed by the federal government as being critical features of special education programs offered to children and youth with disabilities (U.S. Department of Education, 1999):

- A free appropriate public education (FAPE)
- An individualized education program (IEP)
- The least restrictive environment (LRE)
- Appropriate evaluations

- Parent and student participation in decision making
- Procedural safeguards

Let's briefly review these fundamental provisions of IDEA, the foundations for individualized education programs offered through special education. Then we will turn our attention to information about who ensures that these provisions are delivered.

- *Free Appropriate Public Education (FAPE)* IDEA guarantees all children and youth with disabilities and their families a **free appropriate public education (FAPE)** regardless of where they receive their education (e.g., school for the Deaf, general education classroom). This also applies to students in the juvenile justice system (National Center on Education, Disability, and Juvenile Justice, 2002). The word *education* here is broadly defined to include all types of supportive services and a curriculum that may differ from that presented in general education. To be appropriate, the program must be highly individualized, or, as some are now calling it, "customized" (Smith et al., 2001). Few special education graduates, particularly those with cognitive disabilities, successfully complete the traditional secondary general education curriculum. This may be because they drop out of school, participate in an alternative curriculum, or cannot pass the final competency tests. The concept of an array of curricular options fits with the concept of FAPE. For some students with disabilities, it may include a functional curriculum where the traditional emphasis on academics is less important than focusing on adult outcomes, such as living and working in the community satisfactorily (Hanson et al., 2001). For some youngsters, FAPE may mean participation in community based instruction that allows students to learn important job and life skills in the natural environment—that is, in the community, not in a general education class. But for most, FAPE means participation in the general education program.

Each student with disabilities is entitled to a tailor-made and individually designed educational program complete with supportive (related) services. The costs of these services are the responsibility of the state and the public school system, not the family. Services delivered are determined by the needs of the child, not the convenience of the school district. Also, the cost of the services cannot be a factor in whether they are provided to a child who requires them. For example, if Samantha requires a special communications device to benefit from special education and to participate in a general education placement, that device and the training in how to use it must be part of her IEP. The school district must provide the equipment for Samantha. (Community leaders often find private funding to help school districts pay for such special equipment.) Teachers and parents must understand that when the school district purchases equipment, the district, not Sam, owns the device. Depending on the district's policy, Samantha may or may not be able to take the equipment home with her or practice using the equipment in a variety of settings. If Sam's insurance company purchases the assistive technology equipment, however, it belongs to Sam.

As a final note about these IDEA requirements, FAPE is a guarantee to all students with disabilities. Therefore, states and schools are obligated to seek out and identify all children with disabilities. This obligation in the law is referred to as **child find** and, particularly in the early days of IDEA, was a major effort in most states. Child find systems are now firmly in place, and states use public information campaigns, direct contact with social service agencies, and other types of outreach efforts to locate and provide services to every child with a disability.

- *Individualized Education Program (IEP)* As we have just noted, for an educational program to be appropriate for each child with a disability, it must be individualized. Therefore, it is clear that there is no single answer to the educational

MAKING **C**ONNECTIONS
Review the "What IDEA Says About FAPE" box in Chapter 1.

Special Education Services

needs of all students with disabilities: no standard program, no single service delivery option, no single place where education is received, and no single curriculum. For these reasons, the expression "no one shoe fits all" has recently become a special education mantra. (More information about IEPs is found later in this chapter.)

When parents, teachers, and students share the results from IEP team meetings, everyone understands goals, expectations, and the purpose of instruction.

• *Least Restrictive Environment (LRE)* The concept of LRE is controversial, and it is at the heart of many of the debates that divide the field of special education. These debates about LRE are not new. Heated discussions about placement issues have raged for decades. Current debates about whether students with disabilities should receive their entire education in general education classes began in 1986. The then director of the federal Office of Special Education Programs, Madeline Will, began the push for more inclusion of students with disabilities into general education (at that time, the idea was called the Regular Education Initiative). Today, many issues related to where and how special education services should be delivered remain unresolved.

MAKING
CONNECTIONS

Review the "What IDEA Says About LRE" box in Chapter 1.

Does LRE always mean placement in the general education classroom? Do feelings of "restriction" and isolation go hand in hand with segregated special education settings? These questions have no simple answers. Educators must be constantly aware of how placement decisions can segregate students by removing them from the role models their peers provide, from diverse social interactions, and from the standard curriculum. Educators must be sensitive to how placement decisions can also brand students as different and fragment their daily lives. Finally, removing a child from the general education classroom has serious implications for today and the future. Special education placements have resulted in lower expectations, a less challenging curriculum, and a self-fulfilling prophecy of reduced educational outcomes. However, general education placement can deny many youngsters specialized instruction with scientifically validated practices (such as community based instruction in job-related skills).

Debate among parents, special educators, general educators, politicians, and the media continually focuses on the concept of LRE and how it should be interpreted. On one side of the issue are those who believe that a full array of options should be available to youngsters with disabilities (Commission on the Deaf, 1988; Crockett, 1999–2000; Deshler, 2001; Vaughn, Elbaum, & Boardman, 2001; Vaughn & Schumm, 1995). They advocate **integration** into general classrooms and general education activities whenever possible, but they also argue that other services, even separate schooling, may sometimes be necessary to meet the individual needs of the child (Crockett, 1999–2000). Agreement on how to make decisions about LRE and integration has not been achieved. As some professionals have pointed out, the general education classroom teacher referred the child in the first place, indicating that at least *this* professional believes that the general education classroom, as it is currently structured, is not the most appropriate placement for the child (Keogh, 1988; MacMillan & Forness, 1998; Smith, 1988). In that teacher's view, the child needs additional support in the general education classroom, supplemental services, or possibly a separate curriculum in order to have a successful educational experience. Also, many parents and professionals, particularly those concerned with blind or deaf students, feel that the array of placement options must include residential center schools. In their view, general education placements can be the most restrictive of settings for those who are often excluded from social and extracurricular activities by their nondisabled peers. On the other side of the issue is the interpretation that LRE is a legal mandate and ethical obligation that ensures the right of those with disabilities to be fully included in general education settings (Sailor, 1991; Snell, 1988; Stainback et al., 1994; Turnbull et al., 2002). The debate about full inclusion and about where students with disabilities should receive their education is one of the hottest and most contentious issues facing parents and educators.

As professionals argue about LRE—what it is, where it can happen, and how it should be determined—the children and youth who are experiencing whatever it is that adults have decided for them are typically left out of the conversation. Many students with disabilities feel concerns about where their special education services are received. For example, some older students with severe disabilities indicate that they are more comfortable attending classes with friends who have similar interests and abilities (Palmer et al., 2001). Students with less severe disabilities, 60 percent in one study, preferred special class placements because of strong negative experiences they had had in general education classes (Lovitt, Plavins, & Cushing, 1999). In another study, 76 percent of elementary school students with disabilities indicated that they liked going to special education classes, and 90 percent believed that the services provided in those classes were beneficial (Padeliadu & Zigmond, 1996). And in yet another study, children with learning disabilities preferred pull-out programs because they thought they received special assistance and could work in a quieter setting (Klingner et al., 1998; Vaughn et al., 2001). Maybe we should listen to the collective voices of students with disabilities to learn about what services they prefer and what practices are effective! At least from the limited studies conducted, it seems that although some students prefer to receive all of their education in general education classes, others do not. This observation certainly supports retaining different options for special education and allowing for a variety of interpretations of LRE.

• *Appropriate Evaluations* Assessments of students' performance have many different purposes. Three types of **evaluation** are particularly important in special education, and each serves a different function:

1. Identify and qualify students for special education.

2. Guide instruction, continually ensuring that the practices implemented are effective, so that a minimal amount of instructional time is wasted using a tactic that is ineffective or has lost its power for an individual child.

3. Determine annual or long-term gains, possibly through statewide or districtwide achievement tests given to entire classes of students, or by assessing progress toward achieving benchmarks listed on IEPs.

Remember, all evaluation instruments or procedures selected should reflect the purpose or intended outcomes of the evaluation process.

Evaluations of students with disabilities usually include a "battery of tests" (more than one test or type of assessment). They often include standardized tests that were normed on large groups of people. (Intelligence and achievement tests are examples of standardized instruments.) The use of standardized tests concerns many educators, because such tests contribute to the overrepresentation of culturally and linguistically diverse students in special education. In an attempt to resolve or at least monitor this problem, the authors of IDEA now require states to collect data and change practices that may be discriminatory.

Also, states now encourage diagnosticians to use a full array of evaluation instruments and procedures, rather than relying exclusively on standardized tests.

For more about identifying students with disabilities see the "Defined" sections of Chapters 3–13.

MAKING CONNECTIONS

See the "What IDEA Says about Nondiscriminatory Testing" box in Chapter 1.

Today, many professionals are advocating the use of **authentic assessments,** which use the work that students generate in classroom settings as the assessment measurements (Fuchs & Deno, 1994; Fuchs & Fuchs, 1998). In other words, evaluation is made directly from the curriculum and the students' work. Results on students' class assignments (spelling tests, math tests), anecdotal records, writing samples, and observational data are examples of authentic assessments. Authentic assessments also include ongoing, frequent evaluations of students' performance. **Curriculum based measurement (CBM),** often thought of as a self-correcting instructional method that incorporates a data collection system, is now being proposed as an evaluation system as well (Bradley, Danielson, & Hallahan, 2002). When using CBM, teachers collect data about a child's daily progress on each instructional task. For example, a teacher instructing a youngster in math would keep a daily record of the number or percentage of problems the child correctly solved. This record helps the teacher judge whether the instructional methods selected are both efficient and effective. With CBM, teachers know how well their students are learning and whether the chosen instructional methods help the child meet the goals and objectives of the individualized plan.

Also considered a form of authentic assessment, **portfolio assessment** gets the students themselves involved in the process. Students can select a variety of samples of their work, over a period of time, to show their growth and development (Curran & Harris, 1996; Hébert, 2001; Salend, 1998). The portfolio may also include prizes, certificates of award, pictures, dictated work, photographs, lists of books read, and selections from work done with others. Finally, a portfolio might include narratives, written by the teacher or by others who work with the child, about challenging situations or patterns of behavior that should be a focus of concern.

Functional behavioral assessment, another type of authentic assessment, is typically used to understand a student's problem behaviors (Fitzsimmons, 1998; Horner, 1994). This well-researched system, which was developed with students with severe disabilities, leads teachers directly to socially validated outcomes and holds much promise for all students (Larson & Maag, 1998). It helps determine the nature of the behavior of concern, the reason or motivation for the behavior, and under what conditions the behavior does not occur. For example, are a student's temper tantrums a result of frustration by academic work that is too difficult? And does the frequency of the disruptive behaviors diminish when the student is assigned a peer tutor who can help with an assignment? Conducting a functional assessment involves the following five steps:

1. Verify the seriousness of the problem.
2. Define the problem behavior in concrete terms.
3. Collect data on possible causes of the problem behavior.
4. Analyze the data.
5. Formulate and test a hypothesis (Fitzsimmons, 1998, pp. 1–2).

IDEA suggests that functional behavioral assessments be conducted when students with disabilities are faced with disciplinary actions.

• *Parent and Student Participation in Decision Making* IDEA stresses the importance of involving families and students with disabilities in the IEP process. A major goal of the IEP meeting is to form a partnership among parents, schools, and professionals. Educators need to recognize, however, that many parents believe the schools control the special education process. They feel disenfranchised or confused about rules, regulations, and the purpose of special education (Cartledge, Kea, & Ida, 2000). For families who do not speak English well enough to understand the complicated language we use to talk about special education issues, participation may seem impossible (Hughes, Valle-Riestra, & Arguelles, 2002). In such instances, schools must welcome family members or people from the community who are flu-

MAKING CONNECTIONS

For more information about parent involvement of diverse families, see these sections in Chapter 3:

- Prevalence
- Causes and Prevention
- Families

CHAPTER 2 *Individualized Special Educational Programs*

ent in the family's native language and also knowledgeable about the special education process. The law encourages the family's maximal participation, and it is the obligation of educators to include and inform parents and students about the efforts that will be made on their behalf.

● *Procedural Safeguards* The IDEA laws prior to 1997 included many **procedural safeguards,** and the 1997 reauthorization expanded some of those protections. The "What IDEA Says" box lists many of these protections, but a few important points that educators should keep in mind are summarized next.

The first point to remember is that it is important to communicate with parents and family members and that communication must be meaningful. Therefore, to ensure that communication with parents about their children's educational programs has occurred, notification about meetings and other important events (change in the IEP, change in the child's placement, plans for evaluation) need to be in writing. Also, parents need to understand the meaning of communications from school, so these interactions must be in the native language of the parents, and they need to be clear and free from special education jargon. Second, many parents do not know their rights or understand the special education process. It is the school's obligation to be sure they know that they have to give permission for their children to be tested or evaluated, that they have a right to participate in the special education planning process, that they have the right to examine their child's records, and that they can obtain an independent educational evaluation of their child.

Parents have a right to challenge any of the school's decisions about the education of their child. The disagreement may then be taken to a **mediation** process. If agreement between the two parties cannot be reached, a **due process hearing** may be called, in which an impartial third party settles the dispute (Ahearn, 2002 April). If either party does not agree with the decision made at the due process hearing, it can appeal to the state education agency. A party who still does not agree, may take the matter to the civil courts and have a **judicial hearing.** These rights include the right to legal counsel and other rights concerning witnesses, written evidence, verbatim documentation of the hearing, and an appeal. The state or school district is obligated to pay the parents' legal costs (possibly at reduced fees, however) if the parents prevail.

Who provides these services?

At the heart of special education are the wonderful professionals who provide multidisciplinary services to students with disabilities and their families. A special educator might be a paraprofessional (teacher's aide), a resource specialist, a consultant, an itinerant teacher, a special education classroom teacher, a job coach, a **home or hospital teacher,** or an administrator. In addition, special education professionals might work in a related service (e.g., adaptive physical education, assistive technology, audiology, occupational therapy, physical therapy, school health services, speech/language pathology) to create the multi- or transdisciplinary team necessary to create the flexible services needed by many students with disabilities. (See Figure 2.1 for a model of how these specialists are coordinated and work together.) The federal government considers the professionals who provide these related services—such as school nurses who perform school health services for students with disabilities and school counselors who provide counseling or guidance

What IDEA Says About

Procedural Safeguards

Parents of each student with a disability have the right to

- Be notified and invited to all meetings held about their child's educational program
- Give permission for their child to be evaluated and to obtain independent evaluations
- Access to their child's educational records
- Participate in all decisions about their child's educational program, placement, goals, and objectives
- Mediation, due process, and civil action

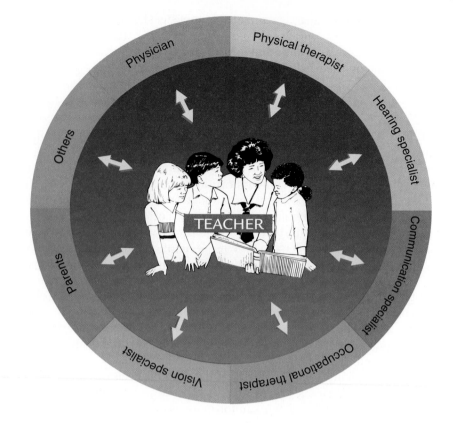

Figure 2.1 Organization of the Transdisciplinary Team. *In this approch, the classroom teacher is the primary service provider and team coordinator.*

Source: From "Customizing instruction to maximize functional outcomes for students with profound multiple disabilities" by P. D. Smith, D. L. Gast, K. R. Logan, and H. A. Jacobs, 1999–2000, *Exceptionality, 9,* p. 137. Reprinted by permission.

MAKING **C**ONNECTIONS

See the "Making Accommodations" boxes in Chapters 3–13 for more ideas about meeting students' unique learning needs.

to children with disabilities and their families (e.g., parent training or support)— part of the special education team whose costs are in part covered by IDEA funding (U.S. Department of Education, 1999). Sometimes special education professionals are **itinerant,** such as itinerant teachers or SLPs who travel from school to school. Others might work at one school delivering a very special set of skills, like some audiologists who only work with Deaf students at one **center school,** a separate school that only students with disabilities attend.

Many people contribute to the appropriate education of students with disabilities but are not considered to offer a related service. General education teachers are one example. Adovates and lawyers are another. Although not listed in IDEA as related services, the services of these professionals are vital to the educational programs for many students with disabilities. Adovates and lawyers, for example, can be helpful in ensuring that students' rights under IDEA are protected (U.S. Department of Education, 1999).

Special education teachers, related service providers, and general education teachers collaborate—work cooperatively—to ensure that each student receives an appropriate education in the least restrictive setting possible. Together they form teams and use a method called collaboration to adapt and modify instruction so that students with disabilities can participate in the general education curriculum to the maximal extent possible. Crucial to positive experiences for students with disabilities are general education teachers. Their attitudes, particularly if they are uneasy with and even reject students with disabilities, influence outcomes for these students (Cook, 2001; Cook et al., 2000). Such negative attitudes are often subtly expressed in the way in which they talk about students with disabilities and the **accommodations** they need to participate successfully in the general education curriculum (Smith, Salend, & Ryan, 2001). Another key person in the collaborative effort at every school is the school principal (Williams & Katsiyannis, 1998). Because principals often coordinate management efforts at their site, they can be most helpful in developing and ensuring the delivery of accommodations and **adaptions** (particu-

CHAPTER 2 *Individualized Special Educational Programs*

larly for large-scale assessments), in monitoring the variety of services indicated on a student's IEP, and in coordinating services throughout the school and across the district.

Where are special education services provided?

Let's look at different models used to deliver special education classroom services. Toward the end of the last century, a model called **full inclusion** gained momentum. One version of this model became known as **pull-in programming.** In this system, children with disabilities receive *all* of their education in the general education classroom. Under this approach, special education and related service therapies (e.g., speech, physical therapy) are provided to the child in the general education classroom (Welch et al., 1995). Recently, other full inclusion models have gained in popularity. For example, team teaching, **co-teaching,** and **consultation/collaborative teaching** are now being tried in the schools (Fennick, 2001; Friend, 2000). One major benefit of such new approaches, as co-teaching is that accommodations for learning differences are developed initially, as part of lesson plans. Here, general and special education teachers to work as a team to modify the curriculum, teaching strategies, and materials for students with learning differences. Results from these new approaches are mixed, some results positive and others not (Fox & Ysseldyke, 1997; Hunt & Goetz, 1997; Klingner et al., 1998; Rea, McLaughlin, & Walther-Thomas, 2002; Salend & Duhaney, 1999). Why might this be so? One reason is that people apply different criteria to judge the merits of special education. Some think that gains in social skills are more important than gains in academic or life skills. Another reason is that what works for some special needs students does not work for others. Regardless, it is clear both from teachers' comments and from research findings that fully including students with disabilities is hard work and succeeds only when teams of professionals commit considerable effort to the endeavor (Kennedy, Shukla, & Fryxell, 1997). Full inclusion and other service delivery options are listed and explained in Table 2.1.

All of these services and placement options come together to form an **array of services** that are flexible and responsive to the needs of each student. Furthermore, these services need not be provided in any rigid, prescribed order. The supports offered through the array of special education services vary in type, intensity, location, personnel, and duration. Special education and related services together form

General and special education teachers work side by side in the pull-in service delivery model.

Special Education Services

Table 2.1 Service Delivery Options

Type	Description	Government Category	Government Criterion
Pull-In Programming (Full Inclusion)	All special education and related services are brought to the student in the general education classroom setting.	Regular (general education) class	No separate government category exists. Although all services are delivered in the general education category, placement data are reflected in the "less than 21%" category.
Co-teaching	General education and special education teachers teach together in the same classroom for the entire school day. Students may be "pulled out" for related services.	Regular (general education) class	No separate government category exists. Although all services are delivered in the general education category, placement data are reflected in the "less than 21%" category.
Consultation/ Collaborative Teaching	General education and special education teachers work together to meet the needs of special needs students. Students are seldom removed from the general education class.	Regular (general education) class	Students receive special education and related services outside the general education class for less than 21% of the school day.
Itinerant or Consultative Services	The teacher and/or student receives assistance from a specialist who may serve many students at many schools.	Regular (general education) class	Students receive special education and related services outside the general education class for less than 21% of the school day.
Resource Room (Pull-Out Programming)	Student attends a regular class most of the day but goes to a special education class several hours per day or for blocks of time each week.	Resource room	Includes students who receive special education and related services for at least 21% and not more than 60% of their school day.
Special Education Class (Partially Self-Contained)	Student attends a special class but is integrated into regular education classes for a considerable amount of time each day.	Separate class	Students receive special education for more than 60% of their day, outside of the general education classroom.
Special Education Class (Self-Contained)	Student attends a special class most of the school day and is included in regular education activities minimally.	Separate class	Students receive special education for more than 60% of their day, outside of the general education classroom.
Special Education Schools (Center Schools)	Center schools—some private, others supported by the state—serve only students with a specific category of disability. Some offer residential services; others do not.	Public separate school facility; private separate school facility; public residential facility; private residential facility	Includes students who receive their education for more than 50% of the day (a) in a separate day school, (b) in a public or private residential facility at public expense, (c) in a hospital setting, or (d) at home.

a support system that includes a rich array of services individually determined and applied. Each student's level of need for each type of service is assessed continually so that children do not go too long without individualized services that are needed, nor is their access to the general education curriculum unnecessarily restricted.

The most common way, however, to describe the educational services and settings available is to use the term **continuum of services.** IDEA reaffirms that a continuum of services must be available to children and youth with disabilities and to their families, and the law does not suggest that one service delivery option (such as the general education class) should be the single alternative. The "continuum" concept implies a full range of alternatives. For example, a continuum of living arrangements for people with disabilities would probably include a large congregate institution, smaller congregate facilities, foster care, structured group homes, independent group homes, apartments with roommates, and independent apartments and homes. For special education, the continuum of educational services includes hospital

CHAPTER 2 *Individualized Special Educational Programs*

and home settings, residential center schools, and general education placements.

An older description of the continuum model is **cascade of services** (Deno, 1970). This concept of special education has many pitfalls, but it was most often criticized because progress was to occur in lock step, and students found it difficult—almost impossible—to move to each successively more integrated placement. As a result, many students who were placed in a separate classroom for special education remained in that setting throughout their school careers, even as their educational needs changed and they reached a point where resource or itinerant services would have been more appropriate. The cascade also became associated with the severity of the student's disability. The incorrect assumption was that youngsters with the most severe disabilities should receive services in a full-time, self-contained classroom. That assumption, however, is often erroneous. It may be that one student with a severe disability is most appropriately served in the general education classroom, whereas another with a moderate disability requires temporary placement in a full-day special education classroom. Another child with a learning disability may not be able to profit from the type of initial reading instruction offered in the general education classroom and, until his basic reading skills are mastered, is better served in an intensive special education program.

The student's age is often a factor that needs to be considered when making placement decisions (Hanson et al., 2001). For example, many students with severe disabilities attend inclusive preschools, with parents universally positive about those experiences. However, as these students get older and their educational goals become more and more different from those of their nondisabled peers (e.g., life and vocational skills versus preparation for college), specialized and more restrictive programs often become the preferred choice. Smaller classes, more specialized therapies and services, peer acceptance, and specialized teaching skills are available outside the general education setting. Also, it becomes more difficult to achieve positive peer relationships with nondisabled classmates as students with severe disabilities progress in age and in school years (Hall & McGregor, 2000). For these reasons, many parents have observed that their children with severe disabilities prefer friendship opportunities with others with similar disabilities—opportunities they find more easily in special education settings (Palmer et al., 2001).

Unfortunately, the problems associated with the cascade model also plague the concept of "continuum of services." Because some criticisms of special education focus on special education segregating students with disabilities from their nondisabled peers, both professionals and parents have to work hard to find ways to provide services needed for an appropriate education without unnecessarily segregating children. To avoid the problems of the past, a flexible approach is necessary when professionals determine services, supports, and placements for students with disabilities. A key factor in this process should be the analysis of the outcomes or goals for each student. For example, careful consideration of the goals of integrated employment, community living, citizenship and involvement, and personal autonomy and life satisfaction should all factor into the decisions about the topics of instruction each individual should receive. In identifying what services an individual requires and where they should be delivered, the student with disabilities and the family should be the focus. The balance between FAPE and LRE can be challenging to achieve, but it is this tension that keeps special education fluid and responsive to individual needs (see Figure 2.2).

Let's consider the special education service delivery options and how often they are used. Here are some important points to keep in mind (U.S. Department of Education, 2001):

1. Nearly all (96 percent) students with disabilities attend school on general education campuses.

2. Almost half (47 percent) attend general education classes for more than 80 percent of the school day.

Figure 2.2 A Special Challenge. *Achieving a balance between FAPE and LRE can be difficult.*

3. Less than 3 percent of all students with disabilities are educated in separate public or private day center schools.

4. Less than 1 percent of students with disabilities attend residental facilities, and about 0.5 percent are educated in home or hospital settings.

Placement rates are changing, reflecting more inclusive practices. For example, in 1984–85 only about 25 percent of students with disabilities attended general education classes for more than 80 percent of the school day, and today that percentage has risen to almost half. Resource room placements are becoming a less common placement option. Additional data indicate that the average class size of resource rooms is rapidly becoming too great for students to be provided, in that setting, with the special instruction they need. These facts worry some learning disabilities, experts who are concerned that an option that many students with disabilities need is disappearing or becoming ineffective (Moody et al., 2000).

Be careful not to make assumptions about data drawn from large groups. It might seem, because each state has about the same proportion of youngsters with disabilities, and because students with disabilities have similar needs for education no matter where they live, that we would see in each state roughly the same percentage of students in each type of educational environment. However, the rates at which states use each type of placement vary tremendously (U.S. Department of Education, 2001). For example, New York's rate of segregated day and residential placements is more than four times Oregon's rate. In Texas, 27 percent of all students with disabilities receive their education in general education classes for most of the school day, whereas in Colorado that percentage was 71. Placement rates also vary widely by state and by disability. For example, in North Dakota 80 percent of all students with visual disabilities receive their education in general education classrooms, whereas in Utah some 24 percent do. Clearly, it is not only students' characteristics that determine their LRE. Such variations may well contribute to some of the criticism leveled at special education. What do you think are some reasons for the differences between states? Do you think that this is a problem the federal and state governments should address?

Do special education students participate in the general education curriculum?

IDEA stresses the importance of students with disabilities having access to the general education curriculum. One criticism of special education is that it is ineffective. Of course, that evaluation is dependent on the goals held for special education: achieving the skills necessary for independent living or passing the state-adopted competency tests that students must pass to be awarded a standard high school diploma. Regardless, of this there is no doubt: The likelihood of passing statewide competency tests is low for those who do not participate in the curriculum the tests reflect. Choices that need to be made about instruction and curriculum are complex and have long-term effects. Let's look at these important requirements of IDEA: participating in the general education curriculum and in statewide or district-wide assessments.

• *Access to the General Education Curriculum* With the 1997 passage of IDEA came the requirement that students with disabilities have access to the general education curriculum and to reforms that occur in general education at the state, district, and local school levels. Each student's IEP must address participation in and access to the general education curriculum (see the "What IDEA Says" box. If a student is removed from this curriculum, the IEP must specifically explain why the student cannot participate at that particular time (U.S. Department of Education, 1999). Students with disabilities should participate in the general education curriculum and should be removed and placed in an alternative curriculum only when *"supplementary support and services can be demonstrated as benefiting the student"* (Yell & Shriner, 1997, p. 7). This change in IDEA may well become a new defining feature of LRE: Rather than access to a place or service, it is access to a curriculum.

Simply attending classes in general education does not ensure participation in the general education curriculum. To succeed in the general education curriculum, most students with disabilities require instructional accommodations that are tailored to the specific strengths and needs of the individual student. Accommodations do not change the content or difficulty of the curriculum; rather, they alter how the student receives information or how the student demonstrates learning (King-Sears, 2001). Here are a few examples of accommodations that were matched to students' specific learning needs:

• Difficulty reading textbooks	Listens to text on audiotape Uses graphics to organize information Outlines text using a standard format
• Problems with eye–hand coordination	Solves every other math problem Tapes class lectures Types a critique

Why did federal lawmakers and advocates for students with disabilities insist that IDEA be changed to include these requirements? Congress had heard too many reports that students with disabilities were not achieving as well as they should and that the gap in both achievement and adult outcomes between students with and those without disabilities was widening (U.S. Department of Education, 1999). The government also had data from across the nation indicating that only 26 percent of students with disabilities receive a standard diploma when they graduate from high school (Office of Special Education Programs, 2000). It is assumed that connecting goals and objectives from the general education curriculum, along with consistently evaluating benchmarks indicating achievement, will raise standards and expectations—and graduation rates—for students with disabilities (Lanford & Cary, 2000). The hope is that when all students are included in state and district assessments, all educators will become accountable for improved academic outcomes. These hopes are shared by many. For example, the Gallaudet Research Institute reports that only 34 percent of hard of hearing and deaf students passed high school graduation competency tests in 1998 (Johnson, 2001). However, with the increased acceptance of

What IDEA Says About

Access to the General Education Curriculum

The IEP of each student with a disability must

■ Indicate how the disability affects involvement and progress in the general education curriculum

■ Include annual goals that reflect inclusion in the general education curriculum

■ Describe how the educational program will be modified

■ Indicate how the student will participate in extracurricular and nonacademic activities

■ Discuss plans for integrating the student with his or her nondisabled peers

MAKING
CONNECTIONS

For more about ASL and
Deaf students' academic
progress, see Chapter 10.

American Sign Language (ASL) and the continual assessment of students' progress, optimism about these students meeting high expectations abounds.

The disconnect between general and special education has been documented time and time again. Perhaps the best example is the absence of special educators in the conversation about general education reforms and the absence of general educators from conversations about special education reforms. The IEP process now requires that professionals who have knowledge about the general education curriculum be made available to students.

MAKING
CONNECTIONS

For a reminder of the major
laws that include requirements for students with disabilities, see Table 1.2 and
the accompanying text in
Chapter 1.

• *Participation in Statewide or District-wide Assessments* Although special education students experience frequent—for many, daily—assessments of their educational progress, they have not consistently participated in the large-scale assessments designed to evaluate the progress of their nondisabled peers. At the end of the last century, general dissatisfaction grew about the educational results of all students attending public schools, particularly those students who attended schools in the inner cities. For these reasons, calls for more assessment of students' progress were heard from the public, in the press, in Congress, and in state legislatures. And, in many states, policymakers have added both incentives and disincentives to schools on the basis of students' overall performance. President Bush (both while campaigning and as president) has brought issues of testing and educational accountability to the forefront. One of the first major education reforms the Bush administration was the set of changes it sought in the reauthorization of the federal Elementary and Secondary Education Act, which is now referred to as the No Child Left Behind Act of 2001. This law requires annual testing of *all* children (Ziegler, 2002). The ultimate expectation is that all children will achieve proficiency in reading and math, and if children's test scores indicate that they do not reach those levels, the schools they attend will experience significant disincentives. What is often called **high stakes testing** has now become a system of rewarding schools for good student achievement on these standardized tests and sanctioning schools that do not meet the mark.

Although the nation has expressed concern about public education and has spent years discussing ways to improve the achievement of America's students, most remarkably, the results of students with disabilities were not part of those discussions (Vanderwood et al., 1998). In fact, in most **statewide** and **district-wide assessments,** students with disabilities were not included. Because they had not been part of these accountability systems, it is not known to what extent they participated in such tests nationally (Thurlow, 1998). We do know that participation rates, even within the same school district, varied widely, all students with disabilities participating at some schools and only a few participating at other schools (VanEtten, 1998). Although many states still do not report data about how many students with disabilities participate in these accountability programs, it appears that the numbers are increasing (American Youth Policy Forum and Center on Education Policy, 2002). Possibly,

Source: Trevor, *Albuquerque Journal.* Reprinted by permission.

CHAPTER 2 *Individualized Special Educational Programs*

less than half of students with disabilities are actually participating, so there is considerable room for more inclusion. Given the difficulties that many students with disabilities have mastering academic subjects, why are experts encouraging more inclusion? Here's one answer: "Assessments frequently serve as the cornerstone of efforts to improve education. If students with disabilities are excluded from the development and administration of statewide assessments, it is less likely that they will benefit from overall school reform improvements" (Landau, Vohs, & Romano, 1998, p. 1).

But some special educators are concerned that general educators will now see a risk to including students with disabilities in their classes. They may fear that they will be held responsible for these students' insufficient progress in the general education curriculum. General educators are worried that including "difficult-to-teach" students at their schools and in their classes will result in disincentives, such as reductions in the school's budget, bad reports in the press, and poor public image. Some experts are concerned that students with disabilities will become less welcome in general education classes and schools and that the end result will be a reversal of the trend of inclusive education. Others say that if students with disabilities participate in the development of these tests (that is, if they are part of the groups used to norm these tests), such concerns will disappear (Thurlow, 1998). Still others believe that if students with disabilities receive proper accommodations while taking these tests, they can and will perform well. Another way to think about accountability is to use **low stakes testing,** wherein schools and teachers do not incur disincentives but, rather, receive more assistance when working with high numbers of "difficult-to-teach" youngsters. And many also believe that the process will become more equitable (Elliott, Kratochwill, & Schulte, 1998). Here are some examples of the types of adaptations of the testing situation that many students with disabilities profit from:

- Braille versions of tests
- Tests read to the student
- Directions explained several ways
- Extended time to take tests
- Breaks in the testing sessions
- Aids or adaptive equipment
- Directions signed to the student
- Dictating answers to an assistant
- Taking tests in a quiet space
- Tests given over several days

INDIVIDUALIZED SPECIAL EDUCATION PROGRAMS

To safeguard the principles embodied in the concept of a free appropriate public education, IDEA requires that an individualized program plan be developed and implemented for every child identified as having a disability and in need of special education. Individualized plans are required by other laws as well. For example, federal regulations, such as those for Medicaid and Social Security, require that individualized plans also be developed and implemented for individuals residing in institutions or community-based living arrangements, such as group homes. Written, individualized rehabilitation plans are also required for people receiving vocational rehabilitation. Individualized plans thus cover a range of educational, social, and vocational goals of people with disabilities. Although the various types of plans respond to different goals, all share some basic principles. For example, such plans typically include a description of the individual's current abilities and disabilities, goals and related objectives, a summary of services to be provided, and the ways these services are to be evaluated. For those concerned with schools and educational systems, it is only IDEA that requires an individual plan for children. So, only students with disabilities have individual programs that detail the services they require for an appropriate education that has been agreed upon by their parents.

How does the IEP process work?

The IEP process is required by law and is systematically applied for every student with disabilities. The process, sometimes called the IEP cycle, is to include considerable participation by the family, the student (whenever possible), and a team of experts (Council for Exceptional Children [CEC], 1999). The IEP process is meant to be deliberate and equitable, and the individualized program plans that it generates are the means by which the educational concepts outlined in IDEA are guaranteed to each student and that student's family. The formation of an individualized program involves seven steps (see also Figure 2.3), beginning with pre-referral and ending with evaluation of a youngster's program. These steps are

1. Pre-referral
2. Referral
3. Evaluation
4. Eligibility
5. Development of the IEP
6. Implementation of the IEP
7. Annual review

Let's look at the seven steps of the IEP process in more detail to get a better understanding of what each means and how they add up to a process or cycle.

- *Step 1: Pre-referral* The IEP process is also sometimes called the IEP cycle (CEC, 1999). It is initiated as a result of a series of pre-referral interventions. The point here is to avoid unnecessary referrals, which are costly in time, money, and resources. Before any special education referral is made, teachers and family members should work together to see whether educational or behavioral difficulties can be resolved in the general education classroom by general education teachers. During this pre-referral period, teachers should try different teaching approaches and make basic accommodations to the instructional program. They can also seek assistance and consultation with resources available at the school (principal, resource room teachers, special educators, district-wide methods and materials

CHAPTER 2 *Individualized Special Educational Programs*

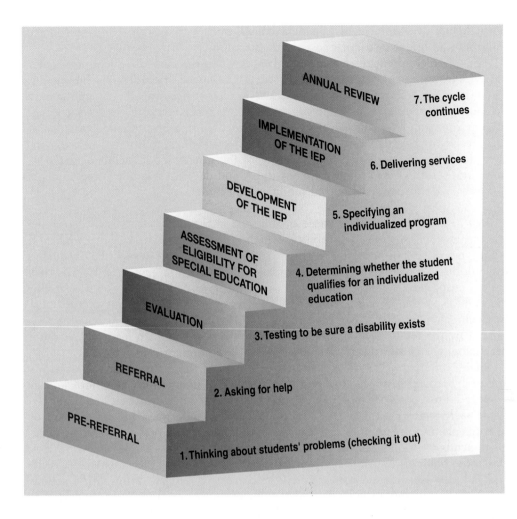

Figure 2.3 The Seven Steps in the IEP Process

teachers). If concerns continue, a referral to special education and the initiation of the IEP process should begin.

• *Step 2: Referral* In this step, a child is actually referred for special education services. The parents must be invited to a meeting where a committee decides whether the student's problems are significant enough to warrant formal assessment. The committee looks at all of the information collected during the pre-referral process, which includes samples of the student's work and descriptions of the effectiveness of changes in teaching style and other accommodations. Parents must give permission for the next step in the IEP process (evaluation) and must be invited to all meetings where their child's **identification**, evaluation, and placement are considered.

Referrals can come from many different sources. For preschoolers, the referral can come from parents, a social service agency, a public health nurse, a day care or preschool teacher, or a doctor. Typically, the referral process begins sooner for children with severe disabilities than for other children with disabilities. For example, some infants with severe disabilities may be identified at birth or early in infancy. Children who are at risk because of improper prenatal care, low birth weight, or accident or trauma during infancy are also often referred for special services by public health nurses or day care professionals. Parents might be concerned about a child who is not walking by age 2 or not talking by age 3. Preschool teachers focus on children who have frequent and excessive bursts of violent behavior or inappropriate displays of temper. Pediatricians may be concerned about children whose physical or motor development is slow. Delayed language, difficulties in eating, inability to locate the source of sounds, and excessive crying are other signals that normal child development may be delayed. All of these indicators can result in the referral of an infant or toddler to special education.

For schoolchildren, referral usually begins when the general education teacher becomes concerned about a particular student's behavior or academic achievement. Candidates for referral are students whose academic performance is significantly behind that of their classmates or who continually misbehave and disrupt the learning environment. Students who are thought to be gifted and talented because of their accelerated academic performance or high levels of creativity may also experience the IEP process. Although education of the gifted is not included in IDEA, many states follow the requirements of IDEA and develop IEPs for gifted students just as they do for students with disabilities.

MAKING CONNECTIONS

For more about identifying students with disabilities, see the "Defined" sections of Chapters 3–13.

• ***Step 3: Evaluation*** The purpose of this step in the IEP process is to determine whether a youngster has a disability, whether special education is required, and what types of special or related services are needed. Evaluations must be conducted by multidisciplinary teams and must assess the student's strengths and needs. If a child is suspected of having a language impairment, an SLP should be a member of the multidisciplinary team. If there may be a hearing problem, an audiologist must be a team member, and so on. All information provided by the parents must be considered by the multidisciplinary team. In many states, the team leader is a **school psychologist,** an educational diagnostician, or a psychometrician.

Many different types of data are used to inform the team about the student's abilities. Medical history, information about social interactions at school and at home, adaptive behavior in the community, educational performance, and other relevant factors are considered. Evaluations must include an array of assessment instruments and procedures. Formal tests—tests of intelligence, academic achievement, **acuity** (vision and hearing), and learning style—and less formal assessments—classroom observations of social behavior, curriculum based measurements (CBM), and samples of academic performance—may be used as well. Information should also be collected about the individual's major life activities: how the child performs at home, at school, in interpersonal relationships, and during leisure time. Thus evaluations may also include interviews of extended family members and of others who know the child well.

Because of the potentially negative effect on the individual and the family if an individual is incorrectly identified as having a disability, IDEA is quite specific, stressing that tests must be nondiscriminatory and must be given in the child's native language or in another mode of communication (such as sign language). The team must give considerable weight to samples of students' classroom work, CBM summaries, and teachers' descriptions of social behavior. The details of the identification procedure are established by each state, and teams of professionals must be involved in establishing that process to ensure that the procedures adopted represent the points of view of all culturally and linguistically diverse groups.

In all cases, evaluation should contribute to the development of an appropriate education for those students identified as having disabilities. The information gathered about the child during this stage is used throughout the rest of the process. Assessment is the foundation of the planning process. The team's thinking and planning should focus on life goals and outcomes so that instruction will be relevant to the individual's long-term needs (living independently, holding a job, participating in the community). And the result should be a baseline of performance that guides the development of the individualized education program and will later be used to judge the effectiveness of the educational program that was implemented.

• ***Step 4: Eligibility*** The assessment process first identifies whether a student has a disability and then classifies that disability (mental retardation, learning disabilities, emotional or behavioral disorders, low vision or blindness, deafness or hard of hearing, speech or language impairment). Although IDEA and its regulations, which

were prepared by the U.S. Department of Education, provide definitions of the special education categories, each state has written its own definitions. Typically, children who are younger than 5 years old are not assigned to a disability category, and not using disability or special education categories for mild disabilities (high incidence disabilities) is being suggested (Finn, Rotherham, & Hokanson, 2001). Regardless, once it is determined that a child has a disability—be it mental retardation, a learning disability, or an emotional or behavioral disorder—the IEP committee needs to determine whether the child also needs special education.

• *Step 5: Development of the IEP* What happens next? A very few of the children who are tested are ineligible for special services because they do not meet the criteria set by individual states (Algozzine, Ysseldyke, & Christenson, 1983; Kroth, 1990). These youngsters continue to be served by general education. Special education is intended only for those students with disabilities. For them, the next step requires decisions about appropriate education, services, and placement. The assessment results are used to help make these decisions. It is at this point that the **IEP Team** begins its work. Representation on the IEP Team is specified by IDEA (see the "What IDEA Says" box). Collectively, the members should be knowledgeable about the student, the resources and services available from the school district, the general education curriculum, implications of evaluation results, and the IEP process. At least one team member should be prepared to explain the process and the student's IEP goals and objectives to the parents. If an interpreter is needed for a family that is not proficient in English, one must be provided.

Now is the time when the parents, the child (if appropriate), and the IEP Team meet to set goals and objectives, to establish **benchmarks,** and to determine what services are necessary to meet the needs of the child. They design the constellation of services and supports that will become part of the student's appropriate education.

• *Step 6: Implementation of the IEP* After development of the IEP, the student's services and individualized program begin. Of course, minor changes in students' goals and objectives, or in the benchmarks that indicate their achievement, do not signal a need for a new IEP or another IEP meeting. The annual IEP meeting sets the stage for a productive year, and no other meetings are necessary. However, any major change in the student's program or placement does require written notification of the parents and may necessitate a meeting. Most actions related to discipline fall into the category of major change.

For students with disabilities who commit serious infractions that would cause a nondisabled peer to be suspended or expelled, implementation of the IEP can become more challenging and confusing (Katsiyannis & Maag, 1998). For example, the school district has to notify parents on the same day that a decision to discipline their child is made. The school district has a number of options available to it when a student with a disability is violent, brings a gun or weapon to school, or is involved with drugs. School officials can, for no more than a total of 10 school days in any one academic year, suspend the student or place the student in another school. However, once those 10 days are exceeded, the IEP Team must meet. At the heart of what many educators and parents believe is unfair is the process that is meant to determine whether the behavior that caused the disciplinary action is a

What IDEA Says About

IEP Team Members

The IEP Team for each student with a disability must include:

■ At least one general education teacher (if the student is participating in general education)

■ At least one special educator or related service provider

■ A representative of the school district

■ The parents

■ The student (if appropriate)

■ Other people whom the school or parents invite

result of the student's disability—**manifestation determination** (Katsiyannis & Maag, 2001). If the team decides that the behavior was not a manifestation of the student's disability and that the special education services specified in the student's IEP were appropriate, then standard disciplinary actions may be taken. If, on the other hand, the misbehavior is determined to have resulted from the student's disability, then the team must see that a functional behavioral assessment is conducted in order to develop and implement a **behavioral intervention plan.** The IEP team may also identify an **interim alternative setting** in which the student will continue to receive services and make progress on IEP goals and objectives, and in which the behaviors that were the cause of disciplinary actions will be addressed (Bear, 1999; Voyles, 1999). IDEA mandates that the interim alternative setting not be used for more than 45 school days, after which a formal request to change the student's placement is necessary. If problems continue beyond that time period, then the school can request a change of placement during a new IEP meeting, where the parents participate. If the parents disagree with the placement change, they are entitled to their procedural safeguards (mediation, due process hearings, and civil action if disagreements continue).

• *Step 7: Annual Review* The IEP is reviewed annually by the IEP Team and the parents. The purpose of the annual review meeting is to be sure the student is meeting the goals and objectives specified in the IEP. Evaluation is conducted to determine whether the student has achieved or at least is making progress toward or the benchmarks specified for each objective. Most educators are careful to specify goals, objectives, and benchmarks in terms that can be evaluated. And, of course, the goals must reflect tasks and skills that the student needs to learn to have greater success with the general education curriculum or for independence and a community presence later in life.

Although the IEP process requires only an annual review, the individualized program—whether it is for an infant or toddler (an IFSP) or a schoolchild (an IEP)—must include frequent evaluations of student performance. A student's individualized program is typically evaluated to guide instruction and to be sure the interventions scheduled are effective; ongoing and frequent assessments in the curriculum are used for these purposes, and to reevaluate the continuing needs of the student. As the student grows and learns, the educational decisions made one year may not be the best for the ensuing years. At the time of the annual review, a new program is developed. Decisions about placement, supportive services, and the goals and objectives for the upcoming year are made. In some cases, a child's progress may have been so great that special services are no longer required. In other cases, the degree of special services may change. For example, a child's progress may indicate that only periodic support from a special educator is necessary to maintain growth and continued progress. In other cases, more intensive special services may be needed. For example, a student with an emotional or behavioral disorder may have been placed in a resource room under a behavior management program. If the student showed insufficient progress over the year, this student may need to spend at least part of the upcoming year in

The preschool at the John F. Kennedy Center at Vanderbilt University—named after Susan Gray, a pioneer in the Head Start movement—remains an active research center. Here, young children with and without disabilities learn together.

CHAPTER 2 *Individualized Special Educational Programs*

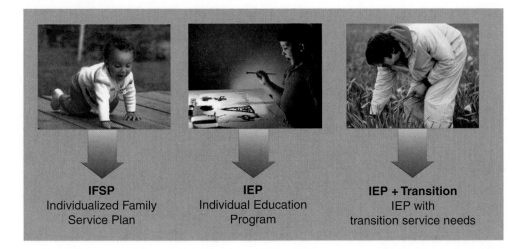

Figure 2.4
The Individualized
Education Sequence

IFSP
Individualized Family
Service Plan

IEP
Individual Education
Program

IEP + Transition
IEP with
transition service needs

a self-contained special education class taught by a teacher who is specially trained to work with children with emotional or behavioral disorders.

What are the different kinds of individualized education plans?

IDEA specifies that an **individualized family service plan (IFSP)** be developed for each infant and toddler with disabilities and that an **individualized education program (IEP)** be developed for all preschool through high school students (students between ages 3 and 21) with disabilities. Older children's IEPs specify the services necessary to help them make successful transitions from school to work. The transition component is initiated at age 14 and continues until the student leaves the public schools. Figure 2.4 shows how these plans fall into a sequence. Let's now look at the IFSP in a little more detail.

• *Individualized Family Service Plans (IFSPs)* Infants or toddlers (birth through age 2) who have disabilities or are at risk for disabilities were originally guaranteed the right to early intervention programs through PL 99-457, which was passed in 1986, and that right continues through IDEA. Children who are age 3 or older receive an IEP and are served through school districts. The process starts with referral and assessment and, for those who qualify for services, results in development of the plan drawn up by the IFSP.

To review the IDEA laws, see Table 1.2 in Chapter 1.

The required contents of the IFSP differ somewhat from those of plans for older children. One key difference is that, like all individualized programs, the plan is evaluated once a year, but the IFSP must also be reviewed with the family every 6 months. The key components of the IFSP include the following descriptions:

• The child's current functioning levels in all relevant areas (physical development, cognitive development, language and speech development, psychosocial development, and self-help skills)

• The family's strengths and needs, to assist them in enhancing the development of their child

• The major outcomes expected, including criteria, procedures, and a time line, so that progress can be evaluated

• The services necessary and a schedule for their delivery

• Projected dates for initiation of services

• The name of the service manager

- A biannual review with the child's family of progress made and of any need for modifications in the IFSP
- Indication of methods for transitioning the child to services available for children ages 3 to 5

MAKING CONNECTIONS

For more about early intervention services, see the "Early Childhood Education" sections in Chapters 3–13.

To many **service managers** and early childhood specialists, the IFSP is a working document for an ongoing process in which parents and specialists work together, continually modifying, expanding, and developing a child's educational program. Children and families who participate in early intervention programs often find these years to be an intense period, with many professionals offering advice, training, guidance, personalized services, and care and concern. The transition to preschool at the age of 3 can be particularly difficult and frightening, so IDEA includes transition efforts for these youngsters and their families (CEC, 1999).

• *Individualized Education Programs (IEPs)* The IEP is a management tool designed to ensure that schoolchildren with special needs receive the special education and related services appropriate to their needs. First required in 1975 by PL 94-142, the IEP remains a cornerstone of every educational program planned for each student with a disability. Congress delineated the minimal contents of the IEP, and it is important that every educator know these key components (CEC, 1999; U.S. Department of Education, 1999):

- The student's present levels of educational performance
- Indications about ways in which the student's disability influences participation and progress in the general education curriculum
- Statement of measurable annual goals, including benchmarks or short-term instructional objectives that are related to participation in the general education curriculum, as well as to meeting other educational needs resulting from the disability
- Specific educational services to be provided, including program modifications or supports that will allow participation in the general education curriculum and in extracurricular activities
- Explanation of the extent to which the child will not participate in general education classes and extracurricular activities with nondisabled peers
- Description of modifications in statewide or district-wide assessments (if the student will not be participating, a statement of the reasons for that nonparticipation and of how the student will be assessed must be included)
- Projected date for initiation of services
- Expected duration of those services
- Beginning at age 14, an annual statement of the transition service needs, and at age 16, a statement of interagency responsibilities to ensure continuity of services when the student leaves school
- Statement of how the student's progress will be measured and how parents will be informed about the progress for at least the same grade-reporting periods as apply to nondisabled peers, as well as how parents will be informed about annual progress made on the IEP.

Five important principles should be followed when developing and implementing IEPs (Bateman & Linden, 1998). These principles are included in the law and have been verified and supported through hundreds of rulings from a variety of agencies and the courts. First, all of the student's needs must be met, not just a selected few. Academic areas may be reflected, but so may areas not typically part of educational programs for students without disabilities (e.g., fine and gross motor skills and functional life skills). Second, whether services are available does not determine whether they are included on the IEP. If a student needs the services of an assistive technologist, those services shall be made available. Third, the services that the IEP indicates must be provided. Through this process, they become legally binding. They cannot be denied without another IEP meeting and mutual approval by the family and the school district. Fourth, the IEP should be individually determined. Not all students who require the services of an SLP, for example, need have identical IEPs.

A fifth important principle should be followed when implementing IEPs: Their contents should be communicated to everyone who should have the information. Too often teachers do not know what the student's IEP comprises, and at the secondary level, many general education teachers of specific students with disabilities do not even know that they have an IEP that spells out accommodations and modifications that should be made (Bateman & Linden, 1998; Lovitt, Cushing, & Stump, 1994; Pautier, 1995). This situation leads one to ask how an appropriate education can be delivered when the educators who interact with students with disabilities do not even know what services, goals, and objectives their education should include. The answer is obvious. An appropriate education cannot be delivered under these circumstances. At least some modifications in instruction and some accommodations in the learning environment are required even for those with the mildest disabilities. Although IEPs are part of the students' school records, they are available to those educators who have legitimate educational reasons for consulting them (Bateman & Linden, 1998).

● *IEP Component for Transitional Services* IDEA included some changes related to transitional services and adolescents with disabilities. Guidelines about transition were initiated in PL 101-476, the 1990 amendments to IDEA, and were expanded in the 1997 reauthorization (see the "What IDEA Says" box). The law stresses the importance of vocational and life skills for these individuals, and it ensures that transitional services are provided throughout the school years (NICHCY, 1998; Patton & Blalock, 1996).

Beginning at age 14 and every year thereafter, students' IEPs must include a statement of transitional services, and at age 16, the IEP must include a statement of interagency responsibilities and linkages to ensure continuity of services when the student leaves school. This feature adds an important dimension to adolescents' educational programs. In the past, there was little dialogue between special educators and the vocational rehabilitation counselors who assume some responsibility for many of these youngsters after their school years. As a result, many young adults with disabilities were ill prepared for community living or the world of work. Collaboration between special education and vocational education has great benefits, including preparation of the individual for independent living and employment. Young adults with disabilities often interact with many different social service agencies, postsecondary job training opportunities, and potential employers, so the transition component of students' IEPs facilitates the process involved in becoming an independent adult (Blalock, 1996).

The transition component supplements and complements the school based IEP process. Whereas the IEP describes the educational goals and objectives that a student should achieve during a school year, the transitional services part of the IEP addresses the skills and the supportive services that will be required in the future (being able to shop, make leisure time choices,

MAKING CONNECTIONS

See the "Transition Through Adulthood" sections in Chapters 3–13.

What IDEA Says About

Transition Services

For every student over the age of 14 who has a disability, the IEP must

■ Include a statement about transitional service needs

■ At the age of 16, add information about the coordination of services across agencies (education, social services, vocational rehabilitation)

■ Describe how the educational program will be modified

■ Indicate how the student will participate in extracurricular and nonacademic activities

■ Include a statement that the student has been informed about the rights that she or he has upon attaining the age of majority

Many businesses are now helping individuals with disabilities find their places in the community and in employment settings. Restaurant work seems to be one of the most popular employment settings for individuals with disabilities.

and cooperate with co-workers). It ensures that the IEP reflects goals and objectives related to skills necessary at work, at home, and in the community. Some goals may be related to desired outcomes (integrated employment, community living, citizenship and involvement, personal autonomy, life satisfaction); others may be specific to skill acquisition (money management, independent travel from home to work, time management), and should reflect a life skills curriculum (Clark, 1996; Patton, Cronin, & Jairrels, 1997).

By the time some youngsters reach high school, their involvement with school and the educational process has lessened. Unfortunately, many adolescents with disabilities find the process used to develop IEPs and transition plans frustrating and meaningless (Lovitt, Cushing, & Stump, 1994). These last years of school, however, can be critical to their achievement of special education outcomes and to their smooth and successful transition to adulthood. Recognizing the importance of these last years of schooling, Congress strongly suggests, in IDEA, that students be involved in the development of their own IEPs. By participating in the IEP meetings, adolescents can be more involved in the process and can become motivated to achieve transitional goals (Lehmann, Bassett, & Sands, 1999). Certainly, the needs and feelings of the students themselves must be considered. At the conclusion of several research projects that focused on high school students with disabilities, the researchers made the following suggestions about educational programs and these adolescents (Hasazi et al., 1999; Lovitt, Plavins, & Cushing, 1999; Sands, 1999):

- Assist them in becoming more independent, self-sufficient, and vocal about their needs.
- Include more instruction on social skills.
- Make them more aware of their IEP goals, the instructional practices being implemented to achieve those goals, and how they are being evaluated.
- Identify and focus on students' strengths that are valued by the student and others.
- Help develop positive self-identities.
- Expand school options to include learning in the community, even for students with mild disabilities.
- Give students information about options they might explore after leaving high school.
- Continue working on the mastery of basic skills, if necessary.

AKING
CONNECTIONS

Look again at the Advance Organizers found at the beginning of the chapter. To help you study the content of this chapter, the answers to the Focus and Challenge questions are provided next. Test yourself to see whether you have mastered the major points of this chapter.

Summary

A cornerstone of the federal laws ensuring all children and youth with disabilities a free appropriate education is the mandated creation of individualized educational programs: the individualized family service plan, the individualized education program, and the supplemental individualized transition plan. Each of these management tools guides the education system as it plans for and delivers an appropriate education to individuals with disabilities.

Self-Test Questions

Focus Questions

What are the seven steps in developing an individualized program for each student with disabilities?

1. Pre-referral
2. Referral
3. Evaluation
4. Eligibility
5. Development of the IEP
6. Implementation of the IEP
7. Annual review

What factors must be considered when determining the least restrictive environment for individual students?

- Student's goals and objectives
- Balance between LRE and FAPE
- Desired adult outcomes for the individual
- Array of special education services required to attain all goals

What role does the IEP Team play?

The multidisciplinary IEP Team: sets goals and objectives, establishes benchmarks, determines necessary services, and designs the constellation of services and supports that constitute FAPE for each individual student.

The Team meets if a change in the student's program or placement is required.

It conducts annual meetings to review and evaluate the effectiveness of the IEP and its special education services.

What are the different educational placement options that make up the continuum of services for special education?

New and innovative placement options and service delivery systems are continually being developed by the creative professionals who work to see special education evolve and improve.

Service delivery options (some recognized and some not recognized by the federal government's accountability and data collection system):

- Pull-in programming
- Co-teaching
- Consultation/collaborative teaching
- Itinerant or consultative services
- Resource room (pull-out programming)
- Partially self-contained special education class
- Separate special education class
- Special education (center) schools

What are the different purposes of IDEA's various program plans?

For infants and toddlers, individualized family service plans (IFSPs) contain the child's current functioning levels, the strengths and needs of the family, measurable goals and objectives, services required and the time of their delivery, assistance when transitioning to preschool, and the name of the person responsible for coordination of these services.

For children with disabilities from ages 3 to 21, individualized education programs (IEPs) serve as the management tool to guide educational programming. They include an assessment of the child's present level of educational performance, annual goals and objectives, the extent of participation in general education, related services to be provided, and the date for initiation of those services.

For students with disabilities who are 14 years old and older, a transitional services plan must be part of the IEP. This plan helps the student prepare for employment and community based independent living and, when the student reaches the age of 16, launches the student's preparation for moving from the schools to other service agencies.

Challenge Question

How should the array of educational services and supports available to students with disabilities be implemented?

- Individually determined

- At the intensity required

- For the duration of time needed to solve the problem

- With participation by the student and the family

- Including partnerships among school officials, the student's teachers, the student, and the family

- Flexibly, rather than in lock step

- Evaluated frequently

MEETING THE STANDARDS AND PREPARING FOR LICENSURE EXAMS

After reading this chapter, you should be able to demonstrate basic knowledge and skills described in the CEC standards and INTASC principles listed below. The section of this chapter most applicable to each standard is shown in parentheses at the end of the knowledge or skill statement.

 Content Standard 1: Foundations

- **Laws, policies and ethical principles** Understanding of laws, policies, and ethical principles including rights and responsibilities of students, parents, teachers, other professionals, and schools related to exceptional learning needs (Individualized Special Education Programs)

- **Due process rights** Issues, assurances, and due process rights related to assessment, eligibility, and placement within a continuum of services (Special Education Services)

- **IEP participation** Assist individuals with exceptional learning needs and their families to become active participants in the educational team. (Individualized Special Education Programs)

- **Collaboration** Collaborate with school personnel and community members in integrating students with exceptional learning needs into various settings (Special Education Services)

 Core Standard 8: Assessment

- **Legal and ethical principles** Legal and ethical principles regarding assessment of the individual with disabilities (Procedural Safeguards)

INTASC Principle 10

The teacher fosters relationships with school colleagues, parents, and agencies in the larger community to support students' learning and well-being.

- **Rights and responsibilities** The teacher understands and implements laws related to students' rights and teacher responsibilities (Special Education Services)

- **Child's well-being** The teacher is concerned about all aspects of a child's well being and is alert to signs of difficulty (Individualized Special Education Programs)

- **Collaborate** The teacher is willing to work with other professionals to improve overall learning for students (Individualized Special Education Programs)

Standards in Practice

These knowledge statements, dispositions, and skills might be demonstrated by effective participation in the IEP process. Understanding the legal, ethical, and professional responsibilities will provide a foundation for you to be a member of the educational team and participate more fully in the planning of educational programs for students with disabilities.

 Go to the companion website (ablongman.com/smith5e) for detailed text correlations to CEC and INTASC standards, PRAXIS II™ exams, and other state-sponsored licensure exams.

SUPPLEMENTARY RESOURCES

Professional Readings and Resources

Bateman, B. D., & Linden, M. A. (1998). *Better IEPs: How to develop legally correct and educationally useful programs* (3rd ed.). Longmont, CO: Sopris West.

Council for Exceptional Children. (1999). *IEP Team Guide*. Reston, VA: Author.

NICHCY (1998, June). The IDEA Amendments of 1997 (Special Issue). *News Digest, 26,* 1–39.

Patton, J. R., & Blalock, G. (1996). *Transition and students with learning disabilities: Facilitating the movement from school to adult life.* Austin, TX: Pro-Ed.

U.S. Department of Education. (1999). *Assistance to states for the education of children with disabilities and the early intervention program for infants and toddlers with disabilities; final regulations (34 CFR Parts 3000 and 3303).* Washington, DC: U.S. Department of Education.

Ziegler, D. (2002, April). *Reauthorization of the Elementary and Secondary Education Act: No Child Left Behind Act of 2001.* Arlington, VA: The Council for Exceptional Children, Public Policy Unit.

Parent, Professional, and Consumer Organizations and Agencies

American Bar Association: Commission on Mental and Physical Disability Law
740 15th Street, NW
9th Floor
Washington, DC 20005
Phone: (202) 662-1570
TTY: (202) 662-1012
E-mail: cmpdl@abanet.org
Web site: http://www.abanet.org/disability

National Association of State Directors of Special Education (NASDSE)
1800 Diagonal Road, Suite 320
Alexandria, VA 22314
Phone: (703) 519-3800
TTY: (703) 519-7008
Web site: http://www.nasdse.org

National Council on Disability
1331 F Street, NW, Suite 850
Washington, DC 20004
Phone: (202) 272-2004
TTY: (202) 272-2074
E-mail: mquigley@ncd.gov
Web site: http://www.ncd.gov

National Association of School Psychologists
4340 East West Highway, Suite 402
Bethesda, MD 20814
(301) 657-0270
TTY: (301) 657-4155
E-mail: publications@naspweb.org
Web site: http://www.nasponline.org/index2.html

NICHCY
P.O. Box 1492
Washington, DC 20013-1492
Voice/TTY: (800) 695-0285
Voice/TTY: (202) 884-8200
E-mail: nichcy@aed.org
Web site: http://www.nichcy.org

Video**Workshop** Extra

If the VideoWorkshop package was included with your textbook, go to Chapter 2 of the Companion Website (www.ablongman.com/smith5e) and click on the VideoWorkshop button. Follow the instructions for viewing Video clip 1 and 3. Consider this information along with what you have read in Chapter 2, while answering the following questions.

Video Clip 1: The IEP (Time 7:31)

1. Pretend that you are sitting at the table during the meeting on the video; you remember reading in your text that IDEA requires family and student involvement in the IEP process. What would you do to make that happen before the meeting ends?

2. On the basis of reading this chapter, what would be your obligation as the special education teacher during implementation of the IEP?

Video Clip 3: The Collaborative Process (Time 4:14)

1. As noted in the text, IDEA stresses the importance of students with disabilities participating in the general education curriculum. However, in order for students with disabilities to gain this access, the special education and general education teachers must work together. How are the teachers in the video providing appropriate access for the students in this elementary classroom?

2. In some special education models, the special education teacher works in the general education classroom. How does the special education teacher in this video deliver service to the students with disabilities? Offer specific examples of services offered.

The Gift by Michael A. Naranjo. Reproduced with kind permission of the artist.
Photo: © Mary Fredenberg.

MICHAEL NARANJO lost his sight during the Vietnam War. Although his mother was a well-know potter from Santa Clara Pueblo in northern New Mexico, he did not dedicate himself to sculpture until he was recovering from the injuries he received in battle. Michael is now a respected sculptor whose work is included in important collections across the nation. He is truly a very special person who contributes his time and work to Very Special Arts and community programs for young artists, particularly those with disabilities.

3 Multicultural and Bilingual Special Education

A PERSONAL PERSPECTIVE

Tanto, tanto, Karisa

Norma Lopez-Reyna is a special education professor at the University of Illinois-Chicago. Her path to a successful academic career is quite remarkable in and of itself. Norma's parents had only a high school education. Her father worked at the "ranch" and earned 90 cents an hour driving a wheat harvester. She is the fourth of nine children, and, therefore, had begun to learn English from her brothers before she entered kindergarten. She remembers that during her first 3 years of school, there were times when she couldn't explain her needs or participate in activities because she hadn't mastered her second language. Norma vividly recalls spending early mornings and summers in the fields picking grapes. Norma did well in school, won scholarships, and went on to college. She made a decision early that "I must serve my people because I can." She dedicated herself to being a special educator. Today she looks back and believes that, without understanding why, she chose this path (out of many exciting choices available to her) because she was preparing for her third child, Karisa, her own child with special needs. (Norma Lopez-Reyna's research is cited in this chapter.)

Karisa was born, just a few years after we had moved for a new job, far away from my large family.

Everything was typical in her developmental milestones except for language. She was kinesthetically and socially above average to average. Because we only spoke and read in Spanish at home, that was also her first language. We were convinced, as our experience thus far had shown us, that children could learn their home language and then, with the appropriate supports (home and school), become fluent and literate in the majority language. Our pediatrician, friends, and family all said that I was being overly concerned when I started to notice at 13 months, that Karisa was not using as much language as had her brother and sister before her. "What do you expect," everyone said, "she hears two languages, her older sibs probably talk for her," and "well, she's the baby." My professional friends said that the use of a language different from the mainstream was confusing her. Everyone had advice, even the nurses and secretaries and store clerks—they all said I should speak English to her, after all I was fluent, why was I holding her back, and I should demand her to speak and not respond if she didn't use appropriate language!

Karisa was a very loving, sociable, physical, curious toddler. It wasn't until about age 3 that her language began to affect her social skills and she began avoiding being around others, preferring one-on-one with family members. She continued to have an immense amount of energy—sleeping no more than 9 hours yet always waking up refreshed, enthusiastic, and ready to take on a new day.

I began to keep notes, on words and phrases she used, on her abilities in other activities and her social skills. This served as a means of organizing my thoughts and ideas and also as a means of staying sane. It had been so straightforward with the first two children, both "gifted" and highly developed socially and linguistically; there just seemed to be so many more details involved in language and the interaction between language and the rest of everyday life that I'd never noticed before.

When I finally approached our district office regarding language services for her, at age 3, it was the beginning of a very long, frustrating, and painful experience. Essentially, it was a collection of professionals ignoring my referring information and telling me, for example, that my child needed to be screened in English first to see if she needed a full assessment and culminating in a session with a "bilingual" language pathologist who couldn't even pronounce words [clearly enough] for my daughter to respond! That was only the beginning, we also went through the "un-testable" conclusions of the school psychologist and the 300-item checklist (normed on children in a small town, Euro-American population) which indicated to the social worker that Karisa was delayed in language and gross motor skills! All the while, I tried to describe Karisa's language, our language, her problem solving skills, her social skills and her tremendous physical agility to those who were bound to standardized measures and refused to interpret from observations the cognition, language, and social abilities and skills that Karisa in fact had. Those abilities, I gently tried to educate [them], are the basis for her needed instruction. The professionals, on the other hand, were interested in finding a label, the one word that could summarize for them my child's needs, her personality, her future prospects, and most importantly, the classroom in which to place her.

It became very evident that we were in this game (and it is a game) alone. No one knew or knows her better than her mother and father and it was up to us to seek out and guide her development every step of the way. We knew that we had a child with a severe language delay—in both Spanish and English—who was also very creative, happy, persistent, brave, and always busy.

The biggest challenge has been balancing between the professional and the mother, between the laissez faire of our culture and the "get a diagnosis" culture in which we live. In my relations with my daughter's school I chose not to be the former school psychologist, now special education professor who prepares teachers and researchers in bilingual special education—first and foremost, I am a parent. In spite of this stance, I suppose because I advocated for an appropriate and complete assessment in our home language as well as English, the district saw fit to have their attorney preside over the MDC meeting and then refused appropriate services. Thus, I sought services independently, via my HMO network and via my professional friends and via our personal bank account. One and a half years later, I went to our home school district directly to the principal and staff that already knew me and Karisa's brother and sister and sought an inclusive setting with language and academic supports. [And while] they set up the appropriate supports, I attended Kindergarten with her— that lasted 4 days. And so it has been for 4 years now. Karisa's language is developing nicely, still delayed of course, she has been diagnosed ADHD for which she takes medication, and she remains excited and very motivated about learning more each day. She has friends, occasionally gets invited to birthday parties, loves swimming and ballet. Going into the fourth grade next year, she is reading at a second grade level. We know it gets more difficult each year, but then Karisa is also understanding more and more language each day.

It's a constant vigil on our part—for each day, and for the future. This means everything from making sure she has the services specified in her IEP to being aware of when one of her teachers is out ill, on vacation, or changing jobs. It also means constantly seeking dialogue with her teachers, via notes, meetings, or quick after-school chats on the playground to talk about things such as, Karisa not responding to a request [being] most likely due to inability to understand what is being requested, not an act of defiance or that saying "tanto, tanto" [so much, so much] meant too much language, please stop, not a mispronounced "tonto" [dummy] in an act of disrespect to her teacher.

Each opportunity I have, I try to guide others in knowing the child we know so well. Because if there is one lesson to be had it is that the parents know their child best. Even if they don't have degrees in psychology and education, they still know the child's temperament, what makes the child smile and be motivated, what frightens the child, and most importantly, that that child is a whole human being, not a collection of special needs.

1. **How do you think Karisa would fare without a mom like Norma? What might be different?**

2. **What do you anticipate for Karisa and her family?**

CHAPTER 3 *Multicultural and Bilingual Special Education*

ADVANCE ORGANIZERS

Overview

The diversity of America's schools is changing more rapidly than ever before. Only about 3 percent of Americans can consider themselves true natives; the rest of us are immigrants or the descendants of immigrants. Schoolchildren today come from hundreds of different cultures and speak almost as many languages. These children are at great risk for being overidentified as having disabilities and underidentified as gifted. Culturally and linguistically diverse students often require many accommodations to achieve their full potential, and those with exceptionalities require special education programs and interventions that address both their diversity and their disabilities.

Self-Test Questions

Focus Questions

- What is multicultural and bilingual special education, and who is served by such programs?
- In what ways can biases occur in the identification and assessment process?
- Why are educators so concerned about culturally and linguistically diverse children?

- What is considered overrepresentation in special education and underrepresentation in education for the gifted?
- How can school personnel integrate children's home cultures and languages into the educational environment and curriculum?

Challenge Question

- What measures can be taken to reduce the overrepresentation of culturally and linguistically diverse students in disability categories and their underrepresentation in education of the gifted?

Use the learning strategy—Advance Organizers—to help focus your study of this chapter's content, and reinforce your learning by reviewing answers to the focus and challenge questions at the end of the chapter.

As confirmed by the 2000 U.S. census, America remains a country whose populace has great and increasing diversity (Goode, 2002). Since the nation's founding, the face of the United States has been one of perpetual change. The demographics of the nation and its schools is one reflection of this evolutionary process. America's schoolchildren are diverse in so many different ways. The languages and cultures they bring with them to school represent cultures from all over the world, not just from several continents. Their heterogeneity is marked along multiple dimensions: language, values, culture, and abilities. And all schools and teachers face the challenge of creating appropriate educational opportunities where instruction is effective for all students who now make up the school population. That the United States is a multicultural country is a given. And we must judge ourselves in terms of what we do with our diversity, how we treat each other, how we understand each other's similarities and differences, and how we learn from one another. By using this diversity to our advantage, we can make the educational environment richer, and all children can flourish.

See the "Prevalence" section later in this chapter.

Advance Organizers

OPPORTUNITIES FOR A BETTER FUTURE

The ways in which Americans have welcomed others to their new homeland have changed across time. At one point, Americans prided themselves on being seen as part of a cultural "melting pot," where everyone was to be incorporated into a new American culture. At other times, cultural pluralism was valued as a way for people to retain their traditions and cultures but still feel part of America. And at still other times, groups of Americans were segregated and denied opportunities. The attitudes of the larger society affect the educational system. As the nation wrestles with increasing diversity of language and cultures, so will the schools. Undoubtedly, those children who do not fit easily into the general education system are likely to experience special education, a system accused of legitimizing segregation and guaranteeing poor outcomes for students at great risk of school failure.

Turning Legacies into Lessons

Associations among poverty, limited access to health care, having a disability, participation in special education, dropping out of school, and renewing a cycle of poverty are now clearer. Regardless of race or ethnicity, poor children have not fared well in America's educational system. And culturally and linguistically diverse children remain at the greatest risk not only for being poor, but also for being disproportionately represented in special education programs and underrepresented in education of the gifted. Educators and policymakers are now bringing these issues to the forefront, but considerable effort will be required to solve these problems.

Thinking About Dilemmas to Solve

As you read this chapter, consider children who are not native speakers of English or are not from the dominant culture in American society. Think about

- How schools and society can create opportunities for children from culturally and linguistically diverse backgrounds to have equal chances to succeed
- How they and their families can become better connected and more involved with schools
- How general education can become more responsive to the needs of diverse learners
- How issues related to disproportionate representation in special education can be resolved
- How special education and programs for education of the gifted can become more effective for diverse learners

MULTICULTURAL AND BILINGUAL SPECIAL EDUCATION DEFINED

Particularly because of factors associated with poverty (e.g., access to health care, exposure to environmental toxins such as lead paint, attending poor schools), culturally and linguistically diverse students are at greater risk for being identified as having a disability (Artiles et al., 2002). Diverse students deserve an educational program that builds on their cultures, holds high expectations, and addresses their unique learning styles and needs. For those diverse students who are at risk of being incorrectly identified as having disabilities, effective multicultural education (education that supports and extends concepts from students' cultural backgrounds) or effective bilingual education (education that develops competence in English and in the native language) can avoid tragic outcomes (Baca & Cervantes, 1998; Gollnick & Chinn, 2002). However, for those diverse students who truly have disabilities, a unique education combining multicultural, bilingual, and special education approaches can provide them with the unique education they need to achieve their potential (see Figure 3.1). As you read this chapter, think about how teachers might use these approaches to better serve all culturally and linguistically diverse children, particularly those with disabilities.

MAKING CONNECTIONS

or more information about the relationships among disabilities and poverty, see

- "Causes and Prevention" in this chapter
- Information about access to health care in Chapter 6 ("Prevention" section)

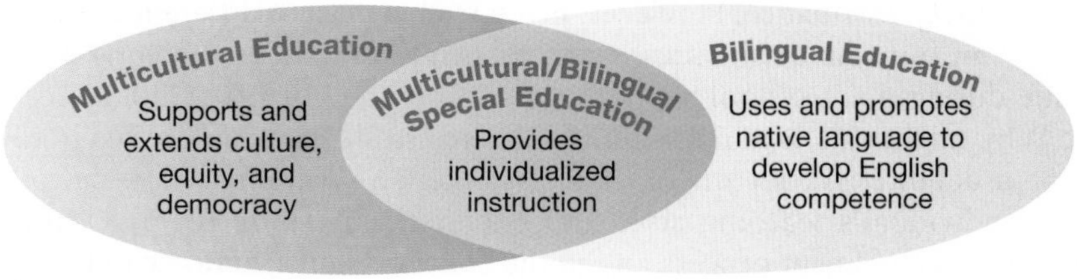

Multicultural Education — Supports and extends culture, equity, and democracy

Multicultural/Bilingual Special Education — Provides individualized instruction

Bilingual Education — Uses and promotes native language to develop English competence

Figure 3.1 Multicultural and Bilingual Special Education

How does the federal government classify people from diverse backgrounds?

The federal government classifies its citizenry and asks people to describe themselves for the purpose of a national census. It uses this system for reports and other official documents and divides citizens into five general ethnic/racial groups:*

1. Asian/Pacific Islander
2. Black (African American)
3. Hispanic (Latino/Latina)
4. American Indian/Alaska Native (Native American)
5. White (non-Hispanic)

Each of these groups contains considerable diversity of culture, language, and identity. In fact, many members of historically underrepresented groups prefer other means of identification. The examples of two Latinas, both experts in education, serve as illustrations: Alba Ortiz refers to herself as Mexican American, and Hinojosa Maldonado-Colon considers herself a Puerto Rican; neither woman finds that the federal term *Hispanic* fits her identify (as reported in Bessent Byrd, 2000). Similar examples can be found within and across groups. Here's another example: Many Asian/Pacific Islanders consider themselves first Native Hawaiians, Chinese Americans, Vietnamese, Japanese Americans, and so on. Clearly, the diversity within each of these groups is enormous along a multitude of dimensions: language, home country, years and generations in the United States, reasons for coming to the United States, ethnicity, and social and economic status (SES).

In addition to classifying students by racial or ethnic groups, educators often base their research and clinical findings on two additional dimensions of diversity: culture and language. Remember that these categories overlap: Many children who are born in the U.S. are not native English speakers. Some families have retained their cultural heritage even though they have been in this country for several generations. Others have not done so. Clearly, it is important not to make any assumptions about individuals or groups of people.

Which students are considered culturally diverse?

Students who are considered culturally diverse come from backgrounds different from American mainstream society, which is predominantly Western European in origin. How many different cultures are represented by America's schoolchildren has not been determined, but it could be over a thousand. Being from a culture different from the dominant American culture does not directly cause disabilities or

---

* Many terms are used to refer to different groups of people in the United States. The federal government uses one set (American Indian/Alaska Native, Asian/Pacific Islander, Black, Hispanic, White); people from specific locales use other specific referents (Anglo, African American, Latino/Latina, Chicano/Chicana); and for broad inclusion, other terms are used (Native American for all Native peoples). Terms used in this text reflect a balance and national preferences.

poor academic performance. However, being from a culture different from the dominant one can put one at significant risk of being identified as having a disability sometime during one's school years (Baca & Cervantes, 1998; Gollnick & Chinn, 2002). Why might this be so? Culturally diverse students are more likely to live in poverty—a definite risk factor for actually having a disability. Also, culture influences an individual's learning style and experiences, failure to take culture into account in the assessment process and in the delivery of instruction can lead to inappropriate placement in special education.

Who are linguistically diverse students?

MAKING CONNECTIONS

More about ELL students is found in this chapter in the section called "Elementary Through High School."

Many culturally diverse students are also linguistically diverse, but certainly not all. **English language learners (ELLs)**, who are still sometimes referred to as **limited English proficient (LEP)**, are generally thought of as those who are linguistically diverse. They represent the most rapidly growing segment of the U.S. student population (Goode, 2002 August). Their native languages are not English. In many school districts, including Chicago, Los Angeles, and Fairfax County, Virginia, students and families use over 100 different languages; New York City reports that over 145 different languages are spoken by its students (Gersten & Baker, 2000). Nationally, however, the majority of English language learners speak Spanish (Escamilla, 1999).

The challenges these students present to school district personnel are great. In classrooms where English is the exclusive language of instruction, their lack of true English mastery usually undermines their ability to excel academically (Ortiz & Yates, 2001). The public, policymakers, and educators seem unable to reach consensus about how best to help these students learn their new language and meet new academic challenges (Rueda et al., in press). Schools also have difficulty providing these students with the supports they need. These students come from many different cultures and speak many different languages. Not enough teachers are available who speak these children's native languages. Thus many children have to rely on a parent, community member, or paraprofessional for translations and language support.

MAKING CONNECTIONS

For more about over- and underrepresentation of diverse learners, see
- Chapter 1
- "Prevalence" in this chapter
- "Causes and Prevention" in this chapter
- Chapter 7

Who are Native students?

Only a very few people—American Indians, Eskimos, Aleutian Islanders, and Native Hawaiians—can claim native status (Tiedt & Tiedt, 1999). Most of these Native students experience the effects of minority status, and many also are linguistically diverse. Native Americans speak some 187 languages, and many of these children, particularly those living in rural areas and on reservations, come to school without previous exposure to the English language (Krause, 1992). They represent hundreds of different tribes, but together they make up less than 1 percent of America's population.

Half of the Native American population is concentrated in five states (Alaska, Arizona, California, New Mexico, and Oklahoma). In seven states (Alabama, Arizona, Montana, New Mexico, North Dakota, Oklahoma, and South Dakota), they constitute over 5 percent of the schoolchildren enrolled (National Center for Education Statistics [NCES], 1997). Of the almost 86,000 public schools in this country, 149 are recognized as tribal or reservation schools, and another 1,260 schools have high enrollments (over 25 percent) of Native American students. However, the majority of the 445,425 American Indian/Alaska Native students attend public schools with a low Native enrollment, leaving them isolated from their home cultures (Amos, 1997).

As a group, Native Americans face many serious challenges, many of which are substantial risk factors for disabilities or poor academic outcomes. First, they are the poorest group in the United States: 88 percent of students attending tribal schools

Learning cultural values and traditions does not need to be separated from school. They can become part of the richness of experiences children bring to school and can be used to anchor instruction in relevance and meaning.

and 61 percent of those attending schools with a high enrollment of American Indians receive free lunches, a signal for poverty status (Amos, 1997). Conditions associated with poverty (e.g., increased health problems, attending poor schools) have truly negative effects on children (Children's Defense Fund [CDF], 2001; National Research Council, 2002). Second, they have a 36 percent dropout rate (25 percent higher than the national average). Third, conflict between teachers' and students' communication styles, cultural preferences, and values is a common experience for Native children (Sparks, 2000). "Caught between two cultures" is a phrase frequently used to describe the experience of most Native students who do not attend a tribal school. As an example, Native children's communication at home tends to be symbolic and filled with nonverbal nuances. To these children, adults at school talk too much, are overly blunt, seek disturbingly direct eye contact, and ask questions that are inappropriately personal. Also, views about what is important often differ between home and school. The result can be disengagement, misidentification as having a disability, and eventual dropout (Amos, 1997).

MAKING **C**ONNECTIONS

For specific dropout data, see "Transition Through Adulthood" in this chapter.

How might diverse students with disabilities be identified more reliably?

To avoid misidentifying diverse students as having disabilities will require new, innovative approaches to the identification process (National Research Council, 2002). Students from ethnic and racial groups that are not part of the dominant American culture are often at a disadvantage when taking standardized tests. Also, students who have not yet truly mastered English cannot demonstrate their abilities in such testing situations (Thurlow & Liu, 2001). Differences in culture and in language contribute to some students being misidentified as having a disability or being excluded from education of the gifted (Ochoa et al., 1999). For other students, test results present an incorrect and depressed picture of their abilities. Despite all of the negative attention and charges of discrimination leveled at IQ tests and other standardized tests, and despite court rulings that bias plagues these testing procedures, educators still rely on what appears to be the simplest and most clear-cut form of student evaluation: the standardized test.

How can discrimination in the assessment process occur? There are many reasons for bias, but some of the major ones are worthy of attention and thought. For

MAKING CONNECTIONS

The theory of multiple intelligences is discussed in the Defined section of Chapter 7.

one thing, the content of the test items might give an advantage to groups with specific experiences and interests. For example, asking a child who has never been fishing to explain how to bait a fishing line might negatively affect the impression others have of that child's expressive language and cognitive abilities. A second reason is that diverse groups are not always represented in the standardization population. Also, opportunities for unfair evaluations are created when an individual untrained in multicultural and bilingual techniques conducts the evaluation. To stress the importance of nonbiased evaluations, IDEA requires that **nondiscriminatory testing** be established in each state. Take a look at the "What IDEA Says" box to see how the law and its regulations address this important issue.

How might this bias be removed? One way might be to rethink and broaden the narrow view of intelligence reflected in standardized tests. A restricted concept of aptitude—reflecting only students' abilities to achieve academically—may be one reason why disproportionate numbers of students from culturally and linguistically diverse groups continue to be unidentified, misidentified as needing special education, and underrepresented in education of the gifted (Ford et al., 2002; Tomlinson et al., 1998). Although the theory is invoked more often when considering gifted children, educators of diverse children have taken a growing interest in Howard Gardner's (1983) theory of **multiple intelligences.** In this model, intelligence consists of eight different intelligences: verbal linguistic, logical/mathematical, visual/spatial, musical/rythmic, bodily/kinesthetic, naturalistic, interpersonal, and intrapersonal (Campbell, Campbell, & Dickinson, 1999; Kagan & Kagan, 1998). To be considered gifted, individuals need demonstrate talent in only one area. June Maker and her colleagues (Maker, Nielson, & Rogers, 1994) originally applied Gardner's theory to children from diverse backgrounds, believing that a multiple approach better reflects talent fostered across cultures. They point out that one's culture may influence how ability is expressed. They give the example that oral storytelling may be a common form of linguistic giftedness in one culture, whereas writing a novel may be a predominant form in another culture. They claim that students identified as gifted through this process often make gains equal to or greater than those of other gifted students identified through the standard IQ testing process. Applying this innovative concept to all special education assessments also may well reduce the number of these students who are inappropriately identified as having disabilities.

Another means of solving the problem may well rest with the use of different assessment procedures. Performance based diagnostic procedures, such as authentic and portfolio assessments, have particular merit for students at risk for over- or underrepresentation in special education (Hébert & Beardsley, 2001). Curriculum based measurement has also been suggested as a means of more fairly evaluating students' abilities because assessment is based on classroom performance (National Research Council, 2002; Reschly, 2002; Reschly, Tilly, & Grimes, 1999).

And yet another solution may require flexible and sensitive identification systems that change depending on the individual's situation, family, culture, length of time in the United States, economic status, and region (Cuccaro, 1996). The referral process could include input from multiple sources, such as parents, extended family members, church and community leaders, and service clubs (Patton, 1998; Patton & Baytops, 1995; Rogers-Dulan, 1998). Experts agree on one thing: Even minor changes in current practice can make a difference (Amos, 1997; Ortiz, 1997; Ortiz & Yates, 2001). Here are some of their recommendations:

- Provide early pre-referral intervention.
- Develop assessment portfolios.
- Conduct assessments in the student's dominant language.
- Use qualified personnel competent in their own and the student's language and culture.
- Use interpreters, if necessary, who are proficient in the child's native language and familiar with the special education system and the assessment process.

What is the impact of inaccurately identifying students as having disabilities?

Parents, policymakers, and educators are concerned about misidentifying students as having disabilities, because the long-term results of special education are not always positive (Rueda et al., 2002; Tyler, Lopez-Reyna, & Yzquierdo, 2002). How could this be so when special education is costly and is supposed to be individualized and to provide intensive educational supports? Unfortunately, when teachers believe students from a language-different background, students of color, and low-income students are unable to attain high levels of academic achievement, their expectations for these students are lower (Baca & Cervantes, 1998; Gollnick & Chinn, 2002). Without high expectations for students, many teachers tend to slow the pace of instruction, select instructional materials that are not challenging, and teach "down" to their students. The result of such negative attitudes and low expectations often is low achievement. Students tend to internalize negative expectations and perceptions. Internalizing negative attitudes can lead to reduced motivation to learn difficult skills and concepts. The problem is compounded because special education is plagued by an excessive number of untrained teachers (those teaching before they are licensed) and by a high attrition rate, leaving these students with a less than adequate education (Tyler, Lopez-Reyna, & Yzquieredo, 2002).

Students who are engaged in learning, using activities that are for them, flourish in the learning environment. Here, students are learning how paper is recycled along with the environmental benefits of reducing solid waste.

Multicultural and Bilingual Special Education Defined

This situation may also explain these students' high dropout rates (Winzer & Mazurek, 1998). Leaving school before completion has serious long-term effects, including an inability to break the poverty cycle. Educators must create positive learning climates in which children are stimulated to do their best, are supported in taking risks, and are encouraged to have fun learning.

HISTORY OF THE FIELD

Education in the United States has been faced with issues of bilingualism and multiculturalism throughout its history. In the late 19th and early 20th Centuries, total exclusion (or separate language schools) began to give way to a new era of "Americanization." Antiforeign feelings and sentiments were on the rise. The guiding principle during the new period was the melting pot model, in which individuals were expected to assimilate and abandon their home languages and cultures as soon as possible for a new, homogenized American experience. But the melting pot model appears to have failed. Instead of creating a harmonious new culture, it led to racism, segregation, poverty, and aggression toward individuals in each new immigrant group. It also led to a loss of some of the richness that can result when a country welcomes many cultures and languages.

Cultural pluralism, a model that was proposed again in the 1960s, actually emerged in the early years of the 20th Century (between 1915 and 1925) as an alternative to the assimilation argument (Banks, 1994). Cultural pluralism does not require abandoning one's home culture, as did the **melting pot** model. Rather, it allows people to maintain their various ethnic languages, cultures, and institutions, while encouraging their participation in society as a whole.

The concern about overrepresentation of culturally and linguistically diverse students in disability categories is not new. This issue was brought to national attention in several ways. In 1968 Lloyd Dunn published an article in which he estimated that about 60 to 80 percent of special education students, particularly those with mental retardation, were culturally and linguistically diverse. In 1970 the President's Committee on Mental Retardation (PCMR) published *The Six Hour Retarded Child,* which dramatically exposed the ways in which cultural differences were causing some children to be inappropriately labeled as having mental retardation. In California, also in 1970, the case of *Diana* v. *State Board of Education* began to bring issues about bias in the assessment process into focus. This case was a class action suit on behalf of Hispanic children placed in classrooms for students with mental retardation on the basis of IQ tests that were argued to be discriminatory. Additionally in California, the case of *Larry P.* v. *Riles* (1971) brought to the attention of the courts and schools the overrepresentation of African American children in classes for students with mental retardation and the possibility of discrimination in intelligence testing. In 1974 the U.S. Supreme Court ruled, in a case brought in San Francisco, on behalf of students with limited English proficiency (LEP) (students who would now be called English language learners) who spoke Chinese (*Lau* v. *Nichols,* 1974). Following the favorable decision in *Lau,* Congress enacted legislation that incorporated the Court's rationale:

> *Public education is not a "right" granted to individuals by the Constitution. But neither is it merely some governmental "benefit" indistinguishable from other forms of social welfare legislation. Both the importance of education in maintaining our basic institutions, and the lasting impact of its deprivation on the life of the child, mark the distinction.... In sum, education has a fundamental role in maintaining the fabric of our society. We cannot ignore the significant social costs borne by our Nation when select groups are denied the means to absorb the values and skills upon which our social order rests. (Citations omitted; p. 2397)*

CHAPTER 3 *Multicultural and Bilingual Special Education*

Source: Reprinted by permission from the *Albuquerque Tribune.*

Nationally normed, standardized tests continue to be at the center of concern about accurate identification of diverse students. In 1973 Jane Mercer was the first to attempt to develop a test aimed at reducing bias in the identification process. Use of the *System of Multicultural Pluralistic Assessment (SOMPA)* significantly decreased the number of African American and Hispanic children placed in special education classes (Gonzales, 1989).

The very special learning needs of this unique and heterogeneous group of learners were brought to the attention of the professional community in the professional literature. The journal of the Council for Exceptional Children, *Exceptional Children,* published in 1974 a special issue on cultural diversity (Bransford, Baca, & Lane, 1974) that brought many authors together to discuss multicultural and bilingual special education issues. Donna Gollnick and Phil Chinn, in their landmark 1983 book, *Multicultural Education in a Pluralistic Society,* helped educators better understand the influence of culture on children's educational performance. Leonard Baca and Hermes Cervantes's textbook *The Bilingual Special Education Interface,* first published in 1984, brought the question of language different youngsters with disabilities to the attention of people in the fields of multicultural education, bilingual education, and special education.

Periodically, the right of diverse children to an education has come into question. In 1982 the Supreme Court decided a Texas case about whether the children of Mexican nationals residing in Texas without proper documentation had a right to free public school education (*Phyler* v. *Doe,* 1982). The Supreme Court ruled that children do have this right. Despite the *Phyler* v. *Doe* decision, California voters in 1994 passed Proposition 187, prohibiting undocumented immigrants from receiving public benefits, including education. This action was later ruled illegal by the federal government. Bilingual education has also come under attack. In 1998 California voters passed a ban on bilingual education through Proposition 227, thereby implementing an almost "English only" policy for the state's schools and to some degree limiting many students' access to a meaningful education.

PREVALENCE

Many policy makers and experts in multicultural and bilingual education believe that the percentage of children and youth from different ethnic groups served by special education and education of the gifted should generally reflect the prevalence of those groups in the general population (Rueda et al., in press). When this situation does not occur, the phenomena are considered:

- **overrepresentation** in disability categories
- **underrepresentation** in education of the gifted

For a general benchmark, let's first look at the percentage of diverse individuals in the general population. According to the most recent census, in the year 2000, the proportional representation of racial and ethnic groups in the United States was 69.5 percent Whites, 12.5 percent Hispanics, 12.1 percent Blacks, 3.7 percent Asian/Pacific Islanders, and 0.7 percent Native Americans. Estimates are that by the year 2050, Whites will make up 53 percent of the U.S. population, Hispanics 24 percent, Blacks 13 percent, Asian/Pacific Islanders 9 percent, and Native Americans 1 percent (Chinn, 2002). Of course, patterns vary by locale. Thus in some school districts—particularly in urban areas—diverse students constitute 80 percent of the district's student body (Burnette, 2000). In these instances, it is difficult to justify referring anywhere from one-third to one-half of the school's population to special education—or even referring to them as minorities!

Another factor to consider is that, as reflected in the census category new to the 2000 study, many Americans are of mixed racial and ethnic identities (Chinn, 2002). Nearly 2 percent of all Americans (some 4.2 million people) identified themselves as "Blended Americans" in the last census, and this is considered an underestimate. Predictions are that by 2050, 21 percent of Americans will belong in this group. What impact multiple ethnicities will have on this discussion is not known.

How many diverse students are there?

Culturally and linguistically diverse students represent a large segment of the school population (NCES, 1997; U.S. Census Bureau, 2000). Here are a few examples of states with large proportions of diverse students in their overall school populations:

The diversity of America's schoolchildren is increasing dramatically. Teachers have wonderful opportunities to enrich their instruction with interesting information and stories from many different cultures and heritages.

CHAPTER 3 *Multicultural and Bilingual Special Education*

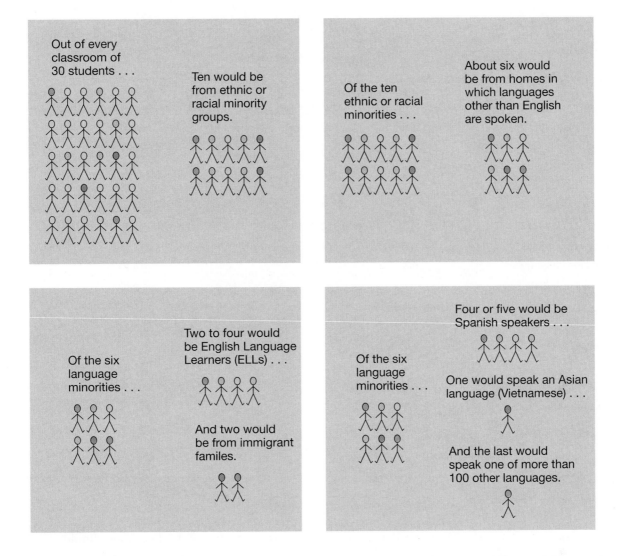

- More than 60 percent—Hawaii and the District of Columbia
- More than 50 percent—Mississippi, New Mexico, New York, and Texas
- Between almost 40 percent and 50 percent—Arizona, California, Georgia, Louisiana, Maryland, and South Carolina

Baca (1998) helps us visualize what a typical American classroom might look like (see Figure 3.2). You might be surprised to learn that 30 percent of the students are culturally or linguistically diverse, 20 percent are from homes where languages other than English are spoken, and about half are themselves ELLs. Of course, it is important to remember that these are national statistics; in some schools nearly all of the students are from diverse backgrounds, in other schools relatively few. And these percentages are likely to change. Hispanic students are the fastest growing ethnically identified group of students (their numbers are almost equal to those of Black students in the educational system), and a large percentage of them are ELL (Yates, Hill et al., & Hill, 2002). In California, one-fourth of all students are ELL (Rueda et al., in press). Of these students, 90 percent speak one of five languages (82 percent Spanish, 3 percent Vietnamese, 2 percent Hmong, 2 percent Cantonese, and 1 percent Filipino). Of the Spanish-speakers, 60 percent are from Mexico. It is important to understand that although the federal government divides Americans into five ethnic/racial groups, Americans identify themselves differently. For example, a teacher may have a class of Asian/Pacific Islanders but will still need to know and understand many very different Asian cultures to avoid making incorrect assumptions about children and their families (Mathews, 2000).

Figure 3.2 Diversity in America's Classrooms
Source: From the Diversity of America's Schoolchildren by L. M. Baca. In R. Thorp (1998) Teaching Alive CD ROM. Santa Cruz, CA: The Center for Research on Education, Diversity, and Excellence, University of California-Santa Cruz. Reprinted by permission.

Table 3.1 Percentage of Students Ages 6 Through 21 Served by Disability and Race/Ethnicity, 1999–2000 School Year [a, b, c]

Disability	American Indian/ Alaska Native	Asian/ Pacific Islander	Black (non-Hispanic)	Hispanic	White (non-Hispanic)
Resident population	1.0	3.8	14.5	16.2	64.5
Specific learning disabilities	1.4	1.6	18.4	16.6	62.1
Speech or language impairments	1.2	2.4	16.1	12.7	67.6
Mental retardation	1.1	1.8	34.2	9.1	53.8
Emotional disturbance	1.1	1.2	27.3	8.9	61.5
Multiple disabilities	1.5	2.3	20.0	11.5	64.8
Hearing impairments	1.3	4.6	16.4	17.9	59.8
Orthopedic impairments	0.8	3.0	14.7	14.8	66.8
Other health impairments	1.1	1.4	14.9	8.0	74.7
Visual impairments	1.1	3.5	18.6	14.0	62.9
Autism	0.7	4.8	20.5	9.2	64.9
Deaf-blindness	2.0	7.5	24.7	11.2	54.6
Traumatic brain injury	1.6	2.4	16.9	10.5	68.5
Developmental delay	0.9	0.8	30.5	4.1	63.7
All disabilities	1.3	1.8	20.3	13.7	62.9

[a] Due to rounding, rows may not sum to 100 percent.
[b] Race/ethnicity distributions exclude outlying areas because current populations estimates by race/ethnicity were not available for those areas.
[c] Population counts are July 1999 estimates from the U.S. Census Bureau

The fact that these children are from diverse backgrounds should not be disturbing. What *should* be disconcerting is the fact that youngsters from diverse groups have a much higher probability of having been born to mothers who did not receive early prenatal care, of living in poverty, of having limited access to health care, and of being raised in a single-parent household (Children's Defense Fund [CDF], 2001). All of these factors put children at great risk of having a disability. In addition, for many, their cultural and language differences increase their chances of failure in the educational system and the likelihood of their being referred for special education.

Are diverse students overrepresented in special education?

Some experts believe that because of the disproportionate numbers of diverse students subject to the ravages of poverty, some over- and underrepresentation is to be expected (Macmillan, Gresham, & Bocian, 1998; Reschly, Tilly, & Grimes, 1999). Others insist that any variation from representation in the general student population is unacceptable (Rueda, et al., in press).

Let's consider the most current national data available from the *Annual Report to Congress on the Implementation of IDEA* (U.S. Department of Education, 2001). Take a look at Figure 3.3 and Table 3.1. (Remember, when reflecting on these data, that percentage data are distorted for groups of relatively small numbers.) On the table, the number appears in color when the representation in a disability category exceeds that group's representation. Obviously, one major concern is the overrepresentation of Black students in the mental retardation category and the emotional or behavioral disorders category.

These national data tend to mask those at the local level. At the local level, more disturbing data are available about the overrepresentation of diverse students in special education programs. Data from Hawaii's Department of Education show why educators are concerned about diverse children's disproportionate participation in special education. Hawaiian and part-Hawaiian children represent about 25 percent of the overall student population, but they represent about 34 percent of the special education student population. Compare this to their peers from Japanese backgrounds, who represent about 12 percent of students in the public education system and only 9 percent of special education students. The situation of Hawaiian students is not much different from that of Native American students in North and South Dakota and in Montana or that of Hispanic students in Arizona (Harry, 1994).

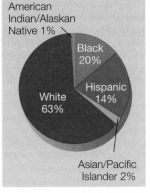

Figure 3.3 Percentage of Students Ages 6 Through 21 by Disability Categories, 1999–2000 School Year
Source: U.S Department of Education. (2001). Office of Special Education, Data Analysis System (DANS), as reported in the *Twenty-third Annual Report to Congress on the Implementation of the Individuals with Disabilities Education Act.* Washington, DC: Government Printing Office

Are diverse students underrepresented in gifted education?

Just as African American, Hispanic, Hawaiian, and Native American students are overrepresented in many special education categories, they are underrepresented in education of the gifted (Bernal, 2000; Ford et al., 2000). But, as we have seen, not all diverse students are included in special education in a proportion greater than their proportion in the overall school population. For example, students from an Asian background are less than half as likely as other diverse students to be identified as having a disability (U.S. Department of Education, 2001). Remember the statistics about Native American students in Alaska, Montana, South Dakota, and Arizona; these students are overwhelmingly identified as having disabilities. In Alaska, for example, Native Americans make up 25 percent of the population, but only 15 percent of them are receiving educational services in programs for the gifted (Harry, 1994).

For more about diverse learners' participation in education of the gifted, see Chapter 7.

CAUSES AND PREVENTION OF DISABILITIES IN DIVERSE STUDENTS

Clearly, diversity, poverty, and disabilities in America today are related. But it is very important to understand how they are related, and how they are not:

- Diversity does not cause disabilities.
- Poverty places students at substantial risk for disabilities.
- Not all diverse students are poor, although they are disproportionately likely to be poor. (The majority of poor children are White.)

Terrible mistakes can be made when people assume that all diverse students are poor or that all poor students have disabilities. Unfortunately, the economic conditions of many families from historically underrepresented groups did not improve greatly in times of prosperity (CDF, 2001). Issues of multiculturalism, bilingualism, cultural and linguistic diversity, and poverty are complex and intertwined. It is important not to oversimplify the causes of disabilities in students from diverse backgrounds or how they can be prevented.

What causes diverse students to be at greater risk of actually having disabilities?

Social and economic inequities have a significant impact on our nation's children (CDF, 2001; Kozol, 1991, 1995; Reed & Sautter, 1990). Two main conditions are of critical concern:

1. Poverty
2. Mobility

Before turning our attention to conditions that contribute to diverse children being mislabeled as having disabilities and to being overrepresented in special education programs, let's take a look at these two causes that contribute as to *actual* disabilities.

MAKING CONNECTIONS

For more information about the importance of access to health care, see "Causes and Prevention" in Chapter 6.

- *Poverty* The rate of childhood poverty is a major problem in the United States. The Children's Defense Fund (CDF, 2001) gives us some alarming facts to consider when we think about the relationship between the conditions under which children live and the incidence of disabilities in children.

- Half (some 50 percent) of children served through IDEA (special education) are also eligible for Title 1 (a federal poverty program).
- Every 44 seconds, an American baby is born into poverty (1 in 4).
- 1 in 3 will be poor sometime during childhood.
- Every minute, a baby is born without health insurance (1 in 7).
- 1 in 4 is born to a mother who did not finish high school.
- 1 in 8 is born to a teenage mother.
- 1 in 5 is born to a mother who did not receive prenatal care during the first 3 months of pregnancy.
- Every 2 minutes, a baby is born at a low birth weight (1 in 13).

Officials from the federal government are certain about the link between poverty and disabilities (U.S. Department of Education, 1998). Considerable data support this notion. First, data from individual states show the higher incidence of disabilities among poor groups. Here's one example. Study Table 3.2, which displays data from Hawaii. Note that in 1997, the proportion of Asian students from three particular groups (Chinese, Japanese, and Korean) who received special education was far less than their proportion in the overall student population. These students also participate less in free lunch programs. Now look at the column for Hawaiian students, and you'll find the opposite relationship: A higher proportion of them than of the general school population participate in free lunch programs and in special education.

Advocacy groups such as the Children's Defense Fund are also convinced that poverty and the factors associated with it place diverse students at incredible risk for needing special education (CDF, 2001). There is no denying the lifelong impact of poor nutrition, anemia (which stops blood cells from carrying oxygen to the brain), lead poisoning (particularly from lead paint), low birth weight, and not receiving immunizations on time during childhood. During the school years, the effects can be seen in learning and behavior problems. Across a life span, the effects can be seen in employment and life satisfaction outcomes.

Causation of disabilities must also be viewed within a cultural context. Different cultures sometimes think about the causes of disabilities in children differently. Because of various conceptions and definitions of what disability is, cultures do not always agree about the presence of a disability (Holman, 1997). In general, people from the dominant American culture believe in a direct scientific cause-and-effect relationship between a biological problem and the developing baby. Those from other cultures may, in contrast, consider fate, bad luck, sins of a parent, the food the mother ate, or evil spirits to be potential causes of disabilities (Cheng, 1995;

Table 3.2 The Link Between Poverty and Disabilities

	Chinese, Korean, and Japanese Students	Hawaiian and Part Hawaiian Students
Percentage of school population	17	25
Percentage of those receiving free lunches	6	37
Proportion of special education	12	34

Source : Hawaii Department of Education. (1999). *Hawaii's state demographics—1997.* Honolulu, HI: Author.

Lynch, & Hanson, 1998). These alternative views affect the way a child with a disability is considered within the culture and the types of intervention services that a family may be willing to pursue to address the child's disabilities and needs.

• *Mobility* Homelessness, which is clearly related to poverty, compounds the risk for many children—and disproportionately so for those who are diverse (Markowitz, 1999). Homeless children and children of immigrants and migrant workers often experience disruption and dislocation, circumstances that can adversely affect their physical, mental, and academic abilities. Those who live in shelters experience daily humiliation at school when peers learn that they have no home (CDF, 2001). These students often change schools every few months, breaking the continuity of their education and leaving gaps in their knowledge that result in reduced academic achievement. Their low academic performance occurs because of many factors, but some of the most important to consider are

• Fractured education

• Absenteeism

• High risk for health care issues

Because many homeless, refugee, or migrant children have little formal experience with school, teachers may need to address years of missed educational opportunities. Estimates about the number of children who are homeless vary widely because such children "fall between the cracks" of different social service agencies and because they are so mobile. What we do know is that there are many of them, they tend not to attend school, and many have disabilities (Walther-Thomas et al., 1996).

Homeless and migrant children with special needs can experience exceptional hardship because they may have to move from a school where these needs were being met (or were in the process of being assessed) to a different school or a series of schools, depending on the shelter(s) to which a homeless child is sent or on the new site(s) of the migrant parents' work. At the schools these children attend, it is not uncommon to note that between 60 and 80 percent have moved on during the school year (CDF, 2001). The stress, hunger, disease, and feelings of hopelessness that often accompany homelessness and mobility can create new special education needs in a child or exacerbate existing ones. The ability of the family to implement aspects of an IEP at home are impaired when the family is separated in large dormitories, for example, or when living conditions are so crowded or dangerous that physical survival demands all the family's energy (Kozol, 1991, 1995).

Being homeless, particularly in a large city, has indelible effects on the lives of children (Markowitz, 1999; Zima et al., 1998). In one study, researchers tested children who were living in an urban shelter and found that 46 percent of all the children had a disability. The most common disability was behavioral disorders or emotional disturbance; these problems afflicted 30 percent of the children identified as having a disability. Diverse children were the most likely to find themselves in this situation: 44 percent of the children were Black and 35 percent were Hispanic. Although the Education for Homeless Children Act of 1994 guarantees children the right to an education and allows them to attend any school the parent requests, many of these youngsters experience a fractured education.

Children of migrant workers also find life difficult. Over 80 percent of migrant and seasonal farm workers are U.S. citizens or legal immigrants (Henning-Stout, 1996). These workers earn less than $7,500 a year, clearly below the federal poverty level. Most migrant families live in Florida, Texas, or California between November and April and move to find agricultural work the rest of the year. Approximately half of million migrant students live in the United States, and about 75 percent are Hispanic. These culturally and linguistically diverse children are very likely to be affected by disabilities because of the poverty and health problems that accompany a migrant lifestyle. This group experiences high rates of tuberculosis, cervical cancer, and hypertension (Henning-Stout, 1996). Although 64 percent of these students are reported as having learning disabilities, they tend to be under-identified and underserved in special education. These children face other hardships as well. Their parents must make a difficult choice: keeping their families together but being highly mobile, or separating the family by leaving their children with relatives for a more stable school experience. Many middle and high school students also work long hours in the fields before and after school. Their high mobility only aggravates their educational problems.

What causes diverse students to be at greater risk of being misidentified as having disabilities?

Many causes contribute to the overrepresentation of diverse students in special education and to their misidentification as having disabilities. Key factors include

- Bias and negative attitudes
- Inconsistency of educational programs
- Nonresponsiveness of educators to differences of language and culture
- Poor schools

Educators often misunderstand culturally and linguistically diverse students and their behaviors (Artiles, 2002; Bessent Byrd, 2000; Neal, McCray, & Webb-Johnson, 2001). One result of such misunderstandings can be low expectations. Children who present language differences often experience an "automatic devaluation of what they bring to school—their language and culture" (Maldonado-Colon, as quoted in Bessent Byrd, 2000, p. 55). To eliminate such bias will require changing "predominant values and attitudes toward language minority students which are held by educators and the general public" (Ortiz, as quoted in Bessent Byrd, 2000, p. 58).

Homeless and migrant children are not the only students who find their education disrupted and without continuity. Because of inconsistent and seemingly ever-changing policies about bilingual education, ELL students can experience a variety of approaches—ranging from bilingual education to full immersion without native language support—during their period of developing English proficiency (Escamilla, 1999). And although some teachers accept verbal and nonverbal behaviors that are at odds with mainstream classroom culture, others do not, and such rigidity leaves some students unable to behave appropriately across different settings and situations (Neal, McCray, & Webb-Johnson, 2001).

Many teachers and schools are not responsive to diverse individuals' differences and are unprepared to work effectively with these students. The root of the problem is usually a lack of understanding about the roles that culture and language play in the learning process (Yates, Hill, & Hill, 2002). Some cultural characteristics and students' resulting behaviors and actions can be at odds with the classroom culture. A mismatch of home and school cultures (sometimes referred to as **cross-cultural dissonance**) may explain why many diverse students seem to be constantly in trouble and why their behavior patterns seem offensive to teachers from America's mainstream culture (Harry, 1992). This mismatch, or dissonance, can result in referrals to special education (Artiles & Harry, 2002). Also, a lack of understanding about acquisition of a second language often results

All children's language skills develop when they are engaged, excited, and are working together on activities that support academic instruction.

in students not being supported long enough while they are acquiring the language skills they need to progress beyond conversational speech to the fluency required for academic learning. Supporting this notion are data about the effectiveness of an approach that does not include language supports: Students who receive the straight English immersion approach have higher rates of special education placement (Rueda et al., in press).

Poor children are also exposed to the poorest of schools, a compounding factor in their low achievement (Artiles et al., 2002). Inner-city and rural schools tend to have fewer human and financial resources. These schools have the lowest budgets, the fewest materials, and the least prepared teachers (who in turn have the highest turnover rates). Poverty-stricken schools have the greatest percentage of inexperienced and uncertified teachers (Ingersoll, 2001). All of these factors put many diverse learners at even greater disadvantage and reduce the probability of their having good educational outcomes.

How can the over- and underrepresentation of diverse students be prevented?

Referral rates and eventual placements of diverse children in special education need to be reduced, and those for education of the gifted must be increased. Of course, removing the risk variables of poverty, improving access to health care, guaranteeing universal vaccinations against disease, and ensuring safe living environments would make an enormous difference in the outcomes of children (CDF, 2001). Of course, effecting such sweeping social changes is beyond the individual educator's capability, but there are actions that teachers can take.

First, it is the responsibility of *all* educators to become culturally sensitive and also to be knowledgeable about acquisition of a second language. America's teachers do not reflect the diversity of their students (Tyler, Lopez-Keyna, & Yzquierdo, 2002). In fact, only 0.04 percent of special education elementary teachers and 2.2 percent of secondary special education teachers are African American males (Voltz,

MAKING CONNECTIONS

For more about over- and underrepresentation of diverse learners, see

- Chapter 1
- "Prevalence" in this chapter
- "Causes and Prevention" in this chapter
- Chapter 7

Fostering Culturally Responsible Classrooms and Schools

1. Post welcome signs in public areas in every language of the school's community.

2. Ensure that communications between home and school are in the family's preferred language.

3. Provide opportunities for students from the same racial/ethnic/language group to work and study together.

4. Assign literature from the students' first cultures.

5. Have students research and share information about special holidays and events.

6. Decorate the school and classrooms with pictures of diverse individuals in the professions and high-status occupations and with objects from the school's cultures.

7. Recruit community leaders to serve as translators at important school events (assemblies, IEP meetings).

8. Seek out family and community members to be active partners in classroom instruction and to connect curriculum to culture.

1998). Thus, all teachers must be better prepared to work with children from many different backgrounds (Obiakor & Utley, 1997; Sileo & Prater, 1998; Voltz, 1998). By developing culturally responsible schools and classrooms, teachers demonstrate respect for children's home cultures, anchor instruction with relevant and interesting content, and motivate students to do their best (Montgomery, 2001). The "Tips for Teachers" box provides a few ideas about how to foster such environments for classrooms and schools.

Second, teachers can provide culturally responsive instruction by "anchoring" their teaching with examples from many American experiences (Castellano & Díaz, 2002; Kea & Utley, 1998). How can a teacher incorporate multicultural and bilingual aspects into a classroom? Instructional materials should reflect the cultural diversity of students (Artiles & Zamora-Duran, 1997). Although it is important not to become "cultural tourists" by celebrating holidays of countries or traditions of places that these students have never visited, cultures can be meaningfully linked to instruction and the classroom experience (Artiles et al., 2000). Some teachers both have students celebrate local holidays and post pictures of events from the local community. Many teachers have found that using magazines (such as *Essence, Ebony, Canales, Latina, Pamir,* or *Indian Country Today*) for supplemental reading activities piques students' interest and can provide them with excellent role models (Connie Chung, the journalist; Michael Chang, the tennis star; Zubin Mehta, the musician) to emulate (Jairrels, Brazil, & Patton, 1999; Sileo & Prater, 1998). Schools can also recognize and value different cultures by supporting their clubs and groups (e.g., ESL clubs, Movimiento Estudiantil Chicano de Aztlan [MEChA] clubs, chapters of African American sororities and fraternities, and arts, music, dance, and crafts clubs).

Third, in attempting to incorporate cultural diversity into the day-to-day activities of a school, teachers must be careful not to use stereotypical images of students' cultures, yet they should select content that reflects central aspects of a culture (Lynch & Hanson, 1998). For example, the assumption that a second-generation, American-born child of Japanese heritage maintains the same cultural belief system as a recent Japanese immigrant is just as erroneous as the assumption that a child of Cherokee heritage who lives in Denver is completely assimilated into the dominant U.S. culture. In other words, children must not be stereotyped, and neither should their education be stereotyped. Students also need to understand that each of them enters the classroom with a unique set of values, beliefs, cognitive and behavioral styles, and verbal and nonverbal communication styles (Sileo & Prater, 1998). These beliefs can be influenced not only by the cultural background of students but also by such factors as the length of time their families have been in the United States; the geographic region of the country in which they live; the age, gender, and birthplace of each child; the language spoken at home; the religion practiced by the family; the proximity to other extended family members; and the socioeconomic level of the family (Gollnick & Chinn, 2002).

Fourth, teachers can select instructional materials that are highly motivating to their students because the content reflects students' race, ethnicity, or culture. Motivated students are more likely to achieve academically, less likely to be mislabeled as having a disability, and more likely to be selected for educational programs for the gifted (Ford & Harris, 2000; Ford et al., 2002). For example, to develop self-understanding, awareness, and pride, teachers can include multicultural literature as reading assignments. Throughout the year, teachers can include information and assignments where students can learn about their countries of origin as well as history sections that appear in textbooks. Such additive approaches can help reduce underachievement due to lack of interest in the curriculum.

CHARACTERTISTICS

Artiles (1998) believes that being seen as different puts people on distinct trajectories before they have an opportunity to display their own strengths, weaknesses, and characteristics. His point is well worth considering. Culturally and linguistically diverse children with special education needs often have problems in several areas.

- Language and communication differences can present challenges.
- Differences between school and home cultures can result in behaviors that result in special education referrals.

Clearly, some of these students' characteristics contribute to their overrepresentation in special education programs and to their not being tapped to participate in education of the gifted.

What is the difference between a language disorder and a language difference?

Both culturally diverse and linguistically diverse children exhibit language and communication differences that often raise educational questions but should not always result in special education (Cheng, 1999). Being able to tell the difference between a speech or language impairment and a language difference is not always easy. Let's first look at differences exhibited by many linguistically diverse students and then turn our attention to the language skills of culturally diverse students.

Some children may speak forms of a language that vary from its literate or standard form (Cheng, 1999). For example, the spoken Spanish used in South Texas usually differs from the spoken Spanish used in New Mexico, both of which may differ from the standard form of Spanish. These variations are dialects and should not automatically be considered language deficiencies. Some languages do not include certain sounds or grammatical structures found in English. For example, the *f, r, th, v,* and *z* sounds do not exist in Korean. Many English consonant sounds do not exist in Chinese, so a Chinese-speaking child's difficulty with some English sounds may reflect the child's inexperience with the sounds rather than a speech or language impairment. Although many of these children are referred for speech therapy for an articulation problem, their distinctive speech is simply an accent, and therapy is unnecessary.

Detecting the difference between a language impairment or a learning disability and a language difference can be difficult, even for well-trained professionals. Sometimes children are wrongly identified and find themselves placed in special education even though they have no language impairment or learning disability (Ruiz, 1995). At other times, children's disabilities are masked by the language difference, and they wait years for the special services they need. The general guideline for determining whether a bilingual child has a speech or language impairment is whether the impairment occurs in *both* English and the child's dominant language. For example, a Spanish-speaking child who converses perfectly in Spanish with his brothers on the playground but who has limited ability to discuss academic subjects in English in the classroom certainly has a problem, but it is not a language impair-

MAKING CONNECTIONS

See Chapter 5:

- "Language Impairments" section (Causes) for more about language differences
- "Speech Impairments" sections (Defined, Causes, Children with Speech or Language Impairments) for more about articulation.

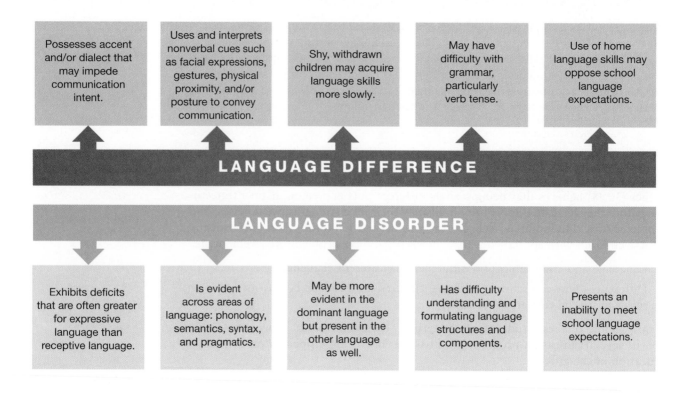

Figure 3.4 Distinctions Between Language Differences and Language Disorders

Source: Courtesy of and thanks to Zina Yzquierdo, Department of Special Education, Vanderbilt University, 2002. Reprinted by permission.

ment. Rather, it is due to a communication difference and an inadequately developed second language. Zina Yzquierdo (2002) helps us visualize these differences (see Figure 3.4).

Although many Hispanic children come to school speaking Spanish, some come to school speaking a combination of two languages (Sileo, Sileo, & Prater, 1996). Native Americans speak over 187 different languages (Krause, 1992), and people from Southeast Asia and the Pacific speak hundreds of different languages and dialects (Cheng & Chang, 1995). And remember that some 20 percent of the current school population does not speak English at home (Baca, 1998). Many of these students use both English and their home language within the same communication. That is, they are code switching (Brice & Rosa-Lujo, 2000). **Code switching** is not a disorder but rather a way for people to achieve mastery of two languages, and it is often a sign that dual language proficiency is developing.

Language is a major issue for many students, even those who speak English at home. Many African American children, for example, come to school speaking a **dialect** of English. Another group of learners and their language differences have come to the attention of educators, Congress, and the public. These children speak a variation of standard English often referred to as **Ebonics**. Interestingly, although this form of American English is often considered substandard, it is used to generate millions of dollars in advertisements, music, television, and film. What is the concern? Should Ebonics be discouraged at school? Most schools and mainstream American institutions do not accept this form of English, and many leaders in the Black community believe its use in inappropriate settings has a negative impact on those individuals who cannot "switch codes." They believe strongly that schools must "teach standard English to all of our nation's children yet celebrate their diversity and their ability to communicate effectively in a variety of settings" (Taylor, 1997, p. 3). Educators must continually find effective ways to teach students who come to school without a basic mastery of English. If they do not succeed, the outcomes are serious (Seymour, Abdulkarim, & Johnson, 1999). Language and communication differences influence students' oral language skills and their overall academic performance. These differences also affect acquisition of the reading skills so crucial to academic success. The overall low achievement of diverse children is very troubling, for, at least in American society, academic achievement is a predictor of future success.

CHAPTER 3 *Multicultural and Bilingual Special Education*

Schoolwide Disciplinary Actions: Consistency

Teachers and administrators at John Murray Elementary School, an inner-city school in a large urban area, were becoming very concerned about many aspects of their school. They felt that they were offering a curriculum with high standards and that they had high expectations for their pupils. They coordinated units and activities so that students across the grades received motivating instruction supported by excellent and engaging activities. They believed they were anchoring their instruction to experiences of their students and that they were sensitive to the many different cultures and backgrounds of their students and families. However, each educator had individual concerns about the educational program they were collectively offering. Concerns stemmed from their own informal observations and from the overall evaluation data about John Murray students' outcomes. John Murray had one of the highest special education referral rates in the city, overall achievement levels were low, many students were being assigned to in-school suspension, and a high number of negative notes were being sent home.

Individually, teachers, support staff, paraprofessionals, and parents voiced their concerns to the school's principal, Ms. Mims. She decided to call for a meeting of the school's community, including elected student representatives, to discuss the problems and see if they could arrive at some solutions. At the first meeting, people discussed both the strengths and the weaknesses of the school's programs and listed their concerns. At the end of the first meeting, everyone agreed that an outside professional was needed to work with the community and create a professional development plan. Using the resources and expertise available in the district, several problem solving meetings made it clear to everyone that each teacher had a set of rules and expectations but that these differed across teachers and settings. Furthermore, the consequences for inappropriate behavior were not consistently applied. One teacher would ignore a fight in the hall, whereas another would assign in-school suspension for such violations. No one wanted a structure that would restrict students' freedom to discover, think creatively, acquire basic knowledge,

or develop personally. But they also wanted to create a positive climate where students were free to learn and disruption was held to a minimum. To achieve their goals, they developed a schoolwide code of conduct, where standards for acceptable behavior in all settings were clear and where consequences for levels of infractions were consistently applied.

Steps Used to Create Schoolwide Discipline

- All stakeholders contribute to a process in which problems are identified and understood.

- All stakeholders participate in developing solutions.

- A plan is developed that includes clear examples of acceptable and unacceptable behaviors in all different settings and situations.

- Levels of consequences for violations of the code of conduct are clearly listed.

- The community—everyone, including students—comes to understand the code and the consequences for infractions.

- The plan is implemented schoolwide.

How can cultural differences lead to students being misidentified as having emotional or behavioral disorders or attention deficit/hyperactivity disorders?

Cultural conflicts may well contribute to some diverse children being identified as having disabilities (Cummins, 1984; Sileo, Sileo, & Prater, 1996). Because behavior is culturally based, children from nondominant cultures are likely to be at variance with the culture of school (Cartledge & Loe, 2001). In other words, when the cultures of school and home collide, the results can be tragic, as evidenced by the substantial overidentification of Black boys for special education programs.

A student's inappropriate behavior can trigger the special education referral process (Rivera & Smith, 1997). Boys who "act out," do not comply with expectations at school, and have trouble controlling their anger are more likely to be

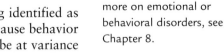

MAKING CONNECTIONS

For more on ADHD, see Chapters 4, 8, and 9; for more on emotional or behavioral disorders, see Chapter 8.

referred for special education services. This may be one important reason why so many Black males are identified as having emotional or behavioral disorders (Hosp & Reschly, 2002). Home and school cultural conflicts may also explain why so many Black youngsters (both boys and girls) screen positively for ADHD, particularly when tested by White teachers (Reid et al., 2001). What establishes this situation for some African American boys may well be their nonverbal behaviors, their movement styles (Neal, McCray, & Webb-Johnson, 2001). Assuming an assertive or defiant posture, arm swinging, and walking with a swagger can all lead to tension between educators and a child.

Sometimes children do not understand that a particular behavior is acceptable in one setting but not in another. And this situation is reciprocal in that many White female teachers do not know what is acceptable in their students' home cultures. For example, having fun with a group of friends, making spontaneous and clever jokes, striking poses, and kidding around by physically touching a peer might bring positive attention and make the child popular after school. However, during class time or during period changes, such behaviors are troubling to teachers and school administrators. Most children learn to sort out the different behavioral expectations across a variety of settings and situations, but many do not and need help to learn. The "Achieving Discipline" box provides an illustration of how educators can help students learn these important skills. Another outcome can be a reduction in the rates of special education referral and placement.

It is important to keep in mind that other issues can arise when behavior appropriate in one environment, such as the home, is inappropriate in another environment, such as the school. A silent child might be behaving in a desirable way according to standards of his home culture, for example, but be characterized at school as "withdrawn" or "anxious." For example, the White culture's focus on individual competitiveness clashes with the standard of cooperation preferred in the Hawaiian culture. A similar point can be made about Native Americans and other diverse learners. For these children, intense competitiveness at home might be interpreted as a behavior disorder, and its absence at school could be interpreted as a lack of motivation. When home and school cultures clash, children can become terribly confused and poorly educated (Obiakor, 1994). Keep in mind that another way to help children sort out the differences between behavioral expectations at school, at home, and in the community is for educators to help students learn and understand what is appropriate in school settings.

EARLY CHILDHOOD EDUCATION

Making Connections

More information about the "at risk" concept is found in Chapter 5.

The federal Headstart program, initiated in 1964 as part of the federal initiative called the War on Poverty, is for children from low-income families. In 1994 the program was expanded to include children from birth to age 3 through the Early Headstart program. Results from these early interventions are outstanding, reflecting positive changes for children and families (Kraft, 2001a). Unfortunately, most Headstart-eligible children do not participate in these programs designed to reduce the impact of risk factors that contribute to disabilities (Currie & Thomas, 1995). Headstart services include a physical examination and full health assessments (immunization status; assessment of growth, vision, hearing, and speech; and screening for anemia, sickle-cell anemia, lead poisoning, tuberculosis, and infections). Remember, access to health care is an important factor in preventing disabilities.

Truly including preschoolers with disabilities, particularly those from diverse backgrounds, in early intervention programs is not always an easy task. The process involves considerable planning and thought, but long-term results clearly justify the effort. Here are a few ideas about how to accomplish good integration in preschool settings (Kraft, 2001b):

- Incorporate pictures of children with disabilities along with pictures of typically developing youngsters into the classroom decor.

- Monitor the accessibility of the physical environment to be sure all children can move around freely and safely.

- Communicate with families consistently and frequently (not just when there is a problem).

- Include adults with disabilities on the staff to provide role models for young children.

- Encourage typical peers to play and interact with their peers with disabilities.

Young children often use toys and dolls to practice and expand language and learn social conventions. They also learn that they are valued when dolls reflect their own appearances. Notice the adaptive devices that accompany these toys.

Other measures can also be taken, to create a positive preschool environment, and make early intervention programs more relevant to diverse young learners. Children have an awareness of cultural differences very early (King, Chipman, & Cruz-Janzen, 1994). They are being taught to be more aware of their own cultural identities early in life. Rather than having a "unit" about each cultural group during a designated week, the history, customs, art, literature, music, and famous people from all cultures should be woven into every curriculum topic presented across the school year (Sexton et al., 1997). The curriculum can be modified to reflect more culturally appropriate components. For example, it could include activities involving creative arts from different cultures—music, artwork, and drama from students' diverse backgrounds and home experiences (Santos et al., 2000). The curriculum can also incorporate stories from a wide variety of cultural and ethnic traditions.

ELEMENTARY THROUGH HIGH SCHOOL

The 21st Century school cannot afford to be either (1) a White *environment nor a* Black *environment; (2) a* Latino *environment nor an* Asian American *environment; (3) a* Native American *environment nor a special environment; (4) a* rich *environment nor a* poor *environment; (5) an environment for* smart people *nor an environment for the* not-so-smart people. *Schools must be a place where all the above flourish, that is, an environment where opportunities and choices for growth are created by well-prepared teachers who understand the true meaning of the teaching profession. (Obiakor, 2001, p. 82)*

Indicators, such as the high dropout rates and low achievement of diverse students, make it clear that America's schools are not meeting the needs of many of these children. This situation can change. For example, poor and Black students achieve large learning gains as a result of reduced class sizes (CDF, 2001). As you read the rest of this section, which includes information about language, cultural diversity, and instruction, be mindful of Artiles's sage advice: "Indeed, special educators must begin to hear the voices of the students we serve" (1998, p. 34).

What special instructional considerations do English language learners (ELLs) need?

First, ELLs need instruction to learn the English language. Second, they need support to use their newly developing English skills to meet the demands of academic instruction. Neither of these learning goals is easily accomplished, so debate about effective programs rages on (Gersten & Baker, 2000).

Language acquisition and the development of enough proficiency to profit from academic instruction in English is a slow and complex process—and, as Gersten and his colleagues point out, it is not an automatic or natural process for many children (Gersten, Brengilman, & Jimnez, 1994). It often requires that teachers help students make explicit connections between what they read and write in one language and their activities in the other language. Teachers also need to understand that the mere ability to translate one language into another is not sufficient (Cheng, 1996). Complete understanding also requires understanding of feelings, anecdotes, and culturally based nonverbal messages. Research conducted by Cummins (1984) highlights these issues and helps us appreciate what true mastery of a language means. The first stages of language proficiency include conversational fluency: the mastery of pronunciation, vocabulary, and grammar. Only later does the individual develop the more complex, conceptual linguistic ability: the deeper functions of language necessary for competent participation in academic settings. (See Figure 3.5, which shows the surface (conversational) and the deeper levels of language proficiency.) Cummins cautions that children first develop face-to-face conversational skills and are then transferred to all-English instruction because they appear to have English proficiency. But then they fall further and further behind academically, because they do not have the more complex linguistic abilities required for academic success. Their **basic interpersonal communicative skills (BICS)** are more developed than their **cognitive/academic linguistic proficiency (CALP)**. Conversational skills in a second language can be acquired within 2 to 3 years, but the more complex language abilities needed for academic work require some 5 to 7 years of meaningful exposure and practice (Collier, 1995; Lessow-Hurley, 2000).

The student's understanding is affected by how many contextual clues accompany the language, such as explanatory pictures, specific people speaking, and tone of voice. Understanding is also affected by how demanding the activity is; if the task is concrete, it is easier to understand than if it is quite complex. Second-language ability must be greater when fewer contextual clues suggest meaning or when the

Figure 3.5 Surface and Deeper Levels of Language Proficiency

Source: From J. Cummins, *Bilingualism and Special Education: Issues in Assessment and Pedagogy,* 1984, p.138. Cleveden, England: Multilingual Matters. Reprinted by permission.

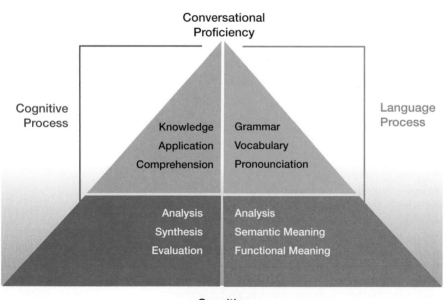

CHAPTER 3 *Multicultural and Bilingual Special Education*

communication requires more cognitive ability. The activities shown in the bottom half of the pyramid in Figure 3.5 require the highest levels of language and cognitive skills.

What, then, is the best way to help ELLs achieve mastery of English? Even after over 20 years of research efforts, this question has no definitive answer. Although bilingual education has come under attack and bilingual approaches are banned or restricted in some states (California is the most widely publicized example), bilingual approaches can be very effective in teaching students both their new language, English, and also academic subjects (Escamilla, 1999; Lemberger, 1996; Lyons, 1998). Not all approaches are effective (e.g., full English immersion results in high special education placement rates), but other language development approaches are available (Gersten & Baker, 2000; Reiss, 2001; Rueda et al., in press).

- **Bilingual education.** Dual language instruction is provided, with the first year of instruction offered solely in the child's native language.

- **Transitional bilingual education.** Academic subjects are taught in the child's native language until sufficient English is mastered for transition; the first phase usually lasts 3 years.

- **Sheltered instruction.** Teachers help students understand difficult concepts presented in English by rephrasing, restating, and providing examples and visuals.

- **English as a second language (ESL)** or **English language development (ELD).** Both focus on teaching the formal structures of language (grammar).

- **Total immersion.** No English instruction or native language instruction is provided; the student is taught entirely in English without supports.

What about ELLs with disabilities? How can teachers meet their learning needs? Like all ELLs, students with disabilities often do not find the typical general education classroom supportive of their developing language skills. However, like their special education peers, ELLs with disabilities often do not find the bilingual education classroom individualized enough to support their academic needs (Fletcher, Bos, & Johnson, 1999). For example, bilingual education teachers tend to use whole-group, undifferentiated instruction rather than an individualized approach. And they do not provide enough accommodations, for they typically only change a child's seating arrangement, adjust the amount of time allowed to complete assignments, lower their expectations, or provide cooperative learning activities.

After considerable study of the issues, Russell Gersten and Scott Baker (2000) are convinced that effective instruction for ELLs includes five critical components:

Many diverse children work well in group situations, like those incorporated in cooperative learning activities, where they can help each other develop language skills and solve problems.

1. *Build vocabulary as an anchor to curriculum:* Teach seven or fewer new words that convey key concepts of the academic content being learned.

2. *Use visuals:* Develop visual aids (graphic organizers,

Elementary Through High School

VALIDATED PRACTICES
Reciprocal Teaching

What Is Reciprocal Teaching?

Reciprocal teaching helps students who can read words but have difficulty with comprehension. Reciprocal teaching includes four components: (1) predicting, (2) questioning, (3) summarizing, and (4) clarifying. At first, the teacher models the method by reading stories and asking questions. Then the student and teacher switch roles.

Why Reciprocal Teaching Is Beneficial

Bilingual students benefit from scaffolding, an instructional process that gives students temporary support as they learn a new skill. Scaffolded instruction increases bilingual students' comprehension skills by providing them with opportunities to play the teacher's role. Students who effectively assume the teacher's role understand the material they have read.

Implementing Reciprocal Teaching

Reciprocal teaching requires you to be very active with your students as they learn the method. You might need to demonstrate the technique several times to be sure the students know the steps. Once they know the procedure, have them become the teacher as you become the student. Here is how the components work:

Predicting

- Read the title of the book to the students and ask them to predict what they think the story is about.
- Ask students to share their background knowledge of the topic.
- Refer to background knowledge and predictions as you read by anchoring examples in the students' culture.

---

concept and story maps, word banks) to help provide a concrete structure for thinking about new information.

3. *Implement cooperative learning and peer tutoring:* Structure groups of students who question each other and provide feedback about content comprehension.

4. *Use the native language strategically:* Use levels of English at which students are fluent, and introduce complexity in students' native language.

5. *Adjust language demands:* Accept varying levels of language output as determined by the cognitive demands of the learning situation.

Let's think about **cooperative learning** and peer tutoring, two strategies that Gersten and Baker believe are critical in the provision of effective instruction to ELLs. Most Americans are not proficient in two languages, and certainly no teacher speaks all the different languages spoken by children attending American schools. Bilingual education or support in a child's native language is not a possibility for many children who come to school not speaking English. What can teachers do when they do not speak the child's native language? One approach often suggested is to create cooperative learning groups, in which children work together on academic tasks (Fletcher, Bos, & Johnson, 1999). This approach is thought to be powerful in several different ways. Children who come from cultures that do not value individual competition will be more comfortable, and peers can help each other learn academic tasks. Of course, merely assigning students to small groups and telling them to help each other does not guarantee desired academic improvement (Lopez-Reyna, 1997). Although classmates can be very helpful to each other, students also need structure and guidance from the teacher. They need instructional prompts to help them learn to write coherent and thoughtful stories, expand their vocabularies, and increase the sophistication of their language use.

Reciprocal teaching—rich with demonstration, careful instruction, and feedback—can be added to direct instruction to improve students' reading comprehension (see the "Validated Practices" box for an example). Another strategy that is proving to be effective for ELLs is direct reading instruction, particularly instruction

MAKING CONNECTIONS

Norma Lopez-Reyna wrote the "Personal Perspectives" at the beginning of this chapter.

- As you are reading, stop at headings from the story and make new predictions.

Questioning

- Ask questions such as "Why do you think the boys were scared?"
- Avoid using fill-in-the-blank questions, because you want to encourage higher-level thinking skills.
- If students have difficulty forming questions, they should summarize first.
- Provide prompts as needed when students assume the teacher's role.

Summarizing

- Identify the main idea and supporting details.
- Provide summaries without looking at the passage.
- You may need to remind students of the following guide-lines for summarizing.
  - Identify the topic sentence, making one up if needed.
  - Disregard trivial or redundant information.

Clarifying

- Clarify when having difficulty with:
  - Referents (such as *she, it, they,* and *you*)
  - Troublesome or novel vocabulary
  - Unorganized text or incomplete information
  - Figurative language

This scientifically validated practice is a teaching method proven by systematic research efforts (Johnson Santamaria, Fletcher, & Bos, 2002; Klinger & Vaughn, 1996; Palinscar & Brown, 1987). Full citations are found in the references for Chapter 3 under "Elementary Through High School."

focusing specifically on basic phonological awareness and decoding skills. Failure to read has significant long-term results. Limited proficiency in English may be partially responsible for the low reading achievement often seen in ELLs, and there has been some question about whether students who are not proficient in English would benefit from instruction in basic decoding skills in their non-native language. The research findings are quite positive in this regard (Gunn et al., 2000). Hispanic students who spoke little or no English profited as much as their English-speaking classmates from systematic instruction in decoding skills (phonemic awareness, sound–letter correspondence, and sounding out and blending words with daily practice reading text).

How can schools become more accountable for diverse learners' outcomes?

Two answers are to include diverse students in high stakes testing and in conversations about educational reform. Growing consensus exists that educational systems need to be accountable for diverse learners' achievement. For such accountability to exist, children must be part of annual assessments, even ELLs not yet proficient in English (Ortiz & Yates, 2001; Thurlow & Liu, 2001). Exclusion from the testing process sends students and their families the message that they are not really a part of the educational community. When this happens, disengagement is a likely outcome. Such a message also runs counter to the key elements Festus Obiakor (2001) identifies as four necessary components of responsible multicultural schools:

1. Schools have a neighborhood feeling.

2. Teachers and students reflect each others' diversity.

3. The school's climate is committed to excellence.

4. Schools foster a sense of belonging, welcoming students instead of conveying a feeling of discrimination and exclusion.

MAKING CONNECTIONS

For other discussion about high stakes testing, see Chapters 1, 2, and 4.

ACCOMMODATING FOR INCLUSIVE ENVIRONMENTS

English Language Learners with Disabilities Participating in State and District-Wide Assessments

Bilingual Testing Opportunities

- Have text passages in both English and native language
- Provide questions in both languages
- Accept answers in either language

Vocabulary Assistance

- Allow English dictionary use
- Permit bilingual dictionary use
- Translate unfamiliar words

Extended Time

- Give extra time for test directions
- Allow extra time to take test

Alternative Test Version

- Simplify test's language
- Deliver the test to the student orally

Alternative Assessments

- Measure growth in language proficiency
- Use portfolio assessment documentation

IDEA requires that *all* students with disabilities participate in state and district assessments, and Title 1 of the Elementary and Secondary Education Act requires that all students covered under that program—those who are poor—also participate. However, alternative assessments and accommodations can and should be provided for those students who have special needs or circumstances. For example, students who have been in the United States less than 1 year are exempted from taking the tests. At present, no accommodations have been specifically designed or adopted for ELLs with disabilities, but some good guidelines (see the "Accommodating for Inclusive Environments" box for some examples) are being implemented across the nation (Thurlow & Liu, 2001). The purpose of these accommodations is giving students an opportunity to demonstrate their knowledge and skills, rather than emphasizing their disabilities or lack of English fluency. How many ELLs with disabilities might warrant these special accommodations? Martha Thurlow and Kristin Liu (2001) estimate that the number approaches half a million students.

What are some of the benefits of including diverse students with disabilities in high stakes testing and other reform agenda? Although both the testing movement and the inclusion of these youngsters is new, some positive outcomes have already been noted (Gersten & Baker, 2000; McLaughlin, Pullin, & Artiles, 2001):

- High stakes accountability has put pressure on schools to get their ELLs to learn English faster and earlier.
- Accountability measures have now brought diverse students' educational needs to the attention of school district administrators, which in turn will bring additional resources and help to these students and their teachers.
- Learning problems are addressed early and intensively.
- An atmosphere of high expectations is created.

COLLABORATION FOR INCLUSION

The word *inclusion* means many different things to different people. Issues related to inclusion are extremely complex and vary from individual to individual and group to group. For homeless children, inclusion might mean gaining access to school (Walther-Thomas et al., 1996). To ELLs, who in general are more likely to attend segregated classes, it might mean attending general education classes alongside their English-speaking peers (Hoff, 1995). For all culturally and linguistically diverse children, it means including their families and their communities in the educational system. This last level of inclusion requires partnerships and the development of collaborative relationships with groups that can provide a network of supports.

Building the right partnerships often requires working in difficult situations, for many of these families and communities are fighting for their own survival, often feel disenfranchised, and are competitive with one another (Garcia, 2001; Walther-Thomas et al., 1996). Collaboration needs to occur in meaningful ways, often with nontraditional partners. For example, innovative approaches for homeless children might bring educators together with staff from shelters. It might mean finding ways for family members who have no means of transportation to get to meetings at schools. Collaboration could take the form of identifying creative ways of communicating with families that have no consistent mailing address. For families that do not speak English well, it means finding interpreters very familiar with the special education process who can explain it to people who have no knowledge of the American educational system and do not speak English. It definitely means finding ways to change attitudes of community members who feel alienated from the educational and social service systems.

Communities are a good source of partnerships because they stand ready to help. Many American Indian communities embrace the idea of "many serving one" (Vraniak, 1998). A related perspective comes from African American communities: "It takes a whole village to raise a child." Unfortunately, educators do not typically tap these valuable resources, which are important, permanent parts of students' lives.

Partnerships with communities can enrich the curriculum and link home communities and schools together in meaningful ways.

Community partnerships have many benefits. For one, they often can provide services after the school day and during the summer months. An excellent example of a service group that offers a full range of services and supports is the Chicago Youth Centers (CYC). CYC enrolls over 700 children in its early intervention programs, programs that have received accreditation from the National Association for the Education of Young Children (only 5 percent of child development centers in the United States have been so acknowledged). CYC's After-School Programs have over 8,000 students. Even more notably, CYC has developed a partnership and collaborative agreement with many Chicago inner-city schools and provides early intervention and prevention programs that uniquely complement the work of public schools while serving the needs of children. CYC approached principals, guidance counselors, and teachers in Chicago public schools, offering to set up innovative programs. That initiative has brought CYC program directors into schools to conduct weekly sessions on basic life skills. Some of the topics discussed have been communication skills, conflict resolution, family relationships and responsibilities, gender stereotyping, cultural diversity, assertiveness techniques (especially in resisting sexual and peer pressure), child and sexual abuse, drug use, alternatives to gangs, goal setting, and sexual relationships and parenthood. Each of these sensitive and volatile issues is addressed through school approved curricula that incorporate CYC's experience and ability to teach through stories and examples, role playing, and videos. CYC also calls upon its own community relationships and sometimes invites guest speakers, as in a recent program that brought in officers from the area Sheriff's Department to speak on dating and violence.

Another innovative program resulting from this partnership is known as Girl Power, which was begun in 1998. This program, offered by Lowell Elementary School in Chicago's tough Humboldt Park neighborhood, has sixth-, seventh-, and eighth-grade girls meet with CYC staff as part of a voluntary after-school program. The girls are encouraged to write their thoughts and questions in journals, which are collected weekly. The journal writings are then used as the basis for open discussions of teen pregnancy, suicide, peer and gang pressure, and relationship issues. The popularity of these programs, both with students and with school personnel, attests to the power of collaborative partnerships between the community and schools.

Other excellent sources for partnerships and assistance exist in inner-city areas. Educators can seek out community leaders as they solicit help from community groups, churches, and volunteer organizations (Rogers-Dulan, 1998). One place to start is with students' parents, who will know of other resources in the local community. Educators must remember, however, that partnerships are forged out of a sense of equity. Community leaders must feel welcome at school, must be allowed to become actively involved at school, and must have a voice in the school's life (Thorp, 1997). Many opportunities for inclusion exist; we just need to be creative and to seize them.

TRANSITION THROUGH ADULTHOOD

The relationships among education, wages, and life outcomes are clear: High school graduates are less likely to be unemployed, and people with college degrees earn more. Every year of high school completed increases lifetime wages by 8 percent and improves job satisfaction (Currie & Thomas, 1995). In 1998, 82 percent of White students, 74 percent of Blacks, and 60 percent of Hispanics completed high school (Harvey, 2001). These trends are improving with more and more students graduating. What about students with disabilities? Overall, some 54 percent of them graduated with a standard diploma and 24 percent dropped out of school (U.S.

MAKING CONNECTIONS

The Native American dropout problem is also discussed in the "Defined" section of this chapter.

CHAPTER 3 *Multicultural and Bilingual Special Education*

Department of Education, 2001). Variations exist across groups, however (48 percent for American Indian/Alaska Native, 57 percent for Asian/Pacific Islanders, 44 percent for Blacks, 53 percent for Hispanics, and 63 percent for Whites). Although the trend across the years shows gains, opportunities for improvement for students with disabilities are obvious.

High school graduation is one criterion for entrance into college. Unfortunately, data indicate that diverse students are underrepresented at colleges and universities. Why might this be so? Remember, poor students often attend poor schools where a rich curriculum is not offered, textbooks are outdated, and teachers are less experienced. In fact, at many inner-city schools, advanced placement courses are not even available (Pachon, 1998). Sometimes, diverse students are advised not to take the core subjects required for admission to college (e.g., enough science, math, and foreign language courses). The result is inadequate preparation for college study. Here's what the data tell us about diverse students' success in higher education. Diverse individuals earned 24 percent of the associate's degrees earned in 1998, 21 percent of the bachelor's degrees, 16 percent of the master's degrees, 4 percent of the doctorates, and 22 percent of the professional degrees awarded that year (Harvey, 2001).

FAMILIES

The strength of families and their involvement in school can make a real difference in the lives of children (Garcia, 2001). Many culturally and linguistically diverse families come to the school situation burdened with alienation, feelings of distrust, and lack of information (Linan-Thompson & Jean, 1997; Parette & Petch-Hogan, 2000; Voltz, 1994). Some teachers accuse these parents of not wishing to be involved in their children's education (Thorp, 1997). Probably as a result of the exclusion these families feel, diverse families tend not to access social services available to them either (Bailey et al., 1999; Little, 1998). This situation may have developed because many of these parents do not feel welcome in a system they do not understand and among professionals whose speech is long on jargon and short on explanation. Many of these families have had negative experiences with the educational system and may appear disinterested and detached from their children's education. But family involvement can lead to improved outcomes for children (Kraft, 2001). It is therefore worthwhile to think about how the situation might be improved.

Why are many families of diverse students accused of being detached from their children's education?

Although it is a common observation of educators that many parents of diverse learners are not engaged in their children's educational programs, it is likely that the barriers the educational system sets up for these families make it difficult for them to participate (Thorp, 1997). Many parents report that educators do not listen to them (Rao, 2001). Teachers and service providers may inadvertently discourage the development of effective partnerships by excluding diverse family members in many different ways (Thorp, 1997). The roots of these barriers include conflict between home and school cultures, poor communication, lack of mutual respect, misunderstandings that lead to people making promises they cannot keep, and lack of sufficient information.

In many school–home relationships, cross-cultural dissonance (acute misunderstanding of fundamental issues and values about education, disability, and home–school interaction) may undermine special education for students with disabilities (Harry, 1992). Teachers may use language and special education jargon that parents do not understand. Even those who speak English may not be proficient enough in this second language to truly understand and communicate with educators using technical language or jargon (Holman, 1997). To them, the word *disability* may mean only a physical or sensory disability or only a severe disability—an interpretation very different from educators' view of disability (Thorp, 1997). For those who speak a language other than English, the interpreter selected might not understand the special education process. Most important, educators must develop trust and respect between home and school.

Teachers often assign parents to an inferior role and, in so doing, convince parents that their beliefs are not valued (Roa, 2001; Thorp, 1997). Family members need to be respected and not to be given assignments they are unable to complete. For example, many parents who are not proficient in English are embarrassed that they cannot help their children with homework (Milian, 1999). To avoid humiliation, they might agree to help their children with schoolwork but then be unable to follow through. Likewise, educators should not make promises they cannot keep. Parents are often limited to playing the role of "consent giver" and "educational planner" rather than being accepted as full partners in the special education of their sons and daughters (Harry, 1992). Instead of assuming that parents will be loyal supporters and passive recipients of information, educators should seek parents' input about how they would like to be involved in their child's educational program (Prater & Tanner, 1995; Thorp, 1997). They need information. In fact, families report that they are more satisfied with the educational system when they receive frequent communications (Hughes, Valle-Riestra, & Arguelles, 2002). They also report that they want more involvement with schools (Hughes, Valle-Riestra, & Arguelles, 2002). Maybe apparent disengagement is simply a communication problem.

How can educators increase diverse families' participation?

Experts have been pondering this question, studying the dynamics of diverse families, and analyzing schools. The following list indicates what they suggest that educators consider when they seek to foster special partnerships with diverse families (Bailey et al., 1999; Kraft, 2001; Linan-Thompson & Jean, 1997; Milian, 1999; Parette & Petch-Hogan, 2000; Roa, 2001; Thorp, 1997).

- Develop an atmosphere of trust and respect.
- Be sure families and communities feel welcome.
- Select and involve community leaders to serve as representatives of both school and home.
- Identify families' preferred means of communication and use it effectively.
- Communicate on a regular, ongoing basis (not just when there is a problem).
- Use interpreters who are knowledgable about schools and their programs for effective communication and participation.
- Incorporate materials that reflect the diversity of the community.
- Seek meaningful ways (e.g., actively sharing culture, art, music, and recreational activities) to involve families and communities (as they feel comfortable).
- Treat families with individual respect, and avoid stereotyping on any base (race, ethnicity, language, or socioeconomic class).
- Hold meetings with families at times and places that are manageable for them.

CHAPTER 3 *Multicultural and Bilingual Special Education*

Parents also need to be asked which family members they would like to be involved in their children's programs. Children from diverse backgrounds may have a family constellation that differs from that of children from the dominant, mainstream culture. Often these **extended family** members play a crucial role in the life of the individual with disabilities. The families of culturally and linguistically diverse children may include many extended family members as well as individuals outside the family. For example, for some African American families, church and community leaders often lend support and resources to the student with disabilities (Rogers-Dulan, 1998). For that child, the concept of extended family may well include key members of the community. For Native American children, these may be tribal elders whose exclusion would be considered an offense (Vraniak, 1998). Before making any decisions about treatments or educational strategies, it may be necessary to consult with these tribal elders and allow time for their response. Without understanding the cultural demands and expectations of the child's family, educators can inadvertently erect unfortunate and unnecessary obstacles.

In part, a child's success in school depends on respect between the school and the family. Children must feel confident that their cultural heritage and language are valued by the teacher and school. To encourage confidence and cooperation, a teacher can bring the strengths, contributions, culture, and language of the family directly into the school experience. For example, a grandfather might teach the class a special skill such as making silver jewelry. A grandmother who creates pottery following ancient techniques might demonstrate her art. A mother who programs computers might teach the class how to make drawings or large signs using the computer. A parent who is a migrant agricultural worker might sing folk songs in the home language or tell traditional stories. An aunt who has recently immigrated might show the class photos, musical instruments, clothing, or other items from her home country to help them dramatize a myth and better understand the customs of the country. A church leader could explain a religious holiday or event. Finally, a tribal leader might be asked to officiate at a school awards ceremony. Any such family participation in school events helps foster home–school partnerships and promote children's success at school.

TECHNOLOGY

Technology has changed all of our lives. And technology will certainly continue to affect the lives of those with disabilities and their families. It seems the possibilities are endless. For example, **computerized language translators** can translate words and phrases into many languages. Seiko, among many other companies, produces not only inexpensive bidirectional dictionaries but also translators that can handle complicated verb conjunctions. Such devices may have a significant impact for special education students with a primary language other than English. For instance, the student may be able to use a computer to write an assignment in his or her primary language, check the spelling and punctuation, and then press a button to translate the work into English and give it to the teacher. Or translators could help students expand their vocabularies. Such devices can also save time for the bilingual teacher or volunteer, who can use them for immediate translations of specific words or explanations of phrases and idioms. And teachers can use language translators to improve communications (both written and oral) between home and school, regardless of the language used at home.

MAKING **C**ONNECTIONS

Look again at the Advance Organizers found at the beginning of the chapter. To help you study the content of this chapter, the answers to the Focus and Challenge questions are provided next. Test yourself to see whether you have mastered the major points of this chapter.

IN CONCLUSION

Summary

Education should reflect the rich diversity of culture and language found in communities across this country, and special education should capitalize on each student's background as an appropriate individualized education program is created. Many exceptional children are bilingual, and many more come from diverse cultural backgrounds. Various combinations of disability, giftedness, cultural diversity, and ELL present many challenges to these children, their families, and educators as schools attempt to ensure that special education services are delivered to children who need and are entitled to them.

Self-Test Questions

Focus Questions

What is multicultural and bilingual special education, and who is served by such programs?

Combination of multicultural education, bilingual education, and special education

- Multicultural education: supports and extends concepts from students' cultural backgrounds
- Bilingual education: develops competence in English and the native language
- Special education: individualized education tailored to the unique learning needs of each student

Multicultural and bilingual special education serves culturally and linguistically diverse students with disabilities.

In what ways can bias occur in the identification and assessment process?

Bias in standardized tests: minority groups are not represented in the standardization population, and content is culturally "loaded"

Bias in the testing process: test administrator is not proficient in students' language or culture, student is not proficient in English, and no accommodations are made for learning differences

Why are educators so concerned about culturally and linguistically diverse children?

These students are at great risk for low educational achievement, being identified as having disabilities, attending poor schools, and dropping out of school.

Many of these risks arise because their families face social and economic inequities: poverty, low birth weight babies, reduced prenatal care for mothers, limited access to health care, lack of timely vaccinations.

Cultural differences between school and home can result in conflict and confusion over the appropriateness of behavior.

It is difficult to become proficient in English as a second language while receiving academic instruction in English.

Teachers are unprepared for the challenges many of these students present.

What is considered overrepresentation in special education and underrepresentation in education of the gifted?

Overrepresentation: percentage identified as having disabilities is greater than the group's percentage in the general student population

Underrepresentation: percentage identified and served in programs for gifted students is less than group's percentage in general student population

How can school personnel integrate children's home cultures and languages into the educational environment and curriculum?

Cultural sensitivity: anchor instruction in different American cultures, reflect students' diversity in instructional materials, incorporate supplemental materials from students' cultures and heritage (magazines, posters, books)

Language sensitivity: ensure parent and family participation and inclusion despite language barriers, encourage cooperative learning and study groups, include community volunteers, learn welcoming phrases in every student's home language

CHAPTER 3 *Multicultural and Bilingual Special Education*

MEETING THE STANDARDS AND PREPARING FOR LICENSURE EXAMS

After reading this chapter, you should be able to demonstrate basic knowledge, dispositions and skills described in the CEC standards and INTASC principles listed below. The section of this chapter most applicable to each standard is shown in parentheses at the end of the knowledge or skill statement.

 Core Standard 1: Foundations

- **Impact of dominant culture.** Impact of dominant culture on shaping school and the individuals who study and work in them. (History of the Field)

- **Identification.** Issues in identification of individuals with exceptional learning needs including those from culturally and linguistically diverse backgrounds (Prevalence)

 Core Standard 3: Individual Learning Differences

- **Cultural influences.** Cultural perspectives influencing the relationships among families, school and communities as related to instructions. (Elementary Through High School)

 Core Standard 5: Learning Environments

- **Creating learning environments.** Ways to create learning environments that allow individuals to retain and appreciate their own and each other's respective languages and cultural heritage. (Elementary Through High School)

 Core Standard #10: Collaboration

- **Communication.** Communicate effectively with families of individuals with exceptional learning needs from diverse backgrounds. (Elementary Through High School)

INTASC Principle 2

The teacher understands how children learn and develop, and can provide learning opportunities that support their intellectual, social and personal development.

- **Individual variation.** Appreciates individual variation with each area of development, shows respect for the diverse talents of all learners and is committed to help develop self-confidence and competence. (Elementary Through High School)

INTASC Principle 3

The teacher understands how students differ in their approaches to learning and creates instructional opportunities that are adapted to diverse learners.

- **Linguistic diversity:** Understands the process of second language acquisition and strategies to support the learning of the student whose first language is not English. (Exceptional Culturally and Linguistically Diverse Children)

- **Cultural diversity:** Has a framework for understanding cultural and community diversity and knows how to learn about and incorporate students' experiences, cultures, and resources into instructions. (Elementary Through High School)

Standards in Practice

These knowledge statements, dispositions, and skills may be demonstrated by beginning teachers in a lesson or unit plan. Consider including examples from diverse cultures into your everyday teaching. The knowledge of various cultural and linguistic backgrounds can provide an important link for your students and their families.

Go to the companion website (ablongman.com/smith5e) for detailed text correlations to CEC and INTASC standards, PRAXIS II™ exams, and other state-sponsored licensure exams.

SUPPLEMENTARY RESOURCES

Professional Readings and Resources

Artiles, A. J., & Ortiz, A. (Eds.). (2003). *English language learners with special needs: Identification, placement and instruction.* Washington DC: Center for Applied Linguistics.

Baca, L. M., & Cervantes, H. T. (Eds.). (1998). *The bilingual special education interface* (2nd ed). Columbus, OH: Merrill.

Castellano, J. A., & Díaz, E. I. (Eds.) (2002). *Reaching new horizons: Gifted and talented education for culturally and linguistically diverse students.* Boston: Allyn & Bacon.

Garcia, E. E. (2001). *Hispanic education in the United States.* New York: Rowman & Littlefield.

Gollnick, D. M., & Chinn, P. C. (2002). *Multicultural education in a pluralistic society* (6th ed.). Columbus, OH: Merrill.

Lynch, E. W., & Hanson, M. J. (1998). *Developing cross-cultural competence: A guide for working with young children and their families* (2nd ed.). Baltimore: Paul H. Brooks.

National Research Council (2002). *Minority students in special and gifted education.* Committee on Minority Representation in Special Education. M. Suzanne Donovan and Christopher T. Cross, editors. Washington, DC: National Academy Press.

Utley, C. A., & Obiakor, F. E. (2001). *Special education, multicultural education, and school. Reform: Components of quality education for learners with mild disabilities.* Springfield, IL: Charles C Thomas Publisher.

Popular Books

Anaya, R. A. (1979). *Tortuga.* Berkeley, CA: Editorial Justa.

Dorris, M. (1989). *The broken cord.* New York: Harper & Row.

Carter, F. (1997). *The education of Little Tree.* Albuquerque: University of New Mexico Press.

Kenzaburo, O. (1994). *The pinch runner memorandum.* London: M. E. Sharpe.

Kozol, J. (1995). *Amazing grace: The lives of children and the conscience of a nation.* New York: Crown.

Ng, F. M. (1993). *Bone: A novel.* New York: Hyperion.

Southgate, D. E. (1996). *The other way to dance.* New York: Laurel-Leaf Books.

Williams-Garcia, R. (1995). *Like sisters on the homefront.* New York: Penguin Books.

Videos and DVDs

Lean on Me (1989). Warner Brothers

An inner-city public school has deteriorated and is suffering from overcrowded classrooms, drug addicted students, gang members, and violence, making it impossible to maintain order. A principal is hired to turn the school around, and he begins by expelling all the proven troublemakers. He is willing to take any measure, legal or illegal, to ensure that his students are safe and prepared for the state's school evaluation test.

This film offers a realistic portrayal of a typical inner-city school from the late 80s and early 90s. It shows that school administrators and principals can have a tremendous impact on the lives of students by helping to engage them in both academics and school life. The result is a reduction in school failure and dropout rates.

The Education of Little Tree (1997). Paramount

Little Tree's parents die during the Great Depression, and he goes to live with his grandparents. They teach this 8-year-old boy the Cherokee ways of East Tennessee. But a complaint is filed against the boy's grandparents because they did not enroll him in school to receive a formal education. Authorities place the boy in a boarding school, where he is abused because he is not familiar with the customs of this new world, so his grandfather liberates him.

This film begins with a young boy acclimating to a completely rural setting, where he is taught to live in harmony with nature. Once Little Tree is enrolled in a boarding school, cultural differences become apparent, and the disparity between this setting and his previous environment becomes intolerable. Each culture holds different things sacred; one reveres nature and the other discipline.

Stand and Deliver (1988). Warner Brothers

Based on the true story of one teacher who has high hopes for his students from a low-income neighborhood in East Los Angeles and who challenges them to take the advanced placement test in calculus. To achieve this goal, they have to attend summer school for several extra hours a day. The students actually get the highest score in the state but then are accused of cheating.

In East Los Angeles, where the majority of residents are Latino/a, the schools are underfunded and the education the students receive is inferior to that available at other schools in the same district. Officials from the Board of Education for the State of California challenged the

CHAPTER 3 *Multicultural and Bilingual Special Education*

students' results because of their preconceptions about Latino/a students. Without the persistence and strength of their teachers, these students could not have overcome low expectations and would have fulfilled the prophecy of failure.

Parent, Professional, and Consumer Organizations and Agencies

Division for Culturally and Linguistically Diverse Exceptional Learners (DDEL) Council for Exceptional Children (CEC)

> 1110 North Glebe Road, Suite 300
> Arlington, VA 22201-5704
> Phone: (888) CEC-SPED; (703) 620-3660
> Web site: http://www.cec.sped.org or
> www.cec.sped.org/dv/ddel

National Association for Bilingual Education (NABE)

> 1030 15th Street, NW, Suite 470
> Washington, DC 20005
> Phone: (202) 898–1829
> Web site: http://www.nabe.org

National Clearinghouse for English Language Acquisition & Language Instruction Education Programs

> 2121 K Street, NW, Suite 260
> Washington, DC 20037
> Phone: (800) 322-6223; (202) 467-0867
> E-mail: askncbe@ncbe.gwu.edu
> Web site: http://www.ncbe.gwu.edu

National Association for Multicultural Education (NAME)

> 733 15th Street, NW, Suite 430
> Washington, DC 20005
> Phone: (202) 628-NAME
> E-mail: name@nameorg.org
> Web site: http://www.nameorg.org

Video**Workshop** Extra

If the VideoWorkshop package was included with your textbook, go to Chapter 3 of the Companion Website (www.ablongman.com/smith5e) and click on the VideoWorkshop button. Follow the instructions for viewing Video clip 4. Consider this information along with what you've read in Chapter 3 while answering the following questions.

Video clip 4: Teaching in Bilingual Classrooms (Time 3:24)

1. The teachers in the video tape suggest repeating and slowing down as strategies to meet the needs of diverse students. Your text suggests several additional strategies. Which of all strategies do you think might work best for your content or grade level? Provide a rationale for your answer.

2. The second grade in the video appears to consist primarily of students who are members of a diverse group and who may not be native English speakers. Your text provides data on the incidence, in U.S. classrooms, of students who are from diverse cultures. How does your community compare to the class in the video and to the data given in the textbook? What does this mean for you as a teacher?

Edouard Manet. *Blowing Soap Bubbles.* Gulbenkian Museum, Lisbon, Portugal

EDOUARD MANET was born in Paris in 1832. His father's ambitions for him were to carry on the family tradition and become a lawyer. Despite outraged protests, Manet became one of the most famous impressionist painters of his day. Possibly he turned to art because of his difficulties at school. One headmaster considered him to be "feeble"; another referred to him as "distracted", not "very studious", and "mediocre" (Schneider, 1968). If his father had not been a highly respected community leader, Manet would have been dismissed from school. To keep Manet from a career as an artist, his father got him a commission in the navy, but Manet failed the naval examination (Bolton, 1989) and turned to art. In the 1800s, the special education category of learning disabilities had not been identified. Whether Manet actually had learning disability or not cannot be verified. Regardless, from all accounts, academic learning was clearly a challenge for him.

4 Learning Disabilities

A PERSONAL PERSPECTIVE

Educating Erin

Megan and Jim Askim and I, although we come from different parts of America, met while on vacation at a cooking school in Italy. Megan and I were attracted to each other almost immediately. It had not occurred to either of us that we would go halfway across the world to meet someone else whose life was immersed in issues related to students with disabilities. After a few days of traveling and cooking together, I asked Megan if she would share her story—the story of her daughter, Erin, who has very serious learning disabilities, the Askim family, and a special mom who exemplifies the modern parent advocate. Megan agreed, but she found the writing task to be more difficult than she had expected. Megan has not had to fight for Erin to be able to go to school, although she continually has to monitor her daughter's education. What you will learn, and may perhaps be surprised to learn, is that services do not automatically kick into place when a child's disability is suspected, nor are they "seamless" as children move through the educational system.

We were a young couple when Erin was born. She was a second child, and we had no reason to suspect problems. But she stayed like a baby for a long time. "Well, it's a good thing we like having a baby," we would say. "She is taking her sweet time growing up. Not too fast for us; that's okay." She was a little slow crawling, a little slow walking, and she talked a funny kind of language—we called it ewock. What we slowly learned was that how Erin is in the world is just different. Our family calls Erin "inside-out, upside-down, and backwards." I realized that Erin

really had difficulties when I sent my son off to kindergarten. I knew that Erin wouldn't be ready for that program in 2 or 3 years. Honestly, I knew there was something wrong from the second day she was with us. She was fretful. She was sleeping and eating, but she would start to cry for no apparent reason. I had a 2-year-old; he didn't do that, and I could comfort him. I looked for help from our pediatrician, but he said, "Erin's fine." I asked family members but only got a lot of opinions that weren't very helpful. I had a friend who was an educator, and her expertise was early childhood development. So I invited her over for lunch and expressed my concern that there was something "not quite right." I asked her straight out what she thought, and she said, "There is something drastically wrong with Erin." Although I knew that, it was hard to accept. Fortunately, with that profound statement I got a helping hand and a list of phone numbers.

Hours, days, and weeks with countless interviews, needs assessments to fill out, and about a million phone calls later (not really; it just felt like it), we had an appointment with the county office of education for the assessment they felt was necessary. Educators, speech and language pathologist, OT, psychologist—all deemed her to be fine. "No way," I said. "There is something wrong!" Luckily, there was one speech pathologist who said, "Well, let's look more." Finally, Erin, at 3 years and 3 months, was eligible to receive special education services. The help meant a special education preschool that had the specialists needed to teach her. Help meant putting a little 3-year-old girl on a little yellow school bus to go 10 miles away to school at 6:50 in the morning. I sent her blanket with her, but that was never enough of a blanket for me. I kept thinking that it wasn't supposed to be like this; Erin's barely out of her crib!

At age 5, Erin's school program changed. She went from that preschool far away to an elementary school in our school district. She attended a special day class for K–2. Here she stayed until age 7. In spite of all the intensive teaching, the speech therapy, and OT, she still couldn't count to 10 or learn the ABCs. The school was truly puzzled. We needed more assessments! This would come in the form of an intense 4-day stay at our state diagnostic center, which included psychologists, speech and language evaluation, occupational therapy, medical evaluation, and numerous educational tests. More reports, and confirmation of many specific learning disabilities, and a very specific plan with the recommended interventions. In order for her to participate in the amount of therapies and the intense intervention needed, she would have to change schools. This move meant a special school, which is considered one of the most restrictive environments in education, but for Erin (at this time) it was the least restrictive environment. She had the program that was necessary for her to learn. She stayed at this school for 4 years. She learned to read and write. She made friends. Erin grew into a confident and motivated learner with a lot of help—and I mean a lot of help—and some very intense learning strategies. However, this school was 20 miles away from home. With all the very positive things going on in her education, she was beginning to realize that she didn't go to school with her friend down the street.

Erin, now a middle school student, told us she was ready for a change, and it was our responsibility to make that happen. The thought of a neighborhood middle school for her was terrifying to us. So the place to start was by reconvening the IEP committee to have discussions from everyone involved about what her program might look like. The details are irrelevant and too numerous, but it is critical for you to know that we ended up being the experts who made decisions about what Erin's program would be. Anyway, Erin did transition to our neighbor-

hood school in seventh grade, into a "full inclusion program." She was now enrolled in all general education classes, like all typical seventh graders, but it seemed like meetings with teachers were endless. For an example, the math teacher was concerned that the curriculum would be too difficult. I recommended that he present the math curriculum as it was, and if Erin "hit a wall" we would be open to alternatives. She has not hit the wall yet. Erin received real grades (for the first time ever), and she has thrived. (She still receives special education services with what the district calls a "one-to-one aide" and also continuing speech and language therapy.)

Erin is now a sophomore in high school, and we have different issues to deal with. My challenge now is to have relationships with all the different teachers. I have to, because her general education teachers do not understand disabilities in general and how they specifically impact individual students. I can plead Erin's case very effectively, but I keep wondering why I still have to. And I worry about those parents who are unable to advocate effectively on their own child's behalf. Our family is still dealing with teachers who actively question our decisions about Erin's education. After all these years—with all the professionals, the educational therapists, the medical evaluations, the IEPs, the team meetings, support from family and friends and teachers, making decisions based on past history and high expectations for the future—how can a teacher say, "Well, Mrs. Askim, I really don't think this is the best class for Erin"? It is my responsibility to advocate on Erin's behalf, but should it be my responsibility to convince teachers that my child deserves to be taught? My response in my own mind is that Erin hasn't "hit the wall" in learning but some teachers have "hit the wall" in teaching. My child has been a challenge to teach all along, and she has been the teacher to many teachers. They are the teachers who admit they don't have all the answers but are willing to be persistent, to be supportive, and to have high expectations for a little girl, and now a young lady, who sees the world "inside-out, upside-down, and backwards."

1. **Why do you think Erin's high school teachers were so concerned about including Erin in the general education curriculum?**

2. **What do you think might be next for Megan and Erin?**

MAKING CONNECTIONS

Use the learning strategy, Advance Organizers, to help focus your study of this chapter's content, and reinforce your learning by reviewing answers to the Focus and Challenge Questions which are found at the end of the chapter.

ADVANCE ORGANIZERS

Overview

Learning disabilities is the largest special education category; well over half of all students with disabilities (some 6 percent of all schoolchildren) are identified as having it as their primary disabling condition. Although these individuals are a heterogeneous group, they all share several defining characteristics: unexpected underachievement and difficulty mastering academic subjects, particularly reading. Many of these students also display characteristics associated with attention deficit/hyperactivity disorder (ADHD). Partly because of the ease of identifying students as belonging to this special education category and the size of this group, much controversy surrounds these children and their educational programs. Although some have questioned whether this disability even exists, considerable evidence indicates not only that it does exist but also that it is a lifelong disability.

Self-Test Questions

Focus Questions

- What are the key features of most definitions of learning disabilities?
- Why is there a call for a new definition, and how might it be different?
- Why is it correct to consider learning disabilities a lifelong condition?
- What are some learning characteristics that contribute to these students' poor academic performance?
- How might the array of services be reconceptualized for students with learning disabilities?

Challenge Question

- What constitutes an appropriate education for these students, and in what setting should it be provided?

We have all had the experience: No matter how hard we try, we have trouble understanding the information presented. In school we might sit through lectures and not understand the messages the instructor is trying to deliver. We may not understand the reading material for a particular class. We find it impossible to organize our thoughts to write a coherent essay or report. Sometimes we stumble over words and are unable to convey our thoughts, feelings, or knowledge. And occasionally we are uneasy and uncomfortable with other people. For most of us, these situations are infrequent. For people with learning disabilities (LD), however, one or more of these situations is commonplace. People with learning disabilities belong to a group of very diverse individuals, but they all share one problem: They do not learn in the same way or as efficiently as their nondisabled peers. Although most possess normal intelligence, their academic performance is significantly behind that of their classmates. Some have great difficulty learning mathematics, but most find the mastery of reading and writing to be their most difficult challenge (Fuchs, Fuchs, Mathes et al., 2001).

In this chapter, you will come to understand learning disabilities. You will learn that because of this group's heterogeneity, there is no single explanation why these otherwise normal individuals have problems learning at the same rate and in the same style as their nondisabled classmates. You will learn that learning disabilities is the largest special education category, one that has come to be applied to some students who do not have this disability. You will also learn about students with learning disabilities who also have ADHD. Despite considerable controversy about learning disabilities, many individuals overcome their learning disabilities through highly specialized, intensive, individualized instructional programs. Unfortunately, for many others, the impact of a learning disability lasts a lifetime.

OPPORTUNITIES FOR A BETTER FUTURE

Although learning disabilities is one of the newest special education categories, having been described in the 1960s, a study of history shows that this condition did not originate in the 20th Century. Rather, the American educational system is finally responding to a disability that had previously been either ignored or misdiagnosed. However, this burgeoning special education category now comprises over half of the children identified as having special education needs, and the numbers continue to increase year after year. Possibly, by the end of the century this category had lost its utility and was no longer serving its original purpose.

Because the operational definition of this disability is so broad, identifying a student who is not succeeding in general education classes as having a learning disability is not difficult. Therefore, because of its ever-growing membership, some education professionals question whether the diagnosis of learning disabilities is simply an educational response to students' failure in the general education curriculum rather than an actual disability. Has it become a "dumping ground" for unsuccessful students? Or could different students described as exhibiting this disability really have different types of problems? (Some might actually have a disability, whereas others might be either low achieving or not performing well for a variety of reasons.)

As you read this chapter, think about children who are unable to achieve to their potential in the general education curriculum and the services and supports they need. Think about whether

- this disability area should be discontinued and replaced with a more general "high incidence" special education category combining all mild disabilities

- the size of the category should be limited

- the operational definition should become more restrictive

- research findings are leading to effective practices for unique sets of learners

- as with other disability areas, learning disabilities range from mild to severe cases

LEARNING DISABILITIES DEFINED

Two definitions of **learning disabilities** are the basis for those developed and implemented in the 50 states and Washington, DC. One is included in the U.S. Department of Education's regulations for IDEA; the National Joint Committee on Learning Disabilities (NJCLD), a coalition of professional and parent organizations concerned with learning disabilities, adopted the other. Let's look at the two approved definitions before we consider the possibility of a new one. Here is the federal government's definition:

> *Specific learning disability means a disorder in one or more of the basic psychological processes involved in understanding or in using language, spoken or written, that may manifest itself in an imperfect ability to listen, think, speak, read, write, spell, or to do mathematical calculations, including such conditions as perceptual disabilities, brain injury, minimal brain dysfunction, dyslexia, and developmental aphasia. The term does not include learning problems that are primarily the result of visual, hearing, or motor disabilities, mental retardation, emotional disturbance, or environmental, cultural, or economic disadvantages. (U.S. Department of Education, 1999)*

The NJCLD definition is as follows:

> *Learning disabilities is a general term that refers to a heterogeneous group of disorders manifested by significant difficulties in the acquisition and use of listening, speaking, reading, writing, reasoning or mathematical skills. These disorders are intrinsic to the individual, presumed to be due to central nervous system dysfunction, and may occur across the life span. Problems in self-regulatory behaviors, social perception, and social interaction may exist with learning disabilities but do not by themselves constitute a learning disability. Although learning disabilities may occur concomitantly with other handicapping conditions (for example, sensory impairment, mental retardation, serious emotional disturbance) or with extrinsic influences (such as cultural differences*

or insufficient or inappropriate instruction), they are not the result of those conditions or influences. (NJCLD, 1994)

The key differences between these two definitions rest in orientation about the causes of the disability and the age of the definition.

1. The federal definition is older and has a medical orientation.
2. The NJCLD definition allows for coexisting disabilities (e.g., learning disabilities and visual disabilities).
3. The NJCLD definition acknowledges problems many of these individuals have with social skills.

Neither of these two definitions directly calls out what has come to be *the* defining characteristic of learning disabilities: **unexpected underachievement.** The predominant problem these students face is developing academic competence, and such problems are unexpected or not predictable from the talents and potential they show in other areas (Fuchs, 2002). And because some individuals show strengths in one area but not in another, in different patterns from those seen in their peers with learning disabilities, this special education category is also defined by its **heterogeneity.**

MAKING CONNECTIONS

See the section on gifted students with disabilities in Chapter 7.

Definitions of learning disabilities used in almost every state share some common features, which are listed in Table 4.1. Many states' definitions indicate that an individual's learning disability may be due to a **central nervous system dysfunction,** but they do not require documentation. Some states' definitions acknowledge problems these students have achieving social competence, but the main characteristic shared by students with learning disabilities is their low academic achievement.

Dissatisfaction exists with current definitions of learning disabilities (Elksnin et al., 2001; Horowitz et al., 2002). One reason is the great inconsistency in the percentage of students included in this category across states: Some states include as few as 2 percent and others as many as 9 percent (U.S. Department of Education, 2001). The cause for national concern stems from this category's sheer size: Over half of all students included in special education are designated as having a learning disability. Thus, the search for a new definition is gaining momentum. Some experts are calling for an entirely new definition, not one that just attempts to fix problems with either the IDEA or the NJCLD definition (Kavale & Forness, 2000). Not all researchers agree, but the Thomas B. Fordham Foundation estimates that with such an approach, learning failure and a diagnosis of learning disabilities could be avoided for some 2 million children (Finn, Rotherham, & Hokanson, 2001). Others are calling for a new system of identification that prevents diagnosis for many children because they receive intensive instruction using validated methods early (Bevilacqua, 2002). What features might a new definition include, or what issues would it address? Of course, it is impossible to know for certain, but the topics most likely to be discussed are:

Table 4.1 Key Features of Definitions of Learning Disabilities
Intelligence scores within the normal range
A significant discrepancy between academic achievement and expected potential
Not caused by other factors, such as cultural differences, lack of educational opportunities, poverty, or other disabilities: the exclusion clause
Often manifested in language-related areas, such as communication, written language, or reading
Problems intrinsic to the individual involving that person's central nervous system, specific deficits in information processing, or the ability to learn
Learning problems specific and confined to one or two cognitive areas

- Changing the criterion so that fewer students are identified as having a learning disability
- Whether students need to demonstrate a significant gap (a discrepancy) between intelligence and achievement

Learning Disabilities Defined

- The term *unexpected underachievement* and its inclusion in the definition
- Early intervention to prevent later reading problems
- The concept of *resistance to treatment* and whether it is a second defining feature of this disability

Because these issues are embedded in how students are identified as having learning disabilities, more explanation is provided in the next sections.

Are there different types of learning disabilities?

Remember that one defining characteristic of learning disabilities is "unexpected underachievement." In other words, these students perform significantly below their peers and below levels teachers and parents would expect from children of their ability. Over the years, debate has focused on whether there is a difference between **low achievers** and students with learning disabilities, and some still maintain that learning disabilities is an artificial category no different from low achievement (Fletcher et al., 2002). The root of the debate is whether learning disabilities actually exist: Are these children experiencing low achievement or underachievement? A small group of researchers even argue that the category of learning disabilities should be disbanded so that the resources available could be spent on preventing reading failure, and that all children who do not profit from typical instruction should be put in a group with other low achieving students (Lyon et al., 2001). This radical view is not widely accepted by most experts, who insist that learning disabilities is severe, pervasive, and chronic—a condition that results in unexpected underachievement and requires intensive intervention (Gerber, 1999–2000; Martin, 2001).

No uniform classification system exists for students with learning disabilities. According to current definitions of the disability, these students are supposed to have normal intelligence, but they do not achieve academically at the levels they should. As a group, these students' most common problem is in the area of reading (Fuchs & Fuchs, 2001). Although some students have problems in only one academic area, such as written communication or mathematics, most have pervasive problems that affect the entire range of academic and social areas (Bryant, Bryant, & Hammill, 2000; Gregg & Mather, 2002). Also, many of these students have coexisting attention deficit/hyperactivity disorders (ADHD), which compounds their academic and social challenges (Mayes, Calhoun, & Crowell, 2000). Schools do not typically further divide this large group of learners into specific types, but to better understand the diversity—the heterogeneity—of these students, we will examine some common profiles next.

- *General Unexpected Underachievement* Although poor academic achievement is the outcome in both low achievement and learning disabilities, they are not the same. Experts are certain that learning disabilities is different from low achievement, which can be explained by cognitive disabilities, poor motivation, or poor teaching (Fuchs, Fuchs, Mathes et al., 2002; Kavale & Forness, 2000). Although no reliable means is available currently to test this notion, learning disabilities probably reflects deficits in the ability to process information or remember it (Torgensen, 2002). What appears to be quite certain, however, is that learning disabilities are **resistant to treatment** or **resistant to intervention** (Fuchs, 2002; Gresham, 2002). This is not a new concept. Frank Gresham applied this idea to the identification of students with emotional or behavioral disorders over 10 years ago (Gresham, 1991). The premise is that if a student receives instruction or intervention typically used in general education programs and does not respond or improve sufficiently, then more intensive individualized intervention is necessary. The evidence is mounting that some students do not learn at the same rate or in the same ways as their classmates; they are resistant to treatment (Bryant et al., 2000; Fuchs, Fuchs, Thompson et al., 2002). Estimates are that as many as 6 percent of all children have unexpected underachievement and also experience resistance to treatment (Learning Disability Summit, 2001). These students with learning disabilities require special education.

• *Reading Disabilities* Students identified as having learning disabilities have much lower reading abilities than students who are low achievers (Fuchs & Fuchs, 2001; Fuchs, Fuchs, Mathes et al., 2002). Often, their academic achievement in reading is significantly below the levels of their nondisabled classmates, and reading difficulty is the most common reason for referrals to special education. Because reading and writing are intimately related, most of these students have problems with written communication as well (Graham, Harris, & Larsen, 2001). Reading and writing, obviously, are important skills; in school, students must be able to read information from a variety of texts (social studies, science, literature) and write in varying formats (essays, reports, creative writing, notes). As the complexity of academic tasks increases, students who are not proficient in reading and writing cannot keep pace with the academic expectations of school settings.

Reading/learning disabilities causes pervasive academic problems because comprehending information gained by reading grows increasingly important as the curriculum becomes more advanced. How great is this problem for students with learning disabilities? It is significant, and here's why. To understand printed text requires proficiency in a number of skills: reading words, comprehending language, and accessing background language (Jenkins & O'Connor, 2002). Students must be able to decode words and read with enough fluency to gain information at a rate close to that of their classmates. Joe Jenkins compared fourth-graders' reading skills and found that those with reading disabilities read at only one-third the rate of their classmates and made many more errors when they read than their counterparts. Evidently, problems in reading occur not just because students are developmentally slow in acquiring the necessary prerequisite skills; they also acquire these skills differently than students without reading disabilities (Compton, 2002).

• *Mathematics Disabilities* Although reading problems are the most common reason for referral, more than 50 percent of students with learning disabilities also have difficulties with mathematics (Fuchs & Fuchs, 2001). **Mathematics/learning disabilities** presents problems for many of these students. A few of these individuals seem to have difficulties with mathematics alone, but for most, this difficulty is part of an overwhelming and pervasive underachievement.

Students with mathematics disabilities have problems that seem to stem from their difficulties retrieving information from long-term memory. These children have problems remembering basic number facts (Robinson, Menchetti, & Torgensen, 2002). Other students' mathematics disabilities seem to stem from their inability to solve multistep problems, such as borrowing in subtraction and solving word problems (Bryant, Bryant, & Hammill, 2000). Because math problem solving places demands on both reading and information processing skills, this area of the mathematics curriculum can be most challenging for both teachers and students. What is helpful is providing structure to different types of problems. In this regard, graphical representations can be most helpful (Jitendra, 2002). When students draw pictures or diagram the word problem, it becomes easier to solve. By learning the rules about key words in problems and then knowing what type of diagram to apply, students place structure and make order out of what would otherwise be just a confusing situation. Another way to help these students is to provide real-world examples of mathematics problems to solve (Fuchs, Fuchs, Hamlett, & Appleton, 2002). The notion is that if word problems are posed in the context of relevant situations (bank balances, credit card statements, shopping allowances), students will be better motivated to think about how the problems are solved.

• *Coexisting ADHD* Learning disabilities and **attention deficit/hyperactivity disorder (ADHD)** often occur in combination. Some studies have shown that 70 percent

MAKING CONNECTIONS

Reading interventions are discussed in the "Early Childhood" and "Elementary Through High School" sections of this chapter.

For more about ADHD, see Chapter 9.

of children with ADHD also have a learning disability (Mayes, Calhoun, & Crowell, 2000). Those students with reading problems only are most likely to be identified as having learning disabilities; those with reading problems *and* uncontrolled temperament tend to be identified as having both learning disabilities and ADHD (Pisecco et al., 2001). Students with ADHD do not score higher on tests of intelligence than other students, including those individuals with learning disabilities and significant reading problems (Kaplan et al., 2000). Studies on whether these students are more likely to have more problems with written communication, reading, math, or spelling have yielded conflicting results (Mayes, Calhoun, & Cromwell, 2000; Willcutt & Pennington, 2000). Some experts believe that these students fall into separate cognitive, biological, and behavioral subgroups (Bonafina et al., 2000). Whether subgrouping has any usefulness to teachers at the moment is unclear. What each of these students requires is an individualized educational program to meet his or her specific learning needs.

ADHD, now a condition included in the "other health impairments" category, is discussed in Chapter 9, but because it often overlaps with other disabilities, it is important to understand the characteristics of this condition early in your studies. What is ADHD? According to the DSM-IV (American Psychiatric Association, 1994), ADHD is "a persistent pattern of inattention and/or hyperactivity-impulsivity that is more frequent and severe than is typically observed in individuals at a comparable level of development" (p. 78). Symptoms of the condition must occur in more than one setting. The DSM-IV also establishes criteria for determining whether a child has ADHD; the main characteristics are inattention, hyperactivity, and impulsivity.

How are learning disabilities identified?

One consistent element of the identification process for students with learning disabilities is the application of what is called **discrepancy formulas.** Such formulas are used to determine whether a student's gap between achievement and potential is significant and accounts for that student's learning failures. Although many different types of discrepancy formulas are applied across the nation, *all* 50 states use at least one version for the purpose of identifying these children (Schrag, 2000). Two test results are needed to apply all discrepancy formulas: an IQ score and the score from a standardized achievement test. Considerable dissatisfaction with discrepancy formulas exists (Fuchs, 2002; Kavale, 2002). Here are a few criticisms of discrepancy formulas:

- IQ tests are not reliable and are unfair to many groups of children.
- Results have little utility in planning a student's educational program.
- The process is not helpful determining which interventions might be successful.
- The outcomes are not related to performance in the classroom, in the general education curriculum, or on district- or statewide assessments.
- Children must fail before they qualify for needed services. Thus early intervention is delayed until the gap becomes great enough for children to meet this criterion.

With such concerns, why are discrepancy formulas still used? One important reason is that they endow the identification process with objectivity. Diagnosticians or school psychologists give a child an IQ test and an achievement test and then apply the formula. Whether the child is included in the learning disabilities category thus becomes a cut and dried, "yes" or "no" answer. This reason may well become a barrier to removing discrepancy formulas from the identification process. Also, some experts maintain that if the requirements for qualifying as having learning disabilities were strictly adhered to, applying the current procedures and rules would be sufficient to reduce the rolls and resolve concerns about the number of

CHAPTER 4 *Learning Disabilities*

students identified with this disability (Scruggs & Mastropieri, 2002).

Most special education categories are stable; that is, they are not experiencing substantial growth (Blair & Scott, 2002). If objective measures are being used, why does the learning disabilities category continue to grow when most others are not? School services committees often ignore strict policies and identify students as having learning disabilities who do not have the required discrepancy between their ability and academic expectations for them (Lester & Kelman, 1997; MacMillan & Siperstein, 2002). Why would such committees violate state and school district guidelines? The answers are many. In some cases, they are attempting to avoid negative labels such as mental retardation. In other instances, they are desperately trying to get extra help to students who might not otherwise qualify for special edu-

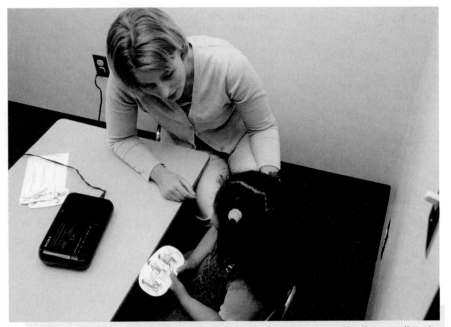

One way to determine whether a child's academic achievement is equal to her overall intellectual abilities is to use standardized achievement tests. Another method is to collect data directly on performance. Here a diagnostician is taping the child's story as she creates it from three pictures she is holding. Her performance evaluation will be used to determine whether her referral for learning disabilities is due to a disability or to her incomplete learning of a second language.

cation. Some of these students might not yet meet the cutoff score. For them, the current difference between achievement and intelligence is not great enough, but because of the growing disparity between these scores, it is only a matter of time before their low academic achievement will qualify them for special services. Other students are low achievers, who perform up to expectations for them and thus demonstrate no discrepancy, but who cannot keep up with their general education classmates. And some other students are linguistically diverse and struggling to master English. For some of them, well-intentioned teachers refer them to special education in hopes of getting them the additional help they need to succeed in school.

What, then, might replace discrepancy formulas and the ways in which children are currently identified as having learning disabilities? Many systems are being proposed. Some systems would "process" children through many stages of learning opportunities to determine how resistant to instructional intervention they are (Horowitz et al., 2002). Others would apply a pre-referral concept, whereby students receive special assistance before an actual referral to special education is made (Fuchs & Fuchs, 2001). And some would use comprehensive informal assessments of students' actual classroom work to determine patterns of errors, levels of performance, and descriptions of specific skills (Gregg & Mather, 2002). The advantage of these systems is that children, parents, and teachers would no longer have to "wait to fail enough" to get the help they need. What will be required is a well-coordinated approach that provides progressively more intensive and individualized education programs to children who are not learning even though they are receiving validated practices.

How might this work? Students who are not profiting from instruction in the general education classroom, while other children are, first receive tutoring, extra attention, peer tutoring, and modified textbooks. If they continue not to profit from instruction, they then receive more intensive instruction carefully matched to their

MAKING CONNECTIONS

For a review of challenges faced by English language learners, see those sections in Chapter 3.

MAKING CONNECTIONS

Review the "Appropriate Evaluation" section of Chapter 1.

skill levels (Fuchs & Fuchs, 2001). Instruction includes active responding, cues, prompts, and direct instruction that is consistently evaluated. If they improve to the levels of other students in the general education classroom, they rejoin their classmates. However, if their academic performance returns to unsatisfactory levels, they receive intensive and sustained special education. Lynn and Doug Fuchs report that over 60 percent of students in a pilot program testing this new identification process could not sustain the improvement made in their first intensive experience and had to return to special education to resume academic growth. Embedded in this new approach are measurement systems, like **curriculum based measurement (CBM)**, that do not rely on infrequently administered standardized achievement tests (McMasters et al., in press). CBM uses direct and frequent measurements of students' performance. Advocates of CBM indicate that this system is sensitive to different students' learning patterns and expectations. It can be used to compare one student's daily achievements with those of classmates and to track trends across time. And it provides useful feedback to teachers about the effectiveness of their instructional methods for the entire class.

What is the impact of this disability?

Individuals with learning disabilities who do not receive early attention for their learning problems have serious, life-long challenges to face (Miller & Felton, 2001). Early, intensive intervention makes a difference, and it is imperative that young children and their families get services as early as possible. Just like other individuals with disabilities, those with learning disabilities range widely in abilities. Some children have a mild learning disability. With assistance, they profit from the standard curriculum offered in general education and enroll in college. Children with severe disabilities, however, require intensive remediation and support throughout their school years and into adulthood. Students with learning disabilities are different from their nondisabled classmates. These students are the lowest of low achievers (MacMillan, Gresham, & Bocian, 1998).

Most children with learning disabilities are not identified as having a learning disability until they have attended school for several years. And what happens in those early school years can set the stage for future success or failure. Parents and researchers are concerned about the growing trend toward grade retention (Cannon, 1998). Although government officials and education policymakers alike are calling for an end to social promotion, research results do not support this policy change. Grade retention does not usually result in academic improvement, and seems also to be related to school dropout. Grade retention does not reduce costs either, and parents argue that for each grade repeated, school districts spend $13,000—money that should be spent on extra services such as summer school, on smaller classes, and on earlier identification for special education (Cannon, 1998; King, 1998). Because the outcomes for those who are retained are not good, and because more and more of these students are being included in general education classes with fewer supports, it is important for educators and parents to change their beliefs about the effectiveness of retention.

HISTORY OF THE FIELD

On April 6, 1963, the term *learning disabilities* was coined by Professor Sam Kirk and others at a meeting of parents and professionals in Chicago. The field of education has since experienced an explosion in the number of pupils identified, teachers trained, and classroom programs offered. Services began in elementary schools, were later extended to high schools, and continue to expand, as programs for post-secondary students and adults with disabilities proceed to develop.

Investigation of learning disabilities, however, put down roots long before 1963 (Hallahan & Mercer, 2002; Wiederholt, 1974). In 1919 Kurt Goldstein began working with young men with brain injuries who had returned to the United States after World War I. He found many of them distractible, unable to attend to relevant cues, confused, and hyperactive. They also could no longer read or write well. Some years later, Alfred Strauss and Heinz Werner expanded on Goldstein's work. Strauss and Werner worked at the Wayne County Training Center in Michigan with pupils who were thought to be brain-injured. They found many similarities to the group of World War I veterans that Goldstein had studied earlier. However, there was one important difference between these two groups: Goldstein's subjects had lost their abilities to read, write, and speak well; Strauss and Werner's group had never developed these abilities. The study of learning disabilities thus originated in the work of these pioneers.

Sam Kirk is considered by many to be the "father" of the field of learning disabilities, in part because he helped coin the term at a meeting in 1963 of what was to become the Learning Disabilities Association of America.

During the 1920s and 1930s, Samuel Orton, a specialist in neurology, developed theories and remedial reading techniques for children with severe reading problems, whom he called "dyslexic" and believed to be brain-damaged. He emphasized the importance of **lateral dominance.** In the late 1930s, Newell Kephart worked with Strauss at the Wayne County School and further studied a group of children who were considered to have mental retardation but behaved like Goldstein's brain-injured subjects. Both Kephart and Laura Lehtinen developed teaching methods for what they thought were a distinct subgroup of children with disabilities. Kephart's approach was motoric; he sought to remediate these children's difficulties through physical exercises. Lehtinen's instructional procedures were systematic and directly sought to teach children academic skills, much like methods used by teachers today. At about the same time, Sam Kirk, who also worked at the Wayne County School, helped to develop a set of word drills and other teaching procedures he referred to throughout his career. In 1961 he and his colleagues published the *Illinois Test of Psycholinguistic Abilities (ITPA),* which sought to identify individuals' strengths and weaknesses and their learning styles and preferences (whether they learned better by seeing or by hearing information presented). This test was used for many years to identify students with learning disabilities.

In the 1960s, Marianne Frostig developed materials designed to improve students' visual perceptual performance. It was thought that many students with learning disabilities were unable to process information accurately through the visual channel, so if their visual perceptual skills were enhanced, their reading abilities would also show improvement. The 1970s saw the field of learning disabilities embroiled in the heated **process/product debate** about perceptual training, or process, approaches and their use in the remediation of students' academic deficits. The dispute was resolved when Don Hammill and Steve Larsen's research analysis showed that perceptual approaches were seldom effective in teaching academic skills but that **direct instruction** techniques did make a difference (Hammill & Larsen, 1974).

People with this disability and their families, possibly more than those affected by any other disability, are vulnerable to fads and invalidated practices that are supposed to solve their problems. Many of these practices become popularized through the press. One fad suggested teaching students with learning disabilities to crawl again, regardless of their age. Others claimed that various diets improved students' academic and behavioral performances. Fluorescent lighting was blamed for learning disabilities. Plants placed on students' desks were given credit for improving the students' academic skills. In most of these instances, people made claims about improvement but offered little scientific evidence of effectiveness. All professionals in special education hope that the use of nonvalidated practices will be relegated to history.

MAKING CONNECTIONS

See again the "Solutions" section of Chapter 1 for the importance of using validated practices.

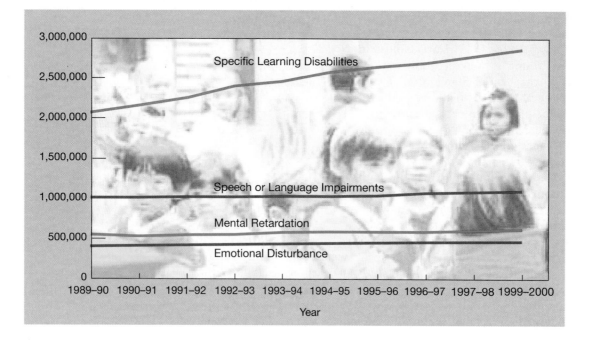

3,000,000

2,500,000

Specific Learning Disabilities

2,000,000

1,500,000

Speech or Language Impairments

1,000,000

Mental Retardation

500,000

Emotional Disturbance

0

1989–90 1990–91 1991–92 1992–93 1993–94 1994–95 1995–96 1996–97 1997–98 1999–2000

Year

Figure 4.1 Children Served Under IDEA

The relationship among the numbers of children with learning disabilities, mental retardation, emotional disturbance, and speech or language impairments served under IDEA, is shown for Ages 6 to 21 and school years 1987–88 through 1999–2000. Source: From the *Twenty Second and Twenty Third Annual Reports to Congress on the Implementation of the Individuals with Disabilities Education Act*, U.S. Department of Education, 2000, 2001. Washington, DC: Government Printing Office.

PREVALENCE

Across the nation, policymakers and parents express great concern about the number of children identified by school personnel as having a learning disability (Finn, Rotherham, & Hokanson, 2001). Three major issues are the basis for concerns about the prevalence of learning disabilities:

1. Size

2. Cost

3. Misidentification

This special education category is by far the largest, including some 6 percent of all schoolchildren and over half of all students identified as having a disability (U.S. Department of Education, 2001). When IDEA was first passed and was being implemented in 1976–1977, only about one-quarter of all students with disabilities were served through the learning disabilities category. In the 10-year period from the 1990–91 to the 1999–2000 school year, the learning disabilities category grew by 34 percent. The rate at which assignment to the learning disabilities category has increased far surpasses that for students with speech or language impairments or emotional or behavioral disorders, and the prevalence of mental retardation among students has decreased slightly over the years. These relationships are shown in Figure 4.1. Could ADHD account for the size of the learning disabilities category? The overlapping characteristics of these two conditions might be an explanation. However, in the 1997 reauthorization of IDEA, the government classified ADHD as part of the health impairments category, possibly in hopes of reducing the size of the learning disabilities category. No reduction in the size of the learning disabilities group occurred, but the health impairments group increased by 351 percent because of the inclusion of ADHD in that definition (U.S. Department of Education, 2001).

Why is there such concern about the size of the learning disabilities category? One reason is cost. Although variation exists across the nation and even district by district, every student with a disability costs more to educate than their classmates without disabilities (Chambers, Parrish, & Harr, 2002). It costs about twice as much to educate a student with disabilities as to educate a student without disabilities. Because the federal government does not fully cover these costs, the public and

CHAPTER 4 *Learning Disabilities*

the media make the case that students with disabilities are being educated at the expense of their classmates without disabilities. This situation has caused many to believe that the special education rolls should be reduced, and because learning disabilities both constitute a high incidence disability that is often milder than others and also constitute the largest group, this category is being scrutinized.

The third concern is whether students are being correctly identified. Some experts have called the category of learning disabilities a "dumping ground" where any student unsuccessful in the general education curriculum can be placed (Reschly, 2002). Thus it is possible that some of these students do not have a disability but simply are failing in the general education curriculum and were given the label so they could get extra attention and special assistance. Which students *are* being included in this category? One very carefully conducted study gives us a hint (MacMillan, Gersham, & Bocian, 1998). These researchers matched the state's guidelines for learning disabilities with 61 actual students who were identified by school districts. Their results indicated that 10 did not meet the criterion for any special education category, 19 had IQ scores below 76 (which should have qualified them for services in the mental retardation category), and 9 also met the criteria for ADHD as a coexisting condition.

CAUSES AND PREVENTION

Just as there are numerous manifestations of learning disabilities, there are multiple causes, levels of severity, and preventive measures. Unfortunately, researchers do not have much concrete information about the causes of learning disabilities (Bender, 2001). Without definitive causes or explanations for the problem, effective prevention will remain illusive.

What can cause learning disabilities?

The field of learning disabilities has been plagued, almost since its inception, by fads and unproven theories. Some theories propose causes for the condition. For example, diet, fluorescent lighting, nonsequential developmental milestones (walking before crawling), and various environmental factors have also been suggested as causes of learning disabilities. Little is actually known about the causes of learning disabilities, but we can presume that students who exhibit them are as diverse as the indicators of the condition. Some may have proven brain damage—caused by an accident or by a lack of oxygen before, during, or after birth—resulting in neurological difficulties that affect their ability to learn. For many years, some theorists have presumed a genetic contribution to learning disabilities (Decker & Defries, 1980, 1981). As we learn more about heredity and genetic links to disabilities, any connections with learning disabilities will become more apparent. Such links with reading disabilities are already becoming obvious (Raskind, 2001; Smith et al., 2001). Some experts are beginning to believe that an interactive relationship among several genes establishes the risk factors for reading disabilities (Wood & Grigorenko, 2001). Neurological problems located in the part of the brain where sounds and symbols are associated may well be the cause of reading disabilities, and some believe that a genetic link causes such problems (Gilger, 2001; Richards, 2001).

A strong relationship exists between learning disabilities and low **socio-economic status (SES)** (Blair & Scott, 2002). Whether factors associated with poverty (such as limited access to health care) or the lack of a supportive environment puts these children at great risk for learning disabilities is not known, but the relationship is clear.

Teachers need to recognize that it is not certain what causes learning disabilities and not make assumptions about the students they teach. In the majority of cases of learning disabilities, there is no physical evidence or actual medical diagnosis of

MAKING CONNECTIONS

To review issues related to disproportionate placement of culturally and linguistically diverse students in special education, see related sections in Chapters 3, 6, 7, and 8.

MAKING CONNECTIONS

For more about poverty and its relationship to disabilities, see Chapter 3.

brain injury or damage to the central nervous system. Using terms such as *assumed brain injury* and *presumed central nervous system dysfunction* may lead to a conclusion that cannot be proved and may be misleading. Using terms that imply brain injury (such as **dyslexia**) instead of terms such as *reading disabilities* can give the impression that nothing can be done about the condition. This impression can lead parents, educators, and the individuals concerned to give up and not try to remediate identified educational difficulties. They might also set expectations too low. We know from research on education that when expectations and goals are set low, they are usually met but rarely exceeded. If goals for a child with a learning disability, are set too low, the child may never reach his or her potential. For these reasons, many special educators oppose the use of medical terms associated with brain injury.

How might learning disabilities be prevented?

Until such time as specific causes for learning disabilities are discovered, definitive prevention strategies cannot be developed. However, the impact of the disability can be lessened, and in some cases the condition remediated or compensated for, through education.

Although poor teaching can cause school failure and may be a factor in the identification of many of the students served as having learning disabilities in today's schools, it is not an actual cause of learning disabilities. However, good teaching can prevent school failure and the manifestation of what either is or looks like a learning disability (Fuchs & Fuchs, 2001; Graham, Harris, & Larsen, 2001).

Specific means of preventing or reducing the effects of this disability are now being implemented. Strong evidence about the power of using early intervention programs as a preventive measure is convincing educators that the foundations for reading should be taught in preschool programs; the notion is "catch them before they fail" (Torgensen & Wagner, 1998). Systematic academic intervention—learning strategies, peer tutoring, and direct instruction—during the school years also make a real difference. For instance, developing early sound–symbol awareness during the preschool years may reduce the degree of a reading disability that would have become apparent during the school years (Compton, 2002). Also, it seems that strong relationships between poor language development and learning disabilities exist (Bakken & Whedon, 2002; Weatherby, 2002). Young children who do not develop good language skills during their early childhood years tend to be at risk for academic problems during their later school years. Children who develop language very late tend to have poor cognition; they do not reason or solve problems well.

CHARACTERISTICS

Unexpected underachievement *is* the defining characteristic of learning disabilities (Fuchs & Fuchs, 1998; Kavale & Forness, 1996; Vaughn, Elbaum, & Boardman, 2001). Even so, the most often cited feature probably is heterogeneity (Haager & Vaughn, 1995). But, despite these students' individual differences, some characteristics are commonly seen with learning disabilities; these are listed in Table 4.2.

What characteristics cause unexpected underachievement?

The precise causes and nature of their academic problems vary widely among students with learning disabilities. Although individuals might differ in their strengths

MAKING CONNECTIONS

See also the "Early Childhood" section in Chapter 5.

CHAPTER 4 *Learning Disabilities*

Table 4.2 Signs or Characteristics of Learning Disabilities

Academic	Social	Behavioral Style
Unexpected underachievement	Immature	Inattentive
Resistant to treatment	Socially unacceptable	Distractible
Difficult to teach	Misinterprets social and nonverbal cues	Hyperactive
Inability to solve problems	Makes poor decisions	Impulsive
Uneven academic abilities	Victimized	Poorly coordinated
Inactive learning style	Unable to predict social consequences	Disorganized
Poor basic language skills	Unable to follow social conventions (manners)	Unmotivated
Poor basic reading and decoding skills	Rejected	Dependent
Inefficient information processing abilities	Naïve	
Inability to generalize	Shy, withdrawn, insecure	
	Dependent	

and weaknesses, learning styles, and personalities, all have learning difficulties that result in poor academic performance that compounds across the school years. Many experts feel that at the root of the academic problems are the following learning characteristics (Rivera & Smith, 1997):

- Lack of motivation or poor attribution
- Inattention
- Inability to generalize
- Faulty information processing
- Insufficient problem solving skills

Depending on where a student's problems lie, altering these characteristics or learning styles can lead to substantial improvement in achievement.

- *Motivation and Attribution* Motivation and attribution are related. **Motivation** is the inner drive that causes individuals to be energized and directed in their behavior. Motivation can be explained as a trait (a need to succeed, a need not to fail, a sustained interest in a topic) or as a temporary state of mind (preoccupation with a test or class presentation tomorrow, a passing interest in a topic). **Attributions** are self-explanations about the reasons for one's success or failure. Differences in motivation and attributions may account for differences in the way people approach tasks and for differences in their success with those tasks (Ring & Reetz, 2000). Assuming responsibility for success is an internal attribution in which individuals understand the relationships among effort, task persistence, ability, and interest.

By contrast, year after year of frustration and failure at school can negatively affect students' motivation and their approach to the task of learning can convince them that there is nothing they can do to be successful. Students can develop a negative attitude and come to believe that their failure is a result of lack of ability, rather than a signal to work harder or ask for help. This cycle can even lead students to believe that external factors—luck, extra help, the teacher giving them a break, or a classmate doing them a favor—are the reasons for the successes they have. Students with ADHD have attributions that undermine success in school (Carlson et al., 2002). They rely more than others on external factors to explain their accomplishments, and therefore they are less persistent, expend less effort, prefer easier work, and take less enjoyment in learning.

MAKING CONNECTIONS

For more on ADHD, see Chapters 8 and 9.

Characteristics

Learning basic reading skills, like sound-to-symbol relationships is essential for reading success. Students who do not learn these skills naturally, must receive direct instruction aimed at achieving mastery. These preschoolers are listening to a story about Willy the gorilla and his adventures.

When people expect to fail, they can also become too dependent on others—a situation referred to as **learned helplessness**—and increase the likelihood of poor performance. They expect failure and see no use in expending more effort (Pearl, 1982; Switzky & Schultz, 1988). Students who have fear of failure or low self-esteem are less likely to have a positive motivation to learn. Teachers can help students overcome these problems by involving them in the learning process, responding positively, praising students, promoting mastery, and creating a challenging and stimulating instructional environment (Dev, 1997).

These characteristics of students with learning disabilities are just the opposite of those of high achievers, who tend to expect success and view it as an incentive to work harder. Thus students with learning disabilities tend to be low achievers. Students who expect academic failure tend to be passive. This trait is seen in many students with learning disabilities, who are said to be **inactive learners** (Torgesen & Licht, 1983). They do not approach the learning task purposefully and are not actively involved in their learning. They do not ask questions, seek help, or read related material to learn more.

By comparing low-achieving students' motivation and attributions with those of high-achieving students, we can better understand the concepts of attribution and learned helplessness. Let's look at a classroom situation, such as writing a social studies term paper, to see how students' motivation affects the way they approach the task. High achievers, when given the assignment of writing a term paper on, say, the Revolutionary War, approach the task with confidence, knowing that they are capable of producing a thorough and well-written paper. They realize that if they read their textbook and other materials available at the library, they will know enough about the topic to prepare the paper. Because of past successes, they know that making an effort results in success. Therefore, these students will proofread their term papers and even add extras (such as maps and diagrams) to the final product. The low-achieving students, in contrast, do not approach this assignment with much vigor. They seem overwhelmed by the assignment and complain that it is too difficult. These children believe that it is useless to ask for assistance, spend time in the library, or read extra materials. Instead, they write a short and incomplete term paper that is probably not developed with care or proofread.

It has been found that students benefit when they are shown the relationship between effort and accomplishment and when they are taught learning strategies they know are effective (Hock, 1997; Sexton, Harris, & Graham, 1998). Attributions and motivation can be altered (Fulk, 1996). With intensive effort on the part of teachers and parents, youngsters can learn that *their* efforts can lead to success.

• *Attention Deficits* Another learning characteristic commonly observed by teachers and researchers is inattention, or **attention deficits** (Mercer, 1997). Children who do not focus on the task to be learned or who pay attention to the wrong features of the task are said to be distractible. One characteristic of students with learning disabilities and also of those with ADHD is **impulsivity.** This factor may explain

MAKING CONNECTIONS

For other useful strategies, see the "Achieving Discipline" boxes found in each chapter.

CHAPTER 4 *Learning Disabilities*

Create a Community of Helpers: Peer Management

Marc, a student with both learning disabilities and ADHD, was a fourth-grader at Pearson Elementary School. He had a terrible time concentrating on his school work, seemed always to be restless, and had poor basic reading and writing skills. Ms. Reilly's general education class was a bit larger than she wanted, particularly with the number of special education students who were included in her class. Marc kept disturbing everyone by interrupting class discussions, Ms. Reilly's presentations, and small group work. It seemed that Marc was getting all of the attention, and instructional time was being reduced. Ms. Reilly feared that the entire class was suffering, not only from Marc's disruptions but also from her being distracted, and he was not the only child who needed special attention!

She decided that she could not accomplish her goals alone. She needed a new plan, one that would first address small group work, a time when chaos seemed to be the greatest. Ms. Reilly held several class discussions about the situation. Students talked about their frustrations with not being able to get their

work done and the difficulties they had when their attention was disrupted. The class agreed that intervention was needed and that they could work together and evaluate the intervention's effectiveness. The students agreed to help each other with their group assignments and also with staying on task. The students wanted their teacher to move from group to group, helping them with the assignments. So Ms. Reilly divided her 30 students into 6 groups of 5, being careful to create groups wherein academically strong students, students with special needs, and youngsters who understood the classroom rules and were well behaved were all represented. She also carefully considered the individual students she assigned to each group, not mixing children who did not get along. Each time the class worked in small groups, she reminded them of their individual commitments to help each other and work together cooperatively. She also had students create records about their progress. The class learned a lot. First, they learned that classmates can help each other in many ways. They can help each other behave more

appropriately, learn, and complete their academic assignments. Most important, students are a key part of the environment that fosters a climate of support for each other. Whether students serve as peer tutors, where they help each other with academic assignments, or as behavioral managers, where they model expected behavior or dispense praise and rewards, students themselves are powerful assets in the instructional setting.

Steps Used to Create a Community of Helpers

- The teacher included her students in describing the problem.
- The teacher and students worked together to identify some solutions.
- Everyone made a commitment to help each other.
- Ability groups were mixed.
- The intervention was phased in, not scheduled for all types of activities across the entire day.
- An evaluation component was included in the intervention process.

---

why these children are unable to focus on the relevant components of problems that need to be solved or of tasks that need to be learned, and why they may disrupt the learning environment for an entire class. (See the "Achieving Discipline" box for a suggestion about how to solve this problem.)

A related problem is developing good organizational skills (Stormont-Spurgin, 1997). Becoming better organized can be taught through a variety of means: classmates helping each other, better communication between home and school, rewards, and structured routines and lists. Clearly, creating structure helps students become better organized and also contributes to their focusing attention so that learning is more probable. Several researchers (Deshler et al., 2001) have found that **advance organizers** or **organizing routines,** such as those found at the beginning of every chapter in this text, help to focus students' attention by providing an introductory overview of the material to be presented. These introductory statements explain why the information is important, create a framework or structure for the content, help students see how parts of a course fit together, and provide a key to the crucial elements of the presentation.

MAKING CONNECTIONS

For examples of advance organizers or organizing routines, look again at the beginning of each of the chapters in this text.

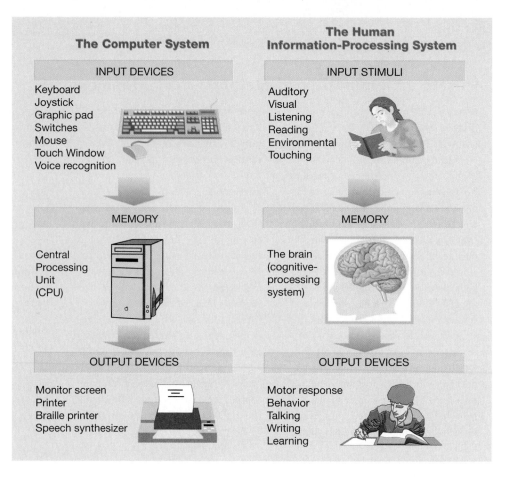

The Computer System

INPUT DEVICES

Keyboard
Joystick
Graphic pad
Switches
Mouse
Touch Window
Voice recognition

MEMORY

Central
Processing
Unit
(CPU)

OUTPUT DEVICES

Monitor screen
Printer
Braille printer
Speech synthesizer

The Human Information-Processing System

INPUT STIMULI

Auditory
Visual
Listening
Reading
Environmental
Touching

MEMORY

The brain
(cognitive-processing
system)

OUTPUT DEVICES

Motor response
Behavior
Talking
Writing
Learning

Figure 4.2 Information Processing Theory and Its Similarities to the Computer System

Source: Janet Lerner, *Learning Disabilities: Theories, Diagnosis, and Teaching Strategies,* Sixth Edition. Copyright © 1993 by Houghton Mifflin Company. Adapted with permission.

● *Generalization* Most students with learning disabilities also have difficulty transferring, or generalizing, their learning to different skills or situations (Rivera & Smith, 1997). They might apply a newly learned study skill in history class but not in English class. Or a child might master borrowing in subtraction when a zero appears in the units column but not apply that rule when borrowing with two zeros. Long-standing research has shown that some teaching methods can actually interfere with students learning the concept of **generalization** (Ellis, 1986). For example, the overuse of feedback on performance (knowledge of results) can reinforce dependency, learned helplessness, and learning inactivity. Another way to encourage generalization is to make connections clearly between familiar problems and those that are new or novel (Fuchs et al., 2002). And when teachers carefully broaden the categories—either the skill or the situation—and point out similar features, students extend their learning more readily. Thus, if a student knows how to solve subtraction problems that require borrowing without zeros in the numerator, teachers should carefully point out the similarities in problems that include zeros—(500 − 354 = ?)—and those that do not—(467 − 189 = ?).

● *Processing Information* Many people with learning disabilities have difficulty learning to read and write, understanding things they are told, and even expressing themselves through oral communication. To explain why, researchers are studying theories of learning and then applying them to the way students with learning disabilities actually learn. Many years ago, Janet Lerner proposed an **information processing theory** that compares the human brain to a computer (Lerner, 1993). In her concept (see Figure 4.2), the flow of information that occurs when people are learning new skills begins with the input of information, continues with the processing of that information, and ends with its output. Like the computer, the human brain takes in information, processes that information (makes associations, stores information, calls it up, acts upon it), and generates responses from it.

How can teachers help students process information and also benefit from the information they receive in class? Educators help when they

- Repeat important information
- Organize content systematically
- Provide students with relevant information
- Anchor examples to the students' experiences
- Associate content with familiar information

Educators can also help students manipulate information by encouraging them to use newly learned information in other assignments, writings, and discussions.

- *Problem Solving and Thinking Skills* Students with learning disabilities are not strategic learners and have poor **problem solving** and thinking skills (Rivera & Smith, 1997). Applying strategies that help organize information in such a way that it is easier to remember can help students study efficiently and remember content (Brigham & Brigham, 2001). For this to happen, students must be proficient in the following thinking skills: classifying, associating, and sequencing. **Classifying** enables the learner to categorize and group items together in terms of the characteristics they have in common. Usually, people remember more items in a list if they approach the task by **chunking,** or clustering, the information presented. For example, if you forget your grocery list and are already at the store, you might try to remember what items you need by thinking about groups of items. You might recall that potatoes and corn were on the list when you think of vegetables and that ice cream, pizza, and TV dinners were on the list when you think of frozen foods.

People are more strategic in their learning and remembering when they relate or associate information by some "common denominator" (for example, softness or hardness, style of painting). **Association** also helps individuals see the relationships that exist among and between different knowledge bases. By associating facts or ideas, the mind is able to find the relationships and connections that units of information possess. By using this thinking skill, people can relate information on different dimensions. **Sequencing** information also facilitates memory and learning. Items can be sequenced in many ways. For example, physical items can be sorted and sequenced by size, weight, or volume. Facts, events, and ideas can be sequenced by time, importance, or complexity. These thinking skills—classifying, associating, and sequencing—help students approach learning tasks more purposefully. With guided practice, these abstract skills can be learned and developed into useful tools for learning.

Are problems with social skills a characteristic of learning disabilities?

Not all individuals with learning disabilities have problems in the realm of social skills (Vaughn, Elbaum, & Boardman, 2001). In fact, about a quarter of them are average or above average range in areas related to social skills and social competence. However, about three-fourths of these individuals have problems with social skills that negatively influence their self-concepts, their ability to make friends, their interactions with others, and even the way they approach schoolwork. Poor social skills contribute to poor academic performance (Elliott, Malecki & Demaray, 2001).

Many students with learning disabilities are not socially competent (Bryan, 1997; Gresham, Sugai, & Horner, 2001). The impact of problems in this area can be great because **social competence** is related, in one way or another, to almost every

MAKING CONNECTIONS

Read the Social Competence Section of Chapter 5.

Although a learning disability is usually thought of in terms of academic problems, many students with this disability lack friends and are excluded from social interactions with classmates. Teachers can help children become more sensitive to each other's feelings and encourage them to play in group activities during recess.

action and skill that people perform. It is the ability to perceive and interpret social situations, generate appropriate social responses, and interact with others. The results of deficits in social skills can be far-reaching. For example, many students with learning disabilities are naïve and unable to judge other people's intentions accurately (Donahue, 1997). They cannot understand nonverbal behaviors, such as facial expressions, and therefore do not comprehend other people's emotional messages (Dimitrovsky, Spector, & Levy-Schiff, 2000). This inability puts them at a great disadvantage when interacting with their peers and with their teachers, and it results in their having low acceptance rates.

Difficulty with social skills, coupled with low achievement and distracting classroom behavior, influences the social status of children with learning disabilities. These children are seen by their peers as overly dependent, less cooperative, and less socially adept (Kuhne & Wiener, 2000). The results are that these children are less likely to become leaders—or even to be included in groups. Children with learning disabilities have low social status, are rejected by their classmates, and have difficulty making friends. Parents believe that social immaturity and inadequate social skills are the reasons for their children's lack of friends (Wiener & Sunohara, 1998). Classmates consistently reject fellow students who have low social status, whether in social or academic situations (Le Mare & de La Ronde, 2000). In other words, students with learning disabilities who have problems in the area of social skills are not included either on the playground or in the classroom. It is not surprising that these students with learning disabilities prefer pullout programs and do not like inclusive classroom situations (Vaughn, Elbaum, & Boardman, 2001).

Signs of these problems begin early, during the preschool years, as these children experience strong feelings of loneliness and lack of friends (Margalit, 1998; Tur-Kaspa, Weisel, & Segev, 1998). Rejection and inadequate social skills persist through adolescence (Le Mare & de La Ronde, 2000). During the later school years, they do not seek the support of peers or friends as do their classmates without disabilities, so feelings of rejection and isolation persist. Of even more concern is their tendency to be victimized—threatened, physically assaulted, subjected to theft of their belongings—more than their peers.

What can be done to improve the social skills of students with learning disabilities? Two lines of attack must be followed: assessment and then intervention (Merrell, 2001). First, specific problem areas must be identified. This assessment phase can be accomplished by using standardized instruments such as the *Walker–McConnell Scales of Social Competence and School Adjustment* and the *School Social Behavior Scales (SSBS-2)*. Problems need to be observed in more than one setting and by more than one person. Then specific intervention plans can be developed. Social skills training programs are one popular response, even though they sometimes have mixed results (Gresham, Sugai, & Horner, 2001). When these programs are effective, they match the intervention to the individual's unique problem areas. For example, if a student has not acquired a social skill, then modeling, coaching, practice, and specific feedback can make development of the missing skill possible. Peer tutoring, reinforcement, and contingencies that reward the entire class (those with and those without disabilities) can help to extend or generalize initial

CHAPTER 4 *Learning Disabilities*

learning. The *Responsive Classroom Approach* is a comprehensive strategy that teaches social skills, provides academic assistance, and also includes social supports for children who do not understand the behavioral and social expectations of school and life (Elliott, Malecki, & Demaray, 2001). What is often needed is direct, structured, and explicit instruction, along with guidance in learning how to set goals for oneself, how to manage time and effort, and how to reward oneself for accomplishments (Harris & Graham, 1999). Also, teachers can play an instrumental role in reducing peer rejection by pairing these students with nondisabled classmates in areas of mutual interest. For example, teachers might plan activities for which students with common interests (sports, music, hobbies) are assigned to work together on an academic task such as a social studies report.

EARLY CHILDHOOD EDUCATION

The importance of the preschool years, when the foundations for learning are developing and become established, cannot be understated. This fact is true for all children. Early childhood is a critical period, in which developmental milestones—the basis for school achievement and life success—need to be accomplished. Most youngsters learn these basic skills naturally; for others they need to be taught directly.

What are the foundation skills for reading?

Reading is crucial to school success, and it is a skill that is difficult for most students with learning disabilities to master. Researchers are now confident that the essential, foundation skills that make for good readers are developed much early than was originally thought (Jenkins & O'Connor, 2002). These first steps on what Joe Jenkins refers to as the ladder to literacy include

- Phonological awareness (being aware of sound segments in words)
- Letter–sound correspondence (knowing the sound each letter or combinations of letters represents)
- Decoding
- Sight word recognition
- Fluency
- Comprehension

Some experts are trying to use this information to predict which children are most at risk for reading failure. Can experts predict which children are most at risk for reading failure during the school years? The answer to this question is "not reliably" (Hammill et al., 2002). Although it appears that **phonological awareness** is the best predictor for young children, not all children who are poor at hearing and identifying sounds in words, or at rhyming, have difficulties later with reading. Regardless, because many of these skills are learned during the early years—preschool, kindergarten, and first grade—educators now advocate early identification and intervention (Learning Disability Summit, 2001).

Can early intervention prevent reading problems?

With growing confidence, researchers are answering this question "yes." It is now understood that the origins of literacy take shape during early childhood, long before children actually begin to read (Dickinson & McCabe, 2001). The relationship

MAKING CONNECTIONS

For more about reading, see the "Early Childhood" or "Elementary Through High School" sections of Chapters 3, 5, and 11.

Peers can alternately read books to each other and work together to learn new words and still have fun in school.

between long-term reading achievement and early instruction in phonological awareness (e.g., *cat* has three sounds, *fall* and *wall* rhyme), letter naming, and decoding is positive (Miller & Felton, 2001; Torgesen, Wagner, & Rashotte, 1994). Most children learn these precursors to reading on their own. Many who do not can be taught these very important skills, and later reading problems can thus be avoided (Jenkins & O'Connor, 2002; Torgesen & Wagner, 1998). For some of these children, direct instruction in the general preschool or general education setting is sufficient; for others intensive intervention is necessary. In either case, a long-term, positive impact on youngsters' reading abilities can be the outcome (Fuchs et al., 2002). Unfortunately, success is not universal, and some 30 percent of these youngsters are still resistant to treatment (Jenkins & O'Connor, 2002).

Why has early reading intervention not been universally available?

Many professionals have been reluctant to identify or label children as having a learning or reading disability in the preschool years or even by first grade. One reason is that young children do not develop at exactly the same rate, and some youngsters are not as ready for school as their classmates. Some children may not have developed as quickly as their peers but do not have a disability and will catch up. Still others are the youngest in their class and are thus not, and should not be, developmentally equal to their classmates.

Educators are reluctant to label preschoolers as having a disability for fear of making a diagnostic mistake. Sometimes, however, the only way to bring intensive services to children is by identifying them as at risk for disabilities or as showing early signs of having a disability. Who might be likely candidates? Children who are not talking by age 3, children with low birth weights, premature babies, poor children, and those with communication problems are at risk for developing learning disabilities and will benefit from good early childhood programs (Blair & Scott, 2002; Shames & Anderson, 2002). Also on this list are young children who are not developing skills related to later reading abilities (Torgesen & Wagner, 1998). Some, such as Reid Lyon, are convinced that these precursors to reading are so important that *all preschool children* should be checked to be sure they have gained phonological awareness and, if they have not, should receive instruction (Lyon et al., 2001).

Preschool and kindergarten teachers should not lose sight of the developing language and "literacy-rich" environments (Katims, 1994). Literacy is not just decoding or even comprehending the printed work; it is a reflection of a greater set of skills and abilities that include reflective thinking (Paul, 2000). Children need to develop a love for reading, gain skills and attitudes that favor future literacy, and come to recognize both that reading is important to them and that it is fun. Through their retelling and reenacting their favorite stories, the important concept that print has meaning is understood early and becomes a foundation for future instruction.

CHAPTER 4 *Learning Disabilities*

ELEMENTARY THROUGH HIGH SCHOOL

As we have seen, one defining characteristic of individuals with learning disabilities is their unexpected underachievement—performance that demands a unique, individualized, and intensive reaction. These students' low achievement separates them more each school year from their classmates without disabilities (Deshler et al., 2001), as is illustrated in Figure 4.3.

Over 30 years of research findings about learning disabilities and those students affected have proved that intervention using validated practices makes a positive difference in these students' performance (Swanson & Sachse-Lee, 2000). In particular, strategy training and direct instruction are most effective. What does this mean? Educational outcomes improve when students are taught

- With proven procedures
- Skills of concern directly (e.g., reading)
- Strategies to organize, comprehend, and remember complex material and information
- Under conditions of frequent evaluation

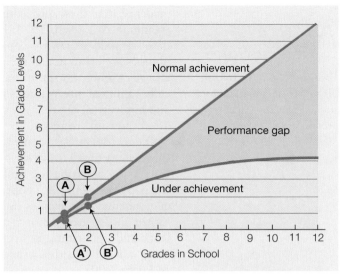

Figure 4.3 The Widening Performance Gap Between Students with and without Learning Disabilities
Source: "Ensuring content-area learning by secondary students with learning disabilities" (p. 96) by D. D. Deshler, J. B. Schumaker, B. K. Lenz, J. A. Bulgren, M. R. Hock, J. Knight, and B. J. Ehren, *Learning Disabilities Research and Practice, 16,* 96–108. Reprinted by permission.

How can education become more effective?

Teachers must become more deliberate, cautious, and intentional in their selection of instructional materials and procedures. They must become better consumers of research and must continuously evaluate the effectiveness of their instructional programs. These students' overall underachievement demands direct and intensive instruction in every academic and content area where their underachievement is a problem. Because of their great individual differences, their teachers cannot assume that a tactic effective with one student will necessarily be effective with another.

Many easy-to-use and proven instructional methods for students with learning disabilities have been verified (Lovitt, 2000). However, some tactics—even some of those used today—have not. The field of learning disabilities, in particular, has a history of advocating one instructional method after another that has not been thoroughly tested first. There are many examples, but let's take sensory integration as a case in point. Sensory integration is based on the importance of sensory (visual, auditory, tactile) stimulation, particularly in the context of motor activity. It is in this theory that perceptual motor training as a prerequisite to reading instruction for students with learning disabilities has its roots. Years ago, children of elementary school age were taught to crawl again, engage in patterning exercises, walk balance beams, make angels in the snow, and draw lines on dittos from one pattern to another. These sensory integration activities were thought to improve reading. Periodically, despite consistent

Cartoon by Mike Lynch. Reprinted by permission.

Elementary Through High School

MAKING **C**ONNECTIONS

For more about the role of sensory (perceptual) motor training, see the "History" section of this chapter.

evidence that these procedures are absolutely ineffective, they gain in popularity (Hammill & Larsen, 1974; Hoehn & Baumeister, 1994). And even today, unvalidated practices that are supposed to "retrain the brain" and "cure" learning disabilities are promoted in the press without any regard for the dearth of data on their efficacy (Soltes, 2002). It may not be as exciting to apply **best practices** or **scientifically validated interventions** that are "tried and true" as to use those that sound new and innovative, but that conservatism may well be our obligation to the students we are responsible to teach.

Educators must become good consumers and "shop" for the instructional tactics they use as they would shop for major personal purchases. Sometimes, a mode of instruction is wrong for students with learning disabilities but is effective for other learners. For example, **cooperative learning** is widely promoted and often applied in general education classes (Slavin, 1996). In this approach, students work in small, mixed-ability groups for reading and content subjects, and they help each other learn and understand information. But despite its popularity, cooperative learning is not always effective, especially for students with learning disabilities (McMaster & Fuchs, 2002).

The whole-language approach is another example of a method that is employed in general education classes but is not useful to students with learning disabilities. This approach emphasizes the "wholeness" of reading and writing and it seeks complete infusion into the entire curriculum. All methods that promote "natural learning" are encouraged, but direct instruction on decoding, isolated vocabulary development, and discrete skills that are components of the reading process is considered unacceptable (Mather, 1992). Teaching independent skills, such as sound–symbol associations, is also not endorsed. Reading is integrated into the entire curriculum, across the school day, for the entire class. For children experiencing reading failure, including those with learning disabilities, "substantial contemporary evidence documents the efficacy of explicit systematic instruction of important reading skills—that is, research supports practices explicitly inconsistent with whole language" (Pressley & Rankin, 1994, p. 161). Research has shown that the whole-language approach alone is not effective for students with learning disabilities (Ehri et al., 2001; Mather, 1992).

Here are some keys to effective instruction for students with learning disabilities (Swanson & Sachse-Lee, 2000; Vaughn, Gersten, & Chard, 2000).

1. Directly teach the subject, skill, or content area.
2. Be certain students have opportunities for drill, repetition, practice, and review.
3. Work in small, active groups.
4. Break learning units into small segments.
5. Use strategy instruction.

Besides using instructional methods that have been subject to the scrutiny of research, it is very important that teachers be certain the tactics they select are actually working with each student. Remember, students with learning disabilities are a heterogeneous group of learners, each possessing different learning needs and styles. Therefore, it is necessary to ensure that the "right" instructional method has been selected, and to do that requires collecting data about how well the student is performing the academic task being taught. The best way to determine whether a specific approach or method is effective for a student is to evaluate performance directly and consistently with systems such as curriculum based measurement (CBM). Students' performance on each learning task is evaluated directly, on their school work, to determine whether the intervention is effective, whether the intervention is effective enough, and whether the child's progress is sufficient to warrant moving on to other tasks.

MAKING **C**ONNECTIONS

Curriculum based measurement (CBM) is also discussed in Chapter 2.

How might the reading skills of these students be improved?

Educators need to be certain that students are actively involved in learning and have many opportunities for direct instruction and a lot of time to practice reading. Of this there is no doubt: Most students with learning disabilities have difficulty learning to read. In some cases, they do not receiving the direct and intensive instruction they require (Vaughn et al., 2002). Too often, the quality of their reading instruction is poor; students spend too much time working independently on worksheets or waiting for instruction.

As has been noted, identification and intervention can begin during the early childhood period. Teachers can help identify preschoolers who are at risk for reading failure and can begin systematic instruction early to help prevent these youngsters from having reading problems during the school years (Jenkins & O'Connor, 2002). But what about those students who continue to have difficulty mastering reading after third grade? Instruction on phonological awareness, decoding, acquisition of sight words, reading accuracy, fluency, spelling, and comprehensive is not limited to younger students (Miller & Felton, 2001; Rashotte, MacPhee, & Torgesen, 2001). By directly addressing these skills, either individually or in small groups, teachers can help students achieve overall reading improvement and, eventually, literacy (Foorman & Torgesen, 2001).

For students who do not learn to read as most of their classmates do, teachers need to select individualized instructional procedures that systematically and explicitly focus on the basic skills (phonics) and component parts (sound blending) of reading (Lyon & Moats, 1997; Vadasy, Jenkins, & Pool, 2000). Fluency (speed of reading) building with a focus on phonics—evaluated directly with CMB procedures—is effective in development reading mastery (Mercer et al, 2000). Many teachers are most excited about PALS, an instructional tactic that was developed by Lynn and Doug Fuchs and that consistently improves the reading performance of many students often referred to as difficult to teach. PALS, which stands for peer-assisted learning strategies, is implemented for entire classes of students. This popular technique is effective with a wide range of students who attend general education classes (Fuchs, 2002; Mathes & Babyak, 2001).

Direct instruction on these basic, reading-related skills helps students learn to decode words, but for many, continued specific instruction aimed at the improvement of reading comprehension is necessary. Here research findings are again helpful. The following tactics have proved useful in improving reading comprehension: teacher-led questioning, text enhancements (such as illustrations and study guides), students restating the content of passages they have just read, skill based instruction (vocabulary development, decoding words) and rewards, and development of increased fluency in oral reading (Bakken, Mastropieri, & Scruggs, 1997; Biemiller & Siegel, 1997; Lebzelter & Nowacek, 1999; Markell & Deno, 1997). Others have found that a technique called **story maps** also promotes greater reading comprehension (Idol, 1987; Swanson & De La Paz, 1998). (See

These students are working together to answer the comprehension and study questions assigned by their teacher. By working as a group, they keep each other on task and engaged in completing the assignment.

Elementary Through High School

VALIDATED PRACTICES
Story Maps

What Are Story Maps?

Story maps are simple diagrams used to assist students, at any grade level, in organizing and recalling elements from stories they have listened to or read. Even first-graders can use simple "who, what, where, when, why" maps, or "first, next, last" sequence maps. More complex maps that incorporate setting, characters, trouble, action, sequence, and outcomes can be used with older students.

Why Story Maps Are Beneficial

Mapping techniques help students remember what they have read by requiring them to paraphrase the information. When students are able to put text into their own words, they are more likely to remember the information.

Implementing Story Maps

Story mapping requires that you provide students with a blank map to complete. Two common story map techniques are the Model–Lead–Test method (Idol, 1987) and Story Frames (Fowler, 1982). The Model–Lead–Test method requires students to be actively engaged in learning and gives students frequent opportunities to practice a new skill while you directly supervise and provide continuous feedback. Here is how the Model–Lead–Test method works:

Model Phase

- Read a story or passage aloud to your students.

- Stop reading when you come to a key element of the story (e.g., character, setting).

- Ask students to identify the key element. You may need to prompt them ("This says Sally woke up one morning. So, Sally must be one of our _____?")

- Model what to do next by writing the information on your map.

- Have students fill in the information on their maps.

the "Validated Practices" box for an example of how to include story maps in instruction.) Children work together in groups and develop a graphic representation of the elements of the story they have just read. Every story map includes information about the main character, the setting, the problem the main character must solve, the major events, and the outcome of the story.

Is it too late by middle or high school to teach students with learning disabilities how to read? It is certainly more challenging, but teachers should not give up (McCray, Vaughn, & Neal, 2001). Motivation is one key to learning success. Even after years of failure and many unsuccessful interventions, it is quite amazing that middle school students with reading disabilities still want to learn to read. In fact, they are described as "craving" to learn to read. These students understand why reading is important to their futures, and educators can capitalize on their motivation and desire. However, they must understand that these students do not want to be embarrassed in front of their friends and classmates. Even those who had previously been resistant to treatment can make impressive improvement in an 8-week program that includes individualized, direct, and structured reading instruction, for 2 hours a day, 5 days a week.

Can learning strategies help compensate for academic problems?

Students with learning disabilities are not strategic learners; they have not learned how to learn. Without instruction in how to approach learning, they are unable to compensate for their learning problems (Vaughn, Gersten, & Chard, 2000). Without a doubt, the **learning strategies** approach is powerful and effective (Swanson & Sachse-Lee, 2000). Don Deshler, Jean Schumaker, and their colleagues at the University of Kansas Center for Research on Learning initially developed the learning strategy approach to help middle and secondary students with learning

Lead Phase

- Students read the story independently.

- Students complete their maps, with your assistance if necessary.

- Review completed maps with your class, adding missed information.

Test Phase

- Students read the story independently.

- Students complete their maps independently.

- Ask your students the following questions: "Who were the main characters?" "Where did the story take place?" "What was the main idea of the story?"

You can use or adapt the story map shown in Figure 1 to help students organize and comprehend reading passages. Regardless of the format you use, remember to review completed story maps to ensure that the information presented is accurate and complete. Provide corrective feedback as needed.

This scientifically validated practice is a teaching method proven by systematic research efforts (Carnine, Silbert, & Kameenui, 1997; Fowler, 1982; Idol,1987; Williams, 1998; Williams et al., 1994). Full citations are found in the references for Chapter 4 under "Elementary Through High School."

Source: From "Group story mapping: A comprehension strategy for both skilled and unskilled readers" by L. Idol, 1987, *Journal of Learning Disabilities, 20,* p. 199. Copyright 1987 by Pro-Ed, Inc. Reprinted with permission.

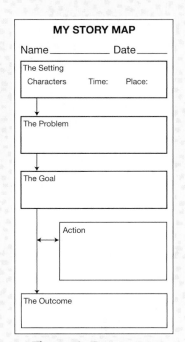

Figure 1 Components of the Story Map

disabililties (Deshler et al., 2001). The results are impressive! Researchers and teachers at the Kansas center, and across the nation, have expanded and further implemented this method. Learning strategies tactics help students learn and remember information more efficiently. For many years, special education teachers practiced "crisis teaching"—that is, they tutored their students with learning disabilities to prepare for imminent academic crises, so that they might have a better chance of receiving a passing grade on tomorrow's test or the term paper due next week. The learning strategies approach goes beyond crisis teaching and helps students meet the demands of the general education secondary curriculum. Another strategy has students group activities by main ideas and details, which helps them remember a great amount of information. Youngsters are also taught how to read difficult passages in high school social studies and science texts and how to write themes and reports in systematic ways. In addition, strategies have been developed that help students study more efficiently and take tests more effectively. Key features of the learning strategies approach are the use of

- Highly structured materials
- Advance organizers (organizing structures)
- Mnemonics
- Built-in systems of direct evaluation

Mnemonics have proved to be effective memory aids (Brigham & Brigham, 2001; Mastropieri & Scruggs, 1997). For example, many people remember the names of the Great Lakes by associating them with the mnemonic HOMES (Huron, Ontario, Michigan, Erie, and Superior). Figure 4.4 is a reminder of this old mnemonic.

Researchers and teachers have developed probably hundreds of teaching tactics extending the work of the team at the University of Kansas. These learning strategies tactics all share several features—advance organizers (organizing routines), mnemonics, systematic instruction, and CBM measures. These powerful interventions

Elementary Through High School

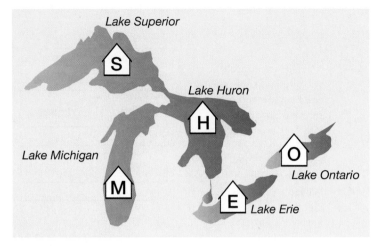

Figure 4.4 The Great Lakes Mnemonics: HOMES

help students compensate for their learning disabilities and help them become "strategic" in their approach to learning (Deshler & Roth, 2002; Hock, 2001). One fairly simple paraphrasing strategy has helped thousands of children remember information from high school texts by studying more efficiently. This strategy is called *RAP:*

Read the paragraph.

Ask yourself the Main Idea and Details in the paragraph.

Put the Main Idea and Details in your own words.

Try *RAP* as you study this chapter. You will probably find that organizing your notes and your thinking around main ideas and details is useful and makes remembering content easier. Another example is the *PEP Road Map Strategy* (Katims & Harmon, 2000). Students are taught to organize their reading of social studies texts around three elements—**P**erson, **E**vent, and **P**lace—and make their notes on a road map that leads to success in comprehending the information presented in their general education textbooks.

COLLABORATION FOR INCLUSION

Most students with learning disabilities receive nearly all of their education in general education classrooms alongside their nondisabled peers. As use of this placement option increases, the number of resource rooms is shrinking, and many parents fear that other options are disappearing. For those who believe that students with learning disabilities should have a continuum or array of services available to them, some data support this concern about fewer resource rooms being available. In 1988–89, 58 percent of students with learning disabilities received special education services through resource room arrangements; in 1999–2000, that figure had dropped to 38 percent (U.S. Department of Education, 1991, 2001). The number of resource rooms is declining, and the size of these classes is increasing to levels that sometimes exceed the general education class size (Moody et al., 2000).

Many parents and professionals worry about the implementation of a full inclusion policy for students with learning disabilities (Vaughn, Elbaum, & Boardman, 2001). They fear that the array of special services now available will disappear and that in the future the general education option, without sufficient supports, will be the only one available. With the move to more and more fully inclusive services, the concern is that students with learning disabilities could be left without the supports they need to realize their potential. Some experts believe it is wrong to assume that placement in general education equals better access to the general education curriculum (Deshler et al., 2001; Kauffman, 1999). To them, policymakers are confused about the concepts of place, services, and instructional conditions. To allay these fears will require not only protection of the array of service delivery options but also more teaming and collaboration between general and special education teachers.

Parents and professionals also worry about the current emphasis on national assessments and high test scores. What is the underlying concern? It is that such efforts will become disincentives to include students with learning disabilities. The

CHAPTER 4 *Learning Disabilities*

outcomes could be higher referrals of students who are not academically competitive to special
education and, ultimately, a
higher dropout rate for students
with learning disabilities. How
can their fears be put to rest? The
only way is to be certain that students with learning disabilities
receive effective instruction
wherein teams of educators collaborate closely to help children
achieve their individual goals and
(eventually) the positive outcomes of adult independence and
fulfillment.

Not all general education
instructional procedures or organizational structures foster positive results for these students
with disabilities. The accommodations necessary to help a student attain the desired outcomes
can demand more of the teacher's

General and special education teachers have many opportunities to help each other evaluate and support instruction, collect data on students' performance, and co-teach.

time and extra planning (see the "Accommodating for Inclusive Environments" box
for some ideas). Sometimes this is more time than a teacher has available to spend
for the benefit of one student. Furthermore, some special education instructional
methods are inconsistent with the philosophy of some general education teachers.
For example, general education teachers use group, rather than individualized,
instruction.

General education placements can be positive for students with learning disabilities, but special educators and general educators must work closely together for this
to occur. Collaboration is one key to the development of successful educational
experiences for students who are difficult to teach (Friend & Bursuck, 2002).
"True" collaboration exists under some important conditions:

- Communication is open and ongoing.
- Participation is voluntary.
- Parity exists in the relationship.
- Goals are shared.
- Evaluation of student performance is continual.
- Decision making is done as a team.
- Resources are pooled.
- Trust and respect are the basis of the partnership.
- Planning time is scheduled.

When these characteristics of collaborative settings exist, all students profit.
General education students can benefit from the unique expertise of the special educator, and students with disabilities find the general education classroom responsive
to their learning needs. However, collaboration alone does not guarantee a successful educational experience for all students with learning disabilities across their
entire educational careers. Individual students' progress must be carefully monitored (Deshler et al., 2001; Vaughn, Elbaum, & Boardman, 2001). Although some
students make excellent progress in general education settings, others do not.
Teachers must be responsive to students' instructional needs; they must recognize

M̶AKING
C̶ONNECTIONS

For more suggestions on
accommodating students'
learning needs in general
education settings, see the
"Accommodating for
Inclusive Environments"
boxes found in Chapters 3
through 12.

ACCOMMODATING FOR INCLUSIVE ENVIRONMENTS

Adjusting Content and Providing Instructional Support

Provide structure and a standard set of expectations:

- Help students develop organizational skills.
- Establish sets of rules for academic and social activities and tasks.
- Adhere to a well-planned schedule.
- Match your language to the comprehension level of the student.
- Be consistent.

Adjust instructional materials and activities:

- Individualize instruction; be sure the reading level is appropriate.
- Break tasks down into smaller pieces (or chunks).
- Begin lessons with advance organizers.
- Supplement oral and written assignments with learning aids (computers).
- Assign a peer tutor.
- Modify tests, allowing the student to take more time or complete the test in a different way (listen to a tape of the test).

- Evaluate the effectiveness of your instructional interventions, and when they are not effective, change them.

Give students feedback and reinforcement for success:

- Tell students when they are behaving properly.
- Reward students for improvement.
- Praise students when they have done well or accomplished a goal.
- Inform students when they are not meeting expectations.
- Encourage students to develop partnerships among themselves, and reinforce those who do so.

Make tasks interesting:

- Develop attention by making assignments interesting and novel.
- Vary the format of instruction and activities.
- Use high-interest curriculum materials.
- Encourage students to work together during extracurricular activities.

when the instructional program needs to be adjusted. They should also be sensitive to the different preferences of the students themselves. Some students with learning disabilities prefer pullout programs; they would rather not participate in general education settings (Le Mare & de la Ronde, 2000). This preference seems to characterize particularly those students who have low social status—those who have been rejected by their classmates either in small work groups or in social situations.

The type of educational and supportive programs that a student with learning disabilities receives must be determined by that child's individual needs, wherever the program is delivered. Most students with learning disabilities who are included in the general education classroom need at least some extra assistance and accommodations, and general and special education teachers who are working together can help ensure that appropriate and effective educational methods are in place. They might require the adaptation and modification of commercially available textbooks and instructional materials. They might need more instructional time for explanations, drill, practice, and feedback. In many cases, these students must learn how to apply a specific strategy to the learning process; others require some tutoring to master academic tasks.

Even with the best collaborative efforts, however, some students with learning disabilities need more intensive instruction than can be offered in the general education setting (Deshler et al., 2001). Sometimes, to actually master a learning strategy, these students need many opportunities for individualized instruction, repeated practice, feedback from the instructor, and extra time to become independent in the learning strategy's use. Often, this instruction needs to be delivered by a specialist. Once the skill or strategy is mastered, the student can apply it in the general education classroom. Here, again, the general education and special education teachers must work closely together to be sure the student actually uses this new information appropriately within the general education content and curriculum. Students who have difficulties transferring knowledge and information to other settings and situations require extra supports from their teachers working as a team. Here's how teachers can help students generalize the application of a study strategy, such as *RAP*, to a general education science class—and also help students take more responsibility for managing their own instructional programs: The special education teacher explains the *RAP* strategy to the science teacher and asks the science teacher (1) to remind the student to apply the strategy while studying and (2) to check to be sure that the student is using *RAP* correctly. The special education teacher then teaches the student to keep a record of the times the strategy was used. Finally, the teacher rewards the student for improved performance in science class.

Some students with learning disabilities do not profit from the standard curriculum used in general education. For them, an educational experience with a life skills, functional, or vocational emphasis is more appropriate. Of this there is no doubt: For students with disabilities to achieve their potential requires many partnerships, along with real collaboration between general and special educators.

TRANSITION THROUGH ADULTHOOD

Some adults with learning disabilities have productive careers and are highly successful adults, but others struggle to meet their potential. Clearly, the experiences of adults with learning disabilities are as varied as the population itself. Evidence— amassed from stories about highly successful adults who had or have learning disabilities—indicates that some people are able to minimize the effects of learning disabilities. For example, several present-day celebrities—Cher, Magic Johnson, Brook Theiss, Bruce Jenner, and Greg Louganis, among others—have acknowledged having a learning disability. Charles Schwab, the millionaire discount broker, has also revealed his lifelong reading problem. And Stephen Cannell, a prolific TV writer and producer (*The Rockford Files, The A-Team, Hunter*) and author, has learning disabilities (Cannell, 1999). Success stories also are told about individuals from previous times who are presumed by many to have had learning disabilities (remember that the field did not exist as such until the 1960s). Debate continues, for example, about whether Hans Christian Andersen and Albert Einstein had the condition (Kihl, Gregersen, & Sterum, 2000; Thomas, 2000). And stories persist that Leonardo da Vinci, Thomas Edison, Nelson Rockefeller, and Woodrow Wilson had learning disabilities. One unfortunate result of such stories is the public's perception that learning disabilities might not be as serious as other disabilities or that they do not have devastating effects on the individuals involved.

What postsecondary education options do individuals with learning disabilities have?

For many individuals with learning disabilities, **postsecondary** education is not an option because they do not complete high school. Only some 63 percent of students with learning disabilities graduate with a standard diploma; the other 27 percent drop out of high school (U.S. Department of Education, 2001). However, for those who are high school graduates, college attendance is now more of a possibility. The

MAKING CONNECTIONS

Graduation and dropout rates are also discussed in Chapters 1, 3, 5, and 8.

Americans with Disabilities Act (ADA) makes it quite clear: Students with disabilities must have access to postsecondary education, and colleges and universities must make reasonable accommodations to ensure such access (Simon, 2001).

Individuals with disabilities are attending 2-year and 4-year colleges (Mull, Sitlington, & Alper, 2001). Whereas in 1978 only 3 percent of college first-year students reported having a disability, some 6 percent of all undergraduates today report that they do, and almost 30 percent of those indicate that they have a learning disability (Greenberg, 2000; National Center for Educational Statistics [NCES], 2000). The number of college students with learning disabilities is increasing. In fact, they are the most rapidly growing group of students with disabilities attending college. In 1988 they represented only 16 percent of all college students with disabilities, but they now represent over 40 percent of first-year college students with disabilities (Henderson, 1999, 2001). About a third of college students with disabilities complete a bachelor's degree, compared to almost half of students without disabilities. Supports and accommodations are also becoming more widely available to assist students during their college experience, which could make an important difference in their completion rates (NCES, 2000; National Joint Committee on Learning Disabilities [NJCLD], 1999). Accommodations for college students with learning disabilities can include

- Alternative exam formats
- Extended time
- Alternative access to oral and written materials
- Tutors
- Readers, classroom notetakers, or scribes
- Registration assistance, priority class registration, course substitutions
- Adaptive equipment and technology (phonetic spellcheckers, speech synthesizers)
- Textbooks on tapes
- Course waivers

The enrollment and graduation rates of students with learning disabilities are increasing, but they must improve. College graduates with learning disabilities have some recommendations to help others succeed (Mooney & Cole, 2000). One important tip is to get organized: Every notebook should have a return address, backpacks and notebooks need a consistent "home" or place to be stored, notes and notebooks should be reorganized weekly, and mental checklists should be completed at the end of every class ("Do I have all of my stuff?" "Did I leave anything under the seat?") Middle and high school teachers can help students master these self-management skills before they enter college.

For all students, picking the right college is one key to a successful outcome. College can be a more positive experience for students with learning disabilities if they plan ahead while in high school and choose a college carefully (Taymans & West, 2001). They should visit different college campuses, investigate what support services are offered, and meet with college staff. Attending special summer programs or taking a college class can help sharpen study skills and time management skills— a problem that plagues most first-year students, not just those with learning disabilities.

Some experts suggest that high school students can best prepare for college by learning which accommodations work best for them and, therefore, what they need to request from a postsecondary educational setting (Mull, Sitlington, & Alper, 2001). As more and more assistive technology becomes available, these students need to know how to use it and how to request access to such aids. On the other

CHAPTER 4 *Learning Disabilities*

side of the accommodations equation are the faculty members who teach college courses (Bourke, Strehorn, & Silver, 2000). Despite their understanding of the importance of adapting instruction for students with disabilities, many college teachers encounter obstacles to their implementing the spirit of ADA. For example, many do not receive support from their administrations in preparing alternative tests or providing alternative settings for students to take tests. Some faculty do not have a budget that permits copying their notes for individual students to use as a resource; other faculty say they have difficulties when too many students with unique learning needs are enrolled in one class. Regardless, it is apparent that colleges and universities are becoming more accepting of students with individual learning needs.

How do adults with learning disabilities fare?

Clearly, many individuals with learning disabilities are successful adults, but all people with disabilities face considerable challenges in their lives. For example, even those who compete well in college experience persistent problems with reading and phonological processing (Wilson & Lesaux, 2001). Many of these individuals explain that they have difficulties understanding what they read, retaining information, and reading quickly enough to feel effective in daily life (Shessel & Reiff, 1999). Many adults with learning disabilities express feelings of constantly being lost, having directional problems, and being challenged with time management (Shessel & Reiff, 1999). They also note that they feel isolated socially and have few friends.

Workers with learning disabilities earn less than their co-workers without disabilities because they tend to be less skilled than their colleagues. Workers with learning disabilities also believe they face discrimination on the job, and they fear that revealing their disability to their employers would result in negative consequences (Dickinson & Verbeek, 2002). These beliefs may stem from their insecurities, negative self-concepts, and internalizations about being "dumb" because they were unable to compete successfully during their school years. Ironically, many employers report that they would offer more supports on the job if they knew of their employees' disabilities.

FAMILIES

Most children with learning disabilities are identified by education professionals, sometimes during the preschool years, but most often at about the third grade. Some of these individuals are not identified until they are in college. In contrast, most deaf children, blind children, and those with severe disabilities are diagnosed by medical professionals when they are very young. Many parents of children with learning disabilities, however, do not suspect that their children have a disability until difficulties at school become apparent, and it is often school personnel who have to deliver the bad news to them. This is a crucial time for parents and for the children who are diagnosed as having a learning disability. It is a time of confusion and concern—and often a time of anger, frustration, and stress.

The challenges that family members of individuals with disabilities face can be great. A disability can affect every aspect of a person's life. Many family members have found that gaining support from others can be helpful. Often, educators offer considerable assistance. Because learning disabilities are academically related disabilities, many parents find that it is crucial to make connections with teachers, school administrators, special education teachers, and whoever else can help their children accomplish realistic goals in school.

Can parent conferencing help school–home relationships?

Educators can develop good relationships with parents if they use good conferencing skills when meeting with them. At least four factors contribute to successful meetings (Kroth & Edge, 1997; O'Shea et al., 2001). First, the area selected should be comfortable and free from interruptions. A desk or table between the parents and the educator can act as a barrier to discussion; a round table might promote better results. Second, the professional must be a good listener. By listening carefully, the professional can help parents solve problems, and parents can come to a better understanding of how the family and the school can develop a partnership. Third, teachers should write down significant information shared by the parents. This note helps the teacher remember and offers the parent evidence of the importance of the meeting. Finally, parents should know how many meetings are planned and how long the meetings will last. Time periods should be adhered to; limiting the number and the length of the meetings seems to enhance their effectiveness. Even under the best of circumstances, where meetings are skillfully conducted, many parents report that they are overwhelmed by the amount and sophistication of the information presented (Dettmer, Dyck, & Thurston, 2002). Because of the emotionally charged nature of parent–teacher meetings, particularly the initial one, parents often indicate that they remember nothing after such terms as *brain-damaged* are used. To solve this problem, educators may need to schedule extra meetings to ensure the following results:

- The purpose of the meeting is specified.
- The information given is clear and precise.
- Information is restated using different words and examples.
- Jargon is not used.
- A professional attitude is maintained.
- Feedback on the child's social and academic performance is provided.
- The results of the meeting are recorded.

Home–school communications can also be improved if educators are flexible in their scheduling to better accommodate parents' other obligations (Jayanthi et al., 1997). For example, meetings can be scheduled during the day if teachers have release time. If teachers can receive extra pay, meetings can be scheduled early in the morning or in the evenings.

How does homework fit into these students' programs?

Homework is a long-standing component of the general education program. It is intended to help students become independent learners. Homework also serves as one communication tool to keep parents informed both about the work being done at school and about their child's progress in the curriculum (Bursuck, Montague, & Vaughn, 2001). However, the word *homework* can strike terror into the parents of students with learning disabilities—and probably into the children as well. The mere mention of the word may revive memories of many long, unpleasant nights spent cajoling a student with learning disabilities to complete unfinished assignments. Such nights often end in shouting matches between parent and child, sometimes with one or both in tears.

Despite the negative situations that homework can create for the family, it accounts for about 20 percent of the time most children spend on academic tasks (Bryan & Sullivan-Burstein, 1997). Although many children and their parents would like to see homework "just go away," it is unlikely that homework will be discontinued. General education teachers place great importance on homework. They consider homework to be a serious part of the instructional program and also to provide opportunities for home–school communication. Many teachers believe that when homework is not completed, parents have not met their expectations (Epstein et al., 1997). How might communication between teachers and parents about homework improve? Some research gives us guidelines (Jayanthi et al., 1997):

- Parents and teachers need to communicate more about homework, with both parties feeling free to initiate the conversation.

- Parents need to tell teachers about homework difficulties.

- Teachers need to tell parents about the quality and completion of homework assignments.

- Parents need to implement consequences when homework is not completed or is unsatisfactory.

- Parents need to know whom to contact at school about homework issues.

Teachers view homework as an important part of school. Parents who actively participate in their children's efforts typically also build partnerships with teachers.

- Teachers need to find ways to communicate with parents who do not speak English.

- Teachers need to determine alternative ways for children to get assistance with homework assignments that their parents do not know how to complete.

Because homework is a reality of school life, some researchers are now attempting to develop methods to make this a more positive experience. First, educators might consider teaching students how to complete homework. Researchers have developed a learning strategy that is most helpful in this regard (Hughes et al., 2002). The PROJECT strategy includes the following steps:

For other examples of learning strategies, see Figure 4.4 and the "Elementary Through High School" section.

Prepare your forms (monthly planning calendar and weekly study schedule).

Record and ask (seek assignment clarification).

Organize (Best).

    Break the assignment into parts.

    Estimate the number of study sessions.

    Schedule sessions.

    Take your materials.

Jump to it.

Engage in work.

Check your work.

Turn in the assignment.

In addition to teaching students how to do homework, there are some other ways in which teachers can be helpful. The "Tips for Teachers" box provides some guidelines that teachers can follow to get more benefits from assigning homework and even use it to forge an improved partnership with families. Also note that middle school students with learning disabilities seem to prefer being assigned homework that can be completed at school, and they do not want assignments different from their classmates'. They are afraid that if they had easier work to do, it would be

Families

Assigning and Adapting Homework

1. Make sure students can complete the homework assignment.
2. Write the assignment on the board.
3. Explain the assignment carefully.
4. Remind students of the due date periodically.
5. Coordinate with other teachers to avoid homework overload.
6. Establish with parents and other teachers a standard policy about late and missed assignments.
7. Provide additional one-on-one assistance.
8. Allow for alternative formats (audio taping rather than written assignments) or the use of learning tools (calculators, word processing, diagrams and charts).
9. Adjust assignment length.
10. Provide access to a peer tutor.

Source: Adapted from "Homework Practices That Support Students with Disabilities" by B. Bursuck, M. Montague, and S. Vaughn, 2001 Spring, *Research Connections in Special Education, 8,* pp. 2–3 (ERIC/CEC).

perceived as unfair and that this might negatively affect their social standing (Nelson et al., 1998). Thus, teachers need to consider their homework assignments as carefully as they consider their lessons, but with planning and instruction, the benefits of homework can be many.

TECHNOLOGY

Today, computers are common in schools and at home. The 1990s saw expanded capabilities of computers as well as substantial price reductions, making access to technology available to all students in most school settings. The benefits to students with disabilities are many, and the possibilities created by technology continue to be discovered. Some educators are suggesting that technology be viewed as a "cognitive prosthesis" for students with learning disabilities (Lewis, 1998). Rapid advances have changed the way educators design instructional opportunities. Let's look at a few of those advances and see how they benefit students with learning disabilities. Technology can

- Augment an individual's strengths
- Compensate for the effects of disabilities
- Provide alternative modes of performing tasks

Specifically, technology can help individuals with disabilities become more efficient and effective learners (Bryant & Bryant, 2003; Raskind & Higgins, 1998). Table 4.3 highlights some of these benefits and suggests how assistive technology can reduce the barriers to success that these individuals face at home, at school, and in daily life. The range of options is great. For example, special software can help students take notes or create such graphic displays as story maps like those described in the "Validated Practices" box on page 132. In other cases, special devices dedicated to one function, such as the *Quicktionary Reading Pen* from Seiko Instruments, which actually rolls over a printed word and both provides a definition and "says" the word for the user, can help students compensate for a particular problem. Of course, more and more complicated—and expensive—systems are available that create entire learning stations for students.

Can classroom computers be an accommodation?

Advances in software and hardware can help students with learning disabilities compensate for their learning challenges. However, consumers must beware: Not all software is equally useful, and not all of it has been carefully evaluated (Higgins, Boone, & Williams, 2000).

Computer assisted instruction (CAI) can supplement or even replace traditional instruction. **Computer enhanced instruction** can provide for more drill and practice opportunities. Some features of CAI can expand learning opportunities. For example, **hypertext** uses pop-up text windows for further explanation of textbook material, allows individuals the options of retrieving definitions of difficult vocabulary words, rewording confusing or complicated text. Hypertext can provide detailed maps and diagrams to further enhance concepts introduced in the text. These features are available to the student at the simple press of a key on the computer keyboard, and this enables teachers to adapt textbooks so that students with learning

Table 4.3 Assistive Technology Options for Students with Learning Disabilities

Barriers	Difficulties	Assistive Technology Solution
Print	Reading	Audiotaped books "Talking" computers Captioned film and videos Semantic mapping software (story mapping) Web based texts Hypermedia and hypertext
	Writing	Word processing programs (including grammar assistance) Desktop publishing Computer based thesauruses Editing aids Planning aids Word prediction software
	Spelling	Spellcheckers Voice input devices
Communication	Organization	Manipulating graphics Presentation packages (e.g., Powerpoint, Persuasion) Semantic mapping software
	Speech	E-mail Voice output systems Sythesized speech
Solving problems	Calculating	Handheld calculators Spreadsheets Graphics programs
Being organized	Daily Life	Personal organizers Electronic calendars Computer "stickies" Electronic address books
	Study Skills	Organizing software (outlines, graphic organizers) Timing devices
Learning	Researching Topics	CD-ROM based reference books Internet databases Computer based instruction (hypermedia, hypertext)
	Remembering	Outlining systems (main ideas from details)

disabilities can have better access to the general education curriculum. **Hypermedia** goes one step further by adding multimedia, such as video clips, and supplements and enriches text with highly interesting visual and auditory presentations (Boone, Higgins, & Williams, 1997).

The Internet, the World Wide Web, and related telecommunications applications (such as e-mail) can help students with learning disabilities participate more fully in the general education curriculum (Byrant & Bryant, 2003). Instead of just reading about art and history in textbooks, students can visit virtual museums and libraries all around the world to experience the content of their teacher's lessons. Students can also do their own independent research and retrieve information to use in class reports and term papers. For an active generation that is used to seeing, doing, and participating actively, the Web offers excitement and enrichment that might otherwise be missing from the curriculum. It also might provide the motivation necessary for the extra effort that students with learning disabilities must invest.

For those students with learning disabilities who find learning to read an insurmountable challenge, assistive technology can help, and more options and devices will soon be available. Some assistance simply requires the purchase of software that works on any computer, such as notetaking software (MacArthur, 2000). Other,

MAKING **C**ONNECTIONS

See again the "Validated Practices" box for an example of creating visual representations of reading content.

Technology

more complicated systems are also available. For example, the <u>Kurzweil 3000</u> system can scan any printed material, including textbooks, pictures, and illustrations, and turn them into an audio output (Kurzweil, 2002). In other words, the computer can "read" parts of the classroom curriculum to the student, using a text-to-speech format. This feature can also be applied to Web pages, which makes Internet searches for research papers more feasible for students with reading disabilities. This program encourages students to read using the computer, which can facilitate the process by defining unknown words with its 175,000-word online dictionary. Students can also gain more information about unfamiliar concepts via the computer's hypertext feature. This computer system also helps students stay organized through its notetaking function. Such systems enable students to compensate for poor reading abilities and help them participate in the general education curriculum alongside their classmates without reading problems.

Advances in technology can serve both as instructional assistants and compensatory aids. Computers with special devices, like this Kurzweil 3000 computer, include voice to print, print to voice, word prediction, and Hypermedia options.

How can word processing technology benefit students with learning disabilities?

Word processing technology can provide the help that many students with learning disabilities need to improve their writing abilities (MacArthur, 2000). The computer seems to support the writing process naturally. For some students, it is physically less tiring. For others, print on a computer screen is easier to see and read than print on paper. The spellchecker, thesaurus, and grammar correction functions available on most word processing programs are of great benefit to those struggling to get a term paper written. Many young students find using the computer fun and interesting. A written paper produced on a computer is more attractive than the often-messy product of students with poor handwriting and visual organizational skills. The computer can also facilitate collaboration between students, making it easier for two or more students to work together and merge their components of a writing task.

Word processing technology makes writing assignments less aversive to many students (Graham, Harris, & Larsen, 2001). The task of writing a term paper and other major assignments can be daunting for students with learning disabilities. Many give up before completing all of the steps necessary to produce a final version: select a topic, generate and organize the content of their paper, create drafts of the text, revise it, proofread it, edit it, and so on. However, the combination of special writing instruction and the use of a computer with a good word processing program improves both the quality and the quantity of these students' writing, and now new software features (e.g., table features, tracking for editing, word predictions) provide even more assistance to students with writing problems (Bryant & Bryant, 2003).

MAKING **C**ONNECTIONS

The answers to the questions posed in the Advance Organizers section at the beginning of the chapter are found here; use them to review the contents of this chapter.

IN CONCLUSION

Summary

Individuals with learning disabilities do not learn in the same way or at the same pace as their nondisabled classmates. Current research is attempting to find better methods of instruction to facilitate further improvement in these students' academic and social performance. When taught by well-trained teachers who are knowledgeable about the newest research findings, many of these individuals should be able to compensate for their disabilities. However, without the best that education can offer, it is unlikely that individuals with learning disabilities will succeed as they should in life.

Self-Test Questions

Focus Questions

What are the key features of most definitions of learning disabilities?

The two national definitions for learning disabilities are the IDEA and NJCLD definitions.

Most states have slightly different versions, but the elements they all share are

- IQ in normal range
- Discrepancy between IQ and achievement
- Problems often manifested in language-related areas (communication, reading, written language)
- Exclusion clause (learning disabilities are *not* due to mental retardation, lack of educational opportunities, poverty, cultural differences, other disabilities)
- Intrinsic to the individual: central nervous system, information processing deficits, inability to learn
- Problems confined to one or two cognitive areas

Why is there a call for a new definition, and how might it be different?

Reasons:

- Inconsistency in who is identified
- Size of the category (6 percent of all school children and half of those with disabilities)

Possible changes in the definition:

- Change criterion so that fewer students are served.
- Remove the discrepancy formula term.
- Include the concept of "unexpected underachievement."
- Include the concept of "resistant to treatment."
- Permit early intervention to prevent later reading problems.

Why is it correct to consider learning disabilities a lifelong condition?

Learning disabilities and their effects present lifelong challenges to these individuals and their families.

Those who continue to have difficulties with reading often find that their postsecondary education opportunities are limited.

High dropout rates negatively influence career choices and employment opportunities.

Across their lives, these individuals tend to lack friends and to feel socially isolated.

What are some learning characteristics that contribute to these students' poor academic performance?

Characteristics that contribute to unexpected underachievement: motivation negatively affected by discouragement and frustration, attribution of outcomes to external factors, attention deficits and inadequately developed generalization, information processing, problem solving, and thinking skills

How might the array of services be reconceptualized for students with learning disabilities?

Much stronger and proactive prevention system of early intervention ("catch them before they fail")

Longer prereferral process

Application of validated practices in the general education program

Provision of more accommodations

Systematic levels of more and more intensive intervention to identify those resistant to treatment

MEETING THE STANDARDS AND PREPARING FOR LICENSURE EXAMS

After reading this chapter, you should be able to demonstrate basic knowledge and skills described in the CEC standards and INTASC principles listed below. The section of this chapter most applicable to each standard is shown in parentheses at the end of the knowledge or skill statement.

 Council for Exceptional Children **Core Standard 2: Development and Characteristics of Learners**

- **Educational Implications:** Educational Implications of characteristics of various exceptionalities (Characteristics)

 Council for Exceptional Children **Core Standard 4: Instructional Strategies**

- **Instructional strategies and materials:** Select adapt and use instructional strategies and materials (Elementary Through High School)

 Council for Exceptional Children **Core Standard 10: Collaboration**

- **Conferences:** Collaborate with school personnel and community members in integrating individuals with exceptional learning needs into various settings. (Collaboration for Inclusion)
- **Conferences:** Plan and conduct collaborative conferences with individuals with exceptional learning needs and their families. (Families)
- **Characteristics:** Communicate with school personnel about the characteristics and needs of individuals with exceptional learning needs. (Characteristics)

INTASC Principle 3:

The teacher understands how students differ in their approaches to learning and creates instructional opportunities that are adapted to diverse learners.

- **Exceptionality in learning:** The teacher knows about exceptionality in learning including—learning disabilities, visual and perceptual difficulties, and special physical or mental challenges. (Characteristics)

- **Appropriate services:** The teacher can identify when and how to access appropriate services or resources to meet exceptional learning needs (Elementary Through High School)

INTASC Principle 4:

The teacher understands and uses a variety of instructional strategies to encourage students' development of critical thinking, problem solving, and performance skills.

- **Instructional Strategies:** The teacher understands principles and techniques along with advantages and limitation associated with various instructional strategies (Elementary Through High School)

INTASC Principle 10:

The teacher fosters relationships with school colleagues, parents and agencies in the larger community to support students' learning and well-being.

- **Consultation:** The teacher is willing to consult with other adults regarding the education and well-being of his/her students.

Standards in Practice

These knowledge statements, dispositions, and skills might be demonstrated in the classroom by presenting lessons using a variety of materials, teaching approaches, and strategies. This will benefit not only the students with learning disabilities, but also all students in the classroom. By adapting or modifying teaching methods, curricula content and assessment approaches it is possible to better meet the educational needs of all learners in the classroom.

 Companion Website

Go to the companion website (ablongman.com/smith5e) for detailed text correlations to CEC and INTASC standards, PRAXIS II™ exams, and other state-sponsored licensure exams.

SUPPLEMENTARY RESOURCES

Professional Readings and Resources

Bender, W. (2001). *Learning disabilities: Characteristics, identification, and teaching strategies* (4th ed.). Boston: Allyn and Bacon.

Bradley, R., Danielson, L., & Hallahan, D. P. (Eds.). (2002). *Identification of learning disabilities: Research to practice*. Mahwah, NJ: Erlbaum.

Lerner, J. (2003). *Learning disabilities: Theories, diagnosis, and teaching strategies* (9th ed.). Boston: Houghton Mifflin.

Lovitt, T. C. (2000). *Preventing school failure* (2nd ed.). Austin, TX: Pro-Ed.

Rivera, D. P., & Smith, D. D. (1997). *Teaching students with learning and behavior problems*. Boston: Allyn and Bacon.

Rodis, P., Garrod, A., & Boscardin, M. (2001). *Learning disabilities and life stories*. Boston: Allyn and Bacon.

Popular Books

Brown, C. (1965). *Manchild in the promised land*. New York: Macmillan.

Gantos, J. (1998). *Joey Pigza swallowed the key*. New York: Farrar, Straus & Giroux.

Mooney, J., & Cole, D. (2000). *Learning outside the lines*. New York: Simon & Schuster.

Moss, P. B. (1989). *An autobiography: P. Buckley Moss: The people's artist*. Waynesboro, VA: Shenandoah Heritage.

Sacks, O. (1985). *The man who mistook his wife for a hat*. New York: Summit Books.

Videos and DVDs

Summer School (1987). Paramount

This light-hearted comedy is about a number of students forced to attend summer school as a consequence their of poor academic performance during the school year. After wasting much of the summer term, in fear of failure and of costing their teacher his job, the students make tremendous effort on their final exam.

One student in the class has reading disabilities, and even though this film is a comedy, it provides an example of how a student with a significant learning disability can slip through the cracks of the educational system. The film shows how not receiving specialized services can affect such students'confidence, and why they fall further behind. The film also shows that once a learning disability is recognized, individualized instruction can aid students.

Parent, Professional, and Consumer Organizations and Agencies

Council for Learning Disabilities (CLD)

P.O. Box 40303
Overland Park, KS 66204
Phone: (913) 429-8755
Web site: http://www.cldinternational.org

Division for Learning Disabilities (DLD) Council for Exceptional Children

1110 North Glebe Road, Suite 300
Arlington, VA 22201-5704
Phone: (703) 620-3660; (888) CEC-SPED
TTY (703) 264-9446
Web site: http://www.cec.sped.org or www.teachingld.org

International Dyslexia Association

Chester Building, Suite 382
8600 LaSalle Road
Baltimore, MD 21286-2044
Phone: (410) 296-0232; (800) 222-3123
Web site: http://www.interdys.org

Learning Disability Association of America (LDA) (formerly the Association for Children with Learning Disabilities [ACLD])

4156 Library Road
Pittsburgh, PA 15234-1349
Phone: (412) 341-1515
E-mail: info@ldamerica.org
Web site: http://www.ldanatl.org

National Center for LD (NCLD)

381 Park Avenue S., Suite 1401
New York, NY 10016
Phone: (212) 545-7510; (888) 575-7373
Web site: http://www.ncld.org

Video**Workshop** Extra

If the VideoWorkshop package was included with your textbook, go to Chapter 4 of the Companion Website (www.ablongman.com/smith5e) and click on the VideoWorkshop button. Follow the instructions for viewing Video clip 6. Consider this information along with what you have read in Chapter 4 as you answer the following questions.

Video clip 6: Learning Disabilities (Time 6:21)

1. Given that Bridget does not want to attend the Resource Room and that Erin (from the "Personal Perspective" at the beginning of this chapter) is meeting some resistance from general education teachers, what should be the role of the special educator and what supports might be provided to insure both young women are successful?

2. Bridget is very concerned that she will not be able to find a job or will make a serious mistake on the job. What does the research tell us about the transition outcomes for students with learning disabilities? How can Bridget's choice of a high school program improve her outcomes?

Princeton University Library. Morris L. Parrish Collection. Department of Rare Books and Special Collections. Princeton University Library. Reprinted by permission.

LEWIS CARROLL is probably best known to all of us for his timeless story *Alice in Wonderland*. Born Charles Lutwidge Dodgson in 1832, he was one of ten children and the eldest son of an Anglican minister. He was recognized at school as possessing "a very uncommon share of genius" and particularly excelled in mathematics. He was a nervous boy who had a chronic stuttering problem and was often ridiculed by his classmates. Although he considered following his father's footsteps as a preacher, his stuttering problem made preaching difficult, and it is suggested that this is why he developed skills as a photographer and pursued a career as a writer (Hinde, 1991). This photograph is of the girl he used as his model for the character Alice.

5 Speech or Language Impairments

A PERSONAL PERSPECTIVE

Talking About Lizzy B

Amy Harris-Soloman is the mother of two daughters, Skye and Lizzy B. Even before Lizzy B was born and 10 months later, diagnosed with cerebral palsy, Amy was involved with children with disabilities. Skye, during her preschool years, had served as a "typical peer model" at an early intervention preschool and at a speech and hearing clinic. Amy is now director of Susan Gray School at the John F. Kennedy Center for Research on Education and Human Development, the same integrated preschool her daughters attended. She is a mom who makes a real difference in the lives of so many children and their families. Amy shares with us the unfolding story of Lizzy B.

My youngest daughter, Lizzy B, was diagnosed with spastic quadriplegic cerebral palsy at 10 months old. Though I had been working in the field of special education for over 15 years at the time Lizzy B was diagnosed, the impact of having my own child diagnosed with a disability hit home, and I felt like I was facing the words *cerebral palsy* for the first time. My doctoral studies had been focused on early childhood communication strategies. I didn't know I would be drawing on all my professional resources to help teach my own child. However, I did know the importance of having a communication system that works for an individual. I had seen all too often the frustrations children can experience if they are not able to communicate their wants, needs, and desires. I set out immediately to ascertain what strategies would facilitate Lizzy B's communication.

It was determined fairly early on that Lizzy B is gifted and has strong cognitive and language abilities, but the severe oral motor deficits made it very difficult to understand her. We were fortunate to have gotten involved with an early intervention system almost immediately after diagnosis.

At 10 months old, Lizzy B began working with Denise, the speech therapist she would have for the next 7 years. Denise started by helping us develop appropriate signs and picture boards for Lizzy B. She stressed how important it was for Lizzy to have some way to communicate what she wanted, and to give her multiple ways to do that. Lizzy B was a quick study and, despite her limited fine motor abilities, developed her own modified sign language very easily, discovering early that using a sign could help her access a desired toy or food item, get her the attention or help she needed, or even prompt a hug.

Unfortunately, almost as quickly as she had picked up a wide variety of signs, she figured out that communication only works if there is a receptive partner. When her Sunday School teachers told me Lizzy B did not communicate with them in class when she was 2, I asked Lizzy B why she didn't talk to her teachers. Her response was that they didn't sign. I think we both realized then that this obstacle, coupled with the fact that her signs were so unique to her, would seriously limit her in what she had to say. Thus began our investigation of augmentative communication systems.

There is a wonderful technology center in Tennessee called the Star Center. When Lizzy B was about 2½, we began making the 4-hour round trip every month to the Star Center for support and information about communication devices. The center worked hard with Lizzy B to determine what device would serve her best. There were numerous evaluations, assessments, consultations, observations, and communications among a team of players that included her therapists at home in order to make this decision. The speech therapist shared information regarding Lizzy B's receptive and expressive skills. The occupational therapist shared information regarding Lizzy B's fine motor skills, and what she could manipulate as far as keys on a keyboard, and switches and isolated buttons on different devices. The physical therapist shared information regarding mobility, and how Lizzy B would need to access the equipment (for example, would it need to have a wheelchair mount or a desktop mounting system, or could she carry it on her walker?).

Though Lizzy B had an augmentative communication device, it was considered a "back-up" system. Her primary means of communication was verbal. She continued to make gains in her expressive language as expected, and as she has gotten older her articulation has improved. However, the augmentative system has allowed her to remain successful in her school experiences. She has attended our neighborhood school since she enrolled in Kindergarten a year early through the gifted program. She has a full-time assistant in her classroom who helps her with transitions to and from wheelchair, walker, or regular chairs. The role of her assistant also includes helping facilitate successful inclusion for Lizzy B. This sometimes requires figuring out the best ways for Lizzy B to communicate what she has learned, and what tools she needs to do assignments. There are many helpful communication technologies available to her, and her assistant helps choose the most practical ones. There is also an intensive 2-week summer camp through the school system in Tennessee designed to assist children who use augmentative communication. This camp allows children to develop new skills and build on their fluency with their devices.

This past year Lizzy B's speech therapist began investigating newer assistive technology that would allow Lizzy B to acquire more sophisticated word processing skills. She is very adept at using the mouse and regular keyboard, and with her strong cognitive abilities, we decided to look for a system that would be more compatible with systems she was already using. She has recently acquired a device that is very similar to a Palm Pilot and is very user-friendly for those who need to help her with it.

Lizzy B is a very social, bright, and happy child. She has a positive self-image, and while she recognizes some of her limitations, she does not let them stop her. She is extremely motivated and challenged to continue learning and growing in her skills. She is active in her school, with her outside therapies, and with extracurricular activities such as chess club, wheelchair cheerleading, Brownie Scouts, and the A.B.L.E. (athletes building life experiences) program at Easter Seals. She was recently crowned Little Miss Wheelchair Tennessee 2002, and she views this title as her personal responsibility to communicate about the needs of children who have disabilities. She is a frequent speaker in classrooms or with medical students at Vanderbilt University and other groups. Her life is rich and full of promise.

Communication has been a key ingredient to her success and will continue to open doors for her. She has much to offer the world, and my hope is that she continues to be happy, full of life and love, and that she maintains her enduring and keen sense of humor. She remains as always my inspiration and my model for life. When I see the challenges she faces on a daily basis and the positive attitude she brings to them, how could I do any less?

1. What do you think the future holds for Lizzy B?

2. How might have Lizzy B's life and learning have been different if she had been born 20 years ago? 30 years ago?

MAKING CONNECTIONS

- For more about augmentative and alternative communication systems, see the "Technology" section of this chapter.

- Learn about Lizzy B's wheelchair-cheerleader coach by reading the Personal Perspective at the beginning of Chapter 9. See a picture of her team in Chapter 1.

Our society places a high value on oral communication, and for most of us, it is the primary method of interacting with others. We talk with each other to share knowledge, information, and feelings. Most of us, in fact, prefer talking to other forms of communication, such as writing. Note the intensity of conversations in cafeterias, college dining halls, and restaurants; think about how often we choose to use the telephone instead of writing a letter. Oral communication enables us to interact with others on many dimensions. Clearly, communication is a crucial part of life. Steven Warren (1999) helps us understand the importance of communication and of the group of professionals who work to remediate speech or language impairments:

> The field of communication and language intervention is truly transdisciplinary due to the fundamental role that these skills play in human functioning. Language is often noted as the most impressive attainment/invention of our species. It is the basis of our culture, of commerce (i.e., the information age), science, religion and so forth. It is what separates us from virtually every other species on this

planet. Individuals' fluency and skill with this tool will to a large extent determine their opportunities and options in our society. (Warren, 1999)

In this chapter, you will learn about students who have difficulty communicating with others because they have either a speech or an oral language impairment. Besides learning about the different types of these impairments, you will learn how they affect children's communication skills, social interactions, and literacy. Specialists, speech/language pathologists, and classroom teachers work together to improve children's communicative abilities.

OPPORTUNITIES FOR A BETTER FUTURE

The vast majority of children with disabilities have difficulties with language and its associated skills. The correlation is particularly high for those individuals who also have cognitive impairments. As preschoolers these youngsters are typically late in developing language, and their acquisition patterns are atypical. As they progress through school, oral language problems are compounded by challenges in learning to read, write, and communicate in social situations with others. Although language development is often the root of their difficulties, it remains the area least directly addressed at school.

Turning Legacies into Lessons

Long before the passage of IDEA in 1975, speech/language pathologists (SLPs) worked in schools and provided support services. However, in those days, the majority of their time was spent with students who had articulation problems, and proportionate little time was devoted to youngsters with cognitive and language disabilities. As the field of special education continued to develop and specialize, teachers assumed responsibilities of educating these students, but they did so with little preparation in the area of language development. Toward the end of the century, SLPs assumed roles as collaborative partners with teachers, helping them create more language development and literacy opportunities in the classroom. Time for these partnerships remains limited, however, because SLPs work with many teachers, many students, and many schools. And SLPs who work intensively with some students with severe language impairments rely on teachers for

follow through with efforts to enhance generalization of skills learned in therapy. Most, general education and special education teachers remain ill-prepared for these duties.

Thinking About Dilemmas to Solve

As you read this chapter, consider your preparation in general and special education. Think about your training in the basic area of language development and about whether the general education curriculum sufficiently addresses language acquisition and fluency. Also, study the interrelationships between language and success in mastering basic academic and social skills. Think about

- What type of training teachers need in the area of language, whether they work with preschoolers, elementary students, or high school students
- What support services SLPs can provide to assist with students' literacy development
- How delivery systems might be changed so that all students would receive a language-rich education
- Whether the general education curriculum should be modified
- Whether more instructional materials should be available that specifically address language development

SPEECH OR LANGUAGE IMPAIRMENTS DEFINED

To understand speech or language impairments, you must first understand the communication process people use to interact with others. At least two people are needed: a *sender* and a *receiver*. The process also requires a *message*. First, the sender has a thought or idea, which then is translated into a *code* the receiver can understand. Communication occurs only when the receiver understands the message as the sender intended it to be understood.

Coding thoughts into signals or symbols is an important part of the communication game. **Communication signals** announce some immediate event, person, action, or emotion. Signals can be gestures, a social formality, or a vocal pattern, such as a gasp or groan. The U.S. Marine Band playing "Hail to the Chief," for example, signals the appearance of the president of the United States. A teacher rapping on a desk announces an important message. **Communication symbols** are used to relay messages. Speech sounds are **vocal symbols**. Letters of the alphabet are **written symbols**. **Sign language** uses gestural symbols. Symbols are used in combination with each other and are governed by rules. Signals, symbols, and the rules that must be followed constitute language and allow language to have meaning. Communication symbols can refer to something: a past, present, or future event; a person or object; an action; a concept or emotion.

Once thought is coded, the sender must select a mechanism for delivering the message. The sender chooses from a number of mechanisms: voice, sign language,

MAKING CONNECTIONS

Sign language, particularly ASL, is discussed in detail in Chapter 10.

gestures, writing tools. The delivery system must be useful to the receiver. For example, selecting voice via telephone to transmit a message to a deaf person is useless (unless that person has a voice-decoding telephone device). Sending a written message to someone who cannot read also results in ineffective communication.

Communication requires the receiver to use eyes, ears, or even tactile (touch) senses (as do those who use braille) to take the message to the brain where it is understood. Receivers must understand the code the sender uses and must be able to interpret the code so that it has meaning. Communication is unsuccessful if the sender or receiver cannot use the signals or symbols adequately. And if either person has a defective mechanism for sending or receiving the information, the communication process is ineffective. Figure 5.1 illustrates the communication process by using an example from a fast-food restaurant.

At this point, it might be helpful to distinguish among 3 important and related terms: **communication, language,** and **speech.**

These children are engaged in the communication process by taking turns sending and receiving messages

- Communication is the process of exchanging knowledge, ideas, opinions, and feelings through the use of verbal or nonverbal (e.g., a gesture) language.

- Language is a rule-based method of communication involving the comprehension and use of the signs and symbols by which ideas are represented.

- Speech is the vocal production of language.

Understanding how the speech mechanisms work together in our bodies to produce speech and language is helpful in understanding what happens when a breakdown in the system results in a speech or language impairment. Refer to the diagram of the head and chest cavity shown in Figure 5.2 as you read the following description of the process of generating speech.

Figure 5.1 The Communication Process

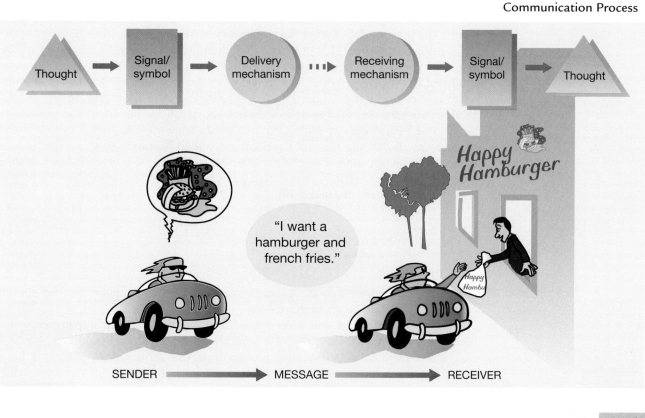

Speech or Language Impairments Defined

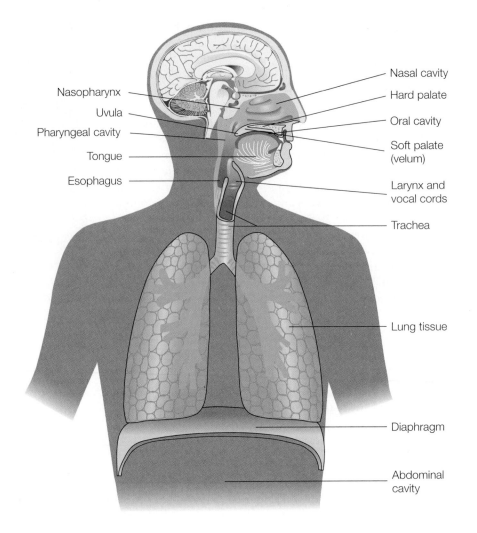

Nasal cavity

Hard palate

Oral cavity

Soft palate
(velum)

Larynx and
vocal cords

Trachea

Lung tissue

Diaphragm

Abdominal
cavity

Nasopharynx

Uvula

Pharyngeal cavity

Tongue

Esophagus

Figure 5.2 The Body's Systems for Generating Voice and Speech

When we want to speak, the brain sends messages that activate other mechanisms. The primary function of the **respiratory system** is to take in oxygen and expel gases from our bodies. However, the diaphragm, chest, and throat muscles of the respiratory system that work to expel air also activate the **vocal system.** Voice is produced in the larynx, which sits on top of the trachea and houses the vocal folds. As air is expelled from the lungs, the flow of air causes the vocal folds to vibrate and produce sounds; the vocal folds lengthen or shorten to cause changes in pitch. The larynx and vocal folds are referred to as the **vibrating system.** As the sounds travel through the throat, mouth, and nasal cavities—the **resonating system**—the voice is shaped into speech sounds by the articulation mechanisms, or **speech mechanisms,** which include the tongue, soft and hard palates, teeth, lips, and jaw. Now, let's discuss impairments in communication.

What are the two types of communication disorders?

Communication disorders are generally divided into two major groups, speech impairments and language impairments.

Although considered one special education category, **speech impairments** and **language impairments** are really two separate, though related, disabilities. Each of these major problem areas is further broken down into more specific problems. Let's look at each type to better understand how a problem with any of the areas influences the effectiveness of communication.

CHAPTER 5 *Speech or Language Impairments*

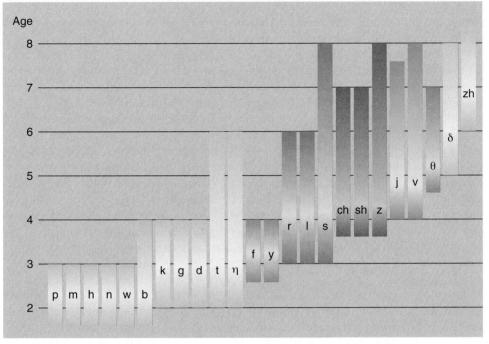

Notes: Average-age estimates and upper-age limits of customary consonant production. The solid bar corresponding to each sound starts at the median age of customary articulation; it stops at the age level at which 90% of all children are customarily producing the sound.

The θ symbol stands for the breathed "th" sound, as in the word *bathroom*. The δ symbol stands for the voiced "th" sound, as in the word *feather*. The η symbol stands for the "ing" sound, as in the word *singing*. The zh symbol indicates the sound of the medial consonant in *measure* or *vision*.

Figure 5.3 Sander's Chart, Indicating When 90% of All Children Typically Produce a Specific Sound Correctly

Source: "When Are Speech Sounds Learned?" by E. K. Sander, 1972, *Journal of Speech and Hearing Disorders, 37,* p. 62. © American Speech-Language-Hearing Association. Reprinted by permission.

• *Speech Impairments* Speech is abnormal when it is unintelligible, is unpleasant, or interferes with communication (Berthal & Bankson, 1998; Hall, Oyer, & Haas, 2001). Any one of the three major types of speech impairments is distracting to the listener and can negatively affect the communication process.

1. Articulation problems, the most common speech impairment, exist when the process of producing speech sounds is flawed, and the resulting speech sounds are incorrect. Articulation is related to the speaker's age, culture, and environment. For example, a young child's errors may be developmentally correct, whereas the same speech product made by an older child may be the result of an articulation problem, a type of speech impairment.

2. **Fluency problems** are associated with the rate and flow pattern of a person's speech. Fluency problems usually involve hesitations or repetitions that interrupt the flow of speech. **Stuttering** is one type of fluency problem. Some young children (ages 3 to 5) demonstrate **dysfluencies** (nonfluencies) in the course of normal speech development, but these are not usually indicative of a fluency problem in need of therapy.

3. **Voice problems,** the third type of speech impairment, is not very common in schoolchildren, but if a child's voice is unusual given the age and sex of the individual, immediate attention from a professional should be arranged. Two qualities of voice are important. **Pitch** is the perceived high or low quality of voice. **Loudness** is the other main aspect of voice.

The receiver of communication must understand the sounds of the words spoken to understand the full message. If speech sounds are incorrectly produced, one sound might be confused with another, either changing the meaning of the message or yielding no meaning. Articulation is also related to the geographic region in which a person lives. Regional differences in speech—dialects—do not need attention from an SLP.

For all three types of speech impairments, age is a critical variable, and it is important that adults not become alarmed or pay too much attention to speech errors during the normal developmental period. For example, correct production does not develop at the same time for all speech sounds (Small, 1999). Thus, articulation behavior that is developmentally normal at one age is not acceptable at another. The chart in Figure 5.3 gives examples of the ages when various speech sounds develop (Sander, 1972). By age 8½ , most children have mastered the last sound (z, as in *was*) at 90 percent accuracy. In the case of stuttering, age is also important; it is normal for very young children (between the ages of 3 and 5) to be dysfluent in their speech production as they master oral communication and language. Dysfluencies are likely to occur in exciting, stressful, or uncommon situations (Conture, 2001; Ramig & Shames, 2002). Young children (below age 6) often exhibit high rates of dysfluencies and may even fit a definition of stuttering. However, the rate of spontaneous recovery is great, possibly as high as 75 percent (Ratner, 1995). And in the case of voice, pitch changes during puberty, particularly for boys. Of course, this pitch change is a normal part of development and disappears as the boy's body grows and voice pitch becomes stabilized.

● *Language Impairments* Language is the complex system we use to communicate our thoughts to others. Oral language is expressed through the use of speech sounds that are combined to produce words and sentences. The use of sounds, letters (symbols), and words is governed by the rules of language. What we know about speech sounds, letters, words (or vocabulary), and rules of language influences the way we speak, read, write, and spell. Other language systems, such as manual communication or sign language, use gestures or other means of communication, but not speech sounds. Let's think about the three aspects of language: form, content, and use.

1. **Form** is the rule system used in all language (oral, written, and sign). Oral language uses sounds or sound combinations, written language uses letters and letter combinations to produce the words and word combinations (sentences) of language, and manual communication uses hand and finger movements. In oral language, form has three components: phonology, morphology, and syntax.

● **Phonology** is the sound system of language and includes rules that govern various sound combinations (Small, 1999). The phonology of language varies according to the language. For example, the speech sounds of Hawaiian are different from those of English. The English language uses 45 different speech sound combinations; the Hawaiian language uses only half that number. Swahili and some Native American languages use "clicking" sounds not found in European languages. Rules in each language govern how vowels, consonants, their combinations, and words are used. The relationship between development of an awareness of sounds in words (phonological awareness) during the preschool years and later ease of learning how to read is now clear (Ball, 1997; Falk-Ross, 2002; Torgesen & Wagner, 1998).

● **Morphology** is the set of rules that govern the parts of words that form the basic elements of meanings and the structures of words. For example, prefixes and suffixes change the meanings of the roots of specific words: An *-ed* at the end of a verb changes the tense to past; a *un-* at the beginning of a word means that something is not. Note the difference in the meanings of the following words: *cover, uncover, covered, uncovered, covers, discovered, discovering, discover, discovery, recover*. The rules governing the structure of words enable us to understand the words' meanings.

● **Syntax** determines where a word is placed in a sentence. Like phonology rules, syntax rules vary in different languages. Compare how a sentence is made negative in the English language to the way this is accomplished in Spanish or in French, if you are familiar with Spanish or French. The rules within a language determine the meaning of the communication. In English, nouns and pronouns generally precede verbs in a sentence, and when they do not, the construction might be a question: "It is one o'clock." "Is it one o'clock?" The placement of the words in sentences can change their meaning. For example, "The car hit the boy" has a meaning very different from "The boy hit the car." Rules also structure our placement of adverbs and other parts of speech. Knowing the difference between "I hardly studied this chapter" and "I studied this chapter hard" requires an understanding of how the elements of the English language are put together. Many of these subtleties can be difficult to master.

2. **Content** reflects the intent and meanings of spoken or written statements. The rules and form of language are important, but for communication to be effective, words must be meaningful. **Semantics** is the system where the intent and meanings of words and sentences make up the content of the communication. The key words in a statement, the direct and implied referents to these words, and the order of the words used all affect the meaning of the message. When senders of messages use indirect or implied referents, the receiver may not understand the message that is intended. When a child comes home and tells his mother, for instance, that he "left it at school," she might be unclear about what the child left at school, unless he is answering a direct question such as "Where is your jacket?"

3. **Use** concerns the application of language in various communications according to the social context of the situation. Use includes **pragmatics,** which is the study of language in context, and focuses in part on the intention of the communication. For example, an individual may request, order, or give an action or some information through a communication; the communication is different depending on the intent or the social context of the communication. Thus the context of discussion between two children talking to each other during free play is quite different from the context of discussion between a teacher and a child. Blank, Rose, and Berlin (1978) brought the importance of pragmatics to the attention of professionals. They pointed out that a child must know what an object is before it can be labeled meaning159fully, described, or referred to in communication. For example, a child must know what a cup is—an object that holds liquid, is picked up, is used to drink from—before that child can develop a concept about cups or use it in conversation.

$\mathcal{M}$AKING
$\mathcal{C}$ONNECTIONS

For the importance of communicative competence, see the "Characteristics" sections in Chapters 4 and 8.

Language, perception, and cognition are key factors in the development of **communicative competence.** Norma Ruiz (1995) helps us understand this important concept: "[Communicative competence] is what a speaker needs to know to communicate appropriately—what may be said and what should not be said; when, where, and by whom; and for what purposes—in addition to the linguistic knowledge necessary to produce grammatical utterances" (p. 477). Students who are not communicatively competent have difficulty understanding teachers' instructions, their lectures, and often interactions with their peers. Ruiz likens this situation to a class being taught in a foreign language the students do not

Children with speech or language impairments need many opportunities to practice their newly acquired skills with their peers.

understand. It may be that they have not mastered the necessary language skills because they are still learning English, or it may be because of an actual language impairment.

To achieve competence in communication, a person must be able to use language correctly in a social context. Social competence and communicative competence are related. Being able to communicate effectively is an essential component of being able socially (Olswang, Coggins, & Timler, 2001). Social conventions or rules are used to initiate conversations and to communicate with others. Thus the way we use language at home or with our friends in a casual conversation is different from the way we speak to an employer, a school principal, or people in authority. Not understanding the social rules of language can have serious consequences, and many students with disabilities have trouble mastering the rules of social interactions.

How are speech or language impairments identified?

Although most people can tell that someone has a speech or language impairment by listening to that person, the formal assessment of speech and language impairments is complicated and is conducted by an SLP. Assessment typically involves the use of both standardized tests, such as the *Test of Language Development (TOLD),* and informal testing in contextual situations, such as free play. If a hearing loss is suspected as a reason for the speech or language impairment, the SLP is joined by an audiologist.

What features of a child's speech or language cause SLPs concern? They look at each and every aspect of speech and language and compare those to the situation (e.g., stressful or not stressful) and the child's age (Hall, Oyer, & Haas, 2002). When testing for speech impairments, they assess the child's articulation, voice, and fluency patterns, and each evaluation requires a different type of assessment. For articulation, four different kinds of articulation errors are possible: substitutions, distortions, omissions, and additions; Table 5.1 defines and provides an example of each type. SLPs consider how seriously communication is negatively affected by poor articulation and the frequency, type, and consistency of the errors a child makes (Bernthal & Banksen, 1998). Most children with articulation problems, even those whose speech is almost unintelligible, have no apparent physiological reason for their articulation difficulties. In fact, some children can correctly pronounce a sound when it is found at the beginning of words but not when it is in the medial position or can pronounce it in some words but not in others (Hall, Oyer, & Haas, 2002). Students with fluency problems may or may not be stuttering. To distinguish between normal dysfluency and stuttering in children, SLPs analyze the specific fea-

Table 5.1 Four Kinds of Articulation Errors

Error Type	Definition	Example
Omission	A sound or group of sounds is left out of a word. Small children often leave off the ending of a word (sounds in the final position).	Intended: *I want a banana.* Omission: *I wanna nana.*
Substitution	A common misarticulation among small children; one sound is used for another.	Intended: *I see the rabbit.* Substitution: *I tee the wabbit.*
Distortion	A variation of the intended sound is produced in an unfamiliar manner.	Intended: *Give the pencil to Sally.* Distortion: *Give the pencil to Sally* (the /p/ is nasalized).
Addition	An extra sound is inserted or added to one already correctly produced.	Intended: *I miss her.* Addition: *I missid her.*

CHAPTER 5 *Speech or Language Impairments*

tures that break the flow of speech (Ramig & Shames, 2002). If words and phrases are repeated, the child is probably not stuttering but, rather, searching for vocabulary and the rules for creating meaningful language. When speech sounds or syllables are repeated, stuttering is a likely diagnosis. Voice problems are not common in young children and can be a sign of a serious laryngeal disease. Therefore, if a child experiences a significant change in voice or has a voice quality that deviates substantially from that of his or her peers, a medical examination should be scheduled.

Difficulties in language often result in more serious learning problems than speech impairments cause. Lack of language competence influences children's ability to

- Learn to read and write at the pace of their classmates
- Communicate orally with others

When assessing children for language impairments, SLPs test all three aspects of language: form, content, and use. To assess the form or structure of an individual's language, the SLP determines how well the child uses the rules of language. Problems with form cause errors in letter or sound formation, in use of grammatical structures, or in sentence formation. Many children who have difficulty with the rules of language also have problems recognizing sounds and understanding the meaning of different grammatical constructions, sentence types, and structural subtleties. For example, a child who has not mastered the rules of language might not be able to tell the difference between "Go to the store" and "Did you go to the store?" The second aspect of language that SLPs assess to determine language competence is content. Children with problems in language content often do not understand the meaning of what is said to them and choose inappropriate words for their oral language communications. They may also have difficulty comprehending the written material presented in textbooks. The third aspect of language competence, use (pragmatics), is assessed to determine how appropriately a child uses language in social contexts and conversations.

What are the distinctions among language impairment, language delays, and language differences?

Before answering this question, let's first look at how language typically develops throughout childhood. The ability to use language and follow its rules increases with a child's age. Although individual children acquire language skills at different times, normal language seems to develop in roughly the same sequence across the first 18 months of life (Owens, 2002). Children with typical language development gain skills in an orderly fashion. Look first at the profile of the normally developing child, which is shown in Table 5.2. Note that most children after age 3 (40 months) can use some fairly sophisticated language. Now compare the language development patterns of the typical child with the profile of the child with language impairments. At the same age, the child with language impairments is speaking in only two-word combinations, while her or his peer is producing fairly complex language. Also note that the two children differ in their pattern or sequence of language acquisition (find when each acquired the use of the *-ing* word ending, for example) Thus it is not just at what rate (how slowly) a child develops language, but also how differently it develops in that child from the way it develops in typical peers, that determines a language impairment.

Children with **language delays** generally acquire language in the same sequence as their peers, but more slowly. Many of these children do not have a disability and catch up with their peers. Some children acquire language in the correct sequence, do so very slowly, and never complete the acquisition of complex language structures. For example, most children with mental retardation have language delays.

MAKING **C**ONNECTIONS

For more information about the relationship between language impairments and learning problems, see these sections:

- Causes and Prevention (Chapters 4 and 6)
- Characteristics (Chapters 3 and 4)
- Early Childhood Education (Chapter 6)

Table 5.2 Pattern of Development Shown by a Child with Language Impairments and by a Normally Developing Child

Child with Language Impairments			Normally Developing Child		
Age	Attainment	Example	Age	Attainment	Example
27 months	First words	*this, mama, bye bye, doggie*	13 months	First words	*here, mama, bye bye, kitty*
38 months	50-word vocabulary		17 months	50-word vocabulary	
40 months	First 2-word combinations	*this doggie, more apple, this mama, more play*	18 months	First 2-word combinations	*more juice, here ball, more TV, here kitty*
48 months	Later 2-word combinations	*Mama purse, Daddy coat, black chair, dolly table*	22 months	Later 2-word combinations	*Andy shoe, Mommy ring, cup floor, keys chair*
52 months	Mean sentence length of 2.00 words		24 months	Mean sentence length of 2.00 words	
55 months	First appearance of -ing	*Mommy eating*		First appearance of -ing	*Andy sleeping*
63 months	Mean sentence length of 3.10 words		30 months	Mean sentence length of 3.10 words	
66 months	First appearance of *is*	*The doggie's mad*		First appearance of *is*	*My car's gone!*
73 months	Mean sentence length of 4.10 words		37 months	Mean sentence length of 4.10 words	
79 months	Mean sentence length of 4.50 words			Mean sentence length of 4.50 words	*Can I have some cookies?*
	First appearance of indirect requests	*Can I get the ball?*	40 months	First appearance of indirect requests	

Source: "Language Disorders in Preschool Children" (p. 147) by L. Leonard, in G. H. Shames, E. H. Wiig, and W. A. Secord (Eds.), *Human Communication Disorders: An Introduction* (4th ed.). Published by Allyn and Bacon, Boston, MA. © 1994 by Pearson Education. Reprinted by permission.

MAKING CONNECTIONS

Review sections about linguistic diversity in Chapter 3.

Their language development will remain below that of their peers who have normal intelligence and are developing at expected rates (Wetherby, 2002).

What of children who are learning English as a second language? Many teachers have difficulty determining whether a child who is not a native speaker of English is merely **language different** or has a language impairment (Gonzalez Brusca-Vega, & Yawkey, 1997; Langdon & Cheng, 1992; Lessow-Hurley, 2000). Truly mastering a second language takes a long time. Many **English language learners (ELLs)** may appear to be fluent in English because they converse with their classmates on the playground and express their basic needs in the classroom, but even so, they may not yet have developed sufficient fluency in their second language to participate fully in academic instruction. These abilities, however, are only some of the language skills acquired on the way toward communicative competence. Cultural differences and family values also influence how individual children learn language skills, and it is important to understand that different interaction styles result in different paths to communicative competence. English being a second language does not result in a disability, but some ELLs may be slow in mastering their second language, particularly because of the impact of poverty, and some do have language impairments (Langdon, 1999; Utley & Obiakor, 2001).

Dialects of American English are not impairments either (Payne & Taylor, 2002). Dialects result from historical, social, regional, and cultural influences and

CHAPTER 5 *Speech or Language Impairments*

are sometimes perceived by educators as inferior or nonstandard (Battle, 1996; van Keulen, Weddington, & DeBose, 1998). Children from diverse backgrounds who use dialects, whether they be from Appalachia or from a predominantly Black inner-city community, are often misidentified as having language impairments. Professionals who can make the distinction between language difference and language impairment are proficient in the rules of the particular child's dialect and in nondiscriminatory testing procedures. It is important that identification procedures be applied to diverse groups of learners carefully.

How can speech or language impairments affect the individuals involved?

Speech impairments can affect how a person interacts with others in all kinds of settings and can influence an individual's success in school, social situations, and employment. Stuttering, for example, can result in emotional problems because listeners—and often the individuals themselves—react to nonfluent speech with embarrassment, guilt, frustration, or anger (Conture, 2001; Ramig & Shames, 2002). The condition can lead to confusion, feelings of helplessness, and diminished self-concept. The long-term effects can be quite serious. Some individuals respond by acting overly aggressive, denying their disability, and projecting their own negative reactions onto their listeners. Others withdraw socially, seeking to avoid all situations in which they have to talk, and ultimately they become isolates. The story of Lewis Carroll is not uncommon among those who stutter. Some spend considerable effort avoiding words that contain letters or sounds that result in dysfluencies, others, such as former Los Angeles Lakers point guard Ron Harper, say what they want to say, despite the product. But clearly, Harper's stuttering influenced him throughout his life. "Kids would mock me and talk behind my back and I was always like 'OK, fine, you want to play me?' That's how I'd get back at everybody" (Plaschke, 2000, p. D13). Harper chose the college team he played on because the school he selected had a good speech department. His basketball success gave him the confidence to be the spokesperson for the team during the 2000 playoffs.

Language impairments have the potential to be even more serious than speech impairments because they can affect all aspects of a child's classroom experiences, including the abilities to speak, to write, and to comprehend what is written and spoken (Wetherby, 2002). Language is a complex system to master: Its rules are not consistent, and it has many subtle conventions to learn and follow. Language is an important foundation to other foundations of classroom learning: reading, writing, thinking, and ultimate literacy. The histories of many children with learning disabilities reveal that they were identified as having a significant language delay or impairment as preschoolers.

Clearly, people who cannot communicate well find that their impairment affects the way they interact with others and how efficiently they communicate and learn. It also influences employment options. For example, a receptionist in an office must be able to talk on the phone, take and deliver messages to the public and to other workers in the office, and give directions to visitors. Thus children with speech or language impairments should be provided with the services they need to enable them to learn how to communicate successfully with others.

HISTORY OF THE FIELD

Records dating before 1000 B.C. reveal that at that time, individuals with disabilities were considered fools, buffoons, and sources of entertainment, often because of their speech or language problems. During Roman times, cages were placed along the Appian Way to display individuals with disabilities. There, Balbus Balaesus the

MAKING CONNECTIONS

Read again the short biographical sketch of Lewis Carroll at the beginning of this chapter to see how his life and career choices were influenced by his stuttering.

MAKING CONNECTIONS

Review the ways people with disabilities were treated across history: read again the section called "The Essence of Disabilities" in Chapter 1.

www.ablongman.com/smith5e
History of the Field

161

Robert West, one of the founders of what is now the American Speech-Language-Hearing Association, is considered by many to be the father of this field.

Stutterer would attempt to talk when a coin was thrown into his cage (Van Riper & Erickson, 1996).

Speech or language impairments have been documented throughout the centuries. Treatment programs also existed, but they were not based in schools, and they yielded mixed results. In the United States, speech correction was not available in the public schools until the 20th Century. In 1910 the Chicago public schools hired an itinerant teacher to help children who "stammered" (Moore & Kester, 1953). In 1913 the superintendent of the New York City schools began a program of speech training for children with speech impairments. The first speech clinic was opened in 1914 by Smiley Blanton at the University of Wisconsin. In 1925 the American Academy for Speech Correction (later called the American Speech and Hearing Association and now called the American Speech-Language-Hearing Association) was formed by a small group of professionals to share their ideas and research. Robert West spearheaded the formation of the academy and is regarded by some (Van Riper, 1981) as the father of his field. Two other pioneers, Lee Travis and Wendell Johnson, developed the program at the University of Iowa and guided this emerging field at the organizational and national level. Through their guidance, the field of speech or language impairments became independent from medicine, psychology, and speech and debate.

In the early part of the 20th Century, public schools hired speech clinicians to work with children who had speech problems, but services were limited. During World War II, the military developed screening procedures to identify persons with speech problems and hearing losses and began their own clinical and research programs. These efforts demonstrated that speech therapy can be effective, and after the war, university programs to train SLPs increased in size and number. Correspondingly, public school programs expanded. By 1959, 39 states had laws allowing or requiring school districts to provide services for students with disabilities, including those with speech or language impairments, and to receive state funding.

Throughout the history of the field, professionals working to remediate children's speech and language problems have had many titles, partly because of their changing roles. At first they were called speech correctionists or speech teachers; these early professionals focused their efforts on remediating stuttering, voice, and articulation difficulties. During the late 1950s and 1960s, professionals began to be called speech therapists and speech clinicians. In this period, they saw more than 200 children per week, primarily in small groups, for as little as 30 minutes a day. However, many children with language problems, with moderate to severe disabilities, with multiple disabilities, or with mental retardation did not receive speech therapy because professionals thought these children were not developmentally able to profit from therapy. During the early 1970s, professionals were called speech pathologists. By the end of that decade, ASHA had coined the term *speech/language pathologist* to reflect the broader view of the services they provide.

The 1970s was a period of transition. ASHA and the professionals it represents sought to improve further the quality of services provided to children. Research data indicated that many articulation problems were developmental and were corrected naturally with age. Therefore, this period of time also saw a shift in the priorities of speech therapy in the schools. SLPs began to work with fewer children with mild articulation problems and concentrated on youngsters with severe speech or language problems. Today, SLPs often consult and collaborate with general education classroom teachers to remediate minor speech or language problems. SLPs can then

CHAPTER 5 *Speech or Language Impairments*

work intensively with 20 or 30 children who have serious speech or language impairments.

PREVALENCE

Official reports show that learning disabilities makes up the largest single category of exceptional learners and that speech or language impairments constitutes the second largest special education category. However, when the primary and secondary disabling conditions are both considered, speech or language impairments is clearly the largest special education category (U.S. Department of Education, 2001). In the only study of its kind, examination of the caseloads of SLPs showed that 42 percent of all the children with communicative difficulties had another primary disabling condition (Dublinski, 1981). For a large proportion of children with speech or language impairments, their primary disabling condition is hard of hearing or deafness, learning disabilities, mental retardation, or health impairments.

Data from the *Twentieth-third Annual Report to Congress on the Implementation of IDEA* (U.S. Department of Education, 2001) indicate that during the 1999–2000 school year, 2.3 percent of the entire school-age population was identified as having a disability because of speech or language impairments or both. Thus more than 2 of every 100 schoolchildren, or a total of 1,081,822 students between the ages of 6 and 17, received services for speech or language impairments as their primary disability. If this represents 58 percent of those school-age youngsters whom SLPs serve, then an additional 454,365 students whose primary disabling condition was not speech or language impairments received supportive services because of speech or language difficulties or both.

Also of interest to educators is the relationship between a student's age and his or her disability classification. Articulation problems, for example, are more common during the preschool and elementary years. Speech or language impairments is definitely the most common label used for children at the ages of 6 (the first year they must be identified as belonging to a special education category), 7, and 8. For example, during the 1999–2000 school year, 191,674 children 8 years old were identified as having speech or language impairments, but that same year, 160,840 children 8 years old were identified as having learning disabilities. Data for 9-year-olds (a time when reading is a greater part of the curriculum), tell a different story: 157,790 were identified with speech or language impairments and 239,255 with learning disabilities. And the trend continues. By the time students are in the 12–17 age group, the learning disabilities category is 1,481,921 larger than the speech or language impairments category (U.S. Department of Education, 2001). Why might this be so?

- Do these problems disappear with age?
- Are early remediation efforts so successful that these impairments are corrected and do not persist through childhood?
- Or are these youngsters reclassified into another group (such as learning disabilities) as they become older?

The answers to these questions probably lie in the expectations and demands of different settings. "The earlier diagnosis of language disability often reflects the expectancies of the preschool curriculum, whereas the later diagnosis of learning disability aligns with the complex demands of a more academic curriculum" (Schoenbrodt, Kumin, & Sloan, 1997, p. 264). Clearly, the association between language impairments, often identified in early childhood, and learning disabilities, often identified as the reading demands of academic learning increase, is strong and now widely accepted (Bakken & Whedon, 2002).

MAKING CONNECTIONS

To see the relationships between language problems and disabilities, scan Chapters 3, 4, 6, and 10.

Children who stutter need to have many experiences to learn that speaking in front of classmates does not have to be stressful. This boy is knowledgeable about the content of his presentation and is allowed to use notes if he becomes uncertain. He was also not forced to make this presentation.

CAUSES AND PREVENTION

Researchers work hard to find factors that cause specific disabilities because finding a cause often leads to preventive measures. Unfortunately, as with so many disability areas, causes for many cases of speech or language impairments are unknown. Consequently, ways to prevent them from occurring in the first place are also as yet unidentified. Despite this fact, many causes *are* well known, and for some of those conditions, impairments are preventable.

What causes speech impairments?

Speech impairments can result from many different conditions, including brain damage, malfunction of the respiratory or speech mechanisms, and malformation of the articulators. Some children make articulation errors because they do not use the right motor responses to form sounds correctly. They make errors because of the way they use the speech mechanisms—tongue, lips, teeth, mandible (jaw), or palate—to form the speech sounds. For others, the cause may be a physical or organic problem, such as a **cleft palate,** where an opening exist in the roof of the mouth.

A cleft lip or palate affects the ability to produce speech. Its incidence varies by race/ethnicity: about 1 of every 500 live births for Asian Americans, about 1 of 750 for Whites, and about 1 of 2,000 for African Americans (McWilliams & Witzel, 1998). The proportions of cleft lips and palates tend to be consistent; about 25 percent involve the lip, 50 percent involve the lip and the palate, and the remaining 25 percent involve the palate. Most cleft lips can be repaired through plastic surgery and do not have a long-term effect on articulation. A cleft palate, however, can present continual problems because the opening of the palate (the roof of the mouth) allows excessive air and sound waves to flow through the nasal cavities. The result is a very nasal-sounding voice and difficulty in producing some speech sounds, such as *s* and *z*. A cleft palate is one physical cause of a speech impairment that requires the intensive work of many specialists (plastic surgeons, orthodontists, and SLPs) to help the individual overcome the resulting speech disability.

Although professionals can describe stuttering, they are unable to pinpoint or agree on a single cause for the problem (Ramig & Shames, 2002). Experts, however, do believe that stuttering episodes are related to stress, particularly when the conversational situation is very complex or unpredictable (Hall, Oyer, & Haas, 2001). Dysfluencies are more likely to occur and reoccur when the situation is challenging or confusing.

Voice problems, which are less common in schoolchildren, can be symptomatic of a medical problem. For example, conditions that interfere with muscular activity, such as juvenile arthritis, can result in a vocal disturbance. Voice problems also can be caused by the way the voice is used: Undue abuse of the voice by screaming, shouting, and straining can damage the vocal folds and result in a voice disorder. Rock singers frequently strain their voices so much that they develop nodules (calluses) on the vocal folds, become chronically hoarse, and must stop singing or have the nodules removed surgically. Teachers who notice changes in children's voices that are not associated with puberty should refer the student to an SLP.

M**AKING**
C**ONNECTIONS**

Read each of the sections about the causes of specific disabilities to understand that the cause of most cases of disabilities is unknown.

What causes language impairments?

Language impairments have multiple causes. Brain injury can cause conditions such as **aphasia,** which interferes with language production. Chronic **otitis media,** or middle ear infection, can cause children to miss hearing auditory models during key developmental periods and may result in difficulties with language development (Roberts & Zeisel, 2002). Many language impairments have a genetic cause and are shared by members of both the immediate and the extended family (Owens, Metz, & Haas, 2000).

Heredity, however, does not explain all language impairments. The quality and quantity of early language input has a definite effect on vocabulary development and language development (Harwood, Warren, & Yoder, 2002). Poor language development can be caused by environmental factors, including lack of stimulation and of the proper experiences for cognitive development and learning language. Some children do not develop language because they have no appropriate role models. Some are left alone too often; others are not spoken to frequently. Some are punished for speaking or are ignored when they try to communicate. Many of these children have no reason to speak; they have nothing to talk about and few experiences to share. Such youngsters are definitely at risk for developing significant language impairments.

How can speech or language impairments be prevented?

Many measures can be taken to prevent speech or language impairments. Many preventive measures have a medical basis and are implemented prior to the birth of a baby. For example, polio and rubella can have devastating effects on an unborn baby; proper immunization protects adults and children from these and other diseases. A nutritional supplement of folic acid during pregnancy can reduce the risk of cleft palates and lips by 25 to 50 percent (Maugh, 1995). Proper prenatal care is important to the health of babies. Good nutrition influences the strength and early development of very young children.

The link between poverty and language disabilities is clear (Utley & Obiakor, 2001). The availability of proper medical care before and after birth is crucial. Access to health care during childhood is important so that conditions like viral encephalitis and otitis media can be avoided or treated early. Although no longer common in the general population, encephalitis is prevalent in poorer communities of our society. If left untreated, encephalitis causes brain damage, which in turn can result in cognitive and language disabilities. Those who are poor are less likely to have access to information and medical programs, which puts them at risk for disease. Better public education programs available to the entire population inform people of the necessity of good prenatal care, nutrition, and medical care. It may be, however, that innovative approaches to the dissemination of information about the importance of protecting children from disease should be implemented. For example, accessing the African American community may require different approaches. Health fairs sponsored by churches, sororities, fraternities, and other community organizations may prove to be more effective ways to communicate important information than are traditional means (CDF, 1997). Teachers can also help in this process. Partnerships between experts in speech and language development and classroom teachers result in appropriate and timely referrals. Such efforts might initially be costly in time and effort, but the positive impact on preventing and overcoming disabilities is significant.

MAKING CONNECTIONS

To learn more about the impact of rubella, read "A Personal Perspective: Making my way in a Hearing World," in Chapter 10.

MAKING CONNECTIONS

Partnerships with members of culturally and linguistically diverse communities are discussed in Chapter 3 (the "Collaboration for Inclusion" and "Families" sections).

CHARACTERISTICS

Children with speech or language impairments are a large and diverse group of youngsters. Some have a speech impairment, others have a language impairment, and still others have both a speech and a language impairment. Naturally, these children have different characteristics and learning needs. For example, a child with a voice problem will have a different remediation program than a child who has difficulty articulating speech sounds correctly. Certainly, those with speech impairments have entirely different characteristics and remediation programs than children with language difficulties. Table 5.3 can be used to compare characteristics across different types of speech or language problems.

What are some common characteristics of students with speech impairments?

Most children whose primary disability is a speech impairment (articulation, fluency, or voice problems) attend general education classes and function well academically with their peers. Usually their disability does not influence their academic learning. If their speech impairment is severe and sustained, however, they may have difficulties with peers in social interactions. Depending on how the peer group reacts to an individual's disability, the person with a severe disability might—or might not—have long-term difficulties with self-concept and independence (Van Riper & Erickson, 1996).

Social difficulties are particularly common for those who stutter (Ramig & Shames, 2002). Stuttering can negatively affect a person's sense of adequacy and confidence. To avoid embarrassment, many people who stutter avoid situations in which they have to talk; others lash out and vent their frustration and anger on others. Consequently, their disability influences the types of jobs they seek, the friends they make, their relationships with others, and their overall quality of life. Think about how you react to people with severe speech impairments. Do you look away from them? Do you try to be helpful to the stutterer by finishing his or her sentence? Do you try to avoid the person? Now think about how young children treat their peers who use different speech sounds, who stutter, or who have a different voice quality. Facing these reactions is an everyday reality for individuals with speech impairments. It is understandable that some would like to withdraw from a society that treats them as different.

Teachers and peers can be most helpful; their actions can make a real difference in the way students with speech or language impairments feel about themselves and others. Environments shape the way people act. Events trigger behavior, which in turn is maintained by the events that follow the behavior's occurrence. If stuttering causes peers to laugh and snicker every time it occurs, the individual who stutters will be negatively affected. This chain of events, however, can be broken through a process called **environmental restructuring**. Peers are taught about behavioral relationships: the causes and effects of actions. They are also taught how to change their behavior to be instructive and supportive. Thus peers learn how to act when

MAKING CONNECTIONS

Read again the story of Ron Harper in the "Speech or Language Impairments Defined" section.

Table 5.3 Possible Signs or Characteristics of Speech and Language Impairments

Speech
- Makes consistent and age-inappropriate articulation errors
- Exhibits dysfluencies (repetitions, prolongations, interruptions) in the flow or rhythm of speech
- Has poor voice quality, such as distracting pitch
- Is excessively loud or soft

Language
- Is unable to follow oral directions
- Is unable to match letters with sounds
- Has an inadequate vocabulary
- Demonstrates poor concept formation
- Has difficulty conveying messages or conversing with others
- Has difficulty expressing personal needs

ACHIEVING DISCIPLINE

Changing the Context: Environmental Restructuring

Marcos is a "class clown." Everyone enjoys his jokes and antics. It's hard not to laugh when he imitates the leader of the school's marching band, particularly when he does so during study hall. He blows a kazoo under a Kleenex, and the resulting chaos lands him in the principal's office. Marcos is not a popular child, and he stutters when called on by the teacher. Possibly, his inappropriate behavior serves to draw attention away from his speech impairment and is also an attempt to gain recognition from his classmates. Marcos's behaviors involve the entire class, for his routines are for their benefit. He seems determined to do whatever it takes to get their attention and to get them to laugh hysterically.

Mr. Tyler, Marcos's sixth-grade teacher, understands that the social climate at school is set by everyone's actions. He decided to discuss Marcos's behavior with his fellow teachers and ask everyone to come up with a united plan of action.

Since Marcos's inappropriate behaviors involved the entire class, the whole class would be involved in the solution. Mr. Tyler discussed the situation with the class. Marcos's peers came to realize that they were partly responsible for encouraging Marcos's inappropriate behavior and that their responsive actions resulted in more silly behavior. Mr. Tyler helped the class understand that they could alter this situation. He taught his students not to respond to Marcos's different and outrageous behaviors. Mr. Tyler also helped the class learn not to laugh at Marcos when he stuttered or when his speech seemed different from typical speech patterns. He also helped them learn how to encourage and reward appropriate behavior in each other and in Marcos. By understanding how they could contribute to the creation of supportive environments and by changing the ways they responded to each other, these classmates came to accept individual differences and

also to help each other behave appropriately and responsibly.

Steps Used in Environmental Restructuring

- Have class discussions that are guided by a teacher or counselor to pinpoint the behaviors that disrupt the learning environment, understand the class's role in encouraging and maintaining them, and develop a helping attitude and concern about the target individual.

- Help class members recognize their role in the dynamic.

- Learn intervention strategies that reduce the likelihood of inappropriate behaviors.

- Role-play scenarios where classmates instruct, ignore, and reward behaviors.

- Reward class members for restructuring their environment.

- Reinforce the target student for acting appropriately.

their classmate stutters, how to encourage that individual to become involved in activities and groups, and how to monitor the effects of their reactions on their peer's behavior.

What are some common characteristics of students with language impairments?

Unlike most speech impairments, language impairments have multiple outcomes beyond the production of oral language. Many youngsters' social competence is affected, and a variety of their social skills are inferior to those of peers without this disability. It is also quite common to find correlated cognitive and academic difficulties in children with language impairments.

- **Social Competence** Language plays a key role in developing and maintaining social relationships; social communication requires linguistic competence (Olswang, Coggins, Timler, 2001). Students with language impairments have a higher-than-average risk of having difficulties with peer relationships (Asher & Gazelle, 1999). Being able to understand messages and to communicate well is important in interactions with peers and adults. For example, part of everyday life at school and in

MAKING CONNECTIONS

For other useful strategies, see the "Achieving Discipline" boxes found in each chapter.

MAKING CONNECTIONS

For more on social competence and language, see Chapters 4 and 8.

Arguments can occur when children do not have sufficient communication competence to explain their needs and discuss solutions.

the community is resolving conflicts. It seems that conflict is an inevitable part of life because individuals have incompatible goals or may understand an event or situation differently. Being able to resolve misunderstandings or disagreements is an important skill that requires abilities to solve problems, understand the viewpoints of others, and clearly present one's feelings. Language impairments, particularly in the pragmatic area, negatively influence the development of skills required for successful conflict resolution (Fujiki et al., 1999).

Problems in the area of pragmatics can result in other difficulties that negatively affect social skills. Many of these youngsters are unable to understand ambiguity in messages (Lloyd, 1994). They seem unable to identify the features that uniquely identify specific objects. For example, they might not be able to successfully play a game in which a target photograph is to be identified by a partner. When the objective is to make as few guesses as possible, the requirement is to describe the distinguishing features of the object using as few clues as possible. How would you help a partner know that it was a photo of a zebra, and not of a giraffe, that was the target? (Try the color of its stripes.)

Children who do not have effective communication skills adjust their interaction patterns to avoid situations wherein they feel uncomfortable or inadequate (Asher & Gazelle, 1999; Rice, 1997). They tend to initiate conversations less. They do not engage in communications and are more likely to rely heavily on adults for their verbal interactions. These students tend to have low social status and are often ignored and rejected by their peers. The results are often extreme feelings of loneliness and overt harsh treatment by their classmates. Many children who experience general peer rejection also do not have friends. Having a close friend—someone with whom to share feelings and from whom to seek advice and gain comfort—is more important for personal adjustment than general popularity (Fujiki et al., 1999).

• *Cognitive and Academic Performance* Whether it be verbal or nonverbal (e.g., sign language), language is at the foundation of cognition. Research finding after research finding provides substantial evidence that children identified as having a language impairment during the preschool years are very likely to have difficulty mastering reading when they are in elementary school and difficulty becoming literate later on (Falk-Ross, 2002; Snow, Scarborough, & Burns, 1999). Early abilities to detect sound segments, to match beginning sounds, to identify sound segments in words and phrases, and to rhyme have been definitively linked to success in learning to read. Students who do not have early phonemic awareness appear to be at great risk for reading failure (Norris & Hoffman, 2002). As already noted, this situation can be corrected. Specific instruction that teaches phonological awareness and sound segmentation provides the prerequisites to learning how to read or, later, results in improved reading abilities. In this regard, SLPs can be most helpful to general and special education teachers who may not feel proficient in these complex language models and related remediation strategies.

Given the connection between language impairments and reading difficulties, it is not surprising that other researchers have discovered a definite connection between language impairments and learning disabilities (Bakken & Whedon, 2002). Some believe that 80 percent of all students with learning disabilities have a concurrent language impairment that is the basis for their academic learning problems (Wiig & Secord, 1998). And it is commonly believed among professionals is that a

M‌AKING C‌ONNECTIONS

For a review of early reading skills, see Chapter 4.

CHAPTER 5 *Speech or Language Impairments*

language impairment diagnosed in a preschooler will result in a diagnosis of learning disabilities during the school years. Because reading skills lead to literacy and are the basis for nearly all academic learning in secondary school settings, it is obvious that students with language impairments are vulnerable to school failure.

EARLY CHILDHOOD EDUCATION

For most very young children identified as having disabilities, it is their late language development patterns that set them apart from their normally developing peers. Preschool programs can make a significant, positive, and long-term difference for young children and their families (Bailey et al., 1999). For example, low birth weight infants who received a customized day care program averaged 15 IQ points higher than the control group (Education of the Handicapped, 1992). Only 2 percent of these youngsters—**at risk** for speech or language impairments, mental retardation, and learning disabilities—were identified as having a disability later on; the control group was nine times more likely to have a disability. During a child's developmental period, the acquisition of good communication and language skills is crucial to the child's later development of academic and social skills. However, it is important to remember that preschool programs must be of high quality, with an appropriate child-to-adult ratio. Evidence now exists that when child-to-staff ratios follow the guidelines set by the American Public Health Association and the American Academy of Pediatrics (3:1 for infants, 4:1 for 2-year-olds, and 7:1 for 3-year-olds), children's readiness for school, particularly in the area of language, is above average (Lombardo, 1999).

How can language development be fostered in preschool settings?

Preschool programs for children with or at risk for speech or language impairments should be provided in accepting and responsive environments that motivate students to communicate. Therefore, instruction should occur in natural settings where children are free to interact and explore. Early intervention programs should foster cooperative play, encourage spontaneous talking, facilitate social interactions with peers, develop responsiveness with conversational partners, and guide parents in the creation of a home environment that fosters language development. Because language—its acquisition and generalization—does not occur in isolation, Plante and Beeson (1999) remind us that social interaction must be integrated into the instructional program.

Settings that promote language production are rich in objects and activities that interest and reward young children (Falk-Ross, 2002). For young children with and at risk for disabilities, good language development does not happen by accident; it occurs through the deliberate actions of preschool teachers and other adults. They must create an environment that fosters language development and thereby promotes early literacy—an environment carefully arranged so that children must imitate, request objects, and obtain the attention of an adult through verbal responses (Ostrosky & Kaiser, 1991; Snow, Scarborough, & Burns, 1999; Warren et al., 1993). These findings give us some ideas about how to stimulate young children's language, encourage its development, and provide a climate where social interaction is fostered. The "Tips for Teachers" box lists some strategies that teachers and family members can arrange to create, directly and indirectly, environments in which language use is necessary and is part of the typical routine.

Promoting Preschoolers' Language

1. Encourage literacy by connecting oral, written, and print language experiences through telling, reading, enacting, and creating stories.

2. Create enthusiasm by making trips to the public library.

3. Arrange classrooms with interesting materials and provide high-interest activities.

4. Provide reasons for oral communication by placing materials within view of the children but out of their reach.

5. Arrange the environment to encourage more communication from children, such as by providing insufficient materials (e.g., paper, paints, or crayons).

6. Create situations in which children do not have all the materials they need to perform an activity (painting without brushes, sandbox pails but no shovels).

7. Make children make choices and request their preferred activity or the materials they want.

8. Develop situations in which children are likely to need help and must communicate their needs to each other or an adult.

9. Create absurd and surprising situations (giving them clay instead of crackers at snack time).

10. Allow children to talk frequently and develop elaborative vocabulary using "make believe" situations that they generate.

MAKING CONNECTIONS

For a review of phonemic awareness and its relationship to later reading, see the "Early Childhood Education" section of Chapter 4.

For students at great risk for communication difficulties, extra attention is often needed to help them develop functional language. Milieu teaching provides language instruction across different settings, including the natural environment of the home, and is delivered by a variety of people: peers and family members, as well as teachers (Kaiser, 2000).

Play is also a key to enhanced language and social interaction skills of preschoolers and young children (Clarke, 1996). Through play, children learn such skills as cooperation and turn taking; they learn to explore shared concerns and to make friends—in short, they learn to communicate and interact with others. Disabilities, particularly language impairments, can be barriers to social interaction and communication. Consequently, teachers must create opportunities for children to have social interactions by prompting them to join groups and play with others. Statements like "Are you going to play with us? Do you want to be a doctor, too?" can serve as invitations to these important learning opportunities.

How can the foundations for literacy be developed through early intervention experiences?

The relationship of environment to language, cognition, and reading abilities is clear (Shames & Anderson, 2002). Preschool environments should be rich in experiences and in literature, including books that are predictable and those that come from children's literature (picture books, storybooks, fairy tales, naming books). Many children begin the reading process by talking about what they think the story says (Katims, 1994). Many come to know every word in the story without being able to read a single word. Such repetitions enhance both early literacy and language development. Language development is also enhanced by children providing oral narratives of stories (Crais & Lorch, 1994). Story reading provides excellent opportunities for language development, vocabulary building, phonemic awareness, and social exchanges (Owens & Robinson, 1997). The process of reading a story and discussing it at the conclusion of the activity can create many learning opportunities, as well as being an enjoyable social event. Children can be encouraged to answer questions about the story, to relate the story to their own experiences, and to build upon each other's responses, and they can be guided to develop good language models for each other. Story reading time can also be a time when basic pre-reading skills, such as phonics and sound–symbol relationships, can be fostered (Hoffman, 1997).

Phonemic awareness seems to be the foundation of reading skills. What skills constitute but phonemic awareness? Here are a few examples: knows alphabet; separates sentences into isolated words, words into syllables, and so on; rhymes; predicts words from sounds; matches letter name with object, sound with object, and so on (Norris & Hoffman, 2002). SLPs can be most helpful in showing teachers how to modify instruction to incorporate activities that promote phonemic awareness. For the most part, teachers do not need assistance if they remember and address some simple

CHAPTER 5 *Speech or Language Impairments*

principles. First, children who are not able to rhyme, cannot identify sounds in words, and cannot hear word–sound patterns have not developed phonemic awareness. Second, such children are at risk for later reading failure. Third, abilities to hear and manipulate individual sounds in spoken words can be fostered through simple games and activities seen in most preschool classes (Flett & Conderman, 2002):

- Teach nursery rhymes.
- Practice simple poems and finger plays that contain rhyming words.
- Point out words that rhyme as they are said in classroom conversations.
- Clap and count syllables.
- Produce words that rhyme with a word that someone said (*Jump: pump, lump, dump*).
- Sort picture cards by initial sounds, medial sounds, and final sounds.
- Have students delete sounds in words (omit the initial sound).
- Read stories that contain rhyming words (e.g., Dr. Seuss books).

ELEMENTARY THROUGH HIGH SCHOOL

Individuals acquire communicative skills at different rates. Before becoming overly concerned about an individual's speech or language abilities, teachers should consider several factors, including age, setting, and stress. However, if problems persist during the early school years, SLPs are valuable in guiding special education and general education teachers, helping them adjust their teaching procedures for students with special needs, and providing therapy.

How can teachers help students develop communication skills?

There are almost endless numbers of ways to enrich classroom environments to help all students, particularly those with disabilities and those who are English language learners (ELLs). In this section, let's focus on four general methods:

1. Instructional supports
2. Content enhancement strategies
3. Direct language instruction and development
4. Language-sensitive environments

One way teachers can help their students develop language skills is to modify their standard instructional procedures by adding instructional supports and including accommodations designed to foster a language-rich instructional environment. Here are a few key elements that effective teachers consider when creating such supportive classrooms (Culatta & Wiig, 2002; van Keulen, Weddington, & DeBose, 1998; Whetherby, 2002):

- Match language with the comprehension abilities of the students.

Teachers can help children develop language by creating exciting learning experiences and encouraging the children to talk about them.

VALIDATED PRACTICES
Semantic Feature Analysis

What Is Semantic Feature Analysis?

Semantic feature analysis (SFA) is a strategy used to increase a student's vocabulary. SFA links a student's prior knowledge with new information by showing the relationships among words from a specific topic. Students are required to complete a matrix (see Figure 1) and to discuss associations among words in a category.

Why Semantic Feature Analysis Is Beneficial

Adults use about10,000 words in their everyday conversations. Students understand and comprehend between 20,000 and 24,000 words by age 6 and more than 50,000 words by age12 (Owens, 2001). Difficulties in content area classes (e.g., science, social studies) are common among students with a low vocabulary base. By using words and features familiar to most students, SFA helps youngsters build their vocabulary by considering how words and objects are related to each other. Discussion is essential to SFA. It increases students' participation, thus increasing their expressive language skills.

Implementing Semantic Feature Analysis

Students may have difficulty understanding the concept of SFA at first. It is important for you to model the process several times before students work independently. First, use categories familiar to the students. As students become accustomed to the strategy, more abstract categories can be added. The following seven-step process is recommended for developing and implementing SFAs.

Select a Category

- Select a familiar category.

List Words

- Down the left side of the grid, list three or four familiar words or objects related to the category.

List and Add Features

- List three or four features in a row across the top of the grid.
- Discuss features with your students, encouraging them to add more to the grid.

- Be responsive to students' language needs by adjusting, modifying, and supplementing instruction.

- Anchor instruction with examples relevant to students' experience and culture.

- Provide multiple examples to illustrate a point or explain a concept.

- Use specific referents (e.g., instead of "Open your book" say "Open the red geography book to page 105"), and avoid indirect expressions.

MAKING CONNECTIONS

For an example of a story map, see the "Validated Practices" box in Chapter 4.

Effective teachers help children with language difficulties in other ways as well. Some use **content enhancement strategies** to help students see relationships among concepts and words (Naremore, 1997; Schoenbrodt , Kumin, & Sloan, 1997). The Semantic Feature Analysis technique (see the "Validated Practices" box for an example) helps students develop vocabulary by using a concrete visual organizer. Here are four other examples of such content enhancement strategies that serve as visual organizers:

1. Attribute web

   - Identifies important aspects of a word

   - Positions the key word in the center of the web

   - Places characteristics of the key word on extensions of the web

   - Groups attributes by similarities

2. Venn diagram

   - Compares and contrasts meanings and characteristics of two concepts

   - Identifies attributes of the two concepts

   - Places attributes in appropriate circles

CHAPTER 5 *Speech or Language Impairments*

Determine Possession

- Guide your students through the matrix, having them determine whether each word on the left side possesses the features listed across the top.
- Students place a plus sign in the box if the word possesses the feature, a minus sign if the word does not.
- Students place a question mark in the boxes if they are unsure of the relationship.

Add More Words and Features

- Students provide additional words that fit the category.
- Students provide additional features.

Complete the Grid

- Students complete the grid by adding plus signs, minus signs, or question marks for the new words and features.

Discuss the Grid

- Students examine the grid and discuss the relationships among the words.

- You should facilitate the discussion only if the students do not recognize the relationships.

Figure 1 shows one SFA for use with young students. Looking at the grid, students quickly realize which vehicles have only two wheels and which vehicles can hold passengers.

This scientifically validated practice is a teaching method proven by systematic research efforts (Bos & Anders, 1992: Owens, 2001; Pittelman et al., 1991). Full citations are found in the references under "Elementary Through High School."

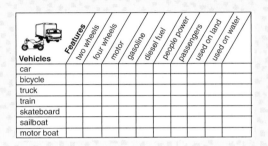

Figure 1

Source: From *Semantic Feature Analysis: Classroom Application* (p. 10) by S. D. Pittelman, J. E. Heimlich, R. L. Berglund, and M. P. French, 1991, Newark, DE: International Reading Association. Reprinted with permission.

- Moves similarities between the two concepts to the overlapping segments of the circles

3. Multiple-meaning tree

- Helps students visualize meanings of words
- Identifies the concept by writing it on the tree's trunk
- Writes different definitions of the word on the branches
- Generates sentences for each meaning

4. Script and story framework

- Organizes knowledge around expected sequences of familiar events
- Develops a framework for remembering event sequences
- Uses a tree-like diagram to arrange a story in a hierarchy
- Orders relationships by groups and sequences

The benefits of content enhancement strategies and instructional supports are many. These instructional techniques improve children's written and oral language skills and their ability to remember information (Hudson & Gillam, 1997). Why do they work so well? Probably because these techniques provide structure for learning concepts on the basis of individuals' experiences. As Naremore (1997) points out, American culture has set expectations for what elements should be included in a story. Stories are supposed to have a point, to be goal-oriented, be "about something." They have a setting and characters and are organized in terms of episodes that tend to have an initiating event, a response, a consequence, and an ending. Teachers can take advantage of these patterns by helping children understand the predictability of stories and teaching them to use organizing tools like the four content enhancement strategies just discussed.

Elementary Through High School

ACCOMMODATING FOR INCLUSIVE ENVIRONMENTS

Creating Language-Sensitive Classrooms

- Give children opportunities to talk and hear talk that is appropriate for different purposes (leading discussions, presenting information) and settings (in small groups, to their class, to other classes).

- Provide students with ideas that give them reasons to talk and to discuss issues.

- Create opportunities for students to interact and use language while they learn academic tasks.

- Give students experience in talking about different subjects with different audiences (build self-confidence).

- Have students work together to plan presentations on topics being taught in content subjects.

- Insist that students take different roles in group presentations.

- Include group debates as part of instructional units.

- Allow students to retell the meaning of difficult reading passages.

- Create a supportive environment where children trust each other and are encouraged to communicate.

- Create a section of the classroom where the physical environment—perhaps a large, round table—encourages sharing and discussion.

- Always consider the developmental stage of each student when setting expectations.

- Collaborate with the SLP to integrate appropriate language development activities in all academic instruction.

- Incorporate activities in class that allow children with language impairments to practice skills mastered in therapy.

- Be alert to the possible presence of speech or language impairments and consult with the SLP when one is suspected.

- Evaluate student progress and outcomes.

Many teachers find that teaching students learning strategies, whether they are based on mnemonics or on content enhancement, is not difficult. What is hard is getting their students to use the technique consistently. For students who forget to use a strategy or cannot remember which strategy to use when, a clever system can help (Edmunds, 1999). The Cognitive Credit Card (CCC), which is laminated and about the size of a credit card, lists the steps for a specific strategy, such as for taking notes for history or creating an attribute web. A student may have many CCCs, one for each subject or each different type of task, hooked together on a key ring.

A third way to help students, particularly those with language impairments, is to teach language skills directly. Language teaching should be part of the curriculum throughout the elementary school years. Just as time is devoted to teaching mathematics, reading, spelling, and social studies, time should be allocated to teaching the language skills that underlie these subjects. During these periods, children should be encouraged to listen, talk, and understand the language of instruction as well as the language of social interactions. All students can benefit from this instruction, but for students with language impairments it is essential.

For teachers who are not trained in oral language development, excellent instructional materials are commercially available. For example, the *Peabody Language Development Kits (PLDK–Revised), Developing Understanding of Self and Others (DUSO–Revised),* and *Classroom Listening and Speaking (CLAS)* include useful activities to increase language and cognitive skills for students in primary grades. *Let's Talk, Conversations, Communicative Competence,* and *Directing Discourse* provide ideas for adolescents. Teachers can use a variety of classroom activities, including games, that encourage children's use of language (Marvin, 1989; Watkins & Rice, 1994). **Barrier games** require children to describe objects while other players guess what they are describing. In a simple version of this game, the teacher could create a game using picture cards, such as those found in the *Peabody Picture Collection (PPC)* or the CD-ROM picture series called *Fast Sort*. The teacher asks the children to tell about a recent experience or make up stories from a set of sequential pictures.

Another language area often in need of direct instruction is the use and understanding of metaphors and analogies (Castillo, 1998). Figures of speech are difficult for many students to comprehend, for they are not literal or direct translations of the words used in such phrases. Here are a few examples: "The president is the head of state," "The eyes are windows to the soul," "He's between a rock and a hard place," "My heart goes out to you," "Time flies." Students whose abstract thinking skills are not well developed, and those who are learning English as a second language, frequently find it difficult to comprehend the meaning of common metaphors and analogies used in texts and in oral presentations. Teachers should not assume that children understand nonliteral language and should help their students develop the flexible thinking skills needed to solve the problems such language use presents. Mere exposure to analogies and metaphors is not enough. Teachers need to include direct instruction about the use of **figurative language;** when they do, students' facility with language grows in a further dimension. As with most language skills, instruction about these conceptually difficult aspects of language use can be integrated into content lessons.

The importance of creating language-sensitive environments cannot be stressed enough. Even slight modifications in teaching style and instructional activities can be most helpful and can have great benefits for all students (Schoenbrodt, Kumin, & Sloan, 1997). Providing opportunities for language use and incorporating them into standard classroom routines is the support many students with language impairments, as well as linguistically diverse students, need; and these goals are not difficult to accomplish. The "Accommodating for Inclusive Environments" box offers some easy and helpful suggestions about how to create classrooms where all students' language development is enriched and supported.

MAKING **C**ONNECTIONS

For more suggestions on accommodating students' learning needs in general education settings, see the "Accommodating for Inclusive Environments" boxes found in Chapters 3 through 13.

How can SLPs assist in bridging language to literacy?

SLPs can encourage teachers to provide instruction on phonics and basic reading skills, and they can also lend their extensive knowledge about sound–symbol relationships to teachers as they impart these fundamental rules to their students. As you have learned, children who are not able to rhyme, cannot identify sounds in words, cannot hear word–sound patterns, and have not developed phonemic awareness are at risk for later reading failure. You have also learned that these skills can be taught and, for many, reading failure avoided (Ball, 1997). However, you have probably also said to yourself, "But how would I teach these skills to children when I'm not sure I understand what needs to be mastered?" SLPs can be very helpful in this regard. They can help special education and general education teachers understand the basic units of words and sounds so that they can develop lessons to teach phonological awareness. And they can help convince educators who do not believe in direct, skill based instruction. They can help them understand that many children will not be successful readers if they are not taught these skills directly, because although many aspects of language development occur naturally, almost spontaneously, often phonological awareness does not (Falk-Ross, 2002). SLPs can help teachers develop language-rich activities that link oral, expressive language with print (Snow, Scarborough, & Burns, 1999).

MAKING **C**ONNECTIONS

Review the sections in Chapter 4 about reading and its necessary precursors.

> *The argument over whether skills-based instruction with code emphasis is best for children with language/learning disabilities or whether whole language better meets their needs is at best an argument we can no longer afford to indulge. It is an argument that has no justification because whole language approaches deprive too many children access to the world of print. (Ball, 1997, p. 24)*

Teachers must offer rich learning environments by creating stimulating instructional settings that encourage oral language and provide the framework necessary for literacy.

Remember, nearly all students with speech and language impairments receive the majority of their educational experiences in the general education classroom. What can teachers do to ensure that students have positive and successful experiences? They can adjust their teaching styles, presentation of content, and expectations for each student in their classes (Geluke & Lovitt, 1992; LaBlance , Steckol, & Smith, 1994). Effective teachers understand the role that language plays in learning and adjust their oral language and adapt their written materials so that students have the best possible chance to understand the message being delivered. Effective teachers also moderate their rate of speech, the complexity of their sentences, and their choice of questions (Gruenewald & Pollack, 1984). Almost naturally, teachers adjust their rate of speech to the age and level of their students (Cuda & Nelson, 1976). For instance, first-grade teachers tend to speak more slowly than fifth-grade teachers. Effective teachers are also careful in their use of referents. They systematically show students the relationships among items and concepts, and they systematically expand discussions about new concepts and ideas. They ask questions at graduated levels of difficulty to help students test the accuracy of their new knowledge.

Many teachers enhance opportunities for discussion and language development by enriching their instruction. For instance, they include activity centers in their classrooms. One center might have electrical components to create circuits so that children can discover cause-and-effect relationships; another center might have magnets and containers of different types of materials. Some part of the day is set aside for children to talk about their exploration of the materials in the activity centers. Teachers could then use discussion time to expand students' learning by having them brainstorm future applications.

COLLABORATION FOR INCLUSION

Teachers and SLPs should work as a team so that all students have positive language learning environments at school and so that students with speech or language impairments have classroom experiences that support and extend therapy. Today, almost every school in the United States has access to an SLP. In some cases, an SLP is a permanent faculty member. In other cases, the SLP works part-time at several schools or is an itinerant teacher, traveling from one school to another. In all cases, the SLP is available to receive referrals, conduct assessments, participate in the development of IEPs, provide therapy, and consult with any teacher concerned about a student's communicative abilities. The role of the SLP has evolved over the last several decades. Today, these professionals collaborate more with teachers, provide less direct services to children (particularly those with mild disabilities), and guide teachers in the implementation of language development and remediation efforts for language based academic areas (e.g., spelling, writing) (Apel & Masterson, 2000).

Collaborative consultation is the shared responsibility for problem definition, planning, provision of services, and evaluation of outcomes (Schoenbrodt, Kumin, & Sloan, 1997). For students with speech or language impairments, this process is critical to good outcomes. The importance of linking speech and language intervention to students' curriculum and classroom experiences is generally accepted by SLPs across the nation. Unfortunately, SLPs have caseloads that do not allow them to work intensively with large numbers of children. They are usually assigned to several different schools and have to allocate their time carefully so that they can provide direct therapy to those individual students who are in the greatest need.

CHAPTER 5 *Speech or Language Impairments*

Nearly all students with speech or language impairments (89 percent) receive their education solely in the general education classroom; an additional 7 percent attend resource rooms for a small part of the school day (U.S. Department of Education, 2001). Obviously, for most cases, SLPs consult and team with special and general education teachers to implement language intervention programs in the general education classrooms. In other cases, teachers support SLPs' therapy efforts by fostering generalization. All of this requires teamwork! Once a child is identified as having a speech or language impairment and is to receive special services from an SLP, teachers work closely and collaborate with the SLP to implement individualized programs for that child. SLPs offer guidance and practical tips to use in the general education class. For example, an SLP might offer teachers the following tips for adjusting their teaching styles:

Students should have many opportunities to expand their language and vocabulary. Class projects or term papers can be used to develop the knowledge base upon which student presentations are made.

- Be an attentive listener.
- Provide more opportunities for children to talk about what they are interested in.
- Ask open-ended questions that encourage children to talk more.

Integrating interventions into the fabric of general education instruction requires SLPs, special educators, and general educators to work closely together to form a team. Increasingly, SLPs work with entire classes of general education students (Owens & Robinson, 1997). How might these three professionals coordinate instruction? Many SLPs and teachers team-teach special units that integrate language instruction into the standard curriculum (Norris, 1997). How might this work? The team members (general educators, special educators, and SLPs) develop goals and plans for the unit they will share (co-teach). During this time, they choose reading selections and supporting materials. They divide the instructional tasks and assign lead responsibilities to each member of the team. For this unit, the SLP might conduct small reading groups where she or he helps students translate the basics of sound–symbol relationships from reading to writing. The special educator might work with small groups as they explore the topics being studied and might use content enhancement strategies to help students comprehend the reading materials more effectively and write coherent reports. The general education teacher could hold editing conferences with groups of students as they refine and improve their written work. The collaborative efforts of SLPs and teachers not only greatly improve the language skills of students with speech and language impairments but also benefit their other students.

TRANSITION THROUGH ADULTHOOD

Adults with speech or language impairments comprise several different subgroups. Some have only a speech impairment, others have only a language impairment, and some have both impairments. Age of onset and causation, however, are what make these subgroups different from one another. Despite having great difficulties as children, the vast majority of them, when adults, experience a lifetime of using normal communication (Owens, Metz, & Haas, 2000). Typically, the problems experienced by adults who were not identified as having speech or language impairments when they were children are caused by disease, accidents, or aging. Those who had some kind of speech or language impairment during childhood represent a small percentage of this adult group. Relatively little is known about how these children fare when they are adults.

In one of the few comprehensive **follow-up studies** of youth with disabilities, students with learning disabilities and speech impairments appeared to have better outcomes than other youth with disabilities (Wagner et al., 1992). They seem to function fairly well some 5 years after graduation. Few are socially isolated. By this time they are beginning to move away from home; 40 percent live independently. They also are employed at about the same rate as their peers without disabilities. Their long-term prospects, however, may not be as good. Although 96 percent are taught almost exclusively in general education classes, only 65 percent of students with speech impairments graduate with a diploma (U.S. Department of Education, 2001). Serious concerns about their success as adults can be raised. Changing this situation will require offering more services while these students are in high school and expanding the roles of SLPs to provide assistance with the development of literacy by linking therapy to the high school curriculum (Ehren, 2002). Also, to remain in academic content courses, these students may require more access to tutoring, more services from guidance counselors, more accommodations and special services, and increased instruction in listening and speaking skills.

FAMILIES

The quality of children's home's language environment has significant and long-term effects in young children (Hart & Risley, 1995). Some families need guidance as they attempt to develop nurturing environments for their children. For these reasons, most preschool programs include a strong family component where professionals help parents implement language-learning lessons at home and help their children transfer (or generalize) their learning from school to home.

Children (and adults) spend less time at home with family than ever before, so involving parents in their children's preschool programs can be challenging. For example, about 7 million children of working parents, as early as 11 weeks old, spend 30 hours per week in child care (Children's Defense Fund, 1996). Parents and children spend less time together today than they did 20 years ago. Regardless, the child's parents and the home environment provide the foundation for these skills. Even for those children who spend most of their days away from home, those whose home environment is rich in language—where parents talk to their children, where children are given the opportunity to explore the use of language, and where experiences are broad—usually develop fine speech and language skills. When children do not have appropriate language models—when they do not hear language used often, when they do not have experiences to share or a reason to talk—it is not uncommon for their language to be delayed and even become impaired.

Educators must not make generalizations about either parents or students. For example, it is unfair and incorrect to assume that parents are responsible for their child's stuttering. Research has shown that parents of stutterers are not consistently different in any characteristics and speech qualities from parents of nonstutterers (Nippold & Rudzinski, 1995; Ramig & Shames, 2002). Generalizations about families from diverse backgrounds are inappropriate as well. Diversity is heterogeneous, and no assumptions are accurate.

When young children do not develop language at the expected rate, intervention is needed. In every community, early intervention programs are available to provide therapy and instruction to children and to assist parents in helping their children acquire language. With training and guidance from SLPs, parents can be excellent language teachers for children with language impairments. In fact, when home

MAKING CONNECTIONS

Graduation and dropout rates are presented in Chapter 1 and in most "Transition Through Adulthood" sections of this text.

MAKING CONNECTIONS

For more suggestions about working with families of students with disabilities, see the "Families" sections in Chapters 3 through 13.

CHAPTER 5 *Speech or Language Impairments*

based intervention is provided by parents, children's language scores improve more than when only clinic based instruction is provided by professionals (Cleminshaw et al., 1996; Hall, Oyer, & Haas, 2001).

What kinds of strategies can parents use at home to improve their child's language skills? Specialists suggest that family members specifically label or name objects in the home. They also suggest that simple words be used more often to describe the objects the child is playing with: "This ball is red. It is round. It is soft." They can encourage repetitions of correct productions of sounds and can repeat the child's error to help the child make a comparison. They can play a game of "fill in the blank" sentences. They can ask the child questions that require expanded answers. The family should include the child in activities outside of the home, too, such as visits to the zoo, the market, or a shopping center, so that the child has more to talk about. Practicing good language skills can be incorporated into everyday events. Family members should model language and have the child imitate good language models. For example, a parent might say, "This pencil is blue. What color is this pencil?" and the child should be encouraged to respond that the pencil is blue. Crais and Lorch (1994) also suggest that parents encourage children to engage in the act of "storytelling." Through these stories, children should describe, explain, and interpret their experiences or the stories they have read. Children need a reason to talk, and the home environment can foster children's oral expression by providing many rich and diverse experiences for children to talk about and good language models for children to imitate.

For a review of how these children are identified and how typical language develops, read again the "Speech or Language Impairments Defined" section of this chapter.

TECHNOLOGY

Many children with speech or language impairments benefit greatly from technology, and the range of applications is considerable. Some applications correct speech mechanisms that are faulty or damaged. For example, an **obturator** can be used to help create a closure between the oral and nasal cavities when the soft palate is missing or has been damaged by a congenital cleft. An artificial larynx can be implanted when the vocal folds become paralyzed or have been removed because of a disease. Other applications of technology can help students communicate with others and participate in mainstream classrooms and society.

Alternative and augmentative communication (AAC) devices provide different means for individuals with speech or language impairments to interact and communicate with others (Kangas & Lloyd, 2002). AAC includes both low-tech devices (such as communication boards) and high-tech equipment (such as speech talkers). AAC devices can be electronic or nonelectronic, they can be constructed for a certain individual, and they can be simple or complex. What all AAC systems have in common is that they are used to augment oral or written language production.

A variety of low-tech AAC devices have been in use for many years (Reichle, Beukelman, & Light, 2002). For example, communication boards have long been available to persons who are unable to speak; the individual who wants to communicate merely points to pictures or words that have been placed on the board. Advances in computer technology, particularly **speech synthesizers,** have changed the mode of communication for many of these individuals. With a computer, a person can type in a message and have it converted into voice or print. Some computers allow the individual to select the voice qualities the machine uses! Some computerized communicative devices are even small enough to be worn on a person's wrist.

The current capabilities of electronic AAC systems are amazing, and the devices continue to improve and become more affordable. Many machines that generate speech and language use an icon system that can be accessed by touch or, for those with limited motor abilities, by switches. However, for some individuals, learning the graphic symbols used with the more sophisticated equipment can be daunting,

For more about technology and students with disabilities, see the "Technology" sections in Chapters 3 through 13

Read again the story of Lizzie B, at the beginning of this chapter, for applications of low- and high-tech ACC devices.

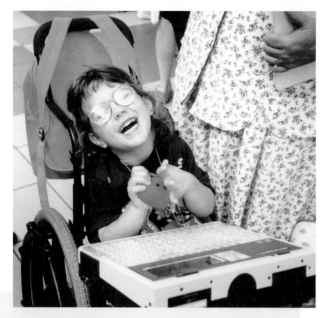

Learning to use assistive communication devices can enable even a student with severe speech or language impairments to engage in a complex interchange of ideas with others. The speech synthesizer once mastered, will "speak" for this child.

requiring considerable effort and instruction (Wilkerson & McIlvane, 2002). Communicating via a speech synthesizer, like learning to produce typical oral language, can take years to master and is best learned in natural environments found at school and home (Harwood, Warren, & Yoder, 2002). Learning how to use ACC in natural environments and through milieu instruction by using peers and family members has great outcomes in the development of functional language skills (Romski et al., 2002).

The demonstrated benefits of ACC are remarkable (Reichle, Beukelman, & Light, 2002; Romski & Sevcik, 1997). Students with little or no speech or language abilities are now able to communicate with others because of AAC devices. Many of these youngsters have developed language abilities that they had not been expected to achieve. The benefits of AAC are still unfolding, but it is clear that they have been underestimated. Most users and their families report great satisfaction with AAC. They believe the child not only develops communicative competence but also gains self-esteem and independence.

IN CONCLUSION

SUMMARY

Communication requires at least two parties and a message. Communication is impaired when either the sender or the receiver of the message cannot use the signs, symbols, or rules of language effectively. Communication occurs only when the message is understood by the receiver as the sender intended. The sender may have an idea or thought to share with someone else, but the sender's idea needs to be translated from thought into some code the other person can then decode and understand. For most of us, oral language is the primary mode of socializing, learning, and performing on the job. Therefore, communicative competence—what speakers need to know about language in order to express their thoughts—is the most important goal for students with speech or language impairments. Because oral communication (or sign language for those who are deaf) occurs in a social context, this ability directly affects an individual's social competence as well.

SELF-TEST QUESTIONS

Focus Questions

What are speech impairments and language impairments?

> A speech impairment is present when the sender's articulation, fluency patterns, or voice (pitch or loudness) impairs the communication.

> A language impairment exists when the sender of the message cannot use the signs, symbols, or rules of language; problems with any one of the three aspects of language—form, content, and use (pragmatics)—can result in a language impairment.

The child's age and the stressfulness of the situation must be considered when determining whether a child should be referred to an SLP for assessment.

What is the prevalence of this disability?

It represents over 2 percent of all students.

It is the largest special education category when primary and second disability categories are both counted.

More young children than older children are included in this category.

How do language delays, language differences, and language impairments differ?

In language delays, the child acquires language in the normal developmental sequence but does so more slowly than the typical learner.

In language differences, English is being learned as a second language, or the child speaks a regional dialect.

In language impairments, language is acquired in an abnormal developmental sequence.

How can teachers enhance language development and help to remediate a language impairment?

Instructional supports: match language to students' level; adjust, modify, and supplement instruction; anchor instruction to students' experiences and culture; give multiple examples; use specific (concrete) referents

Content enhancements: use visual organizers; identify predictable story elements

Language instruction and development: modify curriculum and instructional

programs, create language-rich classrooms
Collaborate with SLPs

What is alternative and augmentative communication, and how does it benefit this population of learners?

ACC devices use technology to help people with speech or language impairments communicate.

Low-tech: communication boards

High-tech: speech synthesizers

Challenge Question

How might the general education and special education curricula be modified to better develop the language and literacy abilities of students? How can speech/language pathologists help?

The curriculum could include more direct instruction for language development and literacy precursors (e.g., phonemic awareness) as specific curriculum areas.

Instruction could be modified to include content enhancements, instructional supports, accommodations for language differences and impairments, language games and activities, and language-sensitive classroom environments.

SLPs could can provide assessment and identification, individualized therapy, consultative and collaborative services, classroom instruction, co-teaching, family intervention and follow-through, and instructional support.

Making Connections

Look again at the Advance Organizers found at the beginning of the chapter; to help you study the chapter's content, the answers to the Focus and Challenge questions are found here. Test yourself to see if you have mastered the major points of this chapter.

MEETING THE STANDARDS AND PREPARING FOR LICENSURE EXAMS

After reading this chapter, you should be able to demonstrate basic knowledge and skills described in the CEC standards and INTASC principles listed below. The section

of this chapter most applicable to each standard is shown in parentheses at the end of the knowledge or skill statement.

 Council for Exceptional Children   **Core Standard 6: Language**

- **Educational Implications:** Effects of cultural and linguistic differences on growth and development. (Causes and Prevention)

- **Technology:** Augmentative, alternative and assistive communication strategies. (Technology)
- **Communication strategies:** Using communication strategies and resources to facilitate understanding of subject matter for students whose primary language is not the dominant language. (Causes and Prevention) See also Chapter 3 of this text.

INTASC Principle 6:

The teacher uses knowledge of effective verbal, nonverbal and media communication techniques to foster active inquiry, collaboration, and supportive interaction in the classroom.

- **Communication theory:** The teacher understands communication theory, language development and the role of language in learning. (Speech or Language Impairments Defined)
- **Language and learning:** The teacher recognizes the power of language for fostering self-expression, identity development and learning. (Characteristics)
- **Effective communication strategies:** The teacher models effective communication strategies in conveying ideas and information and in asking questions (e.g. monitoring the effects of messages, restating ideas and drawing connections using visual, aural and kinesthetic cues, being sensitive to nonverbal cues given and received).
- **Learner expression:** The teacher supports and expands learner expression in speaking, writing, and other media. (Elementary Through High School)

Standards in Practice

These knowledge statements, dispositions, and skills might be demonstrated by the beginning teacher acknowledging the importance of speech and language skills. The teacher may make appropriate referrals to the speech and language pathologist, support the students with speech and language impairments in the classroom, and accept necessary communication technology. The teacher will also use a variety of communication strategies in organizing their instruction and interactions with students, families and colleagues.

 Go to the companion website (ablongman.com/smith5e) for detailed text correlations to CEC and INTASC standards, PRAXIS II™ exams, and other state-sponsored licensure exams.

SUPPLEMENTARY RESOURCES

Professional Readings and Resources

Falk-Ross, F. C. (2002). *Classroom-based language and literacy intervention: A programs and case studies approach.* Boston: Allyn and Bacon.

Hall, B. J., Oyer, H. J., & Haas, W. H. (2001). *Speech, language, and hearing disorders: A guide for the teacher.* Boston: Allyn and Bacon.

Reichle, J., Beukelman, D. R., & Light, J. C. (2002). *Exemplary practices for beginning communicators: Implications for ACC.* Baltimore: Paul H. Brookes.

Owens, Jr., R. E., Metz, D. E., & Haas, A. (2000). *Introduction to communication disorders: A life span perspective.* Boston: Allyn and Bacon.

Shames. G. H., & Anderson, N. B. (Eds.). (2002). *Human communication disorders: An introduction* (6th ed.). Boston: Allyn and Bacon.

Van Keulen, J. E., Weddington, G. T., & DeBose, C. E. (1998). *Speech, language, learning and the African American child.* Boston: Allyn and Bacon.

Popular Books

Butler, S. (1936). *The way of all flesh.* New York: Limited Editions Club.

Caldwell, E. (1948). *Tobacco road.* New York: Grosset & Dunlap.

Johnson, W. (1930). *Because I stutter.* New York: Appleton.

Melville, H. (1962). *Billy Budd.* Chicago: University of Chicago.

Sedaris, D. (2000). *Me talk pretty one day.* New York: Little Brown.

 ### Videos and DVDs

My Left Foot (1989). Miramax

Based on the biography of Christy Brown, a man born with cerebral palsy to a poor Irish family. Brown was able to develop control only of his left foot, which he used as his means of communication because his speech was difficult to understand. His mother's strength and love, along with individual attention from a qualified instructor, helped Christy find his voice both literally and creatively, and he became an acclaimed artist, poet, and author.

This documentary-like film offers insight into the emotional life of someone with disabilities. We see the Christy experience not just physical limitations and difficulty communicating but also because of those universal problems that everyone experiences, such as heartache and grief. Also portrayed is the importance of integrating people with disabilities into mainstream society and of special and individualized instruction. Daniel Day-Lewis and Brenda Fricker won Oscars for Best Actor and Best Supporting Actress.

A Fish Called Wanda (1987). Thames

Four thieves steal diamonds, but two members of the gang, Wanda and Otto, plot to double-cross the others. They rat on George, the leader of the gang, to the police. However, George has already double-crossed them by moving the diamonds without their knowing. Wanda tries to get the location of the diamonds out of George's lawyer; they fall in love and make off with the diamonds.

One member of the gang, Ken, has a nervous stutter. Although this film takes comedic advantage of a person's disability, which could be offensive to some, his stuttering does provide some of the funniest scenes. No one really treats Ken differently, other than Otto who is mean to everyone. Revenge, however, is Ken's at the end of the movie.

Parent, Professional, and Consumer Organizations and Agencies

American Cleft Palate–Craniofacial Association/American Cleft Palate Foundation
104 South Estes Drive, Suite 204
Chapel Hill, NC 27514
(919) 933-9044; (800) 24-CLEFT
E-mail: cleftline@aol.com
Web site: http://www.cleftline.org

American Speech-Language-Hearing Association
10801 Rockville Pike
Rockville, MD 20852
Professionals/Students (800) 498-2071;
Public (800) 638-8255
E-mail: actioncenter@asha.org
Web site: http://www.asha.org

National Institute on Deafness and Other Communication Disorders (NIDCD)

National Institutes of Health
31 Center Drive, MSC 2320
Bethesda, MD 20892-2320
Phone: (800) 241-1044; (301) 496-7243
TTY (301) 402-0252
E-mail: nidcd@aerie.com
Web site: http://www.nidcd.nih.gov

Division for Communication Disabilities and Deafness (DCDD)

The Council for Exceptional Children
1110 North Glebe Road, Suite 300
Arlington, VA 22201-5704
Phone: (888) CEC-SPED; (703) 620-3660;
(770) 540-1158
TTY (703) 264-9946
Web site: http://www.cec.sped.org or
www.gsu.edu/~wwwdhh/

Stuttering Foundation of America
3100 Walnut Grove Road, Suite 603
P.O. Box 11749
Memphis, TN 38111-0749
Phone: (800) 992-9392; (901) 452-7343;
(800) 967-7700
E-mail: stutter@vantek.net
Web site: http://stuttersfa.org/

Video**Workshop** Extra

If the VideoWorkshop package was included with your textbook, go to Chapter 5 of the Companion Website (www.ablongman.com/smith5e) and click on the VideoWorkshop button. Follow the instructions for viewing Video clip 1. Consider this information along with what you have read in Chapter 5 as you answer the following questions.

Video clip 1: The IEP (Time 7:31)

1. Doug has only a few sounds that require correction, yet his friends tease him and he is uncomfortable about his speech. Consider the feelings and social competence of the children who have more severe speech or language disorders. What are areas that may be of concern for these students?

2. Review the discussion in your text about collaboration between the general education teacher and the SLP. As the special education teacher, how can you facilitate that collaboration?

Cats and Kittens (watercolor). No date.
Courtesy of the Courthald Institute Gallery, Somerset House, London.

GOTTFRIED MIND, sometimes called the "Raphael of Cats," depicted cats almost exclusively, and was known to have an obsession with the focus of his work and life. When Mind was not painting or drawing cats, he was carving them out of chestnuts (Foucart-Walter & Rosenberg, 1987). His modest apartment was filled with cats and kittens, and when he worked cats were in his lap and on his shoulders. Mind (1786–1814) was born and lived all his life in Bern, Switzerland. He was known all over Europe, and his work was popular with cat lovers. Most of his work remains in private collections today, and is rarely seen in public. He is probably one of the few artistic masters of the eighteenth and nineteenth centuries with documented mental retardation. He died of a stroke at age 46.

6 Mental Retardation

Independence for Brad

Jean Gibson is one of those very special moms who has never stopped seeing what services are needed and then making certain that they happen. Probably because of her up-beat personality, Jean seems always able to rally resources, energy, and people. Her continuing dedication to her son has benefited so many. Here's the story of how she is creating supportive independent living arrangements for adults who need assistance but do not have moderate or severe cognitive disabilities.

Brad was 5 years old before we became aware officially of his disability—although, as I reflect back, I had noticed his lack of interest in toys, and his vocabulary was extremely limited. However, he was an attractive child. His outward appearance did not suggest a disability and he developed physically without incident. It was our doctor who suggested that we have him tested when we mentioned that Brad didn't seem ready for kindergarten. After many tests and visits to specialists, we were told he had a nonspecific cerebral dysfunction and was neurologically impaired. The realization that something was "wrong" with our son devastated us. I firmly believed that he would "get better" with the right pill.

He was enrolled in nursery school and his vocabulary improved significantly that year. At age 6 he was placed in special education at the local school and was eventually mainstreamed for some classes. The school system was recognized statewide for its Special Needs Program, and as years passed I felt that little by little he was gaining. However, as Brad moved closer and closer to age 21, when all school services end, I began to wonder about his future. In fact, it was a time I didn't want to face.

The first year following his graduation, I tried to find some agency, organization, or group that would continue to provide support or assistance for him. The state of New Jersey is mandated to provide homes and services for citizens with severe disabilities, but there were no services for those with only mild mental retardation.

Two special education teachers at the local school discussed the situation with me and stressed the benefits of a transition program. I knew they were correct, so I kept searching. Finally, after 10 months of attending conferences and meetings where parents were asking about these same issues and wondering why it hadn't happened yet, I began to realize that it wasn't going to happen very soon— and I just couldn't wait any longer. It was then I decided to do it myself. I knew there were others like my son who needed the same kind of support and assistance.

I called parents and special education instructors together, and over coffee and brownies we began to set up our plan and organization. Our group who had mild mental retardation needed a community based transition program that would give them a chance to live and work as independently as possible on their own, and that meant housing as well. Nearly all of the group grew up and went to school in this locality. They knew their community and the community knew them. They were accepted here. Local government and businesses are often more interested in helping local people. It made more and more sense for them to remain in their own community.

We called our not-for-profit organization the South Brunswick Citizens for Independent Living, Inc., or CIL. The first requirement was transportation to job sites, since our participant members could not drive. I approached the local municipality and it was agreed to provide a van and driver through a county grant to the municipality.

While our members were still students at the local high school, they participated in a special education program called STEP (Special Training and Employment Program). The STEP coordinator and the department head became members of our CIL core group. The students were employed at competitive jobs and the coordinator provided on-the-job training at the site. The employer received credit for hiring people with disabilities.

In addition to employment, our group required continual training in living skills to make them self-reliant. When CIL received its first major grant, a director/counselor was hired and a training program was set up. It began in the late afternoon when the participants returned from work. They were taught how to do laundry, cook, clean, manage money, and pay bills. It became clear that managing money and paying bills would be a continual challenge. An Evening Adult School course was set up by the local Board of Education, in which our group was taught how to use the telephone directory, make medical appointments, choose appropriate clothing, and develop additional cooking skills. The class was called Practical Life Skills. Recreation also became a training ground for acceptable social behavior. Health issues were first addressed by a registered nurse through a grant to CIL, and she has remained on as a volunteer.

In just a few short years we began to notice a change in our disabled population. They wanted to do their own shopping lists and purchase their groceries. Even a visit to the local barber shop and washing their own clothes were

major steps forward for them. It was then that affordable housing became an essential part of the CIL program.

I began by writing letters, making speeches, networking at conferences, and talking to state and local politicians and put together a funding package. We purchased four condominiums at scattered sites within a local housing development but within walking distance of stores. Seven of our participant members now rent these CIL-owned condos at 30 percent of their income, a housing provision of the local municipality for people with low incomes and people with disabilities.

However, the need for additional housing was critical, so I approached the local municipal government and requested land so we could build. The desire to help local people became evident again and I put together a larger funding package this time. We called our sister organization CIL Woods, Inc. It took 5 years to complete, and many obstacles were encountered, but they only slowed us down temporarily. This group had to have a chance to live and work and become productive members of society.

Many of the parents, including myself, noticed a difference in themselves as well as their disabled offspring. It was a gradual letting go. Instead of sheltering them, we began to support the independence that they craved. It had to be done!

And what about Brad? He has now lived successfully within the community for 8 years. While math and handling money had always been difficult for him, he has discovered a way to pay for his groceries. Part of his recreation now is a trip by himself to the local food market. Brad's co-workers have nominated him three times for employee of the month. While he has never won, the nomination says it all. Last year, he received a 5-year service award.

Brad's three siblings were all honor roll students in high school and college, one a Phi Beta Kappa graduate. While I am very proud of them, it is Brad who I feel has accomplished the most—and I firmly believe it was due to CIL.

1. **What lessons can be learned about political action and organizing communities from Jean's and Brad's story?**

2. **Where should the responsibility for providing supports for adults with more mild cognitive disabilities rest? What role should the state play in these services?**

3. **What do you think is next for Brad and Jean?**

ADVANCE ORGANIZERS

Overview

Mental retardation is defined by reduced cognitive (intellectual) ability, limited adaptive behavior, and the need for supports for independence in life, at school, and in the community. Mental retardation must first occur during the developmental period (from conception to the 18th birthday). Although people with mental retardation have gained greater access to education, society, and independence over the last 20 years, students with mental retardation still have one of the lowest rates of integration into general education classes.

About 1 percent of all schoolchildren are identified as having this disability. Most of these students have mild cognitive difficulties and require only limited supports for success in the general education curriculum. Academic and social successes for these students with mental retardation are the result of educators and families working closely together. Although relatively few people have severe mental retardation, for them, necessary supports are often intensive, involve many aspects of performance, and come from a variety of sources. For these individuals, planned supports are often required across the life span.

Self-Test Questions

Focus Questions

- What are the key components of the 2002 AAMR definition of mental retardation?
- How are levels of severity and outcomes of mental retardation grouped?
- How are the causes of mental retardation categorized, and what are some major causes?
- What are the four sources of supports?
- What are two specialized instructional approaches for students with mental retardation?
- How can educators be more effective when working with families of students with mental retardation?

Challenge Question

- What are some examples of the four levels of supports, and how do they make a difference in the lives of people with mental retardation?

MAKING CONNECTIONS

Use the learning strategy—Advance Organizers—to help focus your study of this chapter's content, and reinforce your learning by reviewing answers to the Focus and Challenge questions at the end of the chapter.

All disabilities are serious, even when they are considered mild. Those with mental retardation have impaired intellectual or cognitive abilities. These differences in abilities, and the way society reacts to those differences, create obstacles for these individuals and their families. People with this disability must make special efforts to learn, and many need considerable special assistance and support from teachers and others. They are members of families, they have relationships with friends and neighbors, and they have personalities shaped by their innate characteristics as well as by their life experiences. Some of the challenges these individuals face are aggravated by prejudice, lack of information, and discrimination. Children and adults with mental retardation are people first. Youngsters with mental retardation go to school, plan for the future, hope for a good job, wonder whom they will marry, and anticipate adulthood. These people have hopes and dreams like everyone else. They experience joy, sadness, disappointment, pride, love, and all the other emotions that are a part of living.

OPPORTUNITIES FOR A BETTER FUTURE

People with mental retardation have been persecuted since the beginning of history. They have been denied access to education and their rightful places in the community. They face discrimination and prejudice in all walks of life. In the last part of the 20th Century—first because of advocacy by parents and professionals and later as a result of their efforts on their own behalf—they are assuming their places in modern society. But the challenges and the supports they need are great, and it is for civil leaders to ensure that they participate fully and with dignity (Schalock, Baker, & Croser, 2002).

Turning Legacies into Lessons

Some issues related to the education of students with mental retardation are unresolved. For example, there is the question of whether an appropriate education—where they can learn and master skills needed in adult life—requires a separate curriculum that cannot be delivered in the general education setting. A second issue is where these students should receive their education. Some parents and professionals stress the importance of full integration, in which typical role models are a continuing presence. Full participation in the general education classroom, with an emphasis on age-appropriate instructional activities, precludes a special curriculum focusing on job and life skills. This raises questions about what constitutes an appropriate education for these students.

Thinking About Dilemmas to Solve

As you read this chapter, ponder these students' needs, the supports they require, and the outcomes they should achieve. Think about

- How their educational needs can best be met
- How they can be prepared for life's challenges through the general education curriculum
- How the history of their treatment in society cannot be repeated
- How they can achieve a high quality of life
- What the educational system can best provide them

MENTAL RETARDATION DEFINED

A new definition of **mental retardation** has been adopted by the American Association on Mental Retardation (AAMR). This is the tenth definition that this professional organization has developed and supported since 1921. Let's take a look at this new AAMR definition:

> *Mental retardation is a disability characterized by significant limitations both in intellectual functioning and in adaptive behavior as expressed in conceptual, social, and practical adaptive skills. This disability originates before age 18. (Luckasson et al., 2002, p. 1)*

Accompanying this definition, and expanding on how it should be applied, are five assumptions:

1. Limitations in present functioning must be considered within the context of community environments typical of the individual's age peers and culture.
2. Valid assessment considers cultural and linguistic diversity as well as differences in communication, sensory, motor, and behavioral factors.
3. Within an individual, limitations often coexist with strengths.
4. An important purpose of describing limitations is to develop a profile of needed supports.
5. With appropriate personalized supports over a sustained period, the life functioning of the person with mental retardation generally will improve. (Luckasson et al., 2002, p. 1)

What are some differences between this new definition and previous ones? Before 1992, definitions followed a deficit model, describing the limitations of the individual. Modern views conceptualize mental retardation in terms of the levels of supports needed for the individual to function in the community as independently as possible (Polloway, 1997). Old definitions used such terms as: "significantly

MAKING CONNECTIONS

For more about adaptive behavior, see

- Figure 6.2
- The "Defined" section in this chapter: Adaptive Behavior
- The "Elementary Through High School" section in this chapter: Functional Curriculum

subaverage general intellectual functioning," "deficits in adaptive behavior," and "deficits in intellectual functioning." In 1992 AAMR initiated a **paradigm shift**—a change in perspective—and the development of its 1992 definition of mental retardation changed the orientation from the traditional negative or deficit perspective to a more positive one (Luckasson et al., 1992; Polloway, 1997). The 1992 definition addressed the interplay among the capabilities of individuals; the environments in which they live, learn, and work; and how well each person functions with various levels of support. The 1992 definition also moved away from the use of IQ scores to define mental retardation. Instead it grouped individuals by the intensity of supports (intermittent, limited, extensive, or pervasive) that they need in specific areas to function. The 2002 AAMR definition retains the positive outlook developed in the 1992 definition, returns to a cautious use of IQ scores, and strengthens the concepts of adaptive behavior and systems of supports.

What are the components of mental retardation?

The condition of mental retardation is described and defined by AAMR in terms of three major components: (1) intellectual functioning (2) adaptive behavior (3) systems of supports.

Across each of these components, mental retardation varies along a continuum. Most individuals with mental retardation have mild cognitive disabilities, have adequate adaptive behavior to live and work independently in the community, and usually require few supports. Typically, individuals with moderate to severe mental retardation require considerable supports. Let's study each of these components in turn.

● *Intellectual Functioning* In its explanation of the 2002 AAMR definition, the organization stresses that individuals with mental retardation have **intellectual functioning** "significantly below average," or below levels attained by 97 percent of the general population. This level of functioning may be determined by clinical judgment or by a score on a test of intelligence. If a standardized test is used, the individual must score at least two standard deviations below the mean for the test. On IQ tests, intelligence is regarded as a trait that is distributed among people in a predictable manner. This statistical distribution can be represented as a bell-shaped curve, called the **normal curve.** In this curve the majority of a population falls in the middle of the bell, at or around an intelligence quotient (IQ) score of 100, and fewer and fewer people fall to either end of the distribution, having very low or very high intelligence. IQ level is then determined by the distance a score is from the mean, or average, score. To visualize this **theoretical construct** and what is meant by two standard deviations, look at Figure 6.1 which displays the normal curve and the way IQ scores are distributed along it.

MAKING CONNECTIONS

For more about adaptive behavior see

● Figure 6.3
● The "Defined" section in this chapter: Systems of Supports
● The "Characteristics" section in this chapter: Supports
● The "Families" section in this chapter

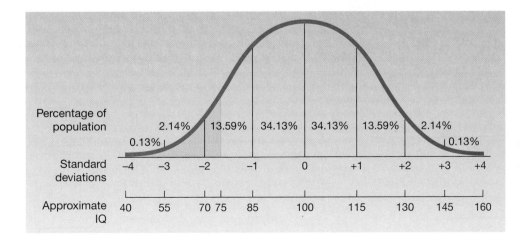

Figure 6.1 The Normal Curve, IQ, and Mental Retardation

The 2002 AAMR definition uses IQ scores as part of the determination of mental retardation, with a cutoff score of about 70 and below. Further, the new definition codes intellectual abilities to express levels of severity in the following ways:

- Mild mental retardation: IQ range of 50 to 69

    Outcomes: learning difficulties, able to work, maintain good social relationships, contribute to society

- Moderate mental retardation: IQ range of 35 to 49

    Outcomes: marked developmental delays during childhood, some degree of independence in self-care, adequate communication and academic skills, require varying degrees of support to live and work in the community

- Severe mental retardation: IQ range of 20 to 34

    Outcomes: continuous need of support

- Profound mental retardation: IQ under 20

    Outcomes: severe limitation in self-care, continence, communication, and mobility, continuous need of supports

- *Adaptive Behavior* "Adaptive behavior is the collection of conceptual, social, and practical skills that have been learned by people in order to function in their everyday lives." (AAMR, 2002, p. 73). **Adaptive behavior** is what everyone uses to function in daily life. People with mental retardation, as well as many people without disabilities, can have difficulties because they do not have the skill needed in specific situations or because they do not know what skill is needed in a particular situation. Or maybe they just do not want to perform the appropriate adaptive behavior when the situation calls for it. Regardless, lacking proficiency in the execution of a wide variety of adaptive skills can impair one's abilities to function independently. What, then, are these "conceptual," "social," and "practical" skills? Practical skills include such activities of daily life as eating, dressing, toileting, mobility, preparing meals, using the telephone, managing money, taking medication, and housekeeping. Take a look at Figure 6.2 for more examples of these three major **adaptive skill areas.**

Figure 6.2 Adaptive Skill Area

- *Systems of Supports* Everyone needs and uses **systems of supports.** We ask our friends for advice. We form study teams before a difficult test. We expect help from city services when there is a crime or a fire. We join together for a neighborhood crime watch to help each other be safe. And we share the excitement and joys of accomplishments with family, friends, and colleagues. For all of us, life is a network of supports. Some of us need more supports than others, and some of us need more supports at different times of our lives.

The 1992 and 2002 AAMR definitions include support as a defining characteristic of this disability and specify four levels of intensity across different types of support needed by people with mental retardation (McDonnell, Mathot-Buchner, & Ferguson, 1996; Luckasson et al., 1992; 2002). Figure 6.3 is a diagram of the supports that people with mental retardation need. It shows areas where supports can be provided and how the

CHAPTER 6 *Mental Retardation*

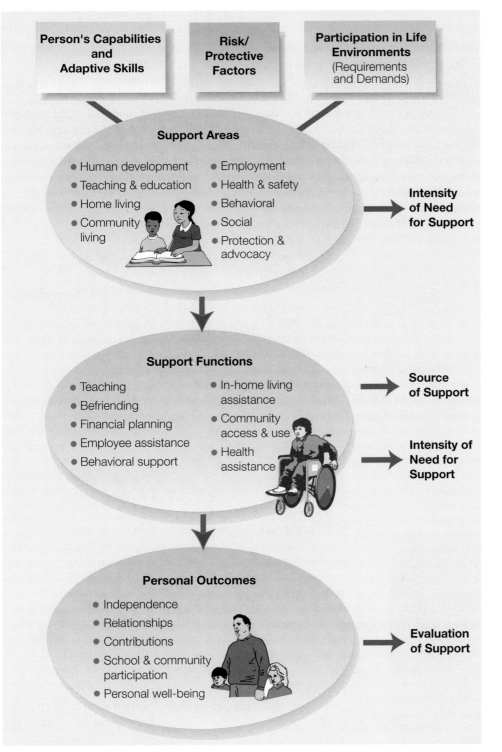

Figure 6.3 Systems of Supports

Source: From *Mental Retardation, Definition, Classification, and Systems of Support,* 10th Edition, by A.A.M.R. Copyright 2002 by American Association on Mental Retardation. Reprinted by permission of American Association on Mental Retardation via Copyright Clearance Center.

support might be delivered. Supports can be offered at any one of four levels of intensity—intermittent, limited, extensive, pervasive. Some people with mental retardation require supports in every area; others might need supports for only one area; and the level of support can vary from one area to another. Finally, Figure 6.3 includes the outcomes (or goals) of this systems approach.

Mental Retardation Defined

How are students with mental retardation identified?

Students with mental retardation are identified by assessing their intellectual functioning and their adaptive skills. Once an individual is identified as having mental retardation, an assessment of that individual's need for supports is conducted to determine the interventions and the intensity of services needed.

Criticism about the use of standardized tests of intelligence has raged for years (Artiles et al., 2002; Reschly, 1997). Tests of intelligence alone do not reliably predict an individual's abilities, they discriminate against culturally and linguistically diverse students, and they do not lead to educationally useable results (National Research Council, 2002). As you have learned, the use of IQ tests with culturally and linguistically diverse students has led to lawsuits, which motivated the state of California to ban their use when diverse students are being identified for mental retardation. Despite the problems they are subject to, IQ tests continue to be used, probably because they are relatively simple to administer and provide a definitive answer—a score for people to use (AAMR, 2002). New ways of determining students' eligibility for special education are on the horizon (National Research Council, 2002). For example, Iowa permits the use of curriculum based measurements (CBM) and other direct measures of student performance (portfolios) to identify students for special education. But until such time as standardized procedures for implementing innovative approaches are universally available, IQ tests will probably remain a common means of assessing intellectual functioning.

Although "mental age" is an outdated and ambiguous concept, it is still used by some professionals to describe the intellectual functioning of an individual, so let's think about it briefly. **Mental age (MA)** is used to describe the developmental level—or level of acquired ability or knowledge—compared with the age of the individual. Mental age is calculated as the chronological age (CA) of children without mental retardation whose average IQ test performance is equivalent to that of the individual with mental retardation. For example, a man of 35 who has an IQ of 57 might be said to have a mental age of 9 years, 5 months. Such a comparison is imprecise and inaccurate, because adults have the physical attributes, interests, and experiences of their nondisabled adult peers. Describing them by mental age underestimates these characteristics. At the same time, the mental age comparison can overestimate certain intellectual skills, such as the use of logic and foresight in solving problems.

Assessment of individuals' adaptive behavior remains a hallmark of the identification of mental retardation. Since 1959, professionals have agreed that IQ scores alone are not enough to qualify individuals for services, to predict their outcomes, or to assist in the development of appropriate educational programs (Kennedy, 2001). Adaptive behavior must also be considered (look again at Figure 6.2). Measures of adaptive skill areas attempt to determine whether the individual actually performs the everyday skills expected of an individual of that age in a typical environment.

Many practitioners have expressed concern about judging individuals' abilities in terms of their adaptive skills because such judgments are typically made by parents and teachers, who may well be biased in their assessment. The tendency to overestimate an individual's skills or to assess them inaccurately against a nonspecified age-relevant standard is great. Standardized assessment instruments are available that specifically assess adaptive behavior. For example, *Assessment of Adaptive Areas (AAA)* is a test that allows the examiner to convert scores to age equivalents across adaptive skill areas. This

MAKING CONNECTIONS

For a review of issues related to overrepresentation of diverse students in special education, see Chapters 1, 3, 4, and 8.

A mastery of an adaptive skill such as cooking has life-long benefits. Often adaptive skills take substantial effort and time to learn.

highly useful instrument brings more objectivity to the determination of individuals' abilities, helps professionals determine what supports are needed, and allows for better communication with families about in these important areas.

What is the impact of mental retardation?

The learning difficulties faced by students with mental retardation are great, particularly because they are usually compounded by communication problems. However, lowered expectations can become self-fulfilling prophecies, dooming people to less independence and autonomy as adults. In addition to the challenges these individuals face because of their disabilities, they also experience the impact of strong negative attitudes and perceptions about themselves and their abilities (Keyes, Edward, & Perske, 2002). Possibly the term *mental retardation* is at the root of much of this stigma (Warren, 2000). Signs of extreme bias appear throughout the history of mental retardation. For example, in 1912 the Kallikak family was portrayed as a threat to society—as a source of crime that could not be eradicated because of the "bad genes" the family carried (Baroff, 2000). Such stories lent support to the **eugenics** approach to mental retardation, wherein these individuals were not allowed to have children and were institutionalized to protect society from them. Some scholars maintain that such attitudes persist in modern society (Kuna, 2001; Smith & Mitchell, 2001). As proof for their argument, they cite the widespread acceptance of terminating pregnancies when medical evidence exists that the baby will have mental retardation and allowing babies to die who have severe disabilities apparent at birth.

Western society places a high value on intelligence, and mental retardation is associated with incompetence (Wickham, 2001). Just think about the comments you hear when someone is being criticized or insulted. Many of these insults—*stupid, dummy, moron, retarded,* or *village idiot*—accuse the person of not being smart. It is not surprising, then, that people whose intelligence is impaired often suffer severe criticism. They may become the victims of prejudice and discrimination solely because of their limited intelligence. It may even be assumed that they are not "good" people (Stainton, 2001). Many uninformed people think of individuals with mental retardation as in a perpetual state of childhood. This belief is not only inaccurate but also unfair, as is demonstrated in Shaun Brewer's case (Loggins, 1999). The courts wanted to force Shaun's mother to uphold visitation rights for his father, even though Shaun is 24 years old. Shaun still lives with his mother. Although Shaun's parents are divorced, and custody and visitation rights are often set by the courts, Shaun is an adult. Is it Shaun's right to decide whether and when he wants to see his father?

The stigma that often accompanies mental retardation can be overpowering. Sometimes, the fear of rejection and stigma leads individuals with mental retardation to pretend that they do not have mental retardation. Or it may cause them to be shy or especially reserved. Some people have even lied about their stay in a mental retardation institution, claiming instead to have been in psychiatric institutions or even prisons (Edgerton, 1967). It should give all of us pause to think that some people are less ashamed of prison than of institutions for mental retardation. Attitudes, even those held by today's high school students, indicate that people with mental retardation are viewed negatively (Krajewski & Flaherty, 2000). It is

Actually, names hurt just as much as sticks and stones.

When you're mentally retarded, you get called all kinds of things. And that's not the worst of it. Because after awhile, you can start believing that what people say is true. And that there really is something wrong with you. Because no matter what anyone says, names really can hurt someone. Permanently.

MAKING CONNECTIONS

- See the "History" section in this chapter for more information about the horrible treatment and discrimination people with mental retardation have experienced.

- Chapter 1 also gives background information about the stigma associated with disabilities and with mental retardation in particular.

important however, to know that high school students who have had more contact with peers with mental retardation, at school and in the community, hold more positive attitudes than those who have been deprived of such opportunities. Possibly one major benefit of the school inclusion movement will be eventually to change the attitudes that result in bias against people with mental retardation. As people with mental retardation take their places in modern society, attitudes will certainly change. Helping in this regard are people like Ashley Wolf—who has Down syndrome—a budding actress and a student at Lesley College in Cambridge, Massachusetts (English, 2000). Ashley demonstrates to everyone that she shares the same hopes and dreams cherished by many young women: a career, home, and family.

HISTORY OF THE FIELD

MAKING CONNECTIONS

Read again the story of Itard and Victor in Chapter 1.

Mental retardation has always been a part of human history. Systematic efforts in education and treatment did not begin until the late 1700s when farmers from the countryside of southern France brought a young boy they had found in the woods to a doctor in Paris. On that landmark day in 1798, when Jean-Marc-Gaspard Itard began working with Victor, "the wild boy of Averyon," the field of special education began (Itard, 1806).

By the mid-19th Century, residential institutions had appeared throughout Europe and Great Britain. In 1848 Samuel Gridley Howe, the first director of the Perkins Institute for the Blind in Boston, expanded the center to include individuals with mental retardation. Later it became a separate institution, the Walter E. Fernald State School. Ironically, Howe clearly saw the dangers of residential institutions: Isolating people with disabilities both geographically and socially from mainstream society resulted in separation, fear, mistrust, and abuse. Despite warnings to keep their numbers down and their size small, institutions spread over the United States. By 1917 all but four states had institutions for people with mental retardation, and many of them were large.

This rise in the number and size of institutions for people with mental retardation was based on unjustified fear of these people and their supposed negative effect on society (Winzer, 1993). In 1877 Richard Dugdale, a member of the New York Prison Association, put forth a story about the Jukes family to illustrate that people with mental retardation were a danger to society. Dugdale believed that mental retardation was a hereditary condition and that people with it were the source of the crime, poverty, and other social ills plaguing the country at that time. The logic worked this way: The Jukes, and families like them, were the source of poverty, immorality, crime, and more "feeblemindedness." They also overpopulated. They were a menace to society, and good people should be protected from them. Members of such families therefore should be cast away, put in institutions, and not allowed to have further offspring. Dugdale was not the only propagator of such theories. In 1912 Henry Goddard released the story of Deborah Kallikak, who came from a family of "feebleminded" people, who were prone to becoming criminals. Goddard maintained that because mental retardation was passed on by heredity, nothing could be done to correct the situation. Goddard's conclusion was that people with mental retardation should be removed from society and their population controlled (Gelf, 1995). Such negative attitudes contributed to the terrible conditions that prevailed in institutions for people with mental retardation—conditions not exposed until 1965 when Burton Blatt wrote *Christmas in Purgatory*.

The oldest U.S. organization in special education dates from 1876. It was first called the Association of Medical Officers of American Institutions and is now named the American Association on Mental Retardation (AAMR). In 1919 the AAMR formed a committee to develop a classification system for mental retardation, and its first definition was published in 1921 (Bryant, Taylor, & Rivera, 1996). AAMR continues to refine the definition of mental retardation as new

CHAPTER 6 *Mental Retardation*

knowledge becomes available. Another important organization, The Arc (formerly the Association for Retarded Citizens), was founded in 1954 by parents. People First, the first **self-advocacy** group, an organization of people with mental retardation, began in the 1970s. It helps people with mental retardation learn about and gain access to their rights as U.S. citizens.

During the 1960s and 1970s, researchers developed and refined new systems of instruction. Behavioral approaches that included token economies, positive reinforcement, direct instruction, and task analysis (breaking tasks down into small, teachable units) proved highly effective, teaching students with mental retardation skills they had never mastered with instructional procedures used previously (Ayllon & Azrin, 1964, 1968; Birnbrauer et al., 1965). Jim Lent and his colleagues at the **Mimosa Cottage Project** demonstrated that children with mental retardation could learn many complex tasks and skills used in daily life and on the job (Lent & McLean, 1976). Procedures developed at this research center in Parsons, Kansas, have since become commonplace in special education programs.

Also in the 1960s, a new philosophy was stimulated by Benjt Nirje in Sweden (Nirje, 1969). The normalization movement was influential all over the world. Normalization emphasizes that people with mental retardation should have available to them "patterns of life and conditions of everyday living which are as close as possible to the regular circumstances and ways of life of society" (Nirje, 1976). About at the same time, Bob Perske formulated the concept of **dignity of risk,** which is based on the premise that people with mental retardation should experience life's challenges and not be overprotected (Perske, 1972). Wolf Wolfensberger used the principle of normalization to call for the closing of all U.S. institutions for people with mental retardation (Wolfensberger, 1972). Court actions and the emergence of the self-advocacy movement also subsequently led to widespread **deinstitutionalization** of people with mental retardation.

Across time, people with mental retardation have been referred to in different ways, including some that now seem cruel. When the first special class was begun in Providence, Rhode Island, in 1896, it was established for "defective children." Since the development of the intelligence (IQ) test, around the turn of the century, people have been grouped, classified, and served on the basis of the score they received on one of these tests. These groupings, or classifications, led to other terms. One classification method, popular among educators in the 1960s and 1970s, distinguished educable mental retardation (EMR)—the category with IQ scores from 50 to 80—from trainable mental retardation (TMR)—the classification for those with IQ scores between 25 and 50. These subgroups were linked solely to IQ scores. The use of EMR and TMR came into disfavor, possibly because educators knew that all people can learn and that education and training should not be separated. Perhaps they also realized that suggesting that certain human beings were merely trainable sounded like comparing them to animals. Since passage of IDEA in 1975, distinctions between education and training have blurred. Today, we understand that all children are capable of learning and have the right to education.

MAKING CONNECTIONS

- Review the "Essence of Disabilities" and the "Origins of Special Education" sections in Chapter 1.

- Compare this old system of classifying levels of mental retardation with one new system, which is described in the "Defined" section of this chapter.

PREVALENCE

The cognitive abilities of students with mental retardation are below the cognitive abilities of 97 percent of their peers (AAMR, 2002). Regardless, the prevalence of mental retardation is much less that 3 percent of the student population. According to the federal government, slightly more than 1 percent (that is, 1 out of every 100) of our nation's schoolchildren between the ages of 6 and 17 are identified and served as having mental retardation as their primary handicapping condition (U.S. Department of Education, 2001). During the 1999–2000 school year, some 546,429 children with mental retardation were served across the country. Most students with mental retardation function at high levels and need few supports. In other words, most fall into the mild range.

Why is the prevalence for this special education category much lower than the 3 percent suggested by using the statistical calculation of two standard deviations from the mean of an IQ test? One reason is that school districts prefer to use other special education categories for students who meet the criteria for mental retardation (MacMillan, Gresham, & Bocian, 1998). Another reason is concern about overrepresentation of diverse students in special education and in this category. In particular, African American students are overrepresented and Hispanics underrepresented in the mental retardation category. Although Black students represent 14.5 percent of the student population, they represent 34.2 percent of students with mental retardation (U.S. Department of Education, 2001). Could this placement rate reflect a relationship between poverty and disabilities? Possibly so. But why, then, are Hispanics not overrepresented as well? Although Latinos/Latinas represent 16.2 percent of the general student population, they represent only 9.1 percent of those served through the mental retardation category.

CAUSES AND PREVENTION

Mental retardation is caused by many factors; many of these are known, but others remain unidentified (The Arc, 2002). The link between identifying specific causes of mental retardation and the development and implementation of preventive measures is clear (Coulter, 1996). When a cause is identified, ways to prevent the debilitating effects of cognitive disabilities have often followed soon after. But it takes action for solutions actually to prevent or reduce the impact of the condition.

What are the major causes of mental retardation?

Many different systems for organizing the causes of mental retardation can be applied. Sometimes they are divided into four groups: socioeconomic and environmental factors, injuries, infections and toxins, and biological causes. AAMR divides them instead into three groups by **time of onset**—that is, when the event or cause occurred (AAMR, 2002):

1. **Prenatal** (before birth)
2. **Perinatal** (during the birth process)
3. **Postnatal** (after birth)

Examples of prenatal causes include genetics and heredity, toxins taken by the pregnant mother, disease, and neural tube defects. Genetics and heredity include conditions such as fragile-X syndrome and Down syndrome, as well as phenylketonuria (PKU). Prenatal toxins include alcohol, tobacco, and drug exposure from the behavior of the mother during pregnancy. Diseases and infection, such as **HIV/AIDS,** can devastate an unborn baby. **Neural tube disorders,** such as anencephaly (where most of the child's brain is missing at birth) and spina bifida (incomplete closure of the spinal column), are also prenatal causes of mental retardation.

Perinatal causes occur during the birthing process. They include birth injuries due to oxygen deprivation (**anoxia** or **asphyxia**), umbilical cord accidents, obstetrical trauma, and head trauma. They also include low birth weight.

Postnatal causes occur after birth. The environment is a major factor in many of these situations. Here are a few examples of postnatal causes: child abuse and neglect, environmental toxins, and accidents. An additional reason for being identified as having mental retardation is societal biases, particularly toward diverse students.

Now let's turn our attention to some major causes of mental retardation across the three periods of onset. In particular, let's think about some genetic causes, both

MAKING CONNECTIONS

For a review of issues related to overrepresentation of diverse students in special education, see Chapters 1, 3, 4, and 8.

CHAPTER 6 *Mental Retardation*

prenatal and postnatal toxins, low birth weight, and child abuse. Finally, the situation of Black youngsters and their risk for being identified as having mental retardation is briefly discussed again.

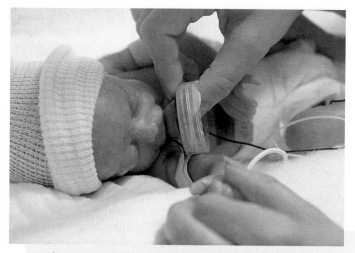

Advances in medical technology can save the lives of infants who previously might not have survived. It can prevent or lessen the impact of disabilities. Medical advances can also result in disabilities.

• *Genetic Causes* More and more causes of mental retardation, many of them rare biological conditions, are being identified (Bailey et al., 1999). Today, more than 500 genetic causes associated with mental retardation have been identified (The Arc, 2002). For example, **fragile-X syndrome**, identified in 1991, is now recognized as the most commonly known inherited cause of mental retardation, affecting about 1 in 4,000 males (Mazzocco, 2000; Sudhalter & Belser, 2001). It results from a mutation on the X chromosome. A common associated condition is recurrent otitis media (middle ear infection) with resulting hearing and language problems. Cognitive disabilities can be severe, and it is believed that some 86 percent of fragile-X-affected males have mental retardation. Many of these individuals are challenged by limited attention spans, hyperactivity, stereotypic behaviors (such as hand flapping or hand biting), and an inability to relate to others in typical ways. It is now thought that some 6 percent of boys with autism also have fragile-X. Many of these individuals also have repetitive speech patterns (Belser & Sudhalter, 2001).

Down syndrome is another example of retardation due to a chromosomal abnormality. Each human cell normally contains 23 pairs of chromosomes (a total of 46) in its nucleus. In the most common type of Down syndrome, trisomy 21, the 21st set of chromosomes contains 3 chromosomes rather than the normal pair. Certain identifiable physical characteristics, such as an extra flap of skin over the innermost corner of the eye (an **epicanthic fold**), are usually present in cases of Down syndrome. The child's degree of mental retardation varies, depending in part on the speed with which the disability is identified, the adequacy of the supporting medical care, and the timing of the early intervention. The great majority of people with Down syndrome have multiple problems (Stoel-Gammon, 1997). For example, estimates of hearing loss in this group of individuals are as high as 78 percent, and because the loss often goes undetected, related problems arise in language acquisition and development of phonemic awareness and later reading abilities. Although individuals with Down syndrome have cognitive disabilities and problems with language and short-term memory, they have fewer adaptive behavior challenges than many of their peers with mental retardation (Chapman & Hesketh, 2000). These individuals do, however, have a higher prevalence of obesity, despite typically consuming fewer calories (Roizen, 2001). These facts are linked to commonly observed outcomes. Possibly their reduced food consumption explains why individuals with Down syndrome are less active and less likely to spend time outdoors than their brothers and sisters. In turn, their opportunities for satisfying friendships, social outlets, and recreation are reduced.

Phenylketonuria (PKU), also hereditary, occurs when a person is unable to metabolize phenylalanine, which builds up in the body to toxic levels that damage the brain. If untreated, PKU eventually causes mental retardation. Changes in diet (eliminating certain foods that contain this amino acid, such as milk) can control PKU and prevent mental retardation, although cognitive disabilities can be seen in both treated and untreated individuals with this condition (Dyer, 1999; Koch & de la Cruz, 1999). Because of the devastating effects of PKU, it is critical that the diet of these individuals be strictly controlled. Here, then, is a condition rooted in

Causes and Prevention

genetics, but it is a protein in milk that becomes toxic to the individuals affected and causes the mental retardation. And both prompt diagnosis and parental vigilance are crucial to minimizing retardation. Now let's look at some toxins that do not have a hereditary link.

- *Toxins* Toxins are both prenatal and postnatal causes of mental retardation. These are two reasons why toxins deserve special attention:

1. Toxins abound in our environment.
2. Toxic exposures are preventable.

Many believe that the increased prevalence of attention deficit/hyperactivity disorder, learning disabilities, and even autism is due to some interplay of genetics, environmental factors, and social factors (Office of Special Education Programs, 2000; Schettler et al., 2000). Clearly, exposures to toxins harm children and are a real source of disabilities. Mothers who drink, smoke, or take drugs place their unborn children at serious risk for premature birth, low birth weight, and mental retardation (Ball, 1999). One well-recognized cause of birth defects is **fetal alcohol syndrome (FAS)**, which is strongly linked to mental retardation and a result of the mother's drinking alcohol during pregnancy (Bauer, 1999). The average IQ of people with FAS is 79; very close to the cutoff score for mental retardation. This means that almost half of those with FAS qualify for special education because of cognitive disabilities. This group's average adaptive behavior score is 61, indicating a strong need for supports. These data explain why some 58 percent of individuals with FAS have mental retardation and why some 94 percent require supplemental assistance at school. Unfortunately, most of these people are not free of other problems in the areas of attention, verbal learning, and self-control (Kerns et al., 1997). Estimates are that some 5,000 babies with FAS are born each year, and an additional 50,000 show symptoms of the less serious condition **fetal alcohol effects (FAE)** (Melner et al., 1998).

Toxins abound in our environment. All kinds of hazardous wastes are hidden in neighborhoods and communities. One toxin that causes mental retardation is lead. Two major sources of lead poisoning can be pinpointed. One is exhaust fumes from leaded gasoline, which is no longer sold in the United States. The other source is lead based paint, which is no longer manufactured. Unfortunately, however, it remains on the walls of older apartments and houses. Children can get lead poisoning from a paint source by breathing lead directly from the air or by eating paint chips. For example, if children touch paint chips or household dust that contains lead particles and then put their fingers in their mouths or touch their food with their hands, they ingest the lead. And lead is not the only source of environmental toxins that government officials should be worried about; other concerns include: mercury found in fish, pesticides, and industrial pollution from chemical waste (Schettler et al., 2000).

- *Low Birth Weight* Low birth weight is a major risk factor for disabilities and is definitely associated with poverty and with little or no access to prenatal care (Children's Defense Fund [CDF], 2001). Medical advances of the 1980s have greatly increased the likelihood that infants born weighing under 2 pounds will survive and this has led both to a new cause of mental retardation and to increased numbers of individuals with mental retardation (Ball, 1999). For example, low birth weight babies are 25 percent more likely to have cerebral palsy. They are 50 percent more likely to be enrolled in special education when they reach school age. And 31 percent of them will have repeated a grade by the time they are age 10. Here are some results from another study of children who had an average birth weight of 11/2 pounds (Haney, 1994): Whereas only 15 percent of the general population has IQs under 85, half of these children did. Whereas 2 percent of full-term babies have mental retardation, 21 percent of these children did. Whereas only 2 percent of full-term babies have exceptionally poor eyesight, 25 percent of this group of children had significant visual problems. Fortunately, not all of these infants grow up to have a disability.

• *Child Abuse and Neglect* Abused children have lower IQs and reduced response rates to cognitive stimuli (CDF, 2001). In a study conducted in Canada that compared abused children with nonabused children, the results of abuse became clear (Youth Record, 1995). The verbal IQ scores were very different between the two groups of otherwise matched peers: The abused children had an average total IQ score of 88, whereas their nonabused peers' average overall IQ was 101; and the more abuse, the lower the IQ score. The link between child abuse and impaired intellectual functioning is now definite, but the reasons for the damage are not. Rather than resulting from brain damage, the disruption in language development caused by the abusive situation may be the source of permanent and profound effects on language ability and cognition. Or the abuse may itself be a result of the frustration often associated with raising children with disabilities. Remember, the connection between neglect and mental retardation has long been recognized and is part of the early history and documentation of this field.

Thousands of children across the nation attend schools within a mile of industrial plants. Children placed in these schools are at great risk for disabilities and health problems. Eliminating environmental toxins can reduce these threats.

Many parents with mental retardation do not understand the basic needs of children and can unintentionally produce negative outcomes in their children. Many of these parents do not understand basic child care principles, nutritional needs, or the importance of positive interactions. Probably because of frustration with the responsibilities of raising children, these parents have higher rates of being abusive. The overall result is that children of parents with mental retardation have problems beyond what one might normally expect (Feldman & Walton-Allen, 1997). These findings help to build a clear case that students with disabilities—and maybe all students— should take courses on child development and parenting during their high school years.

• *Discrimination and Bias* It is important to remember that many subjective reasons account for students' placement in special education. There is little doubt that poverty and its risk factors are clearly linked to disabilities (Birenbaum, 2002; National Research Council, 2002). It is also true that culturally and linguistically diverse children are overrepresented in special education (Hosp & Reschly, 2002; U.S. Department of Education, 2001). This situation is particularly true for Black students, who are almost three times more likely to be identified as having mental retardation than their White peers (National Alliance of Black School Educators, 2002). Specifically, a definite relationship exists between poverty and three other factors: ethnicity, gender, and mental retardation (Oswald et al., 2001). However, this relationship may be somewhat different from what one might initially suspect: The risk factors of poverty (access to health care, poor living conditions) do not entirely explain this disproportionate representation (CDF, 2001). Rather, "the increased rate of identification among students of color may be attributable to systemic bias (Oswald et al., 2001, p. 361). Black students who live in a predominantly White neighborhood are more likely to be identified as having mental retardation than those who live in a neighborhood with more diversity. One conclusion is that students are more vulnerable to discrimination when they represent a minority.

Many strategies can be undertaken to reduce mistakes in the identification process, including pre-referral intervention, appropriate and meaningful curricula, and instruction anchored in culturally relevant examples.

How can mental retardation be prevented?

MAKING CONNECTIONS

For a review of the risk factors associated with poverty, see the "Causes" section of Chapter 3.

Many cases of mental retardation can be prevented by directly addressing the cause. According to The Arc (2002), because of advances in research over the last 30 years, many cases of mental retardation are prevented annually. For example, 9,000 cases of mental retardation have been prevented via the measles and Hib vaccines, 1,250 cases via newborn screening for phenylketonuria (PKU) and congential hypothyroidism, and 1,000 cases via the anti-RH immune globulin. Even more cases are preventable. The President's Committee on Mental Retardation (n.d.) reports that more than 50 percent of all cases of mental retardation could have been prevented through known intervention strategies. Most of these strategies (see Table 6.1) are simple and obvious, but the effects can be significant. For example, in the case of child abuse, teachers now have a legal (and, many believe, a moral) responsibility to report suspected cases so that further damage to the child might be avoided (Lowenthal, 1996).

Education and access are at the heart of many prevention measures. For example, education about the prevention of HIV/AIDS can be effective with all adolescents, including those with mental retardation (Johnson, Johnson, & Jefferson-Akers, 2001). Public education programs can also help pregnant women understand the importance of staying healthy. Other prevention strategies involve testing the expectant mother, analyzing the risk factors of the family (genetic history of disabilities or various conditions), and taking action when necessary; screening infants; protecting children from disease through vaccinations; creating positive, nurturing, and rich home and school environments; and implementing safety measures. Note that not all of these strategies are biological or medical. It is important to look at all aspects of the child and the environment (Coulter, 1996).

The importance of immunization programs to protect children and their mothers from disease cannot overemphasized (The Arc, 2002; CDF, 2001). The incidence

Table 6.1 Prevention of Mental Retardation

For Pregnant Women	For Children	For Society
Obtain early prenatal medical care.	Guarantee universal infant screening.	Eliminate the risks of child poverty.
Seek genetic counseling.	Ensure proper nutrition.	Make early intervention programs universally available.
Maintain good health.	Place household chemicals out of reach.	Provide parent education and support.
Avoid alcohol, drugs, and tobacco.	Use automobile seatbelts, safety seats, and cycle helmets.	Protect children from abuse and neglect.
Obtain good nutrition.	Provide immunizations.	Remove environmental toxins.
Prevent premature births.	Prevent or treat infections.	Provide family planning services.
Take precautions against injuries and accidents.	Have quick and easy access to health care.	Provide public education about prevention techniques.
Prevent or immediately treat infections.	Prevent lead poisoning.	Have universal access to health care.
Avoid sexually transmitted diseases.	Guarantee proper medical care for all children.	Vaccinate all children.
	Provide early intervention programs.	
	Eliminate child abuse and neglect.	

CHAPTER 6 *Mental Retardation*

of disabilities, including mental retardation, has been greatly reduced because viruses such as rubella, meningitis, and measles are prevented. However, immunization is still not provided universally. Despite more federal and state programs to assist families in protecting their children, only some 78 percent of 2-year-olds had received all recommended immunizations in 1999. Why might this be so? Some families do not have access to immunizations, because a health care facility is unavailable or is too far from home, or because the immunizations are too expensive. Some families ignore or are uninformed about the risks of skipping vaccinations, and other families avoid immunizations for religious reasons or believe that the risk of getting the disease from the vaccination itself is greater than the risk of being unprotected. As a result, easily preventable cases of mental retardation due to infection still occur.

People must not underestimate the importance of prenatal care. Staying healthy means taking proper vitamins and eating well, and there are good examples of why this is essential. For example, folic acid reduces the incidence of neural tube defects. By eating citrus fruits and dark, leafy vegetables (or taking vitamin supplements), one receives the benefits of folic acid—a trace B vitamin that contributes to the prevention of conditions such as spina bifida and anencephaly (Sells, 1998).

Infant screening has proved effective in preventing PKU. Using a procedure developed by Robert Guthrie in 1957, a few drops of the newborn's blood are taken from the heel to determine whether the infant has the inherited genetic disorder that prevents metabolizing phenylalanine, a naturally occurring amino acid found in milk. This test, which costs 3 cents, prevents mental retardation because the baby's diet can be changed before the effects of PKU can begin. Guthrie developed the test because his son and his niece had PKU, and he wanted to prevent the condition from affecting others. In the past, PKU was responsible for 1 percent of all severe cases of mental retardation, nearly all of which are now prevented (Schettler et al., 2000). New automated screening programs are accurate, cost-effective, and comprehensive, identifying many different types of causes for mental retardation (Chace & Naylor, 1999).

Couples can take certain actions before the woman becomes pregnant to reduce the risk of biologically caused mental retardation. For example, gene therapy may soon be available to families who know they are at risk for having offspring with PKU (Eisensmith, Kuzmin, & Krougliak, 1999). Some couples have medical tests before deciding to conceive a child. These tests, combined with genetic counseling, help couples determine whether future children are at risk for certain causes of mental retardation. In one study, the majority of women who received genetic counseling either because of their age or because of an abnormal blood test indicated that they would terminate the pregnancy if a test was positive for a disability (Roberts, Stough, & Parrish, 2002). Tay-Sachs disease, for example, is a cause of mental retardation that can be predicted through genetic testing. Other couples take tests for defects after they find out that the woman is pregnant. These tests can determine, in utero, the presence of approximately 270 defects. It is possible that prenatal gene therapy, now in experimental phases, will one day correct such abnormalities before babies are born (Ye et al., 2001).

Let's look at yet another type of preventive technique that has saved children from mental retardation. **Hydrocephaly** is the buildup of fluids in the brain ventricles, causing them to expand. This in turn stretches the child's head outward and squeezes and compresses the brain and nerves. After some time, the result is brain damage. Medical procedures can prevent this damage. Figure 6.4 shows how a **shunt,** or tube, drains excess spinal fluid from the child's brain to another place in the child's body (e.g., the abdomen), where the body can safely absorb, process, and eliminate the fluid. Before this technique was available, children with this condition had irreversible medical problems and mental retardation. And, remarkably, this surgery can now be performed before birth (Snyder & Sandoval, 1999). Doctors at Vanderbilt University Hospital used this fetal surgery technique for the first time on

MAKING CONNECTIONS

The role of immunizations in the prevention of disabilities is discussed in Chapter 5.

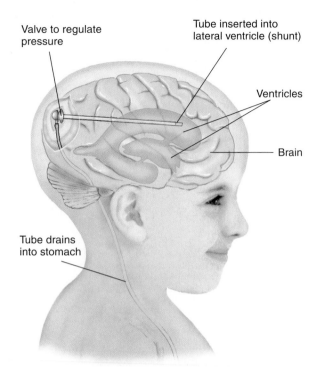

Figure 6.4 How a Shunt Draws Fluid from the Brain

Valve to regulate pressure

Tube inserted into lateral ventricle (shunt)

Ventricles

Brain

Tube drains into stomach

Making Connections

- Fragile-X is also discussed in the "Defined" section of this chapter.

- See Chapter 9 for more information about ADHD.

March 2, 1999, on baby James Neal Borkowski. In a procedure that took about an hour, a shunt was inserted in this unborn baby's brain and the excess fluid then drained into his mother's uterus. After Neal was born on May 12, he received a more traditional shunt (like the one shown in Figure 6.4). Such corrective surgery will become common in the future, increasing the positive outcomes for families at risk for having children with disabilities.

Remember that not all conditions or factors that cause mental retardation can be prevented. In 70 percent of the cases of severe mental retardation, the cause is known (The Arc, 2002). However, for most of these situations the cause is genetic, and at the moment such conditions are not curable. Genetic causes account for about 20 percent of mental retardation, infections for about 11 percent, **trauma** (injury) for another 11 percent, and prematurity for about 4 percent; other individual causes make up the total. Until more causes are identified, we must wait for new preventive measures to be developed.

CHARACTERISTICS

The three defining characteristics of mental retardation are

1. Problems with cognition
2. Problems with adaptive behavior
3. Need for supports to sustain independence

Although every person is an individual, and stereotypes can be unfair and inaccurate when applied to individual people, it is helpful to understand some characteristics educators frequently encounter when working with students with mental retardation and their families. Some specific conditions compound these main effects. For example, those with fragile-X syndrome also have difficulties in social communications and in being engaged in academic learning (Sudhalter & Belser, 2001; Symons et al., 2001). They avoid eye contact, turn away from face-to-face contacts during conversations, and have stylized and ritualistic greetings. However, when teachers make specific efforts to involve youngsters with fragile-X in ongoing academic activities, these students' stereotypic behaviors and engagement levels approximate those of their classmates. Many educators and researchers have noted that individuals with mental retardation have difficulty recognizing emotions, which might explain some of the challenges they experience in social situations (Moore, 2001). It has recently been discovered that some students with mental retardation also have attention deficit/hyperactivity disorder (ADHD) (Kennedy, Caruso, & Thompson, 2001; Pearson et al., 2000). It could be that ADHD is connected to some conditions, such as Prader-Willi, and it could be that ADHD is distributed across individuals with mental retardation as it is across the general population. Future efforts will help sort these issues out for educators who are planning instruction for these students.

How is cognition affected?

The most common, and perhaps the most defining, characteristic of people with mental retardation is impaired cognitive ability. This trait has pervasive effects, whether the disability is mild or severe. It makes simple tasks difficult to learn. It can interfere with communicative competence, because the content of the message is harder to deliver and comprehend. It influences how well one can remember and how flexible one is in the application of knowledge and skills already learned. Ultimately, the degree of cognitive impairment determines the types of curriculum content these individuals are taught: academic or life skills.

Learning new skills, storing and retrieving information (memory), and transferring knowledge to either new situations or slightly different skills are challenges for individuals with mental retardation. Memory, especially short-term memory, is often impaired. The student may also have trouble with long-term memory, finding it hard to remember events or the proper sequence of events, particularly when the events are not clearly identified as important. Even when something is remembered, it may be remembered incorrectly, inefficiently, too slowly, or not in adequate detail. Teachers can assist students in developing memory strategies and help them compensate for their lack of abilities in this area in many ways. For example, the student can learn to create picture notebooks that lay out the sequence of steps in a task that needs to be performed, elements of a job that needs to be done, or a checklist of things to do before leaving the house.

One characteristic mental retardation is that individuals with this disability are frequently less able than their peers to acquire knowledge through incidental learning—that is, to acquire learning as an unplanned result of their ordinary daily experiences. For some, it seems that direct instruction is required for almost every task to be learned. Teachers must plan for the generalization (transfer) of learning so that newly learned skill are applied in a variety of settings (school, home, neighborhood), performed with and for different people, and expanded to similar but different contexts. The "Tips for Teachers" box offers some ideas about how to help children generalize their learning of new skills and knowledge.

What skills make up adaptive behavior and how can it be improved?

Adaptive behavior comprises the skills one uses to live independently, and through direct instruction and the delivery of supports, adaptive behavior can improve. Review Figure 6.2 again, and think about each skill and its importance to independent functioning in the community. Adaptive behavior is not a problem area only for people with mental retardation. Think about some people you know who are very smart, get great grades in school, but cannot manage daily life. These individuals probably have difficulties with some adaptive skill areas. Now think about people you know who are highly successful on the job but have no social skills. Or those who have great personal hygiene and grooming skills but are unable to balance their personal budgets. All of these people have problems in at least one adaptive skill area. Adaptive skills are not skills that people, regardless of ability or disability, always master without instruction. Many IEP goals for the adaptive behaviors stress independence. However, Craig Kennedy wisely cautions that this direction may be somewhat misguided: "Simply put, people with severe disabilities have to depend on other people" (2001, p. 123). He suggests that goals should be thought of in terms of interdependence, where at least two peers work together, providing assistance and support to each other.

• *Supports* Four sources of supports can be made available to people with mental retardation. They are

- Natural supports
- Nonpaid supports
- Generic supports
- Specialized supports

MAKING
CONNECTIONS

Review Figure 6.3 for information about systems of support.

MAKING
CONNECTIONS

For information about a new Best Buddies program, read about e-Buddies in the "Technology" section of this chapter.

Natural supports are the individual's own resources, family, friends, and neighbors (Bradley, Ashbough, & Blaney, 1993). Natural supports can also come from co-workers on the job or peers at school (Chadsey & Beyer, 2001; Kennedy, 2001). These natural, supportive relationships exist among people in almost every setting and in almost every aspect of life. People help each other in simple and complex day-to-day tasks. **Nonpaid supports** are ordinary neighborhood and community supports. Examples of these kinds of supports include clubs, recreational leagues and groups, and private organizations. **Generic supports** are the type that everyone has access to, such as public transportation and states' human services systems. **Specialized supports** are those that are disability-specific, such as human services delivered to families of children with disabilities, special education, special early intervention services, and vocational rehabilitation services. The amount of support needed can vary for each individual and can change over time. Think of support as a fluid concept that is responsive by providing only as much assistance as needed, when it is necessary.

In 1989 Anthony K. Shriver (a nephew of President Kennedy) initiated an innovative way to provide students with mental retardation supports they need. He established a program called **Best Buddies.** This program links college students with individuals with mental retardation. The goal is for these people to become friends, whereby companionship becomes natural supports. Many relationships that developed through Best Buddies have continued for years, with the pairs going to movies, sporting events, and concerts together (Best Buddies, 2002). Best Buddies started on a single campus and now includes more than 40,000 people per year at over 750 middle and high schools. Many other groups are following the lead of Best Buddy programs. For example, UCLA has implemented a program to match college students with youngsters with mental retardation who live and go to school in the local area.

College students working through Best Buddies or through other service programs can improve community participation and provide important supports for students with mental retardation.

• *Friendships* Making friends has received considerable attention during the last decade (AAMR, 2002). This attention has been directed at the development of friendships between people with mental retardation and people without disabilities. Research findings show that children of elementary school age with and without mental retardation can become real friends who play together, express positive feelings for each other, and respond to each other reciprocally (Freeman & Kasari, 2002). However, these friendships do not happen spontaneously. During middle school, children without disabilities tend to form friendships with others of similar backgrounds (e.g., age, gender) and with others who can maintain interactions that can be characterized as equalitarian, enjoyable, balanced, cooperative, and reciprocal (Siperstein, Leffert, & Wenz-Gross, 1997). Even so, these might not be true friendships. Children do not exchange roles of

CHAPTER 6 *Mental Retardation*

leader and follower, and they do not work together to make decisions. They do not have fun together, laugh, or mutually share "secrets." These relationships might better be described as acquaintances. And as children get older, the odds of real friendships developing between nondisabled students and classmates with disabilities seem to diminish (Hughes et al., 1999). For example, little social interaction happens in inclusive lunchrooms. Evidently, mere proximity does not make the difference that is necessary.

The benefits to individuals with mental retardation of having nondisabled friends seem obvious, but what might be the benefits to individuals without disabilities or to society in general? The attitudes of individuals who attend school alongside students with disabilities may well be different from the attitudes of those who have less contact (Ash et al., 1997; Krajewski & Flaherty, 2000). They seem to have more positive attitudes and a better understanding of the challenges that peers with disabilities face.

As work continues in this area, more and more interesting and even perplexing findings are being noted. For example, students with more severe disabilities are often viewed as more desirable peers than students with milder disabilities (Cook & Semmel, 1999). Children with mental retardation who are not very friendly and outgoing seem to be accepted more readily by their classmates without disabilities than children with mental retardation who are assertive, friendly, and outgoing (Siperstein & Leffert, 1997). Clearly, teachers need to help all students—those with and without disabilities—learn how to interact with each other positively and effectively.

MAKING CONNECTIONS

Communicative competence is discussed in Chapter 3 and also in Chapter 5.

EARLY CHILDHOOD EDUCATION

Early identification and intervention are important to children with mental retardation and their families. Early intervention can limit the severity of mental retardation or even prevent it (Guralnick, 1998; U.S. Department of Education, 2001). Preschool experiences provide the foundation for the development of important skills later in school and in life, and they occur at a time when the family is beginning its long involvement in the education of their child with a disability. The power of early intervention is remarkable, and it is now well recognized that early childhood education programs are essential for young children with disabilities and young children who are at risk for developmental delay.

MAKING CONNECTIONS

The importance of early intervention programs is stressed in every "Early Childhood Education" section in Chapters 3–12.

It is quite probable that inclusive education is more of a reality at preschools across the nation than at elementary, middle, or high schools. The preschool curriculum is conducive to inclusive practices, and worries about achieving high scores on state and district achievement tests are not of concern with this age group. Findings from the long-standing program at the University of North Carolina–Chapel Hill show clear benefits from high-quality inclusive preschools (Manuel & Little, 2002):

1. Children with and those without disabilities play together.
2. Children with disabilities show higher rates of social interactions.
3. Typically developing children have no negative consequences.
4. Typically developing children show a greater appreciation and respect for individual differences.

However, not all preschool programs achieve equally. What are some of the features of effective preschool settings? Here is a list of some of their key features:

- Full day program
- Accredited

- Well prepared teachers
- About a third of the student population has disabilities
- Positive interactions with children
- Family partnerships
- Multidisciplinary team approach (including SLPs, special educators, PTs, behavior analysts)
- Fun

Policymakers, parents, and educators recognize the importance of comprehensive and sustained services for these children while they are toddlers and preschoolers. They also understand that students participating in early intervention programs are very diverse in their types of disabilities and in the severity of their disabilities. These factors influence students' short term and long-term results.

ELEMENTARY THROUGH HIGH SCHOOL

Most students with mental retardation have mild disabilities. Increasingly, these students are included in general education classes. These students' learning goals are often similar or identical to those of their peers without disabilities. Of course, in these situations teachers have to adapt their techniques and adjust the curriculum somewhat to accommodate these students' special learning needs. Some teachers modify worksheets, provide more careful instructions about how assignments are to be completed, include students in setting goals, and have students participate in the evaluation of their own work (Copeland et al., 2002). The "Accommodating for Inclusive Environments" box provides for more ideas about how to foster participation in the general education curriculum.

Many students with mental retardation, however, have very complex learning needs. They might require intensive, specialized instruction from a variety of professionals in settings away from the traditional school building—for example, learning how to ride a bus by using public transportation. Merely making accommodations to the general education curriculum is not sufficient. Many students with mental retardation require a different curriculum that includes daily living skills, so that their long-term goal of independent living can be met. Others need more direct and concrete instruction. Let's examine some of these issues.

Children learn a lot from each other when they have opportunities to play together.

Does a functional curriculum address adaptive skill areas?

A **functional curriculum** focuses on life skills. Why might a different curriculum be needed by students who require instruction in adaptive behavior? Carolyn Hughes answers this question for us: "Unfortunately, the traditional secondary school curriculum does not address the needs many students have in order to achieve adult outcomes that many of us

CHAPTER 6 *Mental Retardation*

ACCOMMODATING FOR INCLUSIVE ENVIRONMENTS

Steps for Success in the Academic Curriculum

Specify the Instructional Objectives

- List the objectives in observable terms such that they will communicate to others.
- Focus the objectives on what is directly the instructional target.
- Plan how the objectives will be evaluated to ensure continued student progress.

Sequence Skills

- Be sure prerequisite skills are mastered first.
- Sequence easy skills before more difficult ones.
- Plan to teach confusing concepts separately.

Match Instructional Tactic with Topic or Skill to Be Taught

- Select a tactic that has been proven through rigorous research.

- Monitor its effectiveness continuously.
- Change tactics when it is no longer effective.

Provide Many Opportunities for Practice

- Have students apply their learning in different settings.
- Have students apply their learning with slightly different or expanded tasks or skills.

Be Certain That the Skill Is Truly Mastered

- Have the student demonstrate mastery when performing the skill independently.
- Have the student demonstrate mastery in a variety of settings.

take for granted such as maintaining personal relationships, having a job, or owning a car" (Hughes, 2001, p. 85). A functional curriculum teaches skills that are used in everyday life or that prepare students for life after graduation (Brolin, 2002). These should include the skills required for personal maintenance and development, homemaking and community life, work and career, recreational activities, and travel within the community (Hickson, Blackman, & Reis, 1995). Students' reading, writing, and mathematics instruction focuses on practical skills. The reading program would include reading for protection and information. Here, survival words (street signs: *walk, don't walk, stop;* safety words: *danger, poison, keep out*) might be the topics of instruction. Such sight words can be taught by using a procedure called **time delay,** where students are instructed by using a technique often applied when teaching a foreign language. In the case of language instruction, the word is said, and then the student is given a short period of time to provide the correct answer. If the answer is not provided quickly enough, the instructor provides it as a model. The "Validated Practices" box offers an example of time delay used to teach sight words.

Writing instruction could center on taking phone messages, writing directions for getting to a restaurant, or taking notes on how to do a job. Mathematics instruction would include such topics as telling time, making change, money skills, and cooking measures. All instruction using this system is practical. For example, counting is taught by taking inventory of books in the library rather than by absentmindedly reciting numbers from one to 20. A unit on measurement becomes an opportunity to teach cooking, rather than having the students solve problems in a workbook.

Another topic that is often included in a functional curriculum is learning how to make choices, an important component of self-determination (Wehmeyer, Kelchner, & Richards, 1996). People with mental retardation are allowed fewer choices than other people with disabilities and their nondisabled peers (Wehmeyer

VALIDATED PRACTICES
Progressive Time Delay

What Is Progressive Time Delay?

Progressive time delay (PTD) is an instructional procedure that systematically increases the number of seconds between a stimulus (e.g., "What's this word?") that cues a student to perform a task (e.g., read the word) and the prompt(s) that enable the student to respond correctly. Prompts (feedback such as the correct answer) are faded by systematically inserting increasing amounts of time between the request for a response and the prompt.

Students can give one of five different types of responses: (1) unprompted correct, the student gives the correct answer before it is provided; (2) prompted correct, the student gives the correct answer after the prompt (answer) has been given; (3) unprompted error, the student gives an incorrect response before the prompt is provided; (4) prompted error, the student gives an incorrect answer after the correct answer is presented; and (5) no response, student does not respond.

Why Progressive Time Delay Is Beneficial

PTD has been shown to be effective in teaching students tasks such as reading words, setting tables, doing laundry, and completing job applications. PTD requires you to interact with your student on a constant basis. This, coupled with an effective data collection system, will ensure that you are providing your students with consistent feedback. Because of this high level of student–teacher interaction and immediate feedback, students learn quickly with few errors.

Implementing Progressive Time Delay

Here is a brief description of nine steps followed to teach the word *danger*. Figure 1 is an example of a completed data collection chart for a student learning this word through PTD.

Student	Joe	Instructor	S. L.	Date	6/1	Session	3
Start time	2:00	Stop time	2:10	Total time	10 min.
Task	Counting dollar bills

Trial/ Step	Stimulus/Task Analysis	Delay	Unprompted Correct	Prompted Correct	Unprompted Error	Prompted Error	No Response
1	$5	4"		✔			
2	$3	4"		✔			
3	$4	4"		✔			
4	$1	4"	✔				
5	$2	4"	✔				
Number of Each Response Type			2	3	0	0	0
Percent of Each Response Type			40	60	0	0	0

Key: ✔ = occurrence

Figure 1 Sample Data Collection Sheet

& Metzler, 1995). Every day, people make choices for themselves. They decide where to sit, where to eat, what to eat, how long to stay, where to go, and with whom to interact. For people with mental retardation, particularly those who were allowed to make few choices while they were growing up, the need to make decisions is unfamiliar. Other people make even the simplest decisions for them. It is not uncommon for people who are paid to be escorts for people with mental retardation to make all of the choices, such as what movie to see, at what restaurant to eat, or in what recreational event to participate (Belfiore & Toro-Zambrana, 1994). To avoid such situations, educators may have to teach decision-making skills and ensure that these individuals can apply them in a variety of community and home settings.

When teaching functional or life skills, teachers often find that they need to create their own instructional programs because none are available from commercial publishing houses. In these circumstances, teachers find that **task analysis** is helpful when they are breaking skills down into teachable units and that it can provide a guide for the sequence of instruction. Simple, linear tasks are easily applied to this system. For example, buttoning a shirt, zipping a jacket, tying shoes, cooking, using public transportation, making change, and telling time are all examples of skills that are often part of these students' IEPs and that are easily submitted to task analyses. Teachers can select two different sequences for **chaining.** In forward chaining, students are taught to perform the first step in the chain first. In the task of zipping a jacket, for example, students would be taught to engage the tab first. Each step up the chain of steps is taught and mastered before the next step in the chain is introduced. In some cases (tying shoes: learning to complete the bow first), the teacher

Identify the stimulus that cues the student to respond.

- You say "Jeff, read this word."

Identify the controlling prompt (the correct answer).

- Jeff is to say "danger."

Determine the student's ability to wait for the prompt.

- Identify a task your student **does not** know how to do.
- Provide the student with a prompt to complete the unfamiliar task.
- Determine how long the student can wait before doing the task unprompted.

Identify the number of 0-second-delay trials needed.

During this stage, you will present the word and say it simultaneously, so there is no time for errors.

- "Jeff, what is this word? Danger."

Use your judgment to determine or set the number of times for the no-time-for-errors presentations.

Determine the length of the prompt delay interval.

- To ease the demand on the student's memory, increase the length of the prompt by 1 second.

Determine the schedule for increasing the prompt delay interval.

- Increase the prompt delay with each session.

Determine the consequences for each student response.

- For each prompted and unprompted correct response, the student should receive one token or reward.
- For each unprompted incorrect response, say "Wrong, the word is danger."
- For each prompted error or no response, say "Jeff, say danger."

Select a data collection system.

- Select a system you can use to record the five types of responses (see Figure 1).

Implement, monitor, and adjust the program on the basis of student patterns.

- Use the data you have collected to adjust your teaching and the intervention you are using.

This scientifically validated practice is a teaching method proven by systematic research efforts (Browder & Xin, 1998; Collins & Stinson, 1994; Mechling & Langone, 2002; Wolery, Ault, & Doyle, 1992). Full citations are found in the references under "Elementary Through High School."

Source: From M. Wolery, M. J. Ault, and P. M. Doyle, *Teaching students with moderate to severe disabilities: Use of response prompting strategies* (p. 60). Published by Allyn and Bacon, Boston, MA. © 1994 by Pearson Education. Reprinted by permission of the publisher.

might elect to teach the steps in reverse order, which is called backward chaining or reverse chaining. Table 6.2 gives you an example of a skill (zipping a jacket,) that was task-analyzed and taught to a young child with mental retardation through direct instruction techniques. To complete their instruction, teachers make certain that their students can apply their newly learned skills in real-life situations. For example, the teacher would be sure that the student zips up the jacket when going outside to play on a cold day. In some cases, these practical applications should also occur away from the school setting, and this is why the concept of community based instruction was developed.

How can community based instruction improve adaptive skill areas?

The strategy for teaching functional skills and adaptive behaviors in the environments in which they should occur naturally is called **community based instruction (CBI).** Remember, that generalization is difficult for many students with a disability, and CBI is designed to help students learn to apply skills in all appropriate settings. Like task analysis, CBI is a crucial teaching tool for many students with mental retardation. Let's look at some examples. Learning how to make change is more natural when using real coins at the neighborhood store than when using paper cutouts of coins in the classroom. Learning how to use public transportation to get from home to work is more effective when actually making such trips on a city bus than when pretending to do so at school. Also, rather than addressing a specific

Table 6.2 Task Analysis for Zipping a Jacket

1. Engage zipper

    a. Student stands with unzipped coat on.

    b. Left fingers grasp bottom of jacket on left side near zipper.

    c. Right hand (thumb and first finger) grasp talon, with talon pointing down

    d. Right hand pulls down firmly.

    e. Left hand lifts slider and slides it into the zipper stop.

2. Pull up zipper

    a. Left hand maintains downward pull.

    b. Right hand pulls up on talon to top of jacket.

3. Set zipper

    a. Bend talon down.

curriculum area, such as self-help or language skills, in artificial settings, CBI allows for these skills to be taught in at least four important situations: vocational, community, recreation and leisure, and home and family.

CBI also assists students with transferring learning across situations, people, and places by teaching skills in the environment where the behavior is typically expected. Students have the opportunity to learn and practice generalizing their learning from one person to the next. Of what use is it to be able to make change with the teacher if the students forget the skill and cannot make change with the local shopkeeper or a stranger? Generalizing from one place to another can be enhanced by purchasing items in a store, rather than from an old refrigerator carton on which the teacher has painted the word STORE. Think of more examples of how incidental learning can occur in natural settings through the application of CBI. For instance, a trip to the store can include crossing streets, reading road signs, locating the store, finding the items, purchasing them, and interacting politely with the clerk. For those trips beyond walking distance, students learn about bus routes, change for the bus, locating the stop, and similar tasks.

CBI is very effective with students who need to learn adaptive behaviors and have generalization difficulties. However, CBI poses a dilemma for some educators because it is not compatible with inclusive education in age-appropriate general education placements. When a student is learning in the community while other students of the same age are learning in the school building, the student with mental retardation is deprived of inclusion opportunities with peers. How can the benefits of CBI be weighed against the benefits of inclusive settings? How should this dilemma be resolved?

COLLABORATION FOR INCLUSION

Successful integration of people with mental retardation at school and in society requires considerable teamwork and effort. Teachers of students with moderate to severe disabilities, from preschools to high schools, will increasingly work with a greater array of professionals, particularly those from the field of medicine (Bailey et al., 1999). And, of course, collaboration with SLPs to develop and expand these individuals' speech and language abilities will continue to be a major activity in instructional programs. To develop effective partnerships with professionals from an array of disciplines will require teachers to learn more about science, genetics, neurology, and biology. Teachers need to understand the vocabulary and concepts of multidisiplinary team members to ensure that each student's instructional program is balanced and appropriate.

Of course, teachers supporting each other is one means by which educators become more aware of ways to adapt instruction, modify the curriculum, and provide an appropriate education to students who are difficult to teach. Teaching and including students with cognitive disabilities does not always come naturally. Unfortunately, students with disabilities are often ignored by teachers, who typically call on more able students for class discussion. However, students can be taught to facilitate their own participation in the instructional setting. In a novel study, researchers demonstrated that students with disabilities can solicit attention from their teachers by actually prompting teachers to provide them with feedback (Alber & Heward, 1997; Craft, Alber, & Heward 1998). The students were taught to ask

CHAPTER 6 *Mental Retardation*

Keeping Students informed: Positive Feedback

Michael had moderate cognitive disabilities and attended his neighborhood school. He spent most of his schoolday in Ms. Dismuke's fourth-grade class and was supported by a special education teacher, an SLP, and an adaptive physical educator. Michael's overall academic performance placed him at about the first-grade level, so keeping up with his classmates was a continuing challenge. Michael was a hard worker and wanted to participate in class activities, but when the level of discussion moved beyond his level of receptive language, he often became distracted, fidgeted, and eventually bothered his peers who were seated near him. The longer he could not keep up with the class, the more disruptive he became. He even began wandering around the room, opening other people's backpacks or rearranging items at various workstations. Ms. Dismuke discussed

the problem with Michael's other teachers and found that all of them experienced the same pattern of behavior.

All of his teachers had observed that when Michael was actively involved in group activities, he did not bother anyone. They all decided that before more punitive consequences for Michael's inappropriate behavior were implemented, they would try to keep him involved in class activities by providing him with feedback about when he was behaving properly. They decided to implement an intervention that had three components: frequent prompts about what was the expected behavior in the instructional situation, systematic requests for participation, and feedback at the end of the period about his overall performance. The result was a definite reduction in Michael's "off task" behaviors, though occasionally a more serious conse-

quence still needed to be implemented when he was interfering with other students' learning environment.

Keeping Students Engaged Through Feedback

- Make the behavioral expectations clear
- Prompt or remind students about how they are suppose to behave
- Remember to continually involve them in the instruction or group activity
- Let the students know how well they are doing
- Be certain that the students understand what will happen if they continually disrupt the learning environment
- Be prepared to resort to more punitive measures

their teachers questions like "How am I doing?" and to make statements such as "Look, I'm finished." The result was better academic performance and a substantial increase in teachers' rates of praising students with disabilities. This direct approach can also help reduce behavior problems that arise because the curriculum, instruction, or materials are too challenging for included students. Some smart teachers prompt their students with cognitive disabilities to keep them actively involved in the instructional program; others, as in the example found in the "Achieving Discipline" box, use positive feedback to avoid behavior problems and maintain students' interest in class activities.

For many years, efforts at inclusion have been discussed and implemented at schools, but the degree and amount of participation of students with mental retardation in general education classes is not what you might expect. Keep in mind that the concept of "inclusion" means different things to different people. To some it means participating in public education; to others, it means all-day placements in general education classes (McGregor & Vogelsberg, 1998). And to some, if "it" is not successful, then "it" must not have been done right (Mamlin, 1999). Surprisingly, even after all this discussion and debate, the majority of students with mental retardation—even those with mild cognitive disabilities—still attend school in segregated settings. Only about 14 percent of students with mental retardation use the general education classroom as their primary educational placement option, and some 51 percent receive over 60 percent of their education outside of the general education class (U.S. Department of Education, 2001).

Functional skills are very important to individual outcomes. Without good life skills, for example, achieving independence in the community is almost impossible.

For this reason, some are calling for the curriculum to be judged more important than the placement or setting where students receive instruction (Sandler, 1999). Students with disabilities learn skills that are directly taught to them; they seldom master skills that are not directly taught. And, with the increased demands for high academic outcomes, some special educators are concerned that less time will be available in the general education classroom for instruction in functional skills and for applied learning activities in the community (Benz, Lindstrom, & Yovanoff, 2000).

TRANSITION THROUGH ADULTHOOD

MAKING CONNECTIONS

For more about inclusive classroom placements, see the "Special Education Services" section in Chapter 2 and the "Accommodating for Inclusive Environments" sections in Chapters 3–12.

Individuals with mental retardation can lead satisfying lives as adults. They can work in jobs, establish close relationships with friends and family, live in their home communities, and pursue desired activities. Some may require assistance only from time to time during their lives, whereas others with more significant cognitive disabilities may always need assistance and supports. What should be the general goals for people with moderate to severe mental retardation? Parents and professionals have been grappling with this important question, because its answer could provide a framework for the curriculum, instruction, and experiences offered to students with mental retardation. This question has stimulated an important discussion about quality of life and people with mental retardation. Before talking about employment and community adjustment (the more traditional topics related to transition issues), let's spend just a little time thinking about quality of life and how this concept could guide instruction and decisions about adult living arrangements.

How can we judge the concept of quality of life?

Quality of life is related to one's satisfaction with life and with the circumstances of one's life. It is associated with a sense of contentment that must result in part from feelings of dignity, value, worth, and respect (Wolfensberger, 2002). Quality of life is multifaceted and is affected by many different factors. This elusive concept has been described as being subjective and individually determined (Taylor & Bogdan, 1996). It is certainly complex, and judgments about quality of life must be made by each individual, for what one person perceives as "good" may not be perceived as "good" by another. In other words, no single standard can be applied to all people (Edgerton, 1996).

Why might this concept be important to understand? Thinking about issues related to quality of life can affect decisions and evaluations made about individual people with mental retardation, about their community and vocational placements, and about their instructional programs (Campo et al.,1997). These factors can also help us judge the merits of an individual's outcomes. In this regard, one set of researchers asked people with disabilities about their desires (Gardner, Nudler, & Chapman, 1997). When asked to identify priority outcomes, which could easily be interpreted as quality-of-life indicators, the people who were questioned listed these as their top six desires:

- Have economic resources
- Experience security

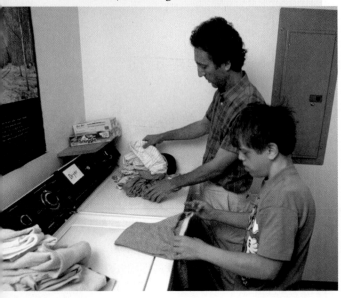

Learning a life skill such as washing clothes in an actual laundry room can improve the likelihood that a student will master the skill and be able to use it in a number of real settings.

- Have personal possessions
- Be free from abuse and neglect
- Participate in the community
- Choose free time

Achieving these outcomes is not always guaranteed for people with mental retardation, and the transition from school to life as an independent adult can be difficult. And as they increasingly join the community and experience integration into society, transition goals and instruction assume greater importance.

The Court Jesters are a group of entertainers with mental retardation. This troupe of magicians performs illusion tricks for audiences across the country.

Do people with mental retardation hold jobs?

Yes, but unfortunately, not as many people with mental retardation (particularly those with moderate and severe mental retardation), who want jobs have them. Some 27 percent are at home with no job, 54 percent work in seg-regated environments such as in sheltered workshops or day activity centers, and only 19 percent are working in the community in some kind of supported employ-ment situation (Kraemer & Blacher, 2001). Restaurants are the most common employment setting for those with paid work.

Just as it is for most people, having a good job is important to people with mental retardation. Jobs give them the opportunity to earn money, to form friendships, to engage in the social activities of the community, and to develop a sense of self-satis-faction about making a contribution. Achieving success on the job can be challenging for many people with moderate to severe mental retardation, but success can be facil-itated in two ways: through supported employment and through natural supports.

Supported employment not only provides work experience but also can improve the wages of people with mental retardation (Mank, Cioffi, & Yovanoff, 2000; Rusch, Heal, & Cimera, 1997). Through this system, students are helped in locat-ing a job, learning the skills needed to be successful in that position, and keeping the job. Many students with mental retardation may need the help of a **job developer** who can discover or even design work that they can accomplish. A **job coach** might also be necessary to work alongside the individual, helping the person to learn all parts of the job. Supported employment can have excellent outcomes for many peo-ple, even those with very severe disabilities. However, in successful situations, co-workers were trained by job coaches to assist people with severe disabilities as they worked alongside them (Mank, Cioffi, & Yovanoff, 1998; Mank, Cioffi, & Yovanoff, 2000). With this extra step, co-workers become natural supports who further assist their peers with mental retardation continue to grow and learn on the job (Butterworth et al., 2000). The positive by-products of developing co-workers as natural supports are the creation of good work environments for everyone and increased social relationships among all employees. An additional result often is the development of friendships that exist at work and after hours—something impor-tant to everyone (Chadsey & Beyer, 2001).

Is living independently in the community a result for most people with mental retardation?

Most people with mental retardation do not have severe disabilities, and living inde-pendently in the community is an expectation. Historically, those with moderate,

Transition Through Adulthood

Jessie

Down syndrome Originals © dolls made by Downi Creations provide children with lovely toys that they can identify with and that lessen the stigma of this disability on the children and their families.

severe, and profound disablilities found themselves confined to residential institutions. During the last half of the 20th Century, the deinstitutionalization movement sought to close all institutions and bring all people with mental retardation to community settings. That movement was partially successful (Holburn, 2000). Some 40 years ago, almost 200,000 people with mental retardation lived in state-run institutions. Today, over 52,000 live in institutions and almost 36,000 live in nursing homes.

Living independently in the community is related to being satisfied with life, but it requires a vast array of skills (Cummins, 2001). For many adults with mental retardation, community living has positively replaced less satisfactory experiences with residential institutional life (Emerson et al. 2001). However, merely living in a community setting, such as a group home or some other supportive housing arrangement, does not guarantee life satisfaction. In some cases, the number of people living in the setting makes a difference in quality of life. Interestly, the optimal number appears to be around six; people come to develop natural supports and friendships with each other when there are neither too few nor too many to develop a talent network.

People need to be prepared for adult life, and instruction to help individuals who have mental retardation learn to make choices and decisions for themselves leads to their being able to assume control of their own lives (Stancliff, 2001). Greater choice is associated with higher levels of adaptive behavior, so **self-determination** has become a target of instruction (Kennedy & Lewin, 2002; Wehmeyer & Metzler, 1995). Self-determination comprises the attitudes and abilities required to act on one's own behalf, to make decisions for oneself, and to make choices. Such a curriculum embodies four basic principles: freedom, authority, support, and responsibility (Moseley & Nerney, 2000). These principles are applied across all adaptive areas and are taught through meaningful and real experiences. Although the normalization movement is well established, people with mental retardation typically do not have the experience or opportunities to make their own decisions, be independent, or assume the role of self-advocate (Cone, 2001). They often do not even get a chance to make simple decisions (what movie to see, what restaurant to eat at, whether to go to church, or whom to visit), even when the person making the decision was hired to help the person with mental retardation accomplish his or her goals. Parents, in particular, express concern about their children's need to learn how to make choices and good decisions (PACER, 2002, May). Individuals with disabilities can assume their rights at majority—that is, at age 21. With this birthday come responsibilities and obligations for which they need to be prepared.

FAMILIES

M AKING C ONNECTIONS

A section about self-determination can be found in Chapter 8.

The families of individuals with mental retardation face special challenges. Most of these families require additional services and supports at some time, especially during periods of transition. These supports might include personal care, family support, respite care, financial allowances, subsidies, counseling and guidance, and in-home assistance. Many families also gain strength and information from organizations such as The Arc and other parent support and advocacy groups. However, it is the families themselves who provide the required day-to-day supports. Educators must recognize that families provide lasting and sustaining life connections for their family members with disabilities long after the schooling years are over. When the school years end, educators' work is done, but the family's work is not. As you learned from Jean Gibson (see the "Personal Perspective" at the beginning of this chapter), although issues change across time, it often seems that families simply move from one challenge to another. For many families, the last major challenge is where their adult family member with mental retardation will live

CHAPTER 6 *Mental Retardation*

(Freedman, Krauss, & Seltzer, 1997). And the fear and worry associated with residential arrangements make many families put off choices until it is almost too late to make good choices and easy transitions. The dilemmas faced by the families of individuals with mental retardation can be complex and confusing, and resolving them requires the efforts of the entire family (Thorin, Yovanoff, & Irvin, 1996).

Elizabeth

What kind of family support comes from dads?

Fathers are very important in the lives of their children, and this is no less true for children with disabilities. Fathers of children with disabilities are as involved and spend about the same amount of time with their children as fathers whose children do not have disabilities (Beach Center, 2002a&b). They just do things differently. These fathers spend more time doing child care. They watch more TV and spend more time at home than other fathers. Those fathers who do take part in the rearing of their children with disabilities also tend to have higher levels of satisfaction with their marriages (Willoughby & Glidden, 1995).

Fathers of these children, however, have a serious complaint about service providers: They believe that they are treated like second-class citizens (Beach Center, 1995a&b). They get the clear impression that mothers are assumed to be the "experts" about their children. One father even reports that a social worker thanked him for his cooperation and said that the worker would check the accuracy of his answers with his wife. Some fathers believe that the professionals, predominantly female, who work with children with disabilities are not sensitive to fathers' emotional perspectives about their children with disabilities. Most fathers seem to understand the importance of their roles. They, more than service providers, know that it takes "two of us to handle all that was happening; service providers would just have to get to know me and learn to accept, if not like, the fact that I was involved with my daughter's life" (p. 4). Children who have positive relationships with their fathers tend to have higher achievement, to be more motivated, and to have better social skills than those who do not have a dad active in their lives (Beach Center, 1995b). Educators need to remember that fathers are an important part of the family support team. Fathers need to be involved and included in their children's educational programs.

What kind of family support comes from brothers and sisters?

Siblings of people with disabilities do not receive much attention from social service agencies, educators, researchers, or policymakers. However, strong and close family ties are important to quality of life, and brothers and sisters often assume responsibility for their siblings with mental retardation when their parents are no longer able (Seltzer & Krauss, 2001). Brothers and sisters play an important role in the lives of their siblings with disabilities, particularly those with mental retardation (Orsmond & Seltzer, 2000). These individuals maintain regular and personal contacts with their less able brothers or sisters and stand ready to assume the role of caregiver (Hannah & Midlarksy, 1999). Many—36 percent in one study—even intend to co-reside when their parents' health or status prevents their continuing to care for their son or daughter with disabilities. This is particularly true when the adult with mental retardation is in poor health. It is interesting that in most of these cases, the parents are making plans for their adult child with disabilities to live in publicly supported residential services, not co-reside with a sibling (Freedman, Krauss, & Seltzer, 1997). Policymakers and community service providers must come to understand and better appreciate the roles that siblings intend to play in the care of their brothers and sisters with disabilities.

TECHNOLOGY

MAKING CONNECTIONS

- For more information about assistive technology and augmentative devices, see the "Technology" section in Chapter 5.

- See the "Characteristics" section of this chapter for background information on the Best Buddies program.

Many of us spend increasing portions of our day on the computer. Papers are prepared, budgets maintained, information sought, and friends kept close. E-mail now keeps people corresponding with each other at a relatively high frequency, and until recently students with mental retardation were often excluded from this exchange. Thanks to a Best Buddies program called **e-Buddies,** e-mail is now an important part of school and daily life for students with mental retardation (e-Buddies, 2002). This program has helped students with mental retardation connect with each other across the nation, and it also facilitates the development of friendships between people with and people without disabilities.

Other applications of technology assist individuals with mental retardation. For example, Herb Rieth and Chuck Kinzer use technology to "anchor" instruction with relevant and meaningful examples, which help enhance students' attention and memory (Williams, Glaser, Rieth, & Kinzer, 1999; Rieth & Colburn, 2003). The computer, combined with instructional materials that are interesting and relevant to the individual, helps students with short attention spans focus their attention. The four phases of the instructional method that Rieth and Kinzer developed are as follows:

1. *Watch the anchor.* Classes watch a video together and discuss real-world issues and propose possible solutions.
2. *Retelling and segmenting.* Students are divided into two large groups to retell the video theme in their own words. These segments are recorded, spliced, and developed into a "broadcast."
3. *Characterization.* Students are divided into smaller groups to analyze and critique the class's video.
4. *Student research.* Study groups are formed to resolve conflicts found in the class's video or to expand and develop related concepts.

Other examples of how technology can help students with mental retardation are as simple as the use of a calculator to perform arithmetic tasks. This enables such students to compensate successfully for the difficulties they often face when they have to solve mathematical problems used in important life skills such as balancing a checkbook. Computer based video instruction is being used to teach words found on grocery aisles (Mechling, Gast, & Langone, 2002). Computer technology also allows many individuals with severe disabilities to communicate, and communication devices that provide speech output can provide great benefits (Romski, Sevcik, & Adamson, 1999). They enable the individual to convey more information in a more understandable fashion. The result can be better access to and participation in the community.

MAKING CONNECTIONS

Look again at the Advance Organizers at the beginning of the chapter; to help you study the content of this chapter, the answers to the Focus and Challenge questions are found in the Self-Test Questions that follow. Test yourself to see if you have mastered the major points of this chapter.

Summary

People with mental retardation have significantly impaired intellectual functioning, have problems with adaptive skills, and require a variety of supports to achieve independence as adults and assume their rightful places in society. Their disability must have been manifested during the developmental period, from birth to age 18. But people with mental retardation are people first, with all the emotions, motivations, and complexities of any human being. Thus, attempts to provide education and habilitation to students with mental retardation must be based on awareness of the fundamental similarities of all people.

Self-Test Questions

Focus Questions

What are the key components of the 2002 AAMR definition of mental retardation?

Intellectual functioning

Adaptive behavior

Systems of supports

How are levels of severity and outcomes of mental retardation grouped?

Mild mental retardation: IQ range of 50 to 69
Outcomes: learning difficulties; able to work, maintain good social relationships, contribute to society

Moderate mental retardation: IQ range of 35 to 49
Outcomes: marked developmental delays during childhood, some degree of independence in self-care, adequate communication and academic skills, require varying degrees of supports to live and work in the community

Severe mental retardation: IQ range of 20 to 34
Outcomes: continuous need of supports

Profound mental retardation: IQ under 20
Outcomes: severe limitation in self-care, continence, communication, and mobility; continuous need of supports

How are the causes of mental retardation categorized, and what are some major causes?

Causes can be grouped in terms of time of onset: prenatal, perinatal, postnatal.

Major causes include the following:

- Genetic: Fragile X syndrome, Down syndrome, phenylketonuria (PKU)
- Toxins: Prenatal (drugs, alcohol, tobacco) and postnatal (environmental, such as lead and other chemicals)
- Low birth weight
- Child abuse and neglect
- Discrimination and bias

What are the four sources of supports?

Natural (the individual's own resources, family, friends, neighbors, co-workers, classmates)

Nonpaid (clubs, recreational leagues, private organizations)

Generic public (transportation, state's human services)

Specialized (special education, early intervention preschools, vocational rehabilitation services)

What are two specialized instructional approaches for students with mental retardation?

Functional curriculum: teaches life skills and adaptive skills

Community based instruction: teaches vocational and adaptive skills in natural settings (in the community and on the job)

How can educators be more effective when working with families of students with mental retardation?

Develop meaningful partnerships with their students' families.

Recognize *all* significant members of the family unit, including immediate family members and extended family members.

Understand that the support that family members provide extends far beyond the schoolday and into the years after school is completed.

Include the entire family unit in informational and planning meetings about a student's educational programs.

Challenge Question

What are some examples of the four levels of support, and how do they make a difference in the lives of people with mental retardation?

The primary goal for most individuals with mental retardation is to achieve a life of autonomy and self-direction with normalized living arrangements and satisfying personal relationships.

To achieve these aims requires, supports, some that are naturally available and some that need to be arranged at varying levels of intensity limited, intermittent, extensive, or pervasive.

The intent is to create a flexible and responsive system of supports that allows the person to live, work, and play in the community with as much independence as possible.

Making Connections

To see how films depict people with disabilities, see the "Supplementary Resources" sections of Chapters 3–13.

MEETING THE STANDARDS AND PREPARING FOR LICENSURE EXAMS

After reading this chapter, you should be able to demonstrate basic knowledge and skills described in the CEC standards and INTASC principles listed below. The section of this chapter most applicable to each standard is shown in parentheses at the end of the knowledge or skill statement.

 Core Standard 1: Foundations

- **Role of families:** Family systems and the role of families in the educational process (Families)

- **History:** Historical points of view and contribution of culturally diverse groups (History of the Field)

 Core Standard 2: Development and Characteristics

- **Educational characteristics:** Educational implications of characteristics of various exceptionalities (Characteristics)

 Core Standard 4: Instructional Strategies

- **Inclusive strategies:** Use strategies to facilitate integration into various settings. (Accomodating for Inclusive Environments)

- **Transition planning:** Use strategies that promote successful transitions for individuals with exceptional learning needs. (Transition Through Adulthood)

 Core Standard 5: Learning Environments and Social Interactions

- **Management:** Effective management of teaching and learning (Elementary Through High School)

- **Social skills:** Social skills needed for educational and other environments (Characteristics)

 Core Standard 7: Instructional Planning

- **Task analysis:** Use task analysis. (Elementary Through High School)

- **Social skills:** Social skills needed for educational and other environments (Characteristics)

INTASC Principle 2

The teacher understands how children learn and develop and can provide learning opportunities that support their intellectual, social, and personal development.

- **Cognitive factors and learning:** The teacher understands that students' physical, social, emotional, moral, and cognitive development influence learning and knows how to address these factors when making instructional decisions. (Elementary Through High School)
- **Cognitive development impact on learning:** The teacher is aware of the expected developmental progressions and the ranges of individual variation within each domain (physical, social, emotional, moral and cognitive); can identify levels of readiness in learning, and understands how development in one domain may affect performance in others. (Elementary Through High School)

INTASC Principle 5

The teacher uses an understanding of individual and group motivation and behavior to create a learning environment that encourages positive social interaction, active engagement in learning, and self-motivation.

- **Social skills:** The teacher understands how social groups function and influence people and how people influence groups. (Characteristics)

INTASC Principle 7

The teacher plans instruction based on knowledge of subject matter, students, the community, and curriculum goals.

- **Learning styles:** The teacher creates lessons and activities that operate at multiple levels to meet the developmental and individual needs of diverse learners and help each student progress. (Elementary Through High School)

INTASC Principle 10

The teacher fosters relationships with school colleagues, parents, and agencies in the larger community to support students' learning and well-being.

- **Consulting:** The teacher makes links with other learning environments on behalf of students by consulting with parents, counselors, teachers of other classes and activities within the schools, and professionals in other community agencies. (Collaboration for Inclusion)
- **Community resources:** The teacher can identify and use community resources to foster student learning. (Collaboration for Inclusion)

Standards in Practice

These knowledge statements, dispositions, and skills might be demonstrated by the beginning teacher who understands that not all children learn in the same way or at the same rate. The teacher is able to modify the classroom lessons so each child may benefit. The beginning teacher would be willing to work with a team of professionals to include students with cognitive impairments in the classroom.

Go to the companion website (ablongman.com/smith5e) for detailed text correlations to CEC and INTASC standards, PRAXIS II™ exams, and other state-sponsored licensure exams.

SUPPLEMENTARY RESOURCES

Scholarly Readings and Resources

The Arc. (2002, June 30). Introduction to mental retardation. In *Frequently Asked Questions*. Retrieved from http://www.tharc.org/faqs/mrqa.html

American Association on Mental Retardation (AAMR) (2002). *Mental retardation: Definition, classification, and systems of support* (10th ed.). Washington, DC: AAMR.

Bos, C., & Vaughn, S. (2002). *Strategies for teaching students with learning and behavior problems* (5th ed.). Boston: Allyn and Bacon.

Kennedy, C. H., & Horn, E. (Eds.). (2003). *Inclusion of students with severe disabilities*. Boston: Allyn and Bacon.

Schalock, R. L., Baker, P. C., & Croser, M. D. (Eds.). (2002). *Embarking on a new century: Mental retardation at the end of the 20th century*. Washington, DC: American Association on Mental Retardation.

Schettler, R., Stein, J., Reich, F., Valenti, M., & Wallinga, D. (2000). *In harm's way: Toxic threats to child development*. Cambridge, MA: Greater Boston Physicians for Social Responsibility. (www.igc.org/psr)

Popular Books

Arrigoni, R. (1997). *Casa Angelica: Arlene's legacy*. Albuquerque: University of New Mexico Press.

Bérubé, M. (1996). *Life as we know it: A father, a family, and an exceptional child*. New York: Merrill.

Meyers, R. (1978). *Like normal people*. New York: McGraw-Hill.

Perske, R. (1986). *Don't stop the music*. Nashville, Abingdon Press.

Sachs, O. (1987). *The man who mistook his wife for a hat and other clinical tales*. New York: Harper & Row.

Simon, R. (2002). *Riding the bus with my sister*. Boston: Houghton Mifflin.

Steinbeck, J. (1937). *Of mice and men*. New York: Viking Press.

What's Eating Gilbert Grape (1993). Paramount

Gilbert lives in a small town with his younger sister, his extremely obese mother, and his brother who has mental retardation. Gilbert is forced to be the patriarch, providing for his dysfunctional family and acting as the primary caretaker of his brother. However, Gilbert falls in love with Becky, who is passing through town with her grandmother. Gilbert readjusts his priorities and deals with the guilt of putting himself before the needs of his family.

This film attempts to depict the level of supports, care, and attention that teenagers with mental retardation require. The feelings that Gilbert experiences are similar to those felt by many brothers and sisters of individuals with disabilities—responsibility, love, resentment, guilt, and dedication. Leonardo DiCaprio gives an incredible performance as the younger brother.

Forrest Gump (1994). Paramount

This epic tale follows the life of the fictional Forrest Gump, a person with cognitive disabilities. Forrest performs extraordinary feats throughout his life. His disability does not prevent him from becoming an All-American football player, the recipient of a medal of honor in the Vietnam War, a successful shrimp boat captain, and a father.

This uplifting story depicts the unpredictability of life and gives everyone hope of achieving the unimaginable. It is also a reminder that people do not have to be cut from a certain mold to be successful or happy, and it offers a positive portrayal of a person with disabilities. This film won six Oscars, including Best Picture. Tom Hanks won the Oscar for Best Actor in the title role.

Sling Blade (1996). Miramax

Karl, an adult with mental retardation, was placed in an institution for killing his mother and her lover. He was released after 20 years and returns to the town where he grew up. He gets a job that suits his talent at fixing things such as lawnmowers. After a couple of days, he befriends a boy named Frank, whose mother is dating a mean, abusive drunk. Karl decides to act on behalf of Frank and his mother before one of them ends up getting killed, by murdering the mother's boyfriend. Because of his disability, he is again placed in the same institution where he had spent most of his life.

Throughout this story, it is clear that Karl's compassion is in no way limited by his limited intellectual function. Despite his retardation, Karl was a suitable father figure to the young boy. This film also deals with the bias experienced by someone who looks and behaves differently. Billy Bob Thorton won an Oscar for his performance as Karl in this film, which he also directed.

I am Sam (2001). New Line Cinema

Sam, who has significant cognitive disabilities, is raising his young daughter independently. However, some social workers believe that Sam will not be capable of raising an adolescent. Rita, an accomplished lawyer, takes Sam's case *pro bono* and helps him fight for the custody of his daughter.

This film is contrived, but it does raise interesting questions about people with mental retardation and their ability to assume adult responsibilities. Sam and his daughter have a loving relationship, but the question is whether that alone is enough for the court of law to award him custody.

Something About Mary (1998). Twentieth Century Fox

In this comedy, Ted has the opportunity to go to the prom with his dream date, Mary, but circumstances prevent their going to the dance, and they go their separate ways. Some 13 years later, Ted decides to hire a private detective to find Mary. As it turns out, she is even more enchanting than she was before, and Ted has to compete with several other men who also love Mary, including the private detective.

In this highly successful movie, Mary has a brother, Warren, with disabilities for whom she cares very deeply. The film shows how siblings often become very active in organizations that support individuals with disabilities. Warren does have some strange characteristics. For example, he wears earmuffs and attacks anyone who approaches his ears. The film does not make fun of the person with the disability, but it does exploit encounters with Mary's brother for comical situations.

Parent, Professional, and Consumer Organizations and Agencies

American Association on Mental Retardation (AAMR)
444 N. Capitol Street NW, Suite 846
Washington, DC 20001-1512
Phone: (800) 424-3688: (202) 387-1968
Web site: http://www.aamr.org

The Arc (formerly the Association for Retarded Citizens of the United States, ARC-US)
1010 Wayne Avenue, Suite 650
Silver Spring, MD 20910
Phone: (301) 565-3842
E-mail: info@thearc.org
Web site: http://www.thearc.org

Association of University Centers on Disabilities (AUCD)
8630 Fenton Street, Suite 410
Silver Spring, MD 20910
Phone: (301) 588-8252
Web site: http://www.aucd.org

Division on Mental Retardation & Developmental Disabilities (MRDD)

Council for Exceptional Children
1110 North Glebe Road, Suite 300
Arlington, VA 22201-5704
Phone: (703) 620-3660; (888) CEC-SPED
TTY: (703) 264-9446
Web site: http://www.cec.sped.org or www.mrddcec.org

Video**Workshop** Extra

If the VideoWorkshop package was included with your textbook, go to Chapter 6 of the Companion Website (www.ablongman.com/smith5e) and click on the VideoWorkshop button. Follow the instructions for viewing Video clip 7. Consider this information along with what you have read in Chapter 6 as you answer the following questions.

Video Clip 7: Mental Retardation (Time 5:08)

1. In the discussion of the preschool child with mental retardation, there is a statement that the individual's personality can affect cognitive abilities. Judging on the basis of the research findings noted in the text and what we can see happening in the video, what might we expect in Carlyn's case?

2. What types of functional skills will Carlyn need to learn in the next several years in order to be successfully integrated into an inclusive kindergarten?

Beauford Delaney, *Washington Square,* 1949. Oil on canvas.
Courtesy of Michael Rosenfeld Gallery, New York, NY.

BEAUFORD DELANEY, the gifted and talented son of a minister and one of ten children, was born in Knoxville, Tennessee in 1901. In 1924 he moved to Boston to study art. In 1929 he moved to the Harlem section of New York City. During this time in New York, he developed his style using radical colors and became a well-known artist in Greenwich Village art circles. In 1953, like many African Americans of his time, he became an expatriate living in Paris and southern France. He died in 1979 after four difficult years in St. Anne Hospital for the Insane in Paris. James Baldwin, his closest friend, said of Delaney, "he has been starving and working all of his life—in Tennessee, in Boston, in New York, and now in Paris. He has been menaced more than any other man I know by his social circumstances and also by all the emotional and psychological stratagems he has been forced to use and survive; and, more than any other man I know, he has transcended both the inner and outer darkness" (Powell, 2002, p. 7).

7 Giftedness and Talent Development

A PERSONAL PERSPECTIVE

Gifted Kids Speak Out

Gifted middle school students were interviewed by their teacher. Their responses reveal their feelings about their education and what it is like to be identified as gifted. These children are sixth- and seventh-graders, attend the same school, and have the same teacher of the gifted for their special education classes.

How does it make you feel to be called gifted?

ROBERT MONTANO: It doesn't really feel any different than how I used to feel, but it makes me feel like good and happy when people say I'm smart and gifted.

KIMBERLY SILVER: It feels strange because I'm the same as everybody else—like everybody's gifted somehow.

JOSHUA BARNARD: Kinda funny because the other kids make fun of you. I guess they are kinda jealous.

ROY BERNALES: I don't know—normal. Just feels like when someone calls me by my name—no different, too.

MICHELLE GOMEZ: It feels neat because you're in higher classes and sometimes you have more fun than in general classes.

DECTRA DIXON: Sometimes it makes you feel like you're ahead of other students. Sometimes they call you nerds, but I like the word *gifted* even if they do call me a nerd.

MARTY FREDERICKSON: I feel singled out. I feel pressured.

JESSICA LUCERO: It feels nice because you have a gift and you should be proud of it.

CHRISTY OLLOWAY: Like everybody thinks you're smart and they ask you to do stuff. Sometimes it bugs me because you don't want to answer the questions, but you're expected to.

What do you like best about your time in gifted class?

GUADALUPE VELASQUEZ: I like it because we dissect things, and it's fun in here, and I think that they teach you more.

KIMBERLY SILVER: I can get more help if I need it, and the teacher explains better.

JOSHUA BARNARD: I like being with only a few people, and I like the teacher. It's nice to be with other people who understand you.

ALIMA MILLS: Things you do in this class are interesting and fun, but still learning.

ROY BERNALES: I like it because there aren't a lot of people—it's not noisy.

DECTRA DIXON: You learn more stuff than in your general classes because in the other one they mess around and in the gifted you have to be serious about what you're doing.

JEREMY CORDOVA: Work is challenging, but more fun. Also, I like working in a small group.

CHRISTY OLLOWAY: You have to try to work extra hard and you feel good about being here.

What does it mean to you to be gifted?

GUADALUPE VELASQUEZ: It means you're more educated. You know more in that subject.

KIMBERLY SILVER: Smart in a different way. Like a different way of learning.

ALIMA MILLS: It's easier for you to learn things, and you are a little smarter than others.

ROY BERNALES: You're special. People think you're all smart and stuff.

MICHELLE GOMEZ: It's like you're smarter in some sections than other people, and you get to show it in higher classes instead of hiding it.

DECTRA DIXON: That you have a faster learning ability than other students.

MARTY FREDERICKSON: Being smarter. Being able to do more. Being singled out.

1. **What are the differences between what the children think the term *gifted* means and what it feels like to them to be called gifted?**

2. **What do these children perceive to be the differences between general and special education?**

3. **What do you think being called gifted means?**

ADVANCE ORGANIZERS

Overview

Although educational services for gifted students are neither protected nor funded by IDEA, many of the basic principles of special education apply to this population. In most states, these services are considered part of special education. Currently, professionals in gifted education are questioning the basic tenets of their field: whom they serve, what education should comprise, and where services are delivered. Current discussions focus attention on the development of talent (skills and achievement) with youngsters who possess high potential and abilities.

Self-Test Questions

Focus Questions

- What is the current vision of giftedness and talents?
- Regardless of the definition applied, what descriptors can be used for gifted and talented individuals?
- What factors can inhibit giftedness and talent development?

- Why are educators concerned about issues related to underrepresentation of some subgroups of gifted learners?
- What are two major approaches to education of the gifted, and how do they differ from one another?

Challenge Question

- Why, in the history of the United States, has there been such an inconsistent commitment to education of the gifted?

MAKING CONNECTIONS

Use the learning strategy—Advance Organizers—to help focus your study of this chapter's content, and reinforce your learning by reviewing answers to the Focus and Challenge questions at the end of the chapter.

OPPORTUNITIES FOR A BETTER FUTURE

Gifted and talented people are highly visible in American society. They are credited for advances in medicine, in technology, in business, in theater and cinema, and in the arts. The roads these individuals took to achieve their high levels of contributions to society vary, depending on their families' social class, their socioeconomic status, and the educational opportunities available to them. Unfortunately, opportunities—particularly from the educational system—are inconsistent, and the gifts of many with high potential are lost to society and to themselves.

Turning Legacies into Lessons

Attitudes and beliefs about the needs of gifted children are mixed. The public, policymakers, and education professionals do not agree about these children or about what constitutes an appropriate education. A commonly held belief is that special education for gifted students is unnecessary. Such rationales are typified by these two statements: "These children will make it on their own" or "The enriched education offered to them will benefit the entire class of general education students." On the other hand, many believe that these children are exceptionally vulnerable and cannot achieve to their potential without special efforts. Throughout the last two centuries, the popularity of and commitment to education of the gifted have waxed and waned. This lack of commitment is one reason why IDEA does not include gifted students in its safeguards and protections. Charges that special education for these students is immoral, racist, socially incorrect, and unfair arose again in the last decade, echoing early Americans' feelings that special treatment for gifted youngsters had no place in an egalitarian society. And there is no doubt that current identification practices exclude many talented youngsters. Thus conflict and confusion persist. Even within the "gifted education" community, there is little consensus about how best to educate gifted students and how to develop their talents.

Thinking About Dilemmas to Solve

Without a doubt, many dilemmas surround these children and the educational opportunities they should be provided. Think about whether

- Their educational needs can best be met without special educational programs
- Identification practices can become more flexible and yet not include those who cannot profit from an enriched or accelerated educational program
- Gifted education is unnecessary
- A national law that guarantees these students with a different education is justified

---

Historians and anthropologists have long recognized that concentrations of extraordinary abilities and outstanding achievement can be observed during different periods of history. For example, the Indus civilization in northern India between 2400 and 1800 B.C. demonstrated advanced concepts of city planning and architecture. Indus cities were built on a regular grid with major streets running north and south. A drainage system served an entire city, and each home had a bathroom and toilet connected to a sewer system. During the time of the ancient Greeks, athletic prowess and excellence in the fine arts reached peak levels that are obvious in the legacies of their civilization: their philosophical writings, dramas, architecture, and sculpture. In ancient China, literary works, architecture, music, and art far surpassed the standards of other cultures. During the 2nd century B.C., the Chinese wrote books, at first using silk for paper, on topics such as astronomy, medicine, and pharmacology.

At the height of the Roman civilization, the number of great orators far surpassed the numbers found in many other periods of history. Between A.D. 300 and 750, the Teotihuacan culture in Mexico developed a sophisticated craft industry that produced figurines, pottery, and tools for export throughout the region. During the Renaissance in Europe, a great number of fine artists—Michelangelo, Leonardo da Vinci, Raphael, and others—created beautiful paintings, sculpture, scientific inventions, homes, palaces, churches, and public buildings. Almost 200 years ago, a concentration of musical prodigies (Handel, Haydn, Mozart, Chopin, Liszt) created work that is still valued and enjoyed. Today computer developers, software designers, and Internet innovators amaze us with their brilliance and technical aptitude.

Why have there been periods in history when particular talents are displayed in abundance? One answer is that periods of brilliance result from a combination of excellent early opportunities, early and continuing guidance, and instruction for the individual (Morelock & Feldman, 1997; Simonton, 1997). These features must be coupled with a major societal interest in a particular ability, opportunities to practice continually and progress, close association and interchange with others of similar abilities, and strong success experiences. Certainly, individuals who demonstrate superiority in a particular area must also have innate talent, but it seems that traits valued by a culture emerge with some frequency when importance is placed on them.

GIFTEDNESS AND TALENTS DEFINED

Gifted and talented individuals do not face challenges in the same way that most children who receive special education services do. However, because of their differences (high levels of intelligence, academic achievement, **creativity,** or unique talents), they are often stifled by educational approaches that do not challenge or develop their cognitive abilities or help them achieve to their potential. For these reasons, many parents, policymakers, and education professionals believe that these students need special services. Who are these individuals? Can giftedness and talents be defined in such a way that all of the students who can benefit from gifted education are identified? Next you will learn about different concepts of giftedness and talents. Perhaps Mary Frasier, founder and director of the Torrance Center for Creative Studies, explains giftedness in the simplest and most straightforward way. "I define giftedness as the potential to excel at the upper end of any talent continuum" (Grantham, 2002, p. 50). Now let's see what other experts have to say.

What do the terms *gifted* and *talent development* mean?

Let's start answering this question by coming to an understanding of how the concepts "gifted" and "talented" have been defined and have evolved. Definitions are important because they reflect beliefs about who qualifies and what services they should receive. Across time, the definitions of giftedness have ranged from a narrow view based exclusively on cognition, reasoning, and the score a person receives on a test of intelligence, to a multidimensional view of intelligence, aptitudes, abilities, and talent development.

As early as 1925, Terman studied individuals with exceptionally high cognitive aptitude. He considered children **gifted** who scored in the highest 1 percent (having scores over 140) on an intelligence (IQ) test. Terman's definition reflects a narrow view of giftedness in which high intelligence is closely associated with high academic achievement. In addition to tying giftedness to a score on an IQ test, Terman also believed intelligence is a fixed characteristic—one that people are born with and one that does not change positively or negatively across time. From his perspective, intelligence is determined solely by heredity; it is a trait inherited from one's parents. Lastly, this view of giftedness reflects many biases that were prevalent in Terman's time about women and people of underrepresented ethnic groups.

Today's professional educators are much less confident than Terman was in the results of standardized tests. They now recognize that such tests can be inherently biased against individuals who are not from the dominant American culture or who have not received a strong and traditional educational foundation. Our understanding of intelligence has also changed since Terman's time. Researchers now believe that intelligence, like any other trait, is influenced by both genetics and environment (Sternberg, 2000). In other words, IQ is no longer thought of as a fixed characteristic of the individual.

New definitions and visions of giftedness and talents began to emerge at the end of the last century. In 1988 the *Jacob K. Javits Gifted and Talented Students*

Education Act of 1988 (PL 100-297) included a broader perspective on the concept of gifted education and talent development. That definition is the basis for the current federal definition, which is growing in acceptance:

> *Children and youth with outstanding talent perform or show the potential for performing at remarkably high levels of accomplishment when compared with others of their age, experience, or environment. These children and youth exhibit high performance capability in intellectual, creative, and/or artistic areas, possess an unusual leadership capacity, or excel in specific academic fields. They require services or activities not ordinarily provided by the schools. Outstanding talents are present in children and youth from all cultural groups, across all economic strata, and in all areas of human endeavor.* (U.S. Department of Education, 1994, p. 26)

By expanding and extending traditional curriculum topics, teachers not only enrich instruction but also provide opportunities for students to learn additional skills and have fun in the process.

Note that this definition does not include the word *gifted* but, rather, includes the concepts of outstanding talent and capability for high performance. **Talent development** is gaining acceptance and may well be the focus of new and innovative efforts for able youngsters that center on developing excitement, motivation, and opportunities for learning (Landvogt, 2001). In this orientation, the development of talent rests with family members, stimulating teachers, peers who value developing abilities, and experts who are successful in a variety of fields and serve as mentors to help students develop their aptitudes into outstanding abilities and achievements (Feldhusen, 1995; Treffinger & Feldhusen, 1996).

Since 1990, many states have changed the definitions they use as a guide to identifying and qualifying students for programs in education of the gifted (Stephens & Karnes, 2000). However, the majority of states still use some version of the 1978 federal definition (a modification of the "Marland definition," named after Sidney Marland, the U.S. Commissioner of Education in 1972):

> *[T]he term "gifted and talented children" means children and, whenever applicable, youth, who are identified at the preschool, elementary, or secondary level as possessing demonstrated or potential abilities that give evidence of high performance capability in areas such as intellectual, creative, specific academic or leadership ability or in the performing and visual arts and who by reason thereof require services to activities not ordinarily provided by the school. (PL 95-561, Title IX, sec. 902).*

Compare this older definition with the newer one. You should notice that the term *gifted* is included in the 1978 definition, and the term is still used in most states' definitions. What is the issue here? To many professionals, the term *gifted* means an ability that is formed and finished, rather than a trait that is developing and that needs to be fostered by families and the educational system (Stephens & Karnes, 2000).

Who, then, are young people who are gifted? James Gallagher, a noted expert in the area, believes that some people are born with a "neurological constitution that allows them to learn faster, remember more, process information more effectively, and generate more new and unusual ideas than their age peers" (2000, p. 6). To those who share Gallagher's view, environment can inhibit or facilitate the

Table 7.1 Gardner's Eight Multiple Intelligences

Intelligence	Explanation	Adult Outcome
1. Linguistic	The ability to think in words and use language in complex ways	Author, poet, journalist, lecturer, lawyer, lyricist, newscaster
2. Logical-mathematical	The ability to calculate, quantify, and hypothesize and to recognize patterns	Mathematician, physicist, scientist, accountant, computer programmer
3. Spatial	The capacity to think three-dimensionally	Architect, engineer, mechanic, navigator, pilot, sculptor, painter, sailor
4. Body-kinesthetic	The ability to use the body and hands skillfully	Dancer, athlete, surgeon
5. Musical	Sensitivity to rhythm, pitch, melody, and tone	Musician, composer, singer, conductor, sensitive listener
6. Interpersonal	The ability to understand and act productively on others' actions and motivations	Teacher, therapist, member of the clergy, politician, salesperson
7. Intrapersonal	The abiltity to understand one's own feelings and capabilities	Theologian, psychologist, philosopher
8. Naturalist	The ingenuity to observe patterns, create classifications, and develop and understand systems	Farmer, botanist, hunter, ecologist, landscaper

Source: Adapted from Linda Campbell, Bruce Campbell and Dee Dickinson, *Teaching and Learning Through Multiple Intelligences, 2/e.* Published by Allyn and Bacon, Boston, MA. © 1999 by Pearson Education. Reprinted by permission of the publisher.

development of individuals' talents, but without some innate predisposition for accelerated achievement or performance, exceptional development is not possible. Not everyone agrees with Gallagher's perception of giftedness. Some believe that enhanced educational services should be available to as many students as possible—to all who have potential to be both creative and productive (Renzulli, 1998). Most researchers today believe that giftedness is multidimensional and that high academic aptitude or intelligence being only one facet.

In 1983 Howard Gardner, in a book entitled *Frames of Mind*, proposed a flexible and multidimensional view of intelligence and giftedness that is still hailed today as the best way to think about giftedness (Campbell, Campbell, & Dickinson, 1999). Gardner first proposed seven dimensions of intelligence—eight dimensions are now included—and suggested that a person can be gifted in any one or more of these areas (Gardner, 1993). A summary of the eight multiple intelligences is presented in Table 7.1. By studying this table, you should be able to see how some youngsters can be excluded when traditional views of giftedness are applied, resulting in their not receiving the educational services they need to develop their unique abilities and talents.

How are these students identified— and how should they be?

Although most definitions of giftedness do not include precise criteria to determine eligibility for special programs, IQ tests are probably the most common way in which children are determined eligible for programs in education of the gifted. Perhaps one day, IQ scores will not be used to identify students; perhaps other methods, such as portfolio assessments or teacher nominations, will be relied on (Hunsaker, Finley, & Frank, 1997).

Because the use of IQ scores is a component of most identification systems used today, you should know what these scores mean. Let's look at how intelligence scores are distributed. The assumption is that if measurements of intelligence were given to a large sample of people, the scores obtained would approximate a normal

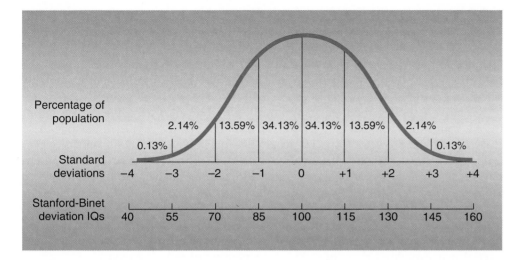

Figure 7.1 Distribution of Intelligence Scores

(bell) curve. The scores would cluster around the mean, or average, in a predictable way. Two commonly used tests of intelligence, the Stanford-Binet and the Wechsler Intelligence Scale for Children III (WISC-III), use the score of 100 as the mean. Each of these tests breaks scores into groups, and each group is called a **standard deviation (SD)**. On the Stanford-Binet, 16 points from the mean equals one standard deviation. On the WISC-III, 15 points from the mean equals one SD. Thus a score of 130 on the WISC-III is two SDs from the mean. Figure 7.1 shows a normal curve that has been divided by SDs and the percentage of the population that falls within each SD grouping. Note that slightly more than 68 percent of the population falls within one SD below and above the mean (of 100). For a criterion of two SDs higher than the mean, slightly more than 2 percent of the population should fall above the score of 130 on the WISC-III. Thus you often hear that gifted students have IQ scores above 130. Remember, though, that this unidimensional (using a single IQ score) approach to identifying gifted students is becoming outdated as theories like Gardner's multiple intelligences are becoming more widely adopted.

Unfortunately, using IQ tests excludes many diverse children and children with disabilities who would qualify if more flexible criteria were applied. To find them, experts suggest that teachers look for such characteristics in children as curiosity, rapid rates of development, extensive vocabulary, motivation, inquisitiveness, keen observation, creativity, thoughtfulness, and innovativeness (Fernández et al., 1998; Smutny, 2000). Note the trend in the area of eligibility toward multiple criteria that include assessment of a variety of skills and abilities: aptitude, academic achievement, past performance, and interest (Gallagher, 2000).

MAKING CONNECTIONS

For another discussion on IQ, see the "Defined" section in Chapter 6.

What is the educational impact of having special gifts or talents?

Gifted individuals are not handicapped by any lack of ability. They can be handicapped, however, by 1) negative attitudes about them, and 2) beliefs that they do not need special services to reach their full potential and develop their talents. Let's look at each of these factors.

Gifted students are often the envy of their typical classmates (Massé & Gagné, 2002). Such attitudes can become a real source of problems, causing worry and influencing the behavior of gifted youngsters. For example, this may be one reason why so many gifted students underachieve; they do not want to call attention to themselves through accelerated academic performance.

Some education professionals and policymakers believe that designing special programs for the gifted is elitist and socially incorrect (Margolin, 1996; Sapon-

Shevin, 1996). To them, education of the gifted should be merged with general education or even eliminated. Such beliefs are probably the reason why access to special services is not guaranteed to gifted students and why their education is not included in IDEA, as education for those with disabilities is. This situation puts the field in a precarious position and results in services being inconsistently available across the nation.

Negative attitudes about education of the gifted seem to stem from myths about the field and the individuals it serves. For example, many people think that these children will thrive without special programs—that they can make it on their own. Quite sadly, this is simply untrue: gifted individuals often do not reach their potential because their educational programs did not meet their needs (Benbow & Stanley, 1996).

Although some gifted children achieve their potential without the benefits of special education, many do not. For example, despite their academic potential, gifted males are three times more likely to drop out of school than gifted females, and overall it is estimated that some 15 to 25 percent of gifted students leave school before finishing (Renzulli & Park, 2000). Research findings about these students' achievement also clearly support the need for special services and a differentiated educational experience for these youngsters (Cornell et al., 1995). These students' statements of "consumer satisfaction" also support such findings. Elementary, middle, and high school gifted students attending general education classes were asked whether their educational programs in general education were appropriate and were meeting their needs (Gallagher, Harradine, & Coleman, 1997). In general, here's what they had to say:

- The curriculum is not challenging.
- The instructional pace is too slow.
- Too much mastered information is repeated.
- Few opportunities are available to study topics of personal interest or in more depth.
- Emphasis on mastery of facts, rather than on thinking skills, predominates.

All children need to develop the motivation to grow and expand. For many gifted children, the general education classroom alone cannot provide the challenges they require to remain motivated or to learn at an accelerated and comfortable pace.

HISTORY OF THE FIELD

Special education for those with exceptional abilities is not a new concept, but it has not been consistently available across time. As early as 3000 B.C., the Egyptians sent the best students (along with royalty) to court schools or assigned mentors to work with them in intensive internships to develop their special talents (Hunsaker, 1995). During the time of Confucius, a Chinese philosopher who lived around 500 B.C., proposed special education for gifted children. By 618 A.D., gifted and talented children were brought to the Chinese imperial court for special education. Because the Chinese valued literacy, leadership, imagination, memory, and reasoning, these topics were part of the curriculum. The Japanese also provided differential educational opportunities to their children. For example, during the Tokugawa period (1604–1868), children born of the samurai nobility were educated in Confucian classics, martial arts, history, moral values, calligraphy, and composition. The children of the poor, however, were educated about the value of loyalty, obedience, humility, and diligence (Davis & Rimm, 1998). In western African cultures, specialized education was provided to children on the basis of the children's status, recognized characteristics, or cleverness.

CHAPTER 7 *Giftedness and Talent Development*

In Western cultures, interest in people's innate and superior abilities was stimulated by the work of Charles Darwin and Sir Francis Galton in the middle 1800s. Charles Darwin is most famous for his theories about natural selection and the evolution of species. Before his time, no one had studied, on a broad scale, individual differences among people or issues related to intelligence and heredity (Clark, 2002). In 1869 Galton proposed his theory that genius was attributable solely to heredity and that **eminence** was due only to two factors: (1) an internal motivation to excel and (2) intellect. Both of these factors were thought to be genetically determined.

In the United States, our wavering commitment to the education of the gifted reflects our national philosophy about equity and social justice. During the 18th century, many leaders of the country leaned toward the view that education was best for the elite. Thomas Jefferson, however, argued against elitism, believing that the purpose of education was to foster democracy. During the 19th century, egalitarianism—the notion that no one should get special treatment—became popular. The egalitarian position was extreme, holding that no individual could be considered better than anyone else, regardless of innate abilities, status, or education. Gardner (1984) suggests that the concept of equal opportunity derived from the egalitarian attitude that special education for gifted children is undemocratic, elitist, unnecessary, and wasteful.

Most chroniclers of education of the gifted in the United States (Clark, 2002; Gallagher, 1988) stress the importance of the development of the Binet Intelligence Test in 1905. Although not originally developed to identify students who are gifted, this test nonetheless marks the beginning, in this country, of interest in such individuals. Some programs for the gifted were established as early as 1866, but real development and growth in educational services for these individuals did not come until the 1920s. Leta Hollingworth, one of the early pioneers in the field of education of the gifted, who joined the faculty at Teachers College, Columbia University, in 1916, taught the first course and wrote the first textbook in this area. One of Hollingworth's major contributions to the field was her proposal that giftedness is affected by both heredity and environment, a concept widely held today.

Another pioneer, Lewis Terman, conducted a classic, long-term follow-up study in 1925 of individuals who were gifted, both as children and as adults. This comprehensive study drew attention to gifted individuals but did not give rise to consistent "gifted education" services nationwide. The promotion of unique educational services can be linked to a specific historical event: Russia's 1957 launching of the space satellite **Sputnik**. This launch was viewed as a risk to national security and a blow to national pride, and the United States vowed to catch up and surpass the competition. Hence federal funding was appropriated to establish programs, develop ways to identify students with high academic achievement, particularly in math and science, and conduct research to find effective methods for providing excellent educational experiences. Gifted students were now seen as a great national resource—the people who would make the United States the leader once again.

Leta Hollingworth, here working in 1938 with students at the Speyer School (the laboratory school of Teachers College of Columbia University), provided the foundation for many of the methods used today in gifted education.

History of the Field

MAKING CONNECTIONS

- For a review of learning disabilities, see Chapter 4.
- For more about gifted students with disabilities see the section "Gifted Individuals with Disabilities" later in this chapter.

During the late 1960s and 1970s, the nation turned its attention to the civil rights movement—to the needs of the culturally and linguistically diverse and poor. Education of the gifted was thought to be yet another advantage showered on already advantaged youth who could make it on their own. During this time, however, June Maker did bring national attention to the needs of one subgroup of gifted students: those with learning disabilities. In 1977 she first published the results of her research, shedding light on this previously ignored group of learners (Maker, 1986).

The late 1980s saw the situation change once again, with renewed interest in education of the gifted. In 1988 Congress passed the *Jacob K. Javits Gifted and Talented Students Education Act*. Many states also invested substantial funding in education of the gifted. However, commitment waxes and wanes, and this cycle will probably continue because of the public's continuing confusion about the vulnerability of these children, along with concerns about equity.

MAKING CONNECTIONS

To review the IDEA law, see the "Necessity for National Intervention" section in Chapter 1.

MAKING CONNECTIONS

For more about Renzulli's approach, see the "Elementary Through High School" section later in this chapter.

PREVALENCE

We do not know precisely how many gifted and talented students are being served by special programs, and we don't know how many would be eligible if programs were available to them. Why? Remember, education of the gifted is not mandated or funded by IDEA, so there is no requirement that states report these statistics to the federal government. We can, however, make some estimates.

The number of students to serve depends on the concept of giftedness that is being applied. For example, if only those who score in the highest 1 percent on an intelligence test are considered gifted, then only 1 in every 100 children will qualify for special services. If we consider those who score in the highest 2 percent, then 2 in every group of 100 children will qualify, and so on. Traditional identification methods used in many schools identify about 2 percent to 5 percent of the school population as gifted (Clark, 2002). But the popularity of more inclusive approaches (such as Renzulli's enrichment model), which do not use a score from a test of intelligence is the sole means of identifying gifted students, increases the percentage receiving at least some special services to somewhere between 10 and 15 percent (Renzulli & Reis, 1997).

Only 25 states mandate that gifted education be offered to those students who qualify (National Center for Educational Statistics, 1994). Thus estimates of the total number of students with IQ scores above a certain level, based on percentages, exaggerate the number of children actually being served. A long-standing problem in education of the gifted is that the number of students who receive special services is much lower than it should be. Considerably less than 3 percent of children receive gifted education. One reason for this is that gifted education is inconsistently offered across the nation. Another reason is that many students from diverse backgrounds, particularly those who live in poor inner-city areas, are overlooked. For example, researchers often find that these children are underrepresented in programs for the gifted (Castellano, 2002; Harry, 1994). Here's one specific example: In one school district where 40 percent of the students are diverse, fewer than 10 percent of the participants in gifted classes were diverse students (Tomlinson et al., 1998). Unfortunately, this situation is repeated consistently across the nation. Recall the statistics about Native American students in Alaska, Montana, South Dakota, and Arizona presented in Chapter 3; these students are overwhelmingly identified as having disabilities. In Alaska, for example, Native Americans make up 25 percent of the population, but only 15 percent of those students receive education of the gifted (Harry, 1994). This is a problem that deserves educators' attention.

MAKING CONNECTIONS

For a review of Native Americans' participation in special education and gifted education, see the "Defined" and "Prevalence" sections in Chapter 3.

CAUSES: FACTORS THAT ENHANCE OR INHIBIT GIFTEDNESS

Both environment and heredity play important roles in the development of the intellect (Reis, 1999; Simonton, 1997). Many factors can affect individuals' outcomes (Brown, 1997; Kitano, 1997, 1998). Attitudes, expectations, and values expressed in different cultures, societies, socioeconomic levels, and families influence the development of talent. Environmental factors correlate with both increased and diminished giftedness. For example, children whose early experiences are not rich and diverse often do not develop outstanding cognitive skills, and children who are not challenged in school tend not to develop their potential fully.

Educators must not underestimate the power of even subtle events that occur in classrooms and at school. For example, every day, girls (and boys) are taught, both directly and indirectly, how to dress and how they are supposed to act. Attitudes and opinions expressed by family, friends, TV, and print media (including textbooks) influence behavior and teach them role expectations (Reis, 1999). Particularly for girls, what is deemed appropriate behavior ("Don't be too aggressive." "Girls don't do well in math.") influences their choices and may limit their ultimate achievement (Rimm & Rimm-Kaufman, 2001). The power of the peer group and of school culture is a critical element that influences all youngsters' behavior (Schroeder-Davis, 1998). For example, 66 percent of high school students say that athletes get more attention, including schoolwide celebration of their accomplishments, than student scholars. "Jocks" and "partyers" are three to five times more popular than "brains." Possibly, educators should seriously reconsider the priorities that some of these celebrations reflect. There is no doubt that schooling and educational experiences can and do make a difference (Parker, 1998). Thus many experts advocate offering special programs to help gifted individuals achieve their potential.

Intellectual and academic achievement are not the only characteristics that can be influenced by attitudes, expectations, and opportunities. Some time ago, Renzulli (1978) observed that many young children are inherently creative, yet relatively few adults are. Creativity is a developed trait and is related to risk taking, which affects the expression of talents (Sternberg, 2000). What happens to children during their preschool and early elementary school years? Is creativity discouraged by the educational process? Teachers tend to favor highly intelligent students who do well academically; they do not consider students who are artistic or creative for special programs. This seems to be particularly true for those who come from different cultures and those who live in rural areas (De Leon, Argus-Calvo, & Medina, 1997). Even children's peer groups criticize divergent, independent, and imaginative behavior among their creative friends. Many educators tend to encourage realism instead of imagination: Dolls talk and act like real children; computerized toys teach children the correct answers to arithmetic problems and the correct way to spell words. College students are advised to select majors that will lead to high-paying jobs. Krippner (1967) made the point that the United States is an achievement-oriented society that rewards individuals merely for being competent. The qualities valued are ability to get along with others, ability to work toward a goal, and ability to adapt, not creativity and individual differences. In fact, the need for acceptance causes many people to repress giftedness. If creativity is not fostered, it can be lost (Kirschenbaum, 1998). Thus many experts believe that it is important to identify not only academically talented children but also those who show promise of creativity (Fishkin & Johnson, 1998).

Educators must come to understand their potential role in inhibiting creativity. Divergent thinking can be a challenge to teachers who are trying to meet the needs

MAKING **C**ONNECTIONS

See the "Characteristics" section of this chapter for more about gifted girls.

MAKING **C**ONNECTIONS

For a review of culturally and linguistically diverse children, see Chapter 3.

Fostering Divergent and Creative Thinking: Flexible Rules

Freesia and Joseph, both highly able and creative mid-schoolers, seemed always to have a different perspective about the content of Ms. Whelan's history lessons. They were easily bored, chatted among themselves, and distracted the class and Ms. Whelan during her lectures and class discussion. Ms. Whelan had implemented strict rules for class conduct. Noise level was to be held to a minimum. Children could speak only when they raised their hands and were called upon, and small-group discussion time was an uncommon occurrence. When the class was asked questions about the historical event being presented, both Freesia and Joseph would often give answers that were interesting but not expected. Their novel contributions often were considered "funny" by their peers, which caused the class to get "out of control." Ms. Whelan had become reluctant to call on either child, for the result seemed to be a loss of instructional time, and it was also hard for her to regain the class's

attention. The less these children were called upon, the more disengaged they became.

Ms. Whelan was worried about loosening the structure she had established. She was afraid that less stringent rules about class conduct would lead to more disruptive behavior. She sought help from the school district's talent development specialist, who came to class to observe the quality of Freesia and Joseph's participation and Ms. Whelan's loss of control. Together, the teachers, despite Ms. Whelan's serious concerns, decided to loosen the class rules. Expectations for "controlled" participation continued, but all of the children were encouraged to think about different views of historical events. Lessons were restructured not only to provide factual presentations, but also to include a multidisciplinary approach (artistic, sociological, and economic perspectives) about the events during the time period being studied. More small-group discussions and time for group projects were allocated across

every week. All students were encouraged to accept and consider divergent analyses of content. Results of these changes in instructional format and delivery were many. The entire class seemed more engaged in learning, class disruption did not increase, and both Freesia and Joseph were able to develop their creative thinking skills.

Fostering Divergent and Creative Thinking by Being More Flexible

- Make the behavioral expectations clear.
- Let students know the "bottom line" for what is considered acceptable behavior.
- Include a range of instructional activities that engage individual students.
- Allow all students to "color outside the lines."
- Encourage divergent thinking.
- Remember that there usually is no single answer to a problem or question.

of children with a wide range of abilities and interests. Particularly in times of high stakes, statewide achievement testing, the pressure to have entire classes attain a standard level of achievement can be overwhelming. Many teachers feel that to create order and to progress through the curriculum at the required pace demand considerable control, and they place greater emphasis on classroom rules. Rules, however, can be too rigid, resulting in stifled creativity. The "Achieving Discipline" box gives you an example of how rules can be applied, while still leaving room for divergent behavior and creative thinking.

CHARACTERISTICS

As with any group of people, it is unfair to generalize group characteristics to individual members. On the other hand, it is easier to understand a group when some commonly observed features are described. Research findings suggest some characteristics that gifted people share (Clark, 2002; Jenkins-Friedman & Nielsen, 1990; Roberts & Lovett, 1994; VanTassel-Baska, 1995; Yong & McIntyre, 1992). These are listed in Table 7.2.

Table 7.2 Common Characteristics of the Gifted Child

Intellectual/Academic	Social/Emotional
Reasons abstractly	Criticizes self
Conceptualizes and synthesizes	Empathizes
Manages and processes information quickly and meaningfully	Plays with older friends
Solves problems	Persists
Learns quickly	Is intense
Shows intellectual curiosity	Exhibits individualism
Has wide interests	Has strength of character
Dislikes drill and routine	Demonstrates leadership abilities
May show unevenness	Is concerned about ethical issues
Generalizes learning	Takes risks
Remembers great amounts of material	Is independent and autonomous
Displays high level of verbal ability	Is highly sensitive to others and self
Prefers learning in a quiet environment	Has mature sense of humor
Adapts to new learning situations	Is nonconforming
Applies varied reasoning and thinking skills	Uses different modes of expression
Uses nonstandard pools of information	Strives for perfection
Is highly motivated by academic tasks	Experiences great stress from failure
Focuses and concentrates on topic or idea for long periods of time	

Do some characteristics require special attention from educators?

Although the gifted and talented students make up a heterogeneous group, some common characteristics are important to monitor. Despite their high levels of talents and abilities, many experts consider gifted students—particularly those who are highly gifted—vulnerable (Brody & Benbow, 1986; Shaywitz et al., 2001). Although gifted students in general are no more likely than typical learners to exhibit disruptive or problem behaviors in classroom settings (or to have emotional or behavioral disorders), they have developed that reputation (Freeman, 1994). And it may be that highly gifted students do exhibit behavior patterns (e.g., hyperactivity, implusivity) similar to those of students with learning disabilities (Shaywitz et al., 2001). However, gifted students complain about being bored at school—a possible explanation for misbehavior. Certainly, keeping these students engaged can be challenging for educators, particularly for those who have a class of students who exhibit a wide range of abilities and achievement levels.

Educators should also be aware of three common characteristics often seen in these youngsters: sensitivity, perfectionism, and intensity (Piechowski, 1997). For example, being highly sensitive may lead some gifted and talented students to over-react to even mild criticism (Freeman, 1994). This, coupled with a need for perfection, causes many of them to experience more negative reactions to what they perceive as failure (Roberts & Lovett, 1994). These tendencies may well contribute to underachievement in some gifted students—an unfortunate situation seen in about half of students with high ability (Peterson, 2000). Another characteristic, intensity,

MAKING CONNECTIONS

For examples of gifted individuals portrayed in film, see the list of DVDs and Videos at the end of this chapter.

can manifest itself both socially and academically (VanTassel-Baska, 1995). Their intensity might also explain why many of these students experience high levels of stress (Nicols & Baum, 2000). On the positive side, this characteristic causes these students to become highly focused on an activity they find fascinating, enabling them to concentrate on an intriguing idea for long periods of time and also to explore curriculum content in depth. Knowledge of these characteristics and learning styles can help the alert educator understand these students' educational needs.

Are there subgroups of gifted students who require special attention?

The answer to this question is a resounding "Yes!" Some gifted and talented children are underachievers and need special intervention to help them achieve their potential. Others, who are not even identified because of bias and different perceptions about what constitutes giftedness, are excluded from education of the gifted. Typically, these children come from one of four subgroups: females, culturally and linguistically diverse children, students with disabilities, and students with ADHD. Let's look at these groups' needs more closely.

MAKING CONNECTIONS

Terman's perspectives on giftedness are presented in the "Defined" section of this chapter.

• *Gifted Females* Since the 1920s, when gifted individuals as a group came to the attention of educators, differences between males' and females' academic achievement and outcomes have been noted. For example, although many of his research associates were women who went on to highly productive academic careers, Lewis Terman included very few women in his study of gifted individuals (Rogers, 1999). During the same time period, Leta Hollingworth argued that the prevailing notion that women were intellectually inferior to men was incorrect; rather, women did not have equal opportunities to excel and realize their potential. Gender differences, particularly girls' poor achievement in math, science, and computer sciences, concern many in the field of gifted education (Reis & Park, 2001). Gifted girls also tend to have lower self-esteem and to lack confidence about their popularity (Kitano & Perkins, 2000). The consensus is that these differences are due to bias both at school and later in the workplace (Noble, Subotnik, & Arnold, 1999).

Although the numbers of preschool boys and of preschool girls identified as gifted are about equal, the proportion of girls to boys in accelerated programs diminishes over time (Silverman, 1995). Why might this be so? Are there innate differences between the genders that cause giftedness to occur more frequently in men than in women? Innate differences have never been proved in research. Rather, are society's expectations for people and the roles they assume the crucial factors in the achievement levels of either gender? It appears that the interplay of society's and people's personal expectations contributes greatly to these differences in outcomes (Rogers, 1999). Gifted girls and boys have different attitudes, likes and dislikes, and achievement across academic subjects. For example, boys favor science, technology, and math, whereas girls tend to favor English, writing, reading, and the

CHAPTER 7 *Giftedness and Talent Development*

arts (Reis & Park, 2001; Swiatek & Lupkowski-Shoplik, 2000). Interestingly, negative attitudes about certain academic subjects increase across the grades: High school girls say they dislike math and science more than do girls in elementary school.

Girls enrolled in education of the gifted are different from girls who attend general education classes (Mendez, 2000). For example, girls in such special programs show high levels of motivation, have greater interest in seeking nontraditional careers, and tend to have more liberal attitudes about the rights and roles of women. Successful women report that it was important during their school years to have friends who valued learning and achievement (Rimm & Rimm-Kaufman, 2001). For these reasons, some researchers conclude that gifted females need special educational experiences to achieve their potential (Noble, Subotnik, & Arnold, 1999).

By expanding concepts of talent to better reflect students' cultures, educators can improve the access of diverse children in programs for gifted students.

- *Culturally and Linguistically Diverse Gifted Students* Culturally and linguistically diverse students face many challenges. Three related issues are of great concern to education professionals and makers of national policy about diverse students (National Research Council, 2002; Renzulli & Park, 2000). Diverse students

- Are overrepresented in disability categories
- Are underrepresented in gifted education programs
- Drop out of school at a high rate

African American, American Indian, and Hispanic students participate in gifted education at rates substantially below what their percentages in the general school population would predict (Ford et al., 2002). National data support the public perception that Asian Americans and Pacific Islanders are overrepresented in education of the gifted, but this assumption is not universally true. Subgroups of Asian Americans and Pacific Islanders vary greatly in their participation rates, and some are considerably underrepresented in gifted education (Kitano & DiJiosia, 2002). Besides raising very important concerns about equity and social justice, over- and underrepresentation result in lost potential to both the individual and society. Let's consider why disproportionate representation happens and what can be done to solve the problem.

Why do African American, American Indian, Hispanic, and some Asian American and Pacific Islander youngsters not participate in programs for gifted students at rates one would expect? One major reason is that children from these groups are at greater risk of being poor, which is clearly related to both overrepresentation in disability categories and underrepresentation in programs for gifted and talented students (National Research Council, 2002). Asian/Pacific Islander children from subgroups that are more likely to live in poverty (Samoans, Hmong) are less likely to be identified as gifted or talented (Kitano & DiJiosia, 2002). Also, many children living in poverty do not have "gifted education" programs in their school districts or at their schools, possibly because some policymakers assume that giftedness and talents do not occur among this group of learners (Baker, 2001). Mary Frasier believes that "people in their heart of hearts really think that when kids are poor they cannot possibly perform at the level of kids who are advantaged (Frasier as quoted by Grantham, 2002, p. 50).

MAKING CONNECTIONS

Discussion of the underidentification of diverse students in education of the gifted is found in Chapter 3.

VALIDATED PRACTICES
Bibliotherapy

What Is Bibliotherapy?

Bibliotherapy uses literature to enhance gifted students' self-awareness, persistence, and social relationships. Bibliotherapy consists of five components: identification, catharsis, insight, universalization, and action. Teachers and students identify areas of need and select a story or novel that will help them understand the problem and generate positive alternatives.

Why Bibliotherapy Is Beneficial

Bibliotherapy helps gifted students deal with issues they face (e.g., anxiety, self-image, working with others). Moreover, the strategy will assist all students in understanding something or someone different from them. Students are provided with ample opportunity to discuss the issues, the solutions generated in the story, and how they themselves can implement positive change in their own situation. These discussions occur in an environment students are familiar with and comfortable in before they apply the strategies in other situations.

Implementing Bibliotherapy

Select a book or novel you feel will assist your students with a current issue they are facing. Follow these five steps to implement bibliotherapy:

Identification

- Guide students to understanding how they are like the character in the story.

Catharsis

- As students read, help them recognize their emotions and begin to discuss them with others.
- If students do not initiate the discussion, you may need to facilitate it.

Insight

- Students make connections with the characters and the issues affecting them.
- Again, they may need some assistance from you at first.

MAKING CONNECTIONS

Review again A Very Special Population: Who are native students? "Defined" section and "Prevalence" section in Chapter 3.

Being poor is also a risk factor for dropping out of school. Almost half of gifted students who drop out are from the lowest socioeconomic levels, whereas less than 4 percent of gifted students who drop out are from the highest socioeconomic levels (Renzulli & Park, 2000). Children of poverty often do not come from families that have an education tradition, and they often do not have access to a computer at home; both of these disadvantages seem to contribute to their lack of interest in staying in school. One result is that Latinos/Latinas and Native Americans are underrepresented in programs for the gifted students.

A number of other reasons contribute to the disproportionately low participation of diverse students in education programs for the gifted (Bernal, 2002; Castellano, 2002; Ford et al., 2002; Harmon, 2002; Kaplan, 2001; Morris, 2002). Let's first look at some explanations advanced for these students' poor participation rates:

- Bias in traditional methods used for testing and identification
- Cultural values at variance with mainstream society and teaching methods used at school
- Barriers created by poverty
- Educators' attitudes toward, and lack of familiarity with, culturally and linguistically diverse students
- Low expectations, bias, and discrimination directed toward diverse individuals
- Limited proficiency in English
- Application of rigid definitions of giftedness and talents

Universalization

- Readers understand that they are not alone and their problem is not unique.

- Students realize that other individuals confront the same issues that they do.

- Students recognize what the characters have done to solve their problems.

Action

- The reader exhibits behavioral and cognitive change.

- Students positively change their thinking and behaviors to influence their actions.

An example of a Bibliotherapy and sample activities for elementary-age students using the story "The Cracked Egg" is presented in Figure 1. (See Ford and Harris [1999] for an extensive annotated bibliography and activities to use with students in grades P–12, plus a list of suggested books to use with gifted African American students.)

This scientifically validated practice is a teaching method proven by systematic research efforts (Ford, Grantham, Harris, 1996; Ford & Harris, 1999; Ford & Harris, 2000; Ford et al., 2002: Ross & Barton, 1994). Full citations are found in the "Characteristic" section of the references for Chapter 7.

- Boil two eggs.
- Paint one of the eggs and cover it with glitter.
- Leave the other egg unpainted.

1. Ask students: "Which egg is pretty"? (Or, "Which is prettier?")

2. Most likely (but not guaranteed), students will choose the painted/colorful egg. Whichever egg is chosen, ask students to explain their choice ("Why do you think it is prettier?").

3. Ask students: "Which egg tastes better? Why?"

4. "What does the outside of the egg have to do with the inside?" "Just because it is pretty outside, does that mean it is pretty inside?"

5. Crack the eggs. Ask students to look for differences on the inside.

6. What do students see? What does this mean?

7. Ask students: "What have you learned about yourself from this activity and book?"

Figure 1 Bibliotherapy Example

Source: From *Multicultural Gifted Education* (p. 142) by D. Y. Ford and J. J. Harris, 1999, New York: Teachers College Press. Reprinted with permission of the publisher. All rights reserved.

Now let's consider what needs to happen for this situation to change. Many culturally and linguistically diverse students do not perform well on tests standardized with students proficient in the dominant American culture. For such students, alternative and innovative measurements—portfolio assessments, peer nominations, authentic assessments (frequent evaluations of students' classroom work), and curriculum based measurements—may allow them to display their talents better (Hébert & Beardsley, 2001). Applying less traditional concepts of giftedness could also result in the inclusion of more diverse learners. For instance, using Gardner's theory of multiple intelligences would allow students with talents in at least one intelligence area to receive special attention (Reid et al., 2000). Clearly, we also need to broaden our search for talent to encompass more artistic and creative individuals, including those who come from rural and remote areas (De Leon, Argus-Calvo, & Medina, 1997). Teachers should consider the background and culture of their students' families. Children whose families have different cultural values, different emphasis on cognitive development, or different expectations often find the classroom situation and the teaching methods used there hostile and confusing (Maker & Schiever, 1989; Tomlinson, Callahan, & Lelli, 1998). For example, children from cultures where working cooperatively in groups is valued, often find it difficult to function well in classes where individual competition is stressed (Bernal, 2002; Kitano, 1997; Kitano & DiJiosia, 2002). Likewise, children who come from homes where being silent and reserved is encouraged are often uncomfortable in American classrooms where individuals are called upon to answer questions and share private feelings.

Teachers can do even more to increase the likelihood of more diverse students succeeding at school. Donna Ford and her colleagues suggest that the books students read, if they are representative of youngsters' culture, can motivate and challenge them to learn (see the "Validated Practices" on page 238 for some examples). Also,

Characteristics

high expectations can make a difference (Harmon, 2002). For example, when teachers perceive diverse individuals as having deficits—when such students are considered "deprived" or "disadvantaged"—the result is reduced access and limited opportunities for challenging work (Ford et al,, 2002). And tragically, if teachers do not expect specific youngsters to excel at school, those students may fulfill that prophecy by not working for good grades on their report cards and doing poorly on class assignments (Kitano, 1998). Another important consideration is the content of the curriculum and whether it is "anchored" with examples relevant to diverse students' experiences and values. When students are central both to instruction and to the curriculum, they gain a sense of belonging and membership that translates into high outcomes (Ford et al., 2000).

Because each culture has different values and norms, it is impossible to generalize from one culture to another. Also, differences exist within cultural groups and even among families. Differences in parent income and education, immigration history, primary language, and access to school in the country of origin vary greatly within each group. All of these factors contribute to individuals' risks of not achieving to their potential. But educational systems have the power to reduce these risk factors and to make a real difference. Here are a few strategies that may work:

- Ensure that all teachers are culturally competent and sensitive.
- Apply flexible identification procedures.
- Adjust instructional methods to the learning styles of students.
- Use culturally appropriate examples to make the curriculum relevant.
- Increase the number of diverse teachers.
- Present knowledge from multiple perspectives.
- Value and respect different cultures.
- Affirm the dignity and worth of all students by holding them to high expectations.

- *Gifted Students with Disabilities* When you think of people with disabilities who are also gifted and have developed outstanding talents, you might think of people like Stephen Hawking, Ludwig van Beethoven, Thomas Edison, Helen Keller, Franklin D. Roosevelt, Stevie Wonder, Itzhak Perlman, and others. Despite their severe disabilities, their genius and major contributions to their respective fields have brought them considerable recognition. Remember that regardless of disability, anyone can have exceptional abilities, talents, or creativity. Never make an assumption about an individual from a casual meeting.

Clearly, society's biases about people with disabilities can overshadow individuals' strengths. In the 1970s, June Maker (1977) began to raise the awareness of educators about the needs of gifted learners with disabilities. At first, those interested in gifted students with disabilities focused almost exclusively on those with learning disabilities, a unique group of learners who came to be called **twice exceptional students** (Nielsen et al., 1993). Today, experts have broadened their views about giftedness further to include groups of individuals with a wide range of disabilities. For example, gifted students with Asperger's syndome are now being recognized (Neihart, 2000). Asperger's syndrome is a disorder that is considered part of the autism spectrum. The characteristics of this disorder include lack of empathy, monotonous speech patterns, social isolation, and inflexibility. And gifted students with Asperger syndrome tend to display inappropriate affect, low tolerance for change, seamless speech, and inability to comprehend humor that requires social reciprocity. Regardless, many of these individuals can rise to eminent positions because of their abilities to compensate for their atypical behaviors, to exhibit extraordinary intellectual powers, and to possess tenacious determination.

Unfortunately, most students with disabilities are not included in education of the gifted. A number of factors contribute to this unfortunate situation:

MAKING CONNECTIONS

See Chapter 12 for more information about Asperger's syndrome.

CHAPTER 7 *Giftedness and Talent Development*

1. Despite the severity of the discrepancy between IQ and achievement, if the level of achievement is sufficiently high, the likelihood of being identified as having a learning disability is low (MacMillan, Gresham, & Bocian, 1998).

2. Students are not allowed sufficient (e.g., enough extra) time or appropriate (e.g., assistive) equipment during the testing situation for them to demonstrate their talents in spite of their disabilities.

3. States' regulations for education of the gifted are not flexible enough (Grimm, 1998).

4. Bias about some disabilities, such as cerebral palsy, overshadow actual abilities and talents (Willard-Holt, 1998).

5. The belief that high abilities and learning problems cannot possibly coexist still survives in some quarters (Brody & Mills, 1997).

Successful gifted students with disabilities tend to share some common characteristics (Willard-Holt, 1998). They often possess skills that allow them to compensate for their disabilities (Dole, 2000). After years of developing alternative ways to learn and keep up with their classmates, they typically have developed exceptional problem solving abilities as well. It is often their persistence and determination that have enabled them to succeed, even with no expert assistance.

Experts agree: Gifted students with disabilities are in desperate need of intervention (Nielsen, 2002; Robinson, 1999). The challenge here is for educators to address aspects of both their talents and their disabilities. For example, these students respond best to an instructional environment that fosters critical thinking and problem solving focused on highly interesting topics. However, direct instruction in areas in need of remediation must also be included in these students' instructional programs. Some experts suggest that students actually be taught (and encouraged) to compensate for their weaknesses (Reis, McGuire, & Neu, 2000). For example, rather than receiving instruction geared to specific content remediation, these students should be taught strategies—such as how to study more effectively and how to advocate for accommodations—that might help compensate for their learning challenges. They also should be encouraged to use a broad array of technologies (word processing, spellcheckers, calculators, database software, and other assistive devices) and other accommodations, such as audio-recorded literature for their reading assignments and tape recorders to take class notes. Elizabeth Nielsen (2002) helps us understand what factors and considerations create successful educational opportunities for gifted students with learning disabilities. The "Tips for Teachers" box reviews some of these important points.

Finally, it is important that these students come to understand the nature of their disabilities. Many of them, particularly those with learning disabilities, come to think of themselves as "not smart"—a belief that, if not corrected, can become a self-fulfilling prophecy (Reis, 2000). These students must be encouraged to accept their personal strengths and weakness, develop a good self-concept, and take pride in their accomplishments. For these goals to be met, support systems and intervention programs are often required. Some professionals argue that at least some of these students may require intensive instruction in separate classes for a part of their educational careers, emphasizing the importance of making an array of educational

TIPS FOR TEACHERS

Creating Success for Gifted Students with Learning Disabilities

1. View such students as gifted first and having a disability second.

2. Provide access to an enriched curriculum in education of the gifted.

3. Allow accommodations through technology.

4. Facilitate a collaborative team approach including general educators, special educators, educators of the gifted, and related service professionals (e.g., school counselors, SLPs).

5. Find opportunities for gifted peers with learning disabilities to interact with each other.

6. Apply a curriculum that incorporates the theory of multiple intelligences.

7. Allow test accommodations.

8. Accelerate when appropriate.

9. Provide opportunities for students to talk about stress and emotional difficulties either in groups or with professionals.

10. Provide students with role models and mentors who are also gifted and have learning disabilities.

MAKING CONNECTIONS

See the "Accommodating" boxes throughout this text for more examples.

Characteristics

For more about ADHD, see Chapters 4, 8, and 9.

alternatives available to gifted students with disabilities (Moon, Swift, & Shallenberg, 2002).

• *Gifted Students with ADHD* Educators are just beginning to focus their attention on students who are gifted and also have attention deficit/hyperactivity disorder (ADHD). How many of these students are there? Remember that many students with ADHD do not meet the criteria for disabilities but still should receive accommodations for their learning difficulties. However, it is difficult to identify those who are gifted, because ADHD is likely to mask intellectual giftedness. Thus most of these youngsters go unidentified (Zentall et al., 2001). Compounding the problem, many gifted students with ADHD are underachievers (Reis & McCoach, 2000). Because of their tendency to be disorganized, distractible, and impulsive, they, like their peers with ADHD, are at greater risk to fail and be retained a year and eventually to drop out.

Many gifted students with ADHD have characteristics remarkably similar to highly creative individuals (Leroux & Levitt-Perlman, 2000). But relatively little is currently known about their leadership, creativity, artistic talents, and musical abilities because educators and researchers have focused on their negative characteristics, which often result in defiance, disruption, low self-esteem, hyperactivity, or anxiety. Such problems result in family stress and problems with peer relationships (Moon et al., 2001). Programs for gifted students with ADHD need to address these issues but must also focus on the development of these learners' unique abilities and talents.

EARLY CHILDHOOD EDUCATION

Recognizing giftedness in young children is important because not responding to their educational needs early could diminish their accomplishments during later school years (Smutny, 2000). Without early identification and the delivery of special services, gifted preschoolers may feel forced to underachieve to remain on a par with their typical classmates (Mooij, 1999). Preschoolers also benefit when their parents receive services from experts in education of the gifted. For example, these parents can be helped to understand better the importance of family during times of play and can learn how to capitalize on these times to build their gifted child's self-esteem, creativity, and communication abilities (Strom, 2000).

Preschool teachers should be aware of differences between gifted and nongifted preschoolers that can lead to a differentiated education program offered as soon as the child is identified. What characteristics are commonly observed in these children? Of course, some of these youngsters are easily recognizable. The 3-year old who reads books, counts to 100, or plays the piano is a prime candidate. But other characteristics are benchmarks. At a young age, gifted and talented children may express talent in art or music or may show high levels of verbal expression, curiosity, concentration, problem solving, theoretical thinking, imagination, and enthusiasm (Smutny, 2000; Tucker & Hafenstein, 1997). These children are likely to be healthier, quicker to learn, larger, emotionally better adjusted, and socially more mature; they persist longer at tasks, resist rules, and enjoy competition (Karnes, Shwedel, & Linnemeyer, 1982). They are also able to handle complex and abstract language relationships earlier than most (Castillo, 1998). They can come to understand metaphors (such as "Presidents are heads of state" and "Time flies") long before their classmates. And recent research has identified another important difference between these youngsters and their more typically learning peers: They gain phonological awareness and the ability to discriminate speech sounds very early. This ability is a predictor of early reading mastery, a skill highly related to school success (McBride-Chang, Manis, & Wagner, 1996).

CHAPTER 7 *Giftedness and Talent Development*

Gifted preschoolers seem to function well in typical early childhood programs. They build things, engage in pretend and dramatic play, and converse with others at the same rate as their nongifted classmates. However, they must be challenged so that their motivation to learn is not dulled. Educators must also understand that sometimes these young children's cognitive abilities far surpass their motor skills (Gallagher & Gallagher, 1994). For example, even those who are able to read may not be able to write well enough to capture their creative ideas. Researchers also caution that children should not be forced to relearn what they have already mastered. Time after time, stories are told about children who come to kindergarten already reading but, instead of being allowed to continue developing their reading skills, are forced to engage in readiness activities with classmates. For these students, instructional time might better be spent on enrichment activities, such as teaching students to classify and organize information or to think critically.

These first grade students are already demonstrating advanced reading and conceptual abilities. Teachers must be alert to continually challenge and support children with giftedness and creativity.

ELEMENTARY THROUGH HIGH SCHOOL

A variety of educational services, varying by locale and in philosophy and orientation, are available to gifted students. In this section, several instructional models or approaches to education of the gifted are discussed. Some approaches are comprehensive and influence the entire school day; others modify a portion of the school day; still others can be easily integrated into any ongoing instructional program. They are examples of how educational systems can offer gifted students a **differentiated curriculum** by modifying the curriculum's content, the learning environment, or the instruction provided (Gallagher, 2000).

What are the two main approaches used in education of the gifted?

Professionals do not agree on a best educational approach for gifted students, and many different models and instructional practices are used across the nation. Although some approaches are eclectic and combine effective strategies, **two—enrichment** and **acceleration**—are widely used across the country. A few of the most commonly applied examples of these approaches are listed in Table 7.3 and discussed next. Remember that regardless of the approach used, such activities always emphasize

- Cognitive processing
- Abstract thinking
- Reasoning
- Creative problem solving
- Self-monitoring

- Content mastery
- Breadth and depth of topic
- Independent study
- Talent development
- Problem based learning

Table 7.3 Approaches to Gifted Education

Approach	Explanation
1. Enrichment	
Interdisciplinary instruction	Teaching a topic by presenting different disciplines' perspectives about the issues involved
Independent study	Examining a topic in more depth than is usual in a general education class
Mentorship programs	Pairing students with adults who guide them in applying knowledge to real-life situations
Internship	Programs that allow gifted students, usually during their senior year in high school, to be placed in a job setting that matches their career goals
Enrichment triad/revolving-door model	An inclusive and flexible model for education of the gifted that changes the entire educational system; exposes students to planned activities that seek to develop thinking skills, problem solving ability, and creativity
Curriculum compacting	Making additional time available for enrichment activities by reducing time spent on traditional instructional topics
2. Acceleration	
Advanced placement	Courses that students take during their high school years for college credit
Honors sections	A form of ability grouping where gifted and nongifted students who demonstrate high achievement in a particular subject are placed together in advanced classes
Ability grouping	Clustering students in courses where all classmates have comparable achievement and skill levels
Individualized instruction	Instruction delivered on a one-to-one basis, with students moving through the curriculum independently at their own pace

• *Enrichment* Broadly speaking, when additional topics or skills are included in the traditional curriculum, the approach is considered **enrichment**. For example, a group of students might spend a small amount of time each week working with instructional materials that enhance creativity or critical thinking. Alternatively, enrichment might consist of studying a particular academic subject in more depth and detail.

To understand the enrichment process better, let's look at an example from a history lesson. This lesson involves interdisciplinary instruction, which encourages students to study a subject from different perspectives. As one application of this instructional technique that incorporates multicultural education, Banks (1994) provides the following example: The students play a game that Banks calls *Star Power*, in which the class is divided into three groups: the stars (who have the most points), the triangles, and the circles (those with the least points). The teacher designs the game so the stars are always in a dominant position, to illustrate the point that highly stratified societies provide little opportunity for mobility. Students study historical examples of groups in positions that are like those of the stars, triangles, and circles. Low-power "circle" groups might include the Pilgrims of 17th-Century England, American colonists in the late 1700s upset with English taxation policies, Cherokee Indians in the Southeast in the 1830s, Jews in Germany during the 1940s, and African Americans in the South during the 1950s and 1960s. Students are then asked to answer questions such as "How might history have been different if the target group had acted differently?" The students' products in these lessons might be oral or written reports that could become part of a class play or short story, or they could be paintings, graphics, or other creative expressions. Throughout this process, students advance their knowledge of a particular historical period, while sharpening their skills in critical thinking.

CHAPTER 7 *Giftedness and Talent Development*

Three of the many other examples of the enrichment approach are independent study, mentorships, and internships. As an enrichment option, **independent study** is generally used within a traditional course where a student studies topics in more depth or explores a topic that is not part of the general education curriculum. Independent study does not mean working alone but, rather, learning to be self-directed and to explore topics in which the individual has an interest. **Mentorships** pair students with special interests with adults who have expertise in those areas. Mentorships need to be carefully arranged by teachers, but the effects are often amazing and may have a long-term and powerful impact on the students' college and career paths (Purcell et al., 2001). The powerful relationship that often develops between a gifted youngster and his or her mentor can reverse stubborn patterns of underachievement (Hébert & Olenchak, 2000). **Internships** are used with many gifted high school students who have expressed interest in a particular career, to enable them to gain experience with that profession.

For her senior-year internship, this student has been matched with a local law firm and has been assigned to a lawyer whose specialty is medical malpractice.

The **enrichment triad/revolving door model,** a popular enrichment approach, seeks to modify the entire educational system by allowing some 15 to 20 percent (instead of just 2 percent to 3 percent) of the school population to participate in advanced activities (Renzulli, 1999; Renzulli & Reis, 1997). Supporters of this approach maintain that it includes students with high potential for creative production *and* a larger pool of culturally and linguistically diverse students. How does the program work? Students "revolve" into and out of different levels of their program into three types of skills categories. Here are a few examples of each type:

Type 1. Enrichment activities expose the entire class of general education students to new and exciting topics of study carried out through a variety of instructional approaches (speakers, field trips, demonstrations, videotapes and films, and interest centers).

Type 2. Activities encourage all students to develop their cognitive and affective abilities through their own expressive skills (writing a play, doing a pen-and-ink sketch, using equipment).

Type 3. Opportunities to apply advanced investigative and creative skills are given to students who are motivated, and those who show great interest are provided with specialized instruction and activities to explore particular topics, issues, or ideas.

How can general education teachers find time in the busy school day to enrich students' curriculum? **Curriculum compacting** helps teachers recapture instructional time by reducing or eliminating coverage of topics that gifted students have mastered or will master in a fraction of the time that their peers need. Saved time can then be reallocated to enrichment activities like mentoring, independent study, internships, or advanced study.

• *Acceleration* Another approach, **acceleration,** enjoys considerable support because it does not require separate or special classes or programs for the gifted and also because it is effective (Lubinski & Benbow, 1995; Witham, 1997). Look again at Table 7.3. Acceleration can take a variety of forms: grade skipping, advanced placement courses, or ability groups such as **honors sections.** High achievers make great gains when they are accelerated, so let's take a look at two of these options.

Advanced placement courses enable students to take classes in high school that earn college credit. Advanced placement allows gifted students and those who are **high achievers** to experience enrichment and acceleration by studying course content in more depth. A side benefit is that they do not have to take these courses over again in college.

Another approach, **ability grouping,** has students of comparable abilities work together in courses or activities in which they excel. Under these conditions, gifted students make great gains in achievement (Kulik & Kulik, 1997). In fact, research indicates that gifted students *need* at least some ability grouping, wherein depth of content, speed and pacing of instruction, and advancement through content match their abilities (Rogers, 2002). Advanced ability groups are easily arranged in middle and high schools, where students attend different sections of classes or where honor sections are available. For example, a ninth-grader might attend a sophomore- or junior-level mathematics class, and a high school senior might take several classes at a local college. Many high schools provide honors sections of academic courses as a form of ability grouping. The criterion for entrance into these classes is outstanding academic achievement in specific subject areas.

What are some benefits of acceleration?

1. Students can complete the traditional general education curriculum in a shorter period of time and may be able to finish high school several years early.

2. Academic material can be completed more quickly, allowing students to study related topics in more depth.

3. Educators see more academic gains from students involved with this approach.

4. Some students develop better self-concepts and more positive attitudes about course content and school.

5. The acceleration approach avoids the criticism that education of the gifted segregates these students from more typical learners, because although they are not placed with students of the same age, they are participating in general education programs.

Despite these benefits, we need to put this approach into perspective: Only 17 percent of gifted students use acceleration (Pendarvais & Howley, 1996).

What service delivery options are used for education of the gifted?

Both enrichment and acceleration are offered in a variety of settings. For example, with **cluster grouping,** the general education teacher is supported by an educator of the gifted and delivers special instructional opportunities (Schuler, 1997). Students might be assigned independent study activities that support and extend topics that are part of the general education curriculum. Sixth-graders, studying state history in social studies, might thus prepare a "Who's Who" book of key figures in their state's history. Or they might prepare a position paper on a current issue, such as water rights, including the historical reasons for the controversy and concluding with possible solutions to the problem.

Cooperative learning, designed for mixed-ability groups of children to work together in small groups, is also typically applied in the general education setting (Slavin, 1990). However, cooperative learning might not be the best answer to the question "What teaching technique is effective for a wide range of student abilities and particularly engages the gifted learner?" Research has revealed that gifted youngsters complain that the pace of cooperative learning is too slow and repetitive

MAKING CONNECTIONS

For a review of special education service delivery options, see the section "Special Education Services" in Chapter 2.

CHAPTER 7 *Giftedness and Talent Development*

and that group instruction is not challenging enough (Gallagher, Harradine, & Coleman, 1997; Ramsay & Richards, 1997). For this strategy to be effective, requires teachers must present complex, problem based, and open-ended tasks (Tomlinson, 2000). The challenge here is to keep gifted students engaged without "losing" the other students because they cannot keep up.

Although they probably still represent the most common placement and administrative arrangement for gifted students, **pull-out programs** are decreasing in number (VanTassel-Baska, 1995). In this service delivery option, students leave the general education class for a portion of the school day to attend a special class. Such programs provide services for either several days a week or an hour or so each day. Some schools combine cluster and pull-out programs. Both cluster and pull-out programs rely heavily on the general education classroom for the majority of a child's education.

Some gifted students attend special classes, and even special schools are growing, once again, in popularity with parents and students (Hishinuma & Nishimura, 2000). Support for separate programs may be due to their unique and comprehensive elements: acceleration, enrichment, counseling, parent involvement, supplemental programs for those with special learning needs, and behavior management. Some students receive the majority of their instruction in a special class, possibly at their neighborhood school, where they are educated in a homogeneous environment in which all the other students have comparable abilities. Some advantaged youngsters receive their education at exclusive private schools. Some students attend special public schools exclusively for students who are gifted. Hunter Elementary, for instance, administered by Hunter College of the City University of New York, is a public elementary school for these students, but such schools are usually at the high school level and stress special areas of education. **Magnet schools** often emphasize a theme, specializing in the performing arts, math, or science, and are available to students who pass qualifying exams or auditions. Finally, although there are only 12 public residential schools for gifted students in the nation, research has documented the social and academic benefits of such separate schools (Coleman, 2001).

COLLABORATION FOR INCLUSION

Most gifted students attend general education classes, receive enrichment activities, and attend "pull-out programs" for a limited portion of the school week, or they participate in standard classes with older peers through the acceleration model. Very few gifted students attend segregated special classes or schools. Thus it is important that gifted education teachers and general education teachers work closely together to ensure an appropriate education is provided and these students' educational and social needs are met. They must collaborate to modify both the general curriculum and instruction for their gifted students so as to preserve educational and social experiences that are at grade level for the majority of their students. As you'll see in the "Accommodating for Inclusive Environments" box, even for twice exceptional students, simple modifications to standard instruction are easy to apply.

In particular, two groups of gifted students deserve extra attention and the development of active partnerships: those with disabilities and those who come from diverse backgrounds. Let's take a closer look at these two groups of students and the types of collaborative arrangements that can make a difference in their educational outcomes. First, for gifted students with disabilities to succeed and profit from education of the gifted (Robinson, 1999), their teachers must work together to

MAKING CONNECTIONS

To review the special needs of gifted students with disabilities, read again that part of the "Characteristics" section of this chapter.

ACCOMODATING FOR INCLUSIVE ENVIRONMENTS

Helping Twice Exceptional Students Demonstrate Their Academic Talents

Supplement Instruction with

- Copies of lecture notes
- Copies of overheads or PowerPoint slides
- Study guides
- Demonstrations
- A highlighted textbook

Provide Extra Practice Opportunities by

- Scheduling peer tutors
- Assigning supplemental homework
- Arranging study sessions

Modify Assignments by

- Using study sheet templates or organizers
- Allowing students to use word processing technology
- Extending due dates for homework
- Abbreviating work requirements

Use Direct and Alternative Assessments Such as

- Portfolios
- Authentic assessments
- Curriculum based measurement (CBM)

MAKING **C**ONNECTIONS

For another discussion of developing partnerships on behalf of diverse students, see the "Collaboration" and "Families" sections in Chapter 3.

- Define the educational problems that individual or groups of students are facing
- Research the problem and identify "best practices" that might be effective
- Identify backup or alternative solutions
- Determine how to evaluate the solution's effectiveness (agree on criteria or level of student performance needed to retain the intervention)
- Develop a plan of action
- Decide on a meeting schedule

Second, students from diverse backgrounds often face different issues and have different educational needs (Castellano & Díaz, 2002; Ford et al., 2002; Harmon, 2002; Kitano & DiJiosia, 2002). School districts' experts in multicultural education and education of the gifted can work together with teachers to address these students' special needs. Then underachievement can be turned into high achievement. Key elements of programs where diverse students remain engaged include or reflect

- Challenging instruction
- High expectations
- A multicultural perspective
- An affirmation of their culture, history, and heritage
- Culturally sensitive techniques and strategies
- Self-affirming experiences and opportunities for better self-understanding
- Social responsibility
- Relevant cultural examples

Of course these points seem self-evident, but they are not easily accomplished, particularly when teachers are working in isolation. Collaboration and partnerships with other educators, community members, and families can make a real difference in the educational lives of gifted and talented children.

TRANSITION THROUGH ADULTHOOD

Possibly because of gifted students' heightened intensity and sensitivity, the transition years can be difficult, particularly as they affirm themselves and seek independence from their families (Peterson, 2001). As previously noted, not all gifted and talented individuals achieve to their potential, and too many become bored and disengaged during the high school years. College attendance and graduation are clearly linked to adult outcomes in American society, and high school achievement is related to success in college (Peterson, 2000). An unexpectedly, high percentage of gifted individuals drop out of high school or college (Renzulli & Park, 2002). Regardless of these findings, **longitudinal studies** do support the common belief: Gifted children tend to grow up to be highly successful, eminent adults (Filippelli & Walberg, 1997; Kitano, 1997, 1998; Kitano & DiJiosia, 2002; Kitano & Perkins, 2000; Terman, 1925; Terman & Oden, 1959; Oden, 1968; Walberg & Zeiser, 1997). However, good outcomes are not guaranteed for all gifted individuals (Benbow & Stanley, 1996).

How can outcomes for more gifted and talented individuals be improved?

Acceleration programs are one way of keeping these students interested and challenged (Benbow & Stanley, 1996). Another suggestion is to offer an array of enrichment activities matched to students' interests so that gifted students can become more engaged in learning (Achter, Lubinski, & Benbow, 1996). Another suggestion is for educators to provide college counseling and career planning to both high and low achievers during the high school years (Peterson, 2000). Evidence indicates that both groups attend college: nearly all high-achieving gifted students and about 50 percent of low achievers. Educators may find that capitalizing on future college plans may motivate youngsters to do well in high school so that they have better choices for college admissions.

A subgroup of gifted students also needs special attention. Tragically, the long-term outcomes for "twice exceptional" students appear not to be as good as they should be (Holliday, Koller, & Thomas, 1999). As adults, these individuals perform more consistently with their learning disabilities than with their intellectual potential. They are more likely to complete high school than their peers with learning disabilities, but they are also more likely than their gifted peers to complete only a few semesters of college. Their earnings-outcomes reflect their school completion rates; many earn close to minimum wage. To avoid this negative pattern will require intervention. Schools should consider including gifted students with learning disabilities in organized transition programs or including them in career exploration opportunities along with their nondisabled gifted peers. Realistic career and college counseling should help these individuals understand their potential and select reasonable alternatives for postsecondary experiences.

FAMILIES

The importance of family is as great in the lives of young gifted and talented individuals as it is for other children. Some experts in gifted education, however, believe that these children's vulnerability and sensitivity often require special attention from family members (Rimm, 2001; Hébert, 2001). Supporting this belief are studies of eminent adults that clearly show how powerful the long-term influence of family is

Information about acceleration and enrichment approaches is given in the "Elementary Through High School" section of this chapter.

To review the special needs of gifted students with disabilities, read again that part of the "Characteristics" section of this chapter.

on gifted children (Filippelli & Walberg, 1997; Hébert, 1998; Kitano, 1997, 1998; Subotnik et al., 1993; Yewchuk, 1995). Definitive common threads run through the early lives of eminent adults. For example, regardless of the father's occupation, learning was valued for its own sake. The family was prepared to commit whatever time and resources were necessary to foster achievement and development of talent. These families arranged for instruction, encouraged and supervised practice and study, were involved in their children's education, and developed open channels of communication between parents and children. Perhaps most important, these parents served as role models by living an achieving lifestyle.

"Sons learn about feelings by watching their fathers and other men" (Hébert, 2001). For gifted boys, learning how to deal with and express emotions is important, particularly because gifted children are often overly sensitive (Piechowski, 1997). Hébert (2001) suggests that fathers can develop more intense relationships with their sons by being certain that they really listen, writing them letters at times of important decisions and times of major disappointments, and also sharing time and experiences. Recall that diverse gifted students are at increased risk for underachievement and underrepresentation. Some believe that Black boys are at the greatest risk (Hébert, 1998). For these children, it is important that parents and family instill a high achievement orientation and a strong belief in self by holding high and reasonable expectations while recognizing accomplishments.

Finally, parents and families also need to guide gifted children to make appropriate choices and to be realistic in their expectations for themselves and others. These children seem to be more mature than others of their age, but appearances can be deceptive (Clark, 2002). One result of the combination of these characteristics can be stress unlike that experienced by their peers (Nichols & Baum, 2000). These children, like others of their age, are not capable of making complex decisions or setting their own goals and directions. Families can help by maintaining open lines of communication through family meetings, talking with their children about values and how to balance life's events, and helping them determine what is important and what is not.

MAKING CONNECTIONS

Cultural diversity and its relationship to mainstream educational systems is presented in the "Characteristics" section of this chapter and also in Chapter 3.

MAKING CONNECTIONS

To compare different types of technology supports across students with special needs, read the "Technology" sections in Chapters 3–12.

TECHNOLOGY

Technology can be a tool, an inspiration, and a means to independent learning for all students. For gifted students, it can also facilitate differentiated instruction (Johnson, 2000). For example, one student can work on a tutorial in chemistry or physics while a classmate can be learning how to program the computer to develop an environmental monitoring and control system. Or these students can work on accelerated or enriched topics while their general education classmates work on their own assignments. For gifted students bored by instruction paced too slowly for them or on topics they have already mastered, technology can allow them to study

CHAPTER 7 *Giftedness and Talent Development*

advanced topics more in depth. And for gifted students, technology could well be considered a functional life skill: desktop publishing, creating multimedia presentations, accessing information via the Internet, word processing, making graphics, managing databases, and building spreadsheets.

Teachers at many schools, such as Central Virginia Governor's School for Science and Technology, have found that technology can be **infused** into the curriculum and need not be taught as discrete skills and applications. Students demonstrate proficiency using software applications in their assignments. For example, they use word processing—along with database, statistical, graphics, and literature search applications—to generate research papers. They also create multimedia presentations for their final reports. Students should be given opportunities to explore robotics, holography, telecommunications, biotechnology, and

The Internet provides opportunities for many enrichment activities. However, students need guidance and practice to become skilled users of databases and critical consumers of information to truly use the web as an efficient tool and resource.

other developing scientific applications of technology. When technology is integrated into the instruction of other disciplines, the computer becomes an intellectual tool used to facilitate learning, to extend the standard curriculum, and to effect its generalization to other settings and skills. For example, students could construct a database to keep records for a science project on air quality. The database could be used to relate different variables—such as time of day, temperature, wind conditions, cloud cover, and season of the year—to the amount of air pollution. By using telecommunications, students could share the database and the results of various comparisons with other students across the nation.

Nearly all of us can attest to the benefits of **telecommunications** in our daily lives. We are now able to communicate with friends efficiently and economically through e-mail. We are able to find important or interesting information "on the Web." Many of you registered for this class online and use Web editions of your college textbooks as you explore topics discussed in class. The practical benefits to all students, particularly gifted students, cannot be overestimated.

Telecommunications enables students who live miles apart, and may not even have met, to work together on joint projects. Students who live in remote areas can access major library facilities and computers that have capabilities to analyze complicated sets of data. They can link up to scientists who work at research laboratories to ask for help in solving a scientific or mathematical problem. Telecommunications can also provide opportunities for dialogue between students and practitioners from all across the nation on real issues and problems. Those who live in rural areas can participate in many courses not available at their home schools and can take advanced courses in math, foreign languages, science, and the arts without leaving their home schools.

For Web links to support your study of disabilities, look at the "Resources" sections at the end of every chapter in this text.

IN CONCLUSION

Summary

Gifted students do not have a disability that presents obstacles to their learning and participating in society. However, they can be handicapped by our social and educational systems, which can present barriers to their achieving to their potential. Gifted individuals possess unique intellectual abilities that can be developed into talents. One challenge facing educators is to develop and put in place a consistent array of educational options that will facilitate these individuals' development.

Self-Test Questions

Focus Questions

What is the current vision of giftedness and talent?

Giftedness is construed as potential for high performance and accomplishments at the upper end of any talent continuum: intellectual, artistic, creative, academic, or leadership.

Talent development: efforts of families, teachers, peers, and mentors to help students develop their aptitudes into outstanding abilities and achievements

Regardless of the definition applied, what descriptors can be used for gifted and talented individuals?

- Demonstrate high intellectual abilities
- Score well on tests of intelligence
- Learn more quickly than peers
- Apply complex thinking skills
- Achieve significantly higher than their classmates academically
- Tend to become leaders
- Are sensitive
- Tend to be perfectionists
- Are intense
- Are successful

What factors can inhibit giftedness and talent development?

Heredity

Environment: deprivation, lack of stimulation, family values, expectations, family's socioeconomic level, individual's birth position

Educational opportunities: availability of programs, bias

Why are educators concerned about issues related to underrepresentation of some subgroups of gifted learners?

Diverse students do not have equal access to programs for education of the gifted.

Fewer African American, Hispanic, and Native American children receive educational services for gifted students than would be expected from their percentage in the general student population.

Identification process is biased and favors students from, and talents encouraged in, the dominant culture.

What are two approaches to education of the gifted, and how do they differ from one another?

Two approaches to gifted education:

- Enrichment: interdisciplinary instruction, independent study, mentorships, internships, enrichment triad/revolving-door model, curriculum compacting
- Acceleration: advanced placement, honors sections, ability grouping, individualized instruction

Acceleration often places gifted students in existing general education programs for older students, whereas enrichment offers gifted students unique and special programs.

The most common educational arrangement is pull-out programs (resource rooms).

Challenge Question

Why, in the history of the United States, has there been such an inconsistent commitment to education of the gifted?

When leaders sense threats to the country's national security, education of the gifted becomes a priority. Because the Russians launched Sputnik in 1957, the 1960s saw programs for gifted students developed and expanded.

Commitment wanes when issues about equity and justice arise and are framed in terms some advantaged citizens being treated as "special."

No federal laws guarantee special education of the gifted.

CHAPTER 7 *Giftedness and Talent Development*

Meeting the Standards and Preparing for Licensure Exams

After reading this chapter, you should be able to demonstrate basic knowledge and skills described in the CEC standards and INTASC principles listed below. The section of this chapter most applicable to each standard is shown in parentheses at the end of the knowledge or skill statement.

Note: The CEC standards for the area of Gifts/Talents represent a combination of the CEC Common Core and Specialty Standards. Only representative standards have been selected. This treatment is unique to giftedness and talents and reflects that not all teachers of these exceptional students are special education teachers as usually defined.

 Combined Standard 1: Foundations

- **Models:** Models, theories and philosophies that form the basis for gifted education (Giftedness and Talents Defined)
- **Role of families:** Family systems and the role of families in the educational process (Families)
- History: Historical points of view and contribution of culturally diverse groups (History of the Field)

 Combined Standard 2: Development and Characteristics of Learners

- **Educational characteristics:** Educational Implications of various gifts and talents (Characteristics)
- **Families:** Family systems and the role of families in supporting development and educational progress for students with gifts and talents (Families)

Combined Standard 3: Individual Learning Differences

- **Diversity:** Impact of diversity on educational placement options for individuals with gifts and talents (Characteristics)
- **Gifts/talents and disabilities:** Academic characteristic of individuals with gifts, talents, and disabilities (Characteristics)

Combined Standard 4: Instructional Strategies

- **Differentiated materials:** Sources of differentiated materials for individual with gifts and talents

Educational strategies: Use strategies to facilitate integration into various settings (Accommodating for Inclusive Environments)

 Combined Standard 5: Learning Environments and Social Interactions

- **Management:** Effective management of teaching and learning for students with gifts and talents (Elementary Through High School)

 Combined Standard 7: Instructional Planning

- **General and differentiated curriculum:** General and differentiated curriculum for individuals with gifts and talents (Elementary Through High School)
- **Social skills:** Social skills needed for educational and other environments (Characteristics)

 Combined Standard 8: Assessment

- **Assessment:** Use and limitations of assessment instruments for students with gifts and talents (Giftedness and Talents Defined)

 Combined Standard 10: Collaboration

- **Families:** Concerns of families of individuals with gifts and talents and strategies to address these concerns (Families)
- **Collaboration:** Models and strategies for consultation and collaboration (Collaboration for Inclusion)

INTASC Principle 2:
The teacher understands how children learn and develop and can provide learning opportunities that support their intellectual, social, and personal development.

- **Cognitive factors and learning:** The teacher understands that students' physical, social, emotional, moral and cognitive development influence learning and knows how to address these factors when making instructional decisions. (Elementary Through High School)
- **Cognitive development impact on learning:** The teacher is aware of expected developmental progressions and ranges of individual variation within each domain (physical, social, emotional, moral and cognitive), can identify levels of readiness in learning, and understands how development in one domain may affect performance in others. (Elementary Through High School)

INTASC Principle 4:

The teacher understands and uses a variety of instructional strategies to encourage students' development of critical thinking, problem solving, and performance skills.

- **Cognitive processes:** The teacher understands the cognitive processes associated with various kinds of learning (e.g. critical and creative thinking, problem structuring and problem solving, invention, memorization and recall) and how these processes can be stimulated. (Elementary Through High School)

- **Critical thinking:** The teacher values the development of students' critical thinking, independent problem solving, and performance capabilities. (Elementary Through High School)

INTASC Principle 7:

The teacher plans instruction based upon knowledge of subject matter, students, the community, and curriculum goals.

- **Learning styles:** The teacher creates lessons and activities that operate at multiple levels to meet the developmental and individual needs of diverse learners and help each progress. (Elementary Through High School)

INTASC Principle 10:

The teacher fosters relationships with school colleagues, parents and agencies in the larger community to support students' learning and well-being.

- **Consulting:** The teacher makes links with other learning environments on behalf of students, by consulting with parents, counselors, teachers of other classes and activities within the schools, and professionals in other community agencies. (Collaboration for Inclusion)

- **Community resources:** The teacher can identify and use community resources to foster student learning. (Collaboration for Inclusion)

Standards in Practice

These knowledge statements, dispositions, and skills might be demonstrated by the beginning teacher who is able to modify instruction and curriculum to accommodate students with gifts and talents. The teacher might also consult with others knowledgeable about educating students with gifts and talents.

Go to the companion website (ablongman.com/smith5e) for detailed text correlations to CEC and INTASC standards, PRAXIS II™ exams, and other state-sponsored licensure exams.

SUPPLEMENTARY RESOURCES

Professional Readings and Resources

Campbell, L., Campbell, B., & Dickinson, D. (1999). *Teaching and learning through multiple intelligences* (2nd ed.). Boston: Allyn and Bacon.

Clark, B. (2002). *Growing up gifted: Developing the potential of children at home and school* (6th ed.). Upper Saddle River, NJ: Merrill/Prentice-Hall.

Castelano, J. A., & Díaz, E. I. (Eds.). (2002). *Reaching new horizons: Gifted and talented education for culturally and linguistically diverse students*. Boston: Allyn and Bacon.

Gallagher, J. J., & Gallagher, S. A. (1994). *Teaching the gifted child* (4th ed.). Boston: Allyn and Bacon.

Davis, G. A., & Rimm, S. B. (1998). *Education of the gifted and talented* (4th ed.). Englewood Cliffs, NJ: Prentice-Hall.

Rimm, S., & Rimm-Kaufman, S. (2001). *How Jane won: 55 successful women share how they grew from ordinary girls to extraordinary women*. New York: Crown Publishers.

Popular Books

Fenner, C. (1995). *Yolanda's genius*. New York: Aladdin.

Fitzgerald, J. D. (1985). *The great brain*. New York: Dell.

Kanigel, R. (1991). *The man who knew infinity: A life of the genius Ramanujan*. New York: Scribner.

Simpson, D. E. (1995). *A matter of color*. Austin, TX: The Inspirational Pen.

Pollack, W. (2000). *Real boys' voices*. New York: Random House.

 Videos and DVDs

Little Man Tate (1991). Orion

Jane directs a school for gifted children and discovers Tate, a 7-year-old boy who is exceptional in a number of fields. Tate had difficulty fitting in with other children his own age and therefore was very unhappy and depressed. Jane, herself a musical prodigy, offers Tate the opportunity to join a school that would allow him to grow both academically and socially.

This film provides insight into the alienation often experienced by gifted youth. Unable to fit in with children his own age, Tate enrolls in a summer college course that challenges him academically but demonstrates that being alienated from an age group can also lead to social isolation. Once Tate enrolls in a program for gifted children, he begins to feel comfortable with his exceptional abilities because many of his classmates come from similar situations.

Good Will Hunting (1998). Miramax

Will is an extremely gifted youth who grew up in foster homes and was abused. One day, working at M.I.T. as a janitor, he anonymously solves some Ph.D-level problems in mathematics, showcasing his intelligence. He is discovered and, because of his police record, is forced to see a psychiatrist as well as practice math with a noted professor. After a time with the psychiatrist, Will enters into a healthy father-son relationship and eventually is able to see his potential in the world by letting old wounds heal.

Even though Will is a genius, his brilliance cannot shelter him from the problems of having been raised in terrible foster homes and having experienced child abuse and a fragmented childhood. In this story, the main character was eventually fortunate enough to wind up in a supportive situation, but the film makes it clear that regardless of Will's intelligence, his life was still filled with tough obstacles. Ben Affleck and Matt Damon won the Academy Award for best original screenplay with this film, and Robin Williams was named Best Supporting Actor.

Amadeus (1984). Republic Pictures
This film depicts the entire life of Wolfgang Amadeus Mozart through the eyes of an extremely jealous, substantially older contemporary, Antonio Salieri. Salieri is the court composer of Vienna, and even though he is talented, his ability cannot be compared to that of Mozart. Salieri sees Mozart as an obscene, repulsive person, and he cannot understand why God would bless such a person with such incredible talent; this infuriates and torments Salieri for his entire life.

Mozart's incredible talent is legendary, and he was a true child prodigy. At 6 he was performing, at 7 he created his first sonata, and at 13 he produced his first full-length opera. His superior talent and potential for a long-lasting career ended tragically at the early age of 33. His downfall was ensured by his hedonistic life, frivolous spending, and alcoholism—and especially by the pressure of continually creating masterpieces.

Searching for Bobby Fisher (1993). Paramount
Josh is typical child, but one day he plays a game of chess with his father, and it soon becomes apparent that Josh is a prodigy at the game. He begins to develop his talent with a traditional instructor, while also honing his skill with a hustler in the park. Josh's father becomes overly competitive, putting too much pressure on his son always to win and to make chess the focal point of his young life. Josh is able to incorporate both of his "teachers' "types of strategies relieving stress and pressure.

This film demonstrates exceptionality in a single field; Josh is clearly a genius but not across all domains. It also shows the difficulties adults have with both talent development and children's giftedness. Children who show talent at an early age often feel fear, insecurity, and pressure. The desire to be "just like everyone else" is common among gifted children.

Parent, Professional, and Consumer Organizations and Agencies

Gifted Child Society
190 Rock Road
Glen Rock, NJ 07452
Phone: (201) 444-6530
Web site: http://www.gifted.org/society

National Association for Gifted Children
1707 L Street NW
Suite 550
Washington, DC 20036
Phone: (202) 785-4268
Web site: http://www.nagc.org

National Office for American Mensa, Gifted Children Program
1229 Corporate Drive West
Arlington, TX 76006-60
Phone: (800) 66-MENSA
Web site: http://www.us.mensa.org

The Association for the Gifted (TAG), Council for Exceptional Children
1920 Association Drive
Reston, VA 22091
Phone: (703) 620-3660; (888) CEC-SPED
Web site: www.cectag.org

The Belin & Blank International Center for Gifted Education and Talent Development
210 Lindquist Center
The University of Iowa
Iowa City, IA 52242
Web site: http://www.uiowa.edu/~belinctr
Phone: (319) 335-6148
(800) 336-6463

National Research Center on the Gifted and Talented
362 Fairfield Road, U-7
Storrs, CT 06269-2007
Phone: (860) 486-4678
E-mail: epsadm06@uconnvm.uconn.edu
Web site: http://www.uconn.edu/nrcgt.html

VideoWorkshop Extra

If the VideoWorkshop package was included with your textbook, go to Chapter 7 of the Companion Website (www.ablongman.com/smith5e) and click on the VideoWorkshop button. Follow the instructions for viewing Video clip 8. Consider this information along with what you have read in Chapter 7 as you answer the following questions.

Video Clip 8 Visual Impairment (Time 4:34)

1. Based on the definitions of giftedness and talent discussed in this chapter of your text, can we consider Kyle gifted or talented even though he has a documented disability? Why?

2. How is Kyle's school experience enhancing the possibility that he will make a successful transition to adulthood? What other opportunities should the school be offering to Kyle?

Edvard Munch, *Angst,* 1984. Oil on canvas 94 × 74 cm. Munch Museum, Oslo.
Artwork © Munch Museum/Munch-Ellingsen Group/ARS 2002;
Photograph © Munch Museum (Andersen/de Jong).

EDVARD MUNCH, the Norwegian painter who is probably best known for the highly emotional and tormented images in his paintings, himself had a tragic childhood and troubled life. Leaving behind what he thought were the emotionless subjects of the impressionists, he sought to record the anguish of modern humanity's psyche. The result was stark and terrifying images of alienation and despair, emotions that Munch himself experienced. For many years, Munch was plagued by nervous disorders and depression. His first documented hospitalization was at a Swiss clinic in 1900 (Bischoff, 1988). During that decade, Munch had long periods of depression and a series of nervous breakdowns. In 1908, after a nervous breakdown in Copenhagen, he spent half a year in a clinic, and recovered after electroshock treatment (Grolier, 1993). Many of his paintings during this period were of the nurses and doctors who took care of him (Messer, 1985). Possibly, his most well-known painting to Americans is *The Scream.*

Anxiety (1894) is a stream of people walking in the evening on a city's main street. Munch explained that he painted these people as though they had masks, behind which they were hiding their suffering, their anxiety.

8 Emotional or Behavioral Disorders

A PERSONAL PERSPECTIVE

The Ivory Tower Goes to School

Tom Catron is a clinical child psychologist who has spent over 20 years working with children with emotional and behavioral problems in classroom settings. He has helped pioneer the development of programs for teachers and families. He is a professor of psychiatry, psychology, and pediatrics at Vanderbilt University and director of the Vanderbilt Community Mental Health Center and the Center for Psychotherapy Research and Policy.

It is seldom the case that a child or adolescent referred to our clinic for mental health services that does not have difficulties at school. This is not surprising given that children spend so much of their time in school.

I remember my first case, a third-grade student referred by his parents for evaluation and treatment. The parents had received numerous "complaints" from the school regarding the child's inattention, disruptiveness, and poor academic progress. I was fortunate that the teacher returned my call that afternoon. She was quite at her wits' end with the student. I made an appointment to go interview the teacher and observe the child in the classroom.

I was quite nervous as I drove up to the school as I didn't really know what to expect. I feared that the teacher was going to resent my presence and attempts to assist (I was the "know-it-all" from the Ivory Tower university). I was concerned that the teacher had formed unalterable opinions and attributions about this student which would create obstacles for a school based intervention. Furthermore, I feared that I would not have a clue as to how to address the student's problems.

To my delight, the meeting could not have gone any better. The teacher was an experienced educator and provided me with important information about the student's behavior and her attempts to address the problems. She answered all of my questions and was quite honest about her frustration with her inability to improve the situation. Mostly, she felt incompetent, rather than angry at the child, and was eager to get some fresh ideas on how to address his problems.

I have observed that some students with challenging problems can negatively influence a parent's, teacher's, and therapist's sense of competency. When we all try very hard and we are not successful, we experience a level of frustration and sense of failure. Sometimes people blame and resent the child who makes them feel this way.

The opportunity to observe this student in the class was extremely useful. I had not yet met the student, nor was he aware that I was there to observe him. He was everything the parents and teacher described. It was possible to be overwhelmed by the complexity and severity of his problems. Where would one start? Previous efforts to address his behavior were met with resistance and increased frequency of difficulty. His peers rejected him and he was socially isolated, though this did not stop him from constantly attempting to gain their attention (and, he must have hoped, their approval). He was a serious disruption to the class and engaged in little academic activity. On the surface, this was a child who was a candidate for a more restrictive, self-contained classroom.

Rather than moving him to a different classroom, the teacher, parents, and I worked together to establish some short-term goals, objectives, and interventions. I helped the teacher and parents establish a behavior modification plan, the teacher developed an educational plan to address his learning deficits, and I developed a social skill training program and therapeutic intervention with the child and parents to address the anxiety and depression.

Fortunately, this was a success story. The student responded quickly to the behavior management and educational plan and later overcame the anxiety and depressive symptoms related to his social failure. For me as a young professional, I was hooked. Working with children in the school setting had tremendous merit and opportunity. It defined my clinical and research career paths.

The chapter that you are about to read on emotional and behavioral disorders (EBD) will provide you with basic information that will help you throughout your career as a teacher. Here are a few other tidbits.

About Parents: Getting parental participation is crucial in efforts to recognize EBD and to treat it successfully. The tendency to blame parents or the children for the problems should be avoided. Parents don't always observe the kinds of problems at home that teachers observe at school. Be patient and find alternative ways to present information so that the parent understands your concerns and can work with you. Avoid developing an adversarial relationship.

About Teachers: There is a tendency to handle EBD problems in ways that are familiar and comfortable. As a result, teachers resort to familiar disciplinary and instructional techniques and abandon the knowledge gained through instruction about effective interventions. It takes effort and energy to practice effective techniques.

About the EBD Classification: There are significant differences in classification and nomenclature between mental health and education. Each discipline should be familiar with the other's vernacular.

And Finally: Teachers, like mental health clinicians, are constantly bombarded with innovations and new intervention techniques. Thus they must sift through a great deal of material and must learn how to tell what is empirically based or validated from what is just ideologically appealing.

1. Why do you hear a consistent and frequent message in this text about professionals' responsibility to use empirically based (scientifically validated) practices?

2. How does Dr. Catron's story explain how related service professionals and educators collaborate and develop partnerships to help families and children?

ADVANCE ORGANIZERS

Overview

Children with emotional or behavioral disorders typically fall into one of two categories: externalizing behavior problems and internalizing behavior problems. Aggressive, coercive, and hostile children have externalizing problems, have the poorest outcome probabilities, are identified at a greater rate, and experience more social rejection than those who are anxious, depressed, and withdrawn and thus have internalizing problems. Fewer than 1 percent of all schoolchildren are identified as having this disability, but this may well reflect an underidentification of youngsters with internalizing problems and the stigma associated with these conditions.

Self-Test Questions

Focus Questions

- How do the IDEA and the National Mental Health and Special Education Coalition definitions of emotional or behavioral disorders compare?

- What are the major subgroups of this disability, and how would you describe the conditions that fall into each subgroup?

- What are the major causes of this disability, and how can it be prevented?

- What outcomes are likely for these children when effective intervention is not provided?

- How can teachers help children with this disability?

Challenge Question

- What educational placement options are used for students with emotional or behavioral disorders, and how can services be improved?

Making Connections

Use the learning strategy—Advance Organizers—to help focus your study of this chapter's content, and reinforce your learning by reviewing answers to the Focus and Challenge questions at the end of the chapter.

Most of us find ways to express our individuality and creativity while keeping our behavior within the boundaries of what is considered appropriate. Most children learn very early that life is easier and more pleasant when they conform to certain standards of behavior. Although these standards are rooted in a long history and tend to be rather inflexible, they do vary somewhat with the situation. Judgments about the appropriateness of a person's actions are often made in terms of behavioral expectations that take into account the individual's age and/or the setting in which the behavior occurs.

Expectations for "proper" behavior vary by environments and settings. Some behavior that is acceptable on the playground or in the neighborhood after school may not match the norms expected at school. Most children learn quickly that at school, they are expected to be generally quiet, orderly, cooperative with other children, compliant with teacher's instructions, and attentive to learning. Children at home are expected to be cheerful, loving, helpful, and obedient to their parents. In their communities, children are expected to respect their neighbors' property, to abide by curfews and traffic rules, and generally to grow into their roles as the new generation of adult leaders of society. Children whose behavior is inconsistent with expectations of normal behavior in these environments are regarded as having problems.

Sometimes problems are not so obvious. They may be hidden, as in teenage girls who constantly diet, starving to the point of endangering their health in an exaggerated effort to be fashion-model slim, or the boy who hides his suicidal depression behind a façade of perfect behavior. These hidden disorders are also serious problems, but their signs are often ignored and the conditions untreated. Don't make the mistake of thinking that all disorders are simple violations of standards of age-appropriate behaviors or societal norms. Some emotional or behavioral disorders appear to be unrelated to either; they would be obvious at any age and in any culture. For example, psychosis—a major departure from normal acting, thinking, and feeling, sometimes expressed in unprovoked physical aggression toward self or others—would be considered disordered behavior at any age and in any society. Teachers and other professionals can play an important part in helping children with this disability to learn in school, to have more satisfying relationships with friends and family, and to assume adult responsibilities in their communities. Let's see how this might be accomplished.

OPPORTUNITIES FOR A BETTER FUTURE

Children with emotional or behavioral disorders and people with mental illness do not fare well in American society. In fact, across most of history they have been persecuted and shunned. When compared with other students, even those with disabilities, this group of students has seemed to pose the greatest challenges to school systems across the nation. And as guns became easier for children to possess and the use of weapons in violent incidents increased at schools, Congress and the public tended to hold children with emotional or behavioral disorders accountable for these threats against public safety.

Turning Legacies into Lessons

Emotional or behavioral disorders commonly occur along with other disabilities and conditions (learning disabilities, ADHD), and this makes the delivery of an appropriate education more complicated. These students are more likely to be retained at least one grade, to fail more courses, to receive their education outside of the general education classroom, and to experience an exceptionally high dropout rate; over half of them leave school before graduating. African American males from poor families are much more likely to be identified as having emotional or behavioral disorders than are affluent white students. Clearly, much work is needed to learn more about prevention techniques and educational procedures that are effective and yield better outcomes for this group of learners.

Thinking About Dilemmas to Solve

As you read this chapter, ponder these students' needs, the supports they require, and the outcomes they should achieve.
Think about

- How to reduce the overrepresentation of African American boys in this special education category

- How some schools achieve high outcomes for these students

- How successful programs can be replicated at other schools

- How to increase school attendance, grade point averages, and these students' positive feelings about school

- How to decrease the dropout rates of these students

Opportunities for a Better Future

EMOTIONAL OR BEHAVIORAL DISORDERS DEFINED

Emotional or behavioral disorders (EBD) are difficult to define. In fact, some think that people are identified as having this disability "whenever an adult authority said so" (Hallahan & Kauffman, 2000, p. 249). In other words, in many cases the application of the definition is subjective. Definitions of this disability, including the one used in IDEA, are based on the one developed by Eli Bower (1960, 1982). Let's first look at the federal definition.

IDEA uses the term **emotional disturbance** to describe children with behavioral or emotional disorders, defining it as follows:

> *The term means a condition exhibiting one or more of the following characteristics over a long period of time and to a marked degree that adversely affects a child's educational performance:*
>
> - *An inability to learn that cannot be explained by intellectual, sensory, or health factors.*
> - *An inability to build or maintain satisfactory interpersonal relationships with peers and teachers.*
> - *Inappropriate types of behavior or feelings under normal circumstances.*
> - *A general pervasive mood of unhappiness or depression.*
> - *A tendency to develop physical symptoms related to fears associated with personal or school problems.*
>
> *The term includes children who are schizophrenic. The term does not include children who are socially maladjusted, unless it is determined that they have an emotional disturbance. (U.S. Department of Education, 1999, p. 12422)*

Old versions of IDEA used the term **serious emotional disturbance** to describe this disability area, but *serious* was dropped in 1999 when the U.S. Department of Education created the regulations for the 1997 version of IDEA. The government did not, however, change the substance of the disability when it changed the term. Here's what it said about the deletion: "[It] is intended to have no substantive or legal significance. It is intended strictly to eliminate the pejorative connotation of the term 'serious'" (U.S. Department of Education, 1999, p. 12542). In addition, some implied parts of the federal definition are important to understand. For example, although only one characteristic listed in the IDEA definition need be present for the student to qualify for special education, whatever the characteristics, the child's educational performance must be adversely affected. Because almost everyone experiences some mild maladjustment for short periods of their lives, the definition also requires that the child exhibit the characteristic for a long time and to a marked degree or significant level of intensity.

The IDEA term and definition have been criticized by many professionals (Kauffman, 2001). To them, using only the word *emotional* excludes students whose disability is only behavioral. The exclusion of students who are "socially maladjusted," which is not defined, contributes to this misunderstanding. And the reference to "educational performance" has been narrowly interpreted to mean only academic performance, not behavioral or social performance, not functional or life skills, and not vocational skills.

Responding to these criticisms, a coalition of 17 organizations, which calls itself the National Mental Health and Special Education Coalition, drafted another definition and continues to lobby federal and state governments to adopt it (Forness & Knitzer, 1992). It is unlikely, however, that this definition will gain uni-

MAKING CONNECTIONS

For a review of IDEA, see Chapters 1 and 2 and also the What IDEA Says boxes found in many chapters of this text.

versal acceptance because it could be used to identify too many children (Kauffman, 2002 July 14, personal communication). Here is the coalition's proposed definition:

> *The term* emotional or behavioral disorder *means a disability characterized by behavioral or emotional responses in school so different from appropriate age, cultural, or ethnic norms that they adversely affect educational performance. Educational performance includes academic, social, vocational, and personal skills. Such a disability:*
>
> - *is more than a temporary, expected response to stressful events in the environment;*
> - *is consistently exhibited in two different settings, at least one of which is school-related; and*
> - *is unresponsive to direct intervention in general education, or the child's condition is such that general education interventions would be insufficient.*
>
> *Emotional and behavioral disorders can coexist with other disabilities.*
>
> *This category may include children or youths with schizophrenic disorders, affective disorders, anxiety disorder, or other sustained disorders of conduct or adjustment when they adversely affect educational performance in accordance with [the opening part of the definition]. (p. 13)*

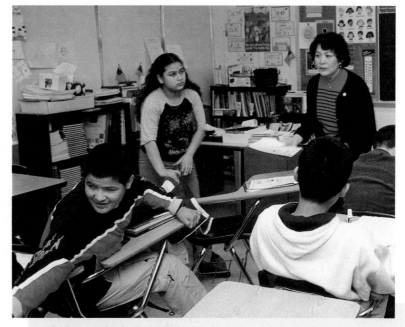

Children in school are expected to pay attention to their schoolwork, but this expectation can be difficult for students with emotional or behavioral disorders.

What are the types of emotional or behavioral disorders?

Emotional or behavioral disorders can be divided into three groups:

1. Externalizing
2. Internalizing
3. Low incidence

Externalizing behaviors can be characterized as an undercontrolled, acting out style that includes behaviors that could be described as aggressive, arguing, impulsive, coercive, and noncompliant. **Internalizing behaviors** can be characterized as an overcontrolled and inhibited style that includes behaviors that could be described as withdrawn, lonely, depressed, and anxious (Gresham et al., 1999).

Students who exhibit externalizing and internalizing behaviors, respectively, are the two main groups of students with emotional or behavioral disorders, but they do not account for all of the conditions that result in placement in this special education category. The *DSM-IV Manual* published by the American Psychiatric Association (1994) provides a section for disorders usually first diagnosed in

Table 8.1 Examples of Externalizing and Internalizing Behavior Problems

Externalizing Behaviors	Internalizing Behaviors
Violates basic rights of others	Exhibits painful shyness
Violates societal norms or rules	Is teased by peers
Has tantrums	Is neglected by peers
Causes property loss or damage	Is depressed
Is hostile	Is anorexic
Argues	Is bulimic
Is defiant	Is socially withdrawn
Is physically aggressive	Tends to be suicidal
Ignores teachers' reprimands	Has unfounded fears and phobias
Steals	Tends to have low self-esteem
Damages others' property	Has excessive worries
Demonstrates obsessive/compulsive behaviors	Panics
Causes or threatens physical harm to people or animals	
Uses lewd or obscene gestures	
Is hyperactive	

children, but not all of these are considered disabilities by the federal government (motor skills disorders, tic disorders, mood disorder, oppositional defiant disorder). Table 8.1 defines and explains some of the common externalizing and internalizing behaviors seen in special education students. Remember, conditions that are more disturbing to other people are identified more often and earlier. Teachers must be alert to internalizing disorders, which are equally serious but are not always identified, leaving children without appropriate special education services. Also, emotional or behavioral disorders can coexist with other disabilities. Therefore, a section is devoted to this disability when combined with ADHD.

• ***Externalizing Behavior Problems*** **Externalizing behaviors** are aggressive behaviors expressed outwardly, usually toward other persons. Some typical examples are hyperactivity, a high level of irritating behavior that is impulsive and distractible, and **persistent aggression.** Young children who have serious challenging behaviors that persist are the most likely to be referred for psychiatric services (Maag, 2000). Table 8.1 lists some examples of externalizing behavior problems. Here three common problems are discussed: hyperactivity, aggression, and delinquency.

MAKING CONNECTIONS

ADHD is also discussed in Chapters 1, 4, and 9, and in the "Coexisting ADHD" section later in this chapter.

Hyperactivity is one of the most common complaints about children referred for evaluations as having emotional or behavioral disorders. Hyperactivity is also a defining symptom of ADHD. Hyperactivity is difficult to define; the judgment about whether a certain level of a specific activity is too much, or "hyper," is often subjective. If, for example, the activity is admired, the child might be described as energetic or enthusiastic rather than hyperactive. Nevertheless, the *DSM-IV* gives some good examples about which there is considerable consensus. See if you can use the *DSM-IV* description to arrive at a definition of hyperactivity:

> *Hyperactivity may be manifested by fidgetiness or squirming in one's seat, by not remaining seated when expected to do so, by excessive running or climbing*

in situations where it is inappropriate, by having difficulty playing or engaging quietly in leisure activities, by appearing to be often "on the go" or as if "driven by a motor," or by talking excessively. (American Psychiatric Association, 1994, p. 79)

Aggression may be turned toward objects, toward the self, or toward others. The *DSM-IV* does not directly define aggression, but it does include elements of aggression in two of the disorders it describes: conduct disorders and oppositional defiant disorder. Of the latter, the manual notes that it includes

Following rules, being a good communicator, and knowing how to resolve disputes are skills many students have problems learning and applying.

a recurrent pattern of negativistic, defiant, disobedient, and hostile behavior toward authority figures . . . and is characterized by the frequent occurrence of at least four of the following behaviors: losing temper, arguing with adults, actively defying or refusing to comply with the requests or rules of adults, deliberately doing things that will annoy other people, blaming others for his or her mistakes or misbehavior, being touchy or easily annoyed by others, being angry and resentful, or being spiteful or vindictive. (American Psychiatric Association, 1994, p. 91)

Aggressive behavior, particularly when it is observed in very young children, is particularly worrisome. This is not just because of the behavior itself—though that should not be minimized—but also because of its strong correlation with long-term problems (dropping out of school, delinquency, violence). A pattern of early aggressive acts beginning with annoying and bullying, followed by physical fighting, is a clear pathway, particularly for boys, to violence in late adolescence (Talbott & Thiede, 1999).

Some 30 to 50 percent of youth in correctional facilities are individuals with disabilities (IDEA Practices, 2002). In this group, learning disabilities and emotional or behavioral disorders are about equally represented (45 and 42 percent, respectively). Delinquency, or juvenile delinquency, is defined by the criminal justice system rather than by the medical or educational establishment. Delinquency consists of illegal acts committed by juveniles, which could include crimes such as theft or assault. Remember that although some children who are delinquent have emotional or behavioral disorders, many do not—just as some children with emotional or behavioral disorders are delinquent but many are not. However, it is very important to understand that many of these children are at great risk for being involved with the criminal justice system (Edens & Otto, 1997). Their rates of contact are disproportionately high. While still in high school, students with emotional or behavioral disorders are 13 times more likely to be arrested than other students with disabilities (Office of Special Education Programs [OSEP], 2001).

M_{AKING} C_{ONNECTIONS}

Juvenile justice is discussed in the "Elementary Through High School" section of this chapter.

• *Internalizing Behavior Problems* Internalizing behaviors are typically expressed by being socially withdrawn. Surprisingly, students who identify themselves as having ADHD also describe themselves as having more internalizing behaviors and are more introspective about their problems (Volpe et al., 1999). Examples of internalizing behaviors include

• Anorexia or bulimia

- Depression
- Anxiety

Anorexia and **bulimia** are serious eating disorders that usually occur during students' teenage years (Manley, Rickson, & Standeven, 2000). These disorders occur because of individuals' (typically girls') preoccupation with weight and body image, their drive for thinness, and their fear of becoming fat. Many causes for these problems have been suggested; they include the media's projection of beauty and health, competition among peers, perfectionism, personal insecurity, and family crisis. Regardless of the cause, teachers can help by spotting these tendencies early and seeking assistance from the school's support team or school nurse.

Depression is often difficult to recognize in children. Its components—such as guilt, self-blame, feelings of rejection, lethargy, low self-esteem, and negative self-image—are often overlooked or may be expressed by behaviors that look like a different problem entirely. Children's behavior when they are depressed may appear so different from the depressed behavior of adults that teachers and parents may have difficulty recognizing the depression. For example, a severely depressed child might attempt to harm himself by running into a busy street or hurling himself off a ledge. An adult might assume this behavior was normal because many children accidentally do those things, or they might minimize its seriousness. In addition, children usually do not have the vocabulary, personal insight, or experience to be able to recognize and label feelings of depression.

Anxiety disorders may be demonstrated as intense anxiety upon separation from family, friends, or a familiar environment, as excessive shrinking from contact with strangers, or as unfocused, excessive worry and fear. Anxiety disorders are difficult to recognize in children. Because withdrawn children engage in very low levels of positive interactions with their peers, peer rating scales may help educators identify these disorders. Children with internalizing behavior problems, regardless of the type, tend to be underidentified, and this leaves many of them at risk of remaining untreated or receiving needed services later than they should.

- *Low Incidence Emotional or Behavioral Disorders* Some disorders occur very infrequently but are quite serious when they do occur. For example, schizophrenia and Tourette's syndrome can have tragic consequences for the individuals involved and their families; thankfully, they do not have high prevalence rates.

Schizophrenia, sometimes considered a form of psychosis or a type of pervavsive developmental disability (American Psychological Association, 1994), is an extremely rare disorder in children, although approximately 1 percent of the general population over the age of 18 has been diagnosed as having schizophrenia. When it occurs, it places great demands on service systems. It usually involves bizarre delusions (such as believing one's thoughts are controlled by the police), hallucinations (such as voices telling one what to think), "loosening" of associations (disconnected thoughts), and incoherence. Schizophrenia is most prevalent between the ages of 15 and 45, and experts agree that the earlier the onset, the more severe the disturbance in adulthood (Newcomer, 1993). Children with schizophrenia have serious difficulties with schoolwork and often must live in special hospital and educational settings during part of their childhood. Their IEPs are complex and require the collaboration of members from a multidisciplinary team.

Another low incidence disorder, which occurs in about 4 to 5 individuals per 1,000, is **Tourette's syndrome.** This disorder is characterized by multiple tics (sudden, rapid, recurrent, and stereotyped motor movements or vocalizations). These individuals may engage in uncontrollable movements at different locations in the body, or they may make strange noises or say inappropriate words or phrases. Or they may have both motor and verbal tics. The verbal tics may be sounds like grunts, yelps, snorts, barks, or obscenities. This disorder causes considerable distress

CHAPTER 8 *Emotional or Behavioral Disorders*

to the individual involved and impairs all aspects of the person's life (American Psychiatric Association, 1994).

• *Coexisting ADHD* Attention deficit/hyperactivity disorder (ADHD) is more likely to be identified in boys, particularly boys who have externalizing behaviors (Reid et al., 2000). As ADHD characteristics (impulsive, talks too much, too intense, too active) increase, antisocial behaviors increase as well, and positive social interactions decrease (Merrell & Boelter, 2001). Researchers now understand that emotional or behavioral disorders often coexist with other disabilities or conditions, and when this happens, students need special help because their problems can be very serious (Bussing et al., 1998). In cases where ADHD and antisocial behaviors both occur, the combination can be dangerous (Gresham, Lane, & Lambros, 2000). Violent behaviors tend to happen infrequently. They also tend to be resistant to treatment, and because events do not occur at a high rate, many of these students do not qualify for special services.

Internalizing behavior problems require intervention but, unfortunately, go untreated because children with these problems are not disruptive.

How common is it for ADHD and emotional or behavioral disorders to coexist? In one study of children with ADHD, it was found that 42 percent received special education services under the emotional or behavioral disorders category (Bussing et al., 1998). It is interesting that 25 percent of the students with ADHD in that study received no mental health services. In another study, researchers learned that, ADHD coexists more often with emotional or behavioral disorders than with learning disabilities (Bussing et al., 1998). More of these students receive medication, such as Ritalin or Concerta, to control their behaviors because research is now showing that a combination of behavioral and medical intervention is most powerful in the treatment of ADHD (Jensen, 2000; Pappadopulos & Jensen, 2001). Concerta will probably become the drug of choice, replacing Ritalin, because its time-release feature makes it unnecessary to take medication during the school day, which relieves school personnel of the duties of distributing and monitoring the use of prescription drugs (Newcorn, 2001).

MAKING CONNECTIONS

ADHD is also discussed in Chapters 1, 4, and 9.

Are some groups specifically excluded from this special education category?

Two groups of children—the **socially maladjusted** and those with **conduct disorders**—are *not* eligible for special education services (unless they have another qualifying condition as well). *Neither* group is included in the IDEA definition (Lane & Wehby, 2002; Walker et al., 2001). Although social maladjustment is widely discussed, particularly as politicians and educators talk about discipline and violence in schools, IDEA does not call it out as a special education category or as a subcategory of emotional or behavioral disorders. In the *DSM-IV*, The American Psychiatric Association defines conduct disorders as "a repetitive and persistent pattern of behavior in which the basic rights of others or major age-appropriate societal norms or rules are violated (1994, p. 85). Section 504 and ADA do not have exclusions for social maladjustment, so the educational system is required to make accommodations for these students even though they do not qualify for special education services (Zirkel, 1999).

Emotional or Behavioral Disorders Defined

Although the law and courts are clear about social maladjustment and conduct disorders not being subsets of emotional or behavioral disorders, practice is not (Costenbader & Buntaine, 1999). Why is there confusion about the educational needs of children who are socially maladjusted or who have conduct disorders? Some explanations are related to definitional issues; others are related to what people think is best for the students involved (Kauffman, 2001; Walker et al., 2000). Here are five reasons:

1. No generally agreed-upon definition of social maladjustment exists.
2. It is very difficult reliably to distinguish students with externalizing emotional or behavioral disorders from students with conduct disorders.
3. A more inclusive definition will increase special education enrollment to levels beyond tolerance and acceptability.
4. Because the needs of students with conduct disorders are best met by specialists prepared to deal with their problems, they should be identified as special education students, even if technically they do not qualify.
5. Many people believe these students are just "naughty" and do not have disabilities.

How are emotional or behavioral disorders identified?

Astute adults almost universally and immediately identify some children with emotional or behavioral disorders. This quick assessment is especially likely in the case of students with externalizing behavior patterns. Why might this be so? Standards for normal behavior change as children grow up and move through the stages of their lives. When children behave outside of what is expected for their age group, it becomes a cause for concern. For example, the behavior of an 8-year-old who suddenly begins to wet the bed, clings to his mother, and stops talking creates great concern. Even though almost identical behavior would be totally accepted in a toddler, an 8-year-old who acts in this way is perceived as having a problem. Think of examples of behavior that provoke concerns about children of one age but, if demonstrated by a child of a different age, do not raise questions at all.

The fact that behavior inappropriate for an individual's age draws attention and can result in the individual's being identified as having an emotional or behavioral disorder makes some experts worry about subjectivity in the assessment process. Also, students with internalizing behaviors are often missed when only teacher referrals are used. Experts recommend that standardized tests or procedures be used in the identification process (Gresham et al., 1999). Some such methods are available. For example, the *Critical Skills Index*, the *Student Risk Screening Scale*, and the *Systematic Screening for Behavior Disorders* are assessment instruments that take the subjectivity out of the identification process. For externalizing behaviors, another very reliable, and simple, measure that is used to identify students is the number of disciplinary referrals to the principal's office (Sugai et al., 2000; Walker, 2000).

Some concerns about this category of special education focus on the disproportionate number of African American males, particularly children who are disruptive, identified as having emotional or behavioral disorders (Townsend, 2000; U.S. Department of Education, 2001). Whereas these boys are overrepresented, other groups, such as Asian Americans and girls, are underrepresented. Some explanations for disproportionate representation center on the lack of reliable methods for identifying these children, particularly those with internalizing behaviors. Current knowledge can guide educators' actions until more accurate assessment procedures are available:

- Evaluation measures should come from at least two different settings.
- Performance in both academics and social skills should be considered.

MAKING CONNECTIONS

For issues about over- and underrepresentation of diverse learners in special education, see Chapter 3.

CHAPTER 8 *Emotional or Behavioral Disorders*

- Information about the child should come from different people who play different roles.
- A variety of methods to assess students' behavior should be used (behavior rating scales, **ecological assessments,** classroom observations, ABC analyses, interviews, projective tests, standardized tests, social work evaluations, psychiatric analyses, functional assessments).

How do emotional or behavioral disorders affect the individuals involved?

These special education students have lower grades, are more likely to fail at least one class during high school (77 percent do), and often experience grade retention. Probably because of their lack of success academically, half of them drop out of school, often by tenth grade—the highest dropout rate of all groups of students with disabilities. And they have a high probability of encountering the juvenile justice system (OSEP, 2001; Oswald & Coutinho, 1996). Their educational programs are also different from those of their peers with and without disabilities. Possibly because of the excessive number of externalizing behaviors they present, their educational programs focus almost exclusively on behavior management and social adjustment. Unfortunately, a balance of these features with either academic or vocational components is typically not achieved. Ironically, research shows that when these students are engaged in academic learning, their disruptive behavior improves as well (Lane, 1999; Lane et al., 2001).

Obviously, emotional or behavioral disorders have grave effects on the life of the individual, whether child or adult, who has the disability. Without intervention, the person is likely to live with emotional pain and isolation and may perhaps even engage in ever-increasing antisocial activity. Once students with behavioral or emotional problems are identified and receive appropriate services, they generally improve their academic skills, enhance their personal relations, and enjoy more satisfying interactions with other people. This disability also affects their relationships with family members, adults, their peers, and their teachers—who have the highest turnover rates in the field of education (U.S. Department of Education, 2001).

MAKING CONNECTIONS

Problems associated with dropping out of school are discussed in Chapter 1 and in most of the "Transition" sections in this text.

HISTORY OF THE FIELD

Throughout history, people have recognized emotional or behavioral disorders, particularly in adults, but this disability was often confused with other disorders (Safford & Safford, 1996). It was probably Leo Kanner's 1957 book *Child Psychiatry* that stimulated the development of services for children in America. In ancient times, people believed that individuals with emotional or behavioral disorders were possessed by the devil or evil spirits. During some periods, such as in ancient Egypt, treatment was enlightened and humane (Deutsch, 1949). However, the mystery surrounding mental illness often fostered negative assumptions about its causes and resulted in horrible treatment. Some societies believed that these disorders were contagious, and the people affected were removed from the community to protect others. Treatments of those days reflected such beliefs and commonly included excessive punishment, imprisonment, placement in poorhouses, beatings, chainings, straitjacketing, and other cruel actions.

The first institution for people with mental disorders was established in London in 1547. Officially named St. Mary of Bethlehem, it became known as Bedlam, a term that now means a place of noise and uproar. Individuals in this institution were chained, starved, and beaten. A popular form of entertainment in London was to take the family, including children, for an outing to view the "lunatics" at Bedlam.

MAKING CONNECTIONS

Review the history of care and treatment of people with disabilities by reading again the section "Origins of Special Education" in Chapter 1 and the "History" sections in Chapters 3–12.

Philippe Pinel, chief physician at Saltpêtrière, freeing patients with mental disorders from their chains.

By the 18th Century, changes began to occur through the efforts of reform-minded individuals. For instance, Philippe Pinel, a French psychiatrist, in 1792 ordered humanitarian reform, including unchaining, for mental patients at the Saltpêtrière, a Paris asylum for the "insane" (Brigham, 1847). In the United States, major reform in the identification and treatment of children and adults with emotional or behavioral disorders began with the efforts of reformers in the 1800s. Benjamin Rush (1745–1813), who is considered the father of American psychiatry, proposed more humane methods of caring for children with these problems. (Rush, a signer of the Declaration of Independence, was not only a leader in the American independence movement but also a founder of the first American antislavery society.)

Samuel Gridley Howe, in addition to his work in blindness and mental retardation, worked to improve the treatment of people with mental disorders. Dorothea Dix influenced the founding of state institutions for people with mental disorders. By 1844 many states had institutions for people with mental disorders, and the Association of Medical Superintendents of American Institutions for the Insane (now the American Psychiatric Association) was founded. But the hope with which early institutions were founded soon gave way to pessimism as the institutions became primarily custodial.

Before the late 1800s and the initiation of public school classes for children with emotional or behavioral disorders, most of these children received no services at all. The passage of compulsory education laws toward the end of that century caused educational services for these students to be developed, even though many attended ungraded classes along with other students who did not adapt well to general education settings. In 1871 a class for students who were regarded as troublemakers was opened in New Haven, Connecticut. It is interesting that many of the early public school classes provided many noneducational services to these students. These multidisciplinary services often included mental health, health care, and other social services, much like the **wraparound services** being proposed today. Thus a "safety net" of school, community, and social services existed to help children and their families (Duckworth et al., 2001). In 1909 William Healy founded the Juvenile Psychopathic Institute in Chicago, where he and Augusta Bronner conducted studies of juvenile offenders (Healy & Bronner, 1926). At about this same time, the theoretical work of Sigmund Freud (1856–1939), the founder of psychoanalysis, and

MAKING CONNECTIONS

Wraparound services are also discussed in the "Collaboration" section of this chapter.

CHAPTER 8 *Emotional or Behavioral Disorders*

his daughter Anna Freud began to influence the education and treatment of children with emotional or behavioral disorders both in Europe and in the United States. In 1944 Bruno Bettelheim began at the University of Chicago to investigate the value of a "therapeutic milieu" for children with severe emotional disturbance. His ideas continue to be used in many classrooms.

The 1960s and 1970s saw many advances for children with emotional or behavioral disorders, as many researchers, scholars, and educational developers created new ways to teach these students. In 1962 Norris Haring and Lakin Phillips published *Educating Emotionally Disturbed Children*, a book that described their experimental work in the public schools of Arlington, Virginia. Their approach stressed behavioral principles, a structured environment, and interactions between the child's home and school environments. Meanwhile, Eli Bower, working in California, developed a definition of behavioral disorders that is the basis for the federal definition and the definitions used in many states today (Bower & Lambert, 1962).

Two highly successful programs were developed in the 1960s. Project Re-Ed was begun in the 1960s by Nicholas Hobbs. This landmark effort, conducted in Tennessee and North Carolina, clearly showed that an ecological approach, in which children attended residential schools for short periods of time and returned to restructured community and family environments, could effect major changes in the lives of very troubled children. Another major demonstration effort was conducted in California at about the same time. In what was known as the Santa Monica Project, Frank Hewett developed the engineered classroom, a highly structured classroom environment based on behavior management principles.

In 1964 the classic applied behavioral analysis study about the effects of teacher attention on a preschooler's social interactions with his peers during playtime was published (Allen et al., 1964). This study launched the generation of new knowledge about the important effects of the environment on people's actions. The development of applied behavioral analysis techniques with children in applied settings—initiated by Montrose Wolf, Don Baer, and Todd Risley—was instrumental to the application of token economies in classroom settings nationwide. Montrose Wolf is also credited with developing the Teaching-Family Model, which was begun at the University of Kansas with boys with emotional or behavioral disorders who were living in group homes and was later extended to a well-known program at Boys Town in Nebraska. These pioneering efforts have been successfully replicated across the nation, both at schools and in residential settings.

Dorothea Dix, the social activist, changed the course of treatment for people with mental disorders across the United States.

PREVALENCE

For two major reasons, it is difficult to estimate accurately the prevalence of emotional or behavioral disorders. First, the definition remains unclear and subjective. Second, because the label is so stigmatizing, many educators and school districts are reluctant to identify many children; a result, less than 1 percent of all schoolchildren are identified as having this disability (U.S. Department of Education, 2001). Some believe that the actual prevalence should be approximately 3 to 6 percent of all students (Kauffman, 2001; Walker et al., 2001).

Important factors in prevalence are gender and race. Clear differences show up in the identification of this exceptionality: Most children (some 74 percent) identified as having emotional or behavioral disorders are male, and this is the highest ratio of boys to girls in special education categories. The reason for this gender difference is not clear, but it is probably linked to boys' higher propensity to be troublesome and violate school rules, coupled with girls' tendency toward less disruptive, internalizing behaviors that are less likely to result in referral. Whereas Asian American and Hispanic students tend to be underrepresented in this special education category, African Americans are overrepresented: 27 percent of students

MAKING CONNECTIONS

For more about the over- and underrepresentation of diverse students in special education, see the "Prevalence" section in Chapter 3.

identified as having emotional or behavioral disorders are Black, even though Blacks represent only about 15 percent of the student population (U.S. Department of Education, 2001). The disproportionate representation by racial variables in this special education category is related both to bias and to culture (Townsend, 2000).

CAUSES AND PREVENTION

As is true of most disabilities, the specific causes of emotional or behavioral disorders remain elusive. However, relationships between some causal factors and this disability are becoming clearer. For example, children who experience physical abuse have a higher probability of being identified with emotional or behavioral disorders (Cauce et al., 2000). A link between the factors of poverty and this disability is apparent as well (Children's Defense Fund [CDF], 2001; Hosp & Reschly, 2002). And it is likely that for many of the children involved, a biological explanation will emerge (Forness & Kavale, 2001).

What can cause emotional or behavioral disorders?

The reasons why such problems arise in a particular child are usually difficult to identify precisely, and the disability is likely to be the result of multiple and overlapping factors (Walker & Sprague, 1999, 2000). At least three general areas can contribute to emotional or behavioral disorders: biology, home and community, and school.

MAKING CONNECTIONS

For more about FAS and Down syndrome, see Chapter 6.

• *Biology* More and more biological and genetic causes for disabilities in general are being identified (e.g., fetal alcohol syndrome [FAS], Down syndrome, Tourette's syndrome). The same is true for emotional or behavioral disorders (Forness & Kavale, 2001). For example, research now tells us that a definite relationship exists between prenatal drug exposure and childhood emotional or behavioral disorders: 53 percent of drug-exposed participants in Headstart preschool programs are identified as having these disabilities as early as kindergarten (Sinclair, 1998). Mood disorders, depression, schizophrenia, and ADHD may have a genetic foundation (American Psychiatric Association, 1994). Knowing whether biological reasons are part of the cause of a disorder can play a role in treatment. For example, knowing that depression has a biological cause allows for the development and use of medications prescribed for specific conditions (Forness & Kavale, 2001). Antidepressants are now an important component in many treatment programs for depression (Pappadopulos & Jensen, 2001). As researchers continue to find biological causes, more medical treatments will become available.

• *Home and Community* Environment and culture set the context for behavior (Maag, 2000). Children, like older people, do not live in a social vacuum. They are members of an immediate family, an extended family, and a variety of communities (neighborhood, church, clubs). All of these environments shape and influence each individual's growth and development, whether positively or negatively. Rarely does a single negative experience lead to or aggravate emotional problems, but combinations of poverty, abuse, neglect, parental stress, inconsistent expectations and rules, confusion, and turmoil over long periods of time can do so. Being poor is a contributing factor (CDF, 2001; Hosp & Reschly, 2002). So, too, are lack of supervision, erratic and punitive discipline, low rate of positive interactions, high rate of negative interactions, lack of interest and concern, and poor adult role models. For example, children whose parents are violent and have arrest records also tend to become violent and to find themselves in trouble with the law (Hallahan & Kauffman, 2000; Rudo, Powell, & Dunlap, 1998). Another link with poverty is clear: Students whose family incomes are in the bottom 20 percent of American families are five times more likely to drop out of school than their peers whose family incomes are in the top 20 percent of American families (National Center for Educational Statistics, 2002).

• *School* Teachers and schools can have a tremendous influence on students (Tolan, Gorman-Smith, & Henry, 2001). Teachers' expectations affect the questions they ask students, the feedback they give, and the number and character of their interactions with students. Problems can get better because of teachers' actions—and they can get worse. In other words, what educators do makes a difference. For example, a teacher who is unskilled in managing the classroom or insensitive to students' individual differences may create an environment wherein aggression, frustration, and withdrawal are common responses to the environment or the teacher. And teachers who are skilled at managing classroom behavior, systematically select interventions that match the students' behavior, and are consistent in their application of those interventions can improve students' outcomes (Rivera & Smith, 1997; Smith & Rivera, 1993). Good teachers are able to analyze their relationships with their students and the learning environment, and they keep close watch on problems and potential problems. Here are some key components of safe and effective schools (McLane, 1997; Walker & Gresham, 1997; Walker & Sprague, 2000):

Many behavior problems can be prevented when all students understand and follow consistent, positive rules in the classroom.

MAKING CONNECTIONS

For other ideas about behavior management, see the "Achieving Discipline" boxes in Chapters 3–12 and the "Effective Discipline" subsection in this chapter.

• Consistency of rules, expectations, and consequences across the entire school

• Positive school climate

• Schoolwide strategies for conflict resolution and dealing with student alienation

• High level of supervision in all school settings

• Cultural sensitivity

• Strong feelings by students of identification, involvement, and bonding with their school

• High levels of parent and community involvement

• Well-utilized space and lack of overcrowding

How might emotional or behavioral disorders be prevented or treated?

Prevention and treatment of emotional or behavioral disorders can be accomplished in many different ways, but the implementation of three different approaches could cause a substantial reduction in the prevalence of this disability:

1. Medical management

2. Reducing overrepresentation

3. School based interventions

Causes and Prevention

• *Medical Management* Medical management can attack issues of prevention on at least two different fronts. For example, the behavioral effects of fetal alcohol syndrome can be prevented if pregnant women do not drink. In other cases, prevention consists of eliminating or ameliorating the symptoms of the disability at its initial onset. And in yet other cases, the condition can be treated through drugs. Because of the publicity surrounding drug management of behavior problems, let's focus on that approach briefly.

Considerable controversy exists about the use of prescription drugs to reduce hyperactivity and the disruption that the condition causes (Zametkin & Earnst, 1999). Considering the fact that American children are prescribed and take drugs, such as Ritalin, at a rate some five times higher than the rest of the world, many educators have been calling for a greater use of classroom management interventions to reduce both inappropriate behavior and the use of medication (Pancheri & Prater, 1999). Some experts who have studied this issue believe that medication is effective (Forness & Kavale, 2001). However, they have also concluded that medication is even more powerful when used in combination with behavior management techniques. In the same study, Steve Forness and Ken Kavale found that the majority of children with school behavior problems have treatable psychiatric disorders, such as mood disorders, anxiety disorders, and schizophrenia. Antidepressants are proving to be successful in some of these cases.

• *Reducing Overrepresentation* The overrepresentation of African American boys in special education concerns educators, policymakers, and parents (National Alliance of Black School Educators [NABSE] & ILIAD Project, 2002). More so than any other group, these youngsters are clearly overrepresented in the emotional or behavioral disorders category (OSEP, 2001). They are also overrepresented in the juvenile justice system; 7 out of 10 youths in secure confinement are from diverse backgrounds (CDF, 2001). One reason for their disproportionate representation is that these students are three times more likely to be suspended from school (Townsend, 2000). Being suspended is part of a vicious cycle that compounds students' problems at school. Let's think about why this is so. Students who are suspended cannot participate in the academic learning opportunities at school. They also miss learning more about the norms of the school culture and the behavior expected because they are "on the streets" engaging in unsupervised activities. This situation then leads to lower academic achievement and higher probabilities of future misbehavior. All of these factors contribute to special education referrals. Educators have a responsibility to become more culturally sensitive and to recognize the importance of helping students understand the rules of the school environment (Cartledge, Kea, & Ida, 2000).

• *School Based Interventions* Standardizing practices used by teachers in their classrooms and across school settings can make a real difference in preventing disruption, violence, and the need for disciplinary actions. Taking a schoolwide approach to solve these problems is proving to be most successful (Hunter & Chopra, 2001; Tolan, Gorman-Smith, & Henry, 2001). One important premise of such programs is prevention (Horner et al., 2001). The aim is to create a school culture where positive behavioral support, social skills instruction, and consistency serve as the foundations for direct intervention when it actually needs to be applied. *All* students are taught what behaviors teachers and the school community expect. They are also taught about what they should expect from each other. Expectations are clear, concise, and simple (e.g., follow directions, be responsible, be safe, be prepared). For those who cannot meet these expectations, direct intervention is provided. In some cases, this entails intense and individualized consequences, including functional assessments to determine the cause of the behavior and to help identify actions that will effectively remediate extreme patterns of behavior. Some educators add a mentorship element, where successful secondary students with emotional or behavioral disorders help elementary students understand classroom expectations and how to act appropriately (Burrell et al., 2001).

MAKING CONNECTIONS

See Chapter 3 for a review of overrepresentation; also see Chapters 1 and 6.

CHAPTER 8 *Emotional or Behavioral Disorders*

It is well documented that early intervention can change patterns of behavior that eventually develop into long-term problems for both the individual and society (Bullis, Walker, & Sprague, 2001; Feil, Walker, & Severson, 1995; Strain & Timm, 1998; Walker & Sprague, 2000). Very young children who exhibit antisocial behavior, set fires, are cruel to animals, and are highly aggressive are most at risk for having serious externalizing behavioral disorders, and they are identified by elementary or middle school. The predictors of this outcome are now known, and structured and intensive preschool programs can in most cases provide the early intervention necessary to prevent disastrous results.

However, even though knowledge exists about how to reduce or prevent some problems associated with emotional or behavioral disorders, the necessary actions are usually not taken. In a provocative commentary, Jim Kauffman (1999) points out that despite discussions about the importance of prevention efforts, actions in the last decade of the 20th century did not keep pace. Possibly for fear of misidentifying children, public systems tend to provide intervention services too late, when the chance of success is reduced. Intervention must begin early and deliberately. Clearly, for most children, particularly those with low risk, classroom interventions can be successful. However, Kauffman estimates that some 5 to 10 percent of students in general education may require intensive, intrusive, individualized help. But the way the education system is set up "prevents prevention." This is how Kauffman thinks it should work:

- Reward desirable behavior.
- Punish, through nonviolent means, undesirable behavior.
- Provide direct instruction for both social and academic skills.
- Correct the environmental conditions that foster deviant behavior.
- Give students clear expectations.
- Standardize responses to children across the entire school setting.
- Monitor students' behavior closely.

In addition to Kauffman's suggestions, other methods can prevent inappropriate behavior. **Functional behavioral assessments** can help teachers determine what events cause the behavior to occur and what other events contribute to the behavior's increase or maintenance (Tobin, Sugai, & Colvin, 1996). Many teachers use a less complicated system that employs the *antecedent, behavior,* and *consequence* events to target behavior for specific interventions. This **ABC model** is further explained in the "Achieving Discipline" box.

What teachers do in school and classroom settings can make a real difference in reducing and preventing behavior problems for both those at risk for emotional or behavioral disorders and those already so identified (Kamps et al., 1999). Here's what works:

- Behavior management, including a point system for appropriate behavior and task completion, wherein good behavior is charted, and students earn rewards
- Systematic intervention plans, where a hierarchy of tactics is used, depending on students' behavior
- Home–school communication that includes notes home and home based reward systems
- Peer involvement
- Classroom structure with guided practice and well-organized transitions from activity to activity
- Supervised free periods (recess, hall changes, lunch)
- Consistent standards applied (by all school staff members) to behavior, with high expectations for academic performance

MAKING CONNECTIONS

See Chapter 13 for more discussion of functional behavioral assessments.

Getting to Know the Behavior: ABC Analysis

Damion lived in a housing project with his mother and four sisters. He attended an inner-city, high-poverty school and was in fourth grade. Damion had been identified as being at risk for emotional or behavioral disorders when he was in kindergarten and was actually identified as having this disability when he was in second grade. Damion's life away from school was in constant turmoil, and his behavior at school seemed to reflect a lack of structure, consistency, and support at home. Some teachers described him as moody. Toward the beginning of the school year, his teachers noticed that his attitude and behaviors were changing; he was becoming more aggressive, hostile, and out of control. He increasingly displayed anger with his peers both in the classroom and during recess and lunch breaks. It seemed to his teachers that his anger began with hostile language and sometimes escalated to a physical action, usually toward an object. He might toss a book, throw a ball away from the sports activity, or even overturn a desk. However, after an incident in which he shoved a classmate, his teachers decided to learn more about this behavior pattern, for they worried that his aggression was accel-erating to a point where he might actually hit a peer. Because the seriousness of his aggression was recent and not yet to a level where the school's management team was concerned, Damion did not have a BIP as part of his IEP.

Damion's special education and general education teachers decided to conduct an ABC Analysis. They wanted to see if there was a definite pattern to Damion's behavior and also to collect more information for the IEP team and others who would conduct a functional behavioral assessment if it was decided that Damion needed a BIP. The first thing they did was to carefully observe Damion's behavior and take notes in an organized fashion. The purposes of this process were to discover the events that "caused" or preceded what his teachers were calling aggressive behavior, to describe precisely what constituted aggression for Damion, and to note the events that followed the inappropriate behaviors. To collect this information, his teachers systematically took notes in a three-column format. The first column was labeled "A" (for Antecedent); the second column, "B" (for the Behavior); and the third column, "C" (for Consequences). Here's what they found: 97% of Damion's aggressive behavior was verbal and resulted from frustration with schoolwork or with a game he was unable to play correctly. And to everyone's surprise, the response to Damion's aggression was very consistent. He received a lot of attention—more than he received at any other time during the day. Armed with this information, his teachers developed a plan and strategy that adjusted schoolwork, provided peer tutoring to help him learn the rules of games played during recess, and set up rewards for academic performance and loss of privileges for even the slightest violation of the classroom rules.

Conducting an ABC Analysis

- Set aside a block of time each day when someone can observe the target student.

- Use a three-column format for collecting information.

- Write down descriptions of the events that preceded the inappropriate behavior, the behavior of concern in behavioral terms, and the events that followed the behavior.

- Fine-tune the descriptions with multiple observations.

CHARACTERISTICS

Students with emotional or behavioral disorders display some common characteristics, which teachers can use to identify them early enough so that intervention can make a difference. Table 8.2 lists typical signs and characteristics that these children often exhibit.

How are social skills affected by this disability?

These students are less socially skilled than their peers. Their antisocial behaviors (impulsivity, poor interpersonal skills with both peers and adults) are prime reasons

CHAPTER 8 *Emotional or Behavioral Disorders*

for their referral to special education (OSEP, 2001). Social skills are the foundation for practically all human activities in all contexts (academic, personal, vocational, and community). We use social skills to interact with others and perform most daily tasks. Possibly more than any other group of children with disabilities, students with emotional or behavioral disorders present problems with social skills to themselves, their families, their peers, and their teachers (Gresham, Lane, & MacMillan, 1999; U.S. Department of Education, 2001).

These students' behavior patterns can be self-defeating, impairing their interactions with others in many negative ways. Some students with externalizing problems are prone to what Frank Gresham and his colleagues call behavioral earthquakes—behaviors that occur rarely but are extreme, such as setting fires, being cruel to others, abusing animals, and assaulting adults. Most students with externalizing behavioral disorders exhibit at least some of the following behaviors *in excess:*

- Tantrums
- Aggression
- Noncompliance
- Coercive behaviors
- Poor academic performance

In this regard, teachers can make a real difference through the instructional procedures they select. By using effective teaching and by engaging students with emotional or behavioral disorders in learning, teachers can bring about improvements in their classroom behaviors, as well as their academic performance. (See the "Validated Practices" box for an example.) Students with internalizing patterns tend to exhibit behaviors that reflect

- Depression
- Withdrawal
- Anxiety

Instruction in social skills can positively influence the development of social competence (Bullis, Walker, & Sprague, 2001). Effective social skills training programs teach specific skills (e.g., how to interact with others) in natural settings—such as classrooms and home—to individuals, rather than teaching global skills (e.g., self-concept, self-esteem) to groups. Key components of effective programs make the difference. For example, instruction in social skills is initiated no later than first grade. Teachers and parents are trained in the use of positive discipline techniques. The instruction is embedded within the general education curriculum and includes considerable demonstration and practice. Peers learn to help and provide support for each other. The outcomes of such a program are outstanding, but it must begin early (Frey, Hirschstein, & Guzzo, 2000; Hawkins et al.,

Table 8.2 Possible Signs or Characteristics of Emotional or Behavioral Disorders

Experiences

Problems with authority figures	Disruption in family life
Peer rejection	Loneliness
Anorexia or bulimia	Academic failure

Demonstrates

Hyperactivity	Agression
Impulsivity	Hostility
Distractibility	Noncompliance
Anxiety	Tantrums
Withdrawal	Coercive behaviors
Depression	Suicidal tendencies

MAKING CONNECTIONS

Look at Table 8.1 again to refresh your memory about externalizing behavior disorders.

Tantrums and behaviors considered as "out of control" can be clear signals for the need for early intervention.

Characteristics

VALIDATED PRACTICES
Effective Teaching Behaviors

What Are Effective Teaching Behaviors?

Effective teaching behaviors are used to increase students' on-task behaviors and academic performance. When effective teaching behaviors are implemented, both you and your students are actively engaged in the learning process.

Why Effective Teaching Behaviors Are Beneficial

When teachers implement effective teaching behaviors, students' engaged learning time is increased; and the more time students are actively engaged in learning, the more they learn. Moreover, when students are engaged in learning, classroom disruption decreases. Several studies have demonstrated that when teachers use praise, call on students often, and engage their students in learning by including questioning and **scaffolding** in their instruction, not only do problem behaviors lessen, but academic achievement increases as well.

Implementing Effective Teaching Behaviors

The five steps of effective teaching behaviors are (1) planning, (2) starting the lesson, (3) presenting the lesson (4) closing the lesson, and (5) reflecting. Each step is described next.

Planning

- Decide what you want your students to know by the end of the lesson; remember that individual students may have different goals.
- Be sure you feel comfortable teaching the topic and answering questions.
- Determine what resources you will need to carry out the lesson.
- Decide how much time you will spend on the lesson.

Starting the Lesson

- Have all your materials ready and close by before beginning your lesson.
- Begin instruction promptly.
- Get the students' attention (e.g., by turning lights on and off and saying, "It's time for math").
- Provide your students with an advance organizer (e.g., "Today, we are going to . . . , and I expect you to . . . .")
- Begin with a review from a previously taught lesson.
- Assess students' background and knowledge of the lesson's topic.

1999). Individuals who participated in social skills training programs as first-graders were, at age 18,

- 20 percent less likely to commit violent crimes
- 38 percent less likely to drink heavily
- 35 percent less likely to become pregnant or contribute to a pregnancy

How do peers perceive these students?

Classmates of students with emotional or behavioral disorders tend to reject them (Bullis, Walker, & Sprague 2001). What do classmates of students with emotional or behavioral disorders think about these peers? The answers to this question are important because they influence educators' efforts to promote inclusion. Unfortunately, the answers are not favorable for youngsters with this disability (Safran, 1995):

1. By the age of 7, young children without disabilities can clearly discriminate externalizing behavioral disorders.
2. Typical children have very negative feelings about peers who act out, exhibit aggressive behavior, or are antisocial. Girls have stricter standards than boys and are more sensitive to aggressive behavior.
3. Children with externalizing behaviors are considered less desirable for friendship.
4. By seventh grade, children without disabilities recognize internalizing behavioral problems, such as being socially withdrawn.

CHAPTER 8 *Emotional or Behavioral Disorders*

esenting the Lesson

Maintain a brisk pace, but one that isn't so fast that you lose your students.

Provide a demonstration and guided practice activities before students work independently.

Allow for independent practice once students have achieved 80 to 90 percent accuracy during the guided practice phase.

Ask factual questions, one at a time.

Ask questions that draw on reasoning skills.

Recognize students' responses by providing praise or corrective feedback.

Probe students for answers and provide scaffolding.

Give specific academic praise (e.g., "I like the way you are reading today").

Be enthusiastic while teaching; show interest (e.g., smile, gesture).

Orient students to the academic task; refocus unrelated talk.

Enforce classroom rules; remind students about the classroom rules.

Be consistent with your consequences (follow through).

Give specific directives (e.g., "Read page 4").

Use surface management techniques (e.g., proximity, redirect, "the look," call out student's name, state expected behavior).

- Give specific praise for good behavior (e.g., "Thank you for raising your hand").

- Circulate among your students while they are working independently.

Closing the Lesson

- Review of the day's lesson.

- Introduce tomorrow's lesson.

Reflecting

- Ask yourself, "How did the lesson go?" "What went well?" "What should I continue?" "What needs to be changed for next time?"

- Evaluate your instruction and the students' performance.

- Decide what, if anything, needs to be retaught.

This scientifically validated practice is a teaching method proven by systematic research efforts (Englert, Tarrant, & Mariage, 1992; Espin, & Yell, 1994; Rosenshine, 1995; Sutherland, 2000; Sutherland, Wehby, & Copeland, 2000; Wehby, Symons, Canale, & Go, 1998). Full citations are found in the "Characteristics" section of the references for this chapter.

5. Children without disabilities have much more compassion and understanding for peers with medical problems than for those with psychological disorders.

How does this disability affect these students' academic performance?

"School failure is the common link between delinquency and disability" (OSEP, 2001, p. II-3). Regardless of intellectual potential, students with emotional or behavioral disorders typically do not perform well academically (Lane & Wehby, 2002). They could be referred to as underachievers, and they lack basic reading and math skills. Of course, the more severe the disability, the greater overall performance is affected, and the greater the likelihood of the child's becoming delinquent and having recurrent problems with the law (Archwamety & Katsiyannis, 2000). Clearly, being in personal turmoil affects one's ability to attend to school tasks and to learning in general. Failure at academic tasks compounds the difficulties these children face not only at school but also in life. Their frustration with the educational system (and its with them) results in these students having the highest dropout rates of all students (National Center for Educational Statistics, 2001). The outcomes of students who do not complete high school are not good. There is also evidence that when students are engaged in academic work, their disruptive behaviors decrease (Lane, 1999). Thus, in addition to helping the child with behavior, a teacher must teach academic skills.

EARLY CHILDHOOD EDUCATION

Most students with emotional or behavioral disorders have poor educational outcomes. The blame for such dismal results rests, in part, with the educational system and its inability to meet the complex needs of these children—needs that must be met beginning when the children are very young.

Some types of emotional or behavioral disorders are difficult to identify in young children. For example, internalizing behavior problems are not usually identified until children are of school age. Severe disabilities, such as a psychosis, sometimes manifest themselves during the early developmental period. However, extreme externalizing behaviors are often obvious by age 4 or 5. Although most preschoolers behave well and learn social rules quickly, some do not (Little, 2002). Indeed, 15 percent of preschoolers engage daily in three or more acts of overt aggressive behavior (e.g., hitting and kicking, pushing, shoving), and 10 percent exhibit daily episodes of serious antisocial behavior (e.g., calling names, playing mean tricks).

The early identification and management of young children with this disability has many benefits (Bullis, Walker, & Sprague, 2001; Feil, Walker, & Severson, 1995; Walker & Sprague, 1999, 2000). First, problem behaviors seen in preschoolers tend to be very stable over time. In other words, they do not go away without intervention, and they may even worsen. The behavior problems seem to follow a progression like the following: disobedient at home, having temper tantrums,

Figure 8.1 The Path to Long-Term Negative Outcomes for At-Risk Children and Youth.
Source: Walker, H. M. & Sprague, J. (1999). The path to school failure, delinquency, and violence: Causal factors and potential solutions. *Intervention in School and Clinic,* 35, 67-73. Copyright 1999 by Pro-Ed, Inc. Reprinted by permission.

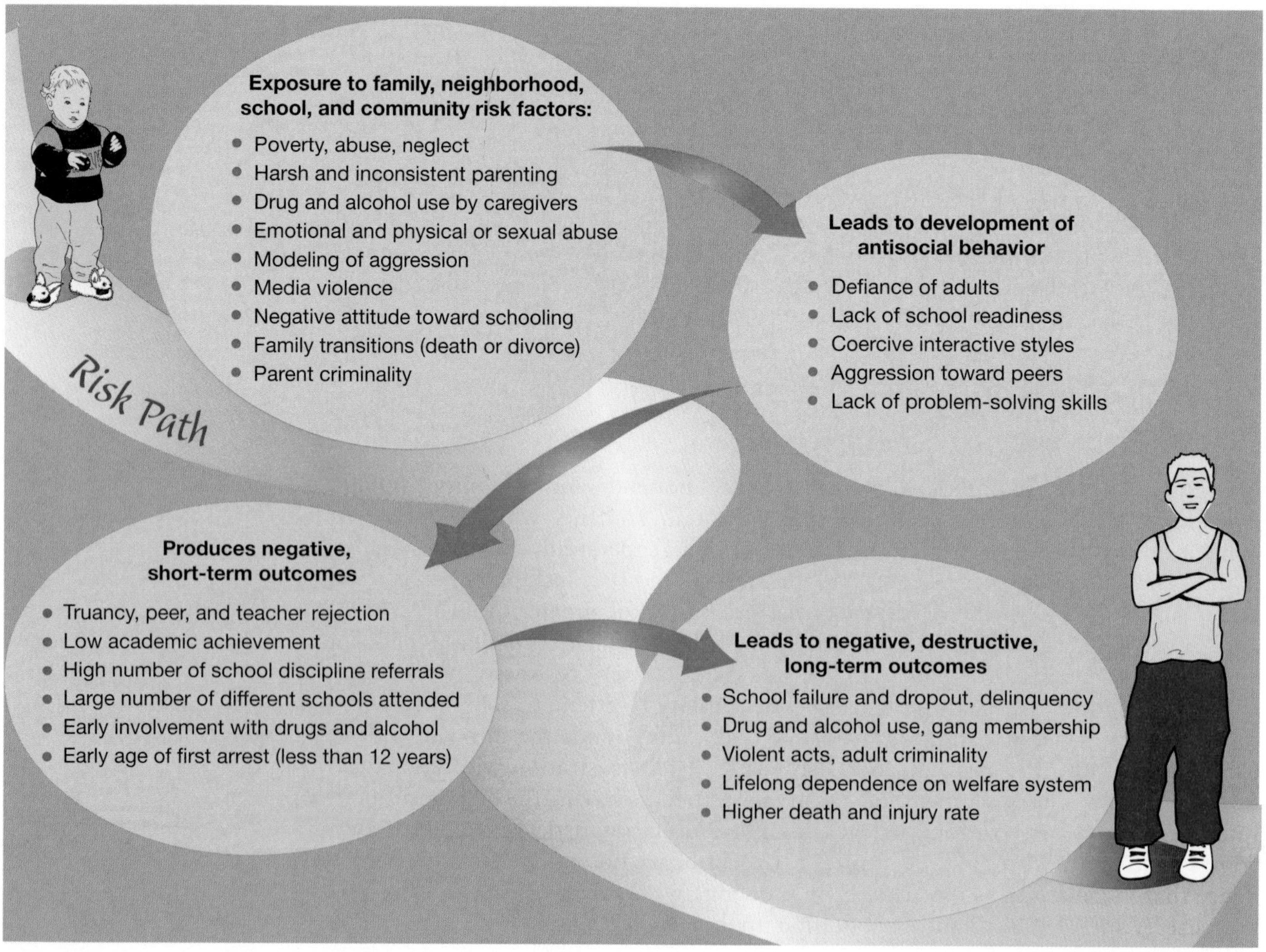

Exposure to family, neighborhood, school, and community risk factors:
- Poverty, abuse, neglect
- Harsh and inconsistent parenting
- Drug and alcohol use by caregivers
- Emotional and physical or sexual abuse
- Modeling of aggression
- Media violence
- Negative attitude toward schooling
- Family transitions (death or divorce)
- Parent criminality

Risk Path

Leads to development of antisocial behavior
- Defiance of adults
- Lack of school readiness
- Coercive interactive styles
- Aggression toward peers
- Lack of problem-solving skills

Produces negative, short-term outcomes
- Truancy, peer, and teacher rejection
- Low academic achievement
- High number of school discipline referrals
- Large number of different schools attended
- Early involvement with drugs and alcohol
- Early age of first arrest (less than 12 years)

Leads to negative, destructive, long-term outcomes
- School failure and dropout, delinquency
- Drug and alcohol use, gang membership
- Violent acts, adult criminality
- Lifelong dependence on welfare system
- Higher death and injury rate

CHAPTER 8 *Emotional or Behavioral Disorders*

teacher reports of fighting or stealing. Second, they are predictive of future learning problems and delinquency. Third, children with early onset of antisocial behavior (e.g., aggression) are only 3 to 5 percent of this population, but they account for 50 percent of all crimes committed by children and youth. Fourth, if children's disorders can be identified early, professionals may be able to intervene with the child and family at an early stage and avoid predictable negative outcomes. Figure 8.1 highlights those markers that are now becoming reliable predictors of long-term negative outcomes for these individuals. Fortunately, quick, direct, and intensive early intervention can alter the path to negative outcomes for many of these individuals.

The path toward emotional or behavioral disorders begins early. Some signs seen during the preschool years include bullying, pushing, shoving, and being cruel and aggressive toward others. Early intervention can alter this boy's probable outcome of problems and trouble.

The relationships among emotional or behavioral disorders, serious juvenile problems, and poor adult outcomes are clear. Signals of later problems in young boys and girls include the following (Day & Hunt, 1996; Miller-Johnson et al., 1999; Strain & Timm, 1998; Walker & Sylvester, 1994):

- Problem behaviors are clearly established at age 4 to 5.
- Overt (e.g., bullying) and covert (e.g., stealing) antisocial activities are becoming behavior patterns.
- Problems happen across settings (at home, at school, and in the community).
- The child is both overactive and inattentive.
- Extreme aggression is frequent.

Of these five characteristics of young children prone to later problems, the single best predictor is aggression. And without intervention, problems tend to persist. For example, sixth-graders referred for special services because of both violent and nonviolent inappropriate social behaviors are likely to present chronic discipline problems during their remaining school years and also to drop out of school (Tobin & Sugai, 1999). Children with the five characteristics listed above are likely candidates for other negative outcomes: substance abuse, teen pregnancy, suicide, AIDS, poor marital relations, chronic unemployment, and psychiatric disorders (depression and personality disorders). Long-term follow-up studies have established the effectiveness of early intervention for these individuals, so it is critical that action be taken when they are preschoolers (Strain & Timm, 1998).

Early intervention can rectify problems before they become more serious or develop into well-established patterns, can help avoid a later need for psychotropic medication to control behavior, can reduce stress in the family, and can effect changes in the young child's behavior when the possibility for change is strongest. In a developing strand of longitudinal research, Phil Strain, Matt Timm, and their colleagues are demonstrating the power of early intervention (Strain et al., 1982; Strain & Timm, 1998, 1999). They have followed up 40 individuals, now in their late twenties and early thirties, who participated in the Regional Intervention Project (RIP), a behavioral intervention preschool program for children at risk for emotional or behavioral disorders. Their results are amazing and very unlike to what would be expected for young children displaying serious aggressive and antisocial behaviors. Two of their subjects are enrolled in doctoral programs, three have earned master's degrees, three have received bachelor's degrees, five others are enrolled in college, three are high school graduates, and the remaining three are high school dropouts. Compare these results with those typically seen for students with emotional or behavioral disorders, who have a 55 percent high school dropout rate. Other studies of early intervention have also shown the power of such programs. For example, the one developed by Hill Walker and his colleagues, "First Step to Success," again shows that early intervention programs can make a real difference (Walker et al., 1998). This is particularly true when the programs have the following components:

- Parent involvement
- Teaching, through examples, about the relationship between behavior and its consequences
- Instruction on appropriate behaviors for different settings (**setting demands**)
- Showing how to make and keep friendships

ELEMENTARY THROUGH HIGH SCHOOL

Many different approaches are used in the education and treatment of school-children with emotional or behavioral disorders. Which approach is selected depends on what conceptual model the professional uses to teach these children. Table 8.3 lists seven major conceptual models of treatment and education. This overview is meant to illustrate the range of options and orientations available—from clinical to

Table 8.3 Conceptual Models in the Treatment of Children with Emotional or Behavioral Disorders

Behavioral approach	Based on the work of B. F. Skinner and other behaviorists, this model focuses on providing children with highly structured learning environments and teaching materials. The student's behaviors are precisely measured, interventions are designed to increase or decrease behaviors, and progress toward goals is measured carefully and frequently.
Psychoanalytic (psychodynamic) view	Based on the work of Sigmund Freud and other psychoanalysts, this model views the problems of the child as having a basis in unconscious conflicts and motivations: based not on the behavior itself, but on the pathology of one's personality. Treatment is generally long-term individual psychotherapy and designed to uncover and resolve these deep-seated problems.
Psychoeducational approach	The psychoanalytic view is combined with principles of teaching, and treatment is measured primarily in terms of learning. Meeting the individual needs of the youngster is emphasized, often through projects and creative arts, through everyday functioning at school and home.
Ecological approach	The problems of the child are seen as a result of interactions with the family, the school, and the community. The child or youth is not the sole focus of treatment; the family, school, neighborhood, and community also are changed in order to improve the interactions.
Social–cognitive approach	The interactions between the effects of the environment and the youngster's behavior are taught to the child. This approach seeks to integrate and reconceptualize behavioral and cognitive psychology. The result is a view that takes into account the interactions among the individual's physical and social environments, personal factors (thoughts, feelings, and perceptions), and the behavior itself.
Humanistic education	Love and trust, in teaching and learning, are emphasized, and children are encouraged to be open and free individuals. The approach emphasizes self-direction, self-fulfillment, and self-evaluation. A nonauthoritarian atmosphere in a nontraditional educational setting is developed.
Biogenic approach	Physiological interventions such as diet, medications, and biofeedback are used, based on biological theories of causation and treatment.

Source: Schema is borrowed from *Characteristics of Behavioral Disorders of Children and Youth* (7th ed., pp. 108–129) by J. M. Kauffman, 2001, Columbus, OH: Merrill.

CHAPTER 8 *Emotional or Behavioral Disorders*

behavioral to holistic to eclectic. Generally, educators incorporate some elements of many of these approaches into the educational programs they design for these children, incorporating the behavioral approach along with a direct focus on academic instruction.

A special education teacher is helping collect data that will be used to discover why behavioral problems are occurring in this general education classroom, and what interventions might be the most successful. Later, teachers will evaluate the effectiveness of the overall program they designed and implemented.

What are some key components of effective programs?

Although many different methods, programs, and curricula exist for students with emotional or behavioral disorders, some features are common to most. These include direct evaluation of success using curriculum based measurement (CBM), functional assessments and BIPs, and the application of an array of interventions aimed at reducing inappropriate behaviors and increasing positive ones.

• *Curriculum Based Measurement (CBM)* CBM is used to measure children's academic gains and thereby evaluate the effectiveness of their instruction (Fuchs & Fuchs, 2000). For example, teachers use CBM to measure the percentage of words spelled correctly, the number of new arithmetic facts memorized, reading fluency (how rapidly the child reads), and the ability to write topic sentences in writing assignments. They also use this method to measure social behaviors of individual children and see whether children improve with the application of various interventions.

To measure progress in complex areas, the teacher first breaks down those areas into precise behaviors. It is important that the behavior specifically of concern be the one targeted for intervention and measurement. Then the appropriate data collection system is selected. The many simple choices for such record keeping include tallies (sheer counts of the frequency of the target behavior's occurrence during a consistent observation period), duration (how long the target behavior lasts during a constant time period), percentage (what proportion of the day the target behavior occurs), and rate (how many times the behavior occurs per minute). Daily measurement of the specific target behavior continues long enough to allow comparisons under different treatments. In other words, how well did the student behave before the teacher implemented a reward system, how well did the student behave while the intervention was in effect, and was that behavior change maintained thereafter.

Let's look at an example. Terrell was a kindergartner who had exhibited extreme externalizing behaviors since coming to school. In particular, the multidisciplinary team (which included the district's school psychologist; a family therapist; a social worker; the school nurse; Ms. Kea, Terrell's special education teacher; Ms. Steppe-Jones, his general education teacher; and members of his family) was concerned about his aggressive behavior. The team discussed what constituted aggression for Terrell, and these are the behaviors they identified: physically attacking others, bullying, and hitting. They decided that the setting to begin intervention was the lunch recess, where the problems seemed to be the worst. They also decided that after a short assessment phase (to be sure they had targeted the right behaviors and to collect a set of data against which to assess future progress), the first intervention they would try was contingent instructions ("Don't hit!" after each act) paired with criterion-specific rewards (5 minutes of free time at the end of the day for "beating" yesterday's score). Every lunch period, Ms. Kea counted the number of aggressive

MAKING CONNECTIONS

CBM is also discussed in Chapters 1 and 4 in the sections on evaluation.

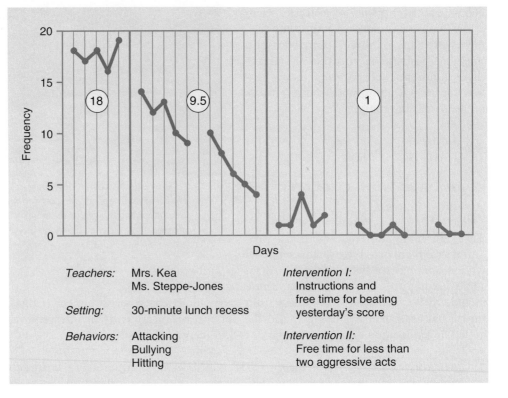

Figure 8.2 Terrell's Evaluation Chart

acts committed by Terrell and noted them on the evaluation chart shown in Figure 8.2. As you, and the members of the multidisciplinary team, can see, systematic and careful intervention planning brought about remarkable improvement in Terrell's behavior.

• *Functional Behavioral Assessments and Behavioral Intervention Plans* Behavioral intervention plans (BIPs) became a requirement of IDEA when it was reauthorized in 1997. See the "What IDEA Says" box for a summary of what the federal government had in mind when it included these plans in the law. Most students with emotional or behavioral disorders, particularly those with externalizing behavior problems, have a BIP as part of their IEP. Although these plans focus on functional behavioral assessments, they should also stress the development of positive social skills (Deveres, 1999a, 1999b).

The process used to develop BIPs can be most helpful when educators are designing individualized instruction for students. The functional behavioral assessment phase helps to clarify the student's preferences for specific academic tasks, as well as when undesirable behavior is likely to occur (Kern et al., 2001). Here's how it works: The goal of the functional assessment is to determine what activities are associated with problem behaviors and to identify the student's interests and preferences. Instructional activities are then modified to incorporate the student's "likes" into activities where problems typically occur. For example, James's behavior during activities that require him to write is highly disruptive. However, he likes to use the computer, so he is allowed to complete written assignments using a word processing program on a computer. The double benefit is that his academic performance is improving and his disruptive behavior has decreased. One caution, however: Functional assessments often miss behaviors that occur rarely (Nichols, 2000). This can be a real problem because many low frequency infractions (e.g., hitting a teacher, setting a fire, breaking a window) are the most dangerous and serious.

MAKING CONNECTIONS

BIPs and functional assessments are also discussed in Chapters 2 and 12.

Why did BIPs become adopted as part of IDEA? The law reflects concerns of Congress and the public about violence, discipline, and special education students. In the early versions of IDEA, students with disabilities could not be expelled if their disruptive behavior was caused by the disability. Students with emotional or behavioral disorders were typically protected by what was called the **stay put provision.** Under that provision, educational services could not be stopped, and these students could not be expelled from school. The 1997 version of IDEA changed that protection. Students with disabilities who violate school rules, particularly in the areas of weapons violence and drugs, are subject to disciplinary actions just like their peers without disabilities. But there are limits, and the end result is that students with disabilities who are violent or "out of control" have BIPs. These plans seek to eliminate undesirable behavior and replace it with appropriate ones. The BIP becomes part of the student's IEP. Here are some guidelines about these plans (Hartwig & Ruesch, 1998). Functional behavioral assessments and BIPs should include descriptions of

1. The problem behavior(s)
2. Events preceding the problem
3. Classroom rules
4. Consequences for infractions
5. Positive behaviors incompatible with the problem behavior

• *Effective Discipline* Discipline is not equivalent to punishment (Maag, 2001). Rather, discipline is training that results in improvement of performance, whereas punishment is supposed to result in decreases in behavior. A systematic discipline strategy, in which a hierarchy of interventions is systematically applied, helps to create safe schools where violence and abuse are eliminated and academic achievement is increased (Myles & Simpson, 1998).

Effective and efficient instruction cannot occur in chaos or in a repressive environment. What is required is a positive learning climate where children can learn, create, discover, explore, expand their knowledge, and apply new skills. When the amount of disruption is high, causing educators to spend time and energy addressing conduct problems, students do not learn either effectively or efficiently. Disruption—whether from several individuals or most of the class—can be held to a minimum without destroying the climate needed for learning. To accomplish this goal, teachers need to be familiar with an array of proven interventions and to know when they are most appropriately applied (Bryant, Smith, & Curren, in press). Interventions applied systematically through a progression, a hierarchy, can lead to effective discipline.

The **Intervention Ladder** (see Figure 8.3) was developed to help teachers better understand how to match interventions with the level and severity of disruptive behavior (Smith, 1984; Smith & Rivera, 1993). The foundation upon which the ladder stands includes basic preventive measures that good teachers incorporate into all of their instruction. For example, educators are encouraged to make school challenging and exciting so that all students are actively engaged in learning and are thus less likely to be disruptive (Nelson et al., 1998). Also, all members of the school community must be aware of the basic rules or standards of behavior, and everyone

MAKING CONNECTIONS

See Chapter 1 for a review of the controversies surrounding discipline and IDEA.

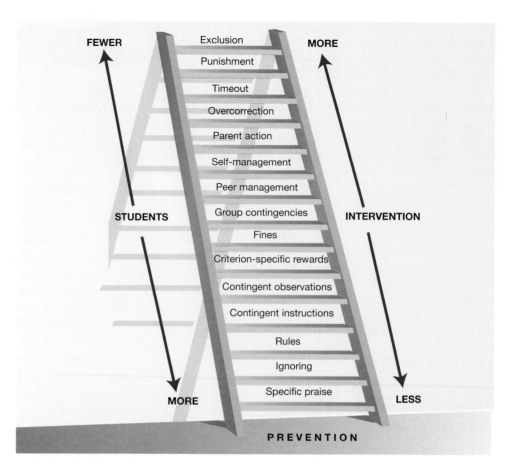

FEWER   Exclusion   MORE
                Punishment
                Timeout
                Overcorrection
                Parent action
                Self-management
                Peer management
STUDENTS   Group contingencies   INTERVENTION
                Fines
                Criterion-specific rewards
                Contingent observations
                Contingent instructions
                Rules
                Ignoring
MORE   Specific praise   LESS

PREVENTION

Figure 8.3 The Intervention Ladder
Source: From *Effective Discipline* (2nd ed., p. 17) by D. D. Smith and D. P. Rivera, 1993, Austin, TX: Pro-Ed. Reprinted by permission.

must consistently apply the same consequences when the standards are violated (Rosenberg & Jackman, 1997, 2002). The Intervention Ladder organizes interventions from the simplest and least intrusive to the most complex and punitive. Only after evaluation procedures indicate that a mild intervention is not successful are more drastic procedures implemented. Some interventions included on the ladder are simple to apply and can positively influence most incidents that occur in classroom settings. Let's look at three of these tactics: behavior-specific praise, positive reinforcement delivered in the form of points, and a group contingency.

It is well documented that **behavior-specific praise** increases the appropriate behavior of disruptive students as well as the time students spend working on class assignments (Brophy, 1981; Hall, Lund, & Jackson, 1968; O'Leary & Becker, 1969). Remarkably, whether in general education or special education classrooms, praise is underutilized, and sometimes students with disabilities receive less than one praise statement per hour (Gable et al., 1983; Wehby, Symons, & Shores, 1995). Moreover, as few as 5 percent of teachers' praise statements are behavior-specific. When used consistently and directly, praise has powerful results, as in the following example: "Robert William, congratulations on studying and staying focused. You earned 90 percent on your fractions test!" (Sutherland, Wehby, & Yoder, 2001). Remarkably, it seems difficult for teachers to change their actions and incorporate more specific praise into their instructional routines (Sutherland & Wehby, 2001). Considering this tactic's simplicity and power, behavior-specific praise should become part of every teacher's repertoire.

Positive reinforcement is a mainstay of behavior management programs. Like praise, this intervention's positive effects are well known and substantially researched (Maag, 2001). Many different versions of positive reinforcement programs have been developed over the years, since their initiation in the 1960s. Many

MAKING CONNECTIONS

For a review of the first reinforcement programs, see the "History" sections of this chapter and Chapter 6.

CHAPTER 8 *Emotional or Behavioral Disorders*

include a system that allows students to earn points for good behavior and then trade in those points for prizes or privileges. Reinforcement systems can be as simple or as complicated as teachers want to make them (Cruz & Cullinan, 2001). In some systems, students earn proportionately more points for behaviors that are more complex or important (completing assignments) than for behaviors deemed easier or less important (speaking nicely to classmates). Privileges (breakfast in the classroom, quiet free reading time) can be purchased with points, and points are deducted for serious offenses (aggression, destruction of property).

Group contingencies are reinforcement systems that involve the entire class and have great applications for general education classroom settings. One version of a group contingency is the **Good Behavior Game** originally developed by Barrish, Sanders, and Wolf in 1969. The technique uses class competition to reduce disruption. The class is divided into teams. In some versions of the game, a tally of infractions is kept to record violations of classroom rules. At the end of the day, the teams with the fewest infractions and therefore the fewest points wins (all teams can win or lose). Students have indicated that they like this approach because of the game-like features, student involvement, and fun (Babyak, Luze, & Kamps, 2000). The "Tips for Teachers" box lists some guidelines for the game's successful application.

TIPS FOR TEACHERS

Playing the Good Behavior Game

1. Class (teacher and students) determines specific behaviors of concern.

2. Class suggests privileges or prizes to win (end of day, end of week).

3. Teacher determines criterion level for winning (cut off scores where more than one team can win or all teams can lose).

4. Teacher divides class into teams.

5. Be sure all students understand the rules.

6. Inform parents, principal, fellow teachers about the game being played.

7. Keep scores as a source of data to evaluate the game's effectiveness.

Is punishment an effective intervention?

The answer to this question is a little more complicated than it first appears. By definition, punishment is punishment only when it decreases the occurrence of the targeted behavior. Thus, if it does not work, technically it isn't punishment. Also, punishment has many different forms (Maag, 2001). Punishment can be fines, restitutional activities (e.g., cleaning the classroom for defacing a wall), suspension, and even corporal punishment. Note that punishment is placed high on the Intervention Ladder because most classroom infractions do not merit such a serious intervention, which can have an overall negative impact on students and the school environment. Unlike positive approaches to managing classroom behaviors, punishment tends to produce an immediate result. Its effects are often short-term, however, and the unwanted behavior may return fairly soon (Axelrod & Hall, 1999).

Taken to its highest level, punishment is very serious and negative. Many states still allow the application of corporal punishment (paddling, spanking, rapping hands). All educators should be aware of the potentially devastating effects that corporal punishment can have on children. But despite all its negative effects and the lack of research to support its use, corporal punishment persists (Lohrmann-O'Rourke & Zirkel, 1998). Those most vulnerable to its application are students with disabilities, students from poverty, and culturally and linguistically diverse boys (Townsend, 2000).

We have just examined many alternatives to corporal punishment. Here, let's review what punishment is. Many people mistakenly believe that punishment must necessarily

Behavior problems are reduced when students are actively engaged in learning.

involve physical hitting, screaming, or embarrassment for the child. Punishment, however, is technically defined as any consequence that reduces the rate or strength of the behavior being punished, which means that many different tactics—including corporal punishment—fall within this category. Some teachers find that certain forms of punishment can be an important part of an effective teaching plan to change unwanted behaviors. For example, mild reprimands, temporary withdrawal of attention, and the loss of certain privileges are all punishing tactics (they are intended to reduce the frequency of the target behavior) but do not have the negative long-term effects of corporal punishment (Bryant, Smith, & Curren, in press; Smith & Rivera, 1993).

Punishment, particularly corporal punishment, should be *avoided* in school settings, because punishment

- Only temporarily stops undesired behaviors
- Does not teach new skills or knowledge
- Causes teachers to become engaged in power struggles with students
- Leads to an unhealthy and negative interaction with students
- Is initiated and dictated by the student
- Can change the classroom to a battleground where the focus is on power and coercion
- Models a negative style of interaction with others

Remember that any form of punishment should always be accompanied by teaching a new behavior. All classrooms must be safe and orderly environments where students can feel secure as they attempt the difficult tasks of learning and can also trust the educators charged with this important responsibility.

What are the relationships among these students, delinquency, the juvenile justice system, and school violence?

Clearly, students served through the emotional or behavioral disorders category have a greater probability than others of running afoul of the law and winding up in the juvenile justice system (Walker & Sprague, 2000). Once they are in the criminal justice system, they are less likely to receive services, supports, and intensive IEPs (National Center on Education, Disabilities, and Juvenile Justice, 2002). Their paths to long-term negative outcomes are taking shape (Walker and Sprague 1999). Look again at Figure 8.1, which highlights some of the major markers or signals for quick and early intervention in an effort to alter predictable patterns of negative results. Interestingly, although 17 percent of violent crimes are committed by juveniles, the most serious crimes at school are *not* committed by students with emotional or behavioral disorders (Lane &

Reprinted with special permission of King Features Syndicate.

CHAPTER 8 *Emotional or Behavioral Disorders*

ACCOMMODATING FOR INCLUSIVE ENVIRONMENTS
Being Prepared for School Violence

Be Alert to

- Whispers and talk of potential confrontation
- Unattended book bags and backpacks
- Students with a history of violence
- Closed classroom doors

Make Plans for

- Teacher buddy systems
- Responding to the sounds of gunshots
- Hostage crises
- All-clear signals

Practice for a Crisis by Knowing

- Where students should go during an incident
- Whom to notify
- Roles for every staff member

Train and Inform All School Staff Members About

- General methods used to resolve conflict
- Standard procedures to follow
- The contents of every behavioral intervention plan

Be Prepared to

- Develop trust and positive relationships with all students.
- Consistently apply behavioral techniques and consequences.
- Dress appropriately (comfortable shoes, loose clothing).
- Put valuables and fragile items out of reach.

Apply These Principles If a Crisis Occurs:

- Remain calm and in control.
- Keep tone of voice steady and firm.
- Seek assistance.
- Ignore accusations.

Wehby, 2002; Nichols, 2000). Some experts surmise that class placements for emotional or behavioral disorders keep some of the most violent and volatile students out of trouble.

In recent years, students' behaviors at school have become increasingly challenging, hostile, and even violent (Bender, Shubert, & McLaughlin, 2001; Maag, 2001). Certainly, acute alarm over school violence is recent; 10 years ago it was not a concern (Furlong & Morrison, 2000). Even today, 95 percent of students attending public school are well behaved and respond to positive reinforcement or simple classroom management interventions. However, some 5 percent—those with the most challenging behaviors—do not respond to traditional tactics.

Despite all the media attention and parents' perceptions that schools are out of control, school violence is actually on the decline, and schools are the safest place children can spend their days (CDF, 2001). Violent incidents, such as the 1999 murders at Columbine High School in Colorado, raise concern, but it is the increase in more frequent and small acts of defiance that has educators worried. Aggression— both verbal and physical—is on the increase. Some scholars and social observers have speculated about why this is so (Begley, 1999; Bender, Shubert, & McLaughlin, 2001):

1. Aggression, violence, and alienation observed in schools simply mirror their presence in society at large.

2. Children who see a high rate of violence become desensitized and devalue life.

3. Fewer hospital and center school placements are available, resulting in more of these students attending general education classes where few supports exist.

4. General education teachers are not trained to deal with violence and aggression.

As Americans puzzle about the "whys" of school violence, educators must ponder the predictors and prevention. Violence is comparatively rare, but even a single case in 5 years demands that schools be prepared, and researchers are turning their attention to the problem and are providing teachers and administrators with information about how to prevent school violence and what actions to take if it does occur (CDF, 2001; Bender & McLaughlin, 1997; Myles & Simpson, 1998). The "Accommodating for Inclusive Environments" box provides some sage guidance.

COLLABORATION FOR INCLUSION

MAKING CONNECTIONS

Wraparound services are also discussed in the "History" section of this chapter.

One defining characteristic of students with emotional or behavioral disorders is school failure, and school failure compounds other problems these individuals face. As you have learned, educational and life-long outcomes can be improved. However, improvement requires the concerted efforts of all partners (school, community, and social services) to assist both families and children (Eber et al., 2002). Let's first take a look at where these students are currently educated and then examine one community agency that is making a difference in the lives of many students with and without this disability.

Where do these students receive their education?

Children with emotional or behavioral disorders receive their education in a variety of settings: general classrooms, separate special education classrooms, special schools, the juvenile justice system, institutions, and hospitals. They live in a variety of settings as well: in family homes, in community based residential group homes, in halfway houses, and with foster families. As far as their education is concerned, these students are included less in general education classrooms than their peers with disabilities. Despite the movement toward inclusion and more integration of special education students into general education classes, the placement rates of students with emotional or behavioral disorders has changed little over the past 10 years. Consider the following placement rates reported by the federal government and others (Edens & Otto, 1997; National Center on Education Disability and Juvenile Justice, 2002; U.S. Department of Education, 2001):

- More than 18 percent of students with emotional or behavioral disorders (compared to less than 4 percent of their peers with disabilities) attend school at segregated settings, either separate schools or separate facilities.

- Around 26 percent attend general education classes for most of the day (compared to 47 percent of all students with disabilities).

- About 50 percent of all students with disabilities in residential programs are identified as having this disability.

- Some 60 percent of students in the juvenile justice system are identified by schools as having emotional or behavioral disorders.

- For these students, separate special education classes are the educational placement option most commonly used.

Issues about inclusion spark controversy in special education. For the group of students with emotional or behavioral disorders, it is no different. One report will raise concerns that so few of these students are integrated with nondisabled peers (U.S. Department of Education, 2001), while another stresses the need to maintain a full continuum of services that includes separate, highly specialized programs (Bussing et al., 1998). Particularly for those who have externalizing behaviors that

CHAPTER 8 *Emotional or Behavioral Disorders*

are aggressive, general educators seem to agree: They are neither trained nor equipped to handle these children, and general education settings are not equipped to control these children's behaviors or to provide necessary therapeutic instruction (Cheney & Barringer, 1995). In addition, some experts question whether placement in general education classrooms benefits these students (Kauffman, 2001). Although many educators and parents of students with disabilities assume that students benefit from being exposed to socially appropriate peer role models, this may not hold true for students with emotional or behavioral disorders. It is only through intensive direct instruction that these children learn correct social behaviors (Walker & Sprague, 1999, 2000).

Thus it may be that inclusion is not desirable in some cases and not possible in others. Students detained by the criminal justice system, for example, are unable to participate in inclusion classes. During the time of their incarceration, it is especially important that their educational needs not be neglected. Students have a right to receive appropriate and individualized special education even if they are in correctional settings such as halfway houses, jails, or prisons. Unfortunately, children in these settings often do not receive the intensive education they need, either in social skills or in academics (Lane, Gresham, & O'Shaughnessy, 2002).

It may take a village to raise a child, but it can take a community to educate one.

How can community partners make a difference?

Making success possible for these students demands the concerted efforts of many. The systematic intervention required to make a difference means that educators must collaborate with each other and also work in partnership with community agencies. Resources available in communities can help children and youth stay out of trouble and succeed at school (Sinclair et al., 1998; Tobin & Sugai, 1999). Let's look at one program that is making just such a difference.

The Chicago Youth Centers (CYC) provides a rich array of programs to over 12,000 youngsters every year (Anderson, 2002; CYC, 2002). Through six content areas (nature and environment/math and science, health/social and physical development, academic support and enhancement, the arts, career exploration/business and community outreach, and leadership development), this independent community agency provides extracurricular activities, after-school tutoring, mentoring, and academic support. Its programs teach youngsters conflict resolution and problem solving skills that can keep inner-city children out of trouble. CYC offers after-school programs in some of the poorest inner-city areas of Chicago, most in partnership with the local schools. One of CYC's programs, Girl Power, helps young girls develop self-esteem and seeks to break the cycle of poverty through education. The program also works to prevent suicides, provides education about problems with teen pregnancy, and encourages and supports its participants to attend postsecondary education programs. Success stories abound. Thousands of former participants have gone on to college and become civic and business leaders. And many have returned to volunteer at CYC. Unfortunately, not enough of these wonderful programs exist.

TRANSITION THROUGH ADULTHOOD

Students with disabilities face daunting obstacles when they enter mainstream society and feel the pressures of independent adult life (Wehmeyer et al., 2000). These obstacles are even more significant for students with emotional or behavioral disorders, whose outcomes are dismal. In most cases, only through timely interventions can the path to an adulthood at the margin be altered and avoided.

What are these students' outcomes?

Outcomes for students with this disability are not good (U.S. Department of Education, 2001). In fact, some think that outcomes are worse for individuals with emotional or behavioral disorders than for any other group of students with disabilities (Chesapeake Institute, 1994; Jolivette et al., 2000; National Center for Educational Statistics, 2002). A review of the data reveals dramatic facts about these students. They

- Have lower grades than any other groups of students with disabilities

- Fail more courses than other students with disabilities

- Fail minimal competence tests more than other students with disabilities

- Are retained more often

- Do not graduate from high school with a diploma at an expected rate (42 percent, compared to 50 percent for all students with disabilities and 76 percent for all students in the general population)

- Miss more days (18 per year) of school because of absenteeism than their peers with disabilities

- Have a high dropout rate (51 percent) compared to other students with disabilities (29 percent) or to peers without disabilities (5 percent)

- Are 13 times more likely to be arrested while in high school than their peers with disabilities and 4 times more likely to be arrested than their classmates without disabilities

- Are very likely (58 percent of them) of being arrested within 5 years of leaving school (compared to 30 percent for all students with disabilities)

How might these dismal outcomes be changed? Treatment and intervention are part of the answer. Students in the criminal justice system do not receive services, supports, or the delivery of intensive IEPs (National Center on Education, Disabilities, and Juvenile Justice, 2002). Also, their transition back to their communities and home schools is problematic (Griller-Clark, 2001). That is, these students do not receive support services (such as pre-placement planning and counseling), their IEPs often include no detailed transition plan, and often, these students' educational records are not even transferred to their receiving schools. Clearly, such lack of transition is not helpful.

Individuals with emotional or behavioral disorders who receive counseling experience improved outcomes (Hunter, 2001; Schoenwald & Hoagwood, 2001). Social skills training (discussed earlier in this chapter), instruction in self-determination (discussed next), and stable home environments also contribute to better results as adults (McConaughy & Wadsworth, 2000; Wehmeyer et al., 2000).

Why might instruction on self-determination make a difference in students' outcomes?

Instruction in self-determination could make the necessary difference in post-secondary outcomes (Test et al., 2000). What is **self-determination?** One way to answer this question is to identify some skills seen in successful individuals. Here are some examples:

- Know how to choose.
- Know what you want and how to get it.
- Choose goals and pursue them persistently.
- Make your needs known.
- Evaluate your own progress toward meeting your goals.
- Adjust your performance and create unique approaches to solve problems.
- Become your own best advocate.

Another way to explore self-determination is to consider what is included in various self-determination curricula. David Test and his colleagues found eight common components in the more than 60 curricula they examined:

- Choice/decision making
- Goal setting/attainment
- Problem solving
- Self-evaluation, observation, and reinforcement
- Self-advocacy
- Inclusion of student-directed individualized education programs (IEPs)
- Relationships with others
- Self-awareness (Test et al., 2000, p. 48)

Many individuals with disabilities do not develop these characteristics. Instead of becoming increasingly independent as they gain years and experience, many become more dependent. Some do not feel comfortable making choices for themselves, whereas others make inappropriate choices because they do not possess the skills or strategies necessary to make wise decisions. Some researchers suggest that this situation may be due in part to the special education experience, wherein students are not given sufficient opportunities to make choices or decisions (Wall & Dattilo, 1995). When opportunities to choose do arise, they are usually too late or students are not systematically guided in how to make decisions (Wehmeyer et al., 2000). Self-determination must become an opportunity for learning, embedded in standard instruction, but it must also become a direct topic for instruction (Serna & Lau-Smith, 1995).

FAMILIES

Parenting a child with emotional or behavioral disorders is usually quite difficult. These families are most likely to be blamed for their children's problems and are also more likely to make significant financial sacrifices to secure services for their children (Ahearn, 1995). Increasingly, though, teachers are paying more attention to both the contributions and the needs of family members and are listening more carefully to parents' concerns. Let's look at two common elements in the family lives of these children: negotiating the mental health care system and foster home placement.

MAKING CONNECTIONS

For a review of self-determination, see "Elementary Through High School" and "Transition" sections in Chapter 6.

How can families better negotiate the mental health care system?

Accessing America's mental health care system can be a daunting experience even for the most capable and most affluent. For those who have limited resources or who distrust the social services system, the barriers can be so great that needed services are not sought or received (CDF, 2001). These barriers may include lack of transportation, lack of child care for other children, lack of information about what services are available and where they can be received, and lack of emotional support. In January of 2001, the Surgeon General's National Action Agenda for Children's Mental Health stressed the importance of coordinating services across many agencies to ensure that children in need of mental health services receive them (Hoagwood, 2001a). Advocating for wraparound services reflects recognition of the importance of supporting children and families in trouble and the knowledge that comprehensive early intervention can prevent a terrible future.

Parent involvement is critical in achieving child mental health and positive outcomes. Parents attending school events, volunteering to help in their child's classroom, and providing follow-up to behavioral intervention programs initiated at school are all necessary components to the development of good child mental health. Engaging families, particularly those from diverse cultures, takes considerable effort and skill (Cartledge, Kea, & Ida, 2000). Communication is one key to developing the trust and respect necessary to make families want to become actively involved at school. Also, children whose families are involved at school have greater academic success. However, for some children, parental efforts alone are not sufficient. Cynthia Lynn and her colleagues found that the mental health needs of students in low income urban communities are twice those of other children. Educators can assist parents in getting the professional help they need if families are connected to schools. As you have learned, parent–school partnerships emerge when educators are culturally competent, respect family members, increase communication, and keep their promises.

What is often the impact of foster care on children?

The U.S. Department of Health and Human Services estimates that some 588,000 children are in the foster care system in this nation (Adoption and Foster Care Analysis and Reporting System, 2002). Although this number represents a 5 percent reduction from the previous year (between 2000 and 2001), it is alarming, especially because social service agencies are reluctant to take children from their families and place them in an alternative home environment.

The numbers of children living in foster care are troubling, but even more so is the percentage of those children who have emotional or behavioral disturbance (Armsden et al., 2000). Estimates range from 35 to 60 percent, almost five times higher than in the general student population. Also, a higher number of these youngsters than would be expected have internalizing problems (anxiety, depression, and poor school performance). Of course, it is not known whether these emotional or behavioral problems are one reason for the children's placement in foster homes or whether the placements and histories of disrupted attachments contribute to—or even cause—these problems.

On another note, the plight these individuals face is compounded by the lack of continuity of services. For example, some 20,000 young people "age out" of foster care programs each year on their 18th birthdays (Ama & Caplan, 2001). Many of them are still in high school, trying to graduate with a high school diploma. However, because few transition programs are available, they end up homeless, facing one more serious challenge in their young lives.

What can be done to improve these individual's situations? Educators can create positive and consistent classroom environments, can be sure students understand

CHAPTER 8 *Emotional or Behavioral Disorders*

the consequences of their actions, and can teach them the skills they need to avoid negative outcomes (O'Dell et al., 2001). It also is important (though not the responsibility of the school) to ensure that these children have access to the mental health services they need to resolve their confusion about family life (Hoagwood, 2001b).

TECHNOLOGY

The computer can be especially helpful to a student with emotional or behavioral disorders (Bryant & Bryant, 2003; Rivera & Smith, 1997). It can serve as an emotionally neutral system with which to interact, have fun, achieve success, and engage actively in learning (Lucent Technologies, 1999).

Computers facilitate learning without the pressure of subjective judgments; a computer does not criticize the child who is using it. Answers are simply right or wrong. Thus a computer serves as a safe environment in which to practice and improve skills. When a teacher incorporates computer-assisted instruction as an individualized learning activity for a child, the computer mirrors many of the attributes of a good teacher. Specifically, it

- Provides immediate attention and feedback
- Customizes (to varying degrees) instruction to the skill level of the child
- Allows students to work at their own pace
- Makes corrections quickly
- Produces a professional-looking product
- Keeps accurate records of correct and error rates
- Ignores inappropriate behavior
- Focuses on the particular response
- Is nonjudgmental

Using a computer is not a substitute for learning to interact appropriately with other people, however, and a teacher should not rely solely on computer interactions with children who have emotional or behavioral disorders. In arithmetic, for example, a teacher might introduce the instruction, allow drill and practice on the computer, and then return periodically to check the student's progress. Many computer learning programs are available at different levels. By consulting with computer specialists, teachers can ensure that their judgments about the learning needs of the students are translated into the appropriate computer materials.

MAKING CONNECTIONS

To compare different types of technology supports across students with special needs, read the "Technology" sections in Chapter 3–12.

MAKING CONNECTIONS

- Look again at the Advance Organization at the beginning of the chapter. To help you study the chapter's content, the answers to the Focus and Challenge questions are given next. Test yourself to see whether you have mastered the major points of this chapter.

- For Web links to support your study of disabilities, look at the "Resources" sections at the end of every chapter in this text.

IN CONCLUSION

SUMMARY

Exactly what constitutes emotional or behavioral disorders reflects, in part, societal standards for behavior and expectations about the development of children. Many behaviors that our society labels as

disordered in a particular individual might be acceptable if that person were a different age, lived in a different society, came from a different culture, or exhibited the behaviors under different circumstances. Of course, some conditions are considered disturbed no matter what the age or the prevailing societal standards. Early screening and intervention with young children who have emotional or behavioral disorders is critical, but unfortunately, it is not consistently available. Therefore, many students with internalizing problems remain unidentified, African American boys who act out are overidentified, and problems that could have been prevented become resistant to change. Schoolwide intervention programs can prevent many problems at school and provide a means of getting intensive services to those in need. Programs that include a balance of academic instruction and social skills instruction lead to more positive results for these students.

SELF-TEST QUESTIONS

Focus Questions

How do the IDEA and the National Mental Health and Special Education Coalition definitions of emotional or behavioral disorders compare?

According to the IDEA definition, emotional or behavioral disorders are indicated when children

- Are unable to develop or sustain positive relationships with peers or teachers
- Have difficulties with academic tasks
- Exhibit inappropriate behaviors
- Experience considerable unhappiness or depression
- Develop physical symptoms related to fears about personal or school problems
- Exibit no other (intellectual, sensory, health) reason for the condition
- Have severe and long-lasting symtoms

In the National Mental Health and Special Education Coalition's definition, the condition

- Is extreme and long-lasting
- Consists of inappropriate behaviors
- Negatively affects educational performance
- Occurs across settings (both school and home)
- Is unresponsive to direct intervention in general education
- Can coexist with other conditions

The IDEA definition has been criticized as too narrow, as placing too much emphasis on emotional problems rather than behavioral

problems, for using the term *emotional disturbance,* and as reflecting an older, academic view of schooling.

What are the major subgroups of this disability, and how would you describe the conditions that fall into each subgroup?

Emotional or behavioral disorders can be divided into three groups:

- Externalizing: aggressive, arguing, impulsive, coercive, and noncompliant
- Internalizing: anorexia or bulimia, depression, anxiety, shyness, withdrawal
- Low incidence: rare but serious (e.g., Tourette's syndrome, schizophrenia)

What are the major causes of this disability, and how can it be prevented?

Biology and genetics, the individual's home and community, and the school can all contribute to these disorders.

Many specific causes of emotional or behavioral disorders or disturbance in a particular individual remain unknown.

Efforts at prevention include medical management, reducing overrepresentation, and school based interventions.

What outcomes are likely for these children when effective intervention is not provided?

Outcomes are not good: they may include academic failure, graduation without a standard diploma, dropping out of school, and high arrest rates.

How can teachers help children with this disability?

Teachers can make a difference by

- Giving direct and systematic instruction
- Conducting regular evaluations to ensure the effectiveness of interventions
- Selecting interventions appropriate for the situation or infraction
- Pairing functional assessment and curriculum based measurement (CBM)
- Avoiding punishment
- Teaching academics to promote interest and engagement
- Partnering with families and communities
- Including self-determination topics, where students learn to make choices and decisions, during the early school years

Challenge Question

What educational placement options are used for students with emotional or behavioral disorders, and how can services be improved?

Services for children and youth with emotional or behavioral disorders are provided in a variety of environments: general education classrooms, special education classrooms, community based residential group homes or halfway houses, foster care, the juvenile justice system, and even institutions or hospitals.

This group of students has the highest rate of educational placements in segregated settings

and the lowest rate of inclusive placements of all groups of students with disabilities. Services can be improved by creating and delivering

- Early identification and intervention programs
- Consistent and positive discipline
- Effective academic instruction
- A system of dealing with dangerous behaviors in the event that violent behavior occurs
- Intensive special education in the juvenile justice system
- Seamless transition services from one placement to another

MEETING THE STANDARDS AND PREPARING FOR LICENSURE EXAMS

After reading this chapter, you should be able to demonstrate basic knowledge and skills described in the CEC standards and INTASC principles listed below. The section of this chapter most applicable to each standard is shown in parentheses at the end of the knowledge or skill statement.

 Core Standard 1: Foundations

- **Behavior management:** Laws and ethical principles regarding behavior management planning and implementation (Elementary Through High School)
- **Role of families:** Family systems and the role of families in the educational process (Families)

 Core Standard 2: Development and Characteristics

- **Families:** Characteristics and effects of the cultural and environmental milieu of the individual with exceptional learning needs and the family; family systems and the role of families in supporting development (Families)
- **Medication:** Effects of medication (Causes and Prevention)

 Core Standard 3: Individual Learning Differences

- **Impact of social abilities:** Impact of learners' academic and social abilities, attitudes, interests and values on instruction and career development (Elementary Through High School)

 Core Standard 4: Instructional Strategies

- **Self-determination:** Use procedures to increase the individual's self-awareness, self-management, self-control, self-reliance and self-esteem. (Elementary Through High School)

 Core Standard 5: Learning Environments and Social Interactions

- **Classroom management:** Basic classroom management theories and strategies for individual with exceptional learning needs (Elementary Through High School)
- **Management:** Effective management of teaching and learning (Elementary Through High School)
- **Social Skills:** Social skills needed for educational and other environments (Characteristics)
- **Learning environment:** Modify the learning environment to manage behaviors. (Elementary Through High School)
- **Behavior management:** Use effective and varied behavior management strategies. Use least intensive behavior management strategy consistent with the needs of the individual with exceptional learning needs. (Elementary Through High School)

 Core Standard 10: Collaboration

- **Collaboration:** Concerns of families of individuals with exceptional learning needs and strategies to help address these concerns (Families)

INTASC Principle 2:

The teacher understands how children learn and develop, and can provide learning opportunities that support their intellectual, social, and personal development.

- **Emotional factors and learning:** The teacher understands that students' physical, social, emotional, moral, and cognitive development influence learning and knows how to address these factors when making instructional decisions. (Elementary Through High School)

- **Social and emotional development impact on learning:** The teacher is aware of expected developmental progressions and ranges of individual variation within each domain (physical, social, emotional, moral, and cognitive), can identify levels of readiness in learning, and understands how development in one domain may affect performance in others. (Characteristics)

- **Identification:** The teacher assesses individual and group performance in order to design instruction that meets learners' current needs in each domain (cognitive, social, emotional, moral, and physical) and that leads to the next level of development (Emotional or Behavioral Disorders Defined)

INTASC Principle 5:

The teacher uses an understanding of individual and group motivation and behavior to create a learning environment that encourages positive social interaction, active engagement in learning, and self-motivation.

- **Classroom management:** The teacher understands the principles of effective classroom management and can use a range of strategies to promote positive relationships, cooperation, and purposeful learning in the classroom. (Elementary Through High School)

- **Classroom environment:** The teacher analyzes the classroom environment and makes decisions and adjustments to enhance social relationships, student motivation and engagement, and productive work. (Elementary Through High School)

- **Monitors:** The teacher organizes, prepares students for and monitors independent and group work that allows for full and varied participation of all individuals (Characteristics)

INTASC Principle 10:

The teacher fosters relationships with school colleagues, parents, and agencies in the larger community to support students' learning and well-being.

- **Child's well-being:** The teacher is concerned about all aspects of a child's well-being (cognitive, emotional, social, and physical), and is alert to signs of difficulties. (Causes and Prevention)

Standards in Practice

These knowledge statements, dispositions, and skills might be demonstrated by the beginning teacher by the structure and management system that is employed in the classroom. Students are better able to learn in an environment where the teacher is able to control the students and manage instruction simultaneously.

Go to the companion website (ablongman.com/smith5e) for detailed text correlations to CEC and INTASC standards, PRAXIS II™ exams, and other state-sponsored licensure exams.

SUPPLEMENTARY RESOURCES

Professional Readings and Resources

Coleman, M. C., & Webber, J. (2002). *Emotional and behavioral disorders: Theory and practice* (4th ed.). Boston: Allyn and Bacon.

Deveres, L. (1999). *A primer on functional behavioral assessments.* Horsham, PA: LRP Publications.

Kauffman, J. M. (2001). *Characteristics of behavioral disorders of children and youth* (7th ed.). Upper Saddle River, NJ: Prentice-Hall.

Kauffman, J. M. (1999). How we prevent the prevention of emotional and behavioral disorders. *Exceptional Children, 65,* 448–468.

Kauffman, J. M., Mostert, M. P., Trent, S. C., & Hallahan, D. P. (2002). *Managing classroom behavior: A reflective, case-based approach* (2nd ed.). Boston: Allyn and Bacon.

Lane, K. L., Gresham, F. M., & O'Shaughnessy, T. E. (2002). *Interventions for children with or at risk for emotional and behavioral disorders.* Boston: Allyn and Bacon.

Rosenberg, M. S., Wilson, R., Maheady, L., & Sindelar, P. T. (1997). *Educating students with behavior disorders* (2nd ed.). Boston: Allyn and Bacon.

Popular Books

Atwood, M. (1996). *Alias Grace.* New York: Doubleday.

Duke, P. (1987). *Call me Anna: The autobiography of Patty Duke.* New York: Bantam.

Kesey, K. (1977). *One flew over the cuckoo's nest.* New York: Penguin.

Pelzer, D. (1995). *A child called "It:" One child's courage to survive.* Deerfield Beach, FL: Health Communications.

Plath, S. (1971). *The bell jar.* New York: Harper & Row.

Sedaris, D. (1997). *Naked.* Boston: Little, Brown.

 Videos and DVDs

One Flew Over the Cuckoo's Nest (1979). United Artists

McMurphy is convicted of a petty crime, and to avoid doing time in jail he convinces everyone that he is insane, so he is sent to a mental institution to serve out his sentence. McMurphy's presence gives the other patients a new lease on life, but all this activity disrupts the hospital routine. Consequently, the head nurse becomes his enemy. She ends up riding him to the breaking point, and she makes certain that this is the last time he challenges the system.

The film tries to imply that the characters in the institution are not as crazy as the world outside, and that if someone does not conform, the system forces the person to obey the rules. This movie shows the horror of institutions and the how much those committed and their caretakers have in common. This film won five Academy Awards in 1976.

A Beautiful Mind (2001). Universal
Based loosely on the life of John Forbes Nash, Jr., a genius in mathematics, who develops a revolutionary economic theory. As Nash is working, he begins to do top-secret code breaking for the FBI, but his wife becomes suspicious of his secretive behavior. She discovers that he is actually schizophrenic and that the FBI agent, along with other people in Nash's life, are all figments of John's imagination.

This story depicts the fine line between genius and insanity, taking a close look at the schizophrenia that effected Nash for his entire life. Nash confronted his illness and spent time in an institution. Through medication, along with the love and support of his wife, he was able to cope with his illness, and in the twilight of his life he was awarded the Nobel Prize. This film won the Oscar for best picture, and Jennifer Connolly won an Oscar for best supporting actress as Nash's wife.

Me, Myself, and Irene (1999). Twentieth Century Fox
This screwball comedy is about a highway patrol officer, Charlie, who develops schizophrenia after years of suppressing anger and abuse. Charlie's other personality, Hank, expresses Charlie's aggressive and hostile side. On the seemingly simple assignment of transporting a female prisoner, Charlie and the woman become caught up in a huge conspiracy, and Hank emerges and re-emerges during times of stress.

This film is not meant to be taken seriously, of course, but even so, its inaccurate portrayal does a disservice to people with a specific emotional or behavioral disorder. Throughout the film, this serious disability is used to evoke laughter. In this irresponsible representation, the main character is battling his other personality, even to the point of physical self-abuse.

Girl Interrupted (1999). Columbia Pictures
After graduation from school, Susanna attempts suicide, so her parents check her into a mental hospital where she is diagnosed with a borderline personality disorder. She is put on a floor for young women who have different emotional or behavioral disorders. Susanna's friendship with the other patients helps her develop a strong sense of self.

This film is based on the memoirs of Susanna Kaysen, who actually spent over a year in an institution during the 1960s. It tells the story of the depersonalization that adolescent treatment centers often inflict and their relatively poor outcomes. Angelina Jolie won the Oscar as best supporting actress for her role as a sociopath and Susanna's closest friend.

Parent, Professional, and Consumer Organizations and Agencies

American Psychiatric Association
1400 K Street NW
Washington, DC 20005
Phone: (888) 357-7924
E-mail: apa@psych.org
Web site: http://www.psych.org

American Psychological Association (APA)
750 First Street NE
Washington, DC 20002-4242
Phone: (202) 336-5500; (800) 374-2721
TTY: (202) 336-6123
Web site: http://www.apa.org

Council for Children with Behavioral Disorders (CCBD)

Council for Exceptional Children
1110 North Glebe Road, Suite 300
Arlington, VA 22201-5704
Phone: (703) 620-3660; (888) CEC-SPED
TTY: (703) 264-9446
Web site: http://www.cec.sped.org or www.ccbd.net

National Alliance for the Mentally Ill (NAMI)
Colonial Place Three
2107 Wilson Blvd., Suite 300
Arlington, VA 22201-3042
Phone: (800) 950-6264; (703) 524-7600
TTY: (703) 516-7227
Web site: http://www.nami.org

National Mental Health Association
1021 Prince Street
Alexandria, VA 22314-2971
Phone: (703) 684-7722; (800) 969-NMHA
TTY: (800) 433-5959
Web site: http://www.nmha.org

The Center for Mental Health Services Knowledge Exchange Network
P.O. Box 42490
Washington, DC 20015
Phone: (800) 789-2647
TTY: (866) 889-2647
E-mail: ken@mentalhealth.org
Web site: http://www.mentalhealth.org

Video**Workshop** Extra

If the VideoWorkshop package was included with your textbook, go to Chapter 8 of the Companion Website (www.ablongman.com/smith5e) and click on the VideoWorkshop button. Follow the instructions for viewing Videoclip 10. Consider this information along with what you've read in Chapter 8 as you answer the following questions.

Video clip 10: Behavioral Disorders (Time 4:22)

1. Nick's teacher, Ms. Naputi, noted that he has academic strengths and that although he has behavior problems, he is manageable and responds to feedback and redirection. Review the "Prevention" section of your text to select a strategy or management system that could be used to prevent Nick's problematic behavior. Provide a specific example in your answer.

2. Often special education teachers are required to construct and implement, as part of the IEP for students with behavior problems, behavior intervention plans (BIPs) that include development of positive social skills. What social skills strategies would you include in a BIP for Nick? Provide a rationale for your choices.

Collection of the Roswell Museum and Art Center, Henriette Wyeth,
Dona Nestorita, oil on canvas, 1940, Gift of Mr. and Mrs. Donald Winston.

HENRIETTE WYETH, an extremely prominent artist in her own right, came from a family of very successful and well-known artists. Her father was the famous artist and illustrator N.C. Wyeth; her brother, Andrew, and her sister, Carolyn, also were well-known artists; and her husband was Peter Hurd, the renowned Western painter. Henriette Wyeth faced many challenges during her youth. She grew up in a high-achieving family that had exceptional expectations for her. She often spoke of the path she took to find the right outlet for her own creativity and talents and how her own special physical challenge helped to shape her future: "I wanted to be a singer. Due to polio at three, I couldn't play the piano. I wanted to be an actress, too. By the age of sixteen I was hooked on painting. I thought everyone drew—like having salt and pepper on the table" (Horgan, 1994, p. 30).

The very special piece shown here was painted in 1940. Doña Nestorita, a blind Mexican woman of 90 years, had lived most of her simple life in the rural Southwest. Wyeth described her as "charming, of great dignity, in a pitiful, tiny, blind person" (Horgan, 1994, p. 58).

Physical Impairments and Special Health Care Needs

Three Cheers for Bethany

Bethany A. Hoppe coaches the first-ever wheelchair cheer-leading and dance squad. The team is sponsored by the Easter Seals of Middle Tennessee and affiliated with A.B.L.E. (Athletes Building Life Experience.) The squad, which cheers for the Music City Wheelchair Basketball team, consists of individuals 5 to 17 years old who use wheelchairs at least 50 percent of the time. Lizzy B., whose story was told in Chapter 5, is a member of this squad. The cheerlead-ers' disabilities vary from cerebral palsy, spinal cord injuries, and orthopedic development issues to spina bifida, the condi-tion that Bethany has. Her story and the story of "her girls" is one that should be repeated across the country. And it could—if more remarkably talented and dedicated people like Bethany decided to devote their spirit and energy to developing teams like the Music City Lightning Wheelcheerleaders. Here's how Bethany puts it:

I believe that simple logic played the greatest role in forming the squad: Young people with disabilities are just as interested in the same extra- curricular activities that interest their able-bodied peers. It's just that the programs aren't as readily available, funded, or even perceived as socially "cool." I recall growing up and being asked to be a part of different after-school group activities for kids with disabilities and not enjoying them. They weren't doing the things I was interested in, and I recall feeling more segregated than ever by being part of such groups. I

wanted to be a cheerleader, to dance, socialize, and hang out with friends as naturally as everyone else did.

Recalling those feelings growing up, we asked parents, recreational workers, and the kids them-selves, "What do most young girls want to do?" We found that they want to attend sporting events, make the cheer squad, and wear the pins, sweaters, and jackets that go along with the after-school scene, and most particularly the "see-and-be-seen" aspect of public school life. So ... if there was wheel-chair football and basketball, then there ought to be wheelchair football and/or basketball cheerleaders to complete the package. The Wheelcheerleaders were born!

The changes in the girls have been visual. I see them sit straighter in their chairs. I see them work very hard physically to get dance moves down. They do more of the "girlie-girl" things: fussing with their hair, wearing make-up, giggling in huddles. Their level of confidence has been noticed by their parents, teachers, and the general public. To me, there lies the success of this program. Their friends are asking about it; they're wearing the pins, tee-shirts, and logos—the emblems of teen socializing.

I'd love to see the Music City Wheelcheerleaders inspire the formation of similar groups across the nation. Each time we've appeared at basketball tournaments, girls have approached us with a gleam in their eye, asking how to get a cheer squad for themselves. Perhaps one day soon, we'll see a National Wheel-cheerleading Association begin. I think it's more than possible and that it would be on a par with the American Cheerleaders Associations that are already established. From the squad here in Middle Tennessee are the seeds of future coaches and facilitators as they move on to college and life after high school. The more society sees girls with disabilities being *just girls,* the closer we'll come to bridging

social gaps and accessing opportunities for women with disabilities in the workplace, within entertainment and media, politics, education, industry, literature ... anywhere! Why not dance and cheer in the meantime?

1. Why do you think such opportunities are not available consistently across the nation? And, how might this situation be changed?

2. How will life be different for Bethany's cheerleaders?

ADVANCE ORGANIZERS

Overview

Despite the fact that the special education category "other health impairments" is the fastest growing disability area, the combined categories of physical impairments and special health care needs are low incidence disabilities (representing slightly more than one-half of 1 percent of all schoolchildren with disabilities). These groups comprise hundreds of conditions and diseases, including ADHD—the primary reason for the large increase in the numbers of children counted in this disability area. Most children with physical impairments attend their neighborhood schools, but they require modifications in the physical environment. Those with special health care needs tend to have high rates of absenteeism, and they require flexibility and modifications in their instructional programs. Some of these children may present

crises to their teachers and require emergency techniques. Children with ADHD can present a wide range of behavioral and academic challenges to themselves and their teachers.

Self-Test Questions

Focus Questions

- How are physical impairments and special health care needs classified and organized?

- What are some steps teachers should take to assist a child who is having a seizure?

- What are the different types of cerebral palsy?

- How do students with ADHD qualify for special education services?

- How can the learning environment be modified to accommodate students with physical impairments and special health care needs?

Challenge Question

- What are the barriers to the full participation of these individuals in society, and how can such barriers be minimized?

Making Connections

Use the learning strategy—Advance Organizers—to help focus your study of this chapter's content, and reinforce your learning by reviewing answers to the "Focus and Challenge" questions at the end of the chapter.

Youth, beauty, and physical fitness are obsessions of modern American society. Through singers, dancers, and actors, the entertainment industry projects ideals of beauty that are not within the reach of most adolescents. The advertising industry urges us to purchase certain styles of clothes, special cosmetics and hair products, new exercise equipment, and even cars to make ourselves more attractive. Have you noticed messages about physical perfection in television shows, commercials,

music videos, and movies? Have you or your friends assigned popularity ratings to others on the basis of physical appearance? Sometimes we even equate physical perfection with virtue or goodness, imperfection and deformities with evil. Think, for example, of the deformed Darth Vader, always dressed in black in the Star Wars films. This symbolism has been repeated in many books and movies, including *The Hunchback of Notre Dame, Dark Crystal, The Lion King,* and *The Wizard of Oz.*

CHAPTER 9 *Physical Impairments and Special Health Care Needs*

Children whose health is precarious or who have physical challenges often do not conform to the standards of strength and energy emphasized by the fashion, advertising, sports, and entertainment industries so admired by our society. Unfortunately, the prejudices of society frequently are reflected in schools as well. These children—whose appearance is unusual because of deformities or muscle problems, or whose very walking ability, to say nothing of athletic prowess, is challenged by wheelchairs or braces—may suffer prejudice and discrimination in school. How can educators eliminate these prejudices in order to provide appropriate learning environments for all children? How can educators address the individual learning needs of children who face physical challenges and require special accommodations because of their health care needs? These are some of the questions and related issues discussed in this chapter.

OPPORTUNITIES FOR A BETTER FUTURE

Historically, children with physical disabilities and special health care needs were excluded from neighborhood schools. Since the original passage of IDEA, access to these schools and to participation in the general education curriculum has progressively improved. Particularly for students with physical disabilities, most states no longer provide separate schools. However, inclusion is not consistent, and the pattern of placements varies widely across states.

Turning Legacies into Lessons

More medically fragile children are receiving their education in general education classrooms. Many teachers were concerned about these placements because they felt unprepared to deal with medical crises in their classes and also feared that the time they had to spend caring for these children would reduce the amount of instructional time they could devote to typical learners. The Supreme Court ruled that school districts would have to bear the costs of medical assistants for those whose needs were greater than a teacher could provide. School administrators are fearful that these costs will substantially affect overall school budgets. A second issue that has arisen is how many more students will need to be served because ADHD is included as a condition in the health impairments category.

Thinking About Dilemmas to Solve

As you read this chapter, ponder these students' needs, the supports they require, and the outcomes they should achieve. Think about

- How the educational system can best respond to their needs

- Why some states use separate special education schools for students with physical disabilities, whereas others do not

- The impact, on all of those directly and indirectly involved, of fully including all medically fragile students in general education classrooms

- The implications of including ADHD as a condition in the health impairments category

- How teachers should be prepared to work with children with these special needs

PHYSICAL IMPAIRMENTS AND SPECIAL HEALTH CARE NEEDS DEFINED

The federal government considers physical impairments and special health care needs separate special education categories. IDEA uses the term **orthopedic impairments** to refer to conditions that in this text are called physical impairments. Children with these disabilities have problems with the structure or the functioning of their bodies. IDEA notes that **physical impairments** adversely affect a child's educational performance and adds that the term

includes impairments caused by congenital anomaly (e.g., clubfoot, absence of some member, etc.), impairments caused by disease (e.g., poliomyelitis, bone tuberculosis, etc.), and impairments from other causes (e.g., cerebral palsy, amputations, and fractures or burns that cause contractures). (U.S. Department of Education, 1999, p. 12422)

The federal government uses the term **other health impairments** to describe, collectively, conditions and diseases that create special health care needs for children. IDEA defines children with special health care needs as those individuals

having limited strength, vitality or alertness, including a heightened alertness to environmental stimuli that results in limited alertness with respect to the educational environment, that is due to chronic or acute health problems such as asthma, attention deficit hyperactivity disorder, diabetes, epilepsy, a heart condition, hemophilia, lead poisoning, leukemia, nephritis, rheumatic fever, and sickle cell anemia; and adversely affects a child's educational performance. (U.S. Department of Education, 1999 p. 12422)

These two special education categories are not as separate or discrete as they might appear by their definitions. For example, some conditions typically grouped under physical or orthopedic impairments also result in long-term health problems. One child with cerebral palsy may face physical challenges and need considerable assistance from a physical therapist (PT) to learn how to control movement, and yet that child might have no special health care needs. Another child also with cerebral palsy may have both physical limitations and serious health care needs. Many children with health-related disabilities also have limitations to their physical well-being and require ongoing medical attention. And some combine major health issues with speech or language impairments (Lubker, Bernier, & Vizoso, 1999). Many of them present special needs at school. However, possibly more than any group, many children with physical impairments or health problems require accommodations but do not require special education services.

Note that the federal government currently includes attention deficit/hyperactivity disorder (ADHD) in the "other health impairments" category. This special edu-

M̲aking
C̲onnections

- See Chapter 12 for more information about autism.

- Read remaining chapters of this text to learn more about "low incidence disabilities."

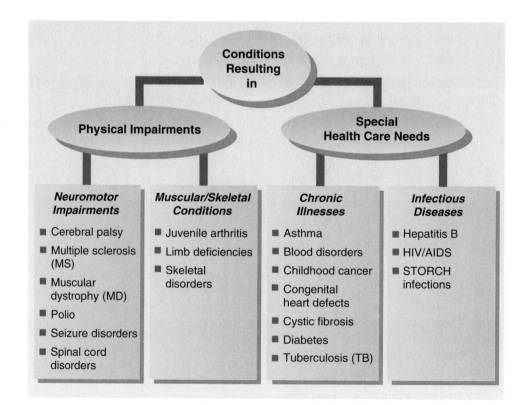

Figure 9.1 An Organizational Scheme. This diagram lists and categorizes the conditions, disorders, impairments, illnesses, and diseases that can result in physical challenges and special health care needs in children.

CHAPTER 9 *Physical Impairments and Special Health Care Needs*

cation category seems to be where future special education categories will originate. For example, autism, which is now a separate disability category, at one time was included in the category of other health impairments, and now it is an independent category. Only time will tell whether ADHD finds its way to another special education category or whether it becomes a category of its own in the future. Presently, the inclusion of ADHD has caused a significant increase in the size of this category (U.S. Department of Education, 2001).

All teachers work with students who need accommodations in the classroom and school environments because of either a physical disability or a special health situation. However, the likelihood of a teacher ever working with children who have some of these conditions is remote. Figure 9.1 displays many of the conditions, impairments, disorders, illnesses, and diseases educators might see at school. It lists a number of different conditions that can result in physical and health impairments but does not include the much less common conditions. Remember, these conditions, even when combined, are "low incidence" disabilities, amounting to slightly more than one-half of 1 percent of all schoolchildren. The number of children to whom this discussion pertains is small, particularly when compared to other catagories, such as learning disabilities, which includes over 6 percent of all schoolchildren.

What are the two major groups of physical impairments seen in children?

The two major groups of physical impairments are

1. Neuromotor impairments
2. Muscular/skeletal conditions

Explanations for many of the conditions and impairments that lead to a physical disability are found in Table 9.1. Some of these diseases, such as polio, are now prevented in the United States; others, such as multiple sclerosis, are found in adults but seldom seen in children; and some, such as muscular dystrophy and spina bifida, have extremely low prevalence rates. Other conditions, such as epilepsy and cerebral palsy, are **neuromotor impairments** that teachers should have knowledge about because they are more prevalent. Neuromotor impairments occur because the central nervous system (the brain and the spinal cord) is damaged, resulting in a **neurological impairment** that limits muscular control and movement. Individuals with **muscular/skeletal conditions** usually have difficulties controlling their movements, but the cause is not neurological. Some need to use special devices and technology even to do simple tasks—walking, eating, or writing—that most of us take for granted. Limb deficiencies and juvenile arthritis are discussed later in this section.

When responsible educators encounter diseases and conditions they know little about, they seek out all the information they need to provide an appropriate education to students involved. Educators also understand that these disabilities range in severity from mild to severe. And, in many cases, they are only one of multiple

ABOUT THE AUTHOR

I am Mattie J. T. Stepanek.
My body has light skin,
Red blood, blue eyes, and blond hair.
Since I have mitochondrial myopathy,
I even have a trach, a ventilator, and oxygen.
Very poetic, I am, and very smart, too.
I am always brainstorming ideas and stories.
I am a survivor, but some day, I will see
My two brothers and my one sister in Heaven.
When I grow up, I plan to become
A daddy, a writer, a public speaker,
And most of all, a peacemaker.
Whoever I am, and whatever happens,
I will always love my body and my mind,
Even if it has different abilities
Then other peoples' bodies and minds.
I will always be happy, because
I will always be me.

From *Journey Through Heartsongs* by Mattie Stepanek. Copyright © 2001 Matthew Joseph Thaddeus Stepanek. Reprinted by permission of VSP Books/Hyperion.

Mattie Stepanek and his mother both have muscular dystrophy. Mattie has been receiving considerable attention for his accomplishments as a poet. Another of his poems appears on p. v.

Table 9.1 Types of Neuromuscular/Skeletal Conditions

Condition	Description
Neuromotor Impairments	
Seizure disorders	*Epilepsy,* the most common type of neuromotor impairment in children, is a condition of recurrent convulsions or seizures caused by abnormal brain electrical activity. It is treated with medications and frequently is well controlled without any effect on learning or motor skills.
Cerebral palsy (CP)	*Cerebral palsy* is an incurable and nonprogressive condition caused by brain injury that sometimes limits the individual's ability to control muscle groups or motor functioning in specific areas of the body or, infrequently, the entire body. It may be associated with multiple disabilities. Physical therapy offers benefits.
Spinal cord disorders	A neural tube birth defect, *spina bifida* is the improper closure of the protective tissue surrounding the spinal cord. It results in limited neurological control for organs and muscles controlled by nerves that originate below the level of the lesion. Increasing numbers of children have suffered traumatic head or spinal cord injuries resulting in permanent disabilities. Typically, the result of injuries from accidents or abuse, *spinal cord injuries* can cause severe motor impairments and even paralysis. Health care needs for both groups include good skin care, management of bladder and bowel care, and physical therapy.
Polio	Caused by a viral infection, almost totally prevented in children immunized in the United States, *polio* attacks the spinal cord and can result in paralysis and motor disabilities. Health care needs parallel those for spinal cord disorders.
Muscular dystrophy (MD)	An exceptionally rare, incurable, and progressive disease, *muscular dystrophy* weakens and then destroys the affected individual's muscles. Health care needs center on lung function support, prevention of pneumonia, and physical therapy.
Multiple sclerosis (MS)	A chronic disease typically occurring in adults, *multiple sclerosis* causes the myelin covering the nerve fibers of the brain and spinal cord to deteriorate, impeding the transmission of electrical signals from the brain to other parts of the body. Health care needs parallel those for MD.
Muscular/Skeletal Conditions	
Juvenile arthritis	*Juvenile arthritis* is a disease caused by an autoimmune process resulting in swelling, immobility, and pain in joints. Health care needs include medication to suppress the process and orthopedic and physical therapy to maintain function in small and large joints.
Limb deficiencies	Skeletal problems in which the individual's limb(s) is shortened, absent, or malformed. They may occur from congenital conditions or from injuries. Health care needs focus on adaptive interventions to support or improve functioning of the missing limb(s).
Skeletal disorders	*Dwarfism,* a condition caused by abnormal development of long bones, may result in varying degrees of motor disabilities. Health care needs may include human growth hormone to improve height. *Osteogenesis imperfecta,* sometimes known as brittle bone disease, is a condition in which normal calcification of the bone does not occur, leading to breakage and abnormal healing of bones with accompanying loss of height. Health care interventions include physical therapy and medical care. *Scoliosis,* a curvature of the spine that occurs in children during puberty, may in severe form limit mobility of the trunk. Health care needs include monitoring of the amount of curvature of the spine and appropriate interventions to arrest the process.

conditions an individual must face (Eriksson, Kivimaki, & Koivikko, 1998; McDonnell, Hardman, & McDonnell, 2003). For example, epilepsy is the additional condition most frequently found in children with mental retardation. But remember never to make the terrible error of associating a health or physical impairment with a cognitive disability. They do not always go hand in hand. Now, let's focus on some specific physical impairments.

AKING CONNECTIONS

See Table 9.2 for tips on what to do in case of a seizure.

• *Neuromotor Impairments* The most common neuromotor impairment encountered at school is **epilepsy** (National Institute of Neurological Disorders and Stroke,

CHAPTER 9 *Physical Impairments and Special Health Care Needs*

2002). This condition is also called a seizure disorder or a convulsive disorder. A person with epilepsy often has recurrent seizures resulting from sudden, excessive, spontaneous, and abnormal discharge of neurons in the brain. This can be accompanied by changes in the person's motor or sensory functioning and can also result in loss of consciousness.

Seizures may involve the entire brain (generalized seizures) or only a portion of the brain (partial seizures). The frequency of seizures may vary from a single isolated incident to hundreds in a day. Some children actually anticipate their seizures because they experience a preictal stage, or an **aura,** and have heightened sensory signals of an impending seizure, such as a peculiar smell, taste, vision, sound, or action. Others might experience a change in their behavior. Knowing about an aura pattern is helpful, because it enables an individual to assume a safe position or warn companions before a seizure begins.

The Epilepsy Foundation of America (2002) identifies four main types of seizures:

1. Absence seizures
2. Simple partial seizures
3. Complex partial (psychomotor) seizures
4. Generalized tonic–clonic seizures

Absence seizures (also called petit mal seizures) are characterized by short lapses in consciousness. It may be difficult to determine that the person is experiencing anything out of the ordinary, and in fact the person may not even realize a seizure has occurred after it is over. Because absence seizures are not dramatic, a teacher might wrongly assume that the child is merely daydreaming or not paying attention. Not all seizures are obvious to those around the individual experiencing them. Such is often the case with **simple partial seizures,** during which children may think that their environments are distorted and strange and that inexplicable events and feelings have occurred. With these seizures, teachers might incorrectly believe that the child is acting out or exhibiting bizarre behavior patterns. With **complex partial seizures** (psychomotor or focal seizures), the child returns to normal activities after a short period. Sometimes, teachers interpret the child's behavior during this type of seizure as misbehavior or clowning. This can be confusing to the child, who is unaware of his or her behavior during the episode. **Generalized tonic–clonic seizures** (formerly referred to as grand mal seizures) are the most serious type of seizure and are characterized by convulsions and loss of consciousness. The dramatic behaviors exhibited during a tonic–clonic seizure may at first be frightening to the teacher and to other students in the class. The child may fall to the floor and experience a stiff (tonic) phase, in which the muscles become rigid, followed by a clonic phase, in which the individual's arms and legs jerk. Table 9.2 describes each type of seizure and explains how teachers can help during and after seizure episodes.

Another neuromotor impairment frequently encountered in schoolchildren is **cerebral palsy.** Cerebral palsy is a result of damage, usually because of insufficient oxygen getting to the brain, that occurred either before (prenatally), during (perinatally), or immediately after (postnatally) the child's birth (Cheney & Palmer, 1997; United Cerebral Palsy Association [UCP], 2002). The condition can also be acquired later, during the first 3 years of life. Acquired cerebral palsy is usually caused by brain damage resulting from accidents, brain infections, or child abuse. Cerebral palsy is not a disease but, rather, a nonprogressive and noninfectious condition that results in severe motor impairments. Regrettably, once it is acquired, it cannot be cured (at least today).

The severity of the condition depends on the precise location of brain damage, the degree of brain damage, and the extent of involvement of the central nervous system. Individuals with cerebral palsy whose motor functioning is affected show these characteristics alone or in combination: jerky movements, spasms, involuntary movements, and lack of muscle tone. Often, individuals with cerebral palsy have

Table 9.2 Managing Seizures at School

Seizure Type	Description	What to do
Absence	Momentary loss of awareness, sometimes accompanied by blinking or movements of the face or arms; may be frequent; fully aware after an episode	Be sure key parts of the lesson are not missed.
Simple partial	Consciousness not lost; unable to control body movements; experiences feelings, visions, sounds, and smells that are not real	Comfort and reassure if the child is frightened.
Complex partial	Consciousness clouded; unresponsive to instructions; inappropriate and undirected behaviors; sleepwalking appearance; of short duration (a minute or two); prolonged confusion after an episode; no recall of seizure	Gently guide child back to seat; speak softly; ensure child's safety; ignore uncontrollable behaviors; ensure full consciousness before changing locations; help child sort out confusions.
Generalized tonic–clonic	Body stiffens and jerks; may fall, lose consciousness, lose bladder control, have erratic breathing, lasts several minutes; can be confused, weary, or belligerent afterwards	Remain calm; reassure classmates; ease child to floor; clear area; rest head on a pillow; turn on side; do not put anything in child's mouth; do not restrain; after jerking ceases, let rest; re-engage in class participation.

Source: Adapted from *Managing Seizures at School,* Epilepsy Foundation Answerplace, www.efa.org, retrieved July 7, 2002. Reprinted with permission.

multiple disabilities, probably caused by the same damage to the brain that caused the cerebral palsy. For example, many individuals who have severe difficulties in motor functioning also have difficulty mastering oral speech. These individuals have a speech impairment and a physical disability. Although some degree of mental retardation is present in about half of the children with cerebral palsy, others are intellectually gifted. It is a tragic mistake to assume that cerebral palsy and mental retardation always occur in combination. Figure 9.2 illustrates four ways in which areas of the body can be affected by cerebral palsy: monoplegia, paraplegia, hemiplegia, and quadriplegia.

Another way in which cerebral palsy is classified is in terms of how the individual's movement is affected:

- Spastic
- Athetoid
- Ataxia

With the **spastic** type of cerebral palsy, movements are very stiff; with the **athetoid** type, involuntary movements are purposeless or uncontrolled, and purposeful movements are contorted; and with **ataxia**, movements such as walking are disrupted by impairments of balance and depth perception. Many individuals with cerebral palsy have impaired mobility and poor muscle development. Even if they can walk, their efforts may require such exertion and be so inefficient that they need canes, crutches, or a wheelchair to get around. Students with cerebral palsy may also need braces to help support the affected limbs and make them more functional or to prevent **contractures** that would eventually lead to bone deformities and further limitations on mobility. Proper positioning of the body also must be considered. Many children need wedges, pillows, and individually designed chairs and worktables so they can be comfortable; can breathe easier; can avoid injuries, contractures, and deformities; and can participate in group activities.

- *Muscular/Skeletal Conditions* **Limb deficiencies** are one of the most common muscular/skeletal conditions seen in children. They can be the result of a missing or nonfunctioning arm or leg and are either acquired or congenital. Regardless of when

CHAPTER 9 *Physical Impairments and Special Health Care Needs*

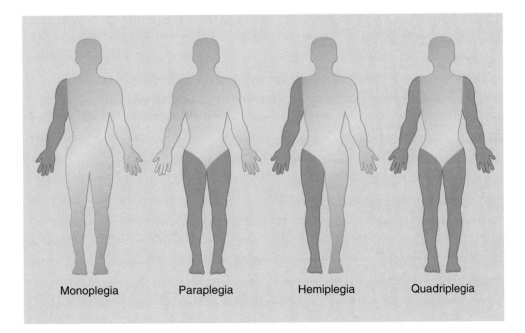

Monoplegia Paraplegia Hemiplegia Quadriplegia

Figure 9.2 Areas of the Body Affected by Cerebral Palsy.

the impairment occurred, the result is a major impediment to normal physical activity and functioning. Although the root of the disability is physical, many individuals with a limb deficiency have difficulties adjusting to their situation. The attitudes of those who work with these youngsters, and of course the support given by family members, can be major contributors to their psychological health. Emerging technology (particularly robotics) now provides great assistance to those with missing limbs. Artificial limbs now make possible movements that only a few years ago were thought to be impossible. And, although it is hard to believe, limb transplants are on the horizon and may become commonplace in the future. In February of 2001, Jerry Fisher became the nation's second recipient of a hand transplant. Both he and Matthew Scott, the first recipient, are successfully using their transplanted hands years after their surgeries, which were performed at Jewish Hospital by University of Louisville surgeons (Kleinert, Kutz and Associates Hand Care Center, 2002).

A relatively common muscular/skeletal condition affecting joints and the function of muscles is **juvenile arthritis.** Although there are many different forms of this disease, it is typically chronic and painful. Juvenile arthritis usually develops in early childhood and can cause many absences from school. These children often need help keeping up with their classmates because they miss so much class instruction. Teachers must understand that their ability to move may be inconsistent (better at different times of the day) and that sitting for extended periods of time can cause them to become stiff and experience considerable pain. These children need to be allowed to move around a lot. Those who have a high rate of absences probably need tutoring and extra help to keep up with their peers (Arthritis Foundation of America, 2002). Some promising medical treatments can reduce the amount of disability from the disease. However, certain medications can have side effects that alter some aspect of personality and physical appearance.

What are the different kinds of special health care needs seen at schools?

In general, there are two major groups of special health care needs:

1. Chronic illness
2. Infectious diseases

Table 9.3 Types of Health Impairments

Condition	Description
Chronic Illnesses	
Asthma	*Asthma,* a condition caused by narrowing of airways accompanied by inflammatory changes in the lining of the airways, may result in severe difficulty in breathing with chronic coughing. Health care needs include appropriate medications, environmental modifications, and monitoring and frequently result in no limitation of activities.
Cystic fibrosis	*Cystic fibrosis* is a genetic birth defect that results in chronic lung infections and digestive difficulties. Health care interventions include replacement of required enzymes for aiding digestion and aggressive care of lung infections and function.
Diabetes	*Diabetes* is the loss of the ability of the pancreas to produce enough insulin, resulting in problems with sugar metabolism. Health care needs include the monitoring of blood sugar levels, appropriate diet and exercise regimens, and knowledgeable response for insulin reactions.
Congenital heart defects	*Congenital heart conditions* can result in high rates of school absences for specialized health care. Most have had surgical intervention and medical monitoring by specialists. Health care needs include taking medications during the school day.
Tuberculosis (TB)	A disease caused by bacterial infection, *tuberculosis* rarely causes severe disease in children older than infancy. Most often the bacteria remain sequestered and harmless until late adulthood or when the body's immune system fails. The rates of infection are on the rise in many parts of the United States.
Childhood cancer	*Cancer,* the abnormal growth of cells, can affect any organ. The most common types of cancer in children are leukemia and lymphomas. While going through treatment, children may feel too ill to profit from classroom instruction.
	Leukemia causes an abnormal increase in the white blood cells, which are important in the body's defenses against infection. It often results in anemia and enlargement of the lymph glands, spleen, and liver.
	Lymphomas are malignant and cause enlargement of the lymph nodes.
Blood disorders	*Hemophilia,* a genetic condition typically linked with males, is characterized by poor blood clotting, which can result in massive bleeding from cuts and internal hemorrhaging from bruises.
	Sickle cell anemia, a hereditary disorder, causes a distortion in the red blood cells that restricts their passage through the blood vessels.
Infectious Diseases	
HIV and AIDS	*Human immunodeficiency virus (HIV),* a potentially fatal viral infection that in school-aged children results from transmission from a mother infected with the virus to her newborn child or from transfusion with blood or blood products carrying the virus, causes *acquired immunodeficiency syndrome (AIDS).* Health care needs include careful monitoring of general health, specialists to care for potentially overwhelming lung infections, and medications that slow or cure infections. The infection is acquired primarily through the exchange of body fluids in older children, through sexual abuse in younger children, through sexual activity in adolescents, and through intravenous drug use. Health care needs include sources of confidential care, counseling, and health education.
STORCH	*STORCH* is the acronym for a group of congenital infections that have the potential of causing severe, multiple impairments. It stands for syphilis, toxoplasmosis, other, rubella, cytomegalovirus, and herpes.
Hepatitis B	A viral disease, *hepatitis B* is infectious and causes inflammation of the liver. It is characterized by jaundice and fever. Cases of this dangerous virus are on the increase.

Table 9.3 includes definitions of illnesses and diseases seen in children. Of course, some general principles apply to all children who are sick, whatever the cause. Before focusing on two **chronic illnesses** (asthma and the blood condition sickle cell anemia) and one **infectious disease** (HIV/AIDS), let's first think about illness and schooling in general. Then, because the federal government has included ADHD in this special education category, a short review of this condition is provided.

All children have episodes of illness during childhood, but most of these are short in duration and not very serious. For a small number of children, however, their illnesses are chronic, lasting for years or even a lifetime. Children with chronic illnesses often do not feel well enough to focus their attention on the instruction being presented. They also experience many absences, causing them to miss a substantial part of their education. For many years the term **medically fragile** was used to describe all children with special health care needs, but it is now more selectively applied. Medically fragile is a status; it is not assigned to any specific condition but rather reflects the individual's health situation. Students can move in and out of fragile status. It is important to understand that because of medical technology, a greater number of medically fragile children survive health crises. In the past, many of these youngsters would not have lived long enough to go to school. Others would have been too sick to attend their neighborhood schools and would have received most of their schooling through hospital based or home based instruction. Even though many are now stable enough to attend school, they require ongoing medical management. For most, it is necessary for teachers to be familiar with procedures that must be followed if an emergency occurs. The "if, thens" must be carefully outlined and planned in collaboration with doctors and the medical profession. Although the contingencies for the "worst case scenarios" must be arranged, in most cases the accommodations required for these children are not terribly dramatic. (However, not having backup power for a child's ventilator could have disastrous results.)

• *Chronic Illnesses* **Asthma,** a pulmonary disease, is the most common chronic illness of children. It is the leading cause of school absences among all the chronic diseases (Getch & Neuharth-Pritchett, 1999; National Institute of Environmental Health Sciences [NIEHS], 2002). A person with asthma usually has labored breathing that is sometimes accompanied by shortness of breath, wheezing, and a cough. A combination of three events causes the wheezing: (1) tightening of the muscles around the bronchial tubes, (2) swelling of the tissues in these tubes, and (3) an increase of secretions in these tubes. Years ago, many people believed that asthma is a psychological disorder. It is not; its origin *is* physical. Many factors (such as chalk dust, dirt in the environment, dust mites, and pollen) can trigger an asthma attack, as can physical activity or exertion. Many students who have asthma are unable to participate in sports or even in physical education activities. Few of these students actually need special education, but they do need special accommodations so that their illness does not hinder their learning.

Sickle cell anemia is a hereditary, life-threatening blood disorder, and 95 percent of all cases occur in the African American population (Guthrie, 2001). This condition causes the red blood cells to become rigid and take on a crescent, or sickle, shape. During what is called a "sickling crisis," this rigidity and the crescent shape of the cells do not allow blood to flow through the vessels, depriving some tissues of oxygen and resulting in extreme pain, swollen joints, high fever, and even strokes. Certain information about this condition is particularly important to educators who

TIPS FOR TEACHERS

Working with Students Who Have Sickle Cell Anemia

1. Frequent hospitalizations are common. Provide students with "make-up" work so they can stay current with assignments when hospitalized or absent from school.

2. Pain episodes are prevented by drinking more water. Let the student keep a water bottle at hand and allow for frequent bathroom breaks.

3. Pain episodes are prevented by avoiding extreme temperatures. Do not let the student get either overheated or exposed to excessive cold.

4. Anemia causes people to tire easily. Encourage rest periods, and let the individual quietly step out of sports and recreational activities.

5. Sickle cell anemia places the individual at risk for other infections. Keep a safe and sterile classroom and school environments.

6. Be alert for instances of fever, headache, chest pain, abdominal pain, numbness, or weakness. If you observe one of these symptoms, call a doctor or the school nurse.

7. Children are sensitive. Avoid calling undue attention to the child.

Source: Adapted from the Georgia Comprehensive Sickle Cell Center, www.SCInfo/teacher.htm, The Sickle Cell Foundation of Georgia, Emory University School of Medicine, Department of Pediatrics, Morehouse School of Medicine, www.emory.edu/PEDS/SICKLE/teacher.htm. Retrieved July 6, 2002.

have students with sickle cell anemia (see Tips for Teachers). First, there seems to be a correlation between the sickling crisis and emotional stress and strenuous exercise (Best, Bigge, & Sirvis, 1994; Heller et al., 1996). Second, many of these children may be absent from school often. To reduce the stress these students experience when they return to school knowing that they have missed assignments and instruction, teachers must work together and develop strategies with the students and their families to compensate for missed school days. For example, a neighborhood child could serve as a peer tutor who brings assignments home to the student and explains important instructions provided during the school day.

• *Infectious Diseases* Human immunodeficiency virus (HIV) is a potentially fatal viral infection transmitted primarily through exchange of bodily fluids in unprotected sex or by contaminated needles. It is the virus responsible for the deadly **acquired immunodeficiency syndrome (AIDS)** and can be communicated to a child by an infected mother. Before blood-screening procedures were instituted, the virus was also transmitted in blood transfusions. The effects of the infection in children include central nervous system damage, additional infections, developmental delay, motor problems, psychosocial stresses, and death. HIV/AIDS is an infectious disease, but unlike most others, such as flu and the common cold, it is serious and life-threatening. For many years, parents and educators were concerned that noninfected children could catch the disease from a classmate. It is now clear that this is highly unlikely. With proper precautions (the use of gloves and normal sanitary procedures), everyone at school is safe and will not catch this disease.

• *Attention Deficit/Hyperactivity Disorder* In the 1997 reauthorization of the IDEA law, ADHD was called out as a disability in the "other health impairments" category. (The "What IDEA Says" box about ADHD gives more information.) Sometimes called attention deficit disorder (ADD), **attention deficit/hyperactivity disorder (ADHD)** has been estimated to affect between 10 and 20 percent of the school-age population in the United States (Shaywitz & Shaywitz, 1992). However, the federal government was confident that very few additional students would be included in special education because of this 1997 action (U.S. Department of Education, 1999). The government came to this conclusion because it believes that most students with ADHD who qualify for special education services are served through either the learning disabilities category or the emotional or behavioral disorders category. The characteristics that define these three conditions tend to overlap. The characteristics that are often associated with ADHD include being hyperactive, impulsive, and distracted. For example, many such children display excessive movement and seem unable to control their behavior. These children are unable to sit or concentrate for very long; their parents and teachers comment that they are in constant motion. Both hyperactivity and impulsivity are frequently associated with other disabilities (traumatic brain injury, emotional disturbance) as well as ADHD. How, then, are students with ADHD served at school?

MAKING **C**ONNECTIONS

For other discussions of ADHD, see Chapters 1, 4, and 8.

• Students with ADHD who do not qualify for special education because their condition does not seriously affect their educational performance receive accommodations for their unique learning needs through Section 504 of the Rehabilitation Act.

• Some students with ADHD qualify for special education services under the "other health impairments" category.

• For many students, ADHD coexists with another disability, and they are identified and served in special education categories such as the learning disabilities category or the emotional or behavioral disorders category.

According to the DSM-IV (American Psychiatric Association, 1994), ADHD "is a persistent pattern of inattention and/or hyperactivity-impulsivity that is more frequent and severe than is typically observed in individuals at a comparable level of

CHAPTER 9 *Physical Impairments and Special Health Care Needs*

development" (p. 78). Symptoms of the condition must occur in more than one setting. The DSM-IV also establishes criteria for determining whether a child has ADHD; those criteria are listed in Table 9.4. As you read this table, think about what ADHD is and what it is not.

Although the DSM-IV definition is widely accepted in the United States, it is not the definition used worldwide. In Europe, particularly in Britain, the World Health Organization's definition is more commonly accepted, which results in fewer students being identified with this condition (Reason, 1999). This definition requires that the individual have both significant inattention *and* hyperactivity. When both characteristics are required, the prevalence falls to between 0.5 percent and 1 percent of the student population, compared to the range of 2 percent to 10 percent identified in the United States. A key difference between these two definitions is the emphasis on problems associated with impulsivity, and British psychologists believe that their more stringent view of ADHD reduces the risk of including children from different cultural backgrounds who come from homes where behaviors expected in school are not instilled from early childhood.

How does a teacher help the student with ADHD? Like their counterparts who have only learning disabilities, students with ADHD respond well to highly

What IDEA Says About

Attention Deficit/Hyperactivity Disorder (ADHD)

- Children with ADHD are not automatically protected by IDEA.

- Not all children with ADHD, not even all those with medical diagnoses and medication, are eligible for special education or related services.

- Some children with ADHD are eligible for special education under categories such as learning disabilities, health impairments, and emotional or behavioral disorders.

- For the student with ADHD to receive special education, the condition must adversely affect educational performance.

- The only category where ADHD is specifically called out is "other health impairments." Not all disabilities or conditions are named in IDEA (e.g., Tourette's syndrome).

structured learning environments where topics are taught directly. Many students with ADHD tend not to be motivated and to lack the persistence to make the extra effort to learn when it is difficult for them (Carlson, et al., 2002). Professionals suggest that carefully planned educational procedures, such as giving rewards, making assignments more interesting, letting students chose their academic assignments from a group of alternatives selected by the teacher, shortening the task, and giving clear and precise instructions, can lead to academic improvement (Powell & Nelson, 1997). Peer tutoring has proved to be very effective for students with ADHD, as well as for those with learning disabilities (DuPaul et al., 1998; Fuchs & Fuchs, 1998). Over 50 percent improvement in academic tasks has been achieved by involving peers in the instructional program. Although it is important for teachers and parents to pay attention to these students' academic problems, it is also imperative that they help these students develop social skills that are acceptable to their peers.

Students with ADHD, whether or not they also have learning disabilities, are often rejected by their peers because of their hyperactivity and poor social skills (Bryan, 1997). Rejection by classmates can leave these children lonely and without friends. They come to judge themselves as social failures and tend to engage in solitary activities (playing computer games, watching television, feeling sorry for themselves). This characteristic contributes to more alienation and withdrawal. Classroom behavior that classmates find more desirable can be encouraged by using direct instruction techniques. For example, self-management strategies that include contingencies for conforming to classroom rules improve behavior (Shapiro, DuPaul, & Bradley-Klug, 1998). For those who do not qualify for special education services, general educators must accommodate their problems and differences in learning styles by providing them with instruction that meets their individual needs.

Many physicians prescribe drugs—such as Ritalin, Dexedrine, or Concerta—to help children with ADHD focus their attention on assigned tasks, and the

Table 9.4 DSM-IV Diagnostic Criteria for Attention Deficit/Hyperactivity Disorder

Either inattention or hyperactivity/impulsivity must have persisted for at least six months. Either condition must be at a level that is both maladaptive and inconsistent with development and must include six (or more) of the following symptoms:

Inattention

- Often fails to give close attention to details or makes careless mistakes in schoolwork, work, or other activities
- Often has difficulty sustaining attention in tasks or play activities
- Often does not seem to listen when spoken to directly
- Often does not follow through on instructions and fails to finish schoolwork, chores, or duties in the workplace (not due to oppositional behavior or failure to understand instructions)
- Often has difficulty organizing tasks and activities
- Often avoids, dislikes, or is reluctant to engage in tasks that require sustained mental effort (such as schoolwork or homework)
- Often loses things necessary for tasks or activities (e.g., toys, school assignments, pencils, books, or tools)
- Is often easily distracted by extraneous stimuli
- Is often forgetful in daily activities

Hyperactivity/Impulsivity

- Often fidgets with hands or feet or squirms in seat
- Often leaves seat in classroom or in other situations in which remaining seated is expected
- Often runs about or climbs excessively in situations in which it is inappropriate (in adolescents or adults, may be limited to subjective feelings of restlessness)
- Often has difficulty playing or engaging in leisure activities quietly
- Is often "on the go" or often acts as if "driven by a motor"
- Often talks excessively
- Often blurts out answers before questions have been completed
- Often has difficulty awaiting turn
- Often interrupts or intrudes on others (e.g., butts into conversations or games)

Also, some hyperactive-impulsive or inattentive symptoms were present before age 7 years.

The symptoms must be present in two or more settings (e.g., at school [or work] and at home).

Clear evidence of clinically significant impairment in social, academic, or occupational functioning must be demonstrated.

The symptoms do not occur exclusively during the course of a pervasive developmental disorder, schizophrenia, or other psychotic disorder and are not better accounted for by another mental disorder (e.g., mood disorder, anxiety disorder, disassociative disorder, or a personality disorder).

Source: Reprinted with permission from the *Diagnostic and Statistical Manual of Mental Disorders,* Fourth Edition (*DSM-IV*), pp. 83–85. Copyright 1994 American Psychiatric Association.

medication is effective for some (Forness & Kavale, 2001). Controversy, however, surrounds the use of behavior control drugs for these youngsters and the roles of educators recommending their use to parents (Gotsch, 2002). Of particular concern is the rapid increase in prescriptions for these drugs—an increase of some 35 percent over a recent 5-year period, to raise the number to some 20 million prescriptions written in 12 months. Although these drugs can be effective in reducing hyperactivity for some of these children, they do not seem to have a positive effect on academic performance. For many, the drugs are unnecessary and can even be harmful (Armstrong, 1995). Instead, behavioral techniques, direct and systematic instruction that is evaluated on a frequent basis, and highly motivating instructional materials have proved successful with many children currently identified as having ADHD.

THE STORY OF JOEY PIGZA

At school they say I'm wired bad, or wired mad, or wired sad, or wired glad, depending on my mood and what teacher has ended up with me. But there is no doubt about it, I'm wired.

This year was no different. When I started out all the days there looked about the same. In the morning I'd be okay and follow along in class. But after lunch, when my meds had worn down, it was nothing but trouble for me.

One day, we were doing math drills in class and every time Mrs. Maxy asked a question, like "What's nine times nine?" I'd raise my hand because I'm really quick at math. But each time she called on me, even though I knew the answer, I'd just blurt out, "Can I get back to you on that?" Then I'd nearly fall out of my chair from laughing. And she'd give me that whitelipped look which meant, "Settle down." But I didn't and kept raising my hand each time she asked a question until finally no other kid would raise their hand because they knew what was coming between me and Mrs. Maxy.

"Okay, Joey," she'd say, calling on me and staring hard at my face as if her eyes were long fingers that could grip me by the chin. I'd stare right back and hesitate a second as if I was planning to answer the question and then I'd holler out really loud, "Can I get back to you on that?" Finally, after a bunch of times of me doing that in a row, she jerked her thumb toward the door. "Out in the hall," she said. And the class cracked up.

So I went and stood in the hall for about a second until I remembered the mini-Superball in my pocket and started to bounce it off the lockers and ceiling and after Mrs. Deebs in the next class stuck her head out her door and yelled, "Hey, cut the racket," like she was yelling at a stray cat, I remembered something I wanted to try. I had seen the Tasmanian Devil on TV whirling around like a top so I unbuckled my belt and pulled on the end really hard, as if I was trying to start a lawn mower. But that didn't get me spinning very fast. So I took out my high-top shoelaces and tied them together and then to the belt and wrapped it all around my waist. Then I grabbed one end and yanked on it and sort of got myself spinning. I kept doing it until I got better and better and before long I was bouncing off the lockers because I was dizzy too. Then I gave myself one more really good pull on the belt and because I was already dizzy I got going really fast and began to snort and grunt like the Tasmanian Devil until Mrs. Maxy came out and clamped her hands down on my shoulders. She stopped me so fast I spun right out of my shoes and they went shooting up the hall.

"You glue your feet to the floor for five whole minutes or you can just spin yourself down to the principal's office," she said. "Now, what is your choice going to be?"

"Can I get back to you on that?" I asked.

Source: From *Joey Pigza Swallowed the Key* (pp. 3–6) by Jack Gantos, 1998, New York: Farrar, Straus, & Giroux.

How are these children identified?

Parents of children with ADHD seek help from their doctors, typically because their child seems hyperactive. These students' inabilities to focus their attention or control their behavior are substantially different from their peers, and are a cause of concern to both parents and teachers. Students with ADHD can qualify for and receive special education services through several different IDEA categories, including "other health impairments." In an attempt to clarify this confusing situation, the U.S. Department of Education (1999) made a number of important points when it developed the regulations explaining IDEA as it was passed in 1997. Here are a few of the points it made:

- A student may become eligible for special education under the "other health impairments" category.

- To qualify for special education services through the other health impairments category because of ADHD, the individual must have heightened alertness to the environment that limits alertness to education, which adversely affects educational performance.

The Music City Lightning Wheelcheerleaders directed by Bethany A. Hoppe (see the "Personal Perspective" on page 297), support the Music City Wheelchair Basketball Team. (Lizzy B. is a member of the cheerleading squad, and her story is told in the "Personal Perspective" in Chapter 5).

- Not all students with ADHD qualify for special education services.
- Many students with ADHD are (and have been) served through other special education categories, such as learning disabilities and emotional or behavioral disorders.

Most students with physical impairments and special health care needs are identified outside of the school setting. Typically, the child's pediatrician identifies the disease or condition. In some cases, however, alert teachers see signs of health concerns in the classroom and request assistance from the school nurse, who should handle the referral process.

Once a child is identified as having ADHD, the school's multidisciplinary team goes into high gear to develop the child's IEP and determine what accommodations and services are required. A broad array of professionals from a wide variety of disciplines work with the child's parents throughout the IEP development and implementation process. Each professional uses a variety of assessment tools and techniques. A complete evaluation for a child with cerebral palsy, for example, includes many professionals, all seeking input and consultation from the parents. The report from the multidisciplinary team for this child can include a physician's evaluation; evaluations by adaptive physical educators, PTs, and OTs; assessments by other professionals, such as SLPs and technology experts (depending on the nature and severity of the disability); and a thorough academic, vocational, and intellectual evaluation by teachers and diagnosticians. Parent involvement throughout the process is crucial, and the family's culture must also be appreciated and considered.

Each related service and its professionals play unique roles in the assessment of these students' needs and in the implementation of their IEPs. For example, PTs evaluate the quality of the person's movement and later teach the student how to compensate for and change inefficient motor patterns. OTs work closely with PTs as they assess and later work with upper-body movement, fine motor skills, and daily living activities. Together, PTs and OTs determine the student's physical characteristics and the assistive devices that will benefit the individual (Best, Bigge, & Sirvis, 1994). Rehabilitation engineers and assistive technologists recommend and devise mobility and special seating systems and can create equipment that will attach other devices (e.g., communication devices) to wheelchairs.

Making Connections

For a reminder about how people with disabilities have been treated across time, and the biases they experienced because they do not meet current standards of physical strength or beauty, see Chapter 1.

What is the impact on the individuals involved?

Think about how you have reacted in the past to people you have met who look different. The reactions of others have been and continue to be a major problem for individuals with physical and health problems and only compound the challenges they face because of their disabilities. Physical differences and health impairments are often obvious, even at first meeting. As a consequence, individuals with these disabilities are forced to deal with the often negative reactions of others in addition to their own feelings about their appearance. Bonnie Mullinax, a special education teacher, meets head on potential reactions to her dwarfism by telling her students that she knows she is little but she expects the respect due all teachers (Ferguson,

2001). Students with these disabilities must address the actual physical and medical requirements of their disabilities to accomplish the tasks of school and daily life. Educators can play an important role in helping these youngsters meet these important challenges and shape satisfying lives for themselves. And the time might now be right, as these students enter a changing society with a much more positive outlook for people with disabilities.

Before 1990, when the Americans with Disabilities Act (ADA) was passed by Congress, many individuals with physical impairments had no opportunity to participate in many aspects of daily life because of physical barriers (e.g., curbs and stairs) and discrimination. Unfortunately, physical barriers still exist in many schools and public buildings that are old and have not yet been renovated. Many school doors are too heavy for students with disabilities to open, school entrances are too steep to negotiate, and many bathrooms are still unsuitable. Even though not all problems are yet resolved, important changes signal a better future of access and inclusion in mainstream society.

The basketball team is coached by Rick Slaughter, director of the Athletes Building Life Experience (A.B.L.E.) program at Easter Seals of Nashville, Tennessee.

Many inclusive and normalized experiences that were not possible only a few years ago are now available to children, as well as adults. The U.S. National Parks Service maintains accessible trails for outdoor adventures, and cruise ship lines now serve passengers with many different kinds of challenges. Special programs are also available, allowing children with disabilities opportunities for recreational activities much like those their brothers and sisters without disabilities enjoy. For example, the A.B.L.E. Program offered by Easter Seals of Middle Tennessee creates many different opportunities for youngsters, taking students on skiing, boating, and camping adventures. Children who use wheelchairs now grow up playing wheelchair basketball, cheered on by cheerleaders who also use wheelchairs. Nationally, Easter Seals supports 140 special camps for children with physical impairments and other disabilities. The Breckenridge Outdoor Education Center (BOEC) provides wilderness programs, expeditions, and instruction in adaptive skiing for children who might not have had such opportunities some 20 years ago (BOEC, 2002). Shake-A-Leg offers a full range of adaptive sailing programs designed to build confidence and self-esteem in children with physical disabilities (Shake-A-Leg, 2002). All of these experiences hold promise for a more active adult life, enhanced by socializing through recreation. Special Challenger Division is often where children with disabilities get their start. These special athletic programs allow participation in sports where children with physical limitations are not typically welcome because giving them a chance to play might make it harder for their team to win. Early access to sports and team activities can set the stage for an adult life that includes physical activity and social involvement in community events.

Resorts and vacation planners are now seeking out and planning to meet the needs of travelers with disabilities. For example, the city of Miami offers a range of usually inaccessible activities—for example, sailing in small boats. The Miami chapter of Shake-A-Leg supports the city's recreation program by offering a free 3-hour ride and even helps in transferring people from wheelchairs to a special boat seat. Some parks have "surfchairs," specialized chairs with "puffy" wheels that allow movement on soft sand. Even the Everglades National Park has an accessible mono-

Kids with
physical disabilities
are getting
too much attention.

Nobody likes to be stared at. Or pointed at. But when you have a disability, that's the kind of thing that happens to you every day. And the worst part is, after awhile, you start believing that there really is something wrong with you. It's time to change that. And start paying more attention to the person. Not the disability.

rail so that visitors with disabilities can visit the park and see all of the wildlife. This is only a sampling of the special accommodations that Miami has created to lure more tourists. Many other sites are seeking out the potentially lucrative tourist business of a previously untapped group of potential travelers. Many business are now also finding that people with disabilities are a large and profitable market for the travel industry.

The impact of ADHD is different from the impact of most other health impairments. In many cases, it is more similar to the impact of learning disabilities or emotional or behavioral disorders. ADHD can be confusing to parents, professionals, and people in the community. The story of Joey Pigza, told in a popular book, also shows the confusion that these individuals themselves experience (see the box on page 313).

HISTORY OF THE FIELD

The history of physical disabilities can be traced back to 11,000-year-old grave sites (Frayer et al., 1987). Evidence of treatment for spinal cord injuries goes back to prehistoric times, the earliest documented treatment being the application of meat and honey to the neck (Maddox, 1987). Beginning with Hippocrates (400 B.C.), treatment usually included traction or even a stretching rack in an attempt to straighten the back or push in a deformity. Even though it was usually not successful, spinal surgery was performed as long ago as A.D. 600, but it was not until the mid-1800s that anesthesia became available and sterile techniques were used.

Hippocrates recognized that epilepsy originated in the brain but believed that it was caused by several factors: blockage of the normal passage of "phlegm" from the brain, the discharge of cold phlegm into warm blood, and unequal heat distribution in the brain from sitting too long in the sun (Scheerenberger, 1983). Descriptions of conditions such as hemophilia, cerebral palsy, and epilepsy can be found in written records as early as 200 B.C. Hemophilia, the most common bleeding disorder, has long been recognized as a hereditary condition; rabbis noted that its transmission was from mothers to sons and was traced through royal and noble families in Spain, Germany, Russia, and England (Heller et al., 1996). William J. Little, an English surgeon, described the condition now known as cerebral palsy in well-researched case studies in 1861.

Perspectives about the best ways to educate students with physical impairments and special health care needs have changed across the years. The first U.S. educational institution for children with physical disabilities was established in Boston in 1893: the Industrial School for Crippled and Deformed Children (Eberle, 1922). The first public school classes for "crippled children" were established in Chicago at the turn of the century (La Vor, 1976). Later, separate schools were established in New York City, Philadelphia, and Cleveland. Special schools for students with disabilities resulted from well-intended motives and reasons. They provided a centralized place where expensive equipment (e.g., therapeutic swimming pools) were housed and where highly skilled professionals could work with all the children with very special physical needs from the area. Providing such treatment, education, and facilities was not feasible when these youngsters were spread across a wide geographical region. They were segregated, however, and students with disabilities

CHAPTER 9 *Physical Impairments and Special Health Care Needs*

were educated together, with no classroom interaction with their neighborhood friends. Today most of these students attend neighborhood schools and participate in the general education curriculum with accommodations. The special services they receive are brought to them.

AMERICANS WITH DISABILITIES ACT: EXPANDING OPPORTUNITIES

Justin Dart, a hero to many in the Disability Advocacy Movement, was instrumental in making the Americans with Disabilities Act (ADA). Many believe that without his political savvy, his persistent advocacy, and his unparalleled commitment to the civil rights of people with disabilities, the law, if passed, would not have had its scope or national impact. Here, in 1998, Dart shakes hands with President Clinton after the signing of an executive memorandum on the ADA.

Advances in medicine have eliminated some diseases and conditions and reduced the impact of others. For example, a text published in 1948, *Helping Handicapped Children in School* (Dolch, 1948), included chapters titled "Crippled Children" and "Health Handicaps." The chapter on "crippled children" focused primarily on heart trouble caused by rheumatic fever, measles, scarlet fever, and diphtheria. These diseases, once common, are now rare. Even when children contract them today, the damage can usually be limited via antibiotics and other medical advances. But other causes of these disabilities now demand our attention. Dolch's 1948 chapter on "crippled children" closes with an appeal to boost efforts at prevention by decreasing the accident rate and by providing prenatal and obstetrical care for all mothers and medical care for all children—pleas that continue to be heard today. The chapter on health disabilities also addressed issues that were a sign of their time: infected and decayed teeth, chronic cold and bronchitis, glandular problems, tuberculosis, and malnutrition.

The history of legislation and advocacy for people with physical disabilities in the United States is long. Congress passed significant legislation concerning these disabilities after World War I and after World War II. The Soldiers Rehabilitation Act was passed in 1918 to offer vocational rehabilitation services to wounded soldiers. Two years later, a similar law for civilians with physical disabilities was passed: the Citizens Vocational Rehabilitation Act (La Vor, 1976). (People with mental illness and mental retardation were not added to this law until 1943.) Additional laws were passed following the Vietnam War. In 1965 the National Commission on Architectural Barriers was established to study the problems faced by people with physical disabilities. Ultimately, this led to a period of advocacy, bringing these people's civil rights to the forefront. Like many underrepresented groups, the disability community needed a catalyst to begin an organized civil rights movement. In the view of many, Ed Roberts was just that catalyst (Shaw, 1995; Stone, 1995). Although Section 504 of the Rehabilitation Act (prohibiting discrimination) was passed in 1973, it took a wheelchair sit-in, orchestrated by Ed Roberts, in the office of Secretary Califano at the Department of Health, Education and Welfare (now Health and Human Services) four years later to bring about implementation of the Section 504 regulations. It took the political influence of Justin Dart, heir to Walgreen Drug Stores and himself a very successful businessman, to get passage of ADA in 1990.

The irony of some of these early personal stories is great. Here's a wonderful example. At the age of 14, Ed Roberts almost died from polio. After considerable

M AKING
C ONNECTIONS

For more about Section 504 of the Rehabilitation Act, the ADA law, and the disability advocacy movement, see the "Necessity for National Intervention" section of Chapter 1.

Ed Roberts, founder of the world Institute on disabilities and a leader in the civil rights movement for people with disabilities, was an aggressive advocate for people with disabilities. His legacy is the community participation people with disabilities expect today.

Making Connections

ADHD is also discussed in Chapters 1, 4, and 8.

struggle and persistence, in the early 1960s he was ready to attend college, but the University of California (UC) at Berkeley declared that he was "too disabled" for the campus to accommodate. Also, the California Department of Vocational Rehabilitation would not pay for his education because he was "too handicapped." Despite this rejection, he paid for the personal care attendants he needed to attend UC, and he became known as one of the "Rolling Quads" on campus. After receiving his bachelor's and master's degrees, he became the director of the agency that had previously refused to support his education. In 1984, with the monetary award he received from being honored as a MacArthur fellow, Roberts cofounded the World Institute on Disability, an event that many mark as the formal beginning of the civil rights movement for people with disabilities. Roberts died in 1995, at the age of 56, but his movement is thriving, and the voices of people with disabilities are heard across the nation, still demanding acceptance, access, and inclusion.

PREVALENCE

Although the low prevalence rates of physical impairments and special health care needs are meaningless to children and their families who are affected, educators should remember that relatively few children have these problems. Also, many with these conditions do not require special education. According to the *Annual Report to Congress,* some 66,574 children between the ages of 6 and 17 have physical impairments, and some 245,098 have special health care needs; together they represent about 0.65 percent of all U.S. schoolchildren (U.S. Department of Education, 2001).

In 1997 IDEA allowed for some children with ADHD to be included in the "other health impairments" category. The federal government was very clear that only a small proportion of additional students with ADHD would be eligible for special education. Officials believed that most who were eligible were already being served (and are still counted) through the learning disabilities and emotional or behavioral disorders categories. They also maintained that many students with ADHD only required some accommodations to profit from the general education curriculum and did not need any special education services. Regardless, the health impairments category has shown marked proportional increases since the law was changed (U.S. Department of Education, 2001). Now that ADHD is included in the "other health impairments" category, it is likely that the numbers in this category will continue to increase.

Let's look at the prevalence rates of a few specific conditions and diseases. Asthma, the leading cause of school absenteeism and the condition that affects the most schoolchildren, is on the rise (Asthma and Allergy Foundation of America, 2002). Over 5 million children have asthma, some 8 to 12 percent of all children (Getch & Neuharth-Pritchett, 1999; National Institute of Environmental Health Sciences [NIEHS], 2002). About 1 percent of all fetuses contract the infection CMV, but only 10 to 15 percent of this 1 percent develop a disability. About 1 percent of the general population has epilepsy, but substantially less than 1 percent of the school population has the condition, and 80 percent of all cases are controlled by medication (Epilepsy Foundation of America, 2002). About 0.03 percent of all children have cerebral palsy, and some of them do not require special education services (United Cerebral Palsy Association [UCP], 2002). Pediatric AIDS is on the decline (National Institute of Allergies and Infectious Disease, 1999). In 1998 a total of 382 cases of pediatric AIDS occurred in the United States. A startling 8 percent of African Americans have inherited sickle cell anemia (Heller et al., 1996; National Human Genome Research Institute, 2002).

Most diseases and conditions that seriously affect children continue to change across time. In some cases this is good news; in others it is not. For example, polio, a viral infection that attacks the nerve cells in the **spinal cord** that control muscle

CHAPTER 9 *Physical Impairments and Special Health Care Needs*

function, is a serious disease that ravaged this country in the 1950s and 1960s, leaving many people with a significant, permanent disability. Hundreds of thousands of Americans contracted the disease; the worst epidemic, some 56,000 new cases, occurred in 1952. Many of the senior advocates with disabilities today had polio as children. Jonas Salk developed a vaccine, and by the end of the 1960s, polio was almost eradicated in the United States. But the prevalence of polio decreased dramatically, some conditions remained stable. For example, the birth prevalence of cerebral palsy has remained about the same for over 40 years (Cheney & Palmer, 1997).

CAUSES AND PREVENTION

There are as many different causes, preventions, and treatments as there are different illnesses, diseases, and conditions that result in disabilities. Instead of discussing these specifically for each condition, some common themes and conditions are examined as examples. Individual students' programs must reflect the impact of the disability on them, their own and their family's priorities, and the skills that must be mastered to achieve independent living as an adult. The summary in Table 9.5 was designed to broaden your understanding of these children's conditions, what caused them, and how they might have been prevented.

MAKING CONNECTIONS

To get an overview of how disabilities are caused and how they can be prevented, review the "Causes and Prevention" sections in this text.

What causes these conditions?

There are almost as many causes for the conditions that result in physical impairments and special health care needs as there are conditions. They can be grouped into some general areas:

- Allergies and infections
- Heredity
- Accidents and injuries
- Multiple factors
- "Unknown"

Infections cause many different kinds of special health care needs. Hepatitis B, HIV/AIDS, CMV, and STORCH are some examples. In children under age 13, the cause of HIV infection can be traced primarily to the risk behaviors of their parents. In contrast, the HIV infections of adolescents are caused primarily by their own risk behaviors. Asthma is most likely to be the result of an allergic reaction to certain substances (allergens) found in the environment. A variety of substances can trigger

Table 9.5 Causes and Prevention of Physical Disabilities and Health Impairments

Causes	Prevention
Motor vehicle accidents	Child restraints Safety belts Auto air bags Motorcycle helmets
Water and diving accidents	Diving safety Swimming safety
Gunshot wounds	Gun control Weapons training Locked storage of ammunition
Sports injuries (boxing, skiing, football)	Headgear and protective equipment Safe fields and slopes Conditioning/training
Child abuse	Family support services Parenting training
Poisoning/toxins	Knowledge of resources in emergencies Safe storage of poisons
Diseases such as polio, measles	Vaccinations
Premature birth	Prenatal care
Infectious diseases	Vaccinations Good hygiene
HIV infection	Abstinence or safe sex Avoidance of drugs Drug equipment not shared Screening of blood and plasma supplies
Genetic disabilities	Genetic screening
Seizures	Medication
Hydrocephaly	Surgery and medical technology
Asthma	Elimination of allergens from the environment

Causes and Prevention

reactions, and they vary with the individual; for some people it may be foods, for others plants, environmental pollutants, chemicals, cigarette smoke, dust mites, cockroaches, or viruses. For others, the cause can be the classroom pet.

Genetic profiles are the cause of many disabilities. Many disabilities for which no cause used to be known are now proving to have a genetic link. Hemophilia, which occurs in only 1 in every 10,000 births, seems to be linked to the X chromosome because it is carried by the mother and passed on to the son. Muscular dystrophy, a relatively rare neuromotor disease (with an incidence of about 2 in every 10,000 people) is another hereditary condition. The most common inherited blood disorder in the United States is sickle cell anemia (National Human Genome Research Institute, 2002). The role of genes in epilepsy is now being revealed. In some cases a single gene deficit may be the culprit, but in other cases a defective gene may be responsible for a condition that itself results in epilepsy as a secondary condition (Stafstrom & Tempel, 2000).

Injuries, both from accidents and from child abuse, can lead to cerebral palsy, seizure disorders, spinal cord injuries, brain damage, and even death. For example, spinal cord injury in young children, which is often caused by automobile accidents, can also result from child abuse. In older children, the most common causes of spinal cord injury are car accidents, falls and jumps, gunshot wounds, and diving accidents. These cases underscore the importance of safety equipment (e.g., seat belts, helmets, protective gear) and of caution.

For seven out of ten cases of epilepsy, no specific cause can be identified. However, it is likely that multiple factors cause seizure disorders; some are congenital and some are acquired (Epilepsy Foundation of America, 2002; National Institute of Neurological Disorders and Stroke, 2002). Congenital cases of epilepsy appear at a young age, usually in families with some history of epilepsy. Often there is a predictable pattern to the seizure and its response to specific medications. Acquired cases may appear at any age and can result from accidents or child abuse, degenerative diseases (such as Sturge-Weber syndrome), brain tumors and abscesses, lesions, head injury, lead poisoning, infections, (such as meningitis or encephalitis) or alcohol or drug withdrawal.

Cerebral palsy is also due to multiple factors. It may be congenital (present at birth) or acquired within the first three years of life. In congenital cerebral palsy, a developing infant may have been deprived of necessary amounts of oxygen when something went wrong during birth. Cerebral palsy may also result from the effects of premature birth; very low birth weight; blood type (Rh) incompatibility; the mother's infection with rubella, CMV, or other viral diseases; and attacks by other dangerous microorganisms (Nelson & Grether, 1997). Most clearly, the later onset of cerebral palsy typically results from vehicle accidents, brain infections such as meningitis, poisoning through toxins such as lead (ingested in paint chips from walls), serious falls, or injuries from child abuse.

MAKING CONNECTIONS

Review the information about cerebral palsy found in the "Physical Impairments and Special Health Care Needs Defined" section in this chapter.

How might these conditions be prevented?

Some physical disabilities and special health care needs are relatively easy to prevent, but others are not. Remember, many disabilities are caused through no one's fault and cannot be avoided. For most conditions that cannot be prevented the effects can be lessened through treatment. You have learned about many of the keys to preventing disabilities. These perennial themes cannot be overemphasized:

- Good prenatal care
- Universal immunization programs
- Avoidance of injuries

Access to health care for pregnant women and later for young children can prevent many disabilities and reduce the impact of those that cannot be avoided (Children's Defense Fund [CDF], 2001). Prenatal care can ensure access to intensive

CHAPTER 9 *Physical Impairments and Special Health Care Needs*

medical care for the mother and infant if problems occur; provide diagnosis and treatment for diseases in the mother that can damage developing infants; and help prevent exposure of the fetus to infections, viruses, drugs, alcohol, and other toxins.

Vaccinations can safeguard children from infectious diseases and avoid millions of dollars in health care costs and millions of lives complicated by disabilities. Vaccines have almost eradicated some diseases in the United States. For example, vaccines have all but eliminated polio in the United States; the last naturally occurring case was reported in 1979 (Neergaard, 1995). This news has led some parents to believe, incorrectly, that it is safer not to immunize their children, an oversight that can lead to unnecessary cases of dangerous diseases (CDF, 2001).

These professionals are part of a multidisciplinary team who are working with other related service experts to design a comprehensive individualized program for this child.

The use of seat belts, air bags, helmets, and other protective devices can reduce injuries from motor vehicle and sports-related accidents. Proper child care, child supervision, and family support can help families avoid household accidents and family stresses that can lead to child injury. Family support services and training in effective parenting techniques can help parents understand the harmful physical and emotional effects of physical punishment.

• *Prevention of Infectious Diseases and Other Illnesses* Although they can help curtail the spread of infection, teachers cannot prevent most cases of infectious diseases. Children can become infected outside of the school and can infect other children before they become sick themselves. However, teachers must become more aware of the risk of infectious disease among schoolchildren and must use preventive techniques in their classrooms. Here are a few measures that can help:

• Refer sick children to the school nurse and to the parents.

• Keep play areas, toys, and other objects in the classroom disinfected (clean) so they will not transmit diseases.

• Have all students wash their hands frequently.

• Use some commonsense hygienic precautions at school.

• Use fresh pairs of disposable gloves when helping a bleeding child or cleaning up an accident, and safely dispose of the soiled gloves.

The frequency of episodes of some illnesses can be reduced through the efforts of teachers. For example, asthma is often triggered by exposure to specific allergens (Getch & Neuharth-Pritchett, 1999; NIEHS, 2002). For some students the chance of an asthma attack is reduced when the classroom is free of chalk dust, plants that generate pollen or mold, cold and dry air, smoke, paint fumes, and chemical smells. Class pets (their fur) can cause an asthma attack. By keeping classrooms free from these sources of pollutants, teachers can help reduce the probability of an attack and of resulting illness and absences from school. Teachers can play a very special role by helping these individuals find physical activities that are safe for them to engage in and by finding activities that can be substituted for physical exertion that would put them at risk.

• *Treatment* Medical advances provide hope for a different future for individuals with physical impairments and special health care needs. For example, Children's

Causes and Prevention

VALIDATED PRACTICES
Graphic Organizers

What Are Graphic Organizers?

Graphic organizers are visual aids used to assist students in organizing and comprehending large amounts of information from expository text. These visual–spatial arrangements connect important words or statements to diagrams. Graphic organizers can include maps, pictures, graphs, charts, diagrams, and photographs.

Why Graphic Organizers Are Beneficial

Students often have difficulty reading and comprehending information presented in content area textbooks (e.g., science, social studies, health). In addition, many books are poorly organized, confusing students even more. Graphic organizers help students by including only the crucial information, making what is important clear and precise. Graphic organizers may illustrate relationships among concepts, show a process, or provide a sequence. When students generate their own graphic organizers, they are demonstrating their comprehension of the course content. One additional benefit of graphic organizers is that they force you, the teacher, to focus on the specific information you are presenting.

Implementing Graphic Organizers

When you begin to use graphic organizers with your class, *you* should develop them. Students can follow along and use your visual aid as a guide to the lecture and an aid to comprehending the content. As students become comfortable using graphic organizers, they should generate their own. Here are four guidelines to follow when constructing graphic organizers:

Select and Divide the Chapters

- Select material that is difficult for students to understand or that is poorly organized.

- Divide the chapter into sections. (Typically, textbooks are organized by sections. If this is true, develop a graphic organizer for each section. If there are no sections, develop a graphic organizer for every 1,500 words.)

Construct an Outline

- Select main ideas from the reading material.

Select the Graphic Organizer's Format

- Formats must match the structure of information and can include diagrams that sequence, that compare and contrast, or that classify.

Healthcare of Atlanta and Emory University Hospital are now performing bone marrow and cord blood stem cell transplants on children with sickle cell anemia (Emory University, 2002). These procedures may herald an eventual cure for this terrible disease. In what some are calling one of the most significant research advances in the fight against HIV/AIDS, a new treatment that consists of giving the infected woman AZT during pregnancy and giving her baby the drug after birth has reduced the maternal transmission of the disease by two-thirds (National Institute of Allergy and Infectious Diseases, 1999). Infants born with spinal column (neural tube) defects have surgery to repair the back and to avoid infection or meningitis, which otherwise could result in mental retardation. Some children with **spina bifida** have hydrocephaly (a buildup of excess fluid in the brain). To avoid mental retardation, a shunt must be surgically implanted to drain excess spinal fluid from the child's brain. And technology to use brain waves to move paralyzed limbs through electrodes implanted under the skin may well be on the horizon (Chase, 2000). New knowledge about the treatment of cerebral palsy also provides a glimmer of hope. Botulinum toxin A (Botox) has been found to help reduce spasticity (Petersen & Palmer, 2001).

Medical treatments by physicians are not covered by IDEA; those costs are borne by insurance, government programs, or the family. Related services provided by the schools are covered by IDEA. Multidisciplinary teams of PTs, OTs, SLPs, and assistive technology experts can make real differences in the outcomes of these children. Supporting their efforts are teachers and paraprofessionals, together designing and implementing an appropriate education.

Remember that treatment does not guarantee a "cure" or an improved situation for all individuals with disabilities. For example, many students with cerebral palsy

- Graphic organizers must be clear, must be easy to follow, and must fit on one page.

Prepare the Graphic Organizer

- Your version should include all of the information and serve as an answer key.
- The version prepared for students should have some information missing: the important facts you want them to focus on.

Graphic organizers can be used either when presenting new material or when reviewing content. If students are working on multiple graphic organizers independently, it may be helpful to have them number their pages. Graphic organizers work well when students are assigned to cooperative learning groups. Once graphic organizers have been completed, discuss and correct them. Graphic organizers with accurate information can serve as great study guides. Figure 1 shows a completed graphic organizer used in a middle school social studies course.

This scientifically validated practice is a teaching method proven by systematic research efforts (Boyle, 1996; Horton, Lovitt, & Bergerud, 1990; Lovitt, & Horton, 1994; Scanlon, Deshler, & Schumaker, 1996). Full citations are found in the "Characteristics" section of the references for this chapter.

Figure 1 Example of a Graphic Organizer
Source: From "The effectiveness of graphic organizers for three classifications of secondary students in content area classes" by S. V. Horton, T. C. Lovitt, and D. Bergerud, 1990, *Journal of Learning Disabilities, 23,* 12–22, 29. Copyright 1990 by Pro-Ed, Inc. Reprinted with permission.

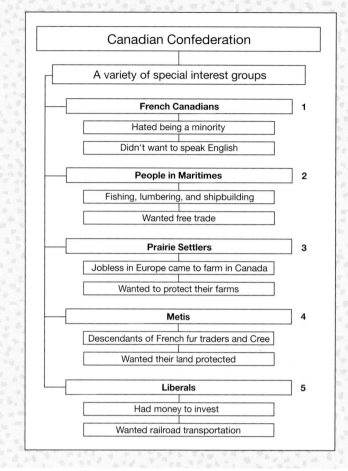

will face significant challenges their entire lives. Only about 80 percent of those with epilepsy have their seizures controlled through medication (Epilepsy Foundation of America, 2002). And asthma cannot be cured, although the factors that trigger episodes can be eliminated or substantially reduced. Even when all precautions have been taken, some asthmatics will still have attacks, and epileptics will still have seizures. Teachers must know what to do for the child during an asthma attack and during a seizure episode. Consultation with the student, the family, and the physician is necessary so that the teacher is prepared to monitor medications, to administer breathing treatment, and to assist the child during a medical crisis.

CHARACTERISTICS

The health care needs of some children are so consuming that everything else becomes a secondary priority. Other students, such as some with physical impairments, require substantial alterations to the physical environment so that learning is accessible to them, but their learning characteristics are quite similar to those of their typical classmates. For others, their health situation requires special accommodations.

What characteristics affect learning?

The treatment goals for many youngsters are to stay strong, healthy, and active and to lead lives as normal as possible. Accomplishing these goals requires considerable attention to many components, including medical management. As with all children, education is also a major component of their childhood, but unlike most of their peers, they face many barriers to efficient learning. Here are a few examples of obstacles that some students experience:

- Fatigue
- Absences
- Inconsistent abilities to pay attention
- Muscle weakness
- Loss of physical coordination

Some symptoms are directly related to medications and treatment, and others are a function of the disease, illness, or condition. For example, children who are receiving cancer treatment go through periods of feeling too sick to profit from much of the instructional day, and during this time they may have frequent absences. Some may require periods of home-bound instruction. In the case of cerebral palsy, symptoms associated with the condition itself should guide instruction (Horn, 1997). Goals for these students must integrate functional skill development into all activities. Because it is best not to teach skills in isolation, students could be taught good posturing positions while reading motivating and interesting books, or they could be taught improved movement skills while playing games or sports. Current thought emphasizes the importance of children with cerebral palsy learning motor skills that have use and function (Barnes & Whitney, 2002; Horn, 1997; Palmer, 1997).

Teachers can help these youngsters in several ways. First, they need to be sensitive to the student's changing degree of wellness. Attentive teachers will be able to notice when the child needs a break. Instructional units might be divided into small, concise elements with key terms and facts emphasized. Long and difficult reading assignments can be shortened. For example, when studying a history unit, classmates often find that summarizing content from a chapter in the textbook, developing time lines, and preparing study notes are good learning exercises for them as well as a great help to their classmate with a special health care need. Teachers can also prepare summary notes and outlines of the information being presented in the history unit as handouts for all students, bearing particularly in mind the learning characteristics of the child with special needs.

For all of these students, organizers to help them focus their learning can be very beneficial. For students with ADHD, graphic organizers can help them identify the important elements of the material being learned. For students whose strength varies across time, graphic organizers can help them return to work more quickly when they are feeling better, because the organizer helps them see where they left off in their studies. An example is shown in the "Validated Practices" box on page 322.

Many accommodations required by children who are medically fragile or chronically ill are rather simple. Remember that for many of these children, education may not be their highest personal priority; they are more preoccupied by their health. This is both understandable and natural. Being sensitive to their physical condition is probably the most important consideration. Sometimes the challenges of being sick affect a child's classroom behavior. An otherwise well-behaved child can become a behavior problem. The "Achieving Discipline" box describes one such case, where the effects of a chronic illness extended far beyond the child's physical well-being. Teachers must be alert to such situations as they develop. Other accommodations, like the ones listed here, can make a real difference to some children:

- Arrange times for naps or rests.
- Monitor medical equipment.
- Keep the child safe.
- Plan for tutors.
- Work with the parents.

MAKING CONNECTIONS

For other ideas about accommodating for the needs of special learners, see the "Accommodating for Inclusive Environments" boxes in Chapters 3–12.

CHAPTER 9 *Physical Impairments and Special Health Care Needs*

Acknowledge the Effort: Rewards

Shaquita has sickle cell anemia and experiences frequent and severe sickling crises. She is capable of doing her schoolwork, but because of her illness she is often absent from school and seldom feels well. Even on the best of days, Shaquita's muscles and joints ache. She is frequently frustrated by schoolwork, and it is not uncommon for her to be defiant, rude, and angry. She breaks classroom rules more than her classmates by talking out of turn, crumpling her papers, and even throwing them across the room. Shaquita's peers were beginning to resent her, and fewer and fewer people were willing to bring Shaquita's homework to her house, explain missed assignments, or tutor her on the classwork she had missed. Her anger was compounded because classmates were forgetting to bring classwork to her home and were not spending time to help her catch up.

Ms. Torres, Shaquita's teacher, had a private conference with Shaquita in which they discussed her behavior, her school progress, and strategies they might use to improve the situation. Shaquita talked with her teacher about her physical condition and how she did not feel that anyone appreciated the pain and exhaustion she experienced. She also talked about how she felt that it was unfair that she was sick, missed school, and could not participate in sports and other school activities like her friends. Ms. Torres and Shaquita discussed how she needed to exert extra effort to keep up with the class assignments and that her friends, who were trying to help her, also were making extra efforts. They decided that people were not appreciating each other. So together they designed a reward system where Shaquita's classmates could earn bonus points toward their grades for helping her, and Shaquita would earn bonus points for each homework and in-class assignment from days when she was absent. They also devised a structured schedule in which Shaquita would earn privileges (being the first in line for recess, being able to stay in the classroom alone during lunch break, getting the assignment of hall monitor) when she behaved appropriately.

Setting up a Reward System

- Define the desired behavior specifically.
- Have the student create a list of privileges or rewards.
- Set criteria for behavior.
- Determine a plan for how rewards will be earned.
- Be sure to give the student the privilege or reward when criteria are met.
- Tell the student why the reward was earned and that you appreciate the effort.

- Consider the complexity and length of homework assignments.
- Accommodate the physical requirements of the student.
- Collaborate with others.
- Keep a sense of perspective as you balance the needs of all of your students.

What physical barriers affect classrooms and schools?

The challenges facing students with physical limitations and special health care needs and their teachers are great. All schools must meet the special architectural codes required by the ADA law and must be "barrier free." Regardless, these students' world is often filled with physical barriers that must be overcome before they can achieve independence and a "normal" life. Surprisingly, students who use wheelchairs still face physical barriers at some schools. Anjali Forber-Pratt, on her first day of high school, found that some of her classes where scheduled on the second floor although no elevator was available for her to use, the bathrooms were not accessible, and many of the passageways were too narrow for her to pass through (Helman, 2002).

Eliminating barriers, even obvious physical ones, can be more difficult than you might think. It certainly was for Mattel Toys. The toymaker was quite embarrassed when it was found that the wheelchair of its 1997 doll, Share a Smile™ Becky®, would not fit through the doorway to the Barbie Dream House (*Newsweek*, 1997).

MAKING **C**ONNECTIONS

Review issues related to accessibility and participation of people with physical disabilities by rereading the "History" section in this chapter and the "Necessity for National Intervention" section in Chapter 1.

Rick Slaughter, director of A.B.L.E. and coach of the Music City Wheelchair Basketball Team, enjoys a skiing experience with one of his team members. This opportunity is now available to them because of accessible resorts and specially designed skiing equipment. Both wish that this could be at least an annual event.

This example shows that even those with the best intentions do not always achieve their goals.

"Discriminating architecture doesn't have to discriminate" (Leibrock & Terry, 1999, p. 17). Technology and advances in architectural design can help everyone live and work better in attractive and accommodating facilities. **Universal design** seeks to accomplish these objectives. Many details are considered when using this design system: lighting, vision panels on doors, spaces for storage, traffic patterns, access to switches and handles, and even wall colors. Some of these elements of universal design are aimed at construction, but others include good tips that teachers can consider. For example, area rugs and entrance mats should be permanently installed, because otherwise they immobilize all types of wheelchairs. Workstations should be placed at the appropriate height, and shelves need to be within reach. The desks and stations need to be stable and sturdy, and the student should be able to have clear view of all instructional opportunities.

When considering ways to make an educational environment accessible to a child with a physical problem, educators should consider all of the places the child needs to go: the bathroom, the lunchroom, the playground, the gymnasium, the music room, the library, the bus, and so on. The child's educational activities should be chosen on the basis of individual learning needs, not just in terms of where a wheelchair can or cannot fit. Every school should have bathroom stalls that accommodate wheelchairs and braces and should have accessible sinks, mirrors, towel dispensers, and door handles. The concept of **accessibility** has many interpretations. It means elevators large enough to hold wheelchairs, handrails along the corridors, chalkboards placed low enough so that children in wheelchairs can write on them, seating arrangements that can accommodate children with a variety of equipment, standing tables so that children can spend time out of wheelchairs, and playground equipment adapted to hold a child with leg braces or in a wheelchair. It also means that all students should be able to participate in school activities to the fullest extent posible. Remember, too, that barriers are not only physical, and integration may necessitate accommodations beyond (the curb cuts, ramps, elevators, and bathroom alterations required by law). Most children will respond warmly and proudly to your subtle reminders that everyone enjoys being included in all aspects of school.

EARLY CHILDHOOD EDUCATION

Whether disabilities are physical or health-related, early intervention programs provide a strong foundation for the child and family. To ensure success of children's intervention programs, parents' efforts and enthusiasm must be supported by the school's team. Motor development and positioning and developing communication skills are often target areas for young children with physical disabilities and special health care needs.

CHAPTER 9 *Physical Impairments and Special Health Care Needs*

For some children, particularly those with physical disabilities, early intervention programs focus primarily on motor development (Barnes & Whinnery, 2002). For example, children born with cerebral palsy may have reflex patterns that interfere with the typical motor development that sets the stage for maximum independence, including body schema, body awareness, purposeful motor use, and mobility. In many cases, direct instruction is necessary, but before teachers and parents become involved in the educational program, they must be trained and supervised to be sure that they do not put the child at risk for injury (Horn, 1997). Enlisting multidisciplinary team members like the OT, PT, and nurse can ensure the development of an effective program delivered by the right people. The student's program usually includes a regimen of special exercises to develop motor skills. The purpose may be to strengthen weak muscle groups through the use of weights or to adapt to and use artificial limbs or orthopedic devices. Once teachers and family members know how to assist the child with the exercises, they should not be afraid and should encourage the youngster to move, play, and interact with the environment.

Because this is a time of tremendous physical and sensorimotor growth, normal motor patterns must be established as early as possible. For those children who already have abnormal motor patterns, repeating those patterns should not be encouraged. The child should always, both at school and at home, be positioned properly so that alignment, muscle tone, and stability are correct during all activities. Specific equipment, such as foam rubber wedges, Velcro straps, and comfortable mats are used to properly position children with physical disabilities. Although some of this equipment is expensive, other items can be made rather inexpensively. Parents and teachers need to keep in touch with therapists to be certain that they are working properly with their children. Teachers must also remember that children should not remain in the same position for too long. They should be repositioned every twenty minutes or so.

Communication is difficult for some of these young children (Langdon, 1999; Owens, Metz, & Haas, 2002). Parents and professionals should acknowledge and reinforce every attempt at communication. Although determining how a child with severe disabilities is attempting to communicate can be difficult, an observant person can learn a great deal about the child's communication abilities, even when others believe that the child cannot communicate at all. A good observer will be able to answer questions like these: In what specific ways does the child react to sounds? How does the child respond to certain smells? Does the child have different facial movements when different people enter the room? Does the child gaze at certain objects more than others? How is anger expressed to the family? Through careful observation and experience, parents, teachers, and family members can recognize meaningful communication even when others believe there is none. Parents and professionals should also remember that communication is a two-way street. Children learn to communicate with others by being communicated with. Talk to the child, express feelings with face and body, play games together, and encourage the child to listen to tapes and the radio.

MAKING CONNECTIONS

For a review of communication, speech, and language, see Chapter 5.

ELEMENTARY THROUGH HIGH SCHOOL

Recall that each child with a physical or a health impairment has individualized needs, even those whose diagnoses seem to be the same. Many of these needs are similar to those of children with other types of disabilities; some, however, require different adjustments to the learning environment. For example, many students with disabilities need flexible schedules, more time to learn academic tasks, and extra assistance. This is also the case for many students with special physical and health care needs. Unlike many of their classmates, some of these students have to have a unique learning environment free from physical barriers that inhibit their movement and their interactions with peers. Remember, classroom space is a very important element of the instructional environment.

What instructional accommodations benefit students with physical impairments and special health care needs?

When the child is ready to enter school, both the child and the child's family become crucial members of the IEP team, providing recommendations for a program. Sometimes simple schedule flexibility is all that is needed. Here's a tip: Ask the students involved to describe their difficulties and what accommodations they need. They are often the best resource when teachers are planning instruction and individualized accommodations.

Some students may often be absent from school because they need medical care or because they are too sick or fragile to come to school on certain days. As mentioned earlier, asthma is the leading cause of school absences, but other conditions are also associated with excessive absences: hemophilia, cystic fibrosis, nephrosis, leukemia, and sickle cell anemia. To help these children keep up with their classmates, schools can

- Provide a home or hospital teacher
- Use television, Internet, or telephone hookups with the child and the classroom
- Make videotapes of special classroom activities
- Allow classmates the opportunity to take turns acting as a neighborhood peer tutor after school
- Incorporate the Web and the Internet into classroom instruction

These methods not only help the child's academic progress but also maintain a social connection to the teacher and other students. They help the child feel more comfortable about returning to the classroom later when the physical condition or illness has improved. Teachers often look for complex answers to difficulties when only simple solutions are required, like using classmates to help each other. Such is often the case when adapting instruction. The keys are to anticipate accommodations and to apply your own problem-solving skills. Let's look at some ways to create accommodations for children who cannot write as fast and efficiently as others (Thompson et al., 2001; Elliott et al., 2000).

- Allow students extra time to complete written assignments.
- Let students use computers for their written work so they can increase their speed and produce pleasing documents.
- Ask a classmate of a student who cannot write to make an extra copy by using carbon paper or photocopying a set of class notes.
- Tape children's work papers to their desks.
- Provide extra-thick pencils.
- Have students tape-record instead of writing their assignments.

These simple adjustments send a threefold message: (1) You are willing to give the student a chance. (2) The student is important to you. And (3) even with adjustments, you have high expectations for the student to produce acceptable schoolwork. The "Accommodating for Inclusive Environments" box provides some more tips about adapting instructional settings.

Test taking is another area in which teachers can make adjustments (Thurlow et al., 2000). Imagine trying to take a timed test while your body goes through uncontrollable jerky movements. This is just one of the difficulties that testing presents to

MAKING CONNECTIONS

To refresh your memory about IEPs, see the "Individualized Special Education Programs" section in Chapter 2.

ACCOMMODATING FOR INCLUSIVE ENVIRONMENTS

Adapting All Aspects of the Classroom

Adapt the Physical Environment

- Remove hazards
- Create more workspace
- Provide storage space for equipment
- Make furniture accessible
- Widen aisles
- Use positioning devices
- Change seating arrangements
- Rearrange furniture

Change Student Response Mode

- Allow speaking instead of writing
- Use a speech synthesizer
- Allow writing instead of speaking
- Allow computer-print output

Alter Materials and Equipment

- Give handouts
- Adapt writing tools
- Use special eating utensils
- Explore assistive and adaptive technology

Modify the Activity

- Allow more time to complete the assignments
- Abbreviate assignments
- Create a flexible schedule

Provide Extra Assistance

- Arrange peer tutors
- Have parents or family members help
- Find volunteers to assist
- Tape record or videotape lessons
- Use e-mail for help sessions

children with physical problems. The risk is that, without accommodations, the test will merely measure the degree of physical difficulty experienced by the individual, rather than her or his actual intellectual or academic abilities. How can a teacher give a fair test? Oral testing is one way to measure students' skill level. And here again, ask each student with special needs what adjustments to the learning environment might be helpful. These students are a vital source of information, because they know what accommodations have been successful in the past.

MAKING **C**ONNECTIONS

For other sections on accommodations for testing, see Chapters 1, 2, 4, and 6.

How can learning environments be better designed to meet the needs of these students?

"Our surroundings affect our moods and temperaments; certain buildings, parks, plazas, and streets lift our spirits; others diminish them" (Sandler, 1989, p. 13). Teachers and children spend a substantial portion of their day in classrooms. Unfortunately, in many classrooms the space and its design restrict learning. For students with physical challenges, poorly designed classroom space can inhibit both academic and social learning. This situation can be remedied, and the process of doing so can become an excellent learning opportunity for the entire class.

Buildings and classrooms need to be safe and accessible. Compliance with various construction codes provides basic safety and accessibility, but those codes do not ensure an environment that is functional, scaled to the size and needs of children, and aesthetically pleasing. The physical environment is often overlooked, ignored, and misused (Taylor, 1990). Although teachers and students cannot alter the structure of the school building, they can redesign the space within a classroom. Students can collect data by using simple frequency counts to study the traffic patterns they use in the classroom. They can redesign the organization of desks, tables, work areas, storage space, and learning centers. They can generate visual design alternatives to their environment as it is currently structured through drawings and models. They can work together as a class to evaluate the functionality of these potential re-creations of their learning environment and, as a unit, can decide how best to use the space allocated to them in what is referred to as a classroom. This experience can help to create a more exciting and useful learning environment for every class member and can be particularly helpful to students who face physical challenges.

As the entire class works to create a better learning environment, everyone's learning styles and needs must be considered. Students with physical problems provide a special opportunity for creativity. The class must become sensitive to the physical environment and to how it can create unnecessary barriers to learning and social interaction. Students with physical problems may require specially fitted chairs, desks, and worktables and perhaps extra space for maneuvering bulky equipment like crutches or wheelchairs. These factors need to be considered when redesigning physical space. Many students with severe physical impairments require bulky language boards or computers for communication, and these may present challenges not only during instruction and small-group work activities but also for storage and security. Space must be allocated so that everybody can interact with the child using assistive technology.

As the class seeks to improve other learning environments, keeping everyone's needs in mind, there are many "consultants" who can provide assistance. Architects and design engineers can serve as valuable resources to the class. How do you find such experts to help? Check with the student's parents and school administrators. Call your local college or university to see whether some architecture, engineering, or interior design students would work with the class for several hours. Explore some options with a local construction company. You might be surprised how willing people from the community are to volunteer their time and expertise to this activity. Also consider professionals who are already working with your students. For example, the OT and PT who are providing direct instruction or itinerant services to the student with physical challenges can also serve as excellent resources to the entire class as they rethink their classroom space.

The benefits of having children participate in creating their classroom learning environment can be great. In addition to designing space conducive to each class member's learning style and physical requirements, the activity itself is a wonderful learning experience that uses many different types of thinking skills, as well as integrating many academic areas (e.g., math, reading, and even history). One class of middle school students applied their academic skills and knowledge about barriers to accessible spaces and built a nature trail at a local park so that classmates could use their wheelchairs on field trips when the class was studying native plants (Long, 1999). Taylor and Warden (1994) believe that this practical application of knowledge helps students develop critical thinking skills, solve problems, work cooperatively, apply knowledge to real-life situations, and develop social responsibility. In others words, it is what we call education.

COLLABORATION FOR INCLUSION

Multidisciplinary teams include an array of professionals from many disciplines who collaborate to develop and deliver a truly appropriate education to students with special physical and health needs. The number of experts who participate in the assessment and planning phases of these students' educational programs seems to expand continually, as new technology and knowledge is developed and as new visions of what constitutes a full education for these students evolve.

And attitudes are changing: More and more students with physical disabilities (46 percent) and those with special health care needs (44 percent) are receiving their education primarily (about 80 percent of the school day) in general education classes (U.S. Department of Education, 2001). In some states, the percentage of general education participation is as high as 80 percent. Increasingly, special center schools for students with physical challenges are closing, and these students are attending neighborhood schools. Successful integration and inclusion for increasing numbers of children, however, requires considerable support from multidisciplinary teams. Depending on the individual needs of students, different related service providers assume the primary responsibility for students' IEP fulfillment. For example, the teacher of a student with a severe physical impairment needs to collaborate closely with the PT; and for the child who also has a speech impairment, the SLP must be significantly involved in the child's educational program. However, for many children with special health care needs, these professionals might not be as crucial to the implementation of an appropriate education as the child's physician and the school nurse. What is very important is that educators seek the help of the family and of those professionals who can assist in designing the best instructional environment possible.

What is the teacher's role in the medical management of children?

What role teachers should play in the medical management of children is a contentious issue (Temple, 2000). In part because of a severe shortage of nurses, in part because the courts continually expand health management duties under IDEA, and despite concerns expressed by the American Federation of Teachers (AFT) and the National Education Association (NEA), teachers are being called on to assume more responsibilities for the medical management of their students (Heller et al., 2000). This is due to several factors. First, more and more of these children are receiving their education alongside their neighborhood peers in the general education classroom. Second, local education budgetary cuts are making a school nurse at every school a rare resource. Teachers are now called on to perform some simple tasks that help children with special health care needs. For example, some children may need assistance with their medication while at school. Coordination among the child, the child's physician, the family, and the school nurse will be necessary to ensure that the child takes the proper dose at the proper times and that the effects of medications are monitored.

Teachers are also being called on to perform duties that historically have not been considered part of their role at school (Heller et al., 2000). Although it is generally understood that all children should attend school, children with fragile health may spend some of their education time at home or in a hospital. When children are in school, teachers may need to provide personal assistance. For example, although older children with paralysis generally are able to attend to their bathroom needs independently through the use of self-administered clean intermittent catheterization (CIC), many younger children need the teacher's assistance. In these cases, it is important to encourage personal privacy when helping a child with hygiene needs, and it is important to maintain the highest of sanitary conditions possible in a school setting. A good start is to have all children wash their hands often. Other children may need extra rest or support devices such as ventilators, feeding tubes, and ostomy supplies, all of which need careful monitoring by the teacher. Here is a list of some of the medically related tasks that school personnel are now being asked to perform: tube feeding, CIC, colostomy care, suctioning, ventilator management,

Collaboration for Inclusion

What excitement after the United States wheelchair basketball team defeated Great Britain in the playoff during the Paralympic Games in Sydney, Australia. Some of the A.B.L.E. basketball athletes aspire to such heights, and starting as young as they are, who can predict the possibilities.

tracheotomy care, oxygen delivery, assistance with insulin medication, and testing for blood glucose (Heller et al., 2000)

All school personnel who work with students with special health care needs must work together, continually informing each other about students' programs and their health care requirements. Here is an example of an accommodation that is important, requires only minor changes to classroom rules, and can prevent major health complications (Rosenthal-Malek & Greenspan, 1999): The general education teacher has a rule that no one will be excused for a bathroom break in the middle of an exam, so when John, who has diabetes, asked to go to the bathroom and also to get a drink, the teacher said no. John, however, told the teacher that he was going anyway and left the classroom. His action could easily have been interpreted as defiant and a major violation of class rules. In John's case, he was probably acting responsibly. He needed to avoid a serious health crisis by keeping his blood sugar at acceptable levels. Better communication among teachers and the multidisciplinary team might have prevented this unfortunate situation.

How are these students included in recreation and extracurricular activities?

Inclusion in recreation has many benefits, including activities where social integration is likely to occur naturally. Participation in sports and recreation sets the pattern of physical exercise that lasts a lifetime. In addition to all the health benefits of recreation and exercise, recreational skills can allow children with physical impairments to have fun with their classmates and can provide opportunities for enjoyment with their families. Many adapted recreational toys and games are available for people with physical impairments. A Frisbee, for example, has been specially adapted with two adjustable clips on the top so that people with limited hand movements can play. And new playgrounds and city parks are being designed so that children with and without disabilities can play alongside each other. Lily's Garden is just such an all-access playground and park, complete with a wheelchair-accessible tree house and elevated sandboxes (Wadhwani, 2001).

Many sports and recreation programs for children and youth with physical disabilities and special health care needs are not inclusive in the sense of having individuals with and without disabilities playing and learning together. However, in many cases, only special programs genuinely allow everyone to participate, even those not athletically able. In fact, many young people report that they enjoy camps and recreational programs that are not integrated because they do not have to fear judgments and can take risks they would not otherwise take (Easter Seals, 2002).

Many special sports and fitness programs are now available for individuals with physical disabilities. For example, America's Athletes with Disabilities offers more than 100 "disability sports events" at its national Victory Games (America's Athletes with Disabilities, 2002). Easter Seals Camping and Recreation Programs are nationwide, with more than 140 different facilities offering special programs

CHAPTER 9 *Physical Impairments and Special Health Care Needs*

(Easter Seals, 2002). Local programs, like the Athletes Building Life Experiences (A.B.L.E) program of Easter Seals of Middle Tennessee extend opportunities, such as special trips to Colorado to learn how to ski. These organizations also offer respite care programs for children who are medically fragile, allowing a break for families and fun for children. They also provide after-school, extracurricular programs; thus when brothers and sisters are at baseball and soccer practices, so are those with physical challenges. And Shake-A-Leg has a successful and long-standing program to help teens with physical problems, particularly those with some paralysis, develop positive body awareness (Shake-A-Leg, 2002).

All teenagers want to drive a car, even if they have to use the bottom of their wheelchair to adapt the seat.

TRANSITION THROUGH ADULTHOOD

About 63 percent of students with physical impairments and 67 percent of students with special health care needs complete high school and earn a standard diploma (U.S. Department of Education, 2001). This rate should be higher! Without a high school diploma, the chance of attending college is small; and particularly for students with physical impairments who do not have cognitive impairments, a college degree may be the ticket to a high-paying job. Many individuals with physical impairments and special health care needs do attend college. In fact, many college freshmen, some 25,000, have identified themselves as having a health-related disability (Edelman, Schuyler, & White, 1998). Many different diseases and conditions have been reported, including severe allergies, arthritis, asthma, cancer, cystic fibrosis, diabetes, epilepsy, and sickle cell anemia. Thus, in addition to providing physical accommodations and barrier-free environments, colleges need to provide other accommodations for students with health problems, such as extra time to take tests, assisted methods for taking class notes, and help in transcribing class tape recordings. The key is for colleges to provide individualized means for these students to accomplish college work. Jean Elison is one example of many college success stories. Jean has been paralyzed from the neck down since a car accident that occurred when she was 11 years old. Using a voice-activated computer, she graduated summa cum laude from Harvard after her four years of study (Hellmich, 2000). Since graduation, she has gone on a speaking tour, talking to school groups, politicians, and community organizations. Her latest crusade is for wheelchair sections to be provided on airplanes (Painter, 2002).

Independent living is the goal for many adults with physical disabilities and health impairments. The "independent living movement"—people helping themselves to live on their own—has had great influence on the lives of people with disabilities. Increasingly, adults with physical disabilities and health impairments take control of their lives and their jobs, establish friendships, have families, and exert political power. Legislation such as ADA has had a tremendous impact on the ability of adults with disabilities to pursue their rights and end discrimination, but people with these disabilities must be prepared to take their places in mainstream society. High school transition programs can be very helpful in this regard, by teaching students how to be responsible for their own needs, advocate for themselves, locate the resources they need, and take active roles in their medical management

MAKING CONNECTIONS

Compare the adult outcomes of individuals with other disabilities to those of individuals with physical disabilities and special health care needs by reading the "Transition" sections in Chapters 3–12.

Transition Through Adulthood

Her specially trained dog Jumar helps Christina Kimm, a special education professor at California State University—Los Angeles, negotiate a large urban college campus and remain as independent as possible despite her continuing problems from polio as a child.

(Edelman, Schuyler, & White, 1998). But IDEA does not apply to students after they have left high school, so this important learning time must not be wasted.

Independence is important to all people but is of vital importance to most adolescents and adults with physical impairments or special health care needs. As time goes on, it appears that more and more types of assistance are becoming available. For example, specially trained service animals sometimes assist individuals, both students and adults, with physical disabilities (Delta Society, 2002). Service animals, like Pam Townsend's service dog Astro and Christina Kimm's Jumar, have been trained to pull a wheelchair, pick things up, open doors, push elevator buttons, turn lights off and on, and bring a telephone receiver. When Pam's muscular dystrophy worsened, Canine Assistants provided her with Astro, a golden retriever who helps in many simple and complex ways, ranging from getting the portable phone when it rings to opening and closing doors (Slaughter, 1999). Dr. Kimm, who is a special education professor at California State University, Los Angeles, has achieved more independence and a more balanced life since Canine Companions of San Diego matched her with Jumar, an able assistant who even hands out papers to Kimm's students (Haynes, 1998). Capuchin monkeys are also used as service animals. Chosen for their small size and ability to perform tasks, they are bred and trained to assist people with physical challenges. These monkeys can feed the individual; dial a speakerphone; get food out of the refrigerator; turn the pages of a newspaper; and turn on the television, stereo, or even a VCR (Ferrer, 1996).

MAKING **C**ONNECTIONS

To compare the challenges these families face with those of families of children with different disabilities, see the "Families" sections in Chapters 3–12.

FAMILIES

The families of children with severe physical and health impairments face special issues as they raise their children (Davis, 1993). Martin, Brady, and Kotarba (1992) document the demands that a child's chronic illness can make on a family, including fatigue and low vitality, restricted social life, and preoccupation with decisions related to the child's illness. Often, the costs of the child's health care are staggering. Thus parents' own career decisions may be driven by questions about maintaining family health insurance. Even when health insurance is available, financial record keeping and filing for reimbursements can be complicated and stressful. If the child is eligible for government medical benefits, eligibility regulations may be complex. Finally, some families find it necessary to move to a larger city in order to obtain necessary health care and therapies, leaving behind a community where they have long-term social ties and an extended family.

If the child's treatment or health problems require absences from school, the family's routine may be disrupted when one adult has to stay home with the child. Similarly, special planning and complicated arrangements may be necessary to accommodate a weekend away, a family vacation, time spent with other children, or time for the parents alone.

Many homes and apartments are not yet designed for the range of physical needs of the entire population. If a child needs large equipment, a special bathtub, ramps, or other accommodations that individuals with physical disabilities typically require, the family may have to move to an accessible apartment or home. Another option for those who are financially able is to remodel their home.

CHAPTER 9 *Physical Impairments and Special Health Care Needs*

Now let's think about families of children with AIDS and HIV. The outcomes for children with HIV are bleak (Beverly & Thomas, 1997), and families of these children often have to educate teachers about their youngsters' prognosis, health conditions, and educational programs. An infectious cause of mental retardation, HIV is devastating to the children affected. It often results in growth, speech, and motor delays; as the disease progresses, skills are lost and functioning levels decline. Of course, at the present time, it results in early death. Families and teachers must work together to develop relevant curricula for these individual children. Teachers and families should evaluate the importance of instructional targets on daily functioning as they make curriculum choices for these students. The instructional program should be balanced to include opportunities for recreation, social interchange, and fun.

Many families of students with special health care needs, especially those of children with AIDS, experience feelings of isolation, rejection, fear, depression, grief, anger, and guilt (Beverly & Thomas, 1997). The burdens on families of children with physical problems and health impairments can be great. As we have just noted, life with a child who has severe physical challenges or who has a chronic illness is very complex, and the stress can be overwhelming. However, many of these parents have difficulty accepting their child's disability. Thus, in addition to dealing with hospitals, insurance companies, an inaccessible world, financial costs, and a sick child, many have to come to grips with their own responses and personal feelings. Patty McGill Smith (1993), executive director of the National Parent Network on Disabilities and the parent of a child with multiple disabilities, suggests that parents take the following constructive actions as they come to accept and deal with their personal dilemmas, their child, and their family situation:

- Seek the assistance of another parent.
- Learn special education terminology.
- Seek information from many different sources.
- Do not be intimidated.
- Maintain a positive outlook.
- Keep in touch with reality.
- Search for a variety of program alternatives.
- Take care of yourself.
- Avoid pity.
- Keep daily routines as normal as possible.
- Recognize that you are not alone.
- Take one day at a time.

Keeping Smith's advice in mind, some parents have found that seeking out others who also have a child with a severe physical or health problem is helpful in many ways. Around the country, these families have joined together in support groups to address common problems and help one another. Often, families share creative ideas for helping the child with the disability to join in the activities of the family, such as inexpensive adaptations of toys, shared baby-sitting, and information exchanges about helpful medical personnel.

TECHNOLOGY

Each day, advances in technology dramatically improve the ability of people with physical impairments and special health needs to gain access to and control the world around them, communicate with others, and benefit from health care.

MAKING CONNECTIONS

AIDS and HIV are discussed in the "Physical Impairments and Special Health Care Needs Defined" section of this chapter.

MAKING CONNECTIONS

To compare different types of technology supports across students with special needs, read the "Technology" sections in Chapters 3–12.

Technology

Assistive technology continues to enhance these individuals' participation in every-day life, and medical technology allows them to engage in activities never dreamt of some 20 years ago.

How does assistive technology influence the lives of individuals with physical disabilities and special health care needs?

Assistive technology includes a wide array of devices and tools that allow individuals to interact with others, benefit from school, and participate in mainstream society (Bryant & Bryant, 2003). The 1990 reauthorization of IDEA and the courts have clarified the role of assistive technology in the schools: It is a related service that is provided so that a student with disabilities can profit from special education. It does not, however, include medical services provided by physicians. The adaptations that technology provides individuals with special physical and health considerations include not only **high-tech devices,** such as computers that control the environment or in flying airplanes, but also **low-tech devices** that assist persons with disabilities, such as simple built-up spoons and communication boards. Not all technology is expensive or even sophisticated. In many cases, creativity and individualization are the keys to solving problems (Bryant & Bryant, 2003).

Deciding what should be considered technology is difficult. Is a wheelchair a piece of technology? What about specially designed chairs for racing or for use in the wilderness? Does a wheelchair become technology if it is motorized or computerized? What if the chair has an electronic switch to permit persons with only partial head or neck control or finger or foot control to move about independently? Should medical advances be considered technology? Certainly, technology is changing the way we think and act. It might even be the cause of a new special education category: **technology-dependent children** (students who use **ventilators** or other medical equipment to survive). And what about **rehabilitation engineering,** which has brought the benefits of science and engineering to bear on movement, seating, and walking problems, such as those created by cerebral palsy? **Gait training** laboratories (special laboratories for walking) help many children by analyzing their weight-bearing patterns and their normal and abnormal movements. With the aid of PTs and other specialists, these laboratories help to improve children's posture and balance.

Computers are used for many skills, including augmentative communication, writing and printing, practicing mathematics, and creating "smart rooms" where the thermostat, lights, music, and doors are controlled by a central computer panel. Many adaptations are available for computers so that people with severe physical disabilities can use them (U.S. Department of the Interior, 2002). For example, computers can be operated by voice, the gaze of an eye, a mouthstick, a sip-and-puff breath stick, a single finger, a toe, a headstick, or other creative method suitable to an individual's abilities. Special keyboards are available for people with limited dexterity or hand strength, and others are wireless so they can be used at some distance from the actual computer. Keyboards can appear on the screen, to be touched with a stylus. And voice recognition software, like *Dragon Naturally Speaking Professional,* lets people who cannot use their hands work on a computer. Jesse Leaman uses this system, and he says that without it, his internship at NASA would have been impossible (Weise, 2000). Jesse is hoping that voice-activated systems will soon be available for almost every aspect of life, remarkably boosting his independence. The Department of the Interior's Accessible Technology Center describes ergonomic workstations that are complete with voice recognition software, include component parts that swivel and adjust for different heights, and can be flexibly designed for each individual's needs.

Computers allow access to other environments and people. This technology can be turned into a great advantage for students who must stay at home for any length of time. Whether an illness requires one day at home or a month, students can use the Internet and e-mail to talk to classmates, get tomorrow's homework assignments, or work with their science group on its project. They can also conduct library research by connecting to an information system and can even communicate with students around the country about information they are gathering from a central database.

How do bionics and robotics influence the lives of people with physical disabilities?

Mobility is an area where the benefits of technology are obvious: freedom of movement, increased privacy, and personal independence. Today, individuals can select artificial limbs that are bionic and resemble human limbs. **Myoelectric limbs** (bionic) are battery-powered and aesthetically pleasing. They are hollow but contain a sensor that picks up electrical signals transmitted from the individual's brain through the limb. Although they are not yet like the **bionic artificial limbs** popularized in the television shows *The Bionic Man* and *The Bionic Woman*, they do allow the individual to control movement and function. Diamond Excell was born without arms, but she can now hug her mom with her new "bionic" arms (Associated Press, 2001). Through community support and donations of over $60,000, her specially made arms move when signals in her brain flex a muscle and activate a motor in her artificial hand. The hand is molded latex with fingernails and a skin tone matching hers.

Rehabilitation engineering has created important devices for people with disabilities. Rudy Garcia-Tolson was a torchbearer carrying the Olympic Flame on one leg of the trip to the 2002 Olympic Games in Salt Lake City.

Robotics is another area that holds promise for the future of people with physical disabilities. Robotics is the use of sophisticated devices to accomplish motor skills such as grasping. For example, robotic arms can manipulate objects in at least three directional movements: extension/retraction, swinging/rotating, and elevation/depression. Other advances in this area include voice-activated robots, which are in the developmental stages but offer great promise of assistance in independent daily living. Manipulator robots have been successfully used in assisting children in such self-help activities as dialing a telephone, turning book pages, and drinking from a cup. Costs, transportability, repairs, and training are currently roadblocks to the widespread use of this type of technology, but popular demand for robots that can do household chores is likely to increase in the future, and this may make robotic technology more economical.

In addition to myoelectric limbs, artificial limbs that are specially designed for various activities are now available and popular. Individuals use a specially designed limb for running, another for daily walking, and another for soccer, and so on. Michael Rinehart was born without feet, but that does not stop him from playing soccer, with his specially designed legs, on his high school team (Humbles, 2000, May). Rudy Garcia-Tolson uses different sets of legs to participate in triathlons (Buckley, 2002). Well, actually, he takes his legs off to swim and uses different legs for running and biking. He holds the U.S. national record among athletes with disabilities for a half-marathon, he runs a mile in 6 minutes and 48 seconds, and also holds the national record for the 200-meter breast stroke. He's hoping to make the 2004 U.S. Paralympics team.

Technology

IN CONCLUSION

Summary

Children with physical impairments and special health care needs can present special difficulties to their parents and teachers. Even when these two special education categories are combined, the number of students involved is small—less than 2 percent of all schoolchildren with disabilities. Therefore, they are considered low incidence disabilities. Many of these youngsters require substantial adjustments and modifications to their learning environments, but their relatively good high school graduation rates indicate that they are capable of competing in the standard curriculum. For many, independent living remains their greatest challenge.

Self-Test Questions

Focus Questions

How are physical impairment and special health care needs classified and organized?

Physical Impairments

- Neuromotor Impairments: seizure disorders, cerebral palsy, spinal cord disorders, polio, muscular dystrophy (MD), multiple sclerosis (MS)
- Muscular/Skeletal Conditions: juvenile arthritis, limb deficiencies, skeletal disorders

Special Health Care Needs

- Chronic Illnesses: asthma, diabetes, cystic fibrosis, congenital heart defects, tuberculosis (TB), childhood cancer, blood disorders
- Infectious Diseases: HIV/AIDS, STORCH infections, hepatitis B

What are some steps teachers should take to assist a child who is having a seizure?

- Seek medical identification.
- Create a safe place free from hazards.

MAKING CONNECTIONS

Look again at the Advance Organizers at the beginning of the chapter. To help you study the chapter's content, the answers to the Focus and Challenge questions are given here. Test yourself to see if you have mastered the major points of this chapter.

- Loosen clothing, particularly around the neck.
- Protect the head from injury.
- Turn the person sideways to ensure free passage of air.
- For seizures lasting longer than five minutes, call for an ambulance.
- Upon return of consciousness, keep the individual calm and offer further assistance.

What are the different types of cerebral palsy?

Classification in terms of how mobility is affected:

- Spastic: stiff movements
- Athetoid: involuntary, purposeless, uncontrolled, and contorted movements
- Ataxia: impaired balance and depth perception leads to disrupted movement

Classification in terms of area of the body affected:

- Monoplegia: one limb
- Paraplegia: both arms or both legs
- Hemiplegia: the arm and leg on one side
- Quadriplegia: all arms and legs

How do students with ADHD qualify for special education services?

All students with ADHD qualify for accommodations to meet their individual learning needs, whether they qualify for special education or not.

Most students with ADHD who qualify for special education have been receiving services through other IDEA categories (e.g., learning disabilities, emotional or behavioral disorders).

Students with ADHD can qualify for special education services if their heightened alertness to the environment adversely affects their educational performance.

How can the learning environment be modified to accommodate students with physical impairments and special health care needs?

Modify the physical environment: create more space, widen aisles, remove hazards, change seating arrangements, create accessible workstations

Alter student response demands: speak instead of write, use a speech synthesizer, write instead of speak, have a computer print or speak the response

Adapt materials and equipment: use handouts to accompany transparencies, assign books with audio versions, allow use of special writing tools and adapted eating utensils

Modify instruction: allow more time to complete assignments, abbreviate assignments, allow for a flexible schedule

Arrange for extra assistance: tutors (peers, parents, volunteers), taperecord or videotape lectures, connect in-class discussions to the Internet, set up an e-chat room

Challenge Question

What are the barriers to the full participation of these individuals in society, and how can such barriers be minimized?

Barriers include

- Coping with inaccessible environments, where their impaired mobility hinders their participation in mainstream society
- Dealing with bias, rejection, and discrimination
- Difficulties living independently
- Difficulties finding jobs
- Social rejection by people without disabilities

Students require

- Accessible physical and learning environments
- Acceptance and understanding
- Goals that foster independence
- Accommodations for their individual learning, physical, and health needs
- Special teaching, scheduling, counseling, therapies, equipment, and technology

MEETING THE STANDARDS AND PREPARING FOR LICENSURE EXAMS

After reading this chapter, you should be able to demonstrate basic knowledge and skills described in the CEC standards and INTASC principles listed below. The section of this chapter most applicable to each standard is shown in parentheses at the end of the knowledge or skill statement.

 Core Standard 2: Development and Characteristics of Learners

- **Development:** Typical and atypical human growth and development. (Physical Impairments and Special Health Care Defined)

 Core Standard 3: Individual Learning Differences

- **Life Span:** Effects an exceptional conditions(s) can have on an individual's life. (Characteristics)

 Core Standard 5: Learning Environments and Social Interactions

- **Learning environments:** Demands of learning environments (Characteristics)
- **Learning environments:** Create a safe, equitable, positive and supportive learning environment in which diversities are valued. (Characteristics)

- **Universal precautions:** Use universal precautions. (Causes and Prevention)

 Core Standard 7: Instructional Planning

- **Inclusive environment:** Identify and prioritize areas of the general curriculum and accommodations for individual with exceptional learning needs. (Accommodating for Inclusive Environments)
- **Technology:** Incorporate and implement instructional and assistive technology into the educational program. (Technology)

INTASC Principle 2

The teacher understands how children learn and develop and can provide learning opportunities that support their intellectual, social, and personal development.

- **Developmental progressions (physical domain):** The teacher is aware of expected developmental progressions and ranges of individual variation within each domain (physical, social, emotional, moral and cognitive), can identify levels of readiness in learning, and understands how development in any one domain may affect performance in others. (Physical Impairments and Special Health Care Defined)

INTASC Principle 3

The teacher understands how students differ in their approaches to learning and creates instructional opportunities that are adapted to diverse learners.

In Conclusion

- **Areas of Exceptionality:** The teacher knows about areas of exceptionality in learning—including learning disabilities, visual and perceptual difficulties, and special physical or mental challenges. (Physical Impairments and Special Health Care Defined)

- **Modifications:** The teacher makes appropriate provisions (in terms of time and circumstances for work, tasks assigned, communication, and response modes) for individual students who have particular learning differences or needs. (Elementary Through High School)

INTASC Principle 5

The teacher uses an understanding of individual and group motivation and behavior to create a learning environment that encourages positive social interaction, active engagement in learning, and self-motivation.

- **Manages resources:** The teacher organizes, allocates and manages the resources of time, space, activities and attention to provide active and equitable engagement of students in productive tasks. (Elementary Through High School)

- **Learning environments:** The teacher maximizes the amount of class time spent in learning by creating expectations and processes for communication and behavior along with a physical setting conducive to classroom goals. (Elementary Through High School)

Standards in Practice

These knowledge statements, dispositions, and skills might be demonstrated by the beginning teacher as she successfully manages the physical arrangement in her classroom and uses universal medical precautions when handling minor first aid duties for the students in her classroom. The teacher would also be accepting of the use of technology to support students with physical disabilities or special health care needs.

Go to the companion website (ablongman.com/smith5e) for detailed text correlations to CEC and INTASC standards, PRAXIS II™ exams, and other state-sponsored licensure exams.

SUPPLEMENTARY RESOURCES

Professional Readings and Resources

Accardo, P. J., Whitman, B. Y., Behr, S. K., Farrell, A., Magenis, E., & Morrow-Gorton, J. (2002). *Dictionary of developmental disabilities terminology* (2nd ed.). Baltimore: Paul H. Brookes.

Haslam, R. H. A., & Valletutti, P. J. (1996). *Medical problems in the classroom: The teacher's role in diagnosis and management* (3rd ed.). Austin, TX: Pro-Ed.

Heller, K. W., Alberto, P. A., Forney, P. E., & Schwartzman, M. N. (1996). *Understanding physical, sensory, and health impairments.* Pacific Grove; CA: Brooks/Cole.

Minskoff, E., & Allsopp, D. (2002). *Academic success strategies for adolescents with learning disabilities and ADHD.* Baltimore: Paul H. Brookes.

Popular Books

Brown, C. (1955). *My left foot.* New York: Simon & Schuster.

Ellison, J. (2002). *Miracles happen: One mother, one daughter, one journey.* New York: Hyperion.

Gallagher, H. G. (1994). *FDR's splendid deception.* New York: Dodd, Mead.

Hawking, S. (2001). *The universe in a nutshell.* New York: Bantam.

Pechinpah, S. E. (1993). *Chester: The imperfect all-star.* Agoura Hills, CA: Dasan Publishing.

Reeve, C. (1998). *Still me.* New York: Random House.

Stepanek, M. J. T. (2001). *Heartsongs.* Alexandria, VA: VSP Books.

Stepanek, M. J. T. (2001). *Journey through heartsongs.* Alexandria, VA: VSP Books.

Videos and DVDs

The Fugitive (1993) **Warner Brothers**

Dr. Richard Kimble is falsely accused, convicted, and sentenced to life in prison for killing his wife. He knows the perpetrator was a man with one arm. Dr. Kimble escapes during an accident that occurs while he is being transferred from one prison to another, but he is tracked by federal marshals. While Dr. Kimble is on the loose, he is able to follow up on leads to expose all the guilty parties and prove his innocence.

This film's central criminal character has a physical disability. At one point, Dr. Kimble is looking for a specific type of prosthetic arm and enters a workroom where these devices are tailored to the individual. Since this film's release, medical advancements in robotics and prosthetics have significantly reduced the impact of the loss of a limb. Today individuals with disabilities are rarely cast in the role of "villain," but here, as in many old story plots, the person with the disability is the antagonist.

Moulin Rouge! (2001). **Twentieth Century Fox**

Christian moves to Paris in 1899 and falls in love with Satine, who works at the infamous nightclub the Moulin Rouge. Satine is promised to the Duke, who is financing a play that Christian is writing, so the love affair between Christian and Satine must be kept secret. At the first performance of the play, which is called "Spectacular Spectacular," the Duke finds out about the two lovers and tries to have Christian killed.

Henri de Toulouse-Lautrec, a well-known artist of that time, is a central character in the story and a friend of Christian. Though considerably smaller in physical stature than the other characters, he is not portrayed as different in other ways, and his disability is not even mentioned.

Notting Hill (1999). **Universal Studios**

This romantic comedy about William Thacker, who owns a travel bookshop, takes place in a small section of London. Thacker falls in love with a woman from the United States, Anna Scott. Their relationship is complicated by the fact that she is a world-famous film star.

One of William's friends is a woman called Bella, who uses a wheelchair. She had fallen down a flight of stairs, which left her paralyzed from the waist down. The film portrays her neither as a victim nor as a person to be pitied. Instead, she is an empowered, pivotal character in the story.

X-Men (2000). Twentieth Century Fox

This film, based on a comic book set in the late sixties, follows "evolved" people called mutants, who are threatened with being rounded up, numbered, and placed in specific centers. A school for mutants, developed by Dr. Xavier and his top mutants (the X-Men), is a safe haven where people and mutants are supposed to live together peacefully. However, a nefarious group of mutants disagree and wage war on "normal" people.

The leader of the X-Men is a man in a wheelchair, but his leadership is not impaired. The underlying meaning of this film is that people who are different should not be viewed as outcasts or ostracized from society. The comic book on which the movie is based dates back about thirty years and tried to promote tolerance.

Mask (1985). Universal/MCA

Rocky Dennis is a teenager who is suffering with an incurable disease that has rendered his skull deformed. He is a gifted youth, who is raised by a caring, loving single mother, who helps her son to cope with the painful side effects of his disease. However, she also has a wild side and regularly carouses with bikers, living a hedonistic lifestyle. Even though his mother is reckless, her perspective allows Rocky to live for the moment, but in the end he cannot overcome the deadly, incurable disease.

In this powerful drama, Rocky's mother does not allow her son to be thought of as different, and she expects him to be given all the same opportunities that everyone else has. This film tellingly reflects how precious life is and how much people take for granted. The prognosis is that Rocky will not survive for long, regardless he attempts to live a full life with typical teenage aspirations, such as pursuing relationship with a blind girl, travel, and independence.

Parent, Professional, and Consumer Organizations and Agencies

Asthma and Allergy Foundation of America (AAFA)
1233 20th Street, NW, Suite 402
Washington, DC 20036
Phone: (800) 7-ASTHMA; (800) 727-8462;
(202) 466-7643
Web site: http://www.aafa.org

Council for Exceptional Children
Division for Physical & Health Disabilities (DPHD)
1110 North Glebe Road, Suite 300
Arlington, VA 22201-5704
Phone: (888) CEC-SPED; (703) 620-3660
TTY: (703) 262-9446
Web site: http://www.cec.sped.org

National Easter Seal Society for Crippled Children and Adults
230 W. Monroe Street, Suite 1800
Chicago, IL 60606
Phone: (312) 726-6200; (800) 221-6827
TTY: (312) 726-4258
E-mail: info@easter-seals.org
Web site: http://www.easter-seals.org

Epilepsy Foundation of America
4351 Garden City Drive
Landover, MD 20785-7223
TYY: (800) EFA-1000; (301) 459-3700
Web site: http://www.efa.org

March of Dimes Birth Defects Foundation
1275 Mamaroneck Avenue
White Plains, NY 10605
Phone: (888) MODIMES
Web site: http://www.modimes.org

United Cerebral Palsy Association
1660 L Street NW, Suite 700
Washington, DC 20036-5602
Phone: (202) 776-0406; (800) 872-5827
TTY: (202) 973-7197
E-mail: national@ucp.org
Web site: http://www.ucpa.org

Video**Workshop** Extra

If the VideoWorkshop package was included with your textbook, go to Chapter 9 of the Companion Website (www.ablongman.com/smith5e) and click on the VideoWorkshop button. Follow the instructions for viewing Video clips 12 & 5. Consider this information along with what you've read in Chapter 9 as you answer the following questions.

Video clip 12: Physical disabilities (Time 4:06)
1. Students like Oscar who have paraplegia typically have support staff assigned to help them. Some general education teachers, unlike the teacher seen in the video, may have concerns about who is actually doing the work during class activities and homework assignments. As the teacher, how can you address those issues before they become a problem? Review the "Collaboration for Inclusion" box in your text and offer two specific examples of what you would do to alleviate teacher concerns.

2. Your text offers an overview of the technology that can be used to support academic work of persons with disabilities. What technologies might be useful for Oscar?

Video clip 5: ADHD (Time 3:33)
1. Judging on the basis of what you see in the video and what you read in this chapter, what outcomes would you predict for Eric? Use examples of Eric's behavior from the video.

2. What strategies or teaching methods would you use to prevent the negative outcomes mentioned in your text? Apply your answer to Eric's case and explain how these strategies or teaching methods would be helpful for him.

Dorothy Brett, *Deer Dancers,* oil on board, 1951, 36 × 24 in. The Albuquerque Museum, gift of Mr. & Mrs. Max L. Ilfeld. Photograph by Damian Andrus.

DOROTHY BRETT was born of a noble British family (Hignett, 1983). Although her childhood was quite sheltered, as a young adult and a student at the Slade Art College in London, she became exposed to young artists like Dora Carrington and the liberal thinking of the day. Her associations with the Bloomsbury Group—two of its more famous members were writer and publisher Virginia Woolf and economist John Maynard Keynes—broadened her horizons. In 1924, Brett followed D. H. Lawrence to New Mexico to be part of a utopian colony. Lawrence returned to England, but Brett remained in America and became part of an artists' colony, often referred to as the Taos Artists. Brett was "partially deaf" almost her entire life; a self-portrait she completed in 1924 shows her with an ear trumpet, which she named Toby, the hearing aid of the day (Hignett, 1983).

10 Deafness and Hard of Hearing

A PERSONAL PERSPECTIVE

Finding My Way in a Hearing World

Susan is a remarkable young woman, full of life, independence, and abilities. Her laughter fills the office, putting office routine into perspective. Susan is truly amazing. Her communication skills are excellent, and it is easy to forget that she is profoundly deaf. That is, until she is through with a conversation, turns her back, and walks away. At that point you know that you've said as much as you're going to say, at least for the moment.

I was 18 months old when it was discovered that I had a profound hearing loss in both ears. My mother walked up behind me one day as I was playing with my toys and started talking to me. I did not respond until she put her hand on my shoulder and I was startled. The doctors confirmed my parents' suspicions and determined the loss to be the result of my mother's mild case of rubella while pregnant with me.

My parents faced many difficult questions and decisions: Would I learn to talk? How would I communicate—oral or sign? Would I have to go away to school? Could I have a "normal" life?

Early on my parents decided that their goal was to provide opportunities that would enable me to be as independent as possible. They traveled to various cities to visit schools that taught either sign or oral communications. Although there were compelling arguments for both approaches, they decided to start me in oral communication because they felt it would best maximize my ability to learn and master the English language.

I was fitted for two hearing aids and immediately started intensive training in reading lips, speech therapy, and learning to recognize sounds that my hearing aids could pick up. There were difficult

moments, but for the most part, I was able to master the English language via oral communication.

When I entered first grade, my parents sent me to a private school with a low teacher/student ratio and small classrooms. While there were no special education services available at the school, the environment was well suited to my needs. It helped that my parents remained actively involved in my education, advocating on my behalf for such needs as front row seating, a different teacher, or tutoring help.

My parents also encouraged me to try everything that interested me. I participated in many activities from competitive swimming to life guarding to cheerleading. Although being involved in mainstream education overall gave me confidence socially, there were also a few experiences that prepared me for the realization that there would always be people who are totally ignorant about hearing loss. However, it has been fun educating others about my loss—especially when I get to shout back at those who shout at me!

After graduating from high school, I attended Mississippi State University. This period of my life was marked by great social acceptance and independence, which prepared me well for the working world. After four years at MSU, I obtained my Bachelor of Business Administration and began to seek employment. My job search was a difficult time because of limitations in using the telephone. After almost two years of being underemployed, I enrolled at the University of Memphis and obtained my Master of Science in Rehabilitation Counseling. This additional education opened the door for me to work for the state of Tennessee as a vocational rehabilitation counselor for almost six years. My work with individuals with all different types of disabilities prepared me for my current job as a program coordinator at Vanderbilt University.

Have I achieved independence? My epiphany came while traveling abroad. I was in my late twenties, visiting a close friend in Madrid, Spain. One day, while my friend was at work, I set out to explore Madrid. At one point, I was so fascinated by the city that I unwittingly allowed myself to become terribly lost. Momentary panic ensued when I realized there were no public TTY's (text tele-

phones), and I could not simply pick up the phone and call my friend to rescue me. An unnerving boldness took hold of me, and I was able to approach complete strangers to ask "Habla Ingles?" It was a defining experience: I realized my disability would never hinder me in finding my way home.

1. Why do you think that Susan's story is not typical among deaf individuals? What in her background and experiences contributed to her success?

2. In what ways do you think Susan's story *is* typical among deaf individuals?

ADVANCE ORGANIZERS

Overview

Hearing, like vision, is a distance sense and provides us with information from outside our bodies. When hearing is limited, it affects the individual in significant ways: limiting communication, access to orally presented information, and independent living. More than any other group of people with disabilities, the Deaf make up a community united by a rich culture and a unique communication system. Deafness and hard of hearing is a low incidence disability for children, affecting about 0.14 percent of schoolchildren.

Self-Test Questions

Focus Questions

- Why is universal screening of newborns such an important issue?
- What variables are used to create different subgroups of deaf and hard of hearing individuals?
- What is meant by the concept of Deaf culture?

- What are major causes of hearing loss?
- How do the major instructional methods for deaf children differ, and how should an individual child's communication style affect the choice of instructional method?

Challenge Question

- What types of technology are available to assist the deaf, and what advances might the future hold?

MAKING CONNECTIONS

Use the learning strategy—Advance Organizers—to help focus your study of this chapter's content, and reinforce your learning by reviewing answers to the Focus and Challenge questions at the end of the chapter.

The process of hearing is remarkable. Sound waves pass through the air, water, or some other medium. They cause the eardrum to vibrate. These vibrations are carried to the inner ear, where they pass through receptor cells that send impulses to the brain. The brain translates these impulses into meaningful sound. The content or associations of sound affect us in different ways. We are warmed by the sound of an old friend's voice, startled by a loud clap of thunder, fascinated by the sound of the wind rushing through trees, lulled by the ocean, excited by the roar of a crowd, consumed by the music of a rock

group, and relaxed by the soothing sounds of a symphony. One important way in which most of us learn about the thoughts, ideas, and feelings of others, is by listening to people tell us their experiences. Through this exchange, we expand our knowledge, share ideas, express emotions, and function in typical workplaces and social settings. Many deaf and hard of hearing people participate fully in mainstream society in part because of advances in education and technology. However, some people cannot be helped by technology such as hearing aids and thus have much more restricted access to mainstream society.

OPPORTUNITIES FOR A BETTER FUTURE

Only a few years ago, most children with even profound hearing loss were not identified early enough to benefit from critical early intervention programs. When deaf and hard of hearing children are not identified until they are 2 to 3 years old (the average identification age in the late 1990s), important periods for language development are missed. With inexpensive early detection methods now available, hearing loss can be detected in all newborns. However, not all states have yet passed legislation requiring universal hearing screening of newborns, and this leaves many children and families without opportunities to obtain services they require.

The Deaf community has become a visible part of American society, claiming its status as a minority group that should be valued and treasured as an important part of the mix that makes America unique. Awareness of their rich culture, which includes dance, literature, arts, and theater, was brought to public attention through Deaf individuals' advocacy efforts. Despite the abilities and talents shared by many members of this community, their employment options and overall outcomes are below expectations because they and their culture remain misunderstood, which results in bias and discrimination—a problem shared by other minority groups in this country.

Turning Legacies into Lessons

Controversy has probably surrounded deaf and hard of hearing people since the beginning of time, and it continues today. Throughout the last two centuries, the education community and policymakers have been embroiled in debates about how and where hard of hearing and deaf children should be educated. At the heart of today's continuing debates are communication (a uniquely distinguishing feature of humans) and values about oral means of interacting with others and the culture that develops from language and social interaction. The use of American Sign Language, a language of manual communication, has become the focal point of the controversy: whether it should become the native language for all deaf children (and English become the second language). New technologies—possibly future versions of cochlear implants—that might someday eradicate deafness are seen by some in the Deaf community as a threat and a devaluation of themselves and their culture. These unresolved controversies influence how children are taught, where they eventually live, with whom they interact easily, and employment outcomes.

Thinking About Dilemmas to Solve

As you read this chapter, there are many things to consider about deaf and hard of hearing children, their education, and their lives. Think about

- How language influences human behavior
- Ways to ensure that all babies with hearing loss and their families receive early intervention programs immediately upon early diagnosis
- The role of Deaf culture in American society
- Special issues that hearing families face with the birth of a deaf child
- How underachievement and poor employment outcomes of many deaf and hard of hearing people can be overcome

DEAFNESS AND HARD OF HEARING DEFINED

People who are **deaf**,[1] (those with profound hearing **loss**, have hearing abilities that provide them with little useful hearing even if they use hearing aids. Although nearly all deaf people perceive some sound, they cannot use hearing as their primary way to gain information. **Hard of hearing** people can process information from sound, usually with the help of a hearing aid.

MAKING CONNECTIONS

For more information, see the "History" and "Characteristics" sections in this chapter.

---

[1]In this chapter, people with severe and profound hearing losses are referred to in different ways. Sometimes they are called, people who are deaf, and at other times they are called deaf people. Many people in the Deaf community prefer the latter term because they believe it better reflects their Deaf culture and identity. The use of the capital letter *D* signifies affiliation with Deaf culture; a small *d* refers to deafness.

Both the degree of hearing loss *and* the age when the hearing loss occurs are important. Individuals who become deaf before they learn to speak and understand language are referred to as **prelingually deaf.** They either are born deaf or lose their hearing as infants. Approximately 95 percent of all deaf children and youth are prelingually deaf. Their inability to hear language seriously affects their abilities to communicate with others and to learn academic subjects taught later in school. One in ten of those who are prelingually deaf have at least one deaf parent. Children in this group typically learn to communicate during the normal developmental period. However, instead of learning oral communication skills, many learn through a combination of manual communication (sign language) and oral language. Those whose severe hearing loss occurs after they have learned to speak and understand language are called **postlingually deaf.** Many are able to retain their abilities to use speech and communicate with others orally.

What is hearing loss? Hearing loss results when the ear and hearing mechanism are damaged or obstructed in such a way that sounds cannot be perceived or understood. To better understand impaired hearing, let's first see how the process of hearing works when the hearing mechanisms are functioning properly. Refer to Figure 10.1, a diagram of the ear, to trace how sound moves through the ear to produce normal hearing. A person speaks, and the sound waves that make up the words pass through the air or some other medium. The sound waves are caught by the pinna or auricle (what we commonly call the ear) and funneled down the auditory canal of the listener; the pinna and the auditory canal are the two parts of the **outer ear.** Sound waves then travel to the **middle ear,** which is an air-filled chamber. This chamber contains the eardrum and is connected to the eustachian tube, which equalizes the pressure on the two sides of the eardrum. Sound waves cause the **eardrum (tympanic membrane)** to vibrate. Those vibrations cause the **hammer (malleus)** and **anvil (incus)** to move and the **stirrup (stapes)** to oscillate. These three tiny bones together are called the **ossicles;** they are also part of the middle ear. The eardrum converts pressure variations to mechanical vibrations, which are then transmitted to the fluid contained in the compartments of the **cochlea.**

The **inner ear** includes the semicircular canals and the cochlea, which is a hollow, spiral-shaped bone that actually contains the organs of hearing. The mechanical vibrations caused by variations in the pressure that the stirrup exerts on the fluid are transmitted to the basement membrane of the cochlea. This membrane supports the **hair cells,** which respond to different frequencies of sound. Each hair cell has about a hundred tiny, rigid spines, or cilia, at its top. When these hair cells move, they displace the fluid that surrounds them and produce electrochemical signals, which are sent through nerve cells along the **auditory nerve** (the eighth cranial nerve) to the brain where the signals are perceived as tones. When these hair cells vibrate, they also create sounds of a very low level called **otoacoustic emissions (OAEs).** OAEs are a relatively new discovery. The ability to recognize them with special computer equipment is what makes possible the ready identification of hearing loss in newborns (Ross & Levitt, 2000).

Now let's look at the qualities of sound that are measured in the assessment process. Sound is the vibration of molecules through some medium such as air, water, or wires. The number of vibrations per second determines the **frequency of sound.** High frequencies are perceived through our ears as high pitch or tone; low frequencies are perceived as low pitch. Frequency is measured in a unit called the **hertz (Hz).** The normal ear hears sounds that range from approximately 20 Hz to 20,000 Hz; rpeech sounds fall about in the middle of the human hearing range (between 250 Hz and 4,000 Hz). Those of you who have some knowledge of music might find Lowenbraun's (1995) explanation of hertz helpful. The frequency of middle C on the piano is approximately 250 Hz. The next vertical line on the audiogram, 500 Hz, is approximately one octave above middle C; 1,000 is two octaves above middle C; and so on. (See the scale in Figure 10.2 on page 350). Humans, however, cannot perceive

CHAPTER 10 *Deafness and Hard of Hearing*

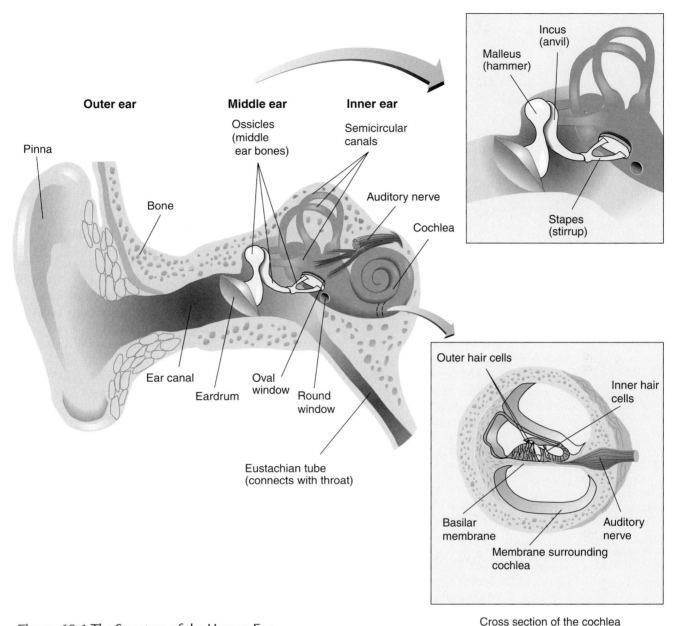

Figure 10.1 The Structure of the Human Ear
Source: From N. R. Carlson, *Physiology of Behavior,* 6th ed. Published by Allyn and Bacon. © 1998 by Pearson Education. Adapted by permission of the publisher.

Cross section of the cochlea

some sounds, regardless of their hearing abilities. For example, some dog whistles use high frequencies that are beyond humans' hearing range.

Intensity, or loudness, of sound is measured in **decibels (dB).** Softer, quieter sounds have lower decibel measurements; louder sounds have higher decibel numbers. A decibel level of 125 or louder is painful to the average person. Decibel levels ranging from 0 to 120 dB are used to test how well an individual can hear different frequencies; a child with normal hearing should be able to perceive sounds at 0 dB. The scale used to assess hearing has been adjusted so that 0 indicates no loss and numbers greater than 0 indicate the degree or amount of loss. Small numbers indicate mild losses; large numbers indicate moderate to severe or profound losses.

What are the two types of hearing loss and how do they differ?

There are two general types of hearing loss:

1. Conductive
2. Sensorineural

Conductive hearing loss is due to blockage or damage to the outer or middle ear that prevents sound waves from traveling (being conducted) to the inner ear. Generally, someone with a conductive hearing loss has a mild to moderate disability. Some conductive hearing losses are temporary; in fact, we have all probably experienced a conductive hearing loss at some point in our lives. For example, you may have experienced a temporary loss of hearing as a consequence of a change in air pressure when flying in an airplane or riding in a car in the mountains. Children often experience head colds and ear infections that result in a temporary loss of conductive hearing. Therefore, it is likely that on any given day, 20 percent of elementary students have a mild conductive hearing loss, and some 80 percent of all children experience such hearing problems at some time between kindergarten and fifth grade (Gordon-Langbein & Metzinger, 2000). Remember that with a mild loss, the individual can still hear almost all speech sounds and can hear most conversations (Moores, 2001). If the hearing loss was caused by a head cold, once the ear infection clears up, the hearing difficulties also disappear. Other causes of conductive hearing losses can usually be corrected through surgery or other medical techniques.

Sensorineural hearing loss, which occurs when there is damage to the inner ear or the auditory nerve, usually cannot be improved medically or surgically. Some people refer to this type of hearing loss as "nerve deafness." Individuals affected by a sensorineural loss are able to hear different frequencies at different intensity levels; their hearing losses are not flat or even. Sensorineural losses are less common in young children than the conductive types, but teachers need to understand that hearing aids can have mixed results with sensorineural losses.

How are hearing losses identified?

People's hearing abilities can be assessed by different methods. The discovery of AOEs allows for **universal infant screening** (also called newborn infant hearing screening and universal screening). Ears that are working normally produce AOEs (a low level of sound) when the hair cells in the middle ear vibrate. Ears that are not working normally do not produce AOEs. The discovery of AOEs allows for easy and cost-effective assessment of all newborn infants for hearing loss (Ross & Levitt, 2000). It is to be hoped that soon all newborns' hearing will be tested, so every baby with hearing problems will have immediate access to early intervention programs.

Children's hearing is usually tested differently. Audiologists use **pure sounds**—sound waves of specific frequencies—at various combinations of hertz and decibels and also at various bands of pitch and loudness. They usually conduct their assessments in soundproof rooms so that distractions like those found in classrooms are eliminated by using an **audiometer,** an instrument that produces sounds at precise frequencies and intensities. The results of these audiological assessments are plotted on an **audiogram,** which is a grid or graph. Along the top of the graph are hertz levels; the vertical lines represent different levels of sound frequency or hertz. Each ear is tested separately. A **hearing threshold** is determined by noting when the person first perceives the softest sound at each frequency level. Sometimes, hearing threshold is reported only for the better ear, and sometimes an average of an individual's scores at three different frequencies (500, 1,000, 2,000 Hz) is used. Any score falling below the 0-dB line on an audiogram represents some degree of hearing loss, because the audiometer is set to indicate that a person has no hearing loss at 0 dB for various hertz levels.

Most children's hearing is assessed by the **air conduction audiometry method,** which uses pure-tone sounds generated by an audiometer. Earphones are placed over the child's ears, and the child raises his or her hand when hearing a sound. Such testing is usually done by a pediatrician at a well-child checkup or by a school nurse. When a hearing loss is suspected, audiologists use an additional procedure to determine whether the loss was due to damage in the outer, middle, or inner ear. The **bone conduction audiometry method** uses a vibrator placed on the forehead so that sound can bypass the outer and middle ear and go directly to the inner ear. When the bone conduction thresholds are normal (near 0 dB) and the air conduction thresholds are abnormal, the hearing loss is conductive. Now let's review the audiograms of two children, Travis and Heather. Because Travis and Heather were suspected of having hearing losses, the audiologist used both the air conduction and the bone conduction methods.

An audiologist is using the air conduction audiometry method to test this young child's hearing to determine if she has a hearing loss.

Travis's audiogram, shown in Figure 10.2, indicates that he has a **conductive hearing loss.** The loss, of about 40 dB, is in the mild range with the amplification of hearing aids. Note how flat the profile is for Travis's air conduction test. However, the bone conduction test reveals that when the middle ear is bypassed, his hearing is much closer to 0 dB. Travis's hearing loss either is temporary or can be corrected through surgery or other medical treatment. Note also that a different code is used for Travis's right and left ears: O for the right ear and X for the left ear. Remember that each ear is tested independently. Travis's hearing threshold for each ear is marked on his audiogram. Most children with normal hearing have auditory thresholds (the points when they first perceive sound) at approximately 0 dB; Travis's thresholds are considerably below 0.

Travis's hearing abilities are plotted on an audiogram form designed by Northern and Downs (1984) a long time ago. This form graphically shows where various speech and other sounds occur and helps us visualize how sounds at different frequencies come together for meaning. If the child's threshold falls below the picture, then the sound pictured cannot be perceived by that child. Without a hearing aid, Travis, for example, can perceive only a few sounds (ng, el, and u).

Heather has a sensorineural hearing loss, as indicated in her audiogram, which is shown in Figure 10.3. A **sensorineural hearing loss** is caused by a defect in or damage to the inner ear and can be more serious than conductive hearing losses. Heather has a 30-dB loss. Note the similarity between her scores from the air conduction and bone conduction tests. Heather's hearing was also tested with her hearing aids on. Note that with the use of aids, Heather's hearing loss is no longer so serious; it is now at a mild functional level. The shaded area on this audiogram (sometimes called the "speech banana" because of its shape) marks the area where speech sounds fall. Because Heather's hearing abilities lie above this area on her audiogram (see the top of the audiogram), the audiologist knows that Heather can hear the speech sounds at the sound intensities measured during audiological assessment. Along the side of the graph are intensity levels measured in decibels, so horizontal lines represent different levels of loudness.

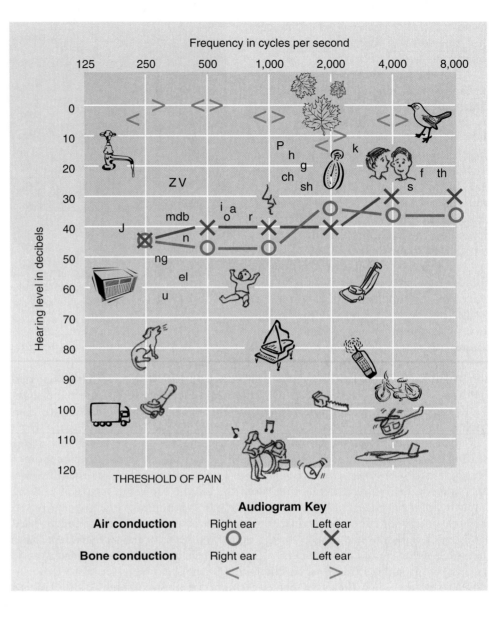

Figure 10.2 Travis's Audiogram

Source: Hearing in Children (p. 7) by J. L. Northern and M. P. Downs, 1984, Baltimore: Williams & Wilkins. Reprinted by permission.

MAKING **C**ONNECTIONS

To review otoacoustic emissions, and why it is now possible to test all newborns' hearing, see the "Defined" section of this chapter.

When should identification occur? The simple answer is as soon as possible. Children who are identified as having hearing problems and receive services before they are 6 months old have better results in speech, language, reading comprehension, and general development than children identified after they are 18 months old (Yoshinaga-Itano & Apuzzo, 1998). One reason for these improved outcomes is that infants even as young as 3 months old can now be fitted with hearing aids so that they will not miss out on important opportunities to learn at the right developmental ages (Hoover, 2000). Unfortunately, despite continued calls for early identification, children with profound hearing losses are typically not identified between the ages of 1½ and 2½ years old in those states without universal hearing screening of newborns. Those with mild and moderate sensorineural hearing losses are reported to be identified at an average of 5 to 6 years, and many hard of hearing students are never identified by schools (Easterbrooks, 1999). Why is this so? Babies are not universally screened for hearing loss, and even those with definite risk factors are not always tested (American Speech-Language-Hearing Association, [ASHA], 2002). Procedures that are simple, nonintrusive, and relatively inexpensive (between $25 and $60, a cost that would decrease if the tests were universally

CHAPTER 10 *Deafness and Hard of Hearing*

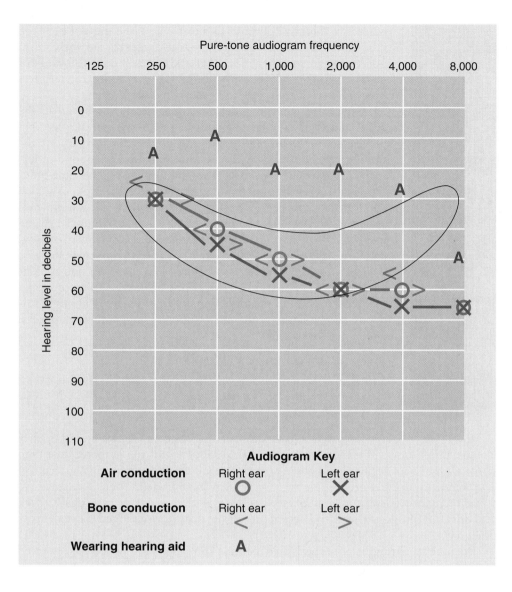

Pure-tone audiogram frequency

Audiogram Key

	Right ear	Left ear
Air conduction	O	X
Bone conduction	<	>
Wearing hearing aid	A	

Figure 10.3 Heather's Audiogram

applied) can be done before babies leave the hospital and could result in improved overall outcomes for all children with hearing losses and their families (Gordon-Langbein, 1998, 1999).

How can hearing losses affect the individuals involved?

Hearing losses affect children in many ways. Depending on the type and degree of loss, development of language, means of communication, educational opportunities, and participation in social situations can all be affected. Sometimes, people do not think about how some teenagers can be embarrassed by their hearing problems and the assistive devices they use (Davis, 2001). By thinking about some of the situations that Minda Huebner (2002) describes in her writings, teachers and classmates might become more sensitive to the feelings of students with hearing problems. For example, Minda was the only person at her high school who used a special listening device (an FM transmission system where she wore a receiver and the teacher used a microphone). To her, that was embarrassing enough, but when the teacher forgot to turn on the mike, she hated having to call attention to herself by asking the teacher to activate the system. She felt that everyone was staring at her. She laughs

To learn more about FM transmission devices, read about assistive listening devices in the "Technology" section of this chapter.

Even a deaf kid can hear what's being said.

when she thinks about a track meet where she did not hear the false-start gun and ran around the track an extra lap with everyone trying to stop her. Teachers and peers should think about how sensitive students with disabilities are about their differences and what they believe others think about them.

Experts vary in their definitions of hearing loss and in the point at which they believe it has educational significance. No precise score on an audiogram can guide educators about the significance of a hearing loss because individuals respond differently. Of course, all hearing losses are serious, and at some point the level of severity substantially influences the way in which children need to be taught and how well they understand oral communication. The amount and type of an individual's hearing loss affect how a student is best taught and what types of services are needed. Such students may need help from assistive devices and special accommodations. For example, one student with a moderate loss might not profit from typical instructional methods (lectures, oral directions) alone, whereas another student with the same profile might function well without supports.

HISTORY OF THE FIELD

As long ago as the days of the ancient Greeks and the early Roman Empire, social leaders such as Aristotle, Plato, and the emperor Justinian wrote about issues facing deaf people of their time. Over the history of Western civilization, attitudes toward people who were deaf have varied. Some societies protected them; others ridiculed and persecuted them and even put them to death. Even in America, attitudes toward and acceptance of the deaf have changed greatly across time.

Documents dating back to the 1500s mention physicians in Europe who worked with people who were deaf. Pedro Ponce de Leon (1520–1584), a Spanish monk believed to have been the first teacher of deaf students, had remarkable success teaching his students to read, write, and speak. William Holder and John Wallis, who lived during the 1600s, are credited with instituting educational programs in England for deaf individuals. Like the Spanish before, they advocated using writing and manual communication to teach speech. By the 1700s, schools for the deaf had been established by Henry Baker in England, Thomas Braidwood in Edinburgh, Abbé Charles Michel de l'Epée in France, and Samuel Heinicke in Germany.

The first school in the United States for deaf students was started in 1817 in Hartford, Connecticut. (Many of the Deaf children of Martha's Vineyard attended this school.) Thomas Hopkins Gallaudet, a young divinity student, went to study in England and France in order to start the first special school for the deaf in this country. At that time, the French at the school begun by l'Epée were experimenting with methods of manual communication, mainly sign language. Gallaudet was greatly influenced by the effectiveness of these methods, and he brought Laurent Clerc, a deaf Frenchman and a well-known educator of the deaf, to the United States. Clerc is often credited with being the father of education for the deaf in the United States. Other Americans interested in education of the deaf also went to Europe and were impressed by the results of oral approaches. This is why some people discouraged the use of any form of manual communication or sign language.

The debate about the oral method versus the manual method of instruction and communication originated early in the history of this field. Although some argument about the best means for communication continues today, the period between the

MAKING **C**ONNECTIONS

Compare the story about the Deaf communities on Martha's Vineyard in Chapter 1 with the history of deaf people recounted in this section.

352

1860s and the 1960s saw the most heated conflict between those who advocated an oralist approach and those who were proponents of manual signed language. Some even refer to this period of time as the "Hundred Years' War" (Drasgow, 1998). The battles were initiated and fueled through the debates of Edward Gallaudet, Thomas Gallaudet's son, and Alexander Graham Bell (Alby, 1962; Adams, 1929). Each of these men had a deaf mother and a highly successful father. Bell invented the telephone and the audiometer and worked on the phonograph. Gallaudet was the president of the nation's college for the deaf and was a renowned legal scholar. These two men clashed. Bell believed that residential schools and the use of sign language fostered segregation. He also felt that communities of deaf people would lead to more deaf people marrying each other and that the result would eventually be a deaf variety of the human race (Campbell, 1999).

I. King Jordan, the first Deaf President of Gallaudet University, has become a symbol of Deaf advocacy and Deaf culture.

Therefore, he proposed legislation to prevent two deaf adults from marrying, eliminate residential schools, ban the use of manual communication, and prohibit the deaf from becoming teachers of deaf students. Gallaudet strongly opposed these positions, and he won support from Congress for the manual approach and for separate center schools. But these conflicts were far from settled.

Formal education for the deaf in the United States in the 19th Century took place primarily in residential schools. Deaf students were sent to boarding schools, as were many students without disabilities in that day. From 1817, when the first school was started, to the eve of the Civil War in 1864, 24 schools for the deaf were in operation. **Gallaudet University** (first called the National Deaf–Mute College) was founded in 1864 on the principle of the right of all deaf students to high expectations and a quality education.

The development of the hearing aid had a significant impact on the lives of deaf and hard of hearing people, particularly those with conductive hearing losses. The hearing trumpet (the name for the first hearing aids), like the one used by Dorothy Brett, made sounds a little louder. At the end of World War II, battery-operated hearing aids were developed, but these early devices were difficult to use because they were bulky. Behind-the-ear (BTE) hearing aids were created after the development of the transistor in the 1950s.

Deaf pride and Deaf culture have gained in popularity since the late 1980s. The Deaf President Now Movement, which galvanized the Deaf community (Gannon, 1989), began in 1988 when a hearing president was appointed to lead Gallaudet University. After protests from Deaf Gallaudet students and the Deaf community, which closed the campus and included a march on the nation's Capital, the newly appointed president (who could not sign) stepped down and I. King Jordan became the first Deaf college president for Gallaudet and in the nation.

For a review of the increased risks for disabilities among diverse groups, read again the "Causes and Prevention" section in Chapter 3.

For a picture of a hearing trumpet, see the photo of Dorothy Brett in the "Technology" section.

The *D* in Deaf has been capitalized here to reflect that deafness here is associated with Deaf culture.

PREVALENCE

Hearing loss in children is the number-one birth defect in the United States (ASHA, 2002). Approximately 1 in every 1,000 babies is born profoundly deaf, and another 2 to 3 have less severe hearing loss. Many people have hearing problems, but almost half of them are over age 65.

Also see the discussion about prevalence rates when students have multiple disabilities in the "Prevalence" section of Chapter 11.

Obtaining reliable statistics about the number of deaf and hard of hearing schoolchildren is difficult because states use different criteria for counting who is deaf, is hard of hearing, and/or has multiple disabilities. In addition, the U.S. Department of Education reports children by their primary disability. Thus students with mental retardation who also have a hearing loss may be reported only in the mental retardation category, or possibly in the multiple disabilities category, but usually not in the deafness and hard of hearing category. Also, these counts do not include those hard of hearing students who do not need special education because hearing aids allow them to hear well enough to participate in typical classroom activities without additional assistance. Considering these factors, the number of deaf and hard of hearing students is probably underestimated. Regardless, according to the *Twenty-third Annual Report to Congress on the Implementation of the Individuals with Disabilities Education Act* (U.S. Department of Education, 2001), during the 1999–2000 school year, 0.14 percent of the resident population between the ages of 6 and 17, or 66,624 students, were classified as deaf or hard of hearing.

Almost 44 percent of deaf schoolchildren are from diverse backgrounds (Gallaudet Research Institute, 1998). Programs for deaf and hard of hearing children serve fewer White and Black students but substantially more Hispanic and Asian/Pacific Islanders. In fact, the rate of Hispanic students identified as having hearing losses has more than doubled since 1974; a rate greater than the rate of increased Hispanic population in the United States (Andrews & Martin, 1998). What is of great concern is that some of these students are not diagnosed and are not identified before the age of 4 and often are not provided with hearing aids (Walker-Vann, 1998). Being without services during the early years has long-term negative effects that often cannot be overcome.

CAUSES AND PREVENTION

For more about these early controversies, see the "History of the Field" section of this chapter.

It is not a surprise to learn that hearing loss can result from illness or injury. For example, sustained loud noise can cause a hearing loss. In addition, some types of deafness are the result of heredity. This was the reason why Alexander Graham Bell, in the late 1800s, proposed legislation to ban marriage between two deaf people; fortunately, he was unsuccessful. For educators, understanding the causes of hearing loss can be useful, for the type of loss can have a bearing on the accommodations necessary for effective instruction. For everyone, knowing how to prevent hearing loss or minimize its effects is important.

What can cause a hearing loss?

CMV is also discussed in the "Prevalence" and the "Causes and Prevention" sections in Chapter 9.

The five most common causes for deafness and hearing problems are listed at the end of this section. However, the "cause" associated with the largest group of children with hearing loss is "unknown," accounting for well over half of the cases of childhood deafness (Gallaudet Research Institute, 1998). As more and more causes are identified, it is likely that heredity and genetics will be found to account for most of the hearing losses currently in the "unknown" category.

Of course, other causes of hearing problems fall outside of these groups. For example, we now know that congenital cytomegalovirus (CMV) infection, a herpes virus, affects about 2 percent of all newborns and can cause mild to profound sensorineural hearing losses and other disabilities as well. At present, no vaccine or cure is available to prevent or treat CMV; however, avoiding persons affected with the virus, ensuring the safety of blood used in transfusions, and good hygiene are important preventive measures (Gallaudet Research Institute, 1998). Let's look at five known, major causes of hearing problems.

CHAPTER 10 *Deafness and Hard of Hearing*

1. **Hereditary conditions** are the most common known causes of deafness and profound hearing loss in children. Genetic causes can be documented as being responsible for more than 150 different types of deafness. As time goes on, it is likely that more "unknown causes" will be identified as having a hereditary origin. Genetic causes can be both congenital and sensorineural. Most children whose deafness is inherited are less likely to have multiple disabilities.

2. **Meningitis,** the second most common known cause of deafness in children, is a disease that affects the central nervous system (specifically the meninges, the coverings of the brain and spinal cord, and their circulating fluid). Most cases that involve a hearing loss are bacterial infections rather than the more lethal viral meningitis. This disease is the most common cause of postnatal deafness in schoolchildren and is one major cause of profound sensorineural hearing losses that are not present at birth. These individuals' hearing losses are acquired, and they may have developed some speech and language before they developed the hearing loss. Vaccines do exist that will prevent the disease, but at present there is no national immunization program for meningitis.

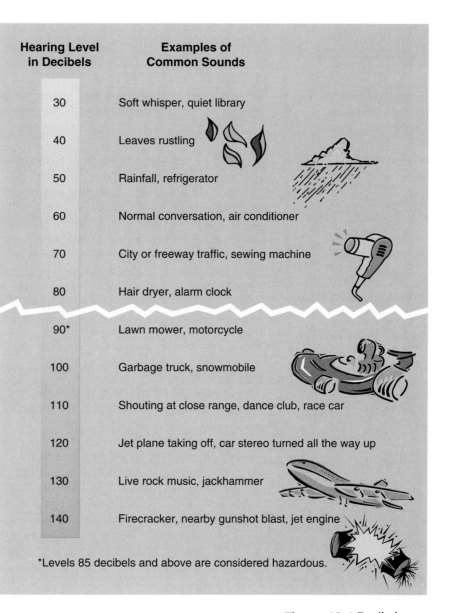

Hearing Level in Decibels	Examples of Common Sounds
30	Soft whisper, quiet library
40	Leaves rustling
50	Rainfall, refrigerator
60	Normal conversation, air conditioner
70	City or freeway traffic, sewing machine
80	Hair dryer, alarm clock
90*	Lawn mower, motorcycle
100	Garbage truck, snowmobile
110	Shouting at close range, dance club, race car
120	Jet plane taking off, car stereo turned all the way up
130	Live rock music, jackhammer
140	Firecracker, nearby gunshot blast, jet engine

*Levels 85 decibels and above are considered hazardous.

Figure 10.4 Decibel Levels of Noise in American Environments
Source: U.S. Congress Select Committee on Children, Youth, and Families.

M**AKING**
C**ONNECTIONS**

For other disabilities that have known hereditary origins, see the "Causes and Prevention" sections of Chapters 4, 6, and 9.

3. **Otitis media** is an infection of the middle ear and an accumulation of fluid behind the eardrum. The condition can be corrected and treated with antibiotics and other medical procedures. If sustained for long periods of time or not detected in very young children, the condition may result in a language impairment that could affect future academic learning. Chronic otitis media can cause a conductive hearing loss by damaging the eardrum and in about 84 percent of such cases results in a mild to moderate hearing loss. Typically these youngsters are hard of hearing, and they profit from hearing aids because their hearing loss is conductive.

4. **Maternal rubella** (German measles), once a major cause of deafness in newborns, has been dramatically reduced in prevalence (from 10.6 percent of known causes in 1972 to 1 percent in 1998). Because vaccines are available to prevent women of childbearing age from contracting this disease, the incidence of deafness caused by maternal rubella has declined dramatically and could be eliminated. Maternal rubella is contracted by a pregnant woman and is devastating to an unborn child. Depending on when the expectant mother contracts the virus, the child may be born with a profound hearing loss, a visual disability, or other disabilities alone or in combinations. Like other congenital hearing losses (those

AKING
CONNECTIONS

To review an account of how even a mild case of maternal rubella can seriously affect an unborn child, re-read Susan story's at the beginning of this chapter.

present at birth), those caused by maternal rubella are typically sensorineural, with damage to the inner ear or the auditory nerve. The children affected are prelingually deaf.

5. **Noise** has not traditionally been included as a major cause of hearing loss, but employers, federal agencies, and researchers are becoming more aware of its dangers. It is now known that noise is the major cause of hearing loss in this country (Dawson, 1997), but it is unclear how many children are affected. Although European countries take legal steps to ensure noise abatement, the United States seems to be getting noisier. The U.S. Occupational Safety and Health Administration (OSHA) has set standards indicating that exposure to noise louder than 105 dB for longer than an hour is unhealthful, and some believe that this level is way too high (Koran & Oliva, 1997). Imagine the damage caused by the sound levels of a rock concert (which often reach 125 dB), a car stereo, or a personal tape player. Indications are that young males are more likely to acquire noise-induced hearing losses because they frequently engage in activities such as mowing the lawn, firing a gun, riding a motorcycle, and fixing a car engine. Even infants and toddlers can sustain irreversible noise-induced hearing losses. Hearing loss from noise occurs without any pain or notice and accumulates slowly across years of exposure. Figure 10.4 shows what sounds are considered in the danger zone.

Can some hearing losses be corrected or prevented?

The answer, of course, is yes. In some cases, the steps needed for prevention are simple; in other cases, complicated medical technology is required. In many cases, no preventive measures exist today. One cause that can be prevented—noise—requires only some simple measures. People can wear ear protectors when they are around loud sounds. Another preventive measure is to have makers of personal stereos, power lawn mowers, and other noisy equipment install noise-limiting devices or graphic warning lights on their products. Although many preventive measures are simple and seem to be "common sense," other measures are complicated and costly. In the following sections, you will learn how early detection, medical technology, and public awareness can reduce the number of individuals with hearing loss. And for those whose hearing loss cannot be prevented, many preventive measures can lessen the impact.

AKING
CONNECTIONS

Review the two earlier sections on universal screening in the "Defined" section of this chapter.

• *Early Detection* Universal screening of newborns for hearing losses is now reliable, cost-effective, and a reality in 36 states and Washington, DC (ASHA, 2002). Early detection is critical because very young children with significant hearing losses who receive early intervention services have much better outcomes than those who do not (Magnuson, 2000). Children identified before they are 6 months old experience half the delays of those identified after they are 18 months old (Yoshinaga-Itano & Apuzzo, 1998). When children with cognitive impairments are removed from the analysis, the deaf and hard of hearing children who were identified early perform at nearly the same level as children without hearing losses. In states where universal screening is not implemented, even children with profound deafness are not typically identified until they are 2½ years old, and early intervention often does not begin until a year later. The impact of universal screening is tremendous and positively affects many individuals and their families. The personal and financial costs of not identifying children early are great. ASHA (2002) estimates that the lifetime cost of each case of congenital deafness is over $1,000,000. They also maintain that the relatively low costs of new universal screening and early intervention are a good investment.

• *Medical Technology* Medical technology can be used to prevent conditions and diseases that result in significant hearing loss. Medical technology can also be used

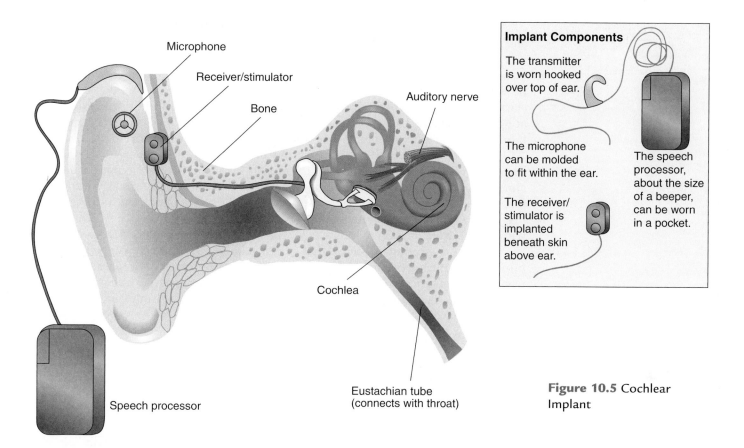

Microphone

Receiver/stimulator

Bone

Auditory nerve

Cochlea

Eustachian tube
(connects with throat)

Speech processor

Implant Components

The transmitter is worn hooked over top of ear.

The microphone can be molded to fit within the ear.

The receiver/stimulator is implanted beneath skin above ear.

The speech processor, about the size of a beeper, can be worn in a pocket.

Figure 10.5 Cochlear Implant

to treat or cure damaged or impaired hearing mechanisms in cases where hearing loss has already occurred. Here are a few examples of medical technology in action.

Some infections can cause hearing loss but, if diagnosed and treated early, do not result in deafness or significant hearing problems. In other words, sometimes hearing loss resulting from infection can be prevented. Most hearing problems that involve the middle ear (e.g., conductive hearing losses) can be either treated medically or corrected surgically. For example, delicate surgical procedures can repair or replace poorly functioning small bones in the middle ear. And yet another example is the laser treatment, OtoLAM, that may become the method customarily used to drain fluid from babies' ears, reducing the number of cases where tubes need to be surgically inserted (Marsa, 1999).

Approved by the U.S. Federal Food and Drug Administration in 1990, **cochlear implants** were once thought to be able to "cure" deafness. To many, the great hope was that cochlear implants would be bionic ears, whereas many in the Deaf community, feared that cochlear implants would make Deaf culture obsolete. Neither outcome—a cure for deafness or a real threat to the Deaf community—is occurring (Easterbrooks & Mordica, 2000). Many members of the Deaf community vehemently oppose cochlear implants, particularly for children (Laborit, 1998; Lane, 1995). This hard-line position, however, is softening because some are beginning to view implants as they view hearing aids: an acceptable means of gaining access to the hearing culture, "helping them enlarge their scope of awareness without destroying their identities as deaf people" (Johnson, 2000, p. 7). Possibly, there is another reason why the conflict between the medical and Deaf communities is subsiding. Despite earlier assumptions that young children with implants should grow up in an oral-only environment, data now have shown that these children make greater progress in language, communication, and later academic achievement when they are taught to communicate using both sign and oral language (Christiansen & Leigh, 2002; Peters, 2000).

What is involved in a cochlear implant? The cochlear implant procedure involves an incision made behind the ear; when that heals, a wire is wound through the cochlea. The wire is connected to a very small receiver that is placed under the skin behind the ear; then wire and receiver are connected to a small computer, which can be worn on a belt. In the hearing process, the computer detects sound and sends electrical signals to the implanted receiver, which stimulates the auditory nerve, creating sound. Figure 10.5 shows a typical cochlear implant, which converts acoustic information to electrical signals that stimulate the remaining auditory nerve fibers.

Cochlear implants have not proved to be bionic ears, nor do they cure deafness. The results from cochlear implants are mixed; for some they are reported to be almost miraculous, but for others they do not result in useable hearing. What factors might influence whether implants work well? First, it is important to recognize that no pre-implant predictors reliably help parents and doctors decide which child will benefit from implants and which will not (Owens, Metz, & Haas, 2000). Second, it is important to know that it can take years before implants actually provide their intended benefits, because the brain has to learn to translate the electronic impulses generated by implants into meaningful messages (Marschark, 2001). Some specific factors may account for the huge differences in implant outcomes across individuals (Lundy, 1997):

- Age at the time of implantation
- Length of time the individual was deaf
- How long the implant has been worn
- The communication mode of the individual
- Whether the person knew speech before becoming deaf

For children, results seem to be better when the child receives the implant before the age of five; therefore, younger and younger children are now receiving implants (Alexander Graham Bell Association, 2002). But regardless of age, not everyone with implants is able to translate the impulses received into meaningful messages. This may be why almost half of prelingually deaf children who have received implants have stopped using them altogether (Easterbrooks & Mordica, 2000). Another reason may be that it can take years of practice (anywhere from 6 months to 2 years) and lots of effort to glean meaning from the impulses received from the implants. Effective cochlear implants have many benefits. Speech and language can noticeably improve (Kluwin & Stewart, 2000; McCaffrey et al., 2000). Improved reading achievement is another benefit (Pisoni et al., 1999; Spencer, Tomblin, & Gantz, 1997). However, new concerns about implants have arisen. For example, people with implants are at greater risk for meningitis, which has caused the death of two toddlers with implants (Associated Press, 2002).

What medical technology is on the horizon? Work is being done to approve the sale of already developed middle ear implants (surgically implanted hearing aids). Several kinds of these implants have been developed, but their purpose is to cause the middle ear bones to vibrate and thereby transmit sound to the inner ear (Chasin, 2000). In some versions, the entire aid is implanted; others require that the microphone and amplifier be worn externally. Other research efforts will not yield results that can be applied for pubic benefit for many years to come. Here's an example. About 80 percent of irreversible hearing loss is caused by damage to the hair cells in the inner ear. Consensus among researchers has been that in mammals, these cells do not regenerate; however, researchers recently found that in chickens, hair cells can regenerate (Wyngate, 2001). This finding has led other researchers to explore the possibility of using stem cells to trigger the growth of new, working hair cells in humans (Gregoret, 2002).

- *Increased Public Awareness* The impact of some conditions that lead to severe hearing loss can be reduced with early identification and intervention. Otitis media

CHAPTER 10 *Deafness and Hard of Hearing*

is one example. In some cases, medical treatment can halt damage to the hearing mechanism, and when damage cannot be prevented, early intervention can make a significant difference in the individual's overall outcomes, not only in terms of expressive and receptive language abilities, but also in terms of overall development and lower levels of family stress (Calderon & Naidu, 2000; Drasgow, 1998).

A more knowledgeable public, availability of good health care for all children, and better-prepared preschool teachers can prevent some hearing losses and provide treatment for others. All parents need to understand the importance of proper immunization. For example, although the number of children with hearing problems due to maternal rubella has been reduced drastically, this disease has not been eliminated. The public needs to be continually reminded of the importance of immunizations. Public service advertisements on television help remind parents and the public about the importance of protecting young children from disease.

CHARACTERISTICS

Deaf and hard of hearing children cannot be stereotyped. They are individuals with different learning styles and abilities, but they do share one characteristic: Their ability to hear is limited. As we have noted, the severity of the hearing loss and the age at which the loss occurred determine how well a person will be able to interact with others orally. Another factor is whether the individual has cognitive impairments along with the hearing loss. Estimates are that at least 25 percent of deaf and hard of hearing children have additional disabilities (Karchmer & Allen, 1999). Additional disabilities may include visual disabilities, mental retardation, learning disabilities, behavior disorders, or cerebral palsy. These accompanying disabilities are often caused by the same disease or accident that caused the hearing loss. For example, rubella (German measles), blood type (Rh) incompatibility between mother and child, and trauma at birth often result in more than one disability. Students whose deafness is inherited tend not to have multiple disabilities. Clearly, for whatever reason, students who cannot hear the communications of others well have a more difficult time learning through traditional instructional methods.

How does Deaf culture influence the lives of Deaf individuals?

Deaf persons may be Deaf or deaf, depending on whether they use ASL and associate with **Deaf culture** and the Deaf community. Many consider the Deaf a minority group, much like ethnic and racial minorities in this country (Drasgow, 1998; Lane,

MAKING **C**ONNECTIONS

For more about multiple disabilities, see those sections in Chapter 13.

MAKING **C**ONNECTIONS

For a review of the differences between being handicapped and having a disability, see "Disabilities Defined" section of Chapter 1.

Using American Sign Language, wooden hands spell out "ASD 185" to celebrate the 185th anniversary of the American School for the Deaf in West Hartford, Connecticut. This is the nation's oldest school for deaf and hard of hearing students.

Characteristics

A deaf troupe of dancers from China tours the United States. Deaf theater groups perform throughout America, and deaf students refine their acting abilities in school plays as young hearing actors do. Many Deaf theater productions express Deaf culture and are performed using American Sign Language.

MAKING CONNECTIONS

For a review of the Deaf President Now Movement, see the "History" section in this chapter.

MAKING CONNECTIONS

To refresh your memory about the Deaf communities on Martha's Vineyard, read again the "Disability Does Not Equal Handicap" box in Chapter 1.

1995). There are many concepts and nuances to understand when learning about the culture of the Deaf; it is important that teachers understand and respect every student's home culture.

Deafness is viewed in different ways by different individuals and groups. Many hearing people consider deafness a disability, a pathological condition. To many Deaf people, however, deafness is one aspect binding a minority group together, a minority group rich in culture, history, language, and the arts. The language of the Deaf community is **American Sign Language (ASL),** a language that uses signs, has all of the elements (grammar, syntax, idioms) of other languages, and is not parallel to English in either structure or word order. ASL is not a mere translation of oral speech or the English language (as is **Signed English**); it is a fully developed language. In fact, many states allow ASL as an option to meet the high school foreign language requirement, and the same is true at many colleges and universities. As the language of the Deaf community, ASL is used in all aspects of their culture. For example, plays are written in ASL and performed by deaf theater groups around the world, and a base of folk literature has also developed over the years. This community unites in many ways by coming together socially and for the purpose of advocacy, such as when they began the Deaf President Now Movement in 1988.

For many deaf people, being Deaf of Deaf (being born Deaf of Deaf parents), or even a CODA (Child of a Deaf Adult) is a source of considerable pride (Soloman, 1994). Although they clearly represent a minority within a minority, life can be substantially easier for these individuals. They learn sign language as their native language, which they develop naturally just as hearing babies develop oral language. These children are not preoccupied by their deafness but, rather, are engaged in childhood and play (Sheridan, 2001). For these individuals, their deafness is a language difference, not a disability (Drasgow, 1998; Lane, 1995). They are much like those who grew up in the Deaf communities that thrived on Martha's Vineyard during the 1800s (Groce, 1985; Kageleiry, 2002). Because everyone on the island of Martha's Vineyard at that time knew sign language (a precursor to ASL), the Deaf there were not handicapped by their inability to hear or communicate orally. Most of these individuals consider themselves part of the Deaf community and are active in its activities and clubs, attend Deaf Theater, travel in groups, use ASL as their language, and believe that it is important to learn about their culture. Of course, for those who became deaf later in life, do not know ASL, and live in the hearing world, deafness is a disability—one that disconnects them from friends and family. For these people, there is no debate: Deafness is a disability.

What is different in the situation of the Deaf is that only about 5 percent of these individuals were born of Deaf parents and learn ASL as their native language. The vast majority of others are assimilated into the culture later in life, often at residential schools for the Deaf (Fletcher, 1994). What about the majority of the prelingually deaf? Recall that 95 percent of deaf children are born of hearing parents. Many of these youngsters do not develop language (either aural or manual) at the time when they should developmentally, which can be devastating to the individual's development of cognitive and social skills. The challenges for these youngsters

The wonderful and engaging story of Dina, the Deaf dinosaur, teaches the importance and acceptance of ASL to those who use it as their primary language.

and their families are great. Many parents are afraid that if their children learn ASL as their first language, they will be excluded from mainstream society, seek out the Deaf community, and be lost to their natural family (Goldberg, 1995).

How can deafness and hearing loss influence academic achievement?

A long-term problem for deaf individuals is their academic achievement, particularly in the area of reading (Gallaudet Research Institute, 1994; Johnson, 2001–2002; Moores, 2001). For example, by age 20, half of the students tested read below the mid-fourth-grade level, leaving them unable to read most newspapers, which are written at least at the fifth-grade level. Of deaf high school graduates, 15 percent of White students, 6 percent of Black graduates, and 5 percent of Latinos/as could read above the sixth-grade level (Goldin-Meadow & Mayberry, 2001). These outcomes may well improve with earlier identification and intervention and with new approaches, such as bilingual/bicultural instruction (Marschark, 2001). However, today, even for deaf students attending college, educators are concerned about their reading comprehension skills (Kelly, Albertini, & Shannon, 2001). Evidently, these college students tend to pay more attention to the words they are reading than to the meaning of the text. To improve this situation, educators suggest that students:

1. Focus on the text's meaning rather than on vocabulary
2. Identify main ideas
3. Think about related knowledge
4. Practice with "real" textbooks
5. Think about the whole message

Reading and literacy have become major concerns, so in recent years, literacy and academic achievement have received increased attention from teachers and researchers. And deaf children's reading performance has been improving. This is due in part to new instructional methods and also to early intervention efforts (Calderon & Naidu, 2000). Also, more motivation might exist for deaf people to learn to read. Many technological advances developed to benefit people with hearing loss, such as captioned television and films, require an ability to read well, for instance.

Bestowing Rewards Rather than Inflicting Punishment

Teresa was 8 years old and attended a neighborhood school. She did very well learning English but had much left to learn. She had been in school for only three years and had not yet mastered her new language. She was able to converse with her peers and teachers, express her feelings, and—with periodic assistance from a bilingual paraprofessional—learn academic subjects. Members of her multidisciplinary team disagreed about Teresa's level of English proficiency. Some of the confusion stemmed from her difficulties with oral speech and how intelligible her speech was to others. Teresa was a quick learner, but her moderate hearing loss limited her receptive language abilities. Like many immigrant children, she was not diagnosed early and also did not get hearing aids soon after she was diagnosed. When Teresa was 4 years old, the family's social worker suspected a problem and referred her to a local clinic, where her hearing loss was discovered. After months of delays, Teresa was fitted with hearing aids.

Teresa had great difficulties getting along with her classmates. She accused them of being unfair to her, and they felt that she did not take turns either on the playground or in group activities. Her peers accused her of being demanding and short-tempered. Her teacher, Ms. Tomas, set up a system where Teresa lost privileges for misbehavior, arguments, and bursts of temper. The result was that Teresa remained inside for most recesses and lunch breaks and was always the last to leave the classroom. Her behavior worsened as she became more frustrated. The "behavior specialist" for Teresa's school, Ms. Garcia, was a special education teacher who served on the IEP teams for children with behavior problems. Ms. Garcia had not been part of Teresa's multidisciplinary team but asked if she could help resolve the growing crisis. Ms. Garcia discussed the situation with Teresa and also talked with her classmates separately. Teresa felt that the punishment was unfair and that everything at school was unfair. Her classmates agreed; most believed the punishment

system arranged was too harsh. Instead, they suggested that Teresa earn privileges (not lose them) for getting along and for talking about events that frustrated her. They further suggested that Teresa earn privileges for asking questions when she did not understand the rules of a game. They also thought that they should earn rewards for including Teresa in games that she "ruined." Once the behavior management program was perceived as fair by all, Teresa's interactions with her classmates became positive.

Being Fair When Implementing Behavior Management Systems

- Consider the current functioning levels of the student.
- Include the target student when setting consequences for inappropriate behavior.
- Seek suggestions from classmates about behaviors of concern and how they should be handled.
- Monitor behavior patterns to be certain that positive outcomes result from interventions.

MAKING CONNECTIONS

For a review of communicative competence and speech and language development, see Chapter 5.

How does deafness affect individuals' speech abilities?

Being able to hear is related to the ability to speak intelligibly. When comparing two groups of children between the ages of five and ten—those with profound hearing loss and those with mild to severe hearing loss—the case is clear. The speech of those with profound losses was not intelligible. For those with mild to severe losses, 82 percent were intelligible (Yoshinaga-Itano & Sedey, 2000). What makes the difference? Intelligibility of speech is related to a number of factors:

- Degree of hearing loss
- Age of the individual
- Communication mode used by the family
- Presence of another disability

Being able to understand someone's speech is also partly determined by the listener's experience (Most, Weisel, & Lev-Matzky, 1996). The resulting inconsistency in the ability to understand the speaker is one reason why data about the intelligibility of deaf children's speech is confusing. Unfortunately, a relationship also exists between a person's speech ability and the way the person is perceived by others: As ratings of intelligibility go down, ratings of cognitive competence and personality decline. Learning to speak is a difficult and arduous task for children who are deaf, requiring years of effort and systematic instruction. Because it is so easy to misjudge the intentions and actions of students who have difficulty communicating, teachers must be careful not to interpret deaf students' behaviors harshly. The "Achieving Discipline" box provides an example of how a situation that a deaf child thought was unfair was turned into a learning situation. We all need to be careful not to judge people unfairly. Clearly, judging a person's abilities and character on the basis of how well he or she can speak is an example of how *not* to make decisions about a person.

EARLY CHILDHOOD EDUCATION

Early intervention positively affects the lifelong outcomes of deaf and hard of hearing children (Marschark, 2001; Yoshinaga-Itano & Sedy, 2000). Obviously, early identification is a prerequisite to early intervention, and now with more and more states requiring hearing screening for all newborns, the promise of early childhood programs is more of a reality for these children and their families. Why are early identification and the resulting intervention so important?

M AKING
  C ONNECTIONS

To review how language typically develops, see the sections on language impairments in the "Defined" section of Chapter 5.

1. Early identification allows children to be fitted with hearing aids as soon as possible, which can be as early as four weeks old.

2. Early intervention, before the age of six months, pays off in better reading achievement and speech abilities in later years.

3. Preschool programs allow deaf and hard of hearing students to develop language at the right periods of their lives.

4. Early intervention programs also help families better understand and meet the very special needs of their deaf family members.

Evidence connecting language development and academic achievement for deaf children is mounting. You just learned that deaf and hard of hearing students have significantly low academic achievement. New research indicates that this outcome can be avoided (Marschark, 2001; Yoshinaga-Itano & Apuzzo, 1998). Deaf children of deaf parents learn sign language during their infancy. For those of them without cognitive impairment, by the time they reach school age, they are reading at two grade levels above deaf children of hearing parents (Marschark, 1993). This difference occurs because these children of deaf parents learned language during the proper developmental period, whereas most deaf children of hearing parents are not identified until age 3—an age when language development should be well under way. Building upon findings from earlier studies, new research supports great optimism. When deaf children learn sign language during infancy, they develop communication skills "on time," and when they then receive instruction that is in their "native" language, they are able to read and write at about the same level as their hearing classmates (Andrews et al., 1997).

Children learn and practice many skills through imaginary play. Dolls, like this signing Barbie, that reflect one's culture and language can send important messages about approval to children.

VALIDATED PRACTICES
Just Plain Common Sense

What Are Just Plain Common Sense Instructional Practices?

Simple, inexpensive, down-to-earth teaching methods can help deaf or hard of hearing students become successful in the general education curriculum. In other words, complicated or expensive procedures are not always required. Also, you are not expected to be familiar with every possible modification or accommodation. Rather, rely on the assistance of a teacher of the deaf and hard of hearing and/or on a deaf interpreter. Their jobs are to help you make the proper adjustments to the classroom routine, instructional procedures, or curriculum.

Why Just Plain Common Sense Instructional Practices Are Beneficial

Deaf and hard of hearing students often need help to learn effectively in the general education setting. Most of these students do not have multiple disabilities and profit greatly from the general education experience when proper, simple modifications are made.

Implementing Classroom Modifications

Hearing loss can range from a mild deficit to complete deafness. Many students have hearing problems that place them at a disadvantage, particularly when participating in group instruction.

Listening

Excessive background noise is often a problem for students with hearing loss. Here are some suggestions you can use to alleviate some background noise:

- Have a rug in your classroom. If the floors are bare, put tennis balls on the bottom of chair legs.
- Make sure your heating/cooling system and lights are in good working condition so they are as quiet as possible.
- Decrease sound vibration with curtains or blinds on windows.

Many hearing families, once their child's deafness is identified, choose to learn and use some combination of oral language and a manual communication system so that they can communicate more fully with their child. Some professionals (Drasgow, 1998) propose that infants and their families be taught ASL so that these children can acquire it as their "native" language. However, it is important to recognize that, like mastering any second language, becoming fluent in ASL is no easy task (Kemp, 1998). Once universal screening is available across the nation, all infants—even those without risk factors—will be screened for hearing losses, and those found to have hearing loss will be able to benefit from early intervention and, it is hoped, will be able to follow a course of language development similar to that of their hearing peers. Like deaf children of deaf parents, they would use their hands to babble at about the same time that hearing infants make babbling sounds. They would produce two-word utterances at about the same time as their hearing brothers and sisters but would probably learn English as a second language.

ELEMENTARY THROUGH HIGH SCHOOL

Differences in the way hard of hearing and deaf students are taught can be dramatic. For example 43 percent of hard of hearing students are taught using the oral-only approach and do not use sign language. The majority of deaf and hard of hearing students, 51 percent, use a combination of sign and speech, and only 5 percent use ASL (Gallaudet Research Institute, 1998). In this section, those differences, along with specific educational options for both deaf and hard of hearing students, are discussed.

- Seat students where they can see everyone who may be speaking.
- Seat students away from air conditioners, pencil sharpeners, computer centers, and any other areas with high noise levels.
- Do not seat deaf or hard of hearing students in a "special area" away from their peers.

Instructional Tips

These simple, easy-to-implement strategies can benefit all students:

- Seat your students where they can see everyone who may be speaking.
- Be alert to classroom noise and seek to reduce it.
- Use visual displays (e.g., graphic organizers, story maps, semantic features analyses) in your teaching. Give specific directions, and be sure to ask your students to clarify what you have said.
- Define key vocabulary words slowly and carefully.
- Use manipulatives to explain math concepts.
- Show multimedia presentations with subtitles.
- Have students share their notes.

- Use maps, globes, and charts to demonstrate key concepts.
- Use familiar, concrete objects and examples when presenting abstract concepts.
- Provide students with ample opportunities for discussion.
- Teach and practice using elaboration (e.g., provide analogies, paraphrase material, identify main ideas, summarize key points).

Speaking

- Be aware of your pace, and slow down if students appear to be confused.
- Keep your hands away from your face when speaking.
- Always face deaf and hard of hearing students when speaking.
- Keep the use of figurative language to a minimum.

This scientifically validated practice is a teaching method proven by systematic research efforts. (DiSarno, Schowalter, & Grassa, 2002; Kaderavek, & Pakulski, 2002; Luetke-Stahlman, 1999). Full citations are found in the "Elementary Through High School" section of the references for this chapter.

What instructional accommodations are needed by many hard of hearing students?

MAKING CONNECTIONS

For more about technology that assists deaf and hard of hearing people, see the "Technology" section of this chapter.

Since the advent of PL 94-142 in 1975, more and more deaf and hard of hearing students have been educated in general education classes with generally positive results, particularly for hard of hearing students (Easterbrooks, 1999). Remember that most students with hearing loss can hear satisfactorily with amplification (that is, a hearing aid) and therefore can attend school and function well with their nondisabled classmates. In most schools, information is presented orally, and students learn through a combination of textbooks, lectures, and class discussions. Teachers can help students with hearing problems gain better access to the general education curriculum and participate in class activities by incorporating some simple features to their instruction (see the "Validated Practices" box for some examples). Most hard of hearing children can cope quite well with these methods as long as an array of supplemental services, supports, accommodations, and assistance are available.

Along with acquiring educational benefits, many students learn important social skills in general classroom settings. However, teachers should not assume that social acceptance goes hand in hand with general education placements. Unfortunately, research findings indicate otherwise: Normally, hearing peers tend not to exhibit high social acceptance of deaf or hard of hearing classmates (Antia & Kreimeyer, 1996). Teachers must be proactive, helping to foster good peer relationships among all their students.

With certain modifications to the environment, deaf and hard of hearing students benefit from general education class placements. A number of simple techniques and procedures can help students profit in oral communication situations; some of these methods are listed in the "Accommodating for Inclusive

ACCOMMODATING FOR INCLUSIVE ENVIRONMENTS

Modifying the Delivery of Instruction

1. Place the child as close to the speaker as possible.

2. Make certain the child's hearing aid is turned on and functioning properly by listening through it.

3. Reduce the background noise as much as possible.

4. Articulate clearly, but do not talk louder unless you have an unusually soft voice.

5. Make certain to have the student's attention before talking or starting a lesson.

6. Do not exaggerate your lip movements.

7. Do not chew gum or cover your mouth when talking.

8. Do not turn your back to the class.

9. Use an overhead projector instead of a blackboard so that the student can see your mouth.

10. Avoid moving around the classroom while talking.

11. Speak slowly.

12. Repeat and restate information by paraphrasing.

13. Spend time talking to the child alone so that you become accustomed to each other's speech.

14. Avoid glare when talking or signing by not standing near a light source such as a window.

15. Do not bounce or move around while talking.

16. Bend down so that you are at students' eye level when you talk to individuals or small groups.

17. Use class handouts to convey important information from lectures, guest speakers, field trips, and instructional films.

18. Ask classmates to volunteer to be peer assistants, possibly one classmate per class, unit, or topic.

19. Ask classmates to rotate as note takers who make an extra set of lecture notes by using carbon paper as they write, thus freeing the deaf student to watch the teacher more closely.

20. Consult with a certified teacher of the deaf.

Environments" box. Another modification to the classroom routine is to provide handouts listing important points from lectures, films, or movies. Also, a classmate can be asked to help by using carbon paper to make an extra set of lecture notes.

Teachers should seek the help of specialists and others who can provide guidance in making the learning environment as effective as possible for all students in the class. For example, classroom teachers have found that the SLP assigned to their school can offer many good ideas about activities that foster better speech and language. The specialist can also provide suggestions about classroom organizers that will help these students gain more from traditional classroom settings. Parents are another important source of information. The child's parents can help teachers come to a better understanding of their child's preferred learning styles and special needs. For instance, one child might profit from having a classmate serve as a resource to ensure that homework and other assignments are correctly understood. Another child might prefer to tape lectures and listen to them carefully in a quiet setting at home in the evening. Yet another student might benefit from being able to do extra outside reading on specific topics. Teachers must remember that each child is unique and must capitalize on each child's strengths, not just attend to that student's disabilities.

What special instructional methods have been developed for deaf students?

Best educational practices for deaf students are still developing. Overall, deaf students' academic achievement is improving, but more progress must be made. One factor that makes a difference is the communication system used to convey instruction. Generally, four different approaches are used to deliver instruction to deaf children:

1. The **oral-only approach** (or speech) teaches children to use as much of their residual hearing as possible. This method was the most popular for deaf students until the 1970s, and a few programs still use it. Using amplification, children learn how to speech-read (lip-read) and how to speak. The oral approach does not allow children to use any form of manual communication such as finger spelling or signing. In fact, even natural signing, such as using gestures, is discouraged. Those who follow the oral approach believe that individuals who are deaf must live and work in a world where most people hear normally and communicate through oral expression. This is the method typically used with children who have cochlear implants, and of course it is the method used in general education classes with most hard of hearing students.

2. The **total communication approach** incorporates aspects of both oral speech and **manual communication** (signing). Total communication allows the child to communicate through whatever mode is easiest and most effective. The philosophy behind this approach is that every child should be able to use whatever channels are available to learn and comprehend messages. About 72 percent of deaf students are now taught using this method (Moores, 2001), as are about 51 percent of all deaf and hard of hearing students (Gallaudet Research Institute, 1998).

3. **Cued speech** uses hand signals to accompany oral speech. These hand signals help deaf people read lips to determine, for example, whether the word spoken was *pan* or *bat,* which look alike to the person reading lips (Roffé, 2000). Cued speech is popular with hearing parents because it is easy to learn and follows the format and structure of the English language (which ASL does not).

4. The **bilingual–bicultural approach,** the newest method, is gaining popularity and research verification (Easterbrook & Baker, 2002; Stewart, 1997). Research findings indicate that achievement levels for many deaf youngsters exposed to this approach are close to those of their hearing peers (Andrews et al., 1997; Easterbrooks, 1999; Marschark, 2001).

Although you might hear a lot about ASL, it is important to recognize that most elementary and secondary school teachers of the deaf do not use ASL. Only about 5 percent of teachers of the deaf use ASL in their school classes (Gallaudet Research Institute, 1998). About 55 percent of deaf and hard of hearing students are taught through a combination of sign and speech, but the sign language used is not typically ASL. Often, a type of manual communication that more closely matches the grammatical form and structure of standard English is used. **Finger spelling,** a form of manual communication different from ASL, assigns each letter of the alphabet a sign. This system is efficient and has been used for centuries; an accomplished person can finger-spell at a rate equivalent to that of typical speech. Signed English uses finger spelling exclusively to translate English: Words are spelled out, but the rules of grammar and language are the same as for English speech. Finger spelling is often used along with ASL when no sign exists for a word or name.

MAKING CONNECTIONS

For another look at bilingual special education methods, reread the "Elementary Through High School" section in Chapter 3.

What content areas need special attention?

As you have learned, the poor academic achievement of deaf and hard of hearing students is a concern. In particular, these students' low levels of reading ability must be improved, not only because literacy is important to everyone, but also because being able to read makes it possible to comprehend **captions** (e.g., text translations of the audio portions of films and TV shows. Viewing TV captions requires being able to read between 100 and 180 words per minute (Jensema, Danturthi, and Burch, 2000). Despite the definite motivation associated with captions, developing these high levels of proficiency is hard to obtain.

Table 10.1 Placement and IEP Considerations

	Type of Hearing Loss	
	Hard of Hearing	**Deaf**
Severity of loss	Youngsters with mild to moderate hearing loss can remain in the general education curriculum with consultative or supportive services from various experts such as SLPs and audiologists.	Students with severe to profound hearing loss require intensive instruction in communication skills and need assistance from an array of related services.
Potential for using residual hearing	Most of these students profit from hearing aids, thereby allowing them to benefit, with some adaptations, from typical oral methods of instruction.	Most deaf students have little useful residual hearing and require considerable accommodations to benefit from oral instructions.
Academic achievement	The academic achievement levels of deaf and hard of hearing students tend to be lower than levels of their hearing peers. Students with less hearing loss and no multiple disabilities are usually close to grade level but might need some additional academic instruction.	The academic achievement levels of deaf students are considerably below those of their hearing peers. These students need considerable instruction in basic language and communication skills, as well as intensive academic remediation.
Communicative needs	Many of these students go undetected for a long time. If the loss occurred before or during the youngsters' development of language, it is likely that they will require SLP services as well as academic assistance.	Total communication is the most commonly used approach with deaf youngsters, but the help of educational assistants is necessary, and in many rural regions this expertise is not available.
Preferred mode of communication	Most of these students should be expected to become proficient using oral language.	Most postlingually deaf students learn (or retain) their use of oral language. Intelligible speech and lipreading are typically unattainable goals for most prelingually deaf children, so for them manual communication is preferred.
Placement preference	The vast majority of these students attend their neighborhood schools with their hearing peers.	Many deaf students also attend their neighborhood schools. However, a significant number of them prefer center schools where their classmates share their deafness and their mode of communication.

COLLABORATION FOR INCLUSION

MAKING CONNECTIONS

For a review of the array of professionals who work with special education students, see the Special Educational Services section of Chapter 2.

At the national level, a full array of educational services and placements is available for deaf and hard of hearing elementary and secondary students. These educational programs typically include the services of audiologists, SLPs, interpreters, teachers of the deaf, and, for those with multiple disabilities, OTs and PTs. Nationally, placement options include general education classrooms, resource rooms, special classes, special day schools, and residential center schools. When thinking about school placements, the types of accommodations needed by these students, and the professionals who are brought together to form multidisciplinary teams, remember that the educational needs of every student with hearing loss are unique. School placements and methods of instruction are also determined for individual students and their families (Luetke-Stahlman, 1998). And, most important, these decisions must be reconsidered at various points across the students' school careers. Let's first look at how the least restrictive environment (LRE) is determined for these students, and then let's consider one particular group of professionals, educational interpreters, who specifically serve many deaf and hard of hearing students and also work collaboratively with general educators.

CHAPTER 10 *Deafness and Hard of Hearing*

How should LRE be determined for Deaf and hard of hearing students?

IDEA mandates that all students with disabilities receive a free appropriate education (FAPE) in the least restrictive environment (LRE). What is the least restrictive environment for deaf children? The law states that what constitutes an appropriate education and what environment is the least restrictive must be individually determined. Many parents and members of the Deaf community believe that the general education classroom is not the least restrictive setting for deaf children (Fielder, 2001).

> *The general education classroom with an interpreter can be a restrictive environment if the student cannot communicate with peers and with staff in the school. The residential school settings where students live in dorms and attend school with peers who are deaf and hard of hearing have a 24-hour communication environment. That educational environment might be the least restrictive environment—one that does not restrict the student as he or she communicates with peers and staff and participates in extracurricular activities without communication barriers. (p. 58)*

For students who rely on sign language as their primary means of communication, the general school environment where administrators, teachers, and classmates are not fluent in sign language can result in considerable isolation. It is important to recognize that 45 percent of general education classes where deaf students attend use an auditory/oral-only approach (Gallaudet Research Institute, 1998). Deaf students who attend general education classes are often not included in nonacademic activities by their hearing classmates; the major reason for exclusion and rejection is difficulty with communication (Most, Weisel, & Lev-Matzky, 1996). Of course, isolation does not have to be the outcome of general education placements.

The Deaf community advocates strongly for residential schools as a placement option. What is at issue? At the same time that advocacy groups for people with mental retardation fought to close institutions, the Deaf community fought to keep residential center schools for deaf students open and fully funded. Remember that deafness in children is a low incidence disability; in the general school-age population, only a few children have this disability. The result can be that there is only one deaf child at a neighborhood school or even in an entire school district. Without a critical mass of these youngsters, they often feel isolated and rejected because few others use or understand their method of communication. This situation leads the Deaf community, some educators, and many parents to conclude that a separate program best meets the needs of deaf students and is also the least restrictive option (Ramsey, 1997).

Some deaf students and their families, particularly during the high school years, select the educational option of a residential center school. Although they have been declining in enrollment over the last 15 years, the 57 all-deaf schools are considered, particularly by members of the Deaf community, an important part of the array of services that should be available to this group of students. Eighty-two percent of students attending residential center schools have severe to profound hearing losses, and they report great satisfaction with their school placements (Byrnes & Sigafoos, 2001).

Determining the LRE for students with disabilities can be difficult, particularly for deaf students. A team of professionals, possibly the student, and the student's

Interpreters and classroom teachers work side-by-side in integrated educational settings. To have access to information, deaf children who use ASL need interpreters for every instructional activity, whether in a classroom or on a field trip.

MAKING
CONNECTIONS

For a review of FAPE and LRE, see the "Special Education Services" section in Chapter 2.

MAKING
CONNECTIONS

To review the educational placement options available through special education, see the "Special Educational Services" section in Chapter 2.

Table 10.2 Roles and Responsibilities of Educational Interpreters, Teachers, and Deaf Students

The Interpreter	The Teacher	The Deaf Student
Holds long conversations with the student after class	Introduces the interpreter to the class	Makes certain the interpreter uses preferred mode of communication
Asks for clarification when the teacher speaks too fast or was not heard	Talks to the student, not to the interpreter	Notifies the interpreter when there is going to be a change in schedules or when that person will not be needed
Considers teaching hearing students some basic signs	Adjusts pace of speech to allow for the translation	Is clear about whether the interpreter should speak for the student
Only interprets; does not tutor or provide assistance with assignments	Arranges for peers to take notes for their deaf peer	Determines desired role with peers
Maintains confidentiality of personal and private information	Seeks assistance of interpreter when working with others (e.g., SLPs)	Meets with the interpreter on a regular basis to provide feedback, resolve problems, and evaluate progress

parents come together to create a team that solves this problem. The team makes the decision on the basis of answers to the following questions:

- How severe is the student's hearing loss?
- Is the student able to use speech?
- Can appropriate educational services be made available locally?
- Are the necessary support services available?

Clearly, many factors must be considered when professionals make decisions about a child's educational placement program and develop an IEP (Cohen, 1994; Schildroth & Hotto, 1994). Some of the factors that affect placement are given in Table 10.1. Meeting these goals requires that a full array of educational services and placements be available.

How should teachers collaborate with educational interpreters?

One essential service needed by many deaf students enrolled in general education programs is delivered by **educational interpreters.** These professionals convert spoken messages into the student's preferred communication system, which may be a signed system such as ASL or signed English. For many teachers, working with the assistance of an interpreter is a novel experience that might occur only once in their teaching career. For the teacher inexperienced in working with students who use sign language, there is much to learn, plan for, and coordinate. The smooth inclusion of this related service provider as part of the educational team can require considerable communication and teamwork. And for many interpreters, working with students in school settings is also a unique experience (Linehan, 2000). A close working relationship is required between this related service provider and teachers, where the interpreter needs to learn academic content and the teacher needs to learn how to work with a translator.

The teacher and the interpreter need to coordinate efforts to ensure that they understand each other's roles. As responsibilities and duties are defined, it should be clear that the teacher has the primary responsibility and the interpreter plays a supporting role (Antia & Kreimeyer, 2001). In other words, the teacher should deliver instruction and remediation (when necessary), and the interpreter should be present to facilitate communication. Because the interpreter may not be an expert in the content of the curriculum, the teacher should give the interpreter copies of

Working with Interpreters

1. Set up standard times to meet. Be sure sufficient time is protected for these meetings, and do not cancel these meetings because of pressures of other events or students.

2. Define and understand each other's roles and responsibilities. Clarify (during noninstructional time) when necessary.

3. Arrange for an interpreter to participate in all meetings about the student.

4. Plan room arrangement together so that both the deaf student and the interpreter have appropriate and sufficient space and that they do not interfere with other students' learning environments.

5. Create a safe space for the interpreter's materials and belongings. This may include space that can be used for short-term storage of materials and equipment.

6. Test out classroom arrangements to be sure that lighting is appropriate, view of instruction is not restricted for any student, and the interpreter is not distracting to hearing students. Modify according to all class members' input.

7. Share lesson plans and supporting materials at least several days in advance. Be sure that textbooks are available for teacher and for interpreter.

8. Arrange for hearing classmates to help the deaf or hard of hearing student by sharing notes, or being available to answer questions about lectures and assignments.

9. Set up a system so interpreter can ask for clarifications or for slower pace with minimum of interruption during instruction.

10. Talk to deaf student directly, not the interpreter. Provide instructional feedback or reminders about appropriate classroom behavior and rules to the student.

11. Do not expect the interpreter to manage disruptive behavior.

12. Invite the interpreter to teach the class signs and finger spelling, share Deaf literature and culture, or arrange for Deaf cultural experiences where the interpreter "interprets" culture to hearing classmates.

lesson plans, lists of key terms, and textbooks to ensure clear and accurate translation of the teacher's lectures and instructions. The teacher and interpreter must also work together on a number of issues, many of which are minor but quite important. For example, the interpreter should sit in a glare-free, well-lit, solid-colored background location that does not block view of the blackboard or of the teacher. Teachers and interpreters also need to agree on and understand each others' roles—how much extra help the teacher provides the student and how much extra help the interpreter provides. Some other guidelines for inclusion of interpreters in classroom settings are found in Table 10.2. Some tips that may be useful when developing partnerships with these professionals are provided in the "Tips for Teachers" box.

TRANSITION THROUGH ADULTHOOD

The purpose of school-to-work transition programs for students who are deaf or hard of hearing is to improve the adult outcomes for these individuals. Of crucial importance are obtaining equitable employment, being able to obtain and hold a job commensurate with one's abilities, earning a fair wage, and being satisfied with the

MAKING **C**ONNECTIONS

For other information about the outcomes of individuals with disabilities, review the "Transition" sections in Chapters 3–12.

job. Deaf and hard of hearing people must also be able to participate in their community and in society. Let's consider some issues of transition next.

What postsecondary options are used by deaf and hard of hearing individuals?

For reminders about ASL and the Deaf community, see these sections of this chapter: "History" and "Characteristics."

Like many college students and their families, many deaf people wonder whether college is worth the effort and expense. The answer is a resounding yes. Data supporting the benefits of college education are available for Gallaudet alumni, who, in general, could be considered relatively affluent. The 1998 median annual income of Gallaudet alumni was $31,700 for those with an associate's degree, $40,000 for those with a bachelor's degree, and $50,000 for those with a master's degree (Schroedel & Geyer, 2000). College graduates were very satisfied with their lives, even though some of them faced challenges to success. For example, one-third fewer women were graduates, and more of them were in clerical positions than in the profession.

Deaf and hard of hearing students have many college opportunities that provide specialized support, but unfortunately, 71 percent of deaf college students drop out, compared to 43 percent of their nondisabled peers (www.jsu.edu, 2002). State and privately funded universities and colleges offer special programs for deaf and hard of hearing students. *College and Career Programs for Deaf Students* (King et al., 2001) lists about 125 postsecondary accredited programs designed specifically for deaf students. The federal government also supports a range of postsecondary schools and programs across the nation. Gallaudet University serves both undergraduate and graduate students, the National Technical Institute for the Deaf (NTID) at the Rochester Institute of Technology in New York offers technical and vocational degrees, and there are four federally funded postsecondary schools (Seattle Community College, California State University-Northridge, St. Paul Technical College, and the University of Tennessee Consortium).

What barriers do deaf people need to overcome?

To review the ADA law, see the "Necessity for National Intervention" section in Chapter 1.

Just as for many nondisabled college graduates, life after school is an adjustment. For the deaf and hard of hearing, the adjustments can be more significant because, despite the ADA law, the accommodations readily available in college often are not found in the workplace. Although many signs indicate that the situation is improving, some experience significant barriers in their adult lives. And, unfortunately, bias and discrimination are issues that deaf people have long had to face:

> *There yet remains a large fund of prejudice to overcome, of false sentiment to combat, of narrow-minded opposition to triumph over. But there is no uncertainty as [to] the final outcome. (From "The Intellect of Women," Agatha M. Tiegel, first woman graduate of Gallaudet, 1893, as cited in W. Tiefenbacher (Ed.), 2002, p. 4)*

Discrimination and bias can affect individuals' livelihood. Federal laws such as the *Americans with Disabilities Act* attempt to eliminate bias and require employers to provide reasonable accommodations—determined on an individual basis—such as sign language interpreters, reduced-noise workspace, special phones, and extra phone lines to allow for real-time translations (Deykes, 2002).

FAMILIES

Although language, social and emotional development, and technology are important to the overall development of deaf and hard of hearing children, possibly the

CHAPTER 10 *Deafness and Hard of Hearing*

most important factor in these children's lives is acceptance and inclusion by their families. Some parents and other family members (grandparents, siblings, extended family members) adjust quickly to the demands presented by a child with hearing loss. This is particularly true for children whose parents are deaf. To Deaf parents, the birth of a Deaf child is typically cause for great celebration and also a great relief (Blade, 1994). These parents know ASL, use it as their native language, and will teach it to their infant through the normal developmental process. However, the birth of a deaf child to hearing parents can be frightening, even devastating to some (Calderon & Greenberg, 1999). However, with support and services, families typically come to welcome their new member with joy and acceptance.

Although one would imagine that hearing families of deaf and hard of hearing children experience substantial stress because of their child's hearing loss, this stress is not overwhelming (Sheridan, 2001). Stress typically arises from concern about their ability to communicate with their children, but these families develop coping strategies fairly quickly. The strategies that they use, however, differ by cultural and ethnic group. In other words, White, African American, and Hispanic families use different coping and problem solving strategies. Regardless, what is most important to all families is developing effective communication modes with their youngsters and receiving effective support services (Moores, Jartho, & Dunn, 2001).

The artist Dorothy Brett is shown here with her hearing trumpet, "Toby," which is an early version of a hearing aid.

TECHNOLOGY

Technology and **assistive devices** can be credited with much of the improved access to mainstream society experienced by people with disabilities, but the promise for tomorrow hints at participation not even dreamed of a generation or two ago. Minda Huebner (2002) helps us see into the future. "In my vision of tomorrow's world, I see many technological advancements that will . . . enable people with hearing loss to understand things that do not have lips, like televisions, telephones, and intercoms" (p. 9). Here are some of the advances she envisions:

- Special glasses that show movie captions that are invisible to everyone else
- Telephones that show the words of conversations on mini screens
- Waterproof hearing aids that let everyone participate in water fights, soccer in the rain, and swim meets
- Home computers that make all of the lights in the house flash and alarm clocks vibrate when the smoke alarm goes off
- Lights on all cars' dashboards to indicate when an emergency vehicle is near

Clearly, the possibilities are endless, but barriers can make it impossible for many to experience Minda's dreams about tomorrow. The costs of assistive devices, although they decrease across time, limit people's access to helpful equipment. Table 10.3 shows the typical costs of assistive devices commonly used today. As you might imagine, cost is a major issue for deaf and hard of hearing people; many are unable to afford improved hearing aids, and government agencies are usually not of much assistance (Trychin, 2001). Assistive devices can be grouped into four categories: assistive listening devices, telecommunication devices, computerized speech-to-text translations, and

MAKING CONNECTIONS

To compare different types of technology supports across students with special needs, read the "Technology" sections in Chapters 3–12.

Reprinted with permission from Tribune Media Services.

Table 10.3 Sample Costs of Assistive Devices Designed for Deaf and Hard of Hearing Individuals

Telephone Devices

TTY	$250
Portable TTY Cellular package	$599
Amplified cordless phone with caller ID	$169
Portable phone amplifier	$ 30
Loud phone ringer	$ 37
Visual (lamp) phone ringer	$ 40
Talkabout T900 2-way pager	$150 + $30 mothly service fee
VCO dialog phones	$190

Alerting Devices

Alarm clock with bed shaker	$ 70
Vibrating alarm wrist watch	$ 40
Visual fire alarm	$130
Doorbell transmitter	$ 60
Visual doorbell	$100
Alertmaster signal system	$ 70
Baby cry signaler	$ 50
Smoke detector	$189
Carbon monoxide detectors with strobe light	$180

Automobile Warning Devices

Blinker Buddy II Turn Signal Reminder	$100
Emergency response indicator (ERI)	$200

Listening Systems

Wireless FM Systems	$650
Analog hearing aids	$600–$1,200
Digital hearing aids	$2,500–$6,000
Cochlear implants	$30,000

Entertainment and Information

TV/VCR with superior captioning	$429

alerting devices. Let's see how they can be beneficial.

What are assistive listening devices?

Assistive listening devices (ALDs) include hearing aids and other equipment that help people make better use of their residual hearing. The **hearing aid** is the most commonly used assistive device for this group of people; it amplifies sound so that the person can hear more easily. Hearing aids allow many individuals to hear well within the normal range. They have eliminated the need for special education for many children who are hard of hearing; with their hearing aids, they can profit from general education classes and participate fully in mainstream society. Even when hearing aids are carefully matched and programmed to the individual, however, they do not completely overcome the limitations of an impaired ear (Ross, 2002; Sweetow & Luckett, 2001). Teachers and parents must recognize that hearing aids do not solve all problems associated with hearing loss.

Because most conductive losses can be corrected with medicine or surgery, people with sensorineural hearing losses typically use hearing aids. Appearance is particularly important to children and teenagers. Four different kinds of hearing aids are available: **behind the ear (BTE)**, **in the ear (ITE)**, **in the canal (ITC)**, and **completely in the canal (CIC)**. For cosmetic reasons, few select BTEs, even though they tend to be somewhat more effective.

Because a hearing aid is a sensitive electronic device, it needs special care. Teachers can assist students who use hearing aids by helping them master the care and handling of these devices:

- Avoid dust, dirt, and humidity.
- Do not drop the hearing aid.
- Keep the ear mold clean.
- Avoid hair spray.
- Do not leave the hearing aid in a hot place.
- Be sure the child and the aid are checked frequently by an audiologist.

A new type of hearing aid is gaining in popularity, possibly because of issues related

CHAPTER 10 *Deafness and Hard of Hearing*

to keeping hearing aids clean and undamaged. The Songbird Disposable Hearing Aid (SDHA), which now also comes in a digital version, costs about $1 per day it is worn (Ross, 2002). Certainly, disposable aids have great advantages for children who often damage their aids and find it impossible to keep them clean.

Most newer hearing aids are digital. **Digital hearing aids** are designed to address each individual's hearing profile by automatically adjusting volume and amplifying sounds only to the degree necessary to compensate for the loss at each frequency of sound. These aids aim to reduce background noise, a significant problem with older, analog models that amplify all sounds equally, making it impossible to discriminate speech from noise. Unfortunately, they can be very expensive (up to $7,000), but over time, the price will come down and effectiveness will improve as well. The cost of digital hearing aids places them out of the reach for many students with hearing loss.

Background noise is a major problem in many classrooms, lecture halls, theaters, auditoriums, recreational centers, cafeterias, and other large rooms. One answer to this problem lies with **FM** (frequency-modulated) **transmission devices.** FM technology helps overcome the distance and noise problems that nearly always arise in general education classrooms (Flexer, 2000). When using this ALD technology, the teacher speaks into a small microphone either on a headset or clipped to a shirt. The student receives sound directly through a desktop receiver (particularly useful to children with cochlear implants) or hearing aid. Background noise is reduced, and teachers are free to move around the classroom without worrying about having their faces in full view of all their students. Teachers are enthusiastic about FM technology (Gordon-Langbein & Metzinger, 2000). They report that students' attention span improves (both hearing students and those with hearing loss), that using FM technology it is easier on their voices, and that they are less fatigued at the end of the day. Students report that this system of hearing amplification makes learning more fun, that listening is easier, and that teachers don't have to raise their voices.

Another answer is the **audio loop.** This ALD routes sound from its source directly to the listener's ear through a specially equipped hearing aid or earphone. Sound may travel through a wire connection or through radio waves. Audio loops are inexpensive and are easy to install in rooms that seat up to 100 persons. Since passage of the ADA law, audio loops are found in most concert halls, theaters, airports, and churches, giving people with hearing loss greater access to events.

Another problem area for many hearing aid and cochlear implant users is the telephone and the interference that is caused between the phone and the aid (DeVilbiss, 2001). Such problems are particularly acute with wireless phones (Harkins, 2000). The **telecoil** (also called an induction coil) was designed to reduce acoustic feedback noise from the hearing aid, sound distortions, and background noise heard on most telephones. Telecoils allow sounds to be brought directly into hearing aids from analog telephones (the kind found in most homes). Despite their benefits, telecoils are underutilized, primarily because people do not know how to use them (Ross, 2002). Teachers can help by connecting children with the school district's audiologist, who can instruct students in the telecoil's use and application. Regardless, telecoils do not help with digital phones. When digital wireless phones are being used, a loud buzzing sound from the hearing aid commonly makes all communication unintelligible (Kozma-Spyteck, 2000). Because analog cell phones are rarely available and current telecoils do not resolve the problem, new assistive devices are rapidly being devised to address the problem of interference.

FM transmission devices, like the Desktop Sound Pak™, can help students who use hearing aids profit more from their teachers' lessons. These assistive listening devices reduce background noise found in most general education classrooms.

MAKING CONNECTIONS

For a fuller discussion of cochlear implants, see the "Prevention" section in this chapter.

How do telecommunication devices benefit deaf people?

Captioning is an assistive telecommunication system that takes advantage of sight and hearing to improve communication and also enjoyment of cinema and television. **Captions** are printed words that appear at the bottom of a TV screen (like the subtitles that translate dialog in foreign films). "The French Chef with Julia Child" was the first captioned television show, appearing on public television in 1972. It used **open captions,** which are seen by all viewers, but they were unpopular with the general public. In the 1980s another system was developed that allows the viewer to chose whether the captions are seen on the TV screen. These captions are called **closed captions.** The Television Decoder Circuitry Act, introduced in 1990 and signed into law in July 1993, requires all television sets sold in the United States to be equipped with an internal, micro-sized **decoder** that allows captions to be placed anywhere on the screen (to avoid interfering with on-screen titles or other important information in the program) and to appear in different colors. Because these devices are mass-produced, they add only a few dollars to the cost of each TV set. Thus the option of selecting closed captions is now available on the equipment, and soon all TV programming will include closed captions as well (Baker, 2001). Captioning is an important tool for deaf people, because it allows them to have equal access to public information, emergency broadcasting, and entertainment. Data indicate that deaf people use captions. They spend some 84 percent of their viewing time reading the captions, 14 percent watching the video picture, and only 2 percent not watching the video (Jensema, Danturthi, and Burch, 2000).

Captioning has been much slower in coming to the movie theaters, making deaf people wait to see films until they are available in captioned video. Of course, FM sound systems have become increasingly available since passage of the ADA law, but remember that they benefit only those individuals who profit from amplification. Experiments with different captioning systems for movie theaters have been conducted for years to develop more ways for deaf people who desire captions to see them while the rest of the audience is not distracted by them. Rear window captioning (RWC) is one example. RWC projects captions from a message board on the theater's rear wall onto a clear plastic screen that attaches to the moviegoer's seat; the individual looks at a transparent Plexiglas panel to see the captions and forward to see the movie (Stanton, 1999). Once a captioning system is developed that satisfies the movie industry, the hearing public, and the deaf and hard of hearing people who use captions, deaf people will have one more way to participate in American life alongside hearing people.

Another important piece of equipment, the **text telephone (TTY),** formerly referred to as the telecommunication device for the deaf (TDD), enables those who are deaf to make and receive telephone calls. The first such device was created by Robert Weitbrecht, a deaf physicist, and used a teletypewriter along with a radio or telephone. TTY prints out the voice message for the person with a hearing loss and can be used to send messages. TTYs are now lightweight (about 1 pound). They come in portable, battery-operated, and cellular versions and are commonly available in public buildings (see Table 10.3 again to find sample prices for TTYs). The next generation of TTYs, the video TTY videophone, is already available. It allows the "listener" to see sign language or even read lips. The system uses a standard television set and a camcorder.

Most TTYs have one major drawback: A unit is required at both the sending and the receiving end. There are two solutions to this problem. First, the Federal Communications Commission now requires all states to have a **telecommunications relay service (TRS),** which allows a person using a TTY to communicate with someone who is using a standard telephone. By using an 800 phone number, the relay service allows deaf individuals to use the phone for everything from calling a doctor to ordering a pizza. When the person who is deaf uses a TTY in a relay system, an operator at a relay center places the call on a voice line and reads the typed message to the non-TTY user. Although a full conversation can be carried on by using a relay system, it is not very private and thus makes phone calls strained and impersonal. However, for making a doctor's appointment, arranging for a car to be fixed, or checking on a homework assignment, the relay system is invaluable.

Most deaf and hard of hearing people prefer to use their voice on a phone call, and a new device is now available. The **voice carry over (VCO)** is a TTY that includes the option of using both voice and text. For those who want to use their voices but need to receive telephone communication through print, these phones allow for both voice and text transmissions. A relay operator types what the hearing person says, which is then displayed on the text phone. VCOs have many advantages, particularly for hearing people with deaf family members or friends, for businesses that want both options but do not want to invest in two different phones, and for public places so that everyone has access to the telephone system. For those who want quicker response times and the option for both parties to talk at the same time, a two-phone-line VCO system is now available (Holbrook, 2000). And there is even a TTY/voice answering machine that takes messages in either format.

On another front, wireless technology designed for use by the general public has many applications for hard of hearing and deaf people. For example, devices that send and receive e-mail messages allow people to communicate at a distance. Susan, who wrote the story at the beginning of this chapter, uses the device created by Blackberry to communicate with the office staff when she is away. This small device vibrates when she has a new e-mail message. She can read the e-mail on its screen and reply immediately by typing in her response.

How can computerized speech-to-text translations benefit deaf students?

Deaf workers attending conferences and meetings often experience the same frustrations as college students during college lectures. It is difficult to take notes and watch a sign language interpreter simultaneously. **Real-time captioning (RTC)** can help deaf people in such situations. Several systems have been developed. **C-Print™** uses a laptop computer, a specially developed word abbreviation software program, and a computer visual display. The specially trained C-Print™ captionist listens to the lecture and types codes that represent words into the computer; the transcription is instantly shown on a monitor or on the individual's laptop. C-Print, which can translate up to 300 words a minute, is the fastest translation system currently available. It is ideal for lectures, though it is not as beneficial in small group work (Stinson et al., 2001). Once the lecture is completed, students can also get a printout—a benefit that lots of class members can appreciate. Many students who attend traditional colleges and universities and who would otherwise have to rely on an interpreter report that RTC does not make them feel different and even improves social interactions (Kramlinger, 1996).

Another system that holds great promise for the future is **automatic speech recognition (ASR)**. New technology now enables the computer automatically to convert speech at rates below 160 words per minute to text with error rates of less than 3 to 4 percent (Davis, 2001). ASR was not developed for the deaf; rather, it was developed for dictation (not access). Therefore, the system does not recognize multiple speakers and is not beneficial for group discussion periods. Regardless, the benefits to persons with disabilities are great.

Although not technically a speech-to-text translator, Ryan Patterson's new invention holds promise for improved communication between the Deaf and hearing people (Thomas, 2002). Ryan, age 17, won more than $300,000, which he received at a meeting in Sweden with Nobel laureates, and top honors at a technology

MAKING CONNECTIONS

- To help you study the chapter's content, the answers to the Focus and Challenge questions from the "Advance Organizers" are given next. Test yourself to see if you have mastered the major points of this chapter.

- Resources to extend your learning about people who are deaf or hard of hearing are found at the end of the chapter, and a fuller listing is available in the Students' Resource Manual.

competition for his translator glove, which translates sign language and finger spelling into print. For those who do not use oral language, the possibilities of broader access to mainstream society that such technological developments offer are clear.

What is an alerting device?

Alerting devices make people who are deaf aware of an event or important sound in their environment by using the sense of sight or touch. A flashing light, loud gong, or vibration can signal a fire alarm, doorbell, alarm clock, or telephone. Some such devices attach to a lamp that flashes on and off for a signal. Others attach to vibrators (in the bed for an alarm clock or on a person's belt as a personal signaler). Some alerting devices include sound-sensitive monitors that let the deaf person know about a baby who is crying or an out-of-the-ordinary sound. Signal dogs (or service dogs) also can help alert deaf people to important sounds in their environments (Delta Society, 1999; Ogden, 1992). These dogs are trained to act as "ears." They can distinguish between noises and alerts and can even recognize specific sounds.

IN CONCLUSION

Summary

Most of us communicate with others through a process of telling and listening. This process is one important way in which we learn about the world we live in, subjects at school, and others' perspectives on issues and concerns. The deaf have a more restricted ability to communicate—a difference that should shape the way these students are taught, the content of their curricula, and the related services they require for an appropriate education.

Self-Test Questions

Focus Questions

Why is universal screening of newborns such an important issue?

Universal screening allows for the identification of hearing loss at birth, reducing the (previous) average age of identification from 2½ to 3 years of age.

Early identification allows for services to children and their families to begin immediately and sets the stage for better language and cognitive development.

What variables are used to create different subgroups of deaf and hard of hearing individuals?

Amount of loss: deaf and the hard of hearing

Age of onset: prelingually deaf and postlingually (after the age of 2) deaf

Type of loss: conductive and sensorineural

What is meant by the concept of Deaf culture?

To many, particularly the Deaf who use American Language (ASL) and who live in the Deaf community, deafness is not a disability but, rather, a characteristic of a historically misunderstood minority group.

To the Deaf community, ASL, a bona fide language, is at the heart of a proud heritage of history, traditions, and art.

What are major causes of hearing loss?

The five major causes of hearing loss are hereditary conditions, meningitis, otitis media, maternal rubella, and noise.

The majority of causes are still unknown, but more and more genetic causes are being identified.

How do the major instructional methods for deaf children differ, and how should an individual child's communication style affect the choice of instructional method?

The major instructional methods are the oral-only approach, the total communication approach, cued speech, and the bilingual–bicultural approach.

Most deaf children do not develop oral language without effort.

Most hard of hearing children benefit from hearing aids, use oral language, and participate as full members of general education classrooms.

Challenge Question

What types of technology are available to assist deaf people, and what advances might the future hold?

Assistive listening devices: both digital and analog hearing aids (BTE, ITE, ITC, CIC), FM transmission devices, audio loop, telecoil

Telecommunication devices: captioning, text telephone (TTY), telecommunications relay service, voice carry over

Speech-to-text translations: real-time translations (college lectures, courtroom proceedings, business meetings), real-time captioning, C-Print™, speech recognition

Alerting devices: special signaling devices for alarms, doorbells, telephone rings

Advancements in digital hearing aids that mask out background noise and adjust to an individual's unique hearing pattern will become less expensive and even more effective. More developments of the speech recognition systems that allow for the participation of multiple speakers are on the horizon.

MEETING THE STANDARDS AND PREPARING FOR LICENSURE EXAMS

After reading this chapter, you should be able to demonstrate basic knowledge and skills described in the CEC standards and INTASC principles listed below. The section of this chapter most applicable to each standard is shown in parentheses at the end of the knowledge or skill statement.

 Core Standard 1: Foundations

- **Points of view:** Historical points of view and contribution of culturally diverse groups (History of the Field)

 Core Standard 2: Development and Characteristics of Learners

- **Educational implications:** Educational implications of characteristics of various exceptionalities (Characteristics)
- **Similarities and differences:** Similarities and differences among individuals with exceptional learning needs. (Deafness and Hard of Hearing Defined)

Core Standard 3: Individual Learning Differences

- **Beliefs and values:** Variations in beliefs, traditions, and values across and within cultures and their effects on relationships among individual with exceptional learning needs, family and schooling. (Families)

Core Standard 4: Instructional Strategies

- **Adapt instructional strategies:** Select, adapt and use instructional strategies and materials according to the characteristics of the individual with exceptional learning needs. (Elementary Through High School)
- **Transition planning:** Use strategies that promote successful transitions for individuals with exceptional learning needs. (Transition Through Adulthood)

 Core Standard 5: Learning Environments and Social Interactions

- **Integration supports:** Identify supports needed for integration into various program placements. (Elementary Through High School)
- **Learner environments:** Design learner environments that encourage active participation in individual and group activities. (Elementary through High School)

 Core Standard 6: Language

- **Effects of linguistic differences:** Effects of cultural and linguistic differences on growth and development (Elementary through high School)
- **Support communication:** Use strategies to support and enhance communication skills of individuals with exceptional learning needs. (Elementary Through High School)

 Core Standard 7: Instructional Planning

- **Technology:** Incorporate and implement instructional and assistive technology into the educational program. (Technology)

INTASC Principle 2:

The teacher understands how children learn and develop and can provide learning opportunities that support their intellectual, social and personal development.

- **Individual variation within areas of development:** The teacher appreciates individual variation within each area of development, shows respect for the diverse talents of all learners, and is committed to help them develop self-confidence and competence. (Elementary Through High School)

INTASC Principle 3:

The teacher understands how students differ in their approaches to learning and creates instructional opportunities that are adapted to diverse learners.

- **Cultural norms:** The teacher is sensitive to community and cultural norms. (Opportunities for a Better Future)

INTASC Principle 4:

The teacher understands and uses a variety of instructional strategies to encourage students' development of critical thinking, problem solving, and performance skills.

- **Multiple perspectives:** The teacher brings multiple perspectives to the discussion of subject matter, including attention to students' personal family and community experiences and cultural norms. (Elementary Through High School)

INTASC Principle 6:

The teacher uses knowledge of effective verbal, nonverbal, and media communication techniques to foster active inquiry collaboration and supportive interaction in the classroom.

- **Language and learning:** The teacher understands communication theory, language development, and the role of language in learning. (Elementary Through High School)

Standards in Practice

These knowledge statements, dispositions and skills might be demonstrated by the beginning teacher who acknowledges the importance of language development and communications skills to the teaching and learning process. The teacher might incorporate multiple teaching strategies including technology to effectively reach students that are deaf or hard of hearing. The teacher would also demonstrate understanding of the differing cultural perspectives on hearing loss.

Go to the companion website (ablongman.com/smith5e) for detailed text correlations to CEC and INTASC standards, PRAXIS II™ exams, and other state-sponsored licensure exams.

SUPPLEMENTARY RESOURCES

Professional Readings and Resources

Bergman, E., & Batson, T. (1997). *Angels and outcasts: An anthology of Deaf characters in literature* (3rd ed.). Washington, DC: Gallaudet University Press.

Davis, J. M. (Ed). (2001). *Our forgotten children: Hard of hearing pupils in the schools.* Bethesda, MD: SHHH Publications.

Lane, H. (1995). Construction of deafness. *Disability & Society,* 10, 171–187.

Moores, D. F. (2001). *Educating the deaf: Psychology, principles, and practices* (5th ed.). Boston: Houghton Mifflin.

Owens, R. E., Metz, D. E., & Hass, A. (2000). *Introduction to communication disorders: A life span perspective.* Boston: Allyn and Bacon.

Tharpe, A. M. (1999). Disorders of hearing in children. In E. Plante & P. M. Beeson (Eds.), *Communication and communication disorders: A clinical introduction.* (pp. 85–116). Boston: Allyn and Bacon.

Popular Books

Davis, L. J. (Ed.). (1999). *Shall I say a kiss: The courtship letters of a Deaf couple, 1936–1938.* Washington, DC: Gallaudet University Press.

Dunai, E. C. (2002). *Surviving in silence: A deaf boy in the Holocaust.* Washington, DC: Gallaudet University Press.

Golan, L. (1995). *Reading between the lips.* Chicago: Bonus Books.

Tiefenbacher, W. (Ed.). (2001). *Deaf girls rule.* Washington, DC: Gallaudet University Press.

Walker, L. A. (1986). *A loss for words: The story of deafness in a family.* New York: Harper & Row.

Whilestone, H., & Hunt, A. E. (1997). *Listening with my heart.* New York: Doubleday.

Wright, M. H. (1999). *Sounds like home: Growing up Black and Deaf in the South.* Washington, DC: Gallaudet University Press.

Videos and DVDs

Hear No Evil, See No Evil (1989). TriStar Pictures

In this comedy, the two main characters are accused of a murder they did not commit, so they have to elude the police, find the real killers, and prove their innocence. However, both of the main characters have disabilities: one is blind, the other deaf. These two work together and minimize each other's disabilities to prove their innocence and help the police capture the real criminals.

This farfetched comedy puts an interesting spin on an unlikely partnership. The deaf character does not use sign language; instead he is able to read lips, which aids him in functioning in the hearing world. This also sets up comedic situations when he sees only partial lip movements because he cannot look directly at the person speaking. The movie does attempt to show the capabilities of those with disabilities, but it also uses people's differences for silly comedy.

CHAPTER 10 *Deafness and Hard of Hearing*

Mr. Holland's Opus (1995). Buena Vista

Mr. Holland is a high school music teacher who connects with his students through music. His greatest challenge occurs when his child is born deaf. His wife enrolls their son in a special school and learns sign language, while Mr. Holland is hesitant and distant. He believes he cannot share his passion for music with his deaf son. Once his son convinces him that he is not so different, Mr. Holland dedicates himself to learning sign language and finding a way to introduce his son to music.

This film sets up a situation in the extreme, where one person's entire life revolves around sound and the other is completely unable to hear. But even so, it is possible for these two to find common ground. One technique that Mr. Holland employs is to use coordinated lights to help his son gain a sense of how dynamic and electric music can be.

Parent, Professional, and Consumer Organizations and Agencies

Alexander Graham Bell Association for the Deaf and Hard of Hearing

3417 Volta Place NW
Washington, DC 20007
Phone: (202) 337-5220
TTY: (202) 337-5221
E-mail: info@agbell.org
Web site: http://www.agbell.org

American Speech-Language-Hearing Association (ASHA)

10801 Rockville Pike
Rockville, MD 20852
Phone toll free/ Voice/TTY: (800) 638-8255
E-mail: actioncenter@asha.org
Web site: http://www.asha.org

Deafpride, Inc.

1350 Potomac Avenue SE
Washington, DC 20003
Voice or TTY: (202) 675-6700

Cochlear Implant Education Center

Laurent Clerc National Deaf Education Center
Kendall School, Room 2418
Gallaudet University
800 Florida Avenue, NE
Washington, DC 20002-3695
Phone: (202) 651-5638
E-mail Debra.Nussbaum@gallaudet.edu

Laurent Clerc National Deaf Education Center

800 Florida Avenue NE
Washington, DC 20002-3695
TTY/Voice: (202) 651-5638
Web site:
http://clerccenter.gallaudet.edu/InfoToGo/index.html

John Tracy Clinic

806 W. Adams Boulevard
Los Angeles, CA 90007-2505
Voice: (213) 748-5481
TTY: (213) 747-2924

Voice/TTY: (800) 522-4582
Web site: http://www.jtc.org

Self-Help for Hard of Hearing People (SHHH), Inc.

7910 Woodmont Avenue, Suite 1200
Bethesda, MD 20814
Voice: (301) 657-2248
TTY: (301) 657-2249
E-mail: National@shhh.org
Web site: http://www.shhh.org

National Institute on Deafness and Other Communication Disorders (NIDCD)

Information Clearinghouse
National Institutes of Health
1 Communication Avenue
Bethesda, MD 20892-3456
Voice: (800) 241-1044
TTY: (800) 241-1055
E-mail: nidcdinfo@nidcd.nih.gov
Web site: http://www.nidcd.nih.gov

The National Theater of the Deaf

55 Van Dyke Avenue, Suite 312
Hartford, CT 06106
Voice/TTY: (860) 724-5179
Toll Free Voice & TTY: (800) 300-5179
E-mail: info@ntd.org
Web site: http://www.ntd.org

Video**Workshop** Extra

If the VideoWorkshop package was included with your textbook, go to Chapter 10 of the Companion Website (www. ablongman.com/smith 5e) and click on the VideoWorkshop button. Follow the instructions for viewing Video clip 8. Consider this information along with what you've read in Chapter 10 as you answer the following questions.

Video clip 8: Hearing impairment (Time 1:51)

1. In the video the student has an aide/interpreter. You may need to supervise and assign tasks if a specific student in your classroom has an interpreter. On the basis of what you saw in the video and what you read in your text, what should you consider when using an interpreter?

2. There may be times when an interpreter is not available to students with hearing impairments, so alternative communication methods may be needed. The "Technology" section of the chapter provides information about telecommunications devices that benefit persons who have hearing impairments. What devices might assist the students in the video? Explain when these devices might be used to maximize learning in a general education class.

Auguste Rodin. *The Burghers of Calais*
© Super Stock

FRANÇOIS AUGUSTE RENÉ RODIN was born and raised on the Left Bank of Paris. His father was a clerk in the police department. Although the family was not rich, the environment in which Rodin grew up in was. His neighborhood was a community for artists, poets, writers, and creative people. He is said to have once remarked that his native Paris gave him *"millions de pensées"* (millions of thoughts) (Hale, 1969, p. 37). Rodin was probably drawn to art because of his poor success at school. His first school experiences were not positive. It is said that after three years he still could not spell, a problem that followed him the rest of his life. At age 10 he was sent off to a country school, but again was unsuccessful and dropped out of school by the age of 13. It is thought that his frustration and failure at school was because of a severe vision problem, for it is reported that he was so nearsighted that he could not see the blackboard (Hale, 1969). It is probably for these reasons that he chose sculpture as his medium of expression, one that is more tactile than visual. He is considered one of the best sculptors of all time.

The Burghers of Calais, begun in 1884 and completed in 1886, shows the emotions these six city leaders must have felt when they surrendered their lives and city to the conquering English. Rodin broke with tradition, by not depicting these Frenchmen as marching nobly to their deaths, but rather with the weight of defeat showing in their bodies and the fear of death on their faces. These sculptured figures demonstrate Rodin's understanding of the human condition.

11 Low Vision or Blindness

The Making of a Professional

Dr. Anne Corn is a nationally famous and respected expert in the area of low vision and blindness. She is professor of special education and also the coordinator of the teacher training program in low vision and blindness at Peabody College of Vanderbilt University. She is a dedicated professional and a tireless advocate for students with visual disabilities and for their families. Because she speaks from both personal experience and professional knowledge, Dr. Corn is an effective and powerful member of this community, a woman who has made a real difference in the lives of children.

At six weeks of age I was diagnosed with congenital nystagmus, a condition that makes it difficult for the eyes to focus and results in low visual acuity. In the 1950s there were no infancy or early childhood services for children with visual impairments, and my parents were only told by the ophthalmologist to return before I was ready for school. They were given no specific information about my condition or what to do for me. They knew of no other parents with children with visual disabilities. Instinctively, they held high expectations for me and sought help from experts, things we ask parents to do today.

I entered the local elementary school, but in first grade the principal suggested that I go to another school where there was a special class for children with visual disabilities. I recall visiting the class and feeling that I didn't belong. The only attribute the children had in common was their visual disability. They just didn't seem to be like the children in my school. My ophthalmologist agreed with my parents that I should attend a regular school. I couldn't see chalkboards, and as the print in my textbooks became smaller, I struggled to read.

I had a range of experiences with teachers, from those who understood and were kind enough to read aloud as they wrote on the board, to teachers who wouldn't make any accommodations. I would walk up to the chalkboard after everyone finished copying and write down as much as I could before the teacher was ready to erase that section of the board. My reading came slowly but my math skills were quite good. Although my grades were toward the top of the class, testing procedures were not appropriate for me. The IQ test that determined my eligibility to attend advanced placement courses was a small-print, group test. So in sixth grade my parents were told that I couldn't attend advanced classes because teachers and administrators said my IQ score was below criteria. Because there were no other real options, I attended a special program for middle school. In ninth grade, I wasn't even allowed to take the entrance tests for New York's special magnet schools, like the Bronx School of Science. And although this is hard to believe, the assistant principal even tried to stop me from reading an essay at honors assembly because I wasn't the "image" she wanted on stage!

For high school I chose to attend my local school rather than a school with a resource class. Within a few weeks the administrators became upset when they learned I was legally blind. Following a flurry of calls and meetings, one of the first itinerant teachers for New York City was sent to help out one day each week after school, but this was short-lived. By the beginning of the next school year I was told that if I wanted services I had to attend another high school that had a resource program. Thankfully, I could stay at my local high school because of my itinerant teacher was truly committed and was very supportive of me. He was available to me by phone, on his own time, to discuss everything from how to order adapted versions of the SAT test to how to handle teachers who did not want me in their classes. He prepared me for obtaining summer jobs and helped me through a time when colleges rejected me because I didn't meet visual requirements for graduates majoring in education in order to obtain licensure.

Today, as a professor of special education and also with an appointment in the Department of Ophthalmology and Visual Sciences at Vanderbilt University Medical Center, I am working to see that children with low vision and blindness have opportunities to receive an appropriate education. Unfortunately, there is a critical shortage of specialized teachers, and many children with visual disabilities don't get the services they need. Today's children and their families are facing the very same issues my family and I faced fifty years ago.

While I did not always have a supportive school experience, I sincerely believe I was appropriately educated in general education classes. Today I strongly support placements for children with visual impairments in general education classes with appropriate educational support services from certified teachers of students with visual disabilities and also from orientation and mobility specialists. These supports refer to both the quality and the quantity of services based on students' assessed educational needs. However,

I also support, when appropriate, placement at special schools for students. Many students benefit from intense services that address their unique educational needs throughout the day, when all personnel understand the impact of visual impairments on learning as well as the importance of developing social and independent living skills. For some students, attending a special school may be their only option for meeting peers with a similar disability. Some schools offer short-term placements to provide special skills training (e.g., orientation and mobility instruction) not available in the local schools. IDEA requires that local options be available when a local school is an appropriate placement. Although my parents chose to enroll me in my local school even without services, I sometimes wonder how life might have been different had I known other children with low vision or learned to read from someone who knew how to instruct a child who couldn't see well.

1. **Dr. Corn suggests that supports for families of children with visual disabilities have not improved much since she was a child. Why do you think this is so? How might this situation improve?**

2. **What accommodations did Dr. Corn receive during her school years, and what additional accommodations would have helped Dr. Corn achieve her potential more easily?**

ADVANCE ORGANIZERS

Overview

Vision is a distance sense that provides us with information from outside our bodies. When vision is limited, it affects the individual in significant ways, limiting mobility, access to printed information, and independent living. People with visual disabilities also face many stereotypes, social stigma, and barriers to full participation in mainstream society. Some believe that blindness is met with more negative attitudes than is any other physical disability. Visual disabilities (low vision and blindness) in children is a low incidence disability, affecting about 0.05 percent of all schoolchildren.

Self-Test Questions

Focus Questions

- How can the category of visual disabilities be divided into subgroups?
- What are the major causes of visual disabilities?
- What are some ways in which the learning environment can be modified to accommodate

students with visual disabilities?

- Why must orientation and mobility be long-term curriculum targets for many low vision students and most blind students, and what specific skills must be included?

- What technological advances can assist people with visual disabilities at school, in the workplace, and in independent living?

Challenge Question

- Why has braille literacy become such an emotionally charged debate, and how do you think it should be resolved?

MAKING CONNECTIONS

Use the learning strategy—Advance Organizers—to help focus your study of this chapter's content, and reinforce your learning by reviewing answers to the "Focus and Challenge" questions at the end of the chapter.

CHAPTER 11 *Low Vision or Blindness*

Although we act on information gained through our sight, we seldom give much thought to the process of seeing. Sometimes, we stop to reflect on the beauty of a particular sunset, the stars at night, a flower in bloom, or the landscape after a snowstorm. We use our sense of sight all of our waking hours, yet we do not think about vision and how it functions. Most of us use vision in our work. For example, people use sight when they use the Internet, write memos, look up telephone numbers, or direct people to various offices. We use our vision for recreation when we watch a movie, view television, or read a book. Some of us actually prefer learning by reading or looking at information, rather than listening to a lecture or instructions. Such people are known as visual learners. We also use our vision for self-defense; for example, we look in all directions before crossing a street on foot or entering an intersection when driving a car. Unlike touch and taste, vision and hearing are **distance senses,** senses that provide us with information outside our bodies. These senses developed to alert us to the presence of helpful as well as dangerous elements in the environment.

Clearly, those of us with unimpaired vision profit from this sense. We learn by observing events, we use our vision to move freely in our environment, and we are alert to danger by using our sight. People with visual disabilities have limited use of their sight, but with systematic instruction, advances in technology, and elimination of barriers associated with stereotypes and discrimination, most can lead fully integrated and independent lives.

OPPORTUNITIES FOR A BETTER FUTURE

When the Deaf community became united through its culture and was acknowledged as an American minority group because of its political action, an example was set for people with visual disabilities. Although not until the late 1990s, they sought the assistance of the federal government to ensure that braille literacy was renewed as an educational option for students with visual disabilities. They were also not silent about the bias and discrimination they experience in society and in the workplace, for despite their skills and abilities, they face chronic unemployment, at levels even below those experienced by other groups of people with disabilities.

Turning Legacies into Lessons

As more and more blind and low vision children were educated at neighborhood schools and in general education settings, fewer of them learned to use braille as their method of reading. As a group, their literacy rates dropped to alarming levels. At the very end of the 20th Century, policymakers learned that many school districts were not providing the option of learning braille as a reading method. Three reasons explain this situation: (1) Very few students need this skill, (2) they attend many different neighborhood schools across school districts, and (3) so few special teachers are available who can teach braille. Accordingly, in IDEA, Congress included learning braille as a necessary option. However, policymakers remain concerned because they know that federal mandates can be difficult to implement, a fact made clear by the problems that blind workers have had in finding appropriate jobs despite the Americans with Disabilities Act (ADA).

Thinking About Dilemmas to Solve

People with visual disabilities face unique challenges at school, at home, and across their lives. As you read this chapter, consider

- How, when there are insufficient numbers of teachers available who know how to teach this skill to students, school districts will meet IDEA's, mandate to offer braille instruction to those who need it

- How the general literacy levels of blind and low vision students who read print can be increased

- Ways to eliminate bias and discrimination experienced by people with visual disabilities

- How instruction in life skills can be included when students are fully participating in the general education curriculum

- Methods of improving the employment rates for this group of people

MAKING CONNECTIONS

For more about the bias and discrimination people with disabilities face, see Chapter 1 and the "Defined" and "Transition" sections in Chapters 6, 8, and 10.

Advance Organizers

VISUAL DISABILITIES DEFINED

When people see normally, four elements must be present and operating:

1. Light
2. Something that reflects light
3. An eye processing the reflected image into electrical impulses
4. A brain receiving and giving meaning to these impulses

As you read the next paragraph, use the picture of the eye in Figure 11.1 to trace how the normal visual process works.

Light rays enter the front of the eye through the **cornea.** The cornea is transparent and curved. The **iris,** the colored part of the eye, expands and contracts in response to the intensity of light it receives. In the center of the iris is an opening, the **pupil.** Light rays pass through the pupil to the **lens,** which is behind the iris. The lens brings an object seen into focus by changing its thickness. The process of adjustment by the lens to bring things that are close and those that are far away into focus is called **accommodation.** The lens focuses light rays onto the **retina,** the inside lining at the back of the eye. It is made up of photosensitive cells that react to light rays and send messages along the **optic nerve** to the visual center of the brain.

How well people can use their sight—their **visual efficiency**—is influenced by many factors, including the person's acuity and peripheral vision, environmental conditions, and psychological variables. **Visual acuity** is how well a person can see at various distances. The width of a person's field of vision, or the ability to perceive objects outside the direct line of vision, is called **peripheral vision.** This aspect of vision helps people move freely through their environment. It helps them see large objects and movement. Severe limitation in peripheral vision is sometimes called **tunnel vision** or restricted **central vision.** Some people with visual disabilities have little functional use of sight, but the great majority have substantial use of their vision, particularly with correction (glasses or contact lenses).

Although many people do not realize it, the vast majority of people with visual disabilities use vision as their primary method of learning, and for many the amount

Figure 11.1 How Vision Works
Source: Physiology of Behavior, 5th ed. by N. R. Carlson, 1994, Boston: Allyn and Bacon, Figures 6.4 and 6.12. Adapted by permission.

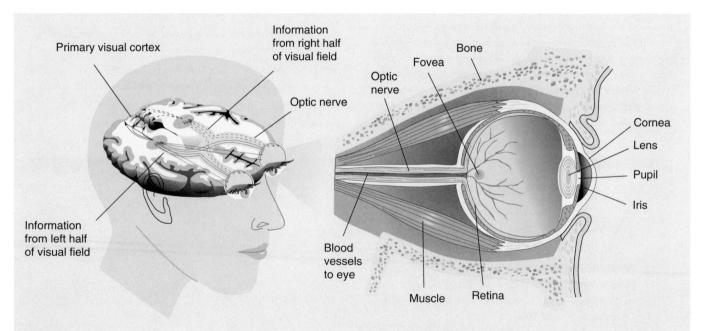

Primary visual cortex

Information from right half of visual field

Bone

Fovea

Optic nerve

Optic nerve

Cornea

Lens

Pupil

Iris

Information from left half of visual field

Blood vessels to eye

Muscle   Retina

CHAPTER 11 *Low Vision or Blindness*

of vision they have left—their **residual vision**—can be further developed. The vision of some is static, remaining the same from day to day, whereas others find that their ability to see varies by the day, time of day, or setting (Levin, 1996). For some, higher or lower levels of illumination affect how well they can see, but for others, lighting level makes little difference. For some individuals, distance and contrast significantly affect how well they can process information presented through the visual channel. Some are color blind; others are not. For most, optical aids such as glasses have a positive effect.

The eye is a very complicated mechanism. Damage to any part of the eye can result in serious limitations in one's abilities to see and process information through the visual channel. Table 11.1 lists conditions that affect various parts of the eye by using an organizational system suggested by Tuttle and Ferrell (1995). These conditions can result in blindness or severe visual disabilities. Many disorders can be corrected or reduced through medical technology, but not all can be resolved by medical treatment.

What are the different types of visual disabilities?

Many professionals divide persons with visual disabilities into two subgroups:

1. Low vision
2. Blindness

Individuals with **low vision** use sight to learn, but their visual disabilities interfere with daily functioning. **Blindness** means that the person uses touch and hearing to learn and does not have functional use of sight. Parents and professionals now tend to use functional definitions for these two subgroups. Remember, this classification system is based on how well people can use their sight, even if its use is severely limited.

Anne Corn, the author of the "Personal Perspective" at the beginning of this chapter, developed the commonly accepted definition of low vision more than 20 years ago:

> *a level of vision which, with standard correction, hinders an individual in the planning and/or execution of a task, but which permits enhancement of the functional vision through the use of optical or nonoptical devices, environmental modifications and/or techniques. (Corn, 1989, p. 28)*

Table 11.1 Types of Visual Disabilities

Type	Definition
Conditions of the Eye	
Myopia	Nearsightedness; condition allows focus on objects close but not at a distance.
Hyperopia	Farsightedness; condition allows focus on objects at a distance but not close.
Astigmatism	An eye disorder that produces images on the retina that are not equally in focus.
Conditions of the Eye Muscles	
Strabismus	Improper alignment of the two eyes causes two images to be received by the brain, with the possible result of one eye becoming nonfunctional.
Nystagmus	Rapid, involuntary movements of the eye that interfere with bringing objects into focus.
Conditions of the Cornea, Iris, and Lens	
Glaucoma	Fluid in the eye is restricted, causing pressure to build up and damage the retina.
Aniridia	Undeveloped iris, due to lack of pigment (albinism), results in extreme sensitivity to light.
Cataract (opacity of the crystalline lens)	A cloudy film over the lens of the eye.
Conditions of the Retina	
Diabetic retinopathy	Changes in the eye's blood vessels are caused by diabetes.
Macular degeneration	Damage to a small area near the center of the retina results in restricted fine central vision and difficulties in reading and writing.
Retinopathy of prematurity (ROP)	Excess oxygen to infants causes retinal damage; was called retrolental fibroplasia.
Retinal detachment	Detachment of the retina interrupts transmission of visual information to the brain.
Retinitis pigmentosa	Genetic eye disease leads progressively to blindness; night blindness is the first symptom.
Retinoblastoma	Tumor.
Condition of the Optic Nerve	
Atrophy	Reduced function of the optic nerve.

In other words, children with low vision use their sight for many school activities, including reading.

Blind children do not have functional use of their vision and may perceive only shadows or some movement. These youngsters must be educated through tactile and other sensory channels and are considered functionally blind. Blindness can occur at any age, but its impact varies with age.

Another way to group individuals with visual disabilities, as with deaf and hard of hearing students, is in terms of the age of onset (when the disability occurred):

- **Congenitally blind** (at birth or during infancy)
- **Adventitiously blind** (after the age of 2)

This distinction is important because people who lose their sight after age 2 remember what some objects look like. The later the disability occurs, the more they remember. Visual memory is an important factor in learning, for it can influence one's development of concepts and other aspects important to learning.

Another way to categorize people with visual problems—as **"legally blind"**—allows them to receive special tax benefits and materials from the federal government and private agencies. Despite the movement toward functional definitions of visual disabilities and despite the fact that many people who meet the qualifications for the classification of legally blind use print to read and gain information, the clas-

sification remains. Here are the criteria: central visual acuity of 20/200 or less in the better eye, with best correction, or a diameter of visual field that does not subtend an angle greater than 20 degrees at its widest point.

How are these disabilities identified?

Professionals and parents use information from assessments to decide whether a child should learn to read print or to read braille, to specify the level and type of education placements the child will receive, and to determine which assistive services will be included in the child's IEP. Such decisions determine what types of special education services a student receives and also have other lifelong implications.

Although parents and professionals are advocating for the use of functional definitions of visual disabilities, many states still use measures of acuity to qualify youngsters for special education services. Normal visual acuity is measured by how accurately a person can see an object or image 20 feet away. Normal vision is thus said to be 20/20. A person whose vision is measured at 20/40 can see at 20 feet what people who do not need visual correction (glasses or contact lenses) can see at 40 feet away. Field of vision is measured in degrees. As we have noted, those whose visual field is restricted to no more than 20 degrees are classified as legally blind. Although states and school districts vary in the criteria they use to determine eligibility for special services, typically people with visual acuity measuring 20/70 to 20/200 in the better eye, with correction, are considered to have low vision (Heller et al., 1996). Acuity below 20/200 classifies an individual as legally blind.

Most states require that all schoolchildren have a visual screening test. Children's visual acuity can be tested in the school nurse's office or by a pediatrician using the Snellen chart. The **Snellen chart,** originally developed by a Dutch ophthalmologist in 1862, comes in two versions. One test uses the letter E placed in various positions in different sizes; the other uses alphabet letters in different sizes. For the screening of substantial numbers of people, a more efficient adaptation of the Snellen chart uses the E version projected on a television monitor placed 10 to 20 feet away from the viewer. The viewer matches a key on a computer with the direction or placement of the E on the screen, and the computer analyzes the data.

Assessing functional vision can be complicated, imprecise, and inaccurate. Information must be gathered from multiple sources. For example, diagnosticians, the children affected, their parents, general educators, teachers of blind and low vision students, school nurses, and eye specialists can all provide important information employed in the comprehensive assessment of useful vision. Another source of information is the children themselves, but it may be surprising to learn that they are often very unreliable. Many parents report that their blind children, possibly motivated by the desire to please a doctor or a diagnostician, both report and simulate a different level of blindness than they actually possess when in the assessment situation (Erin & Corn, 1994). For example, some children indicate that they can see things they cannot: a car coming, the moon at night, the color of an object. Decisions about visual status must be made from accurate information, but

MAKING CONNECTIONS

For a review of IEPs and the services that can be included in special education, review Chapter 2.

Table 11.2 Possible Signs of Visual Disabilities

- Eyes water excessively.
- Eyes are red or continually inflamed.
- Eyes are crusty in appearance.
- Eyes look dull, wrinkled, or cloudy.
- Eyes look swollen.
- One or both pupils (black center of the eye) look gray or white.
- One or both eyes cross, turn in or out, or move differently from the other.
- Baby of three months or more does not look directly at objects.
- Child bumps into or trips over things.
- Child has difficulty seeing after the sun sets (night blindness).
- Child has difficulty reading small print.
- Child has difficulty identifying details in pictures.
- Child has difficulty going up or down stairs, throwing or catching a ball, buttoning clothes, or tying shoes.
- Child is excessively clumsy.
- Child is unable to discriminate letters.
- Child rubs eyes often.
- Child squints.
- Child complains of dizziness or headaches after a reading assignment.
- Child often tilts head.
- Child uses one eye, possibly shutting or covering the other eye when reading.
- Child dislikes or avoids close work.
- Child holds objects abnormally close to the eyes.

MAKING CONNECTIONS

- For suggestions about adapting the classroom setting for blind and low vision students, see the "Accommodating for Inclusive Environments" box in this chapter.

- Read again the story of Michael Hingson and his guide dog Roselle. Before the ADA law was passed, he probably would not have been working in the Trade Towers.

surprisingly, collecting such information can prove to be quite challenging.

Two types of eye specialists provide diagnosis and treatment:

1. Ophthalmologists (medical doctors who specialize in eye disorders)
2. Optometrists

Ophthalmologists conduct physical examinations of the eye, prescribe corrective lenses and medicines, prescribe drugs, and perform surgery. **Optometrists** measure vision, prescribe corrective lenses, and also make functional recommendations. An **optician** fills the ophthalmologist's or optometrist's prescription for glasses or corrective lenses.

Schoolwide visual screenings can help identify children with visual disabilities and get them needed services early. Alert teachers and parents, familiar with the possible signs of a visual problem (see Table 11.2 for a list), can help identify such students even sooner and ultimately reduce the impact of the disability. Children who exhibit one or more of these characteristics should be checked by a school nurse, pediatrician, or ophthalmologist. Although this is not a requirement, each child's visual screening should include teachers' observations about classroom behaviors and performance. For example, teachers should indicate whether a particular child complains about scratchy or itchy eyes or headaches, rubs the eyes excessively, or has difficulty discriminating letters or symbols when completing classroom assignments. Such information is especially helpful when recommendations are made about placement and the types of special assistance a child should receive.

What is the impact of this disability?

People with visual disabilities vary widely in their abilities. With the growing number of low birth weight babies, the number of these individuals with multiple disabilities is increasing as well, making their diversity even greater (Hatton, 2001). You have learned so far that visual efficiency is an important concept. Think about it as you continue to learn more about this disability and how it impacts the people affected by it. Interestingly, even individuals with the same visual acuity or the same amount of peripheral vision may differ in their abilities to use their sight. Visual efficiency influences how individuals learn best (through visual, tactile, or auditory channels) and what accommodations students require. For example, a child's visual efficiency could affect how the classroom needs to be organized, where the child should sit, whether additional equipment (microcomputers, braillers) is required, and whether adapted materials (texts with enlarged print) are necessary.

Because of advances in technology and the passage of the ADA law, many blind and low vision people are assuming their places in the mainstream of society. Remember the story, in Chapter 1, of Michael Hingson and his guide dog, Roselle, who helped co-workers escape the collapsing World Trade Center Towers? He probably would not have had a job there some 15 years ago. Many other blind workers hold important and interesting jobs. Dave Shell is the crew chief and engine builder for the international Hot Rod Association car that is a contender for the championship (Wood, 2000 July 20). Laura Sloate, a New York money manager who heads an investment firm with a $405 million portfolio and is in charge of the Srong Value fund remembers the blatant discrimination she faced when she began her career in the late 1960s. And, unbeknownst to many, the Italian singer Andrea Bocelli, now celebrated in the United States, is blind.

Unfortunately, the stereotyping of and discrimination against blind people are not confined to history (Almon, 2000; Verplanken, Meijnders, & van de Wege, 1994). A team of Dutch researchers found that sighted people tended to have unfavorable feelings about blind people with whom they had interacted; unfortunately, more experience and contact did not improve the situation. Verplanken and his Dutch team maintain that blindness is met with more negative attitudes than other physical disability. Evidently, sighted persons often feel uneasy, afraid, or uncomfortable when interacting with blind people, even if they assess the individual as extremely competent (Almon, 2000). Negative attitudes—which can result in bias in the community, in the workplace, and at school—can be reduced through disability-sensitivity training. Clearly, bias and negative attitudes can lead to discrimination and missed opportunities for participation in the mainstream of society.

David Shell and his guide dog Rye work side-by-side to build competitive hot rods.

HISTORY OF THE FIELD

Records from ancient Egypt confirm that people with visual disabilities were accepted in some societies of the ancient world. Homer, the Greek poet who in the 8th-Century B.C. composed the Odyssey and the Iliad, was blind. The ancient Greeks held Homer and his work in the highest regard, considering him a source of wisdom and a model of heroic conduct. Despite evidence of the acceptance of some blind individuals, there is no record of a systematic attempt to educate blind people and integrate them into society until the 18th Century.

In 1784 Valentin Haüy opened the first school for the blind. At this Parisian school, the Institution for Blind Youth, he conceived a system of raised letters on the printed page. The French Revolution in 1789 ended Haüy's work on this innovative reading system, but by the early 1800s, another Frenchman had developed a tactile system for reading and writing. Louis Braille, who was blind, designed an embossed six-dot cell system, the forerunner of the reading and writing method used today.

The first center school for the blind in the United States, the New England Asylum for the Blind (now the Perkins School for the Blind), directed by Samuel Gridley Howe, opened in 1821. Around 1832, the New York Institute for the Blind and the Pennsylvania Institution for the Instruction of the Blind were founded. These 19th-Century schools were private boarding schools, usually attended by children from wealthy families.

The first day classes for students with visual disabilities began in Scotland in 1872. The Scottish Education Act required children who were blind to be educated with their sighted classmates and to attend schools in their local communities. Note that our mainstreaming and "inclusion" movements are not new concepts: Their roots are deep in the history of education of children with disabilities. In the United States, the first concentrated attempts to integrate blind students into local public

Tradition holds that Homer, a blind Greek poet, lived around the time of the Trojan War (8th century B.C.) in either Chios or Smyrma. He made his living as a court singer and storyteller and is credited with writing the earliest epic poems, The Illiad *and* The Odyssey.

MAKING CONNECTIONS

For more discussion about guide dogs, see the mobility subsection in "Elementary Through High School" later in this chapter.

MAKING CONNECTIONS

Read the "Technology" section of this chapter.

schools were made in Chicago. In 1900 Frank Hall, the superintendent for the Illinois School for the Blind, convinced people to allow blind students to attend a local school in a region of Chicago near where they lived. These students attended general classes but also had a special education teacher who taught braille and helped them participate in the general education curriculum. Hall also developed a mechanical writer—a small, portable machine for taking notes and completing other written tasks.

Edward Allen taught the first class for the partially sighted in 1913 in Boston; later that year, Robert Irwin started a class in Cleveland. These programs were modeled after classes in England in which schoolwork was almost exclusively oral. Reading and writing tasks were kept to a minimum, and students attending these classes participated in general education as much as possible. These classes were generally called "sight saving classes." This method was popular for almost fifty years (from about 1915 to 1965), until Natalie Barraga's research on visual efficiency appeared in 1964 (Barraga, 1964; Barraga & Collins, 1979). She proved that people do not have a limited amount of sight that can be used up; rather, vision can become more limited when it is not used.

Although reading and writing present difficult tasks to many individuals with visual disabilities, another major area of difficulty is movement. Between 1918 and 1925, dog guides were trained to help French and German veterans of World War I. Guide dogs (Seeing Eye dogs) were introduced in the United States in 1928, but less than 4 percent of people with visual disabilities use Seeing Eye dogs (Tuttle & Ferrell, 1995). The more popular method of assisting mobility is the long cane, developed around 1860. Richard Hoover, after whom the **Hoover cane** is named, is credited with developing a mobility and orientation system in 1944. Before this time, there was no systematic method for teaching individuals how to move freely in their environments.

During the 1950s, medical advances that helped save the lives of infants born prematurely ironically caused the disease retinopathy of prematurity (ROP), formally known as retrolental fibroplasia, in surviving infants. ROP results in visual disabilities that range from mild visual loss to blindness. During the 1960s, the

CHAPTER 11 *Low Vision or Blindness*

rubella (German measles) epidemic left many children with multiple disabilities, often including visual disabilities. The dramatic increase in blind and low vision children strained the capacity of residential schools, which before World War II had served 85 percent of all schoolchildren with visual disabilities (Sacks & Rosen, 1994). At the same time, parents began to call for their children to attend their local public schools. Today, the majority of children with visual disabilities live at home and attend local public schools.

Advances in technology have significantly influenced the lives of blind and low vision individuals. Over the past thirty years, improvements in computer capabilities have allowed for efficient and inexpensive print enlargements and immediate translation of print to braille. The first print-to-voice translator, the **Kurzweil Reader**, was developed in the 1970s and, though crude and expensive when compared to today's versions of optical scanners, provided immediate access to printed text not available in other formats (braille, enlarged text, audio). This machine provided the breakthrough technology that allows blind individuals immediate access to all printed information, yet it only hinted at the remarkable innovations now developed and still to come.

Natalie Barraga's work on visual efficiency changed the field's research agenda and influenced how low vision and blind children are taught.

PREVALENCE

According to the American Foundation for the Blind (AFB), approximately 1.3 million Americans are legally blind and there are some 10 million with low vision or blindness (AFB, 2002). However, the vast majority of these people are over the age of 65. Worldwide, only 4 percent of *all* blind people are children (Hatton, 2001). Visual disabilities are clearly associated with increasing age. The proportion of children with visual disabilities is much smaller than the proportion of people with this disability in the general population. About 4 of every 10,000 schoolchildren (less than 0.04 percent) have visual disabilities and receive special services (U.S. Department of Education, 2001). Only 14,546 children between the ages of 6 and 17 are receiving special education because of low vision or blindness. Of this entire group of students, about one-third (5 in every 1,000 students) are legally blind (Tuttle & Ferrell, 1995). Also, many children with visual disabilities are not counted in this special education category. About half of young children with visual disabilities have more than one disability and are often included in the multiple disabilities category (Dote-Kwan, Chen, & Hughes, 2001).

CAUSES AND PREVENTION

Visual disabilities may be

- Congenital (present at birth) or
- Acquired

Medical technology is helping to identify more specific causes of disabilities, information that may then lead to either cures or preventive measures. For example, two causes of visual disabilities were reduced dramatically during the last part of the 20th Century: retinopathy of prematurity (ROP) and rubella. Today, precautions are being taken to prevent many cases of ROP in low birth weight babies, but if ROP is not prevented, it often can be corrected with eye surgery. Rubella, a cause of congenital visual disabilities, and also of multiple disabilities, is prevented today by a vaccine.

Almost half of the children who are blind have the disability because of prenatal factors, mostly hereditary. Researchers are working to identify genes that cause some forms of blindness. The gene that causes retinitis pigmentosa has now been located and isolated, and there is hope of a cure in the near future.

MAKING CONNECTIONS

- For information about other low incidence disabilities, see Chapters 8–12.
- See Chapter 13 for more about students with multiple disabilities.

MAKING CONNECTIONS

See the "Causes" sections in Chapters 3 through 13 to compare and contrast the contributing factors to disabilities.

MAKING CONNECTIONS

To review information about low birth weight babies, see

- The "Causes and Prevention" section in Chapter 6
- The "Prevalence" section in Chapter 9

For more about ROP, see

- The "History" section of this chapter
- Table 11.1

Other medical advances—such as laser treatment, surgery, and corneal implants—also help to reduce the incidence of visual disabilities among children or lessen their severity. Although the medical advances have reduced the prevalence of visual disabilities in children, medical technology can cause increases in this disability as well. Today more infants survive premature birth and very low birth weights of even less than two pounds. The result, however, is often the child being left with multiple disabilities, frequently including visual disabilities (Dote-Kwan, Chen, & Hughes, 2001; Hatton, 2001).

In many cases visual disabilities can now be prevented, but more can be done. For example, the incidence of visual disabilities can be greatly reduced by protecting against eye injuries (Prevent Blindness America, 2002). For those visual disabilities that cannot be avoided, their impact can be lessened through early and consistent treatment. Unfortunately, not all U.S. children have early access to health care. In fact, poor children are between 1.2 and 1.8 times more likely to have visual disabilities (Sherman, 1994). Considering the long-term costs to society and to these individuals, the problem of access to health care must be addressed.

CHARACTERISTICS

The process of learning social skills begins in infancy and continues to develop throughout childhood, and visual information plays an important role in the acquisition of social skills (Baird, Mayfield, & Baker, 1997). The infant learns to make eye contact, smile, and touch appropriately. When not stimulated directly, blind infants often withdraw and do not explore their environments as sighted infants do. They often experience a prolonged period of inactivity during their first year, which inhibits their exploration and discovery of their environment. Many develop inappropriate behaviors, such as rocking, or inappropriate hand movements, including eye poking. Babies with visual disabilities may acquire some social problems as a result of insufficient interpersonal interactions early in life, so they need assistance as they develop relationships, particularly during their first two years (Baird, Mayfield, & Baker, 1997). The child learns to gain access to play groups, resolve conflicts, attract and direct attention of peers, play, and maintain friendships. Whereas these skills are learned through typical interactions by sighted children, they need to be directly taught to many blind children (Heller et al., 1996).

Many blind and low vision children do not understand the social behavior of others because they cannot gain this awareness through normal social interactions (Pring, Dewart, & Brockbank, 1998). They seem to be less assertive than their sighted peers, which may disturb the necessary balance and equilibrium in social exchanges (Buhrow, Hartshorne, & Bradley-Johnson, 1998). Many blind youngsters tend to lack play skills, ask too many irrelevant questions, and engage in inappropriate acts of affection (Rettig, 1994). Possibly because of their inappropriate or immature social behaviors, they tend to interact with and make friends with the least popular peers in their general education classes (MacCuspie, 1992). And unfortunately, they tend not to interact with other children naturally or spontaneously (Crocker & Orr, 1996). Being unable to see peers' nonverbal cues, which serve to guide their sighted classmates' social interactions, is a major problem for these youngsters. Next time you are interacting with friends, consider how nonverbal cues (facial expressions, a shrug of the shoulders) affect the meaning of a message. Now think about how the literal message (without the nonverbal cues) of the interaction would be understood by someone who could not use sight during the interaction. Not understanding social situations can lead to unfortunate and disruptive behaviors. One way to improve such situations is to use clear instructions, such as those described in the "Achieving Discipline" box.

Establish Boundaries: Explicit Rules

Ms. Pacheon's third-graders' first week of school was difficult. She held high expectations for her students and planned to use many cooperative learning groups during the year. This freer style of instruction was unfamiliar to her students and would require them to develop independent learning skills and to deal with challenging academic materials. Through a community partnership, the summer saw an installation of an Ethernet system in all of the upper elementary classrooms. Six computers, networked to the district's main computer, were now in her class available for the children to use for research through the Web and for writing and other computer applications. The possibilities for enhanced learning were great, but so were the opportunities for chaos. By the end of the first week of school, everyone realized that achieving a positive learning environment would require cooperation and some structure.

On Monday afternoon, after another frustrating morning, Ms. Pacheon held a class conference. She waited until this time so the students had a clear understanding of the necessity of developing guidelines for their behavior in class. Together, they discussed the opportunities and responsibilities of being able to work in small groups, in pairs, or independently. They discussed how they would share the computers and fairly manage time spent using them across the entire day. They talked about the noise level in the class during group time and shared with each other their own learning styles and needs. They developed a broad, general list of rules. They developed a set of consequences that would be applied when rules were broken and also a reward system for the entire class when standards for their positive learning environment were met. In addition, they all promised to remind each other of the rules during the first-week trial period. Ms. Pacheon told the class that she would hold another class conference on Friday to assess the outcomes, at which time they could review and modify the rules they developed that Monday afternoon.

Steps Used to Create a Positive Learning Environment

- The teacher actively involved her class in the development of rules.
- Together, they generated a list of rules that were broadly and positively stated.
- The teacher promoted everyone's understanding of the rules.
- The rules were consistently applied.
- They were reviewed and modified periodically.
- The teacher reminded the students of the rules before situations became high-probability times for infractions.

Perhaps the way blind children are treated and the negative experiences they have with peers during the school years contribute to the following characteristics often attributed to blind people in the research literature: They are often found to have low self-esteem and to be socially immature, egocentric, self-conscious, isolated, passive, withdrawn, and dependent (Huurre, Komulainen, & Aro, 1999; Tuttle & Ferrell, 1995). What can sighted peers, teachers, and parents do to help?

- Provide opportunities to develop interpersonal skills.
- Be informed about the visual status of the student with visual disabilities.
- Model appropriate behaviors.
- Encourage students to participate fully in all school activities.
- Help students communicate their visual needs in a straightforward fashion.

Teachers can also help these students understand the explicit and implicit rules of games and social interactions. Meanwhile, parents can organize small play groups at home and provide direct feedback about their youngster's interpersonal interactions.

EARLY CHILDHOOD EDUCATION

Increasing Interactions

The goal is for national interactions to occur at school, at home, and in the community, which requires the child to both initiate and respond to communications (Dote-Kwan, 2001).

1. Understand the child's visual functioning capabilities.
2. Identify visual features that enhance the child's visual functions (color, contrast, size).
3. Encourage the child's interest in objects, events, and people (children need to have something they are interested in talking about).
4. Learn the child's nonverbal cues indicating interest.
5. Develop a predictable and understandable system to initiate communications.
6. Add signs and nonverbal signals to enhance communications, if necessary.
7. Design many opportunities for interactions in the child's natural settings.
8. Expand the child's vocabulary and communications by repeating and modeling extensions of the child's interaction.
9. Reduce the reliance on adult initiations, and allow and encourage increased initiations from the child.
10. Make interactions enjoyable for both the child and the adult.

MAKING CONNECTIONS

The importance of play is also discussed in the "Early Childhood Education" section of Chapter 5.

Just as for students with other disabilities, preschool education is vital for those with visual disabilities. During this time, the foundations for social skills, academic success, and independence are laid. Recall that those who are congenitally blind (born blind) and those who became blind at a very early age (adventitiously blind) have little or no memory of how the world looks. These infants are not stimulated like sighted infants and have limited opportunities for learning. They do not see their mother's smile or the toys in their cribs. The right preschool program can give preschoolers with visual disabilities the "right start" so that the disadvantages this disability can cause are minimized. The teacher of a preschooler with visual disabilities should coordinate a multidisciplinary team of specialists, including an ophthalmologist, occupational therapist, physical therapist, orientation and mobility instructor, and social worker. The preschool years provide the foundation for lifelong learning and independence. This is a time when children learn basic communication and interaction patterns, and for blind students this can be a problem area. See the "Tips for Teachers" box for suggestions on how to facilitate the development of these important skills.

Why is play a new and important theme of preschool education?

Researchers are learning that play is a very important part of human development (McGaha & Farran, 2001; Recchia, 1997). Through play, young children learn to socialize, interact with others, and cooperate. Via discovery and exploration, which are encouraged through play activities, young children also learn about their environment, develop motor skills, and often enhance their language skills. Because of their disability, blind and low vision children play very differently from others and are also delayed about two years behind their sighted peers in the development of play skills (Hughes, Dote-Kwan, & Dolendo, 1998).

Many characteristics of their play follow many blind individuals into adulthood: engaging in high rates of solitary play, not playing spontaneously, seeking play with adults rather than other children, not taking conversational turns, and selecting toys that are concrete, familiar items (McGaha & Farran, 2001; Tröster & Brambring, 1992, 1994). Delayed play development might well contribute to later difficulties in social interactions and concept formation (Recchia, 1997). Sighted children often find it difficult to adjust their play to the ability levels of blind children, who prefer noisy play activities to abstract or symbolic ones (Tröster & Brambring, 1994). They often find their play styles in conflict with those of their blind peers. Their quick and sometimes unpredictable movements can disorient children with severe visual disabilities (Rettig, 1994). Some experts are convinced that simply providing inclusive opportunities does not ensure interactions and play among sighted and blind preschoolers; adult intervention may be necessary (Hughes, Dote-Kwan, & Dolendo, 1998; McGaha & Farran, 2001).

How do skills of independence expand the curriculum for students with visual disabilities?

Orientation and mobility are major curriculum targets for students with severe visual disabilities. Because instruction in this area needs to begin as early as possible, parents and professionals are encouraging the introduction of the long cane to children between the ages of 2 and 6 (Pogrund, Fazzi, & Schreier, 1993). Although some orientation and mobility teachers believe that young children should begin learning how to use a long cane with the adult size that they will use later in life (which would be extra long for their present size), research findings indicate that children are better off learning how to use a mobility cane that is cut to their size (Clarke, Sainato, & Ward, 1994). Sometimes called the "kiddy cane" or the Connecticut precane, this homemade version of the long cane is tailored to the size of the user, even a preschooler. It is made of rigid, white PVC pipe and is cut at midchest height. It has a red stripe at the bottom and tape across the top for a grip.

Because the home is the most natural setting for infants' and toddlers' educational programs, most programs for blind infants include home based instruction with considerable parent involvement. One of the most important lessons parents can learn is to encourage later independence by allowing their babies to explore the environment. Research shows that parents can help their infants become more mobile and independent by teaching them to crawl and walk in a structured program (Joffee, 1988). Some parents of infants with visual disabilities, fearful that their baby will fall or be hurt, are overly protective and controlling—attitudes that can foster dependency (Behl et al., 1996).

ELEMENTARY THROUGH HIGH SCHOOL

The educational needs of low vision students differ from those of blind students. Students with low vision might require some extra tutorial assistance to learn the same number of phonetic rules as their classmates or additional time to read their history assignment. Teachers can help blind and low vision students in many ways. They can make adjustments in the way they lecture and present information to students. Students who are blind might require the introduction of entirely different curriculum topics. For example, they might need to learn independent **life skills** so that they can manage an apartment, pay their bills, shop for food, and cook their meals without assistance from others. The crucial factor is that the educational and developmental goals, and the instruction designed to meet those goals, reflect the specific needs of each individual (Spungin, 2002). In the next sections, we discuss two areas of particular concern for students with visual disabilities: developing reading skills and mobility skills.

How do students with visual disabilities read and become literate?

Today, a large percentage (about 52 percent) of students with visual disabilities spend over 79 percent of their school days in general education classrooms. Over 70 percent of low vision and blind students receive their education at their neighborhood school in the general education classroom, possibly with support from a resource specialist or itinerant teacher (U.S. Department of Education, 2001). These students participate in the general education curriculum with their sighted classmates and, if they do not also have multiple disabilities, tend to perform well

MAKING CONNECTIONS

For more information about mobility, see that subsection in "Elementary Through High School" in this chapter.

MAKING CONNECTIONS

For other discussions of reading and literacy, see Chapters 3, 4, 6, 7, and 10.

VALIDATED PRACTICES
Classroom Modifications

What Are Classroom Modifications?

Classroom modifications for students with visual disabilities are important for them to be successful in the general education curriculum. Remember that everyone has different levels of ability, so some students only need simple modifications to the classroom and instruction, whereas others may need more intense accommodations.

Why Classroom Modifications Are Beneficial

With simple modifications beneficial to everyone, most students with visual disabilities learn well alongside their peers in the general education classroom. In these situations, students with and without visual disabilities learn from each other.

Implementing Classroom Modifications

Below is a list of simple things that teachers can do to make their classrooms more adaptable for students with visual disabilities. Vision specialists can guide the implementation of modifications to be sure they are right for the individual child.

Chalkboards and Dry Eraser Boards

- Seat students close to the window for more natural lighting and fewer reflections off shiny surfaces impairing view of writing on the board.

- Encourage blind and low vision students to use their assistive technology devices (e.g., magnifying glasses, telescopes), and create a climate where they are not embarrassed by using them.

- Before lessons, prepare large print or braille versions of what will be written on the board.

- Prior to each lesson, provide students with a copy of your lecture notes.

- Explain your notes as you write them on the board.

Classroom Demonstrations

- Avoid standing with your back to the window, because glare makes it more difficult for students to see.

- Either before or after the lesson, allow students to touch the materials.

- To avoid considerable confusion, be sure your students have all the required materials prior to the lesson.

MAKING CONNECTIONS

For a review of various strategies and methods for students with learning disabilities, see the "Early Childhood" and "Elementary Through High School" sections of Chapter 4.

academically. Many use aids such as glasses or technology that enlarges type to help them enhance their vision for accessing information from printed material, whether it be in text or on the board. Others, even those with low vision, use their tactile senses and employ braille as their reading method, and some rely on audio means for gaining information. One of the singular characteristics of this group of learners is the variety of ways in which they access information, but in all cases, direct instruction is the best means to help them master reading and achieve literacy (Corn & Koenig, 2002).

Many individuals with severe visual disabilities are not proficient readers, regardless of the reading method they use. One obvious reason for these students' reading difficulties is their visual disabilities. Another reason is that many of these individuals have multiple disabilities, which leads some teachers to conclude that braille instruction is not appropriate (Dote-Kwan, Chen, & Hughes, 2001). However, this fact leads others to conclude that braille instruction is still important but that instructional methods need to be adjusted. For example, somewhere between 14 percent and 65 percent of low vision and blind students also have learning disabilities (Erin & Koenig, 1997). These students may require additional instructional strategies, borrowed from the field of learning disabilities, to master reading. Students learning braille may have great success using the phonics approach, and low vision students with learning disabilities who are learning to read print may benefit from learning strategies that emphasize comprehension by skimming passages to look for the main ideas. Literacy is a goal for all Americans and an expectation for all high school graduates, but literacy presents particular and unique challenges for individuals with visual disabilities.

- Provide the vision teacher early with all texts and other materials that need to be adapted.

Writing in the Classroom

- So that their writing is more visible, allow students to use bold-line paper and felt tip pens.
- Remember that your students will need to write larger so that they can read what they have written.

Homework, Tests, and Reproduced Materials

- As with all materials that need to be adapted, give homework assignments to the teacher of visually impaired students far in advance.
- When assigning a bigger project, give your students advance notice so that they will have sufficient time to gather needed materials.
- Provide text-only versions of worksheets because those with graphics are difficult to enlarge.
- Allow students with visual disabilities to take more time on assignments and tests—perhaps time and a half for students with low vision and double time for students who read braille.
- Allow your students to answer their questions on the test form, or have another student or paraprofessional record the answers the student gives orally.

Maps and Charts

- Provide desk copies of charts and maps to your students with visual disabilities.
- Use raised maps with your students with visual disabilities.

Films, Videos, and Multimedia Presentations

- Schedule an individualized session for students with visual disabilities so that they can view multimedia presentations with the vision specialist to ensure they understand visual concepts.
- If presentations have subtitles, have someone read them to students who cannot read print.

Moving Around the School

- Be very specific when giving verbal directions.
- Secure rugs and other floor covering so students don't trip.
- Keep cupboards and closet doors closed.
- Make sure all chairs are pushed under desks.

This scientifically validated practice is a teaching method proven by systematic research efforts (Cox & Dykes, 2001; Spungin, 2002). Full citations are found in the "Elementary Through High School" section of the of the references for this chapter.

- *Printed Materials* The great majority of students with visual disabilities are able to learn to read and write, watch television, and use their vision to function in society. Many low vision students who use their vision to read need specially adapted versions of the texts used in their classes, which should be readily available from materials centers. One complaint, however, is the excessive length of time it often takes to get large-print accommodations (Frank, 2000). Fortunately, this barrier is easily overcome today, thanks to the availability of copiers, scanners, and computers, which can quickly and easily modify print size and format.

As noted, the print in typical books is too small for many students with visual disabilities. If special equipment is not available locally or from the state's or school district's materials center, what other options do these students have? Fortunately, many books and materials are broadly available through bookstores and mail-order sources. Large-type dictionaries, thesauruses, and atlases are now available. The Book-of-the-Month Club maintains a Large Print Library; Reader's Digest produces a large-type version of its magazine every month, as well as a biography and condensed book series; and the *New York Times* publishes a specially edited weekly version of its newspaper in 16-point type and small page size (12-inch by 14-inch). Such accommodations—essential for most individuals with glaucoma, congenital cataracts, or nystagmus—allow greater participation in American society by blind and low vision people.

For individuals with good central vision but a limited visual field, enlargements may be a hindrance, however. For these students, audiocassette versions of textbooks, **personal readers,** or computer-generated print-to-voice systems (described in the technology section of this chapter) may be good alternatives.

MAKING **C**ONNECTIONS

More information about technology for low vision and blind people is found in the "Technology" section of this chapter.

Braille Instruction and Use of Braille

The IEP Team for each student with a visual disability must consider special factors about each child's method of reading:

■ All IEPs for children with visual disabilities must address the issue of braille instruction and the use of braille in classroom settings.

■ Evaluate the child's reading and writing skills, educational needs, and future need for instruction in braille or use of braille.

■ Provide instruction in braille and allow the child to use braille, if that method is deemed appropriate for that student.

■ The braille decision cannot be based on factors such as the availability of alternative reading methods or the availability of braille instruction.

■ Once the decision is made, services and materials must be delivered without undue delay.

• *Braille* Students with very severe visual disabilities may need to learn to read and write using a very different method, a tactile one. **Braille** uses a coded system of dots embossed on paper so that individuals can feel a page of text. Braille has been used by shrinking proportions of low vision and blind people in recent years. In 1963 over 50 percent of persons with severe visual disabilities used braille; in 1978 less than 20 percent did. Today, even though technology makes braille versions of text more readily available, only about 85,000 of the 1 million people who are legally blind in this country use braille (Sinatra, 2002). For children the story is much the same. In 1992 only 10 percent of blind students used braille (American Printing House for the Blind, 1992). Today, although there are some 55,200 legally blind children in the United States, only 5,500 use braille—a figure that remains at the same 10 percent level as a decade ago (American Foundation for the Blind [AFB], 2002).

Concern about low vision and blind students' reading abilities is widespread because the literacy levels of these individuals are alarmingly low. In a study conducted by the American Printing House for the Blind (1992), which included elementary and secondary students attending local public schools and those attending state center schools, it was found that 27 percent were visual readers, 10 percent were auditory readers, another 10 percent were braille readers, 22 percent were considered prereaders because they were reading at a readiness level and had not yet determined a preferred reading mode, and 31 percent were nonreaders. Findings like these have caused concern in the field about the low literacy rate among individuals with visual disabilities. Therefore, Congress addressed the issue of braille instruction in IDEA, which now requires that braille be considered in the development of these students' IEPs (see the "What IDEA Says" box for more information).

Many reasons have been suggested to explain why fewer people are using braille as a reading method today. First, for many, braille can be very cumbersome and slow. Trent and Truan (1997) report that typical braille readers in high school achieve a rate of only 42 words per minute, and the best reader in their study read 103 words per minute. Adults using braille read 30 percent slower (at a rate of about 134) than those who read print (Wetzel & Knowlton, 2000). Becoming even minimally proficient at the braille method of reading takes extensive training and practice. Braille also uses different codes for different types of reading, such as math and music, which makes it even more difficult for students with cognitive impairments to master braille completely.

Can you think of some other reasons why braille is less popular today? Here are a few:

• Teachers not knowing how to use or teach the braille method
• Unavailability of teachers who know how to teach braille
• Increasing availability of audiotapes
• Immediate computerized print-to-voice translations
• Difficulty in both cost and time of getting braille versions of books

Braille literacy has become a concern of educators and policymakers. The unavailability of braille versions of texts used in the general education classroom has been

Table 11.3 Selected Braille Literacy Skill Areas

1. Emergent Braille Literacy

Listen to adults read; develop hand-finger skills; observe proficient braille reading

2. Pre-braille—Early Formal Literacy

Learn hand-finger skills, tactile discrimination, and hand movement; expand conceptual knowledge and vocabulary; develop early reading skills; become motivated

3. Beginning Braille Literacy

Learn braille decoding and word analysis skills; learn braille writing; build fluency; apply literacy skills throughout day

4. Begin Dual Media (print and braille)

Learn print and braille reading concurrently; learn print and braille writing concurrently; develop vocabulary, comprehension, and reading for specific purposes; engage in leisure reading

5. Intermediate Braille Literacy

Use reading as a tool for learning; continue fluency building; incorporate technology into reading experiences

6. Advanced Braille Literacy

Learn computer braille and foreign language braille; continue using and developing braille for math and science, continue inclusion of technology; balance literacy tools (braille and recorded material)

7. Braille Literacy for Those with Print Literacy

Learn tactile perception, hand movements, and letter/symbol recognition in braille; begin learning contractions; learn braille writing skills; apply literacy skills daily

8. Listening, Aural-reading and Live-reader skills

Develop auditory skills (e.g., auditory awareness, sound localization); acquire information by listening; learn how to use recorded textbooks; direct activities of live readers

9. Technology Skills

Gain access to printed information through technology; take notes by using braille; use speech-synthesizing devices; use the Internet to gather information

10. Keyboarding and Word-processing

Master touch typing; use word processing software, along with all editing features; apply keyboarding and word processing in daily applications

11. Slate-and-Stylus Skills

Master a variety of slate and stylus equipment; become proficient in their use; apply these skills in practical situations

12. Signature-writing skills

Learn how to write a signature for legal purposes; practice with many different writing tools (e.g., pens, pencils); understand about when and why signatures are necessary; apply skill appropriately

Source: Adapted from "Ensuring high-quality instruction for students in braille literacy programs" by A. J. Koenig and M. C. Holbrook, *Journal of Visual Impairment and Blindness,* 94, pp. 689–690. Copyright © 2000 by American Federation for the Blind. Reprinted with permission of the American Federation for the Blind via Copyright Clearance Center.

a great hindrance to this method's widespread use. Current scanning capabilities and special microcomputer software and printers can now translate standard print into braille almost instantaneously. The U.S. Senate would like to take advantage of this fact and have publishers make electronic versions of textbooks available to schools (U.S. Senate, 2002). Because of the inclusion of braille in IDEA, because of concerns about the literacy rates of this group of learners, and because of the improved availability of braille versions of texts, more experts are thinking about braille instruction with an eye toward the goal of braille literacy. Table 11.3 shows the 12 components of instruction leading to braille literacy, as identified by Koenig and Holbrook (2000), and provides some applications of these instructional targets.

How do people with low visual efficiencies learn to move around independently?

Children with very low visual efficiencies need special orientation and mobility training to increase their abilities to move around independently. **Orientation** can be described as the mental map people have about their surroundings (Hill, 1986). Most of us use landmarks and other cues to get from one place to another. Think about how you get from your house to a friend's home or from one class to another on campus. What cues or landmarks do you use? These cues or landmarks make up our mental maps and our orientation to our environments. Remember that these mental landmarks are learned and that students need to know their schools well.

Learning to use a long cane is part of the school curriculum for these students. Orientation and mobility instruction is part of every school day.

M
AKING
C
ONNECTIONS

- Kiddy canes are discussed in the "Early Childhood" section of this chapter.

- For another example of the use of service animals, see the "Transition" section of this chapter and also Chapter 9.

For example, they need to know emergency evacuation procedures, exit paths from the school buildings, and how to safely move through their environment both during normal school hours and in times of stress (Cox & Dykes, 2001).

Mobility is the ability to travel safely and efficiently from one place to another. According to the Centers for Disease Control's most recent data, 130,000 blind adults use the **long cane** (CDC, 1998). Learning how to be independently mobile by using a long cane is difficult, and proficient use requires many years of instruction and practice. Here's how it works. While a person is walking, the cane is tapped on the ground and makes a sound. It helps the user know when a hallway ends, when stairs begin and end, and when doors are reached. A cane does not always help the individual avoid many obstacles found in modern society. For example, silent traffic signals, escalators, elevators, and public transportation, as well as protruding and overhanging objects that are undetectable with mobility canes, can be very dangerous to persons with visual disabilities. Not all people who need assistance with mobility use long canes; some are assisted by **guide dogs.** The number is relatively small; there are 1.3 million legally blind people, and only about 7,000 use guide dogs (less than 4 percent) to help them move about independently (AFB, 2002).

Besides using a long cane or a guide dog, there are some times, such as when crossing a busy street or entering an unfamiliar building, that blind and low vision people require assistance from sighted people. In such a situation, the sighted person must be sensitive to a number of different issues:

1. Be sure the person wants help.

2. Ask the individual to be sure he or she wants assistance.

3. If the answer is yes, guide the individual by offering your arm, holding it in a relaxed position.

4. The individual usually will gently grasp your arm at or above your elbow and will walk slightly behind or to your side. (Never push or pull as you walk.)

5. Enjoy a conversation, and walk with ease.

In addition to use of the long cane, the orientation and mobility curriculum includes many other skills (Ungar, Blades, & Spencer, 1997). Using maps, particularly **tactile maps,** is one example. These maps can assist the individual with independent movement in the community, as street maps do for sighted people. With recent advances in computers and printers, such as American Thermoform's Swell Form Graphics Machine II, the creation of tactile maps and graphics is inexpensive and simple (Horsfall, 1997).

Sports and recreation programs and activities not only contribute to better orientation and mobility skills but also help students become engaged and active. Blind and low vision people have many special sports programs are available to them. Special skiing, sailing, hiking, baseball, bowling, bicycling, and horseback riding are very popular. However, some people with severe visual disabilities chose not to participate in special programs but, rather, compete with sighted athletes—and excel. One such individual is Erik Weihenmayer. Erik, one of the nation's premier rock climbers, has achieved a great deal, including teaching his father to climb by scaling Wind Ridge in Colorado (Walker, 1999). He was the first blind person to hike the sixty-mile-long Inca Trail in Peru. Among his other accomplishments have been climbing El Capitan in California, Aconcagua in Argentina, and Mt. McKinley in

Alaska. Other blind athletes also serve as role models. Marla Runyan, a gold medal Paralympian, competed in the finals of the 1,500-meter run in the IAAF World Championships of track and field, held in Seville, Spain; qualified for the 2000 Olympics in the 1,500-meter run; and set a U.S. indoor record for the 5,000 meters run (Associated Press, 1999; Patrick, 2001; Starr, 2000). And blind youngsters are learning that they do not have to be superathletes to participate in events. Here's an example. Teams of blind and visually impaired teenages, with guides, took a 4-day, 139-mile bicycling trip from Nashville to the home of Helen Keller via the Natchez Trace (Associated Press, 2002; Duzak, 2002).

Maria Runyan, a track and field star who is legally blind, crosses the finish line as the winner in a 5000-meter U.S. championship race. In 2002 she ran the New York Marathon, her first marathon race, where she placed fifth in a field of world-class women runners. She provides an example to children with visual disabilities showing them that the thrill of victory is not out of reach.

COLLABORATION FOR INCLUSION

Collaborative services from experts in the field of visual disabilities should be available to all blind and low vision students, irrespective of where they go to school. Itinerant vision teachers as well as **outreach services** from a center school can help general educators structure both the physical and the academic environment to ensure the success of inclusive efforts (De Mario & Caruso, 2001). They can help teachers understand about putting furniture and materials in a consistent place and pattern. They can also help reorganize the classroom every month so the student with visual disabilities learns to adjust to changes in the environment. Other modifications to the classroom's physical space can be important as well. For example, some of these students use bulky equipment and aids (optical aids, magnifiers, tape recorders) to facilitate their learning. Some use brailling equipment, and others use portable laptop computers. These students need larger desks or a small table near an electrical outlet. They might even need cabinet space to store their belongings.

Some students with visual disabilities need only minor modifications to succeed in general education classes, whereas other students need substantial accommodations. The suggestions found in the "Accommodating for Inclusive Environments" box can easily be incorporated into classroom situations and can certainly make the general classroom environment more "friendly" to students with substantial visual limitations (Barraga & Morris, 1992; Harley, Truan, & Sanford, 1987; Sacks & Kekelis, 1992; Sacks & Reardon, 1992; Spungin, 2002).

Some adaptations help all students gain more from the learning environment and require only some adjustments in teaching style. One such modification is the careful use of language. For example, many of us, when speaking, use words that substitute for other words, rather than terms that concretely name their referents; we say words such as *it, this, that,* and *there* without naming the things we are discussing. For example, an adult might say, "Go get it. It's over there," instead of saying, "Please get the large book at the end of my desk." Clearly, the more concrete and specific instruction is more helpful to a blind student.

A commonly used accommodation for all students with disabilities is extended time. Many blind and low vision students require more time to complete assignments. Teachers often set a later due date but also insist that this deadline be met. Another common accommodation is the use of a computer for both in-class assignments and homework. Regardless of these accommodations, teachers should not lower their expectations for students with visual disabilities.

MAKING CONNECTIONS

For more suggestions about accommodations general education teachers can make to truly include students with disabilities in the instructional program, see the "Accommodating for Inclusive Environments" boxes throughout this text (Chapters 3–12).

ACCOMMODATING FOR INCLUSIVE ENVIRONMENTS

Making the Classroom a Safe and Positive Learning Environment

1. Place the child's desk close to the teacher's desk, the blackboard, and the classroom door.

2. Reduce distracting glare; arrange the child's desk away from a light source but in a well-lit area.

3. Allow the child to relocate in the classroom for different activities to enhance opportunities to see and hear.

4. Open or close doors fully (a half-open door can be a dangerous obstacle).

5. Eliminate unnecessary noise; do not speak too loudly, for it tends to increase classroom volume level.

6. Eliminate clutter from the room, particularly in aisles and movement paths.

7. Place materials in consistent places so students know where particular items are always located.

8. Keep to routine schedules so students know what to expect on specific days and times.

9. Address students by using their names first to get their attention.

10. Do not leave the classroom without telling the student.

11. Explain the implicit and explicit rules for classroom conduct, games, and social situations.

12. Encourage students with visual disabilities to express their visual needs.

13. Repeat orally information written on a board or an overhead projector, and give the student a printed version. (Remember that enlargements on an overhead projector are not helpful to all blind and low vision students.)

14. Prepare enlarged print or braille handouts, summarizing key points from lectures (an easy task using computers with braillers and adjustable font and type sizes).

15. Audiotape lectures so students can use tapes as study aids at home.

16. Select bright and contrasting colors for bulletin boards and other instructional materials, for those who benefit from such visual contrasts.

17. Increase visual contrast: place yellow plastic overlays over purple ditto worksheets (which will help some students see the worksheets more easily), photocopy dittos, use felt-tip pens.

18. Seek assistance of a specialist in the area of visual impairments, and have high expectations.

Except for children with speech or language impairments, blind and low vision students are the most integrated of all students with disabilities. This was not always true. Before World War II, some 85 percent of all students with severe visual disabilities attended special residential center schools (Sacks & Rosen, 1994). Today, about 8 percent attend public residential center schools, and about 73 percent attend either general education or resource room programs in their local public schools (U.S. Department of Education, 2001). And the trend is toward more inclusive education. For example, in Los Angeles Unified School district, some 900 legally blind students now attend "mainstream classes"—up from 400 in 1982 (Sandoval, 2000).

Although they are not an option used by many, center schools serve individuals with intensive needs, providing concentrated instruction in braille, orientation and mobility, technology, career education, and independent living (Spungin, 1997). Center schools are also viable options for those students who feel excluded in the inclusive setting. For most families, however, having a family member attend a boarding school during the school year is not their first choice (Barton, 1997). For these students, their families, and general education teachers, being able to collaborate with specialists from residential or center schools who deliver outreach courses and summer programs is critical to these students' achieving high outcomes (De Mario & Caruso, 2001).

CHAPTER 11 *Low Vision or Blindness*

TRANSITION THROUGH ADULTHOOD

Some young adults with visual disabilities have a difficult time adjusting to independence and the world of work. Many of these individuals do not possess the level of literacy necessary to be successful in the community or on the job. Many do not possess other skills (e.g., social interaction, job, self-advocacy) needed to be competitive in the workplace. When such deficiencies are coupled with bias and discrimination, the result is underemployment and a group of individuals not achieving to their capabilities. With education specifically directed toward literacy, career education, and job training, this situation can be corrected.

Do these students transition to work successfully?

Although adults with visual disabilities hold jobs at every level (e.g., scientists, engineers, teachers, office workers, managers of business, and laborers), as a group they tend to be underemployed (Rumrill & Scheff, 1997). Blind and low vision students have one of the highest high school graduation rates of all students with disabilities. They also attend college at a rate close to that of their nondisabled peers. Despite these facts, only about 30 percent of them (compared to 57 percent of all students with disabilities and 69 percent of nondisabled recent high school graduates) are able to find competitive employment (Nagle, 2001). Underemployment or unemployment is commonplace, even in times of record levels of employment and active implementation of the ADA law. Reports persist that only 40 percent of clients of the Department of Vocational Rehabilitation are placed in competitive employment, that 79 percent of blind Americans who want jobs cannot find them, and that 30 percent of those who do are working below their abilities (Associated Press, 1999). These unfortunate situations do not have to be the case for people with visual disabilities.

Why are so many blind individuals at a disadvantage in getting good jobs? It may be partly because their high school years are filled with educational tasks: During high school, many sighted classmates hold jobs after school or during the summer. These sighted peers learn about finding and keeping jobs and also about salaries, wages, and benefits. Students with severe visual disabilities, on the other hand, often spend their summers learning important skills (such as orientation and mobility) that they need for independence. Unfortunately, not having practical work experience can later put them at a disadvantage in the job market. Some (Associated Press, 1999; Hanye, 1998; Nagle, 2001) suggest the following ideas:

- Internships in real work settings
- College graduation
- Education of potential employers about the skills and abilities of blind workers
- Information provided to employers about how costs of special equipment can be paid by state, federal, and private programs

Graduating from college has a significant bearing on a person's career and earning power, but less than

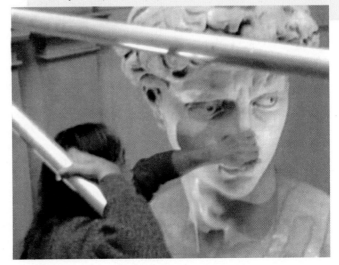

Micheal Naranjo, a blind artist, is shown here "seeing" with his hands Michelangelo's famous sculpture, David. Scaffolding around the statue was erected especially for his benefit. You can see one of Naranjo's sculptures on page 66.

Karen Chasen Spitzberg creates art for blind people to touch and feel. Some of her work includes reproductions of great masterpieces. This woman is from a Henri de Toulouse-Lautrec painting. Spitzberg's contribution of making art truly accessible to those who can only appreciate art tactilely is unique and important to so many.

MAKING CONNECTIONS

See the "Necessity for National Intervention" section of Chapter 1 for more information about including people with disabilities in mainstream society.

half of those with visual disabilities who enter college graduate. Their reasons for leaving college are usually based not on the academic demands but rather on the difficulties of living independently. Fortunately, the skills needed for successful college life can be taught either before or during the college years. The University of Evansville's summer school pre-college program teaches students who are blind the mobility, orientation, academic, and life skills needed for college life (Martin, 1999). Here, students learn how to negotiate a college campus, do their own laundry, live in a dormitory, and take notes during lectures. For students who have participated in this 22-year-old program, college is a less frightening and more successful experience. Other options include programs such as the College-Success Curriculum, which teaches students enrolled in college the skills they need for success (Vancil, 1997). Some topics included in this program are

- Organizational skills
- How to hire a reader
- Gaining access to print material
- Study skills
- Being assertive and advocating for oneself
- Social skills

Regardless of the method, it is clear that blind and low vision students can improve their chances for success in college and in later life by participating in programs specifically designed to develop skills needed for independence.

Do these individuals have ultimate access to the community?

Many adults with visual disabilities feel that their access to recreational, leisure, and cultural activities is limited. Some positive changes are occurring, however. Cultural events are now more accessible. At concert programs of the New York Philharmonic, the Chamber Music Society, and the Great Performances at Lincoln Center, music programs are available in different versions: braille, large-type, and audiotape. Changed attitudes and the ADA law have brought about other opportunities as well. Not only have museums and entertainment centers become more accessible, but so too have zoos. The San Diego Zoo, and most others, once had long-standing bans against guide dogs. These bans existed because many of the wild animals were disturbed by the presence of canines. Now these bans have been relaxed, although some areas of zoos remain off-limits to guide dogs (McCutcheon, 1994). More and more museums are including tactile exhibits for both children and adults. And even children's theater performances are now offering "freeze frames" so young people can feel the costumes and sets of plays (Ansariyah-Grace, 2000).

Increasingly, people with visual disabilities are gaining access to technology and the assistive devices designed to minimize the effects of their disabilities. Although each of these advances adds to the household budget, the diversity of items is remarkable. For example, talking watches, clocks, calculators and food scales, are now plentiful, as are machines that tell you the denomination of paper money. Also,

braille and enlarged-type versions of games can be purchased for about the same price as games without special adaptations. For example, two large-print decks of colorful playing cards can be purchased for $8.95 (Lighthouse International, 2002). Special sets of checkers, chess, Scrabble, poker chips, and many other game items are easy to locate.

FAMILIES

Family members play very special roles as they help their children grow up, particularly mothers of children with visual disabilities. Their responsiveness in complying with their children's requests, repeating or rephrasing their communications, facilitating turn-taking, and giving directions and instructions contributes considerably to positive development in expressive and receptive language (Dote-Kwan, Hughes, & Taylor, 1997; Pérez-Pereira & Conti-Ramsden, 2000). Possibly because of their inability to engage in eye contact, important interactions between parent and child that lay the foundations for social interactions, reciprocal language, and affective behaviors are missing in these children's early experiences (Baird, Mayfield, & Baker, 1997).

As part of understanding their visual differences, these children need to gain knowledge about their visual status, the cause of their vision problem, and the probability of its worsening or improving. Many of the children have great confusion about their disabilities, which is apparent by the questions they ask about their blindness. In one very interesting study, parents were asked to list questions that their children had asked about their vision (Erin & Corn, 1994). Among the frequently asked questions were the following: When would they be able to see? Would they be able to see when they got older? Why did God make them blind? Why could they not see some things (like rainbows)? How do their eyes look? Would anything help them see better? Are they special? Why are they different? What is it like to see? Why did they fail the vision test?

The targets for parents to address with children with severe visual disabilities are many. They must help their children develop many skills across a range of areas: communication, independent living, mobility, sensory development, fine and gross motor skills, cognition, and social skills. And these parents want more help from schools to learn how to teach these skills more effectively to their children (Milian, 2000). The stress that families of low vision and blind children, particularly those with multiple disabilities, feel can be enormous (Tröster, 2000). Their need for social support is great, but they often find supportive networks more difficult to develop than do parents of nondisabled students. Clearly, here is another place where schools can help by facilitating the organization of parent groups.

A family is instrumental in building the confidence of a blind family member. Without such confidence, these children could not make such trips as this 3-day, 139-mile trek from Nashville, Tennessee to Tuscumbia, Alabama, the home of Helen Keller.

To compare the challenges these families face with those of families of children with different disabilities, see the "Families" sections in Chapters 3–12.

Table 11.4 Sample Costs of Assistive Devices Designed for Blind and Low Vision Individuals

Assistive Device	Cost
Visual Aids	
CCTV—portable	$1500
CCTV converter	$450
Clearview Monitor for reading	$3300
Magni-cam	$400
Bar magnifier	$30
Writing guide set	$30
Extra large universal remote control	$40
Audio Aids	
Talking watch	$50
Dialogue phone	$140
Talking alarm clock	$15
Talking calculator	$30
Talking digital thermometer	$15
Emergency dialer	$170
Tactile Aids	
Braille telephone	$60
Braille watch	$160
Braille n' Speak	$1500
Raised map printer	$3000
Kurzeil 1000 DEC talk (thermoform)	$1300
Braille embosser/printer	$1700
Desktop reading system	$800

TECHNOLOGY

The telephone and the phonograph are examples of technological advances that were created for the general population but that have great benefits for people with visual disabilities because they offer inexpensive access to both entertainment and information. Large-print books, computerized versions of popular novels, audiotapes of books, and computers are other examples of items developed for the general population that have increased the access of people with visual disabilities to mainstream society. Everyone now has greater access to printed information through electronic books and laptop computers that allow the reader to increase the size of print or to switch from print to voice easily.

These exciting technological advances open up a new world for people with severe visual disabilities. Clearly, these advances facilitate their participation and give the inde-pendence in all aspects of modern society. However, two major barriers inhibit their access: cost and information. With the average costs of devices ranging from $1,000 to $10,000 and the vast number of options available, careful selection of the right equipment is important. Table 11.4 shows what some of the more popular visual, auditory, and tactile devices cost.

MAKING CONNECTIONS

To compare different types of technology supports across students with special needs, read the "Technology" sections in Chapters 3–12.

What devices give visual input?

Closed-circuit television (CCTV) is one way to enlarge the print found in printed texts and books (American Association of Retired Persons [AARP], 2002; Lighthouse International, 2002). By means of a small television camera with a zoom lens and a sliding reading stand on which the printed materials are placed, greatly enlarged printed material (up to 60 times the original size) can be viewed on a television monitor. Another version, the Magni-Cam, has a TV camera embedded in something that looks like a computer mouse that can roll over printed pages. Such equipment provides immediate access to all types of printed materials, such as magazines, textbooks, and photocopied handouts.

Other equipment can also increase print size. For example, overhead projectors, although they are not useful to most individuals with low vision, can be used to enlarge printed materials. Personal computers can produce large-print displays on the computers' screens, allowing persons with low vision to adjust the size and style of print to match their own visual efficiencies. In addition, accompanying printers allow the user to select different sizes of print for hard-copy printout. These features enable teachers to prepare different versions of handouts—one for students with visual disabilities and one for sighted students. Remember that most standard copy machines can also adjust print size.

CHAPTER 11 *Low Vision or Blindness*

What devices give audio input?

Audio aids enable persons with visual disabilities to hear what others can read. Coming soon are "talking ATMs." Despite much controversy nationally, Bank of America in California will soon make these machines commonplace so that blind patrons can have audio-capable banking machines (Grupé, 2000). **Talking books** are not new and have been available through the Library of Congress since 1934. The American Printing House for the Blind provides compressed-speech (eliminating natural pauses and accelerating speech) versions recorded on tape and compact discs (CD); these can be ordered from regional resource and materials centers. Today, "talking books" are available at most bookstores. Developed for the general public, audio versions of many classics and current best-sellers allow people with visual disabilities greater access to books and print materials.

The Kurzweil 1000, a Stevie Wonder Vision Awards "1998 Product of the Year," changes printed material into synthesized speech. This reading machine is vastly improved over its 1970s predecessor, which was large, cumbersome, very expensive, unable to recognize all words, and difficult to understand. The Kurzweil 1000 is a personal computer as well as a convenient and quick desktop reading system that turns print into speech or print into braille. The listener can select the rate of speech (how fast it is delivered), the pitch, and the gender of the voice-sound the computer generates. This system has many advantages for individuals who cannot read print. Students can use the same books and materials as their sighted classmates; they are not dependent on the availability of braille or audio materials from a regional materials center. Users of this system also do not have to order special materials or wait for their delivery. Even those who are able to read print benefit from this system.

Another technique, **audiodescription,** allows people with severe visual disabilities to enjoy plays, movies, television, and home videos. With audiodescriptions, they hear a narration of the visual cues and nonverbal information presented on the screen or stage. This system, initially developed for television by Margaret Pfanstiehl, uses the added sound track available in stereo televisions to describe aspects (costumes, scenes, sets, body language) important to a fuller understanding of the story. A similar system has been devised for theaters; it uses an earphone and a tiny FM receiver. The explanations occur in the pauses or otherwise silent parts of the film or play. This accommodation is not so common in movie theaters, because many owners of cinema chains do not want to spend the $15,000 it takes to equip a theater, even though new systems, allowing for both captions for deaf movie-goers and audiodescriptions for blind patrons, are now available (McMahon, 2000). TV shows that have audiodescription versions are becoming more common, because the second audio track that is necessary to play the descriptions is now included on most TV sets (Descriptive Video Service [DVS], 2002).

What devices give tactile input?

Those people who use braille as their preferred reading method find the Perkins Brailler to be a compact and portable machine that embosses special paper with the braille code. The Perkins Brailler is inexpensive but not so efficient as electronic versions that use microprocessors to store and retrieve information. For example, Braille 'n Speak functions as an organizer, note taker, calendar, and talking clock. A braille version of a telephone credit card is available; it stores the user's access number so that he or she can charge the toll and call on any phone. Also, microcomputer systems, even those designed for sighted users, can support various types of braille and can even be networked so that many people can use the braille adaptation simultaneously. Access to braille versions of text is becoming less of a challenge because of the Xerox/Kurzweil desktop reading system that can scan printed materials and produce a braille version.

MAKING CONNECTIONS

The Kurzweil Reader is also discussed in the "History" section of this chapter.

MAKING
CONNECTIONS

To help you study the chapter's content, the answers to
the Focus and Challenge
questions from "Advance
Organizers" are given next.
Test yourself to see if you
have mastered the major
points of this chapter.

Personal computers with special printers transform print into braille. When a specially designed braille printer is attached to a microcomputer, standard text can be translated into braille, allowing a teacher who does not know how to use braille to produce braille copies of handouts, tests, maps, charts, and other class materials. And some new printers, such as the ones made by American Thermoform, can produce braille and print on the same page.

Another limitation of braille versions of text is also now eliminated. Only a few years ago, diagrams and illustrations were omitted from braille versions because of the inability of technology to produce them easily. Today a new system, Tactile Assess to Education for Visually Impaired Students (TAEVIS), uses a special type of paper, backed with plastic and coated with a heat-sensitive chemical, to produce raised versions of diagrams (Tennessean, 1999). Clearly, technology continues to improve access to the world of print for individuals with visual disabilities.

IN CONCLUSION

Summary

For most of us, the primary way we learn is through vision. Often, in the process of learning a new skill, we are shown how to do the task. We observe the actions of others and imitate their behaviors. We gain information by watching television or reading a newspaper, book, or magazine. People with visual disabilities have a restricted ability to use their sight, and that can affect how they function as independent adults. For schoolchildren, visual disabilities is one of the smallest special education categories. The incidence of visual disabilities increases with age: the older a person, the higher the likelihood of that person having some visual problems. Although these students have been successfully included in general education for many years, they do not find integration the norm when they are adults. Many have not found competitive employment but work instead in sheltered workshops. They are not included in the mainstream of American society. In fact, stereotypes and old traditions impede their participation in normal activities as adults. Improvement in this area is essential and will require the concerted efforts of adults with this disability, their families, and their advocates. With changed attitudes, this group will participate more fully in society and take their places alongside sighted people.

Self-Test Questions

Focus Questions

How can the category of visual disabilities be divided into subgroups?

Group students on the basis of the severity of the disability or the amount of their functional use of sight: low vision and blind.

Group students by age of onset: congenitally blind (at birth or during infancy) and adventitiously blind (after the age of two).

The category, "legally blind", qualifies people for special tax benefits and materials.

More than half of children with visual disabilities have an additional disability, often placing them in the multiple disabilities category.

What are the major causes of visual disabilities?

Worldwide: poor nutrition and preventable infections

Nationally: increasing age, heredity, and accidents

What are some ways in which the learning environment can be modified to accommodate students with visual disabilities?

Teachers can help by

- Using commonsense teaching strategies such as: advance organizers, oral summaries, printed information, hand-outs of lectures

- Positioning low vision students where they can benefit most from each instructional activity: close to the chalkboard, away from the glare of an unshaded window
- Eliminating dangerous obstacles and hazards
- Providing consistent organization, expectations, and consequences in the physical and instructional environments

Why must orientation and mobility be long-term curriculum targets for many low vision students and most blind students, and what specific skills must be included?

Good orientation and mobility skills are needed for independent living, maintaining a household, personal care, transportation to and from work, mobility within the workplace, and sports and recreation.

Orientation and mobility skills are complex and difficult to master, taking years of instruction and practice.

Challenges in the physical environment include escalators, elevators, public transportation, orientation to new places, and use of maps.

What technological advances can assist people with visual disabilities at school, in the workplace, and in independent living?

Visual aids: enlarged print displays, large-print newspapers, closed circuit television (CCTV) enlargements

Audio aids: talking books, talking watches and clocks, audiodescriptions

Tactile aids: labels for household appliances, tactile maps, braille books, computerized text-to-braille software

Challenge Question

Why has braille literacy become such an emotionally charged debate, and how do you think it should be resolved?

For those who do not read print, braille is their access to the print world and their means of achieving literacy. However, braille literacy is declining because:

- Braille instruction is not uniformly or consistently available
- Not enough teachers are proficient in braille
- Cognitive disabilities may make it difficult to learn

The individual needs and abilities of each individual should be matched to reading style, and appropriate instruction should be delivered.

MEETING THE STANDARDS AND PREPARING FOR LICENSURE EXAMS

After reading this chapter, you should be able to demonstrate basic knowledge and skills described in the CEC standards and INTASC principles listed below. The section of this chapter most applicable to each standard is shown in parentheses at the end of the knowledge or skill statement.

 Core Standard 2: Development and Characteristics of Learners

- **Educational implications:** Educational implications of characteristics of various exceptionalities. (Characteristics)
- **Similarities and differences:** Similarities and differences among individual with exceptional learning needs. (Visual Disabilities Defined)

 Core Standard 3: Individual Learning Differences

- **Lifetime effects:** Effects an exceptional condition(s) can have on a individual's life. (Transition through Adulthood)

 Core Standard 4: Instructional Strategies

- **Adapt instructional strategies:** Select, adapt and use instructional strategies and materials according to the characteristics of the individual with exceptional learning needs. (Elementary Through High School)
- **Transition planning:** Use strategies that promote successful transitions for individuals with exceptional learning needs. (Transition Through Adulthood)

Core Standard 5: Learning Environments and Social Interactions

- **Social skills:** Social Skills needed for educational and other environments (Characteristics)
- **Integration supports:** Identify supports needed for integration into various program placements. (Elementary Through High School, Collaboration)
- **Learner environments:** Design learner environments that encourage active participation in individual and group activities (Elementary Through High School)

 Core Standard 6: Language

- **Support communication:** Use strategies and to support and enhance communication skills of individuals with exceptional learning needs. (Elementary Through High School)

 Core Standard 7: Instructional Planning

- **Social skills:** Integrate affective, social and life skills with academic curricula. (Elementary Through High School)
- **Technology:** Incorporate and implement instructional and assistive technology into the educational program (Elementary Through High School, Technology)

 Core Standard 10: Collaboration

- **Family concerns:** Concerns of families of individual with exceptional learning needs and strategies to help address these concerns. (Families)
- **Collaborate:** Collaborate with school personnel and community members in integrating individuals with exceptional learning needs into various settings. (Accommodating for Inclusive Environments, Collaboration)

INTASC Principle 2

The teacher understands how children learn and develop and can provide learning opportunities that support their intellectual, social, and personal development

- **Individual variation within areas of development:** The teacher appreciates individual variation within each area of development, shows respect for the diverse talents of all learners, and is committed to help them develop self-confidence and competence. (Elementary Through High School)
- **Students' strengths:** The teacher is disposed to use students' strengths as a basis for growth and their errors as an opportunity for learning. (Elementary Through High School)

INTASC Principle 4

The teacher understands and uses a variety of instructional strategies to encourage students' development of critical thinking, problem solving and performance skills.

- **Teaching strategies:** The teacher carefully evaluates how to achieve learning goals, choosing alternative teaching strategies and materials to achieve different instructional purposes and how to meet student needs (e.g. developmental stages, prior knowledge, learning styles and interests). (Elementary Through High School)

INTASC Principle 10

The teacher fosters relationships with school colleagues, parents, and agencies in the larger community to support students' learning and well-being. The teacher values and appreciates the importance of all aspects of a child's experience. (Characteristics, Transitions Through Adulthood)

Standards in Practice

These knowledge statements, dispositions and skills might be demonstrated by the beginning teacher who is able to include a student with visual impairments or blindness in the general education classroom. The teacher would, in consultation with special education professionals, be able to modify curriculum and make teaching accommodations.

 Go to the companion website (ablongman.com/smith5e) for detailed text correlations to CEC and INTASC standards, PRAXIS II™ exams, and other state-sponsored licensure exams.

SUPPLEMENTARY RESOURCES

Professional Readings and Resources
Heller, K. W., Alberto, P. A., Forney, P. E., & Schwartzman, M. N. (1996). *Understanding physical, sensory, and health impairments.* Pacific Grove, CA: Brooks/Cole.

Sacks, S. Z., & Silberman, R. K. (1998). *Educating students who have visual impairments with other disabilities.* Baltimore: Paul H. Brookes.

Spungin., S. J. (Ed.). (2001). *When you have a visually impaired student in your classroom: A guide for teachers.* New York: AFB Press.

Wilson, J. (1995). *Biography of the blind: Including the lives of all who have distinguished themselves as poets, philosophers, artists, & etc., & etc.* Washington, DC: Library of Congress.

Popular Books
Hine, R. V. (1993). *Second sight.* Berkeley: University of California Press.

Hull, J. M. (1990). *Touching the rock.* New York: Pantheon Books.

Keller, H. (1988). *The story of my life.* New York: Sig Classics.

Kuusisto, S. (1998). *Planet of the blind.* New York: Dial Press.

Mehta, V. (1989). *The stolen light.* New York: Norton.

Videos and DVDs

At First Sight (1999). MGM

Based on a true story about a blind masseur, Virgil, who likes to play hockey, met Amy and fell in love. Amy suggests that Virgil have surgery to restore his sight, but because he has been blind since childhood, he cannot connect to the visual world. The real result is that his life spins out of control until his relationship with Amy can provide him with stability.

Once he has the surgery and no longer has a physical disability, he is forced to redefine his entire world. Even his relationship with Amy is altered. Once Virgil's life is changed, he has to start over—socially, emotionally, and psychologically.

Scent of a Woman (1992). Universal/MCA

To earn extra money while on break from an expensive eastern boarding school, Charlie agrees to serve as a personal assistant to an older blind man whose family is away. At first, the two—Charlie and Lt. Col Frank Slade—do not get along because of the blind man's alcoholism and abrasive personality. As their week together proceeds, they both end up saving each other and developing a life-long friendship.

Individuals with disabilities often feel isolated and become detached from people and society, a theme developed in this film. The men's interaction shows both the darker psychological side of this blind person and the unique insights he has to offer. This film also provides a good physical representation of a person with visual disabilities, contributing to Al Pacino's winning the Best Actor Oscar for his portrayal of Slade.

Daredevil (2003). Twentieth Century Fox

This movie is based on a comic book that has been in publication for over thirty years. The title character is a blind lawyer by day and a superhero fighting crime by night. The idea of blind justice is the central premise behind the film, and Daredevil is forced to fight a crime syndicate led by his nemesis Kingpin.

Daredevil has, by far, the biggest budget for any film made about a person with disabilities who is in the lead and title role. Although they represent a myth about blind individuals, the character's heightened senses give him an advantage in making "right" prevail. In an unusual approach, people with disabilities in this film are portrayed as superheroes.

Parent, Professional, and Consumer Organizations and Agencies

American Foundation for the Blind
11 Penn Plaza, Suite 300
New York, NY 10001
Phone: (800) 232-5463; (212) 502-7600
E-mail: afbinfo@afb.net
Web site: www.afb.org

Division of the Blind and Visually Impaired, Rehabilitation Services Administration

U.S. Department of Education
Room 3329-MES
400 Maryland Avenue, SW
Washington, DC 20202-2551
Phone: (202) 205-5465
Web site: www.ed.gov/offices/OSERS/RSA/index.html

American Printing House for the Blind
P.O. Box 6085
1839 Frankfort Avenue
Louisville, KY 40206-0085
Phone: (800) 223-1839; (502) 895-2405
E-mail: info@aph.org
Web site: http://www.aph.org

National Federation of the Blind
1800 Johnson Street
Baltimore, MD 21230
Phone: (410) 659-9314
E-mail: nfb@nfb.org
Web site: www.nfb.org

Division for the Visual Impairments (DVI), Council for Exceptional Children
1110 North Glebe Road, Suite 300
Arlington, VA 22201-5704
Phone: (888) CEC-SPED; (703) 620-3660
TTY: (703) 264-9446
Web site: www.cec.sped.org or
www.ed.arizona.edu/dvi/welcome.htm

Prevent Blindness America
500 E. Remington Road
Shaumberg, IL 60173-5611
Phone: (800) 331-2020
E-mail: info@preventblindness.org
Web site: http://www.prevent-blindness.org

Video**Workshop** Extra

If the VideoWorkshop package was included with your textbook, go to Chapter 11 of the Companion Website (www.ablongman.com/smith5e) and click on the VideoWorkshop button. Follow the instructions for viewing Video clip 8. Consider this information along with what you read in Chapter 11 as you answer the following questions.

Video Clip 8 Visual Impairment (Time 4:34)

1. Very low vision and blindness can affect social skills development during childhood. In the video, Kyle appears to be a very well-adjusted teenager. To what can you attribute his appropriate adjustment? Give specific examples from the video that are supported by your textbook reading.

2. In the video we saw Kyle using braille in a general education setting and participating in extracurricular performing-arts activities. What academic and ancillary support services would you expect to see included in Kyle's IEP?

Stephen Wiltshire, St. Peters, Kensington Park Road.
© Stephen Wiltshire. Reprinted by permission.

STEPHEN WILTSHIRE is an artist with autism. He was mute as a child, and at age 5 he began to communicate by drawing on scraps of paper. He now talks with reporters and others who want to interview him about his work. Wiltshire lives in England, but has made a number of trips to America. These trips gained him much publicity in America and stimulated his "American Dream" series of art. He uses his visual memory to remember scenes he wants to sketch later. Very seldom does he sketch or paint while he is actually seeing the image for the first time. Most of his early work was done with pen and ink, but he has recently completed art school, where he learned the techniques of using color and paint. The drawing here is of St. Peters, Kensington Park Road.

12 Autistic Spectrum Disorders

A PERSONAL PERSPECTIVE

The Bewildering Special Education Maze

Belinda and her husband are well-educated people and loving parents dedicated to their three young children. Everything was going perfectly for them. The business Aneel began after graduate school was becoming highly successful, and they loved being together. They decided it was time to start a family. Their first-born, a beautiful boy, was diagnosed with autism after Belinda was already pregnant with the twins. Here she recounts how her family's course changed when a child was diagnosed with autism and they entered the special education maze.

My husband and I have two boys with autism. Receiving a diagnosis of autism is difficult, in large part because there is no universally accepted treatment protocol at this time. The professional making the diagnosis does not say, "He has autism. This is what you should do . . ." Parents are left to research different interventions on their own, and most choose a course of treatment without much professional advice.

Imagine yourself in a maze—not the simple kind used with rats in the psychology lab, but something bigger and darker with dozens of choices at every turn. The well-being of your child—indeed his very future—rests upon your ability to navigate this maze successfully. You are being timed, and the penalties for standing still are stiff. At the entrance to each corridor is a gate keeper who will charge you time and money to enter. Some of the most promising corridors are too expensive. Others have prohibitively long lines of people waiting to get in. Several corridors look inviting, but after investing your time and money, you find a dead end. Now here's the kicker:

for most, the maze never ends. You can only hope to get as close to the jackpot as possible.

Since our first child was diagnosed two years ago, we have investigated applied behavioral analysis (ABA), speech therapy, occupational therapy, music therapy, auditory integration therapy (AIT), art therapy, and water therapy. We have looked into therapeutic riding, dolphin therapy, the picture exchange communication system (PECS*), megavitamin therapy, chelation, antifungal treatments, serotonin inhibitors, secretin, antiyeast agents, and gluten-free/casein-free diets. We have had the boys tested for chromosomal abnormalities, allergies, lead poisoning, and mercury poisoning. Am I forgetting anything? Oh yes, we spoke with a doctor who prescribes blood thinners for children with autism despite the fact that he has no scientific data to back up his theories.

After two years of navigating the maze, my husband and I have decided that certain corridors are not worth investigating. We do not enter corridors that might be potentially harmful to our children. We steer clear of those choices that might benefit our sons at the expense of the family unit. Most important, we have learned to ignore the ticking of the ever-present clock. We have decided that success at any age is still success.

1. **What needs to happen so that parents of children with autism do not have to face such a confusing maze of people and services?**

2. **What do you think the future holds for this family?**

---

* For more about PECS, see the "Family" section of this chapter and the "Validated Practices" box.

Overview

Autism is a specific diagnosis included under the broader term, autistic spectrum disorders (ASD). In addition to autism, Asperger's disorder, Rett's syndrome, childhood distintegrative disorder (CDD), and pervasive developmental disorder–not otherwise specified (PDD-NOS)—are part of ASD. All conditions included in ASD are characterized by problems in three areas of development: communication, social skills, and range of interests. But, as the word "spectrum" implies, ASD falls along a continuum in each area of development ranging from severe problems to above-average abilities. No facial characteristics or other physical features help to identify children with ASD, so ASD is sometimes thought of as an "invisible" disability. The effects of ASD on children's access to full participation in mainstream society, however, are all too visible. Historically, it was thought that 1 out of 10,000 children would be diagnosed with autism. Recently, however, more children are diagnosed specifically with autism and generally

MAKING CONNECTIONS

Use the learning strategy—Advance Organizers—to help focus your study of this chapter's content, and reinforce your learning by reviewing answers to the Focus and Challenge questions at the end of the chapter.

with ASD, and the increase is dramatic. For example, experts now estimate that 1 out of 500–700 children has autism. Even with this increase, ASD—its syndromes and disorders—comprise a low incidence disability affecting about 0.002% of the population.

Self-Test Questions

Focus Questions

- What is the relationship of autistic disorder, or autism, to autistic spectrum disorders?

- What is meant by the term *spectrum,* and what does this term imply about people diagnosed with ASD?

- What is the cause of autistic disorder? Why is this sometimes a controversial issue?

- What are some ways in which the learning environment can be modified and adapted for students with autism?

- Why should instruction in nonacademic areas such as social skills be included in educational programs for students with autism?

Challenge Question

- What are some of the implications or effects of autism being an "invisible" disability for the child and for the child's family? What are the implications for educators? for other professionals?

Think for a minute about all the things you do throughout the day that involve communicating with other people. Whether going out to buy some new clothes, going to class, or just hanging out with our friends, we communicate with others. Given the proliferation of cell phones and e-mail, one might conclude that communicating is central to the human experience. Through communication with others, we mediate our experiences, articulate our thoughts, describe our needs, express our desires, learn new skills, understand each other's perspectives, and relate to one another. In general, relating to and communicating with others is so effortless, so much a part of who we are and what we do, that we rarely realize how integral it is in our lives.

Now imagine that communication is difficult for you. That is, imagine that even though you hear people talking, you do not understand the words you hear. Imagine that you are unable to produce words and that you do not know how to use other sorts of nonverbal communication strategies, such as gesturing or using your eyes to express yourself. Imagine further that being near another person is difficult for you. That is, when people approach you, even if it's just with their gaze, you are unable to respond. For most of us, this is a world we truly cannot imagine. For many children with autism, however, this may be what life is like. Given a supportive and structured environment, however, children with autism, can learn important communication and interaction skills—skills that will help them lead more independent lives.

CHAPTER 12 *Autistic Spectrum Disorders*

Opportunities for a Better Future

With the 1997 reauthorization of IDEA, autism became an independent special education category*. However, considerable confusion remained about definitions and qualifications of those who can diagnose or label children with autism and the other autistic spectrum disorders (ASD). The independent classification coincided with increased attention on this disability. The results have been more coverage in the popular press and increased funding for research. Current research is focusing on determining the cause, developing new treatments, determining effective treatments, and how best to prepare school personnel to work with children with ASD. Clearly, the future holds promise for these children and their families.

Turning Legacies into Lessons

The study of autism as a field has existed for at least sixty years. In that time, many insights have been gained and advances have improved the quality of life for children with autism and their families. However, missteps have been made along the way. Here's an important example: During the 1960s, Bruno Bettelheim, a psychologist, suggested that autism was caused by the cold interaction styles of mothers with their children. This theory, "the refrigerator mother theory", has

* For a review of IDEA and its reauthorizations, see Chapter 1.

since been proved false, but the tragic, residual effects of this theory, or belief, are still felt today. Sometimes, professionals consciously or inadvertently blame parents for their child's behavior or parents feel guilty thinking that their behavior may in some way have caused their child to become autistic. As scientists become better able to describe the causes for autism, this hurtful, discredited, and inaccurate view of the disability will disappear.

Thinking About Dilemmas to Solve

People with autism have deficits in skill areas that make learning difficult. As you read this chapter, consider

- How the three deficit areas (communication, social skills, and range of interests) affect how and what children with autism learn

- How the wide range of abilities within autism affects educational programming

- How deficits in nonacademic skills influence academic learning

- Ways to educate people about the facts of autism while debunking the myths

- How autism affects families

- How to provide instruction for children with autism so that they can more fully participate in the general education curriculum

Autistic Spectrum Disorders (ASD) Defined

Autistic spectrum disorder (ASD) is a broad term that groups together five specific disorders:

1. Autistic disorder or autism
2. Childhood disintegrative disorder (CDD)
3. Asperger's syndrome
4. Rett's syndrome
5. Pervasive developmental disorder–not otherwise specified (PDD-NOS)

These disorders share similar behavioral traits, characterized by problems with communication, social skills, and patterns of behavior or range of interests. The key word in the term ASD is *spectrum,* which implies similar characteristics but great variance in the actual skills exhibited. The National Research Council describes ASD in this way:

ASD varies in severity of symptoms, age of onset, and the presence of various features, such as mental retardation and specific language delay. The manifestations of ASD can differ considerably across children and within an individual child over time. Even though there are strong and consistent commonalties, especially in social deficits, there is no single behavior that is always typical of autism or any of the autistic spectrum disorders and no behavior that would automatically exclude an individual child from a diagnosis of ASD. (National Research Council, 2001, p. 2)

What differentiates the five types of ASD?

Each disorder included in ASD has specific diagnostic criteria. So, one way to think of ASD is as an umbrella of disorders—one of which is autism—that share a range of behaviors or common traits. Figure 12.1 illustrates ASD in this way. Now, let's examine each condition to gain a clearer understanding of the similarities and differences among them.

● *Autism or Autistic Disorder* Technically, the terms **autism** or **autistic disorder** refer to a specific diagnosis, much like the word *Coke* refers to a specific type of soft drink, rather than generically referring to many brands of cola or all soft drinks. The term *autism* is often used in place of the term ASD to refer to all of the disorders and syndromes included under the ASD umbrella. Through IDEA, the federal government defines autism in this way:

A developmental disability significantly affecting verbal and nonverbal communication and social interaction, generally evident before age 3, that adversely affects a child's performance. Other characteristics often associated with

Figure 12.1 Autism Spectrum Disorders (ASD) Umbrella

CHAPTER 12 *Autistic Spectrum Disorders*

Table 12.1 DSM-IV Diagnostic Criteria for Autistic Disorder

A. A total of six (or more) items from (1), (2), and (3), with at least two from (1) and one each from (2) and (3):

   (1) Qualitative impairment in social interaction, as manifested by at least two of the following:

      (a) Marked impairment in the use of multiple nonverbal behaviors such as eye-to-eye gaze, facial expression, body postures, and gestures to regulate social interaction

      (b) Failure to develop peer relationships appropriate to developmental level

      (c) A lack of spontaneous seeking to share enjoyment, interests, or achievements with other people (e.g., by a lack of showing, bringing, or pointing out objects of interest)

      (d) Lack of social or emotional reciprocity

   (2) Qualitative impairments in communication as manifested by at least one of the following:

      (a) Delay in, or total lack of, the development of spoken language (not accompanied by an attempt to compensate through alternate modes of communication such as gesture or mime)

      (b) In individuals with adequate speech, marked impairment in the ability to initiate or sustain a conversation with others

      (c) Stereotyped and repetitive use of language or idiosyncratic language

      (d) Lack of varied, spontaneous make-believe play or social imitative play appropriate to developmental level

   (3) Restricted repetitive and stereotyped patterns of behavior, interests, and activities as manifested by at least one of the following:

      (a) Encompassing preoccupation with one or more stereotyped and restricted patterns of interest that is abnormal either in intensity or focus.

      (b) Apparently inflexible adherence to specific, nonfunctional routines or rituals

      (c) Stereotyped and repetitive motor mannerisms (e.g., hand or finger flapping or twisting, or complex whole-body movements)

      (d) Persistent preoccupation with parts of objects

B. Delays or abnormal functioning in at least one of the following areas, with onset prior to age 3 years: (1) social interaction, (2) language as used in social communication, or (3) symbolic or imaginative play.

C. The disturbance is not better accounted for by Rett's disorder or childhood disintegrative disorder.

Source: Reprinted with permissioin from the *Diagnostic and Statistical Manual of Mental Disorders*, *Fourth Edition* (pp.70-71). Copyright 1994 American Psychiatric Association.

---

autism are engagement in repetitive activities and stereotyped movements, resistance to environmental change or change in the daily routines, and unusual responses to sensory experiences. The term does not apply if a child's educational performance is adversely affected primarily because the child has a serous emotional disturbance. (U.S. Department of Education, 1999, p. 12421)

The IDEA definition of autism is a general description and lacks the specificity needed to fully understand the disorder. The American Psychiatric Association (1994) in the fourth edition of the *Diagnostic and Statistical Manual of Mental Disorders* (DSM-IV) provides specific diagnostic criteria for autism (see Table 12.1).

Note that according to this description all children with autism have impairments in communication, impairments in social skills, and restricted and repetitive behavioral patterns or range of interests.

Children with autism do not communicate with other people in typical ways. Approximately 50 percent of children with autism do not talk to communicate; these individuals are nonverbal (Sturmey & Sevin, 1994). Of the other 50 percent, some children are verbal, but much of what they say is merely a repetition of what they have just heard, this is called **echolalia** (Wetherby, Yonclas, & Bryan, 1989). Some children with autism generate verbal language, but make errors when using personal pronouns or have a difficult time understanding or forming semantic categories (Ramberg et al., 1996). Here's an example: People with autism have difficulty understanding that the word *dog* refers to a general category of "dogness" as well as to specific examples of dogs. Regardless of the actual verbal abilities of a particular child, *all* children with autism have trouble with the use or pragmatics of language. Typically, they do not understand that communication happens between people nor do they understand that nonverbal cues and personal perspectives are important to successful communication (Wetherby & Prizant, 1993).

Children with autism also have problems with social interactions. They often appear to live in their own world and may not seek out the company of peers or adults. Many children with autism seem to use people as tools (Powers, 2000). For example, a child may lead an adult by the hand to the refrigerator and push the adult's hand towards the juice the child wants. In this way, the child with autism is using the adult as a means to an end. Also, children with autism do not generally initiate social situations and do not engage in social turn-taking just for the pleasure of being part of a social interaction.

Children with autism have repetitive or odd patterns of behavior, **stereotypic behaviors,** unusual interests, or strange responses to the environment (Lewis & Bodfish, 1998). They may be attracted to specific aspects of a toy. For example, a child with autism may be interested only in spinning the wheel of a toy car or may be interested only in wiggling the string of a pull toy. Some children may have rigid or set patterns of behavior. For example, one child might line up his or her toys in a specific way, and might have to follow the same routine every day. If these patterns of behavior are violated, a tantrum might result to protest the disruption. Other children may repeat the same movement over and over again. For example, a child may wave his hand in front of an eye frequently. Not a lot is understood about the function of this type of behavior. Interestingly, children diagnosed with autism at a young age (around the age of 2 years) do not exhibit much of this type of routinized behavior. It is not known, however, if whether children with autism learn this type of behavior in response to their experiences in the world, or whether this aspect of the disorder just does not develop until children are older.

Intelligence scores are not considered in the diagnosis of autism, yet most children (approximately 75 percent) diagnosed with autism also have mental retardation (Strumey & Sevin, 1994). Thus 25 percent of the autistic population has at least a normal level of intelligence. This wide range of cognitive ability has resulted in people using terms such as *low-functioning autism* and *high-functioning autism.* Low functioning autism often refers to children with autism and mental retardation; whereas, high functioning autism often refers to children without mental retardation. The term *high functioning autism* should not be thought a synonym for another type of ASD.

Are there types of autism? As the discussion above has illustrated, the skills that children diagnosed with autism exhibit vary greatly. Some experts think that the different levels of intellectual functioning, variety in the age of onset, and number and severity of symptoms suggest subtypes of autism (Koegel & Koegel, 1995; Wing, 1989). But, other experts do not agree. Currently, no consensus among experts has been achieved about the existence of subtypes of autism or whether subtype distinctions would be useful.

MAKING CONNECTIONS

To review use or pragmatics of language, see the "Defined" section of Chapter 5.

CHAPTER 12 *Autistic Spectrum Disorders*

Regardless, one potential subtype of autism or group of people, **autistic savants,** is of far more interest to the general public than to researchers. The number of autistic savants is very small, only about 5 percent of individuals diagnosed with autism, but the public seems fascinated by the almost bizarre inconsistencies in this group's abilities (Begley & Springen, 1996). For example, some, like the character Raymond in the film *Rain Man*, can instantly count the number of wooden matches that have fallen on the floor, remember the dates of important events, or recall the numbers of all of the winning lottery tickets for the past year. Others have outstanding musical or artistic abilities. But, even in light of these talents, these individuals are unable to initiate or maintain conversations. For example, nine-year-old Alex Mont can solve complicated mathematics problems,

Alex Mont has unusual mathematical abilities, excelling far beyond even many of his gifted peers. However, like many autistic savants, his abilities are not uniform.

even calculus, but has difficulties comprehending social cues. Alex also could not distinguish a horse from a cow until after he finished kindergarten. While these splinter skills are fascinating to the observer, they are rarely functional for the individual.

Table 12.2 DSM-IV Diagnostic Criteria for Childhood Disintegrative Disorder

A. Apparently normal development for at least the first 2 years after birth as manifested by the presence of age-appropriate verbal and nonverbal communication, social relationships, play, and adaptive behavior.

B. Clinically significant loss of previously acquired skills (before age 10 years) in at least two of the following areas:

   (1) expressive or receptive language

   (2) social skills or adaptive behavior

   (3) bowel or bladder control

   (4) play

   (5) motor skills

C. Abnormalities of functioning in at least two of the following areas:

   (1) qualitative impairment in social interaction (e.g., impairment in nonverbal behaviors, failure to develop peer relationships, lack of social or emotional reciprocity)

   (2) qualitative impairments in communication (e.g., delay or lack of spoken language, inability to initiate or sustain a conversation, stereotyped and repetitive use of language, lack of varied make-believe play)

   (3) restricted, repetitive, and stereotyped patterns of behavior, interests, and activities, including motor stereotypes and mannerisms

D. The disturbance is not better accounted for by another specific pervasive developmental disorder or by schizophrenia.

Source: Reprinted with permission from the *Diagnostic and Statistical Manual of Mental Disorders, Fourth Edition* (pp. 74–75). Copyright 1994 American Psychiatric Association.

Table 12.3 DSM-IV Diagnostic Criteria for Asperger's Syndrome

A. Qualitative impairment in social interaction, as manifested by at least two of the following:

  (1) Marked impairments in the use of multiple nonverbal behaviors such as eye-to-eye gaze, facial expression, body postures, and gestures to regulate social interaction

  (2) Failure to develop peer relationships appropriate to developmental level

  (3) A lack of spontaneous seeking to share enjoyment, interests, or achievements with other people (e.g., by a lack of showing, bringing, or pointing out objects of interest to other people)

  (4) Lack of social or emotional reciprocity

B. Restricted repetitive and stereotyped patterns of behavior, interests, and activities, as manifested by at least one of the following:

  (1) Encompassing preoccupation with one or more stereotyped and restricted patterns of interest that is abnormal either in intensity or focus

  (2) Apparently inflexible adherence to specific, nonfunctional routines or rituals

  (3) Stereotyped and repetitive motor mannerisms (e.g., hand or finger flapping or twisting, or complex whole-body movements)

  (4) Persistent preoccupation with parts of objects

C. The disturbance causes clinically significant impairment in social, occupational, or other important areas of functioning.

D. There is no clinically significant general delay in language (e.g., single words used by age 2 years, communicative phrases used by age 3 years).

E. There is no clinically significant delay in cognitive development or in the development of age-appropriate self-help skills, adaptive behavior (other than in social interaction), and curiosity about the environment in childhood.

F. Criteria are not met for another specific pervasive developmental disorder or schizophrenia.

Source: Reprinted with permission from the *Diagnostic and Statistical Manual of Mental Disorders, Fourth Edition* (p. 77). Copyright 1994 American Psychiatric Association.

• *Childhood Disintegrative Disorder* (CDD) Childhood Disintegrative Disorder (CDD) is very rare—far rarer than autism. The DSM-IV description of CDD is found in Table 12.2 on page 421. The most distinguishing aspect of CDD is that these children develop as their nondisabled peers do until they are 5 or 6 years old, at which time a developmental regression begins. In particular, these children lose already acquired language and social skills. Eventually, their behaviors are similar to the behavior patterns of children with autism, however, their long-term outcomes are far worse.

For a review of how children develop speech and language, see the "Defined" section of Chapter 5.

• *Asperger's syndrome* Dr. Hans Asperger was the first to describe and classify **Asperger's syndrome** as a collection of behavioral characteristics. Asperger's syndrome is characterized by problems with social skills and by restricted or unusual behaviors or interests. Table 12.3 provides the DSM-IV description of this type of ASD. Although the communication of children with Asperger's syndrome may be peculiar, this characteristic is not due to a delay in the development of speech or language. In fact, children diagnosed with Asperger's syndrome develop speech and language on a par with children without disabilities. Other aspects of communication, however, are problematic. Some children with Asperger's syndrome understand language very literally, which can make it difficult for them to form conceptual categories, understand jokes, or interpret nonverbal language (such as gestures). For these individuals, the social use of language can be a particular

CHAPTER 12 *Autistic Spectrum Disorders*

challenge, as can be the ability to comprehend other people's feelings or mental states (Safran, 2001).

Unlike children with autism, the majority of children with Asperger's syndrome have normal intelligence, and should not be confused with those individuals with high functioning autism. Because children with autism are diagnosed when a delay in speech or language becomes apparent and children with Asperger's syndrome develop normally, a diagnosis should never change from autism to Asperger's syndrome. The distinction between autism and Asperger's syndrome, however, may turn out to be only a matter of semantics. Presently, there is controversy about whether any meaningful differences in the behaviors or performance of people with high functioning autism and Asperger's syndrome exist. In the future, results from psychological testing, quality of life measures, and brain activity might solve this controversy.

Children with autism are often excluded from social interactions with peers.

• *Rett's syndrome* **Rett's syndrome**, sometimes called Rett's disorder, is a genetic condition discovered more then 40 years ago by Andreas Rett, an Austrian physician. The DSM-IV description of this syndrome is shown in Table 12.4. Signs of Rett's syndrome appear early in life when development appears normal and then stops. Unlike many inherited conditions, Rett's syndrome is more common in girls.

Table 12.4 DSM-IV Diagnostic Criteria for Rett's Syndrome

A. All of the following:

  (1) apparently normal prenatal and perinatal development

  (2) apparently normal psychomotor development through the first 5 months after birth

  (3) normal head circumference at birth

B. Onset of all of the following after the period of normal development:

  (1) deceleration of head growth between ages 5 and 48 months

  (2) loss of previously acquired purposeful hand skills between ages 5 and 30 months with the subsequent development of stereotyped hand movements (e.g., hand-wringing or hand washing)

  (3) loss of social engagement early in the course (although often social interaction develops later)

  (4) appearance of poorly coordinated gait or trunk movements

  (5) severely impaired expressive and receptive language development with severe psychomotor retardation

Source: Reprinted with permission from the *Diagnostic and Statistical Manual of Mental Disorders, Fourth Edition* (pp. 72–73). Copyright 1994 American Psychiatric Association.

Behaviorally, it is characterized by repeated, stereotypic hand wringing; lack of muscle control; along with communication and social deficits. Sometimes misdiagnosed as autism, Rett's syndrome has different characteristics. Autism is not usually characterized by hand wringing. Children with autism tend to have better motor skills than children with Rett's syndrome. Children with Rett's syndrome tend to have better social skills when compared to children with autism. And, while about half of the individuals with autism have mental retardation, most children with Rett's syndrome have mental retardation and those cognitive disabilities are more severe than what is observed in people with autism.

• *Pervasive Developmental Disorder–Not Otherwise Specified (PDD-NOS)* Problems in the areas of communication, social skills, and unusual behaviors including restricted range of interests are the three common characteristics of ASD. Each ASD condition—autism, CDD, Asperger's syndrome, and Rett's syndrome—is different because of the profile of behaviors exhibited by the individual or by the pattern of development observed. (While the DSM-IV describes PDD-NOS, it does not provide a table of its common characteristics.) When children do not display problems in all three areas, or when problems in all three areas are mild, a different diagnosis is made. In these cases, the disorder is identified as **pervasive developmental disorder–not otherwise specified (PDD-NOS)**. The PDD part of the diagnosis signifies deficits similar to those of autism, CDD, Asperger's syndrome, and Rett's syndrome. The NOS part refers to other specified disorders or syndromes. Although they share characteristics, PDD-NOS is distinct from high functioning autism and Asperger's syndrome.

Are there other ways to organize ASD?

Professionals are just beginning to understand ASD, so different views of the conditions themselves, and of their symptoms and severity, are still developing. To some, these different disorders and syndromes represent different types of autism. Others, however, suggest that types of autism may be formed across diagnostic categories and may instead be based on level of intellectual functioning, age of onset, or number or severity of symptoms (Tanguay, Robertson, & Derrick, 1998). Still others suggest that the child's level of activity (e.g., active or passive) is the correct dimension on which to formulate subgroups (Rogers, 1998). And, as understanding of the genetic basis of ASD continues to develop, some suggest that differences in genetics may exist and that these differences should underlie any groupings. As it stands now, no consensus exists among experts about what dimensions should be used to develop subtypes of ASD, or even about whether it is useful to establish such categories.

How are children with autism identified?

Until recently, children with **autism** were not diagnosed until the age of 5, but now it is possible to diagnose children before the age of 3 (Stone et al., 1999). In part because of the development of new assessment tools, some children are even being identified as early as age 2. For example, the *Autism Diagnostic Observation Scale (ADOS)* and the *Screening Test for Autism in Two Year Olds (STAT)*, along with developmental assessments and parent reports, help to identify very young children with autism. Because many typically developing children are just beginning to develop spoken language at the age of 2, and because the diagnostic features of autism include language delay, both the *ADOS* and the *STAT* include measures that also examine other skills, such as children's ability to imitate motor movements. In other words, children with autism seem to also have deficits in motor imitation skills that can be used for diagnosis before other problems (e.g., deficits in language) become apparent.

Although current assessment procedures cannot diagnose children younger than 2, researchers are working to develop valid and reliable assessments to identify even younger children with autism. It is likely that these efforts will be successful, because researchers can now diagnose children retrospectively when they are 1 year old. Specifically, Julie Osterling and Gerry Dawson examined videotapes parents had made of their children's first birthday parties. They recognized that the children who were later diagnosed with autism behaved differently from typically developing children (Osterling & Dawson, 1994). They have identified four major differences that distinguish these children. The children later diagnosed with autism

- Did not use a finger to point at an object
- Did not show their presents to others
- Did not respond to their names
- Did not make direct eye contact with others

Interesting as this information is, it has not yet been incorporated into an assessment instrument that can be used prospectively to diagnosis 1-year-olds with autism.

Efforts are underway to develop methods to detect autism even before a child's first birthday. Around nine months of age, children without disabilities begin to engage in what psychologists describe as joint attention. **Joint attention** involves two people such as a child and a parent. It occurs when first one person looks at an object, then looks at the other person, and finally when the two people simultaneously look at the object. That is, they together (or jointly) look at (or attend) to the same object. Researchers believe that joint attention is important in the development of both language and social skills (Mundy & Neal, 2001). While children with autism do participate in joint attention episodes, their pattern and type of participation is different from that of children without disabilities. (Shienkopf et al., 2000). Why is this information important? Potentially, it can help us understand more about the development of social and language skills as well as the core characteristics of autism. Such information might also lead to earlier identification of children with autism. No diagnostic tools are currently available that address deficits in joint attention, but many psychologists look for a child's joint attention skills when forming their clinical impressions about him or her.

Most assessment instruments used to diagnose children with autism are administered by trained psychologists with experience diagnosing children with autism. One screening tool, the *Checklist for Autism in Toddlers (CHAT)*, was developed to help physicians spot early warning signs. Another measure, the *Childhood Autism Rating Scale (CARS)*, is widely used to confirm a diagnosis and also to monitor the child's growth over time. The *CARS* also describes the severity of problems that a child with ASD demonstrates.

What is the impact of this disability?

Autism is a significant, lifelong disability. Even for those with average intelligence, long-term outcomes in terms of independent living, employment, and life satisfaction are bleak (Sperry, 2001). In fact, most people with autism require comprehensive services and extensive supports for their entire lives. Effective services and supports require high levels of coordination and consistency. Unfortunately, these are difficult goals to achieve through the often fragmented services offered by social service agencies, health care providers, and the educational system.

From the start of life, the skill deficits of children diagnosed with autism affect their learning and development of social relationships. Children with autism do not participate in turn-taking exchanges. This lack of social interaction directly and adversely affects the acquisition and use of preverbal communications (e.g., gestures) as well as the eventual acquisition of speech and language skills (Stone & Yoder, 2001). Most cultural mores are passed from generation to generation via

MAKING CONNECTIONS

For a review of systems of support, see Chapter 6.

INSIGHTS INTO AUTISM

Oliver Sacks, in the foreword to Temple Grandin's (1996) biography, *Thinking in Pictures and Other Reports of My Life with Autism*, underscores the importance of her insights about her disability.

> Unprecedented because there had never before been an "inside narrative" of autism; unthinkable because it had been medical dogma for forty years or more that there was no "inside," no inner life, in the autistic, or that if there was it would be forever denied access or expression; extraordinary because of its extreme (and strange) directness and clarity. Temple Grandin's voice came from a place which had never had a voice, never been granted real existence, before—and she spoke not only for herself, but for thousands of other, often highly gifted, autistic adults in our midst. She provided a glimpse, and indeed a revelation, that there might be people, no less human than ourselves, who constructed their worlds, lived their lives, in almost unimaginably different ways.

> Temple does not romanticize autism, nor does she downplay how much her autism has cut her off from the social whirl, the pleasures, the rewards, the companionships, that for the rest of us may define much of life. But she has a stong, positive sense of her own being and worth, and how autism, paradoxically, may have contributed to this. (pp. 11, 16)

Temple Grandin, an adult with autism, describes her thought processes as being very different from those of most other people:

> I think in pictures. Words are like a second language to me. I translate both spoken and written words into full-color movies, complete with sound, which run like a VCR tape in my head. When somebody speaks to me, his words are instantly translated into pictures. Language-based thinkers often find this phenomenon difficult to understand, but in my job as an equipment designer for the livestock industry, visual thinking is a tremendous advantage. . . . [O]ne third of the cattle and hogs in the United States are handled in equipment I have designed. (p. 19)

She helps us understand autism better by explaining how her senses are too active:

> Overly sensitive skin can be a big problem. Washing my hair and dressing to go to church were two things I hated as a child. . . . Scratchy petticoats were like sandpaper scraping away at raw nerve endings. . . . When I was little, loud noises were also a problem, often feeling like a dentist's drill hitting a nerve.

> They actually caused pain. I was scared to death of balloons popping, because the sound was like an explosion in my ear. Minor noises that most people can tune out drove me to distraction. . . . My ears are like microphones picking up all sounds with equal intensity. (pp. 66–68)

Grandin talks about her emotional differences, which may help us understand different behavior patterns in children with autism:

> Some people believe that people with autism do not have emotions. I definitely do have them, but they are more like the emotions of a child than of an adult. My childhood temper tantrums were not really expressions of emotion so much as circuit overloads. . . . When I get angry, it is like an afternoon thunderstorm; the anger is intense, but once I get over it, the emotion quickly dissipates. . . . I don't know what it is like to feel rapturous joy. I know I am missing something when other people swoon over a beautiful sunset. Intellectually I know it is beautiful, but I don't feel it. . . . [E]motional nuances are still incomprehensible to me, and I value concrete evidence of accomplishment and appreciation. . . . I still have difficulty understanding and having a relationship with people whose primary motivation in life is governed by complex emotions, as my actions are guided by intellect. (pp. 87–90)

Grandin describes typical autistic behaviors not as an observer, but as the participant. In doing so, she gives us guidance about how educational programs should be developed:

> I would tune out, shut off my ears, and daydream. My daydreams were like Technicolor movies in my head. I would also become completely absorbed in spinning a penny or studying the wood-grain pattern on my desktop. During these times, the rest of the world disappeared, but then my speech teacher would gently grab my chin to pull me back into the real world. . . . Autistic children will remain in their own little worlds if left to their own devices. (p. 96)

> [Teachers must] be able to determine whether a tantrum or other bad behavior is caused by fear or pain or a learned avoidance response. Sometimes it's because of pain from sounds that hurt their ears or fear of an unexpected change in routine. . . . Autistics are afraid of the unexpected. (pp. 149–150)

CHAPTER 12 *Autistic Spectrum Disorders*

implicit teaching that involves social interactions and observational learning. Both of these means of learning represent deficit areas for children with autism. Most instruction at school is socially mediated and language-based, again problem areas for children with autism. Thus the social and communication problems faced by children with autism create a cascade of obstacles to learning in general (Carpenter, Pennington, & Rogers, 2002). In this way, autism pervasively affects the child's entire developmental trajectory.

Even high-functioning individuals with autism face considerable challenges. In a fascinating account of her own life, entitled *Thinking in Pictures and Other Reports from My Life with Autism,* Temple Grandin (1995) shares with the world what it is like to experience the pains of isolation and of being very different from her peers. Excerpts from her biography appear in the accompanying box. Dr. Grandin holds a doctorate in animal science from the University of Illinois and is currently a professor at Colorado State University. She is well known for her designs of livestock-holding equipment, and one-third of all such equipment in this country was designed by her. You may be thinking, "How could someone with such a significant disability be such a successful scientist?" Truly, she is unique. However, her insights may help others.

Temple Grandin has received considerable attention for her biographical insights into autism and how it affects individuals.

Dr. Grandin writes about her early frustrations with not being able to talk, even though she understood language. She also mentions her hypersensitivity to sound and touch, which caused her to withdraw from people and the world outside herself. She continues to experience motor problems, having difficulties with balance and with coordinating multiple motor responses simultaneously. Even today, she says, she cannot move two or three levers at the same time. She is a strong advocate of early intervention programs. She maintains that young children with autism must not be allowed to "tune out." She believes that these children must remain engaged with others in activities at least 20 hours per week; they must not be allowed to withdraw into their own worlds and shut everyone and everything out. A lot can be learned from Dr. Grandin's insights, for despite her successful career, she continues to experience many of the symptoms of autism. She certainly is proof that people with autism can function in the community with supports. Unfortunately, most adults with autism do not fare as well.

HISTORY OF THE FIELD

Although autism has probably always been part of the human condition, its discrete identification is relatively recent. In 1943 Leo Kanner, a child psychiatrist at Johns Hopkins University Medical School, first described children and the condition he called "early infantile autism." (Independently, but almost simultaneously, Hans Asperger described a similar condition that would be named Asperger's syndrome.) Kanner's use of *early infantile* reflects his strongly held belief that the condition he was describing was present at or shortly after birth. Kanner borrowed the term *autism* from Eugen Bluer, a Swiss psychiatrist who had coined the term in 1911. Bluer used the term *autism* to describe patients with schizophrenia who actively withdraw into their own world. Unfortunately, the notion of voluntary withdrawal also became associated with children with autism, inviting the fallacious notion that these children were withdrawing because parents, particularly mothers, were cold or uncaring. The outcomes of these ideas were devastating to families and resulted in children being removed from their families and raised in institutions (Powers, 2000).

In the 1960s, the treatment of autism changed. First, enough scientific evidence had been collected to rule out the idea that the "refrigerator mother" (or parent) caused autism. Instead, experts began to believe that autism probably resulted from neurological or biochemical problems. Second, parents organized themselves and advocated for themselves and their children. Bernard Rimland spearheaded this advocacy movement. He was a psychologist who dedicated his career to studying autism after his son was diagnosed with the condition. Rimland helped to collect and organize the information known about autism, but he also joined with other parents to form a parent advocacy group called the National Society for Autistic Children (now called the Autism Society of America). This major advocacy group, armed with data collected by the Autism Research Institute (which Rimland founded in 1967) successfully lobbied for the independent classification of autism in the 1990 reauthorization of IDEA (Rimland, 1994).

Currently, several major parent organizations advocate for the rights of children with autism and their families. These organizations raise money for research, hoping to find a cure for autism. The federal government has also increased funding for research to determine the causes of autism, as well as to develop medical and behavioral/educational treatments for this condition.

PREVALENCE

No precise census, or count of the number, of children with autism has been made, so it is not possible to say exactly how many people have autism. Since 1990, when autism became a separate special education category, the states have reported to the federal government the number of students served in special education programs. In the 1999–2000 school year, some 61,406 students between the ages of 6 and 17 received special education services (U.S. Department of Education, 2001). Although it is not possible to chart prevalence rates of autism across time, parents, professionals, and policymakers tend to agree that many more children are diagnosed with autism today than received this diagnosis in the past (Burton, 2002). Two sources of information are used when reporting prevalence: **epidemiological studies** and the data collected by states about enrollment in special education programs (National Research Council, 2001).

Epidemiological studies conducted in ten countries with approximately 4 million children reveal that the incidence rate of autism has increased from about 2 to 5 children out of every 10,000 diagnosed with autism in the 1970s to 7.5 children out of every 10,000 being diagnosed with autism since 1987 (Fombonne, 1999). When Asperger's syndrome and other ASD diagnoses are included, the incidence rate increases even more.

Exact estimates vary, but data from school districts' special education programs confirm this increase. Figure 12.2 illustrates the numbers of students in California who have received special education services under the state's autism category since 1991. As you can see, there is a dramatic rise in the number of children with autism receiving special education services. Three possible explanations for this increase are

1. Improved diagnostic methods
2. Use of the broader term *ASD* instead of the narrower term *autism*
3. An actual increase in the condition

Although no strong evidence supports any one of these explanations over the others, most experts believe that the increased incidence of autism is due to better diagnostic procedures, along with the use of the broader ASD definition (National Research Council, 2001). This conclusion, however, is controversial. Some experts and many parents believe that an actual increase in the number of children with autism is occurring. However, until a good census is completed or until there is a

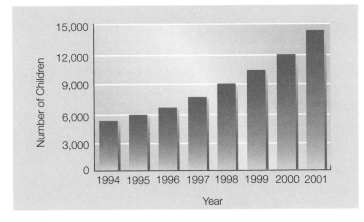

Figure 12.2 Prevalence Rates of ASD in California

Source: From "Scant evidence for an epidemic of autism." (p. 35) by E. Stokstad, 2001, *Science,* 294. Reprinted with permission.

known cause for this disability, the reason for the increased number of children diagnosed with autism will continue to be debated. Remember that even with this increase in diagnosis, ASD remains a low incidence disability. Most pediatricians and general education teachers are likely to have no or little opportunity to meet or work with children who have the disorders or conditions included in this spectrum.

CAUSES OF AUTISM

Experts have been trying to identify the causes of autism, but to date no definitive answers are available. With no specific causes having been identified, it is impossible to develop prevention strategies. This situation is frustrating to people who work with children with autism, but perhaps it is most frustrating to families. Because they want to know the chances of having another child with autism, it is important for researchers to continue their work in determining whether there is a genetic basis for these disorders.

Although precise causes have not been identified, a number of suggestions and reasonable conclusions have been made. First, several suggested causes of autism have been ruled out. Here's one such example: autism is not the result of inadequate parenting. There's something that we know is *not* the reason for the disability. Most experts agree that autism is a lifelong neurological disorder. Some researchers believe that at least some forms of autism are caused by injury to the brain stem (Koegel et al., 1995). Others suggest that autism is basically a failure of the frontal lobe (Dawson et al., 1998). Regardless, it appears that autism probably has a genetic basis (Piven, 2002).

Until such time as more specific causes are identified, speculation about a range of possibilities will persist. The causes suggested in recent years, have included: environmental toxins; gastrointestinal anomalies; and ingredients in the measles, mumps, and rubella vaccines. Such speculation about possible causes of autism creates dangerous situations. For example, some parents believe that the measles/mumps/rubella vaccine causes autism. Although little evidence exists that the vaccine plays any role as a cause of autism, some parents are not protecting their children from these diseases, leaving them vulnerable to conditions that are known to cause disabilities (Cowley, Brownell, & Footes, 2000).

Just as there are few known causes, no consistently effective treatments are available (Seroussi, 2000). The Internet and popular press are littered with stories of children being "cured," but these accounts often involve the use of vitamins, special diets, or medical drugs. The parents and professionals who support these alternative treatments may believe in them and may believe that the treatments help remediate

MAKING **C**ONNECTIONS

For a comparable situation, see the "History" section of Chapter 4 and think about the confusion surrounding the selection of treatments when causes for a disability are not known.

Causes of Autism

Table 12.5 Characteristics of Autism

Impairment in Reciprocal Social Interactions

- Normal attachments to parents, family members, or caregivers do not develop.
- Friendships with peers fail to develop.
- Cooperative or peer play is rarely observed.
- Emotions, such as affection and empathy, are rarely displayed.
- Nonverbal signals of social intent (smiling, gestures, physical contact) tend not to be used.
- Eye contact is not initiated or maintained.
- Imaginative play is seldom observed.
- The lack of social-communicative gestures and utterances is apparent during the first few months of life.
- Preferred interaction style could be characterized as "extreme isolation."
- Understanding of others' beliefs, emotions, or motivations is greatly impaired.
- Joint attention deficits (not being able to cooperate or share interest with others in the same event or activity) impair normal social reciprocation.

Poor Communication Abilities

- Functional language is not acquired fully or mastered.
- Content of language is usually unrelated to immediate environmental events.
- Utterances are stereotypic and repetitive.
- Gestures, facial expressions, and nonverbal cues are poorly understood.
- Conversations are not maintained.
- Spontaneous conversations are rarely initiated.
- Speech can be meaningless, repetitive, and echolalic.
- Many fail to use the words *I* and *yes* and have problems with pronouns in general.
- Both expressive and receptive language are extremely literal.
- Verbal turn-taking, choosing a topic, and contributing properly to a conversation are rare.

Insistence on Sameness

- Marked distress is typically experienced over trivial or minor changes in the environment.
- Aspects of daily routine can become ritualized.
- Obsessive and compulsive behavior is frequently displayed.

- The need to complete self-imposed, required actions is intense.
- Stereotypic behaviors (rocking, hand-flapping) are repeated in cycles difficult to stop.

Unusual Behavior Patterns

- Hypersensitive and/or inconsistent behaviors are the response to visual, tactile, or auditory stimulation.
- Aggression to others is common, particularly when compliance is requested.
- Self-injurious or outwardly aggressive behavior (hitting, biting, kicking, head-banging) is common and frequent.
- Extreme social fears are manifested toward strangers, crowds, unusual situations, and new environments.
- Loud sounds (barking dogs, street noises) can result in startle or fearful reactions.
- Severe sleep problems occur with frequency.
- Noncompliant behavior to requests from others results in disruption to the individual and others (tantrums).
- Self-stimulation (twirling objects, rocking) consumes a considerable amount of time and energy.
- The ability to pretend is lacking.

a child's symptoms, but no scientific evidence validates these claims. Until autism is well understood and consistently effective treatments are developed, the causes and treatments for autism will remain the subject of considerable speculation and conjecture.

CHARACTERISTICS

Despite the heterogeneity of autism, some general statements can be made about characteristics that people with this disorder share (see Table 12.5). Autism is a lifelong disability, and no specific physical features are associated with the conditions. Although identified during early childhood, autism is present from birth or very early in the developmental period. Although autism results in unique profiles of symptoms across individuals and conditions, it typically affects three important areas that help to define the condition (Barnhill, 2001):

This is my family. I have a brother named Evan, in the green shirt. He has autism. It is a complicated problem. My Mom is in the yellow shirt. My Dad is in the red shirt and I am in the orange shirt. Evan can't talk. He has never talked to me or my family using words. Instead he uses pictures and sign language. I wonder what he would say to me if he did talk to me. I have a lot to say to him, and I think he understands most of what I say. 6

Sarah Peralta, eight-year-old sister of Evan who has autism, tells about her family through her drawings and the story she wrote in her book *All About My Brother.*
Source: All About My Brother by Sarah Peralta, © 2002 by Autism Asperger Publishing Co. P.O. Box 23173, Shawnee Mission, Kansas. Reprinted by permission.

1. Communication
2. Social interactions
3. Restricted range of interests or behavioral repertoires

Here are a few more specifics. Among children with autism,

- 75–80 percent have a concurrent diagnosis of mental retardation
- 50 percent never develop functional speech
- 40 percent engage in **self-injurious behavior**
- 4 out of 5 are male
- 33 percent develop seizures (Sturmey & Sevin, 1994)

In addition to these characteristics and the characteristics described by the diagnostic criteria, children with autism may be sensitive to sensory input, such as loud noises or soft touches (Talay-Ongan & Wood, 2000). They have trouble developing the abilities necessary to understanding other people's perspectives or to predicting others' behavior—both important skills for successful communication. (Baron-Cohen, 2001). Regardless, remember that children with autism are children first and thus are more like other children than they are different from their peers.

EARLY CHILDHOOD EDUCATION

While children can be diagnosed with autism before the age of 3, little empirical data suggests which practices and programs are best for these very young children. In other words, the ability to diagnose children with autism has outpaced the

Early Childhood Education

Teach These Skills Directly

1. Attention (by focusing on salient aspects of the environment)
2. Motor imitation
3. Expressive language
4. Receptive language and comprehension
5. How to play with toys
6. Social interaction

validation of effective interventions. A few practices developed for older children with autism and other developmental disabilities have also proven to be effective with toddlers with autism. For example, the increased frequency of making choices causes increases in appropriate engagement and also decreases inappropriate behavior (Reinhartsen, Garfinkle, & Wolery, in press). Similarly, the *Walden Program* is effective with 3-to-5 year-old children with autism, and has been adapted to serve even younger children. Others, like the Inclusive Program for Very Young Children with Autism, are being developed from collective information about child development, the nature of autism, and existing interventions that have been validated with 2-year-olds with autism (Marcus, Garfinkle, & Wolery, 2001).

Educational programs for 3- to 5-year-old children are some of the most developed and best studied, but much is still to be learned (Handleman & Harris, 2000). For example, no one program is consistently effective, so universal recommendations about educational programming cannot be made. Also, no guidelines can suggest whether one type of program would be better than another for a particular child. Finally, few studies have measured the effectiveness of a treatment program using a randomized, experimental study, and no studies have compared the effectiveness of one program against that of another.

Although no programs have been totally validated, research has identified some key features of effective programs for preschoolers. These key features are apparent even across programs that differ in philosophy, theoretical background, intensity of services, and timing of instruction with peers (Dawson & Osterling, 1997; Harris & Handleman, 1994). Key elements of all successful programs include

- Supportive teaching environments
- Plans for generalization
- Predictable and routine schedules
- Functional approaches to address problem behaviors
- Supports for program transitions
- Family involvement and support

These programs also include some common targets for instruction. Students with autism often do not profit from instruction that is not clear, specific, and concrete. The "Tips for Teachers" box identifies some important instructional content that teachers should include in their curriculum for these preschoolers.

Even though most effective programs for young children with autism share some features, significant differences exist across programs. (Some disagreements among the advocates of different programs have been so intense that they have had to be resolved in the courts!) Two particular programs are popular in the education of preschoolers with autism: the *Treatment and Education of Autistic and Communication-Handicapped Children* (TEACCH) and the *Young Autism Program* (YAP). Let's look at some highlights of each program.

What are some features of TEACCH?

TEACCH was developed at the University of North Carolina at Chapel Hill. The program emphasizes the use of **structured teaching** (Lord & Schopler, 1994). Structured teaching involves adapting materials and environments to help children make sense of the world. Once new skills are acquired, children are taught to perform them more and more independently. The program relies on "start-to-finish boxes" as well as visual supports and schedules in teaching. The underlying philosophy of the program is that children with autism are missing skills that they cannot learn but that can be compensated for through visual supports and other forms of structure. TEACCH is an individualized program that supports families through collaboration and training. In this program, parents become co-therapists.

What is the Young Autism Program (YAP)?

The **Young Autism Program (YAP)** grew out of the work of I. Ovar Lovaas at UCLA (Lovaas, 1987). Sometimes it is simply referred to as the "Lovaas Program" or, incorrectly, as ABA (which stands for applied behavior analysis[1]). YAP is an intensive (usually 40 hours a week) program that uses the principles of **applied behavior analysis** (e.g., positive reinforcement) as well as the instructional strategies that have been developed by behavior analysts (e.g., task analysis and discrete trial training). The goal of this program is to teach children, one skill at a time, all the skills the child needs to be able to participate independently in all facets of daily living.

MAKING CONNECTIONS

An example of task analysis is shown in Chapter 6, Table 6.2.

Why are blended programs being developed?

Although the theoretical bases of two popular intervention programs—TEACCH and YAP—are very different from one another, they have many similar components because both include empirically validated strategies. Also, the strategies of both programs target the same skill areas: communication, social skills, toy play, attention, and motor imitation (Dawson & Osterling, 1997). Many researchers, teachers, and parents of children with autism are more interested in effective intervention strategies than in strictly following a particularly philosophy or theory. Thus, combining or blending some elements of established programs, such as structured teaching with discrete trial teaching, is becoming commonplace. One example of a blended program being developed by researchers who are including successful aspects of established early interventions programs is the Developmentally Appropriate Treatment for Autism Project (DATA Project) at the University of Washington in Seattle. In this program, strategies that are effective for a particular child are applied without regard to the theoretical background from which the strategy was initially developed. In other words, they use what works and assess effectiveness through program evaluation. Such types of programs use elements of a variety of procedures (e.g., structured teaching, behavioral principles, discrete trial training, or various combinations) (Schwartz et al., 2001).

ELEMENTARY THROUGH HIGH SCHOOL

Although most established and researched intervention programs for children with autism are designed for preschool children, many of the same principles and strategies are applicable for older children as well. In particular, consistent structure,

---

[1]People often refer to the UCLA program as ABA. This is technically incorrect. ABA stands for applied behavior analysis. Applied behavior analysis is the science of studying observable behavior in settings where people spend time (homes, schools, etc.). The basic principles are those of behaviorism as articulated by B. F. Skinner and others. YAP and other programs for children with autism use ABA principles in designing interventions, but ABA is not synonymous with any one treatment program.

ACCOMMODATING FOR INCLUSIVE ENVIRONMENTS
Creating Situations Where Individuals with Autism Participate Successfully

Make Events Predictable

- Develop a schedule
- Make novel experiences predictable
- Avoid surprises
- Do not make unannounced changes
- Provide structure and a routine
- Know how well the individual handles free time

Communicate Instructions and Consequences Carefully

- Seek consistency in everyone's responses to inappropriate behavior
- Use direct statements

- Do not use slang or metaphors
- Avoid using only nonverbal cues
- Use personal pronouns carefully

Foster Positive Participation

- Provide feedback about the appropriateness of responses
- Remember to tell the individual when behavior is proper
- Arrange tasks that the person can perform
- Translate time into something tangible or visible
- Enhance verbal communications with illustrations or pictures
- Use concrete examples

with autism into inclusive settings at the outset of treatment (Hoyson, Jamieson, & Strain, 1984). Other programs, such as TEACCH and YAP, systematically include peer models in special programs as the child learns interaction and communication skills. Regardless of the approach, many children with autism do well in inclusive environments. But remember that the following elements must be present:

- Sufficient structure
- Supports for functional communication
- A functional approach to problem behaviors
- Supports for social interactions

Accomplishing these aims requires the combined and concentrated efforts and collaboration of teams of professionals.

TRANSITION THROUGH ADULTHOOD

MAKING CONNECTIONS

See Chapter 6 for a review of systems of supports.

Few supports are typically available to persons with autism as they transition into adulthood. Although many persons with autism have skills that would make them employable, their difficulty with social skills and their need for routine often keeps them from being hired or prevents them from being able to remain employed. In general, the difficulties faced by people with autism are similar to those faced by others with severe disabilities. Transition plans can be helpful, but issues such as living and working independently are major problem areas for people with autism and their families. Transition experts have reached consensus about the skills necessary for independent living. Those transition outcomes, which should become some of the goals for these students' education and should be mastered by the time they complete their schooling, are described in Table 12.6.

Table 12.6 Transition Outcomes

Individuals know how to

- ask for help, offer assistance, ask questions.

- answer questions, respond to criticism.

- interact with others socially at work.

- initiate conversations appropriately.

- advocate for themselves.

- interpret and discriminate social cues.

Personal acceptance is demonstrated by co-workers

- voluntarily eating lunch with the individual.

- seeing the individual after work.

- taking breaks with the individual.

- indicating that the individual is a friend.

- encouraging the individual to attend company social events.

Co-workers or the employer

- initiates social interactions with the individual.

- responds to social interactions initiated by the individual.

- advocates for the individual.

- teaches the individual new social skills.

Individuals participate socially by interacting with co-workers

- about work upon arrival, at breaks, during lunch, several times throughout the day, and after work.

- on nonwork topics upon arrival, at breaks, during lunch, and after work.

- at company-sponsored events.

- at social occasions that occur outside of work.

Individuals experience social support as demonstrated by increased

- happiness at work.

- self-esteem.

- friendship network.

- support network.

Individuals are accepted in the workplace as indicated by co-workers

- indicating they like the person.

- advocating for or supporting the person.

- considering the person to be an acquaintance.

- considering the person to be a team player.

- displaying positive, general interactions.

- training the person to perform work tasks better.

Source: From "Building Consensus from Transition Experts on Social Integration Outcomes and Interventions" by J. Chadsey-Rusch and L. W. Heal, 1995, *Exceptional Children,* 62, pp. 170–174. Adapted with permission.

For people with autism, life as an adult can be challenging for themselves and for their families. Many of these individuals, like Jessy Park, seem happy enough, particularly when they are able to retreat to the world they understand—often a world of their own making complete with structure and security in routine patterns and limited contact with others (Park, 2001). Jessy is an artist, whose work is now getting some national attention, but she is unable to live independently or interact with people comfortably enough to live and participate in the community without extensive supports. Anthony Crudale, another recognized artist with autism, is a college graduate and a marathon runner (Raia, 2001). Although he drives a car, at age 24 he still cannot live independently or sustain competitive employment. His mother reports that people do not understand autism and that Anthony's inability to maintain eye contact with other people, his short verbal responses, and his inability to carry on conversations make others uncomfortable. She believes that he, and others with autism, would make excellent employees because of characteristics like focusing on specific tasks, attention to detail, and the need to complete jobs. Thus, although many people with autism are now living in the community (instead of in institutions), their participation in and full access to mainstream society remains distant goals.

FAMILIES

Having a child with autism is difficult even for the most confident parents (Powell, Hecimovic, & Christensen, 1992). These children often lack independent play and leisure skills, which means that parents must spend more time providing direct care

MAKING **C**ONNECTIONS

For a review of natural supports, see Chapter 6.

VALIDATED PRACTICES

The Picture Exchange Communication System

What Is the Picture Exchange Communication System?

The Picture Exchange Communication System (PECS) is a method of providing communication support to nonverbal individuals. PECS uses pictures to represent categories such as clothing, toys, activities, feelings, special events, foods, body parts, and more. The pictures are computer generated or cut out of old magazines. Students begin by using single pictures and eventually form requests using complete sentences.

Why the Picture Exchange Communication System Is Beneficial

It is easy to ask nonverbal individuals what they want, rather than allowing them to tell us. Students who are taught to use PECS are able to request items they need or want. This communication act is initiated by the student, not by you, and allows students to ask for and receive concrete objects within real-life, social situations. Students have also been taught to use PECS to engage in positive peer interactions.

Implementing the Picture Exchange Communication System

Bondy and Frost (2002) provide a detailed description of the PECS program. A brief description of the first four initial phases is given here. For more in-depth procedures and examples, please refer to the articles listed in the research foundation list.

Phase One: Initiating Communication

- Students are taught to request an object, rather than your asking, "What do you want?"

- Two adults are needed (a communicative partner and a physical prompter).

- Select a desired item and don't allow the student to use it for a brief time. This is so the student will "miss" the item and be motivated to ask for it.

- The communicative partner sits directly across from the student with the desired object but provides no verbal prompts.

- The physical prompter guides the student to give the picture to the communicative partner, rather than picking up the item.

- When the student places the picture in the communicative partner's hand, she or he immediately gives the object.

Phase Two: Expanding the Use of Pictures

- The communicative partner no longer sits across from the student. This means the student must find the adult when

to their children. One result is that these parents have less time to take care of other important activities of daily living, such a self-care and household chores.

Perhaps more frustrating for these families are ways their children seem different. Some parents report difficulties connecting with or relating to their child. This experience is common with children who do not like physical affection such as hugs or who are extremely socially avoidant. Parents who believe they are in part responsible for their children's instruction often find it very frustrating when learning is not achieved or is achieved very slowly.

Autism is nevertheless an invisible disability: these children do not have any facial or physical features indicating the disability. Although this may seem fortunate, many families find it a source of stress. For example, one mother was worried that on shopping trips, strangers would say "hi" to her child. The mother worried that her child would ignore the stranger's greeting and the stranger would assume that she was a bad mother because her child was rude. To prevent this from happening, the mother used signs with the child, even though the child did not understand them. The mother thought that her use of signs would cue others that her child had a disability. Another mother kept in her purse a letter from her son's pediatrician, describing her son's autistic diagnosis. Her son was nonverbal but screamed when overstimulated or when the environment was too unpredictable for him. This screaming had happened several times in public, resulting—more than once—in the police being called. This mother was afraid of being arrested for child abuse.

requesting something.

- The items are moved farther from the student, but they must remain in sight and be easy to access.
- The number of items is increased and should span several categories.
- Students are required to place a picture in the adult's hand prior to receiving the item.

Phase Three: Choosing the Message Within PECS

- The main goal is to ensure that students are able to discriminate between pictures, demonstrating that they understand what they are asking for.
- Select one favorite picture (e.g., a toy) and one that the student dislikes (e.g., carrots).
- Say, "What do you want?" and allow the student to select the picture.
- Give the selected item to the student. You will know by the student's reaction if he or she selected the correct picture.
- Add more pictures once students can discriminate between objects they like and those they dislike.
- Students exchange the picture for the desired item.

Phase Four: Introducing Sentence Structure Within PECS

- Provide picture cards that indicate "I want . . ." or "I see. . . ."

- Place the "I want . . ." or "I see . . ." card on the sentence strip.
- Students select the picture of what they want and place it on the strip. See Figure 1 for an example.
- Students give the sentence strip to you.
- You read the sentence, encouraging the student to touch each picture as you read.

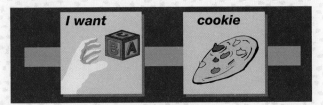

Figure 1 Example of a Sentence Strip

This scientifically validated practice is a teaching method proven by systematic research efforts (Bondy & Frost, 2002; Garfinkle & Scwhartz, 2001; Frost & Bondy, 1994; Schwartz, Garfinkle, & Bauer, 1998). Full citations are found in the "Technology" section of the of the references for this chapter.

Source: From *Topics in autism: A picture's worth. PECS and other visual communication strategies in autism* (p. 90) by A. Bondy and L. Frost 2002, Bethesda, MD: Woodbine House. Reprinted by permission.

The behaviors that define the spectrum of autistic disorders make being a parent challenging. Many programs recognize these difficulties and provide supports for families. Some programs offer support groups and information on how to access such community services as respite care. Other programs help parents develop skills they need to raise their child more effectively. For example, the TEACCH program in North Carolina offers an eight-week course for parents. These "teaching sessions" provide information about the nature of autism, as well as presenting techniques whereby parents can "co-treat" their child with autism. Regardless of the model, support from professionals, support from other parents of children with autism, access to information, and access to high-quality comprehensive services are paramount.

TECHNOLOGY

Children with autism usually do not need the high-tech supports that many children with other disabilities do. Rather, the technology that is useful to these children revolves around two areas:

1. Visual supports to help simplify and structure the environment
2. Augmentative and assistive communication (AAC) to increase language

MAKING CONNECTIONS

To review ACC, see the "Technology" section of Chapter 5.

Autism affects not just the individual involved but the entire family. Alex's brother, Will Masket, is already engaged in charitable contributions and community service. Playing at a benefit—an unusual opportunity for musicians who are still teenagers—his band raised $57,000 for autism research.

Visual supports help simplify and structure the environment and can many forms and serve many purposes. For example, concrete objects, photographs, drawings, or words can create a schedule and cue the child about tasks to complete that day. Baskets, templates, and other visual adaptations can reduce nonessential cues in the environment and draw attention to cues that are useful.

AAC devices are helpful for children with autism because they provide children with an alternative sytem for communication. For example, children with autism have been taught to sign exact English, to point to pictures, and to press a machine's button for a pre-recorded voice message of their intended communication. Only one AAC system, however, was specifically designed for children with autism, although it is also used with children who have other types of disabilities. The **Picture Exchange Communication System (PECS)** combines prompting and fading techniques to help children learn how to use the system, while at the same time teaching the basics of communication. For example, this program teaches that communication is between people, that to be a successful communicator one needs to be persistent, and that communication is about something specific (Frost & Bondy, 1994). PECS has been validated through research and has proved to be an effective and efficient system (Schwartz, Garfinkle, & Bauer, 1998). Nearly all children with autism learn how to use PECS, and more then half of those who master the program also develop some language. An example of the application of PECS is found in the accompanying "Validated Practices" box.

IN CONCLUSION

Summary

Autism, along with several other specific disorders and syndromes, comprises a spectrum of disorders. This implies that even though all children with autism share some common characteristics and common deficits, individuals with autism exhibit very different behaviors. Children with autism vary in terms of severity of deficits and intelligence level. Although the cause is unknown, experts believe that autism is a life-long neurologically based disability. No consistently effective medical or behavioral treatments are currently available, but researchers have identified some key features of high-quality programs. These features include the use of environmental structure, support for functional communication, explicit instruction in social skills, and a functional approach to understanding problem behavior. Families are greatly affected by having a child with autism in the family, and helping families find supports is important. Children with autism, like all children, are individuals who, with proper supports, can learn many skills.

Self-Test Questions

Focus Questions

What is the relationship of autistic disorder, or autism, to autistic spectrum disorders?

Autistic disorder, or autism, is one of five disorders or syndromes now recognized as part of autistic spectrum disorders (ASD).

ASD is the broader term, but people sometimes use *ASD* and *autism* interchangeably, causing considerable confusion.

What is meant by the term spectrum, and what does this term imply about people diagnosed with ASD?

Autistic spectrum disorders (ASD) are defined by the word *spectrum*, which implies that within a particular child and across children with the same diagnosis, a wide range of skills, cognitive abilities, and severity is exhibited.

What is the cause of autistic disorder? Why is this sometimes a controversial issue?

The exact cause of autism is currently unknown.

The cause is probably neurobiological, with a genetic origin.

Lack of known causes leaves room for speculation about other causes.

What are some ways in which the learning environment can be modified and adapted for students with autism?

Learning environments should be predicable and should provide structure. Especially valuable is the use of pictures or symbols to help children organize time, learn new skills, and communicate more effectively.

Why must instruction in nonacademic areas such as social skills be included in educational programs for students with autism?

One of the areas in which children with autism have deficits is social skills. Social skills, however, are critical life skills. Children with autism need instruction in social skills so that they can form friendships and other relationships, so that they can participate in instruction in other content areas, and so that they will have a greater opportunity to qualify for and keep jobs.

Challenge Question

What are some of the implications or effects of autism being an "invisible" disability for the child and for the child's family? What are the implications for educators? for other professionals?

Children with autism physically do not look as though they have a disability.

Parents often find this lack of identifiable characteristics stressful because no cues alert strangers to the disability.

Sometimes, others wrongly assume that the child's inappropriate behaviors are the result of bad parenting, rather than a behavioral manifestation of a disability.

MEETING THE STANDARDS AND PREPARING FOR LICENSURE EXAMS

After reading this chapter, you should be able to demonstrate basic knowledge and skills described in the CEC standards and INTASC principles listed below. The section of this chapter most applicable to each standard is shown in parentheses at the end of the knowledge or skill statement.

 **Core Standard 1: Foundations**

- **Development:** Models, theories, and philosophies that form the basis for special education practice (History of the Field)

- **Family systems:** Family systems and the role of families in the educational process (Families)

 Core Standard 2: Development and Characteristics of Learners

- **Human Growth and Development:** Typical and atypical human growth and development (Characteristics)

- **Educational Implications:** Educational implications of characteristics of various exceptionalities (Early Childhood Education)

 Core Standard 5: Learning Environments and Social Interactions

- **Learning environments:** Design and manage daily routines. (Early Childhood Education and Elementary Through High School)

Council for Exceptional Children Core Standard 6: Language

- **Assistive communication:** Augmentative, alternative, and assistive communication strategies (Technology)

- **Support communication:** Use strategies to support and enhance communication skills of individual with exceptional learning needs. (Early Childhood Education and Elementary Through High School)

 Council for Exceptional Children Core Standard 7: Instructional Planning

- **Functional assessments:** Use functional assessments to develop intervention plans. (Achieving Discipline)

INTASC Principle 2:

The teacher understands how children learn and develop and can provide learning opportunities that support their intellectual, social, and personal development

- **Developmental progressions (physical domain):** The teacher is aware of expected developmental progressions and ranges of individual variation within each domain (physical, social, emotional, moral, and cognitive), can identify levels of readiness in learning and understands how development in any one domain may affect performance in others. (Characteristics)

INTASC Principle 3:

The teacher understands how students differ in their approaches to learning and creates instructional opportunities that are adapted to diverse learners.

- **Teacher expectations:** The teacher believes that all children can learn at high levels and persists in helping all children achieve success (Transition to Adulthood)

- **Valued as people:** The teacher makes students feel valued for their potential as people, and helps them learn to value each other (Defined)

- **Services or Resources:** The teacher can identify when and how to access appropriate services or resources to meet exceptional learning needs. (Collaboration for Inclusion)

INTASC Principle 10:

The teacher fosters relationships with school colleagues, parents and agencies in the larger community to support students' learning and well-being.

- **Collaboration:** The teacher is willing to work with other professionals to improve the overall learning environment for students. (Collaboration for Inclusion)

Standards in Practice

The beginning general education teacher is not likely to encounter a student with autism spectrum disorder. These knowledge statements, dispositions and skills might be demonstrated by the beginning teacher as the ability to be able to search and find appropriate resources. The beginning teacher should also be able to function as a contributing member of an educational team.

 Go to the companion website (ablongman.com/smith5e) for detailed text correlations to CEC and INTASC standards, PRAXIS II™ exams, and other state-sponsored licensure exams.

SUPPLEMENTARY RESOURCES

Professional Readings and Resources

Handleman, J. S., & Harris, S. L. (2000). *Preschool education programs for children with autism.* Austin, TX: Pro-Ed.

Koegel, R. L., & Koegel, L. K. (Eds.). (1995). *Teaching children with autism: Strategies for initiating positive interactions and improving learning opportunities.* Baltimore: Paul H. Brookes.

Myles, B. S., & Adreon, D. (2002). *Asperger's syndrome and adolescence.* Shawnee Mission, KS: Autism Asperger Publishing Co.

National Research Council (2001). *Educating children with autism.* Committee on Educational Interventions for Children with Autism. Division of Behavioral and Social Sciences and Education. Washington, DC: National Academy Press.

Peeters, T. (1997). *Autism: From theoretical understanding to educational intervention.* San Diego: Singular Publishing Group.

Siegel, B. (1996). *The world of the autistic child: Understanding and treating autistic spectrum disorders.* New York: Oxford University Press.

Sperry, V. W. (2001). *Fragile success: Ten autistic children, childhood to adulthood.* Baltimore: Paul H. Brookes.

Popular Books

Grandin, T. (1995). Thinking in pictures and other reports from my life with autism. New York: Viking Books.

Harland, K. (2002). A will of his own. New York: Woodbine House.

Maurice, C. (1994). *Let me hear your voice: A family's triumph over autism.* New York: Fawcett Books

Park, C. C. (2001). *Exiting Nirvana: A daughter's life with autism.* Boston: Little Brown.

Peralta, S. (2002). *All about my brother.* Shawnee Mission, KS: Autism Asperger Publishing Co.

Sacks, O. (1995). *An anthropologist on Mars: Seven paradoxical tales.* New York: Random House.

Videos and DVDs

House of Cards (1993). Miramax

After Ruth's husband's death, her young daughter develops symptoms of autism. Ruth takes her daughter to a specialist in childhood autism named Jake, who employs a strictly traditional approach to therapy at his special school. However, Ruth does not accept that Jake's method is the only treatment, so she attempts to connect with her daughter to see the world through her eyes. Through further examination, Ruth and Jake realize that the little girl was not really autistic but is just coping with her father's death in a very unconventional way.

The little girl presents an example of the detachment exhibited by people with autism. This film offers a good look at a proper specialized educational facility for young children with autism. Autism is a growing concern because very little is really known about autism, including how one contracts it, how to cure it, or how to treat it effectively.

Rain Man (1989). United Artists

Charlie Babbit receives word that his wealthy father has died and that the majority of the estate is bequeathed to an autistic brother, of whom he was unaware. Charlie kidnaps his brother from the institution where he had been living in for over 30 years, in an effort to get custody of Raymond so he can gain access to the inheritance. However, Charlie grows to care for Raymond and comes to realize that Raymond's disability is too overwhelming, requiring professional care.

This film explores a rare form of autism, where in the person is extremely gifted (autistic savant) in mathematics but is extremely low functioning in adaptive skills. Although Raymond is more verbal than most people with autism, many scenes depict the "disconnectedness" they often exhibit. Furthermore, the film demonstrates Raymond's dependence on familiarity and sameness and on an environment providing comfort, routine, and safety. This film won Oscars in the categories of Best Director, Best Original Screenplay, and Best Picture, and Dustin Hoffman's performance as Raymond earned him the Best Actor award.

Parent, Professional, and Consumer Organizations and Agencies

National Autism Hotline/Autism Services Center
Prichard Building
Huntington, WV 25710-0507
Phone: (304) 525-8014

Autism Society of America
7910 Woodmont Avenue, Suite 300
Bethesda, MD 20814-3067
Phone: (800) 3AUTISM; (301) 657-0881
E-mail: info@autism-society.org
Web site: www.autism-society.org

Video**Workshop** Extra

If the VideoWorkshop package was included with your textbook, go to Chapter 12 of the Companion Website (www.ablongman.com/smith5e) and click on the VideoWorkshop button. Follow the instructions for viewing Video clip 13. Consider this information along with what you've read in Chapter 12 as you answer the following questions.

Video Clip 13: Working With Families (Time: 5:22)

1. In the video one parent explains that she spends hours each evening helping her daughter with homework. Family members must wear many hats, serving as parent, teacher, medical caregiver, therapist, friend, and comforter, when they have a relative with a disability. According to your text, what are ways in which teachers can help and support the caregiving family members?

2. Read Temple Grandin's comments. Given her comments and those of the parents in the video, briefly outline the educational program and options you might plan for an elementary school student with autism. How might this program change as the student advanced to high school?

Joanne O'Connell, *College of Life,* 2002 , ink, watercolor on paper.
Reprinted with permission of Gateway Arts, Brookline, Massachusetts.

JOANNE O'CONNELL was born in 1968. From childhood she has
noted her observations through drawing and painting. At the age
of eleven, Ms. O'Connell had a near-drowning accident which put
her into a coma for four months and then in the hospital for more
than a year. Her sense of humor and her positive outlook helped
her through a difficult rehabilitation, but she was left with a number of disabilities including impaired vision and a seizure disorder.

Ms. O'Connell attended Perkins School for the blind in
Watertown, MA and graduated from Boston's Hyde Park High
School in 1989. She began attending the Gateway Arts program in
Brookline, MA in 1992, and since then has made great strides
toward achieving her childhood dream of being an artist.

13 Very Low Incidence Disabilities

Multiple-Severe Disabilities, Deafblindness, and Traumatic Brain Injury

---

A PERSONAL PERSPECTIVE

A Time To Remember

Tom Hehir is the former director of the federal office that administers the programs Congress authorizes through the Individuals with Disabilities Education Act (IDEA). Dr. Hehir, a longtime professional in special education, held this post for most of the Clinton administration. He now works at Harvard University and at the Educational Development Center (EDC) in Boston. Tom's perspective on the way life for children and youth with disabilities has improved across the years, and yet how tenuous are the guarantees that make this improved quality of life possible, is important for all of us. We need to understand how much the situation has improved for children with disabilities and their families, how much improvement is still to be achieved, and why history should not be allowed to repeat itself.

I can still recall the smell, a mix of ammonia and human excrement. I still can recall the sight of rows of metal beds in which were entombed living children and adults with cerebral palsy for almost their entire days and nights. I can still recall the racket that enveloped the ward, created by the simultaneous crying, moaning, yelling, and pleading of the residents. I was an undergraduate taking my first course in special education, "Nature and Needs of the Mentally Retarded." This scene occurred during a field trip to a state school for the mentally retarded. The year was 1971.

It was not only the images that stayed in my mind, but also the attitudes expressed by staff. "This is all you can expect of these people. They're severely brain damaged, vegetables." I kept wondering where the school was. When we returned to the college, we discussed our feelings about what we had seen. Our professor assured us that these children and adults were capable of far more and that we would visit other sites that would prove these kids could learn and have full lives. At that time the more positive sites were special schools and classes in which more fortunate kids were learning to read, write, and laugh. However, though some children were getting a chance at a better life, children with significant disabilities were not guaranteed a right to an education. They could be denied entrance to school.

My professor also predicted that the time would come when all disabled kids would be entitled to public education. He told us about lawsuits and legislative initiatives that were seeking to extend education to all disabled kids. He also showed us a book, *Christmas in Purgatory,* by Burton Blatt, a professor of

445

special education at Syracuse University, which exposed the inhumane treatment of people with mental retardation in state institutions. He made it clear to us special educators in training that our job would be to expand educational opportunity to children with disabilities. It was a heady time for special education, as lawsuits proceeding through the courts were challenging exclusion from school and exposing the miseries of institutionalization.

After graduating from Harvard in 1990, I headed for Chicago as associate superintendent of schools with special education as one of my primary responsibilities. At that time Chicago was undergoing a major reform effort, and students with disabilities were very much part of the effort. Indeed, many of the parent activists in the school reform movement were parents of students with disabilities. Though I was pleased with the role of special education activists in the reform movement, I was dismayed by the lack of compliance with IDEA in the district. Too many children were still being inappropriately segregated, and many children were waiting months to be assessed and placed.

Through hard work and focused activity, the special educators, general educators, disability community, and parents of Chicago demonstrated that a large school district could make progress expanding educational opportunity to students with disabilities while improving education for all. Noncompliance with special education law

dropped markedly, overall performance of students increased. I witnessed in Chicago what many in special education are seeing throughout the country, that the principles upon which IDEA is based—individualization, innovation, and strong parental involvement—can benefit all children.

When I reflect on my decision to pursue a career in special education almost thirty years ago, I consider myself truly fortunate to have entered a field that has been so rewarding. I think back on that institution I visited as a student and now see similar children attending school in their communities with their brothers and sisters and friends. I also agree with the parent who reminds us we have far to go and must be constantly vigilant. I would encourage those of you who are reading this text to seriously consider a career in special education. All good educators liberate the mind. However, in a very real sense, special educators, through their efforts to enable children with disabilities to access education, liberate people.

1. **How has life changed for people with disabilities over the last thirty years?**

2. **Why does Dr. Hehir believe that national protections still need to be in place to ensure good outcomes for students with disabilities? What is your position on this issue?**

MAKING CONNECTIONS

- Burton Blatt's work is also discussed in the "History" section of Chapter 6.

- For comments on the lives of people with disabilities living in institutions, see the "Origins of Special Education" section in Chapter 1 and the "Defined" and "History" sections of Chapter 6.

- In every chapter about an exceptionality, you will find a section devoted to definitions.

ADVANCE ORGANIZERS

Overview

Some disabilities do not occur very often; they are considered very low incidence areas: multiple-severe disabilities, deafblindness, and traumatic brain injury. Deafblindness and traumatic brain injury are separate categories in IDEA, whereas multiple-severe disabilities are included in many different special education categories. Most severe disabilities—with the obvious exceptions of blindness and deafness—present an array of complex problems, often including cognitive

disabilities. Children with deafblindness have very special learning needs because of their dual disabilities. Children with traumatic brain injury (TBI) possess a range of cognitive and behavior problems, which for some are lifelong and for others are only temporary. Most children with these disabilities have very severe problems and require comprehensive, well-coordinated, specialized services from multidisciplinary teams of professionals.

This chapter is organized somewhat differently from the chapters that focus on only one special education category. There are separate sections for each of the three disabilities, followed by combined discussions about early intervention through high school, collaboration, transition through adulthood, families, and technology.

This chapter includes information about three very different disabilities: multiple-severe disabilities, deafblindness, and traumatic brain injury. Two of these areas—deafblindness and traumatic brain injury—are separate special education categories recognized in IDEA. Multiple-severe disabilities can cut across other disability areas but are often considered by schools as one group. One characteristic shared by these three disabilities is their low incidence: They are not very common. It is likely that most educators will not teach many youngsters with these conditions during their careers, in part because of the nature of these disabilities and in part because of their relatively low prevalence. Most typically, children with these disabilities require substantial and intensive special education services and supports.

OPPORTUNITIES FOR A BETTER FUTURE

Confusion has surrounded people with low incidence disabilities since the beginning of time. Their proper place in society has often been denied them, and questions of how to best educate them so that they can achieve their potential continue into this millennium. The challenges they present to themselves, their families, and society are great; these challenges must be met through sustained research and humane consideration.

Turning Legacies into Lessons

During the latter part of the 20th Century, special attention was given to very low incidence disabilities. Two were designated as separate special education categories. Perhaps the federal government's intention was to ensure that special attention would be paid to individuals who meet the criteria for such identification. The complex problems they present, however, have no simple solutions. Perhaps the medical community will one day determine the causes of some of the problems faced by people with these disabilities. But for now, the education community must determine through rigorous research how good outcomes can best be achieved.

Thinking About Dilemmas to Solve

As you read this chapter, ponder these students' needs, the supports they require, and the outcomes they should achieve. Think about

- How their educational needs can best be met
- How they can achieve goals of independent living and full participation in the community
- What supports they require during their school years
- How the curriculum can best provide them with the skills they need
- What technological supports will facilitate their ultimate independence

What's more paralyzing is the way he gets treated.

The hardest part about having a disability is being constantly reminded that you have one. Sometimes that happens when people stare at you. Or point at you. Or don't even think of including you in every day activities. Maybe it's time to start treating people with disabilities like people.

MULTIPLE-SEVERE DISABILITIES

The emphasis for students with **multiple-severe disabilities** is on developing skills that promote independence and community presence (McDonnell, Hardman, & McDonnell, 2003; Snell & Brown, 2000). Ironically, in some cases that means teaching individuals how to depend on others to gain the supports they require to achieve maximal independence. The challenges many students with multiple-severe disabilities present to their families and to the education system can be great because they must have an individualized, intensive, and creative education that truly meets each individual's unique learning needs.

MULTIPLE-SEVERE DISABILITIES DEFINED

The themes emerging from modern perspectives about the education that should be provided for individuals with severe disabilities and goals for them to live, work, and play in community settings have moved away from previous definitions. Instead of describing individuals in terms of deficits—what they cannot do—new orientations focus on what the individual can accomplish through a variety of supports across many of life's dimensions. The Association for Persons with Severe Handicaps (TASH) provides this description of people with severe disabilities:

> Individuals of all ages, races, creeds, national origins, genders, and sexual orientation who require ongoing support in one or more major life activities in order to participate in a integrated community and enjoy a quality of life similar to that available to all individuals. Support may be required for life activities such as mobility, communication, self-care, and learning as necessary for community living, employment, and self-sufficiency. (TASH, 2000a)

People with multiple and severe disabilities require ongoing and intensive supports across their school years and typically across their lives. For some, these supports may well be in only one life activity, but for many of these individuals, supports are needed for access and participation in mainstream society. Supports are necessary because most individuals with multiple-severe disabilities require assistance in many adaptive areas (National Information Center for Children and Youth with Disabilities [NICHCY], 2001). For example, an individual with a cognitive disability might need supports to pay bills and manage a budget. If that individual also has a moderate hearing loss, she or he might need an assistant to facilitate communication at the doctor's office but might function at work with only natural supports from co-workers. The federal government, in its regulations pursuant to IDEA, defines **multiple disabilities** this way:

> Concomitant impairments (such as mental retardation–blindness, mental retardation–orthopedic impairment, etc.), the combination of which causes such severe educational needs that they cannot be accommodated in special education programs solely for one of the impairments. The term does not include deaf-blindness. (U.S. Department of Education, 1999, p. 12422).

MAKING CONNECTIONS

To review the concept of systems of supports, see Chapter 6.

CHAPTER 13 *Very Low Incidence Disabilities*

How are the educational needs of these individuals determined?

Instead of using an array of traditional standardized tests to either determine whether an individual belongs in this group of learners or to plan for instruction, many experts are suggesting that **functional assessments** be used to gather information about the individual's strengths, needs, interests, and preferences (McDonnell, Hardman, & McDonnell, 2003). Functional assessments should include

- Independent living skills
- Natural settings
- Analysis of supports
- Opportunities for learning
- Evaluation of different interventions
- Systematic and frequent measurements of direct activities and skills

What is the impact of this disability?

Possessing more than one major disability presents unique challenges to the individual and the family. The combined effects of two disabilities create a pattern of problems different from those presented by one of the disabilities alone (Laurent Clerc National Deaf Education Center, 2001). For example, deaf children who also have another disability need teachers who are specialists in more than one area and who also understand the special problems that this unique combination of disabilities raises.

Even the hardest work can be fun and can lead to excellent long-term outcomes for students with multiple disabilities.

Today, one major impact of severe disabilities is the cluster of challenges that the individual faces to gain independence and participation in the community. Typically, in order for these goals to be accomplished, intensive and pervasive supports from a wide range of individuals and systems must be in place. The current picture for these individuals is very different from what it was only a few decades ago. Before IDEA was passed in 1975, many of these individuals were excluded from school and had no opportunity to benefit from a special education complete with needed related services. For those who did find access to education, it was often in segregated settings. And it was not until the 1960s and 1970s that researchers began to turn their attention to developing and validating instructional procedures that are effective specifically for these learners. Their education now includes

- Expressions of choice
- Self-determination
- Functional skills
- Social skills training

Not long ago, adults with severe disabilities spent their lives in large residential institutions with no access to the community and no chance to participate in mainstream society. This is why TASH continues to call for the closure of all institutions (TASH, 2000b). Today's situation is quite different, and many live in group homes or in apartments. Many of these individuals hold jobs, and thanks to advances in supported employment, the number of them working in the community is expanding as well. Community based instruction helps these individuals prepare for the challenges of adult living. These efforts and services are still being developed, so the outcomes for the next generations of these students should improve even more.

MAKING CONNECTIONS

For a review of the educational issues related to deafness, see Chapter 10.

MAKING CONNECTIONS

- For comments on the lives of people with disabilities living in institutions, see the "Origins of Special Education" section in Chapter 1 and the "Defined" and "History" sections of Chapter 6.

- For a review of community based instruction, see the "Elementary Through High School" and "Transition" sections of Chapter 6.

PREVALENCE

Relatively speaking, few students have multiple-severe disabilities and require intensive educational opportunities to meet their complex needs. Only 0.18 percent of American students are included in the federal special education category of multiple disabilities, representing some 112,345 students aged 6 to 21 (U.S. Department of Education, 2001). Depending on how states include individuals in one category or another, fewer or more students can be considered as having this disability. For example, some states do not include in this category students with learning disabilities and also a hearing problem; other states do. Some states include students with a mild visual disability who also have substantial cognitive disabilities in the mental retardation category; other states report these students to the federal government as having multiple disabilities. Regardless, all students with severe problems are served by special education, and the overall goal for their education usually focuses on achieving independent living in the community.

CAUSES AND PREVENTION

To get an overall understanding of the causes of disabilities, reread each of those sections in this text.

Multiple factors can cause disabilities. As you have learned throughout this academic term, heredity, problems during pregnancy, problems at birth, and incidents after birth can all lead to a lifelong set of challenges—sometimes even to multiple-severe disabilities. Because of advances in medical technology, many children born with multiple-severe disabilities now have long life expectancies (McDonnell, Hardman, & McDonnell, 2003). For example, increasing numbers of babies with extremely low birth weights—as low as 1,500 grams—are surviving infancy and joining the ranks of schoolchildren (March of Dimes, 2002). Many of these youngsters present multiple problems, including substantial cognitive disabilities, to schools. Although reasons for the majority of birth defects are unknown, many could have been prevented with pre-pregnancy doctor's visits to determine potential risk factors (e.g., hereditary possibilities, health and lifestyle issues) and to ensure good prenatal health care during pregnancy (March of Dimes Perinatal Data Center, 2001). Universal access to health care and raised public awareness of prevention strategies would help to reduce the number of children and families affected (Children's Defense Fund [CFD], 2001).

CHARACTERISTICS OF MULTIPLE-SEVERE DISABILITIES

For a review of generalization, see Chapters 4 and 6. For a review of speech and language, see Chapter 5.

Individuals with multiple-severe disabilities display a wide range of skills and abilities, as well as a wide range of problem areas in need of intensive instruction. According to NICHCY (2001), this group of individuals shares some common characteristics:

- Problems transferring or generalizing learning from one situation to another, one setting to another, and one skill to another
- Limited communication abilities
- Difficulties with memory
- Need for supports for many major life activities (domestic, leisure, community participation, vocational)

CHAPTER 13 *Very Low Incidence Disabilities*

It is important for all children to learn how to play recreational sports early in life. No assumptions should be made about who can learn or enjoy which sports.

Compounding their problems, many individuals with multiple-severe disabilities face other challenges. Many of them experience medical problems, such as seizure disorders, vision or hearing problems, heart disease, and cerebral palsy, along with other health issues. Consequently, they and their families interface with many professionals and disciplines, all with different styles of interaction, terms and jargon, and approaches. Such multiple interactions can complicate an already difficult situation.

DEAFBLINDNESS

When you hear the word *deafblindness,* you probably think of people who have no vision *and* no hearing abilities. Although this is true for some individuals, it is far from true for most of them, because the majority of these individuals have some residual hearing and/or vision. In fact, according to the National Deafblind Census, more of them have some functional use of their vision than have some hearing (DB-Link, 2001). Regardless, the world for children with **deafblindness** can be exceptionally restricted. For those whose hearing and vision fall into the ranges of severe or profound losses, their immediate world may well end at their fingertips (Miles, 2001).

Almost half of these students have enough residual vision to allow them to read enlarged print, see sign language, move about in their environment, and recognize friends and family (Miles, 2001). Some have sufficient hearing to understand some speech sounds or hear loud noises. Some can develop speech themselves, but others have such limited vision and hearing that they profit little from either sense. In addition to their visual and hearing losses, the majority of these individuals have other disabilities, such as mental retardation, that further complicate their education. Most individuals with deafblindness need considerable supports for their worlds to be safe and accessible; these students' educational programs need to be carefully thought through and must be uniquely designed to ensure that each of these children meets his or her potential.

DEAFBLINDNESS DEFINED

A separate funding base for students with deafblindness was initiated in 1969. This period was a time of national crisis. The rubella epidemic had caused dramatic increases in the number of babies with disabilities, particularly blindness, deafness, and deafblindness. Thus deafblindness was created as a special category of disabilities. Although every state acknowledges deafblindness, definitions vary by state. The result is inconsistent identification, service outcomes, and numbers of students with this condition. This confusion is compounded by the fact that most of these youngsters have additional disabilities, such as cognitive disabilities and health impairments (Miles, 2001). For these reasons, many of these youngsters are counted in the multiple disabilities category.

IDEA defines deafblindness in this way:

Deafblindness means concomitant hearing and visual impairments, the combination of which causes such severe communication and other developmental

Deafblindness Defined

HE DIDN'T LISTEN

"Why would you want to adopt him?" the neonatologist asked 8 years ago. "He'll never be more than a vegetable," he stated.

But Alex didn't listen, and now he jumps and shouts and laughs and loves his family.

"Alex may never be able to leave the hospital," the doctor said 7 years ago.

But Alex didn't listen, and it's been 4½ years since he was hospitalized.

"Alex will never eat or drink again by mouth," the experts told us 6 years ago.

But Alex didn't listen, and today he's eating and drinking, his G-tube 3 years removed.

"He may never walk," the therapist said 5 years ago.

But Alex didn't listen, and today he walks, runs, skips, and hops.

"He's profoundly retarded, incapable of much learning," the psychologist said 4 years ago.

But Alex didn't listen, and today he is learning to read.

"Even if he is legally blind and won't keep his glasses on, why are you trying contacts? He won't keep those in either," the vision specialist said 3 years ago.

But Alex didn't listen, and those contacts (that he leaves in) have opened up a new world of discovery.

"We'd like Alex to increase his expressive language vocabulary to ten words," his Mom stated at the I.E.P. meeting.

The teacher for the deaf and hard of hearing laughed! "He will never be able to do that," she stated 2 years ago.

But Alex didn't listen and today signs dozens of words and understands over two hundred.

"Maybe potty training is beyond him cognitively," the therapist said 1 year ago.

But Alex didn't listen, and today he rarely wets himself.

So what will Alex be told he can't do next? Whatever it is, I pray that he won't listen. And I hope that I won't either.

Jack Kemper, Alex's Dad.

Source: From "He Didn't Listen." By J. Kemper, 2002, *Deaf-Blind Perspectives, 9,* p. 1. Reprinted by permission.

---

and learning needs that the persons cannot be appropriately educated in special education programs solely for children and youth with hearing impairments or severe disabilities, without supplementary assistance to address their education needs due to these dual, concurrent disabilities. (U.S. Department of Education, 1999, p. 12422)

Some experts believe that the IDEA definition does not assist in accurate identification of, and ultimately appropriate services for, all children with this disability (Deaf-Blind Link, 2002). They believe a functional definition—one that focuses on the conditions needed for optimal learning and considers the unique challenges imposed by the interplay of two sensory impairments—produces better outcomes. Vic Baldwin proposed this functional definition:

If the deficit in hearing and vision is sufficient to require special adaptations in instruction in both the auditory and visual modes to produce maximum learning, then the person qualifies to be identified as deafblind and should be included in the annual census. (Baldwin, 1995, p. 2)

The criterion universally used to qualify a student as having deafblindness requires that "a person needs, at a minimum, to have a visual acuity of 20/70 in the better eye with correction and an auditory deficit of 30 dB in the better ear" (Baldwin, 1995, p. 5).

CHAPTER 13 *Very Low Incidence Disabilities*

What is the impact of this disability?

The impact of deafblindness is significant in so many ways. Besides the seriousness of the disability itself, unfounded assumptions about these individuals' abilities and potential that can limit their educational opportunities and possible outcomes. Jack Kemper writes about his adopted son, Alex, and the negative attitudes he has experienced (Kemper, 2002). Think about how beliefs can affect an individual (see the accompanying box). Another example comes from Australia, where children with severe disabilities were first included in the public school system only a short time ago (Steer, 1999). There, it was believed that these children could not profit from an education. In fact, many individuals with severe disabilities are still relegated to nursing homes and institutions, receive only minimal services, and are afforded no education. Clearly, prophecies of poor outcomes become self-fulfilled under such conditions!

Deafblindness should not be minimized; it is serious and has significant effects on those involved. It definitely affects these students' education, which is often so individualized and intensive that is does not occur in the general education setting. In the U.S., only 6 percent of these students (fewer than 400 nationally) attend general education classes for most of their school day—11 percent when resource rooms are included. More than a third attend specialized center or hospital schools, and almost 30 percent receive their education in separate special education classes (DB-Link, 2001). Most teachers, then, will never work directly with a deafblind student in their entire careers.

Helen Keller and her teacher, Anne Sullivan, proved that deaf and blind people can achieve beyond most people's expectations.

What might be expected from these individuals?

Probably the most famous person with deafblindness is Helen Keller. Keller was a woman of many accomplishments, but none of her achievements, which included graduating from Radcliffe with honors in 1904, would have been possible without the efforts of her teacher, Anne Sullivan (Holcomb & Wood, 1989). Sullivan's "family tree" is interesting and noteworthy. Samuel Gridley Howe was the founder of the Perkins School for the Blind. Located in Boston, it was the first school for blind students in the United States. One of Howe's pupils was Laura Dewey Bridgman, herself a person with deafblindness, who talked to other people by tapping letters and using a manual alphabet. She used braille for reading. Miss Bridgman became a teacher, and one of her students, Anne Sullivan, was a girl with low vision. When Sullivan grew up, she learned of a 6-year-old girl with deafblindness living in Alabama. Sullivan visited young Helen Keller and brought her a gift, a doll that had been given to her by Laura Bridgman. Sullivan became Helen Keller's teacher and lifelong companion. Of her disabilities, Keller said, "Blindness separates a person from things, but deafness separates him from people" (Miles, 1995, p. 4). Clearly, the case of Helen Keller is unique and remarkable. Although it is unrealistic to expect the outcomes for all individuals with deafblindness to be like hers, her story does remind us all of the importance of high expectations, hard work, intensive instruction, and meaningful support.

MAKING CONNECTIONS

See the "Supplementary Resources" section at the end of this chapter for a review of the film about Helen Keller's life.

Deafblindness Defined

Remember, many individuals with deafblindness have enough vision to move around, recognize familiar faces, read enlarged print, and even read sign language at close distances. Some have sufficient hearing to understand some sounds, recognize familiar voices, and maybe even develop speech. Many of these students also have mental retardation. The compounding effects of all of these disabilities result in the vast majority of these individuals requiring extensive supports throughout their lives.

PREVALENCE

According to the Deafblind Census, some 9,344 students—ages 6 to 21—were identified as having deafblindness and as being in special education programs in 1999 (Deaf-Blind Link, 2001). That same year, the federal government reports that only 1,840 students were included in this category across the entire nation (U.S. Department of Education, 2001). Why might such a large discrepancy exist? The answer is that the federal government insists that states report students' disabilities in only one area, and many deafblind students are reported in other categories because they have so many additional problems. Many students are reported in the multiple disabilities category, some in the mental retardation category, and so on. In fact, more students with both hearing and vision problems are included in the multiple disabilities category than in the deafblind category. Whether we should be concerned about which category a student is counted in is questionable. What is important to understand is that relatively few students have these problems, but when they do it is often very serious.

MAKING CONNECTIONS

To review deafness, see Chapter 10; to review blindness, see Chapter 11; and to review cognitive disabilities or mental retardation, see Chapter 6.

MAKING CONNECTIONS

For another example of the effects of a recessive gene in a small, tight-knit community, see the story of the people of Martha's Vineyard in Chapter 1.

CAUSES AND PREVENTION

As with most other disabilities, the specific cause of most cases cannot be identified. Among the known causes, however, the most common reason for deafblindness is prematurity (DB-Link, 2001). The role of heredity is becoming more clearly understood. In 1994, only 18 different hereditary syndromes had been associated with this disability (Heller & Kennedy, 1994). Today, over 56 genetic causes of deafblindness are identified (DB-Link, 2001).

Usher syndrome is a hereditary cause of congenital deafness and progressive blindness, along with mental retardation. In addition to these three disabilities, many individuals with Usher syndrome also have walking and motor problems (Accardo et al., 1996). This recessive, X-linked genetic syndrome is rare, affecting 3 out of every 100,000 people. However, its prevalence varies by locale. For example, in Louisiana some 15 to 20 percent of students with deafblindness have Usher syndrome, and 30 percent of all deaf individuals in three parishes (counties) have the syndrome (Melancon, 2000). By comparison, nationally 3 percent of deaf students have Usher syndrome. Why the concentration of Usher syndrome in Louisiana? When the Cajuns came to Louisiana from Nova Scotia, they brought with them the gene responsible for the disability. Because Cajun communities are small and tight-knit, the prevalence is higher in this part of the United States. This knowledge makes it possible to prevent some cases.

Deafblindness is associated with other conditions besides Usher syndrome (Miles, 2001). Prematurity is the most common known cause; risk factors, such as poverty and limited access to health care, are now well understood. These risk factors can be reduced or eliminated with systematic national prevention programs (Children's Defense Fund [CDF], 2001).

CHAPTER 13 *Very Low Incidence Disabilities*

CHARACTERISTICS OF DEAFBLINDNESS

From the name of this disability, it is clear that those involved have reduced distance senses: restricted vision and hearing. However, the degree and amount of vision and hearing loss are not uniform, and the combination of these losses affects each individual differently. Also, at least some 60 percent of these students have other disabilities in addition to their deafblindness, and cognitive disabilities are a common problem (DB-Link, 2001).

How serious are these students' visual and hearing disabilities?

Loss of sensory input, particularly if it cannot be corrected through optical aids (e.g., glasses or contact lenses) and assistive listening devices (e.g., hearing aids), can be devastating to the learning process. When these disabilities occur together, the impact is even greater, affecting every aspect of the child's education—the way it is delivered, the accommodations needed, and the adjustments required.

One question that you should be asking is related to the seriousness of these youngsters' visual and hearing disabilities. You should also be wondering how these degrees of loss combine. For example, do most of these children have a mild vision loss but a profound hearing loss? Do they have little or no functional use of either sense? First, some 20 percent have low vision and another 26 percent are legally blind. From these data, one can assume that at least half of these individuals have some functional vision. Second, 28 percent of deafblind students are profoundly deaf (DB-Link, 2001). Hence some 70 percent perceive some meaningful sounds and profit somewhat from amplification.

What are some common problems shared by these learners?

The individuals affected by deafblindness, their family members, and their teachers must address problems with

- Feelings of isolation
- Communication
- Mobility

Let's think about these problem areas and how they might be improved.

• *Isolation* Feelings of isolation are a particular problem for many individuals with deafblindness, and this is an area that educators must address. The world of these individuals is restricted. It is the educator's role to expand their "world view" and connect them with other people and with their environments (Haring & Romer, 1995; Heubner et al., 1995). Casey Cook, a deafblind triathlete, illustrates the connection these individuals can make (Boeck, 1998). Cook, winner of an Arete Award for Courage in Sports, has Voigte–Carnegie syndrome, which resulted in his blindness and severe hearing impairments. Despite his disabilities, he races with training partners and says of himself, "I'm a regular guy. . . . I have a few physical quirks. I'm mystified why others see what I do as a big deal" (p. C3). See the accompanying "Tips for Teachers" for suggestions about including students with severe disabilities, and reducing their feelings of isolation, through everyone becoming more "disability sensitive."

MAKING CONNECTIONS

Review low vision and legally blind individuals' functional use of sight in Chapter 11.

Fostering a Sense of Belonging for Deafblind Students

1. Gently touch the person's nearest hand to indicate you are nearby.

2. Every time you meet the person, identify yourself, perhaps with a special sign.

3. Help classmates come to feel comfortable interacting with their deafblind peer.

4. Communicate directly with the deafblind person; don't ask someone else what the individual wants.

5. Have the individual join in class discussions.

6. Create cooperative teams for academic tasks.

7. Encourage classmates to include their peer with deafblindness in games during recess and free time.

8. Offer assistance only when necessary.

9. Demonstrate respect for the individual.

10. Laugh and play with all students.

MAKING CONNECTIONS

For a review of manual communication systems, including ASL, see Chapter 10.

MAKING CONNECTIONS

To review orientation and mobility, see the "Early Childhood Education" and "Elementary Through High School" sections of Chapter 11.

• *Communication* Possibly the greatest challenge facing individuals with deafblindness is learning to communicate (Miles, 2001). Some never learn to talk (Stremel, 1998). Children with this condition are dependent on others to make language accessible to them and help them join the many adults with this disability who have achieved some level of independence.

For many of these children, the way they approach their world is through touch (Chen, Downing, & Rodriguez-Gil, 2000–2001; Miles, 2001). Thus various forms of manual communication (e.g., sign language, body language, gestures) are their means to express their needs and also to learn and grow. Some of these students learn a different kind of sign language to communicate with others. They use a tactile form of sign language, that is called "hand over hand," where the signs are conveyed through touch. In this system, fingers placed in the other person's palm form the means of interaction.

For those of us without disabilities, much of our learning is almost effortless. Through what is called **incidental learning,** we gain knowledge about our environment, learn the subtle rules and social conventions that govern interactions with others, and come to understand how to access our communities. Efficient incidental learning requires intact vision and hearing, because these channels are used to communicate and convey information. Depending on the degree of visual or hearing loss and the age of onset of the disability, the transfer of this knowledge can be impaired.

Because of the severity of their disabilities, these individuals often do not naturally recognize the importance or the need to interact and exchange information with others. For those who need instruction to acquire communication skills, experts now agree: skills should be taught in the child's home and community, using activities of daily life (Noonan & Siegel, 2003). These students need to understand what others are saying. To do so requires use of their residual senses. Accomplishing good communication skills can require a lot of effort, so teachers often need to provide incentives to motivate these children to communicate with others.

• *Mobility* Movement is important to all of us. We move to exercise, play, get from one location to another for so many purposes, and communicate our emotions. Moving freely in our environments is a natural human behavior, but for those who have significant visual losses, movement is often restricted and can even be dangerous. The components of purposeful movement—becoming aware of one's environment, changing locations, protection from danger, deciding when to move—must become instructional targets for many students with deafblindness (Groce & Isaacson, 1995). The activities used to teach mobility skills should be functional (Whinnery & Barnes, 2002). When teaching functional mobility skills, instructors should aim for

- Age-appropriateness
- Increased independence
- Improved access to the community
- Reduced dependence and custodial care
- Promotion of communication, social, and daily living skills

What should be clear from this discussion is that the significance of deafblindness and its associated problems is great. The impact on the individuals affected is substantial. The work and effort to overcome these challenges is considerable and involves teams of dedicated people, including the individuals themselves, their families, educators, and experts from many disciplines.

MAKING CONNECTIONS

For a reminder of Section 504 of the Rehabilitation Act, see "Necessity for National Intervention" in Chapter 1.

TRAUMATIC BRAIN INJURY

The Council for Exceptional Children (CEC) believes that *every* teacher, at some time during his or her career, will work with a child with **traumatic brain injury (TBI)** (Van Kuren, 2001 March). Prior to the 1960s, most children whose brains were seriously hurt died soon after the trauma. Changes in emergency treatment, imaging technology, and surgical and pharmaceutical treatments now routinely save children's lives, but the results for some include the need for special education.

MAKING CONNECTIONS

Compare the characteristics of TBI and LD by contrasting this section with a review of Chapter 4.

About one million children annually experience a head injury; and about 15,000 to 16,000 of those injuries have lasting effects, and about 500 require hospitalization (Van Kuren, 2001). Some youngsters, after their injuries, require special education or special accommodations under Section 504 of the Rehabilitation Act.

Children with TBI have been served in special education since IDEA was originally passed in 1975. In fact, many children with TBI were served long before then. It is quite possible that some were recognized during the 1940s. In 1947 Strauss and Lehtinen published a groundbreaking book, *Psychopathology and Education of the Brain-Injured Child*, in which they recommended highly structured educational approaches for children they described having many of the characteristics observed in today's students with TBI. This disability, however, was not considered a special education category until the 1990 reauthorization of IDEA (PL 101-476). Before 1990, these students were simply counted in whatever category most closely matched their primary learning needs.

Just as they are today, many students with TBI were educated in general education classes, receiving the same instructional strategies as their peers with learning disabilities. Like their classmates with learning disabilities, these students often exhibit memory deficits, attention problems, language impairments, and reduced academic performance. Many benefit from instructional procedures proven effective with children with learning disabilities: direct instruction, structured school days, and organized classes where expectations are clearly specified. Others, because of their head injuries, experience seizures and receive many of the same accommodations as children with epilepsy. Although specific programs for students with TBI are emerging across the nation (the Weld County TBI Task Force outside of Greeley, Colorado; the Rehabilitation Center in Austin, Texas; the Wisconsin Department of Public Instruction), most are served within existing programs for students with other disabilities.

Besides automobile accidents, bicycle accidents are the most common cause of brain injuries. The seriousness of most of these injuries could be limited with the use of proper protection, such as helmets.

TBI DEFINED

In 1990 Congress added TBI to the list of special education categories. Here's how IDEA defines this disability:

> *Traumatic brain injury means an acquired injury to the brain caused by an external physical force, resulting in total or partial functional disability or psychosocial impairment, or both, that adversely affects a child's educational performance. The term applies to open or closed head injuries resulting in impairments in one or more areas, such as cognition; language; memory; attention; reasoning; abstract thinking; judgment; problem solving; sensory, perceptual, and motor abilities; psychosocial behavior; physical functions; information processing; and speech. The term does not apply to brain injuries that are congenital or degenerative, or to brain injuries induced by birth trauma. (U.S. Department of Education, 1999, p. 12422)*

Like other disabilities, TBI ranges in severity from mild to severe. Table 13.1 provides some explanations of what TBI is and what it is not. The vast majority of cases are mild and do not raise alarm with most doctors (Hux & Hacksley, 1996). Mild episodes of brain injury often result in these symptoms: dizziness, headache, selective attention problems, irritability, anxiety, blurred vision, insomnia, fatigue, motor difficulties, language problems, behavior and emotional problems, cognitive problems, and memory problems (Clark, 1996; Heller et al., 1996). These problems can last for a very short time or for years. In many cases the effects eventually disappear, but some cases of TBI result in lifelong problems. Youngsters with moderate to severe injuries often experience dramatic changes in their cognitive, language, motor, sensory, and behavioral performances. Some of these children are typical learners one day but then, after their injury, have significant disabilities. In these cases, it is also common for the individual to experience depression or withdrawal.

How are children with TBI identified?

It is typically medical professionals who identify children with TBI. What is surprising, however, is the lateness of most diagnoses. Many children with TBI are not identified immediately after their injuries. This happens because many of these youngsters show no visible signs (cuts, bruises) of brain injury (NICHCY, 2002). The impact of what has been sometimes called the "silent epidemic" may go misunderstood for months. How can this be? Think about Ryan, who was not wearing a helmet, despite his mother's warnings, and fell while skateboarding. Because he did not want to tell his mother that he was not wearing his helmet, he also did not tell her about the accident. Instead, he told his mom that he was tired and went off to his room to take a nap.

Even when accidents are serious, injury to the brain may go unnoticed at first. Too often, families bring their children home from the hospital not knowing that long after the broken bones are mended, the head injury could result in long-term disabilities (Singer, 1996). Most families are unaware of the signs associated with TBI, and they may not have been informed by medical staff at the hospital that their children might have long-term cognitive effects from their injuries. Sometimes it is educators who must confirm families' worst (and often unspoken) fears: "The bicycle accident several weeks ago caused more than a broken leg; it might have also caused brain injury. You better take Justin to the doctor again."

In many cases, families do not inform school personnel of the possibility of mild TBI. This might happen if the accident occurred during the summer. It might be that family members did not make the connection between physical injuries sustained in an accident and changes in behavior (Hux & Hacksley, 1996). The result can be serious. Educators may spend unnecessary time trying to determine why a child, who never had academic or behavior problems before, is having great difficulty at

Table 13.1 What Is and What Is Not TBI

TBI	Not TBI
Concussion is another term for TBI.	An internal cause of brain damage—such as a stroke, brain tumor, or infection of the brain—is not TBI.
A TBI can occur without a direct blow to the head—as in shaken baby syndrome and other forms of child abuse.	A medically documented event potentially causing brain damage but not accompanied by a documentable change in educational performance does not justify TBI verification.
A person does *not* have to lose consciousness to sustain a TBI.	
Brain damage resulting from TBI is often *not* visible through medical tests such as EEGs or brain imaging techniques such as computerized tomography scans or magnetic resonance imaging.	
Repeated mild TBIs can have a cumulative effect.	

Source: From "Mild Traumatic Brain Injury: Facilitating School Success" by K. Hux and C. Hacksley, 1996, *Intervention in School and Clinic, 31,* p. 160. Reprinted by permission.

school. Educators may not know that they should be making specific accommodations for the child's academic or social performance.

Most states have developed eligibility criteria for TBI that require a neurological or medical examination and documentation of the adverse effects of the injury on the student's educational performance. One result is that health specialists and physicians are serving on these children's IEP committees and multidisciplinary teams. Using non-school-district personnel, particularly from the health field, can cause difficulties with scheduling meetings, having the designated team members readily available, understanding or being familiar with educational terms, and budgeting for increased costs. Consequently, under these circumstances only students with severe disabilities are identified as having TBI. Regardless, multidisciplinary teams are vital to the successful design and implementation of appropriate educational plans for students with disabilities.

What is the impact of this disability?

The impact of TBI is related to the severity of the injury. In many minor cases, recovery occurs within a few months (Van Kuren, 2001). In devastating situations, recovery and relearning can be a slow and frustrating process. Motor skills usually return first. For those who have already developed speech and language skills, basic communication abilities tend to recover quickly. More complex language use and comprehension of subtle verbal and nonverbal cues remain difficult for some students. High-level cognitive functions (problem solving, memory, and high-level complex-thinking skills) often return later. The pattern seems to be rapid progress during the first few months after the injury, followed by substantial improvement throughout the first year. Then gradual improvement is often noted across even a five-year period (Heller et al., 1996).

Educators can play important roles in the recovery of students with TBI. They can provide considerable assistance during the often difficult period when the student is just returning to school and is still in the process of adjusting to unusual fatigue, reduced energy, and loss of ability. Educators can also help students learn, once again, how to remember information—an ability frequently impaired with TBI (Hutchinson & Marquardt, 1997). Systematic instruction (see the accompanying "Validated Practices") helps in times when a student seems disorganized, forgetful,

MAKING CONNECTIONS

For a review of these procedures, see the "Elementary Through High School" section of Chapter 4.

VALIDATED PRACTICES
Self-Management

What Is Self-Management?

Self-management techniques are a systematic process used to teach students with severe disabilities to manage their own behavior. The three types of self-management are self-monitoring, self-evaluation and self-reinforcement. When teaching self-management skills to students, teachers first model the process of self-management and then provide students with ample opportunities to learn and practice the strategy on their own. Many students require positive and corrective feedback during the learning process in order to master the technique.

Why Self-Management Is Beneficial

It is important for students to take responsibility for their learning and actions. Students who are able to "control" their behavior become independent and are able to generalize this ability to other aspects of their lives. In addition, when students are able to use self-management techniques, you will be able to spend more time teaching instead of managing student behavior.

Implementing Self-Management

A brief description of some self-management procedures follows, and Figure 1 shows an example of a data collection system for a student to use.

Select the Behavior for Self-Management

Identify and define the behavior.

- Select behaviors you can easily describe, define, count, and evaluate.
- Identify functional behaviors with social value important to the student (e.g., staying on-task, completing homework).
- Select behaviors the student has ample opportunities to use.
- Select behaviors manageable for the student to perform and record.

Determine mastery criteria.

- Consider the student's current level of task performance (e.g., on-task 50% of the time).
- Compare that level of performance with that of peers to set goals and criteria (e.g., on-task 90% of the time).

Measure current performance levels.

- Conduct 4–5 observations to determine the student's current level.

Choose self-management component.

- Self-monitoring (e.g., "Am I on-task?")
- Self-evaluation (e.g., "Did I reach my goal today?")
- Self-reinforcement (e.g., "I did a good job today.")

and in need of deliberate instruction. Providing environmental cues, teaching mnemonics, and offering many opportunities to remember information that was known before also contribute to improved performance in students with TBI.

PREVALENCE

More than 100,000 children sustain brain injuries each year, and 30,000 of them have permanent disabilities (Lash & DePompie, 2002). Most of these disabilities are mild. According to the federal government, 12,329 students, aged 6 through 17, were served by special education in the 1999–2000 school year as having TBI (U.S. Department of Education, 2001).

CAUSES AND PREVENTION

The most common cause of TBI is car accidents, but bicycle accidents, sports accidents, and falls on the playground are also major causes of TBI (Lash & DePompie, 2002). These injuries typically occur among older children, particularly teenage boys, who are careless in the street; do not take safety precautions while bicycling, skiing, or skateboarding; engage in high-risk behaviors such as driving too fast, mixing alcohol or drugs and driving; or participate in contact sports (Singer, 1996;

CHAPTER 13 *Very Low Incidence Disabilities*

Develop the Self-Management Component

- Finalize and describe behaviors.
- Be sure others can consistently observe those behaviors.
- Determine when and how data will be collected.
- Develop a simple data-recording system.

Teach Students to Use Self-Management

Introduce the procedure.

- State the behavior and provide both examples of effective use of the procedures and examples of its ineffective use.
- Explain the importance of the behavior.
- Provide ample opportunities for supervised practice using the recording system.
- Discuss criteria for mastery.
- Teach self-recording procedure.

Provide practice and assess mastery.

- Provide guided practice and role-playing.
- Assess mastery during role-playing.
- Discuss when self-management will be implemented.
- Provide independent practice.
- Assess mastery and independence.

Evaluate the Student's Performance

- Assess performance against criteria.

- Assess maintenance.
- Assess generalization.

This scientifically validated practice is a teaching method proven by systematic research efforts. (Connell, Carta, & Baer, 1993; Dunlap et al., 1991; Hall, McClannahan, & Krantz, 1995; Hughes & Boyle, 1991; King-Sears & Carpenter, 1997; Prater, Hogan, & Miller, 1992.) Full citations are found in the "Tramatic Brain Injury" section of the references for this chapter.

Sample Self-Monitoring Form for On-Task Behavior

Student's name: **Erik**   Date: **11–6**

Ask yourself: **"Was I working?"**
Check yes or no when you hear the beep.

	1	2	3	4	5	6	7	8	9	10
☺ YES	✓		✓	✓	✓		✓		✓	✓
☹ NO		✓				✓		✓		

Variations:

Was I **paying attention?**   Did I **turn in my homework?**   I had **a positive attitude.**
Was I **on time?**   Did I **raise my hand?**   I had **appropriate adult**
Was I **listening?**   Did I **wait to be called on?**   **interaction.**
                               Did I **bring my materials?**   I am **on-task.**

Figure 1 Sample Self-Monitoring Form for On-Task Behavior

Source: From *Innovations: Teaching self-management to elementary students with development disabilities* (p. 21) by M.E. King-Sears and S.L. Carpenter, 1997, Washington, DC: American Association on Mental Retardation. Reprinted with permission.

West, Gibson, & Unger, 1996). Less straightforward to address is the sad fact that for children under the age of 2, the most common cause of TBI is child abuse (Heller et al., 1996). Many accidents can be prevented through commonsense measures. For example, wearing helmets when bicycling or skateboarding, not driving a car or motorcycle when using intoxicating substances, and avoiding high-risk behaviors can prevent tragic accidents.

It is obvious that appropriate medical treatment and rehabilitation are critical to preventing the devastating outcomes seen in untreated individuals. Education is also a powerful tool. To ensure responsive educational services, some states have developed interagency initiatives so that children hospitalized with TBI can be transitioned to schools in a seamless fashion (Markowitz & Linehan, 2001).

CHARACTERISTICS OF TBI

Children with TBI and their families face great emotional turmoil during the time shortly after the injury. They must adjust to changes in ability, performance, and behavior (Hux & Hacksley, 1996). Even those with mild cases of TBI must cope with sudden changes in performance and many of the symptoms shown in Table 13.2 on page 463. What came easily one day is filled with frustration and confusion the next. Tasks that were previously easy to perform now present repeated failure. Many youngsters with TBI tend to have uneven abilities, a fact that is confusing to the individuals and to their teachers. These students also often experience reduced stamina, seizures, headaches, hearing losses, and vision problems (Van Kuren, 2001). They get tired easily, so some receive home instruction, often for a year, before returning to school part-time. Many of these youngsters have difficulty adjusting to and accepting their newly acquired disability. Because of the frustrations of having difficulty doing tasks that used to be easy, many display behavior problems and reduced self-esteem.

With some simple adjustments to and accommodations in the classroom routine, though, students with brain injuries can be reintegrated into school settings with relative ease. If students spend only half a day at school, the teacher can schedule instruction on important academic tasks during the morning, when they are alert. Homework assignments can be abbreviated to accommodate their reduced stamina. If some students find that their balance, coordination, and ability to carry materials are more limited than before the accident, the teacher can provide another set of textbooks for home use to make life easier for them and their families. Because many of these students get confused easily, teachers should clearly specify and consistently apply classroom rules and expectations. It is also helpful to use instructional tactics that incorporate a considerable amount of drill and practice to help students remember what is being taught.

MAKING CONNECTIONS

Compare accommodations for students with TBI with those needed by many students with physical impairments.

VERY LOW INCIDENCE DISABILITIES

In the first part of this chapter, specific information—definitions, prevalence, causes and preventive techniques, and characteristic—about three **very low incidence disabilities** was presented. For the rest of this chapter, let's turn our attention to more general information about three issues: educational interventions (early childhood through high school, collaboration, transition through adulthood), families, and technology. Recognize that the following information will not apply to every individual, but it is applicable to many children who require sustained and intensive supports.

An individualized education program for children with severe disabilities must begin early, and be delivered by highly trained professionals who together form a multidisciplinary team.

EARLY CHILDHOOD THROUGH HIGH SCHOOL

The benefits of high quality education for all of us cannot be overestimated. For students with low incidence disabilities, education can determine individuals' outcomes: the number and intensity of supports they will need as adults, their attainment of independence, their level of community presence, and their quality of life.

Table 13.2 Characteristics of TBI

Medical/Neurological	Physical	Cognitive	Behavioral/Emotional
Blurred vision	Decreased motor coordination	Decreased attention	Denial of deficits
Concussion		Decreased organizational skills	Depression
Dizziness	Sensory deficits affecting vision, hearing, taste, or smell	Decreased problem solving	Disinhibition
Headache			Distractibility
Seizure activity		Slowed information processing	Flat affect
Skull fracture		Difficulty with abstract reasoning	Impulsivity
Sleep disorder			Inappropriate laughing or crying
		Memory deficits	Irritability
		Perceptual deficits	Limited initiation
		Poor judgment	Social isolation
		Rigidity of thought	
		Word-finding difficulty	

Source: From "Mild Traumatic Brain Injury: Facilitating School Success" by K. Hux and C. Hacksley, 1996, *Intervention in School and Clinic, 31*, p. 161. Reprinted by permission.

What is unique about these children's early intervention programs?

The first real difference is that more children with low incidence disabilities receive federally funded services for early intervention than any other students with special needs (U.S. Department of Education, 2000a). Unlike the vast majority of students with special needs, such as those with learning disabilities, children with low incidence disabilities are identified during their first years of life. Some 20 percent of all children who receive early childhood special education programs began their school careers by the age of 6 months.

Because of infant screening measures, such as universal hearing screening, and because of better understanding by the medical profession about issues like the long-term impact of low birth weight, babies with severe disabilities are identified earlier than ever before. The number of children and families receiving special services increased from 128,000 in 1988 to almost 200,000 in 1997 (U.S. Department of Education, 2000b). The reason for these early and increased participation rates is the quick response of the medical and social services communities and the widespread awareness of well-documented signals for long-term serious developmental disabilities.

More of these children than ever are now identified early, and more families are receiving services to assist them as they learn how to interact in special ways with their baby with severe disabilities. It is these families that benefit from individualized family service plans (IFSPs) and from the services of many different professionals so that secondary disabilities and problems can be prevented or reduced in severity (McDonnell, Hardman, & McDonnell, 2003). This situation presents many opportunities for early and intensive intervention with the child and with the child's family. Unfortunately, however, the lack of highly trained personnel to work with the challenges presented by babies with multiple-severe disabilities and deafblindness is a barrier to systematic intervention efforts (Chen, Alsop & Minor, 2000).

In what ways do these families need special help? The challenges of raising a child with significant disabilities begin almost immediately. Many of these babies are different from typical infants (McDonnell, Hardman, & McDonnell, 2003).

MAKING CONNECTIONS

For a review of IFSPs, see Chapter 2.

Students with low incidence disabilities often require the expertise of professionals from many disciplines for the development of the IEPs.

Here are a few examples:

- They cry more; their cries sound different from typical infants' cries; and they are harder to sooth.
- They often stiffen and pull away from their caregivers.
- They avoid eye contact.
- They smile later and less often.

Many families need help learning how to cope with such differences. Some families also need help learning how to include their young children with severe disabilities in family outings, which should become opportunities for community participation, friendships, and play (Turnbull & Turnbull, 2000). Some also need help learning how to advocate for accommodations to their children's unique needs so the children can participate in a wide variety of events and activities.

Also, more than ever before, young children with severe disabilities participate in preschool programs. Many of these classes are fully inclusive programs where preschoolers with and without disabilities learn and grown together (McWilliams, Wolery, & Odom, 2001). The benefits of such early intervention programs to individuals with severe disabilities are great in terms of motor development, language skills, social interaction abilities, and academics. The long-term benefits in the lives of these children and their families are inestimable.

Do students with low incidence disabilities share some common goals?

Students with very low incidence disabilities present unique sets of complex profiles to their families and to their teachers. Despite being assigned to a category or group, each student should be considered a unique member of a diverse group of learners, all of whom exhibit different learning styles and characteristics. Accordingly, instructional programs must be designed on an individual basis to meet each student's needs. However, despite their diversity, these children often share many common goals and desired outcomes.

One common goal among children with severe disabilities is the development of communication skills. Some children with low incidence disabilities are able to communicate using oral speech well enough to participate in social interactions and express their needs. Others require intensive therapy and instruction; and some need to use assistive technology and augmentative communication devices. Regardless, a few common themes about instruction to enhance communication skills warrant consideration (Downing, 2001):

- Exploit the environment and capitalize on teachable moments.
- Use as many means for communication as possible (oral speech, gestures, signs).
- Encourage social interactions.
- Provide opportunities for students to share information (not just to receive it).

Another common goal is participation in the community. This goal brings instruction for students with low incidence disabilities to a set of objectives not typical for students without disabilities. Most typical children do not need to learn how to play or take part in recreational activities. However, for many students with com-

Making Connections

See Chapter 2 for more about assistive technology as a related service, and see the "Technology" sections throughout this text for examples.

plex disabilities, direct instruction in leisure time skills is necessary so that they will be able to join in community activities while students and later as adults (Westling & Fox, 2000). Teachers cannot assume that all of these students will enjoy the same activities, and in many cases their students will have had no opportunity to learn what activities they prefer. Thus the first step is often determining preferences. Here parents, family members, and neighbors can be helpful by reporting what activities the child seeks out or participates in with others. Developing skills for those activities at school and then arranging for extracurricular opportunities all lead toward the development of important **life skills** through an alternative curriculum. Skills, such as basketball, tennis, swimming, and bowling often need to be taught in small increments through consistent, systematic, and direct instructional techniques. The end result can be a high quality of life and improved physical fitness.

What tools are available to help teachers design appropriate programs?

One tool available was developed by Rob Horner and George Sugai and is called **functional behavioral assessment** (Sugai & Horner, 1999). Functional behavioral assessments are part of a larger system referred to as **positive behavioral supports,** defined as an "application of a behaviorally-based systems approach to enhancing the capacity of schools, families, and communities to design effective environments that improve the fit or link between research-validated practices and the environments in which teaching and learning occur" (Office of Special Educational Programs, 2000, p. III-8). According to Rob Horner and George Sugai (Smith, 2001), functional behavioral assessment is a process and set of procedures for identifying events that trigger and maintain problem behaviors. Functional behavioral assessment is based on an extensive body of research that has demonstrated that behavior support is more likely to be effective when it is based on information derived from a functional assessment.

This method helps parents and educators better understand the relationship between what happens in the student's environment and how the student behaves (Sugai et al., 1999). One result is a list of target behaviors that require intervention (Condon & Tobin, 2001). Another result is a better idea about interventions that might be successful in improving the behavior of concern (Harris et al., 1994; Kennedy & Meyer, 1998; Mullen & Frea, 1995). Functional behavioral assessments also reveal what causes inappropriate or undesirable behavior to occur and why such behaviors continue. Educators often find that some unproductive behaviors occur for purposes of escape, attention, or communication. For example, a tantrum—for children who do not know how to ask for help—may be a means of escaping schoolwork that is too difficult or frustrating. When such is the case, educators have found that teaching a student to engage in **functionally equivalent behaviors** (e.g., "Is this right?" "I need help") often replaces the disruptive behavior (Koegel et al., 1995). These behaviors serve to teach the student very useful skills.

How does functional behavioral assessment work? Functional behavioral assessments should be conducted anytime a student with a disability presents significant problem behavior that might affect eligibility, placement, or disciplinary actions and/or represent a significant barrier to the student's education. General educators, special education teachers, and all people concerned about the student's performance should participate in the assessment (Kennedy et al., 2001). (See the "Achieving Discipline" box for an example.) The process can involve many different ways to gather information:

- Formal interviews with the student and the people who know the student best
- Direct observations of the student's behavior under different circumstances

MAKING CONNECTIONS

See the "What IDEA Says" box in Chapter 8 for a quick review.

ACHIEVING DISCIPLINE

Planning with the Functional Behavioral Assessment Technique

Kailyn, a 7-year-old girl with multiple-severe disabilities, is included in a second-grade general education class. Although sometimes she focused well and worked hard, she was beginning to exhibit high rates of being off-task, wandering around the classroom, and bothering her peers. She was also becoming distressed five or six times per day, losing control, and displaying anger. Because Kailyn's behavior was so disturbing to her classmates, Ms. Tyler, her general education teacher, was beginning to become concerned about this general education placement. Ms. Tyler felt that if Kailyn could not soon control her behavior and follow classroom rules about disturbing classmates while they were working, another placement option would have to be arranged.

Kailyn's special education teacher, her IEP team, the vice-principal, and Ms. Tyler met to discuss the situation. Kailyn's family joined the school's team for the meeting. Everyone decided to observe Kailyn and take observational notes about her behavior difficulties. Her parents also agreed to document her behavior at home and during after-school play groups. In particular, they all agreed to note carefully when, and under what circumstances, the disruptive

behavior occurred. They also would include descriptions of times when Kailyn behaved appropriately. After a week of careful study, they came back together.

The results of this initial documentation revealed that Kailyn was having particular trouble changing from one activity to another. It also appeared from these notes that she performed better when a peer was working with her on academic tasks. The group decided to have the special education teacher, Mr. Saunders, take direct classroom data to verify these observations. For three days, Mr. Saunders used an observational data collection system. His results clearly verified the observations taken the previous week. Kailyn was having difficulties transitioning from one activity to another, often becoming angry when she had to stop one assignment and move on to the next. He also found that when Kailyn was seated next to a peer who prompted her to finish working and put her things away, Kailyn was less agitated. On the fourth day of data collection, Mr. Saunders also told Kailyn that she could be the first in line for lunch if she followed the classroom rules that morning. She behaved appropriately and earned this privilege.

The IEP team, parents, and teachers all met again and decided that they had learned enough about the problem behaviors and possible interventions to remediate the situation. They then developed an intervention program that included assistance from classmates, a 5-minute warning that an activity was soon to end, a reward system, and a simple way for Kailyn and a peer to collect data. For now, at least, Kailyn remains a member of the general education class; her intervention program and her behavior are being monitored closely.

Outcomes of a Functional Behavioral Assessment

- Operational definition of the problem behavior(s)

- Clear statement of the conditions (routines/events) that set the occasion for the problem behavior(s)

- The consequences that maintain the problem behavior (e.g., attention, escape from aversive events, access to food or desired objects, social status)

- Direct observational data supporting these ideas

- A functional analysis that includes systematic manipulations of conditions in the environment while collecting direct observation data

The next steps are to develop hypotheses about the events that trigger and maintain the problem behavior and then test those hypotheses to determine whether they are correct. The testing always involves either observing the student under typical conditions or setting up conditions and observing the student under those "special" conditions. Functional assessments are meant to improve the efficiency and effectiveness of behavior support. The resulting information should help teachers, special educators, and families modify curricula, social contexts, communication training, social skills instruction, and consequences to improve the behavior of the student. A central focus of functional behavioral assessment is on the features of the environment that affect problem behavior. Functional assessment information is designed to help educators discover how to modify environments so that students are successful and then build on that success to produce durable reduction of problem behavior. Functional behavioral assessment was developed with students who have more severe disabilities, yet during the past 5 years it has proved useful in the design of **behavioral support** for students with a full range of disabilities and types of problem behaviors. In 1997, functional behavioral assessment became a requirement of IDEA for students exhibiting behavior problems at school.

Are students with low incidence disabilities included in high stakes testing?

As you have learned this academic term, IDEA and the No Child Left Behind Act require that students with disabilities be a part of the national accountability system of statewide and district testing. These measures are to ensure that *all* students receive high quality instruction and profit from their education (Ziegler, 2002). Most students with disabilities require some accommodations or other testing options in order to participate in these assessments (Thurlow et al., 2000). And most students with disabilities receive some sort of modification to the standard test given to general education students (Ysseldyke et al., 2001). Such modifications include adjustments to the testing schedule (e.g., breaks, test scheduled at a different time, extended time allowed), the setting, the materials (e.g., large print, braille versions), the presentation (e.g., oral vs. printed questions), and the format in which responses are accepted (e.g., not using the machine-score answer sheet). Although great inconsistencies exist across states, three different testing options are also typically available:

High stakes (district- and statewide) testing is first presented in Chapter 2.

- Partial participation in testing: student takes parts of the test but does not have to take the entire test
- Out-of-level testing: student may take a test from a lower grade-level
- Alternative assessment: student takes a different assessment designed for a unique group of learners or an individually determined assessment

The student's IEP team usually is the group that determines the option used. Let's look at the alternative assessment option, because it most broadly applies to students with severe disabilities.

States and districts are still working out what alternative assessment means and how such results are included in a school's overall performance report (Turner et al., 2000). In Kentucky, students with severe disabilities (some 0.6 percent of all students) are assessed through **alternative portfolios.** Many general education students experience portfolio assessments, wherein their schoolwork becomes part of the documentation about their progress at school. Alternative portfolios are much like traditional ones, except their contents are somewhat different. Instead of including a term paper or summary of a science project, an alternative portfolio might include information about the student's performance in these six areas:

Portfolio assessment is also addressed in Chapter 2 in the discussion about appropriate evaluations.

1. Performance on IEP goals and objectives and student participation in developing the portfolio
2. Use of natural supports
3. Where the student performs the target behavior(s) or skill(s)
4. Number of settings in which the skill is used
5. Social interaction
6. Generalization of skills and knowledge

How well a student performs in these six areas can then be judged and this evaluation included in the school's overall assessment data. Such systems of accountability ensure that all students, even those with the most severe disabilities, are included in discussions about school improvement and accountability (Frase-Blunt, 2000).

COLLABORATION FOR INCLUSION

A wide range of professionals make up the multidisciplinary teams that serve students with low incidence disabilities. Expertise is needed in so many areas that it is impossible for one teacher alone to provide an appropriate education for these students. Clearly, collaboration among many different teachers (general educators, special education teachers, paraprofessionals, teachers of the visually impaired, teachers of the deaf), as well as multidisciplinary team members representing many different related services (assistive technology specialists, SLPs, OTs, PTs), is necessary.

Here are a few more examples. Deafblind students often need sign language interpreters to ensure that they have meaningful linkages to the environment and equal access to information (Morgan, 2001). Today, however, whereas deaf students receive assistance from sign language interpreters, deafblind students are now getting somewhat different services. A new professional role is developing, particularly for deafblind students (Alsop, Blaha, & Kloos, 2000). The **intervener** helps students with this disability gain access to visual and auditory information, develops the use of receptive and expressive communication, and promotes social and emotional well-being. Interveners intercede and work between a child and the environment, helping the child gain access to information that others gain with vision and hearing. Interveners do more than just translating; they typically work on an individual basis with a deafblind student. Part of this new professional's role is to facilitate inclusive efforts, so here is one more member of the collaborative team working with general educators to provide FAPE in the LRE. The "Accommodating for Inclusive Environments" box lists some of the major activities conducted by interveners to make participation in the general education classroom and access to the general education curriculum possible for deafblind students.

When so many professionals need to work together, some special communication problems can occur. Coordination of services and careful instructional planning are sometimes hard to accomplish. Effective teams of professionals seem to follow these six steps when addressing their concerns about target children (Snell & Janney, 2000, p. 480):

1. Identify the problem: "Identify your concern."

2. Gather information: "Watch, think, and talk."

3. Generate potential solutions: "Think and throw out ideas."

4. Evaluate potential solutions: "That sounds good" or "That won't work."

5. Implementation: "Give it a shot."

6. Evaluation: "More watch, think, and talk."

Although integration is clearly important and is necessary to achieve adult independence, concerns about fully inclusive programs across all of the school years are emerging (McDonnell, Hardman, & McDonnell, 2003; Peeters, 1997). Some experts maintain that effective education often requires specially trained teachers who implement carefully designed instruc-

For part of his school day, this student attends a special center for students with brain injury. Here he is learning how to safely free dog cookies from a cutting machine; skills he will be able to generalize to work settings after graduation.

CHAPTER 13 *Very Low Incidence Disabilities*

ACCOMMODATING FOR INCLUSIVE ENVIRONMENTS
The Role of the Intervener

Interveners facilitate deafblind students' participation in the general education classroom by

- Presenting information so that the child can detect and profit from it
- Providing opportunities for tactile exploration and direct learning
- Using assistive listening devices and optical aids to augment the child's vision and hearing abilities
- Providing hands-on activities to develop concepts that others understand through incidental learning

- Directing the student's attention
- Presenting information in ways that match the child's strengths
- Adjusting the pace of instruction

Source: Adapted from "The intervener in early intervention and educational settings for children and youth with deafblindness." By L. Alsop, R. Blaha, and E. Kloos, 2000, *NTAC Briefing Paper*, p. 4. The national Technical Assistance Consortium for Children and Young Adults who are Deaf-Blind, DB-Link, Monmouth, OR. Adapted with permission.

tional programs. Many techniques that have proved effective through research are not compatible with the instruction provided to typical learners. For example, structured class schedules, use of concrete examples, controlled teacher language, reduction or elimination of distractions, instruction in different natural settings, and rigorously applied behavioral tactics often prove effective and necessary. General education placements might not be appropriate at this point in these learners' educational careers. Multidisciplinary teams must evaluate student progress continually to balance the drawbacks and benefits of every educational option available. They must also work together to be sure that the necessary accommodations are in place to ensure successful outcomes in general education settings.

TRANSITION THROUGH ADULTHOOD

Unlike their peers without disabilities and their peers with mild disabilities, most students with very low incidence disabilities do not leave school at high school graduation. In fact, IDEA provides them with educational services until age 21, when these individuals are assisted by their state's vocational rehabilitation services departments. After school, many receive services that include supported living arrangements and supported employment.

One important goal of transition programs is for individuals with severe disabilities to achieve social integration in workplace, residential, and recreational settings (Hughes, 2001; Stuart & Smith, 2002). This, along with two other goals—holding a job and living independently—is the core of many education programs during the transition years. Clearly, being employed, possessing functional life skills, and meeting the requirements of daily life (managing a budget, maintaining a household, cooking, shopping) are important to what is considered successful adulthood. Knowing how to make choices and advocate for preferences is also important.

Many students with low incidence disabilities receive a unique education. As they get older, many participate less in the general education curriculum and more in **community based instruction.** One characteristic shared by many individuals who have severe disabilities is their inability to generalize skills taught in one setting to

MAKING CONNECTIONS

Community based instruction and functional curricula are discussed in Chapter 6.

Most students with severe disabilities require direct instruction to master life skills such as shopping for groceries, maintaining a household, and holding a job. The instruction of students in these important adaptive skills should occur in natural settings.

another setting. Therefore, the benefits of being able to learn and practice important skills used in adult life in real-life settings is critical to later success in living and working in the community. Some experts believe that many students with multiple-severe disabilities spend as much as 90 percent of their school day learning in community settings (NICHCY, 2001). These students then transition to supported employment with the goals of attaining job placements in competitive work rather than in sheltered employment or day activity centers, where the pay is low and the work often artificial and menial.

Transition issues for students with severe disabilities begin at age 14, with the addition of a transition plan to the student's IEP. Consideration of some important transition components should always be part of this process. For work-related goals and objectives, the following topics are part of the conversation (Stuart & Smith, 2002):

- Coordinating sets of activities (e.g., real work experience)
- Moving from school to postschool environments (e.g., school to work)
- Assessing the individual's specific needs
- Determining the individual's preferences and interests
- Developing employment objectives

Making Connections

Transition Plans are also discussed in Chapter 2.

Making Connections

Discussions of self-determination are also found in Chapters 6 and 8.

Everyone performs better in situations where they have the skills necessary to succeed—but also when the tasks are of interest. For these reasons, educators are realizing the importance of the individual's preferences and interests as they relate to living and employment opportunities (Lohrmann-O'Rourke & Gomez, 2001; Stuart & Smith, 2002). The importance of promoting individual choice and self-determination as a precursor to community based instruction is widely acknowledged among experts in this field. For example, careers can be developed in many different areas (e.g., landscaping, food services, office or clerical work). Not everyone enjoys each type of opportunity equally. Some of us prefer being indoors; others enjoy quiet settings; some prefer to sit rather than standing for long periods of time. Some of us prefer to live in urban areas; some want a roommate; others prefer a house to an apartment; and some of us desire proximity to churches, convenience stores, bus routes, doctors, and other resources. Decisions about these and many other factors related to success and happiness should be made with full participation of the individual involved. Community based instruction can then reflect the preferences and choices of the individual, which is likely, to lead to better results when instruction is complete.

FAMILIES

Making Connections

For a review of the AAMR definitions of mental retardation, see the "Defined" section of Chapter 6.

Particularly since the 1992 AAMR definition of mental retardation was formulated, professionals in the field of special education have been reconceptualizing programs and services for people with disabilities (Luckasson et al., 1992). Expanded in the 2002 AAMR definition, concepts about supports emphasize the importance of helping individuals with mental retardation and their families become independent and function in the community (Luckasson et al., 2002). The focus is on the type and amount of supports that individuals need to remain in the community, living,

CHAPTER 13 *Very Low Incidence Disabilities*

working, and playing alongside people without disabilities. The family is one obvious source of natural support for all individuals with disabilities, particularly those with low incidence disabilities. In some cases, support requires more than commitment; it requires a wealth of personal resources and an effective system of supports that assist and sustain families.

Services and programs for individuals with low incidence disabilities must be an integral part of the community (ERIC/Clearinghouse on Disabilities and Gifted Education, 2001). The premise is that sustained family involvement in the lives of those with disabilities increases the probability of their achieving success and independence as adults in the community. For example, instead of living in an institution miles from their home communities, these individuals live in homes, apartments, and neighborhoods like everyone else. In many cases, this cannot occur without considerable support from a variety of sources. To prevent the terrible treatment that has been inflicted on many individuals with disabilities living in institutions far removed from public scrutiny, those who give family support and community support need to be aware of the signs of abuse. To some, not only is the **family system** the best source of support, but family members have some clear roles to fill (Dell-Orto & Power, 1997). If they choose to accept these roles, they should be considered full members of the child's multidisciplinary team. They also can be information providers, active participants in assessment and treatment, and advocates. Individuals from the family system can extend treatment programs to all aspects of the individual's life and assist with generalization. This network of people expresses the hopes and dreams for the achievement of goals for the family member with disabilities.

Despite the normalization movement and the growing systems of family and natural supports, professionals must realize that meeting all the needs of a child with severe disabilities is beyond the resources and capabilities of many families (Bruns, 2000). The daily physical care, medication and pain management, and round-the-clock assistance that some children require, along with financial and logistic difficulties force some families to seek out-of-home placements for their child, particularly when fragile health compounds the child's multiple disabilities. Professionals must assist families and help to create solid systems of supports, but they must not make value judgments about the difficult decisions families end up making about the care of their children. Professionals need to understand that such decisions usually are made because of a "triggering event," such as illness of the primary caregiver, the demands of other children in the family, and the overwhelming nature of the disability.

TECHNOLOGY

The increased availability of technology in school settings and the greater understanding of how technology can support standard instruction is a benefit to children with disabilities, particularly those with multiple-severe problems and those with deafblindness (Buckley, 1999–2000). The federal government has made a considerable investment in technology for students with disabilities. The government continues with this commitment because it is confident that technology has improved outcomes for students with disabilities (Office of Special Education [OSEP], 2000). The data on which the federal government bases these conclusions indicate that technology helps these individuals

- Communicate more effectively
- Increase their levels of independence
- Control their environments
- Have greater mobility
- Gain access to information

MAKING CONNECTIONS

Sections about systems of supports are found throughout Chapter 6.

MAKING CONNECTIONS

To see the strength of families and the impact a child with a disability has on families, read again the "Personal Perspectives" sections of Chapters 3, 4, 5, and 12.

MAKING CONNECTIONS

For a comprehensive understanding of the impact of technology on the lives of people with disabilities, reread all the "Technology" sections Chapters 3–12.

Sound output, screen enlargements, and such assistive devices as switches, sticks, and mouse adaptions all make it easier for students with disabilities to participate in standard instruction found in general education classes. Of course, one ultimate goal for technology is for it to address and compensate for disabilities, and that hope is becoming a reality.

How might technology help students with low incidence disabilities?

To review assistive listening devices and optical aids, see the "Technology" sections of Chapters 10 and 11

A major positive change in the lives of people with disabilities and their families has been the development of technology that can address and compensate for their disabilities (Reichle, Beukelman, & Light, 2002). Computer technology has opened up avenues of communication for many students who are unable to communicate with others through oral speech (Byrant & Bryant, 2003). Many of these technological advances—**augmentative and alternative communication devices (AAC)**, assistive technology, computer-assisted and computer-enhanced instruction—are very beneficial to individuals with low incidence disabilities (Noonan & Siegel, 2003). Whether in the form of simple devices, like **communication boards,** or complicated **speech synthesizers** that actually speak for the individual, technology now allows individuals to make their needs known, express their feelings, and interact with others (McCormick & Wegner, 2003). In the most straightforward systems, words and/or pictures are placed on a flat surface or in books. The student communicates by pointing to the appropriate symbols. Symbols are customized to the individual; the words or symbols on the board reflect the individual and salient features of the environments in which he or she operates. Some boards are simple homemade projects; others use quite sophisticated technology.

The advent of these devices has allowed students with multiple-severe disabilities to participate in classroom activities in new and important ways. Most students raise their hands to get their teachers' attention, to take their turn to participate, or to ask for help. Joey cannot raise his hand, but he has learned to operate a switch that turns on a light instead. He uses another switch to hear a tape-recorded story when classmates are reading silently, and other switches enable him to use a communication device (Sax, Pumpian, & Fisher, 1997). The teacher's job is to encourage and shape these techniques into a reliable system of communication for the student. With reliable communication, learning and social interaction can take place.

How might technology help teachers who work with students with low incidence disabilities?

A major challenge faced by school administrators who work in rural and remote areas is that there are not enough children with low incidence disabilities to support the cost of assembling experts from a variety of disciplines to work with these children and their families. For example, there may be only one deafblind child and one child with TBI in an entire school district that is hundreds of miles from a large metropolitan area and comprehensive medical services. There may be only three or four children with multiple-severe disabilities in adjacent school districts that together cover a thousand square miles. Simply put, it is quite likely that there is insufficient expertise at these school sites to provide an appropriate education for these children, regardless of their age and unique learning needs. Compounding the problem are the difficulties of communicating with many people: parents who live many miles from school, members of the multidisciplinary team who come from different parts of the state, itinerant teachers and related service providers, and the student's school based

CHAPTER 13 *Very Low Incidence Disabilities*

teachers. Table 13.3 lists some ideas about how distance technology can be used to increase communication opportunities with families of students with disabilities.

Today, some of these problems can be solved through technology by using the practices, hardware, and software developed for another purpose: **distance education.** This technology was created to deliver instruction to remote areas, typically a substantial distance from a university campus. Although this technology is a great benefit to students with disabilities and their families, its applications extend far beyond the enhancement of teachers' skills and knowledge. For example, distance education could create "statewide classrooms" where special educators who live even hundreds of miles away can collaborate, team teach, and work together to meet the needs of students with very special learning needs. Consulting teachers and related service providers can work with classroom teachers hundreds of miles away. Through live and interactive television, multidisciplinary teams can evaluate behavior and performance as it is occurring in the classroom. Team members can also help the teacher develop and implement an educational program as it is being tested with the child.

Distance education technology can be applied to work with families. Many families have computers, televisions, and videotape players in their homes or can arrange to borrow the equipment from the school or a neighbor. By using a camcorder, the family can also record behaviors they find problematic at home and seek help from the professionals at school. Many have digital cameras and know how to place clips on a Web site or send them via e-mail. This "digital connection" can enhance the interaction between the family and the school, even when work schedules and distance make it difficult for family members to make frequent school visits. Teachers can use videotapes to introduce members of the multidisciplinary team to the family, even though their visits to school could not be coordinated to occur on the same day when the parents could be present.

Distance education technology can help bridge the gap with families who do not speak sufficient English to understand technical terms and descriptions of how best to work with their child with limited vision and hearing. Lessons might be taped in the family's primary language and sent home with the child. Using this strategy, parents can help with generalization by implementing, at home, school programs that they now understand because they were explained in their primary language (even when none of the teachers at their child's school is proficient in that language).

Table 13.3 Using Distance Technology to Communicate with Families

Exchange Videotapes Between School and Home

The teacher or itinerant specialist might videotape:

- A tour of the school and classrooms the child uses
- An introduction of all of the teachers and related service providers to the family
- Examples of the child's educational programs at school
- Demonstrations of activities for follow-up at home
- Initial performance and "progress" performances
- Activities as a video "report card"
- The child engaged in "excellent levels" of performance as examples or models of results that can be achieved
- Home language and English comparisons for families who might not be proficient in English

The parents or family might videotape:

- Introductions of family members, including the extended family and other caregivers (important neighbors, babysitters, close friends)
- Introductions of important members of the child's community
- The child performing chores and family functions
- Behaviors the family would like help in improving
- The child participating in significant community events
- Messages to the teachers

Use the Internet for More Frequent Communication

Have students create Web sites:

- Include descriptions of the classroom, classmates, and teacher(s)
- Have students talk about themselves (interests, hobbies, favorite subjects)
- Scan photos and pictures into the site
- Add in video clips

Use e-mail frequently to:

- Share daily progress
- Talk about concerns
- Create a distribution list to include all multidisciplinary team members

GLOSSARY

ABC model. A behavioral way to select interventions by analyzing events that occur antecedent to (A) the target behavior, the target behavior (B) itself, and events that occur consequent to (C) the target behavior.

ability grouping. Placing students with comparable achievement and skill levels in the same classes or courses; an approach used in education of the gifted.

absence seizures. Seizures with a short lapse in consciousness (also called petit mal seizures).

acceleration. Moving students through a curriculum or through particular years of schooling in a shorter period of time than usual; an approach used in education of the gifted.

accessibility. Offered by barrier free environments that allow maximal participation by individuals with disabilities.

accommodation. The focusing process of the lens of the eye.

accommodations. Modifications or supports to the instructional or the assessment situation to help compensate for disabilities.

acquired immunodeficiency syndrome. See AIDS.

acuity. Sharpness of response to visual, auditory, or tactile stimuli.

adaptive behavior. Performance of everyday life skills expected of adults.

adaptive skill areas. Targets of instruction that focus on the ability of an individual to function in a typical environment and on successful adult outcomes (independent living, employment, and community participation).

advance organizers. Previews to lectures and organizing structures that acquaint students with the content of a unit of study, its organization, and its importance.

advanced placement courses. High school courses that carry college credit.

adventitiously blind. Having acquired severe visual disabilities after the age of 2.

aggression. Hostile and attacking behavior (which can include verbal communication) directed toward oneself, others, or the physical environment.

AIDS (acquired immunodeficiency syndrome). A usually fatal medical syndrome caused by infection from the human immunodeficiency virus (HIV).

air conduction audiometry method. A method to test hearing that uses pure-tone sounds generated by an audiometer.

alerting devices. Devices that use sight, sound, or vibration to make individuals aware of an occurrence or an important sound.

alternative and augmentative communication (AAC). Assistive technology devices that specifically help individuals communicate, including devices that actually produce speech.

alternative portfolio. A collection of a student's work that presents an overall picture of the student's accomplishments, academic progress, and achievement; used for students with severe disabilities who are not participating in state and district high stakes testing but rather are being evaluated via alternative assessment systems.

American Sign Language (ASL). The sign language or manual communication system preferred by many adults in this country who are Deaf; a signal of Deaf culture.

Americans with Disabilities Act (ADA). Federal disability antidiscrimination legislation passed in 1990 to guarantee basic civil rights to people with disabilities; Public Law (PL) 101-336.

anchored instruction. Using examples through video, lectures, and class assignments to support instruction from students' culture and/or real-life situations so that learning is relevant and meaningful.

anorexia. Intense fear of gaining weight, disturbed body image, chronic absence or refusal of appetite for food, causing severe weight loss (25% of body weight).

anoxia. Inadequate supply of oxygen to the brain, usually at birth, which generally leads to disabilities.

anvil (incus). One of the three tiny bones (ossicles) in the middle ear.

anxiety disorders. Conditions causing painful uneasiness, emotional tension, or emotional confusion.

aphasia. Loss or impairment of language ability as a consequence of brain injury.

applied behavior analysis. Research methodology using single subject designs (e.g., reversal, multiple baseline); paradigms describing human behavior in terms of events (such as positive reinforcement) that stimulate behavior, maintain behavior, and increase its likelihood.

array of services. A constellation of special education services, personnel, and educational placements.

articulation problems. Abnormal production of speech sounds.

Asperger's syndrome. A disorder that is part of the autistic spectrum disorders (ASD) and where cognition is usually in the average or above average range.

asphyxia. Deprivation of oxygen, often through near drowning or smoke inhalation, causing brain damage or neurological problems.

assistive devices. Any equipment or technology that facilitates people's work, communication, mobility, or any aspect of daily life.

assistive listening devices (ALDs). Equipment (e.g., hearing aids, audio loops, and FM transmission devices) that helps deaf and hard of hearing individuals use their residual hearing.

assistive technology. Devices that help individuals with disabilities in their daily lives; such devices include hearing aids, speech-to-text translators, wheelchairs, computers that offer augmentative communication, and a wide array of other high tech equipment and low-tech aids that help compensate for an individual's disabilities.

assistive technology specialists. Related service providers who determine, and sometimes create, assistive devices that reduce barriers to the physical and learning environments for students with disabilities, with the goal of increasing each student's access to the general education curriculum and the typical school environment.

association. In thinking, the ability to see relationships among different concepts or knowledge bases.

asthma. A common, chronic condition resulting in difficulty breathing.

at risk. Children whose condition or situation makes it probable that they will develop disabilities.

ataxia. A type of cerebral palsy in which movement is disrupted by impaired balance and depth perception.

athetoid. A type of cerebral palsy characterized by purposeless and uncontrolled involuntary movements.

attention deficit/hyperactivity disorder (ADHD). A condition now included in the special education category "other health impairments;" students display hyperactive behaviors, have difficulty attending to the task at hand or focusing on relevant features of tasks, and tend to be impulsive; not all students with ADHD qualify for special education services.

attention deficits. A characteristic often associated with learning disabilities in which students either do not pay attention to the task or do not focus on the features of a task that are relevant to learning how to perform the skill well.

attributions. The explanations individuals give themselves for their successes or failures.

audio loop. A device that routes sound from the source directly to the listener's ear through a specially designed hearing aid.

audiodescription. An approach to helping people with visual disabilities access visual and nonverbal information. Trained narrators supply this information orally during pauses in the audio or scripted dialogue of plays, films, and television shows; uses FM transmissions or the extra sound track available on stereo televisions.

audiogram. The grid or graph used to display a person's hearing abilities.

audiologist. A professional trained to diagnose hearing losses and auditory problems.

audiometer. An electrical instrument for measuring the threshold of hearing tests; charts individuals' thresholds of hearing at various frequencies against sound intensities in decibels.

auditory nerve. Nerve that carries messages received through the ear to the brain; known in neurology as the eighth cranial nerve.

augumentative and alternative communication devices (AAC). Alternative methods of communicating, such as communication boards, communication books, sign language, and computerized voices.

aura. A signal of an impending seizure, sometimes called the preictal stage.

authentic assessments. Performance measures that use work generated by the student or observational data on social behaviors for assessment and evaluation purposes.

autism. One of the disorders included in the autistic spectrum disorders (ASD); a disability that manifests itself in problems with communication and social interaction and in repetitive or manneristic behaviors; also known as autistic disorder.

autistic disorder. One of the disorders included in the autistic spectrum

disorders (ASD); a disability that manifests itself in problems with communication and social interaction and repetitive or manneristic behaviors, also known as autism.

autistic spectrum disorders (ASD). A group of disorders with similar characteristics that include difficulties with communication and social interaction, and manneristic behaviors.

autistic savant. An individual who displays many behaviors associated with autism yet also possesses discrete abilities and unusual talents.

automatic speech recognition (ASR). Technology that allows the computer to convert speech (at rates below 160 words per minute) to text.

barrier games. Drill and practice activities, in a game format that require the application of verbal skills to solve problems.

basic interpersonal communicative skills (BICS). Face-to-face conversational language.

behavioral intervention plan (BIP). The plan developed for any student with disabilities who engages in violent or dangerous behavior; includes a functional behavioral assessment and describes individually determined procedures for both prevention and intervention; developed as a result of disciplinary action.

behavioral support. Organizing and arranging environments (schools, homes, workplaces) so that problem behaviors are less likely to occur.

behavior–specific praise. Verbal reward and feedback for correct academic or behavioral performance.

behind the ear (BTE). A hearing aid that cups behind the ear with a cord that runs into the person's ear canal.

benchmarks. Indicators of the accomplishment of IEP goals and objectives.

Best Buddies. A program that pairs college students with people with mental retardation to build relationships, friendships, and opportunities for support.

best practices. Instructional techniques, scientifically based practices, or methods that have been proved through research to be effective.

bibliotherapy. Used in education of the gifted to advance students' awareness, persistence, and social relationships by reading books and articles that are of high interest to students and also are anchored in the students' culture.

bilingual-bicultural approach. The application of ESL and bilingual techniques to education of the deaf, where ASL is the native language and reading and writing in English are taught as a second language.

bilingual education. While affirming the importance of English, the child's native language is developed and used for primary instruction until sufficient command of English is attained.

bilingual special education. Uses home language and culture, along with English, as the foundation for and the means of delivering individualized instruction to English language learners with disabilities.

bilingual transitional approach. Teaching students primarily in English and partly in their home language until they know enough English to learn academic subjects.

bionic artificial limbs. Artificial arms and legs that replace full functioning of nonfunctional limbs.

blindness. Condition of not having functional use of sight.

bone conduction audiometry method. A test for conductive hearing loss in which a vibrator is placed on a person's forehead so that sound bypasses the outer and middle ear and goes directly to the inner ear; tests for conductive hearing losses.

braille. A system of reading and writing that uses dot codes embossed on paper; the concept of tactile reading was promoted in 1824 by Louis Braille, whose method is a precursor to the one used today.

bulimia. Chronically causing oneself to vomit, limiting weight gain.

C-Print™. A real-time, speech-to-text, computer aided service designed to help students understand lectures through the use of special word processing software, a trained typist, and a computer display.

captions. Subtitles that print the words spoken in film or video; can be either closed (so that only those who want to see them see the captions) or open (so that everyone always sees the captions).

cascade of services. A linear and sequential model used to describe educational environments and special education placements from the most to the least restrictive; considered by most special educators as an out-dated and rigid perspective.

categorical approach. A system of classifying disabilities (e.g., learning disabilities, mental retardation).

center schools. Separate schools (some residential), typically dedicated to serving students with a particular disability (e.g., schools for the deaf).

central nervous system dysfunction. Some brain or neurological damage that impedes an individual's motor and/or learning abilities.

central vision. The main field of vision in the eye, usually greater than 20 degrees.

cerebral palsy. A neuromotor impairment caused by insufficient oxygen getting to a child's brain before, during, or immediately after birth; results in motor impairments; often associated with multiple disabilities, communication problems, and mobility difficulties.

chaining. A strategy to teach the steps of skills that have been task analyzed, either first step first (forward chaining) or last step first (backward chaining).

child find. A function or office in each state's department of education that helps seek out and identify children with disabilities.

childhood disintegrative disorder (CDD). One of the disorders included in the autistic spectrum disorders (ASD); a disability that manifests itself in problems with communication, social interaction, and repetitive or manneristic behaviors.

chronic illness. Illness that last for a long period of time.

chunking. Clustering information into smaller pieces so that it can be more easily remembered; a thinking skill.

classifying. The ability to categorize items or concepts by their common characteristics; a thinking skill.

cleft palate. An opening in the roof of the mouth, causing too much air to pass through the nasal cavity when the individual is speaking; results in a speech impairment.

closed captions. Captions that can be seen on the television screen only with the use of a decoder; developed to provide access to auditory information for deaf and hard of hearing people.

closed-circuit television (CCTV). A television used for transmissions not accessible to the general public; sometimes, only one camera and television monitor is used.

cluster grouping. A plan whereby students spend a part of their day in the general education classroom on enriched or accelerated activities; an approach to education of the gifted.

cochlea. Part of the inner ear that contains fluid and hairlike nerve cells that transmit information to the brain.

cochlear implant. Electronic microprocessor, surgically placed in the hearing mechanism, that replaces the cochlea and allows some deaf people to perceive and understand sounds.

code switching. A bridge to mastery of two languages, and a signal of developing dual language proficiency; using vocabulary and phases of two languages in the same communication.

cognitive/academic linguistic proficiency (CALP). The abstract language abilities required for academic work.

collaboration. Professionals working in partnerships to provide educational services.

collaborative consultation. Professionals, often from different disciplines (e.g., general and special education), working together to develop and implement students' educational programs.

communication. The transfer of knowledge, ideas, opinions, and feelings.

communication board. A flat device on which words, pictures, or other symbols are used to expand the interactions of people with limited vocal abilities.

communication competence. Proficiency in the use of language, enabling one to participate in all aspects of communication in social and learning situations.

communication signals. A variety of messages that announce some immediate event, person, action, or emotion.

communication symbols. Voice, letters of the alphabet, or gestures used to relay communication messages.

community based instruction (CBI). A strategy of teaching functional skills in the environments in which they occur; for example, shopping skills are taught in the local market instead of in a classroom "store."

completely in-the-canal (CIC). A hearing aid, assistive listening device, that has no visible components because the entire aid fits in the ear canal.

complex partial seizures. Lapses in consciousness; sometimes called psychomotor or focal seizures; a type of epilepsy.

computerized language translators. Microcomputers that provide translations of written text from one language to another.

conduct disorders. Externalizing behavior patterns, including "acting out" and hyperactivity; not a disability according to IDEA.

conductive hearing loss. Hearing loss caused by damage or obstruction to the outer or middle ear that prevents transfer of sound to the inner ear.

congenitally blind. Having had severe visual disabilities since birth.

consultation/collaborative teaching. General education and special education teachers working together to teach students with special needs.

content. An aspect of language that governs the intent and meaning of the message delivered in a communication; includes semantics.

content enhancement strategies. Visual organizers; methods to help students organize and remember important concepts presented in texts and lectures.

continuum of services. A progressive system of special education services, each level of service leading directly to the next, which is more restrictive than the one before.

contractures. Joint stiffening, often because of muscle shortening, to the point where the joint can no longer move through its normal range; can be associated with cerebral palsy; leads to a physical impairment reducing mobility.

cooperative learning. Small groups of students working together to learn the same material.

cornea. The transparent, curved part of the front of the eye.

co-teaching. General education and special education teachers working together, sharing the same classroom and students for the entire school day.

creativity. A form of intelligence characterized by advanced divergent thought, the production of many original ideas, and the ability to develop flexible and detailed responses and ideas.

cross-cultural dissonance. Conflict between the home culture and the school cultures.

cued speech. Hand signals that accompany oral speech and make it easier to lip-read "difficult to see" speech sounds; manual communication system used by people with severe hearing loss.

cultural pluralism. Prevails when all cultural groups are valued components of the society, and the language and traditions of each group are maintained.

curriculum based measurement (CBM). A method of evaluating students' performance by collecting data on their academic performance directly and frequently.

curriculum compacting. Reducing instructional time spent on typical academic subjects so that enrichment activities can be included in the curriculum; used in education of the gifted.

Deaf culture. The structures of social relationships, language (ASL), dance, theater, and other cultural activities that unite the Deaf community.

Deaf pride. A term used to signify the accomplishments and achievements of members of the Deaf community.

deafblindness. A dual disability wherein the individual has both vision and hearing problems but might not be both profoundly deaf and also blind.

deafness. Inability to perceive sounds usefully in the environment with or without a hearing aid; inability to use hearing as a means to gain information.

decibel (dB). Unit of measure for the intensity of sound.

decoder. A device that allows closed captions to appear on a television screen.

deinstitutionalization. Decreasing the number of individuals with disabilities (e.g., mental retardation) who live in large congregate facilities, with the goal of closing all institutions and segregated settings.

demographics. The racial and ethnic composition of a country or regional area.

depression. A continued and sustained state of dejected mood and despair.

desktop publishing. Use of a microcomputer and special software to prepare written and graphic material in publication format and quality.

dialect. Words and pronunciation from a particular area, different from the form of the language used by the normative group.

differentiated curriculum. The flexible application of curriculum targets to ensure content mastery, in-depth and independent learning, and exploration of issues and themes and also to allow for acceleration when needed; used in education of the gifted.

digital hearing aid. An assistive listening device that automatically adjusts volume of the hearing aid to specific sounds and amplifies sounds only to the level necessary to compensate for the loss.

dignity of risk. The principle that taking ordinary risks and chances is part of growing up and is part of being human.

direct instruction. Instruction specifically focused on the desired, targeted behavior.

disabilities studies. A college course of studies about people with disabilities, and their history, culture, and rights.

discrepancy formulas. Formulas developed by state educational agencies or local districts to determine the difference between a child's actual achievement and, using the student's IQ scores, expected achievement; used to identify students with learning disabilities.

distance education. The use of telecommunications technologies to deliver instruction to many different sites; used especially in remote areas where particular expertise is needed but not available.

distance senses. Senses—both hearing and vision—that provide means to gain information; developed to guard against danger.

Down syndrome. A chromosomal disorder that causes identifiable physical characteristics and usually delays physical and intellectual development.

due process hearing. A noncourt proceeding before an impartial hearing officer that can be used if parents and school personnel disagree on a special education issue.

dysfluencies. Aspects of speech that interrupt the pattern of speech; typical of normal speech development in young children; in older children, dysfluency is more likely to be a speech impairment.

dyslexia. Severely impaired ability to read; presumed to be caused by a central nervous system dysfunction.

eardrum (tympanic membrane). The part of the ear on which sound waves and their vibrations fall and cause the ossicles to move; separates the outer and middle ear.

Ebonics. A learned and rule-governed social dialect of nonstandard English, spoken by many African American children.

e-Buddies. A program, part of Best Buddies, that creates e-mail friendships between people with and people without mental retardation.

echolalia. Repeating words, sounds, or sound patterns with no communicative intent, meaning, or understanding; may occur immediately or even days after they hear the sounds.

ecological assessment. A procedure that includes collecting observational data in the student's natural environments for the purpose of identifying specific events that cause a problem behavior to occur or consequent events that maintain or increase the target behavior; ABC analysis is an example.

Education for All Handicapped Children Act (EHA) or Public Law (PL) 94-142. Passed in 1975 with many provisions to ensure free appropriate public education for all students with disabilities; later renamed the Individuals with Disabilities Education Act (IDEA).

educational interpreters. Related service providers who translate or convert spoken messages to the deaf person's preferred mode of manual communication.

effective teaching behaviors. Instructional methods that engage students in learning, increase students' on-task behavior, and thus increase academic achievement.

e-mail. A computerized mail system allowing people using personal computers, the phone system, and a host mainframe computer to communicate.

eminence. Superiority in ability; a descriptor used for highly gifted individuals.

English language learner (ELL). The preferred term for students who are learning English as their second language; these students are also sometimes called limited English proficient (LEP) students.

emotional disturbance. A term that is often used interchangeably with *emotional or behavioral disorders*.

emotional or behavioral disorders. A condition characterized by disruptive or inappropriate behaviors that interfere with a student's learning, relationships with others, or personal satisfaction to such a degree that intervention is required.

English as a second language (ESL). Instructing students in English in their classrooms or in special classes until English proficiency is achieved; does not provide support in the student's native or primary language.

English language development. An instructional method used with English language learners (ELLs) that focuses on learning the formal structures of language (grammar); another term for English as a second language (ESL).

enrichment. Adding topics or skills to the traditional curriculum or presenting a particular topic in more depth; an approach used in education of the gifted.

enrichment triad/revolving door model. A model for education of the gifted wherein 15 to 20 percent rather than 3 percent of a school's students periodically participate in advanced activities planned to develop thinking skills, problem solving, and creativity.

environmental restructuring. Peers are instructed in, and reinforced for, encouraging appropriate behavior in their classmate who is exhibiting disruptive behavior.

epidemiological studies. Scientific and medical studies of the causes, transmission, and characteristics of diseases or disorders within a population.

epicanthic fold. A flap of skin over the innermost corner of the eye.

epilepsy. A tendency to have recurrent seizures (also called a seizure disorder or a convulsive disorder).

eugenics. The social policy that supports improving the human race through selective "breeding" and protecting society by not allowing people with disabilities to reproduce, live in mainstream society, or, (in some cases) even live.

evaluation. Assessment or judgment of special characteristics such as intelligence, physical abilities, sensory abilities, learning preferences, and achievement.

excess cost. The additional costs, beyond the expenses for typical learners in the general education program, incurred to educate students with disabilities.

extended family. Includes immediate family members (mother, father, and siblings) and other relatives (aunts, uncles, grandparents and others).

externalizing behaviors. Behaviors, especially aggressive behaviors, directed toward others.

family system. Potential sources of support for people with disabilities, including sons and daughters, spouses, parents, siblings, in-laws, aunts and uncles, grandparents, extended family members, and step-family members.

fetal alcohol syndrome (FAS). Congenital cognitive disabilities, behavior problems, and perhaps some physical disabilities, caused by the mother's drinking alcohol during pregnancy.

figurative language. Abstract, nonliteral language in which metaphors and analogies are used in the creation of various figures of speech.

finger spelling. A form of manual communication that assigns each letter of the alphabet a sign; one form of sign language used by deaf people.

fluency problems. Hesitations or repetitions of sounds or words that interrupt a person's flow of speech; stuttering is an example; a speech impairment.

FM transmission device. An assistive

listening device used in many classes for students with severe hearing losses; allows for direct oral transmissions from the teacher to each individual student.

follow-up study. Studies performed to provide later evaluation, diagnosis, or treatment of a condition.

form. The rule system of language; it comprises phonology, morphology, and syntax.

Fragile X syndrome. An inherited genetic disorder associated with disabilities and particularly linked to mental retardation.

free appropriate public education (FAPE). One provision of IDEA; states that students with disabilities must receive necessary education and services without cost to the child and family.

frequency of sound. The number of vibrations per second of molecules through some medium, such as air, water, or wires.

full inclusion. An interpretation of the least restrictive environment concept to mean that all students with disabilities should receive all of their instruction in the general education classroom.

functional assessments. A system that is used to determine special education eligibility, the nature of the needed instructional program, and long-term goals for individuals with severe disabilities and that focuses on independent living and is conducted in natural settings.

functional behavioral assessment. A behavioral evaluation technique that determines the exact nature of problem behaviors, the reasons why they occur, and under what conditions the likelihood of their occurrence is reduced.

functional curriculum. A curriculum focused on life skills.

functionally equivalent behaviors. Appropriate behaviors that can replace inappropriate behaviors because they serve similar purposes.

gait training. Analysis of and instruction in walking.

Gallaudet University. The only liberal arts university in the United States created to serve deaf undergraduate and graduate students.

general education. A typical (regular education) classroom and curriculum designed to serve students without disabilities.

generalization. The transfer of learning from particular instances to other environments, people, times, and events.

generalized tonic–clonic seizures. Seizures characterized by convulsions and loss of consciousness.

generic supports. Non-disability-specific public benefits to which all eligible people have access.

gifted. A term describing individuals with high levels of intelligence, outstanding abilities, and capacity for high performance.

Good Behavior Game. A game-like application of the principles of positive reinforcement and group contingencies. Students are divided into competing teams to encourage improved classroom deportment.

graphic organizers. Visual aids used to help students organize and comprehend large amounts of text and content information.

group contingencies. Reinforcement systems that involve the whole class and wherein rewards are contingent on a group's performance.

guide dog. An animal trained to help blind persons move about independently; a service animal.

hair cells. The structures in the inner ear that produce the electrochemical signals that pass through the auditory nerve to the brain, where these signals, which originated as sound waves, are perceived as tones.

hammer (malleus). One of the three tiny bones (ossicles) in the middle ear.

hard of hearing. Having sufficient residual hearing to be able, with a hearing aid, to comprehend others' speech and oral communication.

hearing aid. A device that intensifies sound to help hard of hearing people process information presented orally.

hearing threshold. The point at which a person can perceive the softest sound at each frequency level.

hereditary conditions. Conditions that have a genetic cause.

hertz (Hz). Unit of measure for sound frequency.

heterogeneity. Variation among members in a group.

high achievers. Students who expect success and view it as an incentive to work harder.

high stakes testing. Placing incentives and disincentives on teachers, schools, and school districts for their students' academic achievement.

high-tech devices. Complex assistive technology devices such as computers.

human immunodeficiency virus (HIV). A microorganism that infects the immune system, impairing the body's ability to fight infections.

home or hospital teacher. A special teacher who teaches in the child's home or hospital when the child must be absent from school because of health problems.

honors sections. Advanced classes for any student who shows high achievement in specific subject areas.

Hoover cane. Long, white cane used in the mobility and orientation system developed in 1944 by Richard Hoover to help people with visual disabilities move through the environment independently.

hydrocephaly. The buildup of fluids in the brain ventricles, resulting in brain damage.

hyperactivity. Impaired ability to sit or concentrate for long periods of time.

hypermedia. Computer programs that incorporate text, graphics, sound, photographic images, and video clips.

hypertext. A computer program that can be used to modify textbook materials through rewording, defining vocabulary, and providing further explanations.

identification. The process of seeking out and designating students with disabilities who require special education and related services.

IEP Team. The multidisciplinary team of education and related services professionals that develops and evaluates, along with students with disabilities and their parents, the individualized education program for each student with a disability.

impulsivity. Impaired ability to control one's own behavior.

in the canal (ITC). A hearing aid that is worn inside the person's ear canal.

in the ear (ITE). A hearing aid that fits inside the person's outer ear.

inactive learners. Students who do not become involved in learning situations, do not approach the learning task purposefully, do not ask questions, do not seek help, and do not initiate learning.

incidental learning. Knowledge and skills that are gained without being directly taught.

independent study. Program in which a student studies a topic in depth on an individual basis; a common approach in education of the gifted.

individualized education program (IEP). A management tool used to identify and organize individualized educational and related services for preschoolers and schoolchildren.

individualized family service plan (IFSP). A written plan that identifies and organizes services and resources for infants and toddlers with special needs who are under age 3 and their families.

individualized transition plan (ITP). A complement of a teenager's IEP, of the transition services; required for coordination and delivery of services as the student moves to adulthood and other agencies.

Individuals with Disabilities Education Act (IDEA). New name given in 1990 to the Education for All Handicapped Children Act (EHA); name used for all reauthorizations of the law that guarantees students with disabilities a right to a free appropriate education in the least restrictive environment.

infectious diseases. Contagious diseases.

information processing theory. Suggests that learning disabilities are caused by an inability to organize thinking and approach learning tasks systematically.

infused. The incorporation of enrichment activities into the general education curriculum.

inner ear. The semicircular canals and the cochlea.

instructional supports. Elements added to instructional routines to accommodate the different learning styles and needs of students with disabilities.

integration. Inclusion in, and full access to, mainstream society.

intellectual functioning. The actual performance of tasks believed to represent intelligence, such as observing, problem solving, and communicating.

interdisciplinary instruction. Guiding students in studying a topic and related issues in the context of several different disciplines; used in education of the gifted.

interim alternative setting. A temporary (no more than 45 days) educational placement for a student with disabilities who is violent, brings a gun to school, or is involved with drugs; this action is not considered a change in educational placement, and a new IEP is not required.

internalizing behaviors. Behaviors that are directed inward, focused on oneself, and expressed by being socially withdrawn.

internship. A program that places students, usually high school seniors, in job settings related to their career goals in order to challenge them and give them a chance to apply knowledge in practicing real-life skills; used in education of the gifted.

intervener. A professional who facilitates access to visual and auditory information by working one-on-one with a deafblind student.

Intervention Ladder. A hierarchy of disciplinary tactics organized from the least intrusive and complex to the most intrusive and complicated.

iris. The colored part of the eye.

itinerant teachers. Teachers who teach students or consult with others in more than one setting.

job coach. An individual who works alongside people with disabilities, helping them to learn all aspects of a job.

job developer. An individual who seeks out, shapes, and designs employment opportunities in the community for people with disabilities.

joint attention deficits. Inability to interact mutually or to share interest in events or objects with another person; a problem for many individuals with autism.

judicial hearing. A hearing before a judge in court.

juvenile arthritis. Chronic and painful muscular and joint condition seen in children.

Kurzweil Reader. One of the first computerized systems designed for people with visual disabilities that translates print into synthesized speech.

language. A rule based method of communication involving the comprehension and use of signs and symbols that represent ideas.

language delay. Development of language skills that is slower than in the majority of peers; may signal that the child will require the assistance of a specialist to use language proficiently.

language impairment. Difficulty in mastering or inability to master the various systems of rules in language, which then interferes with communication.

language different. Children who are not native English speakers, or who speak nonstandard English, and do not have an impairment even though their language is not typical.

lateral dominance. A preference for using either the right or the left side of the body for one's motoric responses; some believe that mixed dominance, or lateral confusion, is associated with poor reading performance.

learned helplessness. A phenomenon in which individuals gradually, usually as a result of repeated failure or control by others, become less willing to attempt tasks.

learning disabilities (LD). Disabilities in which the individual possesses average intelligence but is substantially delayed in academic achievement.

learning strategies. Instructional methods to help students read, comprehend, and study better by teaching them to organize and collect information strategically.

least restrictive environment (LRE). One of the principles outlined in IDEA that must be balanced when considering the best educational placement for an individual student with disabilities.

legally blind. Having visual acuity measured as 20/200 or worse in the better eye, with correction, or peripheral vision no greater than 20 degrees.

legislation. Laws passed by a legislature or the Congress and signed by a governor or the president.

lens. The part of the eye, located behind the iris, that brings objects seen into focus.

life skills. Those skills used to manage a home, cook, shop, and organize personal living environments.

limb deficiencies. Deficiencies resulting from missing or nonfunctioning arms or legs.

limited English proficient (LEP). Having limited ability to read, write, or speak English; the preferred term is English language learner (ELL).

litigation. A lawsuit or legal proceeding.

long cane. White cane used to help blind people be independently mobile, developed by Hoover during World War II.

longitudinal studies. Studies that follow individual subjects over a long period of time.

loudness. An aspect of voice, referring to the intensity of the sound produced while speaking.

low achievers. Students who experience school failure and poor academic achievement, come to expect failure, and develop the attitude that expending effort to learn will not produce results.

low incidence disability. A disability that occurs infrequently; that is, the prevalence and incidence are very low. Examples include visual disabilities, deaf and hard of hearing, deafblindness, autism, multiple-severe disabilities, and traumatic brain injury.

low stakes testing. State and district-wide testing for the purpose of performance evaluation that does not include negative consequences on schools or teachers for poor performance.

low-tech devices. Simple assistive technology devices such as communication boards, homemade cushions, and classroom railings.

low vision. A level of visual disability at which vision is still useful for learning or the execution of a task.

magnet schools. Center schools that serve children who do not live in the immediate neighborhood; some magnet schools are designed to serve children whose parents work in a nearby area; other magnet schools emphasize a particular theme (such as theater arts, math, or science).

mainstreaming. An older term for including students with special needs in general education classrooms for some or all of their school day.

manifestation determination. The result of a process that determines whether a student's disciplinary problems are a result of the student's disability.

manual communication. Using the hands, not the voice, as the means of communication, as in sign language and finger spelling.

maternal rubella. German measles contracted by a pregnant woman.

mathematics/learning disabilities. The condition wherein a student's learning disability is significant in the area of mathematics.

medically fragile. A term that was formerly used to describe children with special health care needs but now reflects an individual's health status.

mediation. A meeting of parents and school officials to resolve disagreements about the IEP and the student's placement and services.

melting pot. The concept of an homogenized United States where cultural traditions and home languages are abandoned for the new American culture.

meningitis. A disease that affects the central nervous system and often causes hearing loss.

mental age (MA). A means of describing an individual's mental ability, derived from an artificial comparison between the individual's IQ score and chronological age; not a preferred means of describing an individual's abilities.

mental retardation. A disability characterized by cognitive impairment, limited adaptive behavior, need for support, and initial occurrence before age 18.

mentorship. A program in which a gifted student is paired with an adult in order to learn to apply knowledge in real-life situations.

middle ear. An air-filled chamber that contains the eardrum, the Eustachian tube, and the three little bones (hammer, anvil, and stirrup) that are called the ossicles.

Mimosa Cottage Project. One of the earliest demonstration and research sites, located at a state-funded institution in Kansas, where institutionalized individuals were shown to be able to learn a variety of tasks.

mnemonic. A learning strategy that promotes the remembering of names by, for example, associating the first letters of items in a list with a word, sentence, or picture.

mobility. The ability to travel safely and efficiently from one place to another; a topic of instruction for students with severe visual problems.

morphology. Rules that govern the structure and form of words and the basic elements of word meanings.

motivation. The inner drive to work hard, achieve, master skills, and learn concepts; internal incentives that are influenced by previous success or failure.

multicultural education. By incorporating concepts of culture, differences, equality, and democracy to develop effective classroom instruction and school environments, this educational strategy supports and extends students' cultural backgrounds.

multiple disabilities. More than one disability in an individual.

multiple intelligences. A multidimensional approach to intelligence, providing an alternative to the concept of IQ, allowing those exceptional in any one of seven areas to be identified as gifted.

multiple-severe disabilities. Exceptionally challenging disabilities where more than one condition influences learning, independence, and the range of intensive and pervasive supports the individual and the family require.

muscular/skeletal conditions. Conditions affecting muscles or bones and resulting in limited functioning.

myoelectric limbs. Artificial limbs powered by batteries and controlled by electric signals transmitted by the individual's brain (sometimes called bionic).

natural supports. Supports that are available to all individuals as a natural result of typical family and community living.

neural tube disorders. Another name for spinal cord disorders, which always involve the spinal column and usually the spinal cord.

neurological impairment. Damage to the central nervous system resulting in limitations in the ability to control muscles and motor movement.

neuromotor impairment. Condition involving the nerves, muscles, and motor functioning.

nondiscriminatory testing. Assessment that properly takes into account a child's cultural and linguistic diversity.

nonpaid supports. Ordinary assistance given by friends and neighbors.

normal curve. A theoretical, bell-shaped construct of the normal distribution of human traits such as intelligence.

normalization. Making available ordinary patterns of life and conditions of everyday living.

obturator. A device that creates a closure between the oral and nasal cavities when the soft palate is missing or damaged; helps compensate for a cleft palate.

occupational therapist (OT). A professional who directs activities that help improve muscular control and develop self-help skills; provides a special education "related service."

open captions. Captions (subtitles) that appear on the television screen for all viewers to see.

ophthalmologist. Medical doctor who specializes in eye disorders.

optic nerve. The nerve that carries messages from the eye to the visual center of the brain.

optician. A person who fills the ophthalmologist's or optometrist's prescriptions for glasses or corrective lenses.

optometrist. Professional who measures vision and can prescribe corrective lenses (eyeglasses or contact lenses).

oral-only approach. One method of instruction proposed for students who are deaf, where-in they learn to communicate (both receiving and sending information) orally, not using sign language.

orientation. The mental map people use to move through environments; a topic of instruction for students with severe visual disabilities.

organizing routines. Activities, including questions, that precede instruction to focus students' attention on the information to be presented, also called advance organizers, always a component of a University of Kansas learning strategy.

orthopedic impairments. Conditions related to a physical deformity or disability of the skeletal system and associated motor function.

ossicles. The three tiny bones in the middle ear that transmit sound waves from the eardrum through the middle ear to the cochlea.

other health impairments. Chronic or acute health problems resulting in limited strength, vitality, or alertness; a special education category that includes attention deficit/hyperactivity disorder along with special health care needs.

otitis media. Middle ear infection that can result in hearing loss, communication impairments, and even learning disabilities if it becomes a chronic condition.

otoacoustic emissions (OAEs). The low level of sound produced when the hair cells inside of the inner ear vibrate; testing for OAEs allows for newborn hearing assessment.

outcomes. The results of decisions and actions; a term used to describe students' achievements.

outer ear. The part of the ear made up of the pinna, which is the structure that most people call the ear, and the auditory canal.

outreach services. Specialized programs offered in local communities by residential schools or centralized agencies serving students with special needs.

overrepresentation. Too many students from a cultural or ethnic group participating in a special education category, beyond the level one might expect from that group's proportion of the overall school population.

perinatal. At the time of birth.

peripheral vision. The outer area of a person's visual field.

personal reader. A person who reads text orally to those who cannot read print.

pervasive developmental disorder–not otherwise specified (PDD-NOS). One of the disorders included in the autistic spectrum disorders (ASD); a disability that manifests itself in problems with communication and social interaction and in repetitive or manneristic behaviors.

phenylketonuria (PKU). A hereditary condition that causes mental retardation and can be avoided by eliminating from the diet, shortly after birth, foods (such as milk) that contain an amino acid that, in these individuals, can build up to toxic levels.

phonological awareness. Understanding of the relationship between sounds and their corresponding parts of words; facilitates the abilities to rhyme and understand sound–symbol relationships; an oral language skill that enables children to understand that words can be represented in print.

phonology. The rules within a language used to govern the combination of speech sounds to form words and sentences.

physical therapist (PT). A professional who treats physical disabilities through many nonmedical means; provides a special education "related service."

picture exchange communication system (PECS). A technique used to teach individuals who are nonverbal, particularly children with autism, to use pictures to make requests.

pitch. An aspect of voice; its perceived high or low sound quality.

portfolio assessment. An alternative form of individualized evaluation that includes many samples of the student's work across all curriculum targets and the reports of teachers and parents about that individual's social skills.

positive behavioral supports. A behavioral approach to link scientifically validated practice applications across settings, such as home, school, work, and community.

positive reinforcement. Rewarding students with praise, prizes, or privileges for correct responses; often includes tokens, points, or other concrete items to emphasize the connection between behavior and the reward.

postlingually deaf. Having lost the ability to hear after developing language.

postnatal. After birth.

postsecondary. Education that comes after high school (e.g., community college, technical/vocational school, college, university, continuing education).

pragmatics. A key element of communication; the relationship among language, perception, and cognition.

prelingually deaf. Having lost the ability to hear before developing language.

prenatal. Before birth.

prevalence. The total number of cases at a given time.

problem solving. Finding answers or solutions to situations.

procedural safeguards. IDEA guarantees students with disabilities and their parents the right to a free appropriate public education (FAPE) in the least restrictive environment (LRE) possible through a process to resolve disagreements and disputes that begins with mediation and ends with civil action.

process/product debate. Argument about whether perceptual training or direct instruction was more effective for instruction; resolved in favor of direct instruction.

progressive time delay. Systematically increasing the period of silence (time delay) before the correct answer (prompt) is provided.

Public Law (PL) 94-142. The number of the first special education law; see Education for All Handicapped Children Act (now IDEA).

pull-in programming. Rather than having students with disabilities leave general education classes for special education or for related services, delivering those services to them in the general education classroom.

pull-out programs. Providing special services outside of the general education classroom; often called a resource room for students with disabilities; the most common educational placement for gifted students.

pupil. Hole in the center of the iris that expands and contracts, admitting light to the eye.

pure sounds. Sound waves of specific frequencies used to test an individual's hearing ability.

quality of life. A subjective and individual-specific concept dependent on a number of life-dimensions, including social relationships, personal satisfaction, employment, choice, leisure, and community adjustment.

reading/learning disabilities. The condition wherein a student's learning disability is significant in reading.

real-time captioning (RTC). Practically instantaneous translations of speech into print; an accommodation for deaf students attending lectures.

reauthorization. The act of amending and renewing a law.

reciprocal teaching. A teaching tactic wherein teachers and students switch roles predicting, summariz-

ing, questioning, and clarifying reading passages.

rehabilitation engineering. Application of mechanical and engineering principles to improve human physical functioning.

related services. A part of special education that includes services from professionals (e.g., OTs, PTs, SLPs) from a wide range of disciplines typically outside of education, all designed to meet the learning needs of individual children with disabilities.

residual vision. The amount and degree of vision that one has functional use of despite a visual disability.

resistant to treatment. A newly emerging and defining characteristic of learning disabilities wherein students do not respond to validated methods that are typically applied in general education settings and require intensive, individualized instruction; lack of change in learning or behavior despite intervention or instruction.

resonating system. The oral and nasal cavities where speech sounds are formed.

respiratory system. The system of organs whose primary function is to take in oxygen and expel gases.

retina. Inside lining at the back of the eye.

Rett's syndrome. One of the disorders included in the autistic spectrum disorders (ASD); a disability that manifests itself in problems with communication and social interaction and in repetitive or manneristic behaviors; has a genetic cause.

robotics. Use of high-tech devices to perform motor skills.

scaffolded instruction. An instructional technique wherein students are given support while learning new skills by systematically building on students' experiences and knowledge.

schizophrenia. A disorder, rare in children, that includes bizarre delusions and dissociation from reality.

school nurses. Professionals who participate in delivering FAPE to students with disabilities by assisting with medical services at school and designing accommodations for students with special health care needs.

school psychologist. A psychologist

trained to test and evaluate individual students' abilities.

scientifically validated interventions. Instructional procedures or methods that careful and systematic research has proved to be effective.

Section 504 of the Rehabilitation Act of 1973. This law set the stage for both the Individuals with Disabilities Education Act, passed in 1975, and the Americans with Disabilities Act, passed in 1990, by outlining basic civil rights of people with disabilities.

seizure. A spontaneous abnormal discharge of the electrical impulses of the brain

seizure disorder. See epilepsy.

self-advocacy. A social and political movement started by and for people with mental retardation who wish to speak for themselves on important issues such as housing, employment, legal rights, and personal relationships.

self-determination. A set of behaviors that is needed for independent living and includes making decisions, expressing preferences, and practicing self-advocacy; a curriculum target for many students with disabilities, particularly those with mental retardation.

self-injurious behavior (SIB). Self-inflicted injuries (head banging, eye poking).

self-management techniques. A set of instructional procedures whereby the individual uses self-monitoring, self-evaluation, and/or self-reinforcement to change behavior.

semantics. The system within a language that governs the content, intent, and meanings of spoken and written language.

semantic feature analysis (SFA). An instructional strategy designed to increase students' vocabulary by using a grid to show relationships and features in common among known and unknown concepts.

sensorineural hearing loss. Hearing loss caused by damage to the inner ear or the auditory nerve.

sequencing. Mentally categorizing and putting items, facts, or ideas in order according to various dimensions; a thinking skill.

serious emotional disturbance. The term formerly used in IDEA to classify students with emotional or behavioral disorders.

service delivery options. Various ways in which special education services are provided to students with disabilities (e.g., full inclusion programs, pull-out programs, special classes, center schools).

service manager. The case manager who oversees the implementation and evaluation of an individualized family service plan (IFSP).

setting demands. The behavioral requirements, both obvious and subtle, of an environment.

sheltered instruction. Restating concepts and instructions, as well as using visuals and concrete examples, to provide language support to English language learners so that they better understand complex and abstract learning. An instructional method used with English language learners (ELLs) that focuses on learning the formal structures of language (grammar); another term for English as a second language (ESL).

shunt. A tube used in a medical procedure that draws excess fluid from the brain and head area and disposes of it in a safe area in the body, such as the stomach; used to prevent cognitive disabilities resulting from hydrocephaly.

sickle cell anemia. A hereditary blood disorder that inhibits blood flow; African Americans are most at risk for this health impairment.

signed English. A signed translation of the English language; not a language of its own, as is ASL.

sign language. An organized, established system of manual gestures used for communication; used by some people with severe cognitive disabilities and by people who are deaf.

simple partial seizures. Seizures that are not always apparent; and often affect behavior and feelings.

Snellen chart. A chart, developed in 1862, used to test visual acuity.

social competence. The ability to understand social situations, respond to others appropriately, and interact with other people.

socially maladjusted. A term applied to a group of children who do not act within society's norms but who are excluded from the definition of children with emotional or behavioral disorders.

socioeconomic status (SES). The status an individual or family unit holds in society, usually determined by job, level of education, and the amount of money available to spend.

spastic. A type of cerebral palsy characterized by uncontrolled tightening or pulling of muscles.

special education. Individualized education for children and youth with special needs.

specialized supports. Disability-specific services to help people with disabilities participate in the community.

speech. The vocal production of language.

speech impairment. Abnormal speech that is unintelligible, is unpleasant, or interferes with communication.

speech mechanisms. The various parts of the body—tongue, lips, teeth, mandible, and palate—required for oral speech.

speech synthesizers. Equipment that creates voice; assistive technology devices.

speech/language pathologist (SLP). A professional who diagnoses and treats problems in the area of speech and language development; a related services provider.

spina bifida. A developmental defect whereby the spinal column fails to close properly.

spinal cord. The cord of nervous tissue that extends through the bony spinal column to the brain.

Sputnik. The Russian satellite that was launched in 1957 and stimulated renewed interest in the education of the gifted in the United States.

standard deviation (SD). A statistical measure that expresses the variability and the distribution from the mean of a set of scores.

statewide and district-wide assessments. Part of the national education reform movement that includes annual achievement testing of all schoolchildren for the purpose of increasing the accountability of schools for children's progress in the curriculum.

stay-put provision. The legal mandate that prohibited students with disabilities from being expelled because of behavior associated with their disabilities.

stereotypic behaviors. Nonproductive behaviors (such as twirling, flapping hands, rocking) that an individual repeats at a high rate; commonly observed in youngsters with autistic spectrum disorders.

stirrup (stapes). One of the three tiny bones (ossicles) in the middle ear.

STORCH infections. Many different congenital viruses fall under this group of congenital infections; the term stands for syphilis, toxoplasmosis, other, rubella, cytomegalovirus, and herpes.

story maps. Simple diagrams that help students organize and recall important elements and features of stories they have heard or read.

structured teaching. A feature of the instructional program TEACCH, developed for students with autism, wherein visual aids (start-to-finish boxes) are used to help students comprehend their environments.

stuttering. The lack of fluency in an individual's speech pattern, often characterized by hesitations or repetitions of sounds or words.

supported employment. An arrangement whereby students with mental retardation are placed in paying jobs and provided with job training. They receive significant assistance and support, and the employer is helped with the compensation.

syntax. Rules that govern the order of words in phrases and sentences.

system of supports. The network of supports that each individual develops to function optimally in life.

tactile maps. Maps that utilize touch to orient people to specific locales; used by people with severe visual disabilities.

talent development. The process of translating ability into achievement; another name for education of the gifted.

talking books. Books available in auditory format.

task analysis. Breaking down problems and tasks into smaller, sequenced components.

technology-dependent children. Children who probably could not survive without high-tech devices such as ventilators.

telecoil. An added option on many hearing aids that allows access to telephones, audio loops, and other assistive listening devices; also called an induction coil.

telecommunications. Various electronic devices that allow students and teachers to access and send materials and information via a computer network system.

telecommunications relay service (TRS). A telephone system required by federal law where an operator at a relay center converts a print-telephone message in to a voice-telephone message.

text telephone (TTY). A piece of equipment, formerly called the telecommunication device for the deaf (TDD), that allows people to make and receive telephone calls by typing information over the telephone lines.

theoretical construct. A model based on theory, not practice or experience.

time delay. The instructional technique of giving students an opportunity to provide a correct answer to a question, read a sight word, or spell a word within a set period of time (e.g., 20 seconds) and then supplying the answer at the end of the time period.

time of onset. When the disability occurred.

tonic–clonic seizures. Seizures characterized by a stiff (tonic) phase in which the muscles become rigid, followed by a jerking (clonic) phase in which the arms and legs snap (formerly referred to as grand mal seizures).

total communication approach. A system of instruction for deaf students that encourages the student to use any and all methods of communication (oral speech, manual communication, ASL, gestures) that the student finds easy and effective.

total immersion. The student is taught entirely in English; all the other students are also non-native English speakers, and the teacher can speak the students' home language.

Tourette's syndrome. A low incidence disability that is characterized by multiple and uncontrollable motor and/or verbal tics.

toxin. A poisonous substance that can cause immediate or long-term harm to the body.

transitional bilingual education. An instructional method used with English language learners (ELLs) wherein academic subjects are taught in the child's native language until sufficient English is mastered for transition; usually last three years.

trauma. Injury.

traumatic brain injury (TBI). The result of a head injury; the individual experiences reduced cognitive functioning, limited attention, and impulsivity.

Treatment and Education of Autistic and Communication-Handicapped Children (TEACCH). An individualized program that helps children with autism compensate, through visual supports and other forms of structure, for skills they cannot learn.

tunnel vision. Severe limitation in peripheral vision; limitations in the width of the visual field.

twice exceptional students. Students who have a disability and who are gifted.

unexpected underachievement. A description associated with learning disabilities because poor school performance cannot be explained by students' intellectual potential.

underrepresentation. Too few students from a cultural or ethnic group participating in a special education category or in programs for the gifted; smaller numbers than would be predicted by that group's proportion in the overall school population.

universal design. Barrier free architectural and building designs that meet the needs of everyone, including people with physical challenges.

universal infant screening. Testing of all newborns to determine whether they have a disability or are at risk for disability; specific term associated with newborn screening for hearing loss.

use. The aspect of language that governs applying language appropriately; includes pragmatics.

Usher syndrome. A genetic syndrome that includes a nonprogressive sensorineural hearing loss, retinitis pigmentosa and a progressively restricted field of vision, loss of the sense of smell, mental retardation, and impaired balance and motor skills.

ventilators. Machines that assist with breathing.

vibrating system. The larynx and vocal folds, which vibrate and produce sounds and pitch.

visual acuity. How well a person can see at various distances.

visual efficiency. How well a person can use sight.

vocal symbols. Oral means of relaying messages, such as speech sounds.

vocal system. The parts of the respiratory system used to create voice.

voice carry over (VCO). A TTY that allows the use of both voice and text.

voice problem. An abnormal spoken language production, characterized by unusual pitch, loudness, or quality of sounds.

wraparound services. A service delivery model whereby all of the child's needs are met through the coordination of the educational system, mental health agencies, social services, and community agencies.

written symbols. Graphic means, such as a written alphabet, used to relay messages.

Young Autism Program (YAP). Developed by I. Lovass at UCLA, this program uses behavioral principles to reduce problems associated with autistic spectrum disorders (ASD); sometimes incorrectly called the ABA program.

REFERENCES

CHAPTER 1
THE CONTEXT OF SPECIAL EDUCATION

Artist's Bio

Foy, E., & Butterfield, C. (1998). *The Courtauld Gallery at Somerset House.*London: Courtauld Institute of Art, University of London, in association with Thames and Hudson.

Murdoch, J. (1988). *The Courtauld Gallery at Somerset House.* London: Courtauld Institute of Art, University with Hudson, LTD.

Stein, S. A. (1986). *Van Gogh: A retrospective.* New York: Park Lane.

Walther, I. F., & Metzger, R. (1993). *Vincent van Gogh: The complete paintings* (Vol. 1). Germany: Benedikt Taschen.

Introduction

Berman, S., Davis, P., Kaufman-Frederick, A. & Urion, D. (2001). The rising costs of special education in Massachusetts: Causes and effects. In C. E. Finn, Jr., A. J. Rotherham, and C. R. Hokanson, Jr., (Eds.), *Rethinking special education for a new century.* (pp. 183–212). Washington, DC: Thomas B. Fordham Foundation and the Progressive Policy Institute.

Clayton, J. (2001, July 30). The thicket of special ed. *Los Angeles Times,* p. B10.

Finn, Jr., C.E., Rotherham, A. J., & Hokanson, Jr., C. R. (Eds.). (2001). *Rethinking special education for a new century.* Washington, DC: Thomas B. Fordham Foundation and the Progressive Policy Institute.

Gartner, A., & Lipsky, D. K. (1987). Beyond special education: Toward a quality system for all students. *Harvard Educational Review, 57,* 367–395

Hungerford, R. H. (1950). On locusts. *American Journal of Mental Deficiency, 54,* 415–418.

Lyon, G. R., Fletcher, J. M., Shaywitz, S. E., Shaywitz, B. A., Torgesen, J. K., Wood, F. B., Schulte, A., & Olson, R. (2001). Rethinking learning disabilities. In C. E. Finn, Jr., A. J. Rotherham, and C. R. Hokanson, Jr., (Eds.), *Rethinking special education for a new century* (pp. 259–288). Washington, DC: Thomas B. Fordham Foundation and the Progressive Policy Institute.

Stainback, S., Stainback, W., East, K., & Sapon-Shevin, M. (1994). A commentary on inclusion and the development of a positive self-identity by people with disabilities.

Townsend, B. L., & Patton, J. M. (2001). The discourse on ethics, power, and privilege and African American learners: Guest editors' post notes. *Teacher Education and Special Education, 24,* 48–49.

The Essence of Disabilities

Artiles, A. J. (1998). The dilemma of difference: Enriching the disproportionality discourse with theory and context. *The Journal of Special Education, 32,* 32–36.

Bennett, V. (1997, December 18). Ill children in Kyrgyzstan used as pawns. *Los Angeles Times,* pp. A24–A25.

Bragg, L. (1997). From the mute god to the lesser god: Disability in medieval Celtic and Old Norse literature. *Disability & Society, 12,* 165–177.

Danforth, S., & Rhodes, W. C. (1997). Deconstructing disability: A philosophy for inclusion. *Remedial and Special Education, 18,* 357–366.

Erevelles, N. (1996). Disability and the dialects of difference. *Disability & Society, 11,* 519–537.

Groce, N. E. (1985). *Everyone here spoke sign language: Hereditary deafness on Martha's Vineyard.* Cambridge, MA: Harvard University Press.

Grossman, H. (1998). *Ending discrimination in special education.* Springfield, IL: Charles C Thomas.

Kauffman, J. M. (1997). Caricature, science, and exceptionality. *Remedial and Special Education, 18,* 130–132.

Longmore, P. (2002). San Francisco State University: Institute on disability. Retrieved June 21, 2002, from http:// online.sfsu.edu/~longmore/

Powell, B., & Dlugy, Y. (1998, December 21). Human Rights: Russia's gulags for children. *Newsweek,* pp. 40–41.

Origins of Special Education

Itard, J. M. G. (1806/1962). *The wild boy of Aveyron* (G. Humphrey & M. Humphrey, Trans.). Englewood Cliffs, NJ: Prentice-Hall.

Kanner, L. (1964). *A history of the care and study of the mentally retarded.* Springfield, IL: Charles C Thomas.

Seguin, E. (1846). *The moral treatment, hygiene, and education of idiots and other backward children.* Paris: Balliere.

State ex. rel. Beattie v. Board of Education, 169 Wis. 231, 172 N. W. 153, 154 (1919).

The summer school for teachers. (1907, February). *Training School Bulletin, 36,* 17.

Winzer, M. A. (1993). *The history of special education: From isolation to integration.* Washington, DC: Gallaudet University Press.

Necessity for National Intervention

Aiello, B. (1976). Especially for special educators: A sense of our own history. *Exceptional Children, 42,* 244–252

Americans with Disabilities Act of 1990, Pub. L. No. 101–336, 104 STAT.327.

Ballard, J., Ramirez, B. A., & Weintraub, F. J. (1982). *Special education in America: Its legal and governmental foundations*. Reston, VA: Council for Exceptional Children.

Biklen, D. (1985). *Achieving the complete school: Strategies for effective mainstreaming*. New York: Teachers College Press.

Brown v. *Board of Education*, 347 U.S. 483 (1954).

de Bettencourt, L. U. (2002). Understanding the differences between IDEA and Section 504. *Teaching Exceptional Children, 34*, 16–23

Descriptive Video Services (DVS). (2002 Winter/Spring). *DVS home video catalogue: Described movies for people who have trouble seeing the screen*. Indianapolis, IN: DVS Home Video.

Freedman, M. K. (2001, June 15). Golf, assessment become similar game in wake of Martin ruling. *The Special Educator, 16*, 1, 6.

Hu, W. (2001, October 7). Survivor heard everything, saw nothing: blind man, guide dog navigated 71 floors to safety before collapse. *The Tennessean*, p. 7A.

Individuals with Disabilities Education Act. Pub. L. No. 104–17, 111 STAT.37.

Johnson, K. (1998). Deinstitutionalization: The management of rights. *Disability & Society, 13*, 375–387.

Katsiyannis, A., & Yell, M. L. (2000). The Supreme Court and school health services: *Cedar Rapids* v. *Garret F. Exceptional Children, 66*, 317–326.

Leibrock, C. A., & Terry, J. E. (1999). *Beautiful universal design*. New York: Wiley.

Longmore, P. K. (1995, September/October). The second phase: From disability rights to disability culture. *Disability Rag & Resource, 16*, 4–22

Mills v. *Board of Education of the District of Columbia,* 348 F. Supp. 866 (1972).

Nirje, B. (1969). The normalization principle and its human management implications. In R. B. Kugel & W. Wolfensberger (Eds.), *Changing patterns in residential services for the mentally retarded* (pp. 179–195). Washington, DC: President's Committee on Mental Retardation.

Nirje, B. (1976). The normalization principle. In R. B. Kugel & A. Shearer (Eds.), *Changing patterns in residential services for the mentally retarded* (Rev. ed., pp. 231–240). Washington, DC: President's Committee on Mental Retardation.

Nirje, B. (1985). The basis and logic of the normalization principle. *Australia and New Zealand Journal of Developmental Disabilities, 11*, 65–68.

Pennsylvania Association for Retarded Children v. *Commonwealth of Pennsylvania,* 343 F. Supp. 279 (E. D. Pa., 1972).

Rehabilitation Act of 1973. Section 504, 19 U.S.C. section 794.

Roos, P. (1970). Trends and issues in special education for the mentally retarded. *Education and Training of the Mentally Retarded, 5*, 51–61.

Treanor, R. B. (1993). *We overcame: The story of civil rights for disabled people*. Falls Church, VA: Regal Direct Publishing.

West, J. (1994). *Federal Implementation of the Americans with Disabilities Act, 1991–1994*. New York: Milbank Memorial Fund.

Wolfensberger, W. (Ed.). (1972). *The principle of normalization in human services*. Toronto: National Institute on Mental Retardation.

Wolfensberger, W. (1995). Of "normalization," lifestyles, the Special Olympics, deinstitutionalization, mainstreaming, integration, cabbages and kings. *Mental Retardation, 33*, 16–169.

Ziegler, D. (2002, April). *Reauthorization of the elementary and secondary education act: No child left behind act of 2001*. Arlington, VA: The Council for Exceptional Children, Public Policy Unit.

Special Education Today

20 U.S.C. section 1400 *(c)*

Dymond, S. K., & Orelove, F. P. (2001). What constitutes effective curricula for students with severe disabilities? *Exceptionality, 9*, 109–122.

Müller, E. & Linehan, P. (2001, July). Federal disability terms: A review of state use. *Quick Turn Around (QTA)*. Alexandria, VA: Project Forum at the National Association for Directors of Special Education.

Nazzaro, J. N. (1977). *Exceptional timetables: Historic events affecting the handicapped and gifted*. Reston, VA: The Council for Exceptional Children.

U.S. Department of Education. (1999). *Assistance to states for the education of children with disabilities program and the early intervention program for infants and toddlers with disabilities; final regulations*. Federal Register, 34, CRF Parts 300 and 303.

Opportunities for a Better 21st Century

Artiles, A. J., Aguirre-Muñoz, Z., & Abedi, J. (1998). Predicting placement in learning disabilities programs: Do predictors vary by ethnic group? *Exceptional Children, 64*, 543–559.

Berman, S., Davis, P., Kaufman-Frederick, A.. & Urion, D. (2001). The rising costs of special education in Massachusetts: Causes and effects. In C. E. Finn Jr., A. J. Rotherham, and C. R. Hokanson, Jr., (Eds.), *Rethinking special education for a new century*. (pp. 183–212). Washington, DC: Thomas B. Fordham Foundation and the Progressive Policy Institute.

Briand, X. (Ed.). (1995, May 17). Suspension, special education data reveal mixed picture. *Special Education Report, 21*, 3–4.

Carlson, E., Schroll, K., & Klein, S. (2001). *OSEP briefing on the study of personnel needs in special education (SPeNSE)*. Rockville, MD: Westat.

Cartledge, G., Tillman, L. C., & Johnson, C. T. (2001). Professional ethics within the context of student discipline and diversity. *Teacher Education and Special Education, 24*, 25–37.

Cassuto, L. (1999, March 19). Whose field is it anyway? Disability studies in the academy. *The Chronicle of Higher Education*, p. A60.

Cedar Rapids School District v. *Garret F.,* 106 F.3rd 822 (8th Cir. 1997), cert. gr. 118 S. Ct. 1793 (1998), aff'd, 119 S. Ct. 992 (1999).

Chambers, J. G., Parrish, T., & Harr, J. J. (2002, March). *What are we spending on special education services in the United States, 1999–2000? Advance report #1*. American Institutes for Research: Special Education Expenditure Project (SEEP).

Clayton, J. (2001, July 30). The Thicket of Special Ed. *Los Angeles Times*, p. B10.

Danforth, S., & Rhodes, W. C. (1997) Deconstructing disability: A philosophy for inclusion. *Remedial and Special Education, 18*, 357–366.

Dymond, S. K., & Orelove, F. P. (2001). What constitutes effective curricula for students with severe disabilities? *Exceptionality, 9*, 109–122.

ERIC Clearinghouse on Disabilities and Gifted Education. (2001, April). *Educating exceptional children: A statistical profile*. Arlington, VA: The Council for Exceptional Children.

Ewing, N. J. (2001). Teacher education: Ethics, power, and privilege. *Teacher Education and Special Education, 24*, 13–24.

Finn, Jr., C. E., Rotherham, A. J., & Hokanson, Jr., C. R. (Eds.). (2001). *Rethinking special education for a new century*. Washington, DC: Thomas B. Fordham Foundation and the Progressive Policy Institute.

Forness, S. R., Kavale, K. A., Blum, I. M., & Lloyd, J. W. (1997). Mega-analysis of meta-analyses: What works in special education and related services. *Teaching Exceptional Children, 29*, 4–9.

Gallagher, H. G. (1994). *FDR's splendid deception* (Rev. ed.). Arlington, VA: Vandamere Press.

Garnett, K. (1996, Spring/Summer). What is wrong with the Senate bill? *The DLD Times, 13*, 7–8.

Gartner, A., & Lipsky, D. K. (1987). Beyond special education: Toward a quality system for all students. *Harvard Educational Review, 57*, 367–395.

Gatley, P. (2001, April 30). Are we wasting money on special needs kids? *The Tennessean*, p. 14A.

Gotsch, T. (2001, August 15). Court: Emotionally disabled entitled to IDEA services. *Special Education Report, 27*, 4.

Gotsch, T. (2001, December 19). Disabled discipline plan fails, but will be back soon. *Special Education Report, 27*, 5.

Grissmer, D., Flanagan, A., & Williamson, S. (1998). Does money matter for minority and disadvantaged students? Assessing the new empirical evidence. In W. J. Fowler, Jr. (Ed.), *Developments in school finance 1997*. Washington, DC: U.S. Department of Education, Office of Educational Research and Improvement, National Center for Educational Statistics.

Hehir, T. (1996, September). *The achievements of people with disabilities because of IDEA*. Paper presented at the meeting of Project SUCCESS for annual project directors, Washington, DC.

Hockenbury, J. C., Kauffman, J. M., & Hallahan, D. P. (1999–2000). What is right about special education. *Exceptionality, 8*, 3–11.

Horn, W. F., & Tynan, D. (2001). Time to make special education "special" again. In C. E. Finn, Jr., A. J. Rotherham, and C. R. Hokanson, Jr., (Eds.), *Rethinking special education for a new century*. (pp. 23–52). Washington, DC: Thomas B. Fordham Foundation and the Progressive Policy Institute.

Kappa/Gallup Poll of the public's attitudes toward the public schools. *Phi Delta Kappan*, 41–56.

Katsiyannis. A., & Yell, M. L. (2000). The Supreme Court and school health services: *Cedar Rapids* v. *Garret F. Exceptional Children, 66*, 317–326.

Kauffman, J. M. (1997) Caricature, science, and exceptionality. *Remedial and Special Education, 18*, 130–132.

Kitchin, R. (1998). "Out of place," "knowing one's place": Space, power and the exclusion of disabled people. *Disability & Society, 13*, 343–356.

Klingner, J. K., Vaughn, S., Schumm, J. S., Cohen, P., & Forgan, J. W. (1998). Inclusion or pull-out: Which do students prefer? *Journal of Learning Disabilities, 31*, 148–158.

Kortering, L. J., & Braziel, P. M. (1999). Staying in school: The perspective of ninth-grade students. *Remedial and Special Education, 20*, 106–113.

Lannon, J. (2001, May 2). Not popular to oppose funding for special kids. *The Tennessean*, p. 10A.

Lloyd, J. W., Forness, S. R., & Kavale, K. A. (1998). Some methods are more effective than others. *Intervention in School and Clinic, 33*, 195–200.

Longmore, P. (2002). San Francisco State University: Institute on disability. Retrieved June 21, 2002, from http://online.sfsu.edu/~longmore/

Lovitt, T. C., & Cushing, S. (1999). Parents of youth with disabilities. *Remedial and Special Education, 20*, 134–142.

Lovitt, T. C., Plavins, M., & Cushing, S. (1999). What do pupils with disabilities have to say about their high school experience? *Remedial and Special Education, 20*, 67–76, 83.

MacMillan, D. L., Gresham, F. M., & Bocian, K. M. (1998). Discrepancy between definitions of learning disabilities and school practices: An empirical investigation. *Journal of Learning Disabilities, 31*, 314–326.

Mitchell, D. T. (2002). University of Illinois-Chicago Ph. D. program in disability studies. Retrieved June 21, 2002, from http://www.uic.edu/depts/idhd/DS/

Oswald, D. P., Coutinho, M. J., Best, A. M., & Singh, N. N. (1999). Ethnic representation in special education: The influence of school-related economic and demographic variables. *The Journal of Special Education, 32*, 194–206.

Patton, J. M. (1998). The disproportionate representation of African Americans in special education: Looking behind the curtain for understanding and solutions. *The Journal of Special Education, 32*, 25–31.

Perlstein, L. (2001, July 11). Schools awash in bad behavior: Area educators complain of students out of control. *Washington Post*, p. B1, B5.

Reschly, D. J. (1997). Utility of individual ability measures and public policy choices for the 21st century. *School Psychology Review, 26*, 234–241.

Rose, L. C., & Gallup, A. M. (1998, September). The 30th Annual Phi Delta Kappa/Gallup Poll of the public attitudes toward the public schools. *Phi Delta Kappan*, 41–56.

Rouse, M., & Florian, L. (2001). Editorial. *Cambridge Journal of Education, 31*, 285–289.

Russ, S., Chiang, B., Rylance, B. J., & Bongers, J. (2001). Caseload in special education: An integration of research findings. *Exceptional Children, 67*, 161–172.

Safran, S. P. (1998). The first century of disability portrayal in film: An analysis of the literature. *The Journal of Special Education, 31*, 467–479.

Safran, S. P. (2000). Using movies to teach students about disabilities. *Teaching Exceptional Children, 32*, 44–47.

Smith, D. D., Tyler, N. C., McLesky, J., & Saunders, S. (2002). *The supply and demand of special education teachers*. Gainesville, FL: Center for Personnel Studies in Special Education.

Townsend, B. L. (2000, Spring). The disproportionate discipline of African American learners: Reducing school suspensions and expulsions. *Exceptional Children, 66*, 381–391.

Townsend, B. L., & Patton, J. M. (2001). The discourse on ethics, power, and privilege and African American learners: Guest editors' post notes. *Teacher Education and Special Education, 24*, 48–49.

U.S. Department of Education. (1998). *The twentieth annual report to Congress on the implementation of the Individuals with Disabilities Education Act*. Washington, DC: U.S. Government Printing Office.

U.S. Department of Education. (1999). *Assistance to states for the education of children with disabilities program and the early intervention program for infants and toddlers with disabilities: final regulations*. Federal Register, 34, CRF Parts 300 and 303.

U.S. Department of Education (2001). *Twenty-third annual report to Congress on the implementation of the Individuals with Disabilities Education Act*. Washington, DC: U.S. Government Printing Office.

United States General Accounting Office. (2001, January). *Report to the committees on appropriations, U.S. Senate and House of Representatives, student discipline, Individuals with Disabilities Act*. Washington, DC: General Accounting Office (GAO-01-210).

Wayzata Independent School District No. 284 v. A.C. No.00-2346 MN, (8th Cir. 2001).

West, J., & Hardman, M. L. (2003). Policy issues. In A. D.

McCray, H. Rieth, and P. T. Sindelar (Eds.), *Critical issues in special education: Access alternative and accountability.* Boston: Allyn and Bacon.

White, R., Algozzine, B., Audette, R., Marr, M. B., & Ellis, Jr., E. D. (2001, September). Unified discipline: A school-wide approach for managing problem behavior. *Intervention in School and Clinic, 37,* 3–8.

Williams, B. T. (2001). Ethical leadership in schools servicing African American children and youth. *Teacher Education and Special Education, 24,* 38–47.

Yell, M. L., Bradley, R., Katsiyannis, A., & Rozalski, M. E. (2000, April). Ensuring compliance with the discipline provisions of IDEA '97. *Journal of Special Education Leadership, 13,* 3–18.

Young, B. A. (2002). *Public high school dropouts and completers from common core of data: School years 1998–99 to 1999–2000.* NCES Report 2002–328. Washington, DC: U.S. Department of Education, OERI, NCES.

CHAPTER 2
INDIVIDUALIZED SPECIAL EDUCATIONAL PROGRAMS: PLANNING AND DELIVERING SERVICES

Henri de Toulouse-Lautrec

Art Institute of Chicago. (1999). *Henri de Toulouse-Lautrec.* [On-line]. Available: www.artic.edu

Denvir, B. (1991). *Toulouse-Lautrec.* London: Thames and Hudson.

Perruchot, H. (1962). *Toulouse-Lautrec.* New York: Collier Books.

Special Education Services

Ahearn, E. (2002, April). Due process hearings: 2001 Update. *Quick Turn Around.* Alexandria, VA: Project Forum at NASDSE.

American Youth Policy Forum and Center on Educational Policy (2002). *Twenty-five years of educating children with disabilities: The good news and the work ahead.* Washington, DC: Authors.

Bloom, L., & Bacon, E. (1995). Using portfolios for individual learning and assessment. *Teacher Education and Special Education, 18,* 1–9.

Bradley, R., Danielson, L. & Hallahan, D. P. (Eds.). (2002). *Identification of learning disabilities: Research to practice.* Mahwah, NJ: Erlbaum.

Cartledge, G., Kea, C. D., & Ida, D. J. (2000, January/February). Anticipating differences—celebrating strengths: Providing culturally competent services for students with serious emotional disturbance. *Teaching Exceptional Children, 32,* 30–37.

Commission on the Education of the Deaf. (1988). *Toward equality: Education of the deaf.* Washington, DC: U.S. Government Printing Office.

Cook, B. G. (2001). A comparison of teachers' attitudes toward their included students with mild and severe disabilities. *Journal of Special Education, 34,* 203–213.

Cook, B. G., Tankersley, M., Cook, L., & Landrum, T. J. (2000). Teachers' attitudes toward their included students with disabilities. *Exceptional Children, 67,* 115–135.

Crockett, J. B. (1999–2000). Viable alternatives for students with disabilities: Exploring the origins and interpretations of LRE. *Exceptionality, 8,* 43–60.

Curran, C. M., & Harris, M. B. (1996). *Uses and purposes of portfolio assessment for general and special educators.* Albuquerque: University of New Mexico.

Deno, E. (1970). Special education as developmental capital. *Exceptional Children, 37,* 229–237.

Deshler, D. (2001). SIM to the rescue? Maybe. . . maybe not! *Stratenotes, 9,* 1–4.

Elliott, S. N., Kratochwill, T. R., & Schulte, A. G. (1998). The assessment accommodation checklist. *Teaching Exceptional Children, 31,* 10–14.

Fennick, E. (2001). Coteaching: An inclusive curriculum for transition. *Teaching Exceptional Children, 33,* 60–66.

Fitzsimmons, M. K. (1998, November). *Functional behavior assessment and behavior intervention plans.* ERIC/OSEP Digest, EDO-EC-98-9. Reston, VA: ERIC Clearinghouse on Disabilities and Gifted Education, Council for Exceptional Children.

Fox, N. E., & Ysseldyke, J. E. (1997). Implementing inclusion at the middle school level: Lessons from a negative example. *Exceptional Children, 64,* 81–98.

Friend, M. (2000, May/June). Myths and misunderstandings about professional collaboration. *Remedial and Special Education, 21,* 130–132, 160.

Fuchs, L. S., & Deno, S. L. (1994). Must instructionally useful performance assessment be based in the curriculum? *Exceptional Children, 61,* 15–24.

Fuchs, L. S., & Fuchs, D. (1998). Treatment validity: A unifying concept for reconceptualizing the identification of learning disabilities. *Learning Disabilities Research & Practice, 13,* 204–219.

Hall, L. J., & McGregor, J. A. (2000). A follow-up study of the peer relationships of children with disabilities in an inclusive school. *Journal of Special Education, 34,* 114–126, 153.

Hanson, M. J., Horn, E., Sandall, S., Beckman, P., Morgan, M., Marquart, J., Barnwell, D., & Chou, H-Y. (2001). After preschool inclusion: Children's educational pathways over the early school years. *Exceptional Children, 68,* 65–83.

Hébert, T. P. (2001). Jermaine: A critical case study of a gifted Black child living in rural poverty. *Gifted Child Quarterly, 45,* 85–103.

Horner, R. H. (1994). Functional assessment: Contributions and future directions. *Journal of Applied Behavior Analysis, 27,* 401–404.

Hughes, M. T., Valle-Riestra, D. M., & Arguelles, M. E. (2002). Experiences of Latino families with their child's special education program. *Multicultural Perspectives, 4,* 11–17.

Hunt, P., & Goetz, L. (1997). Research on inclusive educational programs, practices, and outcomes for students with severe disabilities. *Journal of Special Education, 31,* 3–29.

Johnson, R. C. (2001, Spring/Summer). High stakes testing and deaf students: Some research perspectives. *Research at Gallaudet,* pp. 1–6.

Kennedy, C. H., Shukla, S., & Fryxell, D., (1997). Comparing the effects of educational placement on the social relationships of intermediate school students with severe disabilities. *Exceptional Children, 64,* 31–47.

Keogh, B. K. (1988). Perspectives on the regular education initiative. *Learning Disabilities Focus, 4,* 3–5.

King-Sears, M. E. (2001, November). Three steps for gaining access to the general education curriculum for learners with disabilities. *Intervention in School and Clinic, 37,* 67–76.

Klingner, J. K., Vaughn, S., Schumm, J. S., Cohen, P., & Forgan, J. W. (1998). Inclusion or pull-out: Which do students prefer? *Journal of Learning Disabilities, 31,* 148–158.

Landau, J. K., Vohs, J. R., & Romano, C. (1998). *Statewide assessment: Policy issues, questions, and strategies.* Boston: The Federation for Children with Special Needs.

Lanford, A. D., & Cary, L. G. (2000, May/June). Graduation requirements for students with disabilities. *Remedial and Special Education, 21,* 152–160.

Larson, P. J., & Maag, J. W. (1998). Applying functional assessment in general education classrooms: Issues and recommendations. *Remedial and Special Education, 19,* 338–349.

Lovitt, T. C., Plavins, M., & Cushing, S. (1999). What do pupils with disabilities have to say about their experience in high school? *Remedial and Special Education, 20,* 67–76, 83.

MacMillan, D., & Forness, S. R. (1998). The role of IQ in special education placement decisions: Primary and determinative or peripheral and inconsequential? *Remedial and Special Education, 19,* 239–253.

Moody, S. W., Vaughn, S., Hughes, M. T., & Fischer, M. (2000). Reading instruction in the resource room: Set up for failure. *Exceptional Children, 66,* 305–316.

National Center on Education, Disability, and Juvenile Justice. (2002). Monograph series on education, disability and juvenile justice. Retrieved July 13, 2002, from http://www.edjj.org/monographs/index.html

Office of Special Education Programs. (2000). High school graduation. *Twenty-second annual report to Congress on the implementation of the Individuals with Disabilities Education Act,* (pp. IV-15 to IV-21). Washington, DC: U.S. Department of Education.

Padeliadu, S., & Zigmond, N. (1996). Perspectives of students with learning disabilities about special education placement. *Learning Disabilities Research and Practice, 11,* 15–23.

Palmer, D. S., Fuller, K., Arora, T., & Nelson, M. (2001). Taking sides: Parent views on inclusion for their children with severe disabilities. *Exceptional Children, 67,* 467–484.

Project Forum. (1999, February). *Issue: Linkage of the IEP to the general education curriculum. Quick Turn Around.* Washington, DC: NASDSE.

Rea, P. J., McLaughlin, V. L., & Walther-Thomas, C. (2002). Outcomes for students with disabilities in inclusive and pull-out programs. *Exceptional Children 68,* 203–222.

Rose, L. C., & Gallup, A. M. (1998, September). The 30th annual Phi Delta Kappa/Gallup poll of the public's attitudes toward the public schools. *Phi Delta Kappan,* pp. 41–56.

Sailor, W. (1991). Special education in the restructured school. *Remedial and Special Education, 12,* 8–22.

Salend, S. J. (1998). Using portfolios to assess student performance. *Teaching Exceptional Children, 31,* 36–43.

Salend, S. J., & Duhaney, J. M. G. (1999). The impact of inclusion on students with and without disabilities and their educators. *Remedial and Special Education, 20,* 114–126.

Smith, D. D. (1988). No more noses to the glass: A response. *Exceptional Children, 54,* 476.

Smith, P. D., Gast, D. L., Logan, K. R., & Jacobs, H. A. (2001). Customizing instruction to maximize functional outcomes for students with profound disabilities. *Exceptionality, 9,* 135–145.

Smith, R., Salend, S., & Ryan, S. (2001). Closing or opening the special education curtain. *Teaching Exceptional Children, 33,* 18–23.

Snell, M. E. (1988). Gartner and Lipsky's "Beyond special education: Toward a quality system for all students": Messages to TASH. *Journal of the Association for Persons with Severe Handicaps, 13,* 137–140.

Stainback, S., Stainback, W., East, K., & Sapon-Shevin, M. (1994). A commentary on inclusion and the development of a positive self-identity by people with disabilities. *Exceptional Children, 60,* 486–490.

Thurlow, M. L. (1998). *Assessment: A key component of education reform.* Boston: The Federation for Children with Special Needs.

Turnbull, III, H. R., Turnbull, A., Shank, M., Smith, S., & Leal, D. (2002). *Exceptional Lives: Special education in today's schools* (3rd ed.). Upper Saddle River, NJ: Prentice-Hall.

U.S. Department of Education. (1999). Assistance to states for the education of children with disabilities program and the early intervention program for infants and toddlers with disabilities; final regulations. *Federal Register, 34,* CRF Parts 300 and 303.

U.S. Department of Education (2001). *The twenty-third annual report to Congress on the implementation of IDEA.* Washington, DC: U.S. Government Printing Office.

Vanderwood, M., McGrew, K. S., & Ysseldyke, J. E. (1998). Why we can't say much about students with disabilities during education reform. *Exceptional Children, 64,* 359–370.

VanEtten, S. (1998). *The participation of students with disabilities in large-scale assessments.* Unpublished doctoral dissertation, University of New Mexico, Albuquerque.

Vaughn, S., Elbaum, B., & Boardman, A. G. (2001). The social function of students with learning disabilities: Implications for inclusion. *Exceptionality, 9,* 47–65.

Vaughn, S., & Schumm, J. S. (1995). Responsible inclusion for students with learning disabilities. *Journal of Learning Disabilities, 28,* 264–290.

Welch, M., Richards, G., Okada, R., Richards, J., & Prescott, S. (1995). A consultation and paraprofessional pull-in system of service delivery. *Remedial and Special Education, 16,* 16–28.

Williams, B. T., & Katsiyannis, A. (1998, January). The 1997 IDEA amendments: Implications for school principals. *NASSP Bulletin, 82,* 12–18.

Yell, M. L., & Shriner, J. G. (1997, September). The IDEA amendments of 1997: Implications for special and general education teachers, administrators, and teacher trainers. *Focus on Exceptional Children, 30,* 1–19.

Ziegler, D. (2002, April). *Reauthorization of the Elementary and Secondary Education Act: No Child Left Behind Act of 2001.* Arlington, VA: The Council for Exceptional Children, Public Policy Unit.

Individualized Special Education Programs

Algozzine, B., Ysseldyke, J. E., & Christenson, S. (1983). An analysis of the incidence of special class placement: The masses are burgeoning. *Journal of Special Education, 17,* 141–147.

Bateman, B., & Linden, M. A. (1998). *Better IEPs: How to develop legally correct and educationally useful programs* (3rd ed.). Longmont, CO: Sopris West.

Bear, G. G. (1999). *Interim alternative educational settings: Related research and program considerations.* Alexandria, VA: National Association of State Directors of Special Education (NASDSE).

Blalock, G. (1996). Community transition teams as the foundation for transition services for youth with learning disabilities. *Journal of Learning Disabilities, 29,* 148–159.

Clark, G. M. (1996). Transition planning assessment for secondary-level students with learning disabilities. *Journal of Learning Disabilities, 29,* 79–92.

Council for Exceptional Children (CEC). (1999). *IEP Team Guide.* Reston, VA: Author.

Finn, Jr., C. E., Rotherham, A. J., & Hokanson, Jr., C. R. (Eds.).

(2001). *Rethinking special education for a new century.* Washington, DC: Thomas B. Fordham Foundation and the Progressive Policy Institute.

Hasazi, S. B., Furney, K. S., & Destefano, L. (1999). Implementing the IDEA transition mandates. *Exceptional Children, 65,* 555–566.

Katsiyannis, A., & Maag, J. W. (1998). Disciplining students with disabilities: Issues and considerations for implementing IDEA '97. *Behavioral Disorders, 23,* 276–289.

Kroth, R. (1990). *A report of the referral and identification rate of students in the Albuquerque public schools.* Unpublished manuscript, University of New Mexico, Albuquerque.

Lehmann, J. P., Bassett, D. S., & Sands, D. J. (1999). Students' participation in transition-related actions: A qualitative study. *Remedial and Special Education, 20,* 160–169.

Lovitt, T. C., Cushing, S. S., & Stump, C. (1994). High school students rate their IEPs: Low opinions and lack of ownership. *Intervention in School and Clinic, 30,* 34–37.

Lovitt, T. C., Plavins, M., & Cushing, S. (1999). What do pupils with disabilities have to say about their experience in high school? *Remedial and Special Education, 20,* 67–76, 83.

NICHCY (1998, June). The IDEA Amendments of 1997 (Special Issue). *News Digest, 26,* 1–39.

Patton, J. R., & Blalock, G. (1996). *Transition and students with learning disabilities: Facilitating the movement from school to adult life.* Austin, TX: Pro-Ed.

Patton, J. R., Cronin, M. E., & Jairrels, V. (1997). Curricular implications of transition: Life skills instruction as an integral part of transition education. *Remedial and Special Education, 18,* 294–306.

Pautier, N. F. (1995, April 6). Area high schools flunk in attempt to teach learning disabled. *University Week,* p. 5.

Sands, D. J. (1999). *Best practices in transition: What school professionals can do to promote high student participation in transition services.* Denver: Technology and Special Services Division, College of Education, University of Colorado at Denver.

U.S. Department of Education. (1999). Assistance to states for the education of children with disabilities program and the early intervention program for infants and toddlers with disabilities; final regulations. *Federal Register, 34,* CRF Parts 300 and 303.

Voyles, L. (1999). Special focus issue: A primer on IDEA 1997 and its regulations. *CEC Today, 5,* 1–12.

CHAPTER 3
MULTICULTURAL AND BILINGUAL SPECIAL EDUCATION

Michael Naranjo

Plimpton, G. (1993). *Chronicles of courage: Very special artists.* New York: Random House.

Introduction

Goode, T. (2002, August). *Cultural competence.* Presentation to National Council on Disability, Cultural Diversity Committee. Washington, DC.

Multicultural and Bilingual Special EducationDefined

Amos, R. L. (1997). A review of psychological and educational assessment of Northern American Indian/Alaska Native children. *Rural Special Education Quarterly, 16,* 33–43.

Artiles, A. J., Harry, B., Reschly, D. J., & Chinn, P. C. (2002).

Over-identification of students of color in special education: A critical overview. *Multicultural Perspectives, 4,* 3–10.

Baca, L. M. (1998). The diversity of America's schoolchildren. In R. Tharp, *Teaching alive,* CD Rom. Santa Cruz, CA: The Center for Research on Education, Diversity and Excellence, University of California, Santa Cruz.

Baca, L. M., & Cervantes, H. T. (Eds.). (1998). *The bilingual special education interface* (3rd ed.). Columbus, OH: Merrill.

Bessent Byrd, H. B. (2000, November). Effective provision of educational services to Latino-American children with special needs and gifts. *Multiple Voices, 4,* 54–58.

Campbell, L., Campbell, B., & Dickinson, D. (1999). *Teaching and learning through multiple intelligences* (2nd ed.). Boston: Allyn and Bacon.

Children's Defense Fund (CDF) (2001). *The state of America's children.* Washington, DC: Children's Defense Fund.

Cuccaro, K. (1996, April 3). Teacher observations key in bilingual assessment. *Special Education Report, 22,* 1, 3.

Escamilla, K. (1999, Spring). The false dichotomy between ESL and transitional bilingual education programs: Issues that challenge all of us. *Educational Considerations, 26,* 1–5.

Ford, D. Y., Harris III, J. J., Tyson, C. A., & Trotman, M. F. (2002). Beyond deficit thinking: Providing access for gifted African American students. *Roeper Review, 24,* 52–58.

Gardner, H. (1983). *Frames of mind: The theory of multiple intelligences.* New York: Basic Books.

Gersten, R., & Baker, S. (2000). *Topical summary: Practices for English language learners.* Eugene, OR: National Institute for Urban School Improvement.

Gollnick, D. M., & Chinn, P. C. (2002). *Multicultural education in a pluralistic society* (6th ed.). Columbus, OH: Merrill.

Goode, T. (2002 August). *Cultural competence.* Presentation to National Council on Disability, Cultural Diversity Committee. Washington, DC.

Hébert, T. P., & Beardsley, T. M. (2001). Jermaine: A critical case study of a gifted Black child living in rural poverty. *Gifted Child Quarterly, 45,* 85–103.

Kagan, S., & Kagan, M. (1998). *Multiple intelligences: The complete MI book.* San Clemente, CA: Kagan Cooperative Learning.

Krause, M. (1992). Testimony to the Select Senate Committee on Indian Affairs on S. 2044, *Native American Languages Act of 1991,* to assist Native Americans in assuring the survival and continuing vitality of their languages, pp. 16–18.

Maker, C. J., Nielson, A. B., & Rogers, J. A. (1994). Giftedness, diversity and problem solving. *Teaching Exceptional Children, 27,* 4–18.

National Center for Educational Statistics (NCES). (1997). *Enrollment in public elementary and secondary schools, by race or ethnicity and state: Fall 1986 and fall 1995.* Washington, DC: NCES, Common Core of Data survey.

National Research Council (2002). *Minority students in special education and gifted education.* Committee on Minority Representation in Special Education. M. Suzanne Donovan and Christoper T. Cross, editors. Washington, DC: National Academy Press.

Ochoa, S. H., Robles-Pina, R., Garcia, S. B., & Breunig, N. (1999). School psychologists' perspectives on referrals of language minority students. *Multiple Voices, 3,* 1–14.

Ortiz, A. A. & Yates, J. R. (2001, November). A framework for serving English language learners with disabilities. *Journal of Special Education, 14,* 72–80.

Ortiz, A. A. (1997). Learning disabilities occurring concomitantly with linguistic differences. *Journal of Learning Disabilities, 30,* 321–332.

Patton, J. M. (1998). The disproportionate representation of African Americans in special education: Looking behind the curtain for understanding and solutions. *Journal of Special Education, 32*, 25–31.

Patton, J. M., & Baytops, J. L. (1995). Identifying and transforming the potential of young gifted African Americans: A clarion call for action. In B. A. Ford, F. E. Obiakor, and J. M. Patton (Eds.), *Effective education of African American exceptional learners: New perspectives* (pp. 27–68). Austin, TX: Pro-Ed.

Reschly, D. J. (2002). Minority overrepresentation: The silent contributor to LD prevalence and diagnostic confusion. In Bradley, R., Danielson, L., & Hallahan, D. P. (Eds.) *Identification of learning disabilities: Research to practice* (pp. 361–368). Mahwah, NJ: Erlbaum.

Reschly, D. J., Tilly, III, W. D., & Grimes, J. P. (Eds.). (1999). *Functional and noncategorical identification and intervention in special education.* Longmont, CO: Sopris West.

Rueda, R., Artiles, A. J., Salazar, J., & Higareda, I. (in press). An analysis of special education as a response to the diminished academic achievement of Chicano/Latino students: An update. In R. Valencia (Ed.), *Chicano school failure and success: Research and policy agendas* (2nd ed.). London: Routledge/Falmer Press.

Rueda, R., & Garcia, E. (1997). Do portfolios make a difference for diverse students? The influence of type of data on making instructional decisions. *Learning Disabilities Research & Practice, 12*, 114–122.

Rogers-Dulan, J. (1998). Religious connectedness among urban African American families who have a child with disabilities. *Mental Retardation, 36*, 91–103.

Sparks, S. 2000. Classroom and curriculum accommodations for Native American students. *Intervention in School and Clinic, 35*, 259–263.

Thurlow, M. L. & Liu, K. K. (2001, November). Can "all" really mean students with disabilities who have limited English proficiency? *Journal of Special Education, 14*, 63–71.

Tiedt, P. L., & Tiedt, I. M. (1999). *Multicultural teaching: A handbook of activities, information, and resources* (5th ed.). Boston: Allyn and Bacon.

Tomlinson, C. A., Callahan, C. M., & Lelli, K. M. (1998). Challenging expectations: Case studies of high-potential, culturally diverse young children. *Gifted Child Quarterly, 41*, 5–17.

Tyler, N. T., Lopez-Reyna, N., & Yzquierdo, Z. (2002). Diversifying the special education workforce. Gainesville, FL: University of Florida, COPSSE.

Winzer, M. A., & Mazurek, K. (1998). *Special education in multicultural contexts.* Columbus, OH: Merrill.

History of the Field

Baca, L. M., & Cervantes, H. T. (Eds.). (1984). *The bilingual special education interface.* Columbus, OH: Merrill.

Banks, J. A. (1994). *An introduction to multicultural education.* Boston: Allyn and Bacon.

Bransford, L., Baca, L., & Lane, K. (Eds.). (1974). Special issue: Cultural diversity. *Exceptional Children, 40.*

Diana v. State Board of Education, No. C-70-37 Rfp (N.D. Calif. 1970).

Dunn, L. M. (1968). Special education for the mildly retarded: Is much of it justifiable? *Exceptional Children, 35*, 5–22.

Gollnick, D. M., & Chinn, P. C. (1983). *Multicultural education in a pluralistic society.* New York: Macmillan.

Gonzales, E. (1989). Issues in the assessment of minorities. In H. L. Swanson and B. Watson (Eds.), *Educational and psychological assessment of exceptional children: Theories, strategies, and applications* (pp. 383–402). Columbus, OH: Merrill.

Larry P. v. Riles, Civil Action No. C-70-37 (N.D. Calif. 1971).

Lau v. Nichols, 414 U.S. 563 (1974).

Mercer, J. R., & Lewis, J. F. (1978). *System of multicultural pluralistic assessment: Student assessment manual.* New York: Psychological Corporation.

Phyler v. Doe, 102 S. Ct. 2382 (1982).

President's Committee on Mental Retardation. (1970). *The six hour retarded child.* Washington, DC: U.S. Government Printing Office.

Prevalence

Baca, L. M. (1998). The diversity of America's schoolchildren. In R. Tharp, *Teaching alive,* CD Rom. Santa Cruz, CA: The Center for Research on Education, Diversity and Excellence, University of California, Santa Cruz.

Bernal, E. M. (2000). Three ways to achieve a more equitable representation of culturally and linguistically different students in GT programs. *Roeper Review, 24*, 82–88.

Burnette, J. (2000, Fall). Improving results for culturally and linguistically diverse students. *Research Connections in Special Education, 7*, 1–2.

Children's Defense Fund (CDF). (2001). *The state of America's children.* Washington, DC: Children's Defense Fund.

Chinn, P. (2002). *Changing demographics in America.* Nashville, TN: Vanderbilt University, Alliance Project Course Enhancement Materials Series.

Ford, D. Y., Howard, R. C., Harris III, J. J., & Tyson, C. A. (2000). Creating culturally responsive classrooms for gifted African American students. *Journal for the Education of the Gifted, 23*, 397–427.

Harry, B. (1994). *The disproportionate representation of minority students in special education: Theories and recommendations.* Alexandria, VA: National Association of State Directors of Special Education.

MacMillan, D. L., Gresham, F. M., & Bocian, K. M. (1998). Discrepancy between definitions of learning disabilities and school practices: An empirical investigation. *Journal of Learning Disabilities, 31*, 314–326.

Mathews, R. (2000, November). Cultural patterns of South Asian and Southeast Asian Americans. *Intervention in School and Clinic, 36*, 101–104.

National Center for Educational Statistics (NCES). (1997). *Enrollment in public elementary and secondary schools, by race or ethnicity and state: Fall 1986 and fall 1995.* Washington, DC: NCES, Common Core of Data survey.

Reschly, D. J., Tilly III, W. D., & Grimes, J. P. (Eds.) (1999). *Functional and noncategorical identification and intervention in special education.* Longmont, CO: Sopris West.

Rueda, R., Artiles, A. J., Salazar, J., & Higareda, I. (in press). An analysis of special education as a response to the diminished academic achievement of Chicano/Latino students: An update. In R. Valencia (Ed.), *Chicano school failure and success: Research and policy agendas* (2nd ed.). London: Routledge/Falmer Press.

U.S. Census Bureau. (2000). *Race and Hispanic or Latino: 2000.* Retrieved August 20, 2002, from http://www.factfinder.census.gov/servlet/GCTTable?_ts=47898019790.

U.S. Department of Education (2001). *Twenty-third annual report to Congress on the implementation of the Individuals with Disabilities Education Act.* Washington, DC: U.S. Government Printing Office.

Yates, J. R., Hill, J. L., & Hill, E. G. (February 2002). "A vision for change" but for who?: A "personal" response to the National Research Council report. *DDEL News, 11*, 4–5.

Causes and Prevention

Artiles, A. J. (2002). Culture in learning: The next frontier in reading difficulties research. In R. Bradley, L. Danielson, & D. P. Hallahan (Eds.), *Identification of learning disabilities: Research to policy.* Hillsdale, NJ: Erlbaum.

Artiles, A. J., & Harry, B. (2002). Addressing minority student over-representation in special education. Research to Practice Brief. Washington, DC: Center for Effective Collaboration and Practice.

Artiles, A. J., Harry, B., Reschly, D. J., & Chinn, P. C. (2002). Over-identification of students of color in special education: A critical overview. *Multicultural Perspectives, 4,* 3–10.

Artiles, A. J., Trent, S. C., Hoffman-Kipp, P., & Lopez-Torres, L. (2000, March/April). From individual acquisition to cultural-historical practices in multicultural teacher education. *Remedial and Special Education, 21,* 79–89.

Artiles, A. J., & Zamora-Duran, G. (Eds.). (1997). *Reducing disproportionate representation of culturally diverse students in special and gifted education.* Reston, VA: Council for Exceptional Children.

Bessent Byrd, H. B. (2000). Effective provision of educational services to Latino-American children with special needs and gifts. *Multiple Voices, 4,* 54–58.

Castellano, J. A., & Díaz, E. I. (Eds.). (2002). *Reaching new horizons: Gifted and talented education for culturally and linguistically diverse students.* Boston: Allyn and Bacon.

Cheng, L. L. (Ed.). (1995). *Integrating language and learning for inclusion: An Asian-Pacific focus.* San Diego: Singular Publishing Group.

Children's Defense Fund (CDF) (2001). *The state of America's children.* Washington, DC: Children's Defense Fund.

Escamilla, K. (1999, Spring). The false dichotomy between ESL and transitional bilingual education programs: Issues that challenge all of us. *Educational Considerations, 26,* 1–5.

Ford, D. Y., & Harris III, J. J. (2000, September). A framework for infusing multicultural curriculum into gifted education. *Roeper Review, 23,* 4–10.

Ford, D. Y., Harris III, J. J., Tyson, C. A., & Trotman, M. F. (2002). Beyond deficit thinking: Providing access for gifted African American students. *Roeper Review, 24,* 52–58.

Gollnick, D. M., & Chinn, P. C. (2002). *Multicultural education in a pluralistic society* (6th ed.). Columbus, OH: Merrill.

Harry, B. (1992). Restructuring the participation of African-American parents in special education. *Exceptional Children, 59,* 123–131.

Henning-Stout, M. (1996). "Que Podemos Hacer?": Roles for school psychologists with Mexican and Latino migrant children and families. *School Psychology Review, 25,* 152–164.

Holman, L. J. (1997). Working effectively with Hispanic immigrant families. *Phi Delta Kappan, 78,* 647–649.

Ingersoll, R. (2001). *Teacher turnover, teacher shortages, and the organization of schools.* Seattle, WA: University of Washington, Center for the Study of Teaching and Policy.

Jairrels, V., Brazil, N., & Patton, J. R. (1999). Incorporating popular literature into the curriculum for diverse learners. *Intervention in School and Clinic, 34,* 303–306.

Kea, C. D., & Utley, C. A. (1998). To teach me is to know me. *Journal of Special Education, 32,* 44–47.

Kozol, J. (1991). *Savage inequalities: Children in America's schools.* New York: Crown.

Kozol, J. (1995). *Amazing grace: The lives of children and the conscience of a nation.* New York: Crown.

Lynch, E. W., & Hanson, M. J. (1998). *Developing cross-cultural competence: A guide for working with young children and their families* (2nd ed.). Baltimore: Brookes.

Markowitz, J. (Ed.). (1999). Education of children with disabilities who are homeless. *Proceedings of Project FORUM convened April 5–7, 1999,* 1–24. Alexandria, VA: NASDSE.

Montgomery, W. (2001, March/April). Creating culturally responsive, inclusive classrooms. *Teaching Exceptional Children 33,* 4–9.

Neal, L. I., McCray, A. D., & Webb-Johnson, G. (2001, January). Teachers' reactions to African American students' movement styles, pp. 168–174.

Obiakor, F. E., & Utley, C. A. (1997). Rethinking preservice preparation for teachers in the learning disabilities field: Workable multicultural strategies. *Learning Disabilities Research & Practice, 12,* 100–106.

Reed, S., & Sautter, R. C. (1990, June). Children of poverty: Kappan special report. *Phi Delta Kappan, 71,* K1–K12.

Rueda, R., Artiles, A. J., Salazar, J., & Higareda, I. (in press). An analysis of special education as a response to the diminished academic achievement of Chicano/Latino students: An update. In R. Valencia (Ed.) *Chicano school failure and success: Research and policy agendas* (2nd ed.). London: Routledge/Falmer Press.

Sileo, R. W., & Prater, M. A. (1998). Preparing professionals for partnerships with parents of students with disabilities: Textbook considerations regarding cultural diversity. *Exceptional Children, 64,* 513–528.

Tyler, N. T., Lopez-Reyna, N., & Yzquierdo, Z. (2002). Diversifying the special education workforce. Gainesville, FL: University of Florida, COPSSE.

U.S. Department of Education. (1998). *Twentieth annual report to Congress on the implementation of the Individuals with Disabilities Education Act.* Washington, DC: U.S. Government Printing Office.

Voltz, D. (1998). Cultural diversity and special education teacher preparation: Critical issues confronting the field. *Teacher Education and Special Education, 21,* 63–70.

Walther-Thomas, C., Korinek, L., McLaughlin, V. L., & Williams, B. T. (1996). Improving educational opportunities for students with disabilities who are homeless. *Journal of Children and Poverty, 2,* 57–75.

Yates, J. R., Hill, J. L. & Hill, E. G. (2002, February). "A vision for change" but for who?: A "personal" response to the national research council report. *DDEL News, 11,* 4–5.

Zima, B. T., Forness, S. R., Bussing, R., & Benjamin, B. (1998). Homeless children in emergency shelters: Need for prereferral intervention and potential eligibility for special education. *Behavioral Disorders, 23,* 98–110.

Characteristics

Artiles, A. J. (1998). The dilemma of difference: Enriching the disproportionality discourse with theory and context. *Journal of Special Education, 32,* 32–36.

Baca, L. M. (1998). The diversity of America's schoolchildren. In R. Tharp, *Teaching alive,* CD Rom. Santa Cruz, CA: The Center for Research on Education, Diversity and Excellence, University of California, Santa Cruz.

Brice, A., & Rosa-Lugo, L. I. (2000). Code switching: A bridge or barrier between two languages? *Multiple Voices, 4,* 1–9.

Cartledge, G. & Loe, S. A. (2001). Cultural diversity and social skill instruction. *Exceptionality, 9,* 33–46.

Cheng, L. L. (1999). Moving beyond accent: Social and cultural realities of living with many tongues. *Topics in Language Disorders, 19,* 1–10.

Cheng, L. L., & Chang, J. (1995). Asian/Pacific Islander students in need of effective services. In L. L. Cheng (Ed.), *Integrating language and learning for inclusion: An Asian-Pacific focus* (pp. 3–59). San Diego, CA: Singular Publishing Group.

Cummins, J. (1984). *Bilingualism and special education: Issues in assessment and pedagogy.* San Diego, CA: College-Hill.

Hosp, J. L. & Reschly, D. J. (2002, Winter). Predictors of restrictiveness of placement for African-American and Caucasian students. *Exceptional Children, 68,* 225–238.

Krause, M. (1992). Testimony to the Select Senate Committee on Indian Affairs on S. 2044, *Native American Languages Act of 1991,* to assist Native Americans in assuring the survival and continuing vitality of their languages, pp. 16–18.

Neal, L. I., McCray, A. D., & Webb-Johnson, G. (2001, January). Teachers' reactions to African American students' movement styles, pp. 168–174.

Obiakor, F. E. (1994). *The eight-step multicultural approach: Learning and teaching with a smile.* Dubuque, IA: Kendall/Hunt.

Reid, R., Casat, C. D., Norton, H. J., Anastopoulos, A. D., & Temple, E. P. (2001, Winter). Using behavior rating scales for ADHD across ethnic groups: The IOWA Conners. *Journal of Emotional and Behavioral Disorders, 9,* 210–218.

Rivera, D. P., & Smith, D. D. (1997). *Teaching students with learning and behavior problems.* Boston: Allyn and Bacon.

Ruiz, N. (1995). The social construction of ability and disability: I. Profile types of Latino children identified as language learning disabled. *Journal of Learning Disabilities, 29,* 491–502.

Seymour, H. N., Abdulkarim, L., & Johnson, V. (1999). The Ebonics controversy: An educational and clinical dilemma. *Topics in Language Disorders, 19,* 66–77.

Sileo, T. W., Sileo, A. P., & Prater, M. A. (1996). Parent and professional partnerships in special education: Multicultural considerations. *Intervention in School and Clinic, 31,* 145–153.

Taylor, O. L. (1997). *Testimony of Orlando L. Taylor on the subject of "Ebonics" to the United States Senate Committee on Appropriations Subcommittee on Labor, Health and Human Services and Education.* Washington, DC: United States Senate.

Yzquierdo, Z. (2002). *Distinctions between language differences and language disorders.* Nashville, TN: Peabody College of Vanderbilt University, Department of Special Education.

Early Childhood Education

Currie, J., & Thomas, D. (1995). *Does Head Start make a difference?* Santa Monica: Rand.

King, E. W., Chipman, M., & Cruz-Janzen, M. (1994). *Educating young children in a diverse society.* Boston: Allyn and Bacon.

Kraft, S. G. (2001a, February). Study of EHS shows modest but significant impact for kids and families. *Early Childhood Report, 12,* 1.

Kraft, S. G. (2001b, February). HHS: Full early childhood inclusion maximizes kids' potential. *Early Childhood Report, 12,* 7.

Santos, R., Fowler, S., Corso, R., & Bruns, D. (2000). Acceptance, acknowledgement, and adaptability: Selecting culturally and linguistically appropriate early childhood materials. *Teaching Exceptional Children, 32,* 14–22.

Sexton, D., Lobman, M., Constans, T., Snyder, P., & Ernest, J. (1997). Early interventionists' perspectives of multicultural practices with African-American families. *Exceptional Children, 63,* 313–328.

Elementary Through High School

Artiles, A. J. (1998). The dilemma of difference: Enriching the disproportionality discourse with theory and context. *Journal of Special Education, 32,* 32–36.

Cheng, L. R. (1996). Beyond bilingualism: A quest for communication competence. *Topics in Language Disorders, 16,* 9–21.

Children's Defense Fund (CDF) (2001). *The state of America's children.* Washington, DC: Children's Defense Fund.

Collier, V. P. (1995). *Acquiring a second language for school. Directions in Language & Education.* Washington, DC: National Clearinghouse for Bilingual Education.

Cummins, J. (1984). *Bilingualism and special education: Issues in assessment and pedagogy.* San Diego, CA: College-Hill.

Escamilla, K. (1999, Spring). The false dichotomy between ESL and transitional bilingual education programs: Issues that challenge all of us. *Educational Considerations, 26,* 1–5.

Fletcher, T. V., Bos, C. S., & Johnson, L. M. (1999). Accommodating English language learners with language and learning disabilities in bilingual education classrooms. *Learning Disabilities Research & Practice, 14,* 80–91.

Gersten, R., Brengilman, S., & Jimenez, R. (1994). Effective instruction for culturally and linguistically diverse students: A reconceptualization. *Focus on Exceptional Children, 27,* 12–16.

Gersten, R., & Baker, S. (2000). *Topical summary: Practices for English language learners.* Eugene, OR: National Institute for Urban School Improvement.

Gunn, B., Biglan, A., Smolkowski, K., & Ary, D. (2000). The efficacy of supplemental instruction in decoding skills for Hispanic and non-Hispanic students in early elementary school. *Journal of Special Education, 34,* 90–103.

Harvey, W. B. 2001. *Minorities in Higher Education: 2000–2001.* Washington, DC: American Council on Education.

Johnson Santamaria, T., Fletcher, T., & Bos, C. (2002). Effective pedagogy for English language learners in inclusive classrooms. In A. J. Artiles, & A. Ortiz (Eds.), *English Language Learners with special needs: Identification, placement, and instruction.* Washington DC: Center for Applied Linguistics.

Klinger, J. & Vaughn, S. (1996). Reciprocal teaching of reading comprehension strategies for students with learning disabilities who use English as a second language. *Elementary School Journal, 96,* 275–293.

Lemberger, N. (1996). Factors affecting language development from the perspectives of four bilingual teachers. *Journal of Educational Issues of Language Minority Students, 18,* 17–34.

Lessow-Hurley, J. (2000). *The foundations of dual language instruction.* New York: Longman.

Lopez-Reyna, N. A. (1997). The relation of interactions and story quality among Mexican American and Anglo American students with learning disabilities. *Exceptionality, 7,* 245–261.

Lyons, J. (1998, August). *Bilingual education.* Presentation at the BUENO Center and Alliance Project Conference on Language Diversity, Vail, CO.

McLaughlin, M. J., Pullin, D., & Artiles, A. J. (2001, November). Challenges for transformation of special education in the 21st century: Rethinking culture in school reform. *Journal of Special Education Leadership, 14,* 51–62.

Obiakor, F. E. (2001, November). Transforming teaching and learning to improve minority student achievement in inclusive settings. *Journal of Special Education Leadership, 14,* 81–88.

Ortiz, A. A. & Yates, J. R. (2001). A framework for serving English language learners with disabilities. *Journal of Special Education, 14,* 72–80.

Palinscar, A. S., & Brown, A. L. (1987). Reciprocal teaching of comprehension-fostering and comprehension-monitoring activities. *Cognition and Instruction, 1,* 117–175.

Reiss, J. (2001). *ESOL Strategies for teaching content: Facilitating instruction for English language learners.* Columbus, OH: Merrill/Prentice-Hall.

Rueda, R., Artiles, A. J., Salazar, J., & Higareda, I. (in press). An analysis of special education as a response to the diminished academic achievement of Chicano/Latino students: An update. In R. Valencia (Ed.), *Chicano school failure and success: Research and policy agendas* (2nd ed.). London: Routledge/Falmer Press.

Thurlow, M. L. & Liu, K. K. (2001, November). Can "all" really mean students with disabilities who have limited English proficiency? *Journal of Special Education, 14,* 63–71.

Collaboration for Inclusion

Garcia, E. E., (2001). *Hispanic Education in the United States.* New York: Rowman & Littlefield.

Hoff, D. (Ed.). (1995, June 15). New York City special ed suit targets preschoolers. *Special Education Reports, 21,* 2–3.

Rogers-Dulan, J. (1998). Religious connectedness among urban African American families who have a child with disabilities. *Mental Retardation, 36,* 91–103.

Thorp, E. K. (1997). Increasing opportunities for partnership with culturally and linguistically diverse families. *Intervention in School and Clinic, 32,* 261–269.

Vraniak, D. (1998, Summer). Developing systems of support with American Indian families of youth with disabilities. *Health Issues for Children & Youth & Their Families, 6,* 9–10.

Walther-Thomas, C., Korinek, L., McLaughlin, V. L., & Williams, B. T. (1996). Improving educational opportunities for students with disabilities who are homeless. *Journal of Children and Poverty, 2,* 57–75.

Transition Through Adulthood

Currie, J., & Thomas, D. (1995). *Does Head Start make a difference?* Santa Monica: Rand.

Harvey, W. B. 2001. *Minorities in Higher Education: 2000–2001.* Washington, DC: American Council on Education.

Pachon, H. P. (1998, October 15). . . . but the measure's flaws make it hard to implement. *Los Angeles Times,* p. A–2.

U.S. Department of Education (2001). *Twenty-third annual report to Congress on the implementation of the Individuals with Disabilities Education Act.* Washington, DC: U.S. Government Printing Office.

Families

Bailey, Jr., D. B., Skinner, D., Rodriguez, P., Gut, D., & Correa, V. (1999). Awareness, use, and satisfaction with services for Latino parents of young children with disabilities. *Exceptional Children, 65,* 367–381.

Garcia, E. E., (2001). *Hispanic education in the United States.* New York: Rowman & Littlefield.

Harry, B. (1992). Restructuring the participation of African-American parents in special education. *Exceptional Children, 59,* 123–131.

Holman, L. J. (1997). Working effectively with Hispanic immigrant families. *Phi Delta Kappan, 78,* 647–649.

Hughes, M. T., Valle-Riestra, D. M., & Arguelles, M.E. (2002). Experiences of latino families with their child's special educa-

tion program. *Multicultural Perspectives, 4,* 11–17.

Kraft, S. G. (2001, February). Study of EHS shows modest but significant impact for kids and families. *Early Childhood Report, 12,* 1.

Linan-Thompson, S., & Jean, R. E. (1997). Completing the parent participation puzzle: Accepting diversity. *Teaching Exceptional Children, 30,* 46–50.

Little, L. (1998, Summer). Toward a more diverse cultural community. *Early Developments, 2,* 8–9.

Milian, M. (1999). Schools and family involvement: Attitudes among Latinos who have children with visual impairments. *Journal of Visual Impairment & Blindness, 93,* 277–290.

Parette, H. P. & Petch-Hogan, B. (2000, November/December). Approaching families: Facilitating culturally/linguistically diverse family involvement. *Teaching Exceptional Children, 33,* 4–10.

Prater, L. P., & Tanner, M. P. (1995). Collaboration with families: An imperative for managing problem behaviors. In F. E. Obiakor & R. Algozzine (Eds.), *Managing problem behaviors: Perspectives for general and special educators* (pp. 178–206). Dubuque, IA: Kendall/Hunt.

Rao, A. (2001). Put to the test. *Perspectives: Research, scholarship, and Creative Activity at Ohio University, 5,* 18–21.

Rogers-Dulan, J. (1998). Religious connectedness among urban African American families who have a child with disabilities. *Mental Retardation, 36,* 91–103.

Thorp, E. K. (1997). Increasing opportunities for partnership with culturally and linguistically diverse families. *Intervention in School and Clinic, 32,* 261–269.

Vraniak, D. (1998, Summer). Developing systems of support with American Indian families of youth with disabilities. *Health Issues for Children & Youth & Their Families, 6,* 9–10.

Voltz, D. (1994). Developing collaborative parent–teacher relationships with culturally diverse parents. *Intervention in School and Clinic, 29,* 288–291.

CHAPTER 4
LEARNING DISABILITIES

Edouard Manet

Bolton, L. (1989). *Manet: The history and times of great masters.* Secaucus, NJ: Chartwell.

Fuchs, D., Fuchs, L. S., Mathes, P. G., Lipsey, M. W., & Roberts, P. H. (2002). Is "learning disabilities" just a fancy term for low achievement? A meta-analysis of reading differences between low achievers with and without the label. In R. Bradley, L. Danielson, & D.P. Hallahan (Eds.), *Identification of learning disabilities: Research to practice.* Mahwah, NJ: Erlbaum.

Schneider, P., & the Editors of Time-Life Books (1968). *The world of Manet: 1832-1883.* New York: Time-Life Books.

Learning Disabilities Defined

American Psychiatric Association. (1994). *Diagnostic and statistical manual of mental disorders* (4th ed.) (DSM-IV). Washington, DC: American Psychiatric Association.

Bevilacqua, S. (2002, May 3). Racial disparity: Reduce LD population regardless of IDEA reforms to come. *The Special Educator, 17,* 1, 6.

Blair, C., & Scott, K. G. (2002). Proportion of LD placements associated with low socioeconomic status: Evidence for a gradient? *Journal of Special Education, 36,* 14–22.

Bonafina, M. A., Newcorn, J. H., McKay, K. E., Koda, V. H., &

Halperin, J. M. (2000, May/June). ADHD and reading disabilities: A cluster analytic approach for distinguishing subgroups. *Journal of Learning Disabilities, 33*, 297–307.

Bryant, D. P., Bryant, B. R., & Hammill, D. D. (2000, March/April). Characteristic behaviors of students with LD who have teacher-identified math weakness. *Journal of Learning Disabilities, 33*, 168–177, 199.

Bryant, D. P., Vaughn, S., Linan-Thompson, S., Ugel, N., Hamff, A., & Hougen, M. (2000, Fall). Reading outcomes for students with and without reading disabilities in general education middle-school content area classes. *Learning Disability Quarterly, 23*, 238–252.

Cannon, L. (1998, March/April). To promote or to retain: NJCLD Responds. *LDA Newsbriefs, 33*, 1.

Compton, D. (2002). The relationships among phonological processing, orthographic processing, and lexical development in children with reading disabilities. *Journal of Special Education, 35*, 201–210.

Elksnin, L. K., Bryant, D. P., Gartland, D., King-Sears, M., Rosenberg, M. S., Scanlon, D., Stronider, R., & Wilson, R. (2001, Fall). LD summit: Important issues for the field of learning disabilities. *Learning Disability Quarterly, 24*, 297–305.

Finn, Jr., C. E., Rotherham, A. J., & Hokanson, Jr., C. R. (Eds.). (2001). *Rethinking special education for a new century.* Washington, DC: Thomas B. Fordham Foundation and the Progressive Policy Institute.

Fletcher, J. M., Lyon, G. R., Barnes, M., Stuebing, K. K., Francis, D. J., Olson, R. K., Shaywitz, S. E., & Shaywitz, B. A. (2002). Classifications of learning disabilities: An evidence-based evaluation. In R. Bradley, L. Danielson, & D. P. Hallahan (Eds.), *Identification of learning disabilities: Research to practice* (pp. 185–250). Mahwah, NJ: Erlbaum.

Fuchs, D. (2002, July 17). *Identification of students with LD: From IQ-achievement discrepancy to response-to-treatment.* Paper presented at Kansas University's Center for Research on Learning International SIM Trainers Conference, Lawrence, KS.

Fuchs, L. S., & Fuchs, D. (2001). Principles for the prevention and intervention of mathematics difficulties. *Learning Disabilities Research & Practice, 16*, 85–95.

Fuchs, L. S., Fuchs, D., Hamlett, C. L., & Appleton, A. C. (2002, May). Explicitly teaching for transfer: Effects on the mathematical problem-solving performance of students with mathematical disabilities. Learning Disabilities Research & Practice, 17, 90–106.

Fuchs, D., Fuchs, L. S., Mathes, P. G., Lipsey, M. W., & Roberts, P. H. (2002). Is "learning disabilities" just a fancy term for low achievement? A meta-analysis of reading differences between low achievers with and without the label. In R. Bradley, L. Danielson, & D. P. Hallahan (Eds.), *Identification of learning disabilities: Research to practice* (pp. 747–762). Mahwah, NJ: Erlbaum.

Fuchs, D., Fuchs, L. S., Thompson, A., Al Otaiba, S., Yen, L., Yang, N. J., Svenson, E., & Braun, M. (2002). Exploring the importance of reading programs for kindergarteners with disabilities in mainstream classrooms. *Exceptional Children, 68*, 295–311.

Gerber, M. M. (1999–2000). An appreciation of learning disabilities: The value of blue-green algae. *Exceptional Children, 8*, 29–42.

Graham, S., Harris, K. R., & Larsen, L. (2001). Prevention and intervention of writing difficulties for students with learning disabilities. *Learning Disabilities Research & Practice, 16*, 74–84.

Gregg, N., & Mather, N. (2002, February). School is fun at recess: Informal analyses of written language for students with learning disabilities. *Journal of Learning Disabilities, 35*, 7–22.

Gresham, F. (1991). Conceptualizing behavior disorders in terms of resistance to intervention. *School Psychology Review, 20*, 23–36.

Gresham, F. (2002). Responsiveness to intervention: An alternative approach to the identification of learning disabilities. In R. Bradley, L. Danielson, & D. P. Hallahan (Eds.), *Identification of learning disabilities: Research to practice* (pp. 467–519). Mahwah, NJ: Erlbaum.

Jenkins, J. R., & O'Connor, R. E. (2002). Early identification and intervention for young children with reading/learning disabilities. In R. Bradley, L. Danielson, & D.P. Hallahan (Eds.), *Identification of learning disabilities: Research to practice* (pp. 99–149). Mahwah, NJ: Erlbaum.

Jitendra, A. (2002, March/April). Teaching students math problem-solving through graphic representations. *Teaching Exceptional Children, 34*, 34–38.

Kaplan, B. J., Crawford, S. G., Dewey, D. M., & Fisher, G. C. (2000, September/October). The I.Q.s of Children with ADHD are normally distributed. *Journal of Learning Disabilities, 33*, 425–432.

Kavale, K. A. (2002). Discrepancy models in the identification of learning disability. In R. Bradley, L. Danielson, & D.P. Hallahan (Eds.), *Identification of learning disabilities: Research to practice* (pp. 369–426). Mahwah, NJ: Erlbaum.

Kavale, K. A., & Forness, S. R. (2000, May/June). What definitions of learning disability say and don't say. *Journal of Learning Disabilities, 33*, 239–256.

King, P. (1998, June 15). Politics of promotion: An old idea—keeping kids back—is hot again. *Newsweek*, p. 27.

Learning Disability Summit. (2001, November 29, 30). *Consensus report.* Lawrence, KS: University of Kansas.

Lester, G., & Kelman, M. (1997). State disparities in the diagnosis and placement of pupils with learning disabilities. *Journal of Learning Disabilities, 30*, 599–607.

Lyon, G. R, Fletcher, J. M., Shaywitz, S. E., Shaywitz, B. A., Torgesen, J. K., Wood, F. B., Schulte, A., & Olson, R. (2001). Rethinking learning disabilities. In C. E. Finn, A. J. Rotherham, & C. R. Hokansan (Eds.), *Rethinking special education for a new century* (pp. 259–288). Washington DC: Thomas B. Fordham Foundation and the Progressive Policy Institute.

MacMillan, D. L., Gresham, F. M., & Bocian, K. M. (1998). Discrepancy between definitions of learning disabilities and school practices: An empirical investigation. *Journal of Learning Disabilities, 31*, 314–326.

MacMillan, D. L., & Siperstein, G. N. (2002). Learning disabilities as operationally defined by schools. In R. Bradley, L. Danielson, & D. P. Hallahan (Eds.), *Identification of learning disabilities: Research to practice* (pp. 287–333). Mahwah, NJ: Erlbaum.

Mayes, S. D., Calhoun, S. L., & Crowell, E. W. (2000, September/October). Learning disabilities and ADHD: Overlapping spectrum disorders. *Journal of Learning Disabilities, 33*, 417–424.

McMasters, K., Fuchs, D., Fuchs, L., & Compton, D.L. (2000). Monitoring the academic progress of children who are unresponsive to generally effective early reading intervention. *Assessment for Effective Intervention, 27*, 23–33.

Miller, L. L., & Felton, R. H. (2001). "It's one of them. . . I don't know": Case study of a student with phonological, rapid naming, and word-finding deficits. *Journal of Special Education, 35*, 125–133.

National Joint Committee on Learning Disabilities (NJCLD). (1994). *Collective perspectives on issues affecting learning disabilities*. Austin, TX: Pro-Ed.

Pisecco, S., Baker, D. B., Silva, P. A., & Brooke, M. (2001, March/April). Boys with reading disabilities and/or ADHD: Distinctions in early childhood. *Journal of Learning Disabilities, 34*, 98–106.

Robinson, C. S., Menchetti, B. M., & Torgesen, J. K. (2002, May). Toward a two-factor theory of one type of mathematics disabilities. *Learning Disabilities Research & Practice, 17*, 81–89.

Schrag, J. A. (2000, October). Discrepancy approaches for identifying learning disabilities. *Quick Turn Around*, pp. 1–11.

Scruggs, T. E., & Mastropieri, M. A. (2002). On babies and bathwater: Addressing the problems of identification of learning disabilities. *Learning Disability Quarterly, 25*, 155–169.

Torgesen, J. K. (2002). Empirical and theoretical support for direct diagnosis of learning disabilities by assessment of intrinsic processing weaknesses. In R. Bradley, L. Danielson, & D. P. Hallahan (Eds.), *Identification of learning disabilities: Research to practice*. Mahwah, NJ: Erlbaum.

U.S. Department of Education. (1999). *Assistance to states for the education of children with disabilities program and the early intervention program for infants and toddlers with disabilities: Final regulations*. Federal Register, 34, CRF Parts 300 and 303.

U.S. Department of Education (2001). *The annual report to Congress on the implementation of IDEA*. Washington, DC: U.S. Government Printing Office.

Willcutt, E. G., & Pennington, B. F. (2000, March/April). Comorbidity of reading disability and attention-deficit/hyperactivity disorder: Differences by gender and subtype. *Journal of Learning Disabilities, 33*, 179–191.

History of the Field

Hallahan, D. P., & Mercer, C. D. (2002). Learning disabilities: Historical perspectives. In R. Bradley, L. Danielson, & D. P. Hallahan (Eds.), *Identification of learning disabilities: Research to practice* (pp. 1–67). Mahwah, NJ: Erlbaum.

Hammill, D., & Larsen, S. (1974). The effectiveness of psycholinguistic abilities. *Exceptional Children, 41*, 5–14.

Wiederholt, J. L. (1974). Historical perspectives on the education of the learning disabled. In L. Mann and D. Sabatino (Eds.), *The second review of special education* (pp. 103–152). Philadelphia: Journal of Special Education Press.

Prevalence

Chambers, J. G., Parrish, T., & Harr, J. J. (2002, March). *What are we spending on special education services in the United States, 1999-2000? Advance report #1*. American Institutes for Research: Special Education Expenditure Project (SEEP).

Finn, Jr., C. E., Rotherham, A. J., & Hokanson, Jr., C. R. (Eds.). (2001). *Rethinking special education for a new century*. Washington, DC: Thomas B. Fordham Foundation and the Progressive Policy Institute.

MacMillan, D. L., Gresham, F. M., & Bocian, K. M. (1998). Discrepancy between definitions of learning disabilities and school practices: An empirical investigation. *Journal of Learning Disabilities, 31*, 314–326.

Reschly, D. J. (2002). Minority overrepresentation: The silent contributor to LD prevalence and diagnostic confusion. In R. Bradley, L. Danielson, & D. P. Hallahan (Eds.), *Identification of learning disabilities: Research to practice* (pp. 361–368). Mahwah, NJ: Erlbaum.

U.S. Department of Education (2000). *The twenty-second annual report to Congress on the implementation of IDEA*. Washington, DC: U.S. Government Printing Office.

U.S. Department of Education (2001). *The twenty-third annual report to Congress on the implementation of IDEA*. Washington, DC: U.S. Government Printing Office.

Causes and Prevention

Bakken, J. P., & Whedon, C. K. (2002). Teaching text structure to improve reading comprehension. *Intervention in School and Clinic, 37*, 229–233.

Bender, W. (2001). *Learning disabilities: Characteristics, identification, and teaching strategies* (4th ed.). Boston: Allyn and Bacon.

Blair, C., & Scott, K. G. (2002). Proportion of LD placements associated with low socioeconomic status: Evidence for a gradient? *Journal of Special Education, 36*, 14–22.

Compton, D. (2002). The relationships among phonological processing, orthographic processing, and lexical development in children with reading disabilities. *Journal of Special Education, 35*, 201–210.

Decker, S. N., & Defries, J. C. (1980). Cognitive abilities in families of reading disabled children. *Journal of Learning Disabilities, 13*, 517–522.

Decker, S. N., & Defries, J. C. (1981). Cognitive ability profiles in families of reading disabled children. *Developmental Medicine and Child Neurology, 23*, 217–227.

Fuchs, L. S., & Fuchs, D. (2001). Principles for the prevention and intervention of mathematics difficulties. *Learning Disabilities Research & Practice, 16*, 85–95.

Gilger, J. W. (2001, December). Current issues in the neurology and genetics of learning-related traits and disorders: Introduction to the special issue. *Journal of Learning Disabilities, 34*, 490–491.

Graham, S., Harris, K. R., & Larsen, L. (2001). Prevention and intervention of writing difficulties for students with learning disabilities. *Learning Disabilities Research & Practice, 16*, 74–84.

Raskind, W. H. (2001). Current understanding of the genetic basis of reading and spelling disability. *Learning Disability Quarterly, 24*, 141–157.

Richards, T. L. (2001). Functional magnetic resonance imaging and spectroscopic imaging of the brain: Application of fMRI and fMRS to reading disabilities and education. *Learning Disability Quarterly, 24*, 189–203.

Smith, S. D., Kelley, P. M., Askew, J. W., Hoover, D. M., Deffenbacher, K. E., & Gayan, J. (2001, November/December). Reading disability and chromosome 6921.3: Evaluation of MOG as a candidate gene. *Journal of Learning Disabilities, 34*, 512–519.

Torgesen, J. K., & Wagner, R. K. (1998). Alternative diagnostic approaches for specific developmental reading disabilities. *Learning Disabilities Research & Practice, 13*, 220–232.

Wetherby, A. M. (2002). Communication disorders in infants, toddlers, and preschool children. In G. H. Shames and N. B. Anderson (Eds.), *Human communication disorders: An introduction* (6th ed, pp. 186–217). Boston: Allyn and Bacon.

Wood, F. B., & Grigorenko, E. L. (2001). Emerging issues in the genetics of dyslexia: A methodological preview. *Journal of Learning Disabilities, 34*, 503–511.

Characteristics

Bryan, T. (1997). Assessing the personal and social status of students with learning disabilities. *Learning Disabilities*

Research & Practice, 12, 63–76.

Brigham, R., & Brigham, M. (2001, Summer). A focus on mnemonic instruction. *Current Practice Alerts, 5*, 1–4.

Carlson, C. L., Booth, J. E., Shin, M., & Canu, W. H. (2002). Parent-, teacher-, and self-rated motivational styles in ADHD subtypes. *Journal of Learning Disabilities, 35*, 104–113.

Deshler, D. D., Schumaker, J. B., Lenz, B. K., Bulgren, J. A., Hock, M. F., Knight, J., & Ehren, B. J. (2001). Ensuring content-area learning by secondary students with learning disabilities. *Learning Disabilities Research & Practice, 16*, 96–108.

Dev, P. C. (1997). Intrinsic motivation and academic achievement: What does their relationship imply for the classroom teacher? *Remedial and Special Education, 18*, 12–19.

Dimitrovsky, L., Spector, H., & Levy-Shiff, R. (2000, September/October). Stimulus gender and emotional difficulty level: Their effect on recognition of facial expressions of affect in children with and without LD. *Journal of Learning Disabilities, 33*, 410–416.

Donahue, M. L. (1997). Beliefs about listening in students with learning disabilities: "Is the speaker always right?" *Topics in Language Disorders, 17*, 41–61.

Elliott, S. N., Malecki, C. K., & Demaray, M. K. (2001). New directions in social skills assessment and intervention for elementary and middle school students. *Exceptionality, 9*, 19–32.

Ellis, E. S. (1986). The role of motivation and pedagogy on the generalization of cognitive strategy training. *Journal of Learning Disabilities, 19*, 66–70.

Fuchs, D., & Fuchs, L. S. (1998). Researchers and teachers working together to adapt instruction for diverse learnings. *Learning Disabilities Research & Practice, 13*, 126–137.

Fuchs, L. S., Fuchs, D., Hamlett, C. L., & Appleton, A. C. (2002, May). Explicitly teaching for transfer: Effects on the mathematical problem-solving performance of students with mathematical disabilities. *Learning Disabilities Research & Practice, 17*, 90–106.

Fulk, B. M. (1996). The effects of combined strategy and attribution training on LD adolescents' spelling performance. *Exceptionality, 6*, 13–17.

Gresham, F. M., MacMillan, D. L., & Bocian, K. M. (1996). Learning disabilities, low achievement, and mild mental retardation: More alike than different? *Journal of Learning Disabilities, 29*, 570–581.

Gresham, F. M., Sugai, G., & Horner, R. H. (2001, Spring). Interpreting outcomes of social skills training for students with high-incidence disabilities. *Exceptional Children, 67*, 331–344.

Haager, D., & Vaughn, S. (1995). Parent, teacher, peer, and self-reports of the social competence of students with learning disabilities. *Journal of Learning Disabilities, 28*, 205–231.

Harris, K. R., & Graham, S. (1999). Programmatic intervention research: Illustrations from the evolution of self-regulated strategy development. *Learning Disability Quarterly, 22*, 251–262.

Hock, M. (1997, June). Student motivation and commitment: A cornerstone of strategy instruction. *Strategram, 9*, 1–2.

Kavale, K. A., & Forness, S. R. (1996). Social skill deficits and learning disabilities: A meta-analysis. *Journal of Learning Disabilities, 29*, 226–237.

Kuhne, M., & Wiener, J. (2000, Winter). Stability of social status of children with and without learning disabilities. *Learning Disability Quarterly, 23*, 64–75.

Lerner, J. (1993). *Learning disabilities: Theories, diagnosis, and teaching strategies* (6th ed.). Boston: Houghton Mifflin.

Le Mare, L., & de la Ronde, M. (2000, Winter). Links among social status, service delivery mode, and service delivery preference in LD, low-achieving, and normally achieving elementary-aged children. *Learning Disability Quarterly, 23*, 52–62.

Margalit, M. (1998). Loneliness and coherence among preschool children with learning disabilities. *Journal of Learning Disabilities, 31*, 173–180.

Mercer, C. D. (1997). *Students with learning disabilities* (5th ed.). Columbus, OH: Merrill.

Merrell, K.W. (2001). Assessment of children's social skills: Recent developments, best practices, and new directions. *Exceptionality, 9*, 3–18.

Pearl, R. (1982). LD children's attributions for success and failure: A replication with a labeled LD sample. *Learning Disabilities Quarterly, 5*, 173–176.

Ring, M. M., & Reetz, L. (2000). Modification effects on attributions of middle school students with learning disabilities. *Language Disabilities Research & Practice, 15*, 34–42.

Rivera, D. P., & Smith, D. D. (1997). *Teaching students with learning and behavior problems.* Boston: Allyn and Bacon.

Sexton, M., Harris, K. R., & Graham, S. (1998). Self-regulated strategy development and the writing process: Effects on essay writing and attributions. *Exceptional Children, 64*, 295–311.

Stormont-Spurgin, M. (1997). I lost my homework: Strategies for improving organization in students with ADHD. *Intervention in School and Clinic, 32*, 270–274.

Switzky, H. N., & Schultz, G. F. (1988). Intrinsic motivation and learning performance: Implications for individual educational programming for learners with mild handicaps. *Remedial and Special Education, 9*, 7–14.

Torgesen, J. K., & Licht, B. G. (1983). The learning disabled child as an inactive learner: Retrospect and prospects. In J. D. McKinney and F. Feagan (Eds.), *Current topics in learning disabilities* (Vol. 1, pp. 3–31). Norwood, NJ: Ablex.

Tur-Kaspa, H., Weisel, A., & Segev, L. (1998). Attributions for feelings of loneliness of students with learning disabilities. *Learning Disabilities Research & Practice, 13*, 89–94.

Vaughn, S., Elbaum, B., & Boardman, A. G. (2001). The social function of students with learning disabilities: Implications for inclusion. *Exceptionality, 9*, 47–65.

Wiener, J., & Sunohara, G. (1998). Parents' perceptions of the quality of friendship of their children with learning disabilities. *Learning Disabilities Research & Practice, 13*, 242–257.

Early Childhood Education

Blair, C., & Scott, K. G. (2002). Proportion of LD placements associated with low socioeconomic status: Evidence for a gradient? *Journal of Special Education, 36*, 14–22.

Dickinson, D. K., & McCabe, A. (2001). Bringing it all together: The multiple origins, skills, and environmental supports of early literacy. *Learning Disabilities Research & Practice, 16*, 186–202.

Fuchs, D., Fuchs, L. S., Thompson, A., Al Otaiba, S., Yen, L., Yang, N. J., Svenson, E., & Braun M. (2002). Exploring the importance of reading programs for kindergarteners with disabilities in mainstream classrooms. *Exceptional Children, 68*, 295–311.

Hammill, D. D., Mather, N., Allen, E. A., & Roberts, R. (2002, March/April). Using semantics, grammar, phonology, and rapid naming tasks to predict word identification. *Journal of Learning Disabilities, 35*, 121–136.

Jenkins, J. R., & O'Connor, R. E. (2002) Early identification and intervention for young children with reading/learning disabilities. In R. Bradley, L. Danielson, & D. P. Hallahan (Eds.),

Identification of learning disabilities: Research to practice (pp. 99–149). Mahwah, NJ: Erlbaum.

Katims, D. S. (1994). Emergence of literacy in preschool children with disabilities. *Learning Disabilities Quarterly, 17,* 58–69.

Learning Disability Summit. (2001, November 29, 30). *Consensus report.* Lawrence, KS: University of Kansas.

Lyon, G. R, Fletcher, J. M., Shaywitz, S. E., Shaywitz, B. A., Torgesen, J. K., Wood, F. B., Schulte, A., & Olson, R. (2001). Rethinking learning disabilities. In C. E. Finn, A. J. Rotherham, & C. R. Hokansan (Eds.), *Rethinking special education for a new century* (pp. 259–288). Washington DC: Thomas B. Fordham Foundation and the Progressive Policy Institute.

Miller, L. L., & Felton, R. H. (2001). "It's one of them. . . I don't know:" Case study of a student with phonological, rapid naming, and word-finding deficits. *Journal of Special Education, 35,* 125–133.

Paul, P. V. (2000, March/April). A few remarks on the development of early literacy. *Volta Voices,* 18–21.

Shames. G. H., & Anderson, N. B. (2002). *Human communication disorders: An introduction* (6th ed.). Boston: Allyn and Bacon.

Torgesen, J. K., & Wagner, R. K. (1998). Alternative diagnostic approaches for specific developmental reading disabilities. *Learning Disabilities Research & Practice, 13,* 220–232.

Torgesen, J. K., & Wagner, R. K., & Rashotte, C. A. (1994). Longitudinal studies of phonological processing and reading. *Journal of Learning Disabilities, 27,* 276–286.

Elementary Through High School

Bakken, J. P., Mastropieri, M. A., & Scruggs, T. E. (1997). Reading comprehension of expository science material and students with learning disabilities: A comparison of strategies. *Journal of Special Education, 31,* 300–324.

Biemiller, A., & Siegel, L. S. (1997). A longitudinal study of the effects of the Bridge reading program for children at risk for reading failure. *Learning Disabilities Quarterly, 20,* 83–92.

Brigham, R., & Brigham, M. (2001, Summer). A focus on mnemonic instruction. *Current Practice Alerts, 5,* 1–4.

Carnine, D., Silbert, J., and Kameenui, E. J. (1997). *Direct instruction reading* (3rd ed.). Columbus, OH: Merrill.

Deshler, D., & Roth, J. (2002, April). Strategic research: A summary of learning strategies and related research. *StrateNotes, 10,* 1–5.

Deshler, D. D., Schumaker, J. B., Lenz, B. K., Bulgren, J. A., Hock, M. F., Knight, J., & Ehren, B. J. (2001). Ensuring content-area learning by secondary students with learning disabilities. *Learning Disabilities Research & Practice, 16,* 96–108.

Ehri, L. C., Nunes, S. R., Willows, D. M., Schuster, B. V., Yaghoub, Z. Z., Shanahan, T. (2001). Phonic Awareness instruction helps children learn to read: Evidence from the national reading panel's meta-analysis. *Reading Research Quarterly, 36,* 250–287.

Foorman, B. R., & Torgesen, J. (2001). Critical elements of classroom and small-group instruction promote reading success in all children. *Learning Disabilities Research & Practice, 16,* 203–212.

Fowler, G. L. (1982). Developing comprehension skills in primary students through the use of story frames. *Reading Teacher, 36,* 176–179.

Fuchs, D. (2002, July 17). *Identification of students with LD: From IQ–achievement discrepancy to response-to-treatment.* Paper presented at Kansas University's Center for Research on Learning International SIM Trainers Conference, Lawrence, KS.

Hammill, D., & Larsen, S. (1974). The effectiveness of psycholinguistic abilities. *Exceptional Children, 41,* 5–14.

Hock, M. F. (2001, January). Strategy instruction and tutoring. *Strategram, 13,* 1–5.

Hoehn, T. P., & Baumeister, A. A. (1994). A critique of the application of sensory integration therapy to children with learning disabilities. *Journal of Learning Disabilities, 27,* 338–350.

Idol, L. (1987). Group story mapping: A comprehension strategy for both skilled and unskilled readers. *Journal of Learning Disabilities, 20,* 196–205.

Jenkins, J., & O'Connor, R. E. (2002). Early identification and intervention for young children with reading/learning disabilities. In R. Bradley, L. Danielson, & D. P. Hallahan (Eds.), *Identification of learning disabilities: Research to practice.* Mahwah, NJ: Erlbaum.

Katims, D. S., & Harmon, J. M. (2000, May). Strategic instruction in middle school social studies: Enhancing academics and literacy outcomes for at-risk students. *Intervention in School and Clinic, 35,* 280–289.

Lebzelter, S. M., & Nowacek, E. J. (1999). Reading strategies for secondary students with mild disabilities. *Intervention in School and Clinic, 34,* 212–219.

Lovitt, T. C. (2000). *Preventing school failure* (2nd ed.). Austin, TX: Pro-Ed.

Lyon, G. R., & Moats, L. C. (1997). Critical conceptual and methodological considerations in reading intervention research. *Journal of Learning Disabilities, 30,* 578–588.

Markell, M., A., & Deno, S. L. (1997). Effects of increasing oral reading: Generalization across reading tasks. *Journal of Special Education, 31,* 233–250.

Mather, N. (1992). Whole language reading instruction for students with learning disabilities: Caught in the cross fire. *Learning Disabilities Research & Practice, 7,* 87–95.

Mathes, P. G., & Babyak, A. E. (2001). The effects of peer-assisted literacy strategies for first-grade readers with and without additional mini-skills lessons. *Learning Disabilities Research & Practice, 16,* 28–44.

McCray, A. D, Vaughn, S., & Neal, L.V. I. (2001). Not all students learn to read by third grade: Middle school students speak out about their reading disabilities. *Journal of Special Education, 35,* 17–30.

McMaster, K. N., & Fuchs, D. (2002). Effects of cooperative learning on the academic achievement of students with learning disabilities: An update of Tateyama-Sniezek's review. *Learning Disabilities Research & Practice, 17,* 107–117.

Mercer, C. D., Campbell, K. U., Miller, M. D., Mercer, K. D., & Lane, H. B. (2000). Effects of a reading fluency intervention for middle schoolers with specific learning disabilities. *Learning Disabilities Research & Practice, 15,* 179–189.

Miller, L. L., & Felton, R. H. (2001). "It's one of them. . . I don't know:" Case study of a student with phonological, rapid naming, and word-finding deficits. *Journal of Special Education, 35,* 125–133.

Pressley, M., & Rankin, J. (1994). More about whole language methods of reading instruction for students at risk for early reading failure. *Learning Disabilities Research & Practice, 9,* 157–168.

Rashotte, C. A., MacPhee, K., & Torgesen, J. K. (2001, Spring). The effectiveness of a group reading instruction program with poor readers in multiple grades. *Learning Disability Quarterly, 24,* 119–134.

Slavin, R. E. (1996). Research on cooperative learning and achievement: What we know, what we need to know. *Contemporary Educational Psychology, 21,* 43–69.

Soltes, F. (2002, July 23). Making sense of "learning disabilities." *The Tennessean*, 4D.

Swanson, P. N., & De La Paz, S. (1998). Teaching effective comprehension strategies to students with learning and reading disabilities. *Intervention in School and Clinic, 33,* 209–218.

Swanson, H. L., & Sachse-Lee, C. (2000, March/April). A meta-analysis of single-subject-design intervention research for students with LD. *Journal of Learning Disabilities, 33,* 114–136.

Vadasy, P. F., Jenkins, J. R., & Pool, K. (2000, August). Effects of tutoring in phonological and early reading skills on students at risk for reading disabilities. *Journal of Learning Disabilities, 33,* 579–590.

Vaughn, S., Gersten, R., & Chard, D. J. (2000, Fall). The underlying message in LD intervention research: Findings from research syntheses. *Exceptional Children, 67,* 99–114.

Vaughn, S., Levy, S., Coleman, M., & Bos, C. S. (2002). Reading instruction for students with LD and EBD: A synthesis of observation studies. *Journal of Special Education, 36,* 2–13.

Williams, J. P. (1998). Improving the comprehension of disabled readers. *Annals of Dyslexia, 48,* 213–238.

Williams, J. P., Brown, L. G., Silverstein, A. K., and deCani, J. S. (1994). An instructional program in comprehension of narrative themes for adolescents with learning disabilities. *Learning Disability Quarterly, 17,* 205–221.

Collaboration for Inclusion

Deshler, D. D., Schumaker, J. B., Lenz, B. K., Bulgren, J. A., Hock, M. F., Knight, J., & Ehren, B. J. (2001). Ensuring content-area learning by secondary students with learning disabilities. *Learning Disabilities Research & Practice, 16,* 96–108.

Friend, M., & Bursuck, W. D. (2002). *Including students with special needs: A practical guide for classroom teachers* (3rd ed.). Boston: Allyn and Bacon.

Kauffman, J. (1999). Commentary: Today's special education and its message for tomorrow. *Journal of Special Education, 32,* 244–254.

Le Mare, L. & de la Ronde, M. (2000, Winter). Links among social status, service delivery mode, and service delivery preference in LD, low-achieving, and normally achieving elementary-aged children. *Learning Disability Quarterly, 23,* 52–62.

Moody, S. W., Vaughn, S., Hughes, M. T., & Fischer, M. (2000, Spring). Reading Instruction in the resource room: Setup for failure. *Exceptional Children, 66,* 305–316.

Vaughn, S., Elbaum, B., & Boardman, A. G. (2001). The social function of students with learning disabilities: Implications for inclusion. *Exceptionality, 9,* 47–65.

U.S. Department of Education (1991). *The thirteenth annual report to Congress on the implementation of IDEA.* Washington, DC: U.S. Government Printing Office.

U.S. Department of Education (2001). *The twenty-third annual report to Congress on the implementation of IDEA.* Washington, DC: U.S. Government Printing Office.

Transition Through Adulthood

Bourke, A. B., Strehorn, K. C., & Silver, P. (2000, January/February). Faculty members' provision of instructional accommodations to students with LD. *Journal of Learning Disabilities, 33,* 26–32.

Cannell, S. J. (1999, November 22). A writing fool. *Newsweek,* p. 79.

Dickinson, D. L., & Verbeek, R. L. (2002, April). Wage differentials between college graduates with and without learning disabilities. *Journal of Learning Disabilities, 35,* 175–184.

Greenberg, B. (2000, February 14). *Learning disabled advance in school.* Washington, DC: Associated Press.

Henderson, C. (1999). *College freshmen with disabilities. A biennial statistical profile: Statistical year 1998.* Washington, DC: American Council on Education, Heath Resource Center.

Henderson, C. (2001). *College freshmen with disabilities: A biennial statistical profile.* Washington, DC: American Council on Education, George Washington University Heath Resource Center.

Kihl, P., Gregersen, K., & Sterum, N. (2000, November/December). Hans Christian Andersen's spelling and syntax: Allegations of specific dyslexia are unfounded. *Journal of Learning Disabilities, 33,* 506–519.

Mooney, J., & Cole, D. (2000). *Learning outside the lines.* New York: Simon & Schuster.

Mull, C., Sitlington, P. L., & Alper, S. (2001, Fall). Postsecondary education for students with learning disabilities: A synthesis of literature. *Exceptional Children, 68,* 97–118.

National Center for Education Statistics. (2000, June). Postsecondary students with disabilities: Enrollment, services, and persistence. (NCES 2000–092). Washington, DC: U.S. Department of Education, Office of Educational Research and Improvement.

National Joint Committee on Learning Disabilities. (1999, Fall). Learning disabilities: Issues in higher education. *Learning Disability Quarterly, 22,* 263–266.

Shessel, I., & Reiff, H. B. (1999, Fall). Experiences of adults with learning disabilities: Positive and negative impacts and outcomes. *Learning Disability Quarterly, 22,* 305–316.

Simon, J. A. (2001, February). Legal issues in serving postsecondary students with disabilities. *Topics in Language Disorders, 21,* 1–16.

Taymans, J. M., & West, L. L. (2001, December). *Selecting a college for students with learning disabilities or attention deficit hyperactivity disorder (ADHD).* Washington, DC: George Washington University Heath Resource Center (ERIC EC Digest # E620).

Thomas, M. (2000, March/April). Albert Einstein and LD: An evaluation of the evidence. *Journal of Learning Disabilities, 33,* 149–157.

U.S. Department of Education (2001). *The annual report to Congress on the implementation of IDEA.* Washington, DC: U.S. Government Printing Office.

Wilson, A. M., & Lesaux, N. K. (2001, September/October). Persistence of phonological processing deficits in college students with dyslexia who have age-appropriate reading skills. *Journal of Learning Disabilities, 34,* 394–400.

Families

Bryan, T., & Sullivan-Burstein, K. (1998). Teacher-selected strategies for improving homework completion. *Remedial and Special Education, 19,* 263–275.

Bursuck, B., Montague, M., & Vaughn, S. (2001, Spring). Homework practices that support students with disabilities. *Research Connections in Special Education, 8,* 1–5.

Dettmer, P., Dyck, N., & Thurston, L. P. (2002). *Consultation, collaboration, and teamwork for students with special needs* (4th ed.). Boston, MA: Allyn and Bacon.

Epstein, M. H., Polloway, E. A., Buck, G. H., Bursuck, W. D., Wissinger, L. M., Whitehouse, F., & Jayanthi, M. (1997). Homework-related communication problems: Perspectives of general education teachers. *Learning Disabilities Research & Practice, 12,* 221–227.

Hughes, C. A., Ruhl, K. L., Schumaker, J. B., & Deshler, D. D.

(2002). Effects of instruction in an assignment completion strategy on the homework performance of students with learning disabilities in general education classes. *Learning Disabilities Research & Practice, 17,* 1–18.

Jayanthi, M., Bursuck, W., Epstein, M. H., & Polloway, E. A. (1997). Strategies for successful homework. *Teaching Exceptional Children, 30,* 4–7.

Kroth, R. L., & Edge, D. (1997). *Strategies for communicating with parents and families of exceptional children* (3rd ed.). Denver, CO: Love.

Nelson, J. S., Epstein, M. H., Bursuck, W. D., Jayanthi, M., & Sawyer, V. (1998). The preferences of middle school students for homework adaptions made by general education teachers. *Learning Disabilities Research & Practice, 13,* 109–117.

O'Shea, D. J., O'Shea, L. J., Algozzine, R. F., & Hammitte, D. J. (2001). *Families and teachers of individuals with disabilities: Collaborative orientations and responsive practices.* Boston, MA: Allyn and Bacon.

Technology

Boone, R., Higgins, K., & Williams, D. (1997). Computer-based multimedia and videodiscs: Uses in supporting content-area instruction for students with LD. *Intervention in School and Home, 32,* 302–311.

Bryant, D. P., & Bryant, B. R. (2003). *Assistive technology for people with disabilities.* Boston: Allyn and Bacon.

Graham, S., Harris, K. R., & Larsen, L. (2001). Prevention and intervention of writing difficulties for students with learning disabilities. *Learning Disabilities Research and Practice, 16,* 74–84.

Higgins, K., Boone, R., & Williams, D. L. (2000, November). Evaluating educational software for special education. *Intervention in School and Clinic, 36,* 109–115.

Kurzweil Educational Systems. (2002). *Kurzweil 3000 for Macintosh—read it.* Retrieved August 4, 2002, from http://www.kurzweiledu.com/k3000mac-readit.html

Lewis, R. B. (1998). Assistive technology and learning disabilities: Today's realities and tomorrow's promises. *Journal of Learning Disabilities, 31,* 16–54.

MacArthur, C. A. (2000, August). New tools for writing: Assistive technology for students with writing difficulties. *Topics in Language Disorders, 20,* 85–100.

Raskind, M. H., & Higgins, E. L. (1998). Assistive technology for post-secondary students with learning disabilities: An overview. *Journal of Learning Disabilities, 31,* 27–40.

CHAPTER 5
SPEECH OR LANGUAGE IMPAIRMENTS

Lewis Carroll

Hinde, T. (1991). *Lewis Carroll: Looking-glass letters.* New York: Rizzoli.

Introduction

Warren, S. F. (1999). *The transdisciplinary view of communication.* Personal communication.

Speech or Language Impairments Defined

Ball, E. W. (1997). Phonological awareness: Implications for

whole language and emergent literacy programs. *Topics in Language Disorders, 17,* 14–26.

Battle, D. (1996). Language learning and use by African American children. *Topics in Language Disorders, 16,* 22–37.

Berthal, J. E., & Bankson, N. W. (1998). *Articulation and phonological disorders* (4th ed.). Boston: Allyn and Bacon

Blank, M., Rose, S. A., & Berlin, L. J. (1978). *The language of learning: The preschool years.* New York: Grune & Stratton.

Conture, E. G. (2001). *Stuttering: Its nature, diagnosis, and treatment.* Boston: Allyn and Bacon.

Falk-Ross, F. C. (2002). *Classroom-based language and literacy intervention: A programs and case studies approach.* Boston: Allyn and Bacon.

Gonzalez, V., Brusca-Vega, R., & Yawkey, T. (1997). *Assessment and instruction of culturally and linguistically diverse students with or at-risk of learning problems.* Boston: Allyn and Bacon.

Hall, B. J., Oyer, H. J., & Haas, W. H. (2001). *Speech, language, and hearing disorders: A guide for the teacher.* Boston: Allyn and Bacon.

Langdon, H. W. (1999). Aiding preschool children with communication disorders from Mexican backgrounds: Challenges and solutions. In T. V. Fletcher and C. S. Bos (Eds.), *Helping individuals with disabilities and their families: Mexican and U.S. perspectives.* Tempe, AZ: Bilingual Review/Press.

Langdon, H. W., & Cheng, L.-R. L. (1992). *Hispanic children and adults with communication disorders.* Gaithersburg, MD: Aspen.

Leonard, L. (1994). Language disorders in preschool children. In G. H. Shames, E. H. Wiig, and W. A. Secord (Eds.), *Human communication disorders: An introduction* (4th ed., pp. 174–211). New York: Merrill.

Lessow-Hurley, J. (2000). *The foundations of dual language instruction* (3rd ed.). New York: Addison Wesley Longman.

Olswang, L. B., Coggins, T. E., & Timler, G. R. (2001, November). Outcome measures for school-age children with social communication problems. *Topics in Language Disorders, 21,* 50–73.

Owens, Jr., R. E. (2002). Development of communication, language, and speech. In G. H. Shames and N. B. Anderson (Eds.), *Human communication disorders: An introduction* (6th ed, pp. 28–69). Boston: Allyn and Bacon.

Payne, K. T., & Taylor, O. L. (2002). Multicultural influences on human communication. In G. H. Shames and N. B. Anderson (Eds.), *Human communication disorders: An introduction* (6th ed., pp. 106–140). Boston: Allyn and Bacon.

Plaschke, B. (2000, June 18). Look who's talking: Where others might have gotten stuck, Ron Harper showed stick-to-itiveness to overcome his stuttering. *Los Angeles Times,* pp. D11, D13.

Ramig, P. R., & Shames, G. H. (2002). Stuttering and other disorders of fluency. In G. H. Shames and N. B. Anderson (Eds.), *Human communication disorders: An introduction* (6th ed, pp. 258–302). Boston: Allyn and Bacon.

Ratner, N. B. (1995). Language complexity and stuttering in children. *Topics in Language Disorders, 15,* 32–47.

Ruiz, N. T. (1995). The social construction of ability and disability: I. Profile types of Latino children identified as language learning disabled. *Journal of Learning Disabilities, 28,* 476–490.

Sander, E. K. (1972). When are speech sounds learned? *Journal of Speech and Hearing Disorders, 37,* 62.

Small, L. H. (1999). *Fundamentals of phonetics: A practical *guide for students.* Boston: Allyn and Bacon.

Torgesen, J. K., & Wagner, R. K. (1998). Alternative diagnostic approaches for specific developmental reading disabilities. *Learning Disabilities Research & Practice, 13,* 220–232.

Utley, C. A., & Obiakor, F. E. (Eds.). (2001). *Special education, multicultural education, and school reform: Components of quality education for learners with mild disabilities.* Springfield, IL: Charles C Thomas.

van Keulen, J. E., Weddington, G. T., & DeBose, C. E. (1998). *Speech, language, learning and the African American child.* Boston: Allyn and Bacon.

Wetherby, A. M. (2002). Communication disorders in infants, toddlers, and preschool children. In G. H. Shames and N. B. Anderson (Eds.), *Human communication disorders: An introduction* (6th ed, pp. 186–217). Boston: Allyn and Bacon.

History of the Field

Moore, G. P., & Kester, D. (1953). Historical notes on speech correction in the preassociation era. *Journal of Speech and Hearing Disorders, 18,* 48–53.

Van Riper, C. (1981). An early history of ASHA. *ASHA, 23,* 855–858.

Van Riper, C., & Erickson, R. L. (1996). *Speech correction: An introduction to speech pathology and audiology* (9th ed.). Boston: Allyn and Bacon.

Prevalence

Bakken, J. P., & Whedon, C. K. (2002). Teaching text structure to improve reading comprehension. *Intervention in School and Clinic, 37,* 229–233.

Dublinski, S. (1981). Block grant proposal introduced: What does it mean? *Language, Speech, and Hearing Services in the Schools, 12,* 192–199.

Schoenbrodt, L., Kumin, L., & Sloan, J. M. (1997). Learning disabilities existing concomitantly with communication disorder. *Journal of Learning Disabilities, 30,* 264–281.

U.S. Department of Education. (2001). *Twenty-third annual report to Congress on the implementation of the Individuals with Disabilities Education Act.* Washington, DC: U.S. Government Printing Office.

Causes and Prevention

Children's Defense Fund (CDF). (1997). *Child immunizations hit all-time high.* Washington, DC: CDF Reports.

Hall, B. J., Oyer, H. J., & Haas, W. H. (2001). *Speech, language, and hearing disorders: A guide for the teacher.* Boston: Allyn and Bacon.

Harwood, L., Warren, S. F., & Yoder, P. (2002). The importance of responsivity in developing contingent exchanges with beginning communicators. In J. Reichle, D. R. Beukelman, & J. C. Light, (Eds.), *Exemplary practices for beginning communicators: Implications for ACC* (pp. 59–96). Baltimore: Paul H. Brookes.

Maugh, II, T. H. (1995, August 11). Study finds folic acid cuts risk of cleft palate. *Los Angeles Times,* p. A20.

McWilliams, B. J., & Witzel, M. A. (1998). Cleft palate. In G. H. Shames, E. H. Wiig, and W. A. Secord (Eds.), *Human communication disorders: An introduction* (5th ed., pp. 438–479). Boston: Allyn and Bacon.

Owens, Jr., R. E., Metz, D. E., & Haas, A. (2000). *Introduction to communication disorders: A life span perspective.* Boston: Allyn and Bacon.

Ramig, P. R., & Shames, G. H. (2002). Stuttering and other disorders of fluency. In G. H. Shames and N. B. Anderson (Eds.), *Human communication disorders: An introduction* (6th ed, pp. 258–302). Boston: Allyn and Bacon.

Roberts, J. E., & Zeisel, S. A. (2002). *Ear infections and language development.* Washington, DC: U.S. Department of Education and American Speech-Language-Hearing Association.

Utley, C. A., & Obiakor, F. E. (Eds.). (2001). *Special education, multicultural education, and school reform: Components of quality education for learners with mild disabilities.* Springfield, IL: Charles C Thomas.

Characteristics

Asher, S. R., & Gazelle, H. (1999). Loneliness, peer relationships, and language disorder in childhood. *Topics in Language Disorders, 19,* 16–33.

Bakken, J. P., & Whedon, C. K. (2002). Teaching text structure to improve reading comprehension. *Intervention in School and Clinic, 37,* 229–233.

Falk-Ross, F. C. (2002). *Classroom-based language and literacy intervention: A programs and case studies approach.* Boston: Allyn and Bacon.

Fujiki, M., Brinton, B., Hart, C. H., & Fitzgerald, A. H. (1999). Peer acceptance and friendship in children with specific language impairment. *Topics in Language Disorders, 19,* 34–48.

Lloyd, P. (1994). Referential communication: Assessment and intervention. *Topics in Language Disorders, 14,* 55–59.

Norris, J. A., & Hoffman, P. R. (2002, January). Phonemic awareness: A complex developmental process. *Topics in Language Disorders, 22,* 1–34.

Olswang, L. B., Coggins, T. E., & Timler, G. R. (2001, November). Outcome measures for school-age children with social communication problems. *Topics in Language Disorders, 21,* 50–73.

Ramig, P. R., & Shames, G. H. (2002). Stuttering and other disorders of fluency. In G. H. Shames and N. B. Anderson (Eds.), *Human communication disorders: An introduction* (6th ed, pp. 258–302). Boston: Allyn and Bacon.

Rice, M. L. (1997). Specific language impairments: In search of diagnostic markers and genetic contributions. *Mental Retardation and Developmental Disabilities, 3,* 350–357.

Snow, C. E., Scarborough, H. S., & Burns, M. S. (1999, November). What speech-language pathologists need to know about early reading. *Topics in Language Disorders, 20,* 48–58.

Van Riper, C., & Erickson, R. L. (1996). *Speech correction: An introduction to speech pathology and audiology* (9th ed.). Boston: Allyn and Bacon.

Wiig, E. H., & Secord, W. A. (1998). Language disabilities in school-age children and youth. In G. H. Shames, E. H. Wiig, and W. A. Secord (Eds.), *Human communication disorders: An introduction* (5th ed., pp. 185–226). Boston: Allyn and Bacon.

Early Childhood Education

Bailey, Jr., D. B., Aytch, L. S., Odom, S. L., Symons, F., & Wolery, M. (1999). Early intervention as we know it. *Mental Retardation and Developmental Disabilities Research Reviews, 5,* 11–20.

Clarke, J. (1996). Language development in children prenatally drug exposed: Consideration for assessment and intervention. *The Source, 6,* 12–14.

Crais, E. R., & Lorch, N. (1994). Oral narratives in school-age children. *Topics in Language Disorders, 14,* 13–28.

Education of the Handicapped. (1992, February 26). *Early intervention greatly reduces learning problems, study says.* Author, p. 7.

Falk-Ross, F. C. (2002). *Classroom-based language and literacy intervention: A programs and case studies approach.* Boston: Allyn and Bacon.

Flett, A., & Conderman, G. (2002, March). Promote phonemic awareness. *Intervention in School and Clinic, 37,* 242–245.

Hoffman, P. R. (1997). Phonological intervention within story-book reading. *Topics in Language Disorders, 17,* 69–88.

Kaiser, A. (2000). Teaching functional communication skills. In M. E. Snell and F. Brown (Eds.), *Instruction of students with severe disabilities* (5th ed.; pp. 453–492). Upper Saddle River, NJ: Merrill/Prentice-Hall.

Katims, D. S. (1994). Emergence of literacy in preschool children with disabilities. *Learning Disabilities Quarterly, 17,* 58–69.

Leonard, L. (1994). Language disorders in preschool children. In G. H. Shames, E. H. Wiig, and W. A. Secord (Eds.), *Human communication disorders: An introduction* (4th ed., pp. 174–211). New York: Merrill.

Lombardo, L. A. (1999, July). Children score higher on tests when child care meets standards. *Early Childhood Reports, 10,* 4.

Norris, J. A., & Hoffman, P. R. (2002, January). Phonemic awareness: A complex developmental process. *Topics in Language Disorders, 22,* 1–34.

Ostrosky, M. M., & Kaiser, A. P. (1991). Preschool classroom environments that promote communication. *Teaching Exceptional Children, 23,* 6–10.

Owens, Jr., R. E., & Robinson, L. A. (1997). Once upon a time: Use of children's literature in the preschool classroom. *Topics in Language Disorders, 17,* 19–48.

Plante, E., & Beeson, P. M. (1999). *Communication and communication disorders: A clinical introduction.* Boston: Allyn and Bacon.

Shames. G. H., & Anderson, N. B. (2002). *Human communication disorders: An introduction* (6th ed.). Boston: Allyn and Bacon.

Snow, C. E., Scarborough, H. S., & Burns, M. S. (1999, November). What speech-language pathologists need to know about early reading. *Topics in Language Disorders, 20,* 48–58.

Warren, S. F., Yoder, P. J., Gazden, G. E., Kim, K., & Jones, H. A. (1993). Facilitating prelinguistic communication skills in young children with developmental delay. *Journal of Speech and Hearing Research, 36,* 83–97.

Elementary Through High School

Ball, E. W. (1997). Phonological awareness: Implications for whole language and emergent literacy programs. *Topics in Language Disorders, 17,* 14–26.

Bos, C., & Anders, P. L. (1992). Using interactive teaching and learning strategies to promote text comprehension and content learning for students with learning disabilities. *International Journal of Disability, Development and Education, 39,* 225–238.

Castillo, L. C. (1998). The effect of analogy instruction on young children's metaphor comprehension. *Roeper Review, 21,* 27–31.

Cuda, R. A., & Nelson, N. (1976). *Analysis of teacher speaking rate, syntactic complexity and hesitation phenomena as a function of grade level.* Paper presented at the annual meeting of the American Speech-Language-Hearing Association, Houston. As reported in G. Wallach and K. Butler (Eds.). (1984). *Language learning disabilities in school-age children.* Baltimore: Williams & Wilkins.

Culatta, B., & Wiig, E. H. (2002). Language disabilities in school-age children and youth. In G. H. Shames and N. B. Anderson (Eds.), *Human communication disorders: An introduction* (6th ed, pp. 218–257). Boston: Allyn and Bacon.

Edmunds, A. L. (1999). Cognitive credit cards: Acquiring learning strategies. *Teaching Exceptional Children, 31,* 68–73.

Falk-Ross, F. C. (2002). *Classroom-based language and literacy intervention: A programs and case studies approach.* Boston: Allyn and Bacon.

Geluke, N., & Lovitt, T. C. (1992). *Conversations with general education teachers about their work with mainstreamed students.* Unpublished paper, High School Curriculum Project, University of Washington, Seattle.

Gruenewald, L., & Pollack, S. (1984). *Language interaction in teaching and learning.* Austin, TX: Pro-Ed.

Hudson, J. A., & Gillam, R. B. (1997). "Oh, I remember now!" Facilitating children's long term memory for events. *Topics in Language Disorders, 18,* 1–15.

LaBlance, G. R., Steckol, K. F., & Smith, V. L. (1994). Stuttering: The role of the classroom teacher. *Teaching Exceptional Children, 27,* 10–12.

Marvin, C. (1989). Language and learning. In D. D. Smith, *Teaching students with learning and behavior problems* (pp. 147–181). Englewood Cliffs, NJ: Prentice-Hall.

Naremore, R. C. (1997). Making it hang together: Children's use of mental frameworks to structure narratives. *Topics in Language Disorders, 18,* 16–31.

Owens, Jr., R. E. (2001). *Language disorders: A functional approach to assessment and intervention* (5th ed.). Columbus, OH: Merrill.

Pittleman, S. D., Heimlich, J. E., Berglund, R. L. & French, M. P. *Semantic Feature Analysis: Classroom Applications.* Newark, DE: International Reading Association.

Schoenbrodt, L., Kumin, L., & Sloan, J. M. (1997). Learning disabilities existing concomitantly with communication disorder. *Journal of Learning Disabilities, 30,* 264–281.

Snow, C. E., Scarborough, H. S., & Burns, M. S. (1999, November). What speech-language pathologists need to know about early reading. *Topics in Language Disorders, 20,* 48–58.

van Keulen, J. E., Weddington, G. T., & DeBose, C. E. (1998). *Speech, language, learning and the African American child.* Boston: Allyn and Bacon.

Watkins, R. V., & Rice, M. L. (Eds.). (1994). *Specific language impairments in children.* Baltimore: Paul H. Brookes.

Wetherby, A. M. (2002). Communication disorders in infants, toddlers, and preschool children. In G. H. Shames and N. B. Anderson (Eds.), *Human communication disorders: An introduction* (6th ed, pp. 186–217). Boston: Allyn and Bacon.

Collaboration for Inclusion

Apel, K., & Masterson, J. J. (2000, May). Postscript. *Topics in Language Disorders, 20,* 92.

Owens, Jr., R. E., & Robinson, L. A. (1997). Once upon a time: Use of children's literature in the preschool classroom. *Topics in Language Disorders, 17,* 19–48.

Norris, J. A. (1997). Functional language intervention in the classroom: Avoiding the tutoring trap. *Topics in Language Disorders, 17,* 49–68.

Schoenbrodt, L., Kumin, L., & Sloan, J. M. (1997). Learning disabilities existing concomitantly with communication disorder. *Journal of Learning Disabilities, 30,* 264–281.

U.S. Department of Education. (2001). *Twenty-third annual report to Congress on the implementation of the Individuals with Disabilities Education Act.* Washington, DC: U.S. Government Printing Office.

Transition Through Adulthood

Ehren, B. J. (2002, January). Speech-language pathologists contributing significantly to the academic success of high school students: A vision for professional growth. *Topics in Language Disorders, 22,* 60–80.

Owens, Jr., R. E., Metz, D. E., & Haas, A. (2000). *Introduction to communication disorders: A life span perspective.* Boston: Allyn and Bacon.

U.S. Department of Education. (2001). *Twenty-third annual report to Congress on the implementation of the Individuals with Disabilities Education Act.* Washington, DC: U.S. Government Printing Office.

Wagner, M. M., D'Amico, R., Marder, C., Newman, L., & Blackorby, J. (1992). *What happens next? Trends in postschool outcomes of youth with disabilities. The second comprehensive report from the National Longitudinal Transition Study of Special Education Students.* Menlo Park, CA: SRI International.

Families

Children's Defense Fund. (1996). *The state of America's children: Yearbook 1996.* Washington, DC: Author.

Cleminshaw, H., DePompei, R., Crais, E. R., Blosser, J., Gillette, Y., & Hooper, C. R. (1996). Working with families. *ASHA, 38,* 34–45.

Crais, E. R., & Lorch, N. (1994). Oral narratives in school-age children. *Topics in Language Disorders, 14,* 13–28.

Hall, B. J., Oyer, H. J., & Haas, W. H. (2001). *Speech, language, and hearing disorders: A guide for the teacher.* Boston: Allyn and Bacon.

Hart, B., & Risley, T. (1995). *Meaningful differences in the everyday lives of American Children.* Baltimore: Paul H. Brookes.

Nippold, M. A., & Rudzinski, M. (1995). Parents' speech and children's stuttering: A critique of the literature. *Journal of Speech and Hearing Research, 38,* 978–989.

Ramig, P. R., & Shames, G. H. (2002). Stuttering and other disorders of fluency. In G. H. Shames and N. B. Anderson (Eds.), *Human communication disorders: An introduction* (6th ed, pp. 258–302). Boston: Allyn and Bacon.

Technology

Harwood, L., Warren, S. F., & Yoder, P. (2002). The importance of responsivity in developing contingent exchanges with beginning communicators. In J. Reichle, D. R. Beukelman, & J. C. Light, (Eds.), *Exemplary practices for beginning communicators: Implications for ACC* (pp. 59–96). Baltimore: Paul H. Brookes.

Kangas, K. A., & Lloyd, L. L. (2002). Augmentative and alternative communication. In G. H. Shames and N. B. Anderson (Eds.), *Human communication disorders: An introduction* (6th ed, pp. 545–593). Boston: Allyn and Bacon.

Reichle, J., Beukelman, D. R., & Light, J. C. (2002). *Exemplary practices for beginning communicators: Implications for ACC.* Baltimore: Paul H. Brookes.

Romski, M. A., & Sevcik, R. A. (1997). Augmentative and alternative communication for children with developmental disabilities. *Mental Retardation and Developmental Disabilities Research Reviews, 3,* 363–368.

Romski, M. A., Sevcik, R. A., Hyatt, A. M., & Cheslock, M. (2002). A continuum of AAC language intervention strategies for beginning communicators. In J. Reichle, D. R. Beukelman, & J. C. Light, (Eds.), *Exemplary practices for beginning communicators: Implications for ACC* (pp. 1–24). Baltimore: Paul H. Brookes.

Wilkinson, K. M., & McIlvane, W. J. (2002). Considerations in teaching graphic symbols to beginning communicators. In J. Reichle, D. R. Beukelman, & J. C. Light, (Eds.), *Exemplary practices for beginning communicators: Implications for ACC* (pp. 273–322). Baltimore: Paul H. Brookes.

CHAPTER 6
MENTAL RETARDATION
Gottfried Mind

Foucart-Walter, E., & Rosenberg, P. (1987). *The painted cat: The cat in Western painting from the fifteenth to the twentieth century.* New York: Rizzoli.

Introduction

Schalock, R. L., Baker, P. C., & Croser, M. D. (Eds.). (2002). *Embarking on a new century: Mental retardation at the end of the 20th century.* Washington, DC: American Association on Mental Retardation.

Mental Retardation Defined

American Association on Mental Retardation (AAMR). (2002). *Mental retardation: Definition, classification, and systems of support* (10th ed.). Washington, DC: AAMR.

Artiles, A. J., Harry, B., Reschly, D. J., & Chinn, P. C. (2002). Over-identification of students of color in special education: A critical overview. *Multicultural Perspectives, 4,* 3–10.

Baroff, G. S. (2000, February). Eugenics, "Baby Doe," and Peter Singer: Toward a more "perfect" society. *Mental Retardation, 38,* 73–77.

Edgerton, R. (1967). *The cloak of competence.* Berkeley: University of California.

English, B. (2000, March 9). An everyday courage. *Boston Globe,* pp. F1, F8.

Kennedy, C. H. (2001). Social interaction interventions for youth with severe disabilities should emphasize interdependence. *Mental Retardation and Developmental Disabilities Research Review, 7,* 122–127.

Keyes, D., Edward, W., & Perske, R. (2002). People with mental retardation are dying, legally: At least 44 have been executed. *Mental Retardation, 40,* 243–244.

Krajewski, J., & Flaherty, T. (2000, April). Attitudes of high school students toward individuals with mental retardation. *Mental Retardation, 38,* 154–162.

Kuna, J. (2001, April). The Human Genome Project and eugenics: Identifying the impact on individuals with mental retardation. *Mental Retardation, 39,* 158–160.

Loggins, K. (1999, April 4). Adult son wants out of visitation: Ruling may affect many with disabilities. *The Tennessean,* p. B1.

Luckasson, R., Borthwick-Duffy, S., Buntinx, W. H. E., Coulter, D. L., Craig, E. M., Reeve, A., Schalock, R. L., Snell, M. E., Spitalnik, D. M., Spreat, S., & Tassé, M. J. (2002). Definition of mental retardation. Washington, DC: American Association on Mental Retardation.

Luckasson, R., Coulter, D. L., Polloway, E. A., Reis, S., Schalock, R. L., Snell, M. E., Spitalnik, D. M., & Stark, J. A. (1992). *Mental retardation: Definition, classification, and systems of supports.* Washington, DC: American Association on Mental Retardation.

McDonnell, J., Mathot-Buckner, C., & Ferguson, B. (1996). *Transition programs for students with moderate/severe disabilities.* Pacific Grove, CA: Brooks/Cole.

National Research Council. (2002). *Minority students in special education and gifted education.* Committee on Minority Representation in Special Education. M. Suzanne Donovan and Christoper T. Cross, editors. Washington, DC: National Academy Press.

Polloway, E. A. (1997). Developmental principles of the Luckasson et al. (1992) AAMR definition of mental retardation: A retrospective. *Education and Training in Mental Retardation and Developmental Disabilities, 32,* 174–178.

Reschly, D. J. (1997). Utility of individual ability measures and public policy choices for the 21st century. *School Psycology Review, 26,* 234–241.

Smith, J. D. (1997). Mental retardation as an educational construct: Time for a new shared view? *Education and Training in Mental Retardation and Developmental Disabilities, 32,* 167–173.

Smith, J. D., & Mitchell, A. L. (2001, June). Disney's Tarzan, Edgar Rice Burrough's eugenics, and visions of utopian perfection. *Mental Retardation, 39,* 221–225.

Stainton, T. (2001, December). Reason and value: The thought of Plato and Aristotle and the construction of the intellectual disability. *Mental Retardation, 39,* 452–460.

Warren, S. F. (2000, May/June). Mental retardation: Curse, characteristic, or coin of the realm? *American Association of Mental Retardation News & Notes, 13,* pp. 1, 10–11.

Wickham, P. (2001, April). Images of idiocy in puritan New England. *Mental Retardation, 39,* 147–151.

History of the Field

Ayllon, T., & Azrin, N. H. (1964). Reinforcement and instructions with mental patients. *Journal of Experimental Analysis of Behavior, 7,* 327–331.

Ayllon, R., & Azrin, N. H. (1968). Reinforcer sampling: A technique for increasing the behavior of mental patients. *Journal of Applied Behavior Analysis, 1,* 13–20.

Birnbrauer, J. S., Wolf, M. M., Kidder, J. D., & Tague, C. E. (1965). Classroom behavior of retarded pupils with token reinforcement. *Journal of Experimental Child Psychology, 2,* 219–235.

Bryant, B. R., Taylor, R. L., & Rivera, D. P. (1996). *Assessment of adaptive areas (AAA): Examiner's manual.* Austin, TX: Pro-Ed.

Gelf, S. (1995). The beast in man: Degenerationism and mental retardation, 1900–1920. *Mental Retardation, 33,* 1–9.

Itard, J. M. G. (1806). *Wild boy of Aveyron.* (G. Humphrey and M. Humphrey, translators). (1962). Englewood Cliffs, NJ: Prentice-Hall. Originally published in Paris by Gouyon (1801).

Lent, J. R., & McLean, B. M. (1976). The trainable retarded: The technology of teaching. In N. G. Haring and R. L. Schiefelbush (Eds.), *Teaching special children* (pp. 197–223). New York: McGraw-Hill.

Nirje, B. (1969). The normalization principle and its human management implications. In R. Kugel and W. Wolfensberger (Eds.), *Changing patterns in residential services for the mentally retarded* (pp. 179–195). Washington, DC: President's Committee on Mental Retardation.

Nirje, B. (1976). The normalization principle. In R. Kugel and A. Schearer (Eds.), *Changing patterns in residential services for the mentally retarded* (pp. 231–240). Washington, DC: President's Committee on Mental Retardation.

Perske, R. (1972). The dignity of risk. In W. Wolfensberger (Ed.), *The principle of normalization in human services* (pp. 194–200). Toronto: National Institute on Mental Retardation.

Winzer, M. A. (1993). *The history of special education: From isolation to integration.* Washington, DC: Gallaudet University Press.

Wolfensberger, W. (1972). *The principle of normalization in human services.* Toronto: National Institute on Mental Retardation.

Prevalence

American Association on Mental Retardation (AAMR). (2002). *Mental retardation: Definition, classification, and systems of support* (10th ed.). Washington, DC: AAMR.

MacMillan, D. L., Gresham, F. M., & Bocian, K. M. (1998). Discrepancy between definitions of learning disabilities and school practices: An empirical investigation. *Journal of Learning Disabilities, 31,* 314–326.

U.S. Department of Education. (2001). *Twenty-third annual report to Congress on the implementation of the Individuals with Disabilities Education Act.* Washington, DC: U.S. Government Printing Office.

Causes and Prevention

American Association on Mental Retardation (AAMR). (2002). *Mental retardation: Definition, classification, and systems of support (10th ed.).* Washington, DC: AAMR.

Bailey, Jr., D. B., Aytch, L. S., Odom, S. L., Symons, F., & Wolery, M. (1999). Early intervention as we know it. *Mental Retardation and Developmental Disabilities Research Reviews, 5,* 11–20.

Ball, W. (1999, April). Examining the link between tobacco use and low birth weight. *Early Childhood Reports, 10,* 3.

Bauer, C. R. (1999). Perinatal effects of prenatal drug exposure: Neonatal aspects. *Clinics in Perinatology, 26,* 87–106.

Belser, R. C., & Sudhalter, V. (2001, September). Conversational characteristics of children with Fragile X syndrome: Repetitive speech. *American Journal on Mental Retardation, 106,* 28–38.

Birenbaum, A. (2002, June). Poverty, welfare reform, and disproportionate rates of disability among children. *Mental Retardation, 40,* 212–218.

Chace, D. H., & Naylor, E. W. (1999). Expansion of newborn screening programs using automated tandem mass spectrometry. *Mental Retardation and Developmental Disabilities Research Reviews, 5,* 150–154.

Chapman, R. S., & Hesketh, L. J. (2000). Behavioral phenotype of individuals with Down syndrome. *Mental Retardation and Developmental Disabilities Research Reviews, 6,* 84–95.

Children's Defense Fund (CDF). (2001). *The state of America's children.* Washington, DC: Children's Defense Fund.

Coulter, D. L. (1996). Prevention as a form of support: Implications for the new definition. *Mental Retardation, 34,* 108–116.

Dyer, C. A. (1999). Pathophysiology of phenylketonuria. *Mental Retardation and Developmental Disabilities Research Reviews, 5,* 104–112.

Eisensmith, R. C., Kuzmin, A. I., & Krougliak, V. A. (1999). Prospects for treatment of phenylketonuria by gene therapy. *Mental Retardation and Developmental Disabilities Research Reviews, 5,* 150–154.

Feldman, M. A., & Walton-Allen, N. (1997). Effects of maternal mental retardation and poverty on intellectual, academic, and behavioral status of school-age children. *American Journal on Mental Retardation, 101,* 352–364.

Haney, D. Q. (1994, September 22). Disabilities plague the tiniest preemies: Medical miracle has a dark side. *Albuquerque Journal,* p. A4.

Hosp, J. L., & Reschly, D. J. (2002 Winter). Predictors of

restrictiveness of placement for African-American and Caucasian students. *Exceptional Children, 68,* 225–238.

Johnson, G., Johnson, R. L., & Jefferson-Aker, C. R. (2001). HIV/AIDS prevention: Effective instructional strategies for adolescents with mild mental retardation. *Teaching Exceptional Children, 33,* 28–32.

Kerns, K. A., Don, A., Mateer, C. A., & Streissguth, A. P. (1997). Cognitive deficits in nonretarded adults with fetal alcohol syndrome. *Journal of Learning Disabilities, 30,* 685–693.

Koch, R., & de la Cruz, F. (1999). Historical aspects and overview of research on phenylketonuria. *Mental Retardation and Developmental Disabilities Research Reviews, 5,* 101–103.

Lowenthal, B. (1996). Educational implications of child abuse. *Intervention in School and Clinic, 32,* 21–25.

Mazzocco, M. M. M. (2000). Advances in research on the Fragile X syndrome. *Mental Retardation and Developmental Disabilities Research Reviews, 6,* 96–106.

Melner, J., Shackelford, J., Hargrove, E., & Daulton, D. (1998). *Resources related to children and their families affected by alcohol and other drugs* (3rd ed.). Chapel Hill, NC: NEC*TAS.

National Alliance of Black School Educators. (2002). *Addressing over-representation of African American students in special education.* Arlington, VA: Council for Exceptional Children.

National Research Council. (2002). *Minority students in special education and gifted education.* Committee on Minority Representation in Special Education. M. Suzanne Donovan and Christoper T. Cross, editors. Washington, DC: National Academy Press.

Office of Special Education Programs. (2000, December). *Prenatal exposure to alcohol and nicotine: Implications for special education. Twenty-second annual report to Congress on the implementation of the Individuals with Disabilities Education Act.* (pp. 1–34). Washington, DC: U.S. Department of Education.

Oswald, D. P., Coutinho, M. J., Best, A. M., & Nguyen, N. (2001, October). Impact of sociodemographic characteristics on the identification rates of minority students as having mental retardation. *Mental Retardation, 39,* 351–367.

President's Committee on Mental Retardation. (n.d.). *A guide for state planning: For the prevention of mental retardation and related disabilities.* Washington, DC: Author.

Roberts, C. D., Stough, L. M., & Parrish, L. H. (2002). The role of genetic counseling in the elective termination of pregnancies involving fetuses with disabilities. *Journal of Special Education, 36,* 48–55.

Roizen, N. J. (2001). Down syndrome: Progress in research. *Mental Retardation and Developmental Disabilities Research Reviews, 7,* 38–44.

Schettler, R., Stein, J., Reich, F., Valenti, M., & Wallinga, D. (2000). *In harm's way: toxic threats to child development.* Cambridge, MA: Greater Boston Physicians for Social Responsibility. (www.igc.org/psr)

Sells, C. J. (1998). Overview: Neural tube defects. *Mental Retardation and Developmental Disabilities Research Reviews, 4,* 239–240.

Snyder, B., & Sandoval, E. (1999, June 19). Fetal patient an emerging joy: Experimental surgery shows hope. *The Tennessean,* pp. 1A, 8A.

Stoel-Gammon, C. (1997). Phonological development in Down syndrome. *Mental Retardation and Developmental Disabilities Research Reviews, 3,* 300–306.

Sudhalter, V., & Belser, R. C. (2001, September). Conversational

characteristics of children with Fragile X syndrome: Tangential language. *American Journal on Mental Retardation, 106,* 389–400.

The Arc. (2002, June 30). Introduction to mental retardation. In *Frequently Asked Questions.* Retrieved from http://www.tharc.org/faqs/mrqa.html

U.S. Department of Education. (2001). *Twenty-third annual report to Congress on the implementation of the Individuals with Disabilities Education Act.* Washington, DC: U.S. Government Printing Office.

Ye, X., Mitchell, M., Newman, K., & Batshaw, M. L. (2001). Prospects for prenatal gene therapy in disorders causing mental retardation. *Mental Retardation and Developmental Disabilities Research Reviews, 7,* 65–72.

Youth Record. (1995, August 15). *Child abuse leads to lower IQ and body responsiveness,* p. 1.

Characteristics

American Association on Mental Retardation (AAMR). (2002). *Mental retardation: Definition, classification, and systems of support* (10th ed.). Washington, DC: AAMR.

Ash, A., Bellew, J., Davies, M., Newman, T., & Richardson, L. (1997). Everybody in? The experience of disabled students in further education. *Disability and Society, 12,* 605–621.

Best Buddies. (2002). Retrieved July 3, 2002, from http://www.bestbuddies.org/about/index.asp

Bradley, V. J., Ashbough, J. W., & Blaney, B. (Eds.). (1993). *Creating individual supports for people with developmental disabilities: A mandate for change at many levels.* Baltimore: Brookes.

Chadsey, J., & Beyer, S. (2001). Social relationships in the workplace. *Mental Retardation and Developmental Disabilities Research Reviews, 7,* 128–133.

Cook, B. G., & Semmel, M. I. (1999). Peer acceptance of included students with disabilities as a function of severity of disability and classroom composition. *Journal of Special Education, 33,* 50–61.

Freeman, S. N., & Kasari, C. (2002, January). Characteristics and qualities of the play dates of children with Down syndrome: Emerging or true friendships? *American Journal on Mental Retardation, 107,* 16–31.

Hughes, C., Rodi, M. S., Lorden, S. W., Pittken, S. E., Derer, K. R., Hwang, B., & Xinsheng, C. (1999). Social interactions of high school students with mental retardation and their general education peers. *American Journal on Mental Retardation, 104,* 533–544.

Kennedy, C. H. (2001). Social interaction interventions for youth with severe disabilities should emphasize interdependence. *Mental Retardation and Developmental Disabilities Research Review, 7,* 122–127.

Kennedy, C. H., Caruso, M., & Thompson, T. (2001). Experimental analyses of gene-behavior relations: Some notes on their application. *Journal of Applied Behavior Analysis, 34,* 539–549.

Krajewski, J., & Flaherty, T. (2000, April). Attitudes of high school students toward individuals with mental retardation. *Mental Retardation, 38,* 154–162.

Moore, D. G. (2001, September). Reassessing emotion recognition performance in people with mental retardation: A review. *American Journal on Mental Retardation, 106,* 481–502.

Pearson, D. A., Lachar, D., Loveland, K. A., Santos, C. W., Faria, L. P., Azzam, P. N., Hentges, B. A., & Cleveland, L. A. (2000). Patterns of behavioral adjustment and maladjustment in mental retardation: Comparison of children with and without ADHD. *American Journal on Mental Retardation, 105,* 236–251.

Siperstein, G. N., & Leffert, J. S. (1997). Comparison of socially accepted and rejected children with mental retardation. *American Journal on Mental Retardation, 101,* 339–351.

Siperstein, G. N., Leffert, J. S., & Wenz-Gross, M. (1997). The quality of friendships between children with and without learning problems. *American Journal on Mental Retardation, 102,* 111–125.

Sudhalter, V., & Belser, R. C. (2001, September). Conversational characteristics of children with Fragile X syndrome: Tangential language. *American Journal on Mental Retardation, 106,* 389–400.

Symons, F. J., Clark, R. D., Roberts, J. P., & Bailey, Jr., D. B. (2001). Classroom behavior of elementary school-age boys with Fragile X syndrome. *Journal of Special Education, 34,* 194–202.

Early Childhood Education

Guralnick, M. J. (1998). Effectiveness of early intervention for vulnerable children: A developmental perspective. *American Journal on Mental Retardation, 102,* 319–345.

Manuel, J., & Little, L. (2002, Spring). A model of inclusion. *Early developments, 6,* 14–18.

U.S. Department of Education. (2001). *Twenty-third annual report to Congress on the implementation of the Individuals with Disabilities Education Act.* Washington, DC: U.S. Government Printing Office.

Elementary Through High School

Belfiore, P. J., & Toro-Zambrana, W. (1994). *Recognizing choices in community settings by people with significant disabilities.* Washington, DC: American Association on Mental Retardation.

Brolin, D. (2002). *Life centered career education, a competency based approach,* (5th ed.). Arlington, VA: Council for Exceptional Children.

Browder, D. M., & Xin, Y. P. (1998). A meta-analysis and review of sight word research and its implications for teaching functional reading to individuals with moderate and severe disabilities. *Journal of Special Education, 32,* 130–153.

Colins, B. C., & Stinson, D. M. (1994–1995). Teaching generalized reading of product warning labels to adolescents with mental disabilities through the use of key words. *Exceptionality, 5,* 163–181.

Copeland, S. R., Hughes, C., Agran, M., Wehmeyer, M. L., & Fowler, S. E. (2002, January). An intervention package to support high school students with mental retardation in general education classrooms. *American Journal on Mental Retardation, 107,* 32–45.

Hickson, L., Blackman, L. S., & Reis, E. M. (1995). *Mental retardation: Foundations of educational programming.* Boston: Allyn and Bacon.

Hughes, C. (2001). Transition to adulthood: Supporting young adults to access social, employment, and civic pursuits. *Mental Retardation and Developmental Disabilities Research Reviews, 7,* 84–90.

Mechling, L. C., Gast, D. L., & Langone, J. (2002). Computer-based video instruction to teach persons with moderate intellectual disabilities to read grocery aisle signs and locate terms. *Journal of Special Education, 35,* 224–240.

Wehmeyer, M. L., Kelchner, K., & Richards, S. (1996). Essential characteristics of self-determined behavior of individuals with

mental retardation. *American Journal on Mental Retardation, 100,* 632–642.

Wehmeyer, M. L., & Metzler, C. A. (1995). How self-determined are people with mental retardation? The national consumer survey. *Mental Retardation, 33,* 111–119.

Wolery, M., Ault, M. J., & Doyle, P. M. (1992). *Teaching students with moderate to severe disabilities: Use of response prompting strategies.* New York: Longman.

Collaboration for Inclusion

Alber, S. R., & Heward, W. L. (1997). Recruit it or lose it! Training students to recruit positive teacher attention. *Intervention in School and Clinic, 32,* 275–282.

Bailey, Jr., D. B., Aytch, L. S., Odom, S. L., Symons, F., & Wolery, M. (1999). Early intervention as we know it. *Mental Retardation and Developmental Disabilities Research Reviews, 5,* 11–20.

Benz, M. R., Lindstrom, L., & Yovanoff, P. (2000, Summer). Improving graduation and employment outcomes of students with disabilities: Predictive factors and student perspectives. *Exceptional Children, 66,* 509–529.

Craft, M. A., Alber, S. R., Heward, W. L. (1998). Teaching elementary students with developmental disabilities to recruit teacher attention in a general education classroom: Effects on teacher praise and academic productivity. *Journal of Applied Behavior Analysis, 31,* 399–415.

McGregor, G., & Vogelsberg, R. T. (1998). *Inclusive schooling practices: Pedagogical and Research Foundation.* Billings, MT: Consortium on Inclusive Schooling Practices, University of Montana.

Sandler, A. G. (1999). Short-changed in the name of socialization? Acquisition of functional skills by students with severe disabilities. *Mental Retardation, 37,* 148–150.

U.S. Department of Education. (2001). *Twenty-third annual report to Congress on the implementation of the Individuals with Disabilities Education Act.* Washington, DC: U.S. Government Printing Office.

Transition Through Adulthood

Butterworth, J., Hagner, D., Helm, D. T., & Whelley, T. A. (2000, August). Workplace culture, social interactions, and supports for transition-age young adults. *Mental Retardation, 38,* 342–353.

Campo, S. F., Sharpton, W. R., Thompson, B., & Sexton, D. (1997). Correlates of the quality of life of adults with severe or profound mental retardation. *Mental Retardation, 35,* 329–337.

Chadsey, J., & Beyer, S. (2001). Social relationships in the workplace. *Mental Retardation and Developmental Disabilities Research Reviews, 7,* 128–133.

Cone, A. A. (2001, February). Self-reported training needs and training issues of advisors to self-advocacy groups for people with mental retardation. *Mental Retardation, 39,* 1–10.

Cummins, R. A. (2001). Living with support in the community: Predictors of satisfaction with life. *Mental Retardation and Developmental Disabilities, 7,* 99–104.

Edgerton, R. B. (1996). A longitudinal-ethnographic research perspective on quality of life. In R. L. Schalock (Ed.), *Quality of life: Conceptualization and measurement* (pp. 83–90). Washington, DC: American Association on Mental Retardation.

Emerson, E., Robertson, J., Gregory, N., Hatton, C., Kessissoglou, S., Hallam, A., Järbrink, K., Knapp, M., Netten, A., & Walsh, P. N. (2001, September). Quality and costs of supported living residences and group homes in the United Kingdom. *American Journal on Mental Retardation, 106,* 401–415.

Gardner, J. F., Nudler, S., & Chapman, M. S. (1997). Personal outcomes as measures of quality. *Mental Retardation, 35,* 295–305.

Holburn, S. (2000, December). New paradigm for some, old paradigms for others. *Mental Retardation, 38,* 530–531.

Kennedy, M., & Lewin, L. (2002). Fact sheet: Summary of self-determination. From the Center of Human Policy, Syracuse University. Retrieved on July 3, 2002, from http://soeweb.syr.edu/thechp

Kraemer, B. R., & Blacher, J. (2001, December). Transition for young adults with severe mental retardation: School preparation, parent expectations, and family involvement. *Mental Retardation, 39,* 423–435.

Mamlin, N. (1999). Despite best intentions: When inclusion fails. *Journal of Special Education, 33,* 36–49.

Mank, D., Cioffi, A., & Yovanoff, P. (1998). Employment outcomes for people with severe disabilities: Opportunities for improvement. *Mental Retardation, 36,* 205–216.

Mank, D., Cioffi, A., & Yovanoff, P. (2000). Direct support in supported employment and its relation to job typicalness, coworker involvement, and employment outcomes. *Mental Retardation, 38,* 506–516.

Moseley, C., & Nerney, T. (2000, November/December). Emerging best practices in self-determination. *AAMR News and Notes, 13,* 4–5.

PACER. (2002, May). *Parent brief.* Minneapolis, MN: PACER Center, Inc.

Rusch, F. R., Heal, L. W., & Cimera, R. E. (1997). Predicting the earnings of supported employees with mental retardation: A longitudinal study. *American Journal on Mental Retardation, 101,* 630–644.

Stancliff, R. (2001). Living with support in the community: Predictors of choice and self-determination. *Mental Retardation and Developmental Disabilities Research Reviews, 7,* 91–98.

Taylor, S. J., & Bogdan, R. (1996). Quality of life and the individual's perspective. In R. L. Schalock (Ed.), *Quality of life: Conceptualization and measurement* (pp. 11–22). Washington, DC: American Association on Mental Retardation.

Wehmeyer, M. L., & Metzler, C. A. (1995). How self-determined are people with mental retardation? The national consumer survey. *Mental Retardation, 33,* 111–119.

Wolfensberger, W. (2002, June). Social role valorization and, or versus, "empowerment." *Mental Retardation, 40,* 252–258.

Families

Beach Center on Disability. (2002a). Introduction to our research. Retrieved July 4, 2002 from http://www.beachcenter.org

Beach Center on Disability. (2002b). Fathers. Retrieved July 4, 2002, from http://www.beachcenter.org/main.php3?page_id=64#68

Beach Center on Families and Disability. (1995a). Dads feel left out. *Families and Disability Newsletter, 6,* 4.

Beach Center on Families and Disability. (1995b). How to involve fathers more with their children with special needs. *Families and Disability Newsletter, 6,* 5–6.

Freedman, R. I., Krauss, M. W., & Seltzer, M. M. (1997). Aging parents' residential plans for adult children with mental retardation. *Mental Retardation, 35,* 114–123.

Hannah, M. E., & Midlarsky, E. (1999). Competence and adjustment of siblings of children with mental retardation. *American Journal on Mental Retardation, 104,* 22–37.

Orsmond, G. I., & Seltzer, M. M. (2000). Brothers and sisters of adults with mental retardation: Gendered nature of the sibling relationship. *American Journal on Mental Retardation, 105,* 486–508.

Seltzer, M. M., & Krauss, M. W. (2001). Quality of life of adults with mental retardation/developmental disabilities who live with the family. *Mental Retardation and Developmental Research Reviews, 7,* 105–114.

Thorin, E., Yovanoff, P., & Irvin, L. (1996). Dilemmas faced by families during their young adults' transitions to adulthood: A brief report. *Mental Retardation, 34,* 117–120.

Willoughby, J. C., & Glidden, L. M. (1995). Fathers helping out: Shared child care and marital satisfaction of parents of children with disabilities. *American Journal on Mental Retardation, 99,* 399–406.

Technology

e-Buddies. (2002). Retrieved July 3, 2002, from http://www.ebuddies.org/

Glaser, C., Rieth, H. J., Kinzer, C. K., Prestidge, L. K., & Peter, J. (1999). A description of the impact of multimedia anchored instruction on classroom interactions. *Journal of Special Education Technology, 14,* 27–53.

Mechling, L. C., Gast, D. L., & Langone, J. (2002). Computer-based video instruction to teach persons with moderate intellectual disabilities to read grocery aisle signs and locate items. *Journal of Special Education, 35,* 224–240.

Rieth, H. J., & Colburn, L. K. (2003). Anchoring instruction for students with disabilities. In D. P. Bryant & B. Bryant (Eds.), *Technology in special education.* Boston: Allyn and Bacon.

Romski, M. A., Sevcik, R. A., & Adamson, L. B. (1999). Communication patterns of youth with mental retardation with and without their speech-output devices. *American Journal on Mental Retardation, 104,* 249–259.

CHAPTER 7

GIFTEDNESS AND TALENT DEVELOPMENT

Introduction

Morelock, M. J., & Feldman, D. H. (1997). High IQ children, extreme precocity, and savant syndrome. In N. Colangelo and G. A. Davis (Eds.), *Handbook of gifted education* (2nd ed., pp. 439–459). Boston: Allyn and Bacon.

Simonton, D. K. (1997). When giftedness becomes genius: How does talent achieve eminence? In N. Colangelo and G. A. Davis (Eds.), *Handbook of gifted education* (2nd ed., pp. 335–349). Boston: Allyn and Bacon.

Giftedness and Talents Defined

Benbow, C. P., & Stanley, J. C. (1996). Inequity in equity: How "equity" can lead to inequity for high-potential students. *Psychology, Public Policy, and Law, 2,* 249–292.

Campbell, L., Campbell, B., & Dickinson, D. (1999). *Teaching and learning through multiple intelligences* (2nd ed.). Boston: Allyn and Bacon.

Cornell, D. G., Delcourt, M. A. B., Goldberg, M. D., & Bland, L. C. (1995). Achievement and self-concept of minority students in elementary school gifted programs. *Journal for the Education of the Gifted, 18,* 189–209.

Feldhusen, J. F. (Ed.). (1995). Talent development: The new direction in gifted education. *Roeper Review, 18*, 92.

Fernández, A. T., Gay, L. R., Lucky, L. F., & Gavilan, M. R. (1998). Teacher perceptions of gifted Hispanic limited English proficient students. *Journal for the Education of the Gifted, 21*, 335–351.

Gallagher, J. J. (2000, Winter). Unthinkable thoughts: Education of gifted students. *Gifted Child Quarterly, 44*, 5–12.

Gallagher, J., Harradine, C. C., & Coleman, M. R. (1997). Gifted students in the classroom: Challenge or boredom? Gifted students' views on their schooling. *Roeper Review, 19*, 132–136.

Gardner, H. (1983). *Frames of mind: Theory of multiple intelligences.* New York: Basic Books

Gardner, H. (1993). *Multiple intelligences: The theory in practice.* New York: Basic Books.

Grantham, T. C. (2002, Winter). Underrepresentation in gifted education: How did we get here and what needs to change? *Roeper Review, 24*, 50–51.

Hunsaker, S. L., Finley, V. S., & Frank, E. L. (1997). An analysis of teacher nominations and student performance in gifted programs. *Gifted Child Quarterly, 41*, 19–24.

Jacob K. Javits Gifted and Talented Students Education Act of 1988 (PL 100–297).

Landvogt, J. (2001, June). Affecting eternity: Teaching for talent development. *Roeper Review, 23*, 190–196.

Margolin, L. (1996). A pedagogy of privilege. *Journal for the Education of the Gifted, 19*, 164–180.

Massé, L., & Gagné, F. (2002, Winter). Gifts and talents as sources of envy in high school settings. *Gifted Child Quarterly, 46*, 15–29.

Renzulli, J. S. (1998, October). A rising tide lifts all ships: Developing the gifts and talents of all students. *Phi Delta Kappan, 80*, 104–111.

Renzulli, J. S., & Park, S. (2000, Fall). Gifted dropouts: The who and the why. *Gifted Child Quarterly, 44*, 261–271.

Sapon-Shevin, M. (1996). Beyond gifted education: Building a shared agenda for school reform. *Journal for the Education of the Gifted, 19*, 192–214.

Smutny, J. F. (2000, May). *Teaching young gifted children in the regular classroom.* (Report No. E595-EDO-EC-00-4). ERIC Digest, Reston, VA: The Council for Exceptional Children.

Stephens, K., & Karnes, F. (2000). State definitions for the gifted and talented revisited. *Exceptional Children, 66*, 219–238.

Sternberg, R. J. (2000, December). Identifying and developing creative giftedness. *Roeper Review, 23*, 60–64.

Treffinger, D. J., & Feldhusen, J. F. (1996). Talent recognition and development: Successor to gifted education. *Journal for the Education of the Gifted, 19*, 181–193.

U.S. Department of Education. (1994). *National excellence: A case for developing America's youth.* Washington, DC: U.S. Government Printing Office.

History of the Field

Clark, B. (2002). *Growing up gifted: Developing the potential of children at home and school* (6th ed). Upper Saddle River, NJ: Prentice-Hall.

Davis, G. A., & Rimm, S. B. (1998). *Education of the gifted and talented* (4th ed.). Boston: Allyn and Bacon.

Gallagher, J. J. (1988). National agenda for educating gifted students: Statement of priorities. *Exceptional Children, 55*, 107–114.

Gardner, J. W. (1984). *Excellence: Can we be equal and excellent too?* (Rev. ed.). New York: Norton.

Hunsaker, S. L. (1995). The gifted metaphor from the perspective of traditional civilizations. *Journal for the Education of the Gifted, 18*, 255–268.

Maker, C. J. (1986). Education of the gifted: Significant trends. In R. J. Morris and B. Blatt (Eds.), *Special education: Research and trends* (pp. 190–221). New York: Pergamon.

Prevalence

Castellano, J. A. (2002). Renavigating the waters: The identification and assessment of culturally and linguistically diverse students for gifted and talented education. In J. A. Castellano and E. I. Díaz (Eds.). *Reaching new horizons: Gifted and talented education for culturally and linguistically diverse students* (pp. 94–116). Boston: Allyn and Bacon.

Clark, B. (2002). *Growing up gifted: Developing the potential of children at home and school* (6th ed.). Upper Saddle River, NJ: Prentice-Hall.

Harry, B. (1994). *The disproportionate representation of minority students in special education: Theories and recommendations.* Alexandria, VA: National Association of State Directors of Special Education.

National Center for Education Statistics. (1994). *Digest of education statistics.* Washington, DC: U.S. Government Printing Office.

Renzulli, J. S., & Reis, S. M. (1997). The schoolwide enrichment model: New directions for developing high-end learning. In N. Colangelo and G. A. Davis (Eds.), *Handbook of gifted education* (2nd ed., pp. 136–154). Boston: Allyn and Bacon.

Tomlinson, C. A., Callahan, C. M., & Lelli, K. M. (1998). Challenging expectations: Case studies of high-potential, culturally diverse young children. *Gifted Child Quarterly, 41*, 5–17.

Causes: Factors That Enhance or Inhibit Giftedness

Brown, C. N. (1997). Legal issues and gifted education: Gifted identification as a constitutional issue. *Roeper Review, 19*, 157–160.

De Leon, J., Argus-Calvo, B., & Medina, C. (1997). A model project for identifying rural gifted and talented students in the visual arts. *Rural Special Education Quarterly, 16*, 16–23.

Fishkin, A. S., & Johnson, A. S. (1998). Who is creative? Identifying children's creative abilities. *Roeper Review, 21*, 40–46.

Kirschenbaum, R. J. (1998). The creativity classification systems: An assessment theory. *Roeper Review, 21*, 20–26.

Kitano, M. K. (1997). Gifted Asian American women. *Journal for the Education of the Gifted, 21*, 3–37.

Kitano, M. K. (1998). Gifted Latina women. *Journal for the Education of the Gifted, 21*, 131–159.

Krippner, S. (1967). The ten commandments that block creativity. *Gifted Child Quarterly, 11*, 144–151.

Parker, J. (1998). The Torrance Creative Scholars Program. *Roeper Review, 21*, 32–35.

Reis, S. (1999, March). Overcoming barriers to girls' talent development. *Parenting for High Potential*, pp. 18–21.

Renzulli, J. (1978). What makes giftedness? Reexamining a definition. *Phi Delta Kappan, 60*, 180–184, 261.

Rimm, S., & Rimm-Kaufman, S. (2001). *How Jane won: 55 successful women share how they grew from ordinary girls to extraordinary women.* New York: Crown Publishers.

Schroeder-Davis, S. (1998, December). Parenting high achievers: Swimming upstream against the cultural current. *Parenting for High Potential*, pp. 8–10.

Simonton, D. K. (1997). When giftedness becomes genius: How

does talent achieve eminence? In N. Colangelo and G. A. Davis (Eds.), *Handbook of gifted education* (2nd ed., pp. 335–349). Boston: Allyn and Bacon.

Sternberg, R. (2000, June). Patterns of giftedness: A triarchic analysis. *Roeper Review, 22,* 231–235.

Characteristics

Baker, B. (2001, Winter). Measuring the outcomes of state policies for gifted education: An equity analysis of Texas school districts. *Gifted Child Quarterly, 45,* 4–15.

Bernal, E. (2002, Winter). Three ways to achieve a more equitable representation of culturally and linguistically different students in gt programs. *Roeper Review, 24,* 82–88.

Brody, L. E., & Benbow, C. P. (1986). Social and emotional adjustment of adolescents extremely talented in verbal or mathematical reasoning. *Journal of Youth and Adolescence, 15,* 1–18.

Brody, L. E., & Mills, C. J. (1997). Gifted children with learning disabilities: A review of the issues. *Journal of Learning Disabilities, 30,* 282–296.

Castellano, J. A. (2002). Renavigating the waters: The identification and assessment of culturally and linguistically diverse students for gifted and talented education. In J. A. Castellano, & E. I. Díaz (Eds.), *Reaching new horizons: Gifted and talented education for culturally and linguistically diverse students.* Boston: Allyn and Bacon.

Clark, B. (2002). *Growing up gifted: Developing the potential of children at home and school* (6th ed.). Upper Saddle River, NJ: Prentice-Hall.

De Leon, J., Argus-Calvo, B., & Medina, C. (1997). A model project for identifying rural gifted and talented students in the visual arts. *Rural Special Education Quarterly, 16,* 16–23.

Dole, S. (2000, December). The implication of the risk and resilience literature for gifted students with learning disabilities. *Roeper Review, 23,* 91–96.

Ford, D. Y., Grantham, T. C., & Harris, J. J. (1996). Multicultural gifted education: A wakeup call to the profession. *Roper Review, 19,* 72–78.

Ford, D. Y., & Harris, J. J. (1999). *Multicultural Gifted Education.* New York: Teachers College Press.

Ford, D. Y., & Harris, J. J. (2000). A framework for infusing multicultural curriculum into gifted education. *Roper Review, 23,* 4–10.

Ford, D. Y., Harris, J. J., Tyson, C. A., & Trotman, M. F. (2002, Winter). Beyond deficit thinking: Providing access for gifted African American students. *Roeper Review, 24,* 52–58.

Ford, D. Y., Howard, T. C., Hattis, J. J., & Tyson, C. A. (2000). Creating culturally responsive classrooms for gifted African American students. *Journal of Education of the Gifted, 23,* 397–427.

Freeman, J. (1994). Some emotional aspects of being gifted. *Journal for the Education of the Gifted, 17,* 180–197.

Grantham, T. C. (2002, Winter). Underrepresentation in gifted education: How did we get here and what needs to change? *Roeper Review, 24,* 50–51.

Grimm, J. (1998). The participation of gifted students with disabilities in gifted programs. *Roeper Review, 20,* 285–286.

Harmon, D. (2002, Winter). They won't teach me: The voices of gifted African American inner-city students. *Roeper Review, 24,* 68–75.

Hébert, T., & Beardsley, T. (2001, Spring). Jermaine: A critical case study of a gifted black child living in rural poverty. *Gifted Child Quarterly, 45,* 85–103.

Jenkins-Friedman, R., & Nielsen, M. E. (1990). Gifted and talented students. In E. L. Meyen (Ed.), *Exceptional children in today's schools* (2nd ed., pp. 451–493). Denver, CO: Love.

Kaplan, S. (2001, September). Building bridges: Teaching gifted emergent English-language learners. *Teaching for High Potential, 3,* 1–2.

Kitano, M., & DiJiosia, M. (2002, Winter). Are Asian and Pacific Americans overrepresented in programs for the gifted? *Roeper Review, 24,* 76–80.

Kitano, M., & Perkins, C. (2000). Gifted European American women. *Journal for the Education of the Gifted, 23,* 287–313.

Kitano, M. K. (1997). Gifted Asian American women. *Journal for the Education of the Gifted, 21,* 3–37.

Kitano, M. K. (1998). Gifted Latina women. *Journal for the Education of the Gifted, 21,* 131–159.

Leroux, J., & Levitt-Perlman, M. (2000). The gifted child with attention deficit disorder: An identification and intervention challenge. *Roeper Review, 22,* 171–176.

MacMillan, D. L., Gresham, F. M., & Bocian, K. M. (1998). Discrepancy between definitions of learning disabilities and school practices: An empirical investigation. *Journal of Learning Disabilities, 31,* 314–326.

Maker, C. J. (1977). *Providing programs for the gifted handicapped.* Reston, VA: Council for Exceptional Children.

Maker, C. J., & Schiever, S. W. (1989). Defining the Hispanic population. In C. J. Maker and S. W. Schiever (Eds.), *Critical issues in gifted education: Defensible programs for cultural and ethnic minorities* (Vol. 2, pp. 1–4). Austin, TX: Pro-Ed.

Mendez, L. (2000). Gender roles and achievement-related choices: A comparison of early adolescent girls in gifted and general education programs. *Journal for the Education of the Gifted, 24,* 149–169.

Moon, S., Swift, M., & Shallenberger, A. (2002, Winter). Perceptions of a self-contained class for fourth- and fifth-grade students with high to extreme levels of intellectual giftedness. *Gifted Child Quarterly, 46,* 64–79.

Moon, S., Zentall, S., Grskovic, J., Hall, A., & Stormont, M. (2001). Emotional and social characteristics of boys with AD/HD and giftedness: A comparative study. *Journal for the Education of the Gifted, 24,* 207–247.

Morris, J. (2002, Winter). African American students and gifted education: The politics of race and culture. *Roeper Review, 24,* 59–62.

National Research Council. (2002). *Minority students in special education and gifted education.* Committee on Minority Representation in Special Education. M. Suzanne Donovan and Christoper T. Cross, editors. Washington, DC: National Academy Press.

Neihart, M. (2000, Fall). Gifted children with Asperger's syndrome. *Gifted Child Quarterly, 44,* 222–230.

Nielsen, M. E. (2002). Gifted students with learning disabilities: Recommendations for identification and programming. *Exceptionality, 10,* 93–111.

Nielsen, M. E., Higgins, L. D., Hammond. A. E., & Williams, R. A. (1993). Gifted children with disabilities: The twice-exceptional child project. *Gifted Child Today, 16,* 9–12.

Nichols, H. J., & Baum, S. (2000, December). High achievers: Keys to helping youngsters with stress reduction. *Parenting for High Potential,* pp. 9–12.

Noble, K. D., Subotnik, R. F., & Arnold, K. D. (1999). To thine own self be true: A new model of female talent development. *Gifted Child Quarterly, 43,* 140–149.

Peterson, J. (2000, June). A follow-up study of one group of achievers and underachievers four years after high school graduation. *Roeper Review, 22,* 217–224.

Piechowski, M. (1997). Emotional giftedness: The measure of intrapersonal intelligence. In N. Colangelo and G. A. Davis

(Eds.), *Handbook of gifted education* (2nd ed., pp. 366–381). Boston: Allyn and Bacon.

Reid, C., Romanoff, B., Algozzine, B., & Udall, A. (2000). An evaluation of alternative screening procedures. *Journal for the Education of the Gifted, 23*, 378–396.

Reis, S. (2000, March). Overcoming barriers to girls' talent development. *Parenting for High Potential*, pp. 18–21.

Reis, S., & McCoach, D. B. (2000). The underachievement of gifted students: What do we know and where do we go? *Gifted Child Quarterly, 44*, 152–170.

Reis, S. M., McGuire, J. M., & Neu, T. W. (2000, Spring). Compensation strategies used by high-ability students with learning disabilities who succeed in college. *Gifted Child Quarterly, 44*, 123–134.

Reis, S., & Park, S. (2001). Gender differences in high-achieving students in math and science. *Journal for the Education of the Gifted, 25*, 52–73.

Renzulli, J. S., & Park, S. (2000, Fall). Gifted dropouts: The who and the why. *Gifted Child Quarterly, 44, 261*–271.

Rimm, S., & Rimm-Kaufman, S. (2001). *How Jane won: 55 successful women share how they grew from ordinary girls to extraordinary women.* New York: Crown Publishers.

Roberts, S. M., & Lovett, S. B. (1994). Examining the "F" in gifted: Academically gifted adolescents' physiological and affective responses to scholastic failure. *Journal for the Education of the Gifted, 17*, 241–259.

Robinson, S. M. (1999). Meeting the needs of students who are gifted and have learning disabilities. *Intervention in School and Clinic, 34*, 195–204.

Rogers, K. B. (1999). The lifelong productivity of the female researchers in Terman's genetic studies of genius longitudinal study. *Gifted Child Quarterly, 43*, 150–169.

Shaywitz, S. E., Holahan, J. M., Fletcher, J. M., Freudenheim, D. A., Makuch, R. W., & Shaywitz, B. A. (2001, Winter). Heterogeneity within the gifted: Higher IQ boys exhibit behaviors resembling boys with learning disabilities. *Gifted Child Quarterly, 45*, 16–23.

Silverman, L. K. (1995). Gifted and talented. In E. L. Meyen and T. M. Skrtic (Eds.), *Exceptional children and youth: An introduction* (4th ed., pp. 377–414). Denver, CO: Love.

Swiatek, M., & Lupkowski-Shoplik, A. (2000). Gender differences in academic attitudes among gifted elementary school students. *Journal for the Education of the Gifted, 23*, 360–377.

Tomlinson, C. A., Callahan, C. M., & Lelli, K. M. (1998). Challenging expectations: Case studies of high-potential, culturally diverse young children. *Gifted Child Quarterly, 41*, 5–17.

VanTassel-Baska, J. (1995). The development of talent through curriculum. *Roeper Review, 18*, 98–102.

Willard-Holt, C. (1998). Academic and personality characteristics of gifted students with cerebral palsy: A multiple case study. *Exceptional Children, 65*, 37–50.

Yong, F. L., & McIntyre, J. D. (1992). A comparative study of the learning style preferences of students with learning disabilities and students who are gifted. *Journal of Learning Disabilities, 25*, 124–132.

Zentall, S., Moon, S., Hall, A., & Grskovic, J. A. (2001). Learning and motivational characteristics of boys with AD/HD and/or giftedness. *Exceptional Children, 67*, 499–519.

Early Childhood Education

Castillo, L. C. (1998). The effect of analogy instruction on young children's metaphor comprehension. *Roeper Review, 21*, 27–31.

Gallagher, J. J., & Gallagher, S. A. (1994). *Teaching the gifted child* (4th ed.). Boston: Allyn and Bacon.

Karnes, M. B., Shwedel, A. M., & Linnemeyer, S. A. (1982). The young gifted/talented child: Programs at the University of Illinois. *Elementary School Journal, 82*, 196–213.

McBride-Chang, C., Manis, F. R., & Wagner, R. K. (1996). Correlates of phonological awareness: Implications for gifted education. *Roeper Review, 19*, 27–30.

Mooij, T. (1999). Integrating gifted children into kindergarten by improving educational processes. *Gifted Child Quarterly, 43*, 63–74.

Smutny, J. F. (2000, May). Teaching young gifted children in the regular classroom. (Report No. E595-EDO-EC-00-4). ERIC Digest, Reston, VA: The Council for Exceptional Children.

Strom, R. D. (2000, March). Too busy to play? *Parenting for High Potential*, pp. 18–22.

Tucker, B., & Hafenstein, N. L. (1997). Psychological intensities in young gifted children. *Gifted Child Quarterly, 41*, 66–75.

Elementary Through High School

Banks, J. A. (1994). *An introduction to multicultural education.* Boston: Allyn and Bacon.

Coleman, L. J. (2001, Summer). A "rag quilt": Social relationships among students in a special high school. *Gifted Child Quarterly, 45*, 164–173.

Gallagher, J. J. (2000, Winter). Unthinkable thoughts: Education of gifted students. *Gifted Child Quarterly, 44*, 5–12.

Gallagher, J., Harradine, C. C., & Coleman, M. R. (1997). Gifted students in the classroom: Challenge or boredom? Gifted students' views on their schooling. *Roeper Review, 19*, 132–136.

Hébert, T. P., & Olenchak, F. R. (2000, Summer). Mentors for gifted underachieving males: Developing potential and realizing promises. *Gifted Child Quarterly, 44*, 196–207.

Hishinuma, E. S., & Nishimura, S. T. (2000, June). Parent attitudes on the importance of success of integrated self-contained services for students who are gifted, learning disabled and gifted/learning disabled. *Roeper Review, 22*, 241–250.

Kulik, J. A., & Kulik, C. L. C. (1997). Ability grouping. In N. Colangelo and G. A. Davis (Eds.), *Handbook of gifted education* (2nd ed., pp. 230–242). Boston: Allyn and Bacon.

Lubinski, D., & Benbow, C. P. (1995). Optimal development of talent: Respond educationally to individual differences in personality. *The Educational Forum, 59*, 381–392.

Pendarvis, E., & Howley, A. (1996). Playing fair: The possibilites of gifted education. *Journal for the Education of the Gifted, 19*, 215–233.

Purcell, J. H., Renzulli, J. S., McCoach, D. B., & Spottiswoode, H. (2001, December). The magic of mentorships. *Parenting for High Potential*, pp. 22–26.

Ramsay, S. G., & Richards, H. C. (1997). Cooperative learning environments: Effects on academic attitudes of gifted students. *Gifted Child Quarterly, 41*, 160–168.

Renzulli, J. S. (1999, October). A rising tide lifts all ships: Developing the gifts and talents of all students. *Phi Delta Kappan, 80*, 104–111.

Renzulli, J. S., & Reis, S. M. (1997). The schoolwide enrichment model: New directions for developing high-end learning. In N. Colangelo and G. A. Davis (Eds.), *Handbook of gifted education* (2nd ed., pp. 136–154). Boston: Allyn and Bacon.

Rogers, K. B. (2002). Grouping the gifted and talented: Questions and answers. *Roeper Review, 24*, 102–107.

Schuler, P. A. (1997). *Cluster grouping coast to coast*. National Research Center on the Gifted and Talented Winter Newsletter, pp. 11–14.

Slavin, R. E. (1990). Ability grouping, cooperative learning and the gifted. *Journal for the Education of the Gifted, 14,* 3–8.

Tomlinson, C. A. (2000, April). Complex instruction: A powerful cooperative strategy. *Teaching for High Potential,* pp. 1–3.

VanTassel-Baska, J. (1995). The development of talent through curriculum. *Roeper Review, 18,* 98–102.

Witham, J. H. (1997). Public or private schools: A dilemma for gifted students? *Roeper Review, 19,* 137–141.

Collaboration for Inclusion

Castellano, J. A., & Díaz, E. I. (Eds.). (2002). *Reaching new horizons: Gifted and talented education for culturally and linguistically diverse students.* Boston: Allyn and Bacon.

Ford, D., Harris III, J., Tyson, C., & Trotman, T. (2002, Winter). Beyond deficit thinking: Providing access for gifted African American students. *Roeper Review, 24,* 52–58.

Harmon, D. (2002, Winter). They won't teach me: The voices of gifted African American inner-city students. *Roeper Review, 24,* 68–75.

Kitano, M. & DiJiosia, M. (2002). Are Asian and Pacific Americans overrepresented in programs for the gifted? *Roeper Review, 24,* 76–80.

Robinson, S. M. (1999). Meeting the needs of students who are gifted and have learning disabilities. *Intervention in School and Clinic, 34,* 195–204.

Transition Through Adulthood

Achter, J. A., Lubinski, D., & Benbow, C. P. (1996). Multipotentiality among the intellectually gifted: "It was never there and already it's vanishing." *Journal of Counseling Psychology, 43,* 65–76.

Benbow, D. P., & Stanley, J. C. (1996). Inequity in equity: How "equity" can lead to inequity for high-potential students. *Psychology, Public Policy, and Law, 2,* 249–292.

Filippelli, K. A., & Walberg, H. J. (1997). Childhood traits and conditions of eminent women scientists. *Gifted Child Quarterly, 41,* 95–103.

Holliday, G. A., Koller, J. R., & Thomas, C. D. (1999). *Journal for the Education of the Gifted, 22,* 266–281.

Kitano, M. K. (1997). Gifted Asian American women. *Journal for the Education of the Gifted, 21,* 3–37.

Kitano, M. K. (1998). Gifted Latina women. *Journal for the Education of the Gifted, 21,* 131–159.

Kitano, M., & DiJiosia, M. (2002, Winter). Are Asian and Pacific Americans overrepresented in programs for the gifted? *Roeper Review, 24,* 76–80.

Kitano, M., & Perkins, C. (2000). Gifted European American women. *Journal for the Education of the Gifted, 23,* 287–313.

Oden, M. H. (1968). The fulfillment of promise: 40-year follow-up of the Terman gifted group. *Genetic Psychology Monographs, 77,* 3–93.

Peterson, J. (2000, June). A follow-up study of one group of achievers and underachievers four years after high school graduation. *Roeper Review, 22,* 217–224.

Peterson, J. S. (2000, Fall). Gifted and at risk: Four longitudinal case studies of post-high-school development. *Roeper Review, 24,* 31–39.

Renzulli, J. S., & Park, S. (2000, Fall). Gifted dropouts: The who and the why. *Gifted Child Quarterly, 44,* 261–271.

Terman, L. (1925). *Genetic studies of genius* (Vol. 1). Stanford, CA: Stanford University Press.

Terman, L. M., & Oden, M. H. (1959). *The gifted group at midlife.* Stanford, CA: Stanford University Press.

Walberg, H. J., & Zeiser, S. (1997). Productivity, accomplishment, and eminence. In N. Colangelo & G. A. Davis (Eds.), *Handbook of gifted education* (2nd ed., 238–334). Boston: Allyn and Bacon.

Families

Clark, B. (2002). *Growing up gifted* (6th ed.) Upper Saddle River, NJ: Merrill.

Filippelli, K. A., & Walberg, H. J. (1997). Childhood traits and conditions of eminent women scientists. *Gifted Child Quarterly, 41,* 95–103.

Hébert, T. P. (1998). Gifted black males in an urban high school: Factors that influence achievement and underachievement. *Journal for the Education of the Gifted, 21,* 385–414.

Hébert, T. (2001, June). Man to man: Building channels of communication between fathers and their talented sons. *Parenting for High Potential,* pp. 18–22.

Kitano, M. K. (1997). Gifted Asian American women. *Journal for the Education of the Gifted, 21,* 3–37.

Kitano, M. K. (1998). Gifted Latina women. *Journal for the Education of the Gifted, 21,* 131–159.

Nicols, H. J., & Baum, S. (2000, December). High achievers: Keys to helping youngsters with stress reduction. *Parenting for High Potential,* pp. 9–12.

Piechowski, M. (1997). Emotional giftedness: The measure of intrapersonal intelligence. In N. Colangelo and G. A. Davis (Eds.), *Handbook of gifted education* (2nd ed., pp. 366–381). Boston: Allyn and Bacon.

Rimm, S. (2001, December). Parents as role models and mentors. *Parenting for High Potential,* pp. 14–15, 27.

Subotnik, R., Kassan, L., Summers, E., & Wasser, A. (1993). *Genius revisited: High IQ children grow up.* Norwood, NJ: Ablex Publishing.

Yewchuk, C. R. (1995). The "mad genius" controversy: Implications for gifted education. *Journal for the Education of the Gifted, 19,* 3–29.

Technology

Johnson, D. T. (2000). Teaching mathematics to gifted students in mixed-ability classrooms. *ERIC Digest, E594.* Reston, VA: ERIC Clearinghouse on Disabilities and Gifted Education, the Council for Exceptional Children.

CHAPTER 8

Emotional or Behavioral Disorders

Edvard Munch

Bischoff, U. (1988). *Edvard Munch: 1863–1944.* Köln, Germany: Benedikt Taschen Verlag GmbH & Co.

Grolier. (1993). *The new Grolier multimedia encyclopedia.* Danbury, CT: Grolier Electronic Publishing.

Messer, T. M. (1985). *Munch.* New York: Harry N. Abrams.

Emotional or Behavioral Disorders Defined

American Psychiatric Association. (1994). *Diagnostic and statistical manual of mental disorders* (DSM-IV) (4th ed.). Washington, DC: Author.

Bower, E. M. (1960). *Early identification of emotionally disturbed children in school* (Rev. ed.). Springfield, IL: Charles C Thomas.

Bower, E. M. (1982). Defining emotional disturbance: Public policy and research. *Psychology in the Schools, 19,* 55–60.

Bussing, R., Schoenberg, N. E., Rogers, K. M., Zima, B. T., & Angus, S. (1998). Explanatory models of ADHD: Do they differ by ethnicity, child gender, or treatment status? *Journal of Emotional and Behavior Disorders, 6,* 233–242.

Bussing, R., Zima, B. T., Belin, T. R., & Forness, S. R. (1998). Children who qualify for LD & SED programs: Do they differ in level of ADHD symptoms and co-morbid psychiatric conditions? *Behavioral Disorders, 23,* 85–97.

Costenbader, V., & Buntaine, R. (1999). Diagnostic discrimination between social maladjustment and emotional disturbance. *Journal of Emotional and Behavioral Disorders, 7,* 2–10.

Edens, J. F., & Otto, R. K. (1997). Prevalence of mental disorders among youth in the juvenile justice system. *Focal Point, 11,* 1, 6–7.

Forness, S. R., & Knitzer, J. (1992). A new proposed definition and terminology to replace "serious emotional disturbance" in IDEA. *School Psychology Review, 21,* 12–20.

Gresham, F. M, Lane, K. L., MacMillan, D. L., & Bocian, K. M. (1999). Social and academic profiles of externalizing and internalizing groups: Risk factors for emotional and behavioral disorders. *Behavioral Disorders, 24,* 231–245.

Gresham, F. M., Lane, K. L., & Lambros, K. M. (2000, Summer). Cormorbidity of conduct problems and ADHD: Identification of "fledgling psychopaths." *Journal of Emotional and Behavioral Disorders, 8,* 83–93.

Hallahan, D. P., & Kauffman, J. M. (2000). *Exceptional children: Introduction to special education* (8th ed.). Boston: Allyn and Bacon.

IDEA Practices. (2002). *Youth with disabilities in the juvenile justice system.* Retrieved July 17, 2002 from www.ideapractices.org

Jensen, P. S. (2000, Winter). ADHD: Advances in understanding its causes, and best treatments. *Emotional and Behavioral Disorders in Youth, 1,* 9–10, 19.

Kauffman, J. M. (2001). *Characteristics of behavioral disorders of children and youth* (7th ed.). Columbus, OH: Merrill.

Lane, K. L. (1999, Winter). Young students at risk for anti-social behavior: The utility of academic and social skills interventions. *Journal of Emotional and Behavioral Disorders, 7,* 211–223.

Lane, K. L., & Wehby, J. (2002). Addressing antisocial behavior in the schools: A call for action. *Academic Exchange Quarterly, 6,* 4–9.

Lane, K. L., O'Shaughnessy, T. E., Lambros, K. M., Gresham, F. M., & Beebe-Frankenberger, M. E. (2001, Winter). The efficacy of phonological awareness training with first-grade students who have behavioral problems and reading difficulties. *Journal of Emotional and Behavioral Disorders, 9,* 219–231.

Maag, J. W. (2000, January). Managing resistance. *Intervention in Schools and Clinics, 35,* 131–140.

Manley, R. S., Rickson, H., & Standeven, B. (2000, March). Children and adolescents with eating disorders: Strategies for teachers and school counselors. *Intervention in School and Clinic, 35,* 228–231.

Merrell, K.W., & Boelter, E. (2001, Winter). An investigation of relationships between social behavior and ADHD in children and youth: Construct validity of the home and community social behavior scales. *Journal of Emotional and Behavioral Disorders, 9,* 260–269.

National Center for Educational Statistics (NCES). (2001). *Quick tables and figures.* www.nces.ed.gov/quicktables

Newcomer, P. L. (1993). *Understanding and teaching emotionally disturbed children and adolescents* (2nd ed.). Austin, TX: Pro-Ed.

Newcorn, J. H. (2001, Summer). New medication treatment for ADHD. *Emotional and Behavioral Disorders in Youth,* pp. 59–61.

Oswald, D. P., & Coutinho, M. J. (1996). Identification and placement of students with serious emotional disturbance. Part I: Correlates of state child-count data. *Journal of Emotional and Behavioral Disorders, 3,* 224–229.

Office of Special Education Programs (OSEP). (2001). Special education in correctional facilities. In U.S. Department of Education, *The twenty-third annual report to Congress on the implementation of IDEA.* Washington, DC: U.S. Government Printing Office.

Pappadopulos, E., & Jensen, P. S. (2001, Spring). What school professionals, counselors, and parents need to know about medication for emotional and behavioral disorders in kids. *Emotional and Behavioral Disorders in Youth,* pp. 35–37.

Reid, R., Riccio, C. A., Kessler, R. H., DuPaul, G. J., Power, T. J., Anastopoulos, A. D., Rogers-Adkinson, D., & Noll, M. B. (2000, Spring). Gender and ethnic differences in ADHD as assessed by behavior ratings. *Journal of Emotional and Behavioral Disorders, 8,* 38–48.

Sugai, G., Sprague, J. R., Horner, R. H., & Walker, H. M. (2000, Summer). Preventing school violence: The use of office discipline referrals to assess and monitor school-wide discipline interventions. *Journal of Emotional and Behavioral Disorders, 8,* 94–101.

Talbott, E., & Thiede, K. (1999). Pathways to antisocial behavior among adolescent girls. *Journal of Emotional and Behavioral Disorders, 7,* 31–39.

Townsend, B. L. (2000, Spring). The disproportionate discipline of African American learners: Reducing school suspensions and expulsions. *Exceptional Children, 66,* 381–391.

U.S. Department of Education. (1999). *Assistance to state for the education of children with disabilities and the early intervention program for infants and toddlers with disabilities: Final regulations.* Federal Register, 64 (48), CFR Parts 300 and 303.

U.S. Department of Education. (2001). *The twenty-third annual report to Congress on the implementation of IDEA.* Washington, DC: U.S. Government Printing Office.

Volpe, R. J., DuPaul, G. J., Loney, J., & Salisbury, H. (1999). Alternative selection criteria for identifying children with ADHD: Observed behavior and self-reported internalizing symptoms. *Journal of Emotional and Behavioral Disorders, 7,* 103–109.

Walker, H. M. (2000, Winter). Investigating school-related behavior disorders: Lessons learned from a thirty-year research career. *Exceptional Children, 66,* 151–161.

Walker, H. M., Nishioka, V., Zeller, R., Bullis, M., & Sprague, J. R. (2001, Summer). School-based screening, identification, and service delivery issues. *Emotional and Behavioral Disorders in Youth, 1,* 51–52.

Zirkel, P. (1999, February 12). How to determine eligibility of students with problem behaviors. *The Special Educator, 17,* 1, 7–8.

History of the Field

Allen, K. M., Hart, B. M., Buell, J. S., Harris, F. R., & Wolf, M. M. (1964). Effects of social reinforcement on isolated behavior of a nursery school child. *Child Development, 35,* 511–518.

Bower, E. M., & Lambert, N. M. (1962). *A process for in-school screening of children with emotional handicaps.* Princeton, NJ: Educational Testing Service.

Brigham, A. (1847). The moral treatment of insanity. *American Journal of Insanity, 4,* 1–15.

Deutsch, A. (1949). *The mentally ill in America: A history of their care and treatment from colonial times* (2nd ed.). New York: Columbia University Press.

Duckworth, S., Smith-Rex, S., Okey, S., Brookshire, M., Rawlinson, D., Rawlinson, R., Castillo, S., & Little, J. et al. (2001, March/April). Wraparound services for young schoolchildren with emotional and behavioral disorders. *Teaching Exceptional Children, 33,* 54–60.

Haring, N. J., & Phillips, E. L. (1962). *Educating emotionally disturbed children.* New York: McGraw-Hill.

Healy, W., & Bronner, A. F. (1926). *Delinquents and criminals: Their making and unmaking.* New York: Macmillan.

Kanner, L. *Child Psychiatry.* Springfield, IL: Charles C Thomas.

Safford, P. L., & Safford, E. J. (1996). *A history of childhood and disability.* New York: Teachers College Press.

Prevalence

Kauffman, J. M. (2001). *Characteristics of behavioral disorders of children and youth* (7th ed.). Columbus, OH: Merrill.

Townsend, B. L. (2000, Spring). The disproportionate discipline of African American learners: Reducing school suspensions and expulsions. *Exceptional Children, 66,* 381–391.

U.S. Department of Education. (2001). *The twenty-third annual report to Congress on the implementation of IDEA.* Washington, DC: U.S. Government Printing Office.

Walker, H. M., Nishioka, V., Zeller, R., Bullis, M., & Sprague, J. R. (2001, Summer). School-based screening, identification, and service delivery issues. *Emotional and Behavioral Disorders in Youth, 1,* 51–52.

Causes and Prevention

American Psychiatric Association. (1994). *Diagnostic and statistical manual of mental disorders (DSM-IV)* (4th ed.). Washington, DC: Author.

Bullis, M., Walker, H. M., & Sprague, J. R. (2001). A promise unfulfilled: Social skills training with at-risk and antisocial children and youth. *Exceptionality, 9,* 67–90.

Burrell, B., Wood, S. J., Pikes, T., & Holliday, C. (2001, January/February). Student mentors and protégés learning together. *Teaching Exceptional Children, 33,* 24–29.

Cartledge, G., Kea, C. D., & Ida, D. J. (2000, January/February). Anticipating differences—celebrating strengths: Providing culturally competent services for students with serious emotional disturbance. *Teaching Exceptional Children, 32,* 30–37.

Cauce, A., Paradise, M., Ginzler, J., Embry, L., Morgan, C. J., Lohr, Y., & Theofelis, J. (2000, Winter). The characteristics and mental health of homeless adolescents: Age and gender differences. *Journal of Emotional and Behavioral Disorders, 8,* 230–239.

Children's Defense Fund (CDF) (2001). *The state of America's children.* Washington, DC: Children's Defense Fund.

Feil, E. G., Walker, H. M., & Severson, H. H. (1995). The early screening project for young children with behavior problems. *Journal of Emotional and Behavioral Disorders, 3,* 194–202.

Forness, S. R., & Kavale, K. A. (2001, Fall). Are school professionals missing their best chance to help troubled kids? *Emotional and Behavioral Disorders, 1,* 80–83.

Hallahan, D. P., & Kauffman, J. M. (2000). *Exceptional children: Introduction to special education* (8th ed.). Boston: Allyn and Bacon.

Horner, R. H., Sugai, G., Lewis-Palmer, T., & Todd, A. W. (2001, Fall). Teaching school-wide behavioral expectations. *Emotional & Behavioral Expectations, 1,* 77–79, 93–95.

Hosp, J. L., & Reschly, D. J. (2002, Winter). Predictors of restrictiveness of placement for African-American and Caucasian students. *Exceptional Children, 68,* 225–238.

Hunter, L., & Chopra, V. (2001, Summer). Two proactive primary prevention program models that work in schools. *Emotional & Behavioral Disorders in Youth, 57–58,* 71.

Kamps, D., Kravits, T., Stolze, J., & Swaggart, B. (1999). Prevention strategies for at-risk students and students with EBD in urban elementary schools. *Journal of Emotional and Behavioral Disorders, 7,* 178–188.

Kauffman, J. M. (1999). How we prevent the prevention of emotional and behavioral disorders. *Exceptional Children, 65,* 448–468.

Maag, J. W. (2000, January). Managing resistance. *Intervention in School and Clinic, 35,* 131–140.

McLane, K. (1997). School-wide behavioral management systems. *Research Connections in Special Education, 1,* 1–5.

National Alliance of Black School Educators [NABSE] & ILIAD Project. (2002). *Addressing over-representation of African American students in special education.* Arlington, VA: Council for Exceptional Children, and Washington, DC: National Alliance of Black School Educators.

Office of Special Education Programs (OSEP). (2001). Special education in correctional facilities. In U.S. Department of Education, *The twenty-third annual report to Congress on the implementation of IDEA.* Washington, DC: U.S. Government Printing Office.

Pancheri, C., & Prater, M. A. (1999). What teachers and parents should know about Ritalin. *Teaching Exceptional Children, 31,* 20–26.

Pappadopulos, E., & Jensen, P. S. (2001, Spring). What school professionals, counselors, and parents need to know about medication for emotional and behavioral disorders in kids. *Emotional & Behavioral Disorders in Youth,* 35–37.

Rivera, D. P., & Smith, D. D. (1997). *Teaching students with learning and behavior problems.* Boston: Allyn and Bacon.

Rudo, Z. H., Powell, D. S., & Dunlap, G. (1998). The effects of violence in the home on children's emotional, behavioral, and social functioning: A review of the literature. *Journal of Emotional and Behavioral Disorders, 6,* 94–113.

Sinclair, E. (1998). Head Start children at risk: Relationship of prenatal drug exposure to identification of special needs and subsequent special education kindergarten placement. *Behavioral Disorders, 23,* 125–133.

Smith, D. D., & Rivera, D. P. (1993). *Effective discipline.* Austin, TX: Pro-Ed.

Strain, P. S., & Timm, M. A. (1998). *The early childhood intervention study. Nashville: Regional Intervention Project (RIP).* Unpublished paper.

Tobin, T., Sugai, G., & Colvin, G. (1996). Patterns in middle school discipline records. *Journal of Emotional and Behavioral Disorders, 4,* 82–94.

Tolan, P., Gorman-Smith, D., & Henry, D. (2001, Winter). New study to focus on efficacy of "whole school" prevention approaches. *Emotional & Behavioral Disorders in Youth, 2,* 5–6, 22–23.

Townsend, B. L. (2000, Spring). The disproportionate discipline of African American learners: Reducing school suspensions and expulsions. *Exceptional Children, 66,* 381–391.

Walker, H. M., & Sprague, J. (1999). The path to school failure, delinquency, and violence: Causal factors and potential solutions. *Intervention in School and Clinic, 35,* 67–73.

Walker, H. M., & Gresham, F. M. (1997). Making schools safer and violence free. *Intervention in School and Clinic, 32,* 199–204.

Walker, H. M., & Sprague, J. R. (2000, Winter). Intervention strategies for diverting at-risk children and youth from destructive outcomes. *Emotional and Behavioral Disorders in Youth, 1,* 5–8.

Zametkin, A. J., & Earnst, M. (1999). Problems in the management of attention-deficit-hyperactivity disorder. *New England Journal of Medicine, 340,* 40–46.

Characteristics

Archwamety, T., & Katsiyannis, A. (2000, May/June). Academic remediation, parole violations, and recidivism rates among delinquent youth. *Remedial and Special Education, 21,* 161–170.

Bullis, M., Walker, H. M., & Sprague, J. R. (2001). A promise unfulfilled: Social skills training with at-risk and antisocial children and youth. *Exceptionality, 9,* 67–90.

Englert, C. S., Tarrant, K. L., & Mariage, T. V. (1992). Defining and redefining instructional practice in special education: Perspectives on good teaching. *Teacher Education and Special Education, 15,* 62–86.

Espin, C. A., & Yell, M. L. (1994). Critical indicators of effective teaching for preservice teachers: Relationships between teaching behaviors and ratings of effectiveness. *Teacher Education and Special Education, 17,* 154–169.

Frey, K. S., Hirschstein, M. K., & Guzzo, B. A. (2000, Summer). Second step: Preventing aggression by promoting social competence. *Journal of Emotional and Behavioral Disorders, 8,* 102–112.

Gresham, F. M., Lane, K. L., & MacMillan, D. L. (1999, May). Social and academic profiles of externalizing and internalizing groups: Risk factors for emotional and behavioral disorders. *Behavioral Disorders, 24,* 231–245.

Hawkins, J. D., Catalano, R. F., Kosterman, R., Abbott, R., & Hill, K. G. (1999). Preventing adolescent health-risk behaviors by strengthening protection during childhood. *Archives of Pediatrics & Adolescent Medicine, 1153,* 226–234.

Lane, K. L. (1999, Winter). Young students at risk for anti-social behavior: The utility of academic and social skills interventions. *Journal of Emotional and Behavioral Disorders, 7,* 211–223.

Lane, K. L., & Wehby, J. (2002). Addressing antisocial behavior in the schools: A call for action. *Academic Exchange Quarterly, 6,* 4–9.

National Center for Educational Statistics (NCES). (2001). *Quick tables and figures.* www.nces.ed.gov/quicktables

Office of Special Education Programs (OSEP). (2001). Special education in correctional facilities. In U.S. Department of Education, *The twenty-third annual report to Congress on the implementation of IDEA.* Washington, DC: U.S. Government Printing Office.

Rosenshine, B. (1995). Advances in research on instruction. *Journal of Educational Research, 88,* 262–268.

Safran, S. P. (1995). Peer's perceptions of emotional and behavioral disorders: What are students thinking? *Journal of Emotional and Behavioral Disorders, 3,* 66–75.

Sutherland, K. S. (2000). Promoting positive interactions between teachers and students with emotional/behavioral disorders. *Preventing School Failure, 44,* 110–115.

Sutherland, K. S., Wehby, J. H., & Copeland, S. R. (2000). Effect of varying rates of behavior-specific praise on the on-task behavior of students with EBD. *Journal of Emotional and Behavioral Disorders, 8,* 2–8, 26.

U.S. Department of Education (2001). *The twenty-third annual report to Congress on the implementation of IDEA.* Washington, DC: U.S. Government Printing Office.

Webhy, J. H., Symons, F. J., Canale, J. A., & Go, F. J. (1998). Teaching practices in classrooms for students with emotional and behavioral disorders: Discrepancies between recommendations and observations. *Behavioral Disorders, 24,* 51–56.

Early Childhood Education

Barrish, H. H., Saunders, M., & Wolf. M. M. (1969). Good behavior game: Effects of individual contingencies for group consequences on disruptive behavior in classroom. *Journal of Applied Behavior analysis, 2,* 119–124.

Bullis, M., Walker, H. M., & Sprague, J. R. (2001). A promise unfulfilled: Social skills training with at-risk and antisocial children and youth. *Exceptionality, 9,* 67–90.

Day, D. M., & Hunt, A. C. (1996). A multivariate assessment of a risk model for juvenile delinquency with an "under 12 offender" sample. *Journal of Emotional and Behavioral Disorders, 4,* 66–72.

Feil, E. G., Walker, H. M., & Severson, H. H. (1995). The early screening project for young children with behavior problems. *Journal of Emotional and Behavioral Disorders, 3,* 194–202.

Little, L. (2002, Winter). In preschool classrooms: Linking research to practice. *Early developments,* pp. 7–9.

Miller-Johnson, S., Coie, J. E., Maumary-Gremaud, A., Lockman, J., & Terry, R. (1999). Relationship between childhood peer rejection and aggression and adolescent delinquency severity and type among African-American youth. *Journal of Emotional and Behavioral Disorders, 7,* 137–146.

Strain, P. S., & Timm, M. A. (1998). *The early childhood intervention study.* Nashville: Regional Intervention Project (RIP). Unpublished paper.

Strain, P. S., & Timm, M. A. (1999). *Preliminary results from the early childhood intervention study.* Nashville: Regional Intervention Project (RIP). Unpublished paper.

Strain, P. S., Steele, P., Ellis, R., & Timm, M. (1982). Long-term effects of oppositional child treatment with mothers as therapists and therapist trainers. *Journal of Applied Behavior Analysis, 15,* 163–169.

Tobin, T. J., & Sugai, G. M. (1999). Using sixth-grade school records to predict school violence, chronic discipline problems, and high school outcomes. *Journal of Emotional and Behavioral Disorders, 7,* 40–53.

Walker, H. M., Kavanagh, K., Stiller, B., Golly, A., Severson, H. H., & Feil, E. G. (1998). First Step to Success: An early intervention approach for preventing school antisocial behavior. *Journal of Emotional and Behavioral Disorders, 6,* 66–80.

Walker, H. M., & Sprague, J. (1999). The path to school failure, delinquency, and violence: Causal factors and potential solutions. *Intervention in School and Clinic, 35,* 67–73.

Walker, H. M., & Sprague, J. R. (2000, Winter). Intervention strategies for diverting at-risk children and youth from destructive outcomes. *Emotional and Behavioral Disorders in Youth, 1,* 5–8.

Walker, H. M., & Sylvester, R. (1994). Where is school along the path to prison? *The Frontline, 1,* 3–6.

Elementary Through High School

Axelrod, S., & Hall, R. V. (1999). *Behavior modification: Basic principles.* Austin, TX: Pro-Ed.

Babyak, A. E., Luze, G. J., & Kamps, D. M. (2000, March). The good student game: Behavior management for diverse classrooms. *Intervention in School and Clinic, 35,* 216–223.

Barrish, H. H., Saunders, M., & Wolf. M. M. (1969). Good behavior game: Effects of individual contingencies for group consequences on disruptive behavior in classroom. *Journal of Applied Behavior analysis, 2,* 119–124.

Begley, S. (1999, May 3). Why the young kill. *Newsweek,* pp. 32–35.

Bender, W. N., & McLaughlin, P. J. (1997). Weapons violence in schools: Strategies for teachers confronting violence and hostage situations. *Intervention in School and Clinic, 32,* 211–216.

Bender, W. N., Shubert, T. H., & McLaughlin, P. J. (2001, November). Invisible kids: Preventing school violence by identifying kids in trouble. *Intervention in School and Clinic, 37,* 105–111.

Brophy, F. (1981). Teacher praise: A functional analysis. *Review of Educational Research, 51,* 5–32.

Bryant, D. P., Smith, D. D., & Curren, C. (in press). *Systematic discipline.* Dallas, TX: Sopris.

Children's Defense Fund (CDF). (2001). *The state of America's children.* Washington, DC: Children's Defense Fund.

Cruz, L., & Cullinan, D. (2001, January/February). Awarding points, using levels to help children improve behavior. *Teaching Exceptional Children, 33,* 16–23.

Deveres, L. (1999a, August 27). Social skills training aids students in life's lessons. *The Special Educator, 15,* 1, 8–9.

Deveres, L. (1999b). *A primer on functional behavioral assessments.* Horsham, PA: LRP Publications.

Fuchs, L. S., & Fuchs, D. (2000). Curriculum-based and performance assessment. In E. S. Shapiro & T. R. Kratochwill (Eds.), *Behavioral assessment in schools: Theory, research, and clinical foundations* (2nd ed., pp. 168–201). New York: Guilford.

Furlong, M., & Morrison, G. (2000, Summer). The *school* in school violence: Definitions and facts. *Journal of Emotional and Behavioral Disorders, 8,* 71–82.

Gable, R. A., Hendrickson, J. M., Young, C. C., Shores, R. E., & Stowitschek, J. J. (1983). A comparison of teacher approval and disapproval statements across categories of exceptionality. *Journal of Special Education Technology, 6,* 15–22.

Hall, R. V., Lund, D., & Jackson, D. (1968). Effects of teacher attention on study behavior. *Journal of Applied Behavior Analysis, 1,* 315–322.

Hartwig, E., & Ruesch, G. (1998). *Discipline in the schools.* Horsham, PA: LRP Publications.

Kauffman, J. M. (2001). *Characteristics of behavioral disorders of children and youth* (7th ed.). Columbus, OH: Merrill.

Kern, L., Delaney, B., Clarke, S., Dunlap, G., & Childs, K. (2001, Winter). Improving the classroom behavior of students with emotional and behavioral disorders using individualized curricular modifications. *Journal of Emotional and Behavioral Disorders, 9,* 239–247.

Lane, K. L., & Wehby, J. (2002). Addressing antisocial behavior in the schools: A call for action. *Academic Exchange Quarterly, 6,* 4–9.

Lohrmann-O'Rourke, S., & Zirkel, P. A. (1998). The case law on aversive interventions for students with disabilities. *Exceptional Children, 65,* 101–123.

Maag, J. W. (2001, Winter). Rewarded by punishment: Reflections on the disuse of positive reinforcement in schools. *Exceptional Children, 67,* 173–186.

Myles, B. S., & Simpson, R. L. (1998). Aggression and violence by school-age children and youth: Understanding the aggression cycle and prevention/intervention strategies. *Intervention in School and Clinic, 33,* 259–264.

National Center on Education, Disability, and Juvenile Justice. (2002). Monograph series on education, disability, and juvenile justice. Retrieved July 13, 2002, from http://www.edjj.org/monographs/index.html

Nelson, J. R., Crabtree, M., Marchand-Martella, N., & Martella, R. (1998). Teaching good behavior in the whole school. *Teaching Exceptional Children, 30,* 4–9.

Nichols, P. (2000, Spring). Role of cognition and affect in a functional behavioral analysis. *Exceptional Children, 66,* 393–402.

O'Leary, K. D., & Becker, W. C. (1969). The effects of the intensity of a teacher's reprimands on children's behavior. *Journal of School Psychology, 7,* 8–11.

Rosenberg, M. S., & Jackman, L. A. (1997). Addressing student and staff behavior: The PAR model. *The Fourth R, 79,* 1–12.

Rosenberg, M. S., & Jackman, L. A. (2002). *Development, implementation, and sustainability of comprehensive school-wide behavior management systems.* Johns Hopkins University: Manuscript submitted for publication.

Smith, D. D. (1984). *Effective discipline.* Austin, TX: Pro-Ed.

Smith, D. D., & Rivera, D. P. (1993). *Effective discipline* (2nd ed.). Austin, TX: Pro-Ed.

Sutherland, K. S., & Wehby, J. H. (2001) The effects of self-evaluation on teaching behaviors in classrooms for students with emotional and behavioral disorders. *Journal of Special Education, 35,* 161–171.

Sutherland, K. S., Wehby, J. H., & Yoder, P. J. (2001). An examination of the relation between teacher praise and students' with emotional/behavioral disorders opportunities to respond to academic requests. *Journal of Emotional and Behavioral Disorders, 10,* 5–14.

Townsend, B. L. (2000, Spring). The disproportionate discipline of African American learners: Reducing school suspensions and expulsions. *Exceptional Children, 66,* 381–391.

Walker, H. M., & Sprague, J. (1999). The path to school failure, delinquency, and violence: Causal factors and potential solutions. *Intervention in School and Clinic, 35,* 67–73.

Walker, H. M., & Sprague, J. R. (2000, Winter). Intervention strategies for diverting at-risk children and youth from destructive outcomes. *Emotional and Behavioral Disorders in Youth, 1,* 5–8.

Wehby, J. H., Symons, F., & Shores, R. E. (1995). A descriptive analysis of aggressive behavior in classrooms for students with emotional and behavioral disorders. *Behavioral Disorders, 20,* 87–105.

Collaboration for Inclusion

Anderson, M. (2002). *About CYC.* Retrieved July 19, 2002, from http://www.chicagoyouthcenters.org/locations/index.html

Bussing, R., Zima, B. T., Belin, T. R., & Forness, S. R. (1998). Children who qualify for LD & SED programs: Do they differ in level of ADHD symptoms and co-morbid psychiatric conditions? *Behavioral Disorders, 23,* 85–97.

Cheney, D., & Barringer, C. (1995). Teacher competence, student diversity, and staff training for the inclusion of middle school students with emotional and behavioral disorders. *Journal of Emotional and Behavioral Disorders, 3,* 174–182.

Chicago Youth Centers. (2002). *Success stories!* Retrieved July 19, 2002, from http://www.chicagoyouthcenters.org/programs/index.shtml

Eber, L., Smith, C. R., Sugai, G., & Scott, T. M. (2002). Wrap-around and positive behavioral supports in the schools. *Journal of Emotional and Behavioral Disorders, 10,* 171–180.

Edens, J. F., & Otto, R. K. (1997). Prevalence of mental disorders among youth in the juvenile justice system. *Focal Point, 11*, 1, 6–7.

Kauffman, J. M. (2001). *Characteristics of behavioral disorders of children and youth* (7th ed.). Columbus, OH: Merrill.

Lane, K. L., Gresham, F. M., & O'Shaughnessy, T. (2002). Identifying, assessing and intervening with children with or at-risk for behavior disorders: A look to the future. In K. L. Lane, F. M. Gresham, and T. E. O'Shaughnessy (Eds.), *Interventions for children with or at risk for emotional and behavioral disorders.* (pp. 317–326). Boston: Allyn and Bacon.

National Center on Education, Disability, and Juvenile Justice. (2002). Monograph series on education, disability, and juvenile justice. Retrieved July 13, 2002, from http://www.edjj.org/monographs/index.html

Sinclair, M. F., Christenson, S. L., Evelo, D. L., & Hurley, C. M. (1998). Dropout prevention for youth with disabilities: Efficacy of a sustained school engagement procedure. *Exceptional Children, 65*, 7–21.

Tobin, T. J., & Sugai, G. M. (1999). Using sixth-grade school records to predict school violence, chronic discipline problems, and high school outcomes. *Journal of Emotional and Behavioral Disorders, 7*, 40–53.

U.S. Department of Education. (2001). *The annual report to Congress on the implementation of IDEA.* Washington, DC: U.S. Government Printing Office.

Walker, H. M., & Sprague, J. (1999). The path to school failure, delinquency, and violence: Causal factors and potential solutions. *Intervention in School and Clinic, 35*, 67–73.

Walker, H. M., & Sprague, J. R. (2000, Winter). Intervention strategies for diverting at-risk children and youth from destructive outcomes. *Emotional and Behavioral Disorders in Youth, 1*, 5–8.

Transition Through Adulthood

Chesapeake Institute. (1994). *National agenda for achieving better results for children and youth with serious emotional disturbance.* Washington, DC: U.S. Department of Education, Office of Special Education Programs.

Griller-Clark, H. (2001, Spring). Transition services for youth in the juvenile justice system. *Focal Point, 15*, 23–25.

Hunter, L. (2001, Spring). The value of school-based mental health programs. *Emotional and Behavioral Disorders in Youth, 27–28*, 46.

Jolivette, K., Stichter, J. P., Nelson, C. M., Scott, T. M., & Liauspin. (2000, August). *Improving post-school outcomes for students with emotional and behavioral disorders.* Reston, VA: ERIC/OSEP Digest. (ERIC Document Reproduction Service No. EDO-EC-00-6).

McConaughy, S. H., & Wadsworth, M. E. (2000, Winter). Life history reports of young adults previously referred for mental health services. *Journal of Emotional and Behavioral Disorders, 8*, 202–215.

National Center for Educational Statistics (NCES). (2001). *Quick tables and figures.* www.nces.ed.gov/quicktables

National Center on Education, Disability, and Juvenile Justice. (2002). Monograph series on education, disability, and juvenile justice. Retrieved July 13, 2002, from http://www.edjj.org/monographs/index.html

Schoenwald, S. K., & Hoagwood, K. (2001, Winter). Effectiveness and dissemination in research: Their mutual roles in improving mental health services for children and adolescents. *Emotional and Behavioral Disorders in Youth, 2*, 3–4, 18–20.

Serna, L. A., & Lau-Smith, J. (1995). Learning with purpose: Self-determination skills for students who are at risk for school and community failure. *Intervention in School and Clinic, 30*, 142–146.

Test, D. W., Karvonen, M., Wood, W. M., Browder, D., & Algozzine, B. (2000, November/December). Choosing a self-determination curriculum. *Teaching Exceptional Children, 33*, 48–54.

U.S. Department of Education. (2001). *The annual report to Congress on the implementation of IDEA.* Washington, DC: U.S. Government Printing Office.

Wall, M. E., & Dattilo, J. (1995). Creating option-rich learning environments: Facilitating self-determination. *Journal of Special Education, 29*, 276–294.

Wehmeyer, M. L., Palmer, S. B., Agran, M., Mithaug, D. E., & Martin, J. E. (2000, Summer). Promoting causal agency: Self-determined learning model of instruction. *Exceptional Children, 66*, 439–453.

Families

Adoption and Foster Care Analysis and Reporting System (2002). *Child welfare statistics.* www.acf.dhhs.gov/programs/cb/dis/afcars/scstats.html

Ahearn, E. (Ed.). (1995, February). *Summary of the 16th annual report to Congress on special education.* Liaison Bulletin, pp. 1–3. Alexandria: NASDSE.

Ama, S., & Caplan, E. H. (2001, Spring). The human face of foster care in America. *Focal Point, 15*, 25–26.

Armsden, G., Pecora, P. J., Payne, V. H., & Szatkiewicz, J. P. (2000). Children placed in long-term foster care: An intake profile using the child behavior checklist/4–18. *Journal of Emotional and Behavioral Disorders, 8*, 49–64.

Cartledge, G., Kea, C. D., & Ida, D. J. (2000). Anticipating differences—celebrating strengths: Providing culturally competent services for students with serious emotional disturbance. *Teaching Exceptional Children, 32*, 30–37.

Children's Defense Fund (CDF). (2001). *The state of America's children.* Washington, DC: Children's Defense Fund.

Hoagwood, K. (2001a). Surgeon general's conference on children's mental health sets out a national action agenda. *Emotional & Behavioral Disorders in Youth, 1*, 33–34, 40–44.

Hoagwood, K. (2001b). Evidence-based practice in children's mental health services: What do we know? Why aren't we putting it to use? *Emotional & Behavioral Disorders in Youth, 1*, 84–87, 90.

O'Dell, K., Alba, L., Lehman, C., Mayer, J., & Hein, M. (2001, Spring). Powerhouse: Empowering young adults as they transition from foster care. *Focal Point, 15*, 27–28.

Technology

Bryant, D. P., & Bryant, B. (2003). *Assistive technology for people with disabilities.* Boston: Allyn and Bacon.

Lucent Technologies (1999). *Reinventing today's classrooms with wireless technology.* Bell Labs Innovations: www.wavelan.com/educational

Rivera, D. P., & Smith, D. D. (1997). *Teaching students with learning and behavior problems* (3rd ed.). Boston: Allyn and Bacon.

CHAPTER 9

PHYSICAL IMPAIRMENTS AND SPECIAL HEALTH CARE NEEDS

Henriette Wyeth

Horgan, P. (1994). *The artifice of blue light: Henriette Wyeth.* Santa Fe: Museum of New Mexico.

Physical Impairments and Special Health Care Needs Defined

American Psychiatric Association. (1994). *Diagnostic and statistical manual of mental disorders* (4th ed.) (DSM-IV). Washington, DC: American Psychiatric Association.

Armstrong, T. (1995). *The myth of the ADD child.* New York: Dutton.

Arthritis Foundation of America. (2002). *Juvenile rheumatoid arthritis: What is it?* Retrieved July 7, 2002, from http://www.arthritis.org/conditions/DiseaseCenter/jra.asp

Best, S. J., Bigge, J. L., & Sirvis, B. P. (1994). Physical and health impairments. In N. G. Haring, L. McCormick, and T. G. Haring, *Exceptional children and youth* (6th ed., pp. 300–341). New York: Macmillan College Publishing.

Breckenridge Outdoor Educational Center (2002). *Adaptive Ski Program.* Retrieved July 7, 2002 from http/www.boec.org

Bryan, T. (1997). Assessing the personal and social status of students with learning disabilities. *Learning Disabilities Research and Practice, 12,* 63–76.

Carlson, C. L., Booth, J. E., Shin, M., & Canu, W. H. (2002). Parent-, teacher-, and self-rated motivational styles in ADHD subtypes. *Journal of Learning Disabilities, 35,* 103–113.

Cheney, P. D., & Palmer, F. B. (Eds.). (1997). Special issue: Cerebral palsy. *Mental Retardation and Developmental Disabilities Research Reviews, 3,* 109–219.

DuPaul, G. J., Ervin, R. A., Hook, C. L., & McGoey, K. E. (1998). Peer tutoring for children with attention deficit hyperactivity disorder: Effects on classroom behavior and academic performance. *Journal of Applied Behavior Analysis, 31,* 579–592.

Epilepsy Foundation of America. (2002). *Managing seizures at school.* Retrieved July 7, 2002, from http://www.efa.org/answerplace/teachers/managing.html

Eriksson, K., Erilä, T., Kivimäki, T., & Koivikko, M. (1998). Evolution of epilepsy in children with mental retardation: Five-year experience in 78 cases. *American Journal on Mental Retardation, 102,* 464–472.

Ferguson, C. (2001, June 17). A lesson in perseverance. *The Tennessean,* Life section, pp. 4–8.

Forness, S. R., & Kavale, K. A. (2001). Are school professionals missing their best chance to help troubled kids? *Emotional & Behavioral Disorders, 1,* 80–83.

Fuchs, D., & Fuchs, L. S. (1998). Researchers and teachers working together to adapt instruction for diverse learnings. *Learning Disabilities Research and Practice, 13,* 126–137.

Getch, Y. Q., & Neuharth-Pritchett, S. (1999). Children with asthma: Strategies for educators. *Teaching Exceptional Children, 31,* 30–36.

Gotsch, T. (2002, March 13). Medication issue could emerge in IDEA debate. *Special Education Report, 28,* 1–2.

Guthrie, P. (2001, October 26). "Gentler" treatment for sickle cell hailed. *Atlanta Journal Constitution* article retrieved July 6, 2002, from http://www.emory.edu/PEDS/SICKLE/bonemarr.htm

Heller, K. W., Alberto, P. A., Forney, P. E., & Schwartzman, M. N. (1996). *Understanding physical, sensory, and health impairments.* Pacific Grove, CA: Brooks/Cole.

Kleinert, Kutz and Associates Hand Care Center, PLLC. (2001, February 16). *Louisville team announces nation's second hand transplant.* Retrieved July 7, 2002, from http://www.handtransplant.com/

Lubker, B. B., Bernier, K. Y., & Vizoso, A. D. (1999, November). *Topic in Language Disorders, 20,* 59–75.

McDonnell, J. J., Hardman, M. L., & McDonnell, A. P. (2003). *Introduction to persons with moderate and severe disabilities: Educational and social issues* (2nd ed.). Boston: Allyn and Bacon.

National Institute of Environmental Health Sciences (NIEHS). (2002). *Fact sheets.* Retrieved July 10, 2002, from http://www. niehs.nih.gov/oc/factsheets/asthma.htm

National Institute of Neurological Disorders and Stroke. (2002). *Seizures and epilepsy: Hope through research.* Retrieved July 6, 2002, from http://www.ninds.nih.gov/health_and_medical/pubs/

Powell, S., & Nelson, B. (1997). Effects of choosing academic assignments on a student with attention deficit hyperactivity disorder. *Journal of Applied Behavior Analysis, 30,* 181–183.

Reason, R. (1999). ADHD: A psychological response to an evolving concept (Report of a working part of the British Psychological Society). *Journal of Learning Disabilities, 32,* 85–91.

Shake-A-Leg, Inc. (2002). *About SAL.* Retrieved July 6, 2002, from http://www.shakealeg.org/AboutSAL.htm

Shapiro, E. S., DuPaul, G. J., & Bradley-Klug, K. L. (1998). Self-management as a strategy to improve the classroom behavior of adolescents with ADHD. *Journal of Learning Disabilities, 31,* 545–555.

Shaywitz, S. E., & Shaywitz, B. A. (Eds.). (1992). *Attention deficit disorder comes of age: Toward the twenty-first century.* Austin, TX: Pro-Ed.

United Cerebral Palsy Association (UCP). (2002). *General information and fact sheets.* Retrieved July 7, 2002, from http://www.ucp.org

U.S. Department of Education. (1999). Assistance to state for the education of children with disabilities and the early intervention program for infants and toddlers with disabilities: Final regulations. *Federal Register, 64* (48), CFR Parts 300 and 303.

U.S. Department of Education. (2001). *Twenty-third annual report to Congress on the implementation of the Individuals with Disabilities Education Act.* Washington, DC: U.S. Government Printing Office.

History of the Field

Dolch, E. W. (1948). *Helping handicapped children in school.* Champaign, IL: Garrard Press.

Eberle, L. (1922, August). The maimed, the halt and the race. *Hospital Social Service, 6,* 59–63. Reprinted in R. H. Bremner (Ed.), *Children and youth in America, A documentary history: Vol. II, 1866–1932* (pp. 1026–1928). Cambridge, MA: Harvard University Press.

Frayer, D. W., Horton, W. A., Macchiarelli, R., & Mussi, M. (1987, November 5). Dwarfism in an adolescent from the Italian late Upper Palaeolithic. *Nature, 330,* 60–61.

Heller, K. W., Alberto, P. A., Forney, P. E., & Schwartzman, M. N. (1996). *Understanding physical, sensory, and health impairments.* Pacific Grove, CA: Brooks/Cole.

La Vor, M. L. (1976). Federal legislation for exceptional persons: A history. In F. J. Weintraub, A. Abeson, J. Ballard, and M. L. La Vor (Eds.), *Public policy and the education of exceptional children* (pp. 96–111). Reston, VA: Council for Exceptional Children.

Maddox, S. (Ed.). (1987). *Spinal network: The total resource for the wheelchair community.* Boulder, CO: Author.

Scheerenberger, R. C. (1983). *A history of mental retardation.* Baltimore: Paul H. Brookes.

Shaw, B. (1995, May/June). Ed Roberts: 1939–1995. *Disability Rag,* p. 25.

Stone, K. G. (1995, March 19). Disability rights pioneer inspired his community. *Albuquerque Journal,* p. C6.

Prevalence

Asthma and Allergy Foundation of America. (2002). *Childhood asthma.* Retrieved July 6, 2002, from http://www.aafa.org/templ/display.cfm?id=2&sub=28

Cheney, P. D., & Palmer, F. B. (1997). Overview: Cerebral palsy. *Mental Retardation and Developmental Disabilities Research Reviews, 3,* 109–111.

Epilepsy Foundation of America. (2002). *Managing seizures at school.* Retrieved July 7, 2002, from http://www.efa.org/answerplace/teachers/managing.html

Getch, Y. Q., & Neuharth-Pritchett, S. (1999). Children with asthma: Strategies for educators. *Teaching Exceptional Children, 31,* 30–36.

Heller, K. W., Alberto, P. A., Forney, P. E., & Schwartzman, M. N. (1996). *Understanding physical, sensory, and health impairments.* Pacific Grove, CA: Brooks/Cole.

National Human Genome Research Institute. (2002). *Learning about sickle cell disease.* Retrieved July 6, 2002, from http://www.genome.gov/page.cfm?pageID=10001219

National Institute of Allergy and Infectious Diseases. (1999, July 8). *Backgrounder-HIV infections in infants and children.* Retrieved July 6, 2002, from http://www.niaid.nih.gov/newsroom/simple/background.htm

National Institute of Environmental Health Sciences (NIEHS). (2002). *Fact sheets.* Retrieved July 10, 2002 from http://www.niehs.nih.gov/oc/factsheets/asthma.htm

United Cerebral Palsy Association (UCP). (2002). *General information and fact sheets.* Retrieved July 7, 2002, from http://www.ucp.org

U.S. Department of Education. (2001). *Twenty-third annual report to Congress on the implementation of the Individuals with Disabilities Education Act.* Washington, DC: U.S. Government Printing Office.

Causes and Prevention

Chase, V.D. (2000, March/April). Mind over muscles. *Technology Review, 103,* 38–45.

Children's Defense Fund (CDF). (2001). *State of America's children.* Washington, DC: Author.

Epilepsy Foundation of America. (2002). *Managing seizures at school.* Retrieved July 7, 2002, from http://www.efa.org/answerplace/teachers/managing.html

Emory University. (2002). *The sickle cell information center.* Retrieved July 8, 2002, from http://www.emory.edu/PEDS/SICKLE/bonemarr.htm

Getch, Y. Q., & Neuharth-Pritchett, S. (1999). Children with asthma: Strategies for educators. *Teaching Exceptional Children, 31,* 30–36.

National Human Genome Research Institute. (2002). *Learning about sickle cell disease.* Retrieved July 6, 2002, from http://www.genome.gov/page.cfm?pageID=10001219

National Institute of Allergy and Infectious Diseases. (1999, July 8). *Backgrounder-HIV infections in infants and children.* Retrieved July 6, 2002, from http://www.niaid.nih.gov/newsroom/simple/background.htm

National Institute of Environmental Health Sciences (NIEHS). (2002). *Fact sheets.* Retrieved July 10, 2002 from http://www.niehs.nih.gov/oc/factsheets/asthma.htm

National Institute of Neurological Disorders and Stroke. (2002). *Seizures and epilepsy: Hope through research.* Retrieved July 6, 2002, from http://www.ninds.nih.gov/health_and_medical/pubs/

Neergaard, L. (1995, July 11). Safer polio vaccines raise fears of new epidemics. *Albuquerque Journal,* pp. A1, A5.

Nelson, K. B., & Grether, J. K. (1997). Cerebral palsy in low-birthweight infants: Etiology and strategies for prevention. *Mental Retardation and Developmental Disabilities Research Reviews, 3,* 112–117.

Peterson, M. C., & Palmer, F. B. (2001). Advances in prevention and treatment of cerebral palsy. *Mental Retardation and Developmental Disabilities Research Reviews, 7,* 30–37.

Stafstrom, C. E., & Tempel, B. L. (2000). Epilepsy genes: The link between molecular dysfunction and pathophysiology. *Mental Retardation and Developmental Disabilities Research Reviews, 6,* 281–292.

Characteristics

Barnes, S. B., & Whitney, K. W. (2002). Effects of functional mobility skills training for young students with physical disabilities. *Exceptional Children, 68,* 313–324.

Boyle, J. R. (1996). The effects of a cognitive mapping strategy on the literal and inferential comprehension of students with mild disabilities. *Learning Disability Quarterly, 19,* 86–98.

Helman, S. W. (2002, May 28). A disabled student's battle could aid others' struggles. *Boston Globe,* pp. B1–2.

Horn, E. M. (1997). Achieving meaningful motor skills: Conceptual and empirical bases of a neurobehavorial intervention approach. *Mental Retardation and Developmental Disabilities Research Reviews, 3,* 138–144.

Horton, S. V., Lovitt, T. C., and Bergerud, D. (1990). The effectiveness of graphic organizers for three classifications of secondary students in content area classes. *Journal of Learning Disabilities, 23,* 12–22, 29.

Leibrock, C. A., & Terry, J. E. (1999). *Beautiful universal design.* New York: Wiley.

Lovitt, T. C., and Horton, S. V. (1994). Strategies for adapting science textbooks for youth with learning disabilities. *Remedial and Special Education, 15,* 105–116.

Newsweek (1997, June 23). Perspectives. Author, p. 27.

Palmer, F. B. (1997). Evaluation of developmental therapies in cerebral palsy. *Mental Retardation and Developmental Disabilities Research Reviews, 3,* 145–152.

Scanlon, D., Deshler, D. D., and Schumaker, J. B. (1996). Can a strategy be taught and learned in secondary inclusive classrooms? *Learning Disabilities Research and Practice, 11,* 41–57.

Early Childhood Education

Barnes, S. B., & Whinnery, K. W. (2002, Spring). Effects of functional mobility skills training for young students with physical disabilities. *Exceptional Children, 68,* 313–324.

Horn, E. M. (1997). Achieving meaningful motor skills: Conceptual and empirical bases of a neurobehavorial intervention approach. *Mental Retardation and Developmental Disabilities Research Reviews, 3,* 138–144.

Langdon, H. W. (1999). Aiding preschool children with communication disorders from Mexican backgrounds: Challenges and solutions. In T. V. Fletcher and C. S. Bos (Eds.), *Helping individuals with disabilities and their families: Mexican and U.S. perspectives.* Tempe, AZ: Bilingual Review/Press.

Owens, Jr., R. E., Metz, D. E., & Haas, A. (2002). *Introduction to communication disorders: A life span perspective.* Boston: Allyn and Bacon.

Elementary Through High School

Elliot, J. L., Erickson, R. N. Thurlow, M. L., & Shriner, J. G. (2000, Spring). State-level accountability for the performance of students with disabilities: Five years of change? *Journal of Special Education, 34,* 39–47.

Long, D. (1999, May 27). *Students plan nature trail for handicapped. The Tennessean*, p. 5B.

Sandler, A. (1989). Learning by design: The AIA elementary and secondary education program. *Art Education, 42,* 13–16.

Taylor, A. (1990). The place of design education in art education. *Design for Arts in Education, 43,* 22–28.

Taylor, A., & Warden, M. G. (1994). Learning environments for the twenty-first century. *Curriculum in Context, 22,* 12–14.

Thompson, S. J., Quenemoen, R. F., Thurlow, M. L., & Ysseldyke, J. E. (2001). *Alternative assessments for students with disabilities.* Thousand Oaks, CA: Corwin Press.

Thurlow, M. L., House, A. L., Scott, D. L., & Ysseldyke, J. E. (2000, Fall). Students with disabilities in large-scale assessments: State participation and accommodation policies. *Journal of Special Education, 34,* 154–163.

Collaboration for Inclusion

America's Athletes with Disabilities. (2002). Victory games. Retrieved July 10, 2002, from http://www.americasathletes.org/event

Easter Seals. (2002). Services: Camping and recreation. Retrieved July 6, 2002, from http://www.easter-seals.org/services/camp/index.asp

Heller, K. W., Frederick, L. D., Best, S., Dykes, M. K., & Cohen, E. T. (2000, Winter). Specialized health care procedures in the schools: Training and service delivery. *Exceptional Children, 66,* 173–186.

Rosenthal-Malek, A., & Greenspan, J. (1999). A student with diabetes is in my class. *Teaching Exceptional Children, 31,* 38–43.

Shake-A-Leg, Inc. (2002). Body awareness therapy program for teenagers. Retrieved July 6, 2002, from http://www.shakea-leg.org/TeenBAT.htm

Temple, L. (2000, February 15). Disputed health duties injected into teaching of disabled. *USA Today,* p. 9D.

U.S. Department of Education. (2001). *Twenty-third annual report to Congress on the implementation of the Individuals with Disabilities Education Act.* Washington, DC: U.S. Government Printing Office.

Wadhwani, A. (2001, December 16). Welcome to Lily's garden: New playground offers access to all. *The Tennessean,* p. 1B.

Transition Through Adulthood

Delta Society Bookstore. Retrieved June 10, 2002, from www.deltasociety.org/dsr000.htm

Edelman, A., Schuyler, V. E., & White, P. H. (1998). *Maximizing success for young adults with chronic health-related illnesses: Transition planning for education after high school.* Washington, DC: American Council on Education, HEATH Resource Center.

Ferrer, S. H. (1996, August 29). Monkeys give helping hand to paralyzed. *Albuquerque Journal,* p. A8.

Haynes, K. A. (1998, June 16). Teacher's pet. *Los Angeles Times,* p. B12.

Hellmich, N. (2000, May 10). The all-Ellison academic team. *USA Today,* pp. 1D–2D.

Painter, K. (2002, January 7). "Miracles" for mom, paralyzed daughter. *USA Today,* pp. 1D–2D.

Slaughter, S. (1999, January 31). Lending a helping paw: Agency's specially trained dogs quickly become partners for disabled clients. *The Tennessean,* pp. F1, F9.

U.S. Department of Education. (2001). *Twenty-third annual report to Congress on the implementation of the Individuals with Disabilities Education Act.* Washington, DC: U.S. Government Printing Office.

Families

Beverly, C. L., & Thomas, S. B. (1997). Developmental and psycho-social effects of HIV in school-aged population: Educational implications. *Education and Training in Mental Retardation and Developmental Disabilities, 32,* 32–41.

Davis, H. (1993). *Counseling parents of children with chronic illness or disability.* Baltimore: Paul H. Brookes.

Martin, S. S., Brady, M. P., & Kotarba, J. A. (1992). Families with chronically ill young children: The unsinkable family. *Remedial and Special Education, 13,* 6–15.

Smith, P. M. (1993). You are not alone: For parents when they learn that their child has a disability. *NICHCY News Digest, 3,* 1–15.

Technology

Associated Press. (2001, March 15). Daughter's new arms let her hug mom at last. *The Tennessean,* p. 6A.

Bryant, D., & Bryant, B. (2003). *Assistive technology for people with disabilities.* Boston: Allyn and Bacon.

Buckley, J. (2002, April 25–May 8). The boy with no legs: A brave heart is a powerful weapon. *Montecito Journal, 8,* 18–21.

Humbles, A. (2000, May 1). Born without feet, Rinehart finds way: Montgomery Central senior plays using prosthetics. *The Tennessean,* Sports, pp. C1–C2.

U.S. Department of the Interior. (2002). *Accessible Technology Center.* Retrieved on July 9, 2002. from http://nbcprod.nbc.gov/nbc/atc1/services.html

Weise, E. (2000, July 25). Devices free workers from disabilities. *USA Today,* p. 3D.

CHAPTER 10

DEAFNESS AND HARD OF HEARING

Dorothy Brett

Hignett, S. (1983). *Brett from Bloomsbury to New Mexico: A biography.* New York: Franklin Watts.

Deafness and Hard of Hearing Defined

American Speech-Language-Hearing Association (2002, May 4). *Facts on hearing loss in children.* Retrieved from www.asha.org

Davis, C. (2001, July/August). Automatic speech recognition and access: 20 years, 20 months, or tomorrow? *Hearing Loss,* 11–14.

Easterbrooks, S. (1999). Improving practices for students with hearing impairments. *Exceptional Children, 65,* 537–554.

Gordon-Langbein, A. L. (1998). What is universal newborn hearing screening and why is it important? *Hearing Loss, 19,* 7–10.

Gordon-Langbein, A. L. (1999). Screening newborns for hearing loss—The time is hear! *Volta Voices, 6,* 7–10.

Gordon-Langbein, A. L., & Metzinger, M. (2000, January/February). Technology in the classroom to maximize listening and learning. *Volta Voices, 102,* 10–13.

Hoover, B. M. (2000). Hearing aid fitting in infants. *Volta Review, 102,* 57–73.

Huebner, M. (2002) Hearing loss: A challenge not a restriction. *Hearing Loss, 23,* 7–9.

Lowenbraun, S. (1995). Hearing impairment. In E. L. Meyen and T. M. Skrtic (Eds.), *Exceptional children and youth: An introduction* (4th ed. pp. 453–486). Denver, CO: Love.

Moores, D. F. (2001). *Educating the deaf: Psychology, principles, and practices* (5th ed.). Boston: Houghton Mifflin.

Ross, M., & Levitt, H. (2000, September/October). Developments in research and technology: Otoacoustic emissions. *Volta Voices, 7,* 30–31.

Yoshinaga-Itano, C. Y., & Apuzzo, M. L. (1998). Identification of hearing loss after age 18 months is not early enough. *American Annals of the Deaf, 143,* 380–387.

History of the Field

Adams, M. E. (1929). 1865–1935: A few memories of Alexander Graham Bell. *American Annals of the Deaf, 74,* 467–479.

Alby, J. F. (1962, Spring). The educational philosophy of Thomas Hopkins Gallaudet. *Buff and Blue,* 17–23.

Campbell, C. D. (1999). The central asylum for the instruction of the deaf and dumb, Canajoharie, New York, 1823–1835. *American Annals of the Deaf, 144,* 365–372.

Drasgow, E. (1998). American Sign Language as a pathway to linguistic competence. *Exceptional Children, 64,* 329–342.

Gannon, J. R. (1989). *The week the world heard Gallaudet.* Washington, DC: Gallaudet University Press.

Prevalence

American Speech-Language-Hearing Association (ASHA). (2002, May 4). *Facts on hearing loss in children.* Retrieved from www. asha. org

Andrews, J. F., & Martin, G. (1998). Hopwood, affirmative action, and deaf education. *American Annals of the Deaf, 143,* 305–313.

Gallaudet Research Institute. (1998, November). *Regional and national summary report of data from the 1997–1998 annual survey of deaf and hard-of-hearing children and youth.* Washington, DC: GRI, Gallaudet University.

U.S. Department of Education. (2001). *Twenty-third annual report to Congress on the implementation of the Individuals with Disabilities Education Act.* Washington, DC: U.S. Government Printing Office.

Walker-Vann, C. (1998). Profiling Hispanic deaf students: A first step toward solving the greater problems. *American Annals of the Deaf, 143,* 46–54.

Causes and Prevention

Alexander Graham Bell Association. (2002, January/February). AG Bell position statement on cochlear implants in children. *Volta Voices, 9,* 6.

American Speech-Language-Hearing Association (ASHA). (2002, May 4). *Facts on hearing loss in children.* Retrieved from www. asha. org

Associated Press. (2002 July 26). Meningitis reported with hearing implants. *The Tennessean,* p. 11A.

Calderon, R., & Naidu, S. (2000). Further support for the benefits of early identification and intervention for children with hearing loss. *Volta Review, 100,* 53–84.

Chasin, M. (2000, May/June). Middle ear implants: What are surgically-implanted hearing aids and who are they for? *Hearing Loss,* 13–15.

Christiansen, J. B., & Leigh, I. W. (2002). *Cochlear implants in children: Ethics and choices.* Washington, DC: Gallaudet University Press.

Dawson, N. (1997). Noise induced hearing loss. *Wired for Sound, 7,* 1–2.

Drasgow, E. (1998). American Sign Language as a pathway to linguistic competence. *Exceptional Children, 64,* 329–342.

Easterbrooks, S. R., & Mordica, J. A. (2000). Teachers' ratings of functional communication in students with cochlear implants. *American Annals of the Deaf, 145,* 54–59.

Gallaudet Research Institute. (1998, November). *Regional and national summary report of data from the 1997–1998 annual survey of deaf and hard-of-hearing children and youth.* Washington, DC: GRI, Gallaudet University.

Gregoret, L. (2002). A conversation with deafness researcher Douglas A. Cotanche, PhD. *Volta Voices, 9,* 13–17.

Johnson, R. C. (2000, Spring). Gallaudet forum addresses cochlear implant issues. *Research at Gallaudet,* 1.

Kluwin, T. N., & Stewart, D. A. (2000). Cochlear implants for younger children: A preliminary description of the parental decision process and outcomes. *American Annals of the Deaf, 145,* 26–32.

Koran, N., & Oliva, G. (1997). Bring your earplugs: Loud aerobics music may be hazardous to your hearing. *Hearing Loss, 18,* 10–13.

Laborit, E. (1998). *The cry of the gull.* Washington, DC: Gallaudet University Press.

Lane, H. (1995). Construction of deafness. *Disability & Society, 10,* 171–187.

Lundy, J. (1997, April 28). *Letter to the author.* Denver, CO: Metropolitan State College of Denver.

Magnuson, M. (2000). Infants with congenital deafness: On the importance of early sign language acquisition. *American Annals of the Deaf, 145,* 6–14.

Marsa, L. (1999, March). Does your child really need ear tubes? *Parents,* 41–44.

McGee, D. (1999). The Newborn and Infant Hearing Screening and Intervention Act of 1999 (HR 1193). *Volta Voices, 6,* 3.

Marschark, M. (2001, June). *Language development in children who are deaf: A research synthesis.* Alexandria, VA: Project Forum, National Association of State Directors of Special Education.

McCaffrey, H. A., Davis, B. L., MacNeilage, P. F., & von Hapsburg, D. (2000). Multichannel cochlear implantation and the organization of early speech. *Volta Review, 101,* 5–29.

Owens, Jr., R. E., Metz, D. E., & Haas, A. (2000). *Introduction to communication disorders: A life span perspective.* Boston: Allyn and Bacon.

Peters, E. (2000). Our decision on a cochlear implant. *American Annals of the Deaf, 145,* 263–267.

Pisoni, D. B., Cleary, M., Geers, A. E., & Tobey, E. A. (1999). Individual differences in effectiveness of cochlear implants in children who are prelingually deaf: New process measures of performance. *Volta Review, 101,* 111–164.

Spencer, L., Tomblin, J. B., & Gantz, B. J. (1997). Reading skills in children with multichannel cochlear–implant experience. *Volta Review, 99,* 193-202.

Wyngate, P. (2001, December). Sound solution. *Columns: The University of Washington Alumni Magazine, 21,* 36–39.

Yoshinaga-Itano, C. Y., & Apuzzo, M. L. (1998). Identification of hearing loss after age 18 months is not early enough. *American Annals of the Deaf, 143,* 380–387.

Characteristics

Calderon, R., & Naidu, S. (2000). Further support for the benefits of early identification and intervention for children with hearing loss. *Volta Review, 100,* 53–84.

Drasgow, E. (1998). American Sign Language as a pathway to linguistic competence. *Exceptional Children, 64,* 329–342.

Fletcher, R. (1994). On deaf culture and cultures. *Border Walking, 2,* 2.

Gallaudet Research Institute. (1994). *Working Papers 89–3.* Washington, DC: Gallaudet University.

Goldberg, B. (1995). Families facing choices: Options for parents of children who are deaf or hard of hearing. *ASHA, 37,* 38–45.

Goldin-Meadow, S., & Mayberry, R. I. (2001). How do profoundly deaf children learn to read? *Learning Disabilities Research & Practice, 16,* 222–229.

Groce, N. E. (1985). *Everyone here spoke sign language: Hereditary deafness on Martha's Vineyard.* Cambridge, MA: Harvard University Press.

Johnson, R. C. (2001–2002, Fall/Winter). High stakes testing and deaf students: Comments from readers. *Research at Gallaudet,* 1.

Kageleiry, J. (2002, February). *The island that spoke by hand.* Martha's Vineyard Chamber of Commerce. Retrieved February 25, 2002 from www. mvy. com/spokehand. htm

Karchmer, M. A., & Allen, T. E. (1999). The functional assessment of deaf and hard of hearing students. *American Annals of the Deaf, 144,* 68–77.

Kelly, R. R., Albertini, J. A., & Shannon, N. B. (2001). Deaf college students' reading comprehension and strategy use. *American Annals of the Deaf, 146,* 385–400.

Lane, H. (1995). Construction of deafness. *Disability & Society, 10,* 171–187.

Marschark, M. (2001, June). *Language development in children who are deaf: A research synthesis.* Alexandria, VA: Project Forum, National Association of State Directors of Special Education.

Moores, D. F. (2001). *Educating the deaf: Psychology, principles, and practices* (5th ed.). Boston: Houghton Mifflin.

Most, T., Weisel, A., & Lev-Matezky, A. (1996). Speech intelligibility and the evaluation of personal qualities by experienced and inexperienced listeners. *Volta Review, 98,* 181–190.

Sheridan, M. (2001). *Inner lives of deaf children: Interviews & analysis.* Washington, DC: Gallaudet University Press.

Soloman, A. (1994, August 28). Defiantly deaf. *New York Times Magazine,* pp. 38–45, 64–68.

Yoshinaga-Itano, C., & Sedey, A. (2000). Early speech development in children who are deaf or hard of hearing: Interrelationships with language and hearing. *Volta Review, 100,* 181–211.

Early Childhood Education

Andrews, J. F., Ferguson, C., Roberts, S., & Hodges, P. (1997). What's up, Billy Jo? Deaf children and bilingual–bicultural instruction in East-Central Texas. *American Annals of the Deaf, 142,* 16–25.

Drasgow, E. (1998). American Sign Language as a pathway to linguistic competence. *Exceptional Children, 64,* 329–342.

Kemp, M. (1998). Why is learning American Sign Language a challenge? *American Annals of the Deaf, 143,* 255, 259.

Marschark, M. (1993). *Psychological development of deaf children.* New York: Oxford University Press.

Marschark, M. (2001, June). *Language development in children who are deaf: A research synthesis.* Alexandria, VA: Project Forum, National Association of State Directors of Special Education.

Yoshinaga-Itano, C. Y., & Apuzzo, M. L. (1998). Identification of hearing loss after age 18 months is not early enough. *American Annals of the Deaf, 143,* 380–387.

Yoshinaga-Itano, C., & Sedey, A. (2000). Early speech development in children who are deaf or hard of hearing: Interrelationships with language and hearing. *Volta Review, 100,* 181–211.

Elementary Through High School

Andrews, J. F., Ferguson, C., Roberts, S., & Hodges, P. (1997). What's up, Billy Jo? Deaf children and bilingual–bicultural instruction in East-Central Texas. *American Annals of the Deaf, 142,* 16–25.

Antia, S. D., & Kreimeyer, K. H. (1996). Social interaction and acceptance of deaf or hard-of-hearing children and their peers: A comparison of social-skills and familiarity-based interventions. *Volta Review, 98,* 157–180.

DiSarno, N. J., Schowalter, M., and Grassa, P. (2002). Classroom amplification to enhance student performance. *Teaching Exceptional Children, 34,* 20–26.

Easterbrooks, S. (1999). Improving practices for students with hearing impairments. *Exceptional Children, 65,* 537–554.

Easterbrooks, S. R., & Baker, S. (2002). *Language learning in children who are deaf and hard of hearing: Multiple pathways.* Boston: Allyn and Bacon.

Gallaudet Research Institute. (1998, November). *Regional and national summary report of data from the 1997–1998 annual survey of deaf and hard-of-hearing children and youth.* Washington, DC: GRI, Gallaudet University.

Jensema, C. J., Danturthi, S., & Burch, R. (2000). Time spent viewing captions on television programs. *American Annals of the Deaf, 145,* 464–468.

Kaderavek, J. N., and Pakulski, L. A. (2002). Minimal hearing loss is not minimal. *Teaching Exceptional Children, 34,* 14–19.

Luetke-Stahlman, B. (1999). *Language across the curriculum: When students are deaf or hard of hearing.* Hillsboro, Oregon: Butte Publications.

Marschark, M. (2001, June). *Language development in children who are deaf: A research synthesis.* Alexandria, VA: Project Forum, National Association of State Directors of Special Education.

Moores, D. F. (2001). *Educating the deaf: Psychology, principles, and practices* (5th ed.). Boston: Houghton Mifflin.

Roffé, S. (2000). Cued speech: Another option. *Volta Voices, 7,* 13.

Stewart, D. A. (1997). Bi-Bi- to MCE. *American Annals of the Deaf, 142,* 106–111.

Collaboration for Inclusion

Antia, S. D., & Kreimeyer, K. H. (2001). The role of interpreters in inclusive classrooms. *American Annals of the Deaf, 146,* 355–365.

Byrnes, L. J., & Sigafoos, J. (2001). A "consumer" survey of educational provision for deaf and hard of hearing students. *American Annals of the Deaf, 146,* 409–419.

Cohen, O. P. (1994). Introduction. In R. C. Johnson and O. P. Cole (Eds)., *Implications and complications for Deaf students of the full inclusion movement* (pp. 1–6). Washington, DC: Gallaudet Research Institute, Gallaudet University.

Fiedler, B. C. (2001). Considering placement and educational approaches for students who are deaf and hard of hearing. *Teaching Exceptional Children, 34,* 54–59.

Gallaudet Research Institute. (1998, November). *Regional and national summary report of data from the 1997–1998 annual survey of deaf and hard-of-hearing children and youth.* Washington, DC: GRI, Gallaudet University.

Linehan, P. (2000). Educational interpreters for students who are deaf and hard of hearing. *Quick Turn Around.* Alexandria, VA: Project Forum, National Association for State Directors of Special Education.

Luetke-Stahlman, B. (1998). Providing the support services needed by students who are deaf or hard of hearing. *American Annals of the Deaf, 143,* 388–391.

Most, T., Weisel, A., & Lev-Matezky, A. (1996). Speech intelligibility and the evaluation of personal qualities by experienced and inexperienced listeners. *Volta Review, 98,* 181–190.

Ramsey, C. L. (1997). *Deaf children in public schools.* Washington, DC: Gallaudet University Press.

Schildroth, A. N., & Hotto, S. A. (1994). Deaf students and full inclusion: Who wants to be excluded? In R. C. Johnson and O. P. Cole (Eds.), *Implications and complications for Deaf students of the full inclusion movement* (pp. 31–40). Washington, DC: Gallaudet Research Institute, Gallaudet University.

Transition Through Adulthood

Deykes, R. (2002). Reasonable accommodations and access technologies in the workplace. *Volta Voices, 9,* 9–19.

Gallaudet Research Institute. (1998). *Who and where are our children with cochlear implants?* Washington, DC: Gallaudet Research Institute Web site.

Jackson State University. *Accommodating deaf and hard of hearing students.* www. jsu. edu/depart/dss/pec

King, S., DeCaro, J. J., Karchmer, M. A., & Cole, K. *College and career programs for deaf.* Washington, DC: Gallaudet University.

Schroedel, J. G., & Geyer, J. J. (2000). Long-term career attainments of deaf and hard of hearing college graduates: Results from a 15-year followup study. *American Annals of Deaf, 145,* pp. 303–314.

Tiefenbacher, W. (Ed.) (2002). *Deaf girls rule.* Washington, DC: Gallaudet University Press.

Families

Blade, R. (1994, October 31). *Sign language is beautiful, close-knit Deaf community says. Albuquerque Tribune,* p. A5.

Calderon, R., & Greenberg, M. T. (1999). Stress and coping in hearing mothers of children with hearing loss: Factors affecting mother and child adjustment. *American Annals of the Deaf, 144,* 7–23.

Moores, D. R., Jatho, J., & Dunn, C. (2001). Families with deaf members: American Annals of the Deaf, 1996 to 2000. *American Annals of the Deaf, 146,* 245–250.

Sheridan, M. (2001). *Inner lives of deaf children: Interviews & analysis.* Washington, DC: Gallaudet University Press.

Technology

Baker, D. (2001, November/December). Television captioning: Frequently asked questions—FAQs. *Hearing Loss,* 18–19.

Davis, C. (2001, July/August). Automatic speech recognition and access: 20 years, 20 months, or tomorrow? *Hearing Loss,* 11–14.

Delta Society. (1999). Information from Delta Society Web site: www. deltasociety. org

DeVilbiss, G. (2001, November/December). The hearing aid interference dilemma. *Hearing Loss,* 26–28.

Flexer, C. (2000, September/October). FM technologies: Enhancing language and learning in home and school environments. *Volta Voices, 7,* 21–25.

Gordon-Langbein, A. L., & Metzinger, M. (2000, January/February). Technology in the classroom to maximize listening and learning. *Volta Voices, 7,* 10–13.

Harkins, J. (2000, May/June). Wireless phones: Making them work for you. *Volta Voices, 7,* 16–19.

Holbrook, P. (2000, January/February). Relay calling with two-line VCO: Communicate with speed and simplicity. *Volta Voices, 7,* 7–8.

Huebner, M. (2002). Hearing loss: A challenge not a restriction. *Hearing Loss, 23,* 7–9.

Jensema, C. J., Danturthi, S., & Burch, R. (2000). Time spent viewing captions on television programs. *American Annals of the Deaf, 145,* 464–468.

Kozma-Spytek, L. (2000, November/December). Digital wireless telephones and hearing aids: Are they compatible yet? *Hearing Loss,* 12–17.

Kramlinger, J. (1996). Making noise in a silent world: A profile of the deaf college experience. *Volta Voices, 3,* 20–21.

Ogden, P. (1992). *Chelsea: The story of a signal dog.* Boston: Little, Brown.

Ross, M. (2002, March/April). Developments in research and technology. *Hearing Loss,* 32–36.

Stanton, J. F. (1999). Captions and the movies: Where we're going. *Volta Voices, 6,* 20–21.

Stinson, M. S., Elliot, L. B., McKee, B. G., & Francis, P. G. (2001, May/June). Accessibility in the classroom: The pros and cons of C-Print. *Volta Voices, 8,* 16–19.

Sweetow, R. W., & Luckett, E. (2001, March/April). Selecting the "best" hearing aids for yourself or child. *Volta Voices, 8,* 18–21.

Thomas, K. (2002, January 16). Glove lends the deaf a hand: Teenager's invention translates sign language into text. *USA Today,* p. 6D.

Trychin, S. (2001, November/December). Why don't people who need hearing aids get them? *Hearing Loss,* 21–23.

CHAPTER 11
LOW VISION AND BLINDNESS
Visual Disabilities Defined

Almon, P. (2000). Mass transportation operators' beliefs about visual impairment. *Journal of Visual Impairments and Blindness, 95,* 5–13.

Corn, A. L. (1989). Instruction in the use of vision for children and adults with low vision: A proposed program model. *RE:view, 21,* 26–38.

Erin, J. N., & Corn, A. L. (1994). A survey of children's first understanding of being visually impaired. *Journal of Visual Impairment and Blindness, 88,* 132–139.

Hatton, D. (2001, July). Model registry of early childhood visual impairment: First-year results. *Journal of Visual Impairment and Blindness, 95,* 418–433.

Heller, K. W., Alberto, P. A., Forney, P. E., & Schwartzman, M. N. (1996). *Understanding physical, sensory, and health impairments.* Pacific Grove, CA: Brooks/Cole.

Levin, A. V. (1996). Common visual problems in classrooms. In R. H. A. Haslam & P. J. Valletutti (Eds.), *Medical problems in the classroom: The teacher's role in diagnosis and management* (pp. 161–180). Austin, TX: Pro-Ed.

Tuttle, D. W., & Ferrell, K. A. (1995). Visually impaired. In E. L. Meyen & T. M. Skrtic (Eds.), *Exceptional children and youth: An introduction* (4th ed., pp. 487–532). Denver, CO: Love.

Verplanken, B., Meijnders, A., & van de Wege, A. (1994). Emotion and cognition: Attitudes toward persons who are visually impaired. *Journal of Visual Impairment and Blindness, 88,* 504–511.

Wood, S. (2000, July 20). He's blind, but he's crew chief. *USA Today,* p. 14C.

History of the Field

Barraga, N. C. (1964). *Increased visual behavior in low vision children*. New York: American Foundation for the Blind.

Barraga, N. C., & Collins, M. E. (1979). Development of efficiency in visual functioning: Rationale for a comprehensive program. *Journal of Visual Impairment and Blindness, 73,* 121–126.

Sacks, S. Z., & Rosen, S. (1994). Visual impairment. In N. G. Haring, L. McCormick, & T. G. Haring (Eds.), *Exceptional children and youth* (6th ed., pp. 403–446). Columbus, OH: Merrill.

Tuttle, D. W., & Ferrell., K. A. (1995). Visually impaired. In E. L. Meyen and T. M. Skrtic (Eds.), *Exceptional children and youth: An introduction* (4th ed., pp. 487–531). Denver, CO: Love.

Prevalence

American Foundation for the Blind (AFB). (2002). *Statistics and sources for professionals.* Retrieved on September 14, 2002 from www. afb. org

Dote-Kwan, J., Chen, D., & Hughes M. (2001, June). A national survey of service providers who work with young children with visual impairments. *Journal of Visual Impairment and Blindness, 95,* 325–337.

Hatton, D. (2001, July). Model registry of early childhood visual impairment: First-year results. *Journal of Visual Impairment and Blindness, 95,* 418–433.

Tuttle, D. W., & Ferrell, K. A. (1995). Visually impaired. In E. L. Meyen and T. M. Skrtic (Eds.), *Exceptional children and youth: An introduction* (4th ed., pp. 487–532). Denver, CO: Love.

U. S. Department of Education. (2001). *Twentieth-third annual report to Congress on the implementation of the Individuals with Disabilities Education Act.* Washington, DC: U. S. Government Printing Office.

Causes and Prevention

Dote-Kwan, J., Chen, D., & Hughes M. (2001, June). A national survey of service providers who work with young children with visual impairments. *Journal of Visual Impairment and Blindness, 95,* 325–337.

Hatton, D. (2001, July). Model registry of early childhood visual impairment: First-year results. *Journal of Visual Impairment and Blindness, 95,* 418–433.

Prevent Blindness America, (2002). *Children with eye problems.* Retrieved on September 30, 2002, from www.preventblindness.org/children/index.html

Sherman, A. (1994). *Wasting America's future: The Children's Defense Fund on the cost of child poverty.* Boston: Beacon Press.

Characteristics

Baird, S. M., Mayfield, P., & Baker, P. (1997). Mothers' interpretations of the behavior of their infants with visual and other impairments during interactions. *Journal of Visual Impairment and Blindness, 91,* 467–483.

Buhrow, M. M., Hartshorne, T. S., & Bradley-Johnson, S. (1998). Parents' and teachers' ratings of the social skills of elementary-age students who are blind. *Journal of Visual Impairment and Blindness, 92,* 503–511.

Crocker, A. D., & Orr, R. R. (1996). Social behaviors of children with visual impairments enrolled in preschool programs. *Exceptional Children, 62,* 451–462

Heller, K. W., Alberto, P. A., Forney, P. E., & Schwartzman, M. N. (1996). *Understanding physical, sensory, and health impairments.* Pacific Grove, CA: Brooks/Cole.

Huurre, T. M., Komulainen, E. J., & Aro, H. M. (1999). Social support and self-esteem among adolescents with visual impairments. *Journal of Visual Impairment and Blindness, 93,* 26–38.

MacCuspie, P. A. (1992). The social acceptance and interaction of visually impaired children in integrated settings. In S. Z. Sacks, L. S. Kekelis, and R. J. Gaylord-Ross (Eds.), *The development of social skills by blind and visually impaired students* (pp. 83–102). New York: American Foundation for the Blind.

Pring, L., Dewart, H., & Brockbank, M. (1998). Social cognition in children with visual impairments. *Journal of Visual Impairment and Blindness, 92,* 754–768.

Rettig, M. (1994). The play of young children with visual impairments: Characteristics and interventions. *Journal of Visual Impairment and Blindness, 88,* 410–420.

Tuttle, D. W., & Ferrell, K. A. (1995). Visually impaired. In E. L. Meyen and T. M. Skrtic (Eds.), *Exceptional children and youth: An introduction* (4th ed., pp. 487–532). Denver, CO: Love.

Early Childhood Education

Behl, D. D., Akers, J. F., Boyce, G. C., & Taylor, M. J. (1996). Do mothers interact differently with children who are visually impaired? *Journal of Visual Impairment and Blindness, 90,* 501–511.

Clarke, K. L., Sainato, D. M., & Ward, M. E. (1994). Travel performance of preschoolers: The effects of mobility training with a long cane versus a precane. *Journal of Visual Impairment and Blindness, 88,* 19–30.

Dote-Kwan, J. (2001). Research to Practice: Teaching with confidence: Facilitating caregiver–child interactions. In D. D. Smith, *Introduction to special education: Teaching in an age of opportunity* (4th ed., p. 480). Boston: Allyn and Bacon.

Hughes, M., Dote-Kwan, J., & Dolendo, J. (1998). A close look at the cognitive play of preschoolers with visual impairments in the home. *Exceptional Children, 64,* 451–462.

Joffee, E. (1988). A home-based orientation and mobility program for infants and toddlers. *Journal of Visual Impairment and Blindness, 82,* 282–285.

McGaha, C., & Farran, D. (2001, February). Interaction in an inclusive classroom: The effects of visual status and setting. *Journal of Visual Impairment and Blindness, 95,* 80–94.

Pogrund, R. L., Fazzi, D. L., & Schreier, E. M. (1993). Development of a preschool "Kiddy Cane." *Journal of Visual Impairment and Blindness, 86,* 52–54

Recchia, S. L. (1997). Play and concept development in infants and young children with severe visual impairments: A constructivist view. *Journal of Visual Impairment and Blindness, 91,* 401–406.

Rettig, M. (1994). The play of young children with visual impairments: Characteristics and interventions. *Journal of Visual Impairment and Blindness, 88,* 410–420.

Tröster, H., & Brambring, M. (1992). Early social-emotional development in blind infants. *Child: Care, Health and Development, 18,* 421–432.

Tröster, H., & Brambring, M. (1994). The play behavior and play materials of blind and sighted infants and preschoolers. *Journal of Visual Impairment and Blindness, 88,* 421–432.

Elementary Through High School

American Foundation for the Blind (AFB). (2002). *Statistics and sources for professionals.* Retrieved on September 14, 2002 from www.afb.org

American Printing House for the Blind. (1992). *Annual report.* Louisville, KY: Author.

Associated Press (1999a, August 28). Blind runner gains finals. *The Tennessean,* p. C5.

Associated Press (2002, June 1). Blind bicyclists to ride the Trace to Keller's home. *The Tennessean,* Local News section, p. B1.

Bielinski, J., Thurlow, M., Ysseldyke, J., Friedebach, J., & Friedebach, M. (2001, April 11). Read-Aloud accommodation: Effects on multiple-choice reading and math items. Technical Report. Minneapolis, MN: University of Minnesota, National Outcomes Center.

Centers for Disease Control (CDC). (1998). Number of persons using assistive technology devices by age of person and type of device: United States, 1994; updated 1998. Retrieved September 14, 2002, from www. cec. gov/nchs/about/major/nhis_dis

Corn, A., & Koenig, A. J. (2002). Literacy for students with low vision: A framework for delivering instruction. *Journal of Visual Impairments and Blindness, 96,* 305–321.

Cox, P., & Dykes, M. (2001). Effective classroom adaptations for students with visual impairments. *Teaching Exceptional Children, 33,* 68–74.

Dote-Kwan, J., Chen, D., & Hughes, M. (2001,). A national survey of service providers who work with young children with visual impairments. *Journal of Visual Impairment and Blindness, 95,* 325–337.

Duzak, W. (2002, June 3). Young cyclists who are blind ride the Trace. *The Tennessean, DAVIDSON,* p. 12B.

Erin, J. N., & Koenig, A. J. (1997). The student with a visual disability and a learning disability. *Journal of Learning Disabilities, 30,* 309–320.

Frank, J. (2000, November). Requests by persons with visual impairment for large-print accommodation. *Journal of Visual Impairment and Blindness, 94,* 716–719.

Hill, E. W. (1986). Orientation and mobility. In G. R. Scholl (Ed.), *Foundations of education for blind and visually handicapped children and youth: Theory and practice* (pp. 315–340). New York: American Foundation for the Blind.

Horsfall, B. (1997). Tactile maps: New materials and improved designs. *Journal of Visual Impairment and Blindness, 91,* 61–65.

Koenig, A., & Holbrook, M. (2000, November). Ensuring high-quality instruction for students in braille literacy programs. *Journal of Visual Impairment and Blindness, 94,* 677–694.

Patrick, D. (2001, February 19). Runyons sets U.S. mark in indoors 5000 meters. *USA Today,* p. 7C.

Sinatra, A. (2002, August 4). *Use of braille declines.* ABCNEWS. com.

Spungin, S. (Ed.). (2002). *When you have a visually impaired student in your classroom: A guide for teachers.* New York: American Foundation for the Blind.

Starr, M. (2000, July 17). I can see the finish line. *Newsweek,* p. 48.

Trent, S. D., & Truan, M. B. (1997). Speed, accuracy, and comprehension of adolescent braille readers in a specialized school. *Journal of Visual Impairment and Blindness, 91,* 494–500.

U.S. Department of Education. (2001). *Twentieth-third annual report to Congress on the implementation of the Individuals with Disabilities Education Act.* Washington, DC: U.S. Government Printing Office.

U.S. Senate (2002, June 28). *Hearing notes: Instructional materials accessibility act.* Subcommittee on Children and Families.

Ungar, S., Blades, M., & Spencer, C. (1997). Teaching visually impaired children to make distance judgments from a tactile map. *Journal of Visual Impairment and Blindness, 91,* 163–169.

Walker, L. (1999, October 31). The day I took my dad up the mountain. *Parade Magazine,* pp. 4–5.

Wetzel, R., & Knowlton, M. (2000, March). A comparison of print and braille reading rates on three reading tasks. *Journal of Visual Impairment and Blindness, 94,* 146–154.

Collaboration for Inclusion

Barraga, N. C., & Morris, J. E. (1992). *Program to develop efficiency in visual function: Source book on low vision.* Louisville, KY: American Printing House for the Blind.

Barton, D. D. (1997). Growing up with Jed: Parents' experiences raising an adolescent son who is blind. *Journal of Visual Impairment and Blindness, 91,* 203–212.

Cox, P., & Dykes, M. (2001). Effective classroom adaptations for students with visual impairments. *Teaching Exceptional Children, 33,* 68–74.

De Mario, N., & Caruso, M. (2001, August). The expansion of outreach services for specialized schools for students with visual impairments. *Journal of Visual Impairment and Blindness, 95,* 488–491.

Harley, R. K., Truan, M. B., & Sanford, L. D. (1987). *Communication skills for visually impaired learners.* Springfield, IL: Thomas.

Sacks, S. Z., & Kekelis, L. S. (1992). Guidelines for mainstreaming blind and visually impaired children in S. Z. Sacks, L. S. Kekelis, and R. J. Gaylord-Ross (Eds.), *The development of social skills by blind and visually impaired students* (pp. 133–149). NewYork: American Foundation for the Blind.

Sacks, S. Z., & Reardon, M. P. (1992). Maximizing social integration for visually impaired students: Applications and practice. In S. Z. Sacks, L. S. Kekelis, & R. J. Gaylord-Ross (Eds.), *The development of social skills by blind and visually impaired students* (pp. 151–170). New York: American Foundation for the Blind.

Sacks, S. Z., & Rosen, S. (1994). Visual impairment. In N. G. Haring, L. McCormick, & T. G. Haring (Eds.), *Exceptional children and youth* (6th ed., pp. 403–446). Columbus, OH: Merrill.

Sandoval, E. (2000, March 27). A's despite his eyes: Mainstreamed blind student learns, excels among sighted peers. *Los Angeles Times,* Valley section, pp. B1–B2.

Spungin, S. J. (1997). Specialized schools still in jeopardy. *JVIB News Service, 91,* 1, 3–5.

Spungin, S. (Ed.). (2002). *When you have a visually impaired student in your classroom: A guide for teachers.* NewYork: American Foundation for the Blind.

U. S. Department of Education. (2001). *Twenty-third annual report to Congress on the implementation of the Individuals with Disabilities Education Act.* Washington, DC: U.S. Government Printing Office.

Transition Through Adulthood

Ansariyah-Grace, T. (2000, August 6). Touched by arts. *The Tennessean,* p. 1F–2F.

Associated Press (1999, July 3). Blind workers idle in desperate labor market. *The Tennessean,* pp. E1, E3.

Hanye, R. (1998). The missing link: Real work experiences for people who are visually impaired. *Journal of Visual Impairment and Blindness, 92,* 884–847.

Lighthouse International. (2002). *Lighthouse catalog.* New York: The Lighthouse Store.

Martin, K. (1999). *Summer college program for students with disabilities on the campus of the University of Evansville.* Evansville, IN: Evansville Association for the Blind.

McCutcheon, C. (1994, May 5). *First guide dog goes to the zoo. Albuquerque Journal,* Metropolitan section, p. C1.

Nagle, K. (2001, December). Transition to employment and community life for youths with visual impairments: Current status and future directions. *Journal of Visual Impairment and Blindness, 95,* 725–738.

Rumrill, Jr., P. D., & Scheff, C. M. (1997). Impact of the ADA on the employment and promotion of persons who are visually impaired. *Journal of Visual Impairment and Blindness, 91,* 460–466.

Vancil, D. (1997). Steps to success in college for students with visual impairments. *Journal of Visual Impairment and Blindness, 91,* 219–223.

Families

Baird, S. M., Mayfield, P., & Baker, P. (1997). Mothers' interpretations of the behavior of their infants with visual and other impairments during interactions. *Journal of Visual Impairment and Blindness, 91,* 467–483.

Dote-Kwan, J., Hughes, M., & Taylor, S. L. (1997). Impact of early experiences on the development of young children with visual impairments: Revisited. *Journal of Visual Impairment and Blindness, 91,* 131–144.

Erin, J. N., & Corn, A. L. (1994). A survey of children's first understanding of being visually impaired. *Journal of Visual Impairment and Blindness, 88,* 132–139.

Milian, M. (2001). School's efforts to involve Latino families of students with visual impairments. *Journal of Visual Impairment and Blindness, 95,* 389–402.

Peréz-Pereira, M., & Conti-Ramsden, G. (2001). The use of directives in verbal interactions between blind children and their mothers. *Journal of Visual Impairment and Blindness, 95,* 133–149

Tröster, H. (2000). Sources of stress in mothers of children with visual impairments. *Journal of Visual Impairment and Blindness, 95,* 122–134.

Technology

American Association of Retired Persons (AARP). (2002). *Gold violin: Thoughtfully designed products for seniors.* Retrieved June, 16, 2002, from www.goldviolin.com

Descriptive Video Service. (2002, Winter/Spring). *DVS Guide, 12.*

Grupé, B. (Ed.). (2000, March 23). *Report on Disability Programs, 23,* 41–48.

Lighthouse International. (2002). *Lighthouse catalog.* New York: The Lighthouse Store.

McMahon, P. (2000, February 4). Hearing-impaired wage fight in theaters. *USA Today,* p. 3A.

The Tennessean (1999, February 16). 'Net lets blind "see" diagrams, p. A4.

CHAPTER 12
AUTISTIC SPECTRUM DISORDERS (ASD)

Steven Wiltshire

Wiltshire, S. (1993). *Steven Wiltshire's American dream.* London: Michael Joseph.

Autistic Spectrum Disorders (ASD) Defined

American Psychiatric Association. (1994). *Diagnostic and statistical manual of mental disorders* (4th ed.). Washington, DC: Author.

Baron-Cohen, S., Alle, J., & Gillberg, C. (1992). Can autism be detected at 18 months? The needle, the haystack, and the CHAT. *British Journal of Psychiatry, 161,* 839–843.

Begley, S., & Springen, K. (1996, May 13). Life in a parallel world: A bold new approach to the mystery of autism. *Newsweek,* p. 70.

Carpenter, J., Peninngton, B. E., & Rogers, S. T. (2002). Interrelations among social-cognitive skills in young children with autism. *Journal of Autism and Developmental Disorders, 32,* 91–106.

Koegel, R. L., & Koegel, L. K. (Eds.). (1995). *Teaching children with autism: Strategies for initiating positive interactions and improving learning opportunities.* Baltimore: Paul H. Brookes.

Lewis, M. H., & Bodfish, J. W. (1998). Repetitive behavior disorders in autism. *Mental Retardation and Developmental Disabilities Research Reviews, 4,* 80–89.

Lord, C. S., Risi, S., Lambrecht, L., Cook, E. H., Leventhal, B. L., DiLavore, P. C., Picheles, A., & Rutter, M. (2000). The autism diagnostic observation schedule-generic: A standard measure of social and communication deficits associated with the spectrum of autism. *Journal of Autism and Developmental Disorders, 30,* 205–233.

Mundy, P., & Neal, A. R. (2001). Neural plasticity, joint attention, and transactional social-orienting model of autism. In L. M. Glidden (Ed.), *International review of research in mental retardation: Autism,* (Vol 23; pp. 139–168). San Diego: Academic Press.

National Research Council. (2001). *Educating children with autism.* Washington, DC: National Academy Press.

Osterling, J., & Dawson, G. (1994). Early recognition of children with autism: A study of first birthday home videotapes. *Journal of Autism and Developmental Disorders, 24,* 247–257.

Powers, M. D. (2000). What is autism? In M. D. Powers (Ed.). *Children with autism: A parent's guide.* Bethesda, MD: Woodbine House.

Ramberg, C., Ehlers, S., Nyden, A., & Johansson, M. (1996). Language and pragmatic functions in school-age children on the autism spectrum. *European Journal of Disorders of Communication, 31,* 387–413.

Rogers, S. T. (1998). Neuropsychology of autism in young children and its implications for early intervention. *Mental Retardation and Developmental Disabilities Research Reviews, 4,* 104–112.

Safran, S. P. (2001). Asperger syndrome: The Emerging challenge to special education. *Exceptional Children, 67,* 151–160.

Schopler, E., Reicheler, J., DeVeillis, R. F., & Daly, K. (1980). Toward objective classification of childhood autism: Childhood Autism Rating Scale (CARS). *Journal of Autism and Developmental Disorders, 10,* 91–103.

Shienkopf, S. J., Mundy, P., Oller, D. K., & Steffens, M. (2000). Vocal atypicality of preverbal autistic children. *Journal of Autism and Developmental Disabilities, 30,* 345–354.

Sperry, V. W. (2001). *Fragile success: Ten autistic children, childhood to adulthood.* Baltimore: Paul H. Brookes.

Stone, W. L., Lee, E. B., Ashford, L., Brissire, J., Hepburn, S. L., Coonrod, E. E., & Weiss, B. H. (1999). Can autism be diagnosed accurately in children under 3 years? *Journal of Child Psychology and Psychiatry and Allied Disciplines, 40,* 219–226.

Stone, W. L., Coonrod, E. E., & Ousley, O. Y. (2000). Brief report: Screening tool for autism in two-year-olds (STAT): Development and preliminary data. *Journal of Autism and Developmental Disorders, 30,* 607–612.

Stone, W. L., & Yoder, P. J. (2001). Predicting spoken language level in children with autism spectrum disorders. *Autism, 5,* 341–361.

Sturmey, P., & Sevin, J. A. (1994). Defining and assessing autism. In J. L. Matson (Ed.), *Autism in children and adults: Etiology, assessment, and intervention* (pp. 13–36). Pacific Grove, CA: Brooks/Cole.

Tanguay, P. E., Robertson, J., & Derrick, A. (1998). A dimensional classification of autism spectrum disorder by social communication domains. *Journal of the American Academy of Child and Adolescent Psychiatry, 37,* 271–277.

U.S. Department of Education. (1999). Assistance to states for the education of children with disabilities and the early intervention programs for infants and toddlers with disabilities: Final regulations. *Federal Register, 64* (48), CFR Parts 300 and 303.

Wetherby, A. M., & Prizant, B. M. (1993). Profiling communication and symbolic abilities in young children. *Journal of Childhood Communication Disorders, 15,* 23–32.

Wetherby, A. M., Yonclas, D. G., & Bryan, E. A. (1989). Communicative profiles of preschool children with handicaps: Implications for early identification. *Journal of Speech and Hearing Disorders, 54,* 148–158.

Wing, L. (1989). Autistic adults. In C. Gillberg (Ed.), *Diagnosis and treatment of autism* (pp. 419–432). New York: Plenum Press.

History of the Field

Kanner, L. (1943). Autistic disturbances of affective contact. *Nervous Child, 2,* 217–250.

Powers, M. D. (2000). What is autism? In M. D. Powers (Ed.), *Children with autism: A parent's guide.* Bethesda, MD: Woodbine House.

Rimland, B. (1994). The modern history of autism: A personal perspective. In J. L. Matson (Ed.), *Autism in children and adults: Etiology, assessment and intervention.* Pacific Grove, CA: Brooks/Cole.

Prevalence

Burton, D. (2002, April 18). *The autism epidemic: Is the NIH and CDC response adequate?* Committee on Government Reform, Opening Statement, U.S. Congress.

Fombonne, E. (1999). *Epidemiological findings on autism and related developmental disorders.* Paper presented at the First Workshop of the Committee on Educational Interventions for Children with Autism, National Research Council, December 13–14, 1999.

National Research Council. (2001). *Educating children with autism.* Washington, DC: National Academy Press.

Stokstad, E. (2002). Scant evidence for an epidemic of autism. *Science, 294,* 35.

U.S. Department of Education. (2001). *Twenty-third annual report to Congress on the implementation of IDEA.* Washington, DC: U.S. Government Printing Office.

Causes of ASD

Cowley, G., Brownell, G., & Footes, D. (2000, July 31). Parents wonder: Is it safe to vaccinate? *Newsweek,* p. 52.

Dawson, G., Mellzoff, A. N., Osterling, J., & Rinaldi, J. (1998). Neuropsychological correlates of early symptoms of autism. *Child Development, 69,* 1276–1285.

Koegel, R. L., Koegel, L. K., Frea, W. D., & Smith, A. E. (1995). Emerging interventions of children with autism: Longitudinal and lifestyle implications. In R. L. Koegel and L. K. Koegel (Eds.), *Teaching children with autism: Strategies for initiating positive interactions and improving learning opportunities.* Baltimore: Paul H. Brookes.

Piven, J. (2002). Genetics of personality: The example of the broad autism phenotype. In J. Benjamin, R. I. Ebstern, & R. H. Belmaher (Eds.), *Molecular genetics and the human personality.* Washington, DC: American Psychiatric Publishers.

Seroussi, K. (2000). *Unraveling the mysteries of autism and pervasive developmental disorder: A mother's story of research and recovery.* New York: Simon and Schuster.

Characteristics

Barnhill, G. P. (2001). What is Asperger syndrome? *Intervention in School and Clinic, 36,* 259–265.

Baron-Cohen, S. (2001). Theory of mind and autism: A review. In G. Lavaine Masters (Ed.), *International review of research in mental retardation.* New York: Academic Press.

Sturmey, P., & Sevin, J. A. (1994). Defining and assessing autism. In J. L. Matson (Ed.), *Autism in children and adults: Etiology, assessment, and intervention* (pp. 13–36). Pacific Grove, CA: Brooks/Cole.

Talay-Ongan, A., & Wood, K. (2000). Unusual sensory sensitivities in autism: A possible crossroads. *International Journal of Disability, Development and Education, 47,* 201–212.

Early Childhood Education

Dawson, G., & Osterling, J. (1997). Early intervention in autism. In M. J. Guralnick, (Ed.), *The effectiveness of early intervention.* Baltimore: Paul H. Brookes.

Handleman, J. S., & Harris, S. L. (2000). *Preschool education programs for children with autism.* Autism, TX: PRO-ED.

Harris, S. L., & Handleman, J. S. (1994). *Preschool education programs for children with autism.* Austin, TX: PRO-ED.

Lord, C., & Schopler, E. (1994). TEACCH services for preschool children. In S. Harris & J. Handleman (Eds.), *Preschool education programs for children with autism.* Austin, TX: PRO-ED.

Lovaas, O. I. (1987). Behavioral treatment and normal educational and intellectual functioning in young autistic children. *Journal of Consulting and Clinical Psychology, 55,* 3–9.

Marcus, L. M., Garfinkle, A. N., & Wolery, M. (2001). Issues in early diagnosis and intervention with young children with autism. In, E. Schopler, N. Yirmiya, C. Shulman, & L. M. Marcus (Eds.), *The research basis for autism intervention.* New York: Kluwer Academic/Plenum Publishers.

Reinhartsen, D., Garfinkle, A. N., & Wolery, M. (in press). Facilitating play in two-year old children with autism: Teacher selected or child choice of toys. *Journal of the Association for Persons with Severe Handicaps.*

Schwartz, I. S., Boulware, G. L., McBride, B. J., & Sandall, S. R. (2001). Functional assessment strategies for young children with autism. *Focus on Autism and Other Developmental Disabilities, 16,* 222–227.

Elementary Through High School

Barnhill, G. P. (2001) What is Asperger syndrome? *Intervention in School and Clinic, 36,* 259–265.

Bondy, A., & Frost, L. (2002). *Topics in autism: A picture's worth. PECS and other visual communication stratagies in autism.* Bethesda, MD: Woodbine House.

Horner, R. H. (1994). Functional assessment: Contribution and future directions. *Journal of Applied Behavior Analysis, 27* 401–404.

Schwartz, I. S., Garfinkle, A. N., & Bauer, J. (1998). The picture exchange communication system: Communicative outcomes for young children with disabilities. *Topics in Early Childhood Special Education, 18,* 144–159.

Scott, J., Clark, C., & Brady, M. (2000). *Students with autism: Characteristics and instructional programming.* San Diego, CA: Singular Publishing Group.

Sugai, G., Horner, R. H., Dunlap, G., Hieneman, M., Lewis, T. J., Nelson, C. M., Scott, T., Liaupsin, C., Sailor, W., Turnbull, R. H., Wickham, D., Ruef, M., & Wilcox, B. (1999, December). Applying positive behavior support and functional behavior assessment in school. Washington, DC: OSEP Center on Positive Behavioral Interventions and Support.

Thiemann, K. S., & Goldstein, H. (2001). Social stories, written text cues, and video feedback: Effects on social communication of children with autism. *Journal of Applied Behavior Analysis, 34,* 425–446.

Collaboration for Inclusion

Hoyson, M., Jamieson, B., & Strain, P. (1984). Individualized group instruction of normally developing and autistic-like children: The LEAP curriculum model. *Journal of the Division of Early Childhood, 1,* 151–171.

Transition Through Adulthood

Chadsey-Rusch, J., & Heal, L.W. (1995). Building consensus from transition experts on social integration outcomes and interventions. *Exceptional Children, 62,* 165–187.

Park, C. C. (2001). *Exiting Nirvana: A daughter's life with autism.* Boston: Little, Brown.

Raia, J. (2001, June 18). Autism doesn't slow this marathoner. *Los Angeles Times,* p. D7.

Families

Powell, T. H., Hecimovic, A., & L. Christensen. (1992). Meeting the unique needs of families. In D. E. Befkell (Ed.), *Autism: Identification, Education and Treatment.* Hillsdale, NJ: Lawrence Erlbaum Associates.

Technology

Bondy, A. S., & Frost, L. A. (1993). Mands across the water: A report on the application of the Picture-Exchange Communication System in Peru. *The Behavior Analyst, 16,* 123–128.

Bondy, A., & Frost, L. (2002). *Topics in autism: A picture's worth. PECS and other visual communication strategies in autism.* Bethesda, MD: Woodbine House.

Garfinkle, A. N., & Scwhartz, I. S., (2001). "Hey! I'm talking to you:" A naturalistic procedure to teach preschool children to use their AAC systems with peers. In M. Ostorsky & S. Sandall (Eds.), *Young Exceptional Children Monograph Series: Teaching strategies No. 3.* Longmont, CO: Sporis West.

Frost, L. A., & Bondy, A. S. (1994). *The picture exchange communication system training manual.* Cherry Hill, NJ: Pyramid Educational Consultants, Inc.

Schwartz, I. S., Garfinkle, A. N., & Bauer, J. (1998). The picture exchange communication system: Communicative outcomes for young children with disabilities. *Topics in Early Childhood Special Education, 18,* 144–159.

CHAPTER 13
LOW INCIDENCE DISABILITIES
Multiple-Severe Disabilities

Children's Defense Fund (CDF). (2001). *The state of America's children.* Washington, DC: Children's Defense Fund.

Laurent Clerc National Deaf Education Center. (2001). *Deaf children with multiple disabilities.* Retrieved May 19, 2002, from http://www.clerccenter.gallaudet.edu/InfoToGo/141.htm

March of Dimes. (2002). *Health library: Infant health statistics.* Retrieved September 1, 2002, from http://www.modimes.org/HealthLibrary/344_1361.htm

March of Dimes Perinatal Data Center. (2001). *Maternal, infant, and child health in the United States,* 2001. Retrieved August 31, 2002, from http://www.modimes.org/HealthLibrary/334_598.htm

McDonnell, J. J., Hardman, M. L., & McDonnell, A. P. (2003). *Introduction to persons with moderate and severe disabilities: Educational and social issues* (2nd ed.). Boston: Allyn and Bacon.

National Information Center for Children and Youth with Disabilities (NICHCY). (2001, December). *Severe and/or multiple disabilities.* Washington, DC: NICHCY.

Snell, M. E., & Brown, F. (2000). *Instruction of students with severe disabilities* (5th ed.). Upper Saddle River, NJ: Merrill an imprint of Prentice-Hall.

TASH. (2000a). *TASH resolution on the people for whom TASH advocates.* Baltimore: Author. Definition orginally adopted April 1975; revised December 1985 and March 2000. Available at http://www.tash.org/resolutions/R21PEOPL.html

TASH. (2000b). *TASH resolution on deinstitutionalization.* Baltimore: Author. Resolution originally adopted October 1979; revised November 1999 and March 2000. Available at http://www.tash.org/resolutions/res02deinstitut.htm

U.S. Department of Education. (1999). Assistance to states for the education of children with disabilities program and the early intervention program for infants and toddlers with disabilities; Final regulations. *Federal Register, 34,* CRF Parts 300 and 303.

U.S. Department of Education. (2001). *Twenty-third annual report to Congress on the implementation of the Individuals with Disabilities Education Act.* Washington, DC: U. S. Government Printing Office.

DeafBlindness

Accardo, P. J., Whitman, B. U., Laszewski, C., Haake, C. A., & Morrow, J. D. (1996). *Dictionary of developmental disabilities terminology.* Baltimore: Paul H. Brookes.

Baldwin, V. (1995). *Annual Deaf-Blind Census.* Monmouth, OR: Teaching Research, Western Oregon State College.

Boeck, S. (1998, November 4). Blind, deaf triathelete honored. *USA Today* Sports Section, p. C3.

Chen, D., Downing, J., & Rodriguez-Gil, G. (2000–2001, Winter). Tactile learning strategies for children who are deaf-blind: Concerns and considerations from Project SALUTE. *Deaf-Blind Perspectives, 8,* 1–6.

Children's Defense Fund (CDF). (2001). *The state of America's children.* Washington, DC: Children's Defense Fund.

DB Link, National Information Clearinghouse on Children Who Are Deaf-Blind. (2002). *Deaf-blindness.* Monmouth, OR: Teaching Research, Western Oregon University. Retrieved from http://www.tr.wou.edu/dblink/index.htm

DB Link, National Information Clearinghouse on Children Who Are Deaf-Blind. (2001). *National deaf-blind census.* Monmouth, OR: Teaching Research, Western Oregon University. Retrieved from http://www.tr.wou.edu/ntac/census.htm

Groce, M. M., & Isaacson, A. B. (1995). Purposeful movement. In K. M. Heubner, J. G. Prickett, R. R. Welch, and E. Joffee (Eds.), *Hand in hand: Essentials of communication and orientation and mobility for your students who are deaf-blind* (pp. 91–110). New York: AFB Press.

Haring, N. G., & Romer, L. T. (Eds.). (1995). *Welcoming students who are deaf-blind into typical classrooms: Facilitating school participation, learning, and friendships.* Baltimore: Paul H. Brookes.

Heller, K. W., & Kennedy, C. (1994). *Etiologies and characteristics of deaf-blindness.* Monmouth, OR: Teaching Research Publications.

Heubner, K. M., Prickett, J. G., Welch, R. R., & Joffee, E. (Eds.). (1995). *Hand in hand: Essentials of communication and orientation and mobility for your students who are deaf-blind.* New York: AFB Press.

Holcomb, M., & Wood, S. (1989). *Deaf woman: A parade through the decades.* Berkeley, CA: DawnSignPress.

Kemper, J. (2002). He didn't listen. *Deaf-Blind Perspectives, 9,* p. 1.

Melancon, F. (2000, Fall). A group for students with Usher syndrome in South Louisiana. *Deaf-Blind Perspectives, 8,* 1–3.

Miles, B. (1995, December). *Overview on deaf-blindness.* Monmouth, OR: DB Link, The National Information Clearinghouse on Children Who Are Deaf-Blind.

Miles, B. (2001, July). *Overview on deaf-blindness.* Retrieved August 29, 2002, from http://tr.wou.edu/dblink/overview.htm

Noonan, M. J., & Siegel, E. B. (2003). Special needs of students with severe disabilities or autism. In L. McCormick, D. F. Loeb, and R. L. Shiefelbusch (Eds.), *Supporting children with communication difficulties in inclusive settings: School-based language intervention* (pp. 409–434). Boston: Allyn and Bacon.

Steer, M. (1999, Spring). In Australia: Placing parents and families at the center of our planning. *Deaf-Blind Perspectives, 6,* 1–4.

Stremel, K. (1998, August). *Communication interactions: It takes two.* Retrieved August 29, 2002, from DB Link, http://tr.wou.edu/dblink/comm.htm

U.S. Department of Education. (1999). Assistance to states for the education of children with disabilities program and the early intervention program for infants and toddlers with disabilities; Final regulations. *Federal Register, 34,* CRF Parts 300 and 303.

U.S. Department of Education (2001). *Twenty-third annual report to Congress on the implementation of the Individuals with Disabilities Education Act.* Washington, DC: U. S. Government Printing Office.

Whinnery, K. W., & Barnes, S. B. (2002). Mobility training using the MOVE curriculum: A parent's view. *Teaching Exceptional Children, 34,* 44–50.

Traumatic Brain Injury

Clark, E. (1996). Children and adolescents with traumatic brain injury: Reintegration challenges in educational settings. *Journal of Learning Disabilities, 29,* 549–560.

Connell, M. C., Carta, J. J., & Baer, D. M. (1993). Programming generalization of in-class transition skills: Teaching preschoolers with developmental delays to self-assess and recruit contingent teacher praise. *Journal of Applied Behavior Analysis, 26,* 345–352.

Dunlap, L. K., Dunlap, G., Koegel, L. K., & Koegel, R. L. (1991). Using self-monitoring to increase independence. *Teaching Exceptional Children, 23,* 17–22.

Hall, L. J., McClannahan, L. E., & Krantz, P. J. (1995). Promoting independence in integrated classrooms by teaching aides to use activity schedules and decreased prompts. *Education and Training in Mental Retardation and Developmental Disabilities, 30,* 208–217.

Heller, K. W., Alberto. P. A., Forney, P. E., & Schwartzman, M. N. (1996). *Understanding physical, sensory, and health impairments.* Pacific Grove, CA: Brooks/Cole.

Hughes, C. A., & Boyle, J. R. (1991). Effects of self-monitoring for on-task behavior and task productivity on elementary students with moderate mental retardation. *Education and Treatment of Children, 14,* 96–111.

Hutchinson, J., & Marquardt, T. P. (1997). Functional treatment approaches to memory impairment following brain injury. *Topics in Language Disorders, 18,* 45–57.

Hux, K., & Hacksley, C. (1996). Mild traumatic brain injury: Facilitating school success. *Intervention in School and Clinic, 31,* 158–165.

King-Sears, M. E., & Carpenter, S. L. (1997). *Innovations: Teaching self-management to elementary students with developmental disabilities.* Washington, DC: American Association on Mental Retardation.

Lash, M., & DePompei, R. (2002). *Kids corner.* Available from the Brain Injury Association of America. Retrieved August 31, 2002, from http://www.biausa.org/children.htm

Markowitz, J., & Linehan, P. (2001, January). *Quick turn around: Traumatic brain injury.* Washington, DC: Project Forum at NASDSE.

NICHCY. (2002). *Traumatic brain injury.* Fact Sheet 18 (FS18). Retrieved September 15, 2002, from http://www.nichcy.org/pubs/factshe/fs18txt.htm

Prater, M. A., Hogan, S., & Miller, S. R. (1992). Using self-monitoring to improve on-task behavior and academic skills of an adolescent with mild handicaps across special and regular education settings. *Education and Treatment of Children, 15,* 43–55.

Singer, G. H. S. (1996). Constructing supports: Helping families of children with acquired brain injury. In G. H. S. Singer, A. Glang, and J. M. Williams (Eds.), *Children with acquired brain injury: Educating and supporting families* (pp. 1–22). Baltimore: Paul H. Brookes.

Strauss, A., & Lehtinen, L. (1947). *Psychopathology and education of the brain-injured child.* New York: Grune & Stratton.

U.S. Department of Education. (2001). *Twenty-third annual report to Congress on the implementation of the Individuals with Disabilities Education Act.* Washington, DC: U. S. Government Printing Office.

U.S. Department of Education. (1999). Assistance to states for the education of children with disabilities program and the early intervention program for infants and toddlers with disabilities; Final regulations. *Federal Register, 34.* CRF Parts 300 and 303.

Van Kuren, L. (2001, March). Traumatic brain injury—the silent epidemic. *CEC Today, 7,* 1, 5, 15.

West, M. D., Gibson, K., & Unger, D. (1996). The role of the family in school-to-work transition. In G. H. S. Singer, A. Glang, and J. M. Williams (Eds.), *Children with acquired brain injury: Educating and supporting families* (pp. 197–220). Baltimore: Paul H. Brookes.

Very Low Incidence Disabilities

Alsop, L., Blaha, R., & Kloos, E. (2000, November). *The intervener in early intervention and education settings for children and youth with deafblindness.* Monmouth, OR: National Technical Assistance Consortium for Children and Young Adults Who Are Deaf-Blind.

Chen, D., Alsop, L., & Minor, L. (2000, Spring). Lessons from project PLAI in California and Utah: Implications for early intervention services to infants who are deaf-blind and their families. *Deaf-Blind Perspectives, 7,* 1–4.

Condon, K. A., & Tobin, T. J. (2001). Using electronic and other new ways to help students improve their behavior: Functional behavioral assessment at work. *Teaching Exceptional Children, 34,* 44–51.

Downing, J. E. (2001). Meeting the communication needs of students with severe and multiple disabilities in general education classrooms. *Exceptionality, 9,* 147–156.

Frase-Blunt, M. (2000, September). High stakes testing a mixed blessing for special students. *CEC Today, 7,* 1, 5, 7, 15.

Harris, S. L., Belchic, J., Blum, L., & Celiberti, D. (1994). Behavioral assessment of autistic disorder. In J. L. Matson (Ed.), *Autism in children and adults: Etiology, assessment, and intervention* (pp. 127–146). Pacific Grove, CA: Brooks/Cole.

Hunt, P., & Goetz, L. (1997). Research on inclusive educational programs, practices, and outcomes for students with severe disabilities. *Journal of Special Education, 31,* 3–29.

Hughes, C. (2001). Transition to adulthood: Supporting young adults to access social, employment, and civic pursuits. *Mental Retardation and Developmental Disabilities Research Reviews, 7,* 84–90.

Kennedy, C. H. (2001). Promoting social-communicative interactions in adolescents. In H. Goldstein, L. Kaczmarek, & K. M. English (Eds.), *Promoting social communication: Children with developmental disabilities from birth to adolescence,* (pp. 307–330). Baltimore: Paul H. Brookes.

Kennedy, C. H., Long, T., Jolivette, K., Cox, J., Tang, J. C., & Thompson, T. (2001). Facilitating general education participation for students with behavior problems by linking positive behavior supports and person-centered planning. *Journal of Emotional and Behavioral Disorders, 9,* 161–171.

Kennedy, C. H., & Meyer, K. A. (1998). Establishing operations and the motivation of problem behavior. In J. Luselli and M. Cameron (Eds.), *Antecedent-based approaches to reducing problem behavior* (pp. 329–346). Baltimore: Paul H. Brookes.

Kennedy, C. H., Shukla, S., & Fryxell, D. (1997). Comparing the effects of educational placement on the social relationships of intermediate school students with severe disabilities. *Exceptional Children, 64,* 31–47.

Koegel, R. L., Koegel, L. K., Frea, W. D., & Smith, A. E. (1995). Emerging interventions for children with autism: Longitudinal and lifestyle implications. In R. L. Koegel & L. K. Koegel (Eds.), *Teaching children with autism: Strategies for initiating positive interactions and improving learning opportunities* (pp. 1–16). Baltimore: Paul H. Brookes.

Lohrmann-O'Rourke, S., & Gomez, O. (2001). Integrating preference assessment within the transition process to create meaningful school-to-life outcomes. *Exceptionality, 9,* 157–174.

McDonnell, J. J., Hardman, M. L., & McDonnell, A. P. (2003). *Introduction to persons with moderate and severe disabilities: Educational and social issues* (2nd ed.). Boston: Allyn and Bacon.

McWilliam, R. A., Wolery, M., & Odom, S. L. (2001). Instructional perspectives in inclusive preschool classrooms. In M. J. Guralnick (Ed.), *Early childhood inclusion: Focus on change* (pp. 503–530). Baltimore: Paul H. Brookes.

Morgan, S. (2001, Fall). "What's my role?" A comparison of the responsibilities of interpreters, interveners, and support service providers. *Deaf–Blind Perspectives, 9,* 1–3.

Mullen, K. B., & Frea, W. D. (1995). A parent-professional collaboration model for functional analysis. In R. L. Koegel & L. K. Koegel (Eds.), *Teaching children with autism: Strategies for initiating positive interactions and improving learning opportunities* (pp. 175–188). Baltimore: Paul H. Brookes.

National Information Center for Children and Youth with Disabilities (NICHCY). (2001, December). *Severe and/or multiple disabilities.* Washington, DC: NICHCY.

Office of Special Education Programs. (2000). Applying positive behavioral support in schools. *Twenty-second annual report to Congress on the implementation of the Individuals with Disabilities Education Act* (pp. III–7 through III–31). Washington, DC: U. S. Department of Education.

Peeters, T. (1997). *Autism: From theoretical understanding to educational intervention.* San Diego: Singular Publishing Group.

Smith, D. D. (2001). *Introduction to special education: Teaching in a time of opportunity.* Boston: Allyn and Bacon.

Snell, M. E., & Janney, R. E. (2000, Summer). Teachers' problem-solving about children with moderate and severe disabilities in elementary classrooms. *Exceptional Children, 66,* 472–490.

Stuart, C. H., & Smith, S. W. (2002, March). Transition planning for students with severe disabilities: Policy implications for the classroom. *Intervention in School and Clinic, 37,* 234–236.

Strauss, A., & Lehtinen, L. (1947). *Psychopathology and education of the brain-injured child.* New York: Grune & Stratton.

Sugai, G., Horner, R. H. (1999). Discipline and behavior support: Preferred procedures and practices. *Effective School Practices, 17,* 10–22.

Sugai, G., Horner, R. H., Dunlap, G., Hieneman, M., Lewis, T. J., Nelson, C. M., Scott, T., Liaupsin, C., Sailor, W., Turnbull, A. P., Turnbull, R. H., Wickham, D., Ruef, M., & Wilcox, B. (1999, December). *Applying positive behavioral support and functional behavioral assessment in schools.* Washington, DC: OSEP Center on Positive Behavioral Interventions and Support.

Thurlow, M. L., House, A. L., Scott, D. L., & Ysseldyke, J. E. (2000, Fall). Students with disabilities in large-scale assessments: State participation and accommodation policies. *Journal of Special Education, 34,* 154–163.

Turnbull, A. P., & Turnbull, H. R. (2000). Fostering family–professional partnerships. In M. E. Snell and F. Brown, *Instruction of students with severe disabilities* (5th ed.) (pp. 70–114). Upper Saddle River, NJ: Merrill/Prentice-Hall.

Turner, M. D., Baldwin, L., Kleinert, H. L., & Kearns, J. F. (2000). The relation of a statewide alternate assessment for students with severe disabilities to other measures of instructional effectiveness. *Journal of Special Education, 34,* 69–76.

U.S. Department of Education (2000a). Characteristics of children and families entering early intervention (pp. IV–1 through IV–13). *Twenty-second annual report to Congress on the implementation of the Individuals with Disabilities Education Act.* Washington, DC: U. S. Government Printing Office.

U.S. Department of Education (2000b). Preschoolers served under IDEA (pp. II–9 through II–17). *Twenty-second Annual*

Report to Congress on the implementation of the Individuals with Disabilities Education Act. Washington, DC: U. S. Government Printing Office.

Westling, D. L., & Fox, L. (2000). *Teaching students with severe disabilities* (2nd ed.). Upper Saddle River, NJ: Merrill/Prentice-Hall.

Ysseldyke, J., Thurlow, M., Bielinski, J., House, A., Moody, M., & Haigh, J. (2001, May/June). The relationship between instructional and assessment accommodations in an inclusive state accountability system. *Journal of Learning Disabilities, 34,* 212–220.

Ziegler, D. (2002, April). *Reauthorization of the Elementary and Secondary Education Act: No Child Left Behind Act of 2001.* Arlington, VA: The Council for Exceptional Children, Public Policy Unit.

Families

Bruns, D. A. (2000, February). Leaving home at an early age: Parents' decisions about out-of-home placement for young children with complex medical needs. *Mental Retardation, 38,* 50–60.

Dell-Orto, A. E., & Power, P. W. (1997). *Head injury and the family: A life and living perspective.* Boca Raton, FL: GR/St. Lucie Press.

ERIC Clearinghouse on Disabilities and Gifted Education. (2001, April). *Educating exceptional children: A statistical profile.* Arlington, VA: The Council for Exceptional Children.

Luckasson, R., Borthwick-Duffy, S., Buntinx, W. H. E., Coulter, D. L., Craig, E. M., Reeve, A., Schalock, R. L., Snell, M. E., Spitalnik, D. M., Spreat, S., & Tassé, M. J. (2002). *Definition of mental retardation.* Washington, DC: American Association on Mental Retardation (AAMR).

Luckasson, R., Coulter, D. L., Polloway, E. A., Reis, S., Schalock, R. L., Snell, M. E., Spitalnik, D. M., & Stark, J. A. (1992). *Mental retardation: Definition, classification, and systems of supports.* Washington, DC: American Association on Mental Retardation.

Technology

Bryant, D. P., & Bryant, B. R. (2003). *Assistive technology for people with disabilities.* Boston: Allyn and Bacon.

Buckley, W. L. (1999–2000, Winter). Computers in our classrooms. *Deaf-Blind Perspectives, 7,* 1–7.

McCormick, L., & Wegner, J. (2003). Supporting augmentative communication. In L. McCormick, D. F. Loeb, and R. L. Shiefelbusch (Eds.), *Supporting children with communication difficulties in inclusive settings: School-based language intervention* (pp. 435–460). Boston: Allyn and Bacon.

Noonan, M. J., & Siegel, E. B. (2003). Special needs of students with severe disabilities or autism. In L. McCormick, D. F. Loeb, and R. L. Shiefelbusch (Eds.), *Supporting children with communication difficulties in inclusive settings: School-based language intervention* (pp. 409–434). Boston: Allyn and Bacon.

Office of Special Education Programs [OSEP]. (2000). Applying positive behavioral support in schools. *Twenty-second annual report to Congress on the implementation of the Individuals with Disabilities Education Act* (pp. III–7 through III–31). Washington, DC: U.S. Department of Education.

Reichle, J., Beukelman, D. R., & Light, J. C. (2002). *Exemplary practices for beginning communicators: Implications for ACC.* Baltimore: Paul H. Brookes.

Sax, C., Pumpian, I., & Fisher, D. (1997, March). *Assistive technology and inclusion.* CISP Issue Brief. Pittsburgh, PA: Allegheny University of Health Sciences.

NAME INDEX

A
Abbott, R., 275–276
Abdulkarim, L., 88
Abedi, J., 28
Accardo, P. J., 454
Achter, J. A., 249
Adams, M. E., 353
Adamson, L. B., 216
Adoption and Foster Care
   Analysis and Reporting
   System, 292
Agran, M., 206, 290, 291
Aguirre-Muñoz, Z., 28
Ahearn, E., 45, 291
Aiello, B., 19
Akers, J. F., 397
Alba, L., 293
Alber, S. R., 210
Albertini, J. A., 361
Alberto, P. A., 310, 316,
   318, 389, 394, 458,
   459, 461
Alby, J. F., 353
Alexander Graham Bell
   Association, 358
Algozzine, B., 28, 57,
   239, 291
Algozzine, R. F., 140
Allen, E. A., 127
Allen, K. M., 269
Allen, T. E., 359
Almon, P., 391
Al Otaiba, S., 112, 128
Alper, S., 138
Alsop, L., 463, 468, 469
Ama, S., 292
American Association of
   Retired Persons, 408
American Association on
   Mental Retardation,
   190, 192, 195, 204
American Foundation for the
   Blind, 393, 400, 402
American Printing House for
   the Blind, 400
American Psychiatric
   Association, 114, 261,
   262–263, 264, 265,
   270, 310, 419–420
American Speech-Language-
   Hearing Association,
   350, 353, 356
American Youth Policy
   Forum and Center on
   Educational Policy, 52
America's Athletes with
   Disabilities, 332
Amos, R. L., 72, 73, 75

Anastopoulos, A. D., 90,
   265
Anderson, M., 289
Anderson, N. B., 170
Andrews, J. F., 354, 363,
   367
Ansariyah-Grace, T., 406
Antia, S. D., 365, 370
Appel, K., 176
Appleton, A. C., 113, 124
Apuzzo, M. L., 350, 356,
   363
The Arc, 196, 197, 200, 202
Archwamety, T., 277
Arguelles, M. E., 44, 100
Argus-Calvo, B., 233, 239
Armsden, G., 292
Armstrong, T., 312
Arnold, K. D., 236, 237
Aro, H. M., 395
Arora, T., 43, 49
Arthritis Foundation of
   America, 307
Artiles, A. J., 6, 28, 70, 72,
   75, 78, 79, 80, 84, 85,
   86, 87, 93, 96, 192
Art Institute of Chicago, 36
Ary, D., 95
Ash, A., 205
Ashbough, J. W., 204
Asher, S. R., 167, 168
Ashford, L., 424
Askew, J. W., 119
Associated Press, 337, 358,
   403, 405
Asthma and Allergy
   Foundation of America,
   318
Audette, R., 28
Ault, M. J., 208–209
Axelrod, S., 285
Ayllon, R., 195
Aytch, L. S., 169, 197, 210
Azrin, N. H., 195
Azzam, P. N., 202

B
Babyak, A. E., 285
Baca, L. M., 70, 72, 75, 77,
   79, 88
Baer, J. J., 460–461
Bailey, D. B., Jr., 99, 100,
   169, 197, 202, 210
Baird, S. M., 394, 407
Baker, B., 237
Baker, D., 376
Baker, D. B., 114
Baker, P., 394, 407

Baker, P. C., 187
Baker, S., 72, 92, 93–94, 96,
   367
Bakken, J. P., 120, 131, 163,
   168
Baldwin, L., 467
Baldwin, V., 452
Ball, E. W., 156, 175
Ball, W., 198
Ballard, J., 13
Banks, J. A., 76, 244
Bankson, N. W., 155, 158
Barnes, M., 112
Barnes, S. B., 324, 327, 456
Barnhill, G. P., 430, 434
Barnwell, D., 41, 49
Baroff, G. S., 193
Baron-Cohen, S., 431
Barraga, N. C., 392, 403
Barringer, C., 289
Barrish, H. H., 285
Barton, D. D., 404
Bassett, D. S., 62
Bateman, B., 60, 61
Batshaw, M. L., 201
Battle, D., 161
Bauer, C. R, 198
Bauer, J., 434, 438–439, 440
Baum, S., 236, 250
Baumeister, A. A., 130
Baytops, J. L., 74
Beach Center, 215
Bear, G. G., 58
Beardsley, T. M., 74, 239
Becker, W. C., 284
Beckman, P., 41, 49
Beebe-Frankenberger, M. E.,
   267
Beeson, P. M., 169
Begley, S., 287, 421
Behl, D. D., 397
Belchic, J., 465
Belfiore, P. J., 208
Belin, T. R., 265, 288
Bellew, J., 205
Belser, R. C., 197, 202
Benbow, C. P., 230, 235,
   245, 249
Bender, W., 119
Bender, W. N., 287, 288
Benjamin, B., 83
Bennett, V., 8
Benz, M. R., 212
Bergerud, D., 322–323
Berglund, R. L., 172–173
Berlin, S. J., 157
Berman, S., 5, 29, 30, 31, 32
Bernal, E., 238, 239

Bernal, E. M., 81
Bernier, K. Y., 302
Berthal, J. E., 155, 158
Bessent Byrd, H. B., 71, 84
Best, A. M., 28, 199
Best, S., 331, 332
Best, S. J., 310, 314
Best Buddies, 204
Beukelman, D. R., 179, 472
Beverly, C. L., 335
Bevilacqua, S., 111
Beyer, S., 204, 213
Bielinski, J., 467
Biemiller, A., 131
Bigge, J. L., 310, 314
Biglan, A., 95
Biklen, D., 20
Birenbaum, A., 199
Birnbrauer, J. S., 195
Bischoff, U., 256
Blacher, J., 213
Blackman, L. S., 207
Blackorby, J., 178
Blade, R., 373
Blades, M., 402
Blaha, R., 468, 469
Blair, C., 115, 119, 128
Blalock, G., 61
Bland, L. C., 230
Blaney, B., 204
Blank, M., 157
Blosser, J., 179
Blum, I. M., 32
Blum, L., 465
Boardman, A. G., 42, 43,
   120, 125, 126, 134, 135
Bocian, K. M., 28, 80, 116,
   119, 196, 241, 266
Bodfish, J. W., 420
Boeck, S., 455
Boelter, E., 265
Bogdan, R., 212
Bolton, L., 106
Bonafina, M. A., 114
Bondy, A. S., 434, 438–439,
   440
Bongers, J., 32
Boone, R., 142, 143
Booth, J. E., 121, 311
Borthwick-Duffy, S., 188,
   190, 470
Bos, C. S., 93, 94–95, 131
Boulware, G. L., 433
Bourke, A. B., 139
Bower, E. M., 260, 269
Boyce, G. C., 397
Boyce, G. C., 397
Bradley, R., 31, 44
Bradley, V. J., 204

SUBJECT INDEX

Page numbers followed by an italic *f* or *t* denote figures or tables, respectively.

A

AAMR. *See* American Association on Mental Retardation

ABC model, for behavioral analysis, 273–274, 435

Ability grouping, in gifted education, 244*t*, 245–246

Absence seizures, 305, 306*t*

Absenteeism
  of students with emotional or behavioral disorders, 290
  of students with special health care needs, 310, 318, 324–325, 328

Abuse
  and emotional or behavioral disorders, 270
  and mental retardation, 199
  and physical impairments or special health care needs, 319*t*, 320
  and traumatic brain injury, 461

Acceleration, in gifted education, 243, 244*t*, 245–246, 249

Accessibility, for people with disabilities, 16–17, 315–316, 325–326, 329–330, 334

Accessible Technology Center, 336

Accidents, 319*t*, 320, 460

Accommodation, visual, 386

Accommodations
  instructional or educational, 28, 46
    for blind or visually impaired students, 403–404
    for culturally and linguistically diverse students, 92–97
    for deaf or hard-of-hearing students, 364–367
    for gifted students, 243–249
    for gifted students with disabilities, 247–249
    for participation in general education curriculum, 46, 51
    for students with ADHD, 311–312, 322–323
    for students with autism, 435–436
    for students with emotional or behavioral disorders, 272–273, 276–277, 280–288
    for students with learning disabilities, 135–138
    for students with mental retardation, 206–210
    for students with multiple-severe disabilities, 449
    for students with physical impairments or special health care needs, 322–323, 328–329

    for students with speech or language impairments, 171–177
    for students with traumatic brain injury, 457, 459–461
    for students with very low incidence disabilities, 468–469
  physical or architectural, 16–17
    for blind or visually impaired students, 398–399, 404
    for people with physical impairments or special health care needs, 315–316, 325–326, 329–330
  in testing situation, 53, 96, 328–329, 467

Achievement, unexpected lower, with learning disabilities, 111–113, 120–125

Achievement-potential discrepancy, in learning disabilities, 114–116

Acquired immunodeficiency syndrome (AIDS), 308*t*, 310
  families of children with, 335
  and mental retardation, 196, 200, 335
  prevalence of, 318
  prevention of, 322

Acuity
  hearing, 56
  visual, 56, 386, 389

ADA. *See* Americans with Disabilities Act

Adaptions, in special education, 46–47

Adaptive behaviors
  definition of, 190
  in mental retardation, 189–190
    assessment of, 192–193
    community based instruction and, 209–210
    methods for improving, 202–205, 209–210

Adaptive skill areas, 190, 190*f*

Additions, in articulation errors, 158, 158*t*

ADHD. *See* Attention deficit/hyperactivity disorder

Adulthood. *See* Transition through adulthood

Advanced placement courses, 244*t*, 245–246

Advance organizers, for students with learning disabilities, 123, 133–134

Adventitiously blind, 388

Advocacy groups, 18–19
  for deaf people, 345, 381
  guiding principle of, 19–20
  for people with autism, 428
  for people with mental retardation, 19, 185–187, 194–195, 214–215

  for people with physical impairments or special health care needs, 19, 317–318

Advocates, role in special education, 46

African American(s), 71
  assessment of, 76–77
  cleft lip or palate among, 164
  demographics for, 78–79
  disabilities identified in, 80*t*
  dropout and graduation rates of, 91–92, 98–99
  gifted, 237–240, 247–248
  family support for, 250
  homeless children, 84
  language difference in, 88
  language impairments in, 165
  males, lack among teachers, 85
  overrepresentation of
    in attention deficit/hyperactivity disorder, 89–90
    in emotional or behavioral disorders category, 81, 89–90, 266, 269–270, 272
    in mental retardation category, 81, 196, 199–200
    in special education, 76, 80–81
  sickle cell anemia in, 309–310, 318
  under-representation in gifted education, 81, 237–240

African cultures, giftedness in, 230

Age
  and hearing loss, 346, 350–351
  mental, 192
  and speech/language impairments, 155*f*, 156, 163
  and visual disabilities, 388, 393

Aggression, 262–263, 275, 279
  in autism, 430*t*, 431

Aging out of foster care, 292

AIDS. *See* Acquired immunodeficiency syndrome

Air conduction audiometry method, 349

Alaska Natives, 71
  disabilities identified in, 80*t*
  graduation rates of, 99

Alcohol, fetal effects of, 198

Alerting devices, for deaf or hard-of-hearing people, 378

Aleutian Islanders, 72

Allen, Edward, 392

Alternative portfolios, 467

Amadeus (1984 film), 255

American Academy for Speech Correction, 162

American Association on Mental Retardation (AAMR), 9, 194–195
  definitions of mental retardation, 188–190

by students with learning disabilities, 121–122
Audiodescription, 409
Audio devices, for blind or visually impaired people, 409
Audiogram, 348–349, 350f–351f
Audiologists, 22
Audio loop, for deaf or hard-of-hearing people, 375
Audiometer, 348–349
Auditory nerve, 346, 347f
Augmentative and assistive communication, 179–180
  for blind of visually impaired people, 393, 398–401, 406–410
  for deaf or hard-of-hearing people, 364, 373–378
  for multicultural and bilingual students, 101
  for students with autism, 434, 438–440
  for students with learning disabilities, 142–144
  for students with mental retardation, 216
  for students with physical impairments or special health care needs, 336–337
  for students with speech or language impairments, 179–180
  for students with very low incidence disabilities, 464, 472–473
Aura, in epilepsy, 305
Authentic assessment, 44
  in gifted education, 239
  in multicultural education, 74–75
Autism, 414–443
  advocates for people with, 428
  alternative treatments for, 429–430
  applied behavioral analysis in, 433
  versus Asperger's syndrome, 423
  augmentative and assistive communication for people with, 434, 438–440
  behavior patterns in, 430t, 431
  causes of, 429–430
  characteristics of, 430t, 430–431
  and communication skills, 420, 425–427, 430t, 431, 434
  definitions of, 418–421
    IDEA, 418–419
  discipline for students with, 434–435
  DSM-IV diagnostic criteria for, 419t, 419–420
  early intervention for, 427, 431–433, 435–436
    blended programs for, 433
    effective, key elements of, 432
    TEACCH program for, 432–433, 436, 439
    YAP program for, 432–433, 436
  in elementary through high school, 433–434
  families of children with, 417, 437–439
    advocacy by, 428
    theories assigning cause to, 417, 427–428
  film portrayals of, 421, 443
  functional behavioral assessment in, 434–435
  high-functioning, 420
  history of field, 417, 427–428
  IDEA classification of, 15, 303, 417, 428
  identification of, 424–425

impact of, 425–427
inclusion of students with, 435–436
insight into, Grandin's autobiographical, 426–427
insistence on sameness in, 430t
instructional accommodations for students with, 435–436
and intellectual functioning, 420–421
joint attention in, 425
low-functioning, 420
personal perspective on, 415
prevalence of, 428–429, 429f
racial/ethnic statistics on students identified with, 80t
"refrigerator mother theory" of, 417, 427–428
self-injurious behavior in, 430t, 431
and social skills, 416, 420, 425–427, 430t, 431
social skills instruction for students with, 434
stereotypic behavior in, 420
structured teaching for children with, 432–433
subtypes of, possibility of, 420
technology for students/people with, 439–440
toxic exposure and, 198, 429
and transition through adulthood, 436–437, 437t
Autism Diagnostic Observation Scale (ADOS), 424
Autism Research Institute, 428
Autism Society of America, 428
Autistic savants, 421
Autistic spectrum disorders, 414–443
  definitions of, 417–424
    National Research Council description of, 417–418
    organizing schemes for, 424
    types of, 418f, 418–424
Automatic speech recognition, 377
AZT, 322

B
Backward chaining, 208–209
Baer, Don, 269
Baker, Henry, 352
Balbus Balaesus the Stutterer, 8, 161–162
Barraga, Natalie, 392–393
Barrier games, 174–175
Basic interpersonal communicative skills, 92
A Beautiful Mind (2001 film), 26, 297
Bedlam, 267
Behavioral approach, in emotional or behavioral disorders, 280t
Behavioral assessment
  ABC model for, 273–274, 435
  applied, in autism, 433
  functional, 44
    for students with autism, 434–435
    for students with emotional or behavioral disorders, 273, 282–283
    for students with very low incidence disabilities, 465–467
Behavioral earthquakes, 275
Behavioral Intervention Plan (BIP), 31, 58
  IDEA requirements for, 282–283
  for students with emotional or behavioral disorders, 282–283
Behavioral supports, for students with very low incidence disabilities, 465, 467

Behavior problems. *See also* Emotional or behavioral disorders
  externalizing, 261–263, 262t, 275
  internalizing, 261, 262t, 263–264, 275
Behavior-specific praise, 284
Behind-the-ear (BTE) hearing aids, 353, 374
Bell, Alexander Graham, 353
Benchmarks, in IEP, 57
Best Buddies, 204, 216
Best practices, for students with learning disabilities, 130
The Best Years of Our Lives (1946 film), 26
Bettelheim, Bruno, 269, 417
Bibliotherapy, 238–239
Bilingual-bicultural instruction, for deaf students, 361, 367
Bilingual education, 67–105
  accountability in, 95–96
  assessment in, 73–75, 95–96
  characteristics of, 87–91
  community partnerships in, 97–98
  definition of, 70–76, 71f
  elementary through high school, 91–96
  family participation in, 99–101
  gifted students in, 237–240, 247–248
  history of field, 76–77
  inclusion in, 97–98
  instructional considerations in, 92–95
  language difference versus language impairment in, 87–88, 88f, 159–161
  language disorder versus language difference in, 87–88, 88f
  opposition to, 77
  personal perspective on, 67–68
  preschool, 90–91
  technology in, 101
  transitional, 93
  and transition through adulthood, 98–99
The Bilingual Special Education Interface (Baca and Cervantes), 77
Binet Intelligence Test, 231
Biogenic approach, in emotional or behavioral disorders, 280t
Bionic artificial limbs, 337
Bionics and robotics, 337
BIP. *See* Behavioral Intervention Plan
Birth injuries, and mental retardation, 196
Birth weight, low
  and mental retardation, 198–199
  and multiple-severe disabilities, 450
Blacks. *See* African American(s)
Blanton, Smiley, 162
Blatt, Burton, 194, 445–446
"Blended Americans," 78
Blind children/students
  braille literacy of, 385, 397–401
    selected skill areas in, 401t
  characteristics of, 394–395
  classroom modifications for, 398–399, 404
  discipline for, 394–395
  early childhood education for, 396–397
  elementary through high school, 397–403
  families of, 407
  inclusion of, 391–392, 397, 403–404
  independence skills of, 397
  instructional accommodations for, 403–404
  play of, 396

nondiscriminatory testing required by, 74

orthopedic impairment definition in, 301–302

other health impairment category in, 22, 300, 302–303, 310

parent and student participation required by, 44–45

participation requirements in
  for general education curriculum, 50–53
  for statewide and districtwide assessment, 52–53

personal perspective on, 445–446

procedural safeguards in, 45

provision for services until age 21, 469

Section 504 and ADA versus, 17

special education definition in, 20

traumatic brain injury classification in, 446–447, 457

traumatic brain injury definition in, 458

Induction coil, 375

Indus civilization, 225

Industrial School for Crippled and Deformed Children, 316

Infectious diseases, 302f, 307–310, 308t, 319, 319t
  prevention of, 321

Information processing, learning disabilities and, 117, 124f, 124–125

Information processing theory, 124f, 124–125

Inner ear, 346, 347f

Institute on Disabilities at San Francisco State University, 23

Institutions
  for people with mental illness, 267–268
  for people with mental retardation, 194–195

Integration, into general education classrooms, 42

Intellectual functioning
  in autism, 420–421
  in mental retardation, 189–190
    assessment of, 192–193

Intelligence(s), multiple, 74, 228, 228t, 239

Intelligence quotient (IQ)
  child abuse/neglect and, 199
  in giftedness, 226, 228–229
  in mental retardation, 189–190
  mismatch with achievement, in learning disabilities, 114–115
  normal curve of, 189, 189f, 228–229, 229f
  standard deviations in, 189, 189f, 229, 229f

Intelligibility of speech, of deaf people, 362–363

Intensity, of gifted children, 235–236

Intensity of sound, 347

Interdisciplinary instruction, in gifted education, 244t

Interim alternative setting, 58

Internalizing behaviors, 261, 262t, 263–264, 275

Internet use
  by gifted students, 251
  by students with learning disabilities, 142
  by students with physical impairments or special health care needs, 337

Internships
  for blind or visually impaired students, 405
  in gifted education, 244t, 245

Interpersonal intelligence, 74, 228t

Interpreters
  for deafblind students, 468
  for deaf students, collaboration with, 370t, 370–371

Interveners, for deafblind students, 468–469

Intervention Ladder, 283–284, 284f

In the canal (ITC) hearing aids, 374

In the ear (ITE) hearing aids, 374

Intrapersonal intelligence, 74, 228t

Iris, 386, 386f
  disorders of, 388t

Irwin, Robert, 392

Isolation, of deafblind people, 455–456

Itard, Jean-Marc-Gaspard, 9–10, 194

Itinerant professionals, 46, 48t
  for blind or visually impaired students, 403

J

Jacob K. Javits Gifted and Talented Students Education Act (1988), 226–227, 232

Japanese culture, giftedness in, 230

Jefferson, Thomas, 231

Job coach, 213

Job developer, 213

Joey Pigza Swallowed the Key (Gantos), 313, 316

Johnson, Wendell, 162

Joint attention, in autism, 425

Jordan, I. King, 353

Judicial hearing, 45

Jukes family, 194

Justice system, students with emotional or behavioral disorders involved in, 262–263, 267, 277, 286–288, 290

Just plain common sense, for instruction of deaf or hard-of-hearing children, 364–365

Juvenile arthritis, 304t, 307

Juvenile delinquency, 262–263, 267, 277, 286–288, 290

Juvenile Psychopathic Institute, 268

K

Kallikak, Deborah, 194

Kanner, Leo, 267, 427

Keller, Helen, 453

Kemper, Jack, 452–453

Kephart, Newell, 117

Kiddy cane, 397

Kinzer, Chuck, 216

Kirk, Sam, 116–117

Korean language, 87

Kurzweil Reader, 144, 393, 409

L

Language
  appropriate, for disabilities, 24–25, 25f
  careful use, for blind or visually impaired students, 403
  content of, 156, 159
  definition of, 153
  figurative, understanding of, 175
  form of, 156–157, 159
  native
    American Sign Language as, for deaf people, 345, 359–361, 364, 373

strategic use of, 94
use of, 156, 159

Language delays, 159–160

Language development
  in blind or visually impaired children, 407
  in deaf children, 346, 363–364
  patterns of, normal versus impaired, 160t
  preschool programs fostering, 169–171

Language difference, 87–88, 88f, 159–161
  deafness as, 360

Language impairments, 148–183
  age and, 163
  autistic disorders and, 420, 424
  causes of, 165
  characteristics of students with, 166t, 167–169
  child abuse/neglect and, 199
  children at risk for, 169
  and cognitive/academic performance, 168–169
  communication skills in students with, support and enhancement of, 171–175
  content enhancement strategies for students with, 171–174
  definitions of, 156–158
  direct instruction for students with, 171, 174–175
  early childhood education for children with, 169–171
  effects of, 161
  in elementary through high school, 171–177
  families of students of, 178–179
  film portrayals of people with, 182–183
  follow-up studies of students with, 178
  history of field, 161–163
  home-based strategies in, 178–179
  identification of, 158–159
  inclusion of students with, 176–177
  versus language delay, 159–160
  versus language difference, 87–88, 88f, 159–161
  and learning disabilities, 163, 168–169
  patterns of language development with, 160t
  personal perspective on, 149–150
  poverty and, 165
  prevalence of, 163
  prevention of, 165
  racial/ethnic statistics on students identified with, 80t
  and social competence, 167–168
  technology for students with, 179–180
  and transition through adulthood, 177–178

Language proficiency, levels of, 92, 92f

Language-sensitive environments, 171, 174–175

Language translators, computerized, 101

Large-print material, 399, 408

Larry P. v. Riles, 76

Larsen, Steve, 117

Lateral dominance, 117

Lau v. Nichols, 76

Lawyers, role in special education, 46

Lydia Shelomentseva

Lydia Shelomentseva